THE AMERICAN PEOPLES ENCYCLOPEDIA

A MODERN REFERENCE WORK

 Grolier

INCORPORATED
NEW YORK

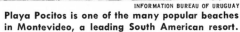

Playa Pocitos is one of the many popular beaches in Montevideo, a leading South American resort.

The Gauchos (cowboys) of Uruguay are renowned for their fine horsemanship. The legendary life of a Gaucho is carefree and filled with romance.

The legislative palace houses Uruguay's senate and chamber of deputies in Montevideo, the capital city. Uruguay's constitution was adopted in 1934.

Cattle from the plains await slaughter at a meat-packing plant in Montevideo. Much of the beef will be frozen and then exported.

URUGUAY, republic, SE South America, bounded on the N by Brazil, on the E by the Atlantic Ocean, on the S by the estuary of the Río de la Plata, and on the W by Argentina, from which it is separated by the Uruguay River; area 72,172 sq. mi.; pop. (1962 est.) 2,800,000. Uruguay is roughly wedge-shaped, and extends 375 miles north-south and 300 miles east-west. Montevideo is the capital. See map in Atlas, Vol. 20. For national flag in color, see FLAG.

PHYSICAL FEATURES

Physiography. The terrain of Uruguay forms a transitional zone between the hilly uplands of southern Brazil to the north and the level prairies, or Pampa, of Argentina to the south. There is a coastal plain in the south varying in width from 80 miles at the Brazilian border to 10 miles at points along the Río de la Plata. In the east the coastal plain is low and marshy; lagoons border the coast, and there are extensive areas of sand dunes and beaches. The largest of the lagoons, Lake Mirim, forms part of the border with Brazil. Inland is a broad hilly plateau, formed from granites, that extends northward from the ranges of the Cuchilla Grande to those of the Cuchilla Haedo. A wide plain, formed mainly on diabase, borders the Uruguay River. Aside from the Uruguay, the longest of the rivers is the Negro, which flows out of Brazil westward to the Uruguay. A dam on the Negro above Paso del Toros forms a lake on the southwestern edge of the central plateau.

Climate. Uruguay has a humid subtropical climate. Precipitation, evenly distributed through the year, averages between 38 inches and 46 inches, increasing toward the interior. Summer temperatures may exceed 100°F when the wind blows from the heated northern interior. In Montevideo, the average temperature is 52°F in winter, 73°F in summer.

Plants and Animals. The principal type of vegetation in Uruguay is grassland, although stream valleys

Location Map of Uruguay

are characteristically wooded with willow, acacia, ceibo and ombu. Uruguay has few good commercial timber stands and must import timber for construction work. Palms and eucalyptus are found along the coast. The tall prairie grasses, native to the country, have a slight purplish cast and have given the name "The Purple Land" to Uruguay.

The wild animals of Uruguay have largely disappeared, although puma and jaguar live along the wooded river banks; 'and tapir, deer, fox, ounce, puma, and wildcat are still found in the remote forests and in the northern mountains. The armadillo is the only remaining representative of the extinct giant land animals that once inhabited the country. Packs of wild hogs and droves of wild horses roam over the sparsely settled territory of the interior. The Isla de Lobos, off the coast of Maldonado, is one of the few places in the world where the common sea lion and southern fur seal are found together in large numbers. The country has numerous rodents, reptiles, and spiders. The bird life of Uruguay includes the stork, crane, ostrich, swan, wild turkey, lapwing, white heron, and various kinds of waterfowl. Among the colorful birds are the hummingbird, cardinal, and parakeet.

SOCIAL FACTORS

Population. Uruguay is the most densely populated South American country. The greatest population concentration is in the south and southwest, particularly in and around Montevideo, where nearly one-third of the country's inhabitants live. Most of the people are of European descent, predominantly of Spanish and Italian stock, with a sprinkling of Portuguese, Brazilian, German, English, and North American. There are small numbers of mestizos, Negroes, and Indians. The language of the country is Spanish. Montevideo is the only large city; other cities with a population of more than 30,000 are Paysandú, Salto, and Rivera.

Education and Religion. Education is free at all levels and compulsory at primary levels. The percentage of literacy is higher than in most other Latin American countries. The University of Montevideo (1849), the only university in Uruguay, is one of the largest in Latin America. Most of the higher technical schools, all affiliated with the University of Montevideo, are mainly grouped together to form the Universidad de Trabajo ("University of Work"). Some, in rural areas, specialize in agricultural training. There are numerous religious seminaries. Church and state are separated in Uruguay, and there is complete religious liberty, but most Uruguayans are of the Roman Catholic faith.

Public Welfare. Special schools are maintained for the blind and the deaf and dumb. Physical, mental, and social defectives are cared for in summer camps or in special institutions. Since the adoption of the Constitution of 1917, Uruguay has had state care for mothers, free medical treatment for the poor, pensions for all persons over 60 years of age, and public housing and public work programs. Both farm laborers and industrial workers are covered by a minimum wage law. Uruguay's eight-hour working-day law (1915) was the first in South America.

ECONOMIC FACTORS

Agriculture. Animal husbandry forms the basis of the Uruguayan economy: more than half of the total area of the country is used for stock raising, an industry initiated, c.1603, by an early colonial governor, Hernando Avias de Saavedra. The excellent natural pastures, moderate climate, and plentiful water supply are favorable to the raising of livestock. In 1961 there were 7.5 million cattle and 21.5 million sheep. Large *estancias* (ranches), some of more than 25,000 acres, are common and are the traditional form of land holding, although some of the large estates were divided into family farms after World

PRINCIPAL CROPS 1961–1962

Item	Area (hectares)	Yield (metric tons)
Wheat	438,427	374,652
Linseed	144,060	102,984
Oats	77,880	52,785
Maize (corn)	236,840	197,421
Sunflower	153,130	97,964
Groundnuts	10,217	7,349
Rice	17,936	61,805
Cotton	1,052	858

Source: *Statesman's Yearbook 1962-63*

War II. Sheep and cattle are frequently raised on the same *estancia*, but stock breeding is more common in the northern areas, while stock fattening is concentrated south of the Negro River, where the pastures are better. The most popular breeds of cattle are Hereford and Shorthorn. Sheep are raised mainly for wool, which is the most valuable single export of the country.

Only about 3 million acres, or less than 10 per cent of Uruguay's total land area, is under cultivation. Agriculture is concentrated in the southwest coastal plain and in the areas bordering the Uruguay River. The landholdings are much smaller than for the *estancias*, averaging only 250 acres. Wheat and flax are grown throughout the agricultural belt. Uruguay is self-sufficient in rice, most of which is grown in the north and east. Vineyards are mainly in the southwest, and production is sufficient for domestic consumption. Other crops are sunflowers, corn, oats, barley, sugar beet, sugar cane, peaches, oranges, and pears. Dairying is concentrated near major towns.

Mining. The mineral resources of Uruguay are not extensive and have been little developed. All mines are the property of the state. Gold, copper, lead, manganese, and talc have been worked, and there is some marble, agate, granite, onyx, and slate. Most mining activity is for construction materials, such as sand and gravel, curb, flag, and paving stone, and limestone, mainly for export to Argentina. Other minerals produced are ground quartz, adapted for glass making, and refractory clay.

Manufacturing. Industrial development in Uruguay has been hampered by a lack of domestic raw materials and the opposition of conservative agricultural interests. Practically all major manufacturing industry, of which meat processing is by far the most important, is concentrated in or near Montevideo. Associated with the meat processing industry is the manufacture of such by-products as leather goods, glue, and fertilizer. Among the well developed food

POLITICAL DIVISIONS

Department	Area	Population
	(sq. mi.)	
Artigas	4,390	63,589
Canelones	1,830	201,359
Cerro-Largo	5,760	110,339
Colonia	2,190	135,038
Durazno	5,570	99,063
Flores	1,750	35,565
Florida	4,670	106,284
Lavalleja	4,810	115,852
Maldonado	1,590	67,933
Montevideo	256	836,165
Paysandú	5,110	92,417
Río Negro	3,270	51,954
Rivera	3,790	91,740
Rocha	4,270	86,334
Salto	4,860	108,030
San José	2,680	96,848
Soriano	3,560	99,927
Tacuarembó	8,110	119,658
Treinta y Tres	3,680	72,068

processing industries are flour milling, sugar refining, and the production of vegetable oils and wine, mostly for domestic consumption. Textile production, using imported machinery, is concentrated in Montevideo, and supplies the local market. Other manufactured goods are rubber tires, chemicals (mainly fertilizers and insecticides), paints, furniture, glassware, building components, electrical appliances, and cigarettes. Power plants, such as that at the Rincón del Bonete dam on the Negro River, provide adequate hydroelectric power.

Commerce. Animal products are by far Uruguay's most important exports, principally to Great Britain, Netherlands, U.S.S.R., United States, West Germany, France, and Brazil. Imports, mainly raw materials and manufactured goods, come principally from the United States, Great Britain, Brazil, and West Germany. The basic unit of currency is the peso (U.S. 66 cents in 1960). Most foreign trade passes through the port of Montevideo, which also provides winter anchorage for several Antarctic whaling fleets owned by British and Scandinavian interests.

Transportation. Uruguay's navigable waterways form the country's oldest form of transportation. From Montevideo, steamship lines radiate to world ports; coastwise traffic is maintained with other river ports, and there are ferry connections with Argentina. Maldonado, Sauce, and Colonia are linked by ferry with Buenos Aires, across the Río de la Plata. The Uruguay River is navigable for ocean-going vessels of 14-foot draft as far inland as Paysandú and for 9-foot vessels as far as Salto. Fray Bentos and Nueva Palmira are other important river ports. The Negro River is open to traffic as far as Mercedes. Uruguay has almost 2,000 miles of standard-gauge railways, all government-owned. Nearly all radiate from Montevideo. They join the Brazilian railways. Uruguay also has an extensive highway network, mainly radiating from Montevideo. Uruguay is served by several international airlines. Montevideo has the most important airport.

GOVERNMENT

The Republic of Uruguay's constitution, adopted in 1934 and amended in 1942 and 1951, provides for three branches of national government: executive, legislative, and judicial. Members of the executive and legislative branches are elected every four years by direct popular vote from among candidates selected by Uruguay's several political parties. For administrative purposes the country is divided into 19 departments, each headed by a mayor.

The Executive Branch, or national council of government, consists of a nine-member college, or commission, each of whose members heads a governmental ministry. The members are restricted to six representatives of the political party receiving the first largest number of votes and three of that receiving the second largest. The chairman of the national council, the head of state, is always a member of the majority party. During the four-year term of govern-

ment, the office of chairman is held for one year by the majority party member who received the largest number of votes, for a year by the member who received the second highest number, and so forth down to the majority party member who received the fourth highest number of votes. The national council is assisted by a nine-member cabinet, whose members the council appoints.

The Legislative Branch, or national assembly, consists of a 31-member senate representing the voters at large, and a 99-member chamber of deputies representing the departments on the basis of their respective populations. Political parties are represented in the national assembly in proportion to the number of votes cast for their candidates. In the senate, however, if the candidates of two political parties together poll more than 50 per cent of the vote, these parties divide all the seats between them proportionately. All citizens of Uruguay 18 years of age and over must vote; aliens who have resided in Uruguay for 15 years may vote.

The Judicial System is headed by a five-judge supreme court, which is elected for a 10-year term by a joint session of the national assembly. The supreme court has original jurisdiction in cases related to the constitution, international affairs, and admiralty. Its appellate powers extend to decisions of four courts of appeal. Original jurisdiction lies with civil, criminal, government, and commercial courts seated at Montevideo and with departmental courts and justice-of-the-peace courts.

The Armed Forces consist of an army, navy, and air force, which are administered by the minister of defense. Each service consists of a small force of regular personnel recruited by voluntary enlistment. There is an army reserve composed of discharged regulars and of civilians who have received military instruction under a system of limited compulsory training. The navy is equipped with patrol ships, motor launches, and a few aircraft. The air force has fighter, bomber, and transport aircraft, which in 1960 were mostly of World War II vintage.

HISTORY

Exploration and Early Settlement. The pre-Columbian history of Uruguay corresponds to that of the south central Atlantic coastal region of South America. The principal Indians living there were the Charrua and the Guarani. Then, in 1516, the Spanish navigator Juan Díaz de Solís sailed up the estuary of the Río de la Plata and claimed the region for Spain, dubbing the area corresponding to Uruguay "Banda Oriental" (east bank). Although there was no notable settlement there for more than 100 years, the Banda Oriental was probably explored further during the sixteenth century. In any case, by the 1620's Roman Catholic missionaries had established missions among the Guarani Indians living inland near the Uruguay River, for which the region was later named. Although the exact origin of the word *Uruguay* is uncertain, it is from the Guarani language, and probably derived

MOORE MC CORMACK LINES

Despite progressive social legislation and economic planning, parts of rural Uruguay remain very poor. In recent years there has been considerable migration to the cities, especially to areas in or about Montevideo.

either from *urugua* (a type of mussel), or from combining the words *uru* (a type of bird), *gua* (from whence it came), and *y* (water).

In ?1603, a number of cattle were shipped to Banda Oriental from Paraguay; by the mid-seventeenth century, these animals having greatly multiplied, there was a thriving ranching economy, operated by the Spanish settlers, on the Argentine side of the Río de la Plata. Soon, however, the Spanish position was threatened by Portuguese settlers from Brazil, who founded the town of Colonia, 1680. Intermittent warfare continued for more than a century, but eventually the Spanish established their hegemony over the entire region. They founded Montevideo, 1726, and in 1776 made Banda Oriental a part of the Spanish Vice-Royalty of Río de la Plata, which also included most of Argentina and Bolivia, part of Chile, and all of Paraguay.

During the Anglo-Spanish wars of the 1790's, several British ships carrying emigrants to Australia were captured by Spanish and French privateers and brought to Montevideo, where many of the emigrants settled. Sensing opportunity for trade and political gain from the then crumbling Spanish Empire the British government subsequently sent naval expeditions into the Río de la Plata. After unsuccessful attempts to capture Buenos Aires, 1806, the British captured and occupied Montevideo, February, 1807. Later the same year further British attempts to capture Buenos Aires failed and the Spanish forces in the Río de la Plata forced the British to evacuate Montevideo.

Independence. The inhabitants of Banda Oriental participated in the general revolt against Spain that broke out along the Río de la Plata, 1810; and by 1814 revolutionary forces, led by José Gervasio Artigas, had driven the Spanish from the region. Brazil, however, subsequently invaded and occupied Banda Oriental, which in 1821 was incorporated into Brazil as the Cisplatine Province. Argentina opposed the Brazilian acquisition and supported a revolution spearheaded by the "Thirty-Three Immortals," a band of Uruguayan exiles in Argentina, led by Juan Antonio Lavallejo. The combined forces of the Uruguayan revolutionists and Argentina drove the Brazilians from Banda Oriental, 1827, and the independence of the area was recognized by both Argentina and Brazil, 1828. Lavallejo was made provisional president of the new state, called Banda Oriental del Uruguay, and a republican constitution was adopted, 1830. Almost from the outset the new republic was beset with political unrest: José Fructose Rivera, who had become Uruguay's first constitutional president, 1830, was succeeded by Manuel Oribe, 1835, but illegally deposed him, 1838, thus initiating a long period of civil strife between two major political factions whose antagonism was to dominate the country's political life for more than a century: (1) the Colorados (reds), established by Rivera, who were usually to be almost exclusively in control of government, and (2) the Blancos (whites), established by Oribe, who were to provide the only significant political opposition.

With the support of Argentine dictator Juan Manuel de Rosas, Oribe laid siege to Montevideo, 1843–51. The civil war ended in Rivera's favor when Rosas was deposed in Argentina by Gen. Justo José Urquiza, 1852, but Venancio Flores, Rivera's successor to the presidency of Uruguay, had to call upon Brazil for aid in maintaining his power against the Blancos. As a result Uruguay became a virtual pawn of Brazil, and subsequently was allied with Brazil and Argentina in their war against Paraguay, 1865–70. See PARAGUAY, History, *Independence.*

After 1870, although Uruguay was largely free of foreign entanglements, its internal affairs continued to be marked by intense political squabbles between the Colorados and Blancos. Nevertheless there were signs of progress: railway construction, begun during the 1860's, proceeded rapidly after 1875 as a result

Coat of Arms of Uruguay

of British investment; free, public education was instituted, 1877; and an electric light plant, the first in South America, was established in Montevideo, 1886.

Political and Social Reform. The election of José Batlle y Ordóñez to the presidency, 1903, marked the beginning of a new era in the social and political life of Uruguay. Batlle, a Colorado, had long believed that Uruguay's traditional dictatorships resulted from too much power in the presidency and the lack of representation in government for the political opposition. He also believed in state ownership of utilities and in separation of church and state, and advocated an extensive program of social welfare, including workmen's compensation and old age pensions. Few of his proposed reforms were adopted during his two terms as president, 1903–07 and 1911–15, but groundwork was laid for their eventual adoption. The Constitution of 1919, for example, provided for a popularly elected executive branch, consisting of a president and a nine-member college, and legislative branch, or national assembly.

During the worldwide depression of the early 1930's the economy of Uruguay suffered. Contending that the constitutional government was unable to cope with the situation, Pres. Gabriel Terra disbanded, 1933, the executive college and the national assembly, and ruled by decree; a new constitution was promulgated, 1934, providing for a single executive office, the presidency. Terra and his successor, Alfredo Baldomir, 1938–43, ruled as dictators, but improved economic conditions and general discontent with arbitrary rule forced the Baldomir government to permit the adoption of constitutional amendments (1942) providing for many social welfare benefits. When the constitution was next amended, 1951, the office of president was abolished and replaced by the collegiate national council of government.

Deteriorating economic conditions during the 1950's resulted, 1958, in the Blanco party being voted into power, replacing the Colorado party for the first time in almost a century.

Foreign Affairs. From the very outset of World War I, 1914–18, Uruguay was sympathetic to the cause of Great Britain, France, and the other Allied powers, and in November, 1917, it declared war against Germany. Uruguay was a signatory of the

Versailles Treaty ending that conflict, and was a member of the League of Nations. At the outbreak of World War II, 1939, Uruguay professed a policy of neutrality, probably because of the considerable pro-German and pro-Italian sentiment in Argentina. The German pocket battleship, *Admiral Graf Spee*, chased by the British Navy, took refuge in Montevideo Harbor, December, 1939, and was scuttled by its crew. Widespread Nazi activities in Uruguay alarmed many in the Uruguayan government, 1940, and soon the United States, then still a nonbelligerent but strongly pro-British, was granted the use of naval air facilities in Uruguay, 1941. Uruguay severed diplomatic relations with Germany, Italy, and Japan in 1942, but did not declare war on Germany and Japan until February, 1945. Uruguay joined the United Nations, 1945, signed the Inter-American Defense Treaty of Rio de Janeiro (1947), and became a member of the Organization of American States, 1948.

Uruguay maintained diplomatic relations with Cuba until September, 1964, and their severance was greeted with widespread protests. Commercial difficulties continued: though for the first half of 1964 Uruguay—unusually—had a favorable balance of payments, trading deficits with its closest economic partners stubbornly persisted. Social unrest, including strikes and riots, hardly assisted economic growth, and factional bickering—with the majority party splitting into four in 1964—made political stability the dream of a few idealists.

BIBLIOG.–Betty De Sherbinin, *River Plate Republics: Argentina, Uruguay, Paraguay* (1947); Russell H. Fitzgibbon, *Uruguay: Portrait of a Democracy* (1954); Simon G. Hanson, *Utopia in Uruguay: Chapters in the Economic History of Uruguay* (1938); William H. Hudson, *Purple Land* (1916); George Pendle, *Uruguay* (1963); *South American Handbook* (Annual); John Street, *Artigas and the Emancipation of Uruguay* (1959); Uruguayan Institute of International Law, *Uruguay and the United Nations* (1958).

URUGUAY RIVER, South America, rises in the Serra do Mar in Brazil, and flows W and S to join the Paraná to form the Río de la Plata; length 1,025 miles. The Uruguay forms the boundary between the Brazilian states of Santa Catarina and Rio Grande do Sul; and between Rio Grande do Sul and the provinces of Misiones and Corrientes in Argentina. In its lower course the Uruguay River forms the boundary between Argentina and Uruguay. Its upper course, in the Brazilian highlands, is interrupted by rapids and is not navigable. In its lower course, across flat and frequently swampy terrain, the river occupies a broad valley and is sluggish and muddy. The most important river ports are Salto, Paysandu, and Fray Bentos in Uruguay, and Concordia and Concepción del Uruguay in Argentina. Wheat, oilseed, fruit, and cattle, raised in the lower valley, constitute most of the river traffic.

URUMCHI (probably Mongol for "grapes"), or Tihwa the Bish Balik of medieval writers, known to the Chinese in the past as Hung Miao Tzu (Red Temple), city, China, the provincial capital of Sinkiang-Uighur Autonomous Region and chief city of Dzungaria; 320 miles E of Kuldja, on the great trade route from W China to Siberia. Its position at the junction of the only highway to Kashgar available for troop movements involving heavy motor vehicles gives the city strategic importance. Urumchi is an oasis town in the north foothills of the Tien Shan (Tien Mountains). There is trade in furs, cotton and silk goods, carpets, and garden produce. The name was changed from Tihwa in 1954. (For population, see China map in Atlas.)

USAK, province, W Turkey, bounded by the provinces of Kütahya on the N, Afyon on the E, Denizli on the S, and Manisa on the W; pop. (1960) 184,888. Uşak is in the western section of the Anatolian Plateau, reaching elevations of more than 7,500 feet above sea level in the northeast. The province is drained by the headwaters of the Gediz and Büyük Menderes rivers. Wheat, barley, and sugar beet, and cattle, sheep, and goats are raised within the province. The capital, which is Uşak, is a highway and railway center. Uşak became a province in 1953.

USE, a legal concept relating to an interest in the profits or rents of land, the legal title to which was held by another. Uses, the forerunners of twentieth century legal trusts, were introduced into England by churchmen during the reign of Edward III, before 1377. They were intended to avoid the statutes of mortmain, which forbade the giving of land to churches, a practice that deprived the crown of revenue (see MORTMAIN). Uses thus allowed the churches to profit from the land without holding title to it. The doctrine and application of uses raised many difficulties, but these were obviated by the famous Statute of Uses, which was passed during the reign of Henry VIII, 1509–47. This statute limited the practice of creating uses, and converted valid uses into absolute ownership. In twentieth century terminology, when uses and trusts are spoken of together, the former are those rights that are of a permanent nature and require no active duty by the trustee and the latter relate to rights under which the trustee has an active duty to perform. See TRUST.

USHANT ISLAND, French Ouessant, NW France, in the department of Finistère, in the Atlantic Ocean 11 miles off the coast of Brittany, some 5 miles long (E-W) and 2 miles wide; pop. about 2,300. The greatest height is 150 feet, and most of the coasts are cliff formations. The chief occupations are market gardening, sheep tending, and fishing. Off Ushant two French-English naval battles were fought: July 27, 1778, between a fleet under Comte d'Orvilliers and another under Adm. Augustus Keppel, the result of which was indecisive; and June 1, 1794, between Adm. Lord Howe and Adm. Villaret-Joyeuse, which was an English victory.

USHAS, in Vedic mythology, the goddess of the dawn. As night draws to a close, Ushas draws open the creaking gates of the sky, drives off the evil night spirits, and leads the prancing white horse of the sun out into the awakening world.

USHER, JOHN PALMER, 1816–89, U.S. lawyer and political figure, was born in Brookfield, N.Y. He studied law, was admitted to the bar, 1839, moved to Terre Haute, Ind., 1840, and there commenced the practice of law, often serving on cases with another midwestern lawyer, Abraham Lincoln. Usher was an unsuccessful candidate for Congress, 1856. He was appointed attorney-general of Indiana, 1861, but resigned, 1862, to become assistant secretary of the Interior in President Lincoln's cabinet; he became head of the department upon Caleb Smith's resignation, 1863. From 1865 Usher was chief counsel for the Union Pacific Railroad.

USHUAIA, city, extreme S Argentina, seat of Tierra del Fuego Province; about 1,450 miles SSW of Buenos Aires. Ushuaia is one of the most southerly settlements in the world. It is on a narrow coastal plain fronting Beagle Channel on the south coast of Isla Grande de Tierra del Fuego. The city is a communications and supply base for Argentine Antarctic operations. There is a small lumbering industry utilizing local stands of oak, and there is a small fish-canning industry. The name Ushuaia which means "inside refuge" in the Yahgan Indian tongue, refers to the city's sheltered harbor. The site was first settled as a Protestant mission in 1868. In 1883, with a population of 150, it became the capital of Argentine Tierra del Fuego. In the period 1889–1944 Ushuaia was a military and (later) civilian prison colony. (For population, see Argentina map in Atlas.)

USK, THOMAS, died 1388, English writer, was probably author of an allegorical prose work, *The Testament of Love*, which for centuries was attributed to Geoffrey Chaucer. Nineteenth century scholars, however, deciphered certain acrostic clues contained within the work and demonstrated to the satisfaction of most, that Usk rather than Chaucer had been the author. When Richard II was forced to impeach his chief counselors, 1387 (see RICHARD II), Usk, who had been appointed undersheriff of London earlier in the same year, shared in their downfall. He was condemned to death, 1388, by the so-called Merciless Parliament.

USK, river, S Wales, rises near Llandovery (Carmarthenshire) and flows E and S to Newport on the Bristol Channel; 67 miles long. It is a famous trout- and salmon-fishing river, flowing through beautiful scenery that recalls the legend of King Arthur.

USPALLATA PASS, Argentina, a pass across the Andes Mountains between Chile and Argentina, at an elevation of more than 12,500 feet. The pass was traversed by a trail, a rough road, and later by the Trans-Andean Railroad. Towering over the pass on the north is the peak of Aconcagua (22,834 ft.). The statue, Christ of the Andes, is located on Uspallata Pass.

USQUE, SAMUEL, sixteenth century Portuguese-born Jewish poet and historian, spent most of his life in Ferrara, Italy, and Safed, Palestine. He is best remembered for his historical prose-poem, *Consalação às Tribulações de Israel* (Consolation for the Sorrows of Israel), 1553, a didactic history of the Jews written to discourage apostasy from the Jewish faith during the time of the Inquisition.

USSHER, JAMES, 1581–1656, Irish divine, was born in Dublin. In ?1605, Ussher (or Usher) was preferred to the chancellorship of St. Patrick's, Dublin; subsequently he was appointed, 1607, Regius Professor of Divinity at Trinity College, Dublin, was nominated Bishop of Meath and Clonmacnoise, 1621, and became Archbishop of Armagh, 1625. He went to England, 1640, and took part in the ecclesiastical questions raised in the Long Parliament. Although Ussher was a well known royalist, he was treated indulgently by Oliver Cromwell after the execution of Charles I. Ussher was buried in Westminster Abbey. Among his writings are *Britannicarum ecclesiarum antiquitates* (1639) and *Annales Veteris et Novi Testamenti* (1650–54). He formulated a biblical chronology, according to which the Creation took place in 4004 B.C.

USSURI RIVER, U.S.S.R., rises in the Sikhote-Alin Mountains near Vladivostok and flows NE through Lake Khanka to join the Amur River at Khabarovsk. It is about 400 miles long. The Ussuri is navigable from Khanka to its mouth, and forms the boundary between Manchuria and the Primorski Territory of the U.S.S.R.

USSURIISK, formerly Voroshilov, city, U.S.S.R., Russian Soviet Federated Socialist Republic, in Primorskiy Territory, about 45 miles by road and rail N of Vladivostok. There are coal mines in the vicinity and the city has railroad shops, a plant for the manufacture of parts for tractors, a sugar-beet refinery, a soybean-oil plant, and other factories. (For population, see U.S.S.R. map in Atlas.)

USTI NAD LABEM, German Aussig, town and river port, Czechoslovakia, capital of the region (*kraj*) of Severočeský, on the Labe (Elbe) river. It is the largest Labe port in the country and has trade in coal, grain, and fruit. An industrial center, Ustí has chemical works and manufactures of glass and textiles. The town was ceded to Germany by the Munich agreement, 1938; after World War II it was returned to Czechoslovakia. (For population, see Czechoslovakia map in Atlas.)

UST-KAMENOGORSK, city, U.S.S.R., E Kazakh Soviet Socialist Republic, in East Kazakhstan Region; on the Irtysh River, 105 miles ESE of Semipalatinsk and 520 miles NE of Alma-Ata. The city is a mining and industrial center. Zinc smelting, metalworking, leather tanning, and the production of chemicals and vegetable oil are the chief industries. Hydroelectric power is provided by a plant at Ablaketka, 10 miles southeast of the city. Ust-Kamenogorsk is connected with the Semipalatinsk-Barnaul section of the Turkestan-Siberian Railroad. (For population,

see U.S.S.R. map in Atlas.)

UST-ORDYNSKY BURYAT, national okrug, S Russian Soviet Federated Republic, in Irkutsk oblast; about 8,000 square miles in area. The district is crossed by the Angara River and extends to within 20 miles NE of Irkutsk and 20 miles NW of Lake Baikal. Wheat, oats, and barley are the chief crops, and dairy and beef cattle are raised. Ust-Ordynski, the capital, is a food processing center. The Trans-Siberian Railway crosses the western end of the district.

USUMACINTA, river, S Mexico, formed by the conjunction of the Pasión with the Chixoy, forming part of the Guatemala-Mexico border. It flows northwest for about 350 miles to the Gulf of Campeche east of Frontera. Most of it is navigable, and it is used for floating logs down to the coast.

USURY, the practice of lending money or goods at a rate of interest deemed by law to be excessive (see INTEREST). The taking of even small interest on loans has been considered ethically unjustifiable and morally wrong in many societies. In the uncomplicated economies of primitive societies, lenders expect only the return of the goods loaned, especially as the usual kinship social structure makes it unthinkable that one individual should weaken another by exacting any sort of interest payment. The Mosaic Law forbade the Hebrews to engage among themselves in the lending of money, victuals, or any other goods "upon usury," but this prohibition did not affect their dealings with non-Hebrews, and as trade became increasingly more important, the ban underwent modifications.

In ancient Greece and Rome, it was generally believed that money itself is unproductive and that taking payment for its use is almost the equivalent of theft; the Roman landed aristocracy, like many later aristocratic groups, considered trade and money lending as beneath its dignity. Early Roman law for the most part opposed the taking of interest, but condoned some form of recompense to lenders for damages resulting from deferred repayments of loans. Roman philosophers, however, were as resolute as their Greek counterparts in the condemnation of usury. Cato the Younger classified usury along with murder.

During the Middle Ages, little capital was needed to finance business enterprise, and borrowing occurred only when individuals needed money for personal use (see CAPITAL). The Roman Catholic church held that it was an evil practice to take advantage of another's misfortune and need by charging interest for loans. This view, embodied in canon law, was based upon the belief that money, like food, is good in its being "consumed" and is not otherwise of value; and that the fact of a loan and the period of time over which the loan is granted neither add nor detract from the value of the money. If interest were to be charged, the lender would derive more in return than had been originally given, and an injustice to the borrower would result. Thus, both canon and (usually) civil law reflected the idea that any interest at all is usurious. If the lender, however, suffered financial losses by reason of his extending the loan, or was forced to forego just profits by reason of having lent the money, he was thought to be entitled to some sort of compensation.

The development of trade and commerce during the fifteenth, sixteenth, and seventeenth centuries and an increasing number of opportunities for the investment of money for the purpose of making money led gradually to the elimination of prohibitions against receiving interest. At first, circumvention of the earlier prohibitions was tacitly ignored by the authorities, except when it suited their convenience to expose and punish a "usurer" to whom they themselves owed money; later, however, the prohibitions against receiving interest were removed from usury laws. Nevertheless, there still remained legal sanctions

Utah

against unjustly high interest. The Protestant Reformation, which included a reaction against church domination of trade and commerce, was partly responsible for this change in attitude, which arose during the long transitional period from feudalism to capitalism.

In England, charging a fixed rate of interest, up to 10 per cent, was made legal in 1545. The maximum rate was reduced to 9 per cent, 1624, to 6 per cent, 1660, and to 5 per cent, 1713; and finally all usury acts were repealed, 1854. The usury acts were abolished in Europe during the 1850's and 1860's. Each of the North American colonies set its own legal rate of interest. As early as 1661, for example, Massachusetts fixed its rate at 8 per cent. In 1692, Maryland set up a 6 per cent rate that later became the prevailing one in many of the other colonies. However, the large demand for capital encouraged many infractions of laws and a chronic failure on the part of the authorities to punish such infractions.

Discussion of the religious and moral ethics of interest-taking continued throughout the seventeenth and eighteenth centuries. The English classical economists were virtually the first ever to theorize on the strictly economic aspects of interest. Adam Smith and the nineteenth century classicists who followed him discussed such things at length, but they did not treat interest as a return on the productive services of capital; instead, the classicists regarded interest as a part of profit, and attempted to determine whether the owners of land and capital make any sacrifice that entitles them to such income (see SMITH, ADAM; PROFIT). In contrast, a leading nonclassical economist of the century, Karl Marx, asserted that not capital, but labor alone creates value; it follows, Marx believed, that collecting interest constitutes "exploitation" of labor as much as does making a profit. Most twentieth century economists regard capital as productive, and its possessors as much entitled to income for its services as are individuals entitled to wages as payment for their work. See INCOME.

During the nineteenth century most states in the United States had laws fixing a maximum legal rate of interest, but no distinction was made between loans for production and loans for consumption. During the latter half of the century, the rise of a large unpropertied wage-earning class led to increased demand for small cash-consumer loans. Extortionate rates of interest were often charged for such loans, leading to a demand for controlling legislation. The Uniform Small Loan Law, devised by the Russell Sage Foundation in 1916, has been adopted by 27 states. In view of the greater risk factor, the statute permits a higher interest than the general statutory rate. See FINANCE; LOAN.

BIBLIOG.—Roger S. Barrett, ed., *Compilation of Consumer Finance Laws and of Usury, Sales Finance, and Allied Laws* (1952); Eugen Böhm von Bawerk, *Capital and Interest* (1959); William T. Cortelyou, *Banking Profit* (1953); Bernard W. Dempsey, *Interest and Usury* (1948), *Frontier Wage: The Economic Organization of Free Agents* (1960); Thomas F. Divine, *Interest: An Historical and Analytical Study in Economics and Modern Ethics* (1959); David W. A. Donald, *Compound Interest and Annuities-certain* (1953); Irving Fisher, *Theory of Interest as Determined by Impatience to Spend Income and Opportunity to Invest It* (1954); Silvio Gesell, *Natural Economic Order* (1958); John P. Kelly, *Aquinas and Modern Practices of Interest Taking* (1946); Jeffrey Mark, *Modern Idolatry: Being an Analysis of Usury and the Pathology of Debt* (1936); S. C. Mukherjee, *Law of Usury and Interest* (1941); Benjamin N. Nelson, *Idea of Usury, from Tribal Brotherhood to Universal Otherhood* (1950); John P. Noonan, *Scholastic Analysis of Usury* (1958); Don Patinkin, *Money, Interest, and Prices: An Integration of Monetary and Value Theory* (1956); Anwar I. Qureshi, *Islam and the Theory of Interest* (1946); Gilbert Stone and Dougall M. Meston, *Laws Relating to Moneylenders* (1952); Edwin F. W. Sumner, *Practical Compound Interest* (1953); Herbert Tate, *Mathematical Theory of Interest* (1947); Richard H. Tawney, *Religion and the Rise of Capitalism* (1947); Max Weber, *Protestant Ethic and the Spirit of Capitalism* (1948); Joseph W. Wickersham, *Introduction to the Theory of Interest* (1960).

UTAH TOURIST & PUBLICITY COUNCIL

Bryce Canyon National Park, with its multicolored limestone formations, provides unsurpassed scenic splendor for more than 100,000 tourists a year.

UTAH, state, W central United States; bounded by Idaho on the N, Wyoming on the NE, Colorado on the E, Arizona on the S, and Nevada on the W; area 84,916 sq. mi. (including 2,570 sq. mi. of inland water); pop. (1960) 890,627. Utah is rectangular in shape except for a deep notch in the northeast; it extends 345 miles north-south and 275 miles east-west. It ranks 11th in area and 38th in population among the states. Utah, popularly known as the Beehive State, was the 45th state to be admitted to the Union. The state motto is *Industry*, the state song *Utah, We Love Thee*. The sego lily is the state flower, the blue spruce is the state tree, and the seagull is the official state bird. Salt Lake City is the state capital. See map in Atlas, Vol. 20. For state flag, see FLAG.

PHYSICAL FACTORS

Topography. Utah is divided into three physiographic regions; the Wasatch-Uinta Mountains, the Colorado Plateau, and the Great Basin. The Wasatch Mountains, which drop as a steep escarpment on the west, form a rugged north-south "backbone" through the central area of the state. The Uinta Mountains extend east-west in the northeast corner of the state. The higher peaks of the Wasatch Mountains generally range between 10,000 and 12,000 feet; the higher Uinta peaks reach to more than 13,000 feet, culminating at Kings Peak (13,498 ft.).

The Colorado Plateau occupies the area south and east of the Wasatch and Uintas. The terrain is highly dissected by multicolored, steep-sided canyons that are hundreds or even thousands of feet below the nearby flat-topped land surface. Isolated clusters of mountains provide further variety and contrast. The Colorado Plateau is drained by the Colorado River and its tributaries.

The Great Basin lies west of the Wasatch Mountains. It contains a series of short north-south mountain ranges and sediment-filled basins, which form a large area of interior drainage with no outlet to the sea. There are marshy areas in some basins, and there are broad areas of salt-encrusted land on the alkali flats and in the Great Salt Lake Desert. In recent geologic history the entire basin was filled with a great fresh-water lake known as Lake Bonneville. Subsequent climatic changes reduced Bonneville to the present briny Great Salt Lake. Lying at 4,200 feet above sea level Great Salt Lake occupies the lowest area in the northern Great Basin region of Utah. Another remnant of Lake Bonneville is Sevier Lake, which is intermittent most years. It receives the Sevier River, one of the state's longest. The largest body of fresh water in the state is Utah Lake, which lies at the foot of the Wasatch Escarpment and empties via the Jordan River into Great Salt Lake. Bear Lake, also fresh water, occupies a mountain valley at the Utah-Idaho border. It also drains, via the Bear River, into Great Salt Lake. The lowest point in Utah, about 2,500 feet above sea level, is in the Virgin River valley in the southwest corner.

Climate. Most of Utah is generally arid, ranging from a subtropical desert in the southwest corner, to subarctic conditions in the higher mountainous northern region. The isolated high mountain masses in the Colorado Plateau and the Great Basin are small islands of increased moisture and cooler temperature in the generally arid surroundings.

Summers are usually hot and dry with an average monthly July temperature of 77°F. Temperatures sometimes exceed 100°F. Because of the low humidity, the high daytime temperatures are not oppressive, and nighttime temperatures are often some 30° cooler. Winters are cold but not severe, with the high Wasatch and Uintas acting as a barrier against the invasions of colder air from the north. Coldest average monthly temperatures are about 27°F in January, although temperatures may decline to as low as 10°F below zero. The freeze-free growing season is generally adequate for maturing crops.

Annual precipitation for the state as a whole averages 11.5 inches. In the high Wasatch and Uinta mountain areas, there is as much as 40 to 50 inches, while some low basin and plateau areas receive 5 inches or less. Northern Utah receives about 75 per cent of its moisture as snowfall from October to April, retaining as much as 5 to 10 feet of snow through most of the winter in the high mountain areas. The low southern area of the state receives most of its annual precipitation from summer rainstorms.

Plants and Animals. The subtropical desert area of southwestern Utah contains many drought-resistant plant forms including giant Saguaro cactus and the Joshua tree. Creosote bush, screwpot, and mesquite are also common. Many colorful annual plants spring into bloom with the early spring rains. Along the streams there are salt cedar tamaracks and willows.

The cold winter, mid-latitude desert of the Great Basin lowlands and much of the Colorado Plateau has sagebrush, rabbit brush, and black brush on the better soils, while shadscale and greasewood are on the more alkaline soils. In the Great Basin, a succession of plants forms concentric rings around barren salt spots according to their salt-tolerant nature. They range from the small succulent salicornia through low, fuzzy-leafed sueda. Cottonwood trees, willows, and cattails line the streams near the mountains and the marshy, fresh water flatlands in the basins.

Upslope, are pigmy forest areas of piñon, Utah juniper, and Rocky Mountain red cedar. On the Colorado Plateau is one of the largest such forests in North America. At still higher elevations there are deciduous shrubs and trees. Scrub oak, dwarf maple, chokecherry, service berry, and hawthorn, and the tree forms of broadleaf maple, red birch, mountain alder, and box elder occur. Cultivated trees include the American elm, locust, sycamore, catalpa, horse chestnut, weeping willow, linden, black walnut, and Lombardy poplar. Blue spruce, Englemann spruce, western yellow pine, lodgepole pine, Douglas and alpine firs, and the limber pine, along with the deciduous quaking aspen grow at still higher elevations. Above the timberline are shrubs and meadows.

There are various wild flowers and grasses throughout the state. The sego lily blooms briefly in early summer in the dry lower mountain and foothill areas. Others are cactus flowers, mallow, sunflower, phlox, lupine, wild rose, geranium, Indian paintbrush, yellow dogtooth violet and red and blue penstimon.

Associated with the multitude of flowering plants are many insects such as bees, wasps, butterflies, and moths. Mosquitoes are numerous for short periods of the year in wet marshy areas; crickets and grasshoppers are common. The woodtick is found in the upland areas. There are many small, burrowing desert animals, some with the apparent ability to survive on only the moisture obtained from the plants or animals they eat. There also are prairie dogs, gophers, kangaroo rats, groundhogs, squirrels, chipmunks, rabbits, horned toads, and varieties of snakes, lizards, and desert tortoise.

Seagulls, pelicans, cormorants, and herons nest on islands in Great Salt Lake, and there are whistling swans, Canadian and snow geese, pintail and canvasback ducks, and green-winged teal in nearby bird refuge areas. The seagull is protected by Utah law as a result of its being credited with having saved the crops of the first settlers from an invasion by grasshoppers. Upland game birds include the ring-necked pheasant, partridge, sage grouse, pine hen, Gambel and California quail, wild turkey and mourning dove. Birds of prey include the golden eagle of mountainous areas and numerous hawks and owls of the desert lowlands. Magpies, blackbirds, crows, jays, and vultures are also common. Characteristic songbirds are robins, sparrows, orioles, meadow larks, swallows, house finches, and warblers.

The mountainous regions of Utah have long been a source of fur-bearing and big-game animals. Furbearers include beaver, mink, marten, weasel, muskrat, badger, skunk, fox, and ringtailed cat. The mule deer is the state's most common big game animal. It ranges over most of the highlands. Elk, moose, bighorn sheep, and pronghorn antelope are also common. There are a few herds of buffalo in some isolated areas. There also are predators such as the black bear, mountain lion, and coyote.

SOCIAL FACTORS

Characteristics of the Population. About 98 per cent of Utah's inhabitants are white, mostly of northern European origin. Most Indians of the state live on the Navajo and the Uintah and Ouray reservations in eastern Utah, while the remainder occupy six smaller reservations in southern and western Utah. About two-thirds of Utah's people are members of the Church of Jesus Christ of Latter-day Saints. See MORMON.

Greatest population density is in the Great Basin lands between the foot of the Wasatch Mountains to the east and Great Salt Lake and Utah Lake to the west. About 75 per cent of Utah's population lives within 50 miles of Salt Lake City, the world center of the Mormon religion, and the largest city of the state. The city lies in the Salt Lake Oasis, where numerous streams from the mountains provide fresh water, while the gently sloping lands of the bottom of ancient Lake Bonneville provide room to cultivate crops, erect cities, and provide adequate transportation routes. About 75 per cent of the state's population is classed as urban.

Education. Public schools in Utah are administered by the popularly elected state board of education and the state superintendent of public instruction, who is appointed by the board. School attendance is compulsory for children between the ages of 6 and 18.

PRINCIPAL CITIES

City	1940 Census	POPULATION 1950 Census	1960 Census
Salt Lake City...	149,934	182,121	189,454
Ogden..........	43,688	57,112	70,197
Provo...........	18,071	28,937	36,047
Logan..........	11,868	16,832	18,731
Orem...........	2,914	8,351	18,344
Kearns.........			17,172 *
Bountiful.......	3,357	6,004	17,039
Murray.........	5,740	9,006	16,806
Brigham City....	5,641	6,790	11,728

* unincorporated

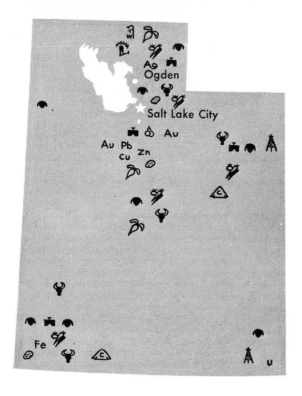

Many of Utah's sandstone outcrops have been carved into weird forms by wind erosion, and the desert sculpture attracts many tourists.

State Seal

PRINCIPAL RESOURCES, INDUSTRIES, AND PRODUCTS

Barley		Potatoes	
Cattle		Sheep	
Coal		Silver	Ag
Copper	Cu	Smelting-ore refining	
Fruit		Sugar beets	
Gold	Au	Truck crops—vegetables	
Iron	Fe	Uranium	U
Irrigation		Wheat	
Lead	Pb	Zinc	Zn
Petroleum			

State Flower
Sego Lily

State Bird — Seagull

The extraction and refining of minerals plays a vital role in the state's economy.

A predominantly arid state, Utah must irrigate its land to insure high productivity.

Since 1893 this temple at Salt Lake City has been the symbolic center of Mormondom.

A large number of children are educated at church-supported schools.

The chief institutions of higher learning are the University of Utah (1850) in Salt Lake City, Utah State University (1888) in Logan, the College of Southern Utah (1897) in Cedar City, all publicly supported. Brigham Young University (1875) in Provo, and Westminster College (1875) in Salt Lake City are both privately financed.

Public Welfare. The state government maintains a prison for men and women near Salt Lake City, an industrial school for boys and girls at Ogden, a school for the deaf, dumb, and blind at Ogden, and mental institutions at Provo and Spanish Fork. The state also has a welfare agency for the aged and infirm, a marriage counseling service, and a state board of health. Juvenile corrective institutions are maintained with state aid throughout the state. The Mormon church and other religious organizations and private agencies also have well developed programs of relief and welfare service.

Economic Factors

Agriculture. Mountain terrain, severe climate, widespread prevalence of alkaline and salty soils, and the lack of readily available water restrict the crop-producing lands of Utah to only 3 per cent of the state's total area. Some cropland is dry-farmed, but most is irrigated. Most crop-producing areas are in the Great Basin. The bulk of the state is used for grazing, about 75 per cent of total agricultural income coming from livestock and livestock products. Dairy and beef cattle, sheep, and poultry are the chief animals. Cattle and sheep are grazed over much of the state except in the arid west. The alpine meadows provide important summer grazing lands. Dairy and poultry farming are chiefly carried on in the irrigated areas, especially in the north central part of the state. The principal field crops are wheat and sugar beets. Others are barley and other grains, dry beans, hay, alfalfa seed, and potatoes. Fruit crops include cherries, apples, peaches, apricots, berries, and melons. The fruit orchards are chiefly on the higher slopes of the Great Basin, where soils and drainage are good. Tomatoes are the principal canning crop, and a wide variety of truck garden vegetables are raised for local consumption.

PRODUCTION OF PRINCIPAL CROPS

Crop	Unit	1964
Barley	short tons	166,000
Corn	bushels	186,000
Hay	short tons	1,378,000
Oats	short tons	19,000
Peaches	short tons	9,100
Potatoes	short tons	68,000
Sugar beets	short tons	522,000 *
Sweet potatoes	short tons	432,000
Wheat	short tons	173,000

* 1965 figure   SOURCE: *U.S. Department of Agriculture*

Forestry and Fisheries. Commercially, forestry and fishing are of minor importance. Both are generally confined to the high mountain and plateau areas in northern and central Utah. Most forests are supervised by the federal government so that the rate of logging does not exceed the rate of growth. Total annual production of lumber is only 70 million board feet, or about one third of the total state demand. Ponderosa pine and Engelmann spruce are the most important commercial species. Fishing for sport is popular, with trout, perch, catfish, carp, whitefish, sucker, and chub the most numerous. State and private fish hatcheries have extensive restocking programs.

Mining. Minerals account for about one third of the total value of production in Utah. The principal

PRODUCTION OF PRINCIPAL MINERALS

Mineral	Unit	1964
Asphalt	short tons	383,000†
Coal	short tons	4,719,843
Copper	short tons	199,588
Gold	troy ounces	287,674
Iron ore	long tons	2,082,000
Lead	short tons	40,249
Natural gas	100,000 cu. ft.	80,175
Petroleum	barrels	28,575,000
Salt	short tons	371,000
Sand and gravel	short tons	10,218,000
Silver	troy ounces	4,551,960
Uranium ore	short tons	761,180
Zinc	short tons	31,428

† 1960 figure   SOURCE: *U.S. Department of the Interior*

minerals by value of production are copper, petroleum, coal, uranium, and iron ore. Utah, ranking 16th among the states in the total value of mineral production in 1964, was second in production of copper and fourth in uranium. Most of Utah's copper comes from the open pit mine at Bingham near Salt Lake City. Most of the lead, zinc, gold, and silver is also produced in the Bingham area. Gold is recovered from the copper ore, and silver is recovered from the copper, lead, and zinc ores. The chief petroleum field and uranium mines are in San Juan County in southeastern Utah. Petroleum production began late in the 1940's and increased rapidly late in the 1950's; oil reserves, estimated at 3 billion barrels, are among the largest in the United States. Shale-oil reserves in the northern Colorado Plateau are also quite large. The major coal field is in Carbon and Emery counties in east central Utah on the Colorado Plateau, and natural asphalt and natural gas are also found in the area. A large portion of the iron ore is mined in Iron County in southwestern Utah.

Nonmetallic minerals, exclusive of mineral fuels, account for about 12 per cent of the value of total mineral production in Utah. Among these are gem stones, carbon dioxide, clay, fluorspar, gypsum, perlite, phosphate rock, potash, pumice, salt, sand and gravel, silica, stone, and rare earths. The phosphate and potash resources on the Colorado Plateau are among the largest in the nation. The total value of mining in Utah was $391 million in 1964 as compared with $248 million in 1954.

Manufacturing in Utah is largely dependent upon the state's mining and agricultural industries. About 40 per cent of the persons employed in manufacturing are concerned with the smelting, refining, or fabricating of minerals; more than 25 per cent are in some type of food or agricultural products processing. The greatest concentration of processing nonferrous metals is west and south of Salt Lake City. Geneva, one of the largest steel mills west of the Mississippi River, is on Utah Lake near Provo. Petroleum and chemical industries are also important to the state's manufacturing economy.

Transportation and Communications. The Salt Lake area is the hub of the state's transportation system, as well as of several transcontinental routes—those between Chicago, Denver, and San Francisco; between Los Angeles and Minneapolis; and between Seattle and Fort Worth. Highways and railroads wind through the rugged mountain topography of northeastern Utah and emerge into the Great Basin via canyons near Salt Lake City and Ogden, the major traffic centers. There are more than 2,000 miles of railroads in the state, the principal ones being the Union Pacific, the Western Pacific, the Southern Pacific (which crosses the northern part of Great Salt Lake via a long causeway), and the Denver and Rio Grande Western. Gas and oil lines feed into the Salt Lake area, with considerable amounts of refined oil products then being piped to the Pacific Northwest.

UTAH

The massive Osler's Castle is one of the numerous imposing structures found in the Bryce Canyon National Park. This sculpturing was a result of countless years of wind erosion.

The livestock on Utah's typically small farms consume approximately 70 per cent of the state's farm products. Above, a farm located in Salt Lake Valley.

The Bingham Utah Copper Mine is the largest in the United States. The copper is worked by electric shovels that scoop loosened rock into the ore trains that run along each tier.

A single road winds through La Sal Canyon, where a number of the state's uranium mines are located. Utah is one of the major uranium-producing states.

The Slaterville Diversion Dam, a part of the Weber Basin Project, restrains the flow of the Weber River. The high snow-capped Wasatch Mountains are seen in the background.

Petroleum is piped directly to Los Angeles. Much irrigation and drinking water in the state is transported by canal and pipeline. There are five daily newspapers, several dozen radio stations, and four television stations in Utah.

Tourist Attractions. Utah's chief tourist attractions are the Mormon Temple Grounds in Salt Lake City, the sites of prehistoric Indian ruins, pioneer trails and forts, and ghost mining towns. Hunting, fishing, skiing, hiking, auto racing on the Bonneville Salt flats, and water sports all attract their seasonal followers. Some of the better known scenic areas are Arches National Monument, a wilderness of unusual natural stone arches; Bryce Canyon National Park, with highly eroded, multicolored rock formations; Capitol Reef National Monument, a colorful cliff site eroded into majestic domes, spires, rock faces, and chasms; Cedar Breaks National Monument, an immense eroded amphitheater carved from a colorful high plateau; Dinosaur National Monument, which includes an in-place fossil exhibit and reconstructions of prehistoric monsters; Hovenweep National Monument, an area of prehistoric Indian dwellings and towers; Natural Bridges National Monument, which includes Indian cliff dwellings and three unusual stone bridges; Rainbow Bridge National Monument, containing one of the largest and most symmetrical stone arches in the world; Timpanoqos Cave National Monument, with a mountainside cavern of varied formations; and Zion National Park, the most popular of Utah parks, displaying huge, highly colored cliffs.   JERRY TUTTLE

GOVERNMENT

Utah is governed under the constitution, as amended, that came into operation when the state was admitted to the Union, Jan. 4, 1896. Proposals to amend the constitution may be introduced at regular sessions of the state legislature, and at special constitutional conventions. In the first instance, an amendment proposal must be approved by a two-thirds vote of the elected members of each house of the legislature and by a majority vote of those voting on the proposal at a statewide referendum. In the second instance, a constitutional convention may be called on the recommendation of two-thirds of the members of the two legislative houses and the approval of a majority of the voters voting at the next general election. Proposed changes must then be ratified by a majority vote at the next general election. Qualifications for voting in general elections in Utah are a minimum age of 21, U.S. citizenship for at least 90 days, and residence in the state for one year, the county for four months, and the election district for 60 days.

The Legislature consists of a Senate of 25 members elected for four years, and a House of Representatives of 64 members elected for two years. Regular sessions are held biennially beginning on the second Monday in January of odd-numbered years, and are limited to 60 days. The state constitution provides for initiative and referendum.

The Governor, who is elected by popular vote every four years, is the chief executive official. There is no limit on the number of terms he may serve. There is no lieutenant governor; in case of the death, removal from office, or incapacity of the governor the secretary of state serves as chief executive. Other elected officials aside from the governor include the secretary of state, the treasurer, the auditor, and the attorney general. The governor has a veto power, which extends to all legislation except laws enacted by the initiative and referendum.

The Judicial Authority is vested in a supreme court composed of five justices who are elected by popular vote for 10 years; in district courts each having from one to five judges elected for 6 years; and in municipal courts and justice-of-the-peace courts.

Utah sends two congressmen to the U.S. House of Representatives.

HISTORY

Early Inhabitants of Utah. Relics such as stone tools found on the Lake Bonneville flats indicate that humans lived in the Utah area before the Christian Era. By the first century B.C. the Anasazi, or Basketmaker, Indians had established a culture over a large region corresponding to much of southwestern United States, including southern Utah. In the sixteenth century the principal Indian tribes living in the Utah region were the Paiute, the Shoshoni, and the Ute. See ARCHAEOLOGY, American Archaeology, *Early Stone Age People;* PUEBLO, *Culture and Economy.*

European Exploration. García Lopez de Cárdenas, a lieutenant of the Spanish explorer, Francisco Vásquez de Coronado, who was then exploring the New Mexico region and the southern Great Plains, set out to the northwest, 1540, and reached the Colorado River in what is now Utah. He soon returned to the main expedition, and gave an unfavorable report of the Utah country; thus, although Spain claimed possession of the vast region, there was no further known exploration there for more than 200 years. Two Franciscan friars, Francisco Athanasio Domínguez and Silvestre Vélez de Escalante visited the region in search of a trail to California, 1776–77. The friars failed to find the trail, but later Spanish hunting and trading parties crossed the southern Utah region and established the Old Spanish Trail from Santa Fe to Los Angeles (see SANTA FE TRAIL). Little was known of the region north of the trail, and the new Republic of Mexico, which claimed the former Spanish territory after 1822, neglected to explore it.

In the meantime, however, trappers and explorerscouts from Canada and the United States such as Étienne Provot, Jedediah S. Smith, Peter Skene Ogden, and James Bridger had begun to penetrate the region. Bridger visited Great Salt Lake, 1824, and at about the same time a Missourian, William H. Ashley, of the Rocky Mountain Fur Company, followed the lower end of the Green River. Expeditions by a Franco-American soldier-explorer, Capt. B. L. E. Bonneville, 1832–36, and U.S. Army Lt. John C. Frémont, 1842–43, were the first to leave permanent records. Frémont named a lake and river for the Ute Indians, whose name he Anglicized as "Utah." The first wagon train crossed, 1841, the northern part of the region on its way to California. See OVERLAND TRAILS, *Western Trails.*

Mormon Settlement. The first persons of European descent to settle the region were the Mormons, a group who had fled from Nauvoo, Ill. to escape religious intolerance. They had crossed the Great Plains and Rocky Mountains in search of a place outside the jurisdiction of the United States where they might worship as they pleased. In July, 1847, a band of 147 Mormons, led by Brigham Young, settled at the foot of the Wasatch Mountains near the southeastern shore of Great Salt Lake. They were joined a few months later by another party numbering 1,500, and before winter the refugees had planted a crop and had built a stockade and a number of adobe houses. The settlement was named Salt Lake City. Within a few years the Mormon settlements in the area had become relatively prosperous, and according to a census taken at Young's direction, 1850, there were 11,350 persons living in the region. Within a year after the arrival of the first Mormons, sovereignty over the Utah area had been transferred from Mexico to the United States by the Treaty of Guadalupe Hidalgo, which ended the Mexican War.

The California Gold Rush of 1849 ended the Mormons' relative isolation as non-Mormons, whom the Mormons categorically called "gentiles", crossed the territory on their way to California. That year the Mormons organized a government over a territory approximating the Mexican Cession, except for California, and petitioned Congress to admit it as a state. They named the proposed state "Deseret," after a

UTAH

Mount Timpanogos, seen from Lake Utah, is the monarch of the Wasatch Range. The range extends from Idaho to central Utah, and forms the southernmost portion of the Rockies.

Intermountain Indian School in Brigham City, once an army hospital, is a boarding school for reservation youngsters.

Cove Fort, a walled ranch constructed 1867, was built by Brigham Young to protect the settlers from Indian attack.

The Manti Morman Temple, completed in 1888 at the cost of the then astronomical sum of $1,000,000, was erected on a site dedicated by Brigham Young shortly before he died.

U.S. 91, running north-south through Utah, is the most traveled road in the state. Here it passes through a valley in the Wasatch Range.

word in the Book of Mormon meaning "honeybee." Congress refused to approve statehood, however, largely because of opposition to polygamous marriage, a practice sanctioned by the Mormons, and instead organized the area as the Territory of Utah, 1850; Salt Lake City was made territorial capital, and Brigham Young was named territorial governor.

Relations with the federal government were seriously strained by Mormon opposition to federal laws that conflicted with the doctrines of their church and the authority of their leaders. Apart from the question of polygamy, for example, the Mormon communal system of land ownership conflicted with federal law on the distribution of land titles in the territories. There were occasional violent clashes between Mormons and non-Mormons, and by 1850, federal-Mormon relations had reached a point near open rebellion (see MOUNTAIN MEADOWS MASSACRE). Except for a few Mormon raids on U.S. Army supply trains, however, there was little violence, and Salt Lake City was peacefully occupied, 1850, by an Army force commanded by Col. Albert Sidney Johnston. The troops remained in Utah until the outbreak of the Civil War, 1861.

Statehood. Although federal control had been established the continued pro-polygamy stand of the Mormon Church resulted in Congress turning down several petitions by Utah for statehood even after Nevada and Wyoming, with smaller populations, had been admitted to the Union. After Mormon church property had been confiscated by the federal government, the church reversed its stand on plural marriage, 1890, and a constitutional convention in the territory drafted a state constitution (1895) that included provisions, as demanded by the U.S. Congress, guaranteeing freedom of religion, forbidding sectarian control of public schools, and prohibiting polygamy. The constitution also granted women the right to vote. Finally, on Jan. 4, 1896, Utah was admitted to the Union as the 45th state.

In the meantime, the area of Utah had been greatly reduced; the organization of Colorado Territory, 1861, changed the eastern boundary to its present location; later the northeast corner of Utah was made part of Wyoming, and the western boundary was moved to form Nevada. The University of Utah was established, 1850, at Salt Lake City and the same year the territory's first newspaper, *The Deseret Evening News*, was established. The joining of the Union Pacific and the Central Pacific railroads at Promontory Point on Great Salt Lake, May 10, 1869, marked the beginning of trans-continental rail service in North America.

Even after it was admitted to the Union, the association of Utah and Mormonism in the minds of many Americans continued to set Utah apart from other states. The U.S. House of Representatives refused, 1899, to seat Utah Congressman Brigham H. Roberts, a Mormon and a polygamist; Reed Smoot, an apostle of the Mormon Church, was elected to the U.S. Senate, 1903, but nearly four years elapsed before he was seated. Anti-Utah feeling in the country diminished during World War I when the state contributed more than 21,000 men and millions of dollars to the war effort.

Although Brigham Young and other early Mormon leaders favored agriculture over mining as a means of livelihood, the mining industry became an important factor in Utah's economy almost from the outset of settlement there. Coal, lead, and iron were mined during the 1850's, and the opening of new markets by the railroads in the 1870's resulted in a great extension of mining activity. The open-out system of extracting copper, developed early in the twentieth century, further boosted the state's mining industry.

BIBLIOG.–J. Cecil Alter, *Utah: The Storied Domain*, 3 vols. (1932); American Guide Series, *Utah: A Guide to the State* (1954); Leonard J. Arrington, *Great Basin Kingdom: An Economic History of the Latter-day Saints, 1830–1900* (1958); Hubert H. Bancroft, *History of Utah* (1890); Robert N. Baskin, *Reminiscences of Early Utah* (1914); Juanita Brooks, *Mountain Meadows Massacre* (1951); Leland H. Creer, *Founding of an Empire: The Exploration and Colonization of Utah, 1776–1856* (1947); John H. Evans, *Story of Utah, the Beehive State* (1933); Norman F. Furniss, *Mormon Conflict, 1850–1859* (1960); LeRoy R. Hafen and Ann W. Hafen, eds., *Utah Expedition, 1857–1858* (1958); Milton R. Hunter, *Utah in Her Western Setting* (1943), *Utah, the Story of Her People, 1540–1947* (1946); George W. James, *Utah, the Land of Blossoming Valleys* (1922); Clyde Kluckhohn, *Beyond the Rainbow* (1933); J. Roderic Korns, ed., *West from Fort Bridger, the Pioneering of the Immigrant Trails Across Utah, 1846–1850* (1951); Gustive O. Larson, *Prelude to the Kingdom: Mormon Desert Conquest* (1947); *Outline History of Utah and the Mormons* (1958); Reuben D. Law, *Utah School System: Its Organization and Administration* (1952); Willard Luce and Celia Luce, *Utah Past and Present* (1955); Andrew L. Neff, *History of Utah, 1847–1869* (1940); El Roy Nelson, *Utah's Economic Patterns* (1956); Elvind T. Scoyen and Frank J. Taylor, *Rainbow Canyons* (1931); Wallace Stegner, *Mormon Country* (1942); Wain Sutton, ed., *Utah, a Centennial History*, 3 vols. (1949); Utah. Laws, Statutes, etc., *Utah Code, Annotated, 1953* (1952); Utah. University. Bureau of Economic and Business Research, *Statistical Review of Utah's Economy* (1960); Utah Foundation, *State and Local Government in Utah* (1954); Noble Warrum, *History of Utah Since Statehood*, 3 vols. (1919); Maurine Whipple, *This is the Place: Utah* (1945); Orson F. Whitney, *History of Utah*, 4 vols. (1892–1904), *History of Utah* (1916); Levi E. Young, *Founding of Utah* (1923).

UTAH, UNIVERSITY OF, a public coeducational institution of higher learning located at Salt Lake City, Utah. The school was founded, 1850, as the University of Deseret, but was renamed the University of Utah, 1892, four years before the state was admitted to the Union. The school's divisions and their founding dates are as follows: college of mines and mineral industries, 1901; college of engineering, 1901; college of education, 1911; library science division, 1912; college of law, 1913; college of business, 1922; graduate school of social work, 1937; the college of medicine, 1942; graduate school, 1946, and the colleges of pharmacy, 1946, fine arts, 1947, nursing, 1948, and letters and science, 1957. The university conducts a summer workshop for writers, and an institute of government and an institute of world affairs, both of which hold special workshops and conferences. Among special collections in the university library are those on Mormon and Utah history, UN and U.S. government documents, the Leichtentritt Collection of music scores, and various materials of Eliza B. Young and John A. Widtsoe. See COLLEGES AND UNIVERSITIES.

UTAH LAKE, a fresh-water lake, Utah, in Utah County, 30 miles SE of the Great Salt Lake, into which it discharges by the Jordan River. It has a length of 25 miles from north to south, an extreme width of 13 miles, and an area of 150 square miles, which makes it the largest body of fresh water in the state. Provo is near its eastern shore.

UTAH TOURIST & PUBLICITY COUNCIL

Delicate Arch in Arches National Monument in southeastern Utah spans 65 feet and is 85 feet in height.

UTAH STATE UNIVERSITY, a coeducational, landgrant college founded in 1888 and known as Utah Agricultural College until 1929, when it was renamed Utah State Agricultural College; the name was changed to Utah State University in 1957. The main campus is at Logan, Utah, with branches at Cedar City (College of Southern Utah) and Ephraim (Snow College). Instruction began in 1890, and most of the schools and colleges in the university were opened early in the 1900's. Among the university divisions are the colleges of agriculture, business and social sciences, education; engineering, family life, forest, range, and wildlife management, and the University College. The school conducts an annual Agriculture-Industry Conference, and carries on research programs for the study of water, nutrition, metabolism, soil, and natural resources. Graduate degrees are offered in most of the biological, physical, and social sciences, and in some of the educational, industrial, and professional divisions. See COLLEGES AND UNIVERSITIES.

UTE, a member of a group of tribes belonging to the original Shoshoni family, first found in the extreme southwestern part of Colorado, eastern Utah, and northern New Mexico. In culture the Utes belonged to the marginal Plains group; they were chiefly hunters and gatherers of wild plant foods, and were habitually nomadic, living in brush shelters and Tepees. They used horses, dressed in skins of deer and antelope, and maintained a Sun Dance and many other customs of the other Plains Indians. The name occurs in other tribe designations, such as Gosiutes, Pai-utes, and so forth, who lived farther west in the deserts of Utah and Nevada. They first signed a treaty with the United States in 1849. Several campaigns were made against them late in the 1870's and early in the 1880's, before they were permanently settled on reservations. The tribe now has a reservation near Ignacio, La Plata County, Colorado, where they number about 1,000. See UTO-AZTECAN FAMILY; SHOSHONI.   CLARK WISSLER

BIBLIOG.–David F. Aberle and Omer C. Stewart, *Navaho and Ute Peyotism: A Chronological and Distributional Study* (1957); Herbert E. Bolton, *Pageant in the Wilderness* (1950); Edward E. Dale, *Indians of the Southwest: A Century of Development Under the United States* (1949); Helen S. Daniels, comp., *Ute Indians of Southwestern Colorado* (1941); Richard I. Dodge, *Our Wild Indians: Thirty-three Years' Personal Experience Among the Red Men of the Great West* (1959); Jacob P. Dunn, *Massacres of the Mountains: A History of the Indian Wars of the Far West, 1815–1875* (1958); Robert Emmitt, *Last War Trail: The Utes and the Settlement of Colorado* (1954); Frederick W. Hodge, ed., *Handbook of the American Indians* (Bureau of American Ethnology Bulletin No. 30, Part 2) (1910); M. Wilson Rankin, *Reminiscences of Frontier Days: Including an Authentic Account of the Thornburg and Meeker Massacre* (1935); Wilson Rockwell, *Utes: A Forgotten People* (1956); Hazen G. Shinn, *Shoshonean Days* (1941); Matthew G. Sniffen, *Meaning of the Ute War* (1915); Marshall Sprague, *Massacre: The Tragedy at White River* (1957); Omer C. Stewart, *Culture Element Distribution: Northern Paiute* (1941); Paul I. Wellman, *Death on Horseback* (1934); Robert M. Zingg, *Reconstruction of Uto-Aztekan History* (1939).

UTERUS. See REPRODUCTIVE SYSTEM.

UTGARD, in Scandinavian mythology, the chief city of Jötunnheim, the land of the giants, which was located along the cold and chaotic shores of the outer world. Utgard was reigned over by Skrymir, who was also known as Utgard-Loki, or Magus of Utgard.

UTICA, city, central New York, a seat of Oneida County, on the Mohawk River and the New York State Barge Canal; on the Lackawanna and the New York Central railroads; on the New York State Thruway, 80 miles NW of Albany.

The city is in a rich dairying and agricultural region. It is an important center for the manufacture of electronics equipment; tools, metal products, aircraft parts and other transport equipment, refrigeration units, air conditioners, and a wide variety of textile goods are also manufactured.

The city is the site of Utica College, a branch of Syracuse University. Utica is the site of a state hospital for the insane, and the state Masonic home. The Munson-Williams-Proctor Institute houses an art collection and also has an art school; the Oneida historical building has a collection of relics. The site of Utica was part of Cosby's Manor, a grant of land made by King George II of England on which the British built Fort Schuyler, 1758; the fort was abandoned a few years before the first settlers arrived at the site, 1773. The completion of the Erie Canal, 1825, stimulated the early growth of Utica, which was incorporated as a city in 1832. Pop. (1960) 100,410.

UTICA, ancient city, N Africa, on the Mediterranean Coast, about 15 miles NW of Carthage. As one of the earliest Phoenician settlements in North Africa, Utica is traditionally to have been founded in ?1100 B.C. It was sometimes a rival of Carthage, sometimes an ally. Utica was captured by Agathocles of Syracuse during his invasion of Africa, ?310 B.C. In the Punic Wars, Utica supported Rome, and after the destruction of Carthage, 146 B.C. it became the capital of the Roman province of Africa. During the period of civil war in Rome, Utica was a center of support for Pompey the Great and of the opposition to Julius Caesar; after Pompey's defeat, Utica was a rallying point for the forces under Cato the Younger, who finally committed suicide at Utica in the face of Caesar's continued success. Utica was a free city under Caesar and was favored by Augustus and Hadrian. The city was taken by the Vandals under Gaiseric, 439, retaken by the Byzantines, 534, and captured by the Arabs, 698, after which the city's population was scattered. Excavations on the site have revealed an amphitheater, baths, theater, fortifications, and aqueducts.

UTILITARIANISM, a system of ethical thought based upon the idea that the greatest happiness for the greatest number of persons is the ultimate good and the sole valid criterion of morality and ethics. According to the utilitarians, "happiness" and "good" are one and the same, namely, pleasure as judged by the individual who experiences it; conventional ethical or social standards are arbitrary, fortuitous, and irrelevant. Thus, "good" is identified with any and all personal motivation, whether it be for conflict or peace, for mental or aesthetic pleasure, for indulgence of the physical appetites or self-denial, or for the pleasure of self-assertion or self-abnegation.

The philosophical aspects of rational freedom as incorporated in utilitarianism were first set down by a clergyman, Richard Cumberland (1631-1718), in his *De legibus naturae*, in which he criticized the earlier philosophy of Thomas Hobbes, who had conceived of the state as a supreme authority that compels man to restrict his hedonistic pleasure seeking, and to which man owes blind obedience. *De legibus naturae* and some later utilitarianist writings were concerned with theological versus secular rule and law as governing man, but David Hume's *Inquiry Concerning the Principles of Morals*, (1751) divorced utilitarianism from theological considerations.

During the eighteenth and nineteenth centuries the reaction of the political economists against state control led to the adoption of utilitarianism as an ethical basis for the principle of laissez faire (see LAISSEZ FAIRE). Jeremy Bentham in seeking a philosophical doctrine that might serve as an objective critical basis for determining public policy and polity, found a solution in Hume's *Essays;* to Bentham it seemed an obvious step from the acceptance of Hume's idea that the individual is the best judge of his own good, to the political theory that maximum freedom (that is, lack of state control) points the way to the greatest good for the greatest number. James Mill, John Stuart Mill, and other laissez faire economists elaborated the theory.

In the nineteenth century, utilitarianism was influenced by certain principles of biology then current;

accordingly pleasure was defined as nature's guide toward physiological health and beneficial evolutionary change. In his *Data of Ethics* (1879), Herbert Spencer formulated certain principles of freedom on a biological-economic basis, and contributed to utilitarianism the so-called quantitative theory of freedom, according to which the prime desideratum is the maximum freedom of any individual that is compatible with equal freedom for all other individuals. During the same period, the marginal utility economists worked out a mechanistic rationale of utilitarian doctrine as applied to economics; the gist of their argument was that good is pleasure, that each pleasure can motivate conduct in direct proportion to its relative intensity to other pleasures, and that desire for a given pleasure decreases compared to desire for other pleasures as more of it is enjoyed (see MARGINAL UTILITY). From this it was deduced that an individual's freedom of choice insures that he will so act as to obtain the maximum pleasure for himself; from this it seemed to follow that voluntary relations among individuals will inevitably result in the greatest good for all. It was assumed, of course, that these principles governed the activities of bargain and exchange upon the open market by which human beings maximize the satisfaction of their economic wants.

Utilitarianism has been criticized on the grounds that it conceives of pleasure and pain as abstract entities; that the doctrine of a direct cause and effect relationship between desire and conduct is psychologically artificial; and that its conception of man's freedom is superficial and mechanical, as is the equating of psychological and ethical hedonism.

UTITZ, EMIL, 1883-   , German aesthetician and philospher, was born in Prague. He was educated at the universities of Prague, Munich, and Leipzig, and taught at the universities of Rostock and Halle. In his aesthetic studies, Utitz was influenced by the phenomonology of Edmund Husserl (see HUSSERL, EDMUND GUSTAV ALBRECHT; PHENOMONOLOGY). Among his principal works are *Grundzüge der aestetischen Farbenlehre* (1908), *Grundlegung der allegemeinen Kunstwissenschaft* (2 vols., 1914-20), *Charakterologie* (1925), *Geschicte der Aesthetik* (1932), and *Mensch und Kultur* (1933).

UTO-AZTECAN FAMILY, a group of North American Indian languages. Early in the twentieth century linguists became aware that several of the original families of Indian languages had been erroneously treated as independent, whereas they were clearly members of a single family. Ultimately it was agreed that the old families of Shoshoni, Pimas, and Aztecs were a single family to which the name Uto-Aztecan was applied. Later the Kiowas, Tanoan, Zuni, and the surviving Mayas of Yucatan were announced as additional members. Thus is recognized a widely distributed family with great diversities of culture as between the great Maya and Aztecan civilizations on the one hand and the lowly Digger Indians of Nevada on the other. There is still some controversy as to the last of these additions to the family.   CLARK WISSLER

UTOPIA, from the Greek *ou* (no), *topos* (a place), and *ia*, a suffix expressing region—hence, "no place" —is an imaginary place of ideal perfection; and, by extension, an impractical scheme of total social reform. The term was coined by Sir Thomas More as a title for a book, *Utopia*, (1516), actually a criticism of English society. More was well aware of the likelihood that if his ideal commonwealth were to come into being, it would be unlivable, and probably little better than the society he was satirizing. Many other creators of utopias-in-print, however, actually hoped and even expected that their proposals might be put into practice. Hence, the term *utopia* and its derivatives came to be used as words of scorn for programs of social reform.

Utopian writings are of two general types, according to whether the ideal place is dislocated temporally or spacially. Utopian works, properly speaking, are those in which the reader is told of an ideal society that is said to exist "now" in some remote part of the world, or perhaps on another planet. Other works, however, transport the reader to another time, usually the remote past or future; such works are more properly called "uchronias" (no time) rather than utopias, but in general usage *utopia* is applied to them.

More's *Utopia* begins with a denunciation of the prevailing penal legislation in England and the tendency toward enclosures (see ENCLOSURE MOVEMENT). The rest of the book is devoted to the description of Utopia, an imaginary island where politics, law, and social life are "perfect." The island has an absolute monarchy; its goods are shared by the community; there is no money or crime; the citizens are peaceful, live a simple existence; religious tolerance is the rule. Plato's *Republic*, also a scheme for an ideal society, was a prime influence on More's work. Tomasso Campanella's *City of the Sun* (1623) is a utopia built around a society led by the Catholic hierarchy. Francis Bacon's *New Atlantis* (1626) stresses the role of technology in bringing about the happiness of society. James Harrington's *Oceana* (1656) elaborates a political utopia in the form of a romance. Jonathan Swift's *Gulliver's Travels* is the most famous of utopian satires. See GULLIVER'S TRAVELS; REPUBLIC.

The nineteenth century saw the publication of a number of utopian writings, some favoring radical social and economic doctrines. The most famous of these are Etienne Cabet's *Voyage en Icarie* (1848); Samuel Butler's satirical books about "nowhere" spelled (almost) backwards, *Erewhon* (1872) and *Erewhon Revisited* (1901); Edward Bellamy's *Looking Backward* (1888); and William Morris' *News from Nowhere* (1891). See COMMUNAL SETTLEMENTS.

In the twentieth century, H. G. Wells wrote several seemingly utopianistic works, but there is good reason to believe that Wells' intention was more satirical than not. Aldous Huxley's *Brave New World* (1932) depicted a grim utopia (actually a uchronia) based on the inventions of the biological sciences; during the later 1940's and after Huxley wrote a number of rueful pieces to the effect that most of the worst things that he had envisaged for the distant future had already taken place or seemed about to do so. His first positive utopian novel, *Island*, was published in 1962. George Orwell's *1984* (1949) was a literal, if somewhat hyperbolic, description of life in a technologically controlled state.

UTRECHT, province, Netherlands, S of the Zuider Zee, and bounded by the provinces of Gelderland on the E, North Brabant on the S, and South and North Holland on the W; area 527 sq. mi.; pop. (1961) 697,450. The western part of the province has clay lands; the northwest part, low fens; the east, sand and gravel; and the south, a fertile soil. Kaiser Wilhelm II, of Germany, following World War I, spent the rest of his life at Doorn. The capital and largest town is Utrecht; the only other town of size is Amersfoort. A bishopric, which included most of the present provincial area, was established in 722. During the fifteenth century the area came under the control of the Duke of Burgundy, and later under that of the Holy Roman emperor, Charles V. In 1559 Utrecht became one of the seven provinces on the Protestant side which signed the Union of Utrecht (1579) against Spain.

UTRECHT, Dutch Oude Trecht (Old Ford), city, the Netherlands, capital of the province of Utrecht; 22 miles SSE of Amsterdam. The old town is bordered by the Singel Canal and intersected by several others which connect it with the Rhine River and the Zuider Zee. Utrecht is a road, water, and rail transportation center. There is trade in velvets, carpets, cottons, chemicals, tobacco, and linens; the chief manufactures are tobacco, chemicals, bricks, and beer.

NETHERLANDS INFORMATION BUR.

The Oudegracht is one of the two main canals that cross the city of Utrecht. The Gothic Cathedral Tower, dating from the fourteenth century, is seen on the right bank.

Noteworthy Buildings in Utrecht are many. Especially important is the Cathedral of St. Martin (1254-67), which marks the site of the church of St. Willibrord (Apostle to the Frisians), built in 720. The nave was destroyed in a storm, 1674, but the 321-foot tower, the transepts, and the lofty choir still stand. St. Martin's has a carillon of 42 bells, the largest of which weighs eight and one-half tons. This cathedral is the seat of the Dutch Old Catholics, who seceded from the Roman Catholic church, 1723. St. Catherine, the Roman Catholic cathedral, of late Gothic architecture, restored in the twentieth century, dates from 1524. St. Jans Church (1050), has a late Gothic choir built in 1539. The university was established in 1636 and enlarged in 1894. The Pope's House (1517) was built by Adrian Thoriszoon Boeyens, who subsequently became pope as Adrian VI. The royal mint of the Netherlands is also in Utrecht, as are the antiquarian and the archiepiscopal museums.

History. Utrecht became important with the establishment there of the See of St. Willibrord. The security offered by the fortifications built to protect the town against the attacks of Frisian and Northmen attracted many residents. When Bishop Balderic ascended the episcopal throne, 819, the city had just been sacked by the Northmen. The bishop succeeded in driving them out, the walls were repaired, and the city prospered. The temporal power of the bishops ended with the sale, 1527, of these rights by Bishop Henry of Bavaria to the Holy Roman Emperor, Charles V. Utrecht took a leading part in the revolt of the Netherlands against Spain; and the union of the seven northern provinces, proclaimed from Utrecht, 1579, led to Dutch independence. Utrecht was taken by the Germans early in World War II and was held by them throughout most of the war, but suffered little damage. Pop. (1959) 252,104.

UTRECHT, TREATY OF, a series of agreements made at Utrecht, United Netherlands, 1713, that provided for ending the War of the Spanish Succession, 1701-13. The war had involved France and Spain as allies against a loose coalition of Austria and

the states of the Holy Roman Empire, England (after 1707, Great Britain), the United Netherlands, Portugal, Prussia, and Savoy. By 1711 the war had reached a virtual stalemate, and at last, in January, 1712, the adversaries met at Utrecht to negotiate a settlement. By the end of the summer, when King Philip V of Spain renounced his claim to the French crown, the main issue over which the war had started was resolved, but the war had subsequently involved substantial territorial and commercial issues as well, and so negotiations continued. See SUCCESSION WARS, *The War of the Spanish Succession.*

On Apr. 11, 1713, France signed separate treaties with Great Britain, the United Netherlands, Savoy, Prussia, and Portugal. In the British treaty, France agreed to the permanent separation of the French and Spanish crowns, recognized the Protestant House of Hanover as the rightful claimant to the British crown as opposed to the claim of the Roman Catholic house of Stuart, agreed to destroy its fortifications at Dunkirk, and ceded to Great Britain the Hudson's Bay country, Newfoundland, Nova Scotia, and St. Kitts. From Great Britain, France received Cape Breton and Prince Edward Islands and fishing privileges off the coast of Newfoundland. In the Dutch treaty, France ceded the forts on the French-Dutch border and the provinces of the Spanish Netherlands, the latter to be given in turn to Austria pending a later settlement between France and Great Britain. By the terms of the other treaties Savoy received Nice and the island of Sicily, Prussia received Neuchâtel and parts of Gelderland, France received the principality of Orange on the Rhône River, and Portugal's sovereignty in Brazil was recognized. In addition, the French treaties with Great Britain and the United Netherlands each contained a most-favored-nation commercial clause.

On July 13, 1713, Great Britain and Spain signed a treaty by which Spain recognized the dynastic provisions of the British-French treaty, ceded Gibraltar and Menorca to Great Britain, and granted Great Britain permission to supply Spanish-American colonies with 4,800 Negro slaves annually for 30 years. In 1714 Austria and France signed treaties at the German town of Rastatt, March 7, and at the Swiss town of Baden, September 7. They first provided for Austrian sovereignty over the Spanish Netherlands, Milan, Naples, and Sardinia, the second established the Rhine River as the boundary between France and the Holy Roman Empire. No formal treaty was concluded between Austria and Spain because the former would not recognize the succession of Philip V to the Spanish throne.

UTRILLO, MAURICE, 1883–1955, French painter, was born in Paris, the illegitimate son of the artist and model, Suzanne Valadon (1865–1938). The man, who was probably his father, disappeared shortly after Maurice was born, and the mother married, 1891, a Spanish artist, Miguel Utrillo, who gave the boy his surname. The young Utrillo lived a wild, uninhibited life, becoming a confirmed alcoholic early in his teens. His life was spent largely in cafes, hospitals, asylums, prisons, and occasional visits to his mother and grandmother. His first drawings and paintings, done only because his mother had convinced him that such work would prove a remedy to his alcoholic ills, were executed without enthusiasm. From the outset, however, his work showed great originality. During the period 1902–04, he produced more than 150 paintings, many of which were later to be regarded as masterpieces. During his so-called White Period, 1909–14, many hundreds of paintings that were later to grace the walls of the world's museums, were sold for just enough to buy Utrillo a few drinks and a night's lodging. Utrillo's mental health steadily declined, and he was interned in asylums numerous times between 1912 and the middle 1920's. Even in confinement, however, he continued to paint —but not as well: by some freak of circumstance, the

COURTESY, MUSEUM OF FINE ARTS. BOSTON

Sacré Cœur de Montmartre et Rue Saint-Rustique
(Detail) by Maurice Utrillo

quality of his art declined as his health improved. In the late 1920's and early 1930's he was a man of temperate habits, married and respectable, and was honored and acclaimed around the world, but he was no longer an artist of genius. Although he never ceased painting, he produced few if any truly significant works during his last two decades of life.

Utrillo's Art. Utrillo learned the rudiments of painting from his mother, a latter-day member of the Impressionist school, and impressionism significantly influenced his early work (see IMPRESSIONISM). Using a palette knife as a trowel, Utrillo applied colors like a mason working with cement, giving his paintings of buildings a zestful yet ominous feel of reality. While sometimes influenced by the cubism of Pablo Picasso and Georges Braque, Utrillo's most effective work was independent of any school. He painted the streets, quays, façades, cathedrals, lanes, and courtyards of Paris with the sure hand and consistent vision of one who seemed to see the things around him as though for the first time with the eyes of a child, discovering in each old building, in each dreary or sunny avenue, its native wonder and simplicity. Utrillo saw people as dwarfed by architecture, and the theme of human isolation was common in his work.

BIBLIOG.–Maurice Utrillo, *Utrillo: Portfolio with Text* (Skira edition); Alfred Werner, *Maurice Utrillo* (1952).

UTTAR PRADESH, state, N India, bounded by Nepal, Tibet, and Himachal Pradesh Territory on the N and Delhi Territory on the W, and by the states of Bihar on the E, Madhya Pradesh on the S, and Rajasthan and Punjab on the W; area 113,400 sq. mi. The capital is Lucknow.

Physical Features. Uttar Pradesh is drained by the Ganges River system and is crossed by the Himalaya Mountains in the north. The mountains have many peaks with an elevation of more than 20,000 feet; the highest is Nanda Devi (25,645 ft.). Glaciers extend down the slopes of the higher ridges; narrow passes such as Niti, Dharma, and Mana La lead northward into Tibet. The foothills south of the Himalayas have an average elevation of 6,000 feet. The many narrow valleys descend into an area covered with extensive talus fans. The Ganges River valley, which covers the bulk of the state, is a broad, flat plain drained by a dense network of tributaries, chief of which are the Gogra, the Gumti, and the Jumna. In the Himalaya foothills the climate is hot and sultry in summer and cool in winter. Precipitation varies from an annual average of 50 inches bordering the plain, to 100 inches on some of the mountain slopes; winter snow is common in areas above 4,000 feet. In the plains the temperatures average 55°F in winter and 90°F in summer. Rainfall averages 35 inches per year, mainly during the summer. Forests are concentrated in the foothills. On the mountain slopes, up to 10,000 feet, rhododendron and forests of evergreen

oak are found; higher up, conifers predominate.

Social Features. The inhabitants of Uttar Pradesh are mostly Hindu, with a small Muslim minority. The predominant language is Hindi. The chief city is Lucknow; other principal cities are Kanpur, Agra, Varanasi, Allahabad, Meerut, Bareilly, Moradabad, Saharanpur, Dehra Dun, Aligarh, and Rampur.

There are nine universities, 150 colleges, and almost 40,000 secondary schools in the state. Nevertheless, the literacy rate is only about 28 per cent for males and 8 per cent for females.

Economic Features. The Ganges Valley in Uttar Pradesh is one of the most highly cultivated regions of India; much of the land is double-cropped, with one harvest in autumn and one in spring. Wheat is the dominant crop in the drier west, where irrigation is used. Rice predominates in the more humid east. Other important food crops are jowar, bajra, gram, and corn. Sugarcane is important in the northwestern section of the plain.

Industry is little developed in Uttar Pradesh. There are a few sugar refineries and oilseed factories. Kanpur is one of India's chief centers for manufacture of consumer goods, especially textiles and leather goods. Agra, Varanasi, and Lucknow are centers for the manufacture of luxury goods such as jewelry, silks, gold and silver embroideries, and ivory products.

History. From antiquity, the region corresponding to modern Uttar Pradesh has been a major center of Indian culture. The Aryans, who settled there sometime during the second millennium B.C., developed the Sanskrit language and Brahmanism, forerunner of the Hindu religion. The sage Gautama Buddha (563?–483? B.C.), spent much of his life in the region. During the first millennium of the Christian era, the region, whose principal political division was known as Oudh, was ruled by Hindu princes, the most notable family being the Gupta. The period of Gupta rule, A.D. 320–535?, was marked as a "golden age" of art, literature, and science. Beginning in the twelfth century, Muslim invaders from Afghanistan and other parts of Central Asia gained political control over the area, but the Hindu religion remained predominant.

Agra was the capital of the Mogul empire, 1526–1658, and the Taj Mahal, a mausoleum built by Mogul Emperor Shah Jahan (1592–1666), is thought to represent the age of Indo-Persian architectural practice. As Mogul power declined during the seventeenth and eighteenth centuries, the empire's provincial governors (nawabs) became sovereign over their respective provinces. They in turn, by treaty or conquest, were brought under the administration of the British East India Company, which from 1600 had engaged in trade in India. In 1858 the nawabs came under the direct sovereignty of the British government. Oudh and Agra were subsequently made a single administrative unit, and in 1902 named the United Provinces of Agra and Oudh. The Government of India Act (1935) gave the provinces a responsible local government and renamed them the United Provinces.

During the 1940's, Jawaharlal Nehru, a native of the area, became the leading exponent of Indian nationalism, and when independence from Great Britain was achieved in 1947, he became the first premier of the new nation. Under the Indian constitution (1950), several princely states, including Banaras, Rampur, and Tehri were joined with the United Provinces to form a single state, Uttar Pradesh. (For population see India map in Atlas.)

BIBLIOG.–Paul R. Brass, *Factional Politics in an Indian State* (1965).

UUSIMAA, southernmost department of Finland, bounded on the S by the Gulf of Finland, and by the departments of Kymi on the E, Häme and Mikkeli on the N, and Turku-Pori on the W; area of the department 4,435 square miles. The department is low-lying, with 10 to 20 per-cent swampland and 60 per-cent forest. Uusimaa was originally settled by Swedes, who called it Nyland, and Swedish influence is still strong. The capital of the department is Helsinki.

UVALDE, city, S Texas, seat of Uvalde County; on the Missouri Pacific and the Southern Pacific railroads and U.S. highways 83 and 90; 80 miles WSW of San Antonio. The city's name is a corruption of the name of Juan de Ugalde, Spanish military leader who, in 1790, defeated the Apaches in what is now Uvalde Canyon. Settled in 1853 by cattlemen, Uvalde was protected by nearby Fort Inge, although Indian raids continued until the 1880's. Located in an important goat-ranching region, Uvalde is nationally important for large shipments of mohair. Cattle, sheep, and wool are also marketed. The city's chief industry is the processing of pecans. Uvalde was the home of John Nance Garner, U.S. vice-president, 1933–41. Pop. (1960) 10,293.

UVULA. See PALATE.

UWAJIMA, city, Japan, Shikoku, Ehime Prefecture, on the Bungo Passage to the Inland Sea. Behind the city lies a height reaching 4,033 feet, around which a rail line swings between Uwajima and the copper-mining town of Yoshinobu. During World War II U.S. bombs destroyed about half of Uwajima. Pop. (1955) 66,154.

UXBRIDGE, town, S Massachusetts, in Worcester County; on the Blackstone River and the New York, New Haven and Hartford Railroad; 30 miles SW of Boston and 4 miles N of the Rhode Island border, in an area of dairy and truck farms and orchards. Uxbridge was incorporated under that name in 1727. There is a granite quarry close at hand, but the town is better known for textiles. Pop. (1960) 7,789.

UXBRIDGE, market town and urban district, England, in Middlesex, on the Colne River near the Grand Junction Canal, about 15 miles from London. There are flour and sawmills, engineering works, and coal and timber docks. In 1645, indecisive negotiations between Charles I and the Parliamentarians were carried on in the Treaty House, a part of which still remains. Pop. (1951) 55,944.

UXMAL, ruined city, Mexico, in the state of Yucatán, about 49 miles S of Mérida. Uxmal has magnificent ruins of arches, terraces, and temples which are said to have been used by the Indians until the end of the sixteenth century. Casa del Governador, the best preserved building is narrow, 322 feet in length and ornamented with a sculptured frieze. The abandonment of the city, some time after the Spanish conquest, is thought to have been caused by bad drainage and other unhealthful conditions, together with a diminishing food supply.

UZBEK SOVIET SOCIALIST REPUBLIC, or Uzbekistan, one of the 15 constituent republics of the Soviet Union; in central Asia, bounded on the N and NW by the Kazakh S.S.R. and the Aral Sea, on the

SOVFOTO

An intricately planned park in the city of Tashkent, the capital city of the Uzbek S.S.R., is one of the favorite gathering places for the many factory workers in the area.

E by the Kirgiz S.S.R., on the SE by the Tadjik S.S.R., on the S by Afghanistan, and on the SW by the Turkmen S.S.R.; extends in a serpentine shape 900 miles E–W and averages 150 miles in width; area 157,500 sq. mi.; pop. (1959) 8,113,000. Uzbekistan is divided into several regions and the Kara-Kalpak Autonomous S.S.R. Tashkent, the capital, is the largest city in all Soviet Asia.

Physical Features. Much of the republic is a plain, whose elevation rises from the delta of the Amu Darya along the Aral Sea in the northwest to the 15,000-foot-high outliers of the Tien Shan in the southeast. Uzbekistan, especially in the western and central areas, is largely desert, although there are a number of important oases. The largest and most significant economically is the Fergana Valley, in the extreme east. Surrounded almost entirely by ranges of the Tien Shan, it is watered by the Syr Darya and its tributaries, the Naryn and the Kara Darya. Fed by heavy rains and snow in the mountains, these rivers provide water for extensive irrigation in the valley. The Tashkent Oasis, to the west, is watered similarly by the Syr Darya and its immediate tributaries, the Chirchik and the Angren. The Zeravshan River waters the Samarkand Bukhara oases, but then disappears into the desert. There are other oases at Termez on the Afghan border, at Karshi, and at Khiva, along the lower Amu Darya.

Average annual precipitation throughout the lowland plain ranges from 4 to 8 inches. Tashkent, on the piedmont plain, receives an average of 13 inches per year. In the mountains precipitation generally averages 40 inches or more annually, with the maximum usually occurring in spring. Summers are dry. Snow falls in winter but is not excessive, except in the higher elevations. For the most part, winter temperatures are low, but at Tashkent the January average is only 31.5° F and the frost does not last long. Summer temperatures are high, and skies are usually clear and sunny. The average July temperature at Tashkent is 81.3°F.

Northeastern Uzbekistan falls within the Kyzyl Kum, or the desert of red sands. The black saxaul, a

Location Map of Uzbek S.S.R.

unique Asian woody plant, is common. Over much of the rest of the republic, including the piedmont plain, is a mantle of loess. The soils are generally fertile, although there are areas of high salinity. Alluvial materials are extensive in the river valleys and in the delta of the Amu Darya, where grasses, reeds, poplars, and vines, including the clematis, are common. Bulbous blue grass, sedges, ephemera, and poplars are found in the piedmont.

Social Factors. Uzbeks, who are a Turkic people, number 5,026,000, or 62 per cent, of Uzbekistan's population. Kara-Kalpaks, a closely related people, number only 168,000. There are also 1,101,000 Russians, primarily in the cities, and many Tatars, Kazakhs, Tadjiks, and other peoples. The densest concentration of population is in the Fergana Valley and in other, smaller, oases. Aside from Tashkent, the principal cities are Samarkand, Andizhan, Namangan, and Kokand. Among the institutions for higher learning are Central Asian V. I. Lenin State University at Tashkent, and numerous technical institutes.

Economic Factors. Throughout much of the republic, crop cultivation is impossible without irrigation which, although practiced for centuries, was greatly expanded during the twentieth century; the building of the Great Fergana Canal, 1939, did much to make the Fergana Valley the cotton bowl of the Soviet Union. Of seven million acres of land in crops, nearly half are in cotton. The use of improved seed and the systematic application of fertilizers resulted in a threefold jump in yield in the period between the early 1930's and the late 1950's. Grain and melons, pomegranates, and other fruits are also grown. Cattle are raised on farms, while sheep and goats are raised on desert pastures and in the mountains.

There are natural gas deposits in the Bukhara-Khiva area and some deposits of oil in the Fergana Valley. Coal is mined at Angren and there also are deposits of sulfur and copper. Hydroelectric power has been developed on some of the rivers, such as on the Syr Darya and the Chirchik. Tashkent, the major manufacturing city of Uzbekistan, is the largest center of machine building in Central Asia. It produces agricultural and textile machinery, and also is major producer of cotton textiles. Steel is produced at Begovat, and chemicals are manufactured at Chirchik. Margelan, in the Fergana Valley, has one of the largest silk-manufacturing plants in the Soviet Union. Little use is made of the rivers for transportation, but the republic is linked by rail to the Caspian Sea, to the southern Urals, to the Afghan border, and to Alma-Ata in Kazakhstan. Within the republic all of the oases have rail facilities. Modern highways link the major cities. Large amounts of cotton, the major export item, are shipped to the textile mills near Moscow and Leningrad.   DOUGLAS JACKSON

History. Much of the area of modern Uzbekistan corresponds to the ancient region of Sogdiana, which was a satrapy of both the Persian and Macedonian empires. Its oldest city, Samarkand, was known to the Macedonian Greeks as Maracanda. Its principal inhabitants were the Parthians, an Iranian people who, beginning in the third century B.C., gradually overthrew Macedonian rule and eventually established hegemony over a vast region stretching from the Indian Ocean to the Hindu Kush (mountains). During the third century of the Christian Era the region was conquered by the Persians, who ruled until the Islamic Arabs overran south central Asia during the seventh century. Bukhara became one of the major religious centers of Islam, and Samarkand, Kokand, and Tashkent flourished as caravan stops along the trade route between Europe and the Far East. During the thirteenth century Mongols from the region of Lake Baykal conquered most of south central Asia, driving before them the various Turkish tribes among whom were the Uzbeks (see TURK). Mongol power endured through the lifetime of Tamerlane (1336?–1405), whose capital was Samarkand.

After Tamerlane's death the unified Mongol domain crumbled and in its place there rose several Turkish kingdoms that encompassed an area historically known as Turkestan. Among these kingdoms was the Uzbek-ruled Bukhara Emirate, which corresponded to large parts of modern Soviet Central Asia. The Bukhara Emirate was sovereign until 1868, when Russia established hegemony over it. After the Russian Revolution, 1917, the new Bolshevik government incorporated within its domains much of the Turkestan region, including Bukhara. In line with the Soviet policy of extending autonomous powers to non-Russian nationalities in the Soviet Union, the Uzbek Soviet Socialist Republic was established, 1924.

UZHGOROD, city, U.S.S.R. in the extreme SW of the Ukrainian Soviet Socialist Republic, capital of the Transcarpathian (Zakarpatskaya) Region, which by treaty (Sept. 29, 1945) Czechoslovakia released to the Soviets. Pop. (1959) 40,000.

UZLOVAYA, city, U.S.S.R., W central Russian Soviet Federated Socialist Republic, Tula Region; 120 miles S of Moscow. The city is in an area in which wheat, rye, corn, and potatoes are grown; lignite is mined in the vicinity. Machinery and metal products are manufactured; the city is a railroad center on the Moscow-Kharkov line. Pop. (1959) 54,000.

UZZA, in the pre-Islamic mythology of the Banu Ghatafan tribe of Arabia, the planet and goddess Venus, who was worshiped in the form of the acacia tree. The worship of Uzza, along with that of Manat and of Allat, or Allatu, or Ilat, the female counterpart of Allah in the pre-Islamic pantheon, was condemned in the Koran.

UZZAH, or Uzza, five persons in the Old Testament of the Bible. (1) A son of Abinadab, was a member of the party led by David to bring the Ark of the Covenant to Jerusalem; he was struck down by God for touching the Ark (II Sam. 6:3-8; I Chron. 13:7-11). (2) The owner of a garden in which two kings of Judah, Manasseh and Amon, were buried (II Kings 21:18, 26). (3) A son of Shimei, a Merarite (I Chron. 6:29). (4) The founder of a family of Nethinims who returned from exile in Babylon with Zerubbabel (Ezra 2:49; Neh. 7:51). (5) A Benjamite, a descendant of Ehud (I Chron. 8:7).

UZZELL, THOMAS ALBERT, JR., 1906–   , U.S. lawyer and public official, was born in New Bern, N.C., and studied law at the University of North Carolina. He was admitted to the North Carolina state bar, 1930, and began practicing law in Asheville, N.C., in 1931. Uzzell was an assistant U.S. attorney for the Western District of North Carolina at Asheville, 1945–48, and was the U.S. district attorney in that area, 1948–53. He was a permanent member of the U.S. Judicial Conference for the Fourth Circuit, and a member of the University of North Carolina Development Council, 1953–54. Uzzell edited the North Carolina *Law Review* for two years.

UZZIAH, or Azariah, in the Old Testament, a king of Judah, the son of Amaziah and Jacoliah, came to the throne in Jerusalem at the age of 16, conjecturally during the eighth century B.C. The period of his reign, which lasted 52 years, was one of great prosperity for Judah. Uzziah warred against the Philistines, encouraged agriculture, and strengthened the defenses of Jerusalem. Uzziah's fame and power were extensive; his army numbered 307,500. His good fortune came to an end, however, when he went into the Temple and attempted to take upon himself the privilege of offering incense to God. Angered at the resistance of the temple priests, Uzziah pressed forward with the censor to the altar of incense, but was suddenly stricken with leprosy. He withdrew from public affairs, and his son Jotham acted as his representative. See II Chron. 26.

UZZIEL, in John Milton's *Paradise Lost*, an angel second in power to Gabriel. In Hebrew the name Uzziel means "my strength is God."

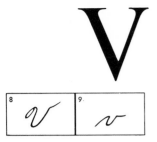

1 No hieroglyph	2 ५	3 Y	4 V	5 u	6 u	7 𝖁
8 𝒱	9 𝓋	10 V	11 v	12 v	13 *V*	14 *v*	15 V	16 v

The letter V has, until about the middle of the seventeenth century, a history identical with that of U, since the two were forms of the same letter. They became differentiated as the V form of the letter began to be used when the letter was initial, and therefore usually consonantal. Correspondingly, the rounded U became identified with the vowel. It is shown in the old Gutenberg black-letter form 7, and in the bottom row in common forms as it appears today. They are handwritten cursive capital 8, handwritten lowercase 9, roman capital 10, roman lowercase 11, roman small capital 12, italic capital 13, italic lowercase 14, sans serif capital 15, and sans serif lowercase 16.

V, the twenty-second letter of the modern English alphabet. Until about the middle of the seventeenth century, *v* and *u* were two forms of the same letter, *v* being used generally at the beginning of a word, *u* within it. When eventually they became separate letters, *u* was restricted largely to the representation of vowels, while *v* was employed as a consonant. In English and French, *v* is a voiced *f*—that is, the voiced lip-teeth spirant. In German, *v* is pronounced as the English *f*. The sound *v* is not liable to much variation.

In Roman numerals, V represents 5, or, with a horizontal line above it, 5,000. In chemistry, V is the symbol for vanadium. The letter *v* is frequently used to abbreviate the Latin *vide* ("see") and also a number of scientific terms, such as *volt* and *velocity*.

VAAL RIVER, Republic of South Africa, main tributary of the Orange River, rises in the Drakensberg Mountains in SE Transvaal Province and flows W and SW to join the Orange after a course of about 750 miles. For much of its course the Vaal forms the boundary between Transvaal and Orange Free State. During the dry season the Vaal is fordable in many places, called drifts. During the wet season the Vaal often floods. The dam at Vaaldam forms a large reservoir which is used for irrigation and as a water supply for the nearby steel mills at Vereeniging. The river valley is a source of alluvial diamonds. Major cities on the Vaal are Standerton, Vereeniging, Christiana, Warrenton, and Douglas.

VAASA, administrative department and city, W Finland. The department is bounded on the W by the Gulf of Bothnia, on the N by Oulu, on the E by Keski-Suomi, and on the S by Turkupori; area 15,062 square miles. Principal occupations are farming and lumbering. The capital and chief port is Vaasa city.

Vaasa city is on the Gulf of Bothnia, some 215 miles NW of Helsinki. Its principal manufactures are wood products, textiles, iron and steel, glass, sugar, and rubber; the chief exports are wood products. Vaasa has both an inner and an outer harbor. The town was founded, 1606, by King Charles IX of Sweden. It played an important part in the Swedish-Russian war of 1808–09. Vaasa was almost totally destroyed by fire, 1852, and was moved closer to the sea in the course of the rebuilding. The name was changed to Nikolaistad, 1855, but the old name was readopted in 1918. During the war of independence, 1917–18, Vaasa was the capital of White Finland. (For populations of department and city, see Finland map in Atlas.)

VACARESCU, a Rumanian family many of whose members made important contributions to their national literature. Its members included Ienache Văcărescu (1654–1714), who was grand treasurer of Walachia; his grandson, also named Ienache (1740–99), author of the first Rumanian vernacular grammar; the younger Ienache Văcărescu's two sons, Alecu (died 1799) and Nikolae (died 1825), both poets of merit; and Alecu's son, Iancu Văcărescu (1792?–1863), who was responsible for inaugurating a Rumanian national poetry and helping to found a national theater. His niece, Elena Văcărescu (1866–1947), wrote verse and prose in both Rumanian and French.

VACCINE, any material that can be injected or inoculated for the purpose of preventing the development of a disease; more particularly, a preparation of killed or weakened organisms which, when introduced into the body, results in the production of active immunity.

Some vaccines are composed of substances that still possess the power to cause disease. An example of such a vaccination is the early method of inoculating a person against smallpox with material obtained from a pustule or pock of someone who has the disease. The virulent germ of typhoid is also used to vaccinate against typhoid fever. It has been shown, however, that typhoid fever can be acquired only when the germ enters the gastrointestinal tract; when the organism is injected under the skin, a local reaction only is produced, and the body manufactures specific antibodies which then circulate in the blood. If the germ is later ingested, its antibody combines with and destroys it.

Most vaccines are made up of killed organisms or of germs that have been weakened by various substances or methods. Included under the general name of vaccines are the products of germ growth from which the germs themselves have been filtered off and which have then been treated with chemical agents. Such preparations are called toxoids. When toxoids are injected, active resistance to the particular disease is built up in the body. Most vaccines are injected just under the skin. In 1960, however, an oral form of poliomyelitis vaccine was developed and used with success.

Diseases for Which Vaccination Is Recommended. There are several diseases against which preventive vaccination or inoculation can be unreservedly recommended. Of these, smallpox is perhaps the most important. This vaccination consists of scratching the skin with material obtained from a pus pocket present in cattle infected with cowpox. In a susceptible person a local reaction of the skin, accompanied by crust formation, usually develops in a few days after vaccination. Although smallpox and cowpox are not identical diseases, vaccination with cowpox confers a great deal of resistance to smallpox. Vaccination is recommended at an early age. Although some immunity after a successful "take" lasts a long time, revaccination is recommended at the time of entering school and again at about the age of 18. Two positive reactions or "takes" are considered to render practically life-long immunity; at least, if the disease should develop after two "takes" it is almost always extremely mild and most unlikely to be fatal.

Diphtheria is another disease against which vaccination of all people is recommended. The vaccine in this case consists of the poison or toxin produced by the growth of the diphtheria bacillus, which has been specially treated. Diphtheria toxoid injections produce a reasonably long period of immunity, and the resistance can be tested or checked by performing a skin test.

A toxoid similar to that for diphtheria is also available for vaccination against tetanus or lockjaw. This toxoid can be combined with diphtheria toxoid or whooping cough vaccine and given at the same time. If an extra, or booster, dose of tetanus toxoid is given at the time of a threatening injury, an active resistance to tetanus is obtained, making it unnecessary to give the tetanus antitoxin or serum in order to combat lockjaw.

Whooping cough vaccine is usually recommended for children. This contains the germs which are known to cause the disease. Whooping cough vaccine can be given alone or combined with diphtheria or tetanus toxoid.

Poliomyelitis was proved to be a disease against which vaccination helped. The vaccine originally was given only in a series of three injections. Later an oral form was developed which was taken in a single dose.

Vaccines of Doubtful Value or Recommended for Special Purposes. A vaccine is available against scarlet fever. Unfortunately the preparation often produces severe reactions and some doubt has been expressed as to its value in producing resistance and how long immunity lasts. For these reasons, scarlet fever preventive inoculation is recommended by some doctors and not by others.

Vaccination against typhoid and the related diseases, paratyphoid A and paratyphoid B, has proved of value. In some countries, notably the United States and Canada, sanitation has been so improved that there is little typhoid in the community and thus little danger of acquiring the disease. In many other parts of the world typhoid is still common and the typhoid vaccine should be given to all those who are likely to be exposed by travel.

Rabies vaccination is desirable for any person who has been bitten by an animal suspected of having the disease. The immunity produced by rabies vaccination develops so rapidly that it can prevent the disease in a person who has been bitten by a rabid animal, if the inoculations are begun soon after the exposure. Rabies vaccination is necessary only for a person whose skin has been broken by an animal harboring the rabies virus.

Various vaccines developed against the several types of influenza have proved valuable. Since a specific vaccine is needed against each of the viruses, however, it is an uncertain immunity that is achieved.

Reasonably successful vaccines have been developed against cholera, typhus, plague, and yellow fever. These diseases are not now common in the continental Americas; hence, vaccines against them are recommended only for those who expect to travel to regions where the diseases in question are common. Similarly, people whose occupations place them in danger of acquiring Rocky Mountain spotted fever can also be inoculated with a reasonably effective vaccine.

Serums and Antitoxins are used for the most part to produce passive or temporary immunity. A great many serums are available to combat various diseases, but their value varies tremendously. A substance called human immune globulin is used particularly against measles. If given after exposure to disease, this serum prevents a severe reaction to measles. The immunity produced does not last long, however.

Antitoxins which are obtained from serums are used with success against diphtheria. Antitoxins are available also for botulism, against certain snake venom, gas gangrene, tetanus or lockjaw, and scarlet fever. Certainly the most effective of these antitoxins is diphtheria antitoxin, but a great deal of its value depends on how early in the course of the disease it is given. Now that diphtheria can be prevented by stimulating active resistance through an inoculation of tetanus toxoid, the disease is becoming more and more rare. There is reason to believe that the administration of scarlet fever antitoxin favorably influences the course of the disease. Serum obtained from patients convalescing from scarlet fever also has value.   EDWIN P. JORDAN, M.D.

BIBLIOG.–John B. Blake, *Benjamin Waterhouse and the Introduction of Vaccination: A Reappraisal* (1957); Henry W. Crowe, *Handbook of the Vaccine Treatment of Chronic Rheumatic Diseases* (1939); Ciba Foundation, *Symposium on Cellular Aspects of Immunity* (1960); Edward F. Dolan, Jr., *Jenner and the Miracle of Vaccine* (1960); Kenneth N. Irvine, *B.C.G. Vaccination in Theory and Practice* (1949); E. J. W. Keuter, *Predisposition to Postvaccinal Encephalitis: Significance of Constitution, Especially the Status Dysraphicus in the Genesis of P.E.* (1960); Henry J. Parish, *Antisera, Toxoids, Vaccines and Tuberculins in Prophylaxis and Treatment* (1958); Sol Roy Rosenthal, *BCG Vaccination Against Tuberculosis* (1957); David Thomson, *Oral Vaccines and Immunization by Other Unusual Routes* (1948); Greer Williams, *Virus Hunters* (1960).

VACHELL, HORACE ANNESLEY, 1861–1955, writer, was born in Sydenham and educated at Harrow and Sandhurst. He resigned an army commission, 1883, and traveled to California, where he became a rancher. He returned to England, 1899, and began his career as a writer. He is best known for his depiction of the English character and countryside. Among Vachell's works are *The Romance of Judge Ketchum* (1894); *John Charity* (1900); *Blinds Down* (1912); a play, *Quinneys'* (1915); *Change Partners* (1922); a mystery, *The Yard* (1923); short stories, *Joe Quinney's Jodie* (1936), *The Black Squire* (1941), *Averil* (1945); reminiscences, *Now Came Still Evening On* (1946), *Twilight Grey* (1948), and *Quests* (1954).

VACHEROT, ÉTIENNE, 1809–97, French philosopher, was born in Langres, was educated at the École Normale, and for a short time, 1838–39, was director of studies there before assuming a professorship of modern philosophy at the Sorbonne. Having already been sharply rebuked by the clerical party for the views he had expressed in his *Histoire critique de l'école d'Alexandrie* (3 vols., 1846–51), Vacherot lost his post at the Sorbonne, 1852, for refusing to swear allegiance to Napoleon III's government, and was imprisoned for three months after the publication of his *Démocratie* (1859). He was elected to the French Academy in 1868. Soon after the fall of the Second Empire, 1870, Vacherot became active in politics, and sat in the national assembly, 1871–73. Among his other works are *La Métaphysique et la science* (1858), *La Religion* (1868), *La Science et la conscience* (1870), and *La Démocratie liberale* (1892).

VACUUM, a space from which a part or most of the material particles have been removed. Although the term means a complete void and the absence of all material particles, such high degree of evacuation is not possible with present-day equipment. The complete absence of all material particles in a space would constitute an absolute vacuum, while in the laboratory today, only a partial vacuum can be achieved. When the term vacuum is now used, it refers to a partial vacuum whose pressure is below that of the atmosphere.

Until the middle of the seventeenth century, the ancient belief that "nature abhors a vacuum" prevailed. Not until Galileo and Torricelli demonstrated experimentally that the rise of liquids in tubes was due to atmospheric pressure and not to nature's abhorrence of a vacuum was this erroneous belief disproved. Galileo's genius was quick to detect a flaw in the argument. He pointed out since water in deep wells could not be raised more than about 32 feet by means of suction pumps, nature's abhorrence for a vacuum had its limitations and did not extend beyond 32 feet. The early fallacy had also led to the conclusion that nature's abhorrence of a vacuum caused the void to be filled by whatever material was available. The suction which caused the material to rush in and occupy the void was explained by Galileo to result from the external atmospheric pressure and not nature's abhorrence of a vacuum. Torricelli succeeded in measuring the atmospheric pressure with a barometer in which he balanced the pressure of the atmosphere against a column of mercury of measurable height. The pressure exerted by such a column of mercury is said to be a measure of the barometric pressure. Its value is about 29.9 inches or 76 centimeters of mercury. This means that the pressure of the atmosphere exerted on the surface of the liquid mercury is equal to that exerted by a column of mercury standing about 30 inches in height. In actual pressure units, the value is expressed in dynes per square centimeter or pounds per square inch. Since there occur from day to day slight variations in the barometric pressure, a standard pressure is defined for purposes of comparison, and it is the pressure exerted by a column of mercury standing 29.92 inches or 76 centimeters in height. This pressure is also known as one atmosphere. These various units are related as follows: 1 atmosphere = 76 cm of mercury = 29.92 in. of mercury = 1033 gm/cm² = 1,013,000 dynes/cm². In modern practice another unit of pressure is also widely used, this unit is the bar and it is equal to 10^6 dynes/cm². One thousandth of a bar, or millibar, is equal to 10^3 dynes/cm². In terms of the millibar, the standard atmosphere is 1013 millibars.

In order for the mercurial barometer to give correct indications, the mercury must be pure and clean and the space above it, which is in a closed cap of the tube, should be free as possible from air and other gases.

Uses. Modern technology demands high vacua for many devices such as electric lamps, x-ray tubes, radio tubes, photoelectric cells, and cathode-ray oscilloscopes. Methods for obtaining the high degree of evacuation required for these devices have been developed as have techniques for producing these devices in quantity. In the field of pure research, high vacua are required in apparatus which demand degrees of evacuation far greater than those of practical devices. Modern requirements of extremely high vacua for scientific research and technical processes have led to the perfection in recent years of two types of air pumps, the rotary pump and vapor-diffusion pump. With the rotary oil pump, known also as the hyvac, and larger models as the megavac and hypervac, it is possible to reduce the pressure to values as low as 10^{-4} mm of mercury. To reduce the pressure below 10^{-3} mm or 10^{-4} mm of mercury, a diffusion pump is employed. The diffusion pump is not effective until a vacuum of about 0.01 mm pressure has been produced by rotary pump used as fore pump. The two pumps, fore and diffusion, can be used together to form a two-stage, high-vacuum pumping system. Such an arrangement makes possible the attainment of pressures of about 10^{-8} mm of mercury, a value close to a hundred-billionth of an atmosphere.

VACUUM CLEANER, a mechanical device for removing dust and dirt from such objects as rugs, carpets, draperies, and fabric upholstery by utilizing the tendency of air to rush into a pipe in which a partial vacuum has been created (see VACUUM). First

successfully used about 1901, early vacuum cleaners were powered either by electric motors or small internal combustion engines. They could be moved about on carts for contract work, the unit being stationed outside of a building, while pipes led into the interior through a door or window. Later, units for large buildings were installed permanently in the basement, with pipes leading to various parts of the building. These installations were of particular value in munitions plants, cement plants, and others where dust constituted an industrial hazard. Such installations have been largely superseded by systems that automatically control the atmosphere within the plant.

From point of numbers, the domestic type of portable vacuum cleaner is the most important. Originally introduced about 1909, these cleaners are designed to operate from the ordinary 110-volt domestic circuit, and may be easily moved about from room to room. Ordinarily, such cleaners consist of a motor-driven pump or turbine for producing the vacuum suction, a rotating brush, piping and nozzle, and dust bag, which can be removed and emptied. In operation, the cleaner picks up the surface dirt swept loose by the rotating brush, together with embedded dust, which is blown into the dust bag with no appreciable scattering of dust into the air. Most modern vacuum cleaners have attachments that permit the cleaning of polished floors, overstuffed furniture, curtains, and draperies. They may also be used to clean furnaces, flues, and heating ducts.

VACUUM PUMP, a device for producing low pressures by displacing gas molecules with the aid of a moving wall, a fluid stream, or electromagnetic forces.

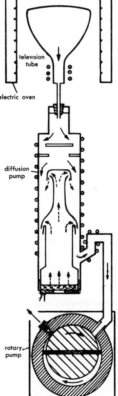

television tube

electric oven

diffusion pump

rotary pump

Two types of vacuum pumps used in series draw air from a tube.

(See VACUUM.) The first practical vacuum pumps were developed by Otto von Guericke and Robert Boyle during the years 1640 to 1670. These pumps employed a moving piston fitting tightly in a cylindrical casing with an intake and an exhaust valve. They were greatly improved by using an oil seal around the piston and the exhaust valve.

In 1643 Evangelista Torricelli discovered that if a mercury-filled tube were inverted in a dish of mercury, the mercury level in the tube fell to about 30 inches above that in the dish, the exact height depending on the atmospheric pressure. (See BAROMETER.) This left a vacuum above the mercury column. The discovery is employed in vacuum pumps first developed by Heinrich Geissler (1855) in which a mercury column serves as the moving piston driving the gas out of the top of a glass bulb through an exhaust valve. The pressure in the system can be measured by the height of the mercury column in the exit tube when the mercury piston is below the intake connection. A "high" vacuum is reached when the height of this column is nearly equal to the barometric value. Other pumps employing liquid mercury are now obsolete because of their slow action, but were important in the early manufacture of incandescent lamps.

Modern high-speed vacuum pumps are of eight general types: improved reciprocating pumps, centrifugal pumps, gear-pumps, rotary oil-sealed mechanical pumps, steam ejectors, oil or mercury vapor ejectors, molecular drag pumps, and mercury or oil diffusion pumps (see PUMP). Reciprocating, centrifugal, gear, and rotary pumps, and steam ejectors produce the moderately low pressures required for such applications as steam turbine exhaust, paper-making machinery, evaporating pans, stills, deodorizers, filters, and impregnators. Oil or mercury ejectors are used in series with rotary pumps and steam ejectors to increase effectiveness. The molecular drag pumps and the mercury or oil diffusion pumps produce the extremely high vacuums required to exhaust the bases from electronic tubes, cyclotrons, and vacuum bottles.

A typical combination of the rotary and steam ejection types of vacuum pumps for the exhaust of television tubes is shown in the illustration. Hot oil vapor in the diffusion pump rises to the nozzles and then issues downward at high velocity and returns to the boiler after condensing on the water-cooled casing. Gas molecules from above are carried by the stream to the space below. The rotary pump sweeps these molecules out to the atmosphere as the inner cylinder revolves the sliding vanes past the intake and exhaust ports. In other forms of rotary pumps a vane slides in the outer cylinder and rests against the inner cylinder, which revolves on an eccentric axis.

Other means of producing low pressures include water aspirators, active metals such as barium, absorbents such as outgassed charcoal, and traps cooled with dry ice or liquid air to condense residual vapors.   BENJAMIN B. DAYTON

VACUUM TUBE, a type of electron tube which has been highly evacuated so that the motion of electrons through it occurs with the minimum number of collisions with the remaining gas molecules. Such tubes make use of the thermionic effect to produce an electron flow which can be controlled by connecting the tube to electronic circuits. A single form of vacuum tube is the two-element diode or thermionic valve. More complex vacuum tubes include the triode, tetrode, pentode, and multigrid tubes.

VAFTHRUDNI, in Scandinavian mythology, one of the wisest of the giants. One day Odin visited him in disguise and proposed a contest in wisdom. Vafthrudni agreed to the contest, but was at last defeated when asked what Odin had whispered in the ear of his dead son Balder, when he laid him on his funeral pyre.

VAGA, PERINO DEL, real name Pietro Buonaccorsi, 1500–47, Italian painter, was born in Florence. He assisted Raphael in the decoration of the loggia in the Vatican. His works deal primarily with historical and mythological subjects.

VAGRANCY, the act of going about from place to place, committed by a person who although being able to work, refuses to do so. A single act, such as begging, may be considered vagrancy, but the condition is usually applied to a way of life.

Anti-vagrancy statutes were first passed in England in the seventh century. Idleness was considered to be a voluntary state, and in law it was held an offense against the public economy. Over the course of years, punishment for vagrancy varied, at times consisting of branding, whipping, commission to slavery, and even execution. With a change in public attitudes toward idleness, punishment changed and vagrants were most frequently jailed for a short time, or fined a small amount.

By mid-twentieth century, most states and municipalities had passed anti-vagrancy laws. Vagrants can be arrested without a warrant, and committed to jail by a police magistrate without a trial by jury. Police are thus legally able to detain criminal suspects on vagrancy charges until proof of other illegal actions can be obtained. In many states, the term vagrancy legally refers to specific acts such as loitering or wandering, and certain people such as prostitutes,

gamblers, drunkards, and their various associates as well may be considered in such cases to be vagrants.

The handling of vagrants is recognized by many experts as an important social problem. The law frequently merely orders the offender to leave the community, and thus the responsibility for the vagrant's actions are merely shifted to another community. A distinction, however, is usually made between persons who are unemployed but willing to work and those who choose not to work. Many social agencies, particularly during the depression years of the 1930's, were active in rehabilitating and relocating vagrants willing to accept such aid.

VAHLEN, JOHANNES, 1830–1911, German philologist, was born in Bonn, at whose university he studied. Because he concentrated all his efforts on the understanding of the Graeco-Roman classical texts, and avoided all of the mental fashions and sensational side ways that tempted and seduced most other philologists (many of whom were overly pre-occupied with the supposed significance of new archaeological excavations, political analogies, new civilizations, religious or philosophical predilections, and so forth), Vahlen came to represent the best achievement of nineteenth century classical philology in Germany. In his academic associations, he taught in Breslau, in Freiburg, in Vienna, and from 1874 in Berlin; thus, the geography of his career encompassed the whole of greater Germany, with its highly varied university traditions. At Berlin, his monographs, written in immaculate Latin, were used to adorn the Lectures Catalogue, which also was printed in Latin in those days; each of these programs was used to restore an ancient mutilated or otherwise "ununderstandable" text to its full splendor and original integrity. A maximum of such restorative skill was shown in Vahlen's interpretations of three important classical writers: the poet Ennius, Aristotle as the author of the *Poetics*, and Cicero on the laws. The three monographs were so admired that, despite their remoteness, they went through several editions. He earned and deserved the title, *Princeps Philologiae* (Prince of Philology).   EUGEN ROSENSTOCK-HUESSY

VAIHINGER, HANS, 1852–1933, German philosopher, was born in Nehren, Würtemberg, and died in Halle, of whose university he had been professor of philosophy from 1884. Of all German thinkers, Vaihinger came closest to espousing the pragmatism of the U.S. philosopher John Dewey, but during much of his career he concealed his own viewpoint of pure sensualism and scientism (we "think" only as means of survival, and can know nothing of the truth) and first established himself as the adroit organizer of the systematic study of the philosophy of Immanuel Kant. Vaihinger founded a series of monographs, the *Kant-Studien*, 1896, and the *Kant-Gesellschaft* (Kant Society), 1904; and he composed a meticulous, but never completed, *Kommentar zu Kants Kritik der reinen Vernunft* (Commentary on Kant's Critique of Pure Reason), 2 vols. 1881–92; ed. 1922. He wrote works on Friedrich Nietzsche (1902) and other thinkers, and he presented a monograph on his own philosophy to the Gesellschaft in 1921. A *Festschrift* for his eightieth birthday showed him that his organizational labors had not been in vain.

As to Vaihinger's own philosophy, he conceived it as early as 1876, but did not dare to publish it until much later, in *Die Philosophie des Als ob, System der theoretischen, praktischen und religiösen Fiktionen der Menschheit auf Grund eines idealistischen Positivismus* (1911; 2nd ed. 1913). In this work, Vaihinger insisted that we cannot really know anything, but must rest content with "fictions" that help bridge the gaps of human sense perceptions; one's awareness of cause-and-effect, for example, is merely a fictitious mental combination of separate experiences. In all the sciences, and in religion and law as well, we act or judge "as if" these or those hypotheses are true; hence, he dubbed his method the "*als ob*" (as if) philosophy. While it is quite satisfactory as an attitude in many aspects of pure research and technology, the *als ob* method is all but useless in matters of life and death where one cannot afford to live by fictions—in matters in which, so to speak, man is not the experimenter, but is the subject of God's Holy Experiment. Although his role paralleled that of John Dewey in many respects, Vaihinger had little influence on education.

EUGEN ROSENSTOCK-HUESSY

VAIL, ALFRED, 1807–59, U.S. inventor, was born in Morristown, N.J. After graduation from the University of the City of New York, 1836, he became a partner of Samuel F. B. Morse in the development of the telegraph, furnished financial assistance for the construction of a complete set of instruments, 1837–38, and assisted in the technical work which was involved in return for a share in the U.S. and foreign rights. As Morse's chief assistant in constructing the experimental Washington-Baltimore telegraph line for the U.S. government, 1843–44, Vail received the monumental first test message, which was "What hath God wrought!"

VAIL, THEODORE NEWTON, 1845–1920, U.S. communications executive, cousin of Alfred Vail, was born near Minerva, Ohio. As general manager of the Bell Telephone Company, 1878–87, Vail consolidated local exchanges; established practical financial, scientific, and manufacturing systems; and helped found the American Telephone and Telegraph Company, 1885. After a period working to promote industrial development in Argentina, 1894–1907, Vail returned to the United States as president of the American Telephone and Telegraph Company, 1907–19. During World War I, he assisted with government control of communications and became chairman of the board of directors of the American Telephone and Telegraph Company when private ownership was resumed after the war.

VAITARANĪ, in Hindu mythology, the river of death flowing between the land of the living and the land of the dead, sometimes identified with the Vaitarani River in northeast India. One could cross Vaitaranī, which was filled with filth, blood, and hair, only by holding on to the tail of a cow. The Hindu hell for destroyers of beehives, and pillagers, was also called Vaitaranī.

VALAIS, canton, S Switzerland, bounded by France on the W, by Italy on the S, and the cantons of Ticino and Uri on the NE, Oberland on the N, and Vaud on the NW; area 2,021 sq. mi.; pop. (1950) 159,178. The canton encloses virtually all the upper valley of the Rhône River; to the north are the Bernese Alps, to the south are the Perrine Alps. In the extreme northwest the canton extends to Lake Geneva. Some of the highest peaks in Switzerland rise on the borders of Valais. They include Jungfrau (13,668 ft.); Matterhorn (14,685 ft.) and Monte Rosa (15,200 ft.). The mountains are breached by spectacular passes and important tunnels. Great St. Bernard Pass, in the southwest, and Simplon Pass, in the southeast, have roadways into Italy, and under Simplon is bored one of the world's longest railroad tunnels, 12.3 miles in length; the Lötschberg Tunnel bores under the Bernese Alps for 9 miles to give rail access to Bern. Wheat and grapes and other fruit are grown in the valleys; stock raising is important. There are many winter sport centers. Sion is the capital.

History. Valais was won by the Romans as a result of their victory at Martigny in 57 B.C. In the ninth century Valais became a part of the Transjurane Burgundy kingdom. After 999 the bishop of Sion ruled the canton as the Count of Valais. In 1798 Valais became part of the newly formed Helvetic Republic. Napoleon I incorporated Valais into France, 1810, but the canton was freed from French rule by an Austrian force, 1813, and became a part of the Swiss Federation, 1815. During the Civil War of 1844, Valais became a member of the Sunderbund; it was the last canton to join the nation in 1847.

VALDAY HILLS, U.S.S.R., in the Kalinin and Novgorod regions of the Russian Soviet Federated Socialist Republic, NW of Moscow. The Valdays are low, morainic hills, ranging in height from 300 to 1,000 feet above sea level. They extend about 200 miles north-south. To the east and west the Valdays are bordered by swamps and lakes such as Lake Seliger, one of the largest. The hills form a low watershed separating the headwaters of the Volga and Dvina rivers on the south from the rivers flowing to the Gulf of Finland on the north.

VALDÉS, JUAN DE, 1500?–41, Spanish Humanist, was born in Cuenca, studied at Alcalá, and soon was in contact with such notable Humanists as Erasmus, with whom he corresponded (see ERASMUS, DESIDERIUS; HUMANISM). Valdés' *Doctrina cristiana* (1529), a kind of Erasmian catechism, was denounced as heterodox and the author, to avoid the persecution of the Inquisition, went to Italy, where he addressed himself to a select group of thinkers. Although he did not preach to the masses, Valdés became one of the principal forces for reform in Italy. In the dialogue *Alfabeto cristiano* (1546), he affirmed the doctrine of justification by faith alone. In the *Ziento i diez consideraziones divinas*, 1550 (*The Hundred and Ten Considerations Treating of Those Most Profitable in Our Christian Profession*, 1638), Valdés expounded the idea of salvation through "interior illumination." His most important literary work, however, is the *Diálogo de la lengua* (written, 1533; first published, 1737), which displays his typical Renaissance sympathy for the "neo-Latin" (that is, Romance) languages, and which is one of the capital books on the history of Spanish philology. ANTHONY KERRIGAN

VALDEZ, town, S Alaska, on an arm of Prince William Sound of the Gulf of Alaska; 115 miles E of Anchorage. The town is connected by the Richardson Highway over the Chugach Mountains to Fairbanks. It is a supply center for gold mines, a shipping point for fur, and an outfitting point for game hunting. Valdez was founded late in the 1890's. Pop. (1960) 555.

VALDIVIA, PEDRO DE, 1498?–?1553, Spanish conquistador of Chile, was born near La Serena, Estremadura. Arriving in the New World, 1534, he joined Hernando Cortés in Mexico; assisted Francisco Pizarro in Peru, 1535–40; and, as Pizarro's lieutenant invaded Chile with 200 Spanish troops and 1,000 Indians, 1540, and for more than two decades enjoyed the success in Chile that had eluded a previous Spanish would-be conqueror, Diego de Almagro, who had tried and failed to subdue that area in 1535. Valdivia founded Santiago, 1541, and when this was attacked by the Araucanian natives, established a second capital, La Serena, on the northern coast. After helping to found Valparaiso, 1544, Valdivia went southward as far as the Bío-Bío River, 1546. He returned to Peru, 1547, to help suppress the revolt of Gonzalo Pizarro, and then returned to Chile as governor. He founded Concepción, 1550, Imperial, 1551, and Valdivia, 1552. Late in 1553 he was captured in a native uprising and put to death by the Araucanians near Tucapel in southern Chile.

VALDIVIA, province, S central Chile; bounded by the provinces of Cautín on the N and Osorno on the S, by Argentina on the E, and by the Pacific Ocean on the W; area 7,723 sq. mi.; pop. (1958 est.) 288,780. The western section of the province lies in the Central Valley. To the east, in the foothills of the Andes Mountains, are several large lakes, which are popular vacation spots. Wheat, oats, potatoes, and apples are grown in the valleys, and cattle raising is important. Lumbering is significant in the south. Valdivia is the capital.

VALDIVIA, city, S central Chile, capital of the province of Valdivia; near the Pacific Ocean, 450 miles SSW of Santiago. The city is a port for the crop-growing and stock-raising region to the east. The chief industrial plants are shipyards, lumber mills, and factories making iron and steel products, machinery, wood products, soap, shoes and leather products, sugar, flour, and beverages. Founded by Pedro de Valdivia, 1552, the city became a Spanish stronghold, and ruins of old colonial forts may still be seen. Many naval engagements between British, Dutch, and other buccaneers took place nearby. (For population, see Chile map in Atlas.)

VAL-D'OR, town, Canada, NW Quebec, Abitibi County; on the Canadian National Railway; 255 miles NW of Montreal. The town is a trade center and shipping point for an area in which gold and zinc are mined. There is some lumbering in the vicinity. Val-d'Or was founded in 1937. (For population, see northern Quebec map in Atlas.)

VALDOSTA, city, S Georgia, seat of Lowndes County; on U.S. highways 41, 84, and 221; 205 miles SSE of Atlanta. The city is a trade and processing center for an area in which cotton, tobacco, vegetables, watermelons, and peanuts are grown. Paperboard, concrete pipe, naval stores, fertilizer, cottonseed oil, and lumber products are manufactured. Valdosta was founded in 1860. (For population, see Georgia map in Atlas.)

VALENCE, city, SE France, capital of the department of Drôme, on the Rhône River, 60 miles S of Lyon. The city is a commercial and manufacturing center for an area in which grapes, olives, and other fruits are raised. There are silk mills, and wineries in the city produce Coté du Rhône wines. Valence is the seat of a Roman Catholic bishopric. The Romanesque Cathedral of St. Apollinaire dates from the eleventh century. Valence was founded by the Romans, 123 B.C., and was known as Valentia Julia. The town fell, in turn, under the power of the dukes of Burgundy, the Franks, the kings of Arles, the dukes of Valentinois, and the counts of Toulouse. In the sixteenth century it was a Protestant stronghold. (For population, see France map in Atlas.)

VALENCE, or oxidation number, the combining capacity of the atoms of an element. It is expressed by a number which indicates the number of hydrogen or chlorine atoms with which one atom of the element combines, or the number of hydrogen atoms that one atom replaces in a compound. Thus in water, H_2O, the valence number of oxygen is 2, because one atom of oxygen is combined with two atoms of hydrogen.

In calcium oxide, CaO, the valence number of calcium is 2, because one atom of calcium is combined with one atom of oxygen and therefore must have the same combining capacity as two atoms of hydrogen, or twice as much as one atom of hydrogen.

According to the electron theory the valence number of an element depends upon the number of electrons that an atom of the element gains, loses, or shares when it reacts with other atoms. In sodium chloride, NaCl, the sodium atom has lost one electron from its outer electron orbit, and the chlorine atom has gained one. The valence of each element is therefore one, but since the charge on the sodium particle is positive, as shown by electrolysis experiments, the valence of sodium is said to be plus one (Na^+), and since the charge on the chlorine is negative, its valence is said to be negative one (Cl^-). This electrovalence results in ion formation.

In the compound methane (CH_4) one pair of electrons is shared by the carbon atom and one of the hydrogen atoms, each contributing one electron to form the pair, and neither atom being able to remove the electron from the other by means of attractive forces—

$$H:\overset{\cdot\cdot}{C}:H$$
$$H$$

. In this process no ions are formed and the type of valency exhibited is called covalence. From the formula CH_4 it is evident that the carbon atom has a valence number of 4.

Experimental Determination. The equivalent weight of an element is defined as the weight of the element which combines with one gram atomic weight (1.008 g.) of hydrogen or its equivalent. Thus 8.0 grams of oxygen or 35.46 grams of chlorine are chemically equivalent to 1.008 grams of hydrogen, and the weight of any given element which combines with these weights of oxygen or chlorine is the equivalent weight of the element. The valence of an element may be determined from the equation,

$$\text{valence} = \frac{\text{atomic weight}}{\text{equivalent weight}}.$$

From the known valences of the elements it is often possible to derive the formulas for their compounds. Thus since the valence of calcium is $+2$ and that of chlorine -1, one atom of calcium will combine with two atoms of chlorine to form the compound calcium chloride,

PARTIAL LIST OF VALENCES, or OXIDATION NUMBERS

	Valence 1		Valence 2		Valence 3		Valence 4	
METALS	Cuprous	Cu^+	Barium	Ba^{++}	Aluminum	Al^{+++}	Platinum	Pt^{++++}
	Mercurous	Hg^+	Calcium	Ca^{++}	Antimony	Sb^{+++}		
	Potassium	K^+	Cupric	Cu^{++}	Arsenious	As^{+++}	Stannic	Sn^{++++}
	Silver	Ag^+	Ferrous	Fe^{++}	Bismuth	Bi^{+++}		
	Sodium	Na^+	Lead	Pb^{++}	Chromium	Cr^{+++}	Thorium	Th^{++++}
	Aurous	Au^+	Magnesium	Mg^{++}	Ferric	Fe^{+++}		
			Mercuric	Hg^{++}				
			Stannous	Sn^{++}	Auric	Au^{+++}		
			Zinc	Zn^{++}				
NON-METALS	Bromide	Br^-	Oxide	$O^=$	Nitride	$N^{\equiv}$		
	Chloride	Cl^-	Sulfide	$S^=$	Phosphide	$P^{\equiv}$		
	Fluoride	F^-						
	Iodide	I^-						
RADICALS	Acetate	$C_2H_3O_2{}^-$	Carbonate	$CO_3{}^=$	Arsenate	$AsO_4{}^=$	Ferrocyanide	$Fe(CN)_6{}^{\equiv}$
	Ammonium	$NH_4{}^+$	Chromate	$CrO_4{}^=$	Arsenite	$AsO_3{}^=$		
	Bicarbonate	$HCO_3{}^-$	Dichromate	$Cr_2O_7{}^=$	Borate	$BO_3{}^=$		
	Bisulfate	$HSO_4{}^-$	Oxalate	$C_2O_4{}^=$	Ferricyanide	$Fe(CN)_6{}^=$		
	Bisulfite	$HSO_3{}^-$	Silicate	$SiO_3{}^=$	Phosphate	$PO_4{}^=$		
	Chlorate	$ClO_3{}^-$	Sulfate	$SO_4{}^=$				
	Hydroxide	OH^-	Sulfite	$SO_3{}^=$				
	Nitrate	$NO_3{}^-$	Tartrate	$C_2H_4O_6{}^=$				
	Nitrite	$NO_2{}^-$						
	Permanganate	$MnO_4{}^-$						

$CaCl_2$. Again, if aluminum is known to have a valence of $+3$ and oxygen -2, two trivalent aluminum atoms will combine with three divalent oxygen atoms to give the compound Al_2O_3.

Electronic Theory of Valence. Compounds fall, in general, into one of two classes, namely the electrolytes, which are substances whose aqueous solutions conduct electricity, and nonelectrolytes. The linking of the atoms which make up these different types of compounds must differ in some important respect. In 1916 W. Kossel proposed the theory that, since the arrangements of the outermost electrons in the inert gases are the most stable structures, combination between atoms occurs in such a way as to cause the attainment of these stable structures—that is a group of two electrons in the case of helium, or of eight in all other cases. The outermost electrons are assumed to be the valence electrons. The inert gas type of structure is attained by the gain or loss of electrons, leaving the atom with the electronic configuration of an inert gas. The ions which result are held together in the solid compound by electrostatic attractions. This theory is clearly inapplicable to substances like O_2, SO_2, and the numerous nonionizable compounds. G. N. Lewis in 1916 proposed the theory that the stable electron configuration of inert gases may be achieved by the sharing of pairs of electrons, the shared electrons contributing to the stability of both the combining atoms. If each of two atoms contributes one electron to form a pair, the bonding is covalent. Neither atom is capable of attracting the electrons away from the other, and therefore no ions can be formed.

The electronic theory of valence has been developed very successfully, and has furnished much useful information. In 1927 the electron theory was extended to include data from the quantum mechanics and the idea of paired and unpaired spins of electrons. They assumed that covalent bonds are pairs of electrons of opposite spins shared between atoms.

Co-ordinate Covalence results from the sharing of a pair of electrons by two atoms, both of the shared pair of electrons having been contributed by the same atom. In ammonia, NH_3, for example, the nitrogen atom shares three pairs of electrons with three hydrogen atoms, H:N̈:H; but if ammonia is passed into the solution of an acid a fourth hydrogen nucleus (a proton, H^+) may be added and share a pair of the electrons of the nitrogen atom

$$H:\ddot{N}:H + H^+ \longrightarrow \begin{bmatrix} H \\ H:\ddot{N}:H \\ \ddot{H} \end{bmatrix}^+$$
ammonia   ammonium ion

Variable Valence. The valences of many of the elements vary in different compounds, i.e., in some the degree of oxidation is higher than in others. The iron atom, for example, forms positive ferric (Fe^{+++}) and ferrous (Fe^{++}) ions. An iron atom contains eight more electrons than an argon atom, but does not lose eight electrons. There are two electrons in the outermost electron orbit, and 14 in the next to the outside orbit. When the two electrons in the outermost orbit are lost, ferrous ion (Fe^{++}) results. If one electron is removed from the next lower layer of electrons, the charge on the ion thus formed is three (ferric ion, Fe^{+++}). Similar variations in valence occur in many elements, such as Cu^+ and Cu^{++}, Mn^{++} and Mn^{+++}, Cr^{++} and Cr^{+++}, Au^+ and Au^{+++}. Loss of electrons from an inside shell can occur only when that shell is not stable (not completely filled); thus in the sodium atom the shell next to the one on the outside contains eight electrons, and consequently does not lose any; hence the sodium atom never has any valence other than $+1$.

Quantum Theory of Valence. This has been used to give a quantitative interpretation to the concept of valence. A covalent bond can be described as two electrons occupying one molecular orbital, the stability of the bond being governed by an effective overlap of the electrons involved and by energy considerations. The shapes of molecules can also be determined by considering that two or more orbitals of comparable energy can be hybridized to give orbitals which are directed in space; these orbitals participate in bond formation. The concept of hybridization has helped to explain the tetravalence of carbon. The electronic structure of carbon, $1s^2\,2s^2\,2p_x^1\,2p_y^1\,2p_z^0$, can be visualized as involving the excitation of one of the $2s$ electrons to the vacant $2p_z$ orbital, giving an arrangement $1s^2\,2s^1\,2p_x^1\,2p_y^1\,2p_z^1$. The $2s$ and $2p$ electrons can be hybridized to give four equivalent orbitals, and overlap with the $1s$ orbitals of four hydrogen atoms will give a molecule of methane (CH_4), in which the hydrogen atoms are tetrahedrally directed, and the bond angles $109°28'$.

HUGH W. PETERSON

VALENCIA, province and city, E Spain. The province is bounded by the Mediterranean Sea on the E, and by the provinces of Castellón de la Plana and Teruel on the N, Cuenca on the NW, Albacete on the SW, and Alicante on the S; area 4,155 sq. mi.; pop. (1960) 1,429,708. The coast has long stretches of sand dunes. There is a broad coastal plain rising inland to the central plateau of Spain. The chief river is the Turia. The province's extensive irrigation works were begun by the Moors, who occupied the area during the twelfth century. Valencia is celebrated for its oranges, dates, and grapes. Other crops are rice, corn, esparto grass, and olives. Fishing in the Mediterranean is an important industry. Manufactures include iron products, spirits, wine, oil, silk, carpets, wool, hemp, linen, glass, pottery and leather. Valencia is the capital and largest city, situated at the mouth of the Turia River, and 190 miles ESE of Madrid. It is a major seaport and important industrial center. Interesting features are the Gothic cathedral, the Palace of the Generality, the museum, university (1411), silk exchange, the Church of San Andrés, originally a mosque; and

SPANISH NATL. TOURIST OFFICE

El Miguelete, the Gothic campanile of the Cathedral of Valencia, is an octagonal tower 157 feet in height, constructed in the first decades of the fifteenth century.

the Alameda, a fashionable, tree-lined promenade. The city was founded, 138 B.C., by Decimus Brutus, a Roman consul. It was taken and partly destroyed by Pompey the Great, the Roman general, in 75 B.C. Valencia was captured by the Visigoths, A.D. 413; was taken by the Moors, 714, who made it their capital, 1021; and became part of the Kingdom of Aragon, 1298, and of the kingdom of Spain, 1479. Pop. (1958) 521,721.

VALENCIA, historic region and former kingdom of Spain, lying along the Mediterranean Coast, and corresponding in area to the modern provinces of Valencia, Castellón de la Plana, and Alicante. The interior is mountainous, but the coastal plain, aided by irrigation, is very fertile, and has been aptly called the garden of Spain. The chief rivers are the Júcar and the Turia. The region was conquered by the Moors, 714; for a time Valencia was part of the Caliphate of Córdoba (see CALIPHATE), but early in the eleventh century it became an independent Moslem kingdom. James I of Aragon conquered it, 1238, and added it to his kingdom. Under the sovereignty of Aragon and, later, the kingdom of Spain, Valencia enjoyed local autonomy. After the expulsion of the Moors, 1609, Valencia suffered an economic and cultural decline; and during the reigns of Philip V of Spain, 1700–24, and 1724–46, it ceased to be politically important.

VALENCIA, city, NW Venezuela, capital of the state of Carabobo; 10 miles W of Lake Valencia and 80 miles W of Caracas. Valencia is an important commercial city and market for cotton, coffee, and sugar grown in the area. Textiles, sugar, iron goods, leather goods, tires, and foodstuffs are manufactured. Founded by the Spanish, 1555, Valencia retains much of its colonial atmosphere. The city has many fine residences owned by wealthy landowners, whose income comes from estates in the Valencia basin. Pop. (1950) 88,701.

VALENCIENNES, city, N France, Nord Department; in Flanders; on the Escaut (Schelde) River, 18 miles NE of Cambrai and 6 miles from the Belgian border. Valenciennes lies in the center of the Anzin coal fields, and is a manufacturing center. Iron and steel products, machinery, beet sugar, spirits, glass, soap, chemicals, hosiery, and cotton textiles are produced. During the seventeenth and eighteenth centuries Valenciennes was famous for the lace produced there. Valenciennes is reputed to have been founded by one of the three Roman emperors named Valentinian. In the sixteenth century the town was a center of Protestantism. Valenciennes became the capital of Hainaut, 1628. Pop. (1954) 43,434.

VALENS, FLAVIUS, A.D. 328?–378, Roman emperor, was born in Pannonia, and became Roman Emperor of the East, 364, ruling with his older brother Valentinian I, who was Emperor of the West. He successfully fought the Visigoths north of the Danube, 367–69; waged an inconclusive war with the Persians, 373–75; and was again involved in a war with the Visigoths, 377–78, after having allowed them to settle south of the Danube in Thrace to escape Hun persecution. He was defeated and killed by Visigoths, under Fritigern at Adrianople, during the worst defeat suffered by a Roman army since Cannae. Flavius Vallens was an Arian and persecuted orthodox Christians during his reign.

VALENTINE, SAINT, a Roman priest, possibly identical with Valentine, bishop of Spoleto, who was martyred Feb. 14, A.D. 271. He is regarded as the patron saint of lovers and his day is celebrated as a lovers' feast. The custom of sending "valentines," missives or tokens of an amatory nature on February 14, probably originated from a pagan ritual celebrating the goddess Juno; some connect it with the medieval belief that birds begin to mate on this day.

VALENTINE, died 827, pope from late August or early September to October in 827, was born in Rome. He became a cleric while still a young man,

and his piety won him the favor of Paschal I, 817–24, who eventually ordained him subdeacon and deacon, and made him archdeacon of Rome. Valentine remained archdeacon during the reign of his predecessor, Eugene II, 824–27.

VALENTINE, city, N Nebraska, seat of Cherry County; on the Niobrara River, the North Western Railway, and U.S. highways 20 and 83; 265 miles NW of Omaha. The city is a trade center for an area in which livestock and grain are raised. Valentine was settled in 1882. Pop. (1960) 2,875.

VALENTINE AND ORSON, a famous romance of the Charlemagne cycle, composed during the reign of King Charles VIII of France, was first printed at Lyons in 1495. Valentine and Orson, twin brothers, are carried off—Orson by a bear, to be reared amid savage surroundings; Valentine by his uncle, King Pepin, who brings him up as a courtier. Many years after their separation, Orson, the epitome of uncouthness, and Valentine, with his courtly good manners and *noblesse oblige*, meet in a forest, and recognize each other despite their apparent differences, whose superficiality is thus demonstrated by the story.

VALENTINIAN I, Latin name Flavius Valentinianus, A.D. 321–375, Roman emperor, was born of humble parentage in Pannonia. Having risen in fame and status through his service in the imperial guard, he was proclaimed emperor, 364; as co-emperor he chose his brother Valens. As Emperor in the West, Valentinian spent much of his time in Gaul, guarding the Rhine defenses against invasions by the Alemanni, who were finally brought to terms, 374. He also sent Theodosius the Elder to put down a Saxon invasion of Britain and a Moorish rebellion in Africa. Valentinian, a Christian, maintained a policy of religious toleration throughout his empire.

VALENTINIAN II, A.D. 371–?392, Roman emperor, the younger brother of Gratianus, with whom he shared the succession to the western part of the Roman Empire upon the death of their father, Valentinian I, A.D. 375. Valentinian II's portion of the western empire, including Italy, Illyricum, and Africa, was administered by his mother Justina until 387, when both mother and son were driven from Milan by the threats of Maximus, and sought protection from the eastern emperor, Theodosius. Supported by Theodosius, Valentinian returned to the West, 388, but he was assassinated in Gaul a few years later, apparently by Arbogast, a Frankish general in the Roman army.

VALENTINIAN III, full Latin name Flavius Placidus Valentinianus, A.D. 419–55, Roman emperor, son of Constantius III, was named Emperor of the West, 425, but his mother, Placidia, daughter of Theodosius I, ruled for him, 425–440. During his reign, Roman Africa, Britain, and parts of Spain, Italy and Sicily were lost to the Suevi, Visigoths and Vandals, 439–40. A Roman victory was won by the general, Aetius, over Attila and the Huns at Châlons, 451; but Attila invaded northern Italy, 452. Valentinian was murdered by followers of Aetius, of whom Valentinian had been jealous and had had assassinated, 454.

VALENTINIUS, in full Basilius Valentinius, Anglicized as Basil Valentine, the purported author of works that were of great importance in the history of chemistry in that they represented a transition from mere alchemy, the attempt to make gold from base metals, to iatrochemistry, the planned production of drugs. To the seven metals known to the ancients—gold, silver, iron, lead, copper, tin, quicksilver—Valentinius added antimony (whose toxic quality he recognized), bismuth, and manganese; he was able to produce sulfuric acid and to open the path to the very difficult production of pure zinc; he also worked with arsenical compounds. To him, the philosopher's stone that the alchemists had sought was not a chemical, but the spiritual experience of

Nature's "inside." This experience was to be reached by a total immobilization of the inner man, an immobility analogous to that of rocks and the like. Valentinius' writings are usually ascribed to the fifteenth century and it has been asserted that he was a Benedictine monk in Saxony who used the admitted pseudonym, Basilius Valentinius. But neither this nor his true name can be proved, and close students of the history of science in this period doubt that Valentinius actually existed. The suspicion is that a chamberlain of the Thuringian town of Frankenhausen, Johannes Thölde, actually composed Valentinius' writings, especially the *Currus triumphalis antimonii,* some time after 1600. The fact that the names Basilius and Valentinius seem to have been chosen arbitrarily from the catalogue of famous second century Christian Gnostics, makes some intentional hoax seem the more probable; such a hoax would have well served the purposes of those who sought to discredit Paracelsus (1493-1541) by suggesting that he had derived many of his more important discoveries and insights from Valentinius' work. See PARACELSUS, *Controversial Figure;* SUDHOFF, KARL.

EUGEN ROSENSTOCK-HUSSEY

VALENTINUS, died A.D. ?160, heretical theologian, was born in Egypt. He gained a great reputation as a philosopher in Rome 140?-?160, entering into controversy with Justin Martyr. The heterodoxy of his teachings led eventually to Valentinus' excommunication, and he retired to Cyprus, ?160. His views were characteristically Gnostic, and his doctrines have been regarded by some as the high-water mark of Gnosticism. Valentinus' followers split into two schools: the Italian, to which Ptolemy and Heracleon belonged; and the Anatolian, which included Bardesanes.

VALERA Y ALCALÁ-GALIANO, JUAN, 1824-1905, Spanish writer, was born in Cabrá, Córdoba Province, studied law at the universities of Granada and Madrid, and by the age of 22 had already made a name for himself in Madrid as a poet, ladies' man, and man of the world. Beginning in the next year he served as a diplomat in Naples, where he read widely, learned Greek, and formed an influential liaison with an Italian marchioness. His first work of literary criticism was *Sobre los cuentos de Leopardi e del romanticismo en España.* He continued his diplomatic career, which was brilliant in itself, and also served as an excuse for his studies: he cultivated Portuguese while serving in Lisbon, for example. He was elected to the Spanish academy, 1861; and was a deputy in the Cortes from 1863, and a senator with tenure for life from 1881. In 1873 he wrote his first and most famous novel, *Pepita Jiménez* (1874). In later life he went blind, but had works in a variety of languages read to him, and wrote until the end. The most European of contemporary Spanish writers, he distinguished himself principally as a novelist, but also wrote excellent poetry, criticism, and historical studies. Among his other novels are *Doña Luz* (1879), *Genio y figura* (1897), and *Morsamor* (1899). In writing his novels he strove only for aesthetic values.

ANTHONY KERRIGAN

VALERIAN, full Latin name Publius Licinius Valerianus, A.D. 193?-?269, emperor of Rome, 253-260. He became princeps senatus, 238, and censor, 251. After the death of Gallus, and the short reign of Aemilianus, the Roman soldiers elected Valerian emperor. With his son Gallienus, he undertook to resist the barbarians who were then threatening the frontiers of the disordered Roman Empire. He recovered Antioch from the Persian, Shapur I, in 257, and drove the Persians back beyond the Euphrates; but, pressing on too fast, he was taken prisoner by Shapur I at Edessa, 260, kept in captivity in Persia for a time, and then put to death.

VALERIUS FLACCUS, GAIUS, died 92?, Roman poet, apparently influenced by Vergil and Ovid, was the author of an epic, *Argonautica,* a retelling, based on the work of Apollonius Rhodius, of the quest for the Golden Fleece. The *Argonautica,* thought to have been begun in the year ?80, was lost from ancient times until early in the fifteenth century, when a manuscript containing three books and a portion of a fourth were discovered.

VALERIUS MAXIMUS, Roman public official and writer during the first century of the Christian Era, went to Asia, A.D. 27, as a member of the retinue of Sextus Pompeius, and later became proconsul of Asia. Utilizing the works of Cicero, Livy, Sallust, Trogus, and others, he compiled a collection of historical anecdotes. The work was apparently intended as a textbook in rhetoric.

VALÉRY, PAUL, 1871-1945, French poet, was born in Sète of a French father and an Italian mother. Much of his youth was spent in Montpellier, where he attended the lycée and the law school, and became an intimate friend of Pierre Louÿs and André Gide. Having completed his studies he went to Paris where he worked in the ministry of war and, later, in the Havas News Agency. After a brief period of literary fertility, during which he wrote a few poems, examined the problem of creativity and responsibility in his *Introduction à la methode de Léonard de Vinci* (1895), and wrote a novel, *La Soive avec Monsieur Teste* (1906), Valéry came to the conclusion that mere literary production, however exalted, was superfluous and, in fact, a betrayal of one's intellectual integrity. For almost 20 years he devoted himself to the study of architecture, mathematics, and psychology. In 1913, however, he reluctantly allowed Gide to publish a collection of his verse and set about composing a poem that would serve as his farewell to writing. Again he found himself fascinated by the problem of the mathematical construction of poetry, as conceived by Edgar Allan Poe and practiced by Stéphane Mallarmé. For four years he worked on the construction and polishing of *La jeune parque* (1917). *Le cimetiére marin,* generally acknowledged to be his masterpiece, appeared in 1920. Nearly all of his poems deal with consciousness, its awakening to an awareness of itself and of the world. Valéry believed with his literary mentors, Poe and Mallarmé, that the real value of pure poetry lies not in the content but in the architectural and musical harmony of its form and in the precision of its style. Even his dialogues, modeled after Plato's, and his essays, were contructed according to the same rigorous technique. Valéry was elected to the French Academy in 1925.

C. W. COLMAN

VALETTA. See VALLETTA.

VALHALLA, a building situated seven miles east of Regensburg, Bavaria, that was erected, 1830–42, by Ludwig I of Bavaria, according to the designs of Franz Karl Leo von Klenze, in honor of German patriotism and liberty. It is of gray marble and is approached by 250 marble steps. It constitutes a German hall of fame.

VALHALLA, or Walhalla, in Teutonic mythology, the great golden hall of the gods, the abode of warriors slain in battle. It had 540 doors, through each of which 800 warriors could march abreast. For sport, the heroes engaged daily in fierce warfare with one another, but each day their wounds were miraculously healed before they sat down to feast with Odin.

VALI, one of the Aesir, gods of Scandinavian mythology, was the son of Odin and a giantess, Rinda. When he was only one night old, he killed his brother Hoth (or Höthr, or Hodur), thus avenging the death of another brother, Balder. The slaying of Balder began Ragnarök, the cataclysmic battle between the gods and the forces of evil; Vali is sometimes named as one of the survivors of Ragnarök.

VALINE. See AMINO ACIDS.

VALKA, city, U.S.S.R., in the Estonian Soviet Socialist Republic, on the Gauja River, on the border of the Latvian S.S.R.; 125 miles SSE of Tallinn. The city is an important railroad junction point. The chief manufactures are liquors, wood products, and flax. Valga adjoins the Latvian town of Valka. Pop. (1959 est.) 25,000.

VALKYRIES, in Teutonic mythology, supernatural maidens of great beauty whose duties included choosing the slain battle heroes to be transported to Valhalla, and handing to the warriors their drinking horns during their daily feast with Odin. The first Valkyrie, and supreme among them, was Freyja, Odin's wife and sister of the god Frey. The number of Valkyries is variously given as three or some multiple thereof. The love of one of them, Brünhilde, and Siegfried is the theme of Richard Wagner's opera *Siegfried*. See NIBELUNGENLIED.

VALLA, LORENZO, or Lorenzo della Valle, Latinized as Laurentius Valla, 1406?–57, Italian Humanist (see HUMANISM), was born and educated in Rome. He was ordained a priest, 1431, and during the same year published his first important work, *De voluptate*. This book, in dialogue form, presents the ethical systems of the Stoics, Epicureans, and Christians in such a manner as to imply that the Epicurean ethic is superior to the Christian. This occasioned the displeasure of some church officials, and Valla prudently left Rome to take teaching positions first at Pavia, later at Milan and Genoa, and eventually at Naples, where he came under the patronage of Alfonso of Aragon. See ALFONSO V.

Throughout these years, 1431–47, Valla continued to attack orthodoxy and tradition. In the *De falso credita et ementita constantini donatione declamatio* (1440), he rather effectively proved the Donation, or Gift, of Constantine (a document purportedly addressed by Emperor Constantine the Great to Pope Sylvester I) to be a forgery, and, in passing, exhorted the people of Rome to rise up and deprive the pope of his political power. In other works Valla accused St. Augustine of heresy, ridiculed the Latin of the Vulgate, denounced scholasticism, denied the perfection of the religious state, and questioned the need of the priesthood in general and of monks in particular. Brought to trial on charges of heresy, Valla was released only upon the vigorous intervention of his patron Alfonso. Shortly thereafter, ?1447, Valla moved to Rome at the request of the new pope, Nicholas V. This surprising indication of papal approval was one of the first official triumphs of the new Humanism over orthodox tradition.

Many of Valla's ideas were later taken up and given a more full expression by the Protestant reformers, especially by Martin Luther, who held Valla in particularly high esteem. Among Valla's less controversial writings are his excellent Latin translations of the Greek historians, Herodotus and Thucydides; and his *De elegantiis linguae latinae* (1442), which long remained a standard work on Latin grammar and style. Valla's New Testament commentary, *Collatio Novi Testamenti* (1444), was edited by Erasmus.

VALLADOLID, province, NW central Spain, in Old Castile; bounded by the provinces of León on the NW, Palencia on the N, Burgos on the NE, Segovia on the SE, Ávila on the S, Salamanca on the SW and Zamora on the W; area 3,222 sq. mi.; pop. (1958) 362,559. Valladolid is a flat limestone tableland drained by the Douro River. The climate is cold in winter and hot and dry in summer, with an average annual rainfall of less than 12 inches. Grain, grapes, and other fruits, and flax are produced, and sheep are grazed. Valladolid, the capital, is the only significant manufacturing center. Valladolid became a province in 1833.

VALLADOLID, city, N central Spain, capital of Valladolid Province; in Old Castile; at the junction of the Esgueva and the Pisuerga rivers, 100 miles NNW of Madrid. Valladolid is the marketing center for a large grain-producing region. The city has railroad shops, tanneries, and flour mills. Hardware, fertilizer, cotton textiles, and beverages are manufactured. Valladolid is the seat of a Roman Catholic archbishop and a university founded in the thirteenth century. Of special interest are the sixteenth century cathedral Renaissance and the thirteenth century Church of Santa Maria la Antigua. The city was the capital of the Kingdom of Castile from the fourteenth to the sixteenth centuries, and capital of Spain, 1600–06. Ferdinand II of Aragon and Isabella of Castile were married in the city, 1469. Christopher Columbus, the navigator, died in Valladolid, 1506, but his remains were later removed to Santo Domingo. Pop. (1958) 137,106.

VALLANDIGHAM, CLEMENT LAIRD, 1820–71, U.S. politician, was born in Lisbon, Ohio. After teaching for a time, he was admitted to the bar, 1842, was a member of the Ohio legislature, 1845–46, and was editor, 1847–49, of the Dayton *Empire*, a Democratic newspaper. He was declared defeated in a contest for a seat in the U.S. House of Representatives, 1856, but before the close of the session he was able to secure the unseating of his rival; he was twice re-elected, 1858 and 1860. When the Civil War broke out, Vallandigham sympathized with the South and denounced the North's policy of coercion in unsparing terms. After the expiration of his term in Congress, he returned to Ohio, where his continued attacks upon the government led to his arrest, 1863. He was convicted by a military court, and sentenced to imprisonment in Fort Warren, but Pres. Abraham Lincoln commuted his sentence to deportation beyond the military lines. Having no desire to remain in the Confederacy, he went to Bermuda on a blockade runner, and from there made his way to Canada. His party in Ohio had, meanwhile, nominated him for governor, but he was defeated by John Brough by about 100,000 votes. Soon permitted to return to the United States, Vallandigham participated in the Democratic national conventions of 1864 and 1868. In 1864 he was elected commander of the Sons of Liberty. In 1871, while counsel in a murder trial at Lebanon, Ohio, he attempted to demonstrate how the shooting had been done, discharged the pistol accidentally, and died instantly.

VALLE D'AOSTA, autonomous region, NW Italy; bounded by the provinces of Novara and Vercelli on the E and Turin on the S, by Switzerland on the N, and by France on the W; area, 1,260 sq. mi.; pop. (1958) 100,276. The region comprises the upper valley of the Dora Baltea River, a tributary of the Po River, and is enclosed by the Pennine Alps on the north and the Graian Alps on the south and west. Most of the region is above 6,000 feet in elevation; Mount Blanc on the west rises to 15,781 feet, Matterhorn on the north to 14,685 feet, Monte Rosa on the northeast to 15,200 feet, and Gran Paradiso on the south to 13,323 feet. The economy is generally agricultural; grains, grapes, and potatoes are grown in the valleys; the uplands are restricted to the pasturing of sheep, goats, and cattle. Aosta is the capital, largest city, and the chief processing center. Most of the inhabitants of the region are French-speaking. Valle D'Aosta Province was formed, 1927, from Turin Province; it was separated from Piedmont Region, becoming autonomous, in 1948.

VALLE DEL CAUCA, department, W central Colombia, bounded by the departments of Chocó and Caldas on the N, Tolima on the E, and Cauca on the S, and by the Pacific Ocean on the W; area 8,085 sq. mi., pop. (1957 est.) 1,460,490. The Pacific Coastal Plain, in the west, is about 15 miles wide and has a hot, wet climate. It is covered by dense jungle. Inland are the ranges of the Cordillera Occidental, which rise to elevations of more than 10,000 feet. The Cauca Valley, farther east, is drained northward by the Cauca River. To the south, the valley floor is covered with soft volcanic ash into which the river has cut a deep gorge; to the north of Cali the river winds across a wide flood plain. Along the eastern border of the department are the ranges of the Cordillera Central, which rise to heights of 12,-000 feet. The coastal plain is sparsely settled, and Buenaventura is the only significant port. The Cauca Valley is a major cattle-grazing area. Sugar cane and grain are important products. The Pan American Highway runs north-south along the eastern slope of the valley.

VALLE-INCLÁN, RAMÓN MARÍA DEL, 1866–1936, major Spanish novelist and poet, was born in the village of Villanueva, Galicia, and died in Santiago de Compostela in the same province. In the interim he had lived in Madrid most of the time from 1895, become one of the most colorful figures of his time, and written some of its finest literary works. In periods away from Madrid, he was a World War I war correspondent from 1916, and director of the Spanish Art Institute in Rome, Italy, from 1931. Personally, he was a living incarnation of bohemianism: perennially short of money, disordered, scandalous, brilliant, paradoxical, talented, garrulous, a political extremist, eccentric of dress (particularly after 1899, when he lost his right arm and took to wearing a long black cape), and extravagant in act. His earliest and most famous works, are erotic "sonatas" of each of the four seasons of the year—*Sonata de otoño* (1902) *Sonata de estío* (1903) *Sonata de primavera* (1904), and *Sonata de invierno* (1905): memoirs of the amorous adventures of the "Marqués de Bradomíro"—the most admirable of Don Juans, "ugly, sentimental and [Roman] Catholic." Soon Valle-Inclán developed a more theatrical style, but from 1921 wrote his famous *esperpentos*, such as *Los cuernos de Don Friolera*. The *esperpento*, a genre invented by Valle-Inclán, involves depicting both individual and social life realistically and yet distorted in such a way as to make the depiction seem all the more real. The best of his work is in the sonatas, which constitute a veritable history of love. They were collected as *El marqués de Bradomín*, 1907 (*The Pleasant Memoirs of the Marqués de Bradomín*, 1924).

VALLEJO, city, W California, Solano County; on San Pablo Bay at the mouth of the Napa River; on the Southern Pacific Railroad and U.S. highway 40; 25 miles NNE of San Francisco. The city is an industrial center in which sportswear, dairy products, boats, flour, sheet metal, window screens, and wood products are manufactured. Many residents are employed at the U.S. Navy yard at Mare Island. The city was settled late in the 1840's and named for the Mexican Gen. Mariano Guadalupe Vallejo. Vallejo was the capital of California, 1851–53. Pop. (1960) 60,877.

VALLÈS, JULES, 1833?–1885, French writer, was born in Le Puy in Auvergne. He was sent to Paris by his father to attend the Lycée Bonaparte, 1848, but soon became involved in revolutionary activities, for which he spent a period in prison, 1853. His series of sketches, *Les réfractaires* (1865) and *La Rue* (1866) depicted the bohemian and street life of Paris. He was exiled for his revolutionary activities, 1871, and lived in England until 1880. On returning to Paris he completed his most noted work, *Jacques Vingtras*, an autobiographical trilogy (*L'enfant*, 1879, *Le bachelier*, 1881, *L'insurgé*, 1886).

VALLETTA, or Valetta, city, capital of Malta; on a rocky promontory extending into a bay on the NE coast of the island and dividing the bay into two deep harbors. On the extremity of the promontory is the lighthouse of Fort St. Elmo; Fort Ricasoli lies on the peninsula enclosing the eastern harbor. The British made Valletta an important naval and military station, with naval dockyards and other installations occupying most of the harbor. During World War II most of the town's buildings, including the Palace of the Grand Master of the Knights of St. John, used as the governor's residence; the library, with its museum of antiquities; the lodges of the Knights; and the Cathedral of San Giovanni (1576) were destroyed. Pop. (1957) 18,202.

VALLEY, the depression between hills, ridges, and mountains through which surface drainage passes. If the depression is more or less bowl-shaped, it is called a basin. Valleys may originate in various ways, such as by folding or faulting of the rocks, or by glacial action, but the majority have been made by the streams which flow through them.

New stream-made valleys have their start on fresh land surfaces which have been raised from beneath the sea, or upon deposits recently laid down by volcanoes, glaciers, winds, or previously existing streams. On such new land surfaces, the first rainfalls form little rills which wash away loose particles, starting small gulleys, the first step in the development of valleys. With continued rainfall, the gulleys grow larger and larger until enormous valleys may result. In the early stages, gulleys and valleys carry water only during rainstorms and for short periods thereafter, but eventually the valleys become eroded to depths where they reach ground water. Thereafter, the streams become permanent because they carry drainage from the ground water as well as from rain. Many tributary valleys are formed simultaneously with the main valleys, and additional ones may start at any time later. A main valley whose tributaries branch from it resembles the trunk and branches of a tree, and is known as a valley system.

The highland area between two valley systems, consisting of ridges or mountains, is known as the watershed. It is here that the rainfall divides into two parts moving in opposite directions into one system or the other. The actual line along which the division takes place is called a divide. If the divide is of such prominence that it sends water not merely into different drainage systems, but into different oceans as well, it is known as a continental divide. The great Continental Divide of North America extends roughly along the crest of the Rocky Mountains, all streams flowing westward from the divide going generally into the Pacific Ocean, and all those flowing eastward going to the Atlantic.

Development. Geologists recognize stages in the development of valleys, which they refer to as youth, maturity, and old age. Very young valleys are **V**-shaped in cross-section, and their floors are no wider than the channels of the streams that flow through them. At this stage the power of the stream is concentrated upon cutting down into the land rather than in widening the valley. If the valley is located in a region that is high above sea level, the down-cutting process is rapid, and the valley sides are steep or almost vertical. Such valleys are known as canyons and gorges, the latter name being applied particularly if the valley is several times deeper than wide.

As time goes on, irregularities in the stream bed throw the current from side to side in the valley, causing the stream to cut laterally as well as downward, thus making the valley wider. After much of the land mass has been eroded away to form the wider valley, and the hills and ridges between have taken on a lower and more rounded appearance, the valley has reached maturity. In old age, the floor of the valley has been cut almost to base level, the hills have been reduced to low elevations, and the stream has become sluggish and meanders widely over its broad floor. The valley is now many times wider than deep, and its sides grade almost unnoticeably upward.

The time required for great valleys to develop is very long, and is dependent upon such factors as height of the original land mass above sea level, distance from the sea, climate, and hardness of the rocks. Studies of the Mississippi Valley System show that it is being eroded, over its entire area, at an average rate of only one foot in about 8,000 years. At this rate, 20,000,000 years or more will be required to wear the entire region down to sea level.

At their lower ends, or mouths, streams may cut their valleys down to the level of the sea, lake, or other stream into which they flow; but the valleys reach this limit only at their lower ends. The upper ends of the valleys are always higher. Thus, throughout the great valley system, such as that of the Mississippi, the Colorado, or the Amazon, a gradual slope, or gradient, exists which extends from near the mountaintops to the sea.   R. E. Janssen

VALLEY CITY, city, SE North Dakota, seat of Barnes County; on the Sheyenne River, the Northern Pacific and the Soo Line railroads, and U.S. highways 10 and 52; 55 miles W of Fargo. The city is a trade and processing center for an area in which wheat, oats, barley, flax, corn, and livestock are raised. It is the site of Valley City State Teachers College. Originally called Worthington the city was incorporated and renamed Valley City in 1881. Pop. (1960) 7,809.

VALLEY FEVER, also known as San Joaquin Valley Fever, or coccidioidomycosis, an acute infection caused by *Coccidioides immitis*. It is usually acquired by inhalation, but also may be contracted through a scratch or abrasion of the skin. If the disease is contracted, it will appear within 7 to 14 days after initial contact. Physical signs may be absent, but when the reaction is severe, the primary symptoms resemble those of pneumonia or acute bronchitis. Other symptoms may include loss of appetite, malaise, chills, fever, headache, backache, night sweats, and pleurisy. The disease may progress to a generalized condition that may involve bones, joints, subcutaneous tissues, internal organs, and the brain. The skin may become inflamed, marked by tender red nodules due to exudation of blood and serum, and accompanied by intense itching and burning.

Infected wild rodents have been found in the southwestern United States, but the cases most frequently encountered are in southern California. Sporadic cases are reported from Hawaii, southeastern Europe, and Italy. Cattle, sheep, and dogs have been found infected. The disease occurs at all ages, and a primary infection is most frequent in hot dusty autumn months. The majority of patients recover in 2 to 3 weeks, if given nothing more than supportive treatment. Chronic infections often present considerable difficulty. Iodides and colloidal copper have been used, but no specific treatment has been developed.

VALLEYFIELD, or Salaberry de Valleyfield, city, Canada, S Québec; Beauharnois County; on the St. Lawrence River and on the Canadian National and the New York Central railroads; 30 miles SW of Montreal. Cotton and rayon textiles, chemicals, paper, flour, and machinery are manufactured. Valleyfield developed from a construction camp at the western terminus of the old Beauharnois Canal, built in the 1850's. Pop. (1956) 23,584.

VALLEY FORGE, located on the Schuylkill River about 23 miles northwest of Philadelphia, Pa., is famous in the history of the American Revolution as the site of the encampment of the Continental army, commanded by Gen. George Washington, from mid-December, 1777 to June 19, 1778. After defeating Washington's forces in the battles of Brandywine and Germantown, the British went into winter quarters in Philadelphia. Washington chose Valley Forge, as the wintering place for his 11,000 troops, because it was readily defensible against attack, and was situated on communication and supply routes between the northern and southern colonies and eastern and western Pennsylvania. Although plans were made for supplying the garrison, the inefficiency of the commissary department and the bitter weather, which set in before it was expected, brought severe material privation upon Washington's army. In January, the melting snow made transport almost impossible, and later the failure of the Continental Congress to furnish matériel aid and reinforcements accentuated the difficulties. Men by the hundreds died of disease induced by malnutrition, inadequate clothing, and the lack of medical supplies; many others were sick, and some deserted. On several occasions, indeed, Washington almost despaired of holding his army together. Despite everything, most of the men stayed at their posts out of loyalty to their commander, and the military training introduced at Valley Forge by Baron Friederich von Steuben, a Prussian soldier serving with the revolutionists, made use of the time to introduce new methods of training and organization that greatly improved the fighting ability of Washington's soldiers. News of the colonies' alliance with France, which reached Valley Forge early in May, greatly encouraged the troops. Finally, on June 19, Washington broke camp at Valley Forge, and advanced against the British, who were evacuating Philadelphia. He engaged the enemy at Monmouth Court House, N.J., June 28, and won a strategic victory.

In commemoration of the ordeal at Valley Forge, which was perhaps the colonists' most trying test in their struggle for independence, Pennsylvania acquired the Valley Forge encampment site, 1893, and made it a 1,500 acre state park. Washington's headquarters was restored and converted into a patriotic shrine. Other features of interest are the Washington Memorial Chapel; a carillon of 13 bells, one for each of the original states; the Valley Forge Museum of American History, many Revolutionary relics; the Old Camp Schoolhouse; the Wayne Statue; the Soldiers' Hut; the Grand Parade Ground; the Lafayette Quarters; and the Washington Inn.

VALLEY STREAM, village, SE New York, Nassau County, on Long Island; on the Long Island Railroad; a residential suburb 17 miles ESE of New York City. Poultry, dairy cattle, and vegetables are raised in the area. The village is the site of Valley Stream State Park. Often called the Gateway to Southern Nassau, it developed rapidly after World War I and was incorporated in 1925. Pop. (1960) 38,629.

VALOIS, name of the ruling French dynasty, 1328–1498. When Charles IV, the last of the Capetians, died without a direct male heir, 1328, the barons of France chose Charles' cousin, Philip VI of Valois, as king; Philip thus became the first of the Valois kings. He was followed by John II, 1350–64, and Charles V, 1364–80. This was the period of the ruinous Hundred Years' War, in which the balance of power gradually but inexorably shifted from France to England. The battles of Crécy, 1346, and Poitiers, 1356, demoralized the chivalry of France, but the worst was still to come: during the reign of Charles VI, 1380–1422, France suffered an even more disastrous defeat at Agincourt, 1415. Subsequently, however, the nation's hopes were raised by the deeds of Joan of Arc, and Charles VII, 1422–61, was crowned at Reims. His successor, Louis XI, 1461–83, enlarged royal power by systematically humbling the great princes and nobles; in sum he added Maine, Anjou, Provence, and part of Burgundy to the crown's possessions. Charles VIII, 1483–98, obtained Brittany through his marriage with Anne of Brittany, but he died without male issue and was the last of the direct Valois line. He was succeeded by Louis, the son of Charles, duke of Orléans, who ascended the throne as Louis XII, 1498–1515, and thus became the first of the Valois-Orléans dynasty. The crown then passed to Francis I, 1515–47, first of the Valois-Angoulême line. See France, History, *Hundred Years' War.*

VALPARAISO, city, NW Indiana, seat of Porter County; on the Grand Trunk, the Pennsylvania, and the Nickel Plate railroads, and U.S. highway 30; 38 miles SE of Chicago. The city is an industrial center in which mica products, magnets, paint and varnish, machinery, bearings, and farm equipment are manufactured. It is the site of Valparaiso University (1859). Valparaiso was founded in the mid-1820's and incorporated in 1865. Pop. (1960) 51,227.

VALPARAÍSO, province, W central Chile; bounded by the provinces of Aconcagua on the NE and Santiago on the SE, and on the W by the Pacific Ocean; area 1,860 sq. mi.; pop. (1958) 618,469. The province is the smallest and the most thickly populated in Chile. It lies on the western slopes of the Coastal Range and has a narrow coastal plain. The province is heavily industrialized. The city of Valparaíso is the capital.

PAUL'S PHOTOS

Valparaíso, the second largest city and major seaport of Chile, was founded on the site of the Indian village of Quintil, 1536, by Spanish conquistador Juan de Saavedra.

VALPARAÍSO, city, central Chile, capital of the province of Valparaíso; on the Pacific Ocean, 60 miles NW of Santiago. Valparaíso is the second largest city of Chile and is the country's major port. It is the western terminus of the Trans-Andean Railroad from Buenos Aires. It has a strikingly beautiful location on the shore of a sweeping bay backed by a crescent-shaped chain of hills. The city is roughly divided into El Puerto (The Port), a section of old buildings and narrow, crowded streets on the northwestern part of the level strip along the bay; El Almendral (Almond Plantation), the commercial section of the southeastern portion of the bayside; and Los Cerros (The Hills), an amphitheater of steep hills rising behind the port to an elevation of 1,000 to 1,400 feet, containing the chief residential section. Communication between the city's two levels is both by improved roads and by several inclined railways. The Chilean Naval Academy and a naval museum are nearby. The Museum of Valparaíso has historical collections. Valparaíso is the seat of the law school of the University of Chile, the Catholic university (1928), and the Santa Maria Technical University (1931).

The city is an important commercial center and is the center of considerable coastwise trade. It has a ship repair yard, a floating dry dock, and several large foundries. Valparaíso is an important industrial center. Tobacco, textiles, clothing, leather goods, and chemicals are manufactured.

History. Valparaíso was founded, 1536, on the site of the Indian village of Quintil, by the Spanish *conquistadore* Juan de Saavedra. Its name meant "Vale of Paradise." During its first century the town suffered from raids by Dutch and English pirates. A Spanish fleet bombarded and destroyed a large part of the town during Chile's war with Spain, 1866. The city was sacked during the anti-Balmaceda revolt, 1891. In 1731, 1822, 1839, 1873, and 1906 Valparaíso suffered from severe earthquakes. The one of 1906 was accompanied by a fire that destroyed the greater part of the business section. Subsequently, Valparaíso was almost completely rebuilt, with wider streets and a modern sewage system. Pop. (1952) 222,000.

VALPARAISO UNIVERSITY, a private, co-educational institution of higher learning, located at Valparaiso, Ind. The university, affiliated with the Lutheran Church, Missouri Synod, was chartered as Valparaiso Male and Female Academy, 1859, and offered its first instruction the same year. The school closed, 1871, but reopened two years later as the Northern Indiana Normal School and Business Institute. The name was changed to Valparaiso College, 1900, and to Valparaiso University in 1907.

Among the university's various divisions are arts and sciences, founded in 1859; law, 1879; and engineering, 1917. Co-operative programs, in which students receive part of their undergraduate training with another university, are conducted, in conjunction with the University of Michigan, Ann Arbor, Mich.; Wagner College, Staten Island, N.Y.; American University, Washington, D.C.; and Carthage College, Carthage, Ill.

VALTIN, JAN, 1905–51, German–American writer, was born Richard Julius Herman Krebs in the German Rhineland. He joined the German Communist party, 1930, was arrested by the Nazi Gestapo, 1934, and sentenced to 13 years in prison, but escaped and fled to the United States, 1938. His account of life under a totalitarian government, *Out of the Night* (1941), became a best-seller in the United States but was banned in Germany, Italy, and the Soviet Union. Valtin lectured in the United States, sold U.S. War Bonds, served in the U.S. Army, 1943–45, and became a U.S. citizen, 1947. Among his other works are *Bend in the River* (1942), *Children of Yesterday* (1946), and *Castle in the Sand* (1947).

VALUE, that property, either in an object or imputed to the object by an appreciative subject, by virtue of which the object is esteemed. Philosophical questions about value were traditionally discussed in terms of "goodness," but in the nineteenth and twentieth century thinkers more commonly discussed such questions in terms of "value theory," axiology, or valuation. Most modern axiologists give special attention to aesthetics and ethics.

The ancient Greek philosopher Plato was perhaps the first to pose what proved to be the central axiological question of subsequent philosophy, namely: is a thing esteemed because it is good or is it good because it is esteemed. His answer was that the Good (or Goodness) is independent of its being appreciated. Aristotle, however, asserted that every good is good for something; the Good is what all desire. This conception of the Good might well have been the starting point of a theory of value, but Aristotle's tendency to structure his theories teleologically (in terms of ends and purposes) led him to explain the Good in terms of metaphysics rather than in terms of a theory of value as such; hence, things are good which man desires, and man desires whatever conduces to man's natural end. Christianity also, with God for an end, could define as valuable whatever conduces to an end, and as most valuable whatever conduces to Him.

Modern thinkers seeking to give a scientific account of reality, generally rejected Plato's notion of intrinsic Good, the ancient-medieval metaphysics that equated values with natural ends, and the Judao-Christian view that made value depend on God. Stripped of exterior sanctions, value systems had to become self-justifying.

English Theories. The earliest autonomous value system in England was that of Thomas Hobbes, who declared that acts and institutions have value insofar as they foster individual self-preservation. Among the Utilitarians (Jeremy Bentham, John Stuart Mill, and others) the supreme value was held to be the greatest good (pleasure) for the greatest number. In reaction to this, S. T. Coleridge, Thomas Carlyle, T. H. Green and F. H. Bradley asserted that human dignity or self-realization is the supreme value. While the religious sanctions of Bishops Butler (conscience) and William Paley (revelation) still continued to exercise a measure of influence, but a declining measure, the majority of thinkers turned to the empirical study of government, psychology, economics, and "humanity itself" in their effort to define value.

German Theories. Immanuel Kant excluded the question of value from scientific study (the domain of pure reason), but retained the idea as religiously significant (practical reason). G. W. F. Hegel identified reality and rationality and regarded value as objective and as in the process of being "realized" as part of reality's own self-realization. Ludwig Feuerbach and E. K. Dühring identified the supreme value as human rationality, and demanded that "obscurantist" religious sanctions be ruled out of order. Later studies of consciousness and its relations to reality led Alexis Meinong, Martin Heidegger and Nicolai Hartmann to hold that value *is* inherent in reality, although science cannot see it.

Value Theory in the United States. Ralph Barton Perry defined value as any object of any interest, thus raising the purely empirical question of what men do desire in fact. More theoretically, John Dewey posited the supreme value of "growth," both social and individual. At mid-twentieth century, perhaps the most active trends in value centered around C. I. Lewis' pragmatic-empirical study of the *act* of valuation; empirical attempts to apply concepts borrowed from economics and sociology; and the logical-positivistic analysis of language.

EDWARD B. COSTELLO

VALUE IN ECONOMICS

In commerce and industry, value is the quantity of one commodity that will be given in exchange for a specified amount of another commodity or service, or for a specified amount of money. The early Greeks believed that the degree to which a commodity contributes to man's needs will determine the price of the commodity, but this idea was eventually discarded by classical economists (see ECONOMICS, *Classical School*), on the objection that many plentiful and useful commodities, such as water or air, do not command a fraction of the price that is commanded by many scarce and often useless commodities, such as diamonds. The eighteenth century economist Adam Smith, in explaining value in terms of the relation between labor and cost, held that the amount of labor involved in its production determines the value of an economic good. Early in the nineteenth century, David Ricardo concluded that the value of an article depends not only on the amount of labor involved in producing it, but also on the amount of time involved.

The neoclassical theory of value, as expounded in the works of the British economist Alfred Marshall, considers the cost of producing an article in terms of the alternate uses that could have been made of the productive facilities involved (see PRODUCTION). In the long run, these alternate uses are determined by demand operating through the price mechanism. See SUPPLY AND DEMAND.

Marginal utility economists of the late nineteenth century, the most notable among whom were Karl Menger, W. Stanley Jevons, and Léon Walras, related value to price and quantity purchased, by assuming a law of satiable wants, or diminishing utility (see MARGINAL UTILITY). According to this law, the satisfaction yielded by each additional unit of a commodity consumed or acquired is less than that yielded by the previous unit acquired. The last unit that an individual can be induced to buy at a given price equates his desire (the value that he ascribes to the commodity) and the price, and is termed the marginal purchase. This concept isolates a given want and its satisfaction from all others. Later economists, however, approached the neoclassical interpretation of value by considering the value of a given good to the individual as relative to the values of all other goods that he might have acquired instead. Thus, value becomes an aspect of choice, and the valuation of one good is a comparison of the values of all goods. This doctrine holds that demand for one commodity is a function of demands for all other commodities and that the individual spends his income in such a way that the last unit purchased of each commodity yields equal satisfaction.

VALVERDE, BATTLE OF, an engagement of the U.S. Civil War that was fought Feb. 21, 1862, at Valverde, a crossing of the Rio Grande in eastern New Mexico Territory, between an invading Confederate force of about 2,600 under Gen. Henry Hopkins Sibley and 3,810 Union troops under Col. Edward Richard Sprigg Canby. Canby's troops were forced to withdraw, with a loss of 68 killed and 160 wounded; the Confederates lost 36 killed and nearly 200 wounded. The invading force went on to capture Albuquerque and Santa Fe, but was forced to withdraw from New Mexico Territory after the Battle of Glorieta, Mar. 27–28, 1862.

VAMPIRE, any being, whether animal or ghost, who actually or allegedly sucks the blood of living beings, man or beast. This habit was first ascribed to the "undead"—dead persons who rise from their tombs at night and drink the blood of young children, supposedly for the purpose of drinking themselves back into existence. The belief in, and fear of, such vampires, was said still to exist even in the 1960's in parts of eastern Europe, where the peasants believe that one can rid oneself of such undead only by unearthing the corpse, impaling it on a stick cut from a tree in full sap, burning its heart, and cutting off its head. The name vampire is of Magyar origin, and the belief in vampires was, and perhaps still is, especially strong in Hungary. In the sixteenth century, the European discoverers of South America rather unfairly applied the appellation *vampirus* to useful and essentially harmless "blood-sucking" bats. In modern American literature, the vampire (and vampirism) was introduced by Edgar Allan Poe. European writers have also written of blood-sucking in a symbolic sense—of people who can only live on the energy or life of others. Hence "vampirism" is often used as a general term for the amoral exploitation of the affection of others.   EUGEN ROSENSTOCK-HUESSY

VAMPIRE BAT, a small tailless blood-feeding animal that has pointed ears and a naked body about four inches long. Belonging to the family *Desmodontidae*, it is represented by two species, *Desmodus rotundus*, which is abundant, and *Diphylla ecaudata*, which is the vampire found in Central and South America. The upper incisors of the vampire are large and sharp and make a painless wound in the skin of an animal from which the blood is taken with the tongue. Vampires prey on livestock, dogs, chickens, and human beings, causing death in some cases by transmitting paralytic rabies. Vampires live in colonies in caves and in old uninhabited houses.

COLIN CAMPBELL SANBORN

VAN, province, SE Turkey, in Armenia; bounded by the provinces of Ağri on the N, Bitlis on the W, Siirt on the SW, and Hakâri on the S, and by Iran on the E; pop. (1960) 211,362. The province lies in an area of high plateaus. Most of the province drains into Lake Van, which forms much of the western border. Wheat, barley, and rye are grown. The capital and principal city is Van. The population is mainly Kurdish, with large Turkish and Armenian minorities. Roads connect the province with western Turkey, and with Khoi in Iran.

VAN, city, SE Turkey, capital of the province of Van, on Lake Van; 450 miles ESE of Ankara, and about 60 miles W of the Iranian border. The city is characterized by flat-roofed mud houses and narrow, winding streets; it is a trading center for the grain, sheep, and cattle raised in the area. Van was taken from the Persians by Alexander the Great and was held at various times by the Arabs, the Seljuks, the Mongols, the Tatars, and finally by the Ottoman Turks. After World War I the city was returned to Turkey by the Russians, who had captured it.

VAN, LAKE, SE Turkey, in Armenia; near the Iranian border; in the provinces of Van and Bitlis; about 5,700 feet above sea level and encircled by mountains. The lake is the largest in Turkey, covering an area of 2,100 square miles; it originated from the blocking of a valley by a lava stream. Its waters are brackish, and there is no apparent outlet. The principal island in the lake is Gadit. The lake has been navigated since earliest times.

VANADINITE, a rare mineral of secondary origin, found associated with veins of lead ores. Vanadinite has the chemical composition $Pb_5Cl(VO_4)_3$, a lead chlorovanadate. Its primary crystal structure is hexagonal; it is comparatively soft with a hardness of 3 (see HARDNESS), and is heavy, with a specific gravity of about 6.9. It is ruby-red to brown and has a high luster. It is a source for vanadium, used to harden steel; and to make vanadium oxide, VO_4, a mordant in dyeing.

VANADIUM, an element which exists as a light gray or white powder and which does not tarnish in air and which is not appreciably affected by moisture at ordinary temperatures. Its symbol is V, its atomic number, 23, and its atomic weight, 50.95. It belongs to group VB of the periodic arrangement of elements (see PERIODIC TABLE). Its density is 5.96 grams per millimeter at 20°C and it melts at 1710°C. It boils at approximately 3000°C. Its principal isotope has a mass number of 51. Other isotopes have a mass number of 50, 47, 48, 49, or 52. The element exhibits in its compounds oxidation numbers, or valences, of 2, 3, 4, and 5.

Vanadium, whose name is derived from Vanadis, the Scandinavian goddess of fortune, was first described as a new element in 1830 and isolated in 1869. The element constitutes about 0.017 per cent of the earth's crust, and although rare, it is more abundant than such metals as copper, tin, and lead. It is widely distributed in nature but rarely in rich deposits. In the United States, the chief vanadium-bearing ore is carnotite, a complex mineral of the formula $K_2O \cdot 2UO_3 \cdot V_2O_5 \cdot 3H_2O$ found in Colorado, Arizona, and Utah. Peru, Mexico, and parts of Africa are the other chief commercial sources of vanadium. The Peruvian ore, a complex vanadium sulfide, is called patronite. Vanadium is generally leached from its ores with acids, as vanadates, and then precipitated with ammonium chloride as the insoluble ammonium vanadate, which, on heating, yields vanadium pentoxide, V_2O_5, as follows:

$$2(NH_4)_3VO_4 \longrightarrow V_2O_5 + 6NH_3 \uparrow + 3H_2O$$
$$\text{Heat}$$

The pure metal can be prepared with difficulty by reducing the pentoxide with hydrogen or aluminum

$$V_2O_5 + 5H_2 \rightarrow 2V + 5H_2O.$$

Generally, vanadium pentoxide and iron oxide, Fe_2O_3, are reduced with carbon, yielding an alloy known as ferrovanadium, which usually contains 25 to 50 per cent of vanadium.

Vanadium is chiefly employed in the production of steels containing approximately 0.5 per cent of vanadium. These steels are resistant to vibrational strain and have high tensile strength. Vanadium pentoxide is used as a catalyst in the preparation of sulfuric acid by the contact process and in the preparation of phthalic anhydride from naphthalene. The pentoxide is used to impart a yellow color to glass and as a developer in photography. Ammonium vanadate has been used as a mordant in the dyeing and printing of fabrics.

VAN ALLEN BELTS, two shells of highly charged particles trapped in the magnetosphere, named for Dr. James A. Van Allen of the State University of Iowa, whose instruments first mapped the belts in 1958. Electrically charged particles streaming toward the earth in the "solar wind" are trapped in the lines of force of the earth's magnetic field that come to earth at 70–75 degrees north and south magnetic latitudes. These particles have maximum density at the equator and taper off to space empty of trapped particles around the North and South poles. Protons and electrons of relatively low energy are found in the trapping area from a few hundred miles out from the earth to the boundary of the magnetosphere. The Van Allen belts are made up of high energy protons trapped in two magnetic fields arching about 2,000 and 10,000 miles out from the earth, respectively.

According to a rule of electromagnetism, a fast-moving charged particle entering a magnetic field is deflected at right angles to both its original course and the lines of force of the field. In the magnetosphere the particle makes an open spiral far out from the earth's magnetic field where the field strength is low, but near the earth the spiral gets tighter until the particle is moving at right angles to the line of force. At this point it "mirrors" and is reflected in the opposite direction along a similar path. The increased strength of the magnetic field nearer the earth causes the particles to drift in longitude around the earth, circling the globe in a few minutes or hours, with electrons moving eastward and protons westward.

Following the discovery of the Van Allen belts, almost every satellite and rocket has carried instruments designed to measure the magnetosphere. An understanding of the behavior of magnetically trapped particles is essential to a manned space flight, since the radiation level of the Van Allen belts exceeds human tolerance. Such an understanding will also yield many valuable new insights into the relation between the earth and the sun.

There are, however, many problems in gathering and assessing data on this subject. The flux of particles is far greater in the outer belt than in the inner belt, and it has been suggested that the two may have different sources. In both belts the spatial distribution and the temporal flux of trapped particles is extremely complex. Furthermore, in addition to the disturbances in the magnetosphere caused by the sun's activity, man has added his own disturbances. In 1958, and again in 1962, the United States and the Soviet Union conducted atmospheric nuclear tests, injecting clouds of high-energy particles into the magnetosphere. Although these tests provided useful information, they have made more difficult the study of certain vital aspects of the natural radiation—its sources and behavior.

VAN BEERS, JAN, called the Elder, 1821–88, Belgian poet, was born in Antwerp. He taught Dutch language and literature at schools in Malines and in Lierre, and in the Antwerp Athenaeum. His Flemish grammar and reading book contributed greatly to a revival of interest in that language, as did his poems, of which the more important are *Jakob van Maerlant* (1860), *Jongelingsdromen* (1853), and *Rijzende Blaren* (1883). Collected editions of his verse appeared in 1873, 1884, and 1921.

VANBRUGH, SIR JOHN, 1664–1726, English architect and playwright, was born in London of Flemish antecedents, and studied architecture in France, 1683–85, before taking a commission in the English army. Arrested and imprisoned for espionage in France, 1690, he turned to writing to pass the time; *The Provok'd Wife*, written in prison, was produced with great success after his return to England. He was a facile writer—*The Relapse* (1696) took him only six weeks—and in addition to producing much original material, translated and adapted plays by Molière for the English stage. Vanbrugh's comedies are of perennial interest for their realistic reflection of the manners of their time. Turning to architecture at the age of 36, Vanbrugh designed Castle Howard, Yorkshire (1701), the Queen's Theatre (1705), and Blenheim Castle (1713), the last probably the most massive domestic structure in England, and certainly Vanbrugh's greatest architectural achievement. After Christopher Wren, Vanbrugh was probably the greatest of the British Baroque architects.

MARTIN GROSZ

ILLINOIS STATE MUSEUM

John Deere's improvements on the plow, in 1839, were a boon to the farmers on the prairie, and made him a wealthy man.

GOODYEAR RUBBER CO.

When Charles Goodyear accidentally dropped rubber treated with sulfur on a hot stove, 1840, he discovered the vulcanizing process which he patented.

Land speculation, state debts, and former Pres. Andrew Jackson's monetary policies caused the Panic of 1837 and a national depression.

N.Y. HISTORICAL SOCIETY

CUNARD WHITE STAR LINE

Grain was first shipped by water to Buffalo, N.Y., 1839, below, and the *Britannia*, above, began a transatlantic mail run, 1840.

CHICAGO HISTORICAL SOCIETY

WESTERN UNION

Samuel F. B Morse was in the process of perfecting his telegraph, which revolutionized communications.

Birthplace: Kinderhook, N. Y.

MARTIN VAN BUREN

Eighth President of the United States

1837—1841

CULVER SERVICE

VAN BUREN, MARTIN, 1782-1862, eighth president of the United States, was born on Dec. 5, 1782, in Kinderhook, N.Y., the eldest son of Abraham Van Buren, a small farmer and tavern keeper. He was educated in local schools, and at the age of 14 went to work in a lawyer's office, and began the study of law. He was admitted to the bar, 1803, and immediately entered politics as an ardent Jeffersonian Republican.

Early Political Career. He was appointed surrogate of Columbia County, 1808, and four years later was elected to the New York state senate on an anti-National Bank platform. During his two terms in the state senate, 1812-20, Van Buren became a leading figure in the Bucktail faction of the Republicans who opposed Gov. De Witt Clinton. Van Buren himself, however, supported Clinton's Erie Canal project. Van Buren was appointed state attorney general, 1815, and served until his removal by Clinton, 1819. Van Buren unsuccessfully opposed Clinton's re-election, 1820, but the Bucktails did win control of the state legislature. Van Buren then helped re-elect the Federalist Rufus King to the United States Senate, and was himself elected to the state's other U.S. Senate seat, 1821. During the same year, having helped organize a convention to revise the New York constitution, he brought about compromises acceptable to both radicals and conservatives on suffrage and on qualifications for office holding. Van Buren was now the chief of a well organized machine descended from the Bucktail faction. Among its other leaders were William Marcy and Silas Wright; their newspaper was the Albany *Argus*. The group, soon known popularly as the Albany Regency, eventually became the New York branch of the Democratic party. Although the Regency developed party discipline through control of public offices (the spoils system), its members faithfully carried out the duties of the offices they were elected to, and—in the words of their chief opponent, Thurlow Weed—were undeniably "men of great ability, great industry, indomitable courage, and strict personal integrity."

In Washington Van Buren became leader of the faction that supported Sen. William H. Crawford of Georgia for the presidency. In the election of 1824, Van Buren received Georgia's nine electoral votes for vice-president. Meanwhile, in the Senate, Van Buren supported state's rights and strict construction of the U.S. Constitution, opposed internal improvements at national expense, and voted for the tariffs of 1824 and 1828. After the election of 1824, Van Buren became a supporter of Andrew Jackson and helped merge the supporters of Crawford, Calhoun, and Jackson into what became the Democratic party. Re-elected to the Senate, 1827, he resigned, 1828, after being elected governor of his home state.

As governor of New York, Van Buren introduced a safety-fund banking system that insured the liabilities of New York banks. He resigned the governorship, March, 1829, to become President Jackson's secretary of state. As such, Van Buren settled a long-standing dispute with England, thereby reopening the British West Indies to U.S. ships; and he negotiated a treaty by which France agreed to pay for damages to U.S. commerce during the Napoleonic Wars. At home, he drafted President Jackson's message vetoing the Maysville Road Bill (1830). Van Buren resigned his post, 1831, to allow Jackson to purge the cabinet of Calhoun supporters, and was appointed minister to England, August, 1831; the Senate, however, with Calhoun casting the tie-breaking vote, refused to confirm the appointment, 1832. Almost directly as a result of this, however, Van Buren was nominated and subsequently elected as vice-president, 1832.

As vice-president, Van Buren supported Jackson's anti-bank policy and his handling of the nullification controversy (see NULLIFICATION). As Jackson's choice as successor, he was nominated for the presidency, May, 1835, and in the election of 1836 he received 170 electoral votes to the 124 obtained by no less than four other candidates.

As President. Shortly after his inauguration, Van Buren was faced with the sharp drop in stock and commodity prices and the serious banking crisis known as the Panic of 1837, among the causes of which were reckless overspeculation in public lands, President Jackson's specie circular of 1836, large state debts, and the calling in of loans by British bankers. Van Buren's program for meeting the crisis involved withholding from the states the fourth installment of the national surplus, so as to offset the expected federal deficit; issuing $10 million in treasury notes to meet the needs of the federal government; and creating, for the first time, an independent treasury (or subtreasury) in which the federal government could keep its funds. This last recommendation was defeated at first, was finally passed in 1840, and was soon repealed by the Whigs, 1841. Van Buren established the 10-hour day, without reduction of wages, on federal public works, 1840.

President Van Buren preserved peace with Great Britain during the Canadian insurrection of 1837, despite the Caroline incident, when a U.S. steamboat, supplying Canadian rebels, was attacked and sunk in United States waters with the loss of one life. This policy lessened his popularity considerably; his failure to support annexation of Texas and the costly second Seminole War in Florida lessened it further. And in the 1840 presidential election Van Buren received only 60 electoral votes, to the 234 obtained by the Whig candidate, William Henry Harrison.

Career After Leaving the Presidency. Van Buren was the leading candidate for the Democratic presidential nomination, 1844, but his continuing opposition to immediate annexation of Texas kept him from getting the necessary two-thirds vote of the delegates—although he did poll a majority—and the nomination finally went to James K. Polk.

During the 1840's Van Buren and his son John led the radical wing, the Barnburners, of the Democratic party in New York. The Barnburners and the conservative Democrats, or Hunkers, ran separate candidates in many state legislature races, 1845. The Barnburners seceded from the Democratic state convention, 1847, and drew up a platform opposing the extension of slavery into "territory now free"— that is, the lands to be acquired from Mexico; and they joined with other antislavery advocates, 1848, to form the Free-Soil party, which nominated Van Buren as its presidential candidate in the election of 1848. While Van Buren received no electoral votes, he did help to defeat the Democratic nominee Lewis Cass by splitting the Democratic vote. Van Buren supported the Compromise of 1850 and returned to the Democratic party in 1852. He soon retired to his estate, Lindenwald, at Kinderhook, but continued to take an active interest in politics until his death at Kinderhook, July 24, 1862.

Van Buren was called "the Red Fox of Kinderhook," "the Wizard of the Albany Regency," "The Flying Dutchman," and "the Little Magician" (he was 5 ft., 6 in.). He married Hannah Hoes (1783–1819) in 1807 and was the father of four sons. His eldest son, John (1810–66), became an important figure in New York state politics. Van Buren wrote an *Inquiry into the Origin and Course of Political Parties in the United States* (1867). His memoirs, up to the year 1833, were published in 1920.   ROBIN OGGINS

BIBLIOG.–Holmes M. Alexander, *American Talleyrand: The Career and Contemporaries of Martin Van Buren, Eighth President* (1935); *Dictionary of American Biography* (1936); Gerald W. Johnson, *American Heroes and Hero-Worship* (1943); Joseph N. Kane, *Facts About the Presidents* (1959); Louis W. Koenig, *Invisible Presidency* (1960); Denis T. Lynch, *Epoch and a Man: Martin Van Buren and His Times* (1929); Robert V. Remini, *Martin Van Buren and the Making of the Democratic Party* (1959); Edward M. Shepard, *Martin Van Buren* (1917); W. Harvey Wise, Jr. and John W. Cronin, comps., *Bibliography of Andrew Jackson and Martin Van Buren* (1935).

VAN BUREN, city, W Arkansas, seat of Crawford County; on the Arkansas River, the Frisco and the Missouri Pacific railroads, and the U.S. highways 64 and 71; a northeast suburb of Fort Smith, 125 miles WNW of Little Rock. The city has railroad shops, and is a canning center for spinach, peaches, and strawberries grown in the area. There are gas wells in the vicinity. The city was settled, 1818, as Phillip's Landing until renamed for Pres. Martin Van Buren, 1838. Pop. (1960) 6,787.

VAN BUREN, town, S Missouri, seat of Carter County; in the Ozarks; on the Frisco Railroad and U.S. highway 60; 115 miles SSW of St. Louis. The town is a resort center. Lumbering is an important industry. Big Spring State Park is 3 miles to the south. Pop. (1960) 575.

VANCE, ARTHUR, known as Dazzy, 1891–1961, U.S. baseball player, elected to the Baseball Hall of Fame, 1955, was born Clarence Arthur Vance in Orient, Iowa. A righthanded pitcher noted for his speed, he was with New York of the American League, 1915 and 1918; and with Pittsburgh, 1915, Brooklyn, 1922–32 and 1935, St. Louis, 1933–34, and Cincinnati, 1934, of the National League. He won 197 games; was the league's leading pitcher, 1924 and 1925, and the league's most valuable player, 1924; and pitched one no-hit game, 1925.

VANCE, ZEBULON BAIRD, 1830–94, U.S. public official and lawyer, was born in Buncombe County, N.C. As a U.S. congressman, 1858–61, he opposed the secession of North Carolina until war became imminent. During the Civil War, he served in the Confederate army as a colonel in the Peninsular Campaign, and as governor of North Carolina, 1862–65. After the war, he returned to legal practice, 1865 and was elected to the U.S. Senate, 1870, but was unable to take his seat because of trouble in having disabilities removed under the Fourteenth Amendment of the U.S. Constitution. Again governor of North Carolina, 1877–78, he put through a number of acts that started the state on its return to prosperity. He was again elected to the U.S. Senate, and was permitted to serve, 1879–94.

VANCEBURG, city, NE Kentucky, seat of Lewis County; on the Ohio River and on the Chesapeake and Ohio Railway; 75 miles ENE of Lexington. The city is a trade center for an area of livestock farms. Shoes, railroad ties, staves, and flour are manufactured. Vanceburg was founded in the mid-1790's and incorporated in 1827. Pop. (1960) 1,881.

VAN CORTLANDT, U.S. colonial family. Oloff Stevense Van Cortlandt (1600–84), U.S. colonist and public official, was born near Utrecht, Netherlands, and emigrated to New Amsterdam (New York) in 1638. He became deputy mayor of New York City, 1667, where his name is perpetuated in Van Cortlandt Park, which was originally a part of his New York City estate. His son, Stephanus Van Cortlandt (1643–1700), U.S. public official, was born in New Amsterdam. He was thrice mayor of New York, 1677, 1686, and 1687, and was for many years a judge of the court of common pleas. He was appointed commissioner of the revenue, 1686, and was chief justice of the colony, 1700. In 1697 his estates were erected into a manor by patent from William III. The grandson of Stephanus, Pierre Van Cortlandt (1721–1814), U.S. public official, was born in Cortlandt Manor, N.Y. He fought in the American Revolution, 1775, and became the first lieutenant governor of the state of New York, 1777–95. His son, Philip Van Cortlandt (1749–1831), U.S. soldier and public official, was born in New York City, served actively in the American Revolution, and was a member of the U.S. House of Representatives, 1793–1809.

VANCOUVER, GEORGE, 1758?–98, British navigator, entered the Royal Navy at the age of 13. An expedition under his command, 1791–95, explored, 1792–94, the Pacific coast of North America from 52° 18' N to 35° N latitude, discovering the Gulf of Georgia, and circumnavigating, 1793, what was later named Vancouver Island. He made two expeditions to the Hawaiian Islands, returning to England, via Cape Horn, 1795. His travel records, completed after his death by his brother John Vancouver and Captain Paget, were published as *A Voyage of Discovery to the North Pacific Ocean and Round the World in the Years* 1790–95 (3 vols. 1798).

VANCOUVER, city, SW Washington, seat of Clark County; on the Columbia River; on the Great Northern, the Northern Pacific, the Spokane, Portland, and Seattle, and the Union Pacific railroads, and on U.S. highways 99 and 830; 8 miles N of Portland and 140 miles S of Seattle. Vancouver, at the head of deepwater navigation on the Columbia River, is an important shipping point for grain and lumber. Chemicals, pulp and paper, wood products, and bricks are manufactured; aluminum is refined, utilizing power from Bonneville Dam; and fruit and fish are canned. The city is the site of Fort Vancouver National Monument. The original settlement grew up around Fort Vancouver, a Hudson's Bay Company post established in 1824. The fort became a U.S. military post, 1848, and was known as Vancouver Barracks after 1879. Vancouver was incorporated in 1857. The city, chartered in 1889, was largely rebuilt after a fire that year. Pop. (1960) 32,464.

VANCOUVER, city, Canada, SW British Columbia; on the Strait of Georgia and a peninsula between Burrard Inlet on the north and the Fraser River on the south; on the British Columbia Electric, the Canadian National, the Canadian Pacific, and the Great Northern railroads; 115 miles NNW of Seattle; pop. (1956) 365,844. Vancouver is the largest city in British Columbia and western Canada and the third largest in the entire country, after Montreal and Toronto.

Vancouver is linked by the Lions Gate and Second Narrows bridges with the north shore of Burrard Inlet. The city's climate is cool in summer and mild and rainy in winter. Vancouver is the commercial and industrial center of British Columbia and the chief distributing point of western Canada. It has an

BRITISH COLUMBIA GOVT.
Vancouver is Canada's third largest city and her largest seaport. Across Burrard's Inlet from the business district is seen the snow-capped West Coastal Range of mountains.

excellent natural harbor, which receives ocean-going vessels from all parts of the world and many smaller ships in coastwise trade. Seaborne trade is especially great when the Great Lakes ports are icebound during winter. The chief commodities handled at the port are wheat, pulpwood, lumber, logs, and firewood, sand and gravel, and petroleum products. Total tonnage averages almost 12 million tons per year, the largest volume handled by any Canadian port except Montreal.

Among the chief industrial concerns of Vancouver are shipbuilding yards, railroad shops, flour mills, sugar refineries, salmon canneries, distilleries, sawmills, and pulp and paper mills. Structural steel, logging equipment, paints, varnishes, and meat products are manufactured. The city is a major grain-storage center. Salmon and halibut fisheries are the main seafood resources. Tourism is also an important source of income for the city.

Of outstanding interest in the city is Stanley Park, on a peninsula extending into Burrard Inlet and containing landscaped gardens, a zoo, and an international memorial commemorating U.S.-Canadian friendship. The University of British Columbia is at Point Gray on a peninsula just west of the city. The Vancouver city museum contains exhibits pertaining to the arts, anthropology, and history of western Canada. Ski lifts at Grouse Mountain or Hollyburn offer outstanding views of the city and harbor.

History. A British expedition led by Capt. George Vancouver explored the Strait of Georgia and Burrard Inlet early in the 1790's. The first European settlements were not made until the 1860's, however, when sawmills were built on both sides of Burrard Inlet. The principal settlements on the site of Vancouver were Granville (popularly called Gastown) near Coal Harbour, and Hastings. The area at Granville was incorporated as the city of Vancouver, 1886, when it was announced that the Canadian Pacific Railway was to be extended from Port Moody to Coal Harbour. Vancouver was rebuilt following a fire that virtually destroyed the city later that year. Rail service began in 1887. With the advantages of a good deep-water harbor, railroad facilities, and the rapid development of natural resources in the area, Vancouver soon became the leading commercial center and shipping point for western Canada.

VANCOUVER ISLAND, Canada, SW British Columbia; separated from the mainland of Canada by the Strait of Georgia, Johnstone Strait, and Queen Charlotte Strait, and from Washington by the Strait of Juan de Fuca and Haro Strait; largest island of the archipelago fringing the Pacific Coast of North America; area 12,408 sq. mi.; pop. (1956 est.) 255,000. The island extends about 275 miles northwest to southeast and is about 80 miles at its greatest width.

The east coast is generally even, but the west coast is deeply indented by numerous bays and inlets.

Among the largest of these are the Alberni Inlet and Nootka, Clayoquot, Kyuquot, and Quatsino sounds. The island is generally mountainous, being an extension of the Coast Range of the United States; several of the highest peaks fall within Strathcona Provincial Park near the center of the island. Golden Hinde (7,219 ft.) is the highest point on the island. The climate is influenced by the warm moist Pacific winds especially on the west, where rainfall is generally in excess of 100 inches annually; on the east it is less than 50 inches. The forested mountains supply a large lumbering industry; fishing is important; farming is sufficiently developed to supply local needs only in the southeast. Considerable fruit is raised, and dairy products are exported. There are deposits of coal, copper, gold, silver, and iron. The island is a summer-resort center. The largest city and chief port of Vancouver Island is Victoria, capital of British Columbia. Other chief cities are Esquimalt, Ladysmith, Nanaimo, and Port Alberni, all on or near the southeastern coast.

Vancouver Island was visited by Capt. James Cook, 1778, and surveyed by Capt. George Vancouver, 1792. It was seized by the Spaniards, 1789, but was relinquished to Great Britain, 1795. British sovereignty over the island was confirmed by the Oregon Treaty with the United States, 1846. Vancouver Island became a crown colony, 1849, and was united with British Columbia, 1866.

VAN CURLER, ARENDT, 1620–67, Dutch colonist in New Netherland, emigrated from Holland to New Amsterdam (New York City) in 1638; was superintendent of Rensselaerwyck, and gained great friendship with the Indians. He founded Schenectady, 1662, and discarded the feudal regulations characteristic of Rensselaerwyck and other patroon estates.

VANDAL, a member of a Germanic people, probably closely akin to the Goths, who inhabited east central Europe from the Baltic Sea southward to the Carpathian Mountains and between the Oder and Vistula rivers, early in the Christian Era. It was probably a southern division of the people who, with the Quadi and the Marcomanni, were subdued by the Roman emperor Marcus Aurelius, A.D. 121–180. Some of the Vandals joined the Goths, ?240, in occupying, first the country north of the Black Sea, then the Roman province of Dacia. A Vandal horde invaded Italy, 405, and was repulsed by the Roman soldier Flauius Stilicho. About the same time other Vandals, together with Alans, Burgundians, and Suevians, overran Gaul, and committed such excesses of barbaric devastation that their name has proverbially since been given to persons causing wanton destruction. They passed into Spain, 409, and took Seville and Carthagena, 422. Andalusia, a historic region of southern Spain is probably named after the Vandals.

On the invitation of Bonifacius, the Roman governor of Africa, the Vandals invaded Africa under their king, Genseric, 429. In Africa they took Hippo Regius (modern Bane, Algeria), 431, and Carthage, 439, which Genseric made his capital. They ruled that part of the North African coast which corresponds to eastern Algeria, Tunisia, and western Libya, and soon built a fleet, and ravaged Sicily, sacking Palermo, and in Spring, 455, landed at the mouth of the Tiber, and plundered Rome, June 15–29, carrying thousands of captives to Carthage. The Vandals continued to harry the Mediterranean coasts. They conquered the island of Sardinia and repulsed a Roman attack on Sicily, 468. Their power was at its height when Genseric died, 477. In Genseric's time the Vandals became Arian Christians, and fiercely persecuted orthodox believers.

The Byzantine general, Belisarius, landed in Africa, 593, defeated the Vandals in several battles, and captured Carthage; Africa, Sardinia, and Corsica were soon restored to the Roman Empire, 534; and the Vandals soon ceased to exist as a nation.

VANDALIA, city, S central Illinois, seat of Fayette County; on the Kaskaskia River, the Illinois Central and the Pennsylvania railroads, and U.S. highways 40 and 51; 65 miles ENE of St. Louis. The city is a trade center for an area of oil wells and in which corn, wheat, soybeans, livestock, and poultry are raised. Furniture and shoes are manufactured. Vandalia was the Illinois state capital, 1820–29. The state capitol building, which then was used as a courthouse, became a museum, 1933. Vandalia was incorporated in 1821. Pop. (1960) 5,537.

VANDAMME, DOMINIQUE RENÉ, COMTE D'UNEBOURG, 1771–1830, French general, was born in Cassel. He fought under Napoleon I in Germany, but was forced by the Russians to surrender, with 10,000 men, at Kulm, 1813, and was imprisoned. Later, back in France, he commanded the third army corps under Grouchy during the Hundred Days, and distinguished himself at Wavre in the Battle of Waterloo, 1815. Exiled, 1816, he lived for a time in the United States before returning to France, 1824.

VANDENBERG, ARTHUR HENDRICK, 1884–1951, U.S. political leader, was born in Grand Rapids, Mich. He began work on the Grand Rapids *Herald*, and later served as editor, 1906–28. Vandenberg became active in state politics, was appointed U.S. senator to fill a vacancy in 1928, was elected to the office that year, and served continuously until his death. Before World War II he was an isolationist, but with the advent of the war he supported the administration of Franklin D. Roosevelt and later strongly supported international co-operation for world peace. He was a delegate to the United Nations Conference in San Francisco, 1945, backed the Marshall Plan and the North Atlantic Treaty Organization, and served as chairman of the Senate Committee on Foreign Relations, 1946–48, in which position he promoted the passage of the European Recovery Program, 1948. He was twice a contender for the Republican presidential nomination, 1940 and 1948.

VANDERBILT, a U.S. family of financiers, of whom the first member to attain wealth and prominence was Commodore Vanderbilt, who was born Cornelius Vanderbilt at Port Richmond, Staten Island, N.Y. in 1794. At the age of 16 he launched a ferry service between Staten Island and New York City. He started a Hudson River steamboat line, 1829, and was soon operating lines on Long Island Sound and between New York and Boston. He eliminated competition through rate wars and greatly increased the size and comfort of the boats he owned. During the Gold Rush of 1849, he established a steamship service to California, cutting two days from the previous traveling time by transferring passengers overland across Nicaragua. In the mid-1850's he started a transatlantic shipping line. At the outset of the Civil War he sold his shipping ventures and gave his yacht *Vanderbilt* to the U.S. government.

Early in the 1860's Vanderbilt began to invest in railroads, and by 1867 he had secured control of the New York and Harlem, Hudson River, and New York Central railroads. He improved equipment and service and by 1872 had merged the three lines into a single system, whose capital was greatly increased by stockwatering. He tried to buy control of the rival Erie Railroad, 1868, but was thwarted by Daniel Drew, Jay Gould, and James Fiske, Jr.; he was successful, however, in acquiring the Lake Shore and Michigan Southern Railway, 1873, and the Michigan Central and Canada Southern railways, 1875, and soon established a through route from New York to Chicago. Late in life he gave $1 million to Central, now Vanderbilt, University, Nashville, Tenn. At his death, 1877, Commodore Vanderbilt left a fortune estimated at $100 million.

William Henry Vanderbilt (1821–85), the eldest son, was born in New Brunswick, N.J., and went into railway business, 1857, as a receiver for the Staten Island Railroad. Later, working under his father, William showed great ability as an administrator. On his father's death, he expanded and improved his railway system, and by the time of his death had doubled his father's fortune. He left four sons: Cornelius Vanderbilt (1843–99), William Kissam Vanderbilt (1849–1920), Frederick William Vanderbilt (1856–1938), and George Washington Vanderbilt (1862–1914). The last of these, a pioneer in scientific forestry, attained success as an agriculturalist and stock breeder on his North Carolina estate, Biltmore. Cornelius Vanderbilt's eldest son Cornelius Vanderbilt III (1873–1942), was among the organizers of New York City's first subway company. William Kissam Vanderbilt's second son Harold Stirling Vanderbilt (1884–), was famous as a yachtsman—he successfully defended the America's Cup, 1930, 1934, and 1937—and as a contract bridge player.   ROBIN OGGINS

VANDERBILT MANSION NATIONAL HISTORIC SITE, SE New York, Dutchess County; area 212 acres. The original estate, much larger than the grounds of the present site, belonged to Peter Fauconnier and dates from early in the eighteenth century. It was first called Hyde Park, from which the town of Hyde Park was named, 1821. The mansion, overlooking the Hudson River, is an example of the type built by financial and industrial leaders late in the nineteenth century. It was completed, 1898, following the purchase of the estate by Frederick W. Vanderbilt, 1895. Vanderbilt Mansion National Historic Site was established in 1940.

VANDERBILT UNIVERSITY, a private, nonsectarian, coeducational institution of higher learning, located at Nashville, Tenn. Chartered, 1872, as Central University of Methodist Episcopal Church, South, the name was changed to Vanderbilt University in 1873, the year in which instruction was first offered.

Among the university's various divisions are law and medicine, founded 1874; arts and science, 1875; and divinity, 1875. Graduate work was first offered in 1875, but a formal graduate school was not established until 1935. The school of Nursing began as a department of the Vanderbilt University Hospital, 1909; its control was transferred to the university in 1925, and it became a professional school in 1930.

The university offers many advanced degrees, including a master of arts in teaching, a doctorate in comparative literature, and master's degrees in nuclear science and nuclear engineering. A special graduate program in economic development, supported by the International Co-operation Administration of the U.S. State Department, is offered primarily for government officials from underdeveloped countries. The university also conducts a radiological physics program in co-operation with the Oak Ridge National Laboratories.

Among the university's publications are the *Vanderbilt Alumnus*, issued bimonthly; the *Vanderbilt Law Review* and *Race Relations Law Reporter*, both issued quarterly; and occasional papers in the series, *Vanderbilt Studies in the Humanities*. See COLLEGES AND UNIVERSITIES.

VANDERGRIFT, borough, SW Pennsylvania, Westmoreland County; on the Pennsylvania Railroad; 25 miles ENE of Pittsburgh. The borough is a center for bituminous coal mining. Sheet metal, machinery, and gloves are manufactured. Vandergrift was laid out in 1895 and incorporated in 1897. Pop. (1960) 8,742.

VANDERLYN, JOHN, 1775–1852, U.S. painter of historical subjects, landscapes, and portraits, was born in Kingston, N.Y. Through the patronage of Aaron Burr, he was able to study under Gilbert Stuart in Philadelphia, and Antoine Paul Vincent in Paris, France, 1796, where he was strongly influenced by the work of Jacques-Louis David. In 1813–15 he painted and exhibited in Paris and Rome, with his close friend Washington Allston. He returned to the United States in 1815. His pictures in the grand manner were for the most part unsuccessful, but his *Ariadne* (1814) was important in freeing the female nude from the ban of American prudery. His *Marius Amid the Ruins of Carthage* (1807) established his reputation. He painted numerous portraits, including those of Zachary Taylor and other U.S. presidents. In his later years, the demand for his work died away, and he was forced to paint panoramas of battles and European cities to keep alive. He died in poverty.

VAN DER MEERSCH, MAXENCE, 1907–1951, French novelist, was born in Roubaix in Flanders. He was educated at Roubaix, Tourcoing, and at the University of Lille, from which he was graduated with degrees in law and literature. Van der Meersch is best known for his pacifist novel *Invasion 14* (1935), which deals with the German occupation of French territory during World War I. He also wrote *La maison dans la dune*, 1932 (*The House in the Dunes*, 1932), *La péché du monde* (The Transgression of the World), 1934, *L'Empreinte du Dieu*, 1936 (*Hath Not the Potter*, 1936), *Corps et âmes*, (Bodies and Souls, 1943), and *Le coeur pur* (The Pure Heart), 1948.

VAN DER WAALS, JOHANNES DIDERIK, 1837–1923, Dutch physicist, was born in Leiden and studied at the University of Leiden, 1862–65. After teaching physics in high schools for some years, he was appointed professor of physics at Amsterdam University, 1877, a position he held until his retirement, 1907. Van der Waals won the Nobel prize in physics in 1910 for his work, begun in the early 1870's, concerning the equation for the state of gases and liquids. See GAS, *Deviations from Ideal, Corresponding States.*

VAN DE VELDE, a family of Dutch painters of the seventeenth century. Esaias Van de Velde (1590?–1630) painted landscapes and military and carnival scenes. His brother Jan Van de Velde (1593?–?1641), painted portraits, landscapes, and historical and genre scenes. Willem Van de Velde, the Elder (1611–1693), the brother of Esaias and Jan, became one of the more prominent members of the family as a painter of seascapes, sea battles, and ships. In 1673 he and his son Willem Van de Velde, the Younger (1633–1707), went to England, where they became painters at the court of Charles II. Adriaen Van de Velde (1636?–1672), another son of Willem the Elder, remained in Holland, where he distinguished himself as an etcher and as a painter of landscapes and animals.

CULVER SERVICE

Willem Van de Velde the Elder, father of the renowned family of Dutch artists, attracts an audience as he paints one of the seascapes for which he was famous.

VAN DIEMEN'S LAND. See TASMANIA.

VAN DOREN, CARL CLINTON, 1885–1950, U.S. poet and historian, was born in Hope, Ill., and studied at the University of Illinois and Columbia University. He taught English at Columbia, 1911–30, and was literary editor of *The Nation*, 1919–22, and staff member of *The Century Magazine*, 1922–25. His biography *Benjamin Franklin* (1938) received the Pulitzer prize, 1939. Van Doren wrote *The Life of Thomas Love Peacock* (1911), *The American Novel* (1921, ed. 1940), *Many Minds* (1924), *Swift* (1930), *A Secret History of the American Revolution* (1941), *Mutiny in January* (1943), *The Portable Carl Van Doren* (1945), *American Scriptures* (with C. Carmer, 1946), and *The Great Rehearsal* (1948). He edited collections of writings of Benjamin Franklin and Richard Jackson, and several anthologies.

VAN DOREN, MARK ALBERT, 1894– , U.S. poet and critic, brother of Carl Van Doren, was born in Hope, Ill., and studied at the University of Illinois and Columbia University. He joined Columbia's English Department, 1920, becoming a professor in 1942. He was literary editor, 1924–28 and movie critic, 1935–38 of *The Nation*. His *Collected Poems* (1939) won the Pulitzer prize, 1940. Among Van Doren's critical works are: *Henry David Thoreau* (1916), *The Poetry of John Dryden* (1920, ed. 1946), *Edwin Arlington Robinson* (1927), *Shakespeare* (1939), *The Noble Voice* (1946), *Nathaniel Hawthorne* (1949), and *Introduction to Poetry* (1951). Among Van Doren's books of poetry are *The Mayfield Deer* (1941), *Our Lady Peace* (1942), *The Seven Sleepers* (1944), *The Country Years* (1945), *Careless Clock* (1947) and *Morning Worship and Other Poems* (1960).

VAN DRUTEN, JOHN WILLIAM, 1901– , English playwright, was born in London. He was graduated at 17 from the University College School, entered a lawyer's office and eventually took an LL.B. degree from London University, 1922. But his greatest interest was in writing, which he had been practicing on the side. He first achieved a literary reputation in the United States, with the play *Young Woodley*, produced in New York, 1925. Van Druten's subsequent career was one success after another; he became a leading writer for the U.S. and British theater and motion picture screen. He was at his best in comedies, and among these were *Chance Acquaintance* (1927), *There's Always Juliet* (1931), *The Distaff Side* (1933), *The Damask Cheek* (with Lloyd Morris 1942), *The Voice of the Turtle* (1943); *Bell, Book and Candle* (1951), *I Am a Camera* (1952), and *I've Got Sixpence* (1953). *I Remember Mama* (1944), another Van Druten play, was adapted from the book by Kathryn Forbes. *The Way to the Present* (1938) is an autobiography. Among his other works are *Playwright at Work* (1953) and *Widening Circle* (1957).

VAN DYCK, SIR ANTHONY, 1599–1641, Flemish painter and etcher, was born in Antwerp. At the age of 10 he became the pupil of Hendrik van Balen and later was admitted, 1619, to the St. Lucas Guild as a master familiar with all the details of his art. Sometime before, probably in 1617, he had held an important position in the workshop of Peter Paul Rubens, who profoundly influenced his early style. Such portraits as those of Frans Snyders and his wife (Frick Collection, New York), and of Jan Wildens and his wife (Detroit Museum), show that Van Dyck was a sensitive portraitist while still in his early 20's.

Titian's Influence. Soon after his father's death, 1622, Van Dyck went to Italy, where he remained for six years. In Venice he admired and studied the work

The Children of Charles I, by Van Dyck

of Titian, and was influenced both by Titian's coloring and by the way he posed his models. In Genoa,
Van Dyck decorated the magnificent palaces of the
Genoese patricians with splendid portraits of their
owners. Some of them still remain in their original
settings; others are now in European museums (*Don
Filippo Spinola*, Munich, *e.g.*). In Rome, Florence,
Mantua, and wherever else he went, the wealthy
wanted their portraits painted by Van Dyck, and
churches commissioned altarpieces by him. Portraits
such as that of the cardinal who later became Pope
Urban VIII, or of the Spanish viceroy, show that no
doors were closed to the successful artist. After his
return to Antwerp, Van Dyck painted many religious
pictures: *St. Augustine in Ecstasy* (Church of St.
Augustine, Antwerp), *The Blessed Herman Joseph
Kneeling Before the Virgin*, and several crucifixions and
lamentations. Van Dyck was by temperament more
lyrical than Rubens; he was better and more himself
when he did not have to present dramatic situations.
It was as a portrait painter that he did his most successful work.

In England. In 1632 Van Dyck entered the service
of Charles I of England, who made him "court
painter to their majesties" and within a few months
knighted him. He painted several pictures of the king
and queen and their children.

After the death of Rubens, who had always overshadowed him on the Continent, Van Dyck went to
his native country. When he returned to England to
settle his affairs there, his health, which had long
been poor, failed completely. He died at his residence
in Blackfriar at the age of only 42.

Significance. Van Dyck exercised a more personal
influence on portrait painting than any artist before
him and certainly laid the foundation for the important British school of portrait painting in the eighteenth century. He holds a unique position as a
portrait etcher. Even before settling permanently in
England, he started what is known as the *Iconography*,
a collection of 100 etched portraits of famous men.

HEDI NIJHOFF

BIBLIOG.–Lionel H. Cust, *Anthony Van Dyck: An Historical
Study of His Life and Work* (1900); Margaret Goldsmith,
Wandering Portrait (1954); Percy R. Head, *Van Dyck and
Hals* (1929).

VAN DYKE, HENRY, 1852–1933, U.S. clergyman, author, and educator, was born in German-

town, Pa. He held a Presbyterian pastorate in New
York City from 1883 until 1900, when he became
professor of English literature at Princeton University,
Princeton, N.J. He served as U.S. minister to the
Netherlands, 1913–16, but was unable to maintain a
neutral viewpoint and resigned to devote himself to
war propaganda. Shortly afterward he became a navy
chaplain. As a writer he was best known for his
inspirational essays and sentimental homilies, such
as *The Story of the Other Wise Man* (1896) and *The
First Christmas Tree* (1897).

VANE, SIR HENRY, called "the Elder," 1589–
1655, English political figure, was born in Kent. He
was a member of Parliament, 1614–42, and served
Charles I as a diplomat during the Thirty Years' War.
He became treasurer of the royal household, 1639, and
secretary of state, 1640. Dismissed from office in 1641,
Vane joined the opposition and represented Kent in
Oliver Cromwell's first Parliament.

VANE, SIR HENRY, called "the Younger," 1613–
62, English political figure, the son of Sir Henry
Vane the Elder (1589–1655), was born in Hadlow,
Kent. The younger Vane began his political career
in the embassies at Leiden, Vienna, and Geneva, but,
as a Puritan from 1628, he emigrated to Massachusetts Bay Colony early in the 1630's and was the
colony's governor, 1636–37. After being succeeded
by John Winthrop (1588–1649), Vane returned to
England, 1637, and became treasurer of the navy. He
served in both the Short and the Long parliaments,
and was knighted, 1640. Although a Puritan and
a leader of the parliamentary party, Sir Henry took a
more benevolent view of the monarchy than did his
compeers; later, although he refused to endorse the
king's execution, Vane was placed on Cromwell's
council of state, 1649. In 1650, while Parliament was
in the act of passing Vane's franchise reform bill,
Cromwell forcibly dissolved Parliament and had Vane
placed under house arrest. Upon Richard Cromwell's
abdication, 1659, Vane was released, and served on
the committee of safety and the council of state. After
the Restoration, 1660, Vane was imprisoned in the
Tower of London and later executed.

VAN HASSELT, ANDRE, 1806–1874, Belgian
librettist, poet, and historian, was born in Maastricht,
the Netherlands. He wrote new librettos for operas by
Wolfgang Amadeus Mozart and Ludwig van Beethoven, and many of his poems were set to music by the
French composer Jules Massenet. Among his works
are *Les primevères* (1834), *Histoire des Belges* (1851),
Poésies (1852), *Poèmes, paraboles, odes, et études rhythmiques*
(1862), *Les quatre incarnations du Christ* (1867), and *Le
livre des ballades* (1872).

VAN HORNE, SIR WILLIAM CORNELIUS,
1843–1915, U.S. railroad executive, was born in
Will County, Ill. He directed the construction of the
Canadian Pacific Railway, 1881–86, supervised the
first years of its operation, and served as president,
1888–89. Van Horne also superintended the construction of railroads in Cuba, 1900–02, and in
Guatemala, 1903–08.

VANIER, GEORGE PHILIAS, 1888–1967,
Canadian political leader, the first French Canadian
and the first Roman Catholic to serve as governor-
general of Canada, was born in Montreal and
studied at Loyola College, Montreal, and Laval University, Quebec. Called to the Quebec bar, 1911, he
practiced law, 1912–14, and saw active duty in
World War I. He was Canada's representative on the
Permanent Advisory Commission for Military, Naval,
and Air Questions to the League of Nations, 1928–31.
He was appointed to the Joint Permanent Board of
Defense of Canada and the United States, 1942, and
was ambassador to France, 1944–53. Vanier became
governor-general in 1959.

VANILLA, a genus of climbing tropical orchids
that bear thick leaves and spikes or racemes of large
fragrant flowers. The most important species are *V.
planifolia*, native to Mexico but most extensively

USDA

The vanilla plant, which is grown in Central America, produces pods that can then be cured and dried for use both as a food flavoring extract and as a base for perfumes.

grown in the West Indies, Java, and other tropical islands, and *V. fragrans*, grown in Mexico and Central America. They are the chief source of commercial vanilla, which is the cured fruit. Vanilla pods are picked and dried before they become ripe. During the drying process vanillin, used extensively as a flavor and perfume base, crystallizes at the surface of the blossom end of the pod, and eventually covers more than half the pod surface.

VANILLIN, an organic compound which occurs naturally in the vanilla bean and in potato skins and which is used as a flavoring agent. Its chemical formula is $C_8H_8O_3$ and its molecular weight, 142.14. It has the chemical name of 3-methoxy-4-hydroxybenzaldehyde. Vanillin can be made synthetically from related organic compounds of eugenol or guaiacol and can also be prepared from the lignin waste of the wood-pulp industry. Vanillin crystallizes in white to slightly yellow needles that have a pleasant aromatic odor and taste. The crystals have a density of 1.056 grams per milliliter and melt at 81°C. Vanillin is soluble to the extent of one gram in 100 milliliters of water. It dissolves readily in alcohol, chloroform, ether and carbon disulfide.

VANINI, LUCILIO, also known by the self-given name of Giulio Cesare or Julius Caesar, 1585?–1619, Italian free thinker, was born at Taurisano, near Naples. He studied philosophy and theology at Naples and Padua and was ordained a priest, but subsequently journeyed through central Europe audaciously preaching antireligious, pantheistic ideas. After fleeing from France and suffering a brief imprisonment in England, Vanini returned to Italy and Genoa, where he tried to teach; again forced to flee for his life, he made his way precariously back to France and there published *Ampitheatrum aeternae providentiae divino-magicum* (1615), an unconvincing and palpably hypocritical treatise against atheism, of which he had often been accused. This book managed temporarily to mollify his persecutors, however, and he was allowed to remain in France long enough to gain a number of disciples and to write another work, *De admirandis naturae reginae deaeque mortalium arcanis* (1616). This latter work, espousing views verging on absolute atheism, was soon con-

demned; as a consequence, Vanini was arrested, tried, and tortured, and, finally, burned at the stake.

VANIR, in Scandinavian mythology, an early race of gods, were at first fertility deities, but were later associated with weather, crops, and commerce. Their home was called Vanaheim. In earliest times they were represented as warring with the Aesir, another race of gods, but the two groups were later merged. Njörd, Freyr, and Freyja were Vanir.

VANITY FAIR, an important and perennially popular novel by William Makepeace Thackeray, was first published in monthly instalments, January, 1847–July, 1848, and then in book form, 1848, with illustrations by the author. The title, an allusion to the fair in John Bunyan's *Pilgrim's Progress*, gave rise to the expression "Vanity Fair," signifying the present world and all its worldliness and meanness. The novel gives a vivid and circumstantial picture of early nineteenth century English society. Probably the greatest characterization in all of Thackeray's works is that amoral heroine of *Vanity Fair*, Becky Sharp, perhaps the cleverest and most devious of the many predatory women in nineteenth century British and Continental fiction.

VAN LERBERGHE, CHARLES, 1861–1907, Belgian dramatist and poet, was born in Ghent. He studied in Ghent and at the University of Brussels, became active in the Symbolist movement in France, and with other Belgian writers sponsored the movement in Belgium. His poetry is filled with delicate, dreamlike imagery. *Chanson d'Eve* (1904) is considered by most critics to be his masterpiece. Among his other works are *Les Flaireurs* (1889) *Entrevisions* (1898), and *Pan* (1906).

VANLOO, a family of French painters prominent during the seventeenth and eighteenth centuries. Jacques Vanloo (1614–70), the son of Jan Vanloo (1585–1630), a Dutch painter, painted portraits, scenes from fashionable life, and mythological pictures. Jean Baptiste Vanloo (1684–1745), grandson of Jacques, acquired a high reputation in France and England as a painter of history, genre scenes, and portraits; among his most important works are a portrait of Louis XV and *Diana and Endymion*, for which he was admitted to the French Academy of Art, 1731. Charles André Vanloo (1705–65), the brother of Jean Baptiste, was well known for his decorative projects, his portraits, and his historical and genre paintings. Louis Michel Vanloo (1707–71), the son of Jean Baptiste, distinguished himself as a court painter to Phillip V of Spain. Charles Amedee Vanloo (1719–96), the brother of Louis Michel, was a court painter to Frederick II of Prussia and a designer of cartoons for tapestries. Jules Cesar Denis Vanloo (1743–1821), son of Charles André, painted landscapes.

VAN LOON, HENDRIK WILLEM, 1882–1944, U.S. author and journalist, was born in Rotterdam, the Netherlands. He emigrated at the age of 21, and studied at Harvard and Cornell Universities, and at the University of Munich, Germany, from which he received his doctorate, 1911. He served as an Associated Press war correspondent during the Russian Revolution of 1905–06 and World War I, and later combined writing with popular lecturing on history, geography, and the arts. His most famous books are *The Story of Mankind* (1921), *The Story of the Bible* (1923), *America* (1927), *R.v.R., the Life and Times of Rembrandt van Rijn* (1931), *Van Loon's Geography* (1932), *The Arts* (1937), and *Van Loon's Lives* (1942). A fragmentary autobiography, *Report to Saint Peter* (1947), was published posthumously.

VANNES, Breton Guened, city, W France, capital of Morbihan Department; in Brittany, 65 miles WNW of Nantes. Vannes is a railway junction. Industrial establishments in the city include shipyards, ironworks, and factories manufacturing textiles, leather goods, rope, and lace. The old city lies on a hill surrounded by fortifications. Of interest are the

Cathedral of St. Peter, burned by the Normans in the tenth century and later rebuilt, and the museum containing a collection of Celtic and Gallo-Roman antiquities. The area around Vannes is noted for its megalithic monuments of the Celts. The Veneti, a powerful Celtic tribe, were the leaders in a league against Rome; and it was not until 56 B.C. that Julius Caesar, the Roman Emperor, took Vannes, which he used as a base to subjugate Brittany and France. During the fifth century the city was ruled by independent counts. It later was under Frank rule. During the tenth century the area came under control of the Duchy of Brittany. Vannes was besieged, 1342, during the Hundred Years' War between France and England; it came under permanent French rule in 1532. (For population, see France map in Atlas.)

VAN RENSSELAER, KILLIAN, 1595–1644, Dutch merchant, was born in Amsterdam. As a wealthy pearl and diamond merchant, he played an important part in creating the Dutch West India Company, 1621, which settled New Netherland (later New York). Having acquired an immense tract of land south of what is now Albany, he established, 1635, the first and largest of the famous patroonships. He himself did not come to North America, but managed his estate through a director.

VAN RENSSELAER, STEPHEN, 1764–1839, U.S. public official, was born in New York City. He was one of the patroons of Rensselaerwyck. He was graduated from Harvard, 1782, and was a member of the assembly, 1789, state senator, 1790–95, lieutenant-governor, 1795–1801, and again member of the assembly, 1808–10. As a major general of New York Militia, 1812, he held a command on the Niagara frontier. As the Federalist candidate for governor, 1813, he was defeated by Daniel D. Tompkins. He was a member of the Erie Canal Commission, 1816–24, and its president, 1824–39. He was a member of Congress, 1823–29. He founded the Rensselaer Polytechnic Institute, Troy, N.Y., 1826, and was a regent, 1819–39, and chancellor, 1835–39, of the University of the State of New York.

VAN'T HOFF, JACOBUS HENDRICUS, 1852–1911, Dutch physical chemist, was born in Rotterdam, and was educated at Delft Polytechnic and at universities in Bonn, Leiden, Paris, and Utrecht. He became a lecturer, 1877, and a professor, 1878, at the University of Amsterdam; he was honorary professor at the Berlin Academy of Sciences from 1896. Van't Hoff was a founder, perhaps the founder, of the science of stereochemistry, or the chemistry of space, which grew out of his researches into the structure of the carbon atom, into the laws of chemical dynamics, and the laws of osmotic pressure. He received the first Nobel prize in chemistry, 1901.

VAN TWILLER, WOUTER, (or Walter), c. 1580–c. 1656, Dutch governor of New Netherland. Snatched from the obscurity of a warehouse clerkship in the Dutch West India Company, of which his uncle, Killian Van Rensselaer, was a director, Van Twiller was named governor in 1633. His blundering stewardship was later burlesqued by Washington Irving in his Knickerbocker's *History of New York*. Van Twiller was removed from his post in 1637.

VANUA LEVU, or Sandalwood Island, the second largest of the Fiji Islands. Fragrant yellow sandalwood is now rarely seen on the island, but the vegetation is still luxuriant and the rugged surface, dotted by boiling springs, still shocked by an occasional earthquake. Hills often rise above 2,000 feet here and the highest peak, Mt. Thurston, reaches 3,139 feet. Gold is dredged from Vanua Levu's mines, and sugar cane and copra are cultivated on its plantations.

VAN VECHTEN, CARL, 1880–1964, U.S. critic, novelist and photographer. Born in Cedar Rapids, Iowa, which he "loathed from the very first," Van Vechten escaped via the University of Chicago—from which he was graduated in 1903—and thence

via a job as crime reporter for Hearst's *Chicago American*, from which he was fired in 1905. In 1906 Van Vechten became assistant music critic for the *New York Times*, which he later served as drama critic. (As a critic, he was unsparing in praise of his favorites. Of Nijinsky he wrote, "His dancing has the unbroken quality of music, the balance of great painting, the meaning of fine literature, and the emotion inherent in all these arts.")

At 40, Van Vechten began writing novels. By 1930 he had written seven—all precious and entertaining—including *Peter Whiffle, His Life and Works* (1922), *The Tattooed Countess* (1922), and *Nigger Heaven* (1926). It was Van Vechten who helped make Harlem nightlife popular with white café society in the 1920's, but his interest in Negro culture went much deeper. Coupled with his passion for collecting, it resulted in his assemblage of photos and manuscripts by Negro authors and early recordings by Negro musicians—which he later gave to the Yale libraries as the James Welden Johnson Memorial Collection. A connoisseur of cats, he wrote *A Tiger in the House* (1922).

At the age of 52 Van Vechten announced he would never publish again, and did not, except for a few letters, short introductions to books by Gertrude Stein and other friends, and brief book reviews. In his later years, Van Vechten spent much of his energy on portrait photography; his subjects include Gene Tunney, William Faulkner, Billy Holliday, Salvador Dali, Alexander Woollcott, and Gertrude Stein.

VAN WERT, city, NW Ohio, seat of Van Wert County; 105 miles NW of Columbus. The city is a processing center for an area in which grain, livestock, and poultry are raised. Cheese, textiles, metal products, and canned foods are manufactured. Van Wert was founded in 1835 and incorporated in 1848. (For population, see Ohio map in Atlas.)

VAPOR, a substance in the gaseous state, or phase, below its critical temperature; above the critical temperature is called a gas. (See CRITICAL POINT.) Vapors depart from the gas laws markedly at temperatures close to the critical temperature; whereas gases considerably above the critical temperature obey gas laws. When the temperature of the substance exceeds the critical temperature, the substance is in the gaseous state and no amount of pressure and compression will alter the phase, even though the density of the vapor may increase considerably and exceed either that of the normal solid or liquid. On the other hand, for values of the temperature below the critical temperature, the pressure on the substance determines whether or not it is in the gaseous phase. For this reason, the substance is referred to as a vapor if it is below the critical temperature. As the pressure on the vapor increases, the volume of the vapor decreases, until condensation to the liquid or solid phase begins.

VAPOR PRESSURE, the pressure at which a liquid and its vapor can coexist in equilibrium at a given temperature. The pressure which is exerted by a saturated vapor at any temperature is the greatest pressure that the vapor can normally exert at that temperature. This pressure is called the saturated vapor pressure, the maximum vapor pressure, or, more simply, the vapor pressure of the liquid at that temperature. The value of the vapor pressure for a substance depends solely on the temperature, and increases with rise in temperature. At the boiling point the vapor pressure equals the external pressure on the liquid. In other words, the liquid boils at the temperature at which the saturated vapor pressure is exactly equal to the external pressure. Solids also show vapor pressures which vary with temperature in a manner similar to those of liquids. A solid substance sublimes, passing directly from the solid to the vapor state, if the vapor pressure of the solid reaches atmospheric pressure at a temperature below the melting point. Sometimes the maximum vapor pressure is referred to as the vapor tension which is the limiting value of the vapor pressure as the space in contact with the liquid approaches complete saturation.

VAR, department, SE France, in Provence; bounded by the Mediterranean Sea on the S, and by the departments of Bouches-du-Rhône on the W, Basses Alpes on the N, and Alpes Maritimes on the E, area of the department totals 2,325 sq. mi. Var is mountainous and has a deeply indented coast, along which there are winter resorts. Wheat is the principal crop in the valleys; there are vineyards and olive groves on the hillsides. Sheep are grazed on the mountains. There are tuna and anchovy fishing fleets along the coast. The capital is Draguignan, and the largest town is the naval base of Toulon. The department was formed in 1790. (For population, see France map in Atlas.)

VARANASI, or Benares, or Banaras, city N India, SE Uttar Pradesh, on the Ganges River, about 75 miles E of Allahabad. The city is a regional center of trade and processing and has cotton and oilseed mills. Manufactured products include brassware, brocades, toys, and jewelry. The city is also one of the great sacred cities of the Hindus. The Ganges River flows in an arc through the city and is bordered by high banks, which for a distance of about four miles are lined by broad flights of steps, or ghats; these ghats are of great religious significance to Hindus and are lined by temples. The city, one of the oldest in India, was an important Hindu center from the sixth to the eleventh centuries, when it was conquered by Muslims. It remained under Muslim rule until 1775, when it was ceded to the British. (For population, see India map in Atlas.)

VARANGIAN, a name given by the Greeks and Slavs to the Northmen, or Scandinavian rovers, who in the ninth and tenth centuries of the Christian Era raided the overland trade routes between the Baltic Sea on the North and the Caspian and Black seas on the South, and threatened the Byzantine imperial capital at Constantinople. Their political centers were at Kiev and Novgorod.

VARDAR RIVER, rises in S Yugoslavia and flows N and E past the city of Skopje, and then S into Greece, to empty into the Aegean Sea at the Gulf of Salonika. The Vardar is about 200 miles long; it is navigable for much of its length, and its valley, now traversed by a railroad, has been a trade route between the Aegean Sea and the Danube River since ancient times. The major tributaries of the Vardar are the Treska, the Pčinja, the Crna, and the Bregalnica rivers.

VARESE, EDGAR, 1885–1965, French-American composer, born in Paris. Although he began his education in preparation for a career in engineering, he entered the Schola Cantorum at the age of 18 and studied with Albert Roussel and Vincent D'Indy. Later, at the Paris Conservatoire, he studied with Charles-Marie Widor. In 1909, he took up residence in Berlin where he developed a close friendship with Ferrucio Busoni whose ideas had a profound influence on him.

Discharged from the French army in 1915 after a serious illness, Varèse went to the United States in 1916 and quickly became prominent in the country that was to be his adopted land for the greater part of his life. There being a scant audience for advanced music in the United States, he and Carlos Salzedo, in 1921, founded the International Composers Guild which, during the six years of its existence, gave the first performances of such works as Stravinsky's *Les Noces* and Schoenberg's *Pierrot Lunaire*.

Until the fashion for electronic music developed in the years following World War II, the greater part of Varèse's work—composed during the twenties and early thirties—was substantially neglected and the composer's output during subsequent years was curtailed. With his "discovery" by the youngsters of the postwar generation, both in Europe and America, his work (like that of Charles Ives and, more cur-

rently, Carl Ruggles) returned to a thoroughly deserved prominence. But in similar fashion to both the Ives and Ruggles revivals, the inclination of current criticism to evaluate the work of Varèse in terms of contemporary identification with his presumed artistic objectives, as opposed to the musical realities of his most celebrated works, would seem to be apparent. For while it was Varèse's objective to eliminate romantic feeling from art, to achieve an objectivity of style, the obvious expressive power of such works as *Amériques* (1932), *Arcana* (1932), *Octandre* (1924), or even *Ionisation* (1931) can be denied only by those who are determined to do so. And while Varèse's preoccupation with novelty "noise instruments"—such as sirens and ingenious percussion originations—were extraordinarily provocative for their day, it is equally clear that the actual musical materials of his more celebrated works are strongly derived from the primitivism of Igor Stravinsky's *Le Sacre du Printemps*.

Varèse is without question the composer of a handful of works that are of supreme artistic importance and originality. That they are as far afield from the mainstream of twentieth-century musical development as is sometimes claimed is open to question.

WILLIAM FLANAGAN

VARESE, province and city, N Italy, Lombardy Region. The province is bounded by Switzerland on the N and the provinces of Como on the E, Milan on the S, and Novara on the W; area 463 sq. mi. It lies on the southern slopes of the Alps, and Lake Maggiore forms most of its western border. The Ticino is the principal river. Chief crops are grapes, cereals, and hay. Silk, leather goods, paper, textile machinery, bicycles, and airplanes are manufactured. Varese, the capital and chief city, is located 30 miles NNW of Milan. The city has canneries, silk and paper mills, and factories producing leather goods, automobiles, and airplanes. It is the site of a sixteenth-century basilica and an archaeological museum and is also a popular resort area. (For population, see Italy map in Atlas.)

VARGAS, GETÚLIO DORNELLES, 1883–1954, Brazilian political leader, became provisional president of Brazil in 1930, following a revolution protesting the election of Julio Prestes. Under the constitution of the second republic, 1934, he became president. He built his political strength by suppressing revolts and by putting through two new constitutions, the second of which, 1937, gave him dictatorial powers. During his ascendancy, he instituted social and economic reforms and gave substantial support to the Allied cause during World War II. Ousted from office by the army in 1945, he was re-elected president in 1950. Forced to give up his power again, he committed suicide in 1954.

VARIABLE STAR, a star that may be broadly defined as one that exhibits observable variations in any of its characteristics. In this sense the sun would be classed as a variable star because of the periodic rise and fall of the number of sunspots on its surface. However, the change in brightness of the sun due to the sunspot cycle amounts to about 0.02 magnitudes only, and many stars may undergo similar undetected variations. Stars classed as variables show changes

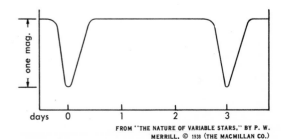

FROM "THE NATURE OF VARIABLE STARS," BY P. W. MERRILL. © 1938 (THE MACMILLAN CO.)

Fig. 1. Light Curve of a Typical Eclipsing Binary

that vastly exceed those exhibited by the sun. A variable star may generally be placed in one of three groups, depending upon the source of the variation: geometric, intrinsic, and extrinsic variables.

Geometric Variables. Many stars, apparently single to the naked eye, or even with the most powerful telescopes, consist of two stars that revolve about their common center of gravity in accordance with the law of gravitation (see DOUBLE STAR). When the line of sight from the earth to such a binary lies close to the plane which contains the orbital motion, each component of the pair will be eclipsed periodically by the other. Stars showing periodic variations in brightness attributable to eclipse by a companion are known as eclipsing binaries. A typical light curve of an eclipsing binary is shown in figure 1. (A light curve is a graph in which brightness, or magnitude, is plotted as the vertical coordinate and time as the horizontal one.)

All eclipsing binaries bright enough to be observed with the spectrograph (see SPECTROSCOPE) are also spectroscopic binaries. This means that the absorption lines in the spectrum of each component shift periodically back and forth with an amplitude in the wave length change that is a measure of the orbital velocity (see DOPPLER EFFECT). In the majority of such stars only the spectrum of the brighter component is visible, but in those in which the two components are of nearly equal brightness, both spectra can be observed. Not all spectroscopic binaries show periodic light variations, however, since in many of them the angle between the line of sight and the orbital plane is sufficiently large to prevent eclipses from being observed. The study of eclipsing spectroscopic binaries is of great importance, for they provide almost the only means for the simultaneous determination of stellar masses, radii, and densities.

Intrinsic Variables, as the name implies, are variable stars whose variations are due to some cause inherent within the stars themselves. The two chief classes of intrinsic variables are the Cepheids (so named after the star Delta Cephei), and the long-period variables. In addition to these there are several smaller groups, usually named after some star typical of the group, which fall under the general classification of irregular or semiregular variables. Novae, or "new stars" should also be included under the general classification of intrinsic variables. See NOVA.

Cepheid variables are marked by constancy of period and almost perfect regularity of behavior. Their periods range from about half a day for the cluster type or RR Lyrae variables, to over a month. The periods of the majority of Cepheids, excluding the RR Lyrae type, fall in the range from one to three weeks. Their amplitudes, that is the range of light variation, are usually somewhat less than one magnitude. Spectroscopic observations of the Cepheids show an alternate approach and recession of the surface layers

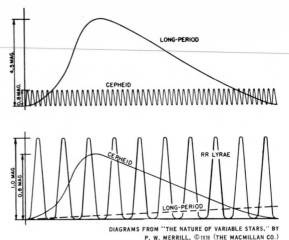

DIAGRAMS FROM "THE NATURE OF VARIABLE STARS," BY
P. W. MERRILL. © 1938 (THE MACMILLAN CO.)

Fig. 3. The chart shows representative light curves of three types of intrinsic variables. The upper graph shows that many cycles occur in the light variation of a Cepheid, while a long-period variable completes only one cycle. In the curve below it is seen that one Cepheid cycle corresponds to many cycles of an RR Lyrae variable and to a small fraction of one cycle of a long-period variable.

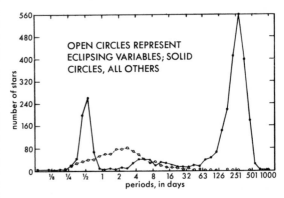

Fig. 4. The number of eclipsing and other type variables are shown in relation to their various periods in days.

of these stars, with the maximum velocity of approach nearly coinciding with maximum light. There is little doubt that the source of the variations of Cepheids is to be found in pulsations of the stars.

Cepheid variables have played an outstanding role in modern astronomy. It has been demonstrated by observation that the periods of these stars are very closely correlated with their absolute magnitudes (intrinsic brightnesses) in the sense that the longer the period, the brighter the star. (See figure 2.) Hence, if the period of such a star can be determined, its absolute magnitude follows at once, and comparison of the absolute with the apparent brightness yields the distance. Thus the Cepheids have provided the basic scale for all the really large astronomical distances measured in recent years, including the distances of the extragalactic nebulae (see GALAXY).

The long-period variables are all red giant and super-giant stars of spectral types M, N, R, and S, of the order of 100 times the luminosity of the sun (see GIANT AND DWARF STARS). Their periods range from about 100 to 500 days and a variation of five magnitudes (100 fold) from maximum to minimum brightness is typical (see MIRA). All of these stars are of low surface temperature, representative values at maximum and minimum being 2400° and 1800°, respectively, above absolute zero on the Centigrade scale. As would be expected for such low temperatures, the spectra are rich in bands due

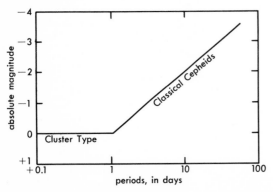

FROM "THE MILKY WAY," BY B. J. AND P. F. BOK
(THE BLAKISTON CO.)

Fig. 2. This schematic diagram indicates the period-luminosity relationship that exists for the Cepheid variables.

to molecules: titanium oxide in class M, carbon in classes R and N, and zirconium oxide in class S. The most surprising feature of the spectra of the long-period variables is the appearance of bright hydrogen lines during a portion of the cycle, and the fact that this emission takes place beneath the regions of the star where the absorption lines are formed. This situation differs from that prevailing in most stars which exhibit bright lines, that is, those of type B where the emission lines seem to arise in an external shell or appendage. Representative light curves of the three types of intrinsic variables described are shown in figure 3, and in figure 4, the number of variable stars classified according to their periods.

Extrinsic Variables. This group is exemplified by a number of dwarf stars in and near the Orion nebulae. It is practically certain that their variability is caused by the passage of the stars behind varying thicknesses of obscuring nebular material. See STAR.

OLIN C. WILSON

VARIATION, in musical composition and improvisation, altering the melody or harmony of a simple basic theme so that at each repetition it appears in a new and usually more complicated, but still recognizable, form. A theme-and-variations may be only a section of work, as in many sonatas; or it may be a composition complete in itself, in which case the last variation is usually in the form of a more or less brilliant coda. Variation form is particularly well-suited to the keyboard instruments.

VARIATION. See PROPORTION, *Proportionality and Variation.*

VARICELLA. See CHICKENPOX.

VARICOSE VEIN, any vein that is increased in length, in caliber, and at first in the thickness of the vessel walls. In severe cases varicose veins become tortuous, knotted, and finally thin-walled. Almost any impediment to the circulation can lead to varicose veins, and occupations which necessitate prolonged standing are extremely conducive to the condition. The veins most apt to be affected are those of the lower limbs. Varicose veins of the rectum may produce hemorrhoids. Varicocele is the varicose state of the veins of the spermatic cord. Varicosity is likely to be progressive, and often results in development of a varicose ulcer, a chronic superficial lesion that is very resistant to treatment. In suitable cases, the affected veins may be closed off by injection of vein-hardening solution. Sometimes surgical removal is practiced. Mild cases may be aided by elastic stockings or bandages.

VARIOLA. See SMALLPOX.

VARIUS RUFUS, LUCIUS, 1st century B.C., Roman poet, wrote during the Augustan Period, 43 B.C.–A.D. 14. His works were highly praised by his contemporaries, Vergil, Horace, and Maecenas. After Vergil's death, 19 B.C., the Emperor Augustus commissioned Varius Rufus to edit Vergil's *Aeneid*, with the assistance of Plotius Tucca. He was the author of the tragedy *Thyestes*, and two epics, *De Morte* and *Panegyric.*

VÄRMLAND, county, SW Sweden, bounded by Norway on the W and by the counties of Kopparberg on the NE, Örebro on the E, and Skaraborg and Älvsborg on the S; area 7,426 sq. mi.; pop. (1958) 291,035. The land descends from the Norwegian border to Lake Vänern on the southern border. There are numerous small lakes, and the county is heavily forested. Lumbering is important, and there is some production of oats, rye, hay, and potatoes, mainly bordering Lake Vänern. Iron ore is mined in the east, part of the Bergslagen Mining District. Karlstadt, the capital, and Kristinehamn are manufacturing centers.

VARNA, city, NE Bulgaria, capital of Varna Province; on the Black Sea, 240 miles ENE of Sofia. Varna is one of the chief Black Sea ports of the country, with a deep and commodious harbor sheltered from northerly winds. Grains and other agricultural produce are exported, and coal, petroleum, machinery, and metals are imported. Cottons and woolens, metal goods, tobacco products, and foodstuffs are manufactured, and fruit and vegetables are grown in the vicinity. Varna is a popular seaside resort. The city, in ancient times, was an important military and trade post. It was the site of the defeat, 1444, of King Ladislas III, of Hungary and Poland, by the Turk, Murad II. The town was occupied by the Russians in 1828. In 1854 Anglo-French forces and their allies occupied Varna during the Crimean War. The Congress of Berlin, 1878, ceded Varna to the Bulgarians. Known as Stalin after World War II, the city was renamed Varna late in the 1950's. Pop. (1956) 119,769.

VARNISH, a solution of a resin or gum in oil or spirit, used to furnish a high glossy coating to wood or metal surfaces so that they will be impervious to air and moisture. This coating is achieved by the evaporation of the spirit or other solvent, or by the oxidation of the oil. The composition of varnishes may be varied widely by using different oils and resin. The presence of the resin gives hardness to the resulting film, or coating. Generally, the more oil that is used with a given amount of resin the more durable is the film, but the film dries more slowly and is less hard. The resins most commonly used are solid at normal temperatures.

Oleoresinous Varnishes are composed of a resin or gum dissolved in a drying oil that hardens as it combines with oxygen from the air. These varnishes are usually prepared by heating a mixture of resin, drying oil, thinner, and drier to about 600°F. The usual resins are ester, gum, rosin esters, synthetic resins, or kauri gum, a resin from a New Zealand pine. Synthetics include cumerone, phenol-aldehyde resins, and maleic acid resins. Fast-drying varnishes made with synthetic resins and tung oil are more durable than those made with natural resins. Linseed oil is in common use refined to remove mucilaginous sediment and undesirable substances. The refined oil bleaches out in the varnish-making process. The most important drying oil for varnish, however, is tung oil from China and the southern United States. Since raw tung oil dries to produce a wrinkled cheesy film, it is first subjected to a special heating and cooling treatment, or thermolizing. The treated tung oil gives a durable, hard, waterproof film on drying. Perilla oil, which is obtained from Manchuria, dries about as quickly as linseed oil but gives a harder film. Other oils used in making oleoresinous varnishes are soybean oil, oiticica oil from Brazil, and castor oil that has been converted into a drying oil by catalytic dehydration at reduced pressure. Oiticica oil dries almost as rapidly as tung oil. Soybean oil, because it bleaches on heating and turns yellow more slowly than other oils, is especially useful in white enamels. Varnishes with asphaltum in place of resin are called baking japans. Spar varnish is a clear, waterproof product for exteriors and boats. It usually contains tung oil and ester gum.

Spirit Varnishes are composed of a resin or gum dissolved in a volatile solvent such as alcohol, petroleum spirit, oil of turpentine, naphtha, or acetone. These varnishes may be colored by the addition of gamboge, cochineal, or an alcohol-soluble dye. Spirit varnishes dry quickly as the solvent evaporates, leaving a thin, bright film. The principal resins used in making these varnishes are shellac, dammar, sandarac, mastic, and such synthetics as urea-formaldehyde, vinyl, and acrylic-acid resins.

Driers are substances such as manganese oxide and compounds, especially soaps, of lead and cobalt, which hasten the drying action. The varnishes are thinned by the addition of turpentine, xylene, toluene, or a hydrogenated naphtha. Hydrated lime neutralizes the acid in the resin, clarifying and hardening the varnish and preventing stickiness in warm weather.

Enamel paints are pigmented varnishes. The vehicle may be an oleoresinous or alkydresin varnish. The latter is used for automobile and truck bodies, but not as widely as lacquer enamels. Duco-spirit varnishes belong to the group of resin lacquers, which, when pigmented, are called resin enamels. Enamel paint gives a durable, glossy surface. Quick-drying in modern production is made possible by baking the surface in ovens or infrared baking tunnels.

Varnish Removers are preparations containing liquid organic solvents or alkaline substances that have a solvent action on varnish. A wide variety of liquid organic solvents, including acetone, methyl ethyl ketone, methylene chloride, and butyl alcohol, may be employed, but since these substances are very volatile, they are usually put into paste form with paraffin wax or cellulose nitrate to retard the rate of evaporation. Alkaline substances used as varnish removers include solutions of trisodium phosphate, sodium carbonate, caustic soda, and ammonium hydroxide. After the varnish has been removed, a 5 per cent solution of oxalic acid is applied to neutralize the alkali and bleach the wood.

VARRO, GAIUS TERENTIUS, died after 200 B.C., Roman public official, was consul at Rome, 216 B.C., with Lucius Aemilius Paulus. As general of the Roman army, Varro fought and lost the Battle of Cannae against Hannibal, 216 B.C.

VARRO, MARCUS TERENTIUS, 116–27 B.C., Roman scholar, was born in Reate. He was propraetor under Pompey the Great in his war against the pirates and later, during the civil war between Pompey and Julius Caesar, he commanded troops for Pompey in Spain, 48 B.C.; however, Varro was reconciled with Caesar, who made him director of the new public library. After the assassination of Caesar, Varro was proscribed by the Second Triumvirate, but friends saved him from execution. He spent the rest of his life in tranquil study. Of his no less than 74 works, among the most important are satires in the style of Menippus, mock tragedies, poems; and the *Antiquitates rerum humanarum et divinarum,* which was much used by St. Augustine in writing his *De civitate dei.* Among Varro's other books are *Imagines* (Portraits) of some 700 Greek and Roman celebrities, and *Disciplinae,* a sort of encyclopedia of the liberal arts.

VARUNA, in Vedic literature, the firmament. In later Indian mythology, Varuna was represented as a white man riding on a sea monster, and came to be identified with the moon, and considered sovereign over the physical and moral orders.

VARUS, PUBLIUS QUINTILIUS, died A.D. 9, Roman general, was consul at Rome, 13 B.C.; governor of Syria 6–4 B.C.; and commander of the Roman army in Germany, A.D. 6–9. His harsh rule provoked the Germans, under Arminius, to revolt, A.D. 9. Entrapped in the Teutoburger Forest, his legions were annihilated after three days of fighting and heavy losses; Varus killed himself by falling on his sword.

VASARI, GIORGIO, 1511–74, Italian art historian, painter, and architect, was born in Arezzo, Tuscany. He was brought to Florence, 1523, where he enjoyed the patronage of the Medici family and studied under Michelangelo Buonarroti, Andrea del Sarto, and other lesser artists. As a painter, Vasari developed as a somewhat anemic imitator of Michelangelo, but he was a brilliant architect, as specimens of his work in Rome, Florence, Arezzo, Pistoja, and Pisa testify. Vasari's fame rests chiefly, however, on his monumental history, *Vite de' piu eccellenti pittori, scultori, ed architetti* (Lives of the Most Eminent Painters, Sculptors, and Architects). This immense work, the first and probably most important history of modern art, was completed in 1547, and published, after extensive stylistic revisions by Annibale Caro and others, in 1550; a second enlarged and much improved edition was issued in 1568. Vasari wrote the book, in his own words, ". . . not to acquire praise as a writer, but to revive the memory of those . . . who do not merit that their names and works should remain the prey of death and oblivion." Vasari's *Lives* is to Italian art history what Plutarch's *Lives* is to the history of ancient Greece and Rome. It not only rescued numerous early painters from complete obscurity, but provides biographical, technical, and anecdotal information nowhere else available.

VASCULAR BUNDLE, a cluster of cells found in plant stems and forming three types of plant tissue: xylem, phloem, and cambium. Vascular bundles allow water and inorganic salts to pass from the roots to all parts of the plant, and carbon and nitrogen compounds to the leaves, where the plant manufactures its food. A cross-sectional cut of a plant stem shows the phloem closest to the outer edge of the stem, followed by the cambium, the tissue that forms new xylem and phloem, and finally, the xylem, composed of tracheid and vessel cells that conduct water and minerals. Vascular bundles extend into the leaves where they are called veins. They perform the same tasks in the leaves as in the stems.

VASE, from the Latin *vas* (vessel), a container whose height is generally greater than its width, which has no spout or lip, and which usually has no lid. It may be made of porcelain, glass, metal, alabaster, marble—among many possible materials. Although originally a strictly utilitarian object used for domestic, sacrificial, ritualistic, or funerary purposes, in modern times the vase was almost invariably used primarily as an ornamental object.

Oriental Vases. All of the great cultures of history developed vase forms. The bronze casters of China were among the finest craftsmen the world has ever known. The earliest examples of Chinese vases date probably from before 3000 B.C. In the historical period called Shang-Yin, 1766?–1122 B.C., a white clay was used to make handsome vessels with designs carved on the surface. In porcelains the Chinese developed some of the simplest forms into high examples of proportion and curve. The decoration was often intricate, but was subordinated to the dynamics of the whole. The note of simplicity implicit in Chinese culture greatly influenced the Japanese and much modern design.

Greek and Roman. The Greeks produced many types of vessels that proved to be the progenitors of vases, and vessels of all types, in later Western culture. The Greeks' immediate source was oriental, but their decoration added a new note to the craft. The most important shapes developed in the Classic culture of the West are as follows:

(1) *Amphora,* a storage jar, widely used throughout the Mediterranean. The amphora was usually of elongated egg shape, with narrow neck, and with handles almost as high as the orifice. Later architects, especially those of the seventeenth century, used them in architectural decoration. The Greeks and Romans had used them in more utilitarian fashion, principally in the transporting of oil, wine, honey, and corn; these most functional amphora were left undecorated, and were pointed at the bottom so that they might be temporarily planted in the earth. Decorated amphora, used as ornaments, had disk-shaped bases.

(2) *Hydria,* which were used for carrying water.

(3) *Crater,* a mixing jar for wine and water. This form was also used in later architectural decoration.

(4) *Cantaros,* a drinking cup, much like a crater.

(5) *Oinochoë,* used in pouring wine, which evolved into the pitcher.

(6) *Lecythos,* an oil flask.

(7) *Cylix* and *Phyton,* were both used for drinking purposes; the former resembled a modern champagne glass, the latter was horn-shaped, often fashioned like a human or animal head, and was obviously the ancestor of the cornucopia vase and the stirrup cup.

The classic Greek vase was made of terra cotta, and was painted red and black, often with touches of white and purple. In Hellenistic times, another type of vase was made of glass, opaque with white reliefs on blueblack. Pottery centers in Etruria produced vases based on Greek prototypes, but heavier in shape and decoration which, especially in black, were called *bucchero.*

Beside the more usual vases with black or red ground, a number of *lekythoi*, usually employed for oil and perfumes, were made at Athens for use in connection with burial of the dead. Since all traces of wall painting in ancient Greece have disappeared, modern knowledge of Hellenic painting is based to a large extent upon the vase decorations.

The urn (Latin *urna*), usually a vase furnished with foot or pedestal, although originally used for various purposes—for storing liquids, or even for holding lots before drawing—is chiefly identified with storage of the ashes of the dead after cremation.

Middle Ages. The main activity in vase manufacture during the Middle Ages took place in the Islamic areas of the Middle and Near East, and in Sicily and Spain. In the thirteenth century, large storage vases of great beauty were produced in Iran; turquoise-blue glaze was common, and ornamentation consisted of Kufic inscription and bands of arabesque scrolls in low relief (see PERSIAN ART AND ARCHITECTURE). A well-known type of Islamic pottery has been long associated with Rakka, on the Euphrates River; some of the pieces, especially those dating from the twelfth century, have great elegance and beauty of design. The luster is usually dark brown, a color which seldom appears in ceramics of other areas. Decoration consists of arabesques and Kufic inscriptions, and occasionally of stylized animals. Some pieces of Rakka pottery, those in black and blue, are regarded as among the masterpieces of Moslem ceramic art. Exportation of Hispano-Moresque pieces carried oriental forms and color schemes through most of Europe. Meanwhile, during the same period, the art of glass blowing was making great progress in Venice.

During the Renaissance, the use of Classical vase forms in tectural decoration spread from Italy to the rest of Europe. Modified amphorae, urns, craters, and cantaros of terra cotta, marble, bronze, and lead were placed in gardens and around fountains. During the seventeenth and eighteenth centuries they became more and more sculptural, and were fantastically adorned with fruits, figures, and flowers. Neo-classic forms were inspired by simpler Greco-Roman models. The importation of Chinese porcelains increased the vogue for vases in house decoration, and the love for odd vessels during the eighteenth and nineteenth centuries led to the creation of porcelain vases in riotous combinations of classical, oriental, and baroque shapes, heavily worked with ornamental detail.

Twentieth Century. Utmost simplicity of design came to be the principal objective in the design of modern vases. Some individual craftsmen often enriched the twentieth century geometric forms, creating objects that transcend the anonymity of mass production. No other foreign influence affected twentieth century Western craftsmen more than did the traditional crafts of Japan. Craftsmen in Sweden, Spain, the United States, Australia, and elsewhere sought to create vases of dynamic simplicity, characteristically employing small asymmetrical distortions and "planned accidents" of color and glaze. See POTTERY.   ANTHONY KERRIGAN

VASELINE. See PETROLATUM.

VASOMOTOR SYSTEM, the system of nerves which controls the expansion and contraction of the blood vessels. The functions of the vasomotor system are to maintain by homeostatic mechanisms an even, but adequate, head of pressure in the capillaries; to make quick adjustments to the needs of the moment in the general level of pressure; and to produce local vasomotor changes, directly or indirectly influencing the blood supply of certain organs or systems in the body. The vasomotor system is concerned with the modification of blood flow through a decrease or an increase in the caliber of the blood vessels brought about through the contraction or relaxation of the visceral muscle in their walls.

There are many ways of determining whether stimulation of a particular nerve to an organ has vasomotor effects: (1) does the organ become blanched or livid? (2) is its temperature lowered or raised? (3) does it shrink or swell? (4) is the flow of blood from its veins increased or decreased? If stimulation of the peripheral stump of the cut nerve leading to the structure produces the same effect as does stimulation of the intact nerve, the fibers in question are efferent, vasoconstrictor or vasodilator, as the case may be. If, on the contrary, only stimulation of the central stump of the cut nerve leading to the nervous system is as effective as is stimulation of the intact nerve, the fibers are afferent, pressor or depressor, depending upon whether they cause reflex vasoconstriction or vasodilation.

Efferent vasoconstrictor fibers are usually sympathetic in origin, while vasodilator fibers are parasympathetic. (See AUTONOMIC NERVOUS SYSTEM.) However, the same nerve may be vasoconstrictor in one species, vasodilator in another. Among the important vasoconstrictors are the splanchnic nerves, whose stimulation produces a generalized decrease of blood flow in the abdominal viscera, indirectly increasing the circulation of blood through the muscles. The center of the vasomotor system, which lies in the medulla oblongata, exerts a continuous tonic influence on the caliber of the blood vessels. This tonic effect occasionally shows a periodicity, resulting in a regular waxing and waning of the blood pressure level.

The activity of the vasomotor center can be influenced in many ways. Afferent impulses, originating in stretch receptors in the walls of the aortic arch and the carotid sinuses, stimulated by a rise in blood pressure and an increased distention of the arteries, cause a reflex general vasodilation. (See CAROTID ARTERY.) In the same regions there are aortic and carotid bodies, containing chemo-receptors, sensitive to changes in the tensions of carbon dioxide and oxygen, as well as to variation in the hydrogen ion concentration of the blood plasma. An increase in carbon dioxide tension leads to reflex vasoconstriction and thus a rise in blood pressure. Similarly, chemical effects are exerted by the variations in the composition of the blood acting directly on the cells of the vasomotor center. The temperature-regulating centers also send nerve impulses to the vasomotor center, cutaneous vasodilation leading to a fall in body temperature, vasoconstriction enabling the organism to conserve heat. Cerebral influences on the vasomotor center are evident in the cutaneous vasodilation in the face and neck region, or blushing, that follows embarrassment. See BLOOD PRESSURE.

There are also vasomotor influences exerted directly on the peripheral arterioles by metabolites and hormones. Again carbon dioxide tension and hydrogen ion concentration appear as causative agents, an increase in either evoking a local vasodilation. Adrenaline and pituitrin each produce a rise in blood pressure through vasoconstriction. Renin, an enzyme formed in the kidney, converts one of the blood plasma protein into angiotonin, the latter producing a general vasoconstriction and a chronic rise in arterial blood pressure.   NATHANIEL KLEITMAN

VASSAL. See FEUDAL SOCIETY; FIEF.

VASSAR COLLEGE, a private institution of higher learning for women, located at Poughkeepsie, N.Y. Chartered as a liberal arts college, 1861, the school offered its first instruction four years later. Originally called Vassar Female College, the name was changed, 1867, to Vassar College at the request of the founder, Matthew Vassar.

The institution's association with the American School of Classical Studies at Athens, Greece, and the School of Classical Studies of the American Academy at Rome, Italy, enables Vassar students to attend either of these schools without paying additional tuition fees. Students in their junior year who are preparing for a teaching career may be selected to participate in a two-year program at Yale University; after the first year of study, these students receive a bachelor of arts degree from Vassar, and after the second year they receive a master of arts in teaching from Yale. Foreign study terms for students in their junior year are conducted in co-operation with Sweet Briar, Smith, Hamilton, and Wayne Colleges, and New York University. The foreign study program includes individually planned studies in English or Scottish universities.

Among the library's special collections are a history of the periodical press, publications of Mitchell Kennerley, the works of Robert Owen and Bliss Carman, materials on the Knights of Malta, and Edna St. Vincent Millay, and the Village Press Collection of fine printing. Publications include the *Vassar Alumnae Magazine*, and the *Vassar Journal of Undergraduate Studies.*

VASSILENKO, SERGEY NIKIFOROVITCH, 1872–1956, Russian composer, was born in Moscow, and studied at the Moscow Conservatory from 1895; as a graduation exercise, he composed the prize-winning cantata, *The Legend of the City of Kietzh* (1901). From 1907 Vassilenko was director of the Moscow Historical Symphony Concerts. Notable among his compositions are a Symphony in G Minor; the vocal works with orchestra, *The Widow* and *The Whirlpool; Epic Poem*, for orchestra; and *The Garden of Death*, a symphonic poem.

VÄSTERÅS, city, S central Sweden, capital of the county of Västmanland; on Lake Mälar, 60 miles WNW of Stockholm. The city is an industrial center; high tension electrical equipment and electric locomotives are the chief manufactures. Västerås, one of the oldest towns of Sweden, dates from the tenth century. The city is the seat of a bishopric dating from the twelfth century; the present cathedral dates from the fourteenth century. Tidö Castle (1640) stands in a large park. Pop. (1958) 74,702.

VÄSTERBOTTEN, county, N Sweden, bounded by Norway on the NW, the Gulf of Bothnia on the SE, and by the counties of Norrbotten on the NE, and Västernorrland and Jämtland on the SW; area 22,838 sq. mi.; pop. (1958) 240,403. The land rises from a coastal plain, which averages 20 miles wide, to mountains of more than 5,000 feet in elevation on the Norwegian border. There are many lakes and rivers, all trending northwest to southeast. There is lumbering in the west. Oats, rye, and hay are the main crops. The Skellefteå district, in the extreme northeast, is one of the major mining areas in Sweden. Gold, silver, nickel, copper, zinc, and lead are produced; Boliden is the major center. The capital of Västerbotten is Umeå.

VÄSTERNORRLAND, county, E central Sweden; bounded by the Gulf of Bothnia on the E, and by the counties of Västerbotten on the N, Gävleborg on the S, and Jämtland on the W; area 9,924 sq. mi.; pop. (1958 est.) 289,050. The coastline is deeply indented and is flanked by a narrow plain rising westward to an upland with scattered lakes. The Angermanälven is the major river. Timber is cut in the upland and floated down the rivers to coastal ports such as Sundsvall, where there are woodworking industries and paper mills. Härnösand, the capital, is a shipbuilding center.

VÄSTMANLAND, county, S central Sweden; bounded by the counties of Kopparberg on the NW, Gävleborg in the N, Uppsala on the E, Södermanland on the S, and Orebro on the W; area 2,611 sq. mi.; pop. (1958) 227,899. The northern section of the country is hilly; the remainder, which extends south to Lake Malar, is flat lowland. Truck farming and dairying are important, particularly in the south. Iron ore mining is important in the northwest. Västmanland is heavily industrialized; iron, steel, and electrical goods are manufactured. The capital is Västerås.

VÄSUKI, in Hindu mythology, one of the three chief serpent kings of the Nāgas, a serpent-worshipping people in Pātāla, the underworld. Vāsuki was a kinsman of Sesha, the thousand-headed serpent-god of the Nāgas. In an effort to prevent the destruction of his people at the hands of Garuda, an inveterate serpent hater, Vāsuki agreed to send him one snake each day to devour; this conciliatory scheme did not attain its end, however, since Garuḍa persisted in eating one Nāga each day as well.

VATEL, FRANÇOIS, died 1671, celebrated French cook in the service of the Great Condé. Vatel is chiefly remembered as the subject of an anecdote, of uncertain authenticity, recounted in one of Mme. de Sévigné's letters. Louis XIV, having heard of Vatel's gastronomic genius, attended a Friday dinner at the Great Condé's villa in Chantilly. Vatel, deeply honored, prepared a magnificent feast for the king. By some mischance, however, the fish he had ordered for the meal failed to arrive, and no substitute was available. In despair, his reputation ruined, Vatel committed suicide.

VATICAN, the independent state in the city of Rome under the rule of the pope. It was established in virtue of the Lateran Treaty accepted on Feb. 11, 1929, by both the papacy and the government of Italy in settlement of the long-standing dispute between the two parties that had arisen over the seizure of vast papal holdings by the Italian partisans during the Risorgimento in 1870. The Vatican, or Vatican City, is the world's tiniest independent state, occupying an area of only 108.7 acres and boasting a citizenry of approximately 1,000 people, of whom only about one-fifth are residents. It is located in the northwestern section of Rome, west of the Tiber River, on a low prominence known from ancient times as the Vatican Hill.

Within the territorial limits of the papal state are to be found many monuments of the history of Christian civilization, such as the world renowned Basilica of St. Peter—which, as recent archaeological excavations attest, was built near the ancient Circus of Nero over a Roman necropolis containing evidences of an early Christian cultus of the Prince of the Apostles; the fabulous art galleries and museum; one of the most richly endowed libraries in the world; and the storied palaces with their famous gardens and artistic treasures. There is also much of the apparatus of modern civilization: a large printing establishment, a radio station for both standard and short-wave broadcasting, a railroad terminal, a college for Ethiopian students, a mint, post office, mosaic factory, administrative offices for the lay governor, up-to-date barracks for a not-so-modern army, the Swiss guards, and an establishment for the papal gendarmerie.

Outside the confines of the city-state, enjoying the rights of extra-territoriality conceded by the Italian government, are other Vatican properties, such as the summer residence of the pope at Castel Gondolfo and the three other major basilicas: St. Mary Major, St. John Lateran, and St. Paul-Outside-the-Walls.

As the official headquarters of the popes, the Vatican is the hub of Roman Catholicism throughout the world. It has been only since relatively recent times, however, that the popes have permanently lived in the Vatican palaces adjacent to St. Peter's Basilica. The official cathedral of the pope as bishop of Rome has always been and still is the Lateran Basilica of St. John.

Nicholas III, 1277–80, was the first pope to abandon the Lateran Palace for the Vatican. Subsequent to the return of the popes to Rome after their long stay at Avignon in France, 1309–77, the Vatican became their permanent residence.

Pope Nicholas V, 1447–55, ordered the razing of the old Basilica of St. Peter, which had been erected by the Emperor Constantine over a primitive shrine of the Apostle, and the construction of the present magnificent structure on the same site. The work was barely initiated when he died, but he managed to secure for it some of the finest architects, including Leon Battista Alberti, Bernardo Rosellino, and Aristotele di Fioravante. During the pontificate of Julius II, 1503-13, Bramante was appointed chief architect. In 1514, under Pope Leo X, Raphael succeeded him, and was himself followed in the position by Antonio da Sangallo, Michelangelo, Giacomo della Porta, and others. It was Michelangelo who altered the original plans of Bramante and built the enormous dome. Sixtus V, 1585-90, gave orders for the basilica to be enlarged with the result that, instead of having four equal arms extending from the transept as originally planned, it assumed the shape of a Latin cross. Under Sixtus V the huge obelisk brought from Hieropolis in Egypt, 39 A.D., by the Emperor Caligula and placed eventually in the Circus of Nero, where according to tradition St. Peter died, was transported and erected in the great square in front of the basilica. Though the name of Paul V appears on its facade, the present structure was completed and consecrated during the pontificate of Urban VIII on Nov. 18, 1626.

The Vatican palaces adjoining the great basilica consist of a number of buildings and courtyards dating from different periods. There is no definitive history of these structures before the twelfth century. According to some authors, Pope Symmachus, 498-514, was the first to live in the Vatican, and did so because an antipope occupied the Lateran. He is supposed to have constructed two palaces, one to the right and the other to the left of the Constantinian Basilica. Additions and modifications in the edifices were reported to have been made under Popes Leo III and Gregory IV. Under Eugene III, 1145-53, and Innocent III, 1198-1216, many of the structures were modernized.

From a cluster of older buildings there rises the renowned Sistine Chapel built in 1473 by Giovanni de' Dolci of Florence under the direction of Pope Sixtus IV. Its walls are decorated with the frescoes of Perugino, Ghirlandaio, Botticelli, and Rosselli. Its vaulted ceiling contains the famous epic of the creation and the fall of man painted by Michelangelo between 1509 and 1512. On the end wall is the enormous panorama of the last judgment by the same artist.

Nearby is the famous Borgia Apartment built by Pope Alexander VI, 1492-1503. Its frescoes are the work of Pinturrichio and his assistants. Not far away are the celebrated Raphael Rooms: living quarters of the sixteenth century popes and decorated with the masterpieces of the artist Raphael. Frescoes in the older Chapel of Nicholas V in this same section were executed by Fra Angelico between the years 1450 and 1455. Pope Sixtus V, 1585-90, commissioned Domenico Fontana to build the newer part of the palaces toward the front of the basilica, and it is this section that has been the residence of his successors.

Across the Belvedere Courtyard from the Vatican Palace lies the Vatican Library; nearby are the museum and art galleries. The library contains more than a half million printed books and a priceless collection of about 60,000 manuscripts. On display are such exhibits as the *Codex Vaticanus*, a manuscript Greek Bible of the fourth century, and classical manuscripts dating from early Christian times. The library was richly endowed with manuscript material by Pope Nicholas V, 1447-55, who is on that account considered by some to have been its founder. See VATICAN LIBRARY.

The Vatican art galleries contain among others, masterpieces by Giotto, Perugino, Pinturricchio, Titian, and Murillo. Notable are one of the first works of Raphael, *The Coronation of the Virgin*, and his last, *The Transfiguration*. The hall of sculptures contains such well known pieces as Laocoön, the Apollo Belvedere, and the Belvedere Torso, which was a source of inspiration to Michelangelo. Important also are the exhibits of Egyptian and Etruscan antiquities.

The Vatican is not only the religious capital of Roman Catholicism, but it is also a sovereign state. As the preamble of the Lateran Treaty implies, it is most desirable that the Holy See have this token territory, sovereign in itself, not only because it is absolutely necessary to assure the pope complete freedom from political pressures of any kind and from the intrigues met with so frequently in the course of history, which have proved detrimental to the church, but also to give the Holy See status among nations, to enable it to deal with them on an equal basis, as one among many, in the common cause of peace. This sovereignty of Vatican City and its status in the world community is acknowledged, especially by those governments that have embassies at the Holy See. Countries that have accredited representatives at the Holy See receive in turn members of the Vatican diplomatic corps, usually archbishops with the title of nuncio or internuncio. Nations that have no representation at the Vatican receive apostolic delegates for the carrying on chiefly of ecclesiastical business; they act as liaison officers between the pope and the episcopate of the country. The United States has no ambassador at the Holy See, but from 1939 to 1950 Myron C. Taylor served as personal representative of the president in the common effort made by the United States and the Vatican to promote international peace.

As in the religious sphere for the whole world, full executive, legislative, and judicial power is legally vested in the pope for the temporal affairs of the Vatican. In practice, however, his task of ruling the city-state is delegated to a number of governmental agencies. Most important of these is the Pontifical Commission for Vatican City. This board is composed of a number of cardinals and a secretary. It was set up on Mar. 20, 1939, by Pope Pius XII. It is charged with the actual civil rule of the Vatican, and has full power to decide routine matters.

Chief executive of the city-state is the governor, a layman appointed by the pope, who is responsible directly to the pope for carrying out the duties of administration. He is assisted by a council composed of the directors of the four departments of administration: secretariat, museum, monuments, and technical services.

In addition to the governor there is a general counsellor who has no direct authority in matters of state, but acts in an advisory capacity to the pope and the governor. He does not have to be a citizen of the Vatican, but, as the governor, he is appointed by the pope and is responsible to him.

The judiciary is composed of a panel of men trained in the law, who also are appointed directly by the pope, and who do not have to be citizens. There are regular courts in which a single judge sits to handle routine penal and civil cases. In addition, there are appeal courts as well as a supreme court. In extraordinary cases an appeal from the supreme court may be made to the supreme ecclesiastical tribunal, the *Segnatura apostolica*.

Foreign affairs of the state as well as certain ecclesiastical affairs are handled through the office of the Cardinal Secretary of State and the diplomatic corps.

CHARLES E. MEYER, S.T.D.

BIBLIOG.-Josef Bernhart, *Vatican as a World Power* (1939); Thérèse Bonney, *Vatican* (1939); Ann Carnahan, *Vatican: Behind the Scenes in the Holy City* (1950); *Catholic Encyclopedia* (Vol. XV); Camille M. Cianfarra, *Vatican and the Kremlin* (1950); Stephen S. Fenichell and Phillip Andrews, *Vatican and Holy Year* (1950); Robert E. G. George, *Genius of the Vatican* (1935); Leone Gessi, *Vatican City* (1950); Robert A. Graham, *Vatican Diplomacy: A Study of Church and State on the International Plane* (1960); Desider Hollisher, *Eternal City: Rome of the Popes* (1943); Karl Ipser, *Vatican Art* (1953); Paul M. Letarouilly, *Vatican* 3 vols. (1954); Albert Lévitt, *Vaticanism: The Political Principles of the Roman Catholic Church* (1960); Anne O. McCormick, *Vatican Journal, 1921-1954* (1957); Geddes MacGregor, *Vatican Revolution* (1957); Avro Manhattan, *Vatican in World Politics* (1949); Jean Neuvecelle, *Vatican: Its Organization, Customs, and Way of Life* (1955); Bartolomeo Nogara, *Art Treasures of the Vatican* (1950); Corrado Pallenberg, *Vatican From Within* (1961); Leon Paul, ed., *Vatican Picture Book* (1957); Charles Pichon, *Vatican and Its Role in World Affairs* (1950); Alec Randall, *Vatican Assignment* (1956); Georges Seldes, *Vatican: Yesterday–Today, Tomorrow* (1941); Donald C. Sharkey, *White Smoke Over the Vatican* (1949).

VATICAN COUNCILS, the twentieth and twenty-first of the ecumenical councils recognized by the Roman Catholic church. The twentieth ecumenical council (Vatican I), noted especially for its decree on the infallibility of the pope, was opened by Pope Pius IX in the Vatican on Dec. 8, 1869. The French garrison that protected the temporal authority of the pope was withdrawn after the Franco-Prussian War began in July, 1870, and the Italian forces of Victor Emmanuel II occupied Rome in September. In October, the pope prorogued the council indefinitely.

More than 700 Roman Catholic bishops, including some 40 from the United States, attended certain sessions of the council. Abbots and superiors-general of religious orders were also summoned. Representatives of the Orthodox and Protestant churches were asked to come, but declined. For the first time, leaders of Roman Catholic states were not invited, with the result that there was little lay interference.

Some 86 general meetings of the assembly took place. There were four public sessions under the presidency of the pope: one for convocation, one for the customary profession of faith, and two for promulgation of the decrees of the council.

In March, 1865, the pope appointed five cardinals to head commissions of theologians and canonists who were to draw up the agenda for the forthcoming meetings. When the council had at length convened and a final prospectus had been prepared, the assembled bishops debated over the various provisions, introduced new ones, proposed modifications of doctrine, and signified their acceptance (*placet*) or rejection (*nonplacet*) of each proposition in the continuously revised schemata. Measures receiving a majority of favorable votes were remanded to the public sessions for promulgation by the pope.

The most notable permanent result of the council was the publication of two dogmatic constitutions, one dealing with faith and the other with the church. The dogmatic constitution *Dei Filius* proclaims the existence of a personal God, absolutely supreme and independent, who freely brought into being all creatures, material as well as spiritual. It declares that certain knowledge of the existence of this Creator is attainable by human reason. Other religious truths, though not beyond human reasoning power, can be known certainly and congruously by the generality of men only through divine revelation. So, too, supernatural revelation, the fonts of which are scripture and tradition, is necessary for the human mind to arrive at certain transcendental truths called supernatural mysteries. Dogmatic faith is to be considered a free and reasonable assent of the mind given under the influence of divine grace to supernatural religious truths, because of the authority of God, who has revealed them. There can be no real opposition between faith and science; on the contrary, they are of mutual aid, for reason demonstrates the foundations of faith, while faith both guards reason from error and furnishes it with truths for contemplation. The second dogmatic constitution, *Pastor aeternus*, sets forth the doctrines of the primacy of jurisdiction of St. Peter over the other apostles, of the transmission of this primacy to his successors in the see of Rome, and of the prerogative of personal infallibility on the part of the pope when teaching the whole church with his full authority (*ex cathedra*) on matters of faith or morals.

The question of the pope's infallibility was violently contested both within and outside the council. Most bishops wholeheartedly supported the doctrine, but many were opposed to a formal definition, either on principle or on the basis that it would not be oppor-

tune. Notable among the group opposing pronouncement was Cardinal Newman. The final vote was: 451 for; 88 against; 62 favorable, but with reservations; 70 abstained from voting.

The twenty-first ecumenical council (Vatican II) was opened by Pope John XXIII on Oct. 11, 1962. The chief aim of the council, as stated by the pope, was the unity of all Christian faiths under the Roman Catholic church. There was discussion of several items on the agenda, but none had been enacted when the first session was adjourned, Dec. 8, 1962. The second session was convened on Sept. 29, 1963, by Pope Paul VI, who was elected pope after the death of John XXIII. Seventeen broad proposals from the more than 70 items on the agenda in the first session were put before the council. A constitution on liturgy, which provides for the use of the vernacular language in the mass, and a decree on communications were voted by the council. There were about 2,400 Roman Catholic delegates at the second session. For the first time women were admitted to the third session of the council in September, 1964. At the same session reforms designed to give the bishops a larger role in administration were enacted.   CHARLES R. MEYER, S.T.D.

VATICAN LIBRARY, the oldest public library in Europe, is famed for its collection of some of the world's most valuable manuscripts. The library forms a part of the Vatican Palace, in Vatican City, Rome. Pope Nicholas V, 1447–55, established the library with 350 volumes contained in collections assembled during the fifteenth century and several earlier papal collections. One of these was the fourth-century *Chartarium ecclesiae Romanae* of Pope Damasus.

Pope Sixtus IV, 1471–84, enlarged the library until it contained 3,500 volumes, more or less. He appointed Bartolommeo Sacchi, or Platina, as its first librarian, 1475. A large number of the selections in the library were lost during the sack of Rome, 1527, but many additions were made shortly thereafter. Pope Sixtus V, 1585–90, ordered the construction of the present library buildings in 1588, and greatly augmented the collection of books and manuscripts. By the Treaty of Tolenino (1798), Pope Pius VI, 1775–99, was forced to surrender to Napoleon Bonaparte all pre-ninth century manuscripts; most of these were returned to the library after the peace of 1815. Numerous rare volumes and collections were added during the nineteenth century, and by mid-twentieth century the library included 60,000 manuscripts, 7,000 incunabula (books printed before A.D. 1501), and 500,000 other printed books. Ancient and valuable collections include manuscripts of Vergil; the original manuscript of the sonnets of the Italian poet Petrarch (1304–74); a copy of Dante's *Divine Comedy* in the handwriting of Giovanni Boccaccio (1313–75); a palimpsest of Marcus Tullius Cicero's (106–43 B.C.) *De republica;* and a fourth century codex of the Bible.

VATTEL, EMERICH DE, 1714–67, Swiss jurist, diplomat, and philosopher, was born near Neuchâtel, the son of a Protestant minister. He studied philosophy at Basel and Geneva, then entered the diplomatic corps of Saxony, serving with distinction in various capacities at Berlin, Dresden, and Bern. Vattel wrote a number of books on philosophy and law, but is best remembered for his *Droit des gens; ou, Principes de la loi naturelle appliqués à la conduite et aux affaires des nations et des souverains*, 1758 (*Law of Nations*, 1760). This work, much indebted to the writings of the German philosophers Gottfried Wilhelm von Leibniz (1646–1716) and Christian von Wolff (1679–1754), asserts the superiority of natural law over artificial (human) legislation, and bases international law on a natural law foundation. By justifying liberal revolutions, the book influenced to a degree both the American and French revolutions.

VÄTTERN, LAKE, S Sweden, extends about 80 miles N-S and 15 miles E-W, the second largest lake in the country; area 730 sq. mi. Lake Vättern divides the counties of Örebro, Östergotland, Jönköping, and Skaraborg. Visingsö, near the south end of the lake, is its only island. Lake Vättern is crossed by a steamer route from Göteborg to Stockholm, and is connected with the Baltic Sea by the Göta Canal. The main city along its shores is Jönköping, at the southern tip of the lake.

VAUBAN, SÉBASTIEN LE PRESTRE, MARQUIS DE, 1633–1707, French military engineer and marshal, was born in Saint Léger de Foucherets (later Saint Léger-Vauban). He served with Condé's troops during the War of the Fronde (see FRONDE), was captured by royal troops, 1653, and transferred his allegiance to the king. He became one of the king's engineers, 1655; governor of the citadel of Lille, 1668; field marshal, 1676; commissary general of fortifications, 1678; and marshal of France, 1703. During his more than 50 years in the king's service, Vauban directed 53 sieges and built or rebuilt 333 forts and citadels. His reputation remained of the highest order until a pamphlet he had written was condemned and suppressed by order of Louis XIV. This pamphlet, calling for a redistribution of wealth through a new system of taxation, foreshadowed many of the ideas that were to be given practical expression by the French Revolution. Vauban, publicly disgraced by the pamphlet, died within a year of its suppression. His memory was honored more than a century later, however, when Napoleon I ordered his heart deposited in the Church of the Invalides, 1808. Vauban wrote numerous treatises on the attack and defense of fortified places. His *Memoirs* fill 12 volumes (1843–46).

VAUCLUSE, department, SE France, in Provence; bounded by the departments of Drôme on the N, Basses Alpes on the E, Bouches-du-Rhône on the S, and Gard on the W; area 1,381 sq. mi.; pop. (1954) 268,318. A small section of Vaucluse, the canton of Valréas, forms an enclave within Drôme. The department rises to the foothills of the French Alps in the east, descending westward to the Rhône River, which forms the western boundary. The principal crops grown are wheat, potatoes, millet, vegetables, grapes, olives, and mulberries. Lignite and sulfur are mined; and local deposits of kaolin, gypsum, and ochre are worked. The capital is Avignon. Vaucluse was formed in 1793.

VAUD, canton, SW Switzerland, bounded by France on the W and S, and by the cantons of Neuchâtel on the N, Fribourg on the NE, Oberland on the E, Valais on the SE, and Geneva on the SW; area 1,239 sq. mi.; pop. (1950) 377,585, most of whom are French-speaking. Vaud extends from the Jura Mountains on the northwest to the Bernese Alps on the southeast. The southern border is formed by Lake Geneva, and Lake Neuchâtel forms part of the northern boundary. Agricultural production is concentrated in the valley of the Rhône River, in the Venoge-Thièle Valley, and along lakes Geneva and Neuchâtel. Cereals, tobacco, and grapes are the chief crops. Cattle are pastured on the slopes of the Alps. The Jura Mountains are heavily forested and are a source of lumber. The principal manufactures are wine, watches, chocolate, chemicals, and musical instruments. Vaud has numerous tourist resorts, including Lausanne, the capital. The Romans conquered the area in 58 B.C.; the canton later came under the Franks and the houses of Zähringen and Savoy. In 1536 the canton was taken by the canton of Bern. It was called Léman under the Helvetic Republic, which was formed in 1798. In 1803 the canton joined the Swiss Confederation under its present name.

VAUDEVILLE, a type of theatrical performance consisting of a series of specialty acts. The word vaudeville is a corruption of the name of a French town, Vau de Vire, where, during the fifteenth century, Oliver Basselin composed a series of satirical ballads that came to be known as *vaux de vire*. Within

a century in France any satirical ballad was called a *vaudeville*, and by the beginning of the seventeenth century the word was commonly used to describe the variety shows offered by strolling players performing in the streets and at fairs. During the eighteenth century in France these shows were often performed in taverns; they retained their spontaneous character, but tradition had established by that time that they would consist of a series of juggling acts, animal acts, comedy sketches, pantomimes, and playlets, interspersed with song and dance routines. The *vaudevilles* were the direct ancestors of the Comédie Française, and many of the stars of the Comédie rose from the ranks of vaudeville to the legitimate stage.

In England a similar development took place. During the eighteenth century variety shows began to be performed in taverns by itinerant players. Later, the tavern owners provided space, usually a room called the music hall, for the performances. The entertainment provided in the music halls was characteristically bawdy, spontaneous, and continuous. There was no definite program—any performer that happened along went on; if his act was well received, he was tipped; if he met with disfavor, he would likely be pelted with garbage; the audience felt free to join in the entertainment. Taverns providing this kind of entertainment were known as free-and-easies, a name that referred as much to the moral tone of the establishment as to the informal entertainment.

The tremendous popularity of the free-and-easies inspired the establishment of more formal variety theaters, and toward the end of the nineteenth century huge music halls, luxuriously appointed, lavishly decorated, and thoroughly respectable, were built in England. In these the convivial atmosphere of the free-and-easies had disappeared, but the techniques and specialized talents of the music hall performers continued to develop in the old tradition.

In the United States the development of the variety show generally followed the pattern established in England. Puritanical Boston was one of the first homes of variety entertainment in the American colonies; its citizens were enjoying the entertainments of strolling players at a time when New Yorkers and Philadelphians were attending performances at legitimate theaters, which were banned by statute in the Massachusetts colony. In the colonies where stage plays were forbidden, performances called exhibitions (usually including a moral lecture) were presented. These mélanges of drama, acrobatics, pantomime, and song and dance acts were the first variety entertainments, and quickly assumed the bawdy characteristics of their European models.

Vaudeville of the type that was to flourish in the United States until the 1930's was born in New York City in 1881, at Tony Pastor's Fourteenth Street Theater. Pastor, himself a performer in beer hall variety shows, was an astute entertainer who reasoned that he could attract a wider audience by cleaning up the bills. His opening night was advertised as a "clean variety show for ladies and gents." Box-office revenue proved that Pastor was correct in his estimation of what the audiences wanted. From that time onward, vaudeville developed rapidly, and great chains of vaudeville theaters, called circuits, were established. Best known among these were the Keith, Orpheum, and Pantages circuits. To play in the Palace Theater on Broadway was the goal of every vaudeville actor, since booking agents for the circuits went there to seek new talent. Unit shows often toured the circuits intact, and as audiences began to rate their favorites, the "headliner" system was developed. Theater managers began the practice of "headlining" their bills with favorite performers, who received top salaries and preferential treatment. The practice of headlining led to the booking of acts for the sake of the name itself. "Names" were usually well known performers in some other field who appeared on the vaudeville stage more as showpieces than as acts. Sarah Bernhardt, Mrs. Patrick Campbell, and Jenny Lind appeared as headliners on several of the circuits. But, apart from such curiosities, the true vaudeville artist continued to develop along his brassy way. Comedy was king during the golden age of vaudeville, from 1890 to 1930. Among the great comedians of this period were Charlie Chase, Joe Cook, Ed. Wynn, W. C. Fields, Bert Williams, Lou Holtz, and Jimmy Durante. Although single artists predominated as headliners, there were favorite teams such as Morton and Ravel, the Howards, Willie and Eugene, and Wheeler and Woolsey. Other favorites were singer Nora Bayes, comedienne Eva Tanguay, and the French *chanteuse* Yvette Guilbert.

The reasons for the decline of vaudeville early in the 1930's were many. Radio, motion pictures, and night clubs all offered competition; the depression dealt a mortal blow. The old vaudeville performers turned to other forms of entertainment, such as television, but it seemed unlikely that new talents of the kind that were fostered on the circuits would ever again be developed.

BIBLIOG.–Herbert M. Alexander, *Strip Tease: The Vanished Art of Burlesque* (1938); Frank H. O'Hara, ed., *Plays, Skits, and Lyrics* (1936); William A. Dillon, *Life Doubles in Brass* (1944); Maurice W. Disher, *Music Hall Parade* (1938); Douglas Gilbert, *American Vaudeville: Its Life and Times* (1940); Maurice A. C. Gorham, *Showmen and Suckers: An Excursion on the Crazy Fringe of the Entertainment World* (1951); Abel Green and Joe Laurie, *Show Biz* (1952); Joe Laurie, *Vaudeville: From the Honky-tonks to the Palace* (1953); Edward B. Marks, *They All Sang: From Tony Pastor to Rudy Vallée* (1934); William M. Marston and John H. Feller, *F. F. Proctor, Vaudeville Pioneer* (1943); Harold Scott, *Early Doors, Origins of the Music Hall* (1946); Constance Tomkinson, *Les Girls* (1956); Bill Treadwell, *50 Years of American Comedy* (1951); Neil Trimble, *Variety Shows and How to Produce Them* (1941); Charles F. Wright, *One Thousand and One One Minute Black-Outs* (1935).

VAUDOIS. See WALDENSES.

VAUDREUIL, a French and French-Canadian family, prominent in military and governmental affairs in the seventeenth and eighteenth centuries. Philippe de Rigaud, marquis de Vaudreuil (1643–1725), was born near Castlenaudary, France. He served as commander of the French military forces in Canada, 1690–98, was appointed governor of Montreal, 1798, and served as governor of Canada, 1705–25. Pierre François de Rigaud, marquis de Vaudreuil-Cavagnal (1698–1765), son of Philippe, was born in Montreal, Québec. He was the last French governor of Canada, serving from 1755 until 1760, when he surrendered the colony to Great Britain. Louis Philippe de Rigaud, marquis de Vaudreuil (1724–1802), son of Louis Philippe and grandson of Philippe, naval commander, was born in Rochefort, France. During the American Revolution he served in action against the British, 1778–83, and commanded a part of Comte de Grasse's fleet that prevented the British from aiding Gen. Charles Cornwallis at Yorktown in 1781.

VAUGHAN, HENRY, known as The Silurist, 1622–95, Welsh poet, was born at Newton-by-Usk, Brecknockshire, South Wales, in the territory of the ancient Silures. He studied law for a time but eventually became a physician at Breçon. As a poet, he wrote secular verse in the style of John Donne and Ben Jonson, but is best known for his religious poetry, much of it rather mystical in tone—as in the famous line: "They are all gone into the world of Light". Among his works are *Poems* (1646), *Olor Iscanus* (1651), *The Mount of Olives* (1652), *Flores Solitudinis* (1654), *Silex Scintillans* (1650; 1655), *Thalia Rediviva; The Pass-Times and Diversions of a Country-Muse* (1678).

VAUGHAN, HERBERT ALBERT CARDINAL, 1832–1903, English Roman Catholic prelate, was born in Gloucester, and was reared in a family circle in which an interest in religion was encouraged: Herbert and five of his eight brothers became Roman

Catholic priests, while all of their sisters entered convents. Soon after his ordination, 1854, Vaughan was appointed vice-president of St. Edmund's College, Ware. He visited the United States twice: first to raise funds for the training of priests for work in foreign missions, 1861, and later to investigate religious education among the Negroes, 1871. He was bishop of Salford, 1872–92, and then succeeded Henry Edward Cardinal Manning as archbishop of Westminster, 1892. Vaughan was created a cardinal in 1893. Vaughan is remembered as the builder of Westminster Cathedral and for his active interest in social and educational programs.

VAUGHAN WILLIAMS, RALPH, 1872–1958, English composer, was born in Down Ampney, Gloucestershire, and was educated at Charterhouse, London; Trinity College, Cambridge; and the Royal College of Music; he received a D. Mus. degree from Cambridge, 1901. He also studied under Max Bruch and Maurice Ravel. His primary ambitions were in the realm of composition, but for practical purposes he studied piano and organ; he was organist for the South Lambeth Church, London, from 1896, and conductor of the London Bach Choir, 1920-28. His long-standing interest in English folk songs is evident in many of his compositions from 1904. His *London Symphony* (1914), program music in symphonic form, and the opera *Hugh the Drover* (1924), full of folk-type music, were especially significant in attracting public attention to Vaughan Williams' work. Among other compositions worthy of special note are the three *Norfolk Rhapsodies* (1906–07), *The Lark Ascending* (1921) and *Concerto Accademico* (1925) for orchestra and violin; *Five Tudor Portraits* (1936); two operas, *Riders to the Sea* (1937) and *Pilgrim's Progress* (1951); and his nine symphonies. In his later years Vaughan Williams, as the "grand old man" of British musical life, did some of his best work; he continued composing music almost to the end.

VAULT, in architecture, a ceiling formed by any of a variety of curved surfaces, usually constructed of masonry. The simplest types are the dome and the barrel vault, which is simply part of a cylinder, longitudinally cut. Two of the most famous domes in the history of architecture are those of the Pantheon in Rome and the Hagia Sophia in Istanbul (see DOME). Barrel vaults were built by the ancient Babylonians, Greeks, and Romans, and in Christian times were frequently used in Byzantine and Romanesque structures. Vaulting that is more complex than the dome or barrel vaults is achieved by the intersection of two or more curved surfaces; the simplest type of intersecting vault is the groin or cross vault, in which two barrel vaults meet at right angles. The ribs seen in more complex forms of intersecting vaults serve both as support and as decoration. See BYZANTINE ARCHITECTURE; GOTHIC ART AND ARCHITECTURE, Architecture; and ROMANESQUE ART AND ARCHITECTURE.

VAUPÉS, commissary, SE Colombia, bounded by the intendencies of Meta on the NW and Caqueta on the W, by the commissaries of Vichada on the N and Amazonas on the S, by Venezuela on the NE, and by Brazil on the E; area 57,857 sq. mi., pop. (1957 est.) 9,870. Vaupés lies on a plateau sloping eastward toward the Orinoco and Amazon River basins. The area has a hot, wet climate, and it is largely undeveloped and sparsely inhabited, mainly by Indian tribes. The few small settlements are along the rivers. Wild rubber and balata gum are produced in small quantities. Mitú is the capital.

VAUVENARGUES, LUC DE CLAPIERS, MARQUIS DE, 1715–47, French moralist, was born in Aix-en-Provence. At the collège in Aix he learned little, and this fact, conjoined with the reduced circumstances of his family, led him to seek a career in the French army. For 10 years he served with distinction as an officer in the Regiment du Roi (King's Regiment), until injuries incurred in the French retreat from Prague, winter, 1741, forced his retirement. At the urging of his friend, Victor Riqueti, the marquis de Mirabeau (1715–89), and encouraged by Voltaire, Luc now undertook to establish himself as a writer. His major work is *Introduction à la connaissance de l'esprit* (1746), but he also is remembered for *Dialogues of the Dead*, which appeared posthumously in the year of his death. Luc's ethics reflect his military background. Revolting against the widespread cynicism and skepticism of his times, he sought to persuade Frenchmen to put aside their concern with material progress and social reform, and return to the stoic practice of courage and honour. For Vauvenargues the noblest of emotions is *la gloire;* the ethical ideal of all should be a humane heroism.

ROBERT WHITTEMORE

VĀYU, in Vedic mythology, the wind god, one of the eight attendants of Indra, god of heaven. Vāyu was sometimes represented as one of the trinity of earth, heaven, and air, a position more generally assigned to Indra. Vāyu was the subject of few myths and he was not a popular figure of worship. He was considered to be the father of other wind gods, and, later, of the Maruts, the storm gods.

VEBLEN, THORSTEIN BUNDE, 1857–1929, U.S. economic theorist and reformer, was born on a farm on the Wisconsin frontier. His father, a Norwegian master builder turned farmer, was a man who valued education, and he saw to it that his 12 children were thoroughly exposed to the life of the mind. As a boy, Thorstein learned German, Greek, and Latin, in addition to Norwegian, and also acquired English. At 17 he entered Carleton College, and afterward did graduate study at Johns Hopkins and Yale universities; Yale granted him a doctorate in philosophy, 1884.

He wanted to teach, but no college wanted this ungainly Scandinavian with the acid wit, and for seven years he brooded in rural Iowa. His first job, a teaching fellowship at the newly founded University of Chicago, materialized in 1892. Here he began the work that was to make his fame as a corrosive critic of U.S. capitalism. In both *The Theory of the Leisure Class* (1899) and *The Theory of Business Enterprise* (1904) the author's concern is with the pernicious social effects of economic waste. The "conspicuous consumption" of the leisure class and the profit taking of the business man, Veblen held, are twin cancers eating away at the economic health of society. The cure, he maintained, must consist in protecting those who make the goods from those who make, and wastefully spend, the money. Thus, in *The Instinct of Workmanship* (1914), he argued that workmanship rather than wastemanship is the essential ingredient in any economically sane civilization.

In his *Imperial Germany and the Industrial Revolution* (1915), and in *An Inquiry into the Nature of Peace and the Terms of Its Perpetuation* (1917), he undertook to apply his theories to explain the economic and political rise of Germany and the decline of Great Britain. In these works he clearly foresaw the conditions that were later to produce nazism. Veblen's criticism of the British, however, made his ideas unpopular, and in the post-World War I boom years his warnings were all but forgotten. The man himself fared little better: his unconventional personal life and public opinions offended his fellow professors and shocked the businessmen who ran the universities. He was, they believed, "not sound," "not scholarly." And so he moved from Chicago to Stanford, and from there to the University of Missouri—always looking for, and never finding, his proper academic niche. What he thought of the academic world that had treated him so shabbily, he expressed in a pitiless dissection of U.S. college education. *The Higher Learning in America* (1918). Shortly before its publication, he had given up teaching to assume the editorship of a New York periodical, *The Dial*. Two series of articles written for it appeared later as *The Vested Interests and the Common Man* (1919) and *The Engineers and the Price System* (1921).

His editorship ended, Veblen returned to teaching at The New School for Social Research, until poor health forced his retirement to a mountain cabin in California, where he died.

ROBERT WHITTEMORE

VECCHI, ORAZIO, 1550–1605, Italian composer, was born in Modena, Italy. He took Holy Orders, and in 1586 was made canon of the cathedral in Corréggio. Vecchi returned to Modena as the *maestro di cappella* (chapel master) of the cathedral, 1596, and assumed the same duties for the court of Modena, 1598. He was deprived of his position at the cathedral in 1604, supposedly for having given musical instruction to nuns. Vecchi is remembered for his *L'amfiparnasso, commedia harmonica* (1594), a composition in madrigal style.

VECTOR. A quantity that requires both magnitude and direction for its complete characterization; for example, the quantities force and velocity are vector quantities. A quantity that requires magnitude only to specify it completely is called a scalar; for

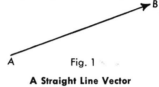

Fig. 1

A Straight Line Vector

example, mass and time. A vector quantity is often represented geometrically by a directed straight line segment whose length represents the magnitude in terms of an arbitrary and convenient scale unit. If the initial point of the segment is denoted by A, and the terminal point by B, the symbol AB indicates the directed segment. Direction is indicated visually by placing an arrowhead at B as in Fig. 1. Vectors are also frequently denoted by single letters in bold face type, as **a, b, c,** or by placing a bar or small arrow above the letters. The magnitude of the vector is then indicated by the same letter in ordinary type, thus the magnitude of the vector **v** is denoted by v. If m is any positive number, the vector **mb** has the same direction as **b,** but is m times as long. The vector **−b** has the same magnitude as **b,** but is opposite in direction.

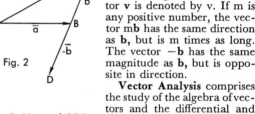

Fig. 2

Simple Vector Addition

Vector Analysis comprises the study of the algebra of vectors and the differential and integral calculus of vectors. Applications of these operations which vectors obey are extremely important in both pure mathematics and mathematical physics.

Elementary operations with vectors are performed according to special rules. Thus in Fig. 2, $\overrightarrow{AC}$ may be regarded as the vector sum of $\overrightarrow{AB}$ and $\overrightarrow{BC}$, that is $\overrightarrow{AB} + \overrightarrow{BC} = \overrightarrow{AC}$, or **a** + **b** = **c.** Then $\overrightarrow{AC}$ is called the sum of $\overrightarrow{AB}$ and $\overrightarrow{BC}$; the latter are components of $\overrightarrow{AC}$. The sum of two or more vectors may be shown geometrically by placing them end to end in succession, each in the proper direction, and then drawing the vector sum from the initial point of the first vector to the terminal point of the last one. Thus **a** + **b** + **c** + **d** = **e** in Fig. 3. The terms of the sum may be taken in any order. This procedure is applicable to vectors in three dimensions as well. The difference of two vectors, **a** − **b,** may be regarded as the sum of **a** and **−b.**

The scalar product, or dot product, of **a** and **b** is a number which is the product of the

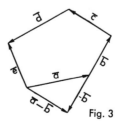

Fig. 3

Adding Several Vectors

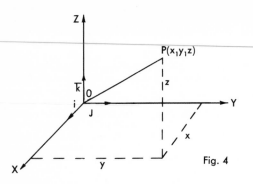

Fig. 4

Vector Analysis in a System of Coordinate Axes

magnitudes of the vectors and the cosine (see TRIGONOMETRY) of the angle between them. This product, denoted by $\mathbf{a \cdot b}$, is commutative, that is $\mathbf{a \cdot b} = \mathbf{b \cdot a}$, and the product is independent of the order of the factors. It is not associative, however: $(\mathbf{a \cdot b}) \cdot \mathbf{c}$ is not the same as $\mathbf{a \cdot (b \cdot c)}$. It is distributive, and thus, $\mathbf{a \cdot (b + c)} = \mathbf{a \cdot b} + \mathbf{a \cdot c}$. As the name implies, this product is a scalar quantity.

The vector product, or cross product, of two vectors, denoted by $\mathbf{a} \times \mathbf{b}$, is equal in magnitude to the product of their magnitudes and the sine of the angle between them. In direction it is perpendicular to their plane and on the side, such that rotation from $\mathbf{a}$ to $\mathbf{b}$ through an angle less than $180°$ appears to be counterclockwise. This product is not commutative, since $\mathbf{b} \times \mathbf{a} = -\mathbf{a} \times \mathbf{b}$. It is not associative, but is distributive, so that $\mathbf{a} \times (\mathbf{b + c}) = (\mathbf{a} \times \mathbf{b}) + (\mathbf{a} \times \mathbf{c})$. Scalar triple products $\mathbf{a} \cdot \mathbf{b} \times \mathbf{c}$, and vector triple products $\mathbf{a} \times (\mathbf{b} \times \mathbf{c})$, are also frequently used.

Vectors may be expressed in terms of components taken in the directions of coordinate axes OX, OY, OZ (see COORDINATES). Arrange the axes so that rotation of OX into OY appears counterclockwise from the side on which OZ is positive (see Fig. 4). Then the components of a vector $\overrightarrow{OP} = \mathbf{r} = x\mathbf{i} + y\mathbf{j} + z\mathbf{k}$ drawn from the origin O to the point $P(x,y,z)$ are $x\mathbf{i}$, $y\mathbf{j}$, and $z\mathbf{k}$. The length r of $\mathbf{r}$ is $\sqrt{x^2+y^2+z^2}$. From the definitions of scalar and vector products above, relations of the following sorts hold:

$$\mathbf{i \cdot i} = \mathbf{j \cdot j} = \mathbf{k \cdot k} = 1$$
$$\mathbf{i \cdot j} = \mathbf{j \cdot k} = \mathbf{k \cdot i} = 0$$
$$\mathbf{j \cdot i} = \mathbf{k \cdot j} = \mathbf{i \cdot k} = 0$$
$$\mathbf{i} \times \mathbf{i} = \mathbf{j} \times \mathbf{j} = \mathbf{k} \times \mathbf{k} = 0$$
$$\mathbf{j} \times \mathbf{k} = -\mathbf{k} \times \mathbf{j} = \mathbf{i}$$
$$\mathbf{k} \times \mathbf{i} = -\mathbf{i} \times \mathbf{k} = \mathbf{j}$$
$$\mathbf{i} \times \mathbf{j} = -\mathbf{j} \times \mathbf{i} = \mathbf{k}$$

By use of these relations, vectors and their sums and products may be expressed in terms of coordinates. For example, if $\mathbf{a} = x_1\mathbf{i} + y_1\mathbf{j} + z_1\mathbf{k}$ and $\mathbf{b} = x_2\mathbf{i} + y_2\mathbf{j} + z_2\mathbf{k}$, then $\mathbf{a \cdot b} = x_1x_2 + y_1y_2 + z_1z_2$ and $\mathbf{a} \times \mathbf{b}$ expressed in determinant form is:

$$\mathbf{a} \times \mathbf{b} = \det \begin{bmatrix} \mathbf{i} & \mathbf{j} & \mathbf{k} \\ x_1 & y_1 & z_1 \\ x_2 & y_2 & z_2 \end{bmatrix}$$

Vector Calculus. A variable vector $\mathbf{F}$ which is a function of a scalar variable (for example, the time t) is indicated by $\mathbf{F}(t)$. Then under suitable conditions it is possible to calculate the derivative $d\mathbf{F}/dt$ (see CALCULUS), to write and solve differential equations involving $\mathbf{F}$, and thus to treat many types of problems in science and engineering by vector methods. In analyses of this type, several operators play important roles. Let $F(x,y,z)$ be an ordinary, or scalar, function of three variables. The vector differential operator, called nabla or del

$$\nabla = \frac{\partial}{\partial x}\mathbf{i} + \frac{\partial}{\partial y}\mathbf{j} + \frac{\partial}{\partial z}\mathbf{k}$$

applied to F is the gradient of F, denoted by ∇F or

grad F. Grad F is a vector whose direction is such that the derivative of F takes its maximum value in that direction and whose magnitude is that value. Moreover, if $\mathbf{F}(x,y,z)$ is a vector function, its derivative in the direction $d\mathbf{r}$ is

$$\frac{d\mathbf{F}}{ds} = \frac{d\mathbf{r}}{ds} \cdot \nabla \mathbf{F}$$

The operator ∇ may be applied to a vector $\mathbf{F}$ in two ways: (1) The scalar

$$\nabla \cdot \mathbf{F} = \mathbf{i} \cdot \frac{\partial \mathbf{F}}{\partial x} + \mathbf{j} \cdot \frac{\partial \mathbf{F}}{\partial y} + \mathbf{k} \cdot \frac{\partial \mathbf{F}}{\partial z}$$

is called the divergence of $\mathbf{F}$ (abbreviated div $\mathbf{F}$); (2) The vector

$$\nabla \times \mathbf{F} = \mathbf{i} \times \frac{\partial \mathbf{F}}{\partial x} + \mathbf{j} \times \frac{\partial \mathbf{F}}{\partial y} + \mathbf{k} \times \frac{\partial \mathbf{F}}{\partial z}$$

is called the curl of $\mathbf{F}$. Expressions of these and many other types, including integrals, are used in hydrodynamic and electromagnetic theory and in various other applications. Thus if $\mathbf{F}$ represents the velocity at the point $P(x,y,z)$ in a moving fluid, the angular velocity about P of an infinitesimal portion is a vector equal to half of curl $\mathbf{F}$; if this is zero, the motion is said to be irrotational, that is, not rotatory.

Other Vector Interpretations. It is often convenient, and particularly so in the theory of alternating currents, to interpret complex numbers as vectors, and conversely. In this interpretation, ordinary algebra is used in which the commutative, associative, and distributive laws hold. If the initial point O of a vector is at the origin of a plane rectangular coordinate system, the terminal point P can be represented by a pair of real numbers x_1 and y_1. See Fig. 5. The number x_1 is the component of the vector in the direction OX, and the number y_1 is the component in the direction OY. If OY is regarded as an axis of pure imaginary numbers, the same point or vector can be represented by the complex number $P_1 = x_1 + iy_1$, where $i^2 = -1$. (Note that this is not the unit vector $\mathbf{i}$ of Fig. 4.) The sum of two such vectors, $P_1 = x_1 + iy_1$ and $P_2 = x_2 + iy_2$, is $P_1 + P_2 = (x_1 + x_2) + i(y_1 + y_2) = P(x_1 + x_2, y_1 + y_2)$. Geometrically, this is consistent with the earlier statement about vector sums. The product $P_1P_2 = (x_1x_2 - y_1y_2) + i(x_1y_2 + x_2y_1)$ is also obtainable by ordinary algebra. If the length $OP_1 = \sqrt{x_1^2 + y_1^2} = r_1$, and angle $XOP_1 = \theta_1$, the complex number P_1 or vector $P_1(x_1y_1)$ can be represented in polar coordinates by $r_1 \cos\theta_1 + ir_1 \sin\theta_1$ or by $r_1 \exp i\theta_1$. (The expression $\exp i\theta_1$ means that $i\theta_1$ is the exponent of the number e, which is the base of the natural system of logarithms.) Similarly, $P_2(x_2y_2) = r_2 \exp i\theta_2$, and hence the product P_1P_2 may also be written as $r_1r_2 \exp i(\theta_1 + \theta_2)$. This may be interpreted as a stretching of r_1 in the ratio $r_2 : 1$ and a rotation of r_1 through an angle θ_2.

In modern algebra a sequence of n numbers $A = (a_1, a_2, a_3, \cdots, a_n)$ is called an n-dimensional vector. The elements $a_1, a_2, \cdots, a_n$ may be interpreted as the coordinates of a point in an n-dimensional space.

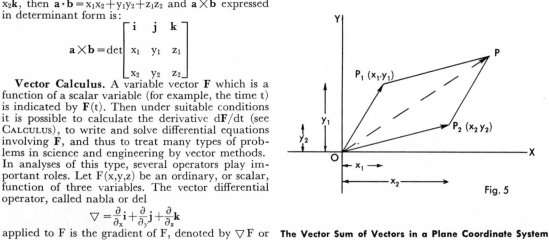

Fig. 5

The Vector Sum of Vectors in a Plane Coordinate System

They may, however, also represent the coefficients in a linear expression $a_1x_2+a_2x_2+\cdots+a_nx_n$, or be given other interpretations. The sum of two such vectors A, and $B=(b_1, b_2, \cdots, b_n)$, is the vector $A+B=(a_1+b_1, a_2+b_2, \cdots, a_n+b_n)$. The elements of the rows, or of the columns, of a matrix or determinant may be called vectors in this sense. Then portions of the theory of modern algebra may be regarded as a generalization of elementary vector concepts.

VECTOR FIELD, a region of space such that with each point there is associated for complete characterization both a magnitude and a direction, that is, a vector quantity. Different points of a vector field have, in general, different vectors associated with them. In a three dimensional space, the vector function describing the field is composed of three quantities corresponding to the components of the vector along the three coordinate axes. (See COORDINATES.) Thus, if to each point (x,y,z) in space, a vector $V=V(x,y,z)$ is assigned, then $V(x,y,z) = V_x(x,y,z)i + V_y(x,y,z)j + V_z(x,y,z)k$, where V_x, V_y, and V_z are the components of the function V along the x, y, and z axes, and each is a function of the coordinates of the point (x,y,z) under consideration. Each vector field is thus equivalent to a triplet of scalar functions of the three variables x, y, and z. Common vector fields are the electric, the magnetic, and the gravitational fields. Examples of vector fields in hydrodynamics are those of fluid velocity and vorticity. In meteorology, the velocity of the wind at each point of the atmosphere is an example of a vector field.

VEDANTA, the most popular of the six orthodox systems of Indian philosophy, takes its name from the Sanskrit *vedānta*, meaning the end or purpose of the scriptures (Vedas). *Vedānta* originally signified only a systematization of the later portion of the Vedas, that is, the Upanishads; in modern Hinduism, however, the term stands for the teaching of the Vedas taken as a whole, plus the *Bhagavadgītā* (The Song of God) and the *Vedānta Sūtra* (Commentary) of Bādarāyana. Since the ambiguity of the sacred texts allows of a variety of interpretations, Vedanta encompasses several schools of thought, the chief of which are the Advaita (non-dualism) of Śankara (probably eighth century), the Viśistādvaita (qualified monism) of Rāmānuja (1016?–?96), and the Dvaita (pluralism) of Madhva (1197–1276).

According to the Advaita Vedānta, all diversity is illusion; only Brahman (Eternal Being) is real. Men, as all other physical complexes, cannot be real (*sat*), since men are not eternal; yet men are not unreal (*asat*), for they are something rather than nothing. As bodies, then, men are neither existent nor nonexistent; the body is rather simply the illusion of the soul (*atman*). As souls men are real, but only insofar as they are Brahman. "Whoever thus knows I am Brahman becomes this All." "That Soul! That art thou [*Tat tvam asi*]." This almost pure monism is modified somewhat by the theologians of the Viśistādvaita, who hold that the world, which Śankara considered mere appearance (*maya*), and soul are not entirely lost in God, but are rather to be thought of as aspects of an embodied whole. Thus Rāmānuja thought that the world and the human soul are bodies of which the soul is God. Moreover, God, as conceived by the Viśistādvaitists is not merely an impersonal Absolute, but Vishnu.

Closer than either of these views to the idea of God and the world as entertained in Western religion is the Dvaita of Madhva. Following the earlier sections of the Vedas, he argued for the reality of the world as known in experience. Not only are individual souls distinct from one another and from physical objects, he averred, but things themselves are independent of our knowledge of them. All, however, depend upon the grace of God, for all would come to nothing were that grace withdrawn even for a moment. In so believing, Dvaita came close to the Advaita viewpoint, since there is little difference between the idea of God

as that supreme entity in and by which all live, and the notion of Brahman as the sole reality. Nevertheless, in this little difference all varieties of Vedanta find their place. ROBERT WHITTEMORE

VEDAS, composed sometime between 2500 and 1500 B.C. by Aryan authors unknown to history, the Vedas (from the Sanskrit word for knowledge) are the world's oldest scriptures. Each consists of mantras (hymns) and brahmanas (prayers) directed to one or more of the various divine powers of nature—Indra (rain), Varuna (sun), and Agni (fire), among others; most are simple pleas that the gods may grant the suppliant prosperity. Conjoined to some, as later additions, are the principal Upanishads. These last set forth the Vedic philosophy of religion, and all are regarded by orthodox Hindus as unerringly authoritative. In modern Hinduism, the Rig-Veda (the Veda of Psalms) is considered the most important, followed in descending order by the Sama-Veda (the Veda of Chants), the Yajur-Veda (the Veda of Sacred Formulas), and the Atharva-Veda (the Veda of Charms, largely a book of sorcery and witchcraft). In older times, what with the prevalence of belief in ritual magic, this order was usually reversed. See HINDUISM; SANSKRIT LANGUAGE AND LITERATURE.

ROBERT WHITTEMORE

VEDDA, one of an aboriginal people of Ceylon. The Vedda has a very long and high skull, long shaggy black hair, low stature (mean 5 ft. 2 in.), and is dark brown in color. The Veddas speak a Singhalese dialect. By some anthropologists they are considered related to the Sakai of the Malay Peninsula, the Dravidians of Hindustan, the Australian aborigines, and possibly other peoples of southeastern Asia.

VEDDER, ELIHU, 1836–1923, U.S. painter and illustrator, was born in New York, N.Y. He studied in Paris under François Picot, 1856, and went to Rome, 1857, where he absorbed much of the spirit of the great decorative painters of the Renaissance. His reputation as an illustrator rests upon his weird and powerful illustrations for an 1884 edition of the *Rubaiyat of Omar Khayyam* and his illustrations for an edition of the *Arabian Nights*. Among his best known paintings are the *Lair of the Sea Serpent*, the *Cumaean Sybil*, *Questioning the Sphinx*, *The Crucifixion*, *The Last Sun Worshipper*, and *African Sentinel*. As a muralist, Vedder accomplished notable work in the Walker Art Building, Bowdoin College, Brunswick, Me., and in the Library of Congress, Washington, D.C. He was elected to the National Academy of Design in 1865.

VEERY, any of the song birds related to the thrushes and noted for their beautiful singing. The veery, *Hylocichla fuscescens*, is approximately 7¼ inches long and has a slender bill about one-half the length of its head. The upper part of its body has a tawny-brown coloration, gradually becoming lighter on the chest and undersides, with dark streaks and spots on its breast. The veery is a shy bird, living deep within woody areas. Its nest, made of leaves and vines and lined with grass, is found on the ground or at the base of small trees and bushes. Clutches usually contain from three to five greenish-blue eggs. It can be found from northern New Jersey to South Dakota and northward into Canada. Being a migratory bird it winters from South Carolina to northern South America. Food consists of wild fruit, insects, beetles, and snails. Another species of the veery, which is known by the name of willow thrush,

ALLAN D. CRUICKSHANK
FROM NATL. AUDUBON SOC.
Veery Thrush

or *H. fuscescens salicicola*, is duller in its coloration, and winters farther south as far as Brazil.

VEGA, GARCILASO DE LA, called the Spanish Petrarch, 1503–36, Spanish poet, was born in Toledo, and before his death in Nice, France, became the incarnation of the ideal young man of his time—a courtier who was equally adept at arms, letters, love, and music. As one of the chief noblemen of the period, Garcilaso de la Vega served in various campaigns under Holy Roman Emperor Charles V, and it was during one such campaign that the poet was killed in the assault on a tower held by the French at Frejus—Garcilaso had led the charge to demonstrate his loyalty to the emperor, who was present. Garcilaso's poetic production was scanty: 3 eclogues in imitation of Vergil, 2 elegies, an epistle, 5 songs (for one of which he invented the strophe that came to be called *lira*), 38 Petrarchian sonnets, a few couplets in the style of the poets of the Spanish *cancionero*, and some Latin verse. His work was published posthumously, 1543, together with the verse of Juan Boscán, who shared with Garcilaso the task of renovating Spanish meter by introducing the hendecasyllable, the Italian meter, and the new spirit of the Italian Renaissance. Garcilaso wrote principally of love, celebrating his liaisons with Isabel Freyre and other court ladies, and of war, in which he also delighted. Garcilaso's influence on Spanish poetry was considerable, especially on the works of Spanish mystic poets.
ANTHONY KERRIGAN

VEGA, LOPE DE, 1562–1635, full name Lope Félix de Vega Carpio, Spanish playwright, was born in Madrid, where his father, Felices de Vega, was an embroiderer. Lope was a child prodigy: he dictated verses before he could write, fenced and danced like a professional, and had two of his plays performed, before his twelfth birthday. After studying for a time at a Jesuit school, he went into the service of Don Jerónimo Manrique, bishop of Ávila, who, impressed by his talent, sent him for four years to the University of Alcalá. He took part in the naval expedition against the Portuguese in the Azores, 1583, and for five years thereafter served the Marquis of Las Navas. In February, 1588, however he was found guilty of circulating criminal libel against his mistress, an actor's wife named Elena Osorio, and was banished from Madrid for eight years and from the whole of Castile for two years.

He withdrew briefly to Valencia, but defiantly returned to Madrid soon afterwards, and eloped with Isabel de Urbina, whom he married by proxy on May 10, 1588. He then joined the so-called Invincible Armada in Lisbon, and participated in several encounters with the British fleet. After a sojourn in Valencia, he entered the service of the Duke of Alba, in Alba de Tormes, and there wrote a pastoral novel, *Arcadia* (1598). See SPANISH LANGUAGE AND LITERATURE, Spanish Literature.

Shortly after the death of his wife Isabel, 1595, he returned to Madrid, where he became secretary to the Marquis of Malpica. His major interest had become the theater: he associated mainly with actors and playwrights and wrote play after play with incredible speed. He married Juana de Guardo, 1598, and lived in Valencia and Toledo before settling down in Madrid, 1610. Four years later, after his second wife's death, 1613, he was ordained a priest, but neither this nor his age subdued him. He went on penning play after play and involved himself in numerous love intrigues. The mounting joy of his successes, however, was marred by heavy family trials: the woman he loved most dearly, Marte de Nevares, lost her sight and reason; one of his daughters, Antonia Clara, ran off with a court gallant; and his son, Lope, was drowned off the coast of Venezuela.

Significance. His life was a mixture of religious piety and paganism and incessant toil. His nondramatic works fill over 20 volumes, and his plays, among which may be mentioned some of the world's greatest

—*La Fuente ovejuna, Peribanez, El caballero de Olmedo*— number well over 1,000. During his lifetime and for generations afterward he was Spain's main source of entertainment, and although none of his dramas attained the perfection of William Shakespeare's the power of his appeal was and continues to be profound among his countrymen.
ANGEL FLORES

VEGA, town, NW Texas, seat of Oldham County; on the Rock Island Railroad and U.S. highways 66 and 385; 35 miles W of Amarillo. The town is a trade center for an area in which grain and livestock are raised. Pop. (1960) 658.

VEGA, *a* Lyrae, the brightest star in the constellation Lyra and fourth brightest star in the sky, is the brightest star in the summer sky visible from mid-northern latitudes. It comes to the meridian at 9 P.M. about mid-August and at 10 P.M. about August 1. Vega is a blue-white star of spectral type A0 and apparent magnitude 0.1. It is not very distant, being only 27 light-years away; from this it can be calculated that its luminosity is 60 times that of the sun. Vega's radial velocity of approach is some eight miles per second. As a result of the phenomenon of precession, Vega will be the pole star 12,000 years from now, as it was 14,000 years ago. Vega is composed of two components, each a telescopic binary. Moreover the brightest of the four stars is itself a spectroscopic binary, so that the entire system is actually a quintuplet.

VEGETABLE, an edible leaf plant or plant part commonly used for food purposes. Some authorities qualify as vegetable the plant part which is not sweet and is usually flavored with salt, pepper, or other condiments before eating. It is also an edible plant in which reserve food is stored in the roots, stems, leaves, and fruits. These plants are cooked before eating, or eaten raw as salad plants. The popular distinction between a vegetable and a fruit places the fruit in the dessert class. Botanically, fruits are vegetables whose edible parts result from the development of pollinated flowers. A clear, sharp distinction between fruits and vegetables is difficult, if not impossible, however.

Vegetables are rich in most of the vitamins, iron, calcium, some copper, proteins, carbohydrates, fats, and minerals. Since all vegetables contain indigestible cellulose, the bulky character of vegetable foods aids in stimulating movements of the digestive tract.

Leafy green and yellow vegetables are valued highly for their vitamin A, vitamin B and iron content. The greener the vegetable, the higher the vitamin B content. Vitamin C, or ascorbic acid, occurs in tomatoes and citrus fruits. Dried beans have a high iron and protein content. The high fuel foods include potatoes, lima beans, peas, and corn.

Classification. Vegetables are conveniently classified as earth vegetables, herbage vegetables, and fruit vegetables.

Earth vegetables are excellent types of storage foods, as they are well protected underground. They assume the forms of true roots and modified stems, such as root stalks, tubers, corms and bulbs. These are valuable, as they are easily digested and have a high energy content. The principal root foods are the beet, carrot, oyster plant, parsnip, radish, turnip, sweet potato, yam, and cassava.

The modified underground stems include the tubers, Jerusalem artichoke, potato, taro and dasheen of the Orient, and the yantia of the tropics; they include the bulbs, such as onion, garlic, leek, chive, and shallot.

The herbage vegetables include their nutrient material in the parts above the ground. They are similar to the earth vegetables in food value and chemical composition and contain less carbohydrates but more water, proteins, mineral salts, and vitamins. Their roughage or bulk value is higher. Vegetables in this group are the artichoke, asparagus, cabbage, kale, collard, Brussels sprout, kohlrabi, cauliflower, broccoli, celery, chicory, endive, lettuce, rhubarb, spinach, Chinese cabbage, dandelion, and watercress.

The fruit vegetables are botanically fruits, but are included as vegetables, as they are either eaten raw in salads or cooked. They include the avocado, breadfruit, jackfruit and chayote (tropical fruits), the cucumber, eggplant, okra, pumpkin, squash, cantaloupe, tomato, pea, and bean.

The best method of transporting fresh vegetables is in refrigerated railroad cars when distances from producing areas to consumers are great. These cars in many places are brought directly to the field and after the products are taken from the ground, vine, or tree, they are immediately immersed in a coldwater bath which reduces the field heat. Cars are iced before leaving the growing area and re-iced every 12 to 24 hours en route to the market.

Vegetables are packed in crates and nested in crushed ice, and finely crushed ice is blown into the refrigerated cars on top of the crates. Such vegetables as tomatoes and cantaloupes are picked a short time before completely ripe and no ice is placed under them. This permits the heat from the bottom of the car to ripen the vegetables en route. A minimum temperature and proper humidity are maintained during the journey to the market. Upon reaching the market the vegetables are unloaded into refrigerated storage rooms or into trucks for final delivery to the retail stores. As a result of these transportation methods, retail sales of vegetables have been at a higher level, as the vital juices, flavor and vitamin content have been retained.

VEGETARIANISM, the practice of eating only fruits and vegetables. Vegetarians exclude meat, fish and fowl from their diets; still others also eliminate animal products such as milk, eggs, and cheese. Their justifications for the practice of vegetarianism are as follows: it is healthier because parasitic and other diseases are communicated to man from animals; it is cheaper; land is put to more economical use when growing plants; and the need of a larger proportion of people to engage in agriculture would result in race improvement. Many vegetarians ardently feel that it is unethical, immoral, and cruel for man to take life of another sentient being. They also believe man's teeth are not adapted to chewing meat.

Vegetarianism is practiced to a great extent in India, especially by the Hindus, and in Japan by the Buddhists. The oldest society, the Vegetarian Society of Manchester in England, celebrated its 110th anniversary in 1958. Other organizations include the London Vegetarian Society, and the New York Vegetarian Society. Attempts to establish a national organization in the United States and a federal society of the world have failed.

VEGREVILLE, town, Canada, E central Alberta; on the Canadian National and the Canadian Pacific railways; 58 miles E of Edmonton. The town is a trade center for an area in which wheat and cattle are raised. Dairy products and flour are manufactured. Vegreville grew from a French settlement originally established, 1890, four miles to the south. The town was moved to its present site when the railway was constructed through the region. Pop. (1956) 2,574.

VEGTAM, a poem contained in the elder Edda, also known as the Lay of Vegtam the Wanderer or as Balder's Dream. The poem explains that Balder, one of Odin's sons, is troubled by dreams of death; the Aesir, the gods of Norse mythology, assemble and appoint Frigga, Odin's wife, to extract a promise from each thing that it will not harm Balder; Odin, dissatisfied with this precaution, arouses the Sybil Völva from her grave to consult with her, but is told that Balder is fated to be killed by his blind brother, Hoth (or Höthr, or Hodur). Loki, the god of evil, having discovered that one thing—mistletoe—had never made its promise to Frigga, makes mischief: one day, while the Aesir are amusing themselves by hurling weapons at the invulnerable Balder, Loki makes Hoth the unwitting cause of his brother's death by inducing him to throw a dart of mistletoe.

VEII, ancient city, Italy, in Etruria, about 11 miles NW of Rome, with which it was at war almost constantly until, after a 10-year seige, it was captured by the Roman soldier and statesman Marcus Furius Camillus, 396 B.C. A town existed on the site during the time of Emperor Augustus, 27 B.C.–A.D. 14. A statue of Tiberius, found in the ruins, was taken to the Vatican. Ruins of an Etruscan house and sixth century B.C. temple exist on the site, which is also notable for the Grotta Campana, a famous Etruscan tomb.

VEIN. See LODE; ORE, *Classification*.

VEIN. See ARTERIES, VEINS, AND CAPILLARIES; CIRCULATION OF THE BLOOD, *Arteries and Veins, Flow in the Veins;* PHLEBITIS; VARICOSE VEIN.

VELA, the Sails, an unimportant southern constellation. This constellation, together with Carina and Puppis, formed the ancient Ptolemaic constellation of Argo, the Ship. Pyxis is sometimes included as the fourth constellation originally comprising

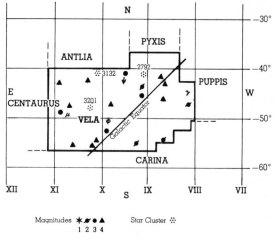

The Constellation Vela

Argo. Because of the vast size of Argo, it was divided into three by B. A. Gould in the nineteenth century. Vela is west of Centaurus and extends in declination from about −40° to −55°. Thirteen stars brighter than the fourth magnitude are included in the constellation, the brightest of which are γ and δ of apparent magnitudes 1.9 and 2.0 respectively. The star γ Velorum is one of the Wolf-Rayet stars of spectral type W, formerly included in spectral class O. Stars of type W are the hottest stars known. The star, γ Velorum, is one of only three Wolf-Rayet stars which can be seen easily with the naked eye. See CONSTELLATION.

VELASCO, LUIS DE, 1500?–64, second viceroy of Mexico and founder of the University of Mexico, 1553, was born in Toledo, Spain. As compared to that of the other *conquistadores,* Velasco's rule was uniquely humane; many Indians were freed from slavery during his administration, and flood-control measures were taken after a disastrous flood of Mexico City, 1553. Velasco sponsored the exploring expedition of Francisco de Ibarra that resulted in the conquest of what later became the Mexican provinces of Chihuahua and Durango.   ALFRED DE GRAZIA

VELÁZQUEZ, DIEGO DE, 1460?–?1524, governor of Cuba, was born in Cuéllar, Spain. He fought in the wars against the Moors, accompanied Christopher Columbus on his second voyage to the New World, and assisted in the conquest of Hispaniola. During 1511–13, he conquered Cuba, and founded Baracoa, Bayamo, Puerto Principe (later Camagüey), Santiago de Cuba, Havana, and other places. In

1518, he sent Hernán Cortés to conquer and plunder Yucatán, but, fearing Cortés' own greed, he tried unsuccessfully to recall Cortés before he departed from Cuba. Cortés conquered Yucatán, invaded Mexico, 1519, and defeated an expedition sent by Velázquez to overtake him, 1520.

VELAZQUEZ, DIEGO RODRIGUEZ DE SILVA Y, 1599–1660, Spanish painter, was born in Seville, the son of a lawyer of Portuguese descent. Young Diego Velázquez (or Velásquez) studied under Francisco de Herrera and Francisco Pacheco, married the latter's daughter, 1618, and in her house met Miguel de Cervantes y Saavedra and other notables of the time. While still in his early twenties, Velázquez moved to Madrid, 1622, and soon was a favorite of King Philip IV; he was appointed court painter, 1623, and held this office throughout his life. Although it is said that his wage was less than that of the court barber, Velázquez at least had a measure of economic security, and had little to fear from the attentions of the Inquisition; he was largely free to paint what he liked at his ease.

The absence of religious themes in his work made him a "modern" before his times as regards realistic subject matter. His early concern with reality is exemplified in *Los Borrachos* (The Drunkards), also and more accurately known as *Bacchus*, since this God of topers figures prominently in the painting which is in the Prado Museum, as are most of his masterpieces. During his first trip to Italy, 1629–31, he painted *Vulcan's Forge* and two landscapes of the Villa Medici gardens; he was to visit Italy again in 1649–51. Velázquez could paint anything he could see, but seems to have been unable to imagine what he could not see; thus he was the very opposite of a later Spanish painter, Pablo Picasso, who chose to paint an inner vision rather than reality as seen. Even Velázquez' earliest work is marked by a vision of the world as it is classically thought to appear, plus a certain hard characterization. Over and above these qualities are his masterful use of color, and his composition; he rendered light and atmosphere as few artists, before or after him, were able to do. Among other paintings of Velázquez' first period are the magnificent *Christ on the Cross*, a dramatic contrast in black and white, and one of the great paintings of all time; *The Water Carrier of Seville*, in which the browns and grays tie together an intensive study in characterization; and *The Old Kitchen*, a profoundly human genre scene.

Characterization. Velázquez' mythological paintings embody an odd note of secular religiosity: his gods are men like other men, with no supermundane qualities. Both in *Vulcan's Forge* and in *The Drunkards*, the mythological persons are peasants in appearance, and their force and impact as individuals seems lessened rather than heightened by their being gods. Velázquez was probably the most earthy painter up to his time, and was perhaps more earthy than any painter of later centuries. His numerous portraits form a gallery of men as superior animals, fully as dignified as trees, but hardly more so; he seems to have had no satirical intent, yet few of the most misanthropic satirists have been more candid. Velázquez' Crucifixion scene is probably the most "human" ever painted; he depicted Aesop and Menippus as two shabby men of letters, not as legendary thinkers living in flights of fancy; his *Mars* is an archetypal top sergeant. One of Velázquez' greatest portraits, however, painted during his later Italian sojourn, is his *Innocent X*, painted in tones of red and white; the pose of this remarkable characterization—the sitter is at an angle to the picture plane, as if to gain depth—was apparently influenced by El Greco's *Portrait of Niño de Guevara*.

During his years as court painter, Velázquez painted some 40 portraits of the king, every one of them well worth study. They show the monarch in many attitudes, but usually sitting or riding on a horse, often in hunting costume, and with dogs in attendance, and sometimes with the queen and other notables close at hand. Also noteworthy is the equestrian portrait of the king's minister, El Conde-Duque de Olivares (Gaspar de Guzmán, duque de Sanlúcar and conde de Olivares or Olivarez).

Other Works. Although much interested in characterization for its own sake, Velázquez was perfectly able to paint a painter's painting, as his *The Venus and Cupid* (National Gallery, London) testifies; this is a study in line and color, in which the face is a mere compositional and decorative element. In *The Spinners*, an interior in which the light-flooded background creates a stunning atmosphere, the figures are all subordinated to the over-all ambience, and the picture is in no sense a figurative study, but rather an interior landscape. Portraiture, landscape, and "pure painting," are combined in another great work, *Las Lanzas* (*The Lances*, also known as *The Surrender of Breda*), 1639–41.

In his later years, Velázquez interested himself in painting beggars, buffoons, idiots, and dwarfs with all the intensity he had lent to his studies of the classical gods on earth. In this he again prefigured a tendency that later modernists were to stress—the vindication of the irrational and the elevation of the ugly to the level of dignified concern. Two of the best known canvases in this series are *El Primo* and *The Jester Called Don Juan de Austria*. One of his last canvases is perhaps his masterpiece, *Las Meninas*, a genre scene in which one watches the king and queen sitting for their portraits; the work is a *tour de force* in the depiction of light—there are four planes of light achieved by subtle gradations of values—and of volume.

Death. From 1652 Velázquez was quartermaster general of the king's household as well as court painter, and he died from over-exertion while helping in the preparations for an elaborate court marriage—that of Louis XIV and the Infanta Maria Theresa.

ANTHONY KERRIGAN

BIBLIOG.–Enrique La Fuente Ferrari, *Velázquez: Biographical and Critical Study* (1960); August L. Mayer, *Velázquez: A Catalogue Raisonné of the Pictures and Drawings* (1936); Pablo Picasso, *Picasso: Variations on Velázquez' Painting 'The Maids of Honor', and Other Recent Works* (1960); Arthur S. Riggs, *Velázquez, Painter of Truth and Prisoner of the King* (1947); Edwin Stowe, *Velázquez* (1929); Elizabeth D. G. Trapier, *Velázquez* (1948); Diego R. de S. y Velázquez, *Paintings and Drawings* (1945), *Six Color Reproductions of Paintings from the Prado Museum* (1946); Diego R. de S. y Velázquez (1955).

VELEZ DE GUEVARA, LUIS, 1579?–1644, Spanish dramatist and novelist, was born in Ecija, Seville Province, married four times, and died in Madrid. He was always poor, to judge by his begging verse, but he had a first-class dramatic talent, an insight into the feeling behind popular legendary verse, and a knack for making effective dramatic use of heroic national themes. In his *La serrana de la Vera*, one of the most delightful of all Spanish comedies, popular and aristocratic elements are nicely combined. His *La niña de Gómez Arias*, telling of a girl's seduction and enslavement, was to be the direct source for a comedy of the same name by Calderón de la Barca. Vélez's *Reinar después de morir*, an impressive tragedy, contains much fine verse. In his one novel, the picaresque satire *El diablo cojuelo* (1641), an imp discloses the fascinating life of the cities to an errant student; this work was to be the principal inspiration of Alain René Lesage's *Le diable boîteux* (1707).

ANTHONY KERRIGAN

VELIA, or Elea, ancient Greek town in Italy, on the SW coast in Lucania (modern Basilicata Region), about 25 miles SE of Paestum and about 40 miles SSE of Salernum (modern Salerno). Velia was founded, c.530 B.C., by seafaring Ionian Greeks from the city of Phocaea, in Asia Minor. It seems, on the basis of numismatic evidence, that the earliest name of the town was Yele; as it prospered and gained in power and prestige, the name was changed to Elea; finally, as a Roman town from early in the first century B.C., it was called Velia. In the period between World Wars I and II archaeologists began extensive excavations of the site; work was interrupted by World War II, but was resumed after the war. Late in the 1950's work was continuing on the excavation of a large *agora* (plaza) at the center of the city. Velia was typically Greek in plan, with part of the city high in elevation and centering around an acropolis, and the rest progressively lower in elevation and extending to the shore line. There were several temples, including ones to Aphrodite, Poseidon, Zeus, and other Greek deities. Four miles of walls and towers aided the inhabitants in defending the city. During the Middle Ages a castle was built on Velia's acropolis, but the castle and the ruins of the ancient city were eventually abandoned until modern times. The city was noted in antiquity for its philosophers. See ELEATIC SCHOOL.

VELIKIYE LUKI, town, U.S.S.R., W Russian Soviet Federated Socialist Republic, Pskov Region; 260 miles W of Moscow. The town is a railroad junction and has textile factories, flour mills, brickworks, dairies, and distilleries. Pop. (1959) 59,000.

VELLETRI, town, W central Italy, Latium Region, Rome Province; at the SE foot of the Alban Hills, 22 miles SSE of Rome. Velletri is an episcopal see, with a cathedral dating from the thirteenth century. The town is in a wine-producing region. It was the scene of Giuseppe Garibaldi's victory over the King of Naples, May 19, 1849. Velletri was heavily bombed in World War II. Pop. (1961) 40,415.

VELLORE, city, SE India, Madras State; on the Palar River, 80 miles WSW of Madras. Vellore is a trade center in a region where rice, sugar cane, cotton, and peanuts are cultivated. Features of interest include a Hindu temple. Vellore's fort was important during the Carnatic Wars. Hyder Ali besieged the city for two years, from 1780 to 1782. Pop. (1961) 113,520.

VELLUTI, GIOVANNI BATTISTA, 1780–1861, last of the great Italian male sopranos, was born in Pausula, Italy. He finished his formal musical education at the age of 20 and achieved his first success, 1804, in Rome singing Nicolini's work, *La selvaggia nel Messico*. His singing was highly praised throughout Europe and in England until 1829, when he lost his voice during a London engagement.

VELOCITY, the time rate of change of distance in a given direction. Velocity is a vector quantity and therefore requires both magnitude and direction for its complete characterization. (See VECTOR.) The magnitude of the velocity, or the scalar portion, is more commonly known as the speed. If the motion of the object is along a straight line, then there is no variation in the direction of motion. In this case, however, the speed may vary. It is convenient to measure the distances from some convenient point on the line taken as the origin, and to adopt a sense of direction as, for example, in the case of the x-axis with abscissae measured positively to the right of the origin. (See COORDINATES.) If the object moves from an initial point s_0 beginning at time t_0 and arrives at a final point s_f at t_f, the average speed is denoted by v and is given by:

$$v = \frac{s_f - s_0}{t_f - t_0}$$

where $s_f - s_0$ is the distance traversed in the elapsed time $t_f - t_0$. Units for the velocity are those of length per time, for example, miles per hour (mi/hr), feet per second (ft/sec), centimeters per second (cm/sec). The instantaneous value of the velocity is given by $\frac{ds}{dt}$ where the first derivative is evaluated at the instant of time under consideration. For straight line motion, ds/dt gives the variation of the speed with respect to time, the direction being fixed along the line s chosen as the axis. With a variable velocity, the acceleration must be taken into account. The acceleration is the time rate of change of the velocity and is the second derivative of the distance with respect to the time, d^2s/dt^2. When velocity is referred to, it is implied to be a linear velocity; otherwise, the velocity of body undergoing rotation about an axis must be specified as the angular velocity.

The motion of a point moving along a plane curve is somewhat more complicated. The velocity of the point is the time rate of change of the distance s from a fixed origin, and is the vector derivative of s with respect to the time. This vector derivative is denoted by ds/dt, and it gives both the speed and direction of motion of the point. In this case the derivative gives for the direction of motion that of the tangent constructed at the point of curve under consideration, and the direction along the tangent corresponds to that in which the point is moving along the curve.

VELOCITY OF ESCAPE, or velocity of liberation, is the velocity that must be imparted vertically to an object at the surface of an astronomical body, such as a planet, satellite, sun, or star, to permit its escape from the gravitational attraction of that body. Since a body projected with such a velocity would theoretically recede an infinite distance in the absence of other bodies, the velocity of escape is also known as the velocity to infinity. This velocity, in centimeters per second, is given by the formula

$$v = \sqrt{\frac{2GM}{r}}$$

where the universal constant of gravitation G equals 6.67×10^{-8}, M is the mass of the astronomical body in grams, and r is its radius in centimeters. The preceding formula gives the velocity of escape under ideal conditions; it does not take into account air drag in the atmosphere enveloping the astronomical body. It can be shown using the preceding formula and assuming a spherical shape for the astronomical bodies, that the velocities of escape for the two bodies are given by

$$\frac{v}{v_1} = \sqrt{\frac{\sigma r^2}{\sigma r_1^2}}$$

where v is the velocity of escape, say for the earth; r, the earth's radius, and σ, its mean density. If the radius r_1 of a second astronomical body is known, and also σ_1, its mean density, then v_1, its velocity of escape, can be determined using the preceding formula, provided the v, σ, and r are known for the earth or some other astronomical body. The velocity needed by a projectile in order for it to escape vertically from the earth's surface under ideal conditions is about 7 miles per second or about 37,000 feet per second. To project a body from the earth to the moon requires a velocity of only about 300 feet per second less than that needed to project it to infinity. The following table shows that there is considerable variation in the range of velocities of escape even among the planets and the moon.

VELOCITIES OF ESCAPE

Astronomical body	Velocity of escape in mi./sec.
Earth	7.0
Moon	1.47
Mercury	2.2
Venus	6.3
Mars	3.1
Jupiter	37.0
Saturn	22.0
Uranus	13.0
Neptune	14.0

VELVET, a warp pile fabric commonly made of silk or rayon woven with cotton. The weave is composed of two sets of warp yarn that run lengthwise on the loom, and one set of filling yarn that is interwoven at right angles with the warp yarn. The filling yarn forms loops that are normally cut apart while still on the loom, producing a short, thick pile surface.

The underside of the fabric is usually plain woven cotton yarn. Poor grades of velvet deteriorate after little use, but better grades are washable, wear well and may be made crush-resistant and water-resistant. There are numerous different kinds of velvet, each suited for a particular use. Bagheera is a crush-resistant, uncut pile velvet of rough texture. Chiffon, or panné, velvet is a lightweight, soft-textured fabric, used for dresses, suits, and evening clothes. Lyons velvet is a stiff, thick pile material used for hats and dresses. Transparent velvet is a lightweight, soft-textured fabric that has a silk or rayon back and that drapes well. Nacre velvet has a back of one color and a pile of another, thus producing a changing appearance. Ciselé velvet has patterns formed by the contrast between cut and uncut loops.

VELVETEEN, a filling pile fabric similiar to velvet. Velveteen has a short pile that is formed by extending an extra set of filling yarn over two or more adjacent threads on the surface of the fabric. This extra filling is bound into the back of the material at intervals by weaving over and under one or more of the warp threads. Velveteen, normally made of cotton, is strong and washable, and is used for draperies, children's clothing, coats, dresses, and suits.

VENANGO, former Indian village in northwestern Pennsylvania, at the junction of French Creek and the Allegheny River, on a site that was later used for a trading post, a military fort, and the modern city of Franklin, Venango County. A British fur trading post was established there, ?1750. The French seized the post, 1753, and made it a link in their chain of forts between Canada and the Ohio Valley (the others being Presque Isle, Le Boeuf, and Duquesne). A few months later, George Washington visited Venango to warn the commandant that he was trespassing on British territory, but the French erected a stronger fort, 1754, which they named Machault. The fort was abandoned and burned, 1759, whereupon the British occupied the site and built, 1760, a new post, which they renamed Venango. At the beginning of Pontiac's War, 1763, the Indians captured the fort by ruse; the garrison was massacred and the stockade burned. Fort Franklin, built on the site as a haven for settlers menaced by hostile Indians, 1787, was abandoned, 1796, as the period of Indian warfare in the area came to an end.

VENDÉE, or La Vendée, department, W France, in Poitou, bounded on the W by the Bay of Biscay of the Atlantic Ocean, and by the departments of Loire-Inférieure on the N, Maine-et-Loire on the NE, Deaux Sèvres on the E, and Charente-Maritime on the S; area 2,709 sq. mi., including the islands of Yeu and Noimoutier; pop. (1954) 395,641. The department consists of a level plain rising to a range of low hills, Haut de Gâtine, on the northeast border. The capital is La Roche-sur-Yon, and Les Sables-d'Olonne is the chief port. Wheat, vegetables, and grapes are the major crops. Cattle grazing is important. Vendée was famous for the stubborn resistance of its people during the peasant uprising known as the Wars of the Vendée, 1793–94.

VENDETTA. See Feud.

VENDING MACHINE. See Coin Machine.

VENDOR AND PURCHASER, the participants in any transfer of real property by sale. Vendors and purchasers differ from buyers and sellers in that the latter are involved in the transfer of personal property. The vendor negotiates the sale and receives some form of compensation from the purchaser, or receiver of the property. The vendor may perform this action for another party or may be the actual owner of the property.

After the prospective vendor and purchaser have agreed upon the terms of the sale, the purchaser frequently orders an examination of the title to the property being transferred. The parties normally bind the bargain by entering into a contract for the sale, the actual passing of title often being postponed to a future date. Under the statute of frauds, a contract or memorandum for the sale of land must be in writing and signed by the purchaser. Thereupon, unless the vendor expressly states otherwise, the law recognizes a complete transfer of title. If there are defects in the property that have not been made known to the purchaser before the transfer of title, he may refuse to accept the contract. If a defect in the property is discovered after the transfer of title, the purchaser must prove that it existed before he accepted the property. Unless a covenant of warranty of title, assuring the purchaser that he has complete and free title to the property, is included in a deed, the purchaser accepts the risk of a defective title. See Title; Title Guaranty Company.

If a certain price is fixed for an area of land, and there is no fraud or mutual mistake, the purchaser cannot refuse to take title, or apply for an annulment of the contract or deed, if it is subsequently discovered that the tract contains less acreage than was originally estimated. If, however, the exact quantity of the land was a material part of the contract, as where a certain number of acres are sold at a certain price per acre, the purchaser is entitled to a return of the excess amount that he has paid. If there is more land than originally estimated, the same rules apply to the vendor. If land not intended to be conveyed is included in a deed by mistake, the vendor may recover it, or its value, from the purchaser. The purchaser may obtain an annulment of the contract upon proof of fraudulent misrepresentations of material facts, such as condition of the land, amount of rental, or existence of certain natural advantages. See Deed; Sale.

VENEER, wood that is cut into thin sheets. It is produced for furniture and finishing materials to overlay cheaper or perhaps stronger woods with the beautiful grain or figure of the rarer and costlier kinds; to assemble into plywood of both structural and decorative types; and to produce containers such as lightweight shipping boxes and crates.

Cutting Veneer. Currently veneer is cut from logs or roughly squared portions of logs by sawing, by slicing against a heavy knife, or peeling against a knife on a rotary veneer lathe. The common range of thicknesses cut is from 1/40 to 5/16 inch, but for special purposes it may be cut as thin as 1/110 inch.

Red gum, yellow pine, birch, cottonwood, tupelo, mahogany, yellow poplar, white and red oak, maple, walnut, spruce, basswood, and Douglas fir are some of the woods cut in quantity. Douglas fir veneer as a component of Douglas fir plywood, is the dominant rotary-cut veneer for construction uses.

In 1960 more than 10 billion square feet of veneer per year were produced. Besides the considerable quantities used in furniture and containers and for

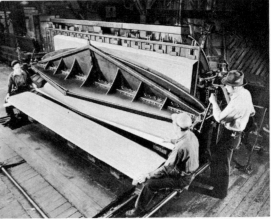

MAHOGANY ASSN., INC.

A panel of mahogany veneer is sliced from a log clamped to the back plate of the veneer machine as the plate swings past the knife edge at an angle to peel off the veneer.

USDA

A peeled birch log is placed in the veneer lathe in the experimental veneer plant of the Forest Products Laboratory of the U.S. Forest Service at Madison, Wisconsin.

general structural purposes, smaller but significant amounts are used in aircraft, railway car interiors, doors, trunks, storage batteries, television and radio cabinets, and sewing machines. A large proportion of furniture is veneered.

VENEREAL DISEASE, any of certain communicable diseases which may be spread through sexual contact. They include syphilis, gonorrhea, and chancroid. See SYPHILIS; GONORRHEA.

The venereal diseases are transmitted by contact of the skin or mucous membrane with infectious material. Infection of the skin requires a break, though it may be so small as to be invisible. Mucous membranes may be infected even if they are intact. The transmission of these diseases is largely by sexual contact, but there are other ways in which they can be acquired. Attendants upon the sick, such as physicians, nurses, and ward orderlies, may become infected in the course of their duties. Syphilis can be transmitted through the saliva, by kissing, or by the transfer of saliva on musical instruments, pipes, eating utensils, and other common home contacts. Gonorrhea is transferable through clothing, bedding, towels, and wash cloths while the infection is fresh. In the case of granuloma inguinale and soft chancre the transmission is always by sexual contact.

Chancroid, or soft chancre, is an infection involving the sex organs and transmitted almost exclusively by sexual intercourse. It is due to a different infection from the hard chancre of syphilis; the responsible organism is known as the bacillus of Ducrey. Owing to similarity in mode of distribution, soft chancres may accompany hard chancres, and may also be found in the presence of gonorrheal infection. The soft chancre differs from the syphilitic sore in the absence of a hard base and in a tendency to spread and become destructive. The hard chancre of syphilis heals spontaneously, leaving only a thin scar, and is painless. The soft chancre does not heal without treatment. The syphilitic chancre is always single, while chancroidal infections may be multiple, starting at various points where the infection has gained entrance to the tissues. The hard chancre of syphilis is the initial indication of an infection which becomes generalized; the soft chancre remains local. Formerly resistant to most forms of treatment, chancroid responds promptly to the antibiotics streptomycin and chloramphenicol, used both internally and locally. Penicillin is ineffective. Frequent cleansing of the affected area is an important adjunct to treatment.

W. W. BAUER, M.D.

VENETI, an ancient tribe of northern Italy and of northwestern France. The Veneti of Italy were referred to by the Greek poet Homer as the Heneti of Paphlagonia, whom the ancients believed to have settled in northern Italy, and who were led by the Trojan leader Antenor; but this is at least doubtful. The Roman historian Cornelius Tacitus wrote of a tribe living on the southern shore of the Baltic as Venedi or Veneti, perhaps identical with the Wends; and it is possible that the Italian Veneti were an offshoot from them. The German classical scholar Theodor Mommsen, however, classed the Veneti as Illyrians, or perhaps Albanians. In any case, the Veneti gradually came under Roman rule, by way of alliance rather than conquest, probably during the second century B.C. The Huns, under Attila, overran Veneti territory, A.D. 452, and destroyed many Veneti towns, including Aquilèia, Padua, and Verona. Their fugitive inhabitants took refuge in the small islands among the lagoons that border the northwesternmost part of the Adriatic Sea; out of these settlements grew Venice.

The Veneti of France were a Celtic people, who inhabited Brittany at the time of Julius Caesar's conquest of northern Gaul, 58–50 B.C. The city of Vannes in Morbihan Department is named for them.

VENETO, region, NE Italy; bounded by Austria on the N and the Adriatic Sea on the SE, and by the regions of Emilia-Romagna on the S, Lombardy on the W, Trentino-Alto Adige on the NW, and Fruili-Venezia Guilia on the E; area 7,098 sq. mi.; pop. (1958) 3,902,173. Veneto includes the provinces of Belluno, Padua, Rovigo, Treviso, Venice, Verona, and Vicenza. The northern part of Veneto lies in the Alps Mountains. The rivers of the region include the Po, the Adige, the Piave, and the Brenta. Veneto's shoreline is rimmed by lagoons and river deltas. The south is a productive agricultural region; the lower mountain slopes support cattle raising. Hydroelectric power is provided by the torrential Alpine streams. Manufacturing of wool, cotton, and silk textiles, and of beet sugar, hemp, paper, and glass are important industries.

Venezuela ranks first in the world in the export of oil and second in its production.

VENEZUELA, republic, N South America; bounded on the N by the Caribbean Sea and the Atlantic Ocean, on the E by British Guiana, on the S by Brazil, and on the W by Colombia; area 352,150 sq. mi.; pop. (1961 est.) 7,431,000. The country averages 930 miles east-west and 790 miles north-south. Included in its territory are a large number of small Caribbean islands, the largest of which is Margarita (460 sq. mi.). Other islands include Tortuga and Blanquilla. Caracas is the capital of Venezuela. See map in Atlas, Vol. 20. For national flag in color, see FLAG.

PHYSICAL FEATURES

Physiography. Venezuela has three major physiographic regions: a mountain and valley region, along

Location·Map of Venezuela

the coast in the north; the plains of the Orinoco River (Llanos), farther south; and the Guiana Highlands, comprising more than half the country's area, in the south. The chief mountains along the coast are the Venezuelan Andes; they trend northeastward from Colombia, one range on either side of Lake Maracaibo, which, together with the Gulf of Venezuela, is a pocket-like bay of the Caribbean. West of the lake, the crest of the Sierra de Perija forms the Colombian boundary and includes peaks exceeding 10,000 feet above sea level. South of the lake, the Cordillera de Mérida has the highest summits in the country, with Pico Bolívar rising to 16,411 feet. To the east, along the Caribbean, the cordillera forms a double range extending, except at Zaraza, to the Gulf of Paria. The northern range rises abruptly from the sea to more than 9,000 feet near Caracas; the southern rises to more than 6,000 feet. The Guiana Highlands are a dissected plateau with several distinct ranges. Among these are the Sierra Parima and the Sierra Pacaraima, both along the Brazilian boundary. The highest summit is Mount Roraima (9,219 ft.), where Venezuela, British Guiana, and Brazil join. Characteristic of the higher elevations of this region, the mountain is flat-topped and has red sandstone strata with sheer slopes.

The Llanos form a shallow trough that slopes gently eastward and terminates in the extensive, forested delta of the Orinoco. They are largely a savanna grassland interspersed with palms and other trees especially along the watercourses. During part of the year extensive areas of the lower Llanos are covered by flood waters, while the higher margins possess a greater slope and more adequate drainage.

Venezuela's coast line is decidedly indented and measures 1,750 miles in length. The Orinoco drains all of southern and central Venezuela. Some of the main tributaries, such as the Meta and the Apure, from the west, and the Caura and Caroní, from the south, are themselves great rivers. Other Venezuelan rivers are quite short.

Aside from Lake Maracaibo, the largest lakes are Valencia and Zulia. There are also many large gulfs and bays along the coast, of which the most important are the gulfs of Venezuela, Unare, Paria, Cariaco, and Coro.

Climate. Venezuela lies wholly within the seasonally rainy tropics. Monthly differences in temperature are slight; temperature variations are mainly influenced by seasonal cloud cover and differences in local elevations. In the Llanos the mean annual temperature is between 81°F and 84°, and average annual rainfall ranges from 25 to 50 inches. The climate of the Andes is tropical to elevations of 3,000 feet, temperate from 3,000 to 6,000 feet, and cool from 6,000 to 10,000 feet. Above 10,000 feet is the *páramo*, a cold, grassy area. Easterly trade winds, which cross the country between November and April, result in a dry season, while convectional thunderstorms of the tropical doldrum belt prevail between May and October. Ciudad Bolívar, at 125 feet above sea level, has an average annual temperature of 80°F, and an average precipitation of 35 inches; Caracas, at 3,415 feet above sea level, averages 67°F and 32 inches.

Plants and Animals. The variations in climate exert a corresponding influence upon plant life, which

PRINCIPAL CITIES

City	Population*
Caracas (greater)	1,336,119
Maracaibo	421,166
Barquisimeto	199,691
Valencia	163,601
Maracay	135,353
San Cristobal	98,777
Cumana	69,630

*1961 census

POLITICAL DIVISIONS

State, Territory, or Federal District	Area	Population*
	Sq. Mi.	
Anzoátegui	16,700	382,002
Apure	29,550	117,577
Aragua	2,700	313,274
Barinas	13,600	139,271
Bolívar	91,900	213,543
Carabobo	1,800	381,636
Cojedes	5,700	72,652
Falcón	9,550	340,450
Guárico	25,100	244,966
Lara	7,650	489,140
Mérida	4,350	270,668
Miranda	3,050	492,349
Monagas	11,150	246,217
Nueva Esparta	450	89,492
Portuguesa	5,900	203,707
Sucre	4,550	401,292
Táchira	4,300	399,163
Trujillo	2,850	326,634
Yaracuy	2,750	175,291
Zulia	24,400	919,863
Amazonas Territory	67,800	11,757
Delta Amacuro Territory	16,100	33,979
Federal Dependencies	46	861
Federal District	745	1,257,515

*1961 census

ranges from alpine shrubs and reindeer moss at the highest elevations to bamboo and orchids in the lowlands. Tropical forests, characterized by palm trees, occupy the Maracaibo Basin, the Orinoco Delta, and much of the Guiana Highlands. The savanna grasslands of the Llanos are also within the tropical zone.

Animal life is abundant. The forests contain many varieties of monkeys, and there are jaguar, puma, ocelot, margay, and bear in the mountains. Sloth and anteater are in the valleys and tapirs in the Orinoco forests. Deer inhabit both the Llanos and the mountains, while horses, donkeys, and cattle roam the plains in a semiwild state. Tropical birds, including the egret, cassique, crested coquette, umbrella bird, manikin, cock-of-the-rock parrot, and macaw, are numerous in the forests. Great flocks of aquatic wild fowl include the pelican, heron, and flamingo, and there are many varieties of eagles. Reptiles are numerous, many of them large and colorful, but few are poisonous. Included are the anaconda, boa, rattlesnake, coral, and bushmaster. Crocodiles and turtles are numerous along the Orinoco River and its tributaries.

Social Factors

Population. Most Venezuelans are mestizos (of mixed Spanish, African, and Indian ancestry), but a small percentage are of unmixed European descent, chiefly Spanish. Negroes, totaling 8 per cent of the population, live mostly along the Caribbean Coast. The official language is Spanish. The population of Venezuela grew slowly until the 1940's. In 1936 it was only 3.5 million, but by 1963 had increased to 8.1 million. The rate of population growth, one of the highest in the world, is more than 3.6 per cent annually. Venezuela's population is largely concentrated in the northern mountain and valley region. Caracas is the largest city; other large cities are Maracaibo, Barquisimeto, Valencia, and Maracay.

Education and Religion. Since 1870, primary education has been free and compulsory for all children over seven years of age. Enforcement, however, is lax in the rural areas. The primary course covers six years. There are two types of secondary schools, the commercial and the academic (the latter only in the cities). In 1963 the school enrollment in Venezuela was: elementary schools, 1,346,751; secondary schools, 197,454; teacher-training and technical schools, about 85,000; and universities about 30,000.

VENEZUELA

For lack of motorized transportation facilities, cattle are usually driven on-the-hoof to the slaughterhouses, losing much valuable weight and inconveniencing motorists in the process.

An intricately piped gas adsorption plant, at La Paz, Venezuela, is one of the industrial operations that has been developed from a skilled exploitation of the nation's natural resources.

Tile, produced in local factories, is used as a roofing material; it is inexpensive to make and a good insulator.

Fruits and vegetables are sold in the outskirts of **Caracas** by a *frutero,* who transports his foods on a horse wagon.

Numerous species of fish are caught in coastal waters of Venezuela; the total annual catch of commercial fishing is more than 75,000 tons.

Largest of the institutions of higher education is Central University, in Caracas, with an enrollment of 9,712 in 1958–59. Other public universities are: Zulia, in Maracaibo; Los Andes, in Mérida; Carabobo, in Valencia; and Oriente, in Cumaná. In addition, there are two private universities, Santa Maria University and Andrés Bello Catholic University, in Caracas.

Roman Catholicism, the predominant religion, is state-supported. Other religions are tolerated, but Protestant churches have a total membership of less than 20,000.

Public Health. The National Ministry of Public Health and Social Welfare supervises the health programs of the country. Separate divisions are organized for maternal and child welfare, school hygiene, social welfare, and control of diseases. Special emphasis is placed upon control of malaria, tuberculosis, and venereal diseases, and maternal and child welfare, and health education. Modern hospitals and dispensaries are distributed throughout the country.

ECONOMIC FACTORS

Mining. Venezuela is rich in minerals, especially petroleum, iron ore, gold, and diamonds. The country also has deposits of asbestos, manganese, bauxite, nickel, copper, and coal. Venezuela ranks among the world's leading producers of petroleum, and is virtually unsurpassed in petroleum exports. The first commercial oil well in the Maracaibo Basin began producing in 1914, but the first major production there began in 1922 with the discovery of La Rosa Field. Output first exceeded 100 million barrels in 1928. Most Venezuelan production comes from the Maracaibo Basin, but the fields in eastern Venezuela, especially in the states of Monagas and Anzoátegui, are of increasing importance.

PRODUCTION OF PRINCIPAL MINERALS

Mineral	Unit	1956	1958
Asbestos....	short ton	5,800	9,100
Coal......	short ton	33,850	40,000
Diamonds..	carat	93,830	89,550
Gold.......	1,000 grams	2,170	2,350
Iron ore....	1,000 short tons	12,215	17,030
Petroleum..	1,000's of 42-gallon barrels	899,200	950,750
Salt.......	short ton	41,400	97,000

SOURCE: *U.S. Department of Commerce*

Iron ore production is concentrated in Bolívar State, almost entirely by subsidiaries of the Bethlehem and United States Steel corporations. The sites include Cerro Bolívar, a vast mountain containing an estimated 600 million tons of ore. Other minerals are mined on a smaller scale. El Callao, in Bolívar State, once one of the world's leading gold-mining centers, ranks first in Venezuela. From more than 8 million grams in 1885, Venezuelan output declined to 2.4 million grams in 1958. Diamonds, chiefly for use in industry, are obtained from alluvial deposits. Asbestos mines are located at Tinaquillo, in Cojedes State; coal at Naricual, in Anzoátegui State; and copper at Aroa, in Yaracuy State.

Agriculture. Almost one half of the Venezuelan labor force is engaged in agriculture. Production is concentrated in the Andean mountains and valleys. Coffee and cacao are raised in sufficient quantities for export, while corn, sugar cane, cotton, bananas, rice, and tobacco are raised extensively for the domestic market. Other crops include rice, wheat, and sesame, and potatoes, beans, onions, and other vegetables. Among the chief fruit crops are tomatoes, oranges, bananas, coconuts, pineapples, papaya, and mangoes. Coffee, introduced from Martinique in 1784, is a major export. The coffee plantations are chiefly in the highlands of the Cordillera de Mérida. Output has declined from the peak of earlier years, but coffee

PRODUCTION OF PRINCIPAL CROPS

Crop	1955	1957
	short tons	
Cacao......................	16,500	16,750
Coffee.....................	50,900	55,400
Corn......................	349,000	374,000
Cotton....................	14,300	15,600
Rice......................	66,000	23,900
Sisal......................	5,000	7,500
Sugar.....................	158,000	212,000
Tobacco...................	7,750	11,900

SOURCE: *U.S. Department of Commerce*

still ranks as one of Venezuela's leading agricultural exports. The growing of cacao for the production of chocolate is important in the central and eastern mountain valleys. The crop is of uniformly high quality and finds a steady export market. Although never an important export, sugar cane has long been a major agricultural product. There are sugar plantations throughout the valleys of the central Andean highlands and the southern Maracaibo Basin.

The basic food crops, corn and beans, are raised throughout Venezuela, and wheat is grown on the high slopes of the Andes. Tobacco is cultivated in the northern margin of the Llanos. Cotton cultivation is concentrated in northeastern Venezuela and in the area around Valencia, which has traditionally been Venezuela's richest agricultural region, although improved transportation and irrigation facilities have helped to increase production in other areas. Notable among these are the Andes-Llanos border of Portuguesa and neighboring states, northern Guárico State, and the southern Maracaibo Basin.

Venezuela was once an important cattle-raising country, but the herds were depleted during the civil wars, and the number of cattle has since fluctuated widely. Cattle are still raised in all parts of Venezuela, particularly in the Llanos. The best animals, both for meat and hides, are supplied from Apure State, where cattle raising is conducted as a modern, scientific enterprise. Dairying has expanded rapidly from Caracas westward to Valencia, and pasteurized milk is supplied to all of the larger cities. The breeding of goats is important in the dry lands of northwestern Venezuela, but sheep and hogs are few in number.

Manufacturing. Venezuela experienced rapid industrial growth after World War II. Important factors in this expansion were the increased revenues from exports of petroleum and iron ore, improved transportation facilities, an influx of skilled immigrants from western Europe, and an expanding domestic market. The investment of U.S. and European capital was also significant. The principal industrial centers are Caracas, Maracaibo, the Valencia Basin, and the Barcelona–Puerto La Cruz area of northeastern Venezuela. In addition, an area of heavy industry centers upon the new iron and steel mill at the junction of the Orinoco and Caroní rivers. Textile manufacturing, one of the nation's largest industries, is centered in Valencia, Maracay, and Caracas. Industries in Caracas produce food and tobacco products, automobiles, shoes, metal goods, and printed matter. Maracaibo industries produce building materials, drugs, soap, shoes, clothing, foodstuffs, and furniture. Valencia and Maracay are centers for the manufacture of products such as textiles, tires, leather, wood and paper goods, foodstuffs, ceramics, and glassware. The nation's oil refining is concentrated near the oil fields, as well as on the Paraguaná Peninsula.

Forestry. The tropical forests of Venezuela support an expanding woodworking industry. Chief source of supply is the Andean foothills area from Acarigua to Barinas, where mahogany, cedar, ceiba, saman, and apamate logs are cut. Some lumber is produced from forests in the Guiana Highlands. Other forestry products include tonka beans, used in perfumes and flavorings; divi-divi, yielding tannic acid; and derivatives from medicinal plants.

Fisheries. Pearl gathering, one of the oldest industries in Venezuela, is concentrated in the islands of Margarita, Coche, and Cubagua. The pearls were a major source of wealth for Europe until depletion early in the 1500's. Sardine fishing in the Gulf of Cariaco supports a canning industry on Margarita Island and at nearby Cumaná, on the mainland. Fifty million cans are marketed annually, including exports to Curaçao, Haiti, and the Dominican Republic. Recent developments in commercial fishing have been concerned with shrimp production which now represents 90 per cent of the total catch.

Transportation. Venezuela's railroads are few in number and of short length. A vigorous period of railroad building during the nineteenth century was followed by a decline and abandonment of much trackage. By 1958 the number of actively operating railroads had been reduced to four: two private lines in Bolívar State for the hauling of iron ore; an antiquated railroad from La Fria to Encontrados, in the Maracaibo Basin; and the 112-mile Gran Ferrocarril de Venezuela between Caracas and Valencia. In 1959, the Venezuelan government inaugurated a new 108-mile line from Puerto Cabello to Barquisimeto, the first segment of a proposed 2,640-mile national railroad network. A seventeen-mile line from the coal mines in eastern Venezuela to the port of Guanta was also opened in 1959.

The Venezuelan highway system, concentrated north of the Orinoco and Apure rivers, connects all major cities. A major segment of this system is the Inter-American Highway leading from Caracas to the Colombian border. Superhighways have been built in the area of greatest traffic, between Caracas and Valencia. By the end of 1951 the total length of roads usable around the year was 15,520 miles, of which 3,926 miles were paved highways, 6,272 miles were gravel-covered, 5,322 were dirt roads. National development plans envisage a considerable amount of new highway construction.

Venezuela's air transport facilities include more than 40 national airfields, and international airports at Maiquetía (near Caracas) and Maracaibo.

Navigable inland waters are limited mainly to the Orinoco and its larger tributaries. The river mouth is dredged to permit passage of the largest iron ore ships upstream to Puerto Ordaz. Most ocean-going vessels can reach Ciudad Bolívar, beyond which smaller vessels penetrate to the falls near Puerto Ayacucho on the Colombian border. Dredging has also given ocean-going vessels access from the Caribbean Sea to Lake Maracaibo.

Commerce. Huge petroleum exports have enabled Venezuela to maintain a favorable balance of trade. Petroleum moves chiefly to the United States, Curaçao, Aruba, Canada, western Europe, Argentina, and Brazil. Iron ore is shipped to the United States, western Europe, and Japan. Other exports include coffee, cacao, gold, diamonds, sisal, corn, and hides. Machinery and other metal goods, foodstuffs, glass, ceramics, and chemicals are the major imports, supplied chiefly by the United States, western Europe, and Canada. La Guaira, an artificial port, is the principal seaport. It is the

Venezuelan Coat of Arms

port for Caracas and is connected with that city by an 11-mile-long superhighway over the Coastal Range. Puerto Cabello, Maracaibo, and Puerto La Cruz are other major Venezuelan ports on the Caribbean, while Ciudad Bolívar and the iron ore ports of Puerto Ordaz and Palua handle most of the Orinoco traffic.

Tourist Attractions. Tourism in Venezuela has developed rather slowly, largely because of high costs. Government promotion has led to some increase, however. Twelve government-owned hotels and numerous private hostelries provide modern accommodations, while improved transportation facilities afford greater accessibility. Major points of interest include Angel Fall, one of the highest in the world (3,700 ft.); Margarita Island and the Caribbean beaches; and five national parks, including the one in the Cordillera de Mérida, which encompasses the highest mountain peaks of the country.

CLARENCE W. MINKEL

GOVERNMENT

Under the constitution of 1953, as amended, Venezuela is a federal republic of 20 states, with a federal district and two territories. The government is divided into three departments—executive, legislative, and judicial.

The Chief Executive is the president, who is elected by direct popular vote for a five-year term. He is assisted by a cabinet which is responsible to him. He is commander in chief of the armed services, and has extensive powers of appointment. The president may propose legislation to the Congress, and has the veto power over legislation; but his veto can be overridden by a two-thirds vote of both houses of Congress. The president must be at least 30 years of age and a native-born citizen of Venezuela. By a 1958 electoral statute, voting was made compulsory for both male and female citizens over 18 years of age. No literacy test is required.

The Legislative Department, the Venezuelan Congress, consists of a senate and a chamber of deputies. Each state and the Federal District are represented by two senators, who are chosen by local state legislatures. Deputies are elected by direct popular vote; and their number in Congress is determined by population. All members of Congress must be native-born citizens of Venezuela; the minimum age for senators is 30, that for deputies 21. The term of Congress is five years.

The Judicial Department is headed by a five member federal court and a 10-member cassation court, whose judges are selected by Congress to terms of five years.

Armed Forces. Venezuela has an army, a navy, and an air force. At the age of 18 all men are required to serve in one of the three services for two years. In 1960 the army numbered 15,000 officers and enlisted men, and included units of infantry, armor, cavalry, and engineers. During the same year the navy was equipped with 29 vessels, including 9 destroyers; the air force had 150 planes including United States and British made jet fighters and propeller-powered, twin-engine bombers and transport craft.

HISTORY

European Discovery and Conquest. The region corresponding to Venezuela became ostensibly part of Spanish America by the Treaty of Tordesillas (1494), which granted the kingdoms of Castile and Portugal the exclusive right to conquer non-Christian lands (see TORDESILLAS, TREATY OF). The coast of Venezuela was seen by the Genoese navigator Christopher Columbus on his third voyage to America, 1498. The Gulf of Maracaibo was entered, 1499, by Alonzo de Ojeda and Amerigo Vespucci who, seeing Indian villages built on piles over the water, named the place Venezuela (Little Venice). The Spaniards made the first permanent European settlement on the South American Continent at Cumaná, 1521. The territory was sold, 1527, by Holy Roman Emperor Charles V (King Charles I of Spain) to the Welsers, a German banking family of Augsburg, but again came into the hands of Spain, 1545, and was made part of the Audiencia (judicial tribunal) of Santo Domingo. The Indians offered a stubborn resistance to the white settlers, but were gradually driven back into the interior. By the end of the sixteenth century several settlements had been established, including Caracas, 1567. During the seventeenth century, Venezuela became part of the Audiencia of New Granada (after 1717 the Vice Royalty of New Granada). During the eighteenth century, there were several unsuccessful revolts against the Spanish viceroy of New Granada.

Independence. A new effort to gain independence, begun in 1797, resulted in the formation of the Republic of Great Colombia, 1819, in which the present Colombia, Venezuela, and Ecuador were included. The war of independence with Spain lasted until 1821, when the Spanish were decisively defeated at Carabobo by the Venezuela-born soldier-patriots Simón Bolívar and José Antonio Páez.

Venezuela seceded from Great Colombia, 1830, and Páez became first president of the independent republic. Slavery was abolished in 1854. Under President Juan Crisóstomo Falcón, a federal constitution was adopted, 1864, naming the country the United States of Venezuela (Estados Unidos de Venezuela).

Foreign Intervention. When Venezuela became a republic, its eastern boundary was fixed somewhere between the Essequibo and Orinoco rivers. English and Dutch settlers had established themselves in this region, however, and there ensued quarrels over the boundary line. In 1850 a treaty was made between Great Britain and Venezuela whereby neither country was to occupy the disputed territory. Mutual accusations of bad faith followed, however, and Great Britain secured a fortified position at the mouth of the Orinoco, 1886. The United States of America then entered into the controversy as a mediator and the upholder of the Monroe Doctrine, and U.S. Pres. Grover Cleveland sent a special message to Congress, 1895, recommending the appointment of a commission to define the true boundary between Venezuela and British Guiana. Great Britain and Venezuela agreed to United States arbitration, 1897, and the boundary of Venezuela and British Guiana was finally established, 1899, giving Venezuela the mouth of the Orinoco.

During the nineteenth century, Venezuela was dominated by a series of dictator-presidents. Of them, Pres. Antonio Guzmán Blanco, 1870–89, was most instrumental in the country's economic development, which he brought about largely by encouraging foreign investment in railroad construction, mining, and agriculture, notably by British, Dutch, German, French, and United States interests. The Venezuelan government became financially indebted to these investors, however, and this proved to be a negative factor in the country's internal and foreign affairs well into the twentieth century.

Revolts against the administration of Pres. Cipriano Castro, 1902–08, damaged much foreign-owned property and the governments of France, Great Britain, Germany, and Italy pressed claims for loans made to the republic and for damages. The French claims were settled, but the other three powers, failing to collect the amounts demanded, blockaded the Venezuelan ports. Through the efforts of U.S. Pres. Theodore Roosevelt, President Castro arranged for a settlement of the claims of the blockading powers according to an agreement known as the Washington Protocols; an international court of arbitration at The Hague, Netherlands, settled the manner in which the claims should be adjusted, 1904, and the United States was commissioned to supervise the agreement. In the meantime, President Castro had embarked upon a policy of canceling concessions granted to foreigners by his predecessor, and had placed heavy levies on other foreign concerns doing business in Venezuela. As a result, the governments of France, Great Britain, the Netherlands, and the United States had, by 1908, broken off diplomatic relations with Venezuela. The "grieved" nations threatened again to blockade Venezuela, but the situation was relieved in November, 1908, when Castro sailed for Europe ostensibly for surgical treatment, leaving Vice-Pres. Juan Vincente Gómez in charge.

Charging that Castro had instigated a plot to assassinate him, Gómez proclaimed himself president and set about to repair the country's foreign relations by assuring creditor powers that Venezuela would meet all of its financial obligations, and by encouraging further foreign investment. As president, 1908–15, 1922–29, and 1931–35, and during the interim years through puppet presidents, Gómez ruled Venezuela with an iron hand, becoming known as "The Tyrant of the Andes." Venezuela's economy expanded, particularly with the exploitation of oil resources after World War I, but except for the liquidation of foreign indebtedness, and internal improvements such as road and building construction, the country as a whole benefited little from the prosperity because most of the profits of Venezuelan enterprises went to foreign investors and to the estates of Gómez and his supporters.

Reform Governments. Upon Gómez's death, 1935, Gen. Eleázar López Contreras succeeded to the presidency for the duration of the Gómez term; he was re-elected to office, 1936. A new constitution was adopted, 1936, and various economic and political reforms were inaugurated, including provisions for an eight-hour work day, social insurance, and employee profit sharing.

World War II and After. Venezuela, which had remained neutral during World War I, declared war on Germany and Japan late in World War II, and in autumn, 1945, joined the United Nations. Venezuela was signatory, 1947, to the Treaty of Rio de Janeiro for inter-American co-operation, and, 1948, became part of the Organization of American States, which was established to settle disputes in the Western Hemisphere.

Meanwhile, however, a revolution, headed by military officers and the liberal Democratic Action (*Acción Democrática*) party, had overthrown the wartime government, 1945, and Rómulo Betancourt had become provisional president. A new constitution (1947) was adopted, providing for direct election of the president, and under it Democratic Action Pres. Rómulo Gallegos was elected to office. In 1948, however, a conservative junta headed by Lt. Col. Marcos Peréz Jiménez ousted Gallegos and imposed a dictatorship. After ruling through several provisional presidents, Jiménez became president in a fraudulent election, 1953, and under a new constitution the country was renamed the Republic of Venezuela.

In 1957 Jiménez was re-elected to office but was deposed in 1958 by a civilian-military junta headed by Rear Adm. Wolfgang Larrazábal. In December of that year Democratic Action party candidate Rómulo Betancourt was elected president. During his term a new constitution was ratified in 1961, providing for a strong central government and limiting the president's term to no more than five years at a time. Diplomatic relations with Cuba were severed and an anti-Castro movement begun. Late in 1963 Raúl Leoni was elected to succeed Betancourt.

BIBLIOG.–Henry J. Allen, *Venezuela: A Democracy* (1940); Edward H. H. W. Bangor, *New El Dorado: Venezuela* (1957); Gustaf Bolinder, *We Dared the Andes: Three Journeys into the Unknown* (1959); Olga Briceño, *Cocks and Bulls in Caracas: How We Live in Venezuela* (1945); Daniel J. Clinton, *Gómez, Tyrant of the Andes* (1948); Jane L. De Grummond, *Envoy to Caracas: The Story of John G. A. Williamson, Nineteenth-Century Diplomat* (1951); Leonidas R. Dennison, *Devil Mountain* (1942), *Caroni Gold* (1943); Erna Fergusson, *Venezuela* (1939); Alfred P. Jankus and Neil M. Malloy, *Venezuela: Land of*

VENEZUELA

CONSULATE GENERAL OF VENEZUELA

The impressive Angel Fall, descending some 3,700 feet, is seen from an aerial view. It drops from the Carrao River in the mountainous eastern region of Venezuela.

BERNADINE BAILEY

The modern Humboldt Hotel, in Caracas, is one of the many new buildings in the Venezuelan capital. The hotel, located on the top of a mountain, can be reached by cable car.

BERNADINE BAILEY

The offices of the Venezuelan president were moved across Urdaneta Avenue in Caracas to this new building in 1956.

GRACE LINE

Caracas, capital and most populous city of Venezuela, is situated on the slope of the Sierra Nevada de Mérida Range, six miles by a highway from the Caribbean Sea.

Although Venezuela has the highest income per capita of the South American nations, squalor may still be found in many of the rural areas.

PAUL'S PHOTOS

Opportunity (1956); Herbert Kirchhoff, *Venezuela* (1956); John Lavin, *Halo for Gómez* (1954); Jonathan N. Leonard, *Men of Maracaibo* (1933); Rodolfo Luzardo, *Venezuela: Business and Finances* (1957); Norman MacDonald, *Orchid Hunters: A Jungle Adventure* (1940); William D. Marsland and Amy L. Marsland, *Venezuela Through Its History* (1954); Heinz P. Ptak, comp., *Venezuela: Heute, Hoy, Today, Aujourd'hui* (1955); William R. Russell, *Bolivar Countries: Colombia, Ecuador, Venezuela* (1949); Anne Spearman, *Take an Island* (1955); Michael Swan, *Marches of El Dorado: British Guiana, Brazil, Venezuela* (1958); Mary Watters, *History of the Church in Venezuela, 1810–1930* (1933); John G. A. Williamson, *Caracas Diary, 1835–1840: The Journal of John G. A. Williamson, First Diplomatic Representative of the U.S. to Venezuela* (1954); George S. Wise, *Caudillo: A Portrait of Antonio Guzmán Blanco* (1951).

VENICE, city, SW Illinois, Madison County; on the Mississippi River, and the Gulf, Mobile, and Ohio, the Illinois Terminal, and the New York Central railroads; 3 miles NE of St. Louis, to which it is connected by the McKinley Bridge. The city is an important industrial center; steel is manufactured. Venice was established as a ferry landing, 1804, platted, 1841, and incorporated, 1873. The name was first used in reference to repeated flooding of the city's streets by the Mississippi prior to the building of the levee in the mid-nineteenth century. Pop. (1960) 5,380.

VENICE, province, NE Italy, Veneto Region; bounded by the provinces of Treviso on the N, Rovigo on the S, and Padua on the W, by Friuli-Venezia Giulia Region on the NE, and by the Gulf of Venice of the Adriatic Sea on the E; area, 950 sq. mi.; pop. (1958) 751,363. Marshland, some of which has been reclaimed, covers much of the province, which extends from the Tagliamento River on the northeast to the Adige River on the southeast. The Brenta, Piave, and Livenza are other major rivers. Grain, sugar beets, fruit, vegetables, and cattle are raised. There is some fishing. The city of Venice, which contains almost half the population of the province, is the capital and main shipping point. Industry is centered in Mestre and Porto Marghera where chemicals, zinc, bauxite, and oil are processed.

VENICE, Italian Venezia, city, NE Italy, Veneto Region, capital of Venice Province; on the Gulf of Venice at the N end of the Adriatic Sea; 245 miles N of Rome; pop. (1958) 341,047. The climate of the city is temperate, with moderately cold winters and fairly hot summers, the average temperatures being 36°F in January and 76°F in July. Venice was the home of many outstanding artists and architects whose works helped make it one of the most beautiful of the Italian cities. Among its many notable artists were Iacopo Bellini and his sons, Carlo Crivelli, Il Giorgione, Palma Vecchio, Sebatiano del Piombo, Paolo Veronese, Titian, Bonifazio Veronese, Paris Bordone, Tintoretto, Giovanni Tiepolo, Antonio Canaletto, and Francesco Guardi. Among the great architects of the city were Sansovino, Palladio, Scarpagnino, and Sanmicheli.

Setting. Venice is situated more than two miles from the mainland on approximately 100 low islands in a shallow lagoon that is protected from the sea by a sand bar. The islands are separated by numerous canals, totaling about 28 miles in length and spanned by more than 400 bridges. The canals link the various sections of the city much as streets do. There are streets on the various islands, many of them extremely narrow and winding. Transportation is chiefly by gondolas and various types of power-driven boats, which are used on the canals and in the lagoon. The 230-foot-wide Grand Canal, the chief waterway, winds through the city for two miles from the Piazza di San Marco to the railroad station. Many of the outstanding palaces and other important buildings of Venice are along the Grand Canal.

The buildings of Venice generally are built on piles driven deep into the soft alluvial mud and secured by large blocks of stone. The heart of Venice is the Piazza and the Piazetta di San Marco. Connecting these squares with the old business district of the Rialto is the Merceria, the principal business street of the city. The industries of Venice include glass making, the production of jewelry and various art objects, shipbuilding, printing, flour milling, cotton spinning, and the manufacture of textiles and lace. The city has an active foreign trade, especially in raw materials, including cotton, coal, and wood. A large portion of the maritime tonnage entering Italy is received at Venice. The harbor facilities of Venice consist of the St. Mark's Canal, the Giudecca Canal, and the Maritime Station, augmented by the development of nearby mainland port facilities at Mestre, to which a shipping channel was constructed, 1922. Lido, a popular resort, is on the sand bar enclosing the lagoon around Venice.

Palaces and Churches. The most famous palace in Venice is the Gothic Palazzo Ducale (Doge's Palace). The building houses an art collection, which includes statues of Mars and Neptune by Jacopo Sansovino and great oil paintings by Tintoretto. Outstanding among the city's Byzantine palaces are the Ca' Molin Farsetti, Loredan, Da Mosto, and Fondaco dei Turchi. One of the most celebrated of the Gothic palaces is the Ca' d'Oro, a fifteenth century structure which is now an art museum containing an outstanding collection of furniture and paintings. Other notable Gothic palaces are the Palazzo Bernardo, the Palazzo Priuli, and the Palazzo Contarini Fasan. Among the principal early Renaissance palaces are the Palazzo Trevisan and the Palazzo Dario. Representatives of the late Renaissance style are the Palazzo Corner della Ca' Grande, the Palazzo Rezzonico, and the Palazzo Pesaro, a baroque palace that contains the Galleria d'Arte Moderna. The most famous of all the Venetian churches is St. Mark's (San Marco), which faces the piazza of the same name. It contains what is reputed to be the tomb of St. Mark.

Among the noted Gothic churches are Santo Stefano, Santi Giovanni e Paolo, San Gregorio, and Santa Maria Gloriosa dei Frari. Early Renaissance churches include San Zaccaria, San Salvatore, and Santa Maria dei Miracoli. Outstanding churches of the late Renaissance style are San Moise, Santa Maria del Giglio, San Giorgio Maggiore, and Santa Maria della Salute, which has a large and beautiful dome.

Other Features of Interest. Of the many bridges in Venice, two are especially famous: the Bridge of Sighs and the Rialto Bridge. The former, dating from the late sixteenth century, connects the Doge's Palace with the state prison. The Rialto Bridge spans the Grand Canal, connecting San Marco Island with the Rialto. The oldest of the bell towers is the eleventh century San Geremia Campanile, but probably the best known is the San Marco Campanile. One of the finest public monuments in the city is the celebrated equestrian statue of Vartolomeo Colleoni, the work of the Florentine sculptor Andrea del Verrocchio.

The scuole (guild halls) are of great interest architecturally. Among them are the Scuola di Santa Maria della Carita, the Scuola di San Giovanni Evangelista, the Scuola di San Teodoro, the Scuola della Misericordia, the Scuola di San Marco, and the Scuola di San Rocco, which contains a splendid group of Tintoretto's paintings. The arsenal of Venice was begun early in the twelfth century. The Biblioteca Nazionale Marciana (National Library of St. Mark) is located in the mint, or Zecca. Among educational institutions in Venice are the University Institute of Architecture and the National Conservatory of Music.

HISTORY

The first historically significant settlement on the site of modern Venice occurred during the fifth century of the Christian Era, when the Veneti, having been expelled from north central Italy by the Lombards and Goths, took refuge in the marshes and islands of the lagoon at the northwest end of the Adriatic Sea. There they established a number of

EWING GALLOWAY

Venetian gondolas pass under the famous Bridge of Sighs, which was designed by Antonio Contino in about 1595 to connect the ducal palace, left, with the state prison.

island communities, each of which maintained a comparatively independent existence until the seventh century, when 12 towns joined in a loose confederation headed by one supreme elected magistrate, called the Doge (see DOGE). Venice, as the confederacy became known, maintained her independence from states of mainland Italy, while the skill of her citizens as sailors enabled it to develop a powerful fleet and to become a great commercial state. By the tenth century, Venice (or Venetia) dominated the Adriatic, and had gradually absorbed most of the carrying trade of Europe and the Middle East, sending her ships as far as England for wool and to the Black Sea for furs. Venetian merchants traveled the caravan routes to India and China. By taking part in the Crusades, late eleventh to the early fourteenth centuries, Venice obtained trading stations in Palestine and, as the Byzantine Empire fell into decrepitude, Venice acquired many of its possessions, establishing colonies in Crete, Cyprus, Peloponnesus, and on many islands in the Aegean Sea.

Venetian power in the Mediterranean was soon challenged, however, by the city-state Genoa. After nearly 200 years of indecisive warfare, Venice crippled Genoa in the War of Chioggia, 1378–81.

Meanwhile, Venice had extended its sovereignty over parts of the Dalmatian Coast, and had, by financially ruining the houses of Della Scala and Carrara, acquired Treviso, Verona, Padua, and other towns on the mainland of Italy; at the expense of the dukes of Milan, Venice obtained Brescia, Bergamo, and Cremona.

Venetian dominance of commerce, seriously challenged when the Ottoman Turks captured Constantinople, 1453, definitely waned after the Portuguese rounded the Cape of Good Hope, 1486, and established an all-water route to the Far East. At about the same time the Holy Roman Empire, France, Aragon, and many of the lesser states in Europe formed the League of Cambrai, 1508, which was designed to check the expansion of Venice in Italy. Allied armies attacked Venice, 1509; during the ensuing two decades of warfare, which devastated much of Italy, Venice lost a large part of her mainland territory.

The struggle with the Turks lasted until 1718, when Peloponnesus, the last of Venice's eastern possessions, was lost. Although politically insignificant, Venice maintained independence until Napoleon Bonaparte conquered northern Italy for France, 1797.

After the fall of Napoleon I, 1815, Venice was made part of Austria. A major Venetian revolt against Austria failed, 1848–49, and the city remained under Austrian rule until it was ceded to the Kingdom of Italy following the Seven Weeks' War, 1866. See ITALY, *Modern Italy, Unification of Italy.*

VENIZELOS, ELEUTHERIOS, 1864–1936, Greek political figure, was born in Crete. Elected to the Cretan assembly, 1887, he became prominently identified with the Cretan movement for independence from Turkey. Venizelos was a leader in the insurrection that led to the Greco-Turkish War, 1896–97, after which the Turks evacuated the island, whereupon it was occupied by British, French, Italian and Russian troops. The forces were withdrawn eventually, 1909, and Crete officially became part of Greece, 1913. In Athens from 1909, Venizelos was appointed premier of Greece, 1910. Under his guidance, Greece passed successfully through the Balkan Wars, 1912–13. During World War I, his vigorous support of the Allies brought him into conflict with pro-German King Constantine, and Venizelos was forced to resign, 1915. He went to Salonika, where he established a "provisional" government that was recognized by the Allies, 1916. When Constantine abdicated in favor of his son, 1917, Venizelos was recalled as premier, but an election defeat turned him out of office, 1920. He returned to power briefly, 1924, but resigned; he was again premier, 1928–32, and for a short time in 1933, when he dissolved parliament and appealed to the electorate, but was defeated. Having instigated an unsuccessful military revolt, 1935, and being forced to flee into exile, Venizelos died in Paris.

VENLO, town, SW Netherlands, Limburg Province; on the Maas (Meuse) River, across from Blerik, 85 miles SE of Amsterdam and 2 miles W of the German border. The town is a commercial and manufacturing center in a region producing dairy goods and vegetables. Optical instruments, incandescent lamps, umbrellas, and soap are manufactured. Venlo is the site of the fifteenth century Gothic church of St. Martin; the town hall dates from the sixteenth century. Pop. (1959) 53,680.

VENOM, in general, a poison, but, specifically, a clear or amber liquid poison secreted by certain reptiles, crustaceans, spiders, and bees. Venomous reptiles, crustaceans, and insects secrete their venom in the form of a fluid and communicate it by biting or stinging. Some poisonous reptiles secrete venom in their salivary glands, communicating it to their enemies through sharp-pointed, darting fangs.

Best known of the poisonous reptiles are the members of the viper family, such as the rattlesnake of North America. Others include the cobra, coral snake, and copperhead. Among venomous spiders is the black widow.

Any venomous bites or stings result in sharp burning, followed by swelling, and often intense pain. Treatment should be administered by a physician, but first aid includes keeping the patient warm and quiet. If it is an appendage that has been bitten, a tourniquet should be applied above the area attacked. Also diagonal incisions in the area of the bite may be made, and suction to draw out the venom applied.

VENTIDIUS, PUBLIUS, 89?–?38 B.C., Roman general, was born in Asculum in Picenum. He was a follower of Julius Caesar and probably served as a military contractor at an early age. Through the patronage of Caesar he entered the Senate. Ventidius was made consul, 43 B.C., as a reward for having led three legions to aid Marcus Antonius against Marcus Brutus in the battle of Philippi. Ventidius' most noted military triumphs were against the Parthians, which he defeated at the Cilician Gates, Mount Amanus, 39 B.C., and Gindarus, 38 B.C.

VENTILATION. See AIR CONDITIONING; HEATING.

VENTIMIGLIA, town, NW Italy, in Liguria Region, Imperia Province; on the Ligurian Sea; 5 miles E of the French frontier and 8 miles SW of San Remo. Ventimiglia is on the Italian Riviera. Its twelfth century Gothic cathedral and the church of San Michele are in the old town, built on a hill above the newer section on the coast. The ruins of Album Intemelium, an ancient town about three miles to the east, include a Roman theater and a number of tombs. The Balzi Rossi grottos, at nearby Grimaldi, and the museum containing prehistoric antiquities uncovered there, were partially destroyed during World War II. Pop. (1958) 21,278.

VENTNOR, city, SE New Jersey, Atlantic County; on Absecon Beach and the Atlantic Ocean; a suburb, 3 miles WSW of Atlantic City. Ventnor is a noted summer resort. It was incorporated early in the 1900's. Pop. (1960) 8,688.

VENTRILOQUISM, the trick of using the voice in such fashion that the sound appears to proceed from a source other than the speaker's mouth. This is done by taking a deep inhalation of breath, and then allowing it to escape slowly, allowing the sounds of the voice to be modified by the muscles of the throat and palate. The illusion is heightened by immobility of the visible muscles usually employed in speech, as well as by gestures and glances that suggest to the onlooker a false source of the sound (misdirection, so-called). Few ventriloquists can deceive in the dark, and most depend upon marionettes with movable lips, to which the attention of the audience is directed. The art owes its name to the erroneous idea of the ancient Romans that the performer produced the voice in the stomach or abdomen (Latin *ventralis*, pertaining to the belly, whence medieval Latin *ventriculus*, "little belly" or ventricle).

VENTRIS, MICHAEL GEORGE FRANCIS, called "The Conqueror of the Mount Everest of Greek History," 1922–56, British architect and linguistic detective, was the scion of an old military British family. He was educated in Switzerland from an early age, where his remarkable talent for languages manifested itself in such feats as teaching himself Polish at the age of six. In England, later, he was a scholarship student at Stowe School. World War II interrupted his studies at the Architectural Association School, London; after war service as navigator in an R.A.F. bomber squadron, he resumed the study of architecture and was graduated with honors, 1948. His subsequent work as an architect showed great promise, but it was for a rather eccentric hobby that he became famous. As a boy of 14, Ventris had attended a lecture by the archaeologist Sir Arthur Evans, the famous excavator of Cnossus, on Crete, where a large number of clay tablets bearing inscriptions in two previously unknown Minoan-Mycenaean scripts (Linear A and Linear B) were unearthed, 1900–08; there and then Ventris decided to devote himself to the decipherment of Linear B—also found on many tablets unearthed in Peloponnesian Pílos—and thus discover the key to Mycenaean history. See AEGEAN CIVILIZATION; ARCHAEOLOGY, *Crete and the Aegean Sea;* MINOAN CIVILIZATION; MYCENAE; PÍLOS.

The task of decipherment seemed almost hopeless, since the language behind the 85 or more semipictorial signs might be any Semitic, Caucasian, or unknown idiom, and there was no Rosetta Stone, or the like, by which the unknown could be linked to the known. About all that the experts agreed on was that the mystery script could not be Greek, for which the earliest testimonies were not older than ?700 B.C.—about seven centuries later than the Linear B script. Using his wartime training as a decoder, and working with a Committee of Correspondents—an international group of scholars who were kept regularly

informed of his tentative steps—Ventris eventually realized his boyhood ambition when, against all expectations (including his own) he found that the mystery language was Greek. Ventris had constructed a grid for a tentative syllabarium, and in terms of it identified three Cretan place names—*Amnisos, Knossos* (Cnossus), *Tylissos;* he then identified, with the help of added pictograms, the spice *koriander*. Greek phonetic values now imposed themselves: *tripod, four, two,* "*so many,*" the divine names of *Poseidon, Paian, Athene, Zeus,* and *Hera,* and heroic names like *Eteocles* or *Achilles*—such were legible. Thus was it demonstrated that at least 500 years before Homer the complete Greek world had existed; and thus was refuted a century or more of "Higher Criticism" with its assertions that Homer's works had not been written until the time of Pisistratus (600?–527) and that the traditional date of the first Olympics, 776 B.C., could not be trusted. As a result of Ventris' discovery, much so-called prehistory, the centuries before 776 B.C., was now articulate history, and the problem of the place of Homer in human history, the famous Homeric Question, had to be reinterpreted.

Ventris vs. the Higher Criticism. Ever since 1795, when Friedrich August Wolf had proclaimed the *Iliad* and *Odyssey* to be no more than a potpourri of independent chansons, the very existence of a poet named Homer had been more often denied than believed, and Homer as a power over history had thereby been eliminated. This was not an accident, but a symptom of the rise of the bourgeois class. In France, this had led to violent revolution. In Germany, however, where neither nobility nor clergy were beheaded, the bourgeois Higher Criticism waged instead a symbolic war against the aristocratic Homer's works and the traditional Bible by asserting that they were composed of meaningless fragments—by asserting that they were as "false" and as "artificial" as the manners and pretensions of French nobles and clergymen. For many decades in Germany, no scholar was considered serious unless he held (1) that the gospel of Mark was older than the "patchwork" of Matthew; and (2) that Homer's works were patchwork. See WOLF, FRIEDRICH AUGUST.

Ventris' discovery did away with the only one of Wolf's arguments that seemed to have a demonstrable character—that Homer could not write—and has changed our whole approach to the place of script in history, since it proves that the ancients experimented with different scripts at various times. Administrative needs apparently caused a change in scripts (Linear A to Linear B), ?1400 B.C.; later in Greece, ?800, the Phoenician alphabet, comprising only consonants, was radically changed by the addition of vowels. As to what could have made such an innovation indispensable, it seems likely that the requirements of the new hexameter verse, with its insistence on treating short and long vowels differently, necessitated the changes in lettering. Prior to Ventris, the addition of the vowels to Greek script had never aroused particular admiration; after Ventris, however, the Homeric Question and the problem of the change in the Greek script became one and the same thing. As one classicist has suggested (H. T. Wade-Gery, *Poet of The Iliad,* 1952): the need for a new alphabet and the desire to write down an epic in Greek hexameter were not two different problems, but were one and the same.

The Significance of Homer in Greek History. If this were true, Homer could not be dismissed as "just a poem" or just folk songs, for he would have to be recognized again as having occupied a central place in the organization of Greek expression. That is, if Homer's 30,000 verses of poetry and the Greek script came into being at the same time, the place of Homer in Greek history would be of prime importance: "Greece" would mean no more and no less than those places where Homer was recited from manuscript—just as the Greeks themselves had believed. In fact, during the last upheaval of Hellenism against Rome, under King Mithridates of Pontus (131?-63 B.C.), the Greeks of Asia Minor demonstrated against Rome by reciting Homer in their theaters. In the light of Ventris' discovery, the argument-from-script that had been used to "prove" the Homeric poems a late patchwork would seem actually to support the earlier Greek tradition of Homer's genius. Before 1200 B.C., before the Trojan War, the Greeks had already used script in organizing the religion of their gods as we know them from Homer.

Ventris was killed in an automobile accident just a few days before the publication of his and John Chadwick's *Documents in Mycenaean Greek* (1956).

EUGEN ROSENSTOCK-HUESSY

BIBLIOG.–John Chadwick, *The Decipherment of Linear B* (1958).

VENTSPILS, Baltic seaport, NW Latvian S.S.R., at the mouth of the Venta River. There was a settlement at Ventspils by the middle ages, and the castle there dates from 1290. Unlike Riga, Ventspils is ice-free the whole year. It has fisheries, sawmills, and foundries, and is a major shipping point for oil from Volga district. (For population, see U.S.S.R. map in Atlas.)

VENTURA, or San Buenaventura, city, SW California, seat of Ventura County; on Santa Barbara Channel of the Pacific Ocean, 60 miles WNW of Los Angeles. The city is a trade and processing center for an area in which citrus fruit, walnuts, vegetables, poultry, and dairy cattle are raised. It is a supply center for a petroleum-producing area. A notable point of interest is the San Buenaventura Mission (1782). Little of the original building remains, due to the incidence of fires, 1791-2, and an earthquake in 1812, but the mission was restored and opened as a museum. Ventura was founded around the mission early in the 1860's and incorporated in 1866. (For population, see California map in Atlas.)

VENTURI TUBE, a smooth constriction in a pipeline for the purpose of increasing the velocity of flow of fluid, thereby causing a decrease in the pressure. The device was invented in 1886 by a U.S. engineer, Clemens Herschel, and named after the Italian physicist G. B. Venturi (1746–1822), who first studied the effect of constricted channels on the flow of liquids.

The internal surface of a venturi (see diagram) consists roughly of two truncated cones connected at their smaller extremities by a very short cylinder, the venturi throat. In accordance with the principle developed by Daniel Bernoulli, when fluids at high velocity move past the surface of a horizontal pipe or tube, the pressure against that surface is lowered. As the velocity of the fluid increases, the pressure decreases in a manner which can be determined by using Bernoulli's principle and the equation of continuity. The application of Bernoulli's principle to the steady incompressible flow of a fluid in a horizontal pipe leads to the statement that pressure is lowest where speed is highest, and conversely.

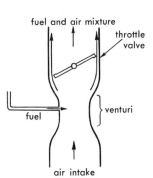

The principle of the venturi tube is used in automobile carburetors where the high velocity and the reduced pressure of the intake draw in fuel at a rate that effects the proper fuel-air mixture.

fuel and air mixture

throttle valve

fuel

venturi

air intake

The venturi tube has many applications in engineering. It is the basis of the venturi meter, used to measure rates of flow. It is used to regulate fuel-air mixtures in the carburetors of internal combustion engines. A small branch tube leading from the fuel chamber is introduced into the air intake at the venturi throat, and fuel is drawn into the fuel line by the suction effect set up by reduced pressures against the throat surface. The accompanying diagram illustrates this action, in the case of the carburetor. The same principle is employed in other devices, including air-speed indicators in aircraft, atomizers, sprayers for paints, suction pumps, and devices for determining the rate of gas and liquid flow.

VENUE, the place in which a suit may properly be brought to trial. A personal action, as for breach of contract or tort, is normally held wherever a proper service of summons is made upon the defendant. In general, actions involving the title to real estate must be tried in the county in which the property is situated. Venue differs from jurisdiction in that the latter connotes the power to decide a case and the former connotes only the place where the suit should be heard. In beginning an action, the plaintiff names the venue. A request for a change of venue may be made on various grounds, as, for example, that the place where the suit was filed is not the proper place to try the case; or that a change would be more convenient for the majority of the witnesses.

VENUS, the second-closest planet to the sun and the earth's nearest planetary neighbor. At favorable times the earth and Venus draw within 25 million miles of each other. Besides the sun and the moon, Venus is the brightest object in the sky; it is readily seen in the early evening or early morning, depending on its orbital position. Viewed through a telescope, Venus often has a crescent appearance like the moon's, since the face toward us at any one time consists in part of the day side and in part of the night side. The illuminated fraction that we see keeps changing as Venus moves in its orbit about the sun. Within a time span of two thirds of a year, Venus changes from a very thin crescent (when we see mostly the night side) to an almost fully illuminated disk (when we see mostly the day side).

Cloud Layer. The eye cannot perceive any obvious markings on the planet. This is one indication that Venus is almost completely covered by clouds, in contrast to the earth, which has only about a 50 per-cent cloud cover. The extensive cloud layer and not the gaseous atmosphere is responsible for most of the sunlight reflected to space. This is indicated by the fact that Venus has a yellow color, whereas sunlight scattered by gases appears blue. On the average, about 75 per cent of the sunlight falling on Venus is reflected to space and only about 25 per cent is absorbed by the atmosphere and the ground.

There has been prolonged debate as to the composition of the cloud layer. Very fine dust and water—in the form of liquid droplets and ice crystals—are the leading candidates. The debate has centered on the variation of the amount of reflected sunlight with wavelength or color. At certain wavelengths a given material will absorb a large amount of sunlight and at these wavelengths a cloud layer composed of this material will reflect comparatively little sunlight. The wavelengths at which such absorption takes place are different for different materials and so may be used as a guide to composition. On the one hand, the clouds over Venus absorb very strongly at infrared wavelengths of 30,000 A and longer, indicative of the presence of water; on the other hand, the same clouds reflect less light in blue light than in red light, which is a typical property of dust. The clouds may, in fact, be mixtures of both dust and water. In 1967 the Russian space probe Venera 4 carried a scientific package through the atmosphere of Venus. Apparently, enough water vapor was detected in the lower atmosphere to imply that condensation takes place at higher, colder altitudes, resulting in the formation of water clouds.

Atmosphere. The gases carbon dioxide, carbon monoxide, hydrogen chloride, and hydrogen fluoride have all been detected in the atmosphere of Venus. They were discovered by the methods used in studying the cloud layer—by finding wavelengths at which more sunlight is absorbed than at neighboring wavelengths. Unfortunately, nitrogen, a major component of the earth's atmosphere, absorbs sunlight only at ultraviolet wavelengths that are presently inaccessible to observers. Venera 4 failed to detect nitrogen, which implies that the nitrogen concentration in the atmosphere is less than 10 per cent. Of the detected gases, carbon dioxide is the most abundant, constituting between 75 and almost 100 per cent of the atmosphere; at least part of the carbon monoxide present may be the result of sunlight breaking up carbon dioxide molecules in the upper atmosphere of Venus. As mentioned above, the Russian space probe experiments apparently indicate the presence of water vapor, which constitutes between 0.1 and 1 per cent of the atmosphere.

The atmosphere of Venus seems to be more massive than that of the earth, but at present its exact volume is somewhat uncertain. Venera 4 measured pressures as high as 20 times the surface pressure on the earth. It is presently unclear, however, whether the space capsule reached the lowest altitudes on Venus, and so typical surface pressures may be several times larger than the above figure. A man standing on the ground might find little light reaching the surface: scattering by air molecules would prevent much blue or yellow light from reaching the surface, and clouds and atmospheric gases would absorb infrared light. Therefore, little sunlight would penetrate directly through the clouds, though some of it might be scattered through. In this sense it would seem like a very overcast day on the earth.

Surface. A remarkable fact about the surface of Venus is its exceedingly high temperature—about 700°F. Because the Venus cloud layer and atmosphere become transparent at very long wavelengths, radio telescopes can "see" it and measure the amount of radio waves it emits. Solid objects emit light at all wavelengths, including radio wavelengths; the higher the temperature the greater is the amount of light emitted. Thus radio telescopes are able to establish that the surface is quite hot. Both the U.S. space probe Mariner V (1967) and Venera 4 confirmed that the surface of Venus is quite hot, though they raised some question as to the exact value of the surface temperature. The last measurement of the Venera 4, which was claimed to be made quite close to the surface, indicated a temperature several hundred degrees cooler than the temperature suggested by radio measurements and by extrapolation of the readings to the surface of Mariner V. Possibly the Venera 4 landed on a very high elevation.

The temperature of Venus is much higher than the temperature of a hypothetical airless planet at Venus's distance from the sun. It is believed that this is a result of the ability of Venus's atmosphere to be much more transparent to sunlight attempting to reach the ground than it is to the bulk of thermal radiation emitted at longer infrared wavelengths. Absorption due to carbon dioxide, water vapor, and perhaps other gases, as well as absorption by suspended dust particles, has been suggested as the source of the selectively high infrared opacity, or "blackness," of the atmosphere.

Rotation and Revolution. Radar observations of the planet indicate rather bizarre rotational behavior: Venus rotates in the "wrong" sense, in a clockwise direction, contrary to that of most planets. Consequently, instead of the sun rising in the east and setting in the west, on Venus it rises in the west and sets in the east. Furthermore, Venus presents the same face to the earth whenever the two planets are closest. This suggests that, in a manner not yet fully understood, tidal forces exerted by the earth control Venus's rate of rotation. The rotation rate with respect to the sun is more than 100 times slower than the earth's, and consequently there are only two "days" in a Venus "year." The pole is only slightly tilted, so there are no "seasons" on Venus.

Venus revolves about the sun once every 225 earth days at an almost constant distance of 67 million miles. Its radius is only 3 per-cent smaller than the earth's radius; its density only 6 per-cent less than the earth's density. Thus, with regard to their solid portions, the two planets bear a strong resemblance to each other.

Life as we know it on the earth, i.e. based primarily on complex structures achievable with carbon molecules, could not exist on the surface of Venus: the temperature is so high that organic matter would decompose. Furthermore, because of the intense heat, any liquid water would quickly evaporate. On the other hand, Venus may have had a more moderate temperature in the past and life might have existed then. If this is true, life could conceivably have evolved to live subsequently in higher portions of the atmosphere where sunlight is abundant, where lower temperatures prevail, and where water might be available in sufficient supply either in vapor form or as cloud particles.

Following is a partial list of the challenging questions about Venus that are as yet unanswered:
1. Why is Venus so hot?
2. What is its cloud layer composed of?
3. What gases make up its atmosphere? In particular, how much nitrogen and how much water vapor are present? How big is its atmosphere?
4. What is its surface composed of? Are there large mountains?
5. Is, or was, life present?

JAMES B. POLLACK

BIBLIOG.–John C. Brandt and Paul Hodge, *Solar System Astrophysics* (1964); Patrick Moore, *The Planet Venus* (ed. 1961); Carl Sagan, Jonathan N. Leonard, and the Editors of *Life*, *Planets* (1965); Harold C. Urey, *Planets* (1952).

NASA

MT. WILSON AND PALOMAR OBSERVATORIES

The cloud covers of the earth (left) and Venus are contrasted. The earth was photographed by a camera-laden Applications Technology Satellite at 10:05 P.M. The varied cloud pattern over the darkened planet is such that, by properly analyzing the photograph, surface configuration on earth can be determined. Venus, on the other hand, presents a much brighter crescent in the sky, but, completely covered by clouds, offers no surface detail.

VENUS, ancient Latin *Uenus*, Medieval Latin *Venus*, was originally the Latin goddess of prosperity, but later became the Roman goddess of love, equivalent to the Greek Aphrodite, and analogous to Astarte in the Orient and to the Germanic goddess Freya and the Old Norse Frigg (compare English *Friday*, Old High German *Friatag*, and modern Italian *Venerdi*).

Venus' original sanctuary was in Artea, Latium, where she was the goddess of fruits and gardens, and of the charm of prosperous growth. The flower season of spring and the season of maturity were both suitable for her cult. Later, when the Romans clashed with the Carthaginians on Sicily, the sanctuary of the female goddess of Mount Eryx made a profound impression on the Latin soldiers, and from this world famous temple they took home, 217 B.C., an enlarged conception of the goddess of Love. The Venus of Rome became much more than the Latin Venus had been and the verb *venerari* (to venerate) and its extensions came to signify all worship and reverence. When Lucius Cornelius Sulla, surnamed Felix, made himself dictator of Rome, 82 B.C., he linked his *felicitas* (luck) to the worship of this more comprehensive goddess, Venus. Sulla's political imitator, Gaius Julius Caesar, declared Venus to be the genetrix (ancestor) of the Julii family; and all of Caesar's descendants claimed to be *progenies veneris* (offspring of Venus). And sometime before 55 B.C. the poet-philosopher Lucretius opened his cosmic poem on *The Nature of Things* (*De rerum natura*) with a wonderful description of Mars and Venus; Mars, the main god of the Latins, and Venus were already, it would seem, the great gods of Roman prosperity.

In her proud new position, the Latin Venus soon came to be identified with the Greek Aphrodite. This identification had vast political consequences, for it enabled the Romans to connect their city with the pre-Greek city of Troy. Aphrodite's mortal lover was the Trojan Anchises; her heavenly lover was Ares, the God of War; and her legitimate Olympic husband was the lame Hephaestus—he of the fiery techniques Once identified with Aphrodite, the Roman Venus, whose priests were of the Julii family, could be believed to connect Troy with Rome since Venus had also, it seems, associated with Anchises, and as a result had given birth to Aeneas, the hero of Vergil's *Aeneid* (see VERGIL, *The Aeneid*). The learned men of Rome soon found for Venus a celestial husband in Vulcanus (analogous to Hephaestus), and also a companion who could compare to the Greek Eros—Cupid became her child. Further, since the meaning of the term *venus* closely compares with the Greek *charis* (graciousness), the Greek Charites could plausibly be made into Venus' companions as the Latin Graces. Among her

EWING GALLOWAY
The Venus de Milo

other companions were the Horae—the Hours of Opportunity. Also from Aphrodite, Venus received the dove as the animal symbolic of her tenderness. In antiquity Venus lent her name to individual diseases spread by sexual intercourse; and sometime before 1550 the French physician James of Bethencourt classified all these diseases as "venereal" diseases.

The blessings of Venus are celebrated in the charming poem, *Pervigilium veneris* (The Wake of Venus), of which little is known except that it must have been written between A.D. 100 and 400 (C. Clementi, *Studies on the Pervigilium Veneris*, 1913). It contains the comforting line, *Cras amet qui numquam amavit; quique amavit, cras amet* (Tomorrow shall love who never has loved; and who has loved, tomorrow shall love).

The common man in Rome probably did not share in the movement of the Roman educated class in its identification of their Latin goddess into the Greek and Asiatic goddess, and so the process of identification remained unfinished. The New Testament furnishes a proof of this lost fact. In the Book of Acts, the Apostle Paul is attacked by the worshipers of the goddess "with the thousand breasts." In Acts, she is called Artemis (Latin Diana), but the goddess referred to was clearly the same as the Sicilian Venus on Eryx.

Among extant examples of ancient sculpture, coinage, and painting there are few genuinely Latin depictions of Venus, and it would seem that the Greek Aphrodite was preferred by artists and artisans. Indeed, the two most famous statues of Venus, the Venus de' Medici and the Venus de Milo (Mílos, or Melos), are typical specimens of the Aphroditic artistic tradition. EUGEN ROSENSTOCK-HUESSY

VENUS DE' MEDICI, a well known statue in the Uffizi Gallery, Florence, found during the sixteenth century in Rome. On its base was the name of Cleomanes, son of Apollodorus of Athens, presumably the name of the sculptor, but this is generally thought to be a forgery. Venus is represented entirely nude, with a beautiful face and form, but with so much self-consciousness as to detract from her charm. The figure is probably copied from the Aphrodite of Praxiteles but is much inferior in conception. On its transportation to Florence the statue was broken into 11 fragments. Its restoration was undertaken after 1667, by Ercole Ferrata, but his modeling of the lower arms, hands, and fingers is not in keeping with the original.

VENUS DE MILO, a famous statue, one of the treasures of the Louvre, considered by some the most beautiful example of ancient sculpture. It was discovered by a peasant farmer in a grotto on the isle of Mílos, in May, 1820, and was purchased by the Marquis de Rivière, French ambassador to Turkey, who presented it to Louis XVIII, who in turn gave it to the Louvre. The statue, which is of heroic size, represents a woman, nude from the waist up, but draped from the hips to the feet. Both arms are missing. With the figure was found an illegibly inscribed fragment bearing a name ending in "sander, of Antioch on the Meander." The character of the writing suggests that its author lived about 100 B.C. This fragment was lost and there has been much controversy as to whether or not it was a part of the original statue. The position of the arms and the date of the masterpiece are also subjects of debate. It is thought that the arms were broken off and lost in the Bay of Mílos at the time of the statue's removal from the island. Undersea exploration for the arms was undertaken as late as 1961, by Myron Kyritsis, a native of Mílos who had made his fortune in America.

VENUS'S-FLYTRAP, a perennial insectivorous plant, *Dionaea muscipula*, belonging to the family *Droseraceae*. It grows wild in a small area in the moist, sandy soil near Wilmington, N.C. It bears short flower clusters in June, but is most remarkable for its hairy leaves, the halves of which are hinged and fold together when the hairs are excited by contact with an insect. After the insect is entrapped, the leaves exude an acid that digests and disintegrates the insect.

VERA, AUGUSTO, 1813–85, Italian scholar and philosopher, was born in Amelia, Umbria, and studied in Rome and Paris. As a teacher in France, Germany, and Italy, and as a writer in French, English, and Italian, Vera was influential in spreading the philosophy of Georg W. F. Hegel. Among his writings are *Problème de la certitude* (1845), *An Inquiry into Speculative and Experimental Science* (1856), and *Essais de philosophie hégélienne* (1864).

VERACRUZ, state, E central Mexico; bounded by the states of Tamaulipas on the N, San Luis Potosí on the NW, Hidalgo and Puebla on the W, Oaxaca on the S, and Chiapas and Tabasco on the SE, and by the Gulf of Mexico on the E; area 27,759 sq. mi.; pop. (1957 est.) 2,392,602. Veracruz extends along the Gulf of Mexico for 430 miles. Its width varies from 30 to 100 miles. The flat coastal region, with a hot, humid climate, is swampy. Toward the west the land rises gradually through a temperate zone to the forested Sierra Madre Oriental traversing the western border. Orizaba (Citlaltepetl), the highest peak in Mexico, rises near the border of Puebla. Veracruz is drained by numerous rivers.

In the plains, rice, bananas, sugar, and rubber are produced. The greatest concentration of population is in the foothill zone, where coffee plantations are common. Cattle grazing is an important industry in the central highlands; cereals are raised in the higher elevations in the west; the forested mountains yield dyewoods, cabinet woods, and chicle. The state has rich deposits of gold, silver, iron, and coal, and valuable oil fields are worked in the south, near Coatzacoalcos, and in the north the fields extend from Tuxpan south to the Tamesí River. The chief urban centers of Veracruz are the inland cities of Córdoba and Orizaba, and the ports of Veracruz, Tuxpan, and Coatzacoalcos. Jalapa is the capital. A development program begun in the Papaloapan River valley, 1947, included flood control and irrigation works, and new hydroelectric plants.

VERACRUZ, city, E Mexico, in the state of Veracruz; on the Gulf of Mexico, 190 miles E of Mexico City. Veracruz is situated on a low coastal plain. The city has road and rail connections with most areas of Mexico. Its harbor is protected by Gallega Island and two breakwaters. The port of Veracruz is served by several steamship lines and coastal shipping routes. It handles a major part of Mexico's foreign trade. Petroleum, dyewoods, sugar, coffee, vanilla, and chicle are exported. Liquors, chocolate, cigars, tiles, and footwear are manufactured. In appearance, Veracruz is an interesting blend of the ancient and modern:

EWING GALLOWAY

The city of Veracruz, bordering on the Gulf of Mexico, was founded by Spaniards in 1519, and many of its older buildings indicate the influence of Spanish architecture.

narrow, cobbled streets and colonial houses contrast with modern buildings and wide thoroughfares. On Plaza Constitución, the center of the city, is an old parish church dating from 1721. On Gallega Island is the Castillo de San Juan de Ulúa (1565), the last Spanish stronghold in Mexico, which served as a prison fort until 1914. The city is the seat of the University of Veracruz (1922).

History. The Spanish *conquistadore*, Hernán Cortés, landed at an Indian village on the site of Veracruz and founded La Villa Rica de la Vera Cruz (Rich Town of the Holy Cross), 1519. The settlement was moved several times before 1599, when a city, Nueva Veracruz, was founded, on the present site. Veracruz was long prominent in Mexican history; it was taken several times by buccaneers; it was captured by the French, 1838 and 1861, and by U.S. Gen. Winfield Scott during the Mexican War, 1847; and was again occupied by U.S. troops in 1914. Pop. (1959 est.) 138,012.

VERATRUM VIRIDE, a drug given to hypertensive patients because it lowers blood pressure. It consists of the dried rhizome and roots of the plant, *V. viride*. The drug has largely been replaced by other hypertensives.

VERB, in traditional grammar, any word that expresses action, being, or state of being. Verbs are classified as transitive or intransitive. The transitive verb is said to carry the action from the subject to the object (*He studied the lesson*), the subject performing the action and the object receiving it. The intransitive verb has no object: that is, it is supposed to imply being or state of being rather than action (*He sings; They ran; She seems healthy; The apples were tart*). Some intransitive verbs (*become, feel,* and *seem* and *be* in the last two examples), which are always followed by a noun or pronoun, are often referred to as copulative or linking verbs, since they link the subject with words which identify or describe it (*she* is linked with *healthy; apples* is linked with *tart*). Some verbs are said to be reflexive because they are often followed by the reflexive pronoun (*The cat is washing itself; Behave yourself!*).

The auxiliary verbs, often called helping verbs, include the forms of *be, have,* and according to some, *do,* and even *shall* and *will,* which are used along with the main verb to form various phrases, or tenses, as they are often called: *is going, was doing, has come, had seen, will return, does sing,* and so forth. Related to the auxiliary verbs are the modal auxiliaries (including *can, could, may, might, must, will, would, shall, should,* and *ought to*), which are said to reflect the speaker's outlook or attitude toward the assertion being made: *I can do it, I must do it, I ought to do it,* etc.

When a verb carries the action from its subject to its object (*He studied the lesson*), it is said to be in the active voice. If the subject receives the action, however, the verb is in the passive voice (*The lesson was studied by him*). Only transitive verbs have voice. The English verb is also said to indicate mood (or mode). The indicative mood is employed for matters of fact (*He studied the lesson; Did he study the lesson?*). The imperative mood is used for commands (*Drive slow!; Quit that!*). The subjunctive mood, in contrast, deals chiefly with matters contrary to fact (*If I were he . . . ; Is it necessary that he have his own car?*). See GRAMMAR; PARTS OF SPEECH.   ARTHUR NORMAN

VERBENA, a genus of herbaceous plants belonging to the family *Verbenaceae,* and commonly called vervain. All are native to the Americas except one European species, *V. officinalis.* Probably the most handsome of uncultivated vervains is *V. canadensis,* a sprawling perennial with flat blue to lilac or purple flower heads. They occur on roadsides, plains, and deserts in Colorado and New Mexico. Some species are cultivated as garden ornamentals.

VERCEL, ROGER, 1894–1957, French novelist, born in Le Mans, the son of a professional military man, completed his elementary studies at La Flèche. He studied for a time at the University of Caen, and then joined the French army at the outbreak of World War I, 1914. After the war he settled in Dinan, and began teaching literature at the local college. He first attained international recognition when he was awarded the 1934 Goncourt prize for his novel, *Capitaine Conan* (1934). Among his other works are the novels *En derive* (1931); *Au large de l'Eden*, 1932 (*In Sight of Eden*, 1934), which won the prize of Comité France-Amerique; *Le Maître du Rêve* (1933); *Léna*, 1936 (Eng. tr., 1937); *Sans le pied de l'Archange*, 1937 (*Tides of Mont St. Michel*, 1938); and *Aurore boréale*, 1947 (*Northern Lights*, 1948).

VERCELLI, province, NW Italy, Piedmont Region, bounded by the provinces of Novara on the N and E, Pavia on the SE, Alessandria on the S, and Turin on the W, and by Valle d'Aosta on the NW; area 1,157 sq. mi.; pop. (1958) 394,160. The province slopes from the Alps Mountains in the north to the Po River plain in the south. The principal rivers are the Po, the Baltea, and the Sesia. The Cavour Canal crosses in the south. Cattle, dairy products, wheat, corn, rice, and cotton are raised. The capital and chief town is Vercelli.

VERCELLI, town, NW Italy, Piedmont Region, capital of Vercelli Province; on the Sesia River, 38 miles WSW of Milan. Corn and rice are milled, and textiles and machinery are manufactured. The church of San Andrea, a Romanesque Gothic building that dates from the thirteenth century, has a museum of Roman antiquities. The cathedral library contains several ancient manuscripts, including the Vercelli Book, or Codex Vercellensis. Among the other churches of Vercelli are several containing examples of the work of Gaudenzio Ferrari. Vercelli was the birthplace of the painter Il Sodoma. Pop. (1958) 47,945.

VERCINGETORIX, died 46 B.C., Gallic chieftain of the tribe of the Arverni, who raised a rebellion against Caesar, 52 B.C. At first he gained several victories over the Romans, but he was eventually besieged in Alesia, and taken prisoner on its capture. He was exhibited in Rome to adorn Caesar's triumph, 46 B.C., and then executed.

VERCORS, 1902– , French writer and, under his own name (Jean Bruller), a typographer and illustrator, was born in Paris. During the German occupation of France in World War II, he founded, 1942, the clandestine *Editions de minuit* which published his *Le silence de la mer*, 1942 (*Put Out the Light*, 1944), and *La marche à l'étoile*, 1943 (*Guiding Star*, 1946). Both of these long stories explored the moral implications of collaboration with the enemy and were influential in French intellectual life during the war. Among his postwar works are *Les armes de la nuit* (1947), and *Les yeux et la lumière* (1948).

VERDANDI, in Scandinavian mythology, one of the three fates: Urd, the past, Verdandi, the present, and Skuld, the future. In the younger Eddas, the Norns are described as the daughters of Davalin, a dwarf. They are sometimes described as sibyls.

VERD ANTIQUE. See SERPENTINE.

VERDI, GIUSEPPE FORTUNINO FRANCES-CO, 1813–1901, Italian composer, was born in Roncole or Le Roncole. His parents, poor village innkeepers, noted the musical leanings of their son, and bought him a spinet. Later he studied with the village organist, Pietro Baistrocchi, for whom he occasionally substituted at church services; and then went to the neighboring musical town of Busseto to study with Ferdinando Provesi, the cathedral organist and conductor of the municipal orchestra. Verdi wrote many compositions for this group, including a symphony at the age of 15. It was arranged, 1832, that he should go to Milan for further study, and though he failed to win a scholarship at the conservatory, he studied privately with Vincenzo Lavigna until 1835, when he returned to Busseto as the *maestro di musica*.

Early operas. His first opera *Oberto* was performed (1839); his next, *Un Giorro di Regno* (1840),

was a failure, but with *Nabucodonosor* (1842) he established himself firmly at Milan's opera house, La Scala. *I Lombardi* (1843) and *Ernani* (1844) carried his fame beyond Italy, but it was with *Rigoletto* (1851) that his real triumphs began, followed closely by *Il Trovatore* (1853) and *La Traviata* (1853). Several other operas that were not to remain for long in the repertory were followed by the favorites *Un Ballo in Maschera* (1859) and *La Forza del Destino* (1862).

Major Works. When he was well past 50 years old, successful and established, Verdi began to feel dissatisfied with the loose and easy operatic conventions under which he had won fame. It was while he was in this state of mind that he accepted the suggestion that he write an opera on an Egyptian subject. The result, *Aïda*, first produced at Cairo, 1871, shows a great gain in orchestral richness and harmonic color over his earlier work. This development is evident also in his *Requiem* (1874), written to honor the great novelist Alessandro Manzoni (1785–1873); it was criticized by some as too dramatic and theatrical for so serious a theme, but it was nonetheless a unique and powerful composition.

Thirteen years were to elapse before the appearance of another work by Verdi, and many assumed that he was through. But when *Otello* was performed at Milan, 1897, it was apparent that Verdi had made another tremendous advance in musical expressiveness. This growth is often attributed to the influence of Richard Wagner (1813–83), and this may be true with respect to the richer harmony and orchestration; but Verdi never adopted Wagner's idea of the leitmotiv (see WAGNER, RICHARD). Much credit must also go to Verdi's friend and librettist, Arrigo Boito, a composer in his own right, who was a powerful stimulus and inspiration.

Finally, at the age of 80, Verdi saw his last opera *Falstaff* into production. Like *Otello*, it was a skillful adaptation from the work of William Shakespeare by Boito, but in musical color, delicacy, and skill it surpasses all of Verdi's other works. Its demands on performers and producers are, however, proportionally great, and this accounts in some measure for the infrequency of its performance. Its fine ensemble scenes, which culminate most naturally and spontaneously in a great contrapuntal finale, are among the most delightful surprises of the operatic stage, and the infectious humor of its characters and situations is perfectly reflected in the music. In his last years Verdi wrote a group of sacred works, performed in Paris, 1898; but his great work was done. He died at Milan three years later, venerated and esteemed by all.

Significance. Verdi was no innovator and in his works committed none of the excesses of innovators. His operas are uneven in merit, but through them all runs the gift of spontaneous melody. The tenacity with which his operas hold their place on the boards and his remarkable development so late in life are ample proofs of the vitality of his genius.

IRWIN FISCHER

BIBLIOG.–Ferruccio Bonavia, *Verdi* (1947); Carlo Gatti, *Verdi, the Man and His Music* (1955); Dyneley Hussey, *Verdi* (1949); Herman Rutters, *Giuseppe Verdi* (1947); Vincent Sheean, *Orpheus at Eighty* (1958); Francis Toye, *Giuseppe Verdi: His Life and Works* (1946); Franz Werfel and Paul Stefan, *Verdi, the Man in His Letters* (1942); Thomas R. Ybarra, *Verdi, Miracle Man of Opera* (1955).

VERDICT, a determination made by a jury upon an issue or issues submitted to them at a trial. A similar determination made by a judge, commissioner, or referee is considered a decision rather than a verdict. A general verdict determines the validity of evidence and the proper application of the law relating to the issues. A special verdict consists solely of a decision as to the truth of the facts presented at the trial; application of the law is left to the judge.

Although the unanimous concurrence of all the members of a jury is normally necessary to render a verdict, it has been held that the parties to a civil action may elect to accept the verdict of less than 12 jurors. In civil cases, the jury's verdict may award damages in an amount that is less than the plaintiff demands, or it may award the plaintiff all he asks, and allow a counterclaim that entitles the defendant to a judgment against the plaintiff for the amount thought to be excessive. In criminal cases, if the accused is tried on a single charge, the jury must submit a verdict of guilty or not guilty. If the defendant is tried on several charges, a partial verdict may be rendered, finding the accused guilty of only some of the charges. Under the statutes of most states, different degrees of various crimes are recognized, and a guilty verdict must include a finding as to the degree of the offense charged.

If a jury disregards the instruction of the court as to the law applicable to the facts under consideration, the verdict may be set aside by the judge. Improper conduct on the part of the jury or any member of it may also be grounds for setting aside a verdict, if such conduct has influenced the jury's consideration of the issues. In most states, if the trial judge is of the opinion that the verdict is against the evidence, he may set it aside and order a retrial. See JEOPARDY; TRIAL.

VERDIGRIS, basic cupric acetate crystals, formed by the exposure in air of metallic copper to acetic acid. The crystals have a deep blue or a green color. Verdigris blue has the approximate formula, $Cu_2O(C_2H_3O_2)_2$, and results from the exposure of copper plates to pure acetic acid; whereas the green variety of verdigris, with the formula, $CuO \cdot 2Cu(C_2H_3O_2)_2$, is derived from exposing copper to vinegar. Verdigris is used as paint pigment and in insecticides and fungicides.

VERDUN, city, Canada, S Québec, Jacques Cartier County; on the St. Lawrence River; residential suburb adjoining S Montreal. The original settlement, Côte de Gentilly was renamed Rivière St. Pierre and incorporated as a village in 1874. The village became known as Verdun in 1876, and was incorporated as a city in 1912. (For population, see southern Quebec map in Atlas.)

VERDUN, town, NE France, in the department of Meuse in Lorraine; on the Meuse River, 38 miles W of Metz. Verdun is an important highway and rail junction. It has been center of an Episcopal see since the fourth century. Hardware, spirits, and confectionery are manufactured in the town. In Roman times the town was known as Verodunum. In 843 the Treaty of Verdun was signed there. This treaty divided the empire of Charlemagne, king of the Franks, into three separate kingdoms. The bishopric of Verdun was then under the rule of the Holy Roman Empire. During the time of Henry II, 1552, Verdun was taken by France, and under Louis XIV the fortifications were planned and built by Sebastien Vauban, the French military engineer. In the Franco-German War of 1870 Verdun made a stout resistance, holding out for 10 weeks, and falling only when supplies failed. After 1871, Verdun was one of the eastern bulwarks of France. See WORLD WAR I; WORLD WAR II. (For population, see France map in Atlas.)

VERDUN, BATTLES OF, in World War I, a series of battles between French and German forces for control of the fortified town of Verdun, Meuse Department, France, comprising (1) the German offensive, from February through the summer and into the fall, 1916, and (2) the French counteroffensive in October, November, and December, 1916, and during late summer and early fall, 1917. In the course of all this, more than a million casualties were sustained by the warring powers.

The Verdun fighting constituted one of the major actions of the war. In January, 1916, the Allies seemed about to take the offensive, having just increased considerably their strength in men and matériel. Germany and Austria, on the other hand, were pressed for men, and the German people were becoming increasingly impatient with victories that

brought no decision, and the prestige of the whole imperial military and bureaucratic system was beginning to wane. As the German leaders viewed the situation, they could either continue a merely defensive war on the Western front so as to be able to concentrate their major effort for victory in the East, or they could attack first in the West and then turn east against Russia. The latter alternative was decided upon, and Verdun was chosen as the objective. If Verdun could be taken quickly, it was hoped, French morale would crumble, and with it effective resistance to a German advance against Paris. In fact, however, just the opposite result occurred.

The German offensive began, Feb. 21, 1916, with an exceptionally intense artillery bombardment, followed by an infantry advance the next day. From the very start the fighting was marked by many casualties on both sides. The German effort to take the observation point of Le Mort-Homme occasioned some of the fiercest fighting of the entire Verdun campaign. As the offensive continued into April, the Germans had yet to make significant headway. Then, toward the end of May, the Germans launched violent assaults along both sides of the river and, by June 7, held Fort Douaumont and Fort Vaux; despite the most strenuous attempts, however, they never succeeded in taking the Mort-Homme hill or the important fort at Souville.

By September the French were beginning to think in terms of a counteroffensive. In four hours, on October 25, the French retook all that the enemy had wrested from them in six months except for Fort Vaux, which the Germans held tenaciously until November 1. By December 15 the French had reestablished themselves in such strongholds as Vacherauville on the Meuse, Pepper Ridge, Louvement, Bézonvaux, and in a number of other places that the Germans had taken only a few months before. Finally, on July 1, 1917, the French took the offensive on the west side of the Meuse, and by early in September had forced the Germans back to a line approximately the same as that which had existed just prior to the German attack of Feb. 21, 1916.

VEREENIGING, city, NE Republic of South Africa, Transvaal Province, on the Vaal River, 37 miles S of Johannesburg. Iron and steel, machinery, nuts and bolts, rivets, copper products, wire, and bricks are manufactured. Sources of power are the hydroelectric project 15 miles upstream on the Vaal River, and coal, which is mined in the vicinity. The city was founded early in the 1890's. The treaty ending the South African War was signed at Vereeniging, May 31, 1902. Pop. (1960) 78,835.

VERENDRYE, PIERRE GAULTIER DE VARENNES, SIEUR DE LA, 1685–1749, French-Canadian explorer, was born in Three Rivers, Québec. He served with the French colonial army and also with the French army in Europe during the War of the Spanish Succession, 1707–11. He obtained a monopoly on the fur trade in the West, 1730, and in succeeding years he and his sons made a number of explorations. They built outposts west of Lake Superior on Rainy Lake, Lake of the Woods, Lake Winnipeg, and the Red and Assiniboine rivers. La Vérendrye reached the Missouri River, 1738, and a lead plate that his sons had buried to claim the upper Missouri Valley for France was discovered, 1913, at Pierre, S.D. La Vérendrye also explored Manitoba, the western plains of Minnesota, and Canada's northwest territory.

VERESHCHAGIN, VASILI VASILIEVICH, 1842–1904, Russian genre and military painter, was born in Tcherepovets, Novgorod, studied at the St. Petersburg Academy and the Ecole des Beaux-Arts, Paris, and was a pupil of Jean Léon Gérôme. Vereshchagin's works are primarily of historical interest. They include a cycle of paintings from the history of India, another depicting the Russian campaign in Turkestan, and one of the Russo-Turkish War. The painter was killed in the sinking of the battleship *Petropavlovsk* in the harbor of Port Arthur, Manchuria.

VERESS, SÁNDOR, 1907– , Hungarian pianist, composer, and folklorist, was born in Kolozsvar (later Cluj, Rumania), and began his musical education at the Music Academy of Buda, Budapest, 1916. At the State Academy of Music, Budapest, 1923–32, he studied under Béla Bartók and Zoltán Kodály, among others, and was graduated as a teacher. He studied music education in Berlin, 1932, London, 1938–39, Amsterdam, 1939, The Hague, 1939, and Rome, 1941–42, and was appointed professor of composition at the Academy of Music, Budapest, 1943. As a musical folklorist he assisted Bartók in editing folk tunes, 1937–40; undertook explorations to the Csangó communities of Moldavia, 1929, 1930, 1932–36, and 1943; and wrote essays and lectured on the subject. Veress became professor of composition at the conservatory of Bern University, 1950. Among his better known works are a ballet, *Terszili Katica* (1934), a violin concerto (1939), *Four Transylvanian Dances* for string orchestra (1944), *Thermos*, in memory of Bartók, and *Sinfonia Minneapolitana* (1954).

VERGA, GIOVANNI, 1840–1922, Italian novelist, was born in Catania, Sicily. His early works are reminiscent of French sensational fiction, but Verga soon found his true element—simple tales and stories dealing with Sicilian village life. Works like *Nedda* (1874) and *Vita dei campi* (1880) made him the acknowledged leader of the Sicilian Realist movement. Among his other works are *Storia di una peccatrice* (1865), *Eva* (1869), *Storia di una capinera* (1869), *I Malavoglia* (1881), *Maestro Don Gesualdo* (1889), and *Pane Nero* (1902). Verga's *Cavalleria rusticana* was used for the libretto of Mascagni's opera of that name (1890). D. H. Lawrence translated many of Verga's works into English.

VERGENNES, CHARLES GRAVIER, COMTE DE, 1717–87, French diplomat, was born in Dijon. As ambassador to Turkey, from 1754, he played a major role in various intrigues against Russia. He was ambassador to Sweden, 1771–74, and aided in the coup by which Gustavus III made his power absolute. Vergennes was appointed minister of foreign affairs, 1774, on the accession of Louis XVI. On the outbreak of the American Revolution, Vergennes' anti-British policy brought about the alliance between France and the United States. He negotiated the Treaty of Paris (1783).

VERGIL, full name Publius Vergilius Maro, 70–19 B.C., Roman poet, was born in Andes, near Mantua, Cisalpine Gaul. Although scholars generally agree that Vergil is the correct spelling of the poet's name, Virgil, a traditional spelling probably based on a fifth century error, is so frequently used that it cannot fairly be called incorrect. Vergil's education was begun in Cremona, continued in Mediolanum (modern Milan), and completed in Rome. It is thought that Vergil lost his estate near Cremona, 42 B.C., when the land in that area was divided among the veterans of the Battle of Philippi. There is evidence in Vergil's *Bucolics* (37 B.C.), however, that his lands were eventually restored to him through the intervention of Octavian (later the Emperor Augustus). From 37 to 29 B.C., Vergil lived in and near Naples, where his shyness, affectionately noted by the Neapolitans, earned for him the nickname Parthenias (The Maiden). He went to Athens, 19 B.C., with the idea of completing his final revision of the *Aeneid* there; but when Augustus appeared in the city and urged him to return to Rome, Vergil gathered up his still unfinished manuscript and joined the imperial party. Before the ship reached Italy he had fallen ill, and he died at Brundisium (modern Brindisi) on September 21.

Scholars have long disagreed, often violently, as to the extent of Vergil's authorship of a group of poems called collectively *Appendix vergiliana*, and often ascribed to Vergil. It is highly probable that some of his earliest poetic efforts are to be found in this collection, but it is almost certain that he did not write all of the pieces. In 37 B.C. he published his *Bucolics* or *Eclogues*. His model for this work were the idylls of the third century Greek poet Theocritus. Most interesting of the *Bucolics* is the fourth, which proclaims the coming of a golden age, to be heralded by the birth of a divine child. For centuries Vergil was believed by many to have prophesied, in this lovely poem, the birth of Jesus.

The Georgics. During Vergil's stay in Naples, he wrote a work of surpassing beauty, the *Georgics*. It was composed at the suggestion of Gaius Cilnius Maecenas, Vergil's friend and Augustus' advisor; its purpose was to aid and support Augustus in the promotion of a back-to-the-country movement. The four books deal, respectively, with agriculture, arboriculture, the rearing of farm animals, and beekeeping. In the fourth book, the poet says that if he were not near the end of his task, and the furling of his sails, he would also sing of gardens.

The Aeneid. The last 11 years of Vergil's life were devoted to the *Aeneid*, an epic in 12 books, on the fall of Troy, the wanderings of Aeneas, and the ultimate establishment of a Trojan settlement in Latium. Again the poet played the role of imperial propagandist: Venus is the mother of Aeneas, and Ascanius, his son, is the progenitor of the Julian line which has now given to the world the great Augustus, its final and perfect flower; moreover, Rome's divine mission as ruler of the races of men is proclaimed with evangelical fervor and passion. Many readers consider Book VI the most beautiful and impressive of the 12; it tells of the descent of the hero Aeneas into Hades, where he finds the shade of his father Anchises in the Elysian Fields, and receives encouragement and counsel for the tempestuous days that lie ahead.

In some ways, Vergil's finest and noblest creation is Dido, queen of Carthage, who graciously welcomes Aeneas' shipwrecked company and establishes them in her newly founded city. As a result of the wiles of Juno and Venus, she falls violently in love with the Trojan leader, who dwells happily in her palace until Jupiter sends Mercury to order him to abandon her and sail on to Italy. This dramatic episode was introduced by Vergil into the narrative in order to supply an explanation of the bitter enmity between Carthage and Rome that produced the Punic Wars.

Another striking and tragic character is Turnus, king of the Rutulians, who is robbed by Aeneas of his promised bride, Lavinia; struggles savagely and heroically against the invaders; but at last falls a victim of Aeneas' invincible might. See AENEAS.

Commentators have vied with one another in extolling Vergil's consummate mastery of meter, his unsurpassed powers of description, his penetrating delineation of character, his haunting tenderness, his unerring choice of the right word, his lofty and lovely imagery. One admirer called Vergil "the chastest poet and the royalest that to the memory of man is known." HUBERT McNEIL POTEAT

BIBLIOG.–Melville B. Anderson, *Fate of Virgil as Conceived by Dante: A Dialogue of the Dead and the Living Between Walter Savage Landor and Willard Fiske* (1931); Cyril Bailey, *Religion in Virgil* (1935); Cecil M. Bowra, *From Virgil to Milton* (1946); Charles R. Buxton, *Prophets of Heaven and Hell: Virgil, Dante, Milton, Goethe* (1945); Domenico P. A. Comparetti, *Vergil in the Middle Ages* (1929); Robert S. Conway, *Harvard Lectures on the Vergilian Age* (1928); Mary M. Diederich, *Vergil in the Works of St. Ambrose* (1931); Dwight L. Durling, *Georgic Tradition in English Poetry* (1935); William W. Fowler, *Death of Turnus* (1919); Tenney Frank, *Vergil: A Biography* (1922); Terrot R. Glover, *Virgil* (1930); Theodore J. Haarhoff, *Vergil, the Universal* (1949); Theodore Haecker, *Virgil, Father of the West* (1934); William F. J. Knight, *Roman Vergil* (1946), *Accentual Symmetry in Vergil* (1951); Francis J. H. Letters, *Virgil* (1946); John W. Mackail, *Virgil and His Meaning to the World of To-day* (1922); Junius S. Morgan, Kenneth McKenzie and Charles G. Osgood, *Tradition of Virgil: Three Papers on the History and Influence of the Poet* (1930); Bruno Nardi, *Youth of Virgil* (1930); Elizabeth Nitchie, *Vergil and the*

English Poets (1919); Henry W. Prescott, *Development of Virgil's Art* (1927); L. Proudfoot, *Dryden's Aeneid and Its 17th-Century Predecessors* (1960); Edward K. Rand, *In Quest of Virgil's Birthplace* (1930), *Magical Art of Virgil* (1931); Homer F. Rebert, *Virgil and Those Others* (1930); William Y. Sellar, *Roman Poets of the Augustan Age: Virgil* (1987); John W. Spargo, *Virgil the Necromancer: Studies in Virgilian Legends* (1934); John H. A. Sparrow, *Half-Lines and Repetitions in Virgil* (1931); Virgil (Publius Vergilius Maro), *Aeneid: A Structural Approach: vol. 1, Bks. 1–2: Edited by Waldo E. Sweet, With a Latin Interpretation and Selected Notes from Servius* (1960); John H. Whitfield, *Dante and Virgil* (1949).

VERGIL, POLYDORE, 1470?–?1555, Italian-British ecclesiastic and historian, was born in Urbino, Italy. He is believed to have been secretary to the Duke of Urbino at Padua some time before 1498, when his work, *Liber proverbium*, appeared. It was followed by *De inventiborus rerum* (1499). After serving as chamberlain to Pope Alexander VI, Vergil was sent to England, 1501, as subcollector of Peter's Pence. He was enthroned as bishop of Bath and Wells, 1504, became naturalized as an Englishman, 1510, and subsequently held several clerical appointments. He was imprisoned for some months, 1515, for having offended Cardinal Wolsey. Vergil returned to Italy, 1538, and died there. His most famous work is *Historia anglica* (1534), on which he worked for nearly 30 years.

VERHAEREN, EMILE, 1855–1916, Belgian poet and art critic, was born in Saint Amand, on the Schelde, near Antwerp. After studying at the College of Sainte Barbe in Ghent, 1869–74, and at the law school of the University of Louvain, 1875–81, he was admitted to the bar of Brussels, 1881, but abandoned law immediately and soon assumed a leading role in the Belgian literary and artistic renascence. His first volume of verse, *Les flamandes* (1883), reveals a robust realism reminiscent of the great Flemish painters. There followed a period of neurasthenia and pessimism, which probably explains his renewed interest in the work of Edgar Allan Poe and Charles Baudelaire and which resulted in *Les débâcles* (1888). His marriage and his interest in humanitarian problems restored his peace of mind.

He allied himself with the French Symbolists, and adapted their technique, save for its hermetic quality, to the principal themes of his later work: the Flemish peasants, their legends, and their customs (*Toute la Flandre*, 1904–11); the great forces of modern social life (*Les villes tentaculaires*, 1895, and *Les forces tumultueuses*, 1902); and his love for his wife—an unusual quality among Symbolist poets—which inspired a trilogy, *Les heures claires* (1896, 1905, 1911). His style was not without its imperfections, but his colorful imagination, his violent intensity, and extreme sensitivity enabled him to become the foremost Belgian poet of his day.   C. W. COLMAN

VERHULST, JOHANNES JOSEPHUS HERMAN, 1816–91, Dutch violinist, conductor, and composer, was born in The Hague, and studied music at the Royal School of Music, The Hague, and at Cologne. Verhulst went to Leipzig, Germany, 1838, and there served as the conductor of the Euterpe Concerts until 1842, when he returned to The Hague. Verhulst was appointed royal music director, conducted orchestras in Amsterdam and Rotterdam, and led the famous Diligentia Concerts, The Hague, 1860–86. In addition, Verhulst spent more than 30 years organizing music festivals throughout Holland. Among his musical compositions, few of which achieved renown outside of Holland, are symphonic works, chamber music, church music, and songs.

VERKHOYANSK, town, U.S.S.R., NE Russian Soviet Federated Socialist Republic, in the Yakut Autonomous Soviet Socialist Republic; on a height above the Yana River; 390 miles NNE of Yakutsk, and about 2,500 miles ENE of Moscow. The town lies north of the Arctic Circle and is noted for its extreme temperature range. In winter temperatures dip below −90°F. The July mean temperature is 60°F, and a maximum of 94°F has been observed. The summer lasts for only 60 or 70 days, and during this short period steamers operating in the Arctic Ocean ascend the Yana to the town. The town was long known as a center for political exiles in Czarist Russia. Since 1900, however, Verkhoyansk has become noted for the development of tin, nickel, molybdenum, lead, and silver mining. It is also a center for the collection of both furs and of mammoth ivory found in the frozen regions. These items are then sent to Yakutsk, on the Lena River. Verkhoyansk has a post office, a school, a hospital, and a government agricultural station. Pop. (1959 est.) 10,000.

VERLAINE, PAUL, 1844–96, French poet, born in Metz in Lorraine, was the son of an army officer. After 1851 the family settled in Paris where Verlaine attended the Lycée Condorcet and the University of Paris. He became a government clerk at the Hôtel de Ville, 1864, and frequented literary circles. His marriage to Mathilde Mauté, 1870, terminated in divorce, 1874. In 1871, Verlaine had come under the sinister influence of the eccentric poet, Arthur Rimbaud (1854–91) and it was their relationship that caused Verlaine's final rupture with his wife. While they were traveling together in Belgium, 1873, Verlaine shot and wounded Rimbaud during a quarrel and was committed to prison for two years at Mons, where he was converted to Catholicism. On terminating his sentence he lived for several years in England and northern France. Returning to Paris, 1885, he enjoyed great popularity and was elected "Prince des Poètes," 1894. Despite his conversion to Catholicism, the honesty of which can hardly be questioned, Verlaine succumbed to debauchery and vice after his mother's death, 1886. In later years he was given to visiting Latin Quarter cafés to recite verses and weep. On his death Paris heaped his bier with lilacs and white orchids. *Poèmes saturniens* (1866) and *Fêtes galantes* (1869), while Parnassian in inspiration, are original in their suggestive melodies. In *La bonne chanson* (1870), dedicated to his wife, Verlaine abandons objectivity for genuine lyric feeling. In his *Romances sans paroles* (1874) the elusive matching of sensation and mood marks the transition to Symbolism. His flowing and supple verse, which approaches but does not become vers libre, renders the vaguest moods with magic spontaneity. Of *Sagesse* (1881) Jules Lemaître writes: "this is the first time that French poetry has truly expressed the love of God."   ERWIN HUGH PRICE

VERMEER, JAN, or Jan van der Meer van Delft, 1632–75, Dutch painter of the Golden Age, was born in Delft, son of an innkeeper and art dealer. From 1653 he was accepted as a master of the Guild of St. Luke. Although esteemed in his lifetime, Vermeer's works were practically unknown throughout the eighteenth century, and only came to light through the persistent research of admirers; at mid-twentieth century his relatively few extant works were classed among the most select in the whole history of art. Most of his works are in the Rijksmuseum, Amsterdam. He apparently worked slowly, and his total production seems not to have exceeded 40 canvases. He probably learned his craft under Carel Fabritius. Vermeer painted both elegant interiors and humble domestic scenes, yet the true mark of his work is not in its themes but in the exceptional clarity of his composition, in which no element dominates, but all boast an eternal appearance. Vermeer's brush stroke reflects his impassive vision. A strange and mysterious silence seems to dominate his canvases, in which the few figures seem to be lost in the absorption of a moment's action, or perhaps are simply hesitating on the border of decision. Thus his *Musicians* have apparently just finished their playing and are listening to the echo, and in *The Letter*, the receiver vacillates before opening the missive. Vermeer's *Little Street* is a subtle composition, broadly handled, in which a masterful composition of rectangles and

Vermiculite

arbitrary color transforms a simple street scene into art of a high order. Most of his paintings are small in size and do not depend on any obvious impact. The famous *Girl with a Water Jug* (Metropolitan Museum, New York) is a study in total color interplay, in which the blue dress of the girl leaves a blue reflection on a pewter jug and modifies the surrounding colors. Vermeer's one mythological scene, *Diana and her Nymphs*, is a quiet, pastoral composition in tones of gold, blue, and red. In color effects, Vermeer's system of underpainting, one of his own invention, consisted in applying a coat of tempera over water color, covering this with light varnish, and then applying color oils; thus he created various effects of sunglow through the entire painting.

One of the great mysteries in art history is how so fine a painter could have dropped from the sight and attention of the art world for more than a century. See FORGERY, LITERARY AND ARTISTIC.

ANTHONY KERRIGAN

VERMICULITE, a foliated hydrous magnesium-aluminum-iron silicate, micaceous mineral, formed as an alteration of biotite. Vermiculite has a monoclinic crystal structure; is extremely soft, having a hardness of only $1\frac{1}{2}$ (see HARDNESS); and a specific gravity of about 2.4. This mineral was given its name by Thomas Webb in 1824 when he observed that, if it was subjected to the heat of the flame of a blowpipe, it expanded and shot out into a variety of wormlike forms. Vermiculite is yellowish to brown in color, and, when calcined at 1750°F, expands to 16 times its original volume. In the calcined state, it is characterized by its lightness and large void volume.

Vermiculite is found in Montana, North and South Carolina, and Wyoming. After the 1920's it became an important source of many industrial products including both thermal and sound insulation. It is also used as a fireproofing component of gypsum and cement, as a soil conditioner and fertilizer, and as a carrier for insecticides. In the late 1950's the U.S. mine production of vermiculite averaged somewhat less than 200,000 short tons, having a value of approximately $2.6 million.

VERMIFORM APPENDIX. See APPENDIX, APPENDICITIS.

VERMILION, town, Canada, E Alberta; on the Vermilion River and the Canadian National Railway; 110 miles E of Edmonton. The town is a trade and processing center for an agricultural area in which grain and livestock are raised. Vermilion has flour and feed mills, a creamery, and an agricultural implement warehouse. Oil and gas are produced south of Vermilion. Pop. (1956) 2,196.

VERMILION, a bright red paint pigment consisting of mercuric sulfide, HgS. It was formerly obtained from the mineral cinnabar, but later was produced artificially by heating mercury and sulfur. The color of vermilion varies from crimson to orange-red, depending on the degree of fineness of grinding. Because the pure vermilion pigment is very expensive, it is commonly adulterated with ferric oxide, red lead, chalk, or gypsum. In addition to its use as a paint pigment, vermilion is employed to color such products as printing inks, rubber, paper, and sealing wax.

VERMILLION, city, SE South Dakota, seat of Clay County; near the Missouri River; on the Milwaukee Railroad, 55 miles S of Sioux Falls. The city is a trade and processing center for an area in which livestock, corn, soybeans, alfalfa, vegetables, and melons are raised. Fort Vermillion was built as a fur-trading post on the site in 1835. Its major growth occurred with settlement in the area after passage of the Homestead Act, 1862. The city is the site of the State University of South Dakota (1882). The university museum, the W. H. Over Museum, has a large natural history collection, and many articles pertaining to the state's history. Pop. (1960) 6,102.

VERMLAND. See VÄRMLAND.

The Green Mountains are home to skiers in winter and campers and hikers in summer.

VERMONT, state, NE United States, in New England; bounded on the N by Québec, on the E by New Hampshire, on the S by Massachusetts, and on the W by New York; area 9,609 sq. mi., including 331 sq. mi. of inland water; pop. (1960) 389,881. Vermont is roughly wedge-shaped, extending 156 miles N–S and varying in width from 89 miles at the northern border to 37 miles at the southern. The Connecticut River forms its entire boundary with New Hampshire, and the Poultney River and Lake Champlain mark about two-thirds of its boundary with New York. Vermont ranks 43rd in area and 47th in population among the states. The state's name is derived from the French *vert mont* (green mountains). "Freedom and Unity" is the state motto; *Hail Vermont* the state song; red clover the state flower; and the hermit thrush the state bird. The capital of Vermont is Montpelier. See map in Atlas, Vol. 20.

PHYSICAL FACTORS

Topography. The land surface of Vermont, generally hilly or mountainous, was greatly affected by glaciation: hence, the state's numerous small lakes, boulder-strewn areas, and drift deposits. The Green Mountains, an old, worn-down range, form Vermont's "backbone" and extend the entire north-south length of the state. The range consists of fairly low, rounded hills in the south but becomes wider and loftier to the north. Major subranges of the Green Mountains are the Northfield Mountains, the Worcester Mountains, and the Cold Hollow Mountains. Notable peaks are Mount Mansfield (4,393 ft.), the highest point in Vermont; Mount Ellen (4,135 ft.); and Camels Hump (4,083 ft.). Into southwestern Vermont extends the Taconic Mountains, which reach their greatest elevation in Equinox Mountain (3,816 ft.).

In the northwest, bordering Lake Champlain, is a discontinuous lowland relieved by low hills. In eastern Vermont are irregular mountains and hills that decline eastward to the Connecticut River valley. Of the many prominent, solitary mountain peaks, or monadnocks, to be seen throughout the state, Ascutney Mountain (3,144 ft.), in the southeast, is perhaps the most notable.

The Green Mountains form a distinct drainage divide between the Connecticut River and Lake Champlain. The westward-flowing rivers include the Missisquoi, the Lamoille, and the Winooski, all of which have cut scenic gorges through the northern Green Mountains, and Otter Creek and the Poultney River. The eastward-flowing rivers include the Passumpsic, the White, the Williams, and the West.

Lake Champlain, partly in New York and Québec, is the largest lake in Vermont. Lake Memphremagog, mainly in Québec, is the second largest. The largest natural body of water wholly within the state is Bomoseen Lake in the west. Other large lakes are Dunmore, Willoughby, St. Catherine, Carmi, and Averill. The many artificial lakes include Somerset, Whitingham, Chittenden, Little River, and Waterbury reservoirs.

Climate. Vermont has a climate of the humid continental, cool summer type. It is characterized by long, fairly severe winters and mild summers. Winter temperatures are frequently well below freezing, with a January mean temperature of 19°F at Burlington, on Lake Champlain, and 19.8°F. at Rutland, in south-central Vermont. July mean temperatures are 69.4°F at Burlington and 69.0°F 'at Rutland. Summer days tend to be quite warm but nights are cool. Winters are cold, with crisp, clear days. Precipitation averages between 35 and 45 inches annually, fairly well spread over the year. Burlington averages 31.9 inches of precipitation annually; Rutland averages 37.4 inches. Winter precipitation in Vermont is mainly in the form of snow. Portions of the Green Mountains average more than 100 inches of snow each winter. The growing season varies from 120 to 150 days in the Champlain Lowlands and Connecticut Valley to less than 100 days in the Green Mountains.

Plant and Animal Wildlife. Forests cover about 60 per cent of Vermont's area, mostly in the uplands. Nearly all is second growth. Predominant tree species are maple, beech, hickory, oak, ash, elm, birch, butternut, and hemlock. In the Connecticut Valley is found white pine, the largest and most valuable tree, which is used as the emblem for the state seal. The dark green color of the Green Mountains is a result of the luxuriant growth of spruce and fir. The numerous broadleaved, deciduous trees of the valleys and lowlands are noted for their brilliant, varied fall colors.

Vermont's forests include a large number of ferns, including several peculiar to this region. The many flowering plants of the state consist mainly of members of the orchid, rose, pea, and heath families. Colorful displays of pussy willows, arbutus, and violets appear early in spring; lilacs and apple blossoms in May; daisies, buttercups, and red clover in summer; and goldenrod and gentians in fall.

Deer are the largest game animals found in the state. Once indiscriminately slaughtered, they are now protected by game conservation measures. Other animals include muskrat, skunk, raccoon, fox, mink, bear, lynx, rabbits, squirrels, woodchucks, and hedgehogs. A wide variety of fresh water fish are found in Vermont's lakes and streams. Speckled, lake, and golden trout, and pike, pickerel, perch, and catfish are native; rainbow and steelhead trout and landlocked salmon have been introduced.

SOCIAL FACTORS

Population. The population of Vermont increased by 12,134, or 3.2 per cent, between 1950 and 1960. Despite growing urbanization, urban dwellers comprise only 38.5 per cent of the total 1960 population. With an average population density of only 42 persons per square mile, Vermont is one of the least densely inhabited of the eastern states. Population densities are greatest in the Connecticut Valley and

PRINCIPAL CITIES

City	Population 1950 census	Population 1960 census
Burlington	33,155	35,531
Rutland	17,659	18,325
Barre	10,922	10,387
Brattleboro	9,606	9,315
St. Albans	8,552	8,806
Montpelier	8,599	8,782
Bennington	8,002	8,023

Champlain Lowlands; least in the Green Mountains. A relatively small number of the population are non-whites. Canadians, many of them French-speaking, form the largest group of foreign-born residents. Roman Catholics constitute the largest single religious group; members of the Congregational, Methodist, Baptist, and Protestant Episcopal churches are also numerous. Burlington is the most populous city.

Education. A commissioner of education, appointed by the state board of education, has general supervision of public schools. School attendance is compulsory for children from 7 to 16 years of age. Institutions of higher education are the University of Vermont (founded 1791), Burlington; Bennington College (1925), Bennington; Champlain College (1878), Burlington; the College of St. Joseph the Provider, Rutland; Goddard College (1863), Plainfield; Green Mountain College (1834), Poultney; Marlboro College (1946), Marlboro; Middlebury College (1800), Middlebury; Norwich University (1819), Northfield; St. Michael's College (1904), Winooski; Trinity College (1925), Burlington; Vermont College (1834), Montpelier; Vermont Technical College, Randolph Center; and Windham College (1951), Putney. Teacher training institutions are located at Castleton, Johnson, and Lyndon Center.

Public Welfare. The Department of Public Welfare has general supervision over state institutions in this category. These include a mental hospital, at Waterbury; a tuberculosis sanatorium, at Pittsford; the Austine Institute for the deaf and dumb, at Brattleboro; and a school for retarded children, at Brandon. There are institutions for dependent and neglected children, a soldiers' home, and such penal institutions as an industrial school for boys and girls, at Vergennes; a prison for women, at Rutland; and a prison for men, at Windsor.

ECONOMIC FACTORS

Agriculture. Vermont is primarily an agricultural state. Dairy cattle raising is the most important branch of agriculture, with more than two thirds of the state's farm area in pasture. Dairying is most important in the north, especially the Champlain Lowland and Connecticut Valley. Milk production, mainly for Boston, New York, and other urban centers, is widespread. Much of the milk and dairy produce is processed and marketed through cooperatives. Some sheep and hogs, and the Morgan work horse, a distinctive breed well adapted to the hilly country, are raised. Vermont has a large poultry industry, particularly turkeys. Livestock in 1964 was valued at $111 million.

PRODUCTION OF PRINCIPAL CROPS

Crop	Unit	1964
Apples	tons	22,100
Corn for Grain	tons	1,700
Hay	tons	1,038,000
Maple Sirup	gallons	486,000
Oats	tons	8,400
Potatoes	tons	18,000

SOURCE: *U.S. Department of Agriculture*

Crops are grown principally in the Lake Champlain Lowland and Connecticut Valley. Hay, corn (for silage), oats, and potatoes are the most important. Apples are also produced. Maple sirup and sugar are important cash crops, some 40 per cent of all U.S. production coming from Vermont. St. Johnsbury is the principal center for this industry.

Forestry. Lumbering was the first major industry of Vermont, the state formerly ranking as one of the major lumber producers in the nation. Despite widespread cutting of the once-virgin forests, there were in 1960 nearly 4 million acres of commercial forest

VERMONT

St. Albans

Burlington

Montpelier

Rutland

Bennington

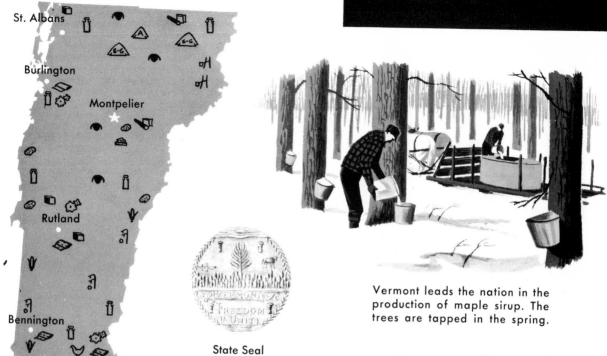

State Seal

Vermont leads the nation in the production of maple sirup. The trees are tapped in the spring.

State Bird—Hermit Thrush

State Flower—Red Clover

PRINCIPAL RESOURCES, INDUSTRIES, AND PRODUCTS

Asbestos		Oats	
Corn		Paper and pulpwood	
Dairying		Potatoes	
Granite		Poultry	
Machinery		Sand and gravel	
Maple sirup		Sheep	
Marble		Textiles	

Vacationists are attracted to the scenic Green Mountains throughout the year.

Dairying, concentrated in northern Vermont, is the major agricultural activity.

Many popular ski resorts are scattered across Vermont's mountainous terrain.

land, yielding considerable amounts of pulpwood, saw logs, veneer wood, railroad ties, poles, piling, and fuelwood. White pine and red spruce are the main species yielding commercial lumber.

Mining. The major mineral products of Vermont are granite, marble, and asbestos. Granite is quarried mainly in the Green Mountains, notably at Barre. Marble quarrying, in which Vermont leads all the states, is done in a number of localities, including Rutland, Swanton, Proctor, Middlebury, and Isle La Motte. The Eden-Lowell District contains the main deposits of asbestos in the United States. Other minerals produced in the state are talc, slate, limestone, kaolin, soapstone, silver, and copper. In 1964, total value of mining in Vermont was $26,127,000 as compared with $20,302,000 in 1953.

PRODUCTION OF PRINCIPAL MINERALS

Mineral	Unit	1957	1964
Sand & Gravel......	short ton	2,215,553	1,764,000
Stone..............	short ton	556,999	2,070,000

SOURCE: *U.S. Department of Interior*

Manufacturing. Vermont's manufacturing industries are limited. Machine tools and machinery rank first in industrial output. Monuments, tombstones, cut stone, and other stone products; lumber, paper, and wood products; food products; textiles, mainly woolens and worsteds; printed matter; chemicals; leather and leather goods; and wide variety of metal goods, are manufactured. Many of the wood, leather, and stone products are made largely by hand. Major industrial centers are Burlington, Barre, Rutland, Bennington, Brattleboro, St. Johnsbury, Springfield, Proctor, Winooski, St. Albans, and Bellows Falls.

Transportation. The main railroad lines are the Central Vermont, the Rutland, the St. Johnsbury and Lake Champlain, the Canadian Pacific, the Grand Trunk, the Barre and Chelsea, the Delaware and Hudson, and the Boston and Maine. Most of the railroads run north-south and provide a fairly close network of lines over the entire state. The state is well served by highways. The main routes are U.S. highways 2 and 4, east and west, and U.S. highways 5 and 7, north and south. Burlington, Montpelier, and Rutland are the main commercial airline centers.

Tourist Attractions. As one of the principal vacation areas of New England, Vermont attracts numerous visitors from a wide area, particularly the large eastern cities. Spring and summer tourists may enjoy the cool, wooded hills and mountains, and the picturesque, green countryside. The Vermont landscape has a distinctive character—hilly farms and patches of woodland against a background of misty green mountains. Dotted here and there are numerous antique buildings, among them old white clapboard houses, severe white churches with open-belfried steeples, and quaint old-fashioned general stores in the villages. More than 200 covered bridges cross Vermont rivers and streams. Fall, because of the brilliant forest hues, is particularly attractive.

Among the notable attractions in the Green Mountains are the Long Trail along the mountains' crest, Mount Mansfield, whose peak is accessible by a 4-mile toll road and aerial chair lift; Smuggler's Notch; Cave of the Winds; and the deep Winooski River Canyon. The Green Mountain National Forest, covering more than 500,000 acres, offers a full range of outdoor recreation facilities. Also renowned for their forests and mountain scenery are the Taconic Mountains, where the summit of Equinox Mountain can be reached by a six-mile toll road. There are extensive facilities for skiing, notably at Stowe, Middlebury, Manchester, and Woodstock.

Vermont contains 25 state forests and 18 state forest parks, with a combined area of about 75,000 acres. All are open to the public, as is Battell Park, a tract of some 10,000 acres at Ripton that is controlled by Middlebury College. Among the many museums and historic buildings that are open to visitors, the following deserve special mention: the Museum of Natural History at Montpelier, containing the Stephen Daye Press, which was the first printing press in North America; Shelburne Village, a reconstructed nineteenth century New England village; the Sheldon Museum (1829), with its early relics of Vermont; the historical museum and art gallery, at Bennington; Old Constitution House, at Windsor, where the Vermont constitution was adopted, 1777; and the Kent Tavern (1835), at Kent Corners, now a country museum.   KENNETH THOMPSON

GOVERNMENT

Constitution. Vermont is governed under the state constitution (1793), as amended. Once every 10 years amendments may be proposed by the state's general assembly. Adoption of an amendment requires the approval of two thirds of the senate and a majority of the house of representatives, of a majority of all members of each house of the next general assembly, and of a majority of the electors. The constitution does not provide for the calling of a constitutional convention.

Voting. Any citizen of the United States, 21 years of age and over, may vote after residence for one year in the state and for three months in the precinct. Vermont sends one congressman to the U.S. House of Representatives.

The General Assembly consists of a senate of 30 members and a house of representatives of 246 members, all elected biennially. The senators are apportioned among the 14 counties according to population, with a minimum of one member per county. Each township elects one representative. Regular sessions of the general assembly are held biennially, beginning in January of odd-numbered years.

The Executive Officials of Vermont—the governor, lieutenant governor, secretary of state, attorney general, treasurer, and auditor—are elected to two-year terms. The governor can veto legislation, but his veto may be overridden by a two-thirds vote of the members present in each house of the general assembly.

Judicial Authority is vested in a supreme court of five justices elected by the general assembly for two-year terms, in six superior judges who preside over the county courts, also elected by the general assembly for two-year terms; in assistant judges, of which two are elected by the freemen of each county to compose a county court with the superior judge; in probate courts; and in justices of the peace.

HISTORY

Exploration and Settlement. The first European known to have entered the Vermont region was the French explorer, Samuel de Champlain, who discovered the lake named for him, 1609, and, at a site on the west bank of the narrows between Crown Point and Ticonderoga, helped the Algonquian Indians to gain a victory over the Iroquois. The first attempted settlement within the borders of modern Vermont was made, ?1666, by the French, who built a fort and shrine to Ste Anne on Isle La Motte in Lake Champlain; the effort was soon abandoned, however. During King William's War, 1689-97, a party of Englishmen from Albany established an outpost at what was later to become Chimney Point, but the fort was abandoned when the emergency ended.

The first permanent settlement was that at Fort Dummer, built by Massachusetts settlers, 1724, near where Brattleboro was later to be founded. Among other early eighteenth century settlements established in and to the west of this region were Chimney Point Stockade, Fort St. Frederick by the French (renamed Crown Point by the British), Bennington,

VERMONT

The Bennington Battle Monument commemorates the victory of American militiamen led by Gen. John Stark over the British forces commanded by Lt. Col. Friedrich Baum.

The state Capitol building in Montpelier, first constructed in 1836, was rebuilt in 1857 after the original structure was destroyed by fire.

Many visitors from all parts of the world have admired scenes such as this one of the Vermont countryside during the brilliant spectacle of a typical New England fall.

Skiing, one of the nation's favorite winter sports, is enjoyed near Stowe at the ski development on Mount Mansfield, the highest peak in the Green Mountains.

At Pres. Warren Harding's sudden death, Calvin Coolidge became U.S. President at his Plymouth home, now a historic landmark.

Fort Carillon (renamed Ticonderoga by the British), Fort William Henry, Fort Edward, Alburg, Swanton, and Colchester. Some of these places were later to be part of New York. During the French and Indian War, 1756-63, the French were driven from the region by the British commander in chief in North America, Jeffrey Amherst.

Disputed Territory. Control of the Vermont country was long disputed by the colonies of New Hampshire and New York. Previously, Massachusetts had also asserted a claim to part of the territory, but this claim had been settled, 1740, in favor of New Hampshire. Most of the early settlers held New Hampshire grants, but in 1764 the claim of New York, based on the grant by King Charles II of England to his brother, the Duke of York, 1664, was upheld by the crown. New York thereupon began making grants in the territory, some of which conflicted with grants previously made by New Hampshire. There was some armed conflict, especially at Bennington, and soon an appeal was made directly to the British government, which issued an injunction against New York, restraining that colony's governor from making further grants until the issue was settled. When this order was disregarded, settlers with New Hampshire grants organized militia to drive out New Yorkers. See GREEN MOUNTAIN BOYS.

The Republic of Vermont. The inhabitants of Vermont, as the region came to be known (from the French *vert mont*, green mountain), took an important and early part in the Revolutionary War. The Green Mountain Boys, under Ethan Allen and Benedict Arnold, captured, May 10, 1775, Ticonderoga, which gave George Washington cannon for his projected assault on Boston; and captured Crown Point, May 12, 1775. Vermont men also took part in the victory in the Battle of Bennington, Aug. 16, 1777, which helped to turn the tide against the British invasion of New York, under Gen. John Burgoyne.

During the war, in January, 1777, a convention at Westminster declared the New Hampshire Grants to be the independent state of New Connecticut. At another convention, that at Windsor, July, 1777, the name was changed to Vermont, and the constitution of New York was adopted with slight changes as the fundamental law of the new state. This constitution was notable in that it made slavery illegal and provided for universal manhood suffrage at a time when every other state had some kind of property qualification for voting. The first state elections were held in March, 1778, and within the month a government was inaugurated with Thomas Chittenden as governor.

Neither New York nor New Hampshire recognized the Vermont government, however, and their influence in the Continental Congress was such that Vermont was refused admission to the Union, 1777-91. Belonging neither with the Thirteen States nor with Great Britain, Vermont remained an independent republic, and as such carried out all the functions of a sovereign state. New Hampshire eventually withdrew her opposition to Vermont statehood, and New York surrendered, 1790, its claims in Vermont for $30,000. Finally, on Mar. 4, 1791, Vermont was admitted to the Union as the fourteenth state. A new constitution was adopted, 1793, and Montpelier was made the state capital, 1805, although the statehouse was not completed until 1808.

Early Statehood. During the early years of statehood the population of Vermont increased rapidly, largely through immigration from the crowded states of southern New England, and by 1810 there were more than 200,000 people in the state. This trend came to a halt with the summer of 1816, a season of unusually low temperatures throughout the Northern Hemisphere, when no crops to speak of were harvested in Vermont; there ensued a temporary but large-scale emigration from Vermont to the newly opened areas of the Middle West. The subsequent gradual increase in the population of Vermont largely resulted from immigration from Québec.

During the War of 1812, Vermont was apathetic, even hostile, to the national cause, partly as a result of its common border with Lower Canada (later Québec). Throughout the war there was widespread smuggling of foodstuffs from Vermont to the British army. The state did, however, contribute materially to the U.S. fleet that defeated the British on Lake Champlain, Sept. 11, 1814.

During the 1820's and 1830's the Anti-Masonic party, a movement marked by its opposition to the Democratic-Republican Pres. Andrew Jackson, gained great strength in Vermont. "Anti-Mason" William Adams Palmer was governor of Vermont, 1831-34, and Vermont was the only state in the Union to give its electoral votes to William Wirt, the Anti-Masonic candidate for president in 1832.

Vermont Republicanism. The people of Vermont took a strong stand against the extension of slavery. The state legislature sent resolutions (1837) to the U.S. Senate protesting against the annexation of Texas and against the admission of any additional slave states; and similar resolutions were passed frequently thereafter, and copies were sent to the legislatures of all the other states. When the new Republican party appeared, 1856, opposing the extension of slavery into the territories, it immediately became the strongest political party in Vermont—a position it was to maintain consistently through the sixth decade of the twentieth century.

During the Civil War, more than 34,000 men from Vermont, most of them volunteers, served with Union armed forces. In October, 1864, a small band of Confederate soldiers, dressed in civilian clothing, entered Vermont from Canada and stole more than $200,000 from banks in St. Albans.

Among the natives of Vermont who gained national prominence during the late nineteenth and early twentieth centuries were U.S. Presidents Chester A. Arthur, 1881-85, and Calvin Coolidge, 1923-29; Vice-President Levi P. Morton, 1889-93; Adm. George Dewey, who defeated the Spanish fleet in Manila Bay, May 1, 1898; and the social philosopher John Dewey (1859-1952).

Twentieth Century Developments were marked by an increase in business and industry. Vermont became the chief source of dairy products for metropolitan Boston; and businesses associated with outdoor recreation—skiing especially—expanded greatly after World War I.

In political affairs on both state and national levels, the Republican party continued to be dominant in Vermont, and in the 1912 and 1936 national elections Vermont (with Utah and Maine, respectively) was one of two states to cast its electoral vote for the Republican nominee for president. During the 1950's, however, the Democratic party became increasingly influential. William H. Meyer, elected to the U.S. House of Representatives, 1958, was the first Vermont Democrat to be elected to Congress in more than 100 years.

BIBLIOG.–American Guide Series, *Vermont: A Guide to the Green Mountain State* (1941); William Brewster, *Fourteenth Commonwealths: Vermont and the States That Failed* (1960); Herbert W. Congdon, *Old Vermont Houses* (1946); Charles E. Crane, *Let Me Show You Vermont* (1937), *Winter in Vermont* (1941); Walter H. Crockett, *Vermont, the Green Mountain State* (1923); Dorothea F. C. Fisher, *Vermont Tradition: The Biography of an Outlook on Life* (1953); William R. Folsom, *Vermonters in Battle, and Other Papers* (1954); Walter Hard and Margaret Hard, *This Is Vermont* (1936); Walter Hard, Jr., *Vermont Guide* (1958); Ralph N. Hill, *Winooski: Heartway of Vermont* (Rivers of America Ser.) (1949), *Contrary Country* (1950), *Yankee Kingdom: Vermont and New Hampshire* (1960); Keith W. Jennison, *Green Mountains and Rock Ribs* (1954), *Vermont Is Where You Find It* (1959); Matt B. Jones, *Vermont in the Making, 1750–1777* (1939); Wallace E. Lamb, *Lake Champlain and Lake George Valleys*, 3 vols. (1940); William S. Lee, *Green Mountains of Vermont* (1955); David M. Ludlum, *Social Ferment in Vermont, 1791–1850* (1939); June B. Mussey, *Vermont Heritage:*

VERMONT

This view of the Vermont countryside, taken from Mill Hill near Northfield, is typical of the scenic spots in Vermont which remain unspoiled by modern progress.

This view of the ski development on Mount Mansfield shows the numerous downhill trails and slopes as irregular white lines and chair and T-bar lifts as straight thin lines.

Because of the nearness of large city markets, small farms such as this one near Mount Mansfield often specialize in dairy production, the state's major agricultural industry.

Visitors observe operations at the granite quarry in Barre, Vt., which supplied the granite for the state Capitol building constructed at Montpelier in 1836.

Around 200 covered bridges similar to this one near Plainfield still exist as an essential part of Vermont's transportation system, and also as a strong tourist attraction.

Picture Story (1947); Earle W. Newton, *Vermont Story: A History of the People of the Green Mountain State* (1949); Wallace Nutting, *Vermont Beautiful* (1936); Vrest Orton, ed., *And So Goes Vermont: A Picture Book of Vermont As It Is* (1937); Lewis D. Stilwell, *Migration from Vermont* (1948); Charles M. Thompson, *Independent Vermont* (1942); Frederic F. Van de Water, *Reluctant Republic, 1724–1791* (1941); Vermont Life (Periodical), *Treasury of Vermont Life* (1956); Viola C. White, *Vermont Diary* (1956); James B. Wilber, *Ira Allen, Founder of Vermont, 1751–1814*, 2 vols. (1928); William J. Wilgus, *Role of Transportation in the Development of Vermont* (1945); Chilton Williamson, *Vermont in Quandary: 1763–1825* (1949).

VERMONT, UNIVERSITY OF AND STATE AGRICULTURAL COLLEGE, a public, coeducational institution of higher learning located in Burlington, Vt. The university was formed, 1865, through the amalgamation of the University of Vermont, a private institution chartered in 1791, and the Vermont Agricultural College, a state institution chartered in 1864.

The school comprises the following divisions: arts and sciences, technology, civil engineering, medicine, education and nursing, and dental hygiene. Selected premedical students, after completing their junior year, are offered a two-year integrated program of courses in both the college of medicine and the college of arts and sciences, before entering their second year of medical study. The university summer program includes an economics course given in the financial district of New York City, the Warren R. Austin Institute in World Understanding, and the Summer Music Institute for high school students.

Among the library's special collections are the George P. Marsh Humanities Library, the Howard-Hawkins Civil War Collection, materials on Vermont, and materials and works of Dorothy Canfield Fisher. Experiment station bulletins are issued periodically, and an alumni magazine is issued quarterly. See COLLEGES AND UNIVERSITIES.

VERMOUTH, a fortified white wine infused with flavoring ingredients such as herbs, barks, roots, seeds, and spices. The two major types of vermouth are French and Italian. French vermouth, produced in the area around Marseilles, is lighter in color, longer aged, and drier than the Italian. Italian vermouth, prepared chiefly in the area around Turin, in northern Italy, usually has a base of muscatel, and is a sweet wine with a musky aroma. Both may be drunk without any additives as an apéritif, but in the United States are more commonly mixed with other beverages to form such cocktails as the Martini and the Manhattan.

VERNAL, city, NE Utah, seat of Uintah County; near the Green River; on U.S. highway 40, 130 miles E of Salt Lake City. The city is a trade and processing center for an area in which there are livestock ranches, coal mines, and oil wells. Leather goods, dairy products, lumber products, and flour are manufactured. Vernal was settled late in the 1870's, and was known as Ashley Center until the 1890's. Pop. (1960) 3,655.

VERNE, JULES, 1828-1905, French novelist, was born in Nantes, studied law in Paris, but began writing for the stage late in the 1840's. In conjunction with Michel Carré, he wrote librettos for two operettas but his work in this vein attained little note. In time, however, he began writing scientific romances (see SCIENCE FICTION), in which his remarkable insight into the trend of current scientific invention was well displayed. The enormously successful, *Five Weeks in a Balloon* (1863), was the first of a long series of imaginative tales exploiting popular interest in the actual and potential achievements of modern science. Many of his imaginary creations, such as the submarine, were later realized. Among Verne's best-known works are *A Voyage to the Center of the Earth* (1864); *From the Earth to the Moon* (1865); *Twenty Thousand Leagues Under the Sea* (1869); *The Mysterious Island* (1872); *Around the World in Eighty Days* (1873),

and *Michael Strogoff* (1876). The adaptations of *Around the World in Eighty Days* and *Michael Strogoff* proved the most successful of Verne's dramas. Verne was a member of the Legion of Honor and several of his works were noted by the French Academy.

VERNER, KARL ADOLPH, 1846–96, Danish philologist, the discoverer of Verner's Law, was born in Aarhus, Jutland. After finishing his studies in Copenhagen, he spent seven years in his father's native country, Germany, as a librarian in Halle. From 1883, however, he lived in Denmark as a teacher of the Slavic languages at the University of Copenhagen. Shy by nature, Verner published little, and made known his discoveries almost accidentally during conversations with other scholars. He did, however, publish an article (*Eine Ausnahme der ersten Lautverschiebung*, 1875) that was to immortalize his name, since it contained Verner's Law, the purpose of which was to account for certain apparent exceptions to Grimm's law. Verner's law says that the position of an accent in pre-Germanic Indo-European influenced the later transformation of consonants as described in Grimm's law. Verner's discovery strengthened the position of a new school of linguistics which proclaimed that linguistic "laws" brook no exceptions. See GRIMM'S LAW.   EUGEN ROSENSTOCK-HUESSY

VERNET, JOSEPH, 1714–1789, French landscape and seascape painter, was born in Avignon, and studied under his father, a coach painter. Impressed by the sea at Marseilles, Joseph studied marine painting under Fergioni in Rome and lived in that city for 20 years, painting unpretentious scenes such as *The Ponto Rotte*, distinguished for its rendering of southern light. The French director of public buildings commissioned him, 1758, to paint a series of views of principal French seaports; it is for the resulting skillfully rendered harbor views that Vernet is principally known. Vernet took 10 years to make wash drawings and take notes for the project, and the paintings suffer from this over-attention to detail, which served to diminish the paintings' quality of immediacy.

Antoine Charles Vernet, called Carle, 1758–1836, French painter and lithographer, studied first with his father Joseph Vernet, winning important honors at an early age. He then went to Rome where, after a period of youthful dissipation, he threatened to reform and become a monk; the father hastily recalled him to France. Carle Vernet's first important work, *The Triumph of Paulus Emilius*, broke with reigning tradition, but won him admission to the academy. After a period of inactivity caused by the French Revolution he turned to painting heroic military subjects such as the *Battle of Marengo* and *Morning at Austerlitz*, for which Napoleon I awarded him the Legion of Honor. But posterity most honors Carle Vernet as a lithographer: his lithographed hunting scenes, race pictures, and caricatures were very popular in their own time and paved the way for future masters of the art.

Emile Jean Horace Vernet, known as Horace, 1789–1863, was born in Paris, the son of Carle Vernet, under whose tutelage he developed his remarkable talent for drawing at an early age. As was his father, Horace was an ardent Bonapartist, and after Napoleon I's downfall, father and son found it expedient to leave France. Soon after returning to Paris from Rome, Horace Vernet sent *Defence of the Barrier of Clichy* to the Salon, where it was rejected, 1822; in defiance, he gave his own exhibition, which proved a great success. He was commissioned, 1824, to paint the portrait of Charles X, and was head of the French Academy in Rome, 1828–33, resigning to go to Algiers with the French army to paint. Visiting Russia, 1842, he painted the Czar and Czarina. In 1855 the French Exhibition devoted an entire gallery to Horace Vernet's famous works. Viewed in retrospect, Vernet's paintings were admirable in their size, their scope, and their dashing execution.

MARTIN GROSZ

VERNIS MARTIN, a lacquer in imitation of Chinese work, made by the brothers Martin, French furniture makers of the eighteenth century. Oriental lacquered work became very popular in France soon after the Dutch established trade with China. Though a great many articles in the Oriental ware were imported, a larger part was made in France by the Martins, who were given a monopoly by the king in 1730. The famous lacquer of transparent green used by them was a skillful adaptation of existing varnishes; and while not equal to the real Oriental lacquer, exhibits the finest work in Europe.

VERNON, EDWARD, known as Old Grog, 1684–1757, English admiral, was born in Westminster. In 1739 he was given command of an expedition against the Spanish possessions in South America, and especially against Porto-Bello, which he captured with only a small squadron. The eldest brother of George Washington, Lawrence, took part in Vernon's later expedition against Cartagena, and named his estate Mount Vernon in the latter's honor. Vernon was dismissed from the service, 1746, on a charge of having published official letters. He was an officer of bravery and ability, but was temperamental and intolerant. It was Vernon who introduced into the British navy the practice of serving out rum mixed with water instead of undiluted rum; the mixture became known as "grog," Vernon having earlier gained the nickname Old Grog from his habit of wearing a grogram coat.

VERNON, town, NW Alabama, seat of Lamar County; 80 miles WNW of Birmingham. Vernon is a trade center for an area in which cotton, corn, potatoes, and livestock are raised. Pop. (1960) 1,492.

VERNON, town, SE Indiana, seat of Jennings County; on the Pennsylvania Railroad; 60 miles SSE of Indianapolis. The town is in an area in which corn, wheat, and livestock are raised. Muscatatuck State Park is to the west. Pop. (1960) 461.

VERNON, city, N Texas, seat of Wilbarger County; near the Red River; on the Fort Worth and Denver and the Frisco railroads, and on U.S. highways 70, 183, 282, and 287; 170 miles NW of Dallas. The city is a trade and processing center for an area in which cotton, wheat, vegetables, and livestock are raised. It is a supply center for oil and gas wells in the area. Meat products, sporting goods, cottonseed products, mattresses, flour, and metal products are manufactured. Vernon was founded, 1880, incorporated, 1901, and chartered a city in 1914. The famous jazz musician Jack Teagarden was born in Vernon. Pop. (1960) 12,141.

VERNON, city, Canada, S British Columbia; on the Canadian National and the Canadian Pacific railways; near the northeast shore of Okanagan Lake; 180 miles ENE of Vancouver. The city is a processing center and shipping point for a diversified and irrigated agricultural area. Apples are the leading crop. Vernon, situated in a lake region, is a popular summer resort. The first settlement was known as Priest's Valley when a postoffice was established there in 1884; it was later called Forge Valley and Centerville; and in 1887 the name was changed to Vernon. Pop. (1956) 8,998.

VERNY. See ALMA-ATA.

VERO BEACH, city, E Florida, seat of Indian River County; on the Indian River, the Florida East Coast Railway, and U.S. highway 1; 130 miles N of Miami. The city is a shipping point for fruit and vegetables grown in the area. It is a winter resort. A major point of interest is McKee Jungle Gardens, 3 miles south. The city was founded late in the 1880's, incorporated as Vero, 1919, and renamed Vero Beach in 1925. Pop. (1960) 8,849.

VEROCCHIO, ANDREA DEL, 1435–88, Italian sculptor, goldsmith, architect and painter, was born Andrea Cioni di Michele in Florence. Many of Verocchio's (or Verrocchio's) sculptures have survived, but there are only two paintings that can positively be ascribed to him. Notable among his sculptures are the bronze *Christ* and *St. Thomas,* for the Orsanmichele Church, Florence. In 1467 he was commissioned to complete the cathedral dome planned by Filippo Brunelleschi. Subsequently Verocchio made the monument of Giovanni and Piero de' Medici, notable for its organic harmony and rhythmic form, and his equally famous *David,* a work full of vibrant life. The Venetians then commissioned him to do the Colleoni Monument, which proved to be one of the two great equestrian statues of the Renaissance; he worked on it from 1481 until his death. A certain agreeable harshness, extreme forcibleness, and superb craftmanship are characteristic of his sculptures. He concentrated on statuesque postures based on naturalistic, incisive drawing.

Of Verocchio's career as a painter little is known, but it is well established that he entrusted much of the work on his paintings to assistants, among whom were Leonardo da Vinci, Il Perugino, Ghirlandaio, Lorenzo di Credi, and probably Sandro Botticelli. The two works definitely attributed to Verocchio are a Madonna (Berlin) and a Baptism (Uffizi Gallery, Florence), the latter a transitional picture prefiguring the High Renaissance; one of its angels, it may be noted, is obviously from the hand of Leonardo.

Verocchio's mastery of plastic values and his rough strength made him the leading artistic figure in fifteenth century Florence and his studio the most famous in that city.   ANTHONY KERRIGAN

VEROIA, or Verria, city, N Greece, in Macedonia, capital of Imathía Province, 40 miles W of Salonika. The city is situated on a plain at the foot of Mount Vérmion. Veroia is a trade and processing center for a region in which wheat, vegetables, and fruit are grown. Textiles are manufactured. Low-grade coal is mined in the locality. The city was formerly called Beroea, or Berea. St. Paul preached there (Acts 17:10). Pop. (1951) 21,844.

VERONA, borough, NE New Jersey, Essex County; on the Erie Railroad; 8 miles NW of Newark. Oil-well equipment, brushes, dairy products, desk calendars, and plastic products are manufactured. Verona was incorporated in 1907. Pop. (1960) 13,782.

VERONA, province, N Italy, in Veneto Region, bounded by the provinces of Trento on the N, Vicenza on the E, Padua and Rovigo on the SE, Mantua on the SW, and Brescia on the NW; area 1,196 sq. mi.; pop. (1958) 661,814. The northwestern boundary is formed by the Alpine Lake Garda; the Adige River crosses the province. The northern section of the plain lies in the Alpine foothills and the southern part lies in the Po River plain. Wheat, corn, rice wine, hemp, sugar beets, and fruits are grown in the province. Silk culture is also carried on. The province has tanneries, distilleries, flour mills, sawmills, and brick and tile works as well as manufactures of textiles and machinery. The capital and principal town is Verona.

VERONA, city, NE Italy, in Veneto Region, capital of the province of Verona, on the Adige River, 65 miles W of Venice. Verona, located on the Po Plain at the foot of Mount Lessini, is a rail and road junction. It is an important trading center and has manufactures of hats, silk, and other textiles, pianos, paper, flour, soap, and candles. Verona is noted for its fine monuments, and Roman ruins. The city is rich in palaces of sculptured marble, some with frescoed walls dating back to the thirteenth century. The most notable is the Palazzo del Consiglio. There are numerous statues, towers, and elaborate tombs. The Gothic cathedral dates from the twelfth century and has a fine *Assumption* by Titian. Also notable is the Romanesque church of San Zeno Maggiore.

Verona was founded by the Celts at least a century before the Christian Era. It became a Roman colony under the name of Augusta in 89 B.C. Verona was the birthplace of the poet Gaius Valerius Catullus. In the later empire it was often the residence of the court. The Roman amphitheater remains in almost perfect condition, and there are also remains of a theater, an ancient gate, and the Wall of Gallienus, erected A.D. 265. Verona at one time led Italy in art, and was the home of a school of painting whose importance was reflected in the name of Paolo Veronese. Pop. (1958) 203,184.

VERONA, CONGRESS OF, the last of the great meetings held in accordance with the terms of the Treaty of Paris (1815), in which France, Austria, Great Britain, Russia, and Prussia agreed to hold meetings at fixed intervals to discuss matters of common interest (see PARIS, TREATIES OF). The representatives of these countries met at the Venetian city Verona, Oct. 20, 1822, to discuss the possibility of French military intervention in Spain in an effort to protect the despotic regime of Ferdinand VII, then threatened by revolution. Russia, Prussia, and Austria declared their readiness to support France, but Great Britain, knowing that Ferdinand was planning to reconquer Spain's former colonies in the Americas, firmly opposed intervention. With the other powers persisting in their position, the British representative Arthur Wellesley, 1st duke of Wellington, refused to take any further part in the congress, and thereby destroyed the possibility of international co-operation. In due course French forces invaded Spain, 1823, and crushed the revolution.

VERONESE, PAOLO, 1528–88, Italian painter and muralist of the High Renaissance, was born Paolo Cagliari or Caliari in Verona, the son of a stone carver, who trained him in this craft. Paolo's first important commission as a painter was executed at Mantua, but from 1555 at the latest he remained in Venice, where a painting of a *Coronation of the Virgin* and other subjects for the Convent of St. Sebastian were among his earliest commissions. To the golden tonalities of the Venetian painters he added the silver tonalities of the north Italian schools. In 1556 he was chosen to decorate the library of St. Mark's.

One of his most characteristic works, *The Marriage at Cana* (Louvre, Paris), is a sumptuous rendition of a religious theme, with little or no religiosity about it. This truly great picture is a study of Venetian magnificence and pomp. It contains some 120 full figures and heads, many of them those of important persons of the time; elaborate architecture sets the scene, with classic columns standing at right angles to the painting and a balustrade running parallel to lend the needed stateliness; brocades blossom everywhere, and the light and shade is rich. An orchestra of artists provides incidental music, with Titian at the double bass, Tintoretto at the cello, Jacopo Bassano playing flute, and Veronese himself at the viola. As are most of his paintings, this work is a masterpiece of technique, perspective, color, composition, and external splendor; also characteristic, however, is its lack of spiritual depth. In 1573, indeed, some 10 years after *The Marriage at Cana*, Veronese was called before the Inquisition to answer charges of blasphemy: he had introduced too many purely decorative elements in a painting of *The Feast of Levi.* He was forced to paint out numerous dwarfs, German mercenaries, and the like, until little was left of the picture except what is now to be seen in the Venetian Academy. After a fire destroyed part of the Doges' Palace, Veronese took a major part in decorating the restored building.

Among other well known works of Veronese are the *Feast in the House of Simon* (Louvre), *Leda and the Swan* (London), and *Death of Adonis* (London). Veronese's use of cool, clear color harmonies greatly influenced later European painting.

ANTHONY KERRIGAN

VERONICA, SAINT, a woman of Jerusalem who is said to have followed Jesus on His way to the Crucifixion, to have taken pity on Him, and to have wiped the sweat from His face with her handkerchief. Tradition has it that the cloth retained the imprint of the Holy Face. During the twelfth century, an image at Rome began to be identified with the legendary one, but Milan and other cities also claimed to possess it. According to French tradition, Veronica was married to Zaccheus, and went with him to Quiercy, where he became a hermit. In the Bordeaux district, Veronica is alleged to have brought relics of the Virgin to Sonlac, where she died and was buried. The name Veronica also appears to have been that of the portrait itself (*vera icon,* true image). St. Veronica's feast is celebrated February 4.

VERRAZANO, GIOVANNI DA, 1480?–?1527, Italian explorer of North America, was born near Florence, but entered the service of France while in his twenties. He is believed to have taken part in raids on the Spanish Indies and to have captured, 1522, two treasure ships that Hernan Cortés had sent to Spain from Mexico. Francis I having put him in charge of an American expedition, 1523, Verrazano arrived in the vicinity of the North Carolina coast, 1524, and explored as far north as Newfoundland, discovering Manhattan Island, the Hudson River, and touching Narrangansett Bay. He returned to France, July, 1524, and gave an account of his discoveries to the French king—the first known description of the North American coast. A French pirate hanged by the Spanish, ?1527, is believed to have been Verrazano, but his fate is not definitely known.

VERRES, GAIUS, 120?–43 B.C., Roman public official, was the son of a Roman senator. When Lucius Cornelius Sulla became dictator, 82 B.C., Verres acquired the post of proquaestor to Cornelius Dolabella, the praetor of Cilicia, 80–79 B.C., and became the governor of Sicily, 73–71 B.C. His subjects protested to Roman authorities about his notorious misgovernment, and Verres was brought to trial by Marcus Tullius Cicero, 70 B.C. His defense counsel, Quintus Hortensius, could not refute Cicero's brilliant oration, and Verres fled to Massilia before the expiration of the nine days required for prosecution under Roman law. In Massilia he lived a life of luxury on the wealth he had accumulated in Sicily. Ultimately, however, he was proscribed and executed at the order of Marcus Antonius who, it is thought, had designs on his wealth.

VERRI, PIETRO, CONTE, 1728–97, Italian economist and writer, was born in Milan. He held a number of important positions in the Milanese government and initiated many administrative reforms. He founded, 1761, the Società dei Pugni, an academy of Milanese nobles dedicated to the principles of the French *Philosophes* (see ENCYCLOPEDISTS), and directed *Il Caffè,* its polemical journal. Among his works are *Sulle leggi vincolanti il commercio dei grani* (1769), *Sull' economia politica* (1771), *Storia di Milano* (2 vols., 1783–97), and *Discorso sull' indole del piacere e del dolore* (1773).

VERRUCA, or wart, a small, round thickening and hardening of the skin, usually found on the fingers. The condition is caused by viruses that invade the epithelial cells of the skin and cause these cells to swell and multiply. Age appears to influence the development and type of wart found. The common wart, or verucca vulgaris, is normally a disease of adolescence and early adulthood, growing from the cells found in the fingers, palm, and forearm. The growths are frequently found in groups, since the virus may infect a wide area of skin. Plantar warts, which develop in the vicinity of a sensory nerve ending, become very painful because of the pressure that they exert on these nerve endings. Another type of wart is the senile wart, or verruca senilis. These growths are found in large numbers on the exposed parts of the body of some people who are past their middle age. The warts are small and often darkly pigmented. They have a soft, greasy surface and because of their appearance are often mistaken for basal cell carcinomas; however, they do not tend to become malignant. The senile wart seems to be inaptly named, since the growth does not necessarily develop in senile individuals but may occur in others as well.

Treatment and Removal. Warts are generally removed from the skin because of their unsightly appearance. Although a number of home remedies are used to eradicate warts, the only effective method requires surgery. Often a person will trim the wart with a knife or other sharp tool and unwittingly irritate the skin area, allowing malignant growths to develop. Radiation, even though it could effectively destroy warts, is not usually suggested as a remedy because tissue damage may result. The patient is usually given local anesthesia for the removal of a wart. If much skin is removed in an attempt to destroy a number of warts, skin is grafted into the area.

VERRUGA, also called bartonellosis and Carrión's disease, is a bacterial disease that is unique in that it occurs in two forms, each displaying symptoms different from those of the other. The initial infection is caused by the microorganism, *Bartonella bacilliformis*, and is characterized by a sudden fever that may range to 104°F, combined with muscle and joint pains, nausea, vomiting, diarrhea, headache, and insomnia. This form of the disease is characterized by anemia. The condition may persist for from one to three weeks and is often fatal. The next phase, or the verruga Peruviana form, may follow the anemic state, but it is possible for a patient to have this form of the disease without exhibiting symptoms of the anemic form. In the case of verruga Peruviana, single or numerous lumps form under the skin in the area of the head and limbs. This form is not fatal and usually subsides within several weeks. The disease is treated most effectively with the antibiotic chloramphenicol (see ANTIBIOTICS).

Verruga is usually found in the valley of the Andes Mountains, primarily in Peru. It has been known to occur in Bolivia, Colombia, and Ecuador, however. It is probably transmitted by sandflies, although the vectors in Colombia are thought to be lice and ticks.

VERSAILLES, town, SE Indiana, seat of Ripley County; on U.S. highways 50 and 421; 65 miles SE of Indianapolis. The town is a trade and processing center for an area in which corn, wheat, tobacco, livestock, and poultry are raised. Wood products are manufactured. Limestone is quarried in the vicinity. Versailles was founded in 1818. Pop. (1960) 1,158.

VERSAILLES, city, central Kentucky, seat of Woodford County; on the Southern Railway and U.S. highways 60 and 62; 13 miles W of Lexington. Versailles has flour and feed mills. Clothing is manufactured. Tobacco, cattle, and horses are raised in the vicinity. Versailles was founded in 1792. Pop. (1960) 4,060.

VERSAILLES, city, central Missouri, seat of Morgan County; on the Rock Island Railroad; 33 miles WSW of Jefferson City. The city is a resort center north of Lake of the Ozarks, and is a trade center for an area of coal mines and lumbering. Versailles was founded in the 1830's. Pop. (1960) 2,047.

VERSAILLES, town, N France, capital of the department of Seine-et-Oise, 11 miles WSW of Paris, of which it is a residential suburb. Versailles is known chiefly for its palace designed by Louis Le Vau, architect to Louis XIV, and completed by Jules Hardouin-Mansart. Among the features of the palace are a Hall of Mirrors, the Royal Apartments, and a miniature opera house. The rooms are hung with well known paintings and contain valuable furniture. The formal gardens, planned by André Le Nôtre for Louis XIV contain magnificent fountains, statuary, wooded groves, and ponds. In the original park are two chateaux: the Grand Trianon, a pink marble palace built for Louis, and the Petit Trianon, given to Marie Antoinette by Louis XVI. Versailles was the residence of the French kings and the center of the French court for more than a century. The treaties ending the American Revolution and World War I were signed in Versailles, and the German Empire was proclaimed from the palace in 1871. Pop. (1954) 84,445.

VERSAILLES, TREATY OF, the peace treaty that ended World War I, was signed at Versailles, France, June 28, 1919, by representatives of the German Weimar Republic and of the Allied powers, headed by France, Great Britain, Italy, and the United States. The treaty had been drawn up by the Peace Congress, which had begun its sessions in the Hall of Mirrors at Versailles, on Jan. 18, 1919, the 48th anniversary of the proclamation of the German Empire in the same place during the Franco-Prussian War, 1870–71.

The Peace Congress, as such, met rarely; most of the work was done by special committees of diplomats and experts, whose reports were passed on to the Congress when it did meet. Most of the decisions were made by the representatives of the "Big Four," that is, French Premier Georges Clemenceau, British Prime Minister David Lloyd George, Italian Prime Minister Vittorio Emanuele Orlando, and U.S. Pres. Woodrow Wilson. The draft of the treaty, as approved by the "Big Four," was ratified by the whole Congress on May 6, 1919. German plenipotentiaries who joined the Congress to discuss the terms, May 7, denounced the treaty as too severe and proposed various amendments. These were rejected by the Allied leaders, and the German government, faced with a severe domestic crisis, was left no alternative but to instruct its delegates to accept the terms.

The Terms of the Treaty provided that Germany would cede Alsace-Lorraine to France, Eupen and Malmédy to Belgium, Memel to Lithuania, and Posen and a strip of West Prussia to Poland. The sovereignty of certain other former German territories was to be decided by plebiscite; the coal-rich, industrial Saar was to be administered by France for 15 years (see SAAR); Germany west of the Rhine River was to be occupied by Allied troops for 15 years, and forever demilitarized; Danzig was to become a free city. All German colonial possessions were to be given up, most of them to become mandates under the League of Nations. In addition, Germany was required to denounce the treaties of Brest-Litovsk and Bucharest, which she had dictated to Russia and Rumania respectively. The German army was limited to no more than 100,000 men; the navy, stripped of its submarines, was limited to six battleships, six light cruisers, and miscellaneous smaller craft. Germany was also made to promise to abolish conscription, to raze her western fortifications, and to abandon military and naval aviation. Furthermore, Germany had to accept responsibility for the war that had occurred and to agree to make financial reparation, the initial payment to be $5 billion—with the total amount left to be decided later. The treaty provided for a League of Nations, Permanent Court of International Justice, and an International Labor Organization. The United States Senate refused to ratify the treaty and that nation did not become a party to it. See UNITED STATES HISTORY, *The Last Peace*.

After the signing of the treaty with Germany, the Allies concluded treaties with the other Central Powers: St. Germain, with Austria; Trianon with Hungary; Neuilly, with Bulgaria; and Sèvres, with Turkey. See ST. GERMAIN, TREATY OF; NEUILLY, TREATY OF; SÈVRES, TREATY OF; TRIANON, TREATY OF.

Failure. From the outset Germans generally protested that the Treaty of Versailles was unduly severe, and this view subsequently was taken up by many groups outside of Germany as well. Pro-German and pacifist groups that had opposed the war from the beginning, and other persons whose feelings of hostility toward Germany had diminished with the passage of time, advocated the reduction or cancellation of reparations, and the return of German colonies.

Whatever the defects of the treaty, it had become almost inoperative by the outbreak of World War II, Sept. 1, 1939. Indeed, it had failed completely in that it did not prevent war. The official German view, promulgated by the National Socialist German Workers' (Nazi) party was that the treaty itself was unjust to Germany, and that its terms should be disregarded (see NATIONAL SOCIALISM). In 1931 Germany reneged on payment of reparations. After the Nazis had come to power, 1933, the German government openly denounced the treaty and where possible violated its terms—reintroducing conscription, re-occupying the Rhineland with troops, building military and naval aircraft, and annexing Austria—with no more than vocal opposition from the former Allied powers.

Opinions outside of Germany as to the fairness or unfairness of the treaty tended to vary with changes in the international situation. During World War II, the official U.S. point of view was that the treaty, if defective at all, had erred in being too lenient, and that World War II might never have occurred if Germany had been kept in its place. Most historians, able to view the situation more objectively, continued to be of the opinion that the treaty was in many respects unfair in its details, but perhaps excusably so, considering all of the circumstances; yet inexcusably unfair (and exceedingly unwise, if the intention of the treaty actually was to make and assure peace) in insisting that the Germans accept full war guilt. This provision was insisted upon by the representatives of France and Great Britain, yet there is little question but that each of these nations was as much responsible for the war as Germany was, and that the two together shared the greater part of the blame. See GERMANY, The Empire and the Republic, *The Republic, the Rise of Hitler, The Nazi Government.*

VERSIFICATION. See PROSODY.

VERTEBRATE, an animal with a vertebral column, or backbone. Vertebrates are classified in the subphylum Vertebrata and are members of the phylum Chordata. All chordates at some time in their lives possess a supporting rod known as the notochord, a dorsal tubular nervous system, and functional or embryonic gill slits in the pharynx.

In fishes and some amphibians these gill slits separate the gills, while in other vertebrates the arches that form between the gill slits further develop into parts of the skeleton and respiratory system. In vertebrates the notochord is replaced either entirely or partially by a vertebral column which may consist of bone or cartilage. In addition to these general chordate characteristics, the vertebrates have many other distinguishing features. Most vertebrates are bilaterally symmetrical, and metamerism, or a series of fairly similar segments, though not pronounced in higher forms, is present. The vertebrate body is divided into head, trunk, and tail regions, the head containing a cartilaginous or bony skull. The nervous system is differentiated into a brain, spinal cord, and a peripheral system; sense organs are highly specialized. The vertebrate animal breathes by means of lungs, gills, or both, and excretion is accomplished through the kidneys. The vertebrate circulatory system is a closed system of vessels through which blood is pumped by the muscular heart; hemoglobin, an oxygen-carrying protein, is present in the red blood corpuscles. The tubular digestive system is divided into a number of parts, such specialization being greatly developed in the higher vertebrates. The body cavity, or coelom, is also separated into several cavities. The form and arrangement of the parts of the appendages are usually paired. The vertebrate body is covered with skin which supplies hair, scales, feathers, horns, glands, and similar structures.

There are seven classes of living vertebrates: class Cyclostomata, including the lampreys and hagfishes; class Chondrichthyes, the sharks, rays, and chimaeras; class Osteichthyes, the bony fishes; class Amphibia, the salamanders, frogs, and toads; class Reptilia, the lizards, snakes, tortoises and turtles, and crocodiles; class Aves, the birds; and class Mammalia, the mammals.

VERTIGO, a giddiness or dizziness. It is the whirling sensation and the inability to maintain balance or equilibrium that one normally experiences following spinning or whirling. There are two types: objective vertigo, in which actually motionless objects appear to move around the individual affected; and subjective vertigo, in which, to the individual involved, it appears that his body is moving in relation to the various stationary objects.

The body maintains its equilibrium by means of a complex system of nerve reflexes and co-ordinated muscle movements. The nervous center controlling the muscle equilibrium is located in the cerebellum. Impulses come to this center from the organs of balance in the inner ear and from the eyes, muscles, joints, and skin. Impulses pass from this center to the centers in the cerebral hemispheres in the brain that control movement of muscles. In addition, the nerves from the organs of balance have connection with the nerve centers which control eye movements.

Any disease condition which affects any of the impulse pathways leading to the equilibrium center in the brain may cause vertigo, as for instance a tumor of the auditory nerve. Vertigo may result from the action of toxins, as from alcohol or tobacco. It occurs frequently in motion sickness. Vertigo occurs also in other ear conditions such as middle ear infections, or when an ear is plugged with ear wax. It may be experienced if the ear canal is washed out with hot or cold water.   HERMAN S. WIGODSKY, M.D.

VERTUE, GEORGE, 1684–1756, English antiquary and engraver, was born in London. He studied under Vandergucht and later, working under Sir Godfrey Kneller, achieved fame as an engraver. He became engraver to the Society of Antiquaries, 1717, and issued a set of *Twelve Heads of Poets* (1730). After his death, Vertue's 40 or more volumes of notes on the history of art in England were bought by Horace Walpole, who used them extensively in compiling his *Anecdotes of Painting in England* (1762–71).

VERVAIN. See VERBENA.

VERY, JONES, 1813–80, U.S. poet and transcendentalist, was born in Salem, Mass., was graduated from Harvard University, 1836, and tutored in Greek there for two years while pursuing divinity studies. Soon he was composing religious sonnets that he claimed had been communicated to him by the Holy Ghost, and at the persuasion of friends, he spent a month in an insane asylum, 1838. His *Essays and Poems* (1839) was published under the patronage of Ralph Waldo Emerson, who along with William Ellery Channing and William Cullen Bryant, was extravagant in praise of Very's work. Very was licensed to preach as a Unitarian minister, 1843, and did so occasionally, but he was never placed over a church.

VESALIUS, ANDREAS, 1514–64, Flemish anatomist, the principal founder of modern anatomy, was born in Brussels, and studied medicine at Louvaine, Montpellier, Paris, and Padua. As a teacher of anatomy at the University of Padua, 1537–44, he soon became a center of controversy over his unorthodox teachings. These teachings, which refuted the traditional concepts of human anatomy handed down by Galen, were based not on theory or dogma, but on observations made during the actual dissection of human bodies (see GALEN). Vesalius demonstrated that Galen's anatomical theories, which had been based almost wholly on the study of animals, were untrustworthy when applied to human anatomy. In 1538 Vesalius published his *Tabulae anatomicae sex,* but this shocking work proved to be but a prelude to his epoch-making *De humani corporis fabrica libri septem* (1543), the first exact and comprehensive treatise on human anatomy, and revolutionary both in its text and in its magnificent engravings by a disciple of Titian, Johann Stephan von Kalkar. The book created a furor amongst scholars, and drew venomous criticism from the Galenists, all of whom denied the truth of Vesalius' statements; the *Fabrica* also incurred the extreme displeasure of ecclesiastical authorities, who became alarmed by Vesalius' insistence that man, although a descendant of Adam, did not have a rib less on one side than on the other, as Genesis 2:21 had led people to suppose must be the case. He also exploded the myth that somewhere in the vertebral column there was a *luz*, or "resurrection bone," from which the body was to be reconstructed after death.

Fearful that charges of heresy might be leveled against him, Vesalius left Padua, 1544, and went to Madrid where he became physician-in-ordinary first to Emperor Charles V, and then to his son, Philip II. Vesalius' reputation followed him, however, and new editions of his *Fabrica* continued to appear throughout Europe. He was convicted of heresy and condemned to death by the Inquisition, 1563, but his patron, Philip II, commuted his sentence, and Vesalius undertook a pilgrimage to Jerusalem as an expiation for his scientific sins. On the return voyage his ship was wrecked off the Ionian island of Zante, and he died of exposure shortly thereafter, not quite 50 years of age.

The influence of Vesalius upon medical science was not entirely beneficial. The successes of Vesalius and later anatomists resulted in the domination of medical science by anatomy and surgery; the scientific theories and discoveries of certain other Renaissance medical men were less immediately useful and their significance was not recognized, in some instances, for centuries. See PARACELSUS.

VESEY, DENMARK, 1767–1822, U.S. mulatto slave and insurgent, was born in the West Indies. As the slave and protégé of a Captain Vesey, "Denmark Vesey" was brought by him to Charleston, S.C., where the slave lived for some 20 years until 1800, when he won $1,500 in a lottery. He bought his liberty for $600, and subsequently worked as a carpenter. He accumulated a considerable estate, allegedly had several wives, and numerous children. He deeply resented, however, the fact that his children were classed as slaves because their mothers were slaves. He sought to foment a slave uprising in and around Charleston, 1818–22, but the plot was betrayed by a Negro. In the ensuing trial Vesey defended himself ably, but he and 34 other conspirators were hanged at Charleston.

VESICANT. See COUNTERIRRITANT.

VESPASIAN, full Latin name Titus Flavius Sabinus Vespasianus, A.D. 9–79, Roman emperor from 69 until his death, was born near Reate, in the country of the Sabines. His father, a man of small means, was a minor tax collector; his mother was the sister of a senator. Titus commanded the second legion, under Aulus Plautius, in Britain, and conquered the Isle of Wight, 47. He was made proconsul of Africa under Nero, 63, and became governor of Judaea, 66. He was well liked by his troops, who proclaimed him emperor at Alexandria, 69. Early in his reign, he suppressed revolts in Batavia, Gaul, and Judaea; Vespasian's son, Titus, ended the last Judaean rebellion with the capture of Jerusalem, 70. After Titus' return to Rome in triumph, the Temple of Janus was closed and the Roman world remained at peace for the ensuing nine years of Vespasian's reign. Under Vespasian, the conquest of Britain continued, the kingdom of Commagne was united to Syria, and a Parthian invasion of Syria was repelled; a new Temple of Jupiter and a temple of Peace were erected and construction of the Colosseum was begun; and Roman taxation was reformed. Vespasian had a great military reputation, and he remained a blunt and forthright soldier throughout his life; personal vanity was not among his weaknesses, and he ridiculed all attempts to conceal or disguise his somewhat humble beginnings. He greatly enjoyed conversation and was not without a sense of humor, showing a preference for rather coarse jokes. He was frugal and simple in his personal life, and his good example was said to have had a strong, if only temporary, influence on Roman morals.

VESPERS, from the Latin *vesper* (evening, or Evensong), is the next to the last of the canonical hours in the Anglican, Roman Catholic, and Orthodox Eastern church services. See BREVIARY.

VESPUCCI, AMERIGO, Latinized Americus Vespucius, 1454–1512, Italian navigator whose given name was to be immortalized in the names of two continents (North and South America), was born in Florence, was educated in *pratiche di mercatura* (commercial science), including detailed studies in geography, cosmography, astronomy, and navigation. As a mercantile agent for the Medici family from 1483, he traveled throughout Italy and several times to Spain and France before eventually establishing himself in Seville, 1492, then a center of mercantile activity, where he became an independent and successful outfitter of ships. He was probably one of those who invested money in the second voyage of Christopher Columbus, 1493. Vespucci was a member of the expedition, 1497, of Vicente Yañez Pinzón that discovered the coast of Central America at about the same time that John Cabot was discovering the mainland of the North American Continent. During a voyage of 1499–1500, Vespucci and Alonsode Ojeda skirted the coast of South America. Later he discovered All Saints' Bay, Brazil, 1503. Vespucci became a Spanish citizen, 1505, and was made pilot major of Spain, 1508. He subsequently planned and put into execution numerous schemes for exploring the as yet unknown latitudes.

To the Medici and others Vespucci sent several accounts of his voyages, but the originals are not extant. While numerous alleged copies of them exist, some of them are actually forgeries, and many are confused and contradictory in many respects. Discrepancies in the documented records of his discoveries led many later students to conclude that Vespucci had been a fraud—a pretender to laurels that were rightfully Columbus'. In *English Traits* (1856), for example, Ralph Waldo Emerson wrote: "Strange that broad America must wear the name of a thief! Amerigo Vespucci, the pickle-dealer at Seville, who went out in 1499 . . . a subaltern . . . in an expedition that never sailed, managed in this lying world to supplant Columbus, and baptize half the earth with his own dishonest name!" Later scholarship, however, found this view of Vespucci to be unfair and tended to restore to him something of the reputation he had enjoyed in his own time. The name "America" was first suggested, 1507, but only for the southern continent, by the eminent cosmographer Martin Waldseemüller, who realized that Vespucci had been the first to understand the discovery of the New World as just that.

VESTA, the brightest asteroid and the fourth to be discovered, was found in 1807, and is the only asteroid that is sometimes visible to the unaided eye. It revolves about the sun at a mean distance of 2.36 astronomical units, which is 219,000,000 miles, in a period of 3.63 years. The diameter is 240 miles. At full phase Vesta reflects more than one-fourth the sunlight incident upon it, and the rate at which the amount of reflected light changes with changes of phase indicates that the surface is probably more rough than the moon's.

VESTA, Roman goddess of the hearth, corresponding to the Greek goddess, Hestia. Vesta was worshiped both at the private family hearth and at the central altar of the city or state. Her shrine in the Roman Forum contained the sacred fire that Aeneas was said to have brought from Troy. The fire was tended by six vestal virgins, who were charged with preventing it from going out. If a vestal let the fire go out, she was beaten. It could only be re-lighted by the pontifex maximus through the friction of two pieces of wood. As to the virginity of the fire girls: if a vestal was found guilty of unchastity, she was buried alive. In early republican Rome, the pontifex maximus took the place of the king for sacred occasions, and the vestals were in his charge. The cult of the vestals continued throughout Roman times until pagan worship was abolished by the Christian emperors.

VEST-AGDER, county, S Norway, bounded on the S by the Skagerrak, W by the county of Rogaland, and N and E by the county of Aust Agder; area 2,815 sq. mi.; pop. (1958) 105,826. The county extends from a narrow coastal plain in the south to the Rjuvem Mountains in the north. Much of the area is forested, and lumbering is an important industy. Agriculture is limited to the narrow valleys and the coastal plain, where wheat, oats, and potatoes are grown and dairy cattle are raised. There are several fishing villages along the deeply indented coast. Molybdenum is mined on the Lista Peninsula.

VESTERÅLEN. See LOFOTEN ISLANDS.

VESTFOLD, county, SE Norway, bounded on the S by the Skagerrak, E by the Oslo Fjord, N by the county of Buskerud, and W by the county of Telemark; area 903 sq. mi.; pop. (1958) 168,341. The county occupies the coastal plain at the mouth of the Oslo Fjord, rising inland to heights of 2,000 feet. Vestfold is one of the smallest and most thickly populated counties of the country. It was formerly known as Jarlsberg-Larvik. Zinc is mined. Oats, potatoes, and hay are the principal crops and dairying is important. Larvik, Sandelfjord, and Tönsberg are ports. Tönsberg is the capital.

VESTMENT, a special garment worn by a person officiating at religious services. The use of certain specific vestments during the performance of official functions is prescribed for the priests of the Old Testament in Exodus 28:4–5 and 29:5–9. The exact nature of these garments cannot be determined from the texts mentioned, but it is clear that their underlying purpose was the same as is common to the use of sacred vestments in general: to excite reverence in the people assisting at the sacred rites, to emphasize the sacred character of the priestly office, and to inculcate by means of religious symbolism certain other lessons.

For many years it was believed that the vestments in use in the Christian church were modifications of the vestments of the Old Testament priesthood, but most authorities agree that their origin is to be found in the ordinary dress worn in the Roman Empire early in the Christian Era, when the officiants at Christian religious services simply wore their everyday dress, or perhaps garments that were somewhat better than the usual, but having the same general character and cut. As the empire declined, fashions in non-clerical dress changed considerably, but the ministers of the Church retained the more traditional types of garments, at least during the performance of their official functions.

Although the vestments in use from early in Middle Ages or before, remained basically the same, everything about them—cut, shape, colors, materials, and styles of decoration—tended to reflect changing fashions and standards of taste over the centuries. The chasuble, the large outer garment worn by the celebrant at the Eucharistic Liturgy or Mass, is perhaps the best illustration of this. The chasuble was originally a simple poncho-like outer garment, or circular piece of cloth of some rather heavy material with a hole near the center through which the head could be passed. In time it tended to become more and more elaborate and richly decorated until, in the Baroque age, when such vestments were heavily embroidered, the chasuble evolved into two large panels of stiff brocade hanging down in front and in back of the wearer. In the East, meanwhile, the development of the corresponding vestment (called in Greek a *phelonion*) proceeded in a different direction: instead of being cut away at the sides to allow for the movement of the arms, it was cut away in front. At mid-twentieth century there was a marked tendency to return to older, simpler, and more ample forms of this particular vestment.

In the Roman Catholic church there are six vestments worn by the celebrant at Mass: (1) the chasuble; (2) the amice, an oblong piece of white linen worn about the neck and fastened by means of cords or tapes that are passed around the chest and tied in front; (3) the alb, also of white linen and sometimes decorated with embroidery or lace, which is a long-sleeved garment reaching to the ankles, and is close-fitting about the neck; (4) the maniple, a band of the same material of which the outer vestments are made, which is worn draped over the left arm just below the elbow; (5) the stole, a long band of the same material, which is worn about the neck and crossed in front over the body; and (6) the cincture, a long cord, often with tassels at the ends, which is of linen or other material, usually white or the color of the outer vestments being worn, and which is used for gathering the alb at the waist and for holding the stole in place.

A prelate who wears a pectoral cross wears the stole hanging straight down, not crossed in front. A deacon wears a stole over his left shoulder with the ends passing under his right arm and there held in place by the cincture, if he is wearing one. The maniple, stole, and chasuble are made of silk, cloth of gold, or some other precious material, and are usually decorated, sometimes rather elaborately, with embroidery or some sort of appliqué work. These three vestments are in one of the so-called liturgical colors—white, red, green, violet, black, and sometimes blue, rose or cloth of gold—the use of which is precisely regulated by the Church.

In addition to these vestments worn by the celebrant at Mass, there are others that are proper to the other ministers, such as the deacon's dalmatic and the sub-deacon's tunicle, at a solemn celebration, and to bishops and other higher prelates. The surplice, a sort of abbreviated alb, is a vestment common to priests and to clerics of lower rank. Finally, the cope, or pluvial, a large capelike garment with a sort of stylized hood at the back and made of the same materials of which the outer Mass vestments are made, is worn by priests and others at many different functions.

In the Eastern Orthodox church the vestments worn by the clergy at various services are similar in origin to those of the Roman Catholic church, but are in many instances quite different in cut and appearance. In the Eastern churches generally, there are not the same sort of strict rules regarding the colors of vestments as in the Roman Catholic church. Even in the latter church, in fact, there are certain local practices, such as the use, in Spanish-speaking countries, of blue vestments for feasts of the Blessed Virgin Mary.

Some of the Protestant churches do not use sacred vestments. Others, particularly those, such as most of the ones within the Anglican Communion, that are more liturgically oriented, adhere to a usage practically identical with that of the Roman Catholic church. Between these two extremes there are many different standards of practice, and even among the various churches of a given communion the practice in regard to the use or nonuse of vestments may not be uniform.   BRENDAN McGRATH, O.S.B., S.T.D.

VESUVIUS, active volcano, S Italy, nine miles SE of Naples, rising 3,842 feet above the Bay of Naples. Vesuvius is the only active volcano on the mainland of Europe. It occupies the site of an older volcano, Mount Somma, whose crater partially surrounds Vesuvius. The name Vesuvius means "the unextinguished." On Aug. 24, 79, it broke into its first recorded eruption, which buried the towns of Herculaneum, Pompeii, and Stabiae under ash and rock. Despite other small eruptions, the mountain was covered by forest, and the crater was overgrown with shrubs. These were swept away by the outbreak of 1631, which destroyed many villages, and many people lost their lives in the streams of hot lava. In

VESTMENT

Former Anglican Archbishop of Canterbury Geoffrey Fisher (sixth from left), wears a long stole, similar to stoles worn by members of the clergy in the Roman Catholic church.

ISRAEL OFFICE OF INFORMATION

Vestments worn by priests of the Greek Orthodox church resemble those worn by Roman Catholic clergymen, but are more elaborate in style.

CORNELL UNIV.

Vestments worn by a rabbi during a Jewish service may be relatively simple, such as a cap, tallith (prayer shawl), and cassock-like robe.

CORNELL UNIV.

The long white alb and the shorter, sleeveless chasuble, are among the vestments worn by Roman Catholic priests when celebrating Mass.

In the Roman Catholic church, red birettas are worn by cardinals; Pope Pius XII places one on Edward Cardinal Mooney's head, Feb. 27, 1946.

the eighteenth and nineteenth centuries eruptions became more frequent. In 1906 the entire top of the crater blew off, and the shape of the mountain was entirely changed. Another disastrous explosion occurred in March, 1944. Explosions and lava flow continued for several days, engulfing the towns of San Sebastino, Arcolo, Massa di Somma, and others. Some of the destruction was caused by molten lava pouring over a gasoline dump used during World War II; an airdrome at the base of the mountain was extensively damaged. Like most lava soils, the sides of the mountains are very fertile and vineyards flourish there.

VETĀLA, an evil spirit in Hindu legend, that haunts graveyards and re-animates corpses. The Vetāla, a mischievous practical joker, is represented in human form, but with its hands and feet backwards and its hair standing on end.

VETCH, SAMUEL, 1668–1732, British colonial army officer, was born in Edinburgh, Scotland. After serving in the Dutch and British armies of William III, he settled in Albany, N.Y., 1699, and later moved to Boston, 1702. He went to England, 1708, to submit a plan for the conquest of French Canada to the British; the project was accepted, and Vetch was authorized to raise troops, 1709. Setting off from Boston as colonel of colonial troops, 1710, he conquered Nova Scotia, and was appointed civilian governor of the new colony within the year; and he became military governor in 1715.

VETCH, or tare, a leguminous herb belonging to the genus *Vicia* of the *Leguminosae* family. It is a climbing plant with pinnate foliage, flat pod, and blue, violet, yellowish, or white flowers. About two dozen species occur in North America. Although most species are weeds, a few are grown for their bright flowers, and many for green manure or cover crops. The plant thrives best in calcareous soils but is also adapted for clays.

VETERANS' AID, assistance, in any of various forms, given to veterans of the military services. Governments have granted many types of aid to veterans, much of it designed to help them adjust to civilian life and to assist them in their education.

As early as 133 B.C. the Roman reformer Tiberius Sempronius Gracchus (167–133 B.C.) was interested in providing aid to men who had served in war to protect their country. Tiberius instituted legislation aimed at redistributing land acquired from the nobles, among the peasants, most of whom had served as Roman soldiers. Sporadically throughout later European history war veterans were compensated for physical and, occasionally, financial loss incurred while in service. Veterans' aid in the United States was based on the English practice of providing compensations and pensions to soldiers as an award for service, as an inducement to enlist in the service, and as compensation for certain types of losses incurred while in the service.

Compensation for disabilities incurred while in military service was first offered in the United States by a colonial enactment, 1636, in Plymouth Colony; similar measures were enacted in other colonies during subsequent years. National aid provisions were first introduced by the Continental Congress for veterans of the Continental army of the Revolutionary War and for dependent survivors of men killed in that war. Later, federal and state compensation programs were made available to veterans of all wars participated in by the United States. Laws providing for compensation were often introduced during time of war and were included in enlistment and draft contracts.

The methods and criteria used to determine the amount of the compensation and the qualifications for receipt of such compensation have varied. Legislation enacted after the Revolutionary War granted compensation only to disabled veterans of the Continental army, in accordance with the degree of

disability they had sustained and for the entire time that such disability existed. Subsequent laws extended the system to cover all veterans of the war, and provided for higher compensations for officers. The General Law system (1862), provided one compensation program for all veterans of all branches of service for an indefinite period of time; the amounts of compensation depended on the service-rank of the veteran and the degree of his disability. This system, which was in effect long enough to cover participants in the Spanish-American War, was replaced by the War Risk Insurance Act (1917), which granted compensation in accordance with disability, regardless of the rank of the veteran, and provided for increased rates for veterans with dependents. Eligible veterans of World War II and the Korean conflict were compensated under similar provisions. See COMPENSATION.

Pensions. Legislation establishing pensions, introduced in several postwar periods, was generally intended to aid veterans without requiring that the recipient of such aid be disabled. The first legislation providing pension benefits for veterans was passed, 1818, for veterans of the Revolutionary War. Payment was made according to need and to rank held while in service. This legislation was superseded by a law (1832) that granted pensions to all Revolutionary War veterans regardless of their health or financial position; pension provisions were also enacted for widows of these veterans, 1836. Pensions to veterans of the War of 1812, the Mexican War, and the various Indian wars were granted on the basis of the 1832 act. The Dependent Pension Act (1890), stated that Civil War veterans were eligible for pension if they were physically unable to earn a living by manual labor. Pension rates under this act were determined solely in terms of the degree of disability, which meant that disabled veterans with substantial incomes were entitled to pensions at the same rate as similarly disabled veterans who were destitute. The law also granted pensions to widows of deceased veterans, and gave additional allowances for dependent children. The National Economy Act (1933), and executive orders issued in accordance with it, limited government pensions to veterans of World War I and all previous wars; veterans whose income exceeded a specified amount or whose disability was not permanent were ineligible. Pension rates were the same for all eligible veterans. The original pension provisions for veterans of World War II and the Korean conflict were similar to those for World War I veterans. Legislation, effective 1960, however, granted pensions in accordance with the veteran's income and number of dependents.

By the mid-twentieth century, federal government pensions and compensation payments to veterans and dependents of all wars and peacetime service had cost the United States close to $25 billion. In addition, many states had awarded pensions and compensation payments to eligible veterans residing within the state. See PENSION, *Military Pensions in the United States*.

Hospital and Medical Care were promised in the War Risk Insurance Act to disabled veterans of World War I. The act included provisions for issuance of artificial limbs in cases of service-incurred losses; outpatient treatment, such as physical examination and medical and dental care; and domiciliary care, designed to aid veterans who suffered from chronic conditions that prevented them from earning a living and who required minimal medical attention. The World War Veterans Act (1924) extended this aid to all veterans with service-connected disease and to all veterans with nonservice-connected disease or disability if facilities for such care were available. Preference was given to those veterans who stated they were unable to finance the care themselves. While the Economy Act was in effect, care was limited to veterans suffering from service-connected disabilities, those who were permanently disabled, and those with no visible means of support. A liberalization of these conditions was enacted in 1935, when hospital and medical care were extended to all veterans who signed an affidavit stating that they were unable to pay for their own medical expenses. Veterans of World War II and the Korean conflict were provided with medical aid, as available, in terms of an established order of priority that covered emergency cases, veterans with service-connected disabilities, and finally, those who stated under oath that they were unable to pay hospital charges for treatment of nonservice-connected disabilities or illnesses.

Other Federal Aid to veterans included life insurance programs, available to veterans of World Wars I and II and the Korean conflict; and loans guaranteed or insured by the government, for veterans of World War II and the Korean conflict, for the purchase, construction, or repair of homes and for the purchase or improvement of farm property or businesses. The Servicemen's Readjustment Act (1944), known as the G.I. Bill of Rights, provided a limited amount of education or training at government expense for veterans of World War II; similar but less generous provisions were extended to veterans of the Korean conflict. Vocational rehabilitation was provided for veterans disabled while in service, and free education was given to veterans in need of training to overcome the handicap of their disability. Specially equipped cars and homes were provided for the disabled who could make use of them, and all veterans were entitled to additional points in Civil Service ratings. See CIVIL SERVICE, *Operation of Civil Service Programs*.

The Veterans Administration. At mid-twentieth century, the U.S. federal government's programs of aid to veterans were operated by the Veterans Administration (VA), an agency created, 1930, to consolidate the work of various federal agencies concerned with the administration of laws pertaining to veterans' benefits. Such agencies included the Pension Bureau, created in 1833 as a part of the War Department, and moved to the Interior Department, 1849; the National Home for Disabled Volunteer Soldiers, created in 1865; and the Veterans Bureau, created in 1921. The VA central office comprises a board of veterans' appeals, information service, department of medicine and surgery, department of insurance, and department of veterans' benefits. There are district and regional offices, benefits offices, hospitals, aid centers, outpatient clinics, domiciliaries, and data-processing centers throughout the United States.

The Controversy over Veterans' Aid. Attempts to secure government-sponsored aid in return for military service have received considerable support throughout U.S. history; general public sentiment has been that former members of the Armed Forces deserved compensation for losses incurred while in service. Considerable controversy exists, however, over the amount and form of aid that should be given. Advocates of extensive aid programs state that all veterans deserve such grants in return for their service to the United States. Others believe that only veterans with service-connected disabilities should receive aid from the federal government. Many of the policies for granting federal aid are based on precedents set in legislation enacted after the Revolutionary War. It has been noted that although the needy veteran of the post-Revolutionary War period often had no alternative forms of aid available to him, the veteran at mid-twentieth century was eligible for various types of aid that were available to all citizens. Scholarships, for example, were available to all qualified citizens, and as a result there were those who felt additional aid to veterans for educational purposes was superfluous. Other opponents of broad-scale aid to veterans held that veterans with non-service-connected disabilities who claimed that they

were unable to provide medical care for themselves should be treated as charity cases by local government agencies. It was further argued that those veterans who might abuse the privilege of free medical care would take up time and money that should have gone to needy veterans with service-connected disabilities.

Veterans have been singularly successful in obtaining broad programs of benefits largely through the efforts of various veterans' organizations. The first such organization, the Grand Army of the Republic, organized after the Civil War, exerted considerable influence on the formation of federal legislation (see GRAND ARMY OF THE REPUBLIC). The American Legion, formed shortly after World War I, succeeded in obtaining even greater financial benefits from the federal government. By mid-twentieth century, veterans' organizations were said to represent only one in every five U.S. veterans, but they operated as one of the major U.S. pressure groups, and their influence was felt in various areas of public affairs that had little or nothing to do with veterans' affairs as such.

BIBLIOG.—American Academy of Political and Social Science, *Our Servicemen and Economic Security* (1943), *Disabled Veteran* (1945); Chicago. University. Committee on Human Development, *American Veteran Back Home: A Study of Veteran Readjustment* (1951); William P. Dillingham, *Federal Aid to Veterans, 1917–1941* (1952); Robert England, *Twenty Million World War Veterans* (1950); Ernest M. Gutman, *Lawyers' Guide: Committees and Guardians: Art. 81-A of the Civil Practice Act, Veterans' Adm.* (1951); Robert T. Kimbrough and Judson B. Glen, *American Law of Veterans: An Encyclopedia of the Rights and Benefits of Veterans and Their Dependents Arising from Service During World War II, the Korean Conflict, and Later, with Statutes, Regulations, Forms, and Procedures* (1954); Frank Mallen, *You've Got it Coming to You: The Guide for Families, Servicemen, Veterans* (1952); Phyllis I. Rosenteur, *Complete Book of Veterans' Benefits* (1965); United States. Laws, Statutes, etc., *Soldiers' and Sailors' Civil Relief Act* (1951); Walter S. Woods, *Men Who Came Back* (1956).

VETERANS OF FOREIGN WARS, in full Veterans of Foreign Wars of The United States, a society of honorably discharged, male veterans of the United States Armed Services who, in time of war or national emergency, served on foreign soil or on the high seas. It was first organized, 1899, at Columbus, Ohio, as the American Veterans of Foreign Service, with membership open only to Spanish-American War veterans. This organization merged, 1913, with the Army of the Philippines under the present name. A V.F.W. auxiliary was founded the next year. Veterans of various foreign expeditions such as the Boxer Rebellion, 1900, and service in Nicaragua, 1910–33, were later admitted. After World War I, eligibility was extended to veterans of that war, and the V.F.W. became the second largest veterans organization in the United States (see AMERICAN LEGION, THE). Other large increases in membership occurred when veterans of World War II and the Korean conflict were made eligible. In 1960 the V.F.W. had about 1.25 million members. During most of its latter-day history, the V.F.W. advocated higher benefits for disabled veterans and for dependents of deceased veterans, and favored a program of universal military training. It publishes the *V.F.W.* magazine, a monthly. The society's national headquarters are at Kansas City, Mo. The V.F.W. is organized territorially by departments, one for each state, for the District of Columbia, the Commonwealth of Puerto Rico, the Panama Canal Zone, and in several foreign countries including France and West Germany. See PATRIOTIC SOCIETIES, *Veterans Organizations*.

VETERINARY MEDICINE, the science and art that deals with the prevention, cure, alleviation, and extermination of diseases among domestic animals. By oath, the veterinarian dedicates himself to maintaining the health of his animal patients and to promoting the welfare of the owners and the public.

At the same time, he commits himself to application of humane techniques and conscientious practice of his profession.

HISTORY

The history of veterinary medicine dates back to the time of Hammurabi, about 2200 B.C., and its developments parallel the domestication of animals. The first author on veterinary subjects was Hippocrates, who is regarded as the father of medicine. Aristotle also discussed many problems of animal as well as human health. Vegetius, who lived in the fifth century, was one of the first who wrote only on veterinary medicine. The father of modern veterinary medicine and of the present educational system was Claude Bourgelat (1712–79). In about 1740 he opened a school of equitation and farriery at Lyón, which, in 1762, he succeeded in having incorporated into the public educational system of France as a school for the training of veterinarians. The opening of this school was followed by the establishment of courses in veterinary medicine at Vienna in 1775, Hanover in 1778, Dresden in 1780, Milan in 1789, London in 1791, and Berlin in 1792.

The growth and recognition of veterinary medicine in North America really began in 1862, with the establishment of the United States Department of Agriculture and the passage of the Morrill Act which provided aid to the land-grant colleges. With the formation of the Bureau of Animal Industry as a branch of the USDA in 1884, veterinary medicine was accorded a much greater degree of importance, since the enabling legislation provided that this bureau must have a veterinarian as its chief.

EDUCATION

American veterinary education began at the Veterinary College of Philadelphia in 1852. Next to open its doors was the Boston Veterinary Institute in 1855, followed by the New York College of Veterinary Surgeons in 1857. Of the schools operating today, all of which are at least partly supported by public funds, the first was Ontario Veterinary College, University of Toronto, Guelph, in 1862. Iowa State College, Division of Veterinary Medicine, Ames, was next in 1879. The University of Pennsylvania, School of Veterinary Medicine, Philadelphia, accepted students in 1884. The Ohio State University began teaching veterinary medicine in 1885, and had a full-scale College of Veterinary Medicine at Columbus in 1895. Next came Québec Veterinary College, in 1886, and it merged with two other schools in 1893. In 1894 the New York State Veterinary College (Cornell) opened; and in 1896 the State College of Washington. Between 1905 and 1961, 13 more veterinary schools, all at land-grant colleges, were opened to make a total of 20 in the United States and Canada. A college of veterinary medicine was also dedicated in 1960 at Purdue University at Lafayette, Ind. Each year the 20 schools graduate approximately 1,000 new veterinarians.

The teaching of veterinary medicine began as a course in farriery. Then, horsemanship, anatomy, physiology, and surgery were added to the curriculum. At first the course was for two terms of about four months each, but by 1908 this educational period had been lengthened to three years of about nine months each. In 1917 the state veterinary colleges increased the course to four academic years. By 1930 all these colleges had a full four-year course plus at least one year of pre-veterinary college training. In 1947 the trend toward a six-year course was well under way and by 1961 all United States schools required two years of pre-veterinary study in addition to the four-year veterinary curriculum.

The Council on Education of the American Veterinary Medical Association inspects all schools of veterinary medicine in the United States and Canada. In order to meet the minimum requirements for recognition as an approved school, the curriculum must provide adequate instruction in the following subjects as applied in the various species of animals: anatomy, including histology and embryology; physiology; pharmacology; microbiology, including bacteriology, mycology, virology, and immunology; pathology; parasitology; biochemistry; internal medicine; preventive medicine and public health; obstetrics; surgery; radiology; biometrics; anesthesiology; ophthalmology; and professional and public relations.

Upon completion of this course of instruction, the candidate receives a degree of Doctor of Veterinary Medicine, or D.V.M. Many diplomates continue their education, acquire other degrees, and specialize in certain phases of veterinary medicine. To practice, the graduate must secure a license in the state or province he has selected by passing an examination.

PRACTICE

Seventy-five per cent of the veterinarians in North America engage in private practice, that is, they work directly with privately owned animals. Many of them devote their efforts to the health and management of farm livestock, principally cattle, swine, sheep, and poultry. Most veterinarians in private practice do some work with dogs, cats, birds, and other household pets, and many, especially in larger cities, deal exclusively with these animals. Some work with race horses and riding horses, with fur-bearing animals, with wild animals held in captivity in zoos and circuses, and with laboratory animals.

Veterinarians may engage in disease eradication and control work or research with the U.S. Department of Agriculture; in meat and poultry inspection for federal, state, or municipal government agencies; in food and sanitary inspection or in biomedical research in the Veterinary Corps of the U.S. Army and the U.S. Air Force; in teaching and research at veterinary, agricultural, or medical colleges; in extension work; and in sales, advertising, or research with producers of veterinary drugs, vaccines, instruments, and feed products.

Veterinary Medicine. Beginning with the problems which plagued North American veterinarians and livestock owners in 1880, many forward steps have been taken in veterinary medicine. The great grasslands of the Southwest were made safe for grazing superior strains of beef cattle, because cattle tick, which transmitted a blood parasite that causes cattle tick fever, was eradicated.

On a less extensive scale, because the eradication program was started before the disease became widespread, veterinarians have stamped out foot-and-mouth disease on the several occasions when it occurred. This disease may affect cattle, hogs, sheep, and all other cloven-footed animals.

Contagious pleuropneumonia was completely eradicated; glanders of horses, once prevalent, is now unknown; dourine of horses was rapidly disappearing; and sleeping sickness of horses was being held in control. The development of an effective vaccine against hog cholera permitted hog raising to develop according to a definite plan and without the periodic epizootics which not only wiped out the potential supplies of pork, but also decimated the foundation stock of superior hog types. Canada completely eradicated this disease, and the United States began, in 1951, a strong move to eradicate it. Vesicular exanthema of swine, reintroduced into the United States in 1952, was eradicated by 1956.

The bovine tuberculosis eradication program led to a more profitable cattle industry; it also resulted in a great decrease in human tuberculosis.

The brucellosis eradication program has continued to make remarkable progress. Twenty-six states have achieved modified-certified brucellosis-free status, that is, a status whereby less than 0.1 per cent of the cattle and less than 0.5 per cent of the herds were infected. New Hampshire, in 1960, became the first state to eradicate brucellosis completely.

Control of other livestock diseases has been improved through development of pesticides, drugs, particularly antibiotics, and vaccines for diseases such as infectious bovine rhinotracheitis, leptospirosis, swine erysipelas, and encephalomyelitis in horses.

To cope with the swine diseases, virus pig pneumonia and atrophic rhinitis, a program of repopulation with pigs, that were pronounced specific pathogen-free, was developed throughout the hog belt of the United States. To produce such stock pigs are obtained from their dams by hysterectomy, or Cesarean section, performed under aseptic conditions two to four days before farrowing. The technique calls for removing the uterus containing the pig and passing it through an aseptic liquid lock into a specially constructed hood. The pigs are then removed from the uterus and transferred to special brooders where they are fed a special ration. They are reared in isolation for 4 weeks and then placed on farms which have been freed from these diseases.

Developments in the field of pet animal medicine have been directed largely at improving diagnostic and surgical procedures and application of new drugs and vaccines. With these improvements have come modern animal hospitals equipped with anesthetic apparatus, X-ray machines, diagnostic laboratories, and many special appliances. Research developments and modern equipment have made possible surgery which is comparable in many respects to surgery performed in human hospitals. Vaccines produced by tissue culture techniques have enabled veterinarians to afford dogs a high level of protection against the dread canine disease, distemper. Development of rapid diagnostic techniques for rabies have helped minimize the dangers from this disease, as have improved rabies vaccines.

With the expansion in the field of biomedical research, many thousands of laboratory animals, including chimpanzees, monkeys, goats, dogs, cats, mice, guinea pigs, rabbits, hamsters, and birds have been delegated to research projects conducted by veterinarians. Veterinary scientific developments using these laboratory animals have made possible improved vaccines and products for use in human as well as veterinary medicine and have provided much of the basic biological information needed to further research in astronautics and nuclear medicine. Using experimental animals, veterinarians have devised a number of surgical appliances now used in human medicine, such as the Stader splint and the Gorman prosthetic hip joint.

Veterinary Surgery must not only save the life of the animal, but restore function in a farm animal to maintain its economic value. The veterinary surgeon clips and shaves the site of the operation, washes the skin with soap and water, and then applies a surface antiseptic. He sterilizes all necessary instruments in steam or boiling water and then restrains his patient in such a way as to produce a minimum of pain and opposition to the actions of the surgery. The most effective restraint in animals is anesthesia, which may be either general or local. The choice of anesthetic is made on the basis of the temperament of the animal, the nature of the operation, the length of time which will be required for its completion, and the advisability of having the patient recumbent or standing during and after the operation. Tranquilizers have been used successfully in animals in conjunction with anesthetics. See AMERICAN VETERINARY MEDICAL ASSOCIATION.   ARTHUR FREEMAN, D.V.M.

BIBLIOG.-Douglas C. Blood and James A. Henderson, *Veterinary Medicine: A Textbook* (1960); George F. Boddie, *Diagnostic Methods in Veterinary Medicine* (1956); Carl A. Brandly and Edwin L. Jungherr, *Advances in Veterinary Science* (1953–61); Harry L. Foust and Robert Getty, *Veterinary Histology and Embryology: Lecture and Laboratory Guide* (1955); Reuben J. Garner, *Veterinary Toxicology: Formerly Lander's Veterinary Toxicology* (1957); Frederick B. Hadley, *Principles of Veterinary Science* (1954); William A. Hagan and Dorsey W. Bruner, *Infectious Diseases of Domestic Animals: With Special Reference to Etiology, Diagnosis, and Biologic Therapy* (1957); Harold W. Hannah and Donald F. Storm, *Law for the Veterinarian and Livestock Owner* (1959); Thomas G. Hungerford, *Diseases of Livestock* (1959); Leo M. Jones, *Veterinary Pharmacology and Therapeutics* (1957); Ellis P. Leonard, *Orthopedic Surgery of the Dog and Cat* (1960); Ival A. Merchant, *Outline of the Infectious Diseases of Domestic Animals* (1957); *Merck Veterinary Manual* (1955); William C. Miller and Geoffrey P. West, eds., *Encyclopedia of Animal Care* (1959); Hermann O. Mönnig, *Veterinary Helminthology and Entomology* (1957); Louis P. Reitz, ed., *Biological and Chemical Control of Plant and Animal Pests* (1960); Ulick F. Richardson, *Veterinary Protozoology* (1958); Stephen J. Roberts, *Veterinary Obstetrics and Genital Diseases* (1956); Russell A. Runnells and Others, *Principles of Veterinary Pathology* (1960); James F. Smithcors, *Evolution of the Veterinary Art: A Narrative Account to 1850* (1958); Reginald H. Smythe, *Veterinary Ophthalmology* (1958), *Clinical Veterinary Surgery*, 2 vols. (1959–60); Gustav W. Stamm, *Veterinary Guide for Farmers* (1957); Hadley C. Stephenson and Stanley G. Mittelstaedt, comps., *Veterinary Drug Encyclopedia and Therapeutic Index* (1958); Denney H. Udall, *Practice of Veterinary Medicine* (1954); United States Dept. of Agriculture. Yearbook of Agriculture, *Animal Diseases* (1956); David Wirth, *Introduction to Veterinary Clinical Diagnosis* (1956); Walter R. Woolridge, *Farm Animals in Health and Disease* (1960); John G. Wright, *Veterinary Anaesthesia* (1958).

VETO, the act of an executive authority in refusing to give approval to a measure approved by a legislative body. Veto power may be either absolute or qualified. An absolute veto completely terminates consideration of the legislation in question; a qualified veto, however, may be overridden in some specified manner, as for example, by a vote of the legislative body. Absolute veto power was exercised by the monarch in England from early in the fifteenth century until 1707, when Queen Anne, 1702–14, became the last British sovereign to veto a petition of the House of Commons. The power of absolute veto was virtually nonexistent in the governments of the twentieth century, although the crown in England theoretically was still capable of exercising such power.

The U.S. Constitution provides that the President have qualified veto power, and the constitutions of all the states except North Carolina endow the governors of those states with qualified veto power. Many municipal charters give qualified veto power to the municipality's chief executive official.

Presidential Vetoes. In instances where the President wishes to withhold his approval from legislation passed by Congress, he returns the bill to the house where it originated, together with a message stating his objections. Congress may override this action by a two-thirds vote in each house. If the President does not return the bill within 10 days, and if Congress is still in session at the end of this time, the bill becomes law without his signature. If, however, Congress adjourns before the 10 days have elapsed, the legislation is considered vetoed, by presidential pocket veto. The President does not have item veto power.

Other Vetoes. In addition to their power of qualified veto, the governors of 41 states have the power of item veto, which permits them to veto selected provisions of proposed legislation, and to approve the remainder. The governors of Washington and South Carolina have the power of item veto over all legislation presented for their approval; other states limit the governor's power of item veto to appropriation bills. In many cities having a mayor-and-council form of government the mayor has absolute veto power over all bills involving budget increases. Each of the five permanent members of the United Nations Security Council—France, Nationalist China, the Union of Soviet Socialist Republics, the United Kingdom, and the United States—has the power to veto the council's proposals, thus blocking action by the body. See UNITED NATIONS.

Use of the Veto. The veto power was used only sparingly by the early Presidents of the United States:

during the first 40 years of the country, the power was exercised only nine times. President Andrew Jackson, however, interpreted the veto provision of the Constitution as a device to forestall congressional action contrary to the President's judgment, and he vetoed more bills during his term of office than had been vetoed by all previous presidents. Subsequently, the veto power was used ever more frequently. Pres. Franklin D. Roosevelt, for example, exercised the veto 631 times during his 13 years in office.

VEUILLOT, LOUIS FRANCOIS, 1813–83, French journalist, and controversialist, was born in Boynes. As a young man, Veuillot served in a law office in Paris and on newspaper staffs in Rouen and Périgueux. Following a visit to Rome during Holy Week, 1838, Veuillot became an aggressive supporter of papal supremacy within the church and of church supremacy within the state. He characterized the "worst" of those who opposed his views, including civil authorities and the French clergy, as "the race of Cain"; those of his opponents for whom he saw some hope were merely lukewarm Christians. He published *Pèlerinage en Suisse* (1839) and *Rome et Lorette* (1841), joined the staff of the Catholic newspaper *L'univers religieux*, 1843, and became its editor, 1848. Because of the violence which characterized Veuillot's writings, the paper was suppressed, 1860. It was revived in 1867, but it was suppressed once again in 1874. Among his other works are *Le Pape et la diplomatie* (1861), *Le Parfum de Rome* (1862), and *L'odeurs de Paris* (1867).

VEVEY, town, W Switzerland, in the canton of Vaud. Located near the eastern shore of Lake Geneva, at the mouth of the river Veveyse, Vevey is a popular resort. It commands a fine view of the vineyards and mountains nearby. The town's industries include metal and leather working, and chocolate manufacture. (For population, see Switzerland map in Atlas.)

VÉZELAY, village, N central France, in the department of Yonne, about 140 miles SSE of Paris. Vézelay is situated on a hilltop, surrounded by the remains of medieval fortifications. The twelfth century abbey-church of La Madeleine is regarded as a masterpiece of Romanesque art. A Benedictine abbey was established there in the ninth century, and the report that the bones of St. Magdalen had been brought to its chapel, attracted thousands of pilgrims. In 1146 St. Bernard of Clairvaux preached there, urging Frenchmen to join the Second Crusade. Richard I of England met Philip II of France there before setting out on the Third Crusade, 1190. Since the Middle Ages, the population of Vézelay has dwindled, and it is now largely dependent on the tourist industry.

VIAREGGIO, town, W Italy, in Tuscany Region, Lucca Province, situated on the coast of the Ligurian Sea, 13 miles NW of Pisa. It is popular as a summer and a winter resort. Percy Bysshe Shelley, the English poet, drowned off the coast of Viareggio in 1822. (For population, see Italy map in Atlas.)

VIBORG, also Wiborg or Wyborg, town, Denmark, on the Jutland Peninsula, seat of Viborg County. Viborg is a highway and railway junction. It is a trade center for an agricultural area in which cattle and pigs are raised and wheat, barley, and tobacco are grown. Viborg is the site of a Gothic cathedral founded in 1130. (For population, see Denmark map in Atlas.)

VIBRATION, rapid, regular, repetitive to-and-fro motion. The time occupied by each to-and-fro motion is termed the period of vibration. The number of vibrations per unit time is called the frequency of vibration. It is equal to 1/period. The plucked string, the struck tuning fork, the swinging pendulum, all vibrate in the medium that surrounds them—the air—in a direction parallel to their own motion: such vibrations are termed longitudinal. When the surrounding medium moves at right angles to the vibrator, the vibration is termed transverse. Light, for

USDA

The maple-leaved viburnum is a decorative wild plant having bright scarlet berries. The berries begin to appear in July, and remain until the following spring.

example, is produced by transverse vibration. See ACOUSTICS; HEAT; SOUND.

VIBURNUM, a genus of about 120 species of hardy shrubs belonging to the family *Caprifoliaceae*. Although some of the species are evergreen, most are deciduous. They bear corymbs or panicles of white or pink flowers followed by berry-like subglobose to oblong, red, dark blue, or black fruits. Many species are cultivated. *V. americanum* is the well known cranberry bush; *V. alnifoleum*, the American wayfaring tree; *V. prunifolium*, the black haw.

VICAR, an ecclesiastical term for a cleric (a priest or minister) acting as a substitute or deputy. In the Roman Catholic church the term is used in this sense in connection with various charges or offices. The representative of the pope in missionary territory is called vicar apostolic, and the territory he administers is known as a vicariate. The vicar capitular is elected by a cathedral chapter to administer a diocese when it becomes vacant, as, for example, upon the death of a bishop. A vicar general acts as a deputy of the bishop throughout the diocese, with all powers the bishop chooses to delegate to him. The vicar forane, also known as rural dean, is a priest appointed by the bishop to supervise the spiritual life of a group of outlying parishes. The pope himself is called the Vicar of Christ because he is regarded as the Lord's representative on earth, acting with authority and powers received from Him.

In the Protestant Episcopal church, a vicar is a clergyman deputized to care for a dependent chapel. In English ecclesiastical law, a vicar is a priest or clergyman in charge of a parish or curacy as a deputy and who receives tithes or a benefice as wages.

VICENTE, GIL, 1465?–?1536, Portuguese poet and dramatist, was born possibly in Lisbon, but more probably in some village of northern Portugal. Owing to the existence of at least half a dozen other contemporary Gil Vicentes, the facts concerning the poet's life are difficult to ascertain. He spoke of himself, possibly in jest, as having been born the son of a pack saddler in Pederneira. The date of his birth is most often listed as 1470, but this date is based on no more than the fact that a judge who figures in one of Gil Vicente's plays, *Floresta de Enganos* (1536), is 66 years old—a dubious means of judging the author's age; most authorities believe that he was born prior to 1470. Another difficulty concerns his profession: there are numerous documentary references to one Gil Vicente, goldsmith, who served the royal court of Portugal, and attained high rank in the Lisbon gild, 1490–1520, a period that coincides to some extent with the court tenure of Gil Vicente, poet and dramatist, who was attached to the royal court in 1502–36. "They" may well have been the same man, a person of diverse talents, but there is no definite link between them.

The earliest documented trace of the poet Gil Vicente dates from 1502, when he presented a 114-line dramatic piece, *Auto da Visitaçam*, before Queen Lianor of Portugal on the occasion of the birth of the Infante (later John or João III). This short presentation won for Vicente the queen's patronage and the court's admiration, and for the next 34 years he remained with the royal court, even accompanying it on its continuous peregrinations between Evora, Lisbon, Coimbra, Almeirim, and Thomar. He wrote, and produced at court, more than 50 plays ranging from simple monologues to elaborately staged pageants, and including sacred and patriotic pieces, comedies, morality plays, satires, farces, tragicomedies, and other types. Of the 44 extant plays, 14 are in Portuguese, 11 in Spanish, and the rest in a mixture of the two languages. In his capacity as poet laureate, Vicente also wrote innumerable poems celebrating state occasions. Among his better known plays are *Auto da Festa* (c.1525), *Auto da Sibila Cassandra* (c.1513), *Farsa da Inés Pereira* (1523), *Auto da Feira* (1527), *Floresta de Enganos* (1536), *Dom Duardos* (c.1525), *Tragicomedia Pastoril da Serra da Estrella* (1527), and the great trilogy, *Barcas* (1518–29), his most ambitious work.

Significance. Vicente is one of the two dominant figures of Portuguese literary history (see CAMOËNS, LUIZ DE). As a lyric poet he was unexcelled; as dramatist he was occasionally powerful, but more often (and more characteristically) incisively brilliant, providing insights into character and situation that, like flashes of lightning, illuminate wherever they fall. He has been called Portugal's Shakespeare. An originator in form rather than subject matter, he defied the academic unities to achieve wholeness of vision (see UNITIES). In the history of world literature, he stands as one of the few who linked the Middle Ages with the new learning of the Renaissance, combining much of the best of both. Unfortunate political and religious conditions prevented the development of a Vicentian school of drama or literature in Portugal; elsewhere, however, such men as Molière, Shakespeare, Calderón, and Lope de Vega owed a considerable debt to his genius.

VICENZA, province, NE Italy, in Veneto Region, bounded by the provinces of Trento on the N, Belluno and Treviso on the NE, Padua on the E and S, and by Verona on the W. The area of the province is 1,051 square miles. In the north are the foothills of the Dolomite Mountains, and in the south Vicenza forms part of the North Italian plain. The plain is broken by the volcanic outliers of the Monti Berici. Cereals, sugar beets, grapes, and tobacco are grown and dairy cattle are raised. For a time in the Middle Ages the province existed as an independent republic. It was taken by the Venetians in 1405.

VICENZA, city NE Italy, in Veneto Region, capital of the province of Vicenza; lying on both banks of the Bacchiglione, 40 miles W of Venice. Vicenza is a highway and railroad center. Iron and steel, machinery, glass, and food products are manufactured. The old town was surrounded by a wall built in the thirteenth century, now mostly demolished. Vicenza has many fine buildings by Andrea Palladio, an Italian architect of the sixteenth century. Among these are the basilica replacing the exterior of the Palazza della Ragione, one of the finest of the Renaissance works; the Torre di Piazza (twelfth to fifteenth centuries); the Loggia del Capitanio (1571); the Monte di Pieta (sixteenth century); and other famous palaces and buildings, some mistakenly attributed to Palladio, who was born in and headed a new school of architecture in Vicenza. Vicenza is frequently known as the City of Palladio. (For population, see Italy map in Atlas.)

VICE-PRESIDENT OF THE UNITED STATES, the second ranking official of the federal government, who succeeds to the presidency if that office is vacated for any reason. The Vice-President appears on the same election campaign ticket with the President and must meet the same legal qualifications (See UNITED STATES PRESIDENT). Along with the President, the Vice-President is elected by a majority vote of the Electoral College. If no candidate for the vice-presidency receives a majority of electoral votes, the Senate must make a selection from the two candidates with the highest popular votes.

Duties. The Vice-President presides over the Senate at all times except during impeachment proceedings against the President. In his role as presiding officer, the Vice-President votes in the Senate only in case of a tie. In 1933, Pres. Franklin D. Roosevelt invited Vice-Pres. John Nance Garner to become a member of his cabinet and from that time vice-presidents regularly attended cabinet meetings, and even conducted such meetings in the absence of the President. The Vice-President's role in national affairs grew more important after 1949, when Alben W. Barkley, Vice-President under Pres. Harry S. Truman, became the first such official to serve as a member of the National Security Council; each succeeding Vice-President served on this body. As Vice-Presidents, Richard M. Nixon and Lyndon B. Johnson were each assigned additional ceremonial, consultative and administrative duties. The latter, for instance, was made chairman of the National Aeronautics and Space Administration council.

Selection. In selecting a candidate for second place on the presidential ticket, political considerations have frequently been controlling. The nomination has often been awarded on the basis of a need to build voting strength in a particular geographic region of the country, or to repay a loyal party worker, rather than to bring to office a leader experienced in national affairs. Originally the Constitution provided that after the choice of the President had been made, the person having the next greatest number of votes of the electors should be Vice-President. In 1796 the operation of this system led to the election of John Adams, a Federalist, as President, and Thomas Jefferson, a Republican, as Vice-President.

The Twelfth Amendment to the U.S. Constitution, adopted in 1804, was intended to prevent such confusion from arising again. It provided that the Electoral College should cast separate ballots for the presidency and the vice-presidency. Thereafter candidates were specifically nominated for the office of Vice-President, and the nomination process evolved into what was, under ordinary circumstances, a simple designation of the choice of a running mate on the part of the presidential nominee, although some presidential nominees indicated that they had no preference in this matter and would accept the person chosen by the nominating convention.

VICEROY, the governor of a country or province who rules in place of the king, as the French derivation of the word indicates (*vice*, in place of, and *roi*, king). The title was officially given to the governors of certain dependencies of the old Spanish monarchy, such as Naples, Peru, and New Spain (Mexico). The British counterpart in India was officially called the Vice-Roy and Governor-General of India.

VICHADA, commissary, E Colombia; bounded by Venezuela on the N and E, by the commissary of Vaupés on the S, by the intendencies of Meta on the W, and Arauca on the NW, and by the department of Boyacá on the NW. The area of the region is 39,764 sq. mi. In the west is a tableland, sloping eastward to the broad Orinoco Valley. The Tomo, Vichada and Guaviare rivers flow eastward to the Orinoco River, which forms the eastern boundary of the commissary. The climate is warm and wet, and the vegetation is mainly grassland with scattered trees. In the south there is a transition into equatorial forest. Vichada is very sparsely settled. There is some Indian settlement along the rivers, however, and here corn, cassava, and bananas are the most common crops. Cattle are grazed, mainly on unfenced pasture. The only town is Puerro Carreño, the capital.

VICHUGA, city, U.S.S.R., in N central Russian Soviet Federated Socialist Republic, in Ivanovo Region; on the Klyazma River, a tributary of the Volga River; on a railway, 40 miles NE of the city of Ivanovo, and 180 miles NE of Moscow. Vichuga is a commercial and industrial center in a region in which wheat and vegetables are grown, and dairy cattle are raised. The city is an important textile center, specializing in cotton goods. Pop. (1959) 51,000.

VICHY, town, S central France, in the department of Allier, on the Allier River, some 70 miles WNW of Lyon and 200 miles SSE of Paris. Vichy is a noted spa and health resort. Vichy water from its hot mineral springs has been known since Roman times. During World War II, Vichy was capital of unoccupied France. See FRANCE, *History*, *World War II*. Pop. (1954) 30,403.

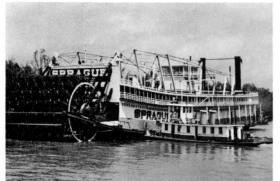

MISSISSIPPI A. & I. BOARD

One of the many tourist attractions of Vicksburg is the 315-foot showboat *Sprague*, a nineteenth century sternwheeler, which has its anchorage at the city waterfront.

VICKSBURG, city, W Mississippi, seat of Warren County; on the Mississippi River at the mouth of the Yazoo River; on the Illinois Central Railroad and U.S. highways 61 and 80; 40 miles W of Jackson. The city is a leading processing and shipping point for cotton, livestock, and lumber produced in the area. Clothing, wood products, chemicals, cottonseed oil, and earth-moving equipment are manufactured. Major points of interest are Vicksburg National Military Park, which adjoins the city; Vicksburg National Cemetery, to the north; the Old Court House Museum, which contains relics of the Civil War siege of Vicksburg; a U.S. Waterways Experiment Station, to the south, which contains a working model of the Mississippi River; and the Sprague, a river boat museum on the Yazoo Diversion Canal.

History. The site of Vicksburg was first prized as a military outpost because of its strategic location on bluffs overlooking the Mississippi. Fort Nogales was established there by the Spanish, 1791. When Spain relinquished its claim to the area, 1795, the name of the outpost was changed to Fort McHenry. Settlement began, 1814, when a Methodist minister, Newitt Vick, established a mission. The town was laid out, 1819, and incorporated and named Vicksburg, 1825. During the Civil War, Union troops occupied the city, July 4, 1863, after a 47-day siege. Pop. (1960) 29,130.

VICKSBURG CAMPAIGN, a major Union military action in the U.S. Civil War; it culminated in the Union's capture of the fortified Confederate city of Vicksburg, Miss., July 4, 1863. Together with the Union's decisive victory over the Confederacy at Gettysburg, Pa., July 1–3, 1863, the Vicksburg Campaign marked the turning point of the war (see

GETTYSBURG, BATTLE OF). The principal general officers involved were, for the Union: Maj. Gen. Ulysses S. Grant, in command of the Department of Tennessee and his corps commanders William T. Sherman, John A. McClenand, Stephen A. Hurlburt, and James B. McPherson—all major generals; and, for the Confederacy: Gen. Joseph E. Johnston, in command of Department of the West, and Lt. Gen. John C. Pemberton, in command of the Department of Louisiana, Mississippi, and Tennessee.

From summer, 1862, Union forces had controlled the Mississippi River, except for a 100-mile stretch between Vicksburg and Port Hudson, La. Between these two points, strongly held by the Confederacy, the Red River empties into the Mississippi, and at this time it was serving as a great highway connecting Texas, Louisiana, and Arkansas with the eastern part of the Confederacy. It was also an important channel to the east. Grant hoped to reduce these Confederate bastions, and thereby gain control of all the Mississippi, and cut the Confederacy in two.

Grant made his first move toward Vicksburg late in November, 1862, advancing from Corinth, Miss., southwest toward Jackson and Vicksburg, while Sherman attempted to effect a landing just north of Vicksburg. Both movements faltered in the face of strong Confederate resistance, and by the year's end Grant had withdrawn from northern Mississippi to Memphis, from where he proceeded to join Sherman at Young's Point, across the river from Vicksburg.

Now aware that Vicksburg was impregnable to direct assault from the west bank of the Mississippi, Grant conceived of several possible plans for attacking the city from the rear without endangering his supply line down the river. He rejected these plans as unsound for either military or political reasons. One, for example, in which he would return to Memphis and from there again advance into northern Mississippi, would, despite its strategic possibilities for success, appear to be a retreat and would further damage Northern morale.

In March, 1863, Grant settled on the audacious plan of cutting loose from his supply line, marching his troops along the west bank of the Mississippi to a point about 30 miles directly south of Vicksburg, and then crossing to dry ground and approaching Vicksburg from the rear. In April, 1863, Union navy gunboats and transport ships, commanded by Rear Adm. David D. Porter, ran the gauntlet of artillery at Vicksburg and joined Grant below the city. There they helped ferry the Federal troops across the river. Marching swiftly, Grant interposed his force between Pemberton and his Confederate troops around Vicksburg, and Johnston, who was attempting to come from the east to Pemberton's aid. With only 45,000 men as against numerically superior Confederate forces—there were 30,000 Confederates around Vicksburg alone—Grant fought five pitched battles—those of Port Gibson, May 1, Raymond, May 12, Jackson, May 13, Champion's Hill, May 16, and Big Black River, May 17—defeating and scattering the enemy forces before they could concentrate.

Siege operations were initiated May 22, 1863, after two Union assaults on Pemberton's lines had failed. Utilizing reinforcements to protect his rear against Johnston's 30,000 men, Grant tightened his grip on the city, where military personnel and civilians alike suffered increasingly from hunger and disease. Pemberton asked for terms, July 3, and surrendered his 37,000 men, 172 cannon, and the city to the Union army, July 4. Five days later Port Hudson surrendered, giving the Union control of all the Mississippi and cutting the Confederacy in two. CIVIL WAR, AMERICAN, *Western Campaign*.

VICKSBURG NATIONAL MILITARY PARK, W Mississippi, adjacent to Vicksburg on the N and E; area 1,650 acres. The park contains well preserved fortifications of the 47-day Siege of Vicksburg in 1863 during the Civil War. It was established in 1899.

VICO, GIOVANNI BATTISTA, 1668–1744, Italian historian and philosopher, father of the philosophy of history, was born and lived all his life in Naples, then a city of more than 200,000 inhabitants, and the capital of the Kingdom of the Two Sicilies. Vico is as remarkable for the conduct of his life as he is for the development of his thought. In both, he was unusually slow. Not until he was 55 years of age did he begin to formulate his own insights, and only after his 64th year did he attain even a moderate amount of social security. It may have been, however, that this tardiness was a condition for his achievement, for a whole mountain of prejudices in Vico's own mind had to be overcome; and, as it happened, there was little need for him to hurry forth with new insights, for almost a century elapsed after his death before the world was prepared to listen to him.

Scienca Nuova. In his enthusiasm, Vico spoke and wrote of his insights as a "new science"; this did not make him popular, and the first version of his major work ran into significant trouble. In Vico's day, it was customary for an author to dedicate his new book to some powerful patron, who would, in turn, pay the printer. When Vico first conceived of his New Science, he had only a short time before endured a humiliation so crushing that later he never could speak of it without weeping: having studied law, philosophy, and history deeply, and finding little opportunity to put this knowledge to the best use as a professor of rhetoric, he had asked for a chair of law at the University of Naples and had been turned down for reasons having nothing to do with the relative abilities of the several candidates. Poverty and drudgery seemed destined to remain his lot. Hence, it required almost a supernatural effort of his whole being for him to concentrate on writing the first exposition of his New Science. But at the very least, Vico assumed, he could count on his sponsor, Cardinal Lorenzo Corsini for expense money. In due course, the cardinal—who later became pope as Clement XII, 1730—proved to be quite willing to accept the dedication, but the money was another matter: he soon sent a note to the effect that "other expenses" prevented his discharging the money for Vico. Whereupon Vico rewrote the long volume (perhaps volumes) into 12 pages, sold a ring from his finger for just the money needed to print that number of pages, and published the pamphlet "complete" with its dedication to his "patron."

Rationalism Versus Marriage. From the vantage point of Vico's plight in his middle fifties, the significant data of his early life can be selected. Son of the poorest bookseller in town, he was nonetheless a cheerful child; but a fall left him weak and saddened, and his phthisic coughing caused his schoolmates to bestow on him the cruel nickname Master Tisicuzzo. Humiliated, he ran from school and subsequently became one of the most persevering of self-taught students. As a tutor on the country estate of the Rocca family at Vatolla, in remote Cilento, Vico kept up this habit until the age of 27, acquiring a fine knowledge of Greek, a good command of Hebrew, Greek philosophy, and so forth. He frequented some of the literary circles (*salotti*, academies) of this period in Italian intellectual and spiritual history, and obviously he shared for a time all the mental fashions of the Cartesian enlightenment (see DESCARTES, RENÉ), for in 1693 he printed a poem, *Affetti d' un Disperato* (Sentiments of a Desperado), of unmitigated gloom. Some 30 years later, however, he was to place himself in precisely the opposite, anti-Cartesian camp. Perhaps the first step beyond the despair that Rationalism engendered was his marriage, 1699, to a brave and illiterate woman, Caterina Destito, who gave birth to eight children and died, 1735, after an exemplary life.

Religious, Heroic, and Human Phases of History. Gradually, as he moved away from the fads of eclectic rationalism, Vico discovered the immense role played in human society by such forces as legislators, cult, poetry, sacrifice, reverence. Gradually, he freed his poetical faculty from subservience to reason's logical concepts. As a result, he immediately saw history in a new way. He could now perceive, for example, that Homer, Shakespeare, Dante, although they lived centuries apart, had served essentially the same poetic function, for each helped enact the "heroic" epoch in the history of Greece, England, and Italy, respectively. Vico taught that history occurs in three successive phases: religious, heroic, human. Without the first two, the third is impossible in any line of achievement. How may science (whether "rational," "experimental," or both) deny the valid reality of faith and heroism, when science itself, to exist fully and historically, must pass through its own religious and heroic phases? By mid-twentieth century, these and others among Vico's insights were to be rather commonplace—except in the United States and the Soviet Union. But in his own day Vico's ideas were unfashionable everywhere and he suffered greatly from the deafness of his contemporaries to his discoveries.

It was the crowning effort of his soul that Vico finally was able to include this very neglect as a part of his conception of history. He came to understand that in his own time he could be tolerated only as a man of exemplary character, as a great Latinist, as a devoted teacher, but that only people of another century would accept his heritage. Having achieved this most difficult of insights, Vico was able to overcome his violent self-criticism and self-distrust sufficiently to undertake to enlarge the first 12 pages of his *Scienza nuova prima* to the *Scienza nuova secunda* in, as he wrote, "a nearly fatal oestrus of passion."

Works. The earliest version of the *Scienza nuova*, as conceived immediately after Vico's rebuff at the hands of the university authorities, was to have been entitled *Dubbi e disideri intorno alla teologia dei gentili,* but was redesignated *Scienza nuova in forma negativa;* soon, however, Vico chose to recast the entire "demonstration" in a more positive way, and in less than a month he rewrote the work as *Principj di una scienza nuova d'intorno alla natura delle nazione per la quale si ritrovano i principj di altro sistema del diritto naturale delle genti* (1725); this was the *Scienza nuova prima*—the First New Science. The Second New Science was published in December, 1730, as *Cinque libri de Giambattista Vico de' principj d'una scienza nuova d'intorno alla comune natura delle nazioni.* By spring, 1731, it is said, Vico was already revising the book again, actually for the fourth time. The result, larger by some 15 chapters and with hardly a page of the 1730 version left unchanged, was issued in July, 1744, six months after Vico's death, as *Principj di scienza nuova di Giambattista Vico d'intorno alla comune natura delle nazioni.* Among Vico's other writings, the following deserve mention: *De ratione studiorum* (1708), *De antiquissima italorum sapientia* (1710), *De universi juris uno principio et fine uno* (1720), and *De constantia jurisprudentis* (1721).

Vico was first resuscitated by Giuseppe Ferrari (1811–76) in an annoted edition of 1837. The complete works, including the autobiography and with the Latin works translated into Italian, were issued at Naples in seven volumes (1858–69). The first German translation of the *Scienza nuova* in its final form was issued in Leipzig, 1822; it, and a French translation (1827), introduced Vico to a Europe that had hardly heard of him before. Not until mid-twentieth century was there an acceptable English translation: *The New Science of Giambattista Vico* (Tr. from the edition of 1744 by T. G. Bergin and M. H. Fisch, 1948).   EUGEN ROSENSTOCK-HUESSY

VICTOR I, SAINT, died ?198, pope from ?190 until his death, was born in Africa. He is remembered for his dispute with the bishops of Asia Minor over the celebration of Easter. The Roman Christians celebrated the holy day on Easter Sunday, while the Asian church followed the custom of marking the death of Christ in keeping with the Jewish Feast of Passover, in accordance with the Hebrew calendar, whether it fell on a Sunday or not. In the course of the dispute Victor threatened to exclude the Asian church, but in the face of strong opposition he did not do so.

VICTOR II, 1018–1057, pope from 1055 until his death, was born Gebhard in Swabia, Germany. After the death of Pope Leo IX, almost a year passed before a candidate for pope could be agreed upon. Through the efforts of the monk Hildebrand (see GREGORY VII), the Romans were persuaded to accept Gebhard, bishop of Eichstätt, as pope. Gebhard was a relative of Emperor Henry III, who met with the Roman faction and agreed that the bishop should be pope. Gebhard accepted the tiara, 1055, and immediately set about his task with a zealousness for reform. He attacked clerical concubinage and simony, and sought general reform of the clergy. His friend, the emperor, was no exception to Victor's demand that all ecclesiastical properties were to be restored to the church. At the deathbed of Henry, 1056, where Victor was summoned to attend, the pope was requested to act as guardian to Henry's son Henry IV, and was appointed regent of Germany. A year later, however, Victor died suddenly in Arezzo.

VICTOR III, 1027–87, pope from 1086 until his death, was born Dauferius or Daufar in Benevento, Italy. Dauferius succeeded Stephen IX as abbot of Monte Cassino, 1057, and, under the name of Desiderius, ruled over the famed monastery during its golden age, contributing personally to the literary output of Monte Cassino with his *Dialogi de miraculis S. Benedicti.* In 1086, against his own wish, the abbot succeeded Gregory VII as pope. During his brief reign, Victor III sent an army to Tunis that defeated the sultan's forces, and excommunicated the antipope Clement III.

VICTOR IV, real name Gregorio Conti, an antipope of the Roman Catholic church, was chosen, 1138, to succeed another antipope, Anacletus II, in opposition to Innocent II. Previously, Victor IV had been cardinal priest of Santi Dodici Apostoli. Two months after his illegal election, Victor IV submitted to the rightful pope.

VICTOR IV, died 1164, antipope of the Roman Catholic church, 1159–64, in opposition to Alexander III, was born Octavian or Octavius in Montecelio, Italy. While cardinal of Santa Cecilia, he was sent as a papal legate to Germany, and there became acquainted with the young Duke of Swabia, later to become Emperor Frederick I (Frederick Barbarossa). When Hadrian IV died, 1159, two popes were elected at the same time—one of them Octavian as Victor IV, the other Cardinal Roland as Alexander III. Frederick supported Victor, but France and England immediately recognized Alexander, who excommunicated Frederick, 1160. Victor IV was only the first of a series of antipopes supported by Frederick against Alexander.

VICTOR AMADEUS I, 1587–1637, duke of Savoy, 1630–37, was born in Turin, and was married to Christine of France, sister of Louis XIII. Having succeeded his father, Charles Emmanuel I, during the War of the Mantuan Succession, Victor Amadeus I allied Savoy with France against Spain by means of the Treaty of Rivoli (1635). He was succeeded by his son Charles Emmanuel II.

VICTOR AMADEUS II, 1666–1732, duke of Savoy, 1675–1732, king of Sicily, 1713–20, and first king of Sardinia, 1720–30, was born at Turin, the son of Duke Charles Emmanuel II. He married Anne Marie of Orléans, a niece of Louis XIV, king of France, who prevailed upon him to fight against the Waldensians; but Victor Amadeus soon joined the league against the French; hostilities with Louis ensued, but ultimately a peace settlement was made. During the War of the Spanish Succession Victor was at first with the French, but again switched sides. By the Treaty of Utrecht, Victor was made King of Sicily, 1713, a title he was later forced to exchange for that of King of Sardinia, 1720. He abdicated, 1730, but his second wife, Anna, widowed contessa dí San Sebastiano, induced him to try to revoke the abdication, whereupon the former king's son had him placed in confinement, where he died.

VICTOR AMADEUS III, 1726–1796, duke of Savoy and king of Sardinia from 1773 until his death, was born at Turin, and succeeded his father, Charles Emmanuel III, as duke and king. As a patron of the arts, Victor Amadeus founded the Academy of Turin. A firm adversary of the French Revolution, he gave asylum to emigrés, fought with France, 1792–96, and was forced to cede Nice, Savoy, and parts of Piedmont to the French under the Treaty of Paris (1796).

VICTOR EMMANUEL I, 1759–1824, king of Sardinia, 1802–21, was born in Turin. He commanded Sardinian forces against the French, 1792–96, and succeeded to the throne when his elder brother Charles Emmanuel IV abdicated in his favor, 1802. The first Peace of Paris (1814) restored Savoy, Nice, and parts of Piedmont to him; the second treaty (1815) gave him Genoa. He abdicated, 1821, in favor of his brother Charles Felix.

VICTOR EMMANUEL II, 1820–78, king of Sardinia from 1849, and king of Italy from 1861, was born at Turin. He ascended the Sardinian throne, 1849, on the abdication of his father, Charles Albert, following the defeat of the Piedmontese army by the Austrians at Novara. He made Camillo di Cavour his chief political adviser, 1852, and in accordance with Cavour's policy, supported France and Britain in the Crimean War, 1854–56. Aided by Giuseppe Garibaldi, Victor Emmanuel had, by the end of 1860, created a new Italian kingdom; he formally declared himself King of Italy in 1861. He received Venice from Austria, 1866, and occupied Rome, 1871, thereby completing Italian unification.

VICTOR EMMANUEL III, 1869–1947, king of Italy, was born in Naples, and succeeded to the Italian throne, 1900, on the assassination of his father, Humbert I. Victor Emmanuel had been trained in military science, and during World War I he remained close to the front, leaving his uncle, Ferdinand, to act as regent; the king was tactful enough throughout the war not to interfere with military decisions. After the armistice, he returned to Rome to rule as constitutional monarch. When the Fascist March on Rome took place, 1922, the king refused to sign a decree of his government for martial law, and thus enabled Benito Mussolini to take power. During the period of Fascist dictatorship, the king played a subservient role, signing laws (such as those suppressing freedom of the press, and the like) that violated his oath as a constitutional monarch. The defeat of Italy in World War II and the collapse of fascism brought the king and his dynasty into disesteem. He named Crown Prince Humbert as lieutenant general of the realm, 1944, and abdicated in favor of his son, May 9, 1946, in an effort to save the House of Savoy; on June 2, 1946, however, the Italian people voted to abolish the monarchy and to establish a republic.

VICTORIA, 1819–1901, queen of Great Britain and Ireland and empress of India, was born in Kensington Palace on May 24, 1819, and was christened Alexandrina Victoria. She was the only child of Edward, duke of Kent, the fourth son of George III, and of Edward's wife, Princess Mary Louise Victoria of Saxe-Coburg-Gotha. Victoria's father died in 1820, and she was brought up carefully sheltered by her mother. She succeeded her uncle William IV on the throne, 1837, one month after her coming of age.

The new queen had no experience of public affairs, and was instructed in her duties by Lord Melbourne (William Lamb, 2nd Viscount Melbourne, 1779–1848), the Whig prime minister, who became her private secretary. In 1839 Melbourne's government was defeated in Parliament, and he resigned. The queen, however, refused to replace the Whig ladies of the bedchamber with Tory ladies. As a result, the Tory leader, Sir Robert Peel, refused to take office, and Melbourne remained prime minister until he resigned in 1841.

In 1840 the queen married her first cousin, Prince Albert of Saxe-Coburg-Gotha. It was a happy marriage, producing nine children: Victoria (1840–1901), who married the crown prince of Prussia and became the mother of Emperor William II; Albert Edward (1841–1910), the future Edward VII; Alice (1843–78), later grand duchess of Hesse-Darmstadt; Alfred (1844–1900), duke of Edinburgh and later duke of Saxe-Coburg-Gotha, who married the daughter of Czar Alexander II; Helena (1846–1923), later princess of Schleswig-Holstein; Louise (1848–1939), later duchess of Argyll; Arthur (1850–1942), duke of Connaught; Leopold (1853–84), duke of Albany; and Beatrice (1857–1944), who married Prince Henry of Battenberg (now Mountbatten). By the end of her long life the queen was an extraordinary matriarch, related by blood or marriage to all the royal families of Europe.

Under Victoria and Albert the royal court took on a strict moral tone, very much in accord with the wishes of their subjects, and in refreshing contrast to the libertine behaviour of George IV and William IV. Albert, who succeeded Melbourne as the queen's private secretary, did much to help develop the new role of the crown. Under George III the crown had taken an active part in politics. Now the crown began to take an ostensibly neutral role above party politics as a sort of constitutional adviser; the queen continued, however, to have a hand in the choice of prime ministers and their colleagues, believing as she did that the crown had the authority to choose its ministers. She recognized that she had to accept a ministry with a clear electoral majority and a solid party backing, but when this did not exist (as was often the case), she felt it was her duty to act. She took a close personal interest in the conduct of policy, notably in foreign affairs. Victoria and Albert carried on what was in fact diplomatic correspondence with the other monarchs of Europe. This sometimes led to difficulties. In the 1840's, for example, the actions of the foreign secretary, Lord Palmerston, were often at cross purposes with those of the queen, and a good deal of tension resulted. The queen finally succeeded in getting Palmerston dismissed, 1851 (see PALMERSTON, HENRY JOHN TEMPLE), but he was soon back in office as home secretary, and was prime minister for most of the period 1855–65.

Prince Albert died in 1861. For two years the queen remained in complete seclusion. She continued to wear mourning for Albert for the rest of her life. In the late 1860's Victoria's popularity reached its lowest point: she was publicly criticized for her seclusion, and her demands for dowries and allowances for her children antagonized both Parliament and the public. The turning point came, 1871, when Prince Edward's narrow recovery from a dangerous illness gained great sympathy for the queen. Her association with the growing imperialist sentiment fostered by Benjamin Disraeli further increased her popularity. The title Empress of India was conferred on her, 1876, and more and more she came to personify the whole idea of Empire. Her jubilees, 1887 and 1897, celebrating the fiftieth and sixtieth anniversaries of her accession, were demonstrations of reverence and affection as well as gigantic "pageants of empire" that captured the imagination of her subjects.

In the 1870's Victoria fell under the personal influence of Disraeli. She came to have a corresponding antipathy to William Gladstone, and to the end of the latter's career in office she harassed him and made his work difficult. Such conduct weakened her political authority, but as her power declined, her status as an institution grew. In a real sense,

Queen Victoria restored the prestige of the monarchy, and so insured its continuance. She died on Jan. 22, 1901, at Osborne, Isle of Wight, after a reign of 63 years, 7 months, and 2 days—the longest reign in English history.

Queen Victoria was under five feet tall. She was not handsome, but she bore herself with dignity and grace. She was impulsive, sentimental (most obviously after Prince Albert's death), and she could on occasion be quite obstinate—as all her prime ministers discovered. She had a strong sense of the importance of her position and was a tireless worker, faithfully performing all the duties of her office. Her favorite residences were Windsor, Osborne, and later in life Balmoral Castle in the Scottish Highlands. She was the author of *Leaves from the Journal of Our Life in the Highlands, from 1848 to 1861* (1868), and *More Leaves . . . from 1862 to 1882* (1884).　　ROBIN OGGINS

BIBLIOG.–Albert, Consort of Victoria, *Letters of the Prince Consort 1831–1861* (1938); Benjamin W. Arnold, *Queen Victoria and Her Chief Ministers* (1927); George C. A. Arthur, *Concerning Queen Victoria and Her Son* (1943); Dorothy J. Baynes, *Youthful Queen Victoria: A Discursive Narrative* (1952); Erica Beale, *Royal Cavalcade* (1939); Edward F. Benson, *Queen Victoria* (1940); Françoise de Bernardy, *Albert and Victoria* (1953); Hector Bolitho, *Reign of Queen Victoria* (1949); Meriel Buchanan, *Queen Victoria's Relations* (1954); Algernon Cecil, *Queen Victoria and Her Prime Ministers* (1953); David S. Duff, *Shy Princess: The Life of Her Royal Highness Princess Beatrice, the Youngest Daughter and Constant Companion of Queen Victoria* (1958); Marion K. W. Flexner, *Drina: England's Young Victoria* (1939); Roger Fulford, *Queen Victoria* (1952), *Hanover to Windsor* (1960); Helmut Gernsheim and Alison Gernsheim, *Victoria R: A Biography with 400 Il. Based on Her Personal Photograph Albums* (1959); Eleanor Graham, *Making of a Queen* (1940); Frank M. Hardie, *Political Influence of Queen Victoria, 1861–1901* (1938); Frank Hird, *Victoria the Woman* (1908); Clare Jerrold, *Early Court of Queen Victoria* (1912); Edith (V.) B.–L. Lytton, *Lady Lytton's Court Diary, 1895–1899* (1961); John A. R. Marriott, *Queen Victoria and Her Ministers* (1934); Frederick E. G. Ponsonby, *Side Lights on Queen Victoria* (1930); David Roberts, *Victorian Origins of the British Welfare State* (1960); Edith Saunders, *Distant Summer* (1947); Edith Sitwell, *Victoria of England* (1949); Lytton Strachey, *Queen Victoria* (1959); Victoria, Princess of Prussia, *Queen Victoria at Windsor and Balmoral* (1959); Victoria, Queen of Great Britain, *Letters: From the Archives of the House of Brandenburg-Prussia* (1939); Vera Watson, *Queen at Home: An Intimate Account of the Social and Domestic Life of Queen Victoria's Court* (1953).

VICTORIA, GUADALUPE, 1789–1843, Mexican soldier and political leader, was born Juán Manuel Félix Fernández in what later became the state of Durango. Having joined the revolutionary movement under Miguel Hidalgo y Costilla, 1810, Fernández changed his name to one suggestive of a Mexico triumphant under Our Lady of Guadalupe. When Agustín de Iturbide set himself up as Emperor Agustín I, 1822, Victoria was imprisoned, but he soon escaped and assisted López de Santa Anna in overthrowing the usurper, 1823. Victoria was elected first president of the federal republic of Mexico, 1824, and held office until 1829. There was much unrest during this period, some of it fomented by factions of Yorkist and Scottish Rite Masons, some of it associated with an unsuccessful revolt led by a Dominican priest who hoped for a restoration of Spanish rule.

VICTORIA, TOMÁS LUIS DE, also known by the Italianized form Vittoria, 1540?–1611, Spanish composer of sacred music, was born at Ávila. He was appointed, 1571, choirmaster of the Collegium Germanicum, Rome, and thenceforth made that city the center of his musical activity, aided by the patronage of Philip II, who had made Victoria's Italian education possible. Victoria's early compositions are among his most noteworthy. An early book of motets (1572), for example, contains most of his works in the free motet form, of which the best known are probably *O quam gloriosum* and *O vos omnes.* He tried to bid farewell to musical labors in a book of masses (1583), dedicated to Philip II, but the composer's retirement was a short one, and he became choirmaster to the Descalzas Reales, Madrid, 1586. One of Victoria's most important publications, *Officium hebdomadae sanctae* (Rome, 1585) contains music for Palm Sunday and the last three days of Holy Week; a second book of masses was issued in 1592. The great folio editions of his works were amplified, 1600, by yet another book, comprising masses, magnificats, motets, psalms and hymns. As tribute to the daughter of Charles V, Empress Maria (died 1603), Victoria composed what is perhaps his masterpiece, an *Officium defunctorum*. After his death, in Madrid, Victoria's works remained in vogue for a time but were all but forgotten during most of the 1800's; toward the end of the century, however, there was renewed interest in his work and a complete edition of his almost 180 pieces was issued, 1896. ANTHONY KERRIGAN

VICTORIA, city, SE Texas, seat of Victoria County; on the Guadalupe River, the Missouri Pacific and the Southern Pacific railroads, and U.S. highways 59, 77, and 87; 120 miles SW of Houston. Victoria is a trade and processing center in a major oil field. Vegetables, cotton, and livestock are raised in the area. Oil refining, cotton ginning, and food processing are leading industries. Chemicals, concrete products, and metal goods are manufactured. Foster Air Force Base is northeast. Victoria was settled by the Spanish, 1824, and was incorporated late in the 1830's. Pop. (1960) 33,047.

VICTORIA, state, SE Australia, bounded by Tasman Sea on the SE, Bass Strait on the S, and by the states of New South Wales on the N and NE, and South Australia on the W; area 87,884 sq. mi.; pop. (1959 est.) 2,796,956.

Physical Factors. The southern section of the state is mainly highland, an extension of the Great Dividing Range of New South Wales to the northeast. In the east of Victoria the mountains are rugged and reach heights of more than 6,000 feet in the Snowy Mountains. The ranges become lower in the west, and terminate in the Grampian Mountains, close to the western border of the state. In the north of Victoria the highlands slope down to the broad Murray River basin. The Murray River rises in the Snowy Mountains and flows northwestward forming the northern boundary of Victoria for some 1,200 miles. Other rivers include the Loddon and the Goulburn, which are tributaries of the Murray; and the Snowy, the Yarra, and the Glenelg, which flow south to the coast. To the south of the highlands is a discontinuous coastal plain. The dominant feature of the coast is the deep indentation of Port Phillip Bay, on which Melbourne, the capital, is located.

In the southern section of the state the climate is moderate, and the rainfall, distributed throughout the year, averages 25 to 30 inches annually. North of the highlands the rainfall averages only 12 inches annually, and the temperatures are higher, frequently reaching 100°F during the summer months. Frost is a rare occurrence.

Much of the highland area is forested, mainly with hardwoods, although there are some stands of planted conifers. Eucalyptus and gum trees are found throughout Victoria. Mallee scrub and salt brush is found in sections of the Murray Valley which are not irrigated.

Economic Factors. Victoria is an important agricultural state. Wheat is the major crop and is grown extensively in the western districts of Mallee, Wimmera, and Western. Oats, barley, and hay are also significant. In the Murray Basin there are large areas of irrigated land, and rice, grapes, fruit, and vegetables are grown. Mildura, on the Murray River, is the center of an important wine-producing region. Apples, pears, and plums are grown in large orchards in Gippsland, on the southeast coastal plain. Wool is one of Victoria's principal exports and a major source of rural income. Sheep are grazed throughout the state, though the finest wool-producing sheep are found in the Western highlands and coastal plain.

AUSTRALIAN NEWS & INFORMATION BUREAU
Collins Street is located in Melbourne, Victoria's capital and second largest city. This tree-lined thoroughfare is named for one of the founders of the city, David Collins.

In the southeast, where the rainfall is higher and the pastures are better, dairying is a major industry.

The state has few important mineral deposits. The discovery of gold played a significant role in the development of Victoria, but production is now declining. Brown coal is mined in the Latrobe Valley, near Yallourn, in the district known as Gippsland, and there is some production of black coal.

Industrial production is concentrated in the area around Port Phillip Bay, in Geelong and Melbourne. Machinery, chemicals, aircraft, automobiles, textiles, food products, and clothing are important manufactures. Victoria has an extensive road and railway network, which is centered at Melbourne.

Social Factors. Victoria's population density is the greatest of any Australian state. The inhabitants are descendants of the peoples of the British Isles. The chief centers and their populations (1959 est.) are Melbourne, 1,777,700; Geelong, 88,160; Balarat, 53,680; and Bendigo, 41,140.

The University of Melbourne, founded in 1855, has five constituent colleges. Primary education is free and compulsory between the ages of 6 and 14.

Since 1875 no religion has received state support, and there is complete religious freedom. The largest single church is the Church of England.

Government. The governor of Victoria is appointed by the British crown, but he is usually a native of the state. The governor is assisted by a cabinet, which does not exceed 14 members. Four of the cabinet members may have seats in the legislative council. The Parliament is made up of two houses: the legislative council with 34 members elected to 6-year terms, half of which are returned every third year, and the legislative assembly with 66 members. Victoria leads in social legislation and has had an old age pension since 1901. Other social benefits include war pensions, maternity allowances, unemployment and sickness allowances, widows' pensions, and child endowments. A state housing commission was established in 1938.

History. Captain James Cook, the English explorer and circumnavigator, sighted the shores of Victoria in 1770 and in 1802 Port Phillip Bay was discovered. A British colony, which was begun, 1804, was abandoned after three months. An attempt to establish a convict settlement at Settlement Point, 1826, proved a failure. However a whaling station established at Portland Bay in 1834 was successful, and sheep and cattle were introduced to the area. In 1835 700,000 acres on the shores of Port Phillip Bay were purchased from Australian aborigines by Tasmanian settlers. This act was repudiated by the British government, but some of the settlers nevertheless remained. The state became part of New South Wales in 1836, but was created as a separate colony in 1851, and was given the name Victoria. A responsible government under

BRITISH COLUMBIA GOVT. PHOTO

These imposing parliamentary buildings are located in Victoria, the provincial capital and second-largest city of British Columbia.

a constitution was established in 1855. The discovery of gold in 1851 increased the size of the settlement considerably. In 1901 Victoria, together with the other states of Australia, became a part of the Commonwealth of Australia.

VICTORIA, city, W Canada, capital of British Columbia; on the Strait of Juan de Fuca at the SE extremity of Vancouver Island; on the Canadian National, the Esquimalt and Nanaimo, and the Canadian Pacific railways; 58 miles SSW of Vancouver. The city is connected to the mainland by ferry.

Victoria is an important shipping point for the products of Vancouver Island, and is the base for an important fishing industry. Forest products make up the bulk of the export trade. The city has shipbuilding yards and railroad shops. Lumber products, tile, cement, bricks, matches, roofing material, paint, clothing, shoes, toys, and bakery goods are manufactured.

Victoria is a popular tourist resort and is noted for its flower gardens, parks, and landscaped parkways. Every year in May, tourists flock to the city to see the Victoria Garden Spring Festival. The Butchart Gardens and Beacon Hill Park, overlooking the strait, are among the noted points of interest. The Parliament buildings, resembling those at Ottawa, are located at the head of the harbor. The Dominion Astrophysical Observatory containing a 72-inch reflector, is north of the city.

Victoria was founded in 1843 as a post of the Hudson's Bay Company. It was incorporated as a city in 1862 after being made capital of the colony of Vancouver Island in 1859. The city was made the capital of British Columbia after the island colony was united with the mainland colony in 1866. (For population, see British Columbia map in Atlas.)

VICTORIA, city, capital of the British crown colony of Hong Kong. The city extends along the northern coastal plain and on the slopes of Victoria Peak on Hong Kong Island. The city is commonly referred to as Hong Kong. (For population, see China map in Atlas.)

VICTORIA, a genus of tropical American aquatic plants belonging to the family *Nymphaeaceae*. There are but two species, the *V. regia*, royal water lily, and *V. Cruziana*, originally found in D'Orbigny, Bolivia. These plants bear oval or orbicular leaves, often six feet or more in diameter. The flowers are very large. The sepals are brownish in color; the outer petals are white and spreading, and the inner petals are rose-colored and filamentous. The flowers are followed by large, green, prickly, fleshy berries containing numerous dark-colored seeds. Where there is light, heat, and a rich, mellow loam, *V. regia* is an annual.

VICTORIA, LAKE, or Victoria Nyanza, E Africa; Africa's largest lake; occupying a shallow basin, whose greatest depth is 270 feet, between the E and W

branches of the Great Rift Valley at an altitude of about 3,700 feet; area 26,200 sq. mi. Lake Victoria is the largest body of fresh water in the world after Lake Superior. The lake lies within former British areas of control, with Uganda to the north, Kenya to the northeast, and Tanzania to the east, south, and west. The lake extends some 250 miles from north to south and 200 miles from east to west. The Kagera River, Lake Victoria's principal tributary, enters the lake in the west. This river is the most remote headstream of the Nile River. The Victoria Nile leaves the northern part of the lake at Napoleon Gulf, flows northward past Jinja, and pours over Owen Falls, where the river has been dammed. The shore of Lake Victoria is deeply indented; on the north is Murchison Bay, with the large port of Entebbe in Uganda. Kavironda Gulf, which is 6 miles wide and 45 miles long, extends eastward into Kenya. At its east is the port of Kisumu, the first terminus of the Kenya and Uganda Railway, which leads to the Indian Ocean port of Mombasa. At the southeast is Speke Gulf and the southwest Emin Pasha Gulf, the former masked by Ukerewe, the largest island. Lake Victoria has a number of shallow reefs and islands, the latter including the Sese Group in the northwest. Most of the islands are well wooded and picturesque. Except for low cliffs fronting the southwest, the shore slopes are low; on the west and north they are swampy. The Lake Victoria area has the greatest population density of east Africa.

Lake Victoria was discovered by J. H. Speke, an English explorer, in 1858, and in 1875 was circumnavigated by Sir Henry Morton Stanley, the Welsh explorer. The lake was originally known as Lake Ukerewe, but was renamed in honor of Queen Victoria. There is regular steamer service to all parts of the lake.

VICTORIA CROSS, a decoration conferred for personal bravery on commissioned officers and enlisted personnel of all ranks of the British armed services. It was founded at the end of the Crimean War, 1856. It consists of a bronze Maltese cross, bearing the royal crown surmounted by a lion, and the inscription, "For Valour." In 1920 its award was extended to civilians for bravery in war.

VICTORIA DE LAS TUNAS, town, E Cuba, in the province of Oriente; on a railroad and the Central Highway, 375 miles SE of Havana. The town is in an important sugar-producing region. During the Cuban Revolution of the nineteenth century, the city was the scene of a decisive battle in which Cuban patriots defeated Spanish forces.

VICTORIA FALLS, E Africa, on the Zambezi River. It is located between Zambia and Rhodesia. The spectacular falls drop 350 feet into a deep, narrow

About 75 million gallons of water per minute tumble over Victoria Falls, which are twice the height of Niagara. A bridge spans the gorge 420 feet above the Zambezi River.

EWING GALLOWAY

fissure which is only about 400 feet wide. The river leaves the chasm through a narrow gorge known as the Boiling Pot and flows through a canyon for 40 miles more. The area around the falls has been made into a national park for wild game. Below the falls a railway bridge 650 feet long was built in 1905. Victoria Falls was discovered by the explorer David Livingstone in 1855 and named by him for Queen Victoria.

VICTORIAVILLE, town, S Québec, in Arthabaska County: on the Nicolet River and the Canadian National Railway; 90 miles ENE of Montreal. The town is a processing center for a timber-cutting and dairy-farming area. The settlement was first named Demersville after Modeste Demers, a Catholic bishop. It was renamed in honor of Queen Victoria in 1861, and incorporated in 1890. Farm machinery, bricks, garments, cheese, and maple-sugar products are manufactured. (For population, see Quebec map in Atlas.)

VICUNA, one of the two wild species of llama. The vicuña, or vicugna, *Lama vicugna*, is smaller and more slightly built than the guanaco, the other species of llama. The vicuña is pale yellow and has an exceptionally soft, silky fleece and hide. It is found at higher altitudes of the Andes, in flocks consisting of 1 male and from 6 to 12 females. Vicuñas are hunted by the Indians for their wool, usually by surrounding a flock and driving it into an enclosure where all are killed. The animal is rarely tamed. See LLAMA.

VIDAL, GORE, 1925-　, U.S. writer, was born in West Point, N.Y. Vidal wrote his first novel, *Williwaw* (1946), at the age of 19, while serving in the U.S. Army during World War II. After the war he spent several years in Guatemala, Europe, and North Africa. In 1960 Vidal was an unsuccessful candidate for a seat in the U.S. House of Representatives from New York. Among his other works are the novels *The City and the Pillar* (1948), *A Search for the King* (1950), *The Judgment of Paris* (1952), and *Messiah* (1954); and the plays *Visit to a Small Planet* (1957) and *The Best Man* (1960).

VIDAL, PEIRE, 1175-1215, Provençal troubadour, was born in Toulouse, France. Among his patrons were Alfonso II, king of Aragon, Alfonso VIII, king of Castile, the Counts of Marseilles and Montferrat, and Richard I of England, whom he accompanied on the Third Crusade, 1189-92. His various travels took him to Italy, Cyprus, Hungary, Spain, and Malta. His songs are excellent examples of troubadour love poetry. See PROVENÇAL LANGUAGE AND LITERATURE.

VIDALIA, town, E Louisiana, seat of Concordia Parish; on the Mississippi River, the Louisiana Midland, the Missouri Pacific, and the Natchez and Southern railroads, and U.S. highway 84; 80 miles NNW of Baton Rouge. The town is a trade and processing center for an area in which timber is cut and cotton is grown. Vidalia was founded in 1801. Pop. (1960) 4,313.

VIDAR, one of the Aesir, the principal gods of Scandinavian mythology, was the son of Odin and the giantess Grid. Vidar, known as the Silent One, rivaled Thor in strength. By some accounts he was a survivor of Ragnarök, the cataclysmic battle between the gods and the forces of evil. During the battle, Vidar avenged his father's death by stepping on the monstrous Fenris wolf's jaw and tearing him in half.

VIDOCQ, FRANCOIS-EUGENE, 1775-1857, French police officer and adventurer, was born in Arras. After an adventurous youth, which included several years at hard labor aboard a prison galley, Vidocq offered his services to the Paris police and was put in charge of a special band of detectives and ex-convicts, 1809. Having saved a small fortune, Vidocq retired from police work, 1827, and opened a paper mill staffed with ex-convicts. The venture failed, and Vidocq returned to the police force, 1832, but was soon discharged when it was discovered that one of the robberies he had investigated had been organized by him in the first place. He organized a private detective agency, but it was only moderately successful and was eventually suppressed. Vidocq spent his later years in poverty. It is doubtful whether the *Memoires de Vidocq* (1828) was actually written by him.

VIEDMA, city, SE Argentina, capital of Río Negro Province, in Patagonia; on the Negro River, 20 miles from the Atlantic Ocean, and 150 miles SSW of Bahía Blanca. Viedma is a commercial and administrative center in an area in which wheat and alfalfa are grown and cattle and sheep are raised.

VIELE-GRIFFIN, FRANCIS, 1864-1937, U.S.-born French Symbolist poet, was born Egbert Ludovicus Vielé in Norfolk, Va., the son of the Union general, Egbert Ludovicus Vielé. The boy was taken by his mother to France, 1872; he spent the rest of his life there and became one of the most prominent of the French Symbolist poets, but he never surrendered his U.S. citizenship. Among his works are *Poèmes et poésies* (1886-93), *La clarté de la vie* (1897), *Phocas le jardinier* (1898), *La partenza* (1899), *La légende ailée de Wieland le forgeron* (1900), *Voix d'Ionie* (1904), *Couronne offerte à la muse romaine* (1922), and *Le domaine royal* (1923). His work is generally elliptical and sensuous. See SYMBOLISTS.

VIENNA, city, S central Georgia, seat of Dooly County; on the Atlantic Coast Line and the Southern railroads, and on U.S. highway 41; 115 miles SSE of Atlanta. The city is a trade and processing center for an area in which timber is cut, and vegetables, pecans, livestock, melons, cotton, and, peanuts are raised. Vienna was incorporated in 1841. Pop. (1960) 2,099.

VIENNA, city, S Illinois, seat of Johnson County; on the New York Central Railroad and U.S. highway 45; 110 miles SE of St. Louis. The city is a trade center for an area in which fruit, corn, and livestock are raised. Vienna was incorporated in 1837. Pop. (1960) 1,094.

VIENNA, town, central Missouri, seat of Maries County; on the Gasconade River and U.S. highway 63; 28 miles SSE of Jefferson City. The town is a trade center for an area in which corn and fruit are grown. Vienna was settled in the mid-1850's. Pop. (1960) 536.

VIENNA, Austrian Wien, city, NE Austria, on the south bank of the Danube River where the Danube leaves the Alps foothills to flow across the Pannonian Plain; 320 miles SSE of Berlin and 460 miles NNE of Rome; pop. (1961) 1,627,566. Vienna is the capital, largest city, and the commercial, cultural, and transportation center of Austria.

Setting. The Inner City (Innere Stadt) of Vienna lies on the Danube Canal northwest of the Vienna River. It is on a river terrace separated from the Danube by a flood plain. The city has a moderate climate with January average temperatures of 27°F and July averages of 68°F. Average annual precipitation is 24.6 inches, three-fifths of it during the summer.

Economy. There is virtually no heavy industry in Vienna. The manufacture of light consumer goods, however, gives employment to about 20 per cent of the city's labor force. Machinery, leather goods, glassware, and luxury goods are the main items manufactured. Industrial plants are concentrated at Leopoldstadt and Floridsdorf, industrial suburbs between the Danube Canal and the Danube River. Almost one-third of the city's labor force is employed in administration, transportation, communications, and the wholesale and retail trades. The Inner City, or central business district, contains the city's major banks, insurance companies, retail stores, and commercial offices. Vienna is also a center for publishing and motion picture production.

The city is one of the leading ports on the Danube, trade with West Germany, upstream, being especially heavy. There are numerous quays on the Danube Canal. In 1960, the Rhine–Main–Danube Canal was slated to be reconstructed so as to improve Vienna's water connections with Western Europe; an Oder-Danube Canal was slated to be dug so as to facilitate the import of coal from Silesia; and an expansion of Vienna's port facilities was planned, a new grain port was to be built at Albern. By the end of 1960 a new oil port at Lobau was already receiving petroleum by pipeline from Zisterdorf, some 30 miles northeast of the city. The leading commodities handled at the port of Vienna are coal, coke, oil, grain, and timber. Riverborne trade totaled more than 5 million tons in 1958.

Social Factors. Vienna is one of Europe's most cosmopolitan cities. Before World War I many persons moved to Vienna from the areas that later became Czechoslovakia, Hungary, Rumania, and Yugoslavia. Most later immigrants came from other parts of Austria, but early in the 1960's Vienna's population still included a large number of non-Austrians. During the 1950's and early 1960's the resident population of the Inner City steadily declined, while the populations of suburbs to the west, southwest, and south expanded rapidly. Despite other changes, the population of Vienna continued to be predominantly of the Roman Catholic faith.

Greater Vienna is a province of the Austrian Federal Republic and, as such, exercises autonomy in its educational system. School attendance is compulsory, and both elementary and secondary institutions are excellently organized. The University of Vienna (1365) is maintained by the Austrian government. There are also two technical high schools, an agricultural college, a veterinary college, and academies of applied arts, music, and dramatic art in the city. The Viennese have paid great attention to welfare facilities such as public housing and recreational areas. The public transportation system is based mainly on buses and trolley cars.

Features of Interest. The relatively simple town plan of Vienna owes much to the fact that at different times the city was enclosed by walls. The innermost of these was replaced by a magnificent 150-foot-wide boulevard, the Ringstrasse; an outer zone is now occupied by the Gürtelstrasse, or belt road. Between the Ringstrasse and the Danube Canal lies historic Vienna, with its wealth of architectural gems. Between the Ringstrasse and the Gürtelstrasse is the nineteenth century town with its largely residential character. Beyond that zone, modern suburbs have spread up the wooded valleys of the nearby hills. Between the canal and the Danube are new industrial suburbs, especially Floridsdorf, with extensive railroad classification yards, docks, and light industries.

Because of its greater age, the Inner City contains most of Vienna's historical buildings. St. Stephen's Cathedral, with its 450-foot-high tower, marble altars, catacombs, and the sarcophagus of Frederick III; the former Imperial Palace (Hofburg), now a museum and library, set in parklike grounds; the old City Hall (Rathaus); and a wealth of museums, art galleries, theaters, and other institutions reflect the importance of Vienna as a great and venerable cultural and administrative center. One of the best known public buildings is the Opera House, which was virtually destroyed during World War II but was rebuilt. Recreational spaces are a major attraction in the city. To the west and southwest are wooded hills, and within the city limits are the Prater Park east of the canal and several ornamental gardens between the Ringstrasse and the Gürtelstrasse.

History. The site of Vienna was settled in pre-Roman times, but the establishment there of the Roman imperial city of Vindobona, during the first century of the Christian Era, marked the first urban settlement. Vienna changed hands frequently among the Huns, Lombards, Franks, and Hungarians until 1278, when it became the seat of the Hapsburg

Dynasty following Rudolph of Hapsburg's defeat of Ottocar of Bohemia. Strongly fortified, the city was able to resist several sieges by the Turks. It was made the capital of the Hapsburg Empire by Francis I, 1745–65, became one of Europe's leading political centers, and was chosen as the site of the Congress of Vienna, 1815. The city was extensively remodeled during the reign of Emperor Francis Joseph I, 1848–1916, and it became one of Europe's principal centers of learning and culture. With the dismemberment of the Austro-Hungarian Empire at the close of World War I, 1918, Vienna became the capital of an Austria greatly reduced in size; the new national frontiers blocked much of the city's previously large trade with eastern Europe. Further restrictions on Vienna's role as a commercial hub arose after World War II from the occupation of the city by the military forces of the United States, Great Britain, France, and the Soviet Union. With the conclusion of the Austrian Peace Treaty (1955), the troops were withdrawn and Vienna once again became the capital of an independent Austria. Its commercial ties with Communist eastern Europe did not regain their prewar importance, however. As a consequence, Vienna's population fell considerably from the 2,031,498 recorded in 1910, and the city became less important.

VIENNA, CONGRESS OF, an assembly of representatives of European states who met at Vienna, Austria, between September, 1814, and June, 1815, for the purpose of reorganizing European political conditions, which had become highly disorganized as a result of the French Revolution and the subsequent wars of conquest by the French Emperor Napoleon I, who had been defeated, spring, 1814, and exiled to Elba. All of the countries that had been involved in wars against Napoleon were represented at the congress, but the principals were Austria, Great Britain, Prussia, and Russia; France was represented by Charles Maurice de Tallyrand-Perigord, foreign minister for the newly restored Bourbon monarch.

The claims of Great Britain against France, and the borders of France as well, had been fixed, May 30, 1814, by treaty; therefore, two bodies were nominated by the congress to debate the German and the general European affairs respectively. The decision as to the distribution of regained territories was supposed to depend upon the recommendations of a special committee, of which France was not a member. Tallyrand, nevertheless, managed to make French interests a strong factor. Smaller nations were disillusioned in the negotiations, which they had believed to have been entrusted to a quasi-European parliament.

The congress, much sidetracked in its business by splendid festivities held by Emperor Francis I of Austria, concerned itself chiefly with Russia's and Prussia's territorial compensations. Russia received the kingdom of Poland, which then embraced Warsaw and the former Russian-Polish provinces. There were embittered negotiations between Austria and Prussia over Saxony and open warfare threatened to break out between Russia and Prussia on the one hand and the followers of Tallyrand and the Austrian Prime Minister Prince Von Metternich on the other, Metternich having gained the support of Great Britain, Bavaria, and smaller German states. In January, 1815, Austria, France and Great Britain concluded a triple alliance with the minor German states joining their pact. Finally, although Prussia and Austria had prepared for a war, concessions were made on both sides; for example, Saxony was divided between Austria and Prussia, with Prussia renouncing approximately one-half of the Saxonian country.

For this loss Prussia was compensated by three new western provinces: Westphalia, Cleve-Berg, and Lower Rhine. There were other territorial reorganizations involving Holland, Bavaria, Hanover, Sweden, and Denmark.

Most German countries retained the status they had gained under Napoleon, and were organized into a confederation to replace the Holy Roman Empire, which had been abolished by Napoleon, 1806. Austria, through the Congress of Vienna, regained sovereignty over much of northern Italy, including Venice, Tuscany, and Parma, and secured new domains in southern Germany, including the city of Salzburg and the Tirol Region. Among other important settlements were the establishment of the Kingdom of the Netherlands and the re-establishment of the Swiss Federation.

In March, 1815, Napoleon left Elba with a small force, landed at Cannes, gained the support of French army forces sent to capture him, and marched on Paris. Talleyrand, acting in the interest of the Bourbons, persuaded Russia, Prussia, and Great Britain to renew their alliance to fight Napoleon, March 25; all nations represented at the congress joined in this alliance, except Sweden and Spain. The return of Napoleon accelerated the negotiations of the congress and its final acts were agreed upon, June 9, 1815.

Napoleon was defeated at Waterloo in the southern Netherlands (Belgium), June 18, 1815, and a new peace treaty, between the Allies and France was signed at Paris on November 20 the same year. See PARIS, TREATIES OF.

The over-all accomplishment of the congress of Vienna was to re-establish among the governments of Europe a balance of power that in effect prevented a major war from breaking out on the Continent for nearly 100 years. On the other hand, its arrangements entrenched monarchial systems of government over many people who either had experienced or were to demand the representative, republican form of government manifested by the French Revolution; in doing so the congress sowed the seeds of revolution.

VIENNA, UNIVERSITY OF, a public institution of higher education in Vienna, Austria. The school was founded, 1365, by Duke Rudolf IV of Austria, and was confirmed by Papal Bull of Urban V. Its original faculties were law, medicine, and arts. Pope Urban VI established the faculty of Roman Catholic theology, 1384. Other divisions, founded later, were faculties of Protestant theology; philosophy, liberal arts, and natural sciences; institutes for a historical research, Austrian archaeology, radium research and nuclear physics, and physical education; and an interpreters institute. The university became a state institution, 1554, and, under twentieth century Austrian law was responsible to the federal ministry of education.

Among the school's several libraries are the main library of the university, and libraries of Roman Catholic theology, Protestant theology, law, and historical research. The university maintains the archives and museum of the University of Vienna, botanical gardens, and collections of materials in the fields of anatomy, archaeology, history of medicine, and astronomy.

VIENNE, department, W France, bounded NW by Maine-et-Loire, N and NE by Indre-et-Loire, E by Indre, SE by Haute-Vienne, S by Charente, and W by Deux-Sèvres; area of the department is 2,720 sq. mi.

Vienne forms part of the region known as Poitou and is a broad plain, sloping gradually northward from the Massif Central to the Loire River. In the south the plain is formed mainly on limestones and sandstones and is less fertile than it is in the north, where it is mainly clay and has rich pastures. The chief river, the Vienne, is a tributary of the Loire. Wheat, oats, and barley are grown, and wine grapes are cultivated. Poultry and livestock are raised. Châtellerault is the main industrial town. Poitiers is the capital. Vienne was formed in 1790 from Poitou and parts of Touraine and Berry.

VIENNE, town, SE France, in the department of Isère, on the Rhône River, 18 miles S of Lyon. Vienne has textile mills, distilleries, iron foundries, and metal refineries. Vienne is noted for its many Roman ruins

including a Roman aqueduct which is still in use. A thirteenth century castle, now in ruins, was built on Roman foundations. A Roman temple, a Roman forum, and Roman theater are other interesting remains. St. Maurice (eleventh-sixteenth centuries), the largest church in Vienne, was formerly a cathedral. Vienne was the capital of the Allobroges. It was made a Roman colony in 47 B.C. and was known as Vienna Senatoria. In 450 it became the see of an archbishopric that endured until 1790. During the early centuries it was the capital of the Kingdom of Burgundy, and later, of the Kingdom of Arles. Vienne was sacked by the Lombards in the sixth century and by the Saracens in the eighth century. In the fifteenth century Vienne became part of Dauphiny. (For population, see France map in Atlas.)

VIENTIANE, city, administrative capital of Laos; on the Mekong River, on the Thailand border; 135 miles SSE of Luang Prabang. Vientiane is connected with the royal capital at Luang Prabang by highway, and by river boat transport on the Mekong River. Vientiane is the most important commercial center in Laos. Silk, cotton, and brocade textiles are manufactured. Food processing and wood working are also important local industries. Vientiane is noted for its Buddhist pagodas. The city became capital of the Kingdom of Vientiane in 1707. In 1827 it was conquered by Thai forces from Siam (Thailand). In 1893 Vientiane sought French protection from the Thai, and the French made it the capital of the Indochinese state of Laos. In 1954 Vientiane became the capital of the newly independent nation of Laos. Pop. (1963 est.) 100,000.

VIERECK, GEORGE SYLVESTER, (1884–1962), U.S. writer, was born in Munich, Germany, and emigrated with his father to the United States when he was 11 years old. He was graduated from the College of the City of New York, 1906, and the following year received national attention through the publication of his first book of English verse, *Nineveh and Other Poems* (1907). His controversial views on U.S.–German relations, expressed at the height of anti-German sentiment in his magazine *The Fatherland* (later the *American Monthly*), brought him into disfavor during World War I, and resulted in his being sent to prison during World War II. Among his other works are *Confessions of a Barbarian* (1910); *Songs of Armageddon* (1916); *My First 2000 Years* (1928) and *Salomé, the Wandering Jewess* (1931), both written with Paul Eldridge; and *Men into Beasts* (1952).

VIERECK, PETER ROBERT EDWIN, (1916–), U.S. Pulitzer prize-winning poet and political writer, the son of George Sylvester Viereck, was born in New York City. He studied at Harvard and Oxford and served with the U.S. Army in the Italian and African campaigns of World War II. He taught at Smith College, 1947–48, and was Fulbright professor in American poetry and civilization at the University of Florence, 1955. His volume of poetry, *Terror and Decorum* (1948), won the 1949 Pulitzer prize. Among his other works of poetry are *Strike Through the Mask!* (1950), *The First Morning: New Poems* (1952), and *The Tree Witch: A Poem and Play* (1960). Among his prose works are *Metapolitics* (1941), and *Conservatism, from John Adams to Churchill* (1956); and *Conservatism Revisited and the New Conservatism: What Went Wrong?* (1962).

VIETE, FRANCOIS, Latin name Franciscus Vieta, 1540–1603, French mathematician, called the father of modern algebra, was born in Fontenay-le-Comte, where he practiced law. As privy councilor to King Henry IV, he broke the code used by the Spaniards during the French civil wars. Viète introduced the use of letters to represent algebraic quantities, the addition and multiplication of algebraic quantities, and the elevation of a binomial to higher powers; he also made valuable contributions to geometry and trigonometry. His *Opera mathematica* (1646) is of continuing interest to mathematicians.

VIETNAM, country, SE Asia, occupying the eastern fringe of the Indochinese Peninsula; bounded on the N by China, on the E and S by the South China Sea, and on the W by Cambodia and Laos; extends 1,200 miles N-S and varies in width from 25 to 300 miles; divided along its narrow neck at about 17°N. latitude between North Vietnam, area 63,360 sq. mi.; pop. (1964 est.) 17,900,000, and South Vietnam, area 65,730 sq. mi.; pop. (1964 est.) 15,715,000. The capital of North Vietnam is Hanoi, of South Vietnam, Saigon. See map in Atlas, Vol. 20.

Physical Features. The dominant topographic feature of Vietnam is the rugged Annamese Mountains, which occupy much of the land area of the nation, and stretch the length of the country between the Yunnan Plateau of China to the Mekong River delta. This rugged highland area has peaks with elevations of more than 8,000 feet, the highest being Fan Si Pan (10,308 ft.), in the extreme northwest. It is essentially a series of westward-tilting high plateaus with rather abrupt eastern slopes. To the south, a covering of sandstone has been largely eroded away to expose ancient crystalline rocks. To the north, beds of sandstone and limestone form the surface rock layers. To the northeast, a structural depression occupied by the Red River, the major stream of the north, separates the Annamese Mountains from the lower Tonkin Mountains.

Between these two mountain areas is the flat Red River Plain, with an area of about 6,000 square miles. Most of the plain embraces the delta of the Red River and is crossed by a maze of distributary channels and canals. In the extreme south is the second major plain of Vietnam, the delta of the Mekong River, with an area of about 14,000 square miles. Between the two lowland plains, along the South China Sea coast, are a number of small deltas separated from each other by spurs of the main

Location Map of Vietnam

mountain range. This section of the coast is fringed by rocky offshore islands and has many fine natural harbors guarded by rocky headlands. The difficulties of travel into the mountainous interior have discouraged port development.

The southern end of Vietnam has a tropical monsoon climate with a hot, humid, wet season from May to October and a dry season the remainder of the year. Saigon, typical of this area, averages 78 inches of rainfall each year, confined almost entirely to the months between April and October, and has an average temperature of 86°F in April, its warmest month, and 79° in December, its coolest month. To the north, onshore winter monsoons and the China Sea typhoons of fall lengthen the rainy season to nine months and add greatly to the precipitation total. In North Vietnam a further variation is provided by middle-latitude cyclones, which bring in spells of cool weather or of drizzly rainfall in mid-winter. This region has a subtropical climate.

Associated with the wet tropical conditions of Vietnam is a native vegetation consisting of tropical evergreen forests on the wetter eastward-facing mountain slopes, tropical semideciduous monsoon forests in well defined wet and dry areas, tropical mountain forests at higher elevations, and swamp forests in the deltaic lowlands. The native forests have been greatly reduced by clearing and burning and have been supplanted over wide areas by scrub and coarse grasses.

Social Factors. The Vietnamese, or Annamese, a Mongoloid people who probably originated in southwestern China, comprise about 90 per cent of the Vietnamese population; and most of them live in the lowland areas, largely as rice growers. There are about 1.5 million representatives of such various peoples as the Thai, Meo, Man, Tho, Nung, Bahner, Rhade, and Jarai, who live in the interior uplands. Most of these groups of late comers from interior China engaged in primitive, nomadic types of agriculture. The Chinese, who number about a million, are mainly urban dwellers, and engage in trade and small industry, as elsewhere in southeastern Asia. Other groups in Vietnam are Cambodians, Chams, and French. The last mainly hold professional and managerial positions.

Buddhism is the dominant religion of Vietnam, and associated with it is Taoism. Other important religious groups are the Caodaists, a cult based upon a synthesis of Christian, Buddhist, and Confucian principles, with about 1.5 million adherents; and Roman Catholics, of whom there are about one million. Minority religious groups have had strong political influence in South Vietnam, and, until 1956, the Caodaists and the Hao (a Buddhist sect) even had their own military forces.

Economic Factors. About 90 per cent of Vietnamese gain their livelihood from agriculture. Rice, mainly for domestic consumption, is the dominant crop in the prevailing small-farm, small-field agricultural system. In some areas, such as the Mekong Delta and the small coastal deltas, rice is almost the sole crop. In the Red River Plain rice is also the leading crop, but there are many varieties of other crops produced in significant amounts. These include corn, sugar cane, sweet potatoes, cotton, and mulberry. On the slopes adjacent to the rice-producing lowlands of the south are commercial plantations producing rubber, tea, and coffee for export. Quinine, cinnamon, vegetable dyes, copra, peanuts, and tobacco are other commercial agricultural products. Cattle, water buffaloes, pigs, and poultry are the common livestock of Vietnam. The most important source of protein in the Vietnamese diet, however, is fish and fish products.

North Vietnam has a variety of valuable minerals. The most important, anthracite, is obtained from open-pit mines near Along Bay. It is used for generation of electric power and for export. Zinc, salt, limestone, gold, iron, tungsten, tin, and antimony are also mined in the north. Mineral deposits in

The scarcity of automobiles in North Vietnam makes bicycles the major mode of transportation. In the capital city of Hanoi residents peddle to work.

A U.S. air cavalry division in South Vietnam holds a training exercise involving a Chinook helicopter. The division is part of the large U.S. force in South Vietnam.

South Vietnam are small and scattered. Although Vietnam is rich in timber resources its forests have not been exploited to any great extent.

North Vietnam, with its mineral resources, variety of agricultural raw materials, and available water power, is the leading industrial area not only of Vietnam but of the whole Indochinese Peninsula. Cement making, metal refining, silk reeling, cotton weaving, and soapmaking are the leading industries. The second industrial area, centered in Saigon, is more typical of southeastern Asia, featuring industries such as rice and lumber milling and sugar refining.

From the beginning of World War II, 1939, Vietnamese trade relationships remained unstable. Although France was important in South Vietnamese trade, the United States, Japan, and Great Britain gradually acquired a large share of the country's commerce. The usual exchange is that of raw or partially processed tropical products from Vietnam for manufactured goods. Saigon, and its twin city of Cholon, is the dominant port and accounts for practically all the foreign commerce of South Vietnam. Saigon is connected with all parts of the Mekong Delta by a network of waterways and to Cambodia and Laos by the Mekong River. Northern Vietnamese trade is mainly oriented toward China. Haiphong, the leading port, is connected with Hanoi, the leading city, by rail.

The railroad system of Vietnam is centered on Hanoi and Saigon, which were at one time connected by a line extending the length of the country. Due to the hostilities between North and South Vietnam the line is cut at about 17° N. latitude and damaged elsewhere.   ALFRED W. BOOTH

History. What is now Vietnam was divided early in the Christian Era into the kingdoms of Annam and Champa. Annam, on the southern border of China, was periodically incorporated into the Chinese empire after the conquest by the Han dynasty, A.D. 111. Although Chinese political control waxed and waned, Chinese culture became dominant; later the influence of Indian culture was felt as well, particularly in religion and art.

South of Annam on the east coast was the kingdom of Champa, founded in the second century A.D. and never conquered by the Chinese. By the seventeenth century Annam had annexed all of Champa and by the beginning of the nineteenth Annamite culture prevailed east of the mountains separating the east coast from the Mekong delta. A vernacular literature was being written in a script different from Chinese and local cults combined with the religions of Buddhism, Taoism, and Confucianism. West of Annam and Champa was the kingdom of Cambodia in the fertile Mekong River delta. The Annamese, gradually spreading west, finally overran the delta by the beginning of the nineteenth century and it was incorporated into the Annam Empire.

Contact with Europe began in the sixteenth century, increasing in the seventeenth with the arrival of numerous merchants and Catholic missionaries, mainly French. One of these missionaries was largely responsible for adapting the Roman alphabet to the Vietnamese language. Late in the eighteenth century the north and south were unified by one emperor with French help. His successors pursued a policy of persecuting Christians, which finally resulted in French military intervention. Concern for missionaries was combined with French commercial and political ambition; in 1862 the eastern half and in 1867 the western half of Cochin China (southern Vietnam) were annexed as a French colony. During this period a French protectorate over Cambodia was established. In 1883, after further military operations, the Annamite government agreed to a French protectorate over Annam (central Vietnam) and Tonkin (northern Vietnam). Although there were periodic Vietnamese revolts until the end of the nineteenth century, France began to administer the country and, together with the French protectorates of Cambodia and Laos, which became a protectorate in 1893, Vietnam formed part of what came to be called French Indochina.

During World War II the Japanese occupied Vietnam and in 1945 declared its independence from France. At the same time a nationalist revolutionary party, the Vietminh, was organized under the leadership of Ho Chi Minh, a Communist, who established an administration for an independent Vietnam (Tonkin, Annam, and Cochin China). From 1946 to 1954 the Vietminh waged a successful guerrilla war against the French, culminating in the capture of Dien Bien Phu.

In July, 1954, as the result of a conference at Geneva, Switzerland, the war between the French and Vietminh forces ended. The country was temporarily divided into North Vietnam, headed by the Communist Ho Chi Minh, and South Vietnam, headed by Emperor Bao Dai. Elections to unite the two sections were scheduled for 1956. They did not take place, however, and Vietnam remained, in effect, two separate countries. North Vietnam, called the Democratic Republic of Vietnam, became associated with the Communist bloc, while South Vietnam became allied with the West.

South Vietnam held a national referendum in 1955 which deposed Bao Dai and established the Republic of Vietnam with Ngo Dinh Diem as president. A new constitution was adopted in 1956, vesting executive power in the president and legislative power in a unicameral national assembly, both to be elected by universal vote.

Tension between South and North Vietnam resulted when fighting broke out between Communist guerrillas (the Vietcong) and South Vietnamese soldiers. As the situation worsened, Diem declared a state of emergency in South Vietnam and accused North Vietnam of arming the Vietcong. In the meantime, the United States began a program of military and economic aid to South Vietnam to bolster the country against alleged Communist aggression.

In November, 1963, President Diem was overthrown by a military coup, climaxing a period of unrest and religious conflict in which the Buddhist majority of the population was subjected to various repressive measures by the government of the president and his close advisers, all Roman Catholics. In May, government troops had fired on and killed nine protesting Buddhists. In a short-lived attempt at conciliation, the government agreed in June to allow greater freedom to Buddhist priests and their followers and to cease arresting and mistreating them. When the government broke this pledge, demonstrations broke out again and the government toppled.

With Diem's downfall the country witnessed a series of military and civilian governments, all trying to cope with the nation's problems. As political instability prevailed in Saigon, the Vietcong grew bolder in the countryside. The United States and the South Vietnamese government charged North Vietnam with not only aiding the Vietcong with arms but with sending North Vietnamese troops into South Vietnam. To reverse the worsening situation, the United States in 1964 began bombing selected military targets in North Vietnam and instituted a massive buildup of U.S. troops in South Vietnam. By 1969 U.S. military forces there numbered over 500,000.

In the meantime, the political situation in South Vietnam had solidified to the extent that air vice marshal Nguyen Cao Ky had assumed the premiership and had supervised the election of a constituent assembly whose job it was to write a new constitution for the country. In October, 1966, Ky went to Manila, Republic of the Philippines, to confer with U.S. Pres. Lyndon B. Johnson and the leaders of other Asian and Pacific nations (South Korea, New Zealand, Australia, the Philippines, Thailand) who,

in some way, were aiding South Vietnam. At the conclusion of the conference President Johnson flew to Cam Ranh Bay, a U.S. air and supply base in South Vietnam, to meet with U.S. troops and to pledge support for the U.S. effort in South Vietnam.

The military regime, meanwhile, progressed with plans to hold national elections on Sept. 3, 1967. Despite widespread charges of fraud, the campaign proceeded vigorously, with 10 civilian candidates arrayed against a military ticket. General Nguyen Van Thieu, running for president, with Ky in the vice-presidential slot, won as expected, but with only 34.7 per cent of the vote.

In February, 1968, the Communist forces launched a massive offensive to topple the South Vietnamese government once and for all. Although the offensive failed, American opposition to U.S. involvement in the war was such that President Johnson announced in March a partial, and later a complete, halt of the bombing of North Vietnam. This cessation of the bombing led to talks in Paris between U.S. and North Vietnamese representatives on ending the conflict. These talks were expanded in 1969 to include delegations from South Vietnam and the Vietcong.

North Vietnam based its first government on the Vietnamese constitution of 1946, framed for the entire country by a specially elected national assembly. The constitution set up a single-chamber parliament to be elected by universal vote. The parliament was to choose a president who would select a prime minister. The French-Vietnamese war intervened and the parliament was never elected. Consequently the national assembly and the Lao Dong (Communist party) became the actual organs of government. Ho Chi Minh was named president in 1945 and continued in the 1960's. A constitution drafted in 1960 provides for a national assembly elected every four years. The assembly elects the president and vice-president, may amend the constitution, and appoints the premier and ministers. North Vietnam has instituted a gradual program of socialization of agriculture and industry. See ANNAM; COCHIN CHINA; INDOCHINA; TONKIN.

BIBLIOG.–Joseph Buttinger, *Vietnam: A Dragon Embattled* (2 vols., 1967); Ann Crawford, *Customs and Culture of Vietnam* (1966); Bernard B. Fall, *Street Without Joy* (1966), *The Two Vietnams: A Political and Military Analysis* (1966); Ellen Hammer, *The Struggle for Indochina, 1940–1955* (1966); Hoang Van Chi, *From Colonialism to Communism: A Case History of North Vietnam* (1964); P.J. Honey, *Communism in North Vietnam, Its Role in the Sino-Soviet Dispute* (1963); George M. Kahin and John W. Lewis, *The United States in Vietnam* (1967); Jean Lacouture, *Vietnam: Between Two Truces* (1966); Donald Lancaster, *The Emancipation of French Indochina* (1961); Douglas Pike, *Viet Cong* (1966); Robert Shaplen, *Lost Revolution: The U.S. in Vietnam, 1946–1966* (1965); Truong Chinh, *Primer for Revolt* (1963); Vo Nguyen Giap, *People's War, People's Army* (1962); Denis Warner, *The Last Confucian: Vietnam, South-East Asia, and the West* (1963).

Women bring produce to the market at Can Tho, a provincial capital of South Vietnam.

JAMES K. LEE-PIX

Most of North Vietnam's Red River Plain is under intensive paddy cultivation. Rice is Vietnam's staple food.

CAMERA PRESS-PIX

Madame Vigée-Lebrun and Her Daughter, a self portrait, reveals the French court painter's ability to present personality in a charming, if somewhat sentimental fashion.

VIGÉE-LEBRUN, MARIE ANNE ÉLISABETH, 1755–1842, French painter, was born in Paris, the daughter of Louis Vigée, a socially prominent portrait painter in pastel, with whom she studied art while still a child. She became so proficient that after her father's death when she was only 13 years of age, she was able to carry on his work, supporting both her mother and herself. She married, 1776, Baptiste Pierre Lebrun, or Le Brun, a wealthy picture dealer, but soon secured a legal separation from him shortly after the birth of their daughter, who appears in many of her pictures, notably the famous *Madame Vigée-Le-brun and Her Daughter* (Louvre). She painted more than 20 portraits of Marie Antoinette (the first in 1779), and was admitted to the French Academy, 1783.

When the French Revolution broke out, 1789, she left Paris under a law protecting artists and allowing them to travel abroad, taking her daughter with her. During a triumphal tour of Italy she was elected to eight academies, and painted a number of portraits, including the notorious *Lady Hamilton as a Bacchante*. Sojourns in Vienna and in St. Petersburg followed; while in Russia she was the special guest of the Empress Catherine II. Back in Paris, 1801, Vigée-Lebrun found her unrepentant devotion to the Bourbons did not endear her to Napoleon Bonaparte, and for the next decade and a half she lived outside of France—in England, Belgium, or Switzerland. Resuming residence in Paris upon the downfall of Napoleon I, she continued to paint until near death at 87. Vigée-Lebrun's outspoken memoirs, *Souvenirs* (2 vols. 1837–39), reveal much about her art and of the scandals through which she lived.

VIGFÚSSON, GÚTHBRANDUR, 1828–89, Icelandic scholar, was born in Breidafjord. He was stipendiary in the Armagnaeic library at Copenhagen, 1849–64, then settled in Oxford, England, 1866, where he was reader in Scandinavian literature from 1884, and anglicized his given name as Gudbrand. Among his publications, which opened a new era in Icelandic scholarship, are *Túnatál* (1855), *Biskopa*

Sögur (1856–78), *Bardar Saga* (1860), and *Forn Sögur* (with Möbius, 1860), *Eybyggia Saga* (1864), *Flateyjarbók* (with Unger, 1860–68), much of the *Icelandic-English Dictionary* (1859–74), *Sturlunga Saga* (1878), and *Corpus poeticum boreale* (with Powell, 1883).

VIGILANTES, an association of private citizens for the preservation of what those comprising the organization regard as law and order, either in the absence of legally established authority, or in defiance of a legally established authority that is deemed corrupt or otherwise unacceptable. On the North American frontier, during the nineteenth century, settlement often occurred in an area long before there were adequate courts and law enforcement officers; at the same time, lawless elements flocked to the frontier, especially into boom communities, such as mining camps. Irregular justice sometimes arose because outlaws had gained control of the local government or had terrorized the officials. In California during the gold rush days, for example, a vigilance committee was formed, 1851, in San Francisco to suppress the criminal elements of the Barbary Coast and the crooked politicians allied with them; the worst offenders were hanged, and many others fled from the community. A second vigilance committee was organized, 1856, to combat similar conditions. Vigilante groups were formed sporadically in nearly all the western states. In the cattle country, vigilante groups were sometimes organized to break up organized groups of horse and cattle thieves, sometimes simply to get rid of sheep ranchers and dirt farmers, who were the natural enemies of cattlemen.

Vigilante "justice" was usually unduly severe and undiscriminating. In their moralistic, self-serving fervor, vigilantes often hanged people thought guilty of any crime, however mild, or even of no crime at all; that is, persons could be, and often were hanged solely on the grounds that they had bad reputations and their mere presence lowered the moral tone of the community.

Vigilantes have also appeared in older communities. The first Ku Klux Klan, for example, was organized in the South during the Reconstruction period as an extralegal method of combating the freed Negroes, Scalawags, and Carpetbaggers who were then dominant; the second Ku Klux Klan, organized after World War I, also engaged in some vigilante activity.

Gangs of hired thugs, or goons, often used in strike-breaking late in the nineteenth century and well into the twentieth century, were often called vigilantes so as to imply that they stood for law and order against the "mob action" of the strikers.

VIGILIUS, died 555, pope from 538 until his death, was born in Rome. He was designated pope by Boniface II. 530–532, but was not recognized as such by the Roman clergy until 538, when his immediate predecessor, St. Silverius, died in exile. Vigilius' reign was beset with troubles over Monophysitism. The Emperor Justinian condemned, 544, the so-called Three Chapters, which were the persons and writings of the three leading opponents of Monophysitism (Theodore of Mopsuestia, Theodoret of Cyrus, and Ibas of Edessa), on the grounds that they smacked of Nestorianism; then, having secured the approbation of the Eastern patriarchs, the emperor sought Vigilius' concurrence in his action and had the pope forcibly brought to Constantinople. In the *Judicatum*, so-called, Vigilius acceded to the emperor's wishes for the sake of peace, whereupon there ensued a storm of protest from the Western bishops; while the pope vacillated, the emperor called a general council of the church at Constantinople, 553. Vigilius at first refused to attend the council, and even made bold to rescind his *Judicatum* and to publish a *Constitutum*, in which he forbade the condemnation of the Three Chapters. The imperial power was brought to bear upon the pope, however, and Vigilius issued a second *Constitutum* upholding the doctrine of the Council of

Chalcedon and condemning the Three Chapters. After having gained his point, the emperor permitted Vigilius to start for Rome, but the pope died at Syracuse before reaching the Eternal City.

CHARLES R. MEYER, S.T.D.

VIGNOLA, real name Giacomo Barozzi, 1507–73, Italian architect, received the name by which he is commonly known from his birthplace near Modena. His first training was in painting, but architecture appealed to him more strongly and he went to Rome to study this subject. Having built the famous Castle of Caprarola (1547) for Alexander Farnese, Vignola was appointed architect to Pope Julius III, 1550, and filled the same office for the entire Farnese family. After the death of Michelangelo, Vignola became the architect in charge of St. Peter's, in which capacity he executed the small lateral domes. He completed, 1550–55, the Casino and the pope's Villa di Papa Giulio, near Rome, works with which Vasari and Michelangelo had been associated. Catering to the then-current taste for worldliness and elegance in architecture, Vignola designed the mother church of the Jesuits in Rome, Church of the Gesù, (1568), whose richness and style were emulated and copied by many architects; on the basis of this one project Vignola is commonly associated with the introduction of the baroque conception in Italy. His book *Treatise on the Orders* (1563) became and remains a guidebook and dictionary for architects; in the book, Vignola carefully stated and explained the proper proportions of the classical (Greek) orders, but often deviated from the rules himself.

VIGNY, ALFRED DE, 1797–1863, French poet and novelist, was born in Loches of a family of minor nobility. He spent his youth in Paris and attended a military school until 1814, when he became an officer in the army. Thirteen years of service left him disillusioned, but appreciative of the honor code, which he characterized in his prose *Servitude et grandeur militaires* (1835) as "the poetry of duty." An anonymous volume of *Poèmes* (1822) had no success. *Cinq-Mars* (1826), France's first serious historical novel, shows the influence of the British novelist Sir Walter Scott, and was better received. Because its characters are obscured by their environment and because its psychological motivation is at times faulty, this work has not the symmetry and vitality of Prosper Mérimée's *Chronique de Charles IX.* During his brief association with Victor Marie Hugo and his circle, Vigny produced several plays and the symbolical prose work *Stello* (1832). His greatest dramatic success, *Chatterton* (1835), presenting the poet as "the perpetual martyr of humanity," is sometimes rated the best of the Romanticist plays. Vigny's poetry, comprising *Poèmes* (1822), *Eloa* (1824), *Poèmes antiques et modernes* (1826), and *Les destinées* (1864), is frequently subjective in conception, but is almost invariably impersonal in execution. To mankind, viewed as inevitably and interminably at grips with hostile nature, Vigny counseled stoical courage and silent labor: gloom does not justify indolence. *Journal d'un poète* (1867) is an important prose record of his thought. Proud, solitary, and intellectual, Vigny was The Thinker of the French Romanticist group. In a vein of innate pessimism, his poems express inner ideas through masterful symbols.

ERWIN HUGH PRICE

VIGO, city, NW Spain, in the province of Pontevedra in Galicia, on the Bay of Vigo, about 150 miles SW of La Coruña, and 18 miles N of the Portugal border. The city is located on a deep inlet of the Atlantic Ocean, sheltered by the Cies Islands. Vigo has an important port and a fishing fleet. The city has a large fish market and is a boat-building center. Fertilizers, paints, cider and wine, food products, canning equipment, and soap are manufactured, and oil is refined. Spanish galleons, carrying cargoes of gold and silver from South America are believed to have been sunk off the coast at Vigo during a pirate raid by an English fleet in 1704. Pop. (1958) 162,114.

VIIPURI, Russian Vyborg, Swedish Viborg, former county, SE Finland, whose area corresponds to the Finnish province Kymi and part of Soviet Karelia. Before the Russo-Finnish War, 1939–40, the area of the county totaled 12,408 square miles; in the peace settlement of 1940 the Soviet Union took the eastern part including the capital city, Viipuri, reducing the county's area to 4,144 square miles. The county was renamed Kymi, 1945. Upon resumption of the war, Finnish and German troops retook the eastern area, 1941, but in the final peace settlement, 1947, the section came definitely into the Soviet Union.

VIIPURI. See VYBORG.

VIJAYAVADA, or Bezwada, city, E India, in Andhra Pradesh State, on the Kistna River, 150 miles SE of Hyderabad. Vijayavada is a railway and highway junction and center of an extensive canal system. The city is an important commercial center and has rice and oilseed mills. To the southwest of the city there are Buddhist caves and a rock temple, which date from the seventh century, a time during which the city was an important religious center. Pop. (1951) 161,198.

VIJAYANAGAR, ancient ruined city, India, Mysore State, on site of the modern village Hampi, 32 miles WNW of Bellary. Its old wall and natural granite precipices protected it against attack. Vijayanagar's temple ruins and other buildings of a pure Hindu style are now preserved by the Indian government. Vijayanagar, founded in the fourteenth century, was for more than 200 years the stronghold of the great Hindu Carnatic Empire, which long withstood Moslem incursions into southern India; eventually, however, a Moslem confederation took and ravished the city, 1564. Vijayanagar, considered a holy place by the Hindu, is the site of an annual festival.

VIKING. See NORSEMAN.

VILAS, WILLIAM FREEMAN, 1840–1908, U.S. public official, was born in Chelsea, Vt., and was educated at the University of Wisconsin and the University of Albany Law School. He practiced law in Wisconsin and served as reviser of the state statutes; was professor of law at the University of Wisconsin, 1868–85 and 1889–92; and served in the state legislature, 1885. Vilas was U.S. postmaster general, 1885–88, and secretary of the interior, 1888–89, in Pres. Grover Cleveland's cabinet, and was a U.S. senator from Wisconsin, 1891–97.

VILLA, FRANCISCO, called Pancho, 1877–1923, Mexican bandit and revolutionary leader, was born Doroteo Arango in Rio Grande, Durango State. Early in life he became the leader of a group of cattle thieves and soon changed his name to that of a former outlaw no longer on the scene. In the course of time Villa and his band came to be admired by the common people of Mexico, to whom he seemed to be something of a modern Robin Hood. Villa joined Francisco Madero and his revolutionary forces against the dictator Porfirio Díaz, 1910. After the murder of Madero, 1913, Villa joined Venustiano Carranza, another revolutionary leader, and with him took Juarez, 1914. The two men soon quarreled, however, and Villa and his men went on to Mexico City, where Villa set himself up as dictator. Early in 1915 Alvaro Obregón forced Villa out of Mexico City; while Villa took refuge in the north, the United States recognized Carranza's government. Embittered, Villa led a Mexican raiding party that looted and partially burned Columbus, N.M., 1916; during the raid 16 people were killed. U.S. Gen. John Pershing was ordered to pursue and capture Villa, even if this meant sending U.S. troops into Mexico. President Carranza was angered by the invasion of Mexico and strained relations between the two governments developed. Pershing, in the meantime, had not succeeded in capturing Villa, and was recalled. Villa continued to be hostile to the administration, but eventually he arranged a peaceful settlement with the Mexican government, 1920. Three years later, however, he was assassinated; the identity of his killers was never established.

VILLA CISNEROS, town, NW Africa, Spanish Sahara administrative center for Río de Oro, the southern section of the colony; on a peninsula between Río de Oro Bay and the Atlantic Ocean; 700 miles NNE of Dakar. Villa Cisneros is a base for fishing boats. It was settled in the mid-1880's. Pop. (1959 est.) 1,100.

VILLAGE COMMUNITY, in the Middle Ages and before, a type of small rural collectivity, the origin and organization of which remains a subject of disagreement among anthropologists and historians. The English historian Frederic Seebohm (1833–1912) believed that in eastern England the village community existed during a period in which the tribal system still prevailed through western England. According to the Russian-English scholar Sir Paul Gavrilovitch Vinogradoff (1854–1925), the communal organization of the peasantry is more ancient than the manorial system. In essence, the village community would seem to have been what the tribal system became after the introduction of agriculture. The village community was probably made up of a mixture of free and unfree men. The tribes were divided into agricultural groups with overlords, to whom tribute was paid. At first the relation between the village and the overlord was probably remote, but the feudal system introduced intermediate lords, who looked not so much for tribute as for the cultivation of the land. Thus, the distant lord ws replaced by a neighboring lord of the manor, and the freedom of the village community gave way to the servitude of the manor. See FEUDAL SOCIETY; MANOR; MARK; TENURE.

VILLAHERMOSA, city, SE Mexico, capital of the state of Tabasco; on the Grijalva River, 460 miles SE of Mexico City. The city is located on a swampy plain, 30 miles from the coast of the Gulf of Mexico. Villahermosa is an important trading and processing center for the sugar, bananas, and rice grown in the region. Rum is manufactured. Villahermosa was founded in 1596. From 1826 to 1915 the city was known as San Juan Bautista. Pop. (1950) 33,587.

VILLA-LOBOS, HEITOR, 1887–1959, Brazilian musician, composer, conductor, and music educator was born in Rio de Janeiro. Villa-Lobos himself was never sure as to the exact year of his birth, but school and birth records found in the 1950's established it as 1887. Villa-Lobos first studied music with his father, an amateur cellist, and after the father's death, 1899, young Villa-Lobos earned a living as a cellist in cafés and restaurants; he later mastered various other instruments, including the guitar and the clarinet. In 1905 he traveled through northern Brazil, collecting folk songs. From 1907 he studied at the [Brazilian] National Institute of Music, where one of his teachers was the composer Francisco Braga (1868–1945). He devoted the years 1912–15 to travels in interior Brazil, again for purposes of collecting folk songs. He lived and worked in Europe, 1923–30, then returned to Brazil, and became director of music education in São Paulo, 1930, and superintendent of musical and artistic education in Rio de Janeiro, 1932. Villa-Lobos composed more than 2,000 works, among the most famous of which are the nine instrumental suites *Bachianas Brasileiras* (1930–45), in which he adapted the counterpoint of Johann Sebastian Bach to Brazilian melodies and rhythms; 14 *Serestas* for voice and piano (1925–41); the symphonic poems *Virapurú* (1917) and *Amazonas* (1917); and a number of instrumental works in the *chôro* form indigenous to Brazil.

VILLA MARIA COLLEGE. See COLLEGES AND UNIVERSITIES.

VILLANI, GIOVANNI, 1275?–1348, Italian historian, was born and educated in Florence. During his early manhood and into middle age he traveled in Italy, France, and the Netherlands as a representative of his father's mercantile firm. After returning permanently to Florence, ?1312, he soon became a prominent businessman and citizen of that city. He was twice elected prior (chief magistrate), 1316 and 1321, and at other times served as chief of the Florence mint and as head of the city's fortifications. An unfortunate fiscal crisis in the mid-1340's reversed his personal fortunes, however, and he was forced into bankruptcy. He died in poverty during the plague of 1348.

Villani is significant as the author of the *Historie fiorentine*, or *Cronica universale*, which is highly esteemed in Italian letters for its purity of style. It is a loosely structured chronicle of Florence, from biblical times until 1348, but is of most value to historians for its wealth of information on Florentine customs, commerce, art, and politics during Giovanni Villani's own time, and that of his brother, Matteo Villani, who continued the chronicle down to the year 1363, and of Matteo's son, Filippo Villani, who brought the chronicle to completion through the year 1410.

VILLANOVA UNIVERSITY, a private institution of higher learning for men, located at Villanova, Pa. Established by the Roman Catholic church, Order of St. Augustine, as Villanova College, 1842, it offered its first instruction the following year. The name was changed to Villanova University in 1953.

Among the university's various divisions, are liberal arts, founded 1843; engineering, 1905; science, 1915; undergraduate part time, 1918; commerce and finance, 1922; graduate school, 1931; nursing, 1951; and law, 1953. Women are admitted to the nursing, engineering, graduate, and part-time divisions. Master's degrees and first and second professional degrees are offered in most divisions.

The university library contains the Joseph McGarrity Irish-American Collection, materials on church and state law, and the Robert Rea Memorial Collection of business materials. An alumni magazine is issued quarterly. See COLLEGES AND UNIVERSITIES.

VILLA PARK, village, NE Illinois, Du Page County; on the North Western and the Great Western railroads; a residential suburb, 18 miles W of Chicago. Food products and fertilizer are its principal manufactures. Pop. (1960) 20,391.

VILLARD, HENRY, 1835–1900, U.S. journalist and financier, was born Ferdinand Heinrich Gustav Hilgard, in Speyer, Rhenish Bavaria. Upon coming to the United States, 1853, he changed his name to Villard. He was a newspaper correspondent during the Civil War, and reported, 1866, the Austro-Prussian War for the New York *Tribune*. Subsequently he represented German bondholders whose U.S. investments had been endangered by the panic of 1873, and formed the "Blind Pool" syndicate that obtained control of the Northern Pacific Railroad, of which Villard became president, 1881. During that same year he bought the New York *Evening Post*, but turned its editorial control over to Carl Schutz, Horace White, and E. L. Godkin. Villard gave financial aid to Thomas A. Edison, and organized and became president of the Edison General Electric Company, 1889.

VILLARRICA, city, S central Paraguay, capital of Guairá Department, on a railway and a highway; 80 miles SE of Asunción. Villarrica has an attractive site on a hilltop in the midst of orange groves. The city was founded, 1576, on the banks of the Paraná River and was named Villa Rica del Espíritu Santo (Rich City of the Holy Ghost). The city was moved to its present site in 1682. Villarrica is the processing and commercial center of a wide region in which stockraising is important and tobacco, fruit, cotton, and yerba maté are produced. Pop. (1950) 26,527.

VILLARS, CLAUDE LOUIS HECTOR, DUC DE, 1653–1734, French soldier and diplomat, was born in Moulins. A cavalry officer under Turenne, Condé, and Luxembourg, he commanded, 1692, in the action of Pforzheim. During the peace of 1698–

1701, Villars was entrusted with a secret diplomatic mission at Vienna, for he shone in society and cabinet as he did on the field. Appointed to the chief command, 1702, he defeated Louis William I of Baden in the Battle of Friedlingen, and was made marshal of France. He won the Battle of Höchstädt, 1703, and then, having been dispatched to the Cevennes, 1704, subdued the Camisards. He was defeated by Marlborough at Malplaquet, 1709. As commander in chief in the Netherlands, he gained a victory over the imperialists at Denain, 1712, and brought about the Peace of Rastatt (1714). He drove the imperialists from Milan and Mantua, 1733. He died in Turin.

VILLEHARDOUIN, GEOFFROI DE, 1160?–?1213, French chronicler, crusader, diplomat, and one of the prototypes of Chaucer's "very parfit gentil knight," was born probably at the Château of Villehardouin near Troyes, in Champagne. Little is known of his life except what he himself recorded in his chronicle of the *Conquête de Constantinople.* He became marshal of Champagne, 1191; joined the Fourth Crusade, 1199; successfully solicited aid for the crusade from the Venetians, 1201; assisted in the Siege of Constantinople, 1204; and was instrumental, as commander of the rear guard, in saving the crusading army at Adrianople from complete destruction at the hands of the Bulgarians, 1205. As a reward for his services, he was granted a rich fief in Thrace, 1207, and received the title Marshal of Romania. This latter title passed to his son Érard in 1213, and it is assumed that Villehardouin died either in that year or the year before.

Villehardouin is most significant as the author of the celebrated *Conquête de Constantinople,* a chronicle of the Fourth Crusade, 1198–1207. Written in a clear, concise, often poetic style, the *Conquête* is an invaluable historical document by virtue of its authenticity, its comprehensiveness, and its usually objective approach. As a work of literature it holds a high place in the history of French letters as the earliest example of French vernacular prose to possess enduring literary merit.

VILLEIN, in feudal law, was a person attached to a manor, who performed menial work upon the manor for the lord, was generally regarded as property, and was unprotected in his rights against the lord of the manor. However, his condition was better than that of a slave in that no person, in the eyes of the law, was a villein except as to his master; to all others, he was a freeman.

VILLE PLATTE, town, S central Louisiana, seat of Evangeline Parish; on the Texas and Pacific Railway and U.S. highway 167; 70 miles WNW of Baton Rouge. The town is a trade and processing center for an area in which timber is cut, and cotton, corn, and rice are grown. Ville Platte was settled early in the 1800's. Pop. (1960) 7,512.

VILLEROI, FRANÇOIS DE NEUFVILLE, DUC DE, 1644–1730, French military leader, was brought up at the court of Louis XIV. He was made a marshal of France, 1693, during a conflict with England. He was given command of the army in Flanders, 1695, but he had little success against the forces of William III of England. His military ineptness became apparent when, during the Wars of the Spanish Succession, he was sent to Italy, 1701, and taken prisoner at Cremona, 1702, by a greatly outnumbered force led by Prince Eugene of Savoy (1663–1736). After John Churchill, 1st duke of Marlborough (1650–1722) defeated him at Ramillies, Belgium, 1706, Villeroi was relieved of his duties. Through the influence of Louis XIV's second wife, Françoise d'Aubigné, Marquise de Maintenon, he was made guardian of Louis XV, but in 1722 he fell into disgrace for plotting against the regent, Philippe II, duc d'Orléans, and died in exile as governor of Lyons.

VILLETA, town, S central Paraguay, in Central Department, on the Paraguay River about 15 miles S of Asunción. The city is a center for tobacco and cotton industries and a port for shipping oranges. It was founded in 1714. Pop. (1950) 14,729.

VILLEURBANNE, city, E central France, in Rhône Department, 3 miles E of Lyon, of which it is a residential and industrial suburb. The city is a center for metallurgical industries. Chemicals, rayon, and food products are manufactured. Pop. (1954) 81,769.

VILLIERS DE L'ISLE-ADAM, JEAN MARIE MATHIAS PHILIPPE AUGUSTE, COMTE DE, 1838–89, French poet, dramatist, and novelist, was born in St. Brieuc, Brittany. Brought up to revere the illustrious history of his impoverished but noble family, and heir to the Breton love of things occult, he became an intense idealist, an uncompromising Catholic, and a haughty aristocrat. In Paris from 1857, he became a familiar, much-talked-about figure in the bohemian cafés of the Left Bank, but he never achieved popular success and always lived in poverty. None of his plays was ever successfully performed, but *La révolte* (1870) clearly foreshadowed the realistic technique of the Théâtre Libre. In *Tribulat Bonhommet* (1867) he satirized the mediocrity of bourgeois life. Edgar Allan Poe's influence appears in his *Contes cruels* (1883), tales of terror, mystery, and fantasy. The count's unquestioned masterpiece, however, is the poetic drama, *Axël* (1890), the story of an idealistic young nobleman (Axël) who persuades a beautiful girl to share a cup of poison with him rather than submit the present perfection of their love to the exigencies of life. Axël's decision typifies the Symbolists' rejection of reality in favor of a subjective world.
C. W. COLMAN

VILLON, FRANÇOIS, 1431–?63, French poet, was born in Paris. He abandoned his given name (de Montcorbier, alias des Loges) and took that of his benefactor, Guillaume de Villon, canon in the church of Saint-Benoît-le-Bétourné, who brought him up from an early age. Villon studied at the University of Paris, and received the degrees of bachelor and master of arts, 1449 and 1452. During a scuffle in the church cloister, 1455, he killed a certain Philippe Chermoye or Sermoise; and not long after that he took part in a robbery at the Collège de Navarre, 1456. During the next few years Villon traveled in the Loire country, composing verse to pay his way and probably living for a while at the court of Prince Charles d'Orléans, a distinguished poet in his own right. During the summer of 1461 Villon languished in the prison of Thibaud d'Auxigny, bishop of Orléans; freed and allowed to return to Paris, he was arrested again for theft, 1462, and again for participation in a fatal brawl, 1463, after which he was condemned to death. The sentence was commuted to one of banishment, but of his life after January, 1463, literally nothing is known.

Works. Villon's first important work, the *Lais* (Legacy) or *Petit Testament* (Little Testament), written in 1456, contains 40 octosyllable eight-line stanzas (*huitains*). It purports to be a last will and testament, made before the author leaves Paris because of unrequited love. Actually, however, it is known that Villon's real purpose for self-imposed exile was fear of the law. The entire poem is filled with lighthearted and yet biting satire, not only of his lady—"lady" in the special context of the tradition of courtly love—but also himself and his friends (see PROVENÇAL LANGUAGE AND LITERATURE, Literature, *Courtly Love*). To his barber, Villon leaves the cuttings from his hair; to imprisoned criminals, a mirror and the jailor's wife; to the mendicant orders, servings of dainty food and drink. This exuberant gayety is matched with an evocation of the lonely student, writing his will in a cold garret room, and then dozing off after having prayed at the sound of the Angelus.

In the *Testament* or *Grand Testament* (Great Testament), written on Villon's return to Paris, 1461–62, the poet enlarged on the *Lais* both in form and content. The *Testament* comprises 173 *huitains* plus several ballads and *rondeaux*. Although much of the earlier satirical spirit is present in such legacies as his body to the earth, two pots and a skillet to his barber, eyeglasses to the House of the Blind, the over-all mood of the *Testament* differs somewhat from that of the *Lais*: a note of personal anguish, an evocation of the poet's own suffering and emotion, creates the dominant tone. In the famous "Ballad of Departed Ladies" and "Regrets of the Belle Heaulmiere," the poet regrets the excesses of his youth and comments on the inevitability of death and physical decrepitude of all human beauty. Although he himself may take little consolation in a Christian world view, that he can appreciate its aesthetic and moral value for those he loves is demonstrated in the "Ballad for Our Lady," which is "bequeathed" to his mother. Yet an unrepentant epicureanism shines through in other ballads, celebrating an old drinking companion, Jehan Cotart, and the Grosse Margot.

Significance. At one time the scholarly world thought of Villon as a romantic figure, poet of the people, unique in his century. Later scholarship showed this view to be false. He reflected perfectly the student-clerical-financial-bureaucratic circles of pre-Renaissance France. All of his themes (the Virgin Mary, Death, Fortune, Woman as Corruption, the "Belle Dame sans Merci") had been sung by previous authors. Yet, with the possible exception of certain thirteenth century *trouvères* such as Colin Muset and Rutebeuf, Villon was the first great "personal poet," that is, the first to fuse these traditional themes into a unified whole bearing the imprint of his own intensely human spirit. Villon was a rebel who attacked courtly love, the world of finance, civil authority, and the church; and the hierarchy of his legacies (good to the good, evil to the evil) represents at least a spiritual reorganization of society as it seemed to be in his time. Essentially, however, the author of the *Lais* and *Testament* was a poet rather than a moralist. He expressed ideas and emotions through the medium of vigorous language, striking images, sudden changes in tone, delicate sound-harmonies: the arsenal of a man who was to remain for 500 years one of the greatest and most popular of French poets.

WILLIAM C. CALIN

BIBLIOG.–Edward F. Chaney, *François Villon in His Environment* (1946); D. B. Wyndham Lewis, *François Villon: A Documented Survey* (1958); Winthrop H. Rice, *European Ancestry of Villon's Satirical Testaments* (1941); Henry D. V. Stacpoole, *François Villon, His Life and Times, 1431–1463* (1917); François Villon, *Complete Poems* (Complete and Unabridged Translation by John Herron Lepper; Together with the Complete John Payne's Version and Versions by Swinburne, Rossetti, etc.) (1926).

VILNA. See VILNIUS.

VILNIUS, Russian Vilna, German Wilna, Polish Wilno, city, U.S.S.R., capital of the Lithuanian Soviet Socialist Republic on the Viliya River; about 80 miles from the Polish border, and 480 miles WSW of Moscow. Vilnius is an important industrial, commercial, and cultural center, and is a major rail junction on the Warsaw-Leningrad and the Moscow Kaliningrad lines. The city is a trade center for the grain and timber industries, and farm machinery, electrical equipment, leather goods, clothing, fertilizers, glass, and foodstuffs are manufactured. The city is almost surrounded by wooded hills. The old section, with narrow, winding streets, lies at the foot of Castle Hill, on which can still be seen traces of a fourteenth century castle. The newer sections have spread into the hills and along the river courses. Vilnius has numerous Roman Catholic, Orthodox, and Protestant churches, as well as a Moslem mosque. The public buildings show Byzantine, German, Roman, and Gothic influences. Notable among them is the Cathedral of St. Stanislaus, which was first erected in 1387. It was subsequently destroyed three times, and the present structure dates from 1801.

Other buildings include the Cathedral of St. Nicholas (1596–1604); the churches of St. Anne (about 1390), St. Theresa (1626), and the Holy Spirit (1592); a sixteenth century gate with a famous image of the Virgin; and the university, founded in 1578.

Vilnius was founded in the tenth century. In 1323 the Grand Duke Gedimin made it the capital of the Duchy of Lithuania. In 1569 Poland and Lithuania were united, and Vilnius came under Polish domination. Late in the eighteenth century, however, Vilnius was annexed by Russia. In 1831 and in 1863 Vilnius was the center of abortive revolutions against the Russians. During World War I it was taken by the Germans, 1915. After the war, Poland demanded the reformation of the Lithuanian-Polish union, but the Western Allies tried to make the city part of an independent Lithuania. The Poles would not accept this disposal. In 1920 the Soviets turned the city over to Lithuanian troops. The Lithuanian-Polish dispute continued in guerrilla warfare, but an armistice was signed in the same year. So-called insurgent Polish troops then violated this armistice by occupying Vilnius. In 1938, under the cover of the German occupation of Austria, the Poles demanded the opening of the closed frontier between Lithuania and Poland, and the Lithuanian evacuation of Vilnius. Along with its seizure of eastern Poland, September, 1939, the Soviet Union took Vilnius, and on October 10 ceded the city and adjoining area to Lithuania. Vilnius then became the capital of Lithuania, succeeding Kaunas. Pop. (1959) 235,000.

VILYUY RIVER, U.S.S.R., in the Yakutsk Autonomous Soviet Socialist Republic of the Russian S.S.R., a west bank tributary of the Lena River; length 1,240 miles. The Vilyuy rises in the Central Siberian uplands and flows generally eastward through the mountains to a low grassy basin which is dotted with lakes and in which grain and livestock are raised. The river joins the Lena below the town of Sangar. The main town along its course is Vilyuysk, center of the iron, coal, gold, and lumber industries of the district.

VIMY RIDGE, a series of hills, NW France, Pas de Calais Department, five miles NE of Arras. Rising to a height of about 475 feet, Vimy Ridge commands an excellent view of the surrounding terrain. It was captured by the Germans early in World War I, and was a major British objective in the second battle of Arras, an offensive against the Hindenburg line, spearheaded, Apr. 9, 1917, by the Canadian Corps under Lt. Gen. Julian H. G. Byng, who was created 1st Viscount of Vimy, 1926. By April 13 the Canadians had captured Vimy Ridge and penetrated more than five miles into the German lines. On the ridge is the Canadian War Memorial in France, sculptured by Walter Allward, and unveiled by King Edward VIII of Great Britain, June, 1936. See ARRAS, *World War I.*

VIÑA DEL MAR, city, central Chile, in the province of Valparaíso, on the Pacific Ocean, adjacent to the city of Valparaíso, of which it is a residential suburb, Viña del Mar, meaning "vineyard of the sea," is a popular seaside resort. It was built on the site of a Spanish estate. The city contains fine parks, plazas, gardens, and landscaped boulevards. It also has fine beaches, golf links, and a race track. An art museum is located in the mansion of José Francisco Vergara, who gave the townsite in 1874. Pop. (1952) 85,281.

VINCENNES, city, SW Indiana, seat of Knox County; on the Wabash River, the Baltimore and Ohio, the Chicago and Eastern Illinois, the New York Central, and the Pennsylvania railroads, and U.S. highway 41; 45 miles N of Evansville. The city is a shipping center for the surrounding agricultural and mining area, and a highly industrialized commercial center with many historical memorials. Flour and paper mills, window-glass plants, shoe factories, canneries, and steel-construction shops are the major industrial establishments. Settled by French fur traders in the late seventeenth century, the area of Vincennes is the site of a fort built in 1732 as part of a French plan to halt English expansion west of the Appalachians. It was named for the first commandant, François Marie Bissot Sieur de Vincennes. The post passed into British hands at the close of the French and Indian War in 1763. George Rogers Clark in command of a small force captured the post from the British, 1778, and after being driven out, recaptured it in the spring of 1779. When Indiana was made a territory in 1800, Vincennes became the capital. At Vincennes, overland travelers crossed the Wabash River on the route later made famous as the National Road. German immigrants began to arrive in the city in great numbers during the late 1840's, and the Creole and American pioneer town changed to an industrial city. Many well marked historical sites are in the city, including a memorial to George Rogers Clark. The territorial legislative hall and the Old Cathedral of St. Francis Xavier are both preserved. The Lincoln Memorial Bridge marks the probable place where Abraham Lincoln and his family drove their ox teams across the river when they moved from Indiana to Illinois in 1830. Pop. (1960) 18,046.

VINCENNES, town, N France, in the department of Seine, 4 miles E of Paris of which it is a residential suburb. The town lies to the north of a large park, the Bois de Vincennes. The chief manufactures of the town are electrical machinery, rubber goods, chemicals, and cartridges. The Château de Vincennes is a large fortress, built in the fourteenth century. It was used as a hunting lodge by kings of France, and in the seventeenth century it became a state dungeon. Pop. (1950) 50,434.

VINCENT, JOHN HEYL, 1832–1920, U.S. Methodist Episcopal bishop, was born in Tuscaloosa, Ala.; studied at Wesleyan Institute, Newark, N.J.; was admitted to the New Jersey conference, 1853, and became a deacon, 1855, an elder, 1857, and a bishop, 1888. He was pastor of churches in Illinois, 1857–65, then founded the *Northwest Sunday School Quarterly*, 1865; and the *Sunday School Teacher*, 1866. He was corresponding secretary of the M.E. Sunday School Union, and editor of the M.E. Sunday School publications, 1868–87. He helped organize the Chautauqua assembly, 1874, and the Chautauqua literary and scientific circle, 1878, and was chancellor of the system after 1878 (see CHAUTAUQUA). From 1900 until his retirement, 1904, Vincent lived in Zürich, Switzerland, heading the European work of his church. Besides preparing numerous works for Sunday School use, Vincent published *The Chautauqua Movement* (1886), *The Church School and its Officers* (1886), *The Modern Sunday School* (1887), *In Search of His Grave* (1893), *Unto Him* (1899), and *Family Worship for Every Day in the Year* (1905).

VINCENT DE PAUL, SAINT, 1580?–1660, French priest, was born of a peasant family in Pouy, Gascony, studied theology in Toulouse and was ordained, 1600, but stayed on in Toulouse to continue his studies, while supporting himself as a tutor. He went to Marseilles to receive a small inheritance, 1605; on the return voyage his ship was captured by Turkish pirates and he was taken to Tunis and sold as a slave. Having converted his Moslem master to Christianity, De Paul escaped, 1607, spent some time at Avignon and Rome, and then settled in Paris, 1609. He became chief almoner (dispenser of alms and charity) for Margaret of Valois, and then tutor and spiritual director in the household of the Count of Gondi, general of the French galleys. During these years, 1613–25, Father De Paul secured a commission as almoner of the galleys, and carried on important and selfless charitable work in that capacity. He also conducted numerous missions among the poor of the Gondi estates and, as curé of the Châtillon les Dombes, established the first conference of charity for the general assistance of the poor. As an outgrowth of his numerous charitable enterprises, he founded the Congregation of Priests of the Missions, 1625, known also as the Lazarist fathers, a charitable and evangelistic religious institute. With St. Louise de Marillac, he founded the Sisters of Charity, 1634, the first association of uncloistered women living by rule and devoted to the care of the sick and poor. During the remaining years of his long and fruitful life, St. Vincent continued in his efforts to alleviate the sufferings of the common people. He was an uncompromising opponent of deviate forms of Roman Catholicism, particularly Jansenism, and made every effort to secure their condemnation. He was beatified, 1729, and canonized as a saint, 1737. His feast day is July 19.

VINCENTIANS, a congregation of secular priests founded, ?1625, by St. Vincent de Paul for organizing and preaching missions to country people and for helping ecclesiastics gain the knowledge and virtues proper to their state. The Congregation of the Mission (C.M.), as it is officially known, was not intended as a religious order. There is no habit and no novitiate as such, but there are "internal seminaries." The priests and brothers take the three religious vows and a fourth vow of service to the poor. They conduct colleges and seminaries as well as mission bands, parishes, and foreign missions. There are about 5,200 Vincentians, of whom more than 850 are in the United States. They are sometimes called Lazarists or Paules.

Also known as Vincentians are any of the congregations of sisters taking their inspiration from the work of St. Vincent de Paul, but particularly the Daughters of Charity of St. Vincent de Paul (D.C.), founded at Paris by the saint and St. Louise de Marillac in the seventeenth century. The Daughters of Charity, whose habit is blue with a distinctive white headdress, engage in almost every type of active service, especially for the poor. There are about 43,000 of these sisters throughout the world including 2,300 in the United States, where they were founded by Mother Elizabeth Seton, 1809. Several independent offshoots from Mother Seton's original foundation engage in work similar to that of the Daughters of Charity. These are called Sisters of Charity of St. Vincent de Paul, or some similar name, and wear a completely different habit. In the United States there are also several congregations of Vincentian sisters that do not trace their origin to Mother Seton's foundation. See RELIGIOUS ORDERS.

VINCENT'S ANGINA. See TRENCH MOUTH.

VINCI. See LEONARDO DA VINCI.

VINCUM. See BINGEN.

VINDELICIA, historic region, S central Europe, corresponding to the northeastern part of Switzerland, the south of Baden-Württemberg and Bavaria states, West Germany, and the north of Tirol Province, Austria. Its Celtic inhabitants, the Vindelici, were subdued by the Roman consul (later emperor), Tiberius, 15 B.C., and the territory was made a part of the Roman province, Rhaetia (Raetia). The chief town of Vindelicia was Augusta Vindelicorum (later Augsburg, Bavaria).

VINDHYA MOUNTAINS, N central India, in Madhya Pradesh State, a well defined though interrupted range, trending WSW to ENE and lying N of the Narbada River. The main ranges of the Vindhyas extend for about 400 miles. They are formed from volcanic lavas in the west, with outcrops of red sandstones in the east. The Vindhyas have an average elevation of 2,500 feet. Many rivers rise in the ranges and flow north to the Ganges River. In the history of India the Vindhyas have prevented Aryan invasions into the north of India from reaching the Deccan.

VINE, any of the climbing shrubs supported by slender tendrils that are attached to surfaces on which the plant grows. These plants belong to the family *Vitaceae* and are characterized by having small, greenish leaves that are arranged in an alternate pattern on the stem. Most of the members of this family are used as ornamental vines or for the food value of their fruits. Four genera containing more than 250 species are found in the family. Members of the genus *Ampelopsis* have shedding bark and a brown pith. They occur in the northern regions of the world. The genus *Cissus* is noted for its beautiful foliage and is most often found in tropical and warm, temperate areas. The genus *Parthenocissus* is composed of high climbing vines, most of which occur in northern regions, although a few species grow in Asia and Mexico. The Virginia creeper is a popular member found in the United States. The genus *Vitis* is economically important because of the edible fruit or grape produced by its species. It is most often found in the temperate countries in the Northern Hemisphere.

VINEGAR, a dilute solution of acetic acid, CH₃COOH. It is usually obtained by the oxidation of dilute ethyl alcohol solutions such as wine or hard cider. This oxidation is accomplished by the oxygen of the air in the presence of an organism known as mother of vinegar, *Bacterium aceti*. In the commercial preparation of vinegar, the fermented fruit juice is allowed to trickle over wood shavings that have been placed in a barrel and have been inoculated with mother of vinegar. Holes in the barrel admit air, permitting the oxidation process to take place. The issuing liquid contains from 5 to 15 per cent of acetic acid besides the natural coloring and flavoring material of the original juices, which differentiate the vinegar as wine, cider, or white. The pungent odor of vinegar is due to the volatility of the acetic acid molecules and the sour, sharp taste is characteristic of its acid properties.

VINEGAR BIBLE, a fine folio edition of the Bible, printed by the king's printer John Baskett at the Clarendon Press, Oxford, England, in 1717 and popularly known since as the Vinegar Bible because of an error in the headline of Luke 20, in which "The Parable of the Vineyard" is mistitled "The Parable of the Vinegar."

VINELAND, borough, S New Jersey, in Cumberland County; on the Jersey Central and the Pennsylvania-Reading Seashore Lines railroads; 33 miles SSE of Philadelphia. The town is a processing center for the fruit and poultry products of the area. Glassware, textiles, chemicals, paint, and candy are manufactured. The Vineland State School and the Home for Disabled Soldiers are there. Vineland was founded and built by James K. Landis, who settled there in 1861. Pop. (1960) 37,685.

VINET, ALEXANDRE RODOLPHE, 1797–1847, Swiss theologian and critic, was born in Ouchy, canton of Vaud. He became professor of French at Basel, 1819, and professor of theology at Lausanne, 1837. In 1845, having associated himself with the Free Church of Vaud, he resigned his professorship. Vinet held a high place as a critic of French literature. His best books in English translation are *Christian Philosophy* (1846), *Vital Christianity* (1846), *Gospel Studies* (1851), *Pastoral Theology* (1852), *Studies in Pascal* (1859), *Outlines of Philosophy and Literature* (1865).

VINGT-ET-UN, a card game, of French origin, better known in the United States as Twenty-One, or Black Jack. A pack of 52 cards may be used or, if there are many players, a double pack of 104 cards. Each player plays individually against the banker, the object being to draw cards whose face values total 21. Picture cards count as 10, aces as 11 or 1. The banker deals 2 cards, in two rounds, to the players and to himself; the first round of cards is dealt face down, the second round face up. If a player is dealt a natural ("Black Jack"), an ace and a picture card (and, in some varieties of the game, the 10 itself), he immediately wins his bet except when the banker also holds a natural, in which case the banker automatically wins all the wagers; if a player

holding a natural does not immediately announce the fact, he forfeits his wager. If the banker does not hold a natural he offers additional cards to each player, these to be dealt face up; the dealer may also deal additional cards to himself, but only after the players have been dealt as many additional cards as they request. If either the banker or the player draws and makes a total of more than 21, he loses his stake. The banker pays the players whose total is closer to 21 than his, and the other players pay him. If the value of the player's hand and that of the banker are equal, the banker wins. In some versions of the game, the dealer may at his option announce before play begins that he will "pay five under twenty-one" (five cards totaling 21 or less) or "four under sixteen" (4 cards totaling 16 or less) even if his own numerical total is higher (but still only 21 or less, of course), or that he will pay both. Thus 5 cards totaling 20 would beat 3 or 4 cards totaling 21; and 4 cards totaling 16 would beat 3 or 4 cards totaling 21.

VINITA, city, NE Oklahoma, seat of Craig County; on the Frisco and the Missouri-Kansas-Texas railroads, U.S. highways 60, 66, 69, and the Will Rogers Turnpike; 57 miles NE of Tulsa. The city is a shipping center for an area which has coal mining and livestock farming. The Will Rogers Memorial Rodeo is held annually at Vinita. The chief industrial establishments of Vinita are machine shops, meat-packing plants, creameries, bottling works, cotton gins, and a chicken hatchery. Grain, livestock, and poultry are raised in the area. Vinita, founded in 1871 as Downingville, was incorporated as a city in 1898. Pop. (1960) 6,027.

VINLAND, the name given by the Norse adventurer Leif Erickson, to the region that he discovered about 1000, and so called because of the wild vines found growing there. The Norsemen had apparently discovered and colonized Greenland a few years previously; the discovery of the North American coast line, told in the Icelandic Norse epic, *Saga of Eric the Red*, occurred when Ericson's ship was driven off its course. Within a decade at least two colonizing expeditions were attempted. The first, ?1005, under Thorfinn Karlsefni, was abandoned because of the severe winter climate and the hostility of the natives. The last expedition was made about 1007, and it is believed that settlers on Greenland kept up their connection with a region in North America called Markland, to secure timber. Since no Norse remains have been found, the areas visited cannot be determined with certainty, but the evidence available in the records indicates that Vinland probably was somewhere along the New England coast line. It has been speculated that the Norse explorations influenced the historic voyage made by the Genoese navigator Christopher Columbus, 1492. See NORSE-MAN, *Norwegian Vikings;* RUNE.

VINNITSA, region, U.S.S.R., in the W central Ukrainian Soviet Socialist Republic; bounded by the regions of Kamenets-Podolskiy on the W, Zhitomir on the N, Kiev on the E, and Odessa on the SE, and by the Moldavian S.S.R. on the S; area 10,600 sq. mi. The region lies in the upper part of the central basin of the Southern Bug River, in the Volyn-Podolian Upland, and is bordered on the south by the Dnestr River. The principal crops are sugar beets, grains, fruit, and tobacco, particularly along the Dnestr. Viticulture is important in the southwest. The region's industries are based mainly on local agricultural produce. There are distilleries, sugar refineries, and food-processing plants. The principal cities include Vinnitsa, the capital, Zhmerinka, and Mogilev-Podolskiy. The region was established in 1932. Pop. (1959) 2,141,000.

VINNITSA, city, U.S.S.R., in the W central Ukrainian Soviet Socialist Republic, capital of Vinnitsa Region; on the Southern Bug River; 120 miles SW of Kiev. Vinnitsa is an industrial center where sugar, flour, meat, and other foodstuffs are produced.

In addition, agricultural machinery, fertilizers, and clothing are manufactured. Vinnitsa was founded in the fourteenth century. Pop. (1959) 121,000.

VINOGRADOFF, SIR PAUL GAVRILO-VITCH, 1854–1925, Russian jurist and English scholar, born near Moscow, was educated at its university, and he taught history there from 1887 until 1901, when his activities in behalf of popular education brought him into conflict with the authorities. He went to the University of Oxford, England, 1902, and was Corpus Professor of Jurisprudence until his death, becoming noted as an authority on medieval English communal life. Among his works are *English Society in the Eleventh Century* (1908), *Roman Law in Medieval Europe* (1909), and *Self Government in Russia* (1915).

VINSON, FREDERICK MOORE, 1890–1953, U.S. jurist, was born in Louisa, Ky., and was educated at Centre College. He was chief judge of the U.S. emergency court of appeals, Mar. 2–May 29, 1943, but resigned to serve as director of the Office of Economic Stabilization, 1943–45. After a few months' service as federal loan administrator, Vinson became director of the Office of War Mobilization and Reconversion, 1945; he left that post within the year, however, to become secretary of the treasury. In 1946, he was appointed chief justice of the United States Supreme Court by Pres. Harry S. Truman, to replace Chief Justice Harlan F. Stone. As a chief justice, Vinson was generally to be found on the conservative side of the Supreme Court balance. He was a close adviser and confidant of President Truman throughout his administration.

VINTON, city, E central Iowa, seat of Benton County; on the Cedar River, the Rock Island Railroad, and U.S. highway 218; 23 miles NW of Cedar Rapids, in a general farming area. Vinton's products include hybrid seed corn and canned corn. Peas, beans, asparagus, lima beans, and pumpkins are raised in the vicinity. Vinton was settled as Northport in 1839 and was later known as Fremont. In 1846, with the establishment of a post office, the name was changed to Vinton. The Iowa School for the Blind is there. Pop. (1960) 4,781.

VINTRAS, PIERRE-MICHEL, 1807–75, religious eccentric and visionary, was born in Bayeux. Early in his career Vintras was, among other things, a tailor, a servant, and a clerk. In 1839, while an assistant manager of a cardboard factory he was visited, or so he claimed, by the Archangel Michael; Vintras then announced that he was the Prophet Elijah, reincarnated to reform the church. He founded a new cult, celebrated a sacrilegious Mass, had more visions, and performed what his followers took to be miracles. The cult was condemned by Pope Pius IX, 1850, and French officials began to investigate Vintras' activities, probably because of his support of Charles Naundorff's dubious pretensions to the throne of France. Vintras retired to England, but eventually returned to France and settled in Lyons.

VIOL, one of a group of stringed instruments that are the antecedents of the present family of the string quartet. Old viols, in common use during the fifteenth century, were played with a bow, like their descendants, and generally made use of six strings, on which the left hand moved up and down to produce the tones desired. In structure, proportions, and size, however, the viols differed from their descendants. There were treble, tenor, and bass viols.

The bass viol, better known as the viola de gamba, was the immediate predecessor of the violoncello, and was a favorite solo instrument up to the time of Johann Sebastian Bach. The viola d'amore, with its ethereal, lovely tone (resulting from the resonance of sympathetic strings not touched by the bow) was much liked as a solo instrument; it was used as such by Giacomo Meyerbeer, Giacomo Puccini, Richard Strauss, Charles Loeffler, Paul Hindemith, and others.

WILLIAM LEWIS AND SON, CHICAGO
Viola

The baryton, for which Franz Joseph Haydn wrote many pieces, was a larger and lower pitched viola d'amore. Still other varities of viols existed. A soft, somewhat nasal sound is common to all types of viols. When the more agile and brilliant violin entered into competition with the viols, the latter lost ground gradually and went out of general use in the eighteenth century.

HUGO LEICHTENTRITT

VIOLA, second most important of the musical instruments of the violin family, is about one seventh larger than the violin, and is held and played in the same manner. Its four strings are tuned in fifths, one fifth lower than the violin: C, G, D′, A′. Music for the instrument is written in the alto clef.

VIOLET, a low perennial herb belonging to the genus *Viola* of the family *Violaceae*. Violets bear alternate or radical leaves and solitary flowers with five irregular petals, the lower one being spurred at the base and the two lateral ones opposite and equal. There are numerous species, all belonging to temperate climates.

The sweet violet, *V. odorata*, is extensively cultivated in the United States. The stems, which are downy or smooth, spring in tufts from a thick rootstock. The leaves are large, and the flowers are generally deep purple, though varieties are cultivated with blossoms of white and of varying shades of blue. Double varieties are also common. In growing violets, the stock plants should be divided, about the end of April, into single crowns, and these should be planted at 9-inch intervals in rows 12 inches apart. Those intended for frame culture are placed in the frames about the end of September. The chief re-

Viola da Gamba

FOREST PRESERVE DIST. COOK COUNTY
Violets

quirements are a rich moist soil and good drainage. A shady location is preferable.

The species *Viola tricolor* is an Old World type of which a strain, *V. tricolor arvensis*, has become naturalized in parts of the United States.

There are more than 80 species of the *Viola* genus that comprise the violets of North America, most of which grow wild; many of the species are also cultivated because of their individual characteristics of coloring, fragrance, or beauty of foliage. Thus they make excellent ornamentals.

VIOLIN, French *violon,* Italian *violino,* German, *Violine* or *Geige,* one of the most important of modern musical instruments, is classified, according to the Sachs-Hornbostel system, as a bowed lute, and as such is one of the chordophonic (Greek *chordos,* string, *phonos,* sound) instruments. In common with the other lutes, the violin has a body with a neck; along most of its length are strung four taut strings that can be plucked but that are normally bowed. Pitch is controlled or chords formed by pressing the strings at proper intervals against the neck of the instrument, thereby shortening or lengthening those portions of the strings that are free to vibrate. As a successor of the viols, the violin was so much better in tone quality, playing power, brilliance, and expressiveness that in the course of the seventeenth century it totally eclipsed the viols and revolutionized the art of playing as well as of composition. This progress was due mainly to the skill and musical instinct of the great violinmakers of Cremona, most notably the Amati, Stradivari, and Guarneri. Shape, proportions, quality of wood, and varnish, founded by them, resulted in an unequaled

WILLIAM LEWIS AND SON. CHICAGO
Violin

beauty, power, flexibility and soulful expressiveness of tone, rivaling the human voice.

The violin's four strings, G, D′, A′, E″, give it a wide range of nearly four octaves, plus the flutelike "flageolet" tones, that can be produced by touching the string only lightly without pressing down the finger to the soundboard. By shifting the hand up and down the soundboard in at least seven positions not only the highest sounds are obtained, but also a great variety of tone color, as the same tones can be played on various strings. Double stops and chords in great variety are possible. The elastic bow permits an abundance of dynamic effects, from pianissimo to fortissimo, and sforzato, with all intermediate grades, and also the effects of legato, marcato martellato, staccato in rapid change. By plucking the strings with the fingers of the right hand, without using the bow, the harplike "pizzicato" effects that are produced increase the variety of sound production still further. HUGO LEICHTENTRITT

BIBLIOG.-Robert Alton, *Violin and Cello Building and Repairing* (1950); Francis D. Ballard, *Appreciation of Rare Violins* (1945); Donald Brooke, *Violinists of Today* (1949); Ernest N. Doring, *How Many Strads? Our Heritage from the Master* (1945); Franz Farga, *Violins and Violinists* (1950); George Fry, *Varnishes of the Italian Violin-Makers of the 16th, 17th, and 18th Centuries and Their Influences on Tone* (1904); Justin Gilbert, *Cremona Violin Technique* (1937); Edward Heron-Allen, *Violin Making: As It Was and Is* (1943); John H. Houghton, *Known Violin Makers* (1942); Karel Jalovec, *Italian Violin Makers* (1957); Edmund S. J. van der Straeten, *History of the Violin: Its Ancestors and Collateral Instruments, From Earliest Times to the Present Day* (1933); Arthur T. Walker, *What Makes a Good Violin* (1960).

VIOLLET-LE-DUC, EUGENE EMMANUEL, 1814–79, French architect, was born in Paris. He studied in Paris, spent two years in Italy, and traveled through most of France on foot for the purpose of making a thorough study of historic buildings and monuments. Becoming probably the strongest advocate of the Gothic revival in France, Viollet-le-Duc gained fame by restoring many French medieval buildings. His first important work was assisting Lassus and Duban in the restoration of Sainte Chapelle, 1840. He and Lassus began the work of restoring Notre Dame, Paris, 1842, and the two worked together on the restoration for 11 years. Lassus died, leaving the remainder of the task to Viollet-le-Duc, who then assumed full responsibility for completing the center spire, chapels, and the high altar. The restoration of the Château of Pierrefonds, 1858, was probably his greatest achievement. He wrote several books, some of them illustrated by himself, which stress the structurally organic nature of Gothic buildings.

VIOLONCELLO, or cello, is the bass and tenor instrument of the violin family, and is descended from the viola da gamba. Its four strings C, G, d, a, are tuned an octave lower than those of the viola. The violoncello is played upright, leaning against the knee of the performer. Its large compass of more than three octaves, its broad, warm tone, and its agility make it equally valuable as an orchestral, chamber music, and solo instrument. Owing to the length of the strings, its fingering differs essentially from that of the violin, but the problems of bowing are very similar for both instruments. The older literature of trios, quartets, sonatas (by Franz Joseph Haydn, Wolfgang Amadeus Mozart, Ludwig van Beethoven, Franz Schubert, Robert Schumann, Felix Mendelssohn, Johannes Brahms, among others), as well as concertos (by Haydn, Schumann, Brahms, Charles

WILLIAM LEWIS AND SON. CHICAGO
Violoncello

Camille Saint-Saëns, Edouard Lalo, Antonín Dvořak Ernest Bloch) reveals the great and varied powers of the violoncello. HUGO LEICHTENTRITT

VIPER, a poisonous snake of the family, *Viperidae.* The family is divided into the true vipers, subfamily, *Viperinae;* and the pit vipers, subfamily, *Crotalinae.*

The true vipers are Old World reptiles, inhabiting Europe, Asia, and Africa. Among them, belonging to the *Vipera* genus, are the European viper, *V. berus,* and the Russell's viper, *V. russelli.*

Pit vipers are found throughout the world except in Australia and New Guinea. Among them are the North American rattlesnakes of the genus *Crotalus,* which includes the eastern diamondback, *C. adamanteus,* the western diamondback, *C. atrox,* the banded variety, *C. horridus.* The pit viper subfamily also includes water moccasins, copperheads, the ferde-lance, and the largest of the pit vipers, the bushmaster of tropical South America.

VIRCHOW, RUDOLF, 1821–1902, German anatomist and pathologist, was born in Schivelbein, Pomerania (later Swindwin, Poland), and studied at the University of Berlin, where he became lecturer on anatomy, 1847. When in 1849 the University of Würzburg offered him the chair of pathology and pathological anatomy, he accepted and remained there until he returned to the University of Berlin as professor of pathological anatomy and director of the Pathological Institute, 1856.

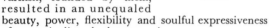

Virdung

In 1858 Virchow completed *Die Cellularpathologie in ihrer Begründung auf physiologische und pathologische Gewebelehre*, in which he extended the work started by François Xavier Bichat (1771–1802) on diseased tissues by applying to them modern cell theory, which was being evolved at that time (see CELL). His doctrine *Omniscellula e cellula* (Every cell from a cell) marked the beginning of the doctrine of germinal continuity, which reached its highest development in the germ-plasm theory of August Weismann (1834–1919).

Virchow was the first to recognize cerebral embolism, and discovered neuroglia and the lymphatic sheaths of the cerebral arteries. A corollary to his work in anatomy was his interest in anthropology and archaeology. He became a liberal leader in the Prussian Landtag, 1862, and in the German Reichstag, 1880–93. As a municipal councilor, 1861, he secured model public health measures.

VIRDUNG, SEBASTIAN, fifteenth-sixteenth century German musician and priest, was born in Amberg, Germany. Little is known of his life. He lived for a time in Eichstätt and became, 1500, a member of the court chapel in Heidelberg. Virdung is remembered as the author of one of the oldest known works on musical instruments, *Musica getutscht und auszgezogen durch Sebastianum Virdung Priesters von Amberg und alles gesang ausz den noten in die tabulaturen diser benanten dryer Instrumenten: der Orgeln, der Lauten, und den Flöten transferieren zu lernen* (Music Germanized and Abstracted by Sebastian Virdung, Priest at Amberg, to Teach to Transfer All Song from the Notes into the Tablatures of these Three Named Instruments: the Organ, the Lute, and the Flute), published at Basel, 1510 or 1511. The work is written as a dialogue between Virdung and his friend Andreas Sylvanus. Virdung also published some German songs at Munich, 1513.

VIRE, town, NW France, capital of the department of Calvados, 34 miles SW of Caen. Vire is a commercial center in a region in which dairy cattle are raised, and is noted for its production of Camembert cheese. Woolen textiles are manufactured. The town is situated on a hilltop set off on three sides by the Vire River. It grew up around a castle erected by Henry I of England in the twelfth century. In a gorge near the town, called Vaux-de-Vire, stood the mill of Olivier Besselin, a fifteenth century author of satiric songs which were later adapted and became known as "vaudevilles." Pop. (1954) 7,963.

VIREO, or greenlet, American bird of the family *Vireonidae*, distributed abundantly in temperate North America, in Central America as far south as Costa Rica, and in the Antilles. There are about 70 species, and 200 varieties. The plumage is prevailingly olive, or olive green, with brown and gray, and buff or whitish underneath, never streaked or spotted. The vireos are mainly insectivorous and they are migratory. The nests are deeply pensile, formed of grapevine bark or similar material, and lined with mosses and lichens. They are hung to the fork of a low branch. The eggs are an elongated oval, and white speckled with red and purple. Some species have a pleasing song; others are noted for the oddity of their notes. The red-eyed vireo, *V. olivaceus*, common throughout temperate North America, is typical of the family.

VIRGINIA, a maiden of ancient Rome. In 449 B.C. Appius Claudius, chief of the decemvirs, ordered a client, M. Claudius, to claim Virginia, the daughter of one of his centurions, Virginius. Virginius, seeing no other escape for his child, snatched up a butcher's knife from a stall and plunged it into her bosom. He then escaped, and inflamed the army with the tale; whereupon soldiers and citizens rose against the decemvirs. Appius was imprisoned, and killed himself. The story is probably only an invention to explain the fall of the decemvirate, but true or not, it is well told in Macaulay's *Lays of Ancient Rome*.

The Old Dominion State preserves a wealth of monuments from a highly treasured past.

VIRGINIA, officially Commonwealth of Virginia, state, E United States; bounded on the NE by Maryland, on the E by the Atlantic Ocean, on the S by North Carolina, on the SW by Tennessee, on the W by Kentucky, on the NW by West Virginia; extends 430 miles E-W and 200 miles N-S, area 40,815 sq. mi., including 922 sq. mi. of inland water; pop. (1960) 3,966,944.

Virginia is shaped roughly like a triangle. It ranks 36th in area and 14th in population among the states. Virginia, one of the original 13 colonies, is popularly called "The Old Dominion." The state motto is *Sic semper tyrannis* (Thus Ever to Tyrants). The state flower is the dogwood, the state bird is the cardinal, and the state song is *Carry Me Back to Old Virginia*. Richmond is the capital city. See map in Atlas, Vol. 20. For state flag in color, see FLAG.

PHYSICAL FACTORS

Topography. Virginia can be divided into three major physiographic regions: from east to west, they are the Atlantic coastal plain, the Piedmont upland, and the Appalachian Mountains.

The Atlantic coastal plain includes that portion of Virginia on the southern tip of the Delmarva Peninsula, known as the Eastern Shore, which is separated from the rest of the state by Chesapeake Bay. The coastal plain is an almost level lowland composed of relatively recent marine gravels, sands, and clays. It rises gently inland to about 300 feet in elevation. Except for areas that have been artificially drained the plain has extensive marshlands such as Dismal Swamp, which extends into North Carolina.

Marking the inland edge of these coastal lowlands is the fall line (see FALL LINE), which separates the marine sediments of the coastal plain from the harder rocks of the Piedmont. The Piedmont upland, a rolling area generally between 300 and 1,000 feet above sea level, widens from about 40 miles in the north to about 175 miles in the south. Its surface is frequently broken by ridges and hills, especially in the west.

Immediately west of the Piedmont upland is the Blue Ridge section of the Appalachians. This rugged mountain area extends in a northeast-southwest direction and, like the Piedmont, is composed of ancient crystalline rocks. The Blue Ridge includes several peaks higher than 4,500 feet, among them White Top Mountain (5,520 ft.) and Mount Rogers (5,720 ft.); the latter is the highest point in Virginia. West of the Blue Ridge is the Great Appalachian Valley, or Valley of Virginia, which includes several smaller valleys, such as the Shenandoah. Farther west is the ridge and valley country, an area of complexly folded parallel ridges and valleys. In the extreme southwest is the Cumberland Plateau, a fairly rugged area of hills averaging about 3,000 feet above sea level.

The coast line of Virginia is of the submergent type—low-lying and deeply indented. The major indentation is Chesapeake Bay, from which extend the estuaries of the Potomac, Rappahannock, York, and James rivers. The Delmarva Peninsula has an irregular coastline, and many small islands line its eastern, or Atlantic, side. Other major rivers of Virginia, aside from those flowing into Chesapeake Bay, are the Roanoke, which flows into North Carolina, and the Shenandoah, which flows into the Potomac in West Virginia. All these rivers rise in the Appalachians and flow across the Piedmont and the coastal plain into the Atlantic. Extreme western Virginia, however, drains westward via rivers such as the New and the Clinch into the Ohio and Tennessee rivers. There are no large natural lakes in Virginia, but there are numerous large reservoirs such as South Holston, which extends into Tennessee, and Buggs Island Lake, which extends into North Carolina on the Roanoke River.

Climate. Lowland Virginia has, for the most part, a climate of the humid subtropical type. Mild winters, warm summers, and abundant precipitation are characteristic. There are cooler and more extreme weather conditions in the uplands, Richmond, at the border between the Piedmont and the coastal plain, has a January mean temperature of 39.1°F, and a July mean temperature of 78.0°. The average annual precipitation at Richmond is 41.9 inches. Winter temperatures often go below freezing, and there are frequent snowfalls in the mountains. The average growing season ranges from about 220 days in extreme southeastern Virginia to less than 150 days in the higher upland areas.

Plant and Animal Wildlife. Pine trees predominate on the coastal plain. There also are oak, red cedar, gum, poplar, beech, hickory, persimmon, ash, walnut, and locust. Cypress and southern white cedar grow in some localities. Along the coasts are expanses of marsh grasses and other marsh vegetation. Coastal-plain flowers include lobelia, bluets, lupine, anemone, violets, May apple, and morning glory.

In the Piedmont and mountain areas, most of the trees are broadleaved and deciduous, although there also are some pine and cedar. These include oak, tulip, poplar, beech, gum, walnut, locust, maple, and basswood. Dogwood and redbud are common in the interior. The upland sections of Virginia are noted for their flowering plants, among them arbutus, rhododendron, azalea, and laurel. Especially characteristic are the pale-yellow St.-John's-wort, purple mountain spurge, Virginia thyme (mountain mint), and trailing wolfsbane.

Virginia has a varied and abundant fauna, despite widespread depredations by man during early settlement of the area. Deer and fox are widespread, as are raccoon, opossum, squirrel, mole, rat, mouse, skunk, ground hog, and rabbit. In the more remote mountains there are some elk, black bear, and wildcat. Game birds of Virginia include quail, which are widely distributed, turkeys, ruffed grouse, doves, and woodcocks. Many migrating waterfowl winter in Virginia, including canvasback, shoveler, goldeye, red head, and blue bill ducks. Canada and brant geese also spend winters in Virginia. Wood, gray, pintail, and mallard ducks nest in the state. Other waterfowl are bitterns, herons, gulls, and numerous species of shore birds. Virginia's largest birds are the bald and golden eagles, and the black and turkey buzzards. There also are species of hawks and owls. The most numerous and widely distributed small birds are crows, bluejays, cowbirds, meadow larks, orioles, martins, swallows, wrens, nuthatches, titmice, woodpeckers, whippoorwills, starlings, sparrows, wood thrushes, cardinals, and mockingbirds.

The extensive inland waters of Virginia contain many species of fish, including bass, bream, perch, pike, carp, and catfish. There are trout in some mountain streams. In tidal waters are croaker, hog fish, spot, white perch, gray and spotted trout, rock-fish, flounder, bluefish, shad, and catfish. Blue crabs and shrimp are also found in tidal waters; clams, in lower Chesapeake Bay; and scallops, in coastal inlets. There are oyster beds in many estuaries and bays.

SOCIAL FACTORS

Population. The population of Virginia increased by 648,269, or 19.5 per cent, in the decade 1950–60. The proportion of the population classed as urban was 55.6 per cent in 1960. In 1950 Negroes comprised 22.1 per cent of the population, foreign-born whites, 1.1 per cent. The most populous areas of Virginia are in the northeast and east, particularly near the estuary of the James River, while the least populous areas are in the west. In 1960 Norfolk was Virginia's largest city, having replaced Richmond, which was the largest in 1950. Major religious denominations in the state are the Baptist and Methodist.

PRINCIPAL CITIES

	Population	
	1950 Census	1960 Census
Norfolk.................	213,513	305,872
Richmond..............	230,310	219,958
Arlington..............	135,449	163,401
Portsmouth.............	80,039	114,773
Newport News...........	42,358	113,662
Roanoke...............	91,921	97,110
Alexandria.............	61,787	91,023
Hampton...............	5,966	89,258

Education. The Virginia school system is administered by a state board of education, whose seven members are appointed by the governor for four-year terms. The superintendent of public instruction is the chief executive officer. Education is free and compulsory for all children between the ages of 7 and 15 years.

Among the state's institutions of higher education are the state-supported University of Virginia (founded 1819), at Charlottesville and Fredericksburg; the College of William and Mary (1693), at Williamsburg, one of the nation's oldest; Virginia Military Institute (1839), at Lexington; Virginia Polytechnic Institute (1872), at Blacksburg; and several state teachers colleges such as Longwood College (1884), at Farmville. Among the privately controlled institutions are Bridgewater College (1880), Bridgewater; Emory and Henry College (1838), Emory; Hampden-Sydney College (1775), Hampden-Sydney; Hollins College (1842), Hollins; Hampton Institute (1868), Hampton; Randolph-Macon College (1830), Ashland; Randolph-Macon Woman's College (1891), Lynchburg; Lynchburg College (1903), Lynchburg; Mary Baldwin College (1842), Staunton; Roanoke College (1842), Salem; Sweet Briar College (1901), Sweet Briar; Washington and Lee University (1749), Lexington; the Medical College of Virginia (1838), Richmond; Union Theological Seminary (1824), Richmond—and not to be confused with Union Theological Seminary, New York City, N.Y.; the University of Richmond (1830), Richmond; Virginia Union University (1865), Richmond; St. Paul's Polytechnic Institute (1888), Lawrenceville; Eastern Mennonite College (1917), Harrisonburg; Madison College (1908), Harrisonburg; Presbyterian School of Christian Education (1914), Richmond; and Virginia State College (1882), Petersburg.

Public Welfare. Among institutions under the direction of the Virginia Board of Charities and Corrections are a school for the deaf and blind, at Staunton; sanitariums for tuberculosis patients, at Catawba, Charlottesville, and Burkesville; mental institutions at Williamsburg, Staunton, Marion, and Petersburg; and a colony for the epileptic and feebleminded, at Colony. Among the state's penal institutions are an industrial school for boys, at Maidens;

VIRGINIA

State Seal

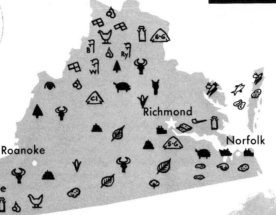

Roanoke

Richmond

Norfolk

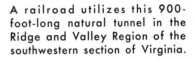

A railroad utilizes this 900-foot-long natural tunnel in the Ridge and Valley Region of the southwestern section of Virginia.

PRINCIPAL RESOURCES, INDUSTRIES, AND PRODUCTS

- Barley
- Cattle
- Chemicals
- Clays
- Coal
- Corn
- Cotton
- Dairying
- Diversified manufacturing
- Fish
- Fruit
- Hay
- Hogs
- Horses
- Fe Iron
- Oats

- Oysters
- Peanuts
- Potatoes
- Poultry
- Rye
- Sand and gravel
- Sheep
- Shipbuilding
- Stone
- Textiles
- Timber
- Tobacco
- Tobacco products
- Truck crops—vegetables
- Wheat
- Zn Zinc

State Flower—Dogwood

State Bird—Cardinal

Virginia has many fine examples of colonial architecture, notably Monticello, home of Thomas Jefferson.

The deeply indented coast affords many good harbors, the chief of which is Hampton Roads at Newport News.

Apples and peaches are grown in interior valleys such as the Shenandoah, seen here from the Blue Ridge Parkway.

industrial school for girls, at Bon Air and Peakes Turnout; a manual-labor school for boys, at Hanover; the state penitentiary, at Richmond; and a state farm for defective misdemeanants, at State Farm.

ECONOMIC FACTORS

Agriculture. Virginia is predominantly an agricultural state, most of whose farms tend to be relatively small in size and diversified in production. Hay, corn, wheat, oats, barley, and rye are the main crops, but tobacco, grown principally in the southern part of the Piedmont, is Virginia's major cash crop, and peanuts are an important crop in the southeast, particularly around Smithfield. Truck farming is important along the coast, especially on the Delmarva Peninsula, where large quantities of potatoes, sweet potatoes, vegetables, and fruits are produced. There is some cultivation of cotton in the extreme southeast. Apples and peaches are grown in the interior Piedmont and in the Shenandoah Valley.

PRODUCTION OF PRINCIPAL CROPS

Crop	Unit	1947–56 average	1957
Apples.............	1,000 bushels	8,917	8,100
Beans, snap.........	1,000 cwt.	311	247
Corn..............	1,000 bushels	37,064	21,120
Hay...............	1,000 tons	1,630	1,512
Peaches............	1,000 bushels	1,331	1,420
Peanuts...........	1,000 pounds	215,035	218,360
Potatoes...........	1,000 cwt.	3,556 *	2,815
Soybeans...........	1,000 bushels	2,997	4,284
Sweet potatoes......	1,000 cwt.	1,291 *	1,656
Tobacco...........	1,000 pounds	160,818	130,610
Wheat.............	1,000 bushels	7,512	4,731

*1949–56 average   SOURCE: *U.S. Department of Agriculture*

Excessive cultivation of certain crops, notably tobacco and cotton, over many decades, resulted in widespread soil depletion and erosion; The Piedmont and hilly areas were especially abused. A widespread program of retiring some land from cultivation, of rotating and diversifying crops, and of other soil-conservation and soil-improvement measures had, by 1960, helped to protect the agricultural resources of the state.

Virginia has a widespread and growing livestock industry. Cattle, hogs, and sheep are the chief animals raised. Cattle raising and dairying are most important in the western and northern parts of the state; most sheep raising is done in the mountain sections; and hog raising is largely confined to the coastal plain, particularly in the southeast, around Smithfield, where the hogs are fed peanuts. Poultry raising is generally important. Horses are bred in the Piedmont.

Forestry. Although there is little virgin timber left in Virginia, the state is extensively forested. Most of the forestland is privately owned and is classed as commercially valuable. The uplands of western Virginia yield both softwoods and hardwoods, but hardwoods predominate on the Piedmont and softwoods predominate on the coastal plain. Timber is cut for lumber, pulpwood, and fuel, and is used for the manufacture of a variety of wood products. Many lumber producers combine their lumbering operations with other economic activities. The chief commercial lumber species are yellow pine, oak, red cedar, gum, yellow poplar, hickory, ash, walnut, beech, birch, maple, tupelo. sycamore, hemlock, and chestnut.

Manufacturing. Industry in Virginia began, 1609, when a glass factory was established in Jamestown; bricks were soon being made in the state, 1611; an iron foundry was opened, 1618; and flour, grist, and weaving mills were common by 1700. By late in the 1950's the total value added by manufacturing in

Virginia exceeded $2 billion per year. The leading industrial product groupings, in order of value added by manufacture, are chemicals, textiles and clothing, tobacco products, food products, transportation equipment, and pulp and paper products. Before World War II the manufacture of tobacco products was the state's leading industry, but subsequently it diminished in relative importance as a result of an unprecedented expansion of other industries during the 1940's and 1950's. The chief tobacco-processing center, Richmond, is one of the world's largest producers of cigarettes. The chemical industry is concentrated in the Norfolk-Portsmouth metropolitan area and in such smaller cities as Hopewell and Waynesboro; synthetic fibers account for much of the total value of the chemical manufactures. The manufacture of clothing and textiles and food products is also widely dispersed. The manufacture of transportation equipment is largely confined to the Hampton Roads area, at Norfolk and Newport News, long one of the nation's leading shipbuilding centers.

Fisheries. The coasts of Virginia, especially in Chesapeake Bay, support an important fishing and shellfish-gathering industry. Oysters, clams, and crabs are taken from lower Chesapeake Bay and its major river estuaries. Menhaden, croaker, shad, alewives, striped bass, sea trout, and mackerel are the more important fish taken. The menhaden are not taken for food uses but for the manufacture of meal, oil, and fertilizer.

Mining. The uplands of Virginia have a variety of mineral resources, but coal is by far the most important. The major coal fields are in the western extremity of the state, in Buchanan, Wise, Dickenson, and Tazewell counties. Virginia's deposits of bituminous and anthracite coal are part of the great Appalachian coal field. Other important mineral products are stone, sand, and gravel; lime, mainly from the limestones of the coastal plain; lead and zinc, from Wythe County; iron ore, from Pulaski County; and clays, mainly from Henrico, Albermarle, and Prince William counties. Significant amounts of feldspar, manganese ore, petroleum, natural gas, aplite, gypsum, kyanite, marl, mica, pyrites, salt, slate, talc and soapstone, and titanium ore are produced in the state.

PRODUCTION OF PRINCIPAL MINERALS

Mineral	1957	1958
	short tons	
Clays....................	893,255	1,152,850
Coal....................	29,505,579	26,826,067
Lime....................	510,216	471,313
Sand and gravel.............	7,046,869	7,158,228
Stone...................	14,243,510	15,412,947
Zinc....................	23,080 *	18,472 *

*Recoverable content of ores
SOURCE: *U.S. Department of the Interior*

Commerce. Hampton Roads, the great roadstead in the James River estuary and one of the world's finest natural harbors, has extensive port facilities, principally at Newport News and Norfolk. Total cargo tonnage handled at these two ports was about 52 million tons in 1958. Exports, especially of coal, comprise the bulk of the cargoes.

Transportation. Virginia has almost 4,000 miles of railroads; principal lines are the Southern, the Atlantic Coast Line, the Chesapeake and Ohio, the Norfolk and Western, and the Seaboard Air Line. Other important lines are the Virginian, the Baltimore and Ohio, the Pennsylvania, and the Richmond, Fredericksburg, and Potomac.

Virginia's dense network of surfaced highways comprises such major north-south routes as U.S. highways 1, 11, 13, 17, 29, and 33, and major east-west routes as 52, 58, 60, and 250. The state is

VIRGINIA

The state capitol at Richmond, completed in 1792, was based on a plan of the Maison Carée obtained by Thomas Jefferson when he was minister to France, 1785–89.

Natural Bridge in Rockbridge County near Lexington, Va., is 236 feet high, 50 feet wide, and 40 feet thick. It supports a highway that spans a footpath and Cedar Creek.

Virginia's largest city is Norfolk, left and center, a major port on the Atlantic, and is adjacent to Portsmouth, right.

This quaint, neatly preserved park is a popular tourist attraction in Williamsburg, Virginia's old Colonial city.

The James River flows past a dolomite plant in which large quantities of ammonium nitrate are processed. The installation is in Hopewell, an industrial center near Richmond.

well served by numerous bus lines and by major airlines. Richmond and Roanoke are the main centers of air transportation.

Tourist Attractions. Virginia, with its rich historical legacy and varied scenic charms, has many attractive features for tourists. Shenandoah National Park, for example, in the heart of the forested Blue Ridge, is traversed by the scenic Skyline Drive and the Blue Ridge Parkway. Near Newport News is the Colonial National Historic Park, which includes part of Jamestown, site of the first successful English settlement in North America, and Yorktown, scene of the critical battle of the American Revolution. A parkway connects these sites with Williamsburg, the restored colonial capital of Virginia.

Among other historical sites in Virginia are the George Washington Birthplace National Monument, near Wakefield; Appomattox Court House National Monument, which preserves the scene of the Confederate surrender at the end of the Civil War; the Fredericksburg and Spotsylvania County Battlefields Memorial National Military Park; Petersburg National Military Park, with its many miles of well preserved earthworks; Manassas National Battlefield (see BULL RUN, BATTLES OF); and Richmond National Battlefield Park.

There are a number of national cemeteries in Virginia. Most outstanding is Arlington National Cemetery, near Washington, D.C. Other national cemeteries are located at Yorktown, Poplar Grove, and Fredericksburg.

Among the many tourist attractions are historically prominent cities such as Richmond, Alexandria, and Charlottesville. In Richmond is the capitol, the Confederate Memorial, the Edgar Allan Poe Shrine, Battle Abbey, and the home of Confederate Gen. Robert E. Lee. Alexandria is the site of Christ Church and the Washington National Masonic Memorial. Charlottesville contains numerous colonial buildings —nearby are Monticello, home of Pres. Thomas Jefferson, and Ash Lawn, home of Pres. James Monroe. Other historic homes in the state are at Stratford, home of the Lee family, and at Berkeley, home of the Harrisons (Pres. William Henry and Benjamin). Virginia has many historic churches, especially in the rural areas; among these are St. Luke's Church (1632), near Smithfield, and Pohick Church (1774), in Fairfax County.

There are excellent recreation facilities in state parks throughout the state. Beaches border much of the Atlantic Coast, notably at Ocean View, Norfolk, Virginia Beach, Cape Henry, and Old Point Comfort. Fishing and sailing are widely available. There are also varied opportunities for hunting.

KENNETH THOMPSON

GOVERNMENT

Constitution. The present Virginia constitution is that adopted in 1902, as amended. There are two procedures for amending the constitution: (1) amendments may be proposed by majority vote of the members of both houses of the general assembly (the state legislature) at two successive sessions, then approved by a majority vote of the people; (2) a constitutional convention may be called by a vote of a majority of the members of the general assembly; adoption of amendments proposed at the convention requires the approval by a majority of the electorate. In order to qualify for voting one must be a U.S. citizen 21 years of age or over, have resided in the state for one year, a county for six months, and a precinct for 30 days, have passed a literacy test, and have paid a poll tax. On the basis of its 1960 population, Virginia sends 10 congressmen to the U.S. House of Representatives.

The General Assembly consists of a senate of not less than 33 nor more than 40 members and a house of delegates of not less than 90 or more than 100 members; the senators are elected for four years and the delegates for two. Membership of both houses is determined by proportional representation. The general assembly must be reapportioned every 10 years. Regular sessions of the assembly open in January of even-numbered years. Legislators are paid for 60 days only. Special sessions may be called upon petition of two-thirds of the general assembly members, and legislators are paid for 30 days only.

The Executive Officials are the governor, lieutenant governor, and the attorney general, all elected for four years; the governor is not eligible for the next succeeding term. The secretary of state, treasurer, commissioner of agriculture, and controller are appointed by the governor with the approval of the general assembly; the auditor is chosen by joint ballot of the general assembly. The governor has a limited power to grant reprieves and pardons. His veto, which extends to items in appropriation bills, may be overridden by a two-thirds vote of the members present in each house of the general assembly.

The Judicial Power is vested in a supreme court of appeals of seven justices chosen for 12-year terms by joint ballot of the general assembly; in 34 circuit courts, each having one judge similarly chosen for 8-year terms of office; in courts of limited jurisdiction such as municipal, and equity courts with judges similarly chosen for terms varying from 4 to 8 years.

HISTORY

European Exploration and Settlement. John Cabot, Italian-born navigator in the service of England, may have been the first European to touch upon the shores of Virginia when he explored the Atlantic Coast of North America, 1498. Another Italian, Giovanni da Verrazano, in the service of France, probably did so when he explored the coast from Cape Fear (N.C.) northward to Cape Breton Island, (Nova Scotia), 1524.

During the reign of Queen Elizabeth I, 1558–1603, England laid claim to the entire coast between Spanish Florida and French Nova Scotia. Courtier adventurers, such as Sir Humphrey Gilbert and Sir Walter Raleigh, made several efforts to establish settlements, but for various reasons their ventures failed (see ROANOKE ISLAND). The region soon came to be called Virginia, probably in honor of the "Virgin Queen," Elizabeth, although the name *Wingina*, chief of an Algonquian Indian tribe living between Albemarle and Pamlico sounds, and the Indian word *wingandacoa* were mentioned by English explorers in their reports to Raleigh. It has been suggested that Elizabeth on perceiving the pronounced likeness of the Indian words to the word "virgin" as it relates to uncultivated land, to spinsterhood, or to both, ordered that the region be named Virginia.

In 1606 the English government chartered the Virginia Company, a joint-stock company, to settle the coast of North America. The Virginia Company established two subsidiary companies, the Virginia of Plymouth (see PLYMOUTH COMPANY) and the Virginia Company of London, for the purpose of colonizing respectively the northern and southern parts of the grant. The Virginia Company of London, or simply the London Company, was granted the stretch of land that included the territory later to become the Old Dominion. In December, 1606, three ships of the London Company under the command of Capt. Christopher Newport set sail on a colonizing expedition. After a circuitous trip the ships reached Chesapeake Bay, May, 1607, and established Jamestown, the first permanent English colony in North America.

The early years of the Jamestown colonists were hard and many died from disease, privation, and from the effects of unaccustomed toil. The colony survived the first two years largely as a result of the arrival of new settlers from England, and the leadership of Capt. John Smith.

After 1610 conditions improved under a series of energetic governors: Thomas West, Baron De La

VIRGINIA

The simple but gracious lines of Oak Hill, home of Pres. James Monroe, are characteristic of many old Virginia mansions. General Lafayette was a guest here in 1824.

Monticello, the home of President Thomas Jefferson, is a red brick home, of classic revival design, that was begun in 1770.

St. Luke's Church in Smithfield is the oldest U. S. church with walls still standing. The Gothic structure was built in 1632.

Agecroft Hall in the Richmond area is an old mansion brought over from England and reconstructed in Virginia. Its design derives from the period of Henry VII.

Richmond's Old Stone House, the oldest in the city, was erected in 1686, and is now dedicated as a memorial to Edgar Allan Poe.

Warr, Sir Thomas Dale, and Sir Samuel Argall. Strong measures were taken to ensure an adequate food supply, and private initiative was stimulated by the abandonment of the original system of working and sharing produce in common and by the granting land ownership to individuals. New settlements were made and the cultivation of tobacco began to furnish a valuable export crop. Changes in the provisions of the Charter, 1609 and 1612, transferred the government of Virginia from the English crown to the company, which in 1618 instructed new governor, Sir George Yeardley, to summon a representative assembly. On July 30, 1619, two representatives from each of the 11 Virginia settlements met in the church at Jamestown; this was the first legislative assembly in English North America (see HOUSE OF BURGESSES). The same year saw the introduction of Negro slavery in the colony. See JAMESTOWN NATIONAL HISTORIC SITE.

A series of Indian attacks, 1622, resulted in the death of some 300 colonists. Two years later King James I revoked the company's charter, and assumed the administration of Virginia. See ROYAL COLONY.

The Colonial Period. Under Sir William Berkeley, governor, 1641–52 and 1659–77, the colony at first continued to prosper in spite of the Civil War in England. A Parliamentary fleet compelled Virginia's submission to the commonwealth and Berkeley's retirement, 1652, but with the approach of the Restoration of the monarchy in England, 1660, Berkeley again became governor. Placing his favorites in all positions of power, he instituted an authoritarian regime that favored a small group of wealthy planters in the tidewater (coastal plain), and neglected the interests of frontier settlers, especially with regard to protecting them from Indians. In a short-lived rebellion, frontier planters, led by Nathaniel Bacon, ousted Berkeley and burned Jamestown, 1676. Bacon died of fever later in the year, however, and Berkeley, having regained control of the situation, inflicted such severe punishment on Bacon's followers that he was soon removed from office by the crown, 1677. See BACON'S REBELLION.

In 1699 the capital of Virginia was moved from Jamestown to Middle Plantation—site of William and Mary College, founded, 1693—which was renamed Williamsburg in honor of King William III of England.

The early eighteenth century marked the beginning of an era which saw the flowering on Virginia's tidewater estates of a leisurely way of life and a culture that still live in that region's traditions. The Virginia gentry, mostly of middle class English backgrounds, took advantage of the favorable soil and climate and the market for tobacco to expand their holdings, so that within one or two generations the leading families were holding plantations that averaged 5,000 acres in size. Although small landholders constituted the great majority of the colony's population, power and wealth rested in the hands of the tidewater aristocrats, whose position was dependent on the labor of indentured servants, mostly immigrants from the British Isles and Northern Europe, and that of Negro slaves, brought to Virginia either directly from Africa or from the West Indies. By 1720 Negro slaves constituted one-fourth of the population of Virginia, about 100,000; by 1775 the colony's population was more than 550,000 persons, about half of them slaves. See INDENTURED SERVANT; SLAVERY, Modern Slavery, *Slavery in the United States*.

In the meantime, Virginians had begun to migrate from the tidewater westward into the Appalachian foothills. An expedition headed by Gov. Alexander Spotswood explored the Shenandoah Valley, 1716, and large sections of it and the Virginia Piedmont were soon opened to settlement. English, Scotch-Irish, and Germans from Maryland and Pennsylvania moved south into the Shenandoah and the Blue Ridge Mountain valleys. A company was formed,

1749, to colonize "beyond the mountains" in a region that, according to the early charters, constituted a part of Virginia (see OHIO COMPANY OF VIRGINIA). The British government's Proclamation of 1763, prohibiting further white settlement west of the Appalachians, was bitterly opposed in Virginia, and was frequently violated by land-hungry settlers. As a result there were clashes between the settlers and Indians, but a force of Virginia militia soundly defeated the Indians who had been harassing the frontier settlements, 1774. See DUNMORE'S WAR.

During the Revolutionary War, 1775–1883, Virginia statesmen were leaders in the fight for independence. George Washington commanded the Continental army. Thomas Jefferson probably wrote the major portion of the Declaration of Independence —at least in its final form—after Richard Henry Lee had made the actual proposal to break with the mother country (see DECLARATION OF INDEPENDENCE). In Virginia itself the new state constitution, adopted June 29, 1776, embodied George Mason's Declaration of Rights, a model for many future fundamental laws. Patrick Henry was the state's first governor, 1776–79. His successor was Jefferson, 1779–81, who pushed the abolition of entail and primogeniture, and later secured passage of the Bill for Religious Freedom. Richmond was made the state capital, 1779. The British navy controlled the Virginia coast throughout most of the war, and there was little fighting on the state's soil until the final Yorktown Campaign, 1781. See YORKTOWN, SIEGE OF.

Early Statehood. After the war, the loss of much of the British tobacco market together with depletion of soil suitable for growing tobacco resulted in a relative decline of Virginia's aristocracy, and migration both to the west and south. The trend continued with the disruption of trade caused by President Jefferson's Embargo Act, 1807, against Great Britain and France, and the War of 1812. As a result vast portions of the state returned to wilderness. Nevertheless, Virginia continued to be politically influential in the new nation, a matter marked by the fact that of the first five U.S. presidents, four—Washington, Jefferson, James Madison, and James Monroe—were Virginians. Furthermore, the tidewater continued to dominate state politics, and in the Constitutional Convention, 1829–30, defeated an attempt by representatives of the Piedmont from instituting universal (white) male suffrage by removing ownership of property as a condition for the right to vote. As a result Negro slavery, which since the Revolution had been under severe criticism by many Virginians, became more firmly entrenched than it had been during the eighteenth century. When universal manhood suffrage was finally granted, 1851, all of Virginia east of the Appalachians had come to regard slavery as essential to its interests.

Civil War and Reconstruction. As late as 1860 most of the people of Virginia opposed secession from the Union, but when Pres. Abraham Lincoln issued his call for troops, Apr. 15, 1861, a Virginia state convention passed an ordinance of secession two days later, and Virginia joined the Confederacy, April 25. These decisions, however, were ratified only by the eastern part of the state, and delegates of 26 western counties met at Wheeling, May 13, and repudiated the ordinance of secession. Late in the year a convention at Wheeling promulgated a state constitution, which in due course was ratified by popular vote in all or parts of 48 western Virginia counties, April, 1862. The new state, West Virginia, was admitted to the Union, June 20, 1863.

The importance of Virginia coal and munitions works and her tradition of political leadership led to the removal of the Confederate capital from Montgomery, Ala., to Richmond, May 21, 1861. As a result, Virginia became the chief battleground of the Civil War. The Confederacy's chief army was the Army of Northern Virginia, and its commander was

U.S. OFFICE OF WAR INFORMATION
One of the many beautiful buildings on the University of Virginia campus at Charlottesville is the Rotunda, which Thomas Jefferson patterned after the Pantheon in Rome.

a Virginian, Robert E. Lee. Among the engagements fought on Virginia soil were the battles of Bull Run, Fredericksburg, Chancellorsville, the Wilderness, Spotsylvania Courthouse, Cold Harbor, Five Forks, the Seven Days' Battles and the Petersburg Campaign. The decisive Confederate surrender took place at Appomattox Court House, Apr. 9, 1865.

After the war, a new constitution was framed in accordance with the Fourteenth and Fifteenth Amendments of the U.S. Constitution (1869), and Virginia was readmitted to the Union, Jan. 26, 1870.

The early post-war years were marked by severe economic distress among the small farmers of Virginia and movements for agrarian reform such as the Farmer's Alliance and the Populist party made headway in the state.

The main political struggle, however, was between the Democratic and Republican parties, the latter having gained the Negro vote. After absorbing most followers of the Populist party in the 1890's, the Democrats gained the upper hand in the general assembly, and brought about the adoption of a new constitution (1902) by which many Negroes were disenfranchised.

Twentieth Century Developments. Virginia politics in the twentieth century were marked by a general conservatism, although the conservative view was determined more by the desire to suppress the Negro politically and socially, than by opposition to economic improvement.

In national politics, Woodrow Wilson, a native Virginian and a noted liberal, was elected President of the United States, 1912 and 1916; Wilson's administrations saw the enactment of many constructively progressive laws. Virginia voters broke their traditional support of the Democratic party in the national elections of 1952, 1956, and 1960, and the state's electoral votes were cast for Republican party presidential candidates. This in part reflected the state's general conservatism.

Various Supreme Court decisions after 1930 modified some of the state's restrictions on Negro political activity. In 1950, however, the state legislature killed a bill to end racial segregation on common carriers, and after the U.S. Supreme Court ruled, 1954, that laws providing for racial segregation in public schools violated the Fourteenth and Fifteenth Amendments to the U.S. Constitution, Gov. Thomas B. Stanley of Virginia announced that the state would oppose desegregation of its schools by every legal means available. Nevertheless, over 1,200 Negro pupils were attending in 1962 previously all-white public schools in the state. In 1959 all public schools in Prince Edward County were made private schools in an effort to avoid integration. The result of this move was that Negro children were without any education whatever

until 1963 when the Prince Edward Free School Association opened its first school to provide for Negro education. Four white children and 800 Negro children were enrolled in 1963.

BIBLIOG.–American Guide Series, *Virginia* (1953); Matthew P. Andrews, *Virginia, the Old Dominion* (1950); Robert B. Bean, *Peopling of Virginia* (1938); Robert Beverley, *History and Present State of Virginia* (1960); John B. Boddie, *Virginia Historical Genealogies* (1954); James Branch Cabell, *Let Me Lie: Being in the Main an Ethnological Account of the Remarkable Commonwealth of Virginia and the Making of Its History* (1947); Helena L. Caperton, ed., *Social Record of Virginia* (1937); Samuel Chamberlain, *Springtime in Virginia* (1947); Richard B. Davis, *Francis W. Gilmer: Life and Learning in Jefferson's Virginia* (1939); Raymond C. Dingledine, Jr., and Others, *Virginia's History* (1956); Evelyn K. Donaldson, *Squires and Dames of Old Virginia* (1950); Clifford Dowdey, *Great Plantation: A Profile of Berkeley Hundred and Plantation Virginia from Jamestown to Appomattox* (1957); Pocahontas W. Edmunds, *Tales of the Virginian Coast* (1950); Emmie F. Farrar, *Old Virginia Houses* (1955); Marshall W. Fishwick, *Virginia: A New Look at the Old Dominion* (1959); Garden Club of Virginia, *Homes and Gardens in Old Virginia* (1953); Robert C. Glass and Carter Glass, *Virginia Democracy*, 3 vols. (1937); Jean Gottmann, *Virginia at Mid-Century* (1955); Nathaniel C. Hale, *Virginia Venturer: A Historical Biography of William Claiborne, 1600–1677: The Story of the Merchant Venturers Who Founded Virginia* (1951); Raus M. Hanson, *Virginians at Work: A Geography of Virginia's Resources and Occupations* (1956); Freeman H. Hart, *Valley of Virginia in the American Revolution, 1763–1789* (1942); William E. Hemphill and Others, *Cavalier Commonwealth: History and Government of Virginia* (1957); Elizabeth V. Huntley, *Peninsula Pilgrimage* (1941); Thomas Jefferson, *Notes on the State of Virginia* (1955); Annie L. Jester and Martha W. Hiden, eds., *Adventures of Purse and Person, Virginia, 1607–1625* (1956); Margaret E. K. Kern, *Trail of the Three Notched Road* (1929); Alfred L. Kocher and Howard Dearstyne, *Shadows in Silver: A Record of Virginia, 1850–1900 in Contemporary Photos* (1954); Alf J. Mapp, Jr., *Virginia's Experiment: The Old Dominion's Role in the Making of America, 1607–1781* (1957); Arthur P. Middleton, *Tobacco Coast: A Maritime History of Chesapeake Bay in the Colonial Era* (1953); Virginia Moore, *Virginia Is A State of Mind* (1943); Edmund S. Morgan, *Virginians at Home* (1959); Richard L. Morton, *Colonial Virginia*, 2 vols. (1960); Blair R. Niles, *James: From Iron Gate to the Sea* (Rivers of America Series) (1945); Percival Reniers, *Springs of Virginia: Life, Love and Death at the Waters, 1775–1900* (1941); Agnes E. Rothery, *Virginia, the New Dominion* (1940), *Houses Virginians Have Loved* (1954); Francis B. Simkins and Others, *Virginia: History, Government, Geography* (1957); Alan Smith, ed., *Virginia, 1584–1607* (1957); William H. T. Squires, *Unleashed at Long Last: Reconstruction in Virginia, April 9, 1865–Jan. 26, 1870* (1939); William O. Stevens, *Shenandoah and Its Byways* (1941); Charles S. Sydnor, *Gentlemen Freeholders: Political Practices in Washington's Virginia* (1952); Morris Talpalar, *Sociology of Colonial Virginia* (1960); Charles W. H. Warner, *Road to Revolution: Virginia's Rebels From Bacon to Jefferson (1676–1776)* (1961); Thomas T. Waterman, *Mansions of Virginia, 1706–1776* (1947).

VIRGINIA, city, W central Illinois, seat of Cass County; on the Baltimore and Ohio Railroad and U.S. highway 67; 90 miles N of St. Louis. The city is a trade center for an area in which corn, wheat, soybeans, poultry, and livestock are raised. Virginia was platted in 1836. During the early years of settlement the county seat alternated between Virginia and Beardstown, but in 1872, when Virginia was incorporated as a city, it became the permanent seat of Cass County. Pop. (1960) 1,669.

VIRGINIA, city, NE Minnesota, in St. Louis County; on the Duluth, Missabe and Iron Range, the Duluth, Winnipeg, and Pacific, and the Great Northern railroads and U.S. highway 53; 55 miles NNW of Duluth; a trade center in the heart of the Mesabi Iron Range and Minnesota's Arrowhead Country. Virginia, founded as a village in 1892, at the height of the iron boom, was named for the home state of Alfred E. Humphrey, president of the Virginia Improvement Company. In 1893 the village was destroyed by fire, but was rebuilt and incorporated as a city in 1895. At one time an important lumbering town, the depletion of surrounding forests and the increase of ore mining made it one of the most important communities of the Minnesota iron ranges. It is the site of the Mesabi Mountain Mine, the world's largest iron ore producing, open-pit mine. The chief industrial establishments of Virginia are the iron mines and foundries, paint factories, bottling works, creameries, and a lumber mill. Pop. (1960) 14,034.

VIRGINIA, UNIVERSITY OF, a public institution of higher learning, located at Charlottesville, Va. The undergraduate divisions of the university are open to men only; women are admitted to the professional and graduate departments. The school also operates Mary Washington College at Fredericksburg, Va., a liberal arts college for women.

The University of Virginia was chartered, 1819, under the sponsorship of Thomas Jefferson, who designed many of its original buildings and planned its original campus. The school's first instruction was offered in 1825. The divisions and their founding dates are: arts and sciences, law, and medicine, 1819; graduate studies, 1859; engineering, 1868; education, 1919; graduate school of education, 1950; commerce, 1952; graduate school of business administration, 1954; architecture, 1954; and nursing, 1956.

The school operates a nuclear information center, a nuclear reactor program, and special educational programs for the orthopedically handicapped. It is the site of the Thomas Jefferson Center for Studies in Political Science, and it administers the Thomas Jefferson Memorial Foundation grants in American history. The university library contains special collections of materials on American literature, Gothic novels, Virginiana, Thomas Jefferson, and Edgar Allan Poe. See COLLEGES AND UNIVERSITIES.

VIRGINIA BEACH, city, SE Virginia, in Princess Anne County; on the Atlantic Ocean, the Chesapeake and Ohio and the Norfolk Southern railways, and U.S. highways 58 and 60; 16 miles E of Norfolk and 5 miles S of Cape Henry. Six miles of white beach with hotel and amusement facilities have made Virginia Beach a popular summer resort. Pop. (1960) 8,091.

VIRGINIA CITY, town, SW Montana, seat of Madison County; on a Northern Pacific bus route; 55 miles SE of Butte. It was founded in 1863 after gold was discovered in Alder Gulch, and in 1864 became the first town in Montana to incorporate. A historical museum, 11 miles southwest, is the leading point of interest. Pop. (1960) 194.

VIRGINIA CITY, town, W Nevada, seat of Storey County; 14 miles NE of Carson City and 20 miles from the California border, at the site of the famous Comstock Lode. The settlement was founded soon after the discovery in 1859 of the Comstock Lode, which drew thousands of gold seekers to the region. Virginia City was an important mining center until resources were exhausted, although some gold and silver ores are still being recovered. During the 1860's Mark Twain worked there as a reporter on the *Territorial Enterprise*. Among the relics preserved from the bonanza days of the settlement are Piper's Opera House (now a museum); the Crystal Bar, named for the multicolored chandeliers; and the Catholic chapel, Saint Mary's in the Mountains, noted for its carved redwood interior. Pop. (1960) 515.

VIRGINIA COMPANY OF LONDON, often called the London Company, the private company that established the English colony in Virginia. It was originally chartered, April, 1606, as a subdivision of a larger company, but was reorganized, 1609, as a separate joint stock company under the official name "The Treasurer and Company of Adventurers and Planters of the City of London for the First Colony of Virginia." The company was dissolved, 1624, when the proprietary colony of Virginia became a royal colony.

VIRGINIA CREEPER, hardy climbing shrubs of the family *Vitaceae*. Similar in appearance to plants belonging to the grape genus, *Vitis*, they may be distinguished from them by the presence of white pith in their branches. That of *Vitis* is brown. The common Virginia creeper, *Parthenocissus quinquefolia*, is usually found on fences, trees, and rocks, sending out delicate

J. HORACE MCFARLAND CO.
Virginia Creeper

trailing branches. It is frequently confused with poison ivy, but its leaves are five-parted instead of three-parted.

VIRGINIA MILITARY INSTITUTE, a public college for men, offering studies in liberal arts, sciences, and engineering, and located at Lexington, Va. The school, chartered by the state of Virginia, 1839, is designated by the U.S. Department of Defense as a military college. All students are required to take four years of military training, and are organized into a corps of cadets. Bachelors' degrees are offered in biology, chemistry, civil engineering, electrical engineering, English, history, mathematics, and physics.

The school conducts an annual Virginia Highway Conference and an annual Industrial Management Conference. Abbreviated courses are offered annually for land surveyors. A planetarium program is conducted weekly throughout the school year. The library contains special collections of materials on the South, the Confederacy, and U.S. military history.

Cadets of the Virginia Military Institute figured prominently in the Civil War. In 1861 the school was closed and the cadet corps was ordered to Richmond to instruct volunteers in military drill. The school was subsequently reopened, and in 1864 the cadets took part in the battle of New Market, Va. The school's buildings and equipment were burned by the advancing Union Army, but instruction continued to be given in temporary quarters until October, 1865, when permanent facilities were reopened. See COLLEGES AND UNIVERSITIES.

VIRGINIA POLYTECHNIC INSTITUTE, a public, coeducational, technological institute located at Blacksburg, Va. The school was chartered as the Virginia Agricultural and Mechanical College, 1872, and offered its first instruction the same year. The name was changed to Virginia Polytechnic Institute in 1944. The divisions and their founding dates are: agriculture, applied science and business administration, and engineering and architecture, 1872; agricultural experiment station, 1888; graduate school, 1890; agricultural extension service, 1914; engineering experiment station, 1923; and Radford College (the women's division of the institution), 1944. Advanced degrees are offered in most departments.

A co-operative work-study program is available in engineering, and special Ph.D. programs are conducted in aeronautical engineering, horticulture, agronomy, and mathematics. Among the institute's publications are *The Bulletin of the Virginia Polytechnic Institute*, prepared by the engineering experiment station, and the quarterly *Mineral Industries Journal.* See COLLEGES AND UNIVERSITIES.

VIRGINIA REEL, an early American variation of the old English country dance, Sir Roger de Coverley, which was brought to North America by the early English settlers in Virginia. The dancers face each other in two rows, each couple executing definite dance steps until all have completed the set. See DANCE, Development of Dance Around the World, *Square Dance;* REEL; SQUARE DANCE. FELIX BOROWSKI

VIRGINIA RESOLUTIONS, nine in number, were resolutions adopted by the Virginia legislature, December, 1798, as a protest against the Alien and Sedition Acts. The resolutions, written by James Madison, were sent to the legislatures of the other states, some of which replied, but none favorably. According to the resolutions, the powers of the federal government result from the compact to which the states are parties, and are limited by that compact; and when the federal government attempts exercise of other powers not granted by the compact, the states that are parties thereto have the right and duty to "interpose so as to maintain within their respective limits the authorities, rights, and liberties appertaining to them." The resolutions are often cited in support of a "strict" interpretation of the Constitution. See IMPLIED POWERS; INTERPOSITION; KENTUCKY RESOLUTIONS; NULLIFICATION; STATES' RIGHTS.

VIRGINIA STATE COLLEGE, a public, coeducational institution of higher learning for Negroes, located at Petersburg, Va. The school was founded, 1882, as the Virginia Normal and Collegiate Institute; offered its first instruction at the college level, 1886; became a land-grant school, 1920; and was renamed Virginia State College in 1946. The school comprises divisions of arts and sciences, agriculture, commerce, education, home economics, industries, general education, graduate studies, and field services. Masters' degrees are offered in agricultural education, biology, chemistry, education, English, history, home economics, mathematics, physics, and psychology and guidance.

The school conducts a general science institute, sponsored by the National Science Foundation; a summer institute for ministers; and a summer institute on conservation of natural resources for teachers. Workshops are conducted in art, music, health, and physical education, and a special education program is conducted for teachers of mentally retarded children. See COLLEGES AND UNIVERSITIES.

VIRGIN ISLANDS, in the West Indies, comprising a group of 100 small islands in the Leeward Islands; lying between the Atlantic Ocean and the Caribbean Sea, about 40 miles E of Puerto Rico; administered by Great Britain and the United States; area 133 sq. mi.; pop. (1960) of Virgin Islands of the U.S., 32,100. See TORTOLA; ST. THOMAS; ST. CROIX; ST. JOHN; LEEWARD ISLANDS.

The major economic activity on the islands is the raising of livestock and sugar cane, the distilling of rum, the servicing of ships, and the fabrication of jewelry. Exports totaled $8,413,000 in 1960.

The Virgin Islands were discovered by Columbus on his second voyage in 1493, and were controlled at various times by Spanish, British, French, Dutch, and Danish forces. The British control of Tortola dates from 1680.

United States Islands. Colonization under the Danish West Indies Company began in 1666; the islands continued under this authority until sold to the Danish monarch in 1755. During the Napoleonic Wars they were held by the British (1801–2, 1807–15) but were restored to the former sovereignty. In 1917, 53 of the islands were purchased by the United States for $25,000,000. In 1936 the United States granted an Organic Act, or constitution, to these islands; in 1954 a new Organic Act consolidated the numerous committees into nine executive departments for more efficient civil administration.

PAUL'S PHOTOS

Charlotte Amalie, picturesque capital and most populous city in the Virgin Islands, is spread out over three hills known to sailors of old as "Foretop," "Main," and "Mizzen."

The tourist trade, halted by World War II, became a major industry after the war. In 1946 the legislature created a Tourist Development Board; in 1947 more than 30,000 tourists visited the islands. The number of tourists increased steadily during the following years, being limited only by the accommodations available. St. Thomas, St. Croix, and St. John, the three largest of the 65 or so islands under U.S. control, receive most of the tourists, many of whom are attracted by such unusual features as the bay-tree forest on St. John, or by the remarkably deep and shifting colors of the Caribbean waters.

VIRGIN ISLANDS NATIONAL PARK, established in 1956 as the twenty-ninth U.S. national park, consists of 9,500 acres on St. John. Within the area are relics of prehistoric Carib Indians and of early sugar plantations, and much tropical flora and fauna.

VIRGINIUS AFFAIR, an international incident that might have led to war between the United States and Spain in the 1870's, but did not. The steamer *Virginius*, a filibustering vessel flying the U.S. flag, while proceeding from Kingston, Jamaica, to Cuba, was captured on the open sea by the Spanish war steamer *Tornado*, Oct. 31, 1873, and taken into Santiago de Cuba, on charges of carrying men and supplies to Cuban insurrectionists. Four of those on board, after an alleged trial, were shot, November 4; the captain of the Virginius, 36 of his crew, and 16 passengers met a like fate, November 7. In the United States, meanwhile, the affair was creating a tremendous furor, and Pres. U. S. Grant authorized the Navy to be put on a war footing. War was averted when the president of Spain was able to show that the executions had been unauthorized by the home government, and that an order to stay proceedings had been dispatched by him, but had arrived too late. Subsequently the matter was settled peaceably through diplomatic negotiation. By the terms of the agreement the *Virginius* and the survivors of her vessel and crew were restored forthwith; the Spanish government proceeded against such of her officials as had infringed on Spanish law or treaty obligations; and Spain was to salute the U.S. flag unless she could prove that the *Virginius*, or any other ship, was not entitled to fly it. England, some of whose subjects had been shot in the course of the affair, exacted an indemnity.

VIRGO, the Virgin, an ancient zodiacal constellation that comes to the meridian at 9 P.M. about May 26, and two weeks earlier, at 10 P.M. It is a large constellation of relatively few stars with a maximum east-west extent of approximately 52° 5', or 3.5 hours in right ascension, and extending from declination 14° 5' north to 22° 5' south. The Virgin has been variously called Astraea, the goddess of justice; Persephone, or Proserpina, wife of Pluto; the Maiden, in India; Ishtar, the Euphratean goddess of love and fertility; and the Egyptian Isis, who threw wheat

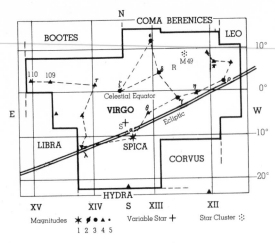

The Constellation Virgo

In Virgo is one of the nearest stars, Ross 128 of spectroscopic type M5, only 11.2 light-years distant. Despite its nearness it is a faint star (magnitude 11.1), indicating that it is very faint intrinsically. Its actual luminosity is 0.00044 times that of the sun. Near the borders of Coma Berenices and Virgo is a region especially rich in spiral nebulae, which Shapley calls the Virgo cluster of galaxies. This cluster, about 7,500,000 light-years distant, numbers more than 100 galaxies brighter than the 13th magnitude. Nearly as many more galaxies are found between the 15th and 13th magnitudes.

Virgo is the sixth sign and the seventh constellation of the zodiac. The signs of the zodiac are considered to share the westward precession of the equinoxes, which is why they no longer coincide with the constellations of the same name. The sun is in the constellation Virgo from mid-September almost to the end of October, but it enters the sign Virgo about August 20. The September 21 equinox is in the sign Libra and the constellation Virgo. See CONSTELLATION.

MOUNT WILSON AND PALOMAR OBS.

A photograph made via a 60-inch reflecting telescope trained for 2¼ hours shows the edge of Virgo, a large constellation of relatively few stars.

heads into the sky to form the Milky Way. Spica, the ear of corn of the Virgin, is the brightest star of the constellation with apparent magnitude of 1.21 It is the sixteenth in order of decreasing brightness of the 20 brightest stars. The second brightest star is γ Virginis, one of the best known of the visual binary systems. Its two components, magnitudes 3.6 and 3.7, revolve in very eccentric orbits in a period of 171.4 years. η Vir is a fourth magnitude spectroscopic binary with a period of 71.9 days. An optical triplet, magnitudes 4, 9, and 10, constitutes the star θ Vir.

There are several long-period red variable stars in Virgo; a Cepheid variable, XX Vir, with a period of 1.35 days. W Vir, with a period of 17 days, has many features characteristic of a Cepheid, such as period, spectral class and regularity of light curve, but the light curve does not match up with the curves of Cepheids of the same period. Moreover, it is located at a remarkable distance from the Milky Way to be considered to be a long-period Cepheid.

VIROQUA, city, SW Wisconsin, seat of Vernon County, on the Milwaukee Railroad and U.S. highways 14 and 61; 85 miles NW of Madison. The city is a trade center for an area in which dairy and tobacco farming are the chief occupations. Viroqua was founded in 1853 and incorporated in 1885. Pop. (1960) 3,926.

VIRTANEN, ARTTURI ILMARI, 1895–   , Nobel prize-winning Finnish biochemist, was born in Helsinki, and educated at the University of Helsinki and at Zürich, Münster, and Stockholm. He taught at the University of Helsinki 1922–48, becoming director of the Institute of Biochemistry there, 1939. Virtanen did important work in the biochemistry of bacteria and nitrogen fixation, and discovered a method of conserving fodder (*The A.I.V. System as the Basis of Cattle-Feeding*, 1943), which won him the 1945 Nobel prize in chemistry "for his researches and inventions in agricultural and nutritive chemistry, especially for his method of fodder preservation."

VIRUS, a small infectious agent, parasitic on living plant or animal material, which by reproduction may cause disease or pathological conditions in the host. Through physical determinations checked by the electron microscope virus sizes have been found to vary about 10 microns to about 300 microns. The ultramicroscopic size, the absolute necessity of living cells as host, and the crystallization of the tobacco mosaic virus have caused much speculation as to whether or not viruses are living organisms. These same conditions have created great difficulty in determining their biological characteristics, important in identification and classification.

Viruses have several qualities that distinguish them from bacteria. Viruses cannot be seen through the ordinary microscope; bacteria may be seen easily. Viruses require a susceptible living host if they are to survive, while almost all bacteria may be cultivated on synthetic organic substances. Moreover, most virus particles are able to pass through mineral or colloidal filters that bacteria cannot penetrate.

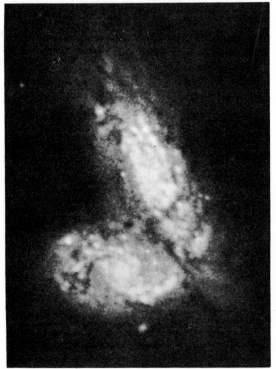

MOUNT WILSON AND PALOMAR OBS.

These twin spiral nebulae occur in a region, called the "Virgo cluster of galaxies," about 7,500,000 light-years distant from the Earth.

Viruses were first discovered in animals, in connection with foot-and-mouth disease, by Frederick Löffler and Paul Frosch in 1898. In 1892 W. P. Ivanow detected the presence of viruses in plants affected by tobacco mosaic. In 1935 W. M. Stanley isolated the rod-shaped tobacco mosaic virus and succeeded in crystallizing it as a nucleoprotein with a high molecular weight. The chief obstacle encountered in the study of viruses was that viruses are intracellular parasites so they require living media upon which to grow. In 1931 Ernest Goodpasture found that viruses would grow luxuriously on fertile eggs into which they were injected through the shell. The smallpox virus was grown in this way, as was the influenza virus and that causing yellow fever, making possible the production of large numbers of viruses for vaccines. The tobacco mosaic virus retains its pathogenic and reproductive powers through crystallization. Less stable viruses have been concentrated and purified by repeated centrifugation at high and low speed in a high-speed vacuum centrifuge. In all viruses purified to date the presence of nucleic acid has been determined. Thus viruses serve as a bridge between the organisms of the bacteriologist and the molecules of the chemist. However, the immediate interest in viruses is not their position between animate and inanimate material but their properties as disease-producing agents.

Virus parasitism is characterized by a specificity not only for species but often for particular types of tissue. However, many animal viruses may infect several hosts. Thus many diseases of animals are known to be transmissible to man. Mutations or changes often occur when the virus enters hosts or tissues other than those it usually invades. These mutations have been closely observed in their effect on various tissues in several laboratory animals. Egg embryo culture of virus was the most important single development in virus history, and makes the laboratory study of animal virus relations and diseases much more simple. Many viruses grow readily on this egg-embryo medium, making possible the production of large quantities of viruses for experimentation.

As Animal Parasites. Animal viruses often produce "inclusion" or "elementary" bodies within the parasitized cell. These bodies contain refractile granules that retain their infectivity when freed from other material. The isolated granules may not be the viruses themselves, but rather particles upon which the virus has been absorbed.

Animal viruses usually produce immune bodies. These viruses are seemingly imprisoned permanently in the parasitized cell and as long as immune bodies are produced in good quantity the host remains immune. Active viruses are believed essential for immunity; therefore, if these parasitized cells are lost, the host loses its immunity. Killed virus does not produce immune bodies in an animal or man, as do killed bacteria. Therefore in the treatment of some virus diseases the living virus is altered, rather than killed, by treatment with chemicals, by passage through another animal host, by growth on egg embryo, or by exposure to X rays or ultraviolet rays. A vaccine made with this attenuated virus may be effective in producing immunity. Sulfa drugs and penicillin have no effect upon viruses, but some antibiotics, such as aureomycin are beneficial in certain virus diseases. Vaccines, however, are still of vital importance in the prevention of smallpox, rabies, and poliomyelitis. Other common virus diseases of man include measles, mumps, chicken pox, yellow fever, and influenza. By means of vaccination, outstanding successes have been achieved in the control of certain animal virus diseases, including hog cholera, fowl pox, and bovine ecthyma of sheep and goats.

As Plant Parasites. Among all bacteria, plants, and animals there are only three groups of plants that have not been found to suffer virus infection.

RADIO CORP. OF AMERICA

An electron microscope photograph of influenza viruses shows the organisms (the large spheres casting shadows) pictured at sixty thousand times their normal diameter.

They are gymnosperms, pteridophytes, and bryophytes. Frequently plant virus diseases are not fatal. The results of infection vary with the virus and with certain host plants. Among the symptoms of virus disease are the mosaic pattern of the leaves, caused by the lack of chlorophyll; ring formation, single or concentric; outgrowths on the underside of the leaves; a stimulation or repression of growth, resulting in leaves abnormally long or wide, or a variation in petal coloration of the flower. Vaccines are not used in the control of plant virus diseases. The control measures include destruction of the diseased plant as soon as possible, and the development of plant varieties that are resistant to virus diseases.

Plants apparently do not produce antibodies. Hence plants do not acquire immunity to virus diseases as do animals. However, there is very limited plant immunity against related viruses. Related strains are those which are strikingly similar in characteristics; and once the plant is infected by a single member of the group the others seem unable to enter. However, a plant may have at the same time infections of several unrelated viruses.

Virus diseases are largely dependent upon insects to transport them to new hosts. Like the mosquito which transmits yellow fever, the aphids and leaf hoppers transport plant sap by their suctorial mouth parts. Whether there is multiplication of the virus within the vector is not known. However, insects may retain their infectivity of some virus diseases for long periods of time without access to a fresh source of virus.

Corresponding to egg embryo culture of animal viruses, the root tip method is used for many plant viruses. The plant viruses are, on the whole, more stable than animal viruses, which permits the use of chemical means for isolation and purification. Plant viruses, particularly tobacco mosaic virus, have been the subject of much physical study in size, sedimentation rate, buoyancy and viscosity. See VACCINE.

R. W. CUMLEY

VISAKHAPATNAM, or Vizagapatam, city, E India, Andhra Pradesh State, capital of Visakhapatnam District; on a highway and railway on the coast of the Bay of Bengal, about 300 miles ENE of Hyderabad. The chief exports are grain, manganese ore, peanuts, and sugar. The city is a trade center for a large area. Food products, coir matting, and textiles are manufactured. The trading station established by the English early in the seventeenth century was taken by the French in 1757, but was recaptured a year later. Pop. (1951) 108,042.

VISALIA, city, S central California, seat of Tulare County; on the Santa Fe and the Southern Pacific railroads; 49 miles SE of Fresno. The town is a processing center for an area in which cotton, fruit, walnuts, and livestock are the chief agricultural products. The Sequoia National Park lies 30 miles to the east of Visalia. Visalia was founded in 1852 and incorporated in 1874. Pop. (1960) 15,791.

VISAYAN ISLANDS, or Bisaya, the central group of the Philippine Islands, lying between the islands of Luzon and Mindanao, and including Mindoro, Masbate, Samar, Leyte, Bohol, Cebu, Negros, Panay, Tablas, Sibuyan, and numerous smaller islands which surround the Sibuyan and Visayan seas; area about 25,000 sq. mi.; pop. about 3,600,000. For the most part the islands are elevated portions of submerged mountain ranges. The highest peak (8,160 ft.) is on Mindoro Island. The islands are peopled for the most part by the Visayan peoples, of Malay stock.

VISBY, or Wisby, city, capital of Gotland County, main settlement on the Baltic Sea, 60 miles E of the coast of Sweden, and about 150 miles SSE of Stockholm. Visby is on the northwest coast of Gotland and has an ice-free port. The roads and railways of that island radiate from the town. The appearance of the town has changed very little since the Middle Ages, and it is still surrounded by a medieval wall, though many of its churches are in ruins. The town is the site of a bishopric. Visby was a commercial center of northern Europe from the tenth to the fourteenth century. The name Visby means "a settlement at a place of sacrifice." Visby received its name in pagan days when it was a religious center. It became one of the first members of the Hanseatic League. During the thirteenth century the Visby Maritime Law was compiled, a code on which the maritime laws of many countries were based. The town was captured by the Danes in 1361 and was a pirate stronghold for several centuries. In 1645 Visby came under Swedish rule. Pop. (1953 est.) 14,962.

VISCACHA, a South American rodent, noted for its unique appearance and belonging to the family *Chinchillidae.* The viscacha has a strong body measuring 20 inches in length with a large head which has large, erect ears. Long, black hairs are tufted under the animal's eyes and two white stripes cross its face. Its short, sturdy forelegs, which are out of proportion to the long hindlegs, cause the animal to move in an awkward manner. The color of the viscacha is a mixture of black, gray, and brown. It lives in burrows, often sharing the community hole with owls and snakes. The viscachas found in the plains are nocturnal animals, but those living in the mountains awaken at sunrise. The rodent can be found in southern Brazil, Uruguay, Paraguay, and the Argentine pampas. Its meals consists mostly of roots.

VISCHER, a family of German Renaissance sculptors, active for about 100 years in the fifteenth and sixteenth centuries, whose members produced numerous masterpieces of late Gothic sculpture, and developed the craft of brassworking to a fine art. The high point in the development of the family style is seen in the Tomb of St. Sebald (1508–19) in the Sebaldus Church, Nürnberg.

Hermann Vischer the Elder (died 1488) began his career in Nürnberg as a brassworker. A baptismal font, in the Wittenberg church, is the only work definitely ascribed to him.

Peter Vischer the Elder (1460?–1529), Hermann's son, furthered the business his father had established. In 1494 he was commissioned to work for Prince Phillip in Heidelberg. The wealthy Fugger family of Augsburg ordered a chapel gate, 1512, but it remained unfinished at Peter's death; most of it was eventually sold for scrap, 1806.

Peter the Elder's sons were: Hermann Vischer the Younger (1486?–1517), who traveled to Rome and brought back *objects d'art* which influenced the family's works; Peter Vischer the Younger (1487–1528), who read the works of poets and historians, studied anatomy, and executed the memorial to the Elector Fredrick the Wise, Wittenberg; Hans Vischer (1489?–1550), who helped Peter the Elder execute the St. Sebald Tomb, was a friend of Dürer, and designed the gate for the Sigmund Chapel in Cracow (Kraków); and Jacob and Paulus Vischer, of both of whom little is known, although it is possible that

Peter Vischer the Elder was commissioned by the wealthy houses of Renaissance Germany to create the Gothic style sculpture and brasswork for which his family was famous.

Paulus (died 1531) executed the wooden Nürnberg Madonna (?1525). George Vischer (1520?–92), the eldest son of Hans Vischer, did the last known work to be produced in the family foundry—an inkwell, dated 1544.

The works of the Vischer family reflect the painstaking, unhurried approach of the Renaissance artist, and their graceful details combine the best features of Gothic and Renaissance art.

VISCONTI, a celebrated family of Italian noblemen of the Ghibelline faction (see GUELPH AND GHIBELLINE), who ruled the city of Milan, 1311–1447. They derived their initial distinction and civil power from Ottone Visconti (1207?–95), a canon from Desio, who was appointed archbishop of Milan, 1262, by Pope Urban IV. The opposition of the Della Torre family, members of the Guelph faction, who were in control of Milan at that time, prevented Ottone from taking possession of his appointed see until 1277. When he finally did take possession, he imprisoned the leading members of the Della Torre family and suppressed, for a time at least, the power of the Guelphs in Milan. Ottone was succeeded as political leader of Milan by his grandnephew Matteo Visconti (1255?–1322). Matteo, who also was opposed by the Guelph faction, was forced to flee Milan by a new uprising of the Della Torre, 1302. After taking refuge in Verona for nearly 10 years, he was restored to the dukedom of Milan, 1311, with the help of Emperor Henry VII, who also conferred the title Imperial Vicar of Lombardy upon him. It was thus Matteo who first firmly established supremacy of the Visconti in Milan, although the Della Torre remained a strong rival faction. Matteo quarreled with the pope over the appointment of a new archbishop of Milan, and was excommunicated from the Roman Catholic church, 1322. He abdicated the same year in favor of his son, Galeazzo I (1277?–1328), and died within a few months.

Galeazzo I ruled Milan for six stormy years, 1322–28. During this time, he defeated an army sent against him by the pope, 1324, but was then imprisoned by his own benefactor, Emperor Louis the Bavarian, who was fearful lest Galeazzo sign a pact with the church. He was succeeded, 1328, by his son, Azzo Visconti (1302–39), who repurchased the title of Imperial Vicar of Lombardy from the emperor, murdered his uncle Marco, 1329, and suppressed a rebellion led by his cousin Lodrisio. He was succeeded by his uncle Lucchino Visconti (1287?–1349), a son of the aforementioned Matteo. An able but tyrannical ruler, Lucchino made temporary peace with the pope, 1341, and brought Parma and Pisa into the Visconti orbit. He was poisoned, 1349, by his wife

Isabella Fieschi, and was succeeded by his brother Giovanni Visconti (1290?–1354), who had been Archbishop of Milan from 1342. In exercising both religious and political rule over Milan, Giovanni was the first of the Visconti to be absolute sovereign over the city. From his time the influence of the emperor in Milan was completely undone, and the power of the Della Torre was so diluted that it ceased to be of significance. By the time of Archbishop Giovanni's death, 1354, the Visconti ruled most of northern Italy.

After Giovanni's demise, the state was partitioned among his brother Stefano's three sons: Matteo II (died 1355), Galeazzo II (1320?–1378), and Bernabò (1319–85). Matteo II was assassinated, 1355, by his brothers, who thenceforth ruled jointly. Galeazzo II, with his court at Pavia, founded the university there and made the city a center of the arts and sciences. Bernabò, with his court at Milan, was more ambitious politically. He waged war and intrigued against the Emperor Charles IV and the popes, Innocent VI and Urban V; Urban went so far as to proclaim a short-lived holy crusade against him. When Galeazzo II died, 1378, Bernabò attempted to assume sole power over the state, but his nephew Gian Galeazzo, son of Galeazzo II, had him assassinated, 1385.

Gian Galeazzo (1351?–1402), as sole ruler of Milan, 1385–1402, was the most powerful of all the Visconti. He consolidated much of north and central Italy, adding by conquest or purchase the cities of Verona, Vicenza, Padua, Pisa, Siena, Perugia, Lucca, Bologna, and Assisi to his territories, and even making inroads in Florence, where he was halted only by the plague. Most of his conquests, however, were lost to the family after his death. His son, Giovanni Maria (1389–1412), ruled Milan from 1402 until his extreme cruelties led Ghibelline partisans to murder him. He was succeeded by his brother Filippe Maria (1392–1447), the last of the direct male line of Visconti. Following his death, Milan became a republic, and Francesco Sforza, husband of Filippo Maria's natural daughter, Maria Bianca, came into power.

VISCOSE. See RAYON.

VISCOSITY, the resistance to flow, due to internal friction when fluids are in motion. When a fluid flows over the flat surface of a solid, that layer of the fluid in contact with the solid remains at rest because of adhesion. The adjacent layer of fluid particles moves slowly over the first layer, the third over the second, and so forth, the speed increasing with the distance from the solid stationary surface. The fluid is thus subjected to a shearing stress.

The coefficient of viscosity is the force in dynes per cm² of fluid surface required to produce motion at the rate of one cm per sec. on a layer one cm from the stationary layer. The coefficient of viscosity is denoted by η and is defined thus:

$$\eta = \frac{F/A}{v/d} = \frac{Fd}{Av} \frac{\text{dynes} \times \text{sec}}{\text{cm}^2}$$

where F/A is the tangential force per unit on the moving layer, and v/d, called the velocity gradient, is the rate at which the velocity changes with distance between layer spaces. The unit of viscosity thus measured is the poise. The following table gives the viscosities of a few common liquids.

I. VISCOSITY OF LIQUIDS

Liquid	Temperature	Viscosity in Poises
Alcohol, Ethyl	20°C.	0.0120
Benzene	20°C.	0.00652
Creosote	20°C.	0.120
Glycerin	20°C.	14.90
Mercury	20°C.	0.0154
Oil, Linseed	30°C.	0.331
Oil, Machine, light	19°C.	1.138
Water	20°C.	0.01005
Water	100°C.	0.002838

Viscosity in gases is much smaller than that in liquids, but it is highly important in its retarding effects on the motions of gases themselves and the motions of other bodies through gases. The frictional resistance of air to the motions of bodies through it increases with the speed of the motion. There is, consequently, a limiting speed for bodies such as rain drops falling through the air. The viscosity for liquids decreases with the rise of temperature, whereas that of gases increases. The following table gives coefficients of viscosity for some common gases.

II. VISCOSITY OF GASES

Gas	Temperature	Viscosity in Poises
Air	0°C.	170.8×10^{-6}
Air	74°C.	210.2×10^{-6}
Ammonia	0°C.	91.8×10^{-6}
Hydrogen	0°C.	83.5×10^{-6}
Mercury vapor	313°C.	551×10^{-6}
Oxygen	0°C.	189×10^{-6}
Water vapor	100°C.	125.5×10^{-6}

VISCOUNT, a title of nobility, most frequently found in the aristocracy of England and France. The rank is the next above that of baron, and the next below count on the continent of Europe, and earl in England. The viscount was an officer who acted in the place of an earl or count. The title has also been used to designate a sheriff. See EARL; NOBILITY.

VISCUM. See MISTLETOE.

VISEU, city, Portugal, capital of Beira Alta Province, on a railway 50 miles SE of Pôrto. The city is located on a plateau, and is a highway junction point. Viseu is a trade and processing center for an area producing grain and fruit, and has tanneries and textile mills. The cathedral in Viseu dates from the twelfth century, and there is a museum with a collection of early Portugese paintings. The city was founded by the Romans, was captured by the Moors, then taken by Ferdinand I of Castile in 1060. It came under Portugese control during the twelfth century.

VISHINSKY, ANDREI YANUARIEVICH, 1883–1954, Soviet lawyer and political leader, was born of bourgeois parents in Odessa, and began to take part in revolutionary activities while yet a student at the University of Kiev. He joined the Bolshevists, fought in the Red army during the Revolution of 1917, joined the Communist party, 1920, and became attorney general of the Russian Soviet Federated Socialist Republic, 1923. In this capacity he figured in many prominent trials, including the famous public hearings on the Trotskyite-Zinoviev terrorist group, 1936–38. Vishinsky became deputy people's commissar for foreign affairs, 1940. After World War II he was the Soviet spokesman at many United Nations meetings and at other international conferences, and became noted for his strongly worded denunciations of the Western powers. He was Soviet minister of foreign affairs, 1949–53.

VISHNU, in Hindu belief, God in the aspect of Savior, as distinguished from the other members of the dominant trinity—Brahma (God as Creator) and Siva (God as Destroyer). According to the mythos of the worshipers of Vishnu, generically known as Vishnuites, whenever the enemies of His rule threatened the serenity of his world, God appears to defend his own. Historically, the Hindus recognize 10 incarnations (avatars) of Vishnu, the last of which, that of Kalki (the Judge of the Final Day), is yet to come. The first four manifestations of Vishnu as the Fish, Tortoise, Boar, and Man-Lion, mark mythical deeds performed in the dawn of Creation. The fifth, or Dwarf, incarnation, refers to a feat mentioned in the *Rig-Veda*, namely: the three cosmic strides wherewith Vishnu measured the basic divisions of the universe. The sixth, seventh, and eighth represent the deification of the three great heroes of Indian mythology; Parasurāma, Rāma, and Krishna. The last two of these are especially important inasmuch as their devotees make up the majority of modern Vishnuites. The ninth incarnation, that of Buddha, represents the recognition by Hinduism of the divine character of the founder of its offshoot, Buddhism.

The almost infinite diversity of Hindu forms and objects of worship make it impossible to determine with any accuracy how many sects of Vishnu there are, but more than 100 are known, most of them reflecting differences in the teachings of the sages and theologians. The largest sect, in point of numbers, is probably that of the Srī Vaishnavas, founded by Ramanuja (1016?–?96). Second largest is the cult of Madhva (1197?–1276), followed by those of Ramananda (1299?–?1410), Vallābhachārya (1479?–?1520), and Chaitanya (1485–1527). Taken all together, the various sects of Vaishnavism constitute the major subdivision of the Hindu religion.   ROBERT WHITTEMORE

VISSER T'HOOFT, WILLEM ADOLF, 1900– , Dutch religious leader and church statesman, was born in Haarlem. He prepared for the ministry at the University of Leiden, and received the doctorate in theology, 1928, and was ordained, 1936, in the Reformed Church in Geneva, Switzerland. Among his various important posts he was secretary of the World Committee of the YMCA, the World Student Christian Federation, and after 1938 of the World Council of Churches. Important among his various books are *Anglo-Catholicism and Orthodoxy* (1933), *The Kingships of Christ* (1948), *The Meaning of Ecumenical* (1953), *The Ecumenical Movement and the Racial Problem* (1954), *The Renewal of the Church* (1957), *Rembrandt and the Gospel* (1958), and *The Pressure of our Common Calling* (1959). He received honorary degrees from many American and European universities.

EASTFOTO

The Vistula, Poland's longest river, is navigable for steamers to the mouth of the San River. Most of the shipping is carried by large river barges.

VISTULA RIVER, Polish Wisła, Poland, rises in the Beskid Range of the Carpathian Mountains and flows across the heart of the country in an S-shaped course to empty into the Baltic Sea at the Gulf of Danzig. It is 630 miles long. The Vistula, with its tributaries the San and the Bug, is one of the most important waterways in Poland. It flows through the cities of Warsaw and Kraków, and the granaries, docks, and warehouses of Danzig are built along its banks. The Vistula is navigable for nine months of the year.

VITALIAN, SAINT, Latin name Vitalianus, died 672, pope from 657 until his death, was born in Segni, Italy. He opposed Monothelitism, but sought to work out a *modus vivendi* with the Monothelite Emperor Constans II. Vitalian is also remembered for having promoted ecclesiastical harmony among the Anglo-Saxons and Britons in England.

VITALISM, in biology and philosophy, a theory of nature which holds that over and above the mechanistically describable features of a living organism there is a "vital principle" that cannot be so described. Vitalism in some senses was accepted without question by almost all philosophers and scientists until the nineteenth century, during which the prevailing view changed as more and more scientists accepted the idea that all phenomena, no matter how complex, could be studied as combinations of simple factors, each acting uniformly. In applying this view to biology, Johannes Peter Müller, Claude Bernard, and others set out to interpret all living processes as combinations of chemical reactions; that life is simply a complex chemical reaction eventually became the prevailing view of U.S. and English scientists and philosophers. Vitalism, however, in refusing to accept this hypothesis and the research program it implies, was represented, at mid-twentieth century, by a small minority of biologists and philosophers of nature, most of them European.   E. B. COSTELLO

VITAL STATISTICS, data on births, deaths, marriages, and divorces. Various types of related information, including the age of the mother and the total number of her children, are usually collected in conjunction with births; data on age of deceased and cause of death are generally collected in conjunction with deaths; statistics on marriages may include age of bride and groom and previous marital status; statistics on divorce may include data on length of marriage and number of children. The ultimate purpose for collecting, tabulating, presenting, and analyzing these statistics is to study the rate of growth of a nation or other area, and the factors affecting this rate.

Problems in the Collection of Data. Vital statistics are collected on a current basis, that is, the event is reported to local authorities as soon as it occurs. The local authorities in turn forward these statistics to a central processing office a short time later. Obviously, if the data are to be of value, all relevant events that occur must be reported. This means that there must be a good reporting system. Most but not all of the major nations of the world have devised reporting systems for births and deaths.

The presence of a reporting system does not, of course, insure the complete reporting of all these events. Probably no country of the world has 100 per cent complete reporting, but a number of nations do come very close to this. Among these are the United States, Canada, and some of the countries of Western Europe.

The Statistical Office of the United Nations, Department of Economic Affairs, receives and compiles official figures on vital statistics from many of its member nations. The publication of this information in a single compilation by that office represents the most complete report on the world's vital statistics available.

Types of Rates. There are two types of birth, death, marriage, and divorce rates—crude and standardized. The crude rate is the number of events per 1,000 population. The difference between the birth rate and the death rate is the crude rate of natural increase of a population. Thus, in the United States, for example, in 1960 the estimated crude birth rate was 22.6 per 1,000, the death rate was 9.9, and the crude rate of natural increase was 12.7. Crude rates have only limited usefulness since the age and sex distribution and other characteristics of a population affect these rates considerably.

The standardized death rate most commonly used is the life table. This table shows how many infants out of 100,000 born alive will live to specified ages. Thus, the life table also shows the death rate at these same ages. It also shows the future life expectancy at any given age. In the United States a white male infant born in 1958 had a future life expectancy of 67.2 years. Life tables of different nations can be compared and generally will afford a more accurate comparison of the true mortality conditions than will the crude death rate.

A standardized birth rate which is utilized considerably is the net reproduction rate. This rate is so constructed that a figure of 1,000 implies that the population in the long run will remain unchanged in size; a rate above 1,000 implies a potentially growing population and a rate below 1,000 a potentially declining population. The net reproduction rate of 1,730 observed in the United States for the year 1958, for example, implies that in the long run the U.S. population, under the specified conditions, would increase by 73 per cent from one generation to the next.

Another type of rate is the morbidity, or sickness rate, which is used to express the extent of sickness and disease in the population. Common morbidity rates are the tuberculosis rate, or the number of tuberculosis cases per 1,000 population, and the venereal disease rate. The compilation of these rates aids greatly in determining the effect of economic, regional, medical, and other factors upon the health of the population.

Registration of Births, Deaths, and Marriages. Until very recent times, records of vital statistics have been incomplete, irregular, and unsystematic. One of the earliest record-keeping authorities was the parish church; hence, throughout the Western world old church files are often found giving this information. Unfortunately, these records can seldom be relied on to give an accurate picture of population trends. Because the records were kept in separate parishes they are not uniform. Moreover, there is the difficulty of getting a sufficient amount of information upon which to base accurate generalizations. Some parishes kept more complete records than others. Many records have been intentionally destroyed after a lapse of time, and others have been lost by fire and other accidents.

In the nineteenth century the keeping of such records was transferred to civil authorities. By the end of the century most states had laws requiring the registration of births, deaths, and marriages, and they were seeking methods to insure accuracy, completeness, and uniformity. England passed a general registration act, 1836, but registration was not made compulsory until 1884. By the beginning of the twentieth century British administration was so perfected that few births, deaths, and marriages went unrecorded. Other European countries followed the British example and by mid-twentieth century most of them had effective systems in use.   A. J. JAFFE

In the United States the authority to inaugurate and administer such registration is a state function. For this reason there continues to be variation in record keeping throughout the country. Before 1900 administration usually depended on the non-compulsory co-operation of physicians; the result was that most rural births and deaths went unrecorded. Most U.S. records antedating 1900 are unreliable. Isolated examples of careful record keeping do exist, as in Massachusetts, 1886–96, but in general the records are fragmentary.

Records kept after 1900 are more reliable. In 1902 the Public Health Association developed a model form for registration. The American Medical Association approved the form, and the U.S. Census Bureau encouraged its adoption by accepting the records of states adopting the model. Even Congress recommended its use, 1903. At the urging of the Census Bureau, the states gradually adopted the approved form, which made for uniform definitions and statistics on a national scale. Birth records were likewise made uniform for the states, and thus greatly simplified the compilation of the national statistics. But even with the use of the model form which was involved, it is doubtful that the records are complete.

Both death and birth records are usually kept in the local public health office, from where most are sent to the state capital. The model law makes the doctor, midwife, or other person present at birth responsible for the registration. In most states the registration must be made shortly after birth. Besides the date and place of birth, the model U.S. law requires the age, nationality, and occupation of the parents as a part of the record.

The delayed registration of births is provided for in many states in order to remedy the laxity of the past. As birth certificates are increasingly required of job applicants and of persons claiming civic benefits, provision is made for the registration of births many years after the actual date. This system of delayed registration requires affidavits and evidence of age and place of birth.

The states have been more successful in enforcing the registration of deaths than they have been in requiring registration of births. The model law requires that a death be recorded and a doctor's statement of the cause of death be filed within 72 hours. If no doctor's certificate can be secured, the report of the coroner is demanded. A body may not legally be buried or moved out of the local jurisdiction without a certificate issued by the registering official insuring that the legal provisions have been met. The name of the deceased, sex, marital status, date and place of birth and of death, occupation, parents' names, cause of death, and place of burial are required in registering deaths.

Except for common law unions, registration of marriages is fairly complete. Before a minister, justice of the peace, or other qualified person can lawfully perform a marriage, he must have in hand an officially issued license. After the ceremony he returns the license with the appropriate signatures to the issuing office, where it is legally recorded. Thus, in practice the information required for registration—names, residences, ages, and previous marriages, if any—is secured before the marriage takes place.

Use of electronic equipment has resulted in earlier availability of data. See CENSUS; POPULATION.

BIBLIOG.–George W. Backman, *Health Resources in the United States: Personnel, Facilities and Services* (1952); Bernard Benjamin, *Elements of Vital Statistics* (1960); Donald J. Bogue, *Structure of the Metropolitan Community* (1949); Louis I. Dublin and Mortimer Spiegelman, *Facts of Life: From Birth to Death* (1951); Percy G. Edge, *Vital Statistics and Public Health Work in the Tropics* (1944); William P. Elderton and Richard C. Fippard, *Construction of Mortality and Sickness Tables* (1947); Marguerite F. Hall, *Public Health Statistics* (1949); Harold A. Phelps and David Henderson, *Population in Its Human Aspects* (1958); Satya Swaroop, *Introduction to Health Statistics* (1960); Pascal K. Whelpton, *Cohort Fertility: Native White Women in the United States* (1954); Hugh H. Wolfenden, *Population Statistics and Their Compilation* (1954); World Health Organization, *Annual Epidemiological and Vital Statistics, 1939–1946* (vol. 1, pt. 1) (1951).

VITAMIN, an organic substance required in minute amount in the diets of animal organisms. Until about the time vitamins were discovered there existed throughout the whole world of biological and medical thought, the tacit assumption that the major chemical constituents of living things, such as water, the proteins, carbohydrates, fats, and the major minerals, constituted the chemical basis for life and were the only chemical constituents of living matter that really made a difference.

It is now known, however, that the importance or significance of the chemical constituents of the human body can by no means be judged on the basis of their relative abundance. Not only vitamins, but the hormones and the trace elements, such as iodine, copper, manganese, cobalt, and molybdenum, are present in living things often in the tiniest amounts; yet they may be absolutely essential to life and well-being, just as vitally necessary as any protein, carbohydrate, fat, or as any major mineral such as calcium or phosphate, could be to existence itself.

The three types of vitally essential "trace" chemicals in the human body, namely, vitamins, hormones, and trace elements, can be readily differentiated. While the vitamins and hormones are both organic in nature, that is, they have the element carbon in their makeup, the hormones are characteristically produced within the body, whereas the vitamins must come from without, that is, in food. Trace elements, which unlike vitamins and hormones are nonorganic in nature, similarly cannot be produced within the body; they, too, must be furnished in the food. See HORMONE. MINERAL.

HISTORY

The question as to when vitamins were discovered can be answered only in vague terms. As far back as 1774, James Lind, a British surgeon, demonstrated clearly that orange juice and lemon juice contained something which had almost miraculous power to cure scurvy, but the clear-cut recognition that this something was a specific chemical substance was very slow in coming. At the time Lind made his observation, cod-liver oil was widely used as a folk remedy. Not until much later were its virtues demonstrated to be the result of its vitamin content.

The term vitamin, which was originally spelled vitamine, was coined by Casimir Funk, a Polish chemist, in 1911, to designate certain protective substances, or vital amines, which he postulated to be present in foods. The lack of these vitamins in specific diets gave rise, he said, to beri-beri, scurvy, rickets, and pellagra. While it is possible to give Funk too much credit (there were many others who had previously contributed pertinent information), there is no question that his bold postulate, which turned out to be almost 100 per cent correct, focused attention on the "vitamin" idea and brought it to the front for serious consideration. The particular "vitamin" which was the starting point for Funk's idea, now known as thiamin or vitamin B_1, was found ultimately to be chemically so constituted that the term "vital amine" could appropriately be applied to it. This designation is, however, quite inappropriate for a large number of those substances which are now called vitamins. While all of them are vital, many of them are farthest removed chemically from anything which chemists call amines. Yet the name is retained with the modified spelling.

CHEMISTRY

The one serious error in Funk's concept was the assumption or implication that vitamins are essentially similar chemically. This is not at all true. Some vitamins contain only carbon, hydrogen, and oxygen; others may contain carbon, hydrogen, oxygen, and nitrogen; still others, including vitamin B_1, contain carbon, hydrogen, oxygen, nitrogen, and sulfur. One vitamin, B_{12}, contains carbon, hydrogen, oxygen, nitrogen, phosphorus, and cobalt. Moreover, the molecular weights of the recognized vitamins vary over about a tenfold range and although most of them are colorless, some are highly colored. Altogether vitamins constitute a highly heterogeneous assortment of organic chemicals. The basis for grouping vitamins together is the similarity of their biological functioning, not their chemical resemblances. They are all organic compounds needed in small amounts in human and animal nutrition.

The number of distinct vitamins generally recognized is not less than thirteen. Uncertainties exist with respect to a number of additional substances suspected of having vitamin activity. Some nutritionally important substances, such as choline and polyunsaturated fatty acids, cannot readily be classified with other nutrients and can at best be grouped only in the fringes of the vitamin category, partly because of the relatively large amounts required and partly

because their functioning appears not to resemble that of well authenticated vitamins.

The enumeration of the known vitamins is complicated by the fact that in some instances there are several substances which serve a particular function, sometimes unequally well for different animals and under different conditions. For example, there is more than one form of vitamin D; each one can function by itself and can take the place of the other forms. Designations such as D_1, D_2, and D_3 are used in such cases. Because of the existence of different forms of essentially the same vitamin, the total number of naturally occurring "vitamin substances," each known to possess vitamin activity, is more than twenty-five.

Nomenclature. The nomenclature of the vitamins is confusing to those not familiar with the history of their discovery. Initially the letters A, B, C, and so forth were used to designate unknown entities which brought about demonstrated nutritional effects. In some cases, notably in the case of B, which was found in such foods as yeast, liver, milk, and rice polishings, the ultimate unraveling of the chemistry of the situation showed clearly that the nutritional effect produced (by the yeast, for example) was not due to any one substance, but to several different substances, each of which was individually essential. Thus when the designations B_1 and B_2 are used, they have an entirely different connotation from those of A_1 or A_2, D_1 or D_2, E_1 or E_2. These latter designations refer to vitamins that can substitute for one another, while B_1 and B_2 are entirely different vitamins, each of which is indispensable, and neither of which can replace the other.

There is a strong tendency in scientific circles to discard the now outworn B designations, and replace them with the names of the specific substances involved: thiamin (B_1), riboflavin (B_2), niacinamide, pantothenic acid, pyridoxin (B_6), inositol (incomplete agreement as to the status of this), biotin, folic acid, cobalamin (B_{12}). This use of names (and discarding of the letter designations) avoids the somewhat embarrassing but logical questions of what are B_4, B_5, B_7, or B_{11}. Actually the use of letter and number designations for vitamins has been far from orderly or systematic. This is due in part to the uncertainties of research findings. An investigator might think he had found a new B vitamin and decide to designate it as B_4. Investigations, perhaps years later, might reveal that the results on which the B_4 designation rested were spurious or were based upon misinterpretation. In the meantime, however, no one would wish to use the B_4 designation for another substance, with the result that it would eventually drop out of the picture.

The advantage of discarding the B designations becomes evident in the case of what has been called vitamin B_6. This vitamin has turned out to be any one of three related substances. Rather than call them vitamin B_{6A}, vitamin B_{6B}, and vitamin B_{6C}, respectively, one gives them names which hold some clue to their nature: pyridoxin, pyridoxal, and pyridoxamine. Any one of these substances functions, although not always equally well, as vitamin B_6.

Classification. Because of gross differences in their chemical nature vitamins are conveniently considered as belonging in fat soluble and water soluble groups. Those that are fat soluble are often associated with fats and include vitamins A, D, E, K; the water soluble group includes ascorbic acid (C), the B vitamins, and the debatable vitamin or vitamins P. Of all of these, vitamin D is unique in that, given a suitable amount of sunlight, or ultraviolet light, the need for an outside source of vitamin D vanishes. It is then produced by the action of the light on sterols in the skin. Vitamin A is unique in another way. Carotenes, which are yellow pigments that occur in carrots and other yellow vegetables and in green leaves, can be transformed into vitamin A in the body. Thus carotenes are often called pro-vitamins.

Function. Losses of vitamins are incurred in the refinement, cooking, and toasting of foods. If vegetables, for example, are cooked with excess water which is discarded, substantial losses occur. Vitamin C is the vitamin most easily destroyed by heat. If the cooking is done in the absence of air, however, as is common in commercial canning practice, loss does not occur.

Initially vitamins were thought of primarily as protective substances useful in preventing specific diseases; while it is true that specific diseases often result from the lack of specific vitamins, it is also true, on the positive side, that in health, vitamins function as essential cogs in many parts of the machinery of living matter. Vitamin A, for example, by furnishing a crucial raw material out of which the visual pigments are produced, makes the phenomenon of sight possible. It is also needed by epithelial tissue throughout the body and helps it resist infection. One of the effects of vitamin A deprivation in male animals is sterility. Pregnant animals fed vitamin A deficient diets often yield highly deformed offspring. Young animals with insufficient vitamin A fail to grow.

In many if not most cases, it is hazardous to try to pinpoint "the disease" which a particular vitamin is supposed to prevent. Certainly it would be inappropriate to designate vitamin A as the anti-blindness vitamin, the anti-infection vitamin, the anti-sterility vitamin, the anti-deformity vitamin, or the anti-stunting vitamin. Vision, resistance to infection, reproduction, and growth are not controlled exclusively by vitamin A, nor can one be sure that vitamin A deprivation may not have manifestations distinct from all these. Even vitamin B_{12} (cobalamin), which when absorbed will prevent or cure pernicious anemia, is more than an anti-anemia vitamin; its lack causes severe lesions of the nervous system, and its need in many tissues of the body is indicated.

Knowledge about how the various vitamins function is uneven. In the case of some vitamins, investigations have been relatively few, or relatively unproductive, with the result that one must remain in ignorance of many fundamental facts. Man's fundamental knowledge about the functioning of the fat soluble vitamins, except, perhaps, in the case of vitamin A, is relatively scanty; the same is also true of ascorbic acid. While ascorbic acid deficiency produces scurvy, this disease affects many tissues, including those of the gums, teeth, bones, capillaries, and the entire network of extracellular protein of the body, and it produces many symptoms: hemorrhages, anemia, lack of appetite, heart enlargement and damage, pain, swelling, and loss of resistance to infection. No satisfactory knowledge exists as to the chemical mechanisms involved in the action of ascorbic acid.

The vitamins for which more complete information is available are members of what may be called the B family. Thiamin in proper combination is essential because it serves as a catalyst for crucial steps in the utilization of pyruvic acid, which is a key intermediate in metabolism. (See Enzyme; Metabolism.) The chemical transformations which thiamin makes possible take place in every cell of the human body and hence there is no cell or tissue which might be expected to be unharmed by its lack. It is true that when thiamin is lacking in the diet of an animal or a human being, nervous symptoms, which include loss of appetite, itching, and loss of co-ordination and reflexes are prominent. If the lack is severe, nerve degeneration can be demonstrated. It was because of observations such as these that this vitamin was early designated the anti-neuritic vitamin. In England and Europe the name aneurin has often been used for it.

From the standpoint of present knowledge, these designations and the implications they carry are unfortunate in that they distort the concept of how vitamins function. The inappropriateness of thinking of thiamin as a nerve vitamin is emphasized by the fact that there are tens of thousands of species of organisms for which thiamin is absolutely essential but which have no nervous systems whatever.

The catalytic functions of several of the B vitamins have been well established. Many of them enter into the makeup of coenzymes which, associated with suitable proteins, constitute indispensable enzymes. These vitamins are thus crucial parts of enzymes or enzyme systems which make possible the many types of chemical transformation that are taking place in the body minute by minute.

These same B vitamins function not only in the biochemistry of animals and human beings, but also in all manner of other organisms of all types. For this reason when one eats any food of plant origin, such as potatoes, carrots, lettuce, or cabbage, he is certain to obtain an assortment of the B vitamins with every mouthful. Unlike animals, however, plants often manufacture these vitamins for themselves, and do not require that they be furnished in the plant food. Moreover, bacteria are in some cases the prime producers of vitamins. Vitamins are also in the flesh of animals; thus the person who eats oysters, or the robin which eats an earthworm, receives an assortment of B vitamins.

In view of their ubiquitous nature, it might seem that obtaining food containing the B vitamins would never be a problem. Indeed obtaining vitamins is no problem, but obtaining them in sufficient quantity is another story. Every organism, as well as every tissue in the body, has distinctive amounts of the various vitamins, and it cannot be safely concluded that any particular food or even mixture of foods will of necessity have the right amounts for the individual.

This is particularly true in terms of cellular nutrition. Cells and tissues can be nourished at various levels of efficiency. Half enough of a given vitamin will, in general, keep a tissue alive, but will not ensure its best functioning. The importance of this concept is emphasized when it is recognized that hundreds of disease conditions involving practically every organ and tissue have been induced in experimental animals by nutritional deficiencies, including those of vitamins. An insufficient amount of one, of pantothenic acid for example, has been found to cause at least twenty-three different disease conditions in different experimental animals.

A large number of human ills, many of which are not yet under control, may have as their basis inadequate cellular nutrition in the affected area. The list of ills which may have, in part, a nutritional origin includes even those of a neurological or psychological nature. It is a striking fact that the frank psychosis observed in pellagra has its roots in the fact that the nervous tissues are not getting enough of the B vitamin niacinamide. When enough of this vitamin is furnished, the psychosis of pellagra disappears. Niacinamide, too, is a nerve vitamin, but it also has vital functions in all manner of organisms which have no nervous systems.

The question of how much of the various vitamins (and other nutrients also) human beings need is a difficult one, complicated by the probability and indeed the certainty that different individuals, for genetic reasons, do not have the same pattern of needs. The unsatisfactoriness of knowledge about the quantitative aspects of human vitamin needs is emphasized by the fact that a pharmaceutical firm in 1932 offered an award of $15,000 to anyone who would determine (as one of three optional questions related to vitamin A) "the vitamin A requirements of human beings." Thirteen years later, when four of the seven original judges were deceased, the award was revoked because no one had answered or was likely to answer any one of the three related questions. Various committees feel obligated to make estimates regarding nutritional needs periodically, but these rest on a highly unsatisfactory basis, particularly insofar as they apply to any individual. The situation with respect to vitamin A is possibly the most unsatisfactory of all because natural diets vary tremendously in their content of vitamin A, and individual human needs probably cover a wide range. See DIET; DEFICIENCY DISEASE.   ROGER J. WILLIAMS

BIBLIOG.–Isaac Asimov, *Chemicals of Life: Enzymes, Vitamins, Hormones* (1954); Association of Vitamin Chemists, *Methods of Vitamin Assay* (1951); Audrey Z. Baker, *Vitamins in Nutrition and Health* (1954); Eustace C. Barton-Wright, *Microbiological Assay of the Vitamin B-Complex and Amino Acids* (1952); Franklin Bicknell and Frederick Prescott, *Vitamins in Medicine* (1953); Biochemical Society, *Biochemistry of Vitamin B12* (1955); Guy W. Clark, *Vitamin Digest* (1953); Katharine H. Coward, *Biological Standardization of the Vitamins* (1948); Walter H. Eddy, *Vitaminology: The Chemistry and Function of the Vitamins* (1949); Edgar S. Gordon and Elmer L. Sevringhaus, *Nutritional and Vitamin Therapy in General Practice* (1947); Ralph Gräsbeck, *Studies on the Vitamin B12-Binding Principle and Other Biocolloids of Human Gastric Juice* (1956); Paul György, ed., *Vitamin Methods* 2 vols. (1950–51); Leslie J. Harris, *Vitamins in Theory and Practice* (1955); International Conference on Vitamin E, *Vitamin E* (1949); Johns Hopkins University. SCHOOL OF HYGIENE AND PUBLIC HEALTH: Department of Biochemistry, *Symposium on Nutrition: The Physiological Role of Certain Vitamins and Trace Elements* (1953); Thomas H. Jukes, *B-Vitamins for Blood Formation* (1952); Thomas Moore, *Vitamin A* (1957); National Vitamin Foundation, *Current Research on Vitamins in Trophology* (1953); National Vitamin Foundation; *Symposium on Vitamin Metabolism* (1956), *Symposium on some Recent Observations on Biological Relationships* (1958); Robert H. A. Plimmer, *Food, Health, Vitamins* (1943); Peter G. Reizenstein, *Vitamin B12 Metabolism* (1959); Frank A. Robinson, *Vitamin B Complex* (1951); Hans R. Rosenberg, *Chemistry and Physiology of the Vitamins* (1954); William H. Sebrell and Robert S. Harris, eds., *Vitamins: Chemistry, Physiology, Pathology* 3 vols. (1954); J. Shafer, *Vitamins in Medical Practice* (1949); Evan V. Shute and Wilfrid E. Shute, *Your Heart and Vitamin E* (1956); Ernest L. Smith, *Vitamin B12* (1960); *Vitamins and Hormones: Advances in Research and Applications* (Annual); Roger J. Williams and others, *Biochemistry of B Vitamins* (1950); John B. Youmans and Ernest W. Patton, *Nutritional Deficiencies: Diagnosis and Treatment* (1943).

VITEBSK, region, U.S.S.R., in the NE Byelorussian Soviet Socialist Republic; bounded by the regions of Mogilev on the S, Minsk on the SW, and Molodechno on the W, and by the Lithuanian S.S.R. on the NW and the Russian Soviet Federated Socialist Republic on the N and E; area 10,000 sq. mi.; pop. (1959) 935,000. Vitebsk lies in the western part of the Smolensk-Moscow upland, and is drained by the Dnepr and the Western Dvina rivers. Agriculture is the principal economic activity, and the major crops are flax, grains, and vegetables. Dairying is important. The region's chief industries are flax processing, sawmilling, glassworking, and the manufacture of foodstuffs. Peat, the chief natural resource, is used to fuel the large power station at Orekhovsk. Vitebsk is the capital and largest city. The region was established late in the 1930's.

VITEBSK, city, U.S.S.R., NE Byelorussian Soviet Socialist Republic, capital of Vitebsk Region; situated amidst high hills on both banks of the Western Dvina River, at its confluence with the Vilba; 140 miles NE of Minsk, and 290 miles WSW of Moscow. Vitebsk is a flourishing road and rail junction, and a manufacturing center noted for its textiles. In addition, glassware, leather goods, agricultural machinery, clothing, linen, wooden products, and tobacco are manufactured. There is an agricultural school and a weather station there. Early in the twelfth century it became the capital of a small principality, and in 1320 came under Lithuania. In the sixteenth century it fell to Poland. It was annexed by Russia in 1772. During World War II Vitebsk was taken by the Germans (1941) and, until it was recovered by Soviet forces (1944), it served the Germans as a pivot for their Baltic and central fronts. Pop. (1959) 148,000.

VITELLIUS, AULUS, A.D. 15–69, Roman emperor, was a favorite of earlier emperors. He was consul, 48, and later proconsul of Africa. Galba gave him command of the troops in lower Germany, 68, and the generous Vitellius soon won their allegiance.

With their support and the urgings of Valens and Caecina, he claimed the imperial power. The senate came to accept Vitellius' claims, but Vespasian had been proclaimed Emperor of the East, and his forces defeated those of Vitellius at the Second Battle of Bedriacum. When the soldiers of Vespasian entered Rome, Vitellius was tortured and killed, and his body was thrown into the Tiber.

VITERBO, province, W central Italy, in Latium Region, bounded by the Tyrrhenian Sea on the W, and by the provinces of Grosseto on the NW, Siena on the N, Terna on the NE, Rieti on the SE, and by Rome on the S; area 1,391 sq. mi.; pop. (1958) 267,964. The province consists of a low coastal plain in the west, rising inland to a range of volcanic hills. In the east of the province is the narrow valley of the Tiber River, which forms part of the eastern boundary. The large lakes of Bolsena and Vico lie in the craters of extinct volcanoes. Wheat, grapes, and olives are the major crops, and cattle and sheep are raised. The buildings of Viterbo are frequently made of volcanic lava blocks. The capital, Viterbo, is the principal town.

VITERBO, town, W central Italy, in Latium Region, capital of Viterbo Province, on a railway connecting with the main Rome-Florence line, 40 miles NNW of Rome. Viterbo is a trade and processing center. It is also the seat of a bishop. Agricultural machinery, food products and furniture are manufactured. Viterbo was founded in the eighth century, and is surrounded by many towered Lombard walls. The town is famous for its many fine medieval churches. Lava was used in much of Viterbo's building and in the paving blocks of the streets. The town was the residence of popes during the thirteenth century. The Romanesque cathedral, dating from the twelfth century, contains the tomb of Pope John XXI; in the Church of San Francesco (1236) are the tombs of Popes Clement IV and Adrian V. In addition to its medieval buildings, the town has Etruscan and Roman relics of interest. Viterbo suffered widespread damage during World War II (1944). Pop. (1958) 47,570.

VITIM RIVER, U.S.S.R., in the Buryat Mongol Autonomous Soviet Socialist Republic, rises in the Vitim Plateau SSE of Lake Baykal, and flows N through a mountainous area to its confluence with the Lena River at the town of Vitim. The river forms part of the boundary between the Chita Region and the Buryat Autonomous Soviet Socialist Republic. The river is about 1,100 miles long and flows through a gold-mining and fur-trapping region.

VITIS. See GRAPE.

VITÓRIA, city, SE Brazil, capital of the state of Espírito Santo; on an island lying in the Atlantic Ocean, a few hundred yards from the mainland, with which it is connected by bridge; 260 miles NNE of Rio de Janeiro. The city, founded in 1535, was rebuilt about 1924. It is connected with the interior Rio Doce Valley and the industrial center of Belo Horizonte, by a railway and a Brazilian air line. The excellent port has a considerable foreign trade; it exports iron ore from inland mines at Itabira, and coffee, cacao, tropical produce, and lumber from the Rio Doce Valley. Vitória has sugar refineries, textile mills, and shoe factories, and also manufactures burlap bags and chocolate. Pop. (1950) 50,922.

VITORIA, city, N Spain, capital of Alava Province, on the Zadorra River, 32 miles SSE of Bilbao. The city is a trade and processing center for a fertile area in which wheat, sugar beets, potatoes, and fruit are grown. Furniture, machinery, leather goods, and clocks are manufactured. Vitoria was founded in 581 by Leovigild, king of the Visigoths, and built on a 1,750-foot hill overlooking the Alava Plain. In 1181 Sancho VI of Navarre, called the Wise, fortified Vitoria. Vitoria is the site of the Cathedral of Santa Maria (1181), and the church of San Miguel (twelfth century). During the Spanish Civil War, which was fought from 1936 to 1939, the city was captured by Nationalists. (For population, see Spain map in Atlas.)

VITRUVIUS, full name Marcus Vitruvius Pollio, first century B.C., Roman architect and engineer, was appointed military engineer by Caesar Augustus. His ten-volume treatise, *De architectura* influenced the development of Renaissance architecture.

VITTORINI, ELIO, 1908–66, Italian writer, was born in Syracuse, Sicily. After working for a time with a road construction company, Vittorini joined the staff of a Florentine daily newspaper and published his first collection of short stories, *Piccola borghesia* (1931). He was imprisoned by the Fascists during part of 1943, and served in the underground during the German occupation of Italy. Among his novels are *Conversazione in Sicilia,* 1941 (*In Sicily,* 1949), *Il sempione strizza l'occhio al frejus,* 1947 (*Twilight of the Elephant,* 1951), and *The Dark and the Light* (Eng. tr. 1961).

VITUS, SAINT, late third and early fourth century, Roman Christian, who suffered under Diocletian and was martyred. His influence is sought against such diseases as chorea (St. Vitus' dance), sudden death, and hydrophobia. He is also the patron saint of comedians and dancers. His festival day is June 15.

VIVALDI, ANTONIO, c. 1675–1741, Italian composer, born in Venice. His father was a violinist at St. Mark's Cathedral, and was responsible for his son's early musical training. While still a youth, Vivaldi completed his studies with Giovanni Legrenzi, who was in charge of the music at St. Mark's. Concurrently with his musical training, Vivaldi studied for the priesthood, and was ordained in 1703. Due to a chronic illness which has never been clearly explained, Vivaldi said Mass for only a year after his ordination, and then devoted himself to his musical activities for the rest of his life.

From 1704 until 1740 he was teacher, director, and composer at the music school-orphan asylum in Venice known as the Conservatorio dell' Ospedale della Pietà. This was one of four such institutions in Venice which trained their inmates almost entirely in music. The students performed in concerts which were famous throughout Europe. The few records that still exist indicate not only that Vivaldi was constantly active at home but that he made several (perhaps extended) trips outside of Italy. He died in Vienna where he had gone to seek service at the Court of Charles VI. His music, widely performed during his lifetime, was known to J. S. Bach, who made transcriptions of it for his own use.

Our knowledge of Vivaldi's music is incomplete and will remain so for some time. The publication of his complete works is progressive, but much music remains in manuscript, and new finds continue to be made. It is noteworthy that the 1879 edition of Grove's *Dictionary of Music and Musicians* lists instrumental works for 12 opus numbers, mentions 28 operas, but devotes half of its discussion to the Bach transcriptions. The 1954 edition of the same work contains a much expanded catalog listing 44 operas, 23 symphonies, 46 concerti grossi, 9 chamber concertos, 446 solo concertos, 73 sonatas, and a large amount of various kinds of church music.

Violinists once looked upon the few available solo concertos for their instrument as fairly simple pieces useful for study, and they felt that they knew Vivaldi. Recently, scholars and musicians have turned their interests to the larger instrumental works, many of which contain unusual instrumental combinations.

Vivaldi was a contemporary of Rameau, Handel, and Bach, whose works mark the climax of the Baroque era. Their composition of music was a daily business; new music was expected for every occasion and little thought was given to the immortality that a few "great" works might procure for the composer.

Vivaldi's music reflects almost every aspect of the first half of the eighteenth century from the early Corelli-like concertos to the later sinfonias which anticipate the early classical symphony. His concertos set the pattern for the contrasting alternation between solo and tutti. The elaboration of the solo parts not only gave the slow movements a new independence, but anticipated the classical solo concerto. The programmatic concertos, of which the group called *The Seasons* is characteristic, represented the same trend that produced Beethoven's "Pastoral" Symphony early in the next century. Programmatic titles, however, never interfered with the clarity of musical structure. He was one of the great composers of his time.   THEODORE M. FINNEY

BIBLIOG.–W.S. Newman, *The Sonata in the Baroque Era* (1959); Marc Pincherle, *Vivaldi* (1962).

VIVARINI, family name of three Italian artists, born on the island of Murano, who were among the lesser masters of the fifteenth century Venetian school of painting. The eldest, Antonio Vivarini (1415?–?76), also known as Antonio da Murano, worked in collaboration with Giovanni d'Alemagna, a German immigrant artist, from 1441 until the latter's death in 1450. The fruits of their collaboration—some 15 altarpieces, triptychs, and polyptychs—strongly demonstrate both Byzantine and northern Gothic influences. After d'Alemagna's death, Antonio collaborated with his younger brother, Bartolommeo Vivarini (1432?–?1499), also known as Bartolommeo da Murano. While Antonio's was the dominant influence in their joint efforts, Bartolommeo's touch, more plastic and flowing than his brother's, is readily evident in their works, particularly when these are compared with the earlier works of Antonio and d'Alemagna. By 1459, or thereabouts, Bartolommeo pursued an independent career, and Antonio's star declined. The younger brother's work thenceforth took on a greater vitality, and was less bound to the Gothic and Byzantine tradition. The influence of his contemporaries—Andrea Mantegna, Carlo Crivelli, Giovanni Bellini—brought a new gaiety of color and flamboyant elegance to his works. It was his nephew, however, Antonio's son Alvise, or Luigi, Vivarini (1446–?1505), who brought the family name to its highest ascendancy. Alvise produced colorful, impassioned works, limpid and flowing, that made him the popular rival of the great Giovanni Bellini.

VIVES, JUAN LUIS, 1492–1540, Spanish philosopher, author of pioneering works on educational theory and psychology, was born Juan Luis Ludovicus Vives in Valencia. At the age of 16 he left his homeland to study at the University of Paris. Five years of Aristotelianism in Paris left Vives convinced of the barrenness of the Scholastic philosophy (see SCHOLASTICISM); and five more years of classics at Louvain University completed his disillusionment with medieval modes of thought. Thenceforward he advocated the direct interrogation of nature, and a reliance upon inductive rather than deductive methods. At the urging of Desiderius Erasmus, Vives undertook, 1522, a new edition of St. Augustine's *City of God;* his notes on the text were condemned as heretical, however, and the book was suppressed. But his dedication of the work to King Henry VIII of England had brought him to the attention of that monarch, and he was invited to become tutor to the Princess Mary. In England, Vives lectured at Oxford and was often at court in the suite of Henry's Spanish queen, Catherine of Aragon. For opposing Henry's divorce from this lady, Vives was imprisoned; upon his release, 1528, he wisely left England and retired to the safety of Bruges where he eventually died, an exile from Spain.

Vives' greatest work, *De Disciplinis* (1531) argues for an educational reform revolutionary for his day, and not entirely commonplace even in the twentieth century. The aims and methods of instruction, Vives thought, must be adapted to the observed needs of the child; the instruction itself, he felt, should be in the language of the child's country rather than in the

Latin of the church; and learning by rote-drill should be replaced by readings of the original authors. Vives believed in education for women, and was the first to attach importance to the study of modern history. In his *De Anima et vita* (1538), he was the first person to probe the structure of the human mind and to investigate the psychology of animals. In consequence, Vives was violently assailed by the Roman Catholic clergy, and his works and his person were banned in Spain.

ROBERT WHITTEMORE

VIVIANI, RENE RAPHAEL, 1863–1925, French statesman, born at Sidi-bel-Abbès, Algeria. In 1893 he was elected Socialist deputy for Paris, and in 1906, when the ministry of labor was formed, Viviani was named its first minister. Strongly committed to the Socialist cause, he was responsible for the passage of the workmen's pension law. He was minister of public information, 1913–14, and premier and minister of foreign affairs, 1914–15. When World War I broke out he withdrew French forces ten kilometers from their borders as a gesture of peace. He resigned the premiership in 1915.

VIVIANITE, a rare mineral occasionally found in association with deposits of tin and copper. It is a soft mineral, having a hardness of $1\frac{1}{2}$ to 2. It has a monoclinic crystal structure, and is characterized by perfect cleavage. Vivianite is a hydrous ferrous phosphate, $Fe_3(PO_4)_2 \cdot 8H_2O$. In its unaltered form it is clear and transparent, but it usually occurs in the weathered, oxidized condition, and in this altered state it is blue to blue-green. It is found in parts of Europe, the U.S.S.R., South America, and Colorado.

VIVISECTION, any form of research done with living animals and using controlled procedures. It is practiced for the purpose of advancing biological science and is better described as animal experimentation. Anti-vivisectionists, who take the position that animal experimentation is cruel and unnecessary, have introduced legislation that would prohibit the use of animals in biological research. Scientists, supported by educators and religious and ethical organizations, hold that the use of animal experimentation has greatly expedited the progress of medical knowledge and biological science.

VIZCAINO, SEBASTIAN, 1550?–1615, Spanish explorer, born in Huelva. He went to Mexico, c. 1586. He led an expedition along the coast from Acapulco to Lower California, 1596–97, and sailed up the California coast to 43°N, 1602–03, discovering and naming Monterey Bay and dropping anchor at Point Reyes, north of San Francisco. While exploring the Pacific Ocean, 1611–14, he tried to institute trade with Japan, but failed.

VIZCAYA, or Biscay, province, N Spain, in the Basque Region; bounded on the N by the Bay of Biscay of the Atlantic Ocean, and by the provinces of Santander on the W, Burgos on the SW, Guipúzcoa on the E, and by Burgos and Alava on the S; area 858 square miles. The province extends from the northern edge of the central Meseta upland to a narrow coastal plain. The plateau is deeply dissected by rivers, the most important of which are the Nervión and the Cadagua. The coast is rocky, with several deep inlets, which form excellent harbors. Unlike most of Spain, Vizcaya has a good and well distributed rainfall, so the corn, hay, and fruit grown in the region need no irrigation. The province is densely populated, and the people are mainly of Basque origin. There are numerous fishing villages along the coast, and important iron-ore mines in the west. Bilbao, the capital, is the major town. (For population, see Spain map in Atlas.)

VIZIANAGARAM, city, SE India, in Andhra Pradesh State, 25 miles NNE of Visakhapatnam on the east coast railway and highway. The city is a commercial and processing center for the hemp, jute, rice and oilseed produced in the area. The Maharaja of Vizianagaram has a palace on the outskirts of the city. (For population, see India map in Atlas.)

VIZIER, or vizir, from Arabic *wazīr* (porter) and *wazara* (to carry a burden), from 750? the title of the chief political officer of the early caliphs. It was adopted in about 1328 by the Ottomans and assigned to the highest official at the Mogul court of Delhi and in other Muslim states.

VLAARDINGEN, city, W Netherlands, in South Holland Province, connected with The Hague by canal, on the Maas River, about 7 miles W of Rotterdam. Vlaardingen has an important port, and is a center of cod and herring fishing in the North Sea. Fertilizer, rope, packing cases, candy, and soap are manufactured. (For population, see Netherlands map in Atlas.)

VLACH, or Walachian, one of a people widely scattered through the Balkans, most of whom live in Rumania. They speak Rumanian or Walachian, a language belonging to the Latin, or Romance, group of the Indo-European language family. They are believed by some to be descended from the Romanized population of Dacia and Moesia. They were named Vlachs by the Slavs. See WALACHIA.

VLADIMIR I, SAINT, called Vladimir the Great, 956?–1015, grand duke of Kiev, was an illegitimate son of a Varangian prince, Svyatoslav. After Svyatoslav's death, his three sons quarreled, and Vladimir fled Kiev, but he later had his brother Yaropolk killed, 980, and seized the throne. In a series of campaigns he defeated tribes that had made inroads into his territory, occupied Bulgaria, and waged war against the Byzantine Emperor Basil II. When Basil and Vladimir made peace, the latter received the emperor's sister Anne as his wife, 989. It is said by some that Vladimir became a Christian in order to marry Anne, but he seems actually to have been baptized some time prior to his marriage. After his own conversion he had his 12 sons baptized, encouraged his people (sometimes by force) to become Christians, and introduced many reforms. The conversion of Russia to Christianity is dated from his reign. The feast day of Saint Vladimir is July 15.

VLADIMIR, city and oblast, U.S.S.R., in the Russian Soviet Federated Socialist Republic. The oblast is bounded on the N by the oblasts of Yaroslavl and Ivanovo, on the E by Gorki, on the S by Ryazan, and on the W by Moscow; area 10,350 square miles; pop. about 1,500,000. The oblast is a plain sloping from the northwest to the southeast, and has some low hills. The major river, the Klyazma, is an important means of transportation. The soils are mainly sandy and the region is fairly heavily forested. More fertile soils occur in the west, and there wheat, potatoes, flax, and tobacco are the major crops. Dairying is important near the manufacturing centers. Industries have been widely developed, and cotton and linen textiles, agricultural machinery, chemicals and glass products are manufactured. The capital, Vladimir, is located on the Klyazma River, 105 miles E of Moscow. Vladimir is a road and rail junction. Automobile accessories, cotton textiles, plastics, and precision instruments are manufactured. The surrounding country has many cherry orchards, and the city has large canneries. The citadel on a hill in Vladimir has two twelfth-century cathedrals. (For population of city, see U.S.S.R. map in Atlas.)

Merchant ships from Pacific ports dock at Vladivostok, the eastern terminus of the Trans-Siberian Railroad.

SOVFOTO

VLADIVOSTOK, city, u.s.s.r., in the Russian Soviet Federated Socialist Republic, capital of the Primorski (Maritime) Territory, on a peninsula in Peter the Great Bay of the Sea of Japan, 450 miles NNE of Seoul (Korea). Vladivostok lies at the eastern terminus of the Trans-Siberian Railroad and has rail connections with Manchuria. The important port at Vladivostok is the base of the Soviet Pacific fleet, which includes crabbing, fishing, and whaling vessels. The city is a manufacturing center, with shipbuilding, fish and other food canning, and lumber milling. Vladivostok has a considerable export trade, shipping coal, grain, lumber, and fish. There are large oil-storage tanks, and power and cold storage plants. The city has research institutes, specializing in oceanography and fisheries. The first Russian settlement was made here in 1860, and Vladivostok became a city under its present name, which means "rule the east," in 1880. The city grew rapidly after the completion of the Trans-Siberian Railroad, 1897. (For population, see u.s.s.r. map in Atlas.)

VLONE, or Valona, town, w Albania, capital of Vlonë Prefecture, on the Bay of Vlonë of the Adriatic Sea, 70 miles ssw of Tirana. The deep inlet is protected by the island of Sazan, and Vlonë has one of the most important ports in Albania. Vlonë,

a commercial center, exports olive oil, soap, and petroleum. The town is at the terminus of an oil pipeline, leading from the Kucovë oil field, and has an oil refinery. In 1912, during the First Balkan War, when Albania was declared independent, Vlonë was bombarded by the Greek fleet. In 1914, at the beginning of World War I, the Italians seized the island of Sazan and occupied the town until 1920. Vlonë was reoccupied by the Italians in 1939; and during the Greek-Italian War (1940–41), the town was heavily bombed. Sazan, commanding the approach to Vlonë, was ceded by the Italians to Albania by the peace treaty (1947) following World War II. (For population, see Balkan states map in Atlas.)

VLTAVA RIVER, or Moldau, Czechoslovakia, E Bohemia. The Vltava rises in the Bohemian forest on the southwest border of Czechoslovakia, and flows past the city of Ceské Budějovice, and northward past Prague until it unites with the Elbe. The Vltava is navigable for river steamers for about 50 miles above its junction with the Elbe.

VOCATIONAL EDUCATION, in the widest sense, is all of the preparation for one's life work; anything one studies, even in a strictly liberal arts program, may be considered vocational education. In a more specific sense, vocational education is special occupational training other than professional education, technical education, or university graduate work. Secretarial training, business education, commercial art training, training in the industrial arts, and agricultural education are usually regarded as vocational education. The emphasis in on training the worker to earn a living in commerce, domestic life, industry, or agriculture. See AGRICULTURAL EDUCATION AND RESEARCH; COMMERCIAL EDUCATION.

The Smith-Hughes Act (1917) established the principle and practice of federal aid for vocational education. The act requires the recipient state and local community to match the federal appropriation. It has operated to extend vocational training to many schools, especially in small towns and villages, where such training would otherwise be impossible. See SMITH-HUGHES ACT.

Vocational guidance has become an important part of the work in vocational schools. The student gains information about careers and occupations, and he makes an inventory of his own occupational assets. He receives experienced counsel in choosing

A young apprentice is taught the fine art of cake decoration at this vocational high school for baking.

Hair styling, a popular career choice among girls, is part of many vocational school curriculums.

By constructing a house in mock-up, these students acquire the basic skills for a career in carpentry.

SYBIL SHELTON-MONKMEYER

BOARD OF EDUCATION-CITY OF NEW YORK

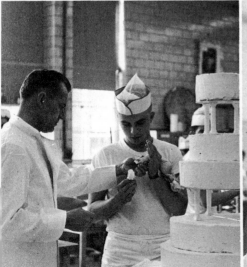

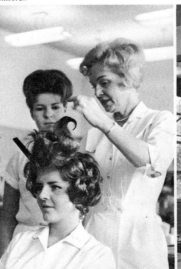

SYBIL SHELTON-MONKMEYER

Typing instruction is an essential preparation for students seeking business or secretarial careers.

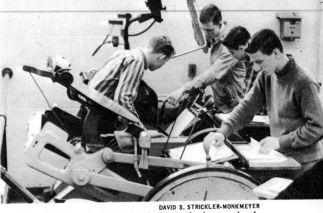

DAVID S. STRICKLER-MONKMEYER

Vocational students learn printing and other mechanical trades by using machines in school workshops.

an occupation and help in finding a job, together with a careful follow-up. See APTITUDE TESTING; VOCATIONAL GUIDANCE.

Other activities of vocational schools include taking indentured apprentices learning trades, giving vocational training to adults in evening and extension classes, and conducting programs of vocational rehabilitation for war veterans. See VOCATIONAL REHABILITATION.

VOCATIONAL GUIDANCE, the process of assisting an individual in the decision-making phases of career development. Career development can be defined as the activities of an individual that result in his entrance into the world of work and his continuous or intermittent performance in it. Ideally, these activities should result in the self-fulfillment of the individual in an occupation, or a series of occupations (a career), useful to society.

By analyzing the work histories of adults in terms of the nature of the problems they faced and the adjustments they needed to make throughout their working lives, researchers have identified five life stages. These stages are: growth, exploration, establishment, maintenance, and decline. With due allowance for overlapping because of individual differences, these stages, each with one or more substages, range as follows: growth—from birth to about fourteen years of age; exploration—fifteen to twenty-five; establishment—twenty-six to forty-five; maintenance—forty-six to sixty-five; and decline—sixty-six and over. These life stages can provide a useful framework for vocational guidance, which can be given according to need at any one or all of these life stages.

Roughly approximating these life stages are agencies designed to assist individuals to enter into and make progress in the world of work. Ideally, the school should provide learning experiences, including vocational guidance, which will enable every high school graduate to enter a suitable institution beyond the high school or suitable employment. For youth out of school and out of work, for unemployed adults, for those who are employed but would like to improve their knowledge and skills, for those who are either physically or mentally handicapped, and for those facing retirement, there are counseling agencies and educational programs. Such agencies in the United States, for example, include: the U.S. Employment Service, adult education programs conducted by the public schools, Youth Opportunity centers, the Job Corps, the Neighborhood Youth Corps, supplementary centers in many communities established with grants from

the U.S. Office of Education, the U.S. Rehabilitation Administration, the Veterans Administration, and many private non-profit and profit counseling centers. Additional institutions with educational programs designed to meet the needs of many of these individuals are: community and junior colleges, technical institutes, area vocational schools, private trade schools, and correspondence schools. Similar offices and institutions are found today in many nations of the world.

Career Decisions. The occupational structure changes rapidly. What seems to be a suitable occupation at one time may suddenly cease to exist. Researchers have estimated that the average U.S. worker could have from six to ten different occupations during his working career. This makes it difficult for high school youth to make choices of occupations with confidence. Thus, the concepts of career development and decision-making counseling have replaced the older concept of matching men and jobs. Such concepts are appropriate when considering vocational guidance for students in elementary and secondary schools. By making decisions first with the assistance of the counselor, the student can learn to make decisions alone and accept the responsibility for the decisions made. The major objective of the school's vocational guidance program is to get individual students to make good decisions concerning career opportunities. With such vocational guidance the chances are good that each student will graduate from the school with a desirable and realistic plan for the next step. This plan may be to take a job at the corner service station or it may be to enter a ten-year educational program leading to a professional career. In any case such a plan is more likely to be expressed in terms of broad occupational fields rather than in terms of a specific job. Employment at the service station may be considered only as the first step in a career. The plan may have to be modified for good reasons such as a change in the occupational structure or because of a desire on the part of the individual; but if the student has learned to make good decisions, he can face such changes with composure. The concepts of career development and decision-making counseling are just as applicable to vocational guidance for adults and out-of-school youth as to students in school. With these groups, however, occupational choices are likely to be narrower and more specific as the need for employment may be more immediate.

Counseling. The heart of vocational guidance is counseling. The counselor assists the individual in evaluating a set of facts about (1) himself (individual appraisal) and (2) about the world of work (occupational information) in the process of making decisions about occupational opportunities and educational programs leading to a career. Decision-making counseling is at its best when both the individual and his counselor learn the significant facts about the individual and his environment and relate this information to his decisions.

Individual appraisal consists of an analysis of the individual's abilities, achievements, special aptitudes, and interests. For this purpose, tests and inventories have been written and standardized. National, regional, and local norms have been prepared on various parts of each test and on the test as a whole to enable the counselee to determine his strengths and weaknesses and to compare himself with others in his locality, his region, and in the nation as a whole. Informal questionnaires and self-rating scales are also used.

The sources of occupational information are: various departments of the u.s. government, state departments of education, commercial publishers, professional and technical societies, businesses, and industries. Information may be in the form of books, brochures, pamphlets, monograms, leaflets, films, filmstrips, kinescopes, filmstrips with tape or record narrator, and reports of local surveys; and individuals may acquire occupational information by free reading or by visits to businesses and industries, work-study programs, work-experience programs, and formal and informal observation.

The effectiveness of vocational guidance depends upon the ability of the counselor. Such a person should be naturally inclined to help. He should be interested in people and concerned about their development. Additionally, he should be well educated as a counselor. To make sure that counseling in public schools shall be of high quality and function within the framework of sound educational policy, each state department of education has established counselor certification requirements for school counselors. These usually require counselors to have both a teaching certificate and a counseling certificate. A counseling certificate requires graduate work in the guidance field and from one to five years of teaching experience. Seventeen states require a master's degree in counseling; and about half the states require some work experience outside the teaching field. Vocational counseling in colleges and universities is usually done at the institution's counseling center which is headed by a counselor with a doctor's degree in counseling psychology. Some federal agencies are staffed by counselors very able in terms of their education and experience; others, not so well staffed, are taking steps to improve the quality of counseling in each agency. Many private counseling centers have excellent counselors.

If vocational guidance services are not available from schools, colleges and universities, the u.s. Employment Service, Youth Opportunity centers, or any of the other governmental agencies, an individual needing help may wish to engage a private counseling agency. To protect individuals from low-quality counseling services, the American Personnel and Guidance Association publishes a yearly directory entitled *Directory of Approved Counseling Agencies* for the American Board on Counseling Services Inc. This Board was created by the American Personnel and Guidance Association to insure high quality counseling by all agencies listed in the directory.

The Background of Vocational Guidance. Vocational guidance has evolved from several sources. The idea of helping individuals to enter and make progress in the world of work is not a modern one, but effective programs of vocational guidance in schools, colleges, and community agencies are relatively recent. Any activity with as broad social implications as those of vocational guidance is difficult to explain historically. It is difficult, for instance, to say precisely at what point the division of labor resulting from the Industrial Revolution became so marked as to indicate a need for vocational guidance.

There are four influences upon the vocational guidance movement to which attention should be directed if its background is to be understood. These are (1) community social service surveys, (2) the scientific measurement approach to human diagnosis, (3) counseling techniques, and (4) gathering and disseminating occupational information.

Early community survey reports by social service agencies emphasized the fact that many young people were neither in school nor at work. They were totally without employment, or they were engaged in short, sporadic periods of employment unrelated to any long-term plans. The need for vocational guidance was apparent and many socially minded citizens became interested in aiding these young people, through schools or other social agencies, to achieve an intelligent selection of vocation.

The first studies on the scientific approach to the measurement of innate abilities and achievements were made shortly before 1900. From these beginnings have come standardized tests that have importantly shaped guidance counseling techniques both in the United States and elsewhere.

The development of counseling techniques has been a continuing process. One of the first organized attempts at offering vocational guidance in the United States was made by Frank Parsons at the Vocational Bureau in Boston (1908). His vocational counseling attracted considerable attention, and the counseling procedure was instituted by many school systems early in the century.

The development and dissemination of information about occupations have grown in importance as the value of vocational guidance has grown in recognition. During the eighteenth and nineteenth centuries there appeared isolated publications that attempted to provide data concerning occupations and advice on the selection of a career. By the 1960's, private publishers, government agencies, school systems, universities, industrial corporations, and trade and professional organizations had produced and disseminated an ever-increasing amount of valuable data useful to those requiring up-to-date and accurate information about occupations.

DOLPH CAMP

BIBLIOG.—Henry Borow, *Man in a World at Work* (1964); Willis E. Dugan, *Counseling Points of View* (1959); Martin Katz, *Decisions and Values* (1963); Charles E. Morehead and Frank G. Fuller, *Career Planning and Development* (1965); Willa Norris, Franklin R. Zeran, and Raymond N. Hatch, *The Information Service in Guidance* (1966); Herman J. Peters and James C. Hansen, *Vocational Guidance and Career Development* (1966); Donald E. Super, Reuben Starishevsky, Norman Matlin, and Jean Pierre Jordaan, *Career Development: Self-Concept Theory* (1963); David V. Tiedeman and Robert P. O'Hara, *Career Development: Choice and Adjustment* (1963); Grant Venn and Theodore J. Marchese, Jr., *Man, Education and Work* (1964); United States Department of Labor, *Occupational Outlook Handbook* (1966–67).

VOCATIONAL REHABILITATION, the services necessary to prepare handicapped people for work that is suited to their abilities. Physical defects, such as blindness, often prevent individuals from working, or limit them in finding employment. Low intelligence and severe personality problems are also employment handicaps.

All of the states, Puerto Rico, and the District of Columbia have a statewide division of vocational rehabilitation, and most have special agencies for the rehabilitation of the blind. The Veterans Administration also carries on an extensive rehabilitation program for disabled veterans. The state programs vary in extent and efficiency but provide a fairly complete rehabilitation service. Aid is given to men and women of working age who have a physical or mental handicap that interferes with their employment. Medical examinations are provided with medical, dental, and psychiatric care, if needed, in order to restore the individual to as near normal a condition as possible. Artificial limbs, hearing aids, and other appliances are furnished. With the aid of aptitude tests, a counselor helps each person to decide upon the type of work best suited to his work abilities, personality, and handicap. Vocational training can be given in any type of school or through apprenticeship. If necessary, training equipment, transportation, and an allowance for living expenses are furnished. The counselor helps the individual to find appropriate work and to adjust to the new employment situation once he has been placed in it. The services of existing schools, organizations, and clinics are used.

Many voluntary organizations also help with rehabilitation of handicapped persons. Among these are the National Society for Crippled Children and Adults, the American Epilepsy League, and the Goodwill Industries of America, all of which operate throughout the United States.

Bibliog.–W. S. Allen, *Rehabilitation: A Community Challenge* (1958); J. S. Cohen and others, *Vocational Rehabilitation and the Socially Disabled* (1966); R. W. Conley, *The Economics of Vocational Rehabilitation* (1965); L. H. Lofquist, *Vocational Counseling with the Physically Handicapped* (1957); L. M. Neuschutz, *Vocational Rehabilitation for the Physically Handicapped* (1959).

VODKA, a distilled alcoholic beverage indigenous to Russia, Poland, and the Baltic states, and popular throughout the Western world. It is commonly made from wheat, but can be, and often is, produced from potatoes, maize, sugar beets, or rye. Distillation of the beer from the cereal mash yields a liquor with an alcoholic content of about 75 per cent (150 proof). For retail sale this is reduced to concentrations ranging from 40 to 60 per-cent alcohol (80 to 120 proof). Vodka is clear in color, and has a smooth but pungent taste. It may be drunk undiluted as an appetizer with food, or mixed with various other beverages as a cocktail or highball.

VOGEL, Sir JULIUS, 1835–99, premier of New Zealand, born in London. He emigrated to Australia, 1852, and to New Zealand, 1861. He was elected to the colonial legislature, 1863, became colonial treasurer, 1869, and was premier, 1873–75 and 1876. Vogel arranged large loans in London to finance public works, and thus encouraged emigration.

VOGLER, GEORG JOSEPH, 1749–1814, German composer and music theorist, born in Würzburg. He studied at Bologna and Padua, and in 1773 became a priest in Rome. In 1784, he became Kappelmeister at the electoral court at Munich, and in 1786 court musical director at Stockholm, where he remained until 1799. In 1807 he settled in Darmstadt, where he accepted the post of Kappelmeister and founded a music school. He composed numerous operas, ballets, organ pieces, and a symphony.

VOGUE, EUGENE MARIE MELCHIOR, VICOMTE DE, 1848–1910, French critic and novelist, born in Nice. He served in the Franco-Prussian War, 1870–81, and was in the diplomatic service, 1871–82. While in St. Petersburg, 1876–82, he became interested in the idealism and mysticism of Russian fiction. His *Le Roman russe*, 1886 (*The Russian Novel*, 1913) helped popularize in France the writings of Aleksandr Pushkin, Nikolai Gogol, Fëdor Dostoevski, and Lev Tolstoi. Among Vogüé's other works are the novels *Les Morts qui parlent* (1899) and *Le Maître de la mer* (1903), and the histories *Histoires orientales* (1879) and *Portraits du siècle* (1883).

VOICE, sound issuing from the throat of living beings, especially human beings. The human body is the instrument of voice production. The lungs and the muscles concerned in breathing are the source of motor power and the breath is the co-ordinating link between the motor power and the vibrator. Primary sound vibrations, the source of vocal sound waves, are produced by the action of the breath upon the vibrator, the vocal cords. Primary vibrations are amplified through the action of the air in the resonance cavities. These resonance cavities are the open cavities of and above the larynx, the lower and upper pharyngeal cavities containing such structures as the ventricular cavities and nasal cavities, and the mouth. The amplification of vocal sounds finds its focal point of concentration and intensification against the hard palate in the mouth. Structures such as the mouth, pharyngeal muscles, lips, and tongue, constitute an articulation apparatus. No two voices are exactly alike in quality, range, or character.

Voice Development. The principal factors in freedom of voice production are correct posture; freedom in breathing; freedom of primary vibrations; amplification, or resonance; articulation; and technical proficiency.

The correct posture ensures the full strength of the body; it permits freedom in breathing; it makes possible the taut approximation of the vocal cords and functional freedom of the larynx without compensatory help; it permits freedom of co-ordination and the development of all muscles and cartilages concerned in voice production.

Breathing exercises are used to attain elasticity and power of distention of the lungs.

Primary vibrations are not audible. They are amplified by resonance before they reach the ear. The sympathetic action of the air in the resonance cavities, induced through intensity of primary sound vibrations, produces resonance.

Purity in intonation in singing and the best quality of vocal sound are achieved when there is freedom in the functioning of the larynx, for then the swing of the vocal cords is without constriction.

Articulation and Vocalization. Words (speech sound) are composed of vowels and consonants. Vowels and vocal tone are synonymous terms. Vowels are vocalized. Consonants are lightly and sharply articulated. Their articulation takes place in and outside the mouth, the effect of tongue, palate, and lip function. They are detached from laryngeal activity. In singing, vocal exercises (songs, arias, roles, etc.) are used to obtain technical proficiency. For facility in the responsiveness of the larynx and vocal cords, staccati exercises, fast arpeggios, fast scales, and various forms of florid music are beneficial. Exercises in sustained tones, in crescendo and decrescendo of sustained single tones gradually extended throughout all ranges of the voice, develop the resistant strength of the vocal cords and of the cartilages of the vocal box.

VOILE, a fine sheer fabric of cotton, silk, wool, or rayon. It is soft and clinging and may be plain or printed. It has a plain weave of hard-twisted combed yarns. It is used in curtains and clothing, lampshades, and bedspreads.

VOIT, KARL VON, 1831–1908, German physiologist, born in Amberg, Bavaria. He studied under Baron Justus von Liebig and Friedrich Wöhler, and after 1863 was professor of physiology at Munich. His work was concerned mostly with nutrition and metabolism. In 1865 he was co-founder of the *Zeitschrift für Biologie* and thereafter contributed numerous articles to it.

VOITURE, VINCENT, 1597–1648, French man of letters, born in Amiens, the son of a wine merchant. He flattered his way into the favor of Gaston, duc d'Orleans, won the support of Cardinal Richelieu by writing a eulogy on the recapture of Corbie, 1636, was made a royal chamberlain by King Louis XIII, 1638, and became one of the first members of the French Academy in 1634. From 1625? he was a principal member of the salon of the Marquise of Rambouillet. He won renown for his poems (ballades, rondeaux, sonnets, and madrigals) and letters, which are distinguished by their wit and delicacy of thought and language. The letters, particularly, furthered the refinement of the French language.

VOJVODINA, or Voyvodina, autonomous province, NE Yugoslavia, part of Serbia, bounded by Hungary on the N, Rumania on the E, and by the Yugoslavian republics of Serbia on the S, Bosnia and Hercegovina on the SW, and Croatia on the W; area 8,407 square miles. Located largely within the fertile valleys of the Danube and Tisza rivers, Vojvodina has much of its area devoted to agriculture. Grains, sugar beets, and tobacco are the chief crops. Industries consist principally of food processing and textile manufacture. The capital and largest town is Novi Sad. Pop. about 1,900,000.

VOLANS, or Piscis Volans, the Flying Fish, a small constellation of the southern skies. It contains no conspicuous stars. It lies south of the constellation Carina and extends in declination from about −65° to −75°. This constellation is not one of the ancient Ptolemaic constellations. See CONSTELLATION.

VOLAPUK, an artificial universal language, originated in 1879 by a German priest, Johann Martin Schleyer. It was based mainly on English, German, and the Romance languages. For about ten years it enjoyed wide popularity; but it was unclear, difficult to learn, and ugly, and when Esperanto was introduced in 1887 many of the supporters of Volapük deserted the language. See ESPERANTO; UNIVERSAL LANGUAGE.

VOLCANO, an opening in the earth's crust from which molten lava, hot rocks, ash, steam, and other gases are erupted; also the geologic formation resulting from such an eruption, usually in the form of a hill, or roughly cone-shaped mountain. An active volcano is one that is in eruption. A volcano is dormant during long periods of inactivity and extinct if eruptive activity has ceased for all time, as nearly as can be determined geologically.

Mount Vesuvius, near Naples, Italy, perhaps the best-known volcano in the world, is an example of the popular conception of an active volcano, in that it consists of a cone-shaped mountain that, from time to time, erupts gases, ash, rock fragments, and lava from a cup-shaped crater at its summit. In addition, however, all volcanoes must have a conduit, or passageway, that leads down from the crater to a reservoir of a solution of molten rock, or magma, located in the interior of the earth. The principal elements of a volcano are shown in the schematic diagram on the following page. See LAVA; MAGMA.

Types of Volcanic Eruptions. The relative proportions of the gaseous, liquid, and solid materials

From the peaceful North Atlantic one wintry day in 1963, a great column of smoke and ash suddenly burst forth. Such volcanic eruptions are not infrequent near Iceland. Sometimes, the accumulated discharge may fill 100 fathoms and create a new island.

Incandescent streams of lava streak the sides of a volcanic crater in Hawaii, where volcanic activity is relatively common. Though the areas of volcanic activity today are closely defined, probably all parts of the world have been affected at some period.

Mount Vesuvius, in Italy, erupted violently in March, 1944. Searing lava spewed from the fiery cone and swept down upon the little town of San Sebastiano. Fortunately, the residents had enough time to escape from the danger zone before their homes were engulfed.

CAMERA PRESS-PIX

WIDE WORLD
UPI

ejected largely determine the character of an eruption. Volcanologists commonly describe any particular phase of volcanic activity, in order of increasing violence, as Hawaiian, Strombolian, Vulcanian, ultravulcanian, or Pelean, accordingly as the eruption possesses the characteristics of one or the other of certain well known volcanoes.

Hawaiian type volcanoes are characterized by the tranquil outflow of highly fluid lava without any explosive discharge of gases and without any ejection of fragments of solid materials. Mauna Loa, in Hawaii, is 13,675 feet high, and rises from an ocean floor about 18,000 feet below the surface of the sea. It has been built up by a series of gentle lava flows. Gases are also emitted, but never with violence. In 1935 a huge lava flow issuing from an elevation of 9,000 feet threatened to destroy the town and harbor of Hilo, but was diverted from its course by a bombing attack carried out by the U.S. Army Air Service. Kilauea, the other active volcano in Hawaii, is located on the eastern slope of Mauna Loa, and has an elevation of 4,088 feet. Before 1924 its crater had a diameter of 1,300 feet and contained a lake of molten basalt, called Halemaumau, which is Hawaiian for "Everlasting House of Fire." This basalt was kept in a state of constant boiling by the copious emission of gases. In 1924 the level of the lava suddenly fell about 700 feet, and a number of explosive eruptions occurred. The pit became much deeper and wider and then began slowly filling up again with lava. The eruption was definitely not Hawaiian in character.

The Strombolian type of activity is named after the volcano Stromboli in the Lipari Islands north of Sicily. This volcano has been in an almost constant state of eruption throughout historic times. Continuous emission of steam from a vent about 1,000 feet below the summit, a series of mild explosions at intervals of 10 or 15 minutes, with ejection of clots or blobs of liquid lava, and a pool of red-hot lava are the chief characteristics of Stromboli.

The Vulcanian type, named from Vulcano, another active volcano in the Lipari Islands, differs from the Strombolian type in that the lava is more viscous and forms a solid surface crust between eruptions. When eruptions occur, the pent-up gases shatter the crust and large angular blocks of solidified lava are ejected along with the fluid lava. When vertical eruptions occur in a volcano that has been long dormant, so that all of the ejected material is old and cold, the activity is described as ultravulcanian.

Pelean type eruptions are named after Mont Pelée on the island of Martinique in the West Indies. In May, 1902, this volcano, after 51 years of inactivity, began to erupt in a series of terrific explosions. On May 8 a tremendous discharge of steam, flame, and hot rock fragments blew out horizontally from the side of the mountain and swept through the town of St. Pierre at the rate of 60 miles an hour, destroying everything in its path. At almost the same time a

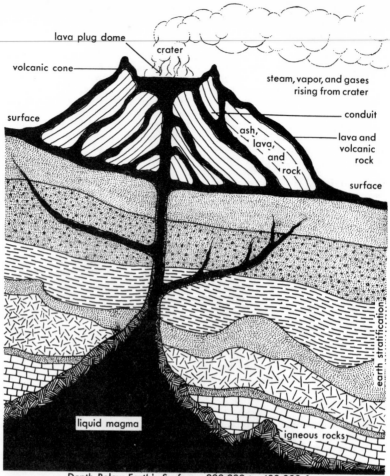

Cross Section of the Structure of a Typical Volcano

similar eruption occurred at the volcano La Soufrière on the island of St. Vincent, 90 miles away.

Volcanic Ejecta. Among the gases ejected by volcanoes are steam, carbon dioxide, hydrogen chloride, hydrogen fluoride, and hydrogen. In some volcanic eruptions sulfur compounds and sublimed sulfur are also emitted. Most abundant of the gases is steam. Some of this steam may represent ground water that has seeped into the path of the rising magma, but much of it is the result of the expansion, with decreasing pressure, of the water contained in the rock magma itself. Most eruptions are accompanied by torrential downpours of rain which are caused by the sudden cooling and condensation of the escaping steam. The presence of considerable quantities of volcanic ash in the surrounding atmosphere turns much of this rain to mud. Liquid lava is the chief material ejected by Hawaiian-type eruptions.

Lavas contain dissolved gases which are often emitted in clouds of steam for weeks after the emission of the lava. In viscous lavas the expansion of these latent gases often produces a veritable rock froth which hardens into the vesicular rock called pumice. (See PUMICE.) In the more fluid basaltic lavas the gas cavities are likely to be large and irregular in shape, producing a rock texture called scoriaceous. When blobs of liquid lava are thrown into the air during an explosive eruption, they generally harden during their flight, forming spherical masses, often with spirally twisted ends, called volcanic bombs. The fragments discharged in solid form are called volcanic dust if less than 0.25 mm in diameter, ash if between 0.25 mm and 4 mm, cinders or lapilli if between 4 mm and 32 mm, and blocks if over 32 mm.

Cones and Craters. When the materials ejected by a volcano are chiefly pyroclastic, the resulting cone is usually high with steeply sloping sides. The steepness of the slope is determined by the "angle of repose" of the material, or the smallest angle at which the mass begins to slide. This angle is often as great as 30°. Such cones are called cinder cones.

Volcanoes built up mainly by repeated lava flows are generally wide at the base and slope gently up to the summit. They are called shield volcanoes. Mauna Loa and Mount Etna are classic examples.

The stratovolcano, intermediate in character between cinder cones and shield volcanoes, is the commonest type of volcano. In this form of volcanic edifice, successive eruptions form overlapping layers of pyroclastic materials and lava which may accumulate to great thicknesses. Mayon in the Philippines, Fuji in Japan, and Hood, Shasta, Adams, and Rainier in western United States are stratovolcanoes.

Volcanic craters that have become enlarged, forming wide, shallow basins, are called calderas. These may result from explosions that blow away the tops of volcanoes, leaving a truncated cone, or from collapse. Crater Lake, in southern Oregon, located on the top of a volcanic mountain in the Cascade Range, is thought to have resulted from a collapse. It is 6 miles wide, 1,996 feet deep, filled with water of a beautiful blue color, and contains an island which is the top of a small volcanic cone that evidently erupted after the collapse of the large original cone.

Craters of extinct and dormant volcanoes frequently furnish sites for mountain lakes of great beauty. Smaller craters produced by volcanic actions that do little more than force a hole through surface rock formations, are called explosion pits. They are surrounded by low ridges, and in most regions generally produce lakes. Many examples are found in the Eifel region in Germany just west of the Rhine River.

Distribution and Extent. There are some 500 active volcanoes in the world and several thousand extinct or dormant ones. Most volcanoes are located in two well defined belts, coinciding very nearly with the zones of earthquake activity. The major belt encircles the Pacific Ocean and contains 60 per cent of the world's active volcanoes. The other belt extends eastward from the West Indies through the Azores, the Canary Islands, and the Mediterranean Sea, to the Arabian Peninsula and the East Indies, and out into the Pacific Ocean. Oceanic volcanoes are generally grouped in lines lying along the various ridges which rise from the ocean floor.

Causation. The manifestations of volcanism in general, indicate quite plainly the existence, at moderate distances under the earth's surface, of great stores of hot, fluid magma. How great the extent of this magma has been throughout geologic time is evidenced by the fact that during the present Cenozoic era, which is a short one and not specially remarkable for volcanism, more than 500,000 cubic miles of lava have been poured out on the surface of the earth. Seismographic evidence on the propagation of earthquake waves shows that the mantle of the earth is rigid, for only rigid bodies can transmit transverse waves. A partial release of the earth's internal pressure in certain localities, due to diastrophic crustal movements (see DIASTROPHISM) is thought to account for the fluidity of the magma in those regions.

There are two well-respected theories to explain the rise of magmas within the earth. One, that seems to account for eruptions from reservoirs not deeply buried, is that the expansive force exerted by confined gases is the prime mover. The other, which explains the tranquil lava flows of the Hawaiian type, is that the weight of the solid rocks overlying the fluid magma causes them to sink into the magma, thus forcing it upward through fissures in the solid rock. See DIKE; EARTHQUAKE; SILL.

VOLCANO ISLANDS, also Sulphur Islands, or Kazan Retto, a group of three small volcanic islands in the W Pacific, 750 miles S of Tokyo, Japan; area 11 sq. mi. The islands are administered by the U.S. Navy (since World War II), but are Japanese territory. The islands are Kita-iwo-jima (north), Iwo Jima (center), and Minami-iwo-jima (south). Kita-iwo-jima and Minami-iwo-jima rise steeply from the sea, but the center island, Iwo Jima, has a flat surface that slopes gently to its west side, where Surabachi Volcano rises to 379 feet. There are sugar plantations on the islands, and sulfur is mined. During World War II, Iwo Jima was used as a Japanese air base. It was taken by U.S. forces in 1945.

VOLGA RIVER, W central U.S.S.R., the longest and most important river in European Russia; rises in the Valday Hills NW of Moscow at an elevation of 750 feet above sea level, and flows 2,215 miles into the land-locked Caspian Sea at Astrakhan at an elevation of 64 feet below sea level. Its basin occupies 530,000 square miles, or about one third of the territory of European Russia.

From the swamps and forests of the glacial Valday Ridge, the river winds eastward across the Russian plain past Yaroslavl and Gorkiy to Kazan; there, it turns south past the great bend at Kuybyshev, past Saratov and through the steppe to Volgograd. From Kazan to Volgograd the west bank of the Volga is lined by bluffs and the east bank is low and flat. Below Volgograd the river flows southeast through the dry steppe and desert to the Caspian Sea. This lower stretch is characterized by numerous braided channels. The Volga's gradient is gentle and the current extremely slow, even at the height of spring flood. The river's large volume of sediment has created a 2,300 square mile delta in the Caspian Sea.

The Volga has many tributaries. Among those of the left, or northeast, bank are the Vetluga, the Unzha, the Vyatka, the Kama, and the Samara. The major right, or southwest, bank tributaries are the Oka and the Sura. Almost the entire course of the Volga is navigable.

The Volga River drains a densely populated and economically developed area. The Volga and its tributaries, comprising less than one-fourth of the Soviet Union's navigable waterways, carry about two-thirds of its water-borne freight tonnage. In 1955 freight tonnage on the Volga system totaled 65.8 million tons and pleasure boats carried 39.9 million passengers. Timber from the north and oil from the south are the chief commodities transported. Grain,

Until 1924 the crater of Kilauea, an active volcano on the east slope of Mauna Loa, contained a lake of boiling basalt called Halemaumau, or "Everlasting House of Fire."
PAUL'S PHOTOS

originating at Volgograd, moves up to various rail-heads on the river for transshipment to western grain-deficient areas, and salt from Lake Baskunchak is shipped to the fish canneries at Astrakhan. After 1952, metals and coal from the Donets Basin moved through the Volga-Don Canal to cities along the Volga.

In its upper course the Volga drains a region characterized by the raising of flax and dairy cattle; in its middle course the cultivation of grain, potatoes, sunflowers, and sugar beets prevails, but farther downstream wheat growing and the raising of livestock are dominant. Below Volgograd, agriculture along the Volga is largely confined to the irrigated cultivation of cotton, fruit, and vegetables. Sturgeon fishing is important in the delta area.

History and Development. The Volga River is famous in Russian folklore as Mat Rodnaia—the mother that has nourished the Russian state. The oldest Russian settlement is Yaroslavl, on the Upper Volga, founded in the eleventh century. Not until the 1550's did the Russians gain the lands of the upper and lower river, when Czar Ivan IV, the Terrible, took Kazan and Astrakhan from the Tatars. The river has been an important trade route for many centuries, linking the cities of the Upper Volga and Oka with the Caspian Sea and central Asian lowlands. Nizhni Novgorod (now Gorkiy) was the site of famous trade fairs in the nineteenth century, an important link between East and West.

Under Stalin's rule several schemes were propounded to utilize more fully the resources of the Volga River by turning it into a series of steplike lakes. A dam and hydroelectric station at Ivanovo made it possible to fill the Moscow-Volga Canal, and gave the city a direct water link with the Volga River. Other dams and hydroelectric stations were built at Uglich and Rybinsk, and the enlargement of the Mariinsk Canal, originally built in 1808, linked the Volga through a series of lakes and rivers with the Baltic Sea. Thus, with the new Baltic–White Sea Canal, Moscow gained access to the Baltic and the Arctic Ocean. The Volga-Don Canal, which Peter I had dreamed of, was started in the 1930's and opened, after a long delay during World War II, in 1952. It runs between Volgograd and Kalach and connects the Volga indirectly with the Black Sea.

Location Map of Volga River

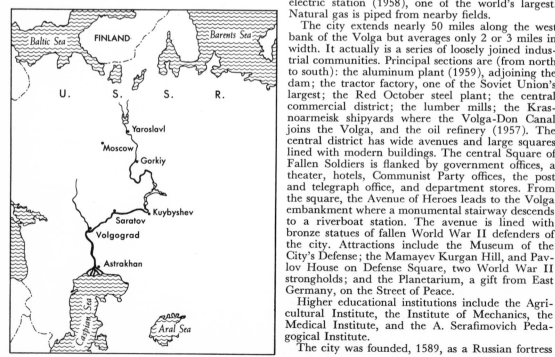

SOVFOTO

The Volga River, famous in Russian legends and songs, is the longest waterway in the Soviet Union; almost the entire 2,215 mile course is navigable throughout the year.

In the 1950's the Volga was dammed above Gorki and at Kuibyshev and Volgograd. The hydroelectric plants at Kuibyshev and Volgograd, each with a capacity of more than two million kilowatts, are among the world's largest. Construction of other great dams was under way at Saratov and Cheboksary early in the 1960's.

VOLGOGRAD, formerly Stalingrad, city and region, U.S.S.R., SW Russian Soviet Federated Socialist Republic.

Volgograd, the city, capital of the region, is on the Volga River 580 miles SE of Moscow; pop. (1959) 591,000. It is one of the largest cities of the Volga Valley and is located at the eastern end of the Volga–Don River Canal (1952). The city is a major railroad and industrial center, producing steel, tractors, machine tools, wood products, aluminum, petroleum products, and rivercraft. Electric power comes from the Volgograd dam and hydroelectric station (1958), one of the world's largest. Natural gas is piped from nearby fields.

The city extends nearly 50 miles along the west bank of the Volga but averages only 2 or 3 miles in width. It actually is a series of loosely joined industrial communities. Principal sections are (from north to south): the aluminum plant (1959), adjoining the dam; the tractor factory, one of the Soviet Union's largest; the Red October steel plant; the central commercial district; the lumber mills; the Krasnoarmeisk shipyards where the Volga-Don Canal joins the Volga, and the oil refinery (1957). The central district has wide avenues and large squares lined with modern buildings. The central Square of Fallen Soldiers is flanked by government offices, a theater, hotels, Communist Party offices, the post and telegraph office, and department stores. From the square, the Avenue of Heroes leads to the Volga embankment where a monumental stairway descends to a riverboat station. The avenue is lined with bronze statues of fallen World War II defenders of the city. Attractions include the Museum of the City's Defense; the Mamayev Kurgan Hill, and Pavlov House on Defense Square, two World War II strongholds; and the Planetarium, a gift from East Germany, on the Street of Peace.

Higher educational institutions include the Agricultural Institute, the Institute of Mechanics, the Medical Institute, and the A. Serafimovich Pedagogical Institute.

The city was founded, 1589, as a Russian fortress

in territory conquered from the Tatars of Astrakhan. It was named Tsaritsyn for the small Tsaritsa River which joins the Volga at the site. Industrial development began in the late nineteenth century and grew because of the city's location on the Volga-Don shipping route. The city was the scene of heavy fighting, 1918, during a civil war following the Bolshevik Revolution, and was abandoned briefly to the White Russians, 1919–20.

It was named Stalingrad, 1925, in honor of Josef Stalin, who led the city's defense during the civil war. Stalingrad expanded during several Five-Year Plans. It became world famous during the winter of 1942–43, when in one of World War II's decisive battles, German troops tried to seize the city (see STALINGRAD CAMPAIGN). The city was almost destroyed but was rebuilt. The city's name was changed to Volgograd in 1961 during destalinization.

Volgograd, the region, is bounded by the Kalmyk Autonomous Soviet Socialist Republic on the S, the Kazakh Soviet Socialist Republic on the E, and by the regions of Saratov on the N, Voronezh on the NW, Rostov on the W, and Astrakhan on the SE; area 47,500 sq. mi.; pop. (1959) 1,849,000. The region is a steppeland. The former Stalingrad Reservoir on the Volga and the Tsimlyanskoye Reservoir on the Don are large artificial lakes. Salt, gypsum, iron, and phosphorite deposits are found in the region. Wheat, cotton, sunflower seeds, pumpkins, and livestock are raised. Industry is centered in the capital city and in Kamyshin. Earliest inhabitants of the region were the Cimmerians, the Iranian Scythians, and the Alans. The region was a battleground for the Caucasian Cossacks and the Mongols, and in the late medieval period the area formed part of the Khanate of Astrakhan. Ivan the Terrible annexed the region to the Russian Empire, 1554. Stalingrad Region was formed in 1934 and renamed in 1961.

VOLLEYBALL, a popular group game, may be played indoors or out by 10 to 40 players. In championship competition there are 6 players on each side. The game is played on a court twice as long as it is wide. It may vary considerably in size but 60×30 feet for men, 40×20 for women are standard indoor sizes; standard outdoor courts are 80×40 feet and 60×30, respectively. A net, three feet high, is stretched across the middle of the court so that its top is 8 feet above the floor. A standard basket ball may be used, but the official volleyball is somewhat smaller, lighter and less highly inflated.

The ball is hit, or volleyed, back and forth across the net by the players using the palms of their hands, or butting it. It may not be kicked, caught, held, or hit with the fist. Service is made from the back court line, as in tennis, and must clear the net. Only the serving team can score, and the service alternates between the contending teams. The player receiving the service can bat it back over the net or can bat it to another member of his team who is in a better position to make a scoring shot. The third player to receive the ball from a team member must bat it across the net or it counts a point for the opposition. Game is 15 points, unless the score becomes tied at 14-all, in which case play continues until the serving side scores two consecutive points.

Volleyball was invented, 1895, by Wm. C. Morgan, physical director of the Holyoke, Mass., Y.M.C.A. The U.S. Volleyball Association governs championship play.

VOLNEY, CONSTANTIN FRANCOIS DE CHASSEBOEUF, COMTE DE, 1757–1820, French scholar, was born in Craon, studied medicine, traveled in Egypt and Syria in the 1780's, and was elected to the constituent assembly, 1789. A supporter of the Girondists, he was imprisoned during the Terror, but was saved from execution by the downfall of Robespierre in July 1794. Volney traveled in the United States, 1795–98, then returned to France and was elected to the senate. He was made a count by Emperor Napoleon I, 1808, and a peer by King Louis XVIII, 1814. Volney's major work is the controversial, anti-Christian survey of the philosophy of history, *Les Ruines, ou méditations sur les révolutions des empires* (1791), in which he tried to show that civilizations collapse because they abandon "natural religion." His other works include *Voyage en Egypte et en Syrie* (1787), and *Tableau de climat et du sol des Estats-Unis* (1803).

VOLOGDA, region and city, U.S.S.R., in N Russian Soviet Federated Socialist Republic.

Vologda, capital of the region, lies on the Vologda River 325 miles ESE of Leningrad and 250 miles NNE of Moscow; pop. (1959) 138,000. The city is a river port, and a highway and rail junction of routes to Moscow, Leningrad, and Archangel. Agricultural implements, riverboats, leather goods, beer, glass, pottery, and cement are manufactured. Landmarks include the sixteenth-century St. Sophia Cathedral and an eighteenth-century bishop's palace, now a museum. The city was founded in 1147 as a colony of Novgorod.

Vologda, the region, is bounded on the NW by the Karelian Autonomous Soviet Socialist Republic and by the regions of Archangel on the N, Kirov on the E, Kostroma, Yaroslavl, and Kalinin on the S. Novgorod on the SW, and Leningrad on the W; area 56,900 sq. mi.; pop. (1959) 1,307,000. The chief river is the Sukhona. The main lakes are the Onezhskoe on the northwest border, the Beloye Ozero, and the Kubenskoe. Vologda region is heavily wooded. Pine and fir timber processed at scattered sawmills is exported from Archangel on the White Sea to western Europe. Dairy farming is the chief agricultural pursuit.

VÓLOS, or Vólo, city, E Greece, in Thessaly, in the department of Magnisía at the head of the Gulf of Vólos, 30 miles SE of Larisa and about 110 miles NNW of Athens. Vólos is located on a small plain at the head of a large, sheltered inlet of the Aegean Sea, and has an important port. It is a commercial and processing center, and exports dried fruit, olive oil, and textiles. The city was founded in the nineteenth century, near the sites of the ancient cities of Demetrias, Iolius, and Pagasae. Pop. (1961) 55,000.

VOLPI, GIUSEPPE, CONTE DI MISURATA, 1877–1947, Italian public official, was born in Venice. He helped frame the Italian-Turkish peace terms, 1912, and was a delegate to the Paris Peace Conference, 1919, and governor of Tripolitana, 1921–25. As minister of finance, 1925–29, he regulated the value of the lira, and settled the Italian debt to the United States and Great Britain.

VOLSCI, an ancient people who inhabited the eastern and southern parts of Latium, a region on the Italian Peninsula. Among their chief towns were Antium (Anzio) Privernum (Priverno), and Arpinum (Arpino). In the fourth century B.C. they became subjects of the Roman republic.

VOLSUNGA SAGA, Old Norse *Volsunga-saga,* an Old Icelandic prose saga derived in large part from the Elder Edda, and first recorded in the twelfth or thirteenth century. The legend it relates is a variation on that of the German *Nibelungenlied.* In the *Volsunga Saga,* the hero Sigurd is raised by the dwarf smith Reginn. At the instigation of Reginn, Sigurd kills the giant Fafnir. Sigurd falls in love with the Valkyrie, Brynhild, whom he finds sleeping in an enchanted forest (see BRUNHILD). But when a magic potion makes him forget her, he marries Gudrun, and arranges Brynhild's marriage to his brother-in-law Gunnar. Grief-stricken, Brynhild has Sigurd stabbed to death by his brother-in-law Guttorm, and kills herself with the same sword; their bodies are burned on the same pyre. Richard Wagner's *Der Ring des Nibelungen* is based more on the *Volsunga Saga* than on the *Nibelungenlied* (see NIBELUNGENLIED; RING DES NIBELUNGEN, DER). William Morris and E. Magnússon translated the *Volsunga Saga* (1870).

VOLT, in the practical system of electrical units, is the unit of difference of potential or electromotive force and is defined as work per unit charge. In this system the unit of work is the joule and the unit of charge the coulomb; hence, the volt, the unit of difference of potential, is the joule per coulomb. This unit is named in honor of the Italian scientist, Alessandro Volta, who invented the electroscope and the voltaic cell. By definition, two points in an electric field are said to be at a difference of potential of one volt, if one coulomb of electricity will do one joule of work in being transported from one point to the other. The volt is also the unit of difference of potential in the meter-kilogram-second, or mks, system of electrical units. This unit can also be defined in terms of current flow. The absolute volt is the steady potential difference which must exist across a conductor which carries a steady current of one absolute ampere and dissipates energy at the rate of one watt. The absolute system of units was adopted on January 1, 1948, and replaced the international system in which the international volt was defined in terms of the international ampere. For purposes of conversion, one international volt = 1.000330 absolute volts.

VOLTA, CONTE ALESSANDRO GIUSEPPE, 1745–1827, Italian physicist, inventor of the electric battery, was born in Como, and educated at the Jesuit College there. He became professor of physics at Como, 1774, and at the University of Pavia, 1779. His first important contribution to electrical science was the invention of an electrophorus, an instrument for producing electric charges by induction; he sent a description of the electrophorus to Joseph Priestley, 1775. Volta next invented a condensing electroscope, a device to detect the presence of electric charges, and he built, 1800, the first primary battery, or voltaic pile, an apparatus for producing regular electric currents of definite strength. The electroscope and battery made possible a great increase in electrical experimentation and inaugurated a new era in electrical science. These discoveries won Volta great renown, and he was summoned, 1801, to Paris by Napoleon Bonaparte, and made a senator and count of the kingdom of Italy. In the field of chemistry Volta made important investigations of the origins of marsh gas and of the expansion of gases. He invented the eudiometer, a device for measuring oxygen content of the air. The volt, or pressure unit of electromotive force, was named in his honor.

VOLTAIC CELL. See Battery, Primary Batteries, *The Voltaic Cell;* Cell, *Voltaic Cells.*

VOLTAIC REPUBLIC. See Upper Volta.

VOLTAIRE, 1694–1778, celebrated French poet, dramatist, historian, novelist, pamphleteer, humanitarian, and leader of the Enlightenment, was born François-Marie Arouet in Paris, the son of a well-to-do notary, François Arouet. Young François-Marie was well educated in Paris at the famous Jesuit Collège de Louis-le-Grand, and by 1718, when he coined the name of Voltaire, he had become well known as a poet, and had already spent 11 months imprisoned in the Bastille because he was thought to be the author of some daring verses satirizing the regent of France.

In 1726 Voltaire was severely beaten by the lackeys of an insolent young nobleman, the Chevalier de Rohan. When Voltaire sought a duel to vindicate his honor, he found that, instead, the relatives of Rohan were able to use their influence at court to have Voltaire imprisoned or exiled, whichever he might choose, but that the chevalier could not deign to duel with the son of a notary. Thus Voltaire learned, and was embittered by the lesson, of the difference between being a commoner and a nobleman. Choosing exile, Voltaire lived in England, 1726–29, and became much interested in the scientific discoveries of Isaac Newton and in the philosophical doctrines of John Locke, and was impressed by what he saw of English religious toleration and political freedom. He also met Alexander Pope and Jonathan Swift, and was influenced by them and by the works of William Shakespeare, which he was later to introduce to Paris.

Back in France, he published some *Lettres philosophiques* (Letters on the English), 1734, praising English ways. This work, with its implicit criticism of French institutions, would probably have caused Voltaire's imprisonment had he not gone to Cirey, a remote estate in Lorraine belonging to Mme du Châtelet, one of the leading physicists and mathematicians in the Europe of that day; Voltaire lived with Mme du Châtelet, mainly at Cirey, until her death, 1749.

Voltaire had, meanwhile, become France's most celebrated poet, dramatist, and historian. The *Henriade* (1728–30), an epic poem celebrating France's first Bourbon king, Henry IV, was Voltaire's most ambitious poem, and was so successful that it permanently established Henry IV in the minds of Frenchmen as their most popular monarch. Voltaire was always a skillful and facile writer of verse. His best plays—*Oedipe* (1718), *Zaïre* (1732), *Mérope* (1743), and *Tancrède* (1760)—are all in verse form; very many of his private letters are interlarded with graceful verses, struck off at a moment; and many of his philosophical and critical works, such as *Le temple du goût* (1733) or the thoughtful *Poème sur le désastre de Lisbonne* (1756), are in verse form. His *La pucelle,* a posthumously published mock-heroic epic poem about Jeanne d'Arc, well illustrates the flexibility and wittiness of Voltaire's verse.

Voltaire's works of history are still read and admired, particularly *Histoire de Charles XII* (of Sweden) (1731), and *Siècle de Louis XIV* (1751); the latter is especially remarkable for its attention to art and literature as well as to war and diplomacy. His very popular and influential *Essai sur les moeurs* (1st ed. in 1756), a sort of universal history, was a vehicle for Voltaire's poking fun at man's absurdities in preceding centuries as well as, by implication, in his own.

Voltaire was appointed royal historiographer, 1745, and was elected to the French Academy, 1746. He went to Berlin and Potsdam, 1750, residing there for several years in close association with Frederick II until the two men, friends since 1736, quarreled most spectacularly. For a while Voltaire stayed in Colmar, in Alsace; from 1754 until his death he lived in Geneva, or at nearby Ferney, just across the border in France.

The terrible earthquake of Nov. 1, 1755, at Lisbon (so like the equally dreadful one that occurred in the same part of the world at Agadir, Morocco, Mar. 1, 1960) shocked Voltaire deeply and caused him to ponder the question of why God permits the existence of evil and allows the innocent to suffer. These ponderings were the origin of what was to remain Voltaire's best known and most loved work, *Candide* (1759), which under the disarming guise of being simply a witty and casual tale of adventure, is also a searching commentary on eighteenth century values and institutions, and a direct attack on the philosophy of Leibniz. In the twentieth century this work was increasingly appreciated as a skillful and subtle work of art. Indeed, Voltaire's "philosophical tales," with their crowded action and fast-moving plots, are the part of his literary remains that has best survived the ravages of time, and stories such as *Zadig* (1748) and *Micromégas* (1752) continued to be read almost as much as *Candide* itself. See Candide.

Voltaire was always a fighter against fanaticism and intolerance, but from ?1759 he was more aggressive in this regard. For example, he began to end most of his letters with the slogan *Ecrasez l'infâme* (Crush the infamous thing). As an upholder of a "natural religion" of habit and expediency (see Deism), Voltaire was by no means an atheist, but critics disagree as to how anti-Christian he really was, and whether he meant by "the infamous thing" simply bigotry in general, or the Roman Catholic church in particular. Perhaps the most glorious thing that Voltaire ever did was to secure, after a great expenditure of money, time, and effort, the reversal of the sentence against Jean Calas. Calas was a Protestant of Toulouse who had been convicted, 1762, on very insufficient evidence, for the murder of his son, the alleged motive having been that the younger Calas had intended to become a Catholic. Voltaire's *Traité sur la tolérance* (1763), written after his vindication of Calas, is a model of polemical rhetoric. Voltaire is famous also for supporting the hapless in other instances of the miscarriage of justice, as in the cases of Admiral Byng, Lally-Tollendal, the Sirvens, and the Chevalier de La Barre, the last a man who had been brutally executed for the "crime" of "free thinking."

Voltaire was an excellent businessman and accumulated a very large fortune, part of it from favorable annuities granted by companies who thought, to look at him, that he would surely die within a very short time; all his long life, however, Voltaire was unexpectedly tough and wiry. His literary production was enormous, as was his correspondence; one edition of his *Oeuvres complètes* fills 18 large volumes.

Voltaire seems really to have enjoyed life, a great deal of the enjoyment coming from plaguing his enemies; it has been said, indeed, that for the better part of a century Voltaire lived, almost literally, on coffee and the joyous flow of his own adrenalin. No "enemy" pamphleteer was too stupid or too obscure to escape Voltaire's attention.

In his later years, when he was called "the Patriarch of Ferney," innumerable visitors sought him out, and he corresponded with eminent persons throughout Europe. In 1778, not having been in Paris since 1750, he made a triumphal trip there, and on this occasion met Benjamin Franklin. Worn out by overexcitement and overwork, however, he died in Paris, May 30, 1778. His ashes were transferred to the Pantheon, 1791, after the French Revolution.

ARTHUR M. WILSON

BIBLIOG.–Albert Bachman, *Censorship in France from 1715 to 1750: Voltaire's Opposition* (1934); Mary M. H. Barr, *Voltaire in America, 1744–1800* (1941); Henry N. Brailsford, *Voltaire* (1935); Georg M. C. Brandes, *Voltaire* (1936); John H. Brumfitt, *Voltaire, Historian* (1958); Cleveland B. Chase, *Young Voltaire* (1926); Francis Espinasse, *Life of Voltaire* (1892); Ruth C. Flowers, *Voltaire's Stylistic Transformation of Rabelaisian Satirical Devices* (1951); Peter Gay, *Voltaire's Politics: The Poet As Realist* (1959); George P. Gooch, *Catherine the Great, and Other Studies* (1954); Evelyn B. Hall, *Life of Voltaire* (1938); Edward B. Hamley, *Voltaire* (1911); Margaret S. Libby, *Attitudes of Voltaire to Magic and the Sciences* (1935); Thomas R. Lounsbury, *Shakespeare and Voltaire* (1902); Robert Lowenstein, *Voltaire As an Historian of Seventeenth Century French Drama* (1935); Marcello T. Maestro, *Voltaire and Beccaria As Reformers of Criminal Law* (1942); André Maurel, *Romance of Mme. Du Châtelet and Voltaire* (1931); André Maurois, *Voltaire* (1952); Adolph E. Meyer, *Voltaire: Man of Justice* (1952); Nancy Mitford, *Voltaire in Love* (1957); Andrew R. Moorehouse, *Voltaire and Jean Meslier* (1936); John Morley, *Voltaire* (1923); Alfred Noyes, *Voltaire* (1939); Kathleen M. J. O'Flaherty, *Voltaire, Myth and Reality* (1945); William R. Price, *Symbolism of Voltaire's Novels: With Special Reference to Zadig* (1911); Constance Rowe, *Voltaire and the State* (1955); Trusten W. Russell, *Voltaire, Dryden and Heroic Tragedy* (1946); Bernard N. Schilling, *Conservative England and the Case Against Voltaire* (1950); Norman L. Torrey, *Voltaire and the English Deists* (1930); *Spirit of Voltaire* (1939); Ira O. Wade, *Voltaire and Madame Du Châtelet: An Essay on the Intellectual Activity at Cirey* (1941), *Search for a New Voltaire* (1958), *Voltaire and Candide: A Study in the Fusion of History, Art and Philosophy* (1959); Mina Waterman, *Voltaire, Pascal, and Human Destiny* (1942).

VOLTA REDONDA, city, SE Brazil, in Rio de Janeiro State, in the Paráiba Valley, on a highway and railway, 55 miles NW of the city of Rio de Janeiro. A steel industry was established at Volta Redonda in 1947, under government sponsorship. Volta Redonda was planned as a model industrial town, and its population increased rapidly after the construction of the steel mills. An expansion and diversification program in 1960 brought production to 1 million tons annually. Pop. (1950) 32,143.

VOLTA RIVER, W Africa; begins as the Black Volta in W Upper Volta and the White Volta in central Upper Volta; becomes the Volta at the confluence of the White and Black Voltas in central Ghana and flows S into the Gulf of Guinea W of Cape St. Paul. Volta's total length, including its longest headstreams, is about 900 miles. The Black Volta forms part of the western boundary of Ghana. The largest tributary of the Volta is the Oti. The Volta is at its lowest level in January. It is navigable all year to about 60 miles above its mouth. Navigation is hindered by a sandbar at the mouth and blocked by rapids beginning 60 miles upstream.

VOLTERRA DANIELE DA, 1509–66, Italian painter, was born Daniele Ricciarelli, in Volterra, and studied painting in Siena, and then in Rome, with Michelangelo Buonarroti, on whose designs some of Volterra's works are based. Volterra's masterpiece is the *Descent from the Cross* in the Trinità de' Monti, Rome; other major works are *David and Goliath* (Louvre, Paris) and *Massacre of the Innocents* (Uffizi Gallery, Florence). Pope Paul IV commissioned Volterra to paint clothing on the nude figures in Michelangelo's *Last Judgment*, whence Volterra's nickname *Il Bracchettone* (breeches maker).

VOLTERRA, ancient Volaterrae, city, N central Italy, in Tuscany Region, in the province of Pisa, 32 miles SSE of the city of Pisa. Volterra is perched on a steep hill, surrounded by well preserved medieval walls. The city is the terminus of a branch rail line connecting with the west coastal trunk railway. Alabaster carvings, metal goods, and salt are manufactured. Volterra is the seat of a bishop and has a fine Romanesque cathedral, consecrated in 1120. Of interest are the Tagassi Palace with an Etruscan collection; a museum; and the town hall (1208–57), formerly a palace. Pop. (1958) 16,991.

VOLTMETER, an electrical instrument for measuring the potential difference, usually calibrated to read in terms of volts or millivolts, between two points along a conductor. The direct current voltmeter is simply a galvanometer of a very high resistance, and when placed across two points of a conductor, it draws a very small current, thus disturbing the current flow in the main circuit only slightly. The voltmeter is connected across or in parallel with the conductor. The small current which is sidetracked through the very high resistance in the voltmeter is, according to Ohm's law, proportional to the potential difference which maintains it, and this is a measure of the potential difference between the points of the conductor to which it is connected. Multirange voltmeters have several high resistances of different values so that the range of the readings may be varied by simply changing the terminals for different scale deflections from say 0 to 5 volts, 0 to 50 volts, and 0 to 150 volts.

The electrostatic voltmeter for measuring electrostatic potentials is simply a gold leaf electroscope equipped with a scale which permits the quantitative measurement of the deflection. Such a scale is calibrated to permit a reading in terms of volts. With such instruments, electrostatic potentials to thousands of volts can be measured. The electrostatic voltmeter, like the vacuum-tube voltmeter, requires an initial flow of charge only and one which is relatively small. Thus it is unlike the swinging coil types of voltmeters, which require for their operation a steady passage of charge, a disadvantage despite the extremely low values of the current drawn by the voltmeter.

VOLUMETRIC ANALYSIS. See CHEMICAL ANALYSIS; TITRATION.

VOLUNTEER, in U.S. military usage, anyone who offers his services to the military, particularly in time of war; or one who, as a member of a military service, volunteers for a particular task or mission, especially one involving extraordinary hazards. During the nineteenth century, militia groups that fought with regular army contingents while retaining their own officers (often appointed by state governors), insignia, and so forth, were known as volunteers. See ARMY OF THE UNITED STATES.

VOLUNTEERS OF AMERICA, a religious and philanthropic organization that carries on a program of welfare by means of day nurseries, health camps, maternity homes and, in addition, homes for children, stranded families, discharged prisoners and the aged. The organization was founded in 1896 by Commander and Mrs. Ballington Booth, partly as a protest against the rigid militarism of the Salvation Army, which had been founded by Commander Booth's father, Gen. William Booth. One of the best known phases of the work of the volunteers is its activity toward improving the conditions in prisons. For this work the Volunteer Prison League was established. The organization also sponsors Sunday school classes. By 1960 it had established 480 service units in the United States, among which were homes, industrial branches, and camps. Its headquarters are in New York City.

VOLVA, in Scandinavian mythology, the sibyl who pronounces the prophecies contained in the Völuspa, a part of the younger Eddas. Völva was the sibyl consulted by Odin about his son Balder's fate. See VEGTAM.

VOLYN, region, U.S.S.R., in the W part of the Ukrainian Soviet Socialist Republic, bounded on the W by Poland, on the N by the Brest Region of the Byelorussian Soviet Socialist Republic, E and S by the Rovno and Lvov regions of the Ukrainian Soviet Socialist Republic. The area of the region is 7,680 sq. mi. The terrain is level, with forests and swampland, part of the Pripet Marshes, in the north. Rye, barley, wheat, oats, and potatoes are the major crops. Cattle raising is important in the north, and lumbering is significant. Industrial production is based on the processing of food products. The capital is Lutsk.

VOLZHSKIY, city, U.S.S.R., in the Russian Soviet Federated Socialist Republic, in Volgograd Region, on the Volga River opposite Stalingrad, of which it is a residential and industrial suburb.

VOMITING, a defensive reflex of the stomach and intestines designed to rid these organs of poisonous substances. When poisonous or irritating objects reach the digestive system, nerve impulses are sent to a nerve center in the brain that controls the vomiting movements. Further impulses are sent down from this center to the muscles of the esophagus, stomach, and intestinal wall which, in a series of strong contractions and relaxations, exert pressure upon the stomach and intestines. This pressure causes the unwanted material to be expelled upward through the esophagus and out of the mouth. It is possible, however, for the vomiting reflex to occur without being caused by a stomach disturbance. Poisonous substances in the blood, mental stress, fatigue, or an interference with the blood supply to the vomiting center may cause the nerve cells in this center to become irritated to such a great extent that they may stimulate the reflex. Nausea usually precedes vomiting although it may exist by itself. It is the unpleasant sensation felt in the throat or stomach resulting in a milder series of muscular movements in the upper digestive tract.

VON BRAUN, WERNHER, 1912– , German engineer and rocket expert, born in Wirsitz. He studied at the institutes of technology in Berlin and Zurich and at the University of Berlin. From 1930 he did research on liquid fuels for rockets and in 1938 developed the first flying bomb for Hitler. He went to the United States in 1945 as adviser to the White Sands Proving Grounds rocket site in New Mexico. In 1956 he was director of development operations of the Redstone Arsenal in Alabama, which was responsible for the Jupiter IRBM and Explorer satellites. In 1960 he was director of the Marshall Space Flight Center. He became a U.S. citizen in 1955.

VONDEL, JOOST VAN DEN, 1587–1679, Dutch dramatist, poet, and translator, was born in Cologne of Anabaptist refugee parents. The family moved to Amsterdam, 1597, where, at his father's death, 1608, Vondel became manager of the family hosiery shop. He married, 1610, and had three sons. Early in life he was a supporter of Maurice of Nassau, but the Synod of Dort and the execution of Jan van Olden Barneveldt, 1619, alienated Vondel from the Calvinist zealots. He was a member and, for a time, a deacon of the Mennonites, but from 1640 was a Roman Catholic. His oldest son having ruined the family business, 1657, Vondel was reduced to working in a pawnshop. The state finally awarded him a small pension, 1668.

Vondel's dramas, translations from the classics, and didactic and lyric verse are among the finest in Dutch literature; indeed, he is often called "the Dutch Shakespeare." He valued most highly his dramas, but his lyrical poems, including the choruses of his plays, were to be even more highly regarded by posterity. His lyrics were collected in *Poëzy* (1647) and *Poëzy of Verscheide gedichten* (1682). Among his 32 plays, most of which are biblical in subject matter, are *Het Pascha* (The Pasha), 1612; *Hierusalem verwoest* (Jerusalem Destroyed), 1612; *Palamedes* (1625), a protest against the judicial murder of Barneveldt (Vondel was fined by the authorities for the play, but he continued writing against the Calvinists); *Gijsbrecht van Aemstel* (1637); *Gebroeders* (Brothers), 1639; *Maria Stuart* (1646); *Lucifer*, 1654 (Eng. trans. by L. C. van Noppen, 1898), one of his finest works; *Koning David herstelt* (King David Restored), 1660; *Adam in ballingschap* (1664); and *Noah* (1667). Among his works of didactic poetry are *Altaargeheimenissen* (Mysteries of the Altar), 1645, and *Johannes de boetgezant* (John the Evangelist), 1662.

VONNOH, ROBERT WILLIAM, 1858–1933, U.S. painter, was born in Hartford, Conn., studied at the Normal Art School in Boston and in Paris, and taught in several art academies. He painted many landscapes, but is best known for his somber, vigorous portraits.

Bessie Potter Vonnoh, 1872–1955, his wife, was born in St. Louis and studied sculpture at the Art Institute of Chicago. She specialized in graceful miniature figures of children and women. The fountain group in the children's garden, Central Park, New York City, is also hers.

VOODOOISM, or Hoodism, a primitive form of religion, prevalent among the Negroes of the West Indies and, to a limited extent, among the Negroes of the southern United States. It is thought by some to be a relic of the fetishistic religion of equatorial Africa, but it contains crude elements of Christian belief. The many gods and demons of voodooism are either beneficent or malevolent spirits of the dead; they can be called upon to protect an individual or to bring harm to an enemy. Voodoo belief holds that disease, or even death, can be inflicted upon an individual by performing certain rites upon any object that the individual has touched, or upon a wax image intended to represent the individual. See MAGIC; WITCHCRAFT.

Voodoo rites are sometimes associated with serpent worship and occasionally with human sacrifice. The secret ceremonies, led by a priest or priestess, are conducted at night, and often culminate in frenzied dancing, incoherent exhortations ("speaking in tongues"), and other abandoned behavior.

The word *voodoo* is thought by some to be derived from *vaudoux*, a Creole form of the French *Vaudois*, or Waldenses, who were represented by their enemies as being addicted to the practice of sorcery and necromancy (see WALDENSES.). A more likely source is Creole French *voudou*, which derives from the African Negro, and more particularly the Dahomey, word *vodu* (a good or bad spirit or demon)—a fetish. See FETISH.

VOORHEES, DANIEL WOLSEY, 1827–97, U.S. political figure and renowned orator, born in Butler County, Ohio. He attended Indiana Asbury (now DePauw) University, and was admitted to the bar in 1851. He was a Democratic member of the U.S. House of Representatives, 1861–66, 1869–73, and Senate, 1877–97. He was chairman of the committee on finance under President Cleveland and was a leader in the struggle for the repeal of the Sherman silver purchase act. During the Civil War he severely criticized both the North and the South. Despite the success of his law practice, he died poor.

VORARLBERG, province, W Austria, bounded by Germany on the N, Switzerland on the NW and S, Liechtenstein on the W, and by the province of Tirol on the E; area of the province totals 1,005 square miles. Lake Constance forms part of the boundary in the northwest corner of the province. Vorarlberg is on the northern flanks of the Alps and is noted for its fine scenery. The chief rivers are the Rhine, which forms part of the western boundary, and the Ill. Only about three per cent of the area is cultivated. Dairying is the most important type of farming, though beef cattle are raised, and wheat, hay and potatoes are grown. Hydroelectric power is well developed along the Ill and Bregenzer Ache rivers. The chief manufactures are textiles and embroidery. The capital is Bregenz. In 1961, the population was 226,323.

VORKUTA, city, USSR, in the Russian Soviet Socialist Republic, in NE Komi Region, on the Usa River, on a northern trunk railway, 240 miles NE of Pechora. Vorkuta lies at the foot of the northern Ural Mountains in the marshy valley of the Usa River. The city lies north of the Arctic Circle, and is in a region with a permanently frozen subsoil. There is some stunted tree growth. Vorkuta is the center of an important coal-mining area, and has some light industries. It increased in importance very rapidly after the railroad was completed, 1942, and became a city in 1943. (For population, see U.S.S.R., map in Atlas.)

VORONEZH, region, U.S.S.R., S Russian Soviet Federated Socialist Republic, bounded by the regions of Lipetsk and Tambov on the N, Saratov on the NE, Volgograd on the E, Rostov on the S, Lugansk on the SW, Belgorod on the W, and Kursk on the NW; area of the region totals 26,400 sq. mi. The terrain is mostly rolling steppe, becoming increasingly hilly in the south. The soils are rich black earth (chernozem), and the region stands high in agricultural production. The Don River flows from north to south through the region and, in the south, forms an important form of transportation for the shipment of grain.

Voronezh is a major region in which spring wheat is produced. Millet, sunflowers (for seed oil), and sugar beets are also important crops. Hogs and sheep are raised. Industries include metallurgical works,

SOVFOTO
Voronezh, on the Voronezh River, is noted in the Soviet Union as a center of engineering industries that manufacture such products as heavy machinery and diesel motors.

machine building, chemical plants, synthetic rubber production, and food processing. The region's rail lines are well developed, and a highway from Moscow reaches Voronezh, the capital. In 1959 the population was 2,363,000.

VORONEZH, city, U.S.S.R., in the Russian Soviet Federated Socialist Republic, capital of the Voronezh Region, on the Voronezh River near its confluence with the Don, 290 miles SSE of Moscow. Voronezh is a commercial and processing center for a rich agricultural region and is a road, rail, and air junction point. Flour, vegetable oils, dressed meat and other food substances, and agricultural machinery and implements are produced. Voronezh is an important industrial city, a center of engineering industries. Heavy machinery, diesel motors, synthetic rubber goods, chemicals, and radios are manufactured. The city has a university, an agricultural institute, and several museums. Voronezh was first known in the eleventh century, but during the fourteenth and fifteenth centuries was deserted. The Russians built a fort here in 1586, and on the river banks in 1695–96 Peter the Great built a fleet of boats on which he floated down the Don to conquer Azov. During World War II, Voronezh was taken by the Germans (1942) and was retaken by the Soviets in 1943, following the German defeat at Stalingrad (since renamed Volgograd). (For population, see U.S.S.R. map in Atlas.)

VOROSHILOV, KLIMENT EFREMOVICH, 1881–   , Soviet military and political leader, was born in Verkhneye, Lugansk Province, Ukraine. From early youth he worked in mines, on farms and in factories. He joined the Bolshevik faction of the Social Democratic party, 1903, was imprisoned several times as a revolutionary, 1907–14, led guerrilla fighters against the Germans in the Ukraine, 1918, fought at the side of Joseph Stalin at Tsaritsyn (Volgograd), 1918–19, and became a member of the

SOVFOTO
Kliment E. Voroshilov

central committee of the Communist party, 1921, and of the Politburo, 1926. He was military commander of the North Caucasus, 1921–24, and the Moscow area, 1924–25. As military and naval commissar, 1925–44, he organized the defense against the German invasion, 1941, but held no field command after that time. He became a marshal, 1935, a member of the supreme soviet, 1937, and of the presidium, 1953. As president of the presidium of the supreme soviet, 1953–60, he was titular chief of state, but real power rested with Nikita Khrushchev. Voroshilov resigned as president because of illness, 1960, and was succeeded by Leonid Brezhnev.

VOROSMARTY, MIHALY, 1800–1855, Hungarian poet, was born in Nyek. He studied law but soon abandoned it for literature. His poems, in which classic restraint and patriotic themes are blended, inaugurated a new era in the literature of Hungary. Among the most important are the epics *Zalán futása* (Zalan's Flight), 1824; *Cserhalom* (1825); and *Két szomséd vár* (1831), and the patriotic song *Szozat* (1836), which became a national anthem. He also wrote a number of dramas and many short lyrics, founded and contributed to two critical journals, and translated the plays of William Shakespeare. Vörösmarty was an original member of the Hungarian Academy.

VORTICISM, a twentieth century art movement that developed as an offshoot of French cubism and Italian futurism. The movement was founded in England, 1914, by the novelist, pamphleteer, and painter Wyndham Lewis, to stir up the British scene as violently as the title of its official journal suggests:

Blast (only two issues published, 1914–15). In addition to Lewis, vorticism's prime movers were Henri Gaudier-Brzeska, a French sculptor and perhaps vorticism's foremost talent; the U.S.–born expatriate agitator and poet Ezra Pound; and the writer Richard Aldington. The characteristic mark of the painting done by this school was its rhythmic fluidity superimposed on a Cubist structure. Lewis's work, for instance, is typically built on a vertical axis with a precise framework that may be geometrical; his *Sunset in the Atlas*, Cubist in structure and fluidly Futuristic in atmosphere, is characteristic of the Vorticist movement. Thus, vorticism used Cubist geometry and mathematics to express more emotional and human values than the Cubists themselves attempted to express. ANTHONY KERRIGAN

VOS, CORNELIS DE, 1585–1651, Flemish painter, was born in Hulst, and became a master of the painters' guild of St. Luke, Antwerp. Peter Paul Rubens often sent his overflow of sitters to De Vos, who was surpassed as a portraitist only by Rubens himself, Anthony Van Dyck, and Jacob Jordaens. Among the finest of De Vos' portraits—which are characteristically very realistic, and soft in color—are *Artist, His Wife, and His Two Daughters* and *Messenger of the Company of St. Luke.*

Paul de Vos, 1590?–1678, his brother, was born in Hulst, and became a painter of brilliantly colored hunting scenes and animals.

VOS, MARTIN DE, also Marten de Vos, 1531?–?1603, Flemish painter, was born in Antwerp. He studied seven years in Italy with Tintoretto, for whose works he often painted the backgrounds; but De Vos' works do not have the beautiful colors and originality of his master's. On returning to Antwerp, he became a member of the painters' guild, 1559, and its dean, 1572. He did many paintings for the churches of Antwerp, but most of them were destroyed during iconoclastic uprisings. His religious paintings, such as the *Incredulity of St. Thomas* and *St. Paul Stung by a Viper*, are inferior to his portraits, of which *Portrait of the Anselmo Family* is one of the most notable.

VOSGES, department, E France, bounded by the provinces of Meuse on the NW, Meurthe-et-Moselle on the N, Bas-Rhin on the NE, Haut-Rhin on the E, Haute-Saône on the S, and by Haute-Marne on the W; area 2,279 sq. mi.; pop. (1954) 372,523. The department extends from the summit of the Vosges Mountains in the east, westward toward the Paris Basin. Forests cover about one third of the area. The chief river is the Moselle, which rises in the southeast of the department. Wheat, beets, oats, tobacco, grapes, hops, potatoes, and hemp are grown and dairy cattle are raised. The industries include sawmills, furniture and woodworking factories, and textile mills, which manufacture cotton, linen, and wool goods. The department has coal mines and stone quarries. The department was formed in 1790 out of territory belonging to Lorraine and small parts of Franche-Comté and Champagne. Épinal, the capital, is the principal town.

VOSGES, mountains, E France, extending about 90 miles from the Saverne Gap (to the N of Strasbourg) on the N to the Belfort Gap (Belfort) at the S, presenting a steep faulted front to the Rhine River on the E and a long gentle slope to the West. The Vosges form part of the western flank of the Rhine Rift valley, which was formed during the late Tertiary period. The mountains are composed of granitic rocks flanked by sandstone and limestone, with an average elevation of 3,000 feet. The timber line is at 4,000 feet. The High Vosges, as the higher slopes are called, are grassy at the summit; the lower slopes are clothed with a dense forest of oak, ash, pine, and beech. There are many valleys, which have deep fertile soils, where wheat, hops, hemp, potatoes, and tobacco are grown. The grasslands of the High Vosges are used to pasture dairy cattle; Münster cheese is made of their milk. Numerous streams rise in the Vosges, including the

Moselle, Meurthe, and Ill. Water power is utilized in the various small factories producing furniture and textiles. There is some mining and quarrying for such materials as lead, iron, marble, slate, potash, and building stone.

VOSS, JOHANN HEINRICH, 1751–1826, German poet and translator, was born in Sommersdorf, Mecklenburg. At the suggestion of Heinrich Boie he went to Göttingen to study, and there became, 1772, a member of the poetic brotherhood *Hainbund*, whose members wrote lyrics in the manner of folk songs, and was editor of the brotherhood's *Musenalmanach*, 1775. Voss taught at Otterndorf and Eutin, 1778–1802, and at Heidelberg from 1805. His finest original work is the hexameter idyll *Luise* (printed complete in 1795), but he is more renowned for his translations of the classics, especially Homer's *Odyssey* (1781; revised 1793), and the *Iliad* (1793). He also translated the works of Vergil, Horace, Hesiod, Aristophanes, Theocritus, Tibullus, Bion, and Moschus and, with his two sons, the plays of William Shakespeare.

VOTING MACHINE. See ELECTION.

VOTING TRUST, an agreement whereby a number of stockholders in a corporation place their stock in the hands of one or more persons with powers of attorney authorizing them to vote the stock at corporate elections, in order to enable them to control the policy of the corporation. This is often done where a corporation is in financial difficulties and one or more men in whom the stockholders have confidence agree to manage it for a certain period on condition of being given control in this way. If the agreement is not for any illegal purpose, as to prevent competition, it may be sustained by the courts, but, in general, voting trusts are viewed with disfavor by the courts. The stockholders receive certificates representing their shares of stock. See TRUST.

VOTKINSK, city, U.S.S.R., in the Udmurt Autonomous Soviet Socialist Republic, on a railway, 10 miles SE of Perm. The city is in the foothills of the western Ural Mountains. Votkinsk is a long-established center of metallurgical industries, with steel mills, and factories producing aircraft, heavy machinery, and metal ware. Peat is mined close to the city, and there is a large hydroelectric power station. Votkinsk is the birthplace of the Russian composer Peter Ilich Tschaikovsky. Pop. (1959) 59,000.

VOULKOS, PETER, 1924– , U.S. artist, began his career as a painter, but later distinguished himself for his complex, abstract ceramic sculptures. His works were exhibited at the Brussels World Fair, 1958, the First Paris Biennale, 1959, the Pasadena Art Museum, 1958–59, and the New York Museum of Art, 1960.

VOW, a voluntary and solemn promise to give up or to do something for God or some other deity in excess of demands, either as a payment or offering, and common in many religions. It may be either public or private. Vows are recorded in both the Old Testament (Gen. 28:20–22; Deut. 23:21–23; I Sam. 1:11; Ps. 61:4–8; 101: 132:2–5; and elsewhere) and in the New Testament (Acts 18:18; 21:23; and elsewhere). Perhaps the most frequently made vow since early Christian times has been the threefold one of poverty, chastity, and obedience taken by persons entering the monastic life of convents and monasteries; among other familiar vows are those of pilgrimage, fasting, prayer, chastity, charity, to cease sinning, to do some duty, and others—either singly or in combination. The Christian sacraments, as Baptism and Marriage, also contain implicit vows.

Some Protestants of the sixteenth century and after minimized the importance of vows, but Roman Catholics and Jews have consistently emphasized them. A vow is usually taken to show that God deserves more than he requires, and to break a vow is a serious offense (Num. 30:1–5) because it implies that He did not deserve the added effort it would have taken to keep the promise.

VOYAGEUR, from the French *voyageur* (traveler), a French Canadian employed by fur traders and trading companies during the eighteenth and nineteenth centuries, for menial tasks such as paddling the canoes and transporting goods overland in the wilds of Canada and northern United States. The voyageurs formed a rather distinct class of men, with their peculiar dress, and distinctive vocabulary and songs. See FUR TRADE.

VRŠAC, city, E Yugoslavia, in Serbia, in Vojuodina Province, 7 miles from the Rumanian border, and 45 miles NE of Belgrade. Vršac is a rail and road junction and a border town. It is a trade and processing center in a fertile region in which wheat, corn, fruit, and vegetables are grown. Red wines and brandies, flour, machinery, and textiles are manufactured. It is the seat of a Greek Orthodox bishop. Pop. (1953) 26,710.

VULCAN, the god of fire in Roman mythology. In early times he was worshiped under various aspects—as the god of destructive fire, of the hearth fire, and of summer heat. Becoming identified with the Greek god Hephaestus, Vulcan came to be regarded as the benign patron of metal work and, by extension, of mechanical creations. On August 23, the festival of Vulcanalia, fish were burned in his honor; doing this was supposed to ward off forest and granary fires. See VENUS.

VULCANIZING. See RUBBER, Natural Rubber Processing, *Vulcanization*.

VULCANO. See LIPARI ISLANDS.

VULGATE, the Latin version of the Bible in common use in the Roman Catholic church since the sixth century. The translation of the Bible into Latin began probably as early as the second century. By the end of the fourth century, the whole Bible was available in Latin, but since there was no one official version, and little control was exercised over the multiplication of manuscripts, there was much confusion and uncertainty. A number of the Fathers, including Augustine of Hippo, applied themselves to the task of producing a correct and uniform Latin text; but the work along these lines that was to be of most permanent value was that of Jerome, 342?–420, with whose name the Vulgate is always associated, although the work as we have it is not entirely his. Jerome was approximately 40 years old when commissioned, ?382, by Pope Damasus, 366–84, to revise and correct the Latin text of the Gospels in accordance with the best available Greek manuscripts. This task was completed in 384. It is often said that he then proceeded to a similar work on the remaining books of the New Testament, but there is no conclusive evidence that the Vulgate version of the rest of the New Testament is in fact Jerome's work. During the time he was working on the gospels, Jerome also made a rather hasty revision of the current Latin version of the Psalter, which was, in turn a translation of the Septuagint Greek. For a long time it was thought that this first Latin Psalter was the Roman Psalter (so-called because of its formerly extensive use in the Roman liturgy), but later research seems to have proved that such is not the case. In 387–88 he made a second, much more thorough revision of the Psalms, which was known as the Gallican Psalter (from its early use in the churches of Gaul). It is this version that was included in the Vulgate and used in the Roman liturgy from the time of Pope Pius V, 1566–72, until the new Latin Psalter of Pope Pius XII, 1939–58. Jerome then proceeded to the revision of a number of books in the Jewish canon of the Old Testament. Of these, only the text of Job survives. It was at about this time that he abandoned the work of mere revision and set out to make a new Latin version directly from the original texts. He translated, 391–405, from the original, all of the books in the Jewish canon (which is identical with the canon represented in the King James or Authorized Version), plus Tobit and Judith. All these translations

are in the Vulgate, except his version of the Psalms from the Hebrew. The rest of the Catholic Old Testament canon in the Vulgate (Wisdom, Baruch, Ecclesiasticus, I and II Maccabees, and the rest of Daniel and Esther) is not the work of Jerome, but simply the Old Latin untouched by him. Whether it was his intention to apply himself to these books as he did to the others is a matter of controversy.

In his works, Jerome appears somewhat inconsistent in his attitude toward these books. Sometimes he seems to regard them as inspired Scripture and at other times, not. Jerome has been criticized for sometimes reading more meaning into the text than is there, but this defect has been much exaggerated. In general, it can be said that his was a truly monumental achievement; his translation is faithful, clear, and elegant.

History. The Vulgate has had a long and complicated history. At first it met with much opposition, but by the end of the eighth century it had all but replaced other Latin versions. The Council of Trent declared it the official Catholic version and "authentic," 1546. It is quite clear that by this it was the intention of the council to state merely that it was free from doctrinal errors. At the same time, moreover, the council directed that a new and correct edition should be prepared, since in the course of centuries and the multiplication of manuscripts the text had become very corrupt, and none of the many attempts at restoring order had enjoyed any permanent success. But it was not until the time of Pope Sixtus V, 1585–90, that the projected official edition appeared. For a number of reasons, however, this was found to be unsatisfactory, and the first edition was withdrawn from sale, and a new, much changed edition was published under the direction of Pope Clement VIII, 1592–1605. Revised in 1598, it remained the official Roman Catholic Latin Bible. In 1889 two Anglican scholars, John Wordsworth, later Bishop of Salisbury, and Henry Julian White, later Dean of Christchurch, Oxford, began the publication of a very highly regarded critical edition of the Vulgate New Testament. Pope Pius X, 1903–14, established a Pontifical Commission for the Revision of the Vulgate. The work of the commission, entrusted to a group of Benedictine scholars and since 1933 centered at the Benedictine Abbey of St. Jerome in Rome, is to re-establish, on a critical basis, the original text of the Latin Vulgate. Genesis appeared in 1926, and by 1960 10 additional volumes, taking the work down to the Song of Songs, had appeared.

BRENDAN McGRATH, O.S.B., S.T.D.

VULPECULA, the Little Fox, a small and unimportant constellation of the northern heavens, lying between Cygnus and Sagitta and extending in declination, is not one of the ancient Ptolemaic constella-

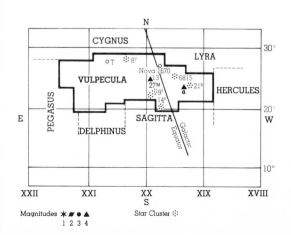

The Constellation Vulpecula

tions; it was delineated by Hevelius. No conspicuous stars are found in this constellation, but it does contain the so-called dumbbell nebula, M-27, which actually has little resemblance in appearance to a dumbbell. This nebula forms an acute triangle with the stars η and γ in the neighboring constellation of Sagitta. This group is also referred to as Vulpecula cum Ansere, the Little Fox with the Goose. See CONSTELLATION.

VULTURE, large preying birds belonging to the family of American vultures, the *Cathartidae*, or to the group of Old World vultures of the family *Accipitridae*. The American vultures are unique in several respects. The hind toe is relatively short and not on the same level with the other toes; the bill is hooked, and the nostrils are perforated, that is, without a partition between them. Characteristic of vultures are such features as a head that is either completely naked or partially covered with down, and large feet with blunt claws. The feet are not adapted for grasping prey but this poses no problem for the birds live exclusively on decaying animal matter. Prey is detected through the bird's use of its keen vision. Close relatives of the vultures are birds of prey, such as the hawks, eagles, falcons, and kites.

ALLAN D. CRUICKSHANK
FROM NATL. AUDUBON SOC.
Turkey Vulture

Vultures are found wherever there is food within their geographical range. They glide with ease in broad circles high above the earth, their powerful wings enabling them to fly gracefully, almost beyond comparison with other birds. Except during the nesting season, vultures live in flocks. They do not build a nest but lay one to three eggs under logs or stumps, on the ground, in caves, or similar places. The young are born naked and are fed by regurgitation. American vultures are separated into six existing species, three of which are North American. The most common and widely distributed form in the United States is the turkey vulture, *Cathartes aura septemtrionalis*.   ALBERT WOLFSON

VUYLSTERE, JULIUS, 1836–1903, Flemish poet and political figure, was born in Ghent. He wrote love poetry and powerful social and political verse. Vuylstere was a political liberal and took an active interest in adult education programs. Among his works are *Zwijgende liefde* (1860) and *Uit het studentenleven* (1868).

VYAZEMSKY, PRINCE PETR ANDREYEVICH, 1792–1878, Russian writer, was born near Moscow. Although a champion of romanticism, his poetry was classical in temper—restrained, lucid, and witty. He wrote critical studies of other Russian writers, and his letters to his friend Aleksander Pushkin continue to be of interest to modern readers.

VYAZMA, town, U.S.S.R., Russian Soviet Federated Socialist Republic, NE Smolensk Region, on the Vyazma River, an affluent of the Dnepr, 90 miles NE of the city of Smolensk and 120 miles WSW of Moscow. The town is a railway junction and on the Moscow-Minsk highway. Vyazma is a food processing and textile center. The town dates from the eleventh century, and received its first charter in the thirteenth century. Pop. (1959) 30,000.

VYBORG, Finnish Viipuri, Swedish Viborg, city, U.S.S.R., in the NW Russian Soviet Federated Socialist Republic, in Leningrad Region; on the Gulf of Finland, an arm of the Baltic Sea; near the Finnish border; 75 miles NW of Leningrad, and 500 miles NW of Moscow. Vyborg is an important port, and commercial center. Agricultural machinery, wood products, woolen goods, and electrical equipment are manufactured. The port handles large shipments of forest products from the city's hinterland. The nearby port of Vysotsk, formerly Uuras, provides Vyborg with additional port facilities. Vyborg, an early Hanseatic port, was incorporated in 1403 and became a part of Russia in 1721 after invasions by Peter the Great. It changed hands again in 1812 and became capital of the Finnish county of Viipuri. After the "Winter War" of 1939–40, the city was ceded to the U.S.S.R. It was retaken by the Finns with the resumption of the war in 1941, but in 1944 was incorporated into the Soviet Union. Pop. (1959) 51,000.

VYCHAN, SIMWYNT, or Simwynt Fychan (Simon the Little), 1530?–1606, Welsh poet. In 1568 at Caerwys, the site of many medieval *eisteddfods* (bardic assemblies), he was elevated to the position of a *pencerdd*—a bard of the highest order, whose task it was to sing the praises of God and the saints and of his lord and the lord's family. He is thought to have been the author of the eloquent *Pum Llyfr Cerddwriaeth*.

VYCPÁLEK, LADISLAV, 1882–   , Czech composer, was born in Prague, took an early interest in music, and studied philology at Charles University, Prague, graduating with a doctorate in 1906. From 1908 to 1912 he studied with the composer Vitězslav Novák (1870–1949), and from 1922 to 1942 he was keeper of the music department of the National Library, Prague. Like many Slav composers, Vycpálek owes much of his inspiration to folk music. Although at first influenced by Novák, Vycpálek soon developed a musical style of great individuality, characterized by an austere eloquence reminiscent of the music of Johann Sebastian Bach. Choral works predominate among his compositions, but he also wrote orchestral works, chamber music, suites for solo instruments, and manys songs. He wrote three cantatas: *O poslednich věcech člověka* (Of the Last Things of Man), 1921, using two Moravian folksongs as a text; *Blahoslavený ten člověk* (Blessed is the Man), 1933, words from the Psalms; and *České rekviem—smrt a vykoupení* (Czech Requiem—Death and Redemption), 1940, words from biblical texts.

VYCPÁLEK, VRATISLAV, 1892–   , Czech composer and music critic, was born in Rychnov nad Kněžnou. He composed many vocal works, was an energetic collector of folk songs, and edited the music revue *Ceská hudba*, 1927–30.

VYSHNEGRADSKY, IVAN, 1893–   , Soviet composer, was born in St. Petersburg (later Leningrad). He studied music at the St. Petersburg Conservatory and in 1922 settled in Paris, where he began his lifelong efforts to promote the quarter-tone system of music (see MUSIC, Modern Techniques, *Quarter-Tone Music*). He published a textbook and many articles expounding the theory and practice of quarter-tone harmony, and built a piano having two keyboards, one tuned a quarter tone higher than the other. In addition to the orchestral work *Dithyramb* (1926) and a number of violin solos and string quartets, Vyshnegradsky wrote predominantly for groups of pianos separated by a quarter tone; among these works are *First Symphonic Fragment, Ainsi parlait Zarathoustra, Etude en forme de scherzo, 24 Preludes in the 13-tone quasi-diatonic quarter-tone scale,* and a symphonic poem, *Cosmos.*

VYSHNIY VOLOCHEK, city, U.S.S.R., Russian Soviet Federated Socialist Republic, in Kalinin Region, 210 miles SE of Leningrad and 170 miles NNW of Moscow. The city is on the main railway and highway from Leningrad to Moscow. Vyshniy Volochek is a cotton-milling center and has sawmills and factories producing construction materials. Peter the Great, between 1703 and 1709, constructed a canal system through there, connecting the Baltic and Caspian basins. Under the Soviets this system was enlarged. Pop. (1959) 66,000.

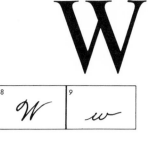

1		2 No Phoenician form	3 No Greek form	4 No Roman form	5 No Irish uncial form	6 No Caroline form	7 No black-letter form
8 *W*	9 *w*	10 W	11 W	12 W	13 *W*	14 *w*	15 W	16 W

W has in its name a description of both its shape and its origin, though both are older than the use of the name. The letter may be found written uu in the early writings of the Roman Empire. Common forms of the letter W as it appears today are illustrated in the bottom row. They are handwritten cursive capital 8, handwritten lowercase 9, roman capital 10, roman lowercase 11, roman small capital 12, italic capital 13, italic lowercase 14, sans serif capital 15, and sans serif lowercase 16.

W, the twenty-third letter of the English alphabet. The English *w* is described phonetically as a bilabial semivowel; it is closely related to the vowel *u* and may be termed consonantal *u*. It is probable that Latin *v*, or *u*, which were undistinguished, had this value after *q*. In the Middle Ages *uu* or *vv* were used to distinguish the consonantal *u*, and it is from this usage that the form of the letter and its English name, double U, derive. In modern Welsh and in thirteenth- and fourteenth-century English, *w* is a vowel with the value of Latin *u*, as well as a consonant; a vestige of this usage appears in such modern English words as *new* and *how*. The capital letter is frequently used as a symbol for the element tungsten and for *west;* the small letter stands for weight, width, or, in aeronautics, velocity of yaw.

WABASH, city, N central Indiana, seat of Wabash County; on the Wabash River, 73 miles NNE of Indianapolis. The Treaty of Paradise Springs, which opened the area to white settlement, was signed in Wabash, 1826. The site was first settled about 1834; it was chartered as a city in 1866. In 1880 Wabash became one of the first cities in the world to be lighted by electricity. Furniture, paper and boxboard, electronic equipment, automotive parts, and asbestos products are among the city's manufactured products. (For population, see Indiana map in Atlas.)

WABASH COLLEGE, a private nonsectarian liberal arts college for men located at Crawfordsville, Ind. The school was founded as the Wabash Teachers Seminary and Manual Labor College, 1832, and offered its first instruction in the following year. It acquired its present name in 1851. Divisions are mathematics and science, humanities, and social studies.

WABASH RIVER rises in Grand Lake in W Ohio and flows 475 miles W and SW across Indiana. A few miles south of Terre Haute the river forms the Indiana-Illinois border until it joins the Ohio. The Wabash drains about 33,000 square miles of fertile farmland. Some historians maintain that LaSalle discovered the Wabash in 1669.

WACE OF JERSEY, c.1100– c.1174, Anglo-Norman chronicler, born on the Isle of Jersey. He studied at Caen and Paris and eventually settled at Caen, c. 1135, where he became a professional poet and translator to the Norman nobility. He received a prebend at Bayeux, c.1170, as a gift from Henry II. Of his many works, all written in the Romance, or Old French, tongue, only six are extant: *Vie de Saint Nicolas, Conception de Nostre Dame, Vie de Sainte Marguerite, Vie de Merlin l'enchanteur, Roman de Brut,* and *Roman de Rou.* His reputation rests chiefly on the last two. The *Roman de Brut* (1155), a history of the British kings, is a metrical paraphrase of the Latin *Historia regum Britanniae* of Geoffrey of Monmouth. It was freely rendered into medieval English by Layamon. The *Roman de Rou* (1160–74), a poetical history of the Norman dukes, is based largely on the writings of Dudo of St. Quentin and William of Jumièges, with a liberal admixture of oral tradition and, very probably, of Wace's own fertile imagination.

WACO, city, E central Texas, seat of McLennan County; on the Brazos River 87 miles S of Dallas. Waco is a leading inland cotton market and a wholesale and retail distributing center for its locale, in which cotton and livestock are raised. Cement, textiles, wood products, tires, machinery, and mattresses are manufactured; dairy and meat products and cottonseed are processed.

The Waco area was once inhabited by the Waco Indians, but their village was burned by the Cherokees in 1829. The present city was platted in 1849 by Jacob de Cordova and incorporated in 1850.

Waco is the seat of Baylor University, Paul Quinn College, a U.S. Veterans Administration facility, and a state home for neglected and dependent children. Nearby is James Connally Air Force Base. The city has a council-manager government. (For population, see Texas map in Atlas.)

WADAI, former Muslim sultanate, N central Africa, since 1958 a part of Chad. The sultanate dated from the seventeenth century; its capital city, Abeshr (later Abéché) was an important station on trade routes leading west to Nigeria and north to Libya. Wadai came into the French sphere of influence late in the nineteenth century and was made a protectorate in 1903. After a series of wars France abolished the sultanate, 1912.

WADDELL, HELEN JANE, 1899– , Irish medieval scholar and translator, born in Tokyo. She studied at Victoria College and Queen's University in Belfast. In addition to translating Latin prose and poetry, she dramatized Antoine François Prevost D'Exiles' *Manon Lescaut* (1931) and wrote a novel, *Peter Abelard* (1933). Among her other works are *Lyrics from the Chinese* (1913), *The Wandering Scholars* (1927), *Medieval Latin Lyrics* (1929), *Beasts and Saints* (1934), *The Desert Fathers* (1936), and *Poetry in the Dark Ages* (1948).

WADE, BENJAMIN FRANKLIN, 1800–78, U.S. political leader born in Feeding Hills, Mass. He was admitted to the Ohio bar and served as state senator, 1837–39 and 1841–43. Elected to the

U.S. Senate as a Whig, 1851, Wade championed anti-slavery legislation; joined the Republican party when it was organized; voted against the (John J.) Critten-den Compromise, 1860; and during the Civil War led the Joint Congressional Committee on the Con-duct of the War, which supported a vigorous war policy. With other Radical Republicans, Wade con-sidered Pres. Abraham Lincoln's proposed Recon-struction policy too lenient. Wade and Sen. Henry W. Davis sponsored a radical Reconstruction bill, 1864; Lincoln pocket-vetoed the bill, whereupon Wade and Davis issued a manifesto accusing Lincoln of "dicta-torship." Later, Wade led opposition to Pres. Andrew Johnson's moderate Reconstruction plan, and for Johnson's impeachment; Wade particularly was criticized for this action, since as president pro tempore of the Senate, he was next in line for the presidency. He was an unsuccessful candidate for the Republican vice-presidential nomination, 1868. He retired from the Senate and resumed private law practice, 1869.

WADENA, city, W central Minnesota, seat of Wadena County, on the Great Northern and the Northern Pacific railroads, and U.S. highways 10 and 71; 130 miles NW of Minneapolis. The city, a live-stock-shipping center, has wholesale houses, a can-ning factory, and an ice-cream manufacturing plant. The Wesley Methodist Hospital is located in the city. Pop. (1960) 4,381.

WADESBORO, town, S North Carolina, seat of Anson County; on the Atlantic Coast Line, the Sea-board Air Line, and the Winston-Salem Southbound railroads; 45 miles ESE of Charlotte. Textile milling is the chief industry. Cottonseed oil and fertilizer are manufactured. The town was settled in 1785. Pop. (1960) 3,744.

WADI HALFA, town, N Sudan, Northern Prov-ince; on the Nile River, six miles below the Second Cataract, 450 miles N of Khartoum, with which it is connected by rail. The town has steamer service to Aswân. It is an important trade and transport center. Pop. (1956) 11,006.

WAD MEDANI, city, E central Sudan, capital of Blue Nile Province; on the Blue Nile River; 110 miles SE of Khartoum. Connected by railroad with Khar-toum, the city serves as an important shipping point for cotton, grain, and livestock. It is located in the Gezira Region, between the White and Blue Nile rivers. The Gezira area produces a large quantity of cotton due to effective irrigation with water from the Sennar Dam. Wad Medani is the site of an agricul-tural research station. Pop. (1956) 47,677.

WADSWORTH, JAMES SAMUEL, 1807–64, U.S. Civil War military figure, was born in Geneseo, N.Y. He was prominent in the Genesee Valley by reason of his large estates and his interest in the development of agriculture. Appointed brigadier general of volunteers, 1861, he commanded the defenses of Washington, 1862, and afterward distin-guished himself (especially at Gettysburg) as a divi-sion commander in the Army of the Potomac. He was mortally wounded in the Battle of the Wilderness, May 6, 1864.

WADSWORTH, city, NE Ohio, Medina County, on the Erie Railroad and U.S. highway 224; 33 miles S of Cleveland. The city is a trade center for a diversi-fied farming area. Valves, matches, dairy products, chemicals, brick and tile, and rubber are manu-factured. Pop. (1960) 10,635.

WAESCHE, RUSSELL RANDOLPH, 1886–1946, U.S. Coast Guard officer, was born in Thur-mont, Md., and graduated from the Coast Guard Academy, 1906. He became a line officer, first chief of the communications division, 1916, chief ordnance officer in Washington, 1928, and rear admiral and commandant of the Coast Guard, 1936. During World War II, Waesche was primarily responsible for the tremendous growth of the Coast Guard, and became the Guard's first admiral, 1945.

WAF. See WOMEN IN THE AIR FORCE.

WAFER, LIONEL, 1640?–1705, English surgeon and buccaneer, was probably born in Wales. He served as a ship's surgeon in the East Indies, practiced medicine in Jamaica, 1677–80, met the English pirate William Dampier, 1679, and went with him to the Isthmus of Panama, 1680. In 1681, probably because of a quarrel with Dampier, he was left behind with four mutineers. After spending four years with the Panamanian Indians, Wafer sailed with a French buccaneer, 1684, and rejoined Dampier, 1685. He lived in either Virginia or Pennsylvania, 1688–90, then returned to England, 1691, where he published his narrative, *A New Voyage and Description of the Isthmus of America* (1699), one of the first good de-scriptions of the Panamanian Isthmus and its Indian inhabitants, and also important because of its cir-cumstantial account of buccaneering.

WAGER, a bet or a contract by which two people may agree that a sum of money or other thing shall be paid or delivered to one of them, upon an uncertain event occurring. In many jurisdictions within the United States, wagers have been made illegal by statute; they were legal at common law. The distinc-tion between a wager and a valid contract is some-times drawn rather fine. In connection with stock, grain, and cotton where there are frequent sales for future delivery the distinction is based on whether there is a delivery of the commodity in the future or merely a settlement on the basis of the differences in market prices. The former is legal and is not con-sidered a wager, but the latter, interpreted by the courts, is a wager. A stake holder may be compelled to deliver the stake, even after the wager is complete by the turn of events, to the one who gave it, con-trary to the wager, or become liable. In some states, the whole transaction is tainted and the courts will not help any party to the wager.

WAGES, that share of the national income going to human labor of all types in return for effort ex-pended in the production of goods and services. Thus, a portion of an employer's income consists of wages received by him for his managerial services, and the same can also be said of a portion of a farm operator's income. In common usage, wages are re-ferred to as weekly remuneration for the services of blue-collar or production workers, in contrast to the monthly or annual "salaries" that are paid for the services of most white-collar, managerial, profession-al, and technical employees.

The economist commonly differentiates *money wages*, the actual dollars and cents paid to labor, from *real wages*, the amount of goods and services that can be purchased with money wages. Real wages depend on the relation between money wages and the cost of living and the movements of these two items respec-tively. After 1930, it also became common in the United States to distinguish "take-home pay," or direct wages, from "fringe benefits," or deferred wages, with the latter signifying wages withheld from the worker by the employer pending the occurrence of various contingencies such as illness, disability, death, and retirement. Take-home pay was subse-quently also affected by the withholding of federal personal income tax from the employee's pay by the employer.

Historical Development. The wage system as it was known at mid-twentieth century was a product of industrialization, although it was anticipated in many of the simpler societies that preceded the in-dustrial society. Wages were not a part of all eco-nomic systems, however. Neither slave labor, such as was much utilized by the ancient civilizations of Egypt, Greece, and Rome, nor the serfdom of the medieval manorial system, required the payment of wages.

As the manorial system gave way to growing trade and commerce in the latter Middle Ages, the payment of wages was increasingly practiced in the towns and cities. The cottage factory system of this period, which was under the control of the craft guilds (gilds), employed some human labor, for which nominal wages were paid (see GUILD). Each cottage factory was owned and operated by a master craftsman who employed apprentices for a stipulated period during which their room, board, and training in the trade constituted their only recompense. From apprenticeship the individual rose to the status of journeyman at which time he was entitled to nominal wages. If he saved his wages and worked hard, the journeyman might become a master craftsman in his own right one day, provided he could meet the guild requirements for master craftsmanship. Journeymen's wages were solely a matter of guild control, with the journeymen possessing no right to bargain over them. In the later stages of the system, however, journeymen, in self defense, organized yeoman guilds, the forerunners of unions, which attempted to better wages and working conditions by bargaining with the craft guilds. The latter had exploited journeymen by lengthening periods of apprenticeship, depressing wages, and raising requirements for the status of master craftsman. See FEUDAL SOCIETY, Towns, *Guilds and Town Government.*

With the coming of the Industrial Revolution in the eighteenth century, the factory system replaced the cottage factory (see INDUSTRIAL REVOLUTION). The resultant interdependent industrial economy, which of necessity evolved a money-exchange system of trade, developed into the wage system. As a result, a modern, mature, industrial country such as the United States is literally a nation of employees since upward of 75 to 80 per cent of its labor force consists of the recipients of wages or salaries. Apart from their importance as a determinant of economic status, wages figure importantly in the determination of the social status of individuals in the mature industrial society. That is, the prestige of an individual in such a society is highly dependent upon how much money he makes.

Wage Theory. Soon after the emergence of the industrial society with its expanding wage system, economists began trying to devise theoretical formulations that would explain the phenomenon of the over-all wage level as well as the matter of wage differentials. Early classical economists, such as David Ricardo in England and the physiocrats in France, advanced the subsistence theory of wages. This theory holds (1) that wages will tend to hover about the level of subsistence for workers, and (2) that workers' families will be maintained at a size sufficient to replenish the nation's labor supply. If, in a short-run period, wages should rise above subsistence, they will be brought back to subsistence level by an increase in the supply of available workers resulting from an increase in the rate of working-class population growth. Similarly, if wages fall below the subsistence level, a decrease in the rate of working-class population growth will bring them up to that level once again. This theory was tied inextricably to the population theory of Thomas R. Malthus, an English political economist who believed that there is an inevitable tendency for population growth to outstrip the ability of society to produce necessities of life, and that this tendency can only be offset by such natural limits on population growth as malnutrition, crime, disease, and war.

The subsistence theory was followed by the wages fund theory, as advanced by John Stuart Mill and others during the 1820's. According to this approach, wages are determined inexorably by the ratio between the supply of labor at a given time and place and the amount of employers' capital available for wages. The latter item was held to be a fixed wages fund whose magnitude cannot be affected by workers, worker organizations, or governmental action; its size is determined by the automatic functioning of economic laws in the labor and commodity markets.

Although Mill subsequently renounced the idea of fixed wages fund, the core of the theory was retained by the U.S. economist F. W. Taussig. Noting that wages were paid out of current production rather than out of some fixed fund, Taussig nevertheless asserted in 1896 that there are limits to which real wages can be expanded in the short run, although over the longer run real wages and other real incomes may seemingly be expanded without any limit except the one posed by the limits of man's ingenuity in improving the methods of production.

Late in the nineteenth century, the U.S. economist John Bates Clark and the English economist Alfred Marshall devised and introduced the marginal productivity theory of wages—the theory that continued to command the most attention and respect of economic theorists at mid-twentieth century. This theory holds that the real income of each factor of production, including labor, tends over the long run to equal the factor's contribution to the production process (see PRODUCTION, *Factors of Production*). In his decisions to employ additional units of factors, such as land, capital, and labor, the entrepreneur will find it most profitable to employ each factor up to the point where the marginal revenue it produces equals its marginal cost (see MARGINAL COST). Factor remuneration, such as the wage paid to labor, will theoretically tend to equal the marginal productivity of the last unit employed. If each factor has been precisely employed up to the point of equilibrium between its marginal cost and marginal revenue, the most efficient, or least costly, combination of the factors will have been achieved, and the result will be maximum profits for the entrepreneur. See MARGINAL UTILITY.

The reformation of the wages fund theory by Taussig, and the productivity theory of wages as advanced by Clark, heightened labor's hopes of achieving a rising real income in a progressive society, contrary to the dismal prospect implied for labor by earlier theories. Because of imperfections of competition in the labor market, however, and the weakness of profit maximization as a motivating force for a firm, wage theory at mid-twentieth century was generally considered to be unsatisfactory as an explanation of short-run wage determination. Insofar as the long run was concerned, many evidences seemed to point to the existence of a meaningful relationship between factor productivity and factor returns.

Short-Run Wage Determination. The shortcomings of wage theory as an explanation of short-run wage determination led to the development in the 1890's of the so-called bargaining theory, by economists Clark, Britain's A. C. Pigou, and others. This theory holds that wages in the short run depend upon the relative bargaining strengths of employers and employees, and that this has always been the case, except for the fact that individual bargaining tends to become "collective bargaining" as the employing unit increases in size. Carrying this analysis further in his range theory of the 1920's, Pigou pictured the two parties coming to collective bargaining with upper and lower bargaining limits in mind. If the two sets of bargaining limits overlap each other, the overlap constitutes an area of practical bargaining and, in most cases, a bargain will result some place within this area. If the two sets of bargaining limits do not overlap, then there is no area of practical bargaining and, assuming no change in the limits, there will be a breakdown in negotiations with a strike or lockout or both resulting. As the strike or lockout wears on, economic pressures will eventually force one or both parties to alter its bargaining limits so that an agreement becomes possible. This may require the services of a third party, such as a governmental mediation agency, which may be able to suggest a settlement acceptable to both parties. Pigou noted that the wage set by this test of bargaining strength will not necessarily be what is, in his definition, a fair or equitable wage. In his judgment, the resultant wage will only be fair if it corresponds to the limits set by labor's marginal productivity. He argued strongly for raising unfair wages—those that are below labor's marginal productivity—through more powerful labor organization, more aggressive bargaining by labor, and governmental intervention in the form of minimum wage legislation. This theory assumed that the employer was in a strategic position to adjust for wages that may be above labor's marginal productivity, by raising the over-all efficiency of the plant, cutting back employment, passing of increased costs on to the consumer, or using some combination of these three alternatives.

Pigou's approach was thought by some to adequately explain short-run wage determination in organized labor markets, which normally include the bulk of employees in major, key industries of the mature industrial economy. It did not, however, necessarily explain the process in unorganized labor markets. In such markets the employer determined wages more or less unilaterally, although he was subject to the influence of economic forces inside and outside his particular market. Under conditions of full employment the employer was thought to be influenced markedly by occurrences in organized labor markets. Hence, under these conditions, or even under conditions of very high-level employment, the collective wage determination process in the organized labor markets exerted a powerful influence on wage determination within unorganized markets.

There is much less inconsistency between the bargaining theory of short-run wage determination and the marginal productivity theory of long-run wage levels than would appear at first glance. The former describes the mechanism that determines the monetary price of labor in the short run; the latter is descriptive of the limits that exist relative to the long-run level of wages. If, in the short-run situation, wages are discovered to be above or below labor's marginal product, this discovery will tend to set in motion adjustments that will move the two toward closer agreement. If the wage is too low, labor may be expected eventually to press for upward adjustments through a more energetic union or union leadership; if the wage is too high, the entrepreneur may attempt to make the adjustments that he hopes will equate the wage with labor's marginal product.

Wage Trends in United States. One of the most obvious wage trends of the twentieth century was the tendency for both money and real wages to rise, with money wages rising faster than real wages. Thus, average hourly earnings of production workers in manufacturing industries rose from 19 cents per hour in 1909 to $2.29 per hour in 1960, an increase of about 1,105 per cent. During the same period average weekly earnings of the same group of workers rose from $9.84 to $91.75, an increase of about 832 per cent. The difference in the two percentages resulted from a 20 per cent decline over the period in the average length of the work week. Although money wages rose much faster than real wages, there was a marked improvement in the latter as well. In 1929–60 average real hourly rates for production workers in manufacturing industries rose by more than 230 per cent; over the century from the 1850's to the 1950's the increase was more than 400 per cent.

Another obvious trend in wages was their tendency to represent a relatively constant, major proportion of national income. Thus, in most of the years between 1920 and 1960, wages and salaries varied within the narrow limits of 65 to 70 per cent of national income in the United States. Highest percentages tended to be registered during periods of depression and unemployment, because profits of business firms dropped at a faster rate than did wages. Thus, in 1932–33, the worst years of the Great Depression, wages accounted for 73 per cent of national income, although about 25 per cent of the labor force was unemployed.

Probably the most spectacular wage trend noted in the years after 1930 was the increasing emphasis that was placed on deferred wages, or fringe benefits, and the relatively smaller emphasis that was placed upon the wage earner's take-home pay. For the economy as a whole, supplements to wages and salaries rose from only 1.1 per cent of total wages and salaries in 1929 to almost 7 per cent by 1960. The most pronounced shifts in wage composition occurred in the mining, communications, public utilities, manufacturing, finance, insurance, and real estate industries, and agriculture and service industries experienced the smallest shifts of this nature.

Between 1955 and 1960 several labor unions were successful in attaining a guaranteed annual wage in such basic manufacturing industries as steel, automobiles, farm equipment, aluminum, and several others. Most such guarantees were merely supplements to unemployment compensation. In the typical plan, the employer contributed to a trust fund a stipulated number of cents per man-hour until a maximum level was reached. Upon being laid off involuntarily, an unemployed worker could draw upon this fund so that for a stipulated period he would receive an amount ranging from 60 to 65 per cent of his regular pay when both unemployment compensation and the guaranteed annual wage benefits were taken into account. See WORKMEN'S COMPENSATION.

Gradually, during the first half of the twentieth century, the wage differential between skilled and unskilled workers narrowed. In 1907 the average skilled worker in the United States received a wage that was about 205 per cent of the average unskilled worker's wage. By 1955 this differential had dropped to about 135 per cent. After 1955, however, a tendency was observed for this trend to level out and to reverse itself slightly in isolated segments of the U.S. economy. Other trends in the U.S. wage structure included some reduction in geographical, industrial, occupation, and racial wage differentials. These differentials, however, still remained somewhat more pronounced than in most European industrial nations.

Methods of Wage Compensation. The traditional wage compensation method involved payment to the worker of a given wage per hour or per day worked; it was known as a straight time wage. Shortly after the advent of scientific management as developed by the U.S. industrial engineer Frederick W. Taylor (1856–1915) in the early 1900's, however, various types of incentive wage plans came into use. Under these plans the worker was paid a premium or bonus for better than standard production attainments. The incentive wage was based on the belief that the worker could be induced to work more efficiently if there was a possibility of increased financial reward. The incentive wage also hinged upon the observation that the speed of work in many situations was under the worker's control and that workers were not uniformly ambitious or efficient. By 1960, it was estimated that more than 25 per cent of all U.S. wage and salary earners were paid through some form of incentive plan. Many observers, however, anticipated a possible decline in the importance of incentive wage plans with the advance in automation, because of the worker's loss of control of the speed of production.

In an effort to keep wages abreast of rising costs of living, many unions secured escalator clauses in their wage contracts. Under such clauses, which covered over four million U.S. workers in 1960, quarterly adjustments were made in basic wage rates, the direction of the adjustment depending upon trends in the Consumers' Price Index. The typical clause usually contained a limit on downward revisions of wage rates in a given year but did not provide a ceiling on upward revisions.

In an effort to bring about greater uniformity of wage rates for the same type of work and to achieve more objective wage determination, many firms after World War I, and many more after World War II set up formal job evaluation programs (see Job Evaluation). Such arrangements typically involved objective evaluations of jobs on the basis of certain factors or characteristics common to all jobs, but present in varying degrees among jobs. On the basis of a ranking of jobs with respect to such factors as responsibility, safety, and mental and physical demands, wage rates that allegedly reflected differences in job content were assigned. Although trade unions often opposed job evaluation plans as being too subjective and as interfering with their right to bargain collectively over wages, such plans were recognized as working well under certain conditions, especially where they had been jointly drawn and administered by labor and management.

Governmental Regulation. Although the United States was originally committed, at least in theory, to a policy of nonintervention by government in the labor market, the twentieth century brought increasing governmental regulation of wages at both state and federal levels. The individual states began enacting minimum wage legislation in 1912, when Massachusetts passed such a law; within 11 years, 14 other states had voted such legislation. These laws, however, were applicable only to the wage rates of women and children who were considered weak bargainers in the labor market. This trend was interrupted, however, when the U.S. Supreme Court took the position that such legislation was unconstitutional, 1923.

The state minimum wage law movement was revived during the early 1930's but again the judiciary held such legislation to be unconstitutional. In 1937, however, the minimum wage law of the state of Washington was upheld in the courts; 32 states enacted minimum wage laws, 1937–60, but approximately two-thirds of them were applicable only to women and children.

Many states enacted legislation affecting the time, place, and method of wage payment. Thus, it was not uncommon to find states requiring that wages be paid at least once every two weeks; that wages not be paid in or near a tavern; and that wages not be paid in company scrip or other paper that would typically circulate at a discount in all but company-owned places of business.

One of the oldest types of state wage legislation, and one that at mid-twentieth century existed in every state, is the mechanics' lien law. This type of legislation, in effect since the mid-1800's in many industrial states, protects the interests of workers on construction projects by giving them a lien on the construction property. In the event of bankruptcy of the construction firm, the interests of unpaid workers are given priority over the claims of the firm's creditors and must be honored in full before the creditors' claims are given attention.

At the federal level, there were, at mid-twentieth century, three principal laws relating to minimum wages. The best known of these is the Wage and Hour Law, or Fair Labor Standards Act, of 1938. This Act applied to most workers employed in the production of goods for interstate commerce. The originally established minimum wage of 25 cents per hour was gradually raised to 40 cents by 1945, 75 cents by 1949, $1 by 1956 and $1.25 by 1961. The other federal minimum wage laws were the Davis-Bacon Act of 1931 and the Walsh-Healey Act of 1936. The former sponsored by Sen. James J. Davis (R-Pa.) and Rep. Robert L. Bacon (R-N.Y.), empowered the secretary of labor to determine prevailing wage rates for given types of labor in various localities and required firms working on government contracts for public works and construction to pay the prevailing rates as announced by the secretary of labor. The Walsh-Healey Act, sponsored by Sen. Thomas J. Walsh (D-Mont.) and Rep. Arthur D. Healey (D-Mass.), made similar provision with respect to firms having government contracts for supplies and equip-

ment in excess of $10,000. The so-called Copeland Kickback Law, sponsored by Sen. Royal S. Copeland (D-N.Y.), and enacted in 1934 to insure the enforcement of the Davis-Bacon Act, prohibited the rebate of legally required wages, or any portion thereof, to the employer or his agents. These laws are administered by the Wage and Hour and Public Contracts Division of the U.S. Department of Labor.

Various federal laws have also been enacted to regulate the methods and certainty of wage payment. Under the Wage and Hour Law, scrip, tokens, credit cards, coupons, and similar media are prohibited as unlawful means of wage payment. The Miller Act of 1935, sponsored by Rep. John E. Miller (D-Ark.), applying to all contracts over $2,000 between the federal government and private firms for the construction, alteration, or repair of any public building or public works, required the prime contractor to furnish a performance bond to protect the U.S. government with respect to fulfillment of the contract, and a payment bond to protect workers who may have wage claims arising under the contract. If such claims were not paid within 90 days after the last day worked, laborers were empowered to sue on the contractor's payment bond for the amounts due.

Finally, during World War II and the Korean conflict, the federal government attempted to freeze wages, profits, and prices in order to curb inflationary tendencies. In democratic, "free enterprise" nations, such action was generally considered appropriate only during wartime emergencies.

Chester A. Morgan

Bibliog.—American Assembly, Graduate School of Business, Columbia University, *Wages, Prices, Profits and Productivity* (1959); Jules Backman, *Wage Determination: An Analysis of Wage Criteria* (1959); David W. Belcher, *Wage and Salary Administration* (1955); Eugene J. Benge, *Compensating Employees* (1953); Irving Bernstein, *Arbitration of Wages* (1954); William G. Bowen, *Wage Behavior in the Postwar Period: An Empirical Analysis* (1961); Charles W. Brennan, *Wage Administration: Plans, Practices, and Principles* (1959); Phil Carroll, *Better Wage Incentives* (1957); Allan M. Cartter, *Theory of Wages and Employment* (1959); Paul H. Douglas, *Theory of Wages* (1957); William J. Fellner, *Competition Among the Few: Oligopoly and Similar Market Structures* (1949); Robert W. Gilmour, *Industrial Wage and Salary Control* (1956); Abraham L. Gitlow, *Wage Determination Under National Boards* (1953); William Gomberg, *Trade Union Analysis of Time Study* (1955); International Economic Association, *Theory of Wage Determination* (1957); John M. Keynes, *General Theory of Employment, Interest and Money* (1936); Adolph Langsner and Herbert G. Zollitsch, *Wage and Salary Administration* (1961); J. Keith Louden, *Wage Incentives* (1959); Lawrence C. Lovejoy, *Wage and Salary Administration* (1959); Charles A. Myers and George P. Shultz, *Dynamics of a Labor Market: A Study of the Impact of Employment Changes on Labor Mobility, Job Satisfactions, and Company and Union Policies* (1951); Benjamin W. Niebel, *Motion and Time Study: An Introduction to Methods, Time Study and Wage Payment* (1958); Jan Pen, *Wage Rate Under Collective Bargaining* (1959); Frank C. Pierson, *Community Wage Pattern* (1953); Ben S. Puchaski, *What You Can Earn in 250 Different Careers* (1959); Lloyd G. Reynolds and Cynthia H. Taft, *Evolution of Wage Structure* (1956); Benjamin C. Roberts, *National Wages Policy in War and Peace* (1958); David R. Roberts, *Executive Compensation* (1959); Donald J. Robertson, *Factory Wage Structures and National Agreements* (1960); Kurt W. Rothschild, *Theory of Wages* (1955); Robert E. Sibson, *Wages and Salaries: A Handbook for Line Managers* (1960); Jack W. Stieber, *Steel Industry Wage Structure: A Study of the Joint Union-Management Job Evaluation Program in the Basic Steel Industry* (1960); George W. Taylor and Frank C. Pierson, eds., *New Concepts in Wage Determination* (1957); Newman A. Tolles and Robert L. Raimon, *Sources of Wage Information: Employer Associations* (1952); John W. Walch, *Complete Handbook on Wage and Price Controls* (1951); Sidney Weintraub, *Approach to the Theory of Income Distribution* (1958); William B. Wolf, *Wage Incentives as a Managerial Tool* (1957); Wladimir S. Woytinsky and Others, *Employment and Wages in the United States* (1953); James S. Youtsler, *Labor's Wage Policies in the Twentieth Century* (1956).

WAGNER, JOHN PETER, called Honus, or the Flying Dutchman, 1874–1955, U.S. baseball player, a member of the Baseball Hall of Fame, was born in Carnegie, Pa. He played with the National League teams of Louisville, 1897–99, and Pittsburgh, 1900–17. Considered the greatest shortstop of all time, he also was the league batting champion eight years, had a lifetime batting average of .329, and set numerous playing records.

WAGNER, RICHARD, 1813–83, German composer, was born Richard Wilhelm Wagner in Leipzig, the ninth child of a police-court clerk. His father died a few months after the child's birth, and a year later his mother married Ludwig Geyer (1780–1830), an actor, writer, and artist who had some influence on the boy. At the age of 14 Wagner was writing a "Shakespearean" tragedy; then, having fallen in love with the music of Karl Maria von Weber and Ludwig van Beethoven, he decided to write music for his drama, and began to study with Gottlieb Müller. He entered the University of Leipzig, 1830, and at the same time continued his music studies with Christian Theodor Weinlig (1780–1842). When he was 20, Wagner became chorus master at Würzburg, and during the next few years he conducted for short periods at Magdeburg, Königsberg, and Riga, meanwhile trying his hand at the composition of opera. In 1836 he married an actress, Minna Planer (died 1866), and the following year became *Kapellmeister* at Riga, where he completed the first two acts of his opera, *Rienzi*. In 1839 he moved to Paris.

Early Career. The years that followed were filled with poverty and struggle for recognition. His *Rienzi* was produced in Dresden, 1842, and this opera, which followed the familiar Italian pattern, was strikingly successful; but *Der fliegende Holländer* (The Flying Dutchman), 1841, produced in Dresden six months later and showing much more of the Wagnerian style, was far less enthusiastically received. In 1843 Wagner became one of the conductors of the Dresden opera; but his *Tannhäuser* (1844), produced in 1845, was too new for the audience. But Franz Liszt, who admired it greatly, produced it in Weimar, 1848, and thus laid the foundation for a one-sided friendship that Wagner repeatedly abused and exploited in later years.

The *Ring*. Annoyed by the fact that the Dresden opera was afraid to produce *Lohengrin* (1848), Wagner took part in the revolutionary agitation of 1848 and soon had to flee Germany, taking refuge in Zürich. During the long years of his exile he was sustained both materially and artistically by Liszt, who produced *Lohengrin* in Weimar, 1850. Meanwhile, Wagner had begun to work on his great tetralogy, *Ring des Nibelungen*, based on legends of the Norse Nibelungs. This work consists of four operas: *Das Rheingold* (1854), *Die Walküre* (1856), *Siegfried* (1869), and *Götterdämmerung* (1874). In 1855 he conducted a series of concerts with the London Philharmonic Orchestra, which found it difficult to accept his musical ideas. *Tristan und Isolde* (1859) was rehearsed in Vienna, 1861, but was dropped because the company found it too difficult; it was finally produced in Munich, 1865. Meanwhile, a performance of *Tannhäuser* in Paris had been received with such hostility that Wagner became a national hero in Germany and was allowed to return; however, recognition and understanding of the merits of Wagner's work as such were slow in coming. Wagner's financial troubles ended in 1864, however, when King Louis II (Ludwig II) of Bavaria became his patron; there followed performances of *Tristan*, *Die Meistersinger von Nürnberg*, *Das Rheingold*, and *Die Walküre*. Wagner's *Siegfried Idyll* (1870) was composed to celebrate the birth of his son Siegfried and the birthday of his second wife, Cosima von Bülow. The music was played for the first time early Christmas morning, her birthday. By 1872 he had finished the other two Nibelung dramas and in 1876 the first great Bayreuth performance of the four operas took place in the famous opera house designed by Wagner himself. This artistic success was followed, 1882, by the tremendous financial triumph of *Parsifal*, based on the Holy Grail legend. The later years of Wagner's life were devoted to production of the operas, every detail of which he personally directed.

Wagner's Musical and Dramatic Theories. His treatment of the opera form consisted not so much of innovations as of a fundamental and revolutionary change in structure. He did not, in fact, even call his works operas, but rather music-dramas. The combination of rhetoric and melodrama in Italian opera gave place in Wagnerian music-drama to a unified art form in which music, action, scenery, and poetry were combined to produce a unified effect of tremendous emotional impact. Wagner enlarged the orchestra and enriched its tonal potentialities, while at the same time giving it tonal unity. Further, the orchestra was to be more than an accompaniment to the singers; both were to be a part of the music and were to be truly a synthesis. The musical and dramatic elements were similarly unified. This striving for unity was characteristic of Wagner's total approach to his drama, no detail of which was too small to merit his attention.

One of Wagner's most enduring contributions to the language of music was his development of the leitmotiv—a theme associated with a particular character and reiterated whenever the character appears. Wagner invented neither the term nor the function of the leitmotiv, but he made it uniquely his. By mid-twentieth century, no composer's use of leitmotivs had surpassed Wagner's in flexibility and power.

His musical theories were set forth in books such as *The Art of the Future* (1849) and *Opera and Drama* (1851). Musically, his work is distinguished by long chromatic developments, thick harmony, and use of brasses and woodwinds; his music has a rich emotional texture that suits the heroic themes and passionate motivations of his operas. His work is considered the epitome of the Romantic movement in music (see ROMANTICISM). His influence on musicians who followed him was great. Critics point out that the greatest of his operas are those of his later period, *Die Meistersinger*, *Tristan*, the Nibelung tetralogy, and *Parsifal*, although these are the most infrequently performed. In them his style found fullest expression. See MUSIC, Historical Evolution of Music, *Romantic Nationalism;* OPERA, Italian Opera the Basic Form, *Wagner*.

Cosima Wagner, 1837–1930, the daughter of Franz Liszt and Countess Marie Agoult, and the wife of Richard Wagner, was born in Como, Italy. She married Hans Guido von Bülow, 1857, but was divorced from him, 1869, whereupon she married Wagner, 1870, having already given birth to three of his children. She was helpful in organizing the Bayreuth festivals and following her husband's death was their artistic director until 1909, when her son Siegfried Wagner succeeded her.   IRWIN FISCHER

BIBLIOG.—Louis Barthou, *Prodigious Lover: New Aspects in the Life of Richard Wagner* (1927); Jacques M. Barzun, *Darwin, Marx, Wagner: Critique of a Heritage* (1958); Paul Bekker, *Richard Wagner: His Life in His Work* (1936); Maurice Boucher, *Political Concepts of Richard Wagner* (1950); Edward Dannreuther, *Wagner and the Reform of the Opera* (1904); W. Ashton Ellis, *The Life of Richard Wagner* 6 vols. (1900–8); Henry T. Finck, *Wagner and His Works; The Story of His Life, with Critical Comment* 2 vols. (1904); Lawrence Gilman, *Wagner's Operas* (1937); James C. Hadden, *Operas of Wagner: Their Plots, Music and History* (1935); Gertrude Hall, *Wagnerian Romances* (1925); Bertita Harding, *Magic Fire: Scenes Around Richard Wagner* (1953); Corinne S.D. Heline, *Esoteric Music Based on the Musical Seership of Richard Wagner* (1948); William J. Henderson, *Richard Wagner, His Life and His Dramas* (1923); George A. Hight, *Richard Wagner: A Critical Biography* 2 vols. (1925); Francis Hueffer, *Richard Wagner, 1813–1883* (1929); Philip D. Hurn and Waverley L. Root, *Truth About Wagner* (1930); Hans Jachmann, *Wagner and His First Elizabeth* (1944); Robert L. Jacobs, *Wagner* (1949); Julius Kapp, *Loves of Richard Wagner* (1952); Gustav Kobbe, *Wagner's Music-Dramas Analyzed With the Leading Motives* (c.1932); Albert Lavignac, *Music Dramas of Richard*

Wagner and His Festival Theatre in Bayreuth (1898); Charles A. Lidgey, *Wagner* (1904); Woldemar Lippert, *Wagner in Exile, 1849–62* (1930); Thomas Mann, *Freud, Goethe, Wagner* (1937); Angelo Neumann, *Personal Recollections of Richard Wagner* (c.1915); Ernest Newman, *Life of Richard Wagner* 4 vols. (1933–1946), *Wagner as Man and Artist* (1924); Guy de Pourtales, *Richard Wagner* (1935); Robert M. Rayner, *Wagner and Die Meistersinger* (1940); Benjamin M. Steigman, *Unconquerable Tristan: The Story of Richard Wagner* (1933); Jack M. Stein, *Richard Wagner and the Synthesis of the Arts* (1960); Leon Stein, *Racial Thinking of Richard Wagner* (1950); Edward M. Terry, *Richard Wagner Dictionary* (1939); Walter J. Turner, *Wagner* (1949); Richard Wagner, *My Life* (1936); William Wallace, *Richard Wagner as He Lived* (1933); Pearl C. Wilson, *Wagner's Dramas and the Greek Tragedy* (1919); H. L. Plaine, ed., *Darwin, Marx, and Wagner: A Symposium* (1962); Robert Donington, *Wagner's "Ring" and Its Symbols* (1963).

WAGNER, ROBERT FERDINAND, 1877–1949, U.S. lawyer and legislator, was born in Hesse-Nassau, Germany, emigrated to the United States in childhood, and studied at the College of the City of New York and the New York Law School. He was a member of the New York senate, 1909–18, a justice of the New York supreme court, 1919–26, and U.S. Senator from New York, 1927–49. He was responsible for the framing of much important New Deal legislation of the 1930's, such as the National Industrial Recovery Act (NIRA), Social Security Act, National Labor Relations Act (generally known as the Wagner Act), and the U.S. Housing Act of 1937.

WAGNER, SIEGFRIED, in full Helferich Siegfried Wagner, 1869–1930, German composer and conductor, only son of Richard Wagner, was born in Liebschen, near Luzern, Switzerland. His father wrote the *Siegfried Idyll* for his infant son. Siegfried studied music with Engelbert Humperdinck and Julius Kniese, conducted often at the Bayreuth festivals from 1896, and succeeded his mother Cosima as administrator and artistic director at Bayreuth, 1909. Among his compositions are symphonic poems, the orchestral scherzo *Und wenn die welt voll teufel wär* (1923), and 15 unremarkable operas.

WAGNER-JAUREGG, JULIUS, 1857–1940, Nobel prize-winning Austrian neurologist and psychiatrist, was born Julius Wagner von Jauregg in Wels; a socialist edict later forced Austrian nobles to drop "von" from their names, hence "Wagner-Jauregg." He was educated at the University of Vienna, and was an assistant in pathology there, 1880–82, and in the psychiatric clinic, 1883–89. He taught psychiatry and neurology at the University of Graz, 1889–93, and in Vienna, 1893–1928. In 1917, 30 years after he had first observed that syphilitic paretics showed improvement when suffering from high fever, Wagner-Jauregg introduced the use of tertian malaria as a fever-producing agent to cure paresis. Although a revolutionary technique, fever therapy soon came to be generally accepted, and won its founder the 1927 Nobel prize in medicine and physiology "for his discovery of the therapeutic value of malaria inoculation in the treatment of dementia paralytica." Among Wagner-Jauregg's other major contributions to medicine were his treatment of cretinism with thyroid gland preparations, his use of iodine in the treatment of goiter, and his interest in forensic psychiatry.

WAGONER, city, E Oklahoma, seat of Wagoner County; on the Missouri-Kansas-Texas, the Missouri Pacific, and the Kansas, Oklahoma and Gulf railroads; 35 miles S of Tulsa. The city is a trade center for an agricultural area. Oil and gas wells are nearby. Wagoner was founded late in the 1880's. Pop. (1960) 4,469.

WAGON TRAINS, in the history of the North American West, were organized for convenience and protection of transportation across the plains. Trains elected a captain and usually hired a guide, who picked camping sites after daily journeys of 15 to 18 miles. To form a corral for stock, and as a protection against Indians, the wagons were usually formed into a close circle at night. Indians attacked fewer wagon trains than is commonly supposed, but there were a few massacres.

Wagons were first taken over the Santa Fe Trail by William Becknell, 1822. Mules were used at first, and always were more plentiful at the western terminus. Maj. Bennett Riley first used oxen, 1827, and they soon became popular with freighters. On the Oregon Trail, M. L. Sublette took a train of 10 five-mule wagons to the trappers' rendezvous on Wind River, 1830, and Capt. B. L. E. Bonneville crossed South Pass with the wagons, 1832. Marcus Whitman brought a wagon—cut down to a two-wheeled cart—in 1836, but within a few years wagons reached Oregon. The first wagon train of emigrants was that led by John Barleson and John Bidwell, 1841; it finally reached California, but the emigrants had been forced to abandon their wagons along the way. In 1843, a train led by Peter H. Burnett, Jesse Applegate, and Marcus Whitman brought most of its 120 wagons to the Columbia River in Oregon. The Stevens-Murphy-Townsend party reached California, 1844, with 5 ox-drawn wagons, having started with 11. A wagon trail from Santa Fe to California was marked by Lt. Col. Philip St. George Cooke with the Mormon Battalion, 1846–47.

Most of the traffic over the Santa Fe Trail was commercial, but an increasing number of emigrants went West, particularly over the Oregon Trail, 1843–48, increasing to many thousands after the discovery of gold in California, 1849. The trains were formed at Independence, Mo., Westport, Mo., Bellevue, Nebr., and other towns that from time to time formed the eastern terminus.

The Prairie Schooner, so-called, was a large wagon with the sides sloping outward and covered with canvas supported by six or seven arching bows. The Murphy Wagons made in St. Louis and Kansas City were also popular. See CONESTOGA WAGON; COVERED WAGON.

After completion of the transcontinental railroad, wagon trains decreased greatly in number, but were still used for freighting and occasional emigrants, sometimes traveling alone as Indian troubles ceased. Few wagon trains were to be seen after 1880. See WEST, THE. DON RUSSELL

WAGTAIL, any of the Old World songbirds belonging to the family *Motacillidae*. The wagtail is approximately six inches in length with a slender, tipped tail. Its plumage is black, gray, and white in color and is not streaked. Its most distinctive characteristic is its walk. Since it is not a hopping bird, it walks or runs on the ground, jerking the latter half of its body and tail. The wagtail favors the edge of streams, eating the insects that it finds in this habitat. The only wagtail found in the Western Hemisphere, the yellow wagtail, *Moticilla flava*, has bright yellow undersides and a long, slender tail. The other species are distributed through Europe and Asia.

WAHABIS, an Islamic sect, founded about the middle of the eighteenth century by Mohammed ibn-Abd-al-Wahab in Nejd, Arabia. He proclaimed anew the sovereign validity of the original Koran; denounced traditional glosses, saint worship, and pilgrimages (except that to the Kaaba at Mecca); condemned luxury in dress and living; and prohibited the use of wine and tobacco. The youthful prophet was driven from city to city until he found asylum with an Arab chief named Mohammed Ibn Saud.

A puritan crusade was undertaken, which was crowned by the conquest of Medina, and resulted in the establishment of a militant church, at issue both with the infidel and with other forms of Islam. After a conflict of nearly 30 years, Ibrahim Pasha of Egypt succeeded in crushing the temporal power of the Wahabis in Arabia, 1818. The Wahabite Kingdom was re-established in central Arabia, 1824; suffered defeat, 1838; was renewed, 1842; was defeated again, 1891; and returned to power again, 1900. At mid-twentieth century, the movement was less militant and puritanic than it had been, and had spread considerably. It played a large part in Muslim life, especially in its propaganda.

WAHIAWA, city Hawaii, central Oahu, located 17 miles NW of Honolulu. The city's business interests serve military personnel from the nearby Schofield Barracks and Wheeler Field. It is also located in one of the world's richest pineapple-producing areas. Pop. (1960) 15,512.

WAHPETON, city, SE North Dakota, seat of Richland County; on the Red River of the North, at the mouth of the Boise de Sioux River. First known as Chahinkapa, the town was renamed Wahpeton in 1893. Wahpeton is a trade center for the surrounding agricultural region. Flour, sheet metal, and dairy products are manufactured. Pop. (1960) 5,876.

WAIKATO RIVER, New Zealand on North Island, rises on the slopes of Ruapehu Mountain and flows N through Lake Taupo, then NW to enter the Tasman Sea after a course of about 200 miles. Four miles below its emergence from Lake Taupo, the river drops 30 feet over picturesque Huka Falls. The river has been dammed in its middle course, forming two lakes, Arapuni and Karapiro. Hamilton and Cambridge are the most important towns on the banks of the Waikato. The river valley was the scene of the chief conflict between the British and the Maori in 1863 and 1864.

WAINEWRIGHT, THOMAS GRIFFITHS, 1794–1852, English art critic, painter, and poisoner, was born in Chiswick. In 1819 Wainewright began to contribute critiques to *The Literary Pocket-Book, Blackwood's Magazine,* and the *Foreign Quarterly Review,* but he is most often associated with the *London Review,* for which he wrote articles, 1820–23, under the pen name Janus Weathercock. He exhibited paintings at the Royal Academy, 1821–25. He insured his sister-in-law's life for a considerable fortune, 1830, but the insurance companies became suspicious when she conveniently died a few months later, and refused to pay. Wainewright spent the next seven years in France. He returned to England, 1837, was promptly arrested, convicted of an 1826 forgery, and sentenced to life imprisonment. It is thought that, in addition to his sister-in-law, he poisoned his uncle, his mother-in-law, and a friend from Norfolkshire. Wainewright's exploits inspired Charles Dickens' novel *Hunted Down* and Bulwer Lytton's *Lucretia,* as well as an essay by Oscar Wilde.

WAINWRIGHT, JONATHAN MAYHEW, 1883–1953, U.S. military figure, was born in Walla Walla, Wash., and was graduated from West Point, 1906. He served in the Jolo Expedition to the Philippines, 1909–10, and in France, 1918. He was promoted to major general and sent to the Philippines, 1940; early in World War II, when Gen. Douglas MacArthur was ordered to Australia, March, 1942, Wainwright succeeded him as commander in the Philippines. He withdrew from Bataan Peninsula into Corregidor Fortress in April, surrendered to the Japanese on May 6 and was kept prisoner in a camp in Manchuria until he was rescued, August, 1945. In the same year he was promoted to general and awarded the Congressional Medal of Honor. After retiring from the army in 1947, General Wainwright became an insurance executive. He was the author of *General Wainwright's Story* (1946).

WAIT, an English street musician. The original waits were town watchmen who played musical instruments to indicate the hour. During the fifteenth and sixteenth centuries many waits organized themselves into bands that played for public occasions and during the Christmas season. Each band developed its own melodies, which came to be named for the group, such as the *Chester Waits.* The musicians usually played hautboys, which were also called waits. In twentieth-century usage, anyone playing music in the streets during the Christmas season is called a wait.

WAITE, MORRISON REMICK, 1816–88, U.S. jurist, was born in Lyme, Conn., was graduated from Yale College, and practiced in Maumee, Ohio, and later in Toledo, gaining a wide reputation in real estate law. He served one term in the Ohio legislature, was a U.S. counsel in the Geneva arbitration of the *Alabama* claims, 1871–72, and was president of the Ohio Constitutional Convention, 1873–74. Appointed chief justice of the U.S. Supreme Court, 1874, he served during the presidencies of U. S. Grant, Rutherford Hayes, James Garfield, Chester Arthur, and Grover Cleveland. Among Waite's more important decisions were those concerning the Granger movement and railroad rates.

WAIVER, the abandonment of certain legal rights. A waiver of rights can be made known either expressly, through words, or implicitly, through conduct. If, for example, a new contract is made about the subject matter of an old contract, a breech of the old contract will be waived; and in legal proceedings a person will be held to waive irregularity if he does not immediately take objection to it. But a man must know what his rights are before he can be held to have waived them. This is an equitable doctrine, and generally the waiver must cause another to change his position, or cause him to neglect to take certain steps in reliance upon it, in order to make it binding. Thus, unless a gift is made, a waiver of one's rights to collect a debt will not be binding, unless there was consideration. See EQUITY; ESTOPPEL.

WAKAMATSU, city, Japan, N central Honshu, Fukushima Prefecture; 125 miles N of Tokyo. The city is located in a hilly, volcanic region, and is five miles W of the volcanic crater lake, Inawashiro. The city is a rail and highway junction center. Silk, lacquer goods, and soy sauce are manufactured. It is the center for large hydroelectric projects. The capture of the Wakamatsu Castle, owned by the Tokugawa family, marked the end of the Japanese civil war, 1868. The castle and most of the city were burned following the surrender, but Wakamatsu's location, guarding the approaches to northeast Honshu, insured its rapid rebuilding. (For population, see Japan map in Atlas.)

WAKAMATSU, city, Japan, N Kyushū, Fukuoka Prefecture, lying on the coast of the Sea of Japan, just E of the Shimonoseki Strait, 95 miles NNE of Nagasaki. The city occupies a narrow coastal strip and reclaimed land as well as adjacent hill slopes. Its port is one of the most important in Japan, its principal export being coal from the nearby Chikuho field, which is shipped in coastal vessels to the ports of southwest Japan. Its imports—metals, machinery, and foodstuffs—exceed its exports. Wakamatsu has a small shipbuilding yard, machine and tool shops, a steel mill, and an oil refinery.

WAKASHAN, a language family of North American Indians, most of whom lived on Vancouver Island, B.C., the nearby shores of British Columbia, and Cape Flattery, Wash. The languages and dialects of the Nootka and Kwakiutl Indians are the principal branches of the stock.

WAKAYAMA, city, Japan, S Honshu, capital of Wakayama Prefecture, on the Kii Peninsula, near the E shore of the Kii Channel leading to the Inland Sea; at the mouth of the Kino River, a railway junction 38 miles SSW of Osaka. Wakanoura, about three miles distant, is its port. The city is a processing center for a region in which oranges, grain, rice, tea, cotton, and mulberries are grown. Wakayama has important spinning, weaving, and dyeing and bleaching industries in cotton, flannel, and silk. Wakayama Castle, in the center of the city, was built in 1585, and belonged to an influential Japanese family. During World War II U.S. bombs destroyed about half of the city. (For population, see Japan map in Atlas.)

WAKE, called Patron Day in Ireland, a festival, involving much merriment and jollity, that was formerly held in Roman Catholic parishes on the anniversary of the dedication of a church to some saint; the practice of having such festivals fell into general disrepute and disuse during the twentieth century.

A similar festival, the lyke or lych-wake, which involved "watching over" a dead body, was once very common in the Highlands of Scotland, in Ireland, and among the Irish residents of the United States, but by mid-twentieth century was being less frequently celebrated. The lych-wake was commonly the occasion for much drinking, dancing, singing of "the old songs," the proposing of elaborate mock-heroic or lachrymose toasts to the memory of the deceased, who was usually laid out in state in another room of the house. The practice was probably related in some way to the so-called Death Watch of antiquity and the Middle Ages, when a number of the deceased's family always remained with a corpse until it was safely buried lest evil spirits enter it and corrupt it in some way, perhaps by stealing the soul and turning it over to the devil. The merriment and jollity of the lych-wake was possibly related to the age-old custom, common to the folk-cultures of parts of Africa, those parts of Europe that border on the Mediterranean Sea, on the islands in the Caribbean Sea, and in parts of the southern United States, that one should cry at the birth and rejoice at the death.

WAKEENEY, city, NW Kansas, seat of Trego County; on the Union Pacific Railroad, and U.S. highways 40 and 283; 82 miles N of Dodge City. The city is a trade center for an agricultural area. Oil wells are in the vicinity. WAKEENEY was incorporated in 1880. Pop. (1960) 2,808.

WAKEFIELD, town, NE Massachusetts, Middlesex County; on the Boston and Maine Railroad; 10 miles N of Boston. Rattan and willow furniture, shoes, knit goods, dies, and electrical goods are manufactured. Wakefield was first settled in 1639 and incorporated in 1812. It was named in honor of Cyrus Wakefield, a pioneer manufacturer. Pop. (1960) 24,295.

WAKEFIELD, county borough, N England, in the West Riding of Yorkshire on the river Calder, 8 miles S of Leeds. Wakefield, an industrial city, is a center of the West Riding woolen industry. Machinery, chemicals, and clothing are manufactured. During the Battle of Wakefield, 1460, Yorkists were defeated by the Lancastrians. Wakefield was incorporated in 1848, became a city in 1888, and was made a county borough in 1915. The Chapel of St. Mary, dating from the twelfth century, is located on a bridge over the Calder.

WAKE FOREST COLLEGE, a private, coeducational institution of higher learning, affiliated with the Baptist Church, and located at Winston-Salem, N.C. The school was chartered as Wake Forest Institute, 1833, and offered its first instruction the following year. It was rechartered as Wake Forest College in 1838. The divisions and their founding dates are the school of law, 1894; the school of medicine, 1941; and the school of business administration, 1949. A master's degree is offered in the school of medicine.

Wake Forest conducts a co-operative five-year program in engineering with Duke University and North Carolina State College of Agriculture and Engineering. A summer institute for high school teachers is sponsored by the National Science Foundation. There is a student-operated radio station. The library contains special collections of materials on the Baptists and on North Carolina. See COLLEGES AND UNIVERSITIES.

WAKE ISLAND, an atoll in the central Pacific, about 2,300 miles W of Honolulu, 1,800 miles ESE of Tokyo; area about 10 sq. mi.; there is no indigenous population. Wake, about 21 feet above sea level and roughly triangular in shape, consists of three sandy islets, Wake, the largest, Wilkes, and Peale, which are situated in a coral reef. The reef and islets enclose a shallow lagoon about four miles long. Wake Islet, on the southeast, is well covered with scrub forest, but the other islets are bare of vegetation. Fish, especially sharks, birds, hermit crabs, and rats are numerous. Because the atoll stands alone and quite low in the ocean, it was many years before its discovery (1796) by the British Captain Wake was verfied. Wake Island was charted by U.S. Commander Wilkes in 1841, but was not annexed by the United States until 1898. Wake Island became a cable station, and later (1935) it was made a stopover on the Pan American Airways route to Guam, when a hotel and other modern facilities were constructed on Peale Islet. After becoming a national defense area in February, 1941, military airfields were constructed on the island.

Wake Island was assaulted by Japanese forces on December 8, 1941, and after a noteworthy defense by the U.S. garrison, surrendered on December 23. Following the war Wake again became a civil and military air base. See WORLD WAR II.

WAKSMAN, SELMAN ABRAHAM, 1888–   , U.S. Nobel prize-winning microbiologist, was born in Priluka, Kiev, Russia. He came to the United States, 1910, studied at Rutgers University and at the University of California, and became a U.S. citizen, 1916. He began to teach at Rutgers, 1918, and was professor of microbiology there, 1942–58. He was microbiologist at the New Jersey Agricultural Experiment Station from 1921, and bacteriologist at Woods Hole Oceanographic Institute, 1930–42. Years of research on soil microbiology led to his discovery of actinomycin, 1940, streptothricin, 1942, and streptomycin, 1943. The discovery of streptomycin, announced in 1944, won him a Nobel prize in medicine and physiology, 1952. Among other antibiotics discovered by Waksman are neomycin, candicidin, and candidin. Waksman assigned most of the royalties from streptomycin to Rutgers for the establishment of the Institute of Microbiology. He wrote *Humus* (1936; 2nd ed. 1938), *Streptomycin, Its Nature and Application* (1949), *Soil Microbiology* (1952), *My Life with the Microbes* (1954), *Neomycin, Nature and Application* (1958). See NEOMYCIN; STREPTOMYCIN.

WALACHIA, a historical region of Rumania, bounded on the N and W by the Transylvanian Alps, on the E by the Dobruja Plateau, and on the S by the Danube River. The region's ancient inhabitants were the Getae, who were largely unaffected by Mediterranean civilization until conquered by the Romans early in the Christian Era. Subsequently they were Latinized so thoroughly that despite their later close association with Slavs, Turks, and other non-Latin peoples, their speech survived as the modern Romance language, Rumanian or Walachian—the latter name being derived from Vlach, the Slavonic name for the Latinized people (see VLACH). Walachia was overrun by many invaders during the centuries following the Roman withdrawal from the area late in the third century, but by the fourteenth century Walachia had emerged as an independent principality. It was then conquered by the Ottoman Turks, 1411, and except for the years 1595–1600, was ruled by Turkish administrators until early in the nineteenth century when, following the Greek revolt of 1821, the Turks sought to avert similar uprisings in Walachia and the nearby principality of Moldavia by granting them the right to elect their own rulers. In 1859 both provinces elected Alexandru Ioan Cuza as their prince, and under his rule they were united to form Rumania, 1861.

WALBRZYCH, German Waldenburg, city, SW Poland, in Wrocław province 40 miles SW of Breslau (Wrocław). The city is in a coal mining district and has manufactures of brick, wire, furniture.

porcelain and pottery, and linen textiles. The city is in the former German district of Lower Silesia, which became part of Poland after World War II. Pop. (1958 est.) 110,900.

WALCHEREN, island, SW Netherlands, in the province of Zeeland, lying at the mouth of the Schelde River, area about 80 sq. mi.; connected by rail and highway bridges with the peninsula of Beveland. Dikes surround much of the island, which is very low-lying, and frequently in danger of inundation by the sea. Sugar beets, vegetables, and wheat are grown. Seepage is controlled by pumps in constant operation. A canal runs across the island and connects the port of Vlissingen with the town of Middleburg, the capital of Zeeland. During World War II Walcheren was held by the Germans, who flooded large parts of the island. The British retook the island in 1944, and the dikes were rebuilt.

WALD, LILLIAN D., 1867–1940, U.S. social worker, was born in Cincinnati, Ohio. She was graduated from the New York Hospital Training School for Nurses, 1891, and entered medical school but gave that up, 1893, to found the Nurses' Settlement House (moved in 1895, and thereafter called the Henry Street Settlement). There she organized a pioneer public health visiting nurse service that by the time of her death employed 300 nurses. At Henry Street she also founded clubs for slum children, home economics classes for women and girls, and art and music workshops. Her other major contributions to social welfare included establishing in New York the first public school nursing service, 1902; urging the creation of a federal children's bureau, which Congress authorized in 1908; and interesting the American Red Cross in undertaking rural public health nursing. She served on many national and international commissions concerned with public welfare, and wrote *The House on Henry Street* (1915) and *Windows on Henry Street* (1934).

WALDECK, former province of Prussia, N central Germany, corresponding to the northern part of Hesse State, West Germany. Arolsen was its principal town. Waldeck was an independent state from the Middle Ages until 1867, when its prince resigned most of his sovereign rights to the king of Prussia. After World War I Waldeck was made a constituent state of the German Weimar Republic. In 1929 it was made a province of Prussia. After World War II, Prussia was dissolved and Waldeck was incorporated into Hesse.

WALDEMAR, or Valdemar, the name of four medieval rulers of Denmark.

Waldemar I, the Great, 1131–82, was born a week after the murder of his father, Canute Lavard, and ascended the throne, 1157. With his extremely able minister, Archbishop Absalon, he increased the power of the monarchy, allayed internal dissensions in the kingdom, and ushered in a period of considerable prosperity. He successfully opposed the Wends, a Slavic people who had long ravaged the Danish coast line from their homeland on the southern Baltic shore, and, after conquering their stronghold on the island of Rügen, 1169, converted them to Christianity. He was succeeded by his son, Canute VI.

Waldemar II, the Victorious, 1170–1241, was the second son of Waldemar I and brother of Canute VI. He came into power, 1202, and within a few years became the most powerful ruler in northern Europe. He hoped to attain *dominum maris baltici*—complete domination of the areas surrounding the Baltic Sea—and almost did so. Although his attempts to reduce Norway and Sweden were unsuccessful, he did manage to gain control of a large part of northwestern Germany, subjugating Holstein, Hamburg, Lübeck, and much of Mecklenburg. He undertook a crusade, 1219, against the heathen Estonians, and defeated them at the Battle of Arvel. On this latter occasion, the *Dannebrog*, now Denmark's national standard, is said to have fallen down miraculously from heaven in

response to the prayers of the Danish bishops. At the height of his power, Waldemar II was seized treacherously by Count Henry of Schwerin, and imprisoned with his son for two years, 1223–25. By the time of his release most of his conquests had been lost, including all of his German territories. Taking up arms again, he was defeated by a coalition of German princes at Bornhöved, 1227. Thereafter, except for intermittent periods of warfare, he devoted himself to domestic reforms within Denmark. It was by his order that the Danish laws were codified into the *Jydske Lov* (Jutland Code), 1241.

Waldemar III, died 1231, was the eldest son of Waldemar II. During the years of his maturity he acted as co-regent, with his father, of Denmark and its dominions.

Waldemar IV, Atterdag, 1320?–75, was the youngest son of Christopher II. He was educated, 1326–40, at the court of Emperor Louis of Bavaria, and returned to Denmark to ascend the throne, 1340. At the time of his accession, the kingdom was largely controlled by German princes. It was Waldemar IV's distinction that, by means of money, arms, and stratagem, he reunited Denmark under monarchial authority. He sold Estonia to the Teutonic Knights, 1346, and regained the old Danish provinces of Scania (Skåne), Halland, and Blekinge in Sweden. Driven by the perennial Danish dream of *dominium maris baltici*, he conquered Gotland, 1361, and returned to Denmark with the treasures of Wisby. This expedition involved him in a war with the Hanseatic states (see HANSEATIC LEAGUE), whose fleet he successfully beat off in 1362. In 1369, however, a coalition of the Hanseatic League with Sweden and Mecklenburg resulted in the burning of Copenhagen and the defeat of Danish troops. In desperation, Waldemar IV signed the humiliating Treaty of Straslund (1370), which subjected his kingdom to the domination of the Hanseatic cities. He was succeeded to the Danish throne, 1375, by his son-in-law, Haakon VI. See DENMARK, History, *Medieval Denmark*.

WALDEN, town, N Colorado, seat of Jackson County; on the Union Pacific Railroad; 95 miles NW of Denver. The town serves as a supply point for the outlying area in which grain and livestock are raised. Located nearby is a shallow, high-grade coal bed that is mined from the surface. Pop. (1960) 809.

WALDEN, a narrative by Henry David Thoreau (1817–62), published in 1854, describes Thoreau's experiences at Walden Pond, near Concord, Mass., where he lived from July 4, 1845, to Sept. 6, 1847, in a small house that he built with logs and second-hand planks and nails. He entered upon the project, he said, because he wished to be free to write a book (later published as *A Week on the Concord and Merrimack Rivers*, 1849), and "to live deliberately, to front only the essentials of life, and see if I could not learn what it had to teach, and not, when I came to die, discover that I had not lived." *Walden* contains Thoreau's careful observations of both nature and man's social, political, and economic life. Of fashions in clothes, for example, he wrote: "Dress a scarecrow in your last shift, you standing shiftless by, who would not soonest salute the scarecrow?" Of furniture: "I had three pieces of limestone on my desk, but I was terrified to find that they required to be dusted daily, when the furniture of my mind was all undusted still, and I threw them out in disgust," and "I would rather sit on a pumpkin and have it all to myself than be crowded on a velvet cushion." Thoreau had three chairs in his house: ". . . one for solitude, two for friendship, three for society. When visitors came in large and unexpected numbers there was but the third chair for them all, but they generally economized the room by standing up." See THOREAU, HENRY DAVID.

WALDEN POND, a small lake, E Massachusetts, near Concord, where Henry David Thoreau, American author and naturalist, lived in seclusion. For two years Thoreau made an intimate study of trees and birds and wrote of them in the journal which was published as *Walden*, one of the classics of American literature. Walden Pond Reservation, with an area of 144 acres surrounds Walden Pond.

WALDENSES, or Vaudois, a heretical Christian sect that developed in the south of France about 1170. It was one of many sects owing something to Manichaean dualism and individualism which were prevalent in the Middle Ages—sects prompted by a spirit of criticism, particularly in towns, against the worldly lives of the clergy.

A rich merchant of Lyons, Peter Waldo, about 1170 sold his property for the benefit of the poor and began a life of poverty so that, like St. Francis, he could be free to preach. For his followers, the Waldenses or "poor men of Lyons," he had a translation of the New Testament made into Provençal, and his preachers expounded the scriptures. Pope Alexander III approved of their poverty, but prohibited preaching without episcopal license in 1179. Waldo refused to obey and was excommunicated by Pope Lucius III in 1184. The sect spread north of the Alps and in Lombardy, though with slight theological differences between the two areas. Like the Cathari, those in the north held that oaths were forbidden by the gospel and that capital punishment should not be allowed. They believed that any layman might consecrate the Sacrament, and that the Roman Church was not the church of Christ. The Lombard group went further, believing that no one in mortal sin could consecrate the Sacrament, and that the Roman church ought not to be obeyed. But, unlike the Cathari, they had no official priesthood and were opposed to asceticism.

Before the onslaught of the Albigensian crusade around Toulouse, many of the Waldenses retreated from the cities and took refuge in the Alps in Piedmont, and gave their name to the valleys of the Vaudois. Their remoteness saved them from several attempts at suppression, though in a crusade against them in 1487 under Alberto de' Capitanei they were only saved by a fog. Even then they suffered severe losses. Under Charles II, duke of Piedmont, they were given freedom, and in 1530 two of their number met the German and Swiss reformers. By this time they were a simple community, accepting the ministrations of the regular priesthood but holding their own services with itinerant preachers. In 1532 the practices of the sect were brought in line with those of the Swiss congregations.

Persecution continued, however, particularly in 1655 when the fanatical attacks on them by Duke Charles Emmanuel II and Louis XIV called forth protests from England, including a sonnet by Milton, and from other Protestant powers. More persecution after the revocation of the Edict of Nantes in 1685 was aimed at complete extermination, but 2,600 were allowed to escape to Geneva. They returned under the protection of Victor Amadeus of Savoy, and, reduced to poverty, were partially maintained by money from England. Napoleon gave them support as a state church, and in the nineteenth century large sums of money were collected in Protestant countries to promote their welfare by building schools and a hospital.   ROBERT W. DUNNING

WALDO, SAMUEL LOVETT, 1783–1861, U.S. portrait painter, born in Windham, Conn. In his early days in Connecticut and Charleston, S.C., he was not a success, but after a three-year stay in London (1806–9), he returned to New York to become very popular. In 1820 he joined with a former pupil, William Jewett, in a successful painting partnership. For forty years, they painted portraits; customarily Waldo painted the face and Jewett the body and clothes. Waldo's best-known works are a portrait of Andrew Jackson and a self-portrait, both in the Metropolitan Museum of Art in New York City.

WALDSEEMÜLLER, MARTIN, Greek Ilacomilus, 1470?–?1521, German geographer and cartographer, was born probably in Radolfzell, on Lake Constance. He studied at the University of Freiburg, became a clerk of the diocese of Constance, and at the time of his death was canon of St. Dié. He was also a printer, and did work for the Humanist Walter Ludd's publishing house at St. Dié. In 1507 Waldseemüller published a small book, *Cosmographiae introductio . . .* (Introduction to Cosmography), containing a treatise on geography, a large (8½ ft. by 4 ft.) map of the world, a smaller map designed to be made into a globe, and a Latin version of Amerigo Vespucci's four voyages. In three places in the treatise Waldseemüller suggests naming the land discovered by Vespucci "America" in his honor, and on both maps he so designated South America. The *Cosmographiae* became so widely known, that when Waldseemüller decided later that Vespucci had not been the first to find South America, the name America had already come into general acceptance. The New York Public Library has a copy of the *Cosmographiae*, and a facsimile edition and study of Waldseemüller's *Cosmographiae introductio* was published by the U.S. Catholic Historical Society (1907). Waldseemüller also published a large *Carta Marina* (1516).

WALES, a country of Great Britain; bounded by England on the E, the Bristol Channel on the S St. George's Channel on the W, and the Irish Sea on the N; area, 8,016 square miles; pop. (1961) 2,644,002. For a description of the geography, economy, and society of modern Wales see the article Great Britain. See also England and Wales map in Atlas.

History. The earliest history of Wales corresponds to that of England—that is, Britain south of the Firth of Forth. By the second century B.C., Celts from the European mainland had settled most of this region (see CELT); and, in the region corresponding to modern Wales, Celts had intermingled with the Silures, a people believed to be of Mediterranean origin, who had settled there previously (it is not known just when). The Romans conquered this part of Britain during the first century of the Christian Era. Among the Roman military posts established in the region corresponding to modern Wales were

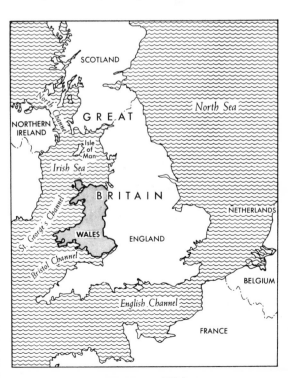

Location Map of Wales

Deva (Chester), Segontium (Caernarvon), and Isca Silurium (Caerleon).

With the decline of Roman authority during and after the fifth century, the Romanized Celts, or Britons, gradually gained dominance over Britain, although they never constituted a united nation or kingdom. In the course of this period they embraced Christianity; the most notable missionary was St. David or Deui (500?–?600), who later became the patron saint of Wales. Beginning in the sixth century, the Britons were either conquered or driven westward by Anglo-Saxon invaders from northern Europe, and early in the seventh century they controlled only western Britain, and a noncontiguous strip of territory along the coast from Scotland to Cornwall. The Anglo-Saxon Conquest, however, resulted in the establishment of political unity among the still independent Britons, who by early in the eighth century controlled an area approximating modern Wales; and it was from the Anglo-Saxon name for the Britons, *waelisc* (foreigner or stranger), that the ethnic identity of the modern Welsh derives. The Welsh warred constantly with the Anglo-Saxon Kingdom of Mercia and it was in defense against the Welsh that King Offa of Mercia (died 796) built his famous dike between the Dee and Wye rivers.

The Normans who invaded the island in 1066 first appeared in Wales in ?1072, and although they met resistance, they did succeed in reducing Wales to nominal submission during the reign of Henry II, 1154–89. During the reign of Henry III, 1216–72, a national revival took place in Wales. The powerful Welsh noble Llewelyn of Gruffydd refused homage to Henry's successor, Edward I, 1272–1307, but during the ensuing struggle Llewelyn was killed. To pacify the Welsh, Edward made his son, Edward of Carnarvon, the "Prince of Wales," 1301, a nonhereditary title subsequently conferred upon most of the eldest sons and heirs-apparent of English sovereigns. During the Wars of the Roses, 1455–85, Welshmen played a prominent part on both sides. For a time, east Wales was mainly Yorkist, the west, Lancastrian. Finally, however, Wales rallied around the Lancastrian prince, Henry Tudor, earl of Richmond, who defeated the Yorkist king, Richard III, and ascended the throne of England as Henry VII, 1485. By the 1536 Act of Union, Wales became a part of England. Nevertheless, the Welsh, by preserving their language and many of their traditional folkways, maintained a strong sense of national identity that persisted into the 1960's.

Bibliog.–George H. Borrow, *Wild Wales* (1955); Emrys G. Bowen, ed., *Wales: A Physical, Historical and Regional Geography* (1957); Country Life, Limited, London, *Picture Book of Wales* (1955); Elwyn Davies and Alwyn D. Rees, eds., *Welsh Rural Communities* (1960); Rhys Davies, *Story of Wales* (Britain in Pictures Ser.) (1943); Tudor Edwards, *Face of Wales* (Face of Britain Ser.) (1950); Louie B. Elwood and J. W. Elwood, *Rebellious Welsh* (1951); Thomas Firbank, *Country of Memorable Honour* (1953); Harry L. V. Fletcher, *North Wales* (Queen's Wales Ser.) (1955), *South Wales* (Queen's Wales Ser.) (1955); Maxwell Fraser, *West of Offa's Dyke*, 2 vols. (1959–60); Eli Ginzberg, *Grass on the Slag Heaps: The Story of the Welsh Miners* (1942); Llewelyn W. Griffith, *Wales in Colour* (1958); James Hanley, *Grey Children: A Study in Humbug and Misery* (1937); George M. Howe, *Wales from the Air* (1957); Cledwyn Hughes, *Royal Wales, the Land and Its People* (1957); Margaret E. Hughes and Arnold J. James, *Wales: A Physical, Economic and Social Geography* (1961); Elisabeth Inglis-Jones, *Story of Wales* (1955); Idris D. Jones, *Modern Welsh History from 1485 to the Present Day* (1960); James I. Jones, *New Geography of Wales* (1960); James Lees-Milne, *National Trust Guide: Buildings* (1948); Eiluned Lewis and Peter Lewis, *Land of Wales* (British Heritage Ser.) (1950); John E. Lloyd, *History of Wales*, 2 vols. (1949); Stuart P. B. Mais, *Highways and Byways in the Welsh Marches* (1939); David C. Marsh, *Changing Social Structure of England and Wales 1871–1951* (1958); Harold J. Massingham, *Curious Traveller* (1950); Henry C. V. Morton, *In Search of Wales* (1955); Litellus R. Muirhead, ed., *Wales* (Blue Guide Series) (1953); Trefor M. Owen, *Welsh Folk Customs* (1959); John Penry, *Three Treatises Concerning Wales* (1960); Hermann A. Piehler, *Wales for Everyman* (1956); William Rees, *Historical Atlas of Wales from Early to Modern Times* (1959); Francis S. Smythe, *Over Welsh Hills* (1941); James A. Steers, *Coast of England and Wales in Picture* (1960); David Williams, *Short History of Wales: 1485 to the Present Day* (1961).

WALES, PRINCE OF, after the conquest of Wales by Edward I, the title borne by most of the eldest sons and heirs-apparent of the reigning sovereign of England. The title was first bestowed upon an English prince, 1301, in the person of the future Edward II, and was regularly borne by the eldest son of the sovereign after being granted to the eldest son of Edward III, Edward, "the Black Prince," 1343. It is not a hereditary title, and in each instance is a fresh creation. Charles, the eldest son of Queen Elizabeth II, was created Prince of Wales on July 26, 1958. The distinguishing badge of the Prince of Wales is the plume of three ostrich feathers, with the motto *Ich dien* (I serve).

WALHALLA, town, NW South Carolina, seat of Oconee County; on the Southern Railway; 38 miles W of Greenville. Cotton textiles, clothing, and mill equipment are manufactured. This Blue Ridge Mountain summer resort town was founded in 1850 by a member of the German Colonization Society of Charleston. Pop. (1960) 3,431.

WALID I, 675?–715, sixth Ommiad caliph, the son of the fifth Ommiad caliph, Abd-al-Malik ibn-Marwān (646?–705), was one of the greatest rulers of his dynasty. Under Walid I, the Moslem Empire made conquests in Europe, western Asia, and India. The most spectacular event of his reign, 705–715, was the conquest of Spain, 711–712, by his generals Tāriq ibn-Ziyād (died 720) and Mūsa ibn-Nusayr (660–714). Walid I was considered a gracious and kind sovereign by his subjects. He built many schools, hospitals, and mosques, gave generously to the poor, and encouraged the arts. He enforced justice and taught his subjects to respect the law.

Walid II, died 744, the son of Yazīd II (died 724), was Ommiad caliph of the Islam Empire, 743–44.

WALKER, FRANCIS AMASA, 1840–97, U.S. economist and educator, was born in Boston, and was graduated from Amherst College, 1860. During the Civil War he rose through the ranks to brevet brigadier general. Appointed chief of the Bureau of Statistics, 1869, he supervised the censuses of 1870 and 1880. He was commissioner of Indian Affairs, 1871–72, professor of political economy and history at the Sheffield Scientific School of Yale University, 1873–81, and president of Massachusetts Institute of Technology from 1881. At Yale and M.I.T., Walker became a leading advocate of independence in economic thought. He encouraged free competition and international bimetallism (but condemned William Jennings Bryan's crusade for unilateral bimetallism), and discredited the wages-fund theory that wages are entirely reliant on the quality of pre-existing capital. He wrote *The Wages Question* (1876), *Money* (1878), *Money in Its Relation to Trade and Industry* (1879), *Land and Its Rent* (1883), *Political Economy* (1883), and *International Bimetallism* (1896).

WALKER, FRANK COMMERFORD, 1886–1959, U.S. businessman and public official, was born in Plymouth, Pa., spent his childhood in Butte, Mont., attended Gonzaga University, Spokane, Wash., 1903–06, was graduated from the University of Notre Dame, 1909, and was admitted to the Montana bar, 1909. He became treasurer of the Democratic National Committee, 1932, and actively supported Franklin D. Roosevelt in his first campaign for the presidency. Walker held various federal offices, 1933–45, including that of postmaster general, 1940–45.

WALKER, FREDERICK, 1840–75, English painter and illustrator, was born in London. He studied at the British Museum, the Royal Academy, and with a wood engraver. From ?1859 he was active as an illustrator for periodicals, such as William Thackeray's *Cornhill* magazine, and he and Thackeray

WALES

Using traditional methods, a farmer in Wales ridges his plot of arable land to retain moisture in the dry spells.

This ruined castle, the most picturesque of all Welsh fortresses, dates from late in the thirteenth century. It is located in the walled town of Conway, Caernarvonshire.

Twin Brecon Beacons are the highest peaks in south Wales.

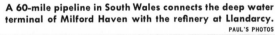

A 60-mile pipeline in South Wales connects the deep water terminal of Milford Haven with the refinery at Llandarcy.

Coal miners of southern Wales gather in neighborhood pubs, there to practice a favorite national pastime: singing.

became good friends. Later Walker devoted himself to oils and water colors of landscapes and genre scenes—works usually distinguished more by their color and depth of feeling than by their composition. Among his best known paintings are *Wayfarers*, *Old Gate*, *The Bathers*, and *Vagrants*.

WALKER, HORATIO, 1858–1938, Canadian painter, was born in Listowel, Ontario, and studied painting in Toronto and New York. Influenced most by the Barbizon school, he painted French Canadian farmers and the Québec countryside. He was a member of the British Royal Institute of Painters in Water Colour and the National Academy of Design. His canvases include *Oxen Drinking* (National Gallery, Ottawa), *Ave Maria* (Corcoran Gallery), and *The Harrower* and *The Sheepfold* (Metropolitan Museum).

WALKER, JOHN, 1732–1807, English lexicographer and actor, was born in Colney Hatch, Middlesex. He became an actor, was a member of David Garrick's company at Drury Lane, and also appeared at Covent Garden and in Dublin. He quit the stage, 1768, conducted a school for two years, and thereafter lectured on elocution. His *Critical Pronouncing Dictionary and Expositor of the English Language* (1791) was for many years a standard work and appeared in many editions, as did his *Rhyming Dictionary* (1775). Walker wrote a number of other books on elocution, rhetoric, and composition.

WALKER, JOSEPH REDDEFORD, 1798–1876, U.S. trapper, explorer, and guide, was born probably in Virginia. He trapped beaver and traded with the Indians in Missouri in the 1820's. In 1832 he led a party from Green River by way of the lake and river named for him over the Sierras to Monterey, Calif. On the return trip, 1832, he crossed the Sierras by what has since been called Walker's Pass. He guided John C. Frémont's second and third expeditions, and prospected for gold in California during the '49 rush, and in Arizona in the 1860's.

WALKER, MARY EDWARDS, 1832–1919, U.S. physician and advocate of women's rights, was born in Oswego, N.Y., was graduated from Syracuse Medical College, 1855, and practiced in Columbus, Ohio, and later in Rome, New York. During the Civil War she served as a U.S. Army nurse, 1861–64, and as an assistant surgeon, 1864–65. Congress awarded her a medal for her valuable services. After the war she practiced in Washington, D.C. An ardent supporter of women's rights, she wore male attire from about 1848, and established, 1897, a colony for women—Adamless Eve.

WALKER, ROBERT JOHN, sometimes called Robert James Walker, 1801–69, U.S. public official and financier, was born in Northumberland, Pa. He was graduated from the University of Pennsylvania, 1819, practiced law in Pittsburgh, 1821–26, and moved to Natchez, Miss., 1826. He became prominent in Democratic politics and, in spite of his opposition to nullification, was elected, 1835, to the U.S. Senate, where he advocated an independent treasury, the independence (and eventual annexation) of Texas, and the nomination of James Polk for President (see NULLIFICATION). While secretary of the treasury in President Polk's cabinet, 1845–49, Walker formulated the antiprotectionist tariff of 1846, which remained in force until 1861; arranged financing of the Mexican War; and helped found the Department of the Interior, 1849. President James Buchanan made Walker governor of Kansas Territory, 1857, but he resigned the same year because of the President's opposition to his plan to admit Kansas as a free state. During the Civil War Walker arranged about $250 million in European loans to the Union.

WALKER, WILLIAM, 1824–60, U.S. soldier of fortune, was born in Nashville, Tenn., studied both medicine and law, then turned to journalism and became, 1848, one of the owners and editors of the New Orleans *Crescent*. He moved to California, 1850, worked for a time on the San Francisco *Herald*, then settled in Marysville, where he practiced law for three years. While there he became interested in the idea of settling North Americans in the Mexican states of Sonora and Lower California; when the Mexican authorities proved to be unreceptive to his scheme, Walker fitted out an armed expedition, 1853, ostensibly to protect the Mexicans against the raids of bands of Apache Indians. In November, Walker and his fellow adventurers landed in Mexico and forthwith proclaimed the republic of Lower California; in January, 1854, he announced the annexation of Sonora. He was soon driven back into the United States, however, and surrendered to the authorities; he was tried at San Francisco for violating the neutrality laws, but was acquitted. See FILIBUSTER.

Walker immediately equipped an expedition to Nicaragua, 1855, at the invitation of one of the warring factions in that country. In July, he and a 57-man force landed in Nicaragua, where he gained the backing of the U.S.-owned Accessory Transit Company, a firm engaged in shipping between the Atlantic and Pacific coasts by way of a land route across Nicaragua. With the company's help, Walker in October conquered the Nicaraguan capital, Granada, bringing the civil war to an end. He now became commander in chief of the Nicaraguan army, which he augmented with recruits from the United States. He defeated the forces of Costa Rica, April, 1856. The new government was recognized by the United States in May, and in July Walker secured his own inauguration as president of Nicaragua.

Walker dreamed of building a canal across Nicaragua and of ruling a Central American empire. As president, he reintroduced African slavery into Nicaragua; of his various actions, this particularly was received with mixed sentiments in the United States: in the South, he was looked on as a hero, but in the North he was thought to be the agent of a Southern plot to expand the institution of slavery.

At this point, Walker involved himself in a struggle between two groups for control of the Accessory Transit Company. He seized the company's Nicaraguan property and turned it over to the group he supported. The other group, led by Cornelius Vanderbilt, then helped organize a military coalition of neighboring republics. Walker was defeated, and took refuge aboard a U.S. ship, May, 1857.

Walker returned to the United States, raised a new expedition, and landed in Nicaragua, November, 1857. He was soon stopped by Commodore Hiram Paulding of the U.S. Navy, however, and was sent back to the United States, where he published the *War in Nicaragua* (1860). In August, 1860, Walker landed with a small group of adventurers in Honduras, planning to proceed by land to Nicaragua. He was intercepted by a British naval officer, who turned him over to the Honduran authorities; Walker was tried by court-martial, convicted, and shot.

ROBIN OGGINS

WALKER, city, N Minnesota, seat of Cass County; on Leech Lake, the Great Northern and Northern Pacific railroads, and U.S. highway 371; 120 miles W of Duluth. The city is a distribution center for dairy products that are produced in the area. Pop. (1960) 1,180.

WALKER-GOODERHAM AND WORTS, one of the largest industrial corporations in Canada, and a leading whisky distiller in Canada, the United States, and Scotland. The company and its subsidiaries also act as agents for the import and sale of whiskies and are leading producers of industrial alcohol.

The company was incorporated in Canada, Dec. 31, 1926, as Hiram Walker's, Ltd., successor to a business founded, 1858, by Hiram Walker. In 1927 it acquired Gooderham and Worts, Ltd., Toronto, the oldest existing distiller in Canada. Subsequently it made other acquisitions of distilleries and related properties. Major facilities are located in Canada, the United States, Scotland, and Argentina. The company markets, besides whiskies, other alcoholic beverages, including gin and rum.

WALKING, the act of propelling oneself on foot at a relatively moderate but steady pace. As a sport, both amateur and professional heel-and-toe walking, wherein one foot must always contact the road, is centuries old.

The stride of the best walking contestants generally averages 40 inches, nearly 1,600 strides per mile, or about four strides per second for top speeds at that distance. The walker steps off the great toe of one foot, landing on the heel of the other, knees locked and arms swinging in rhythm. Competitive walking events normally cover 10 to 50 kilometers.

WALKING STICK INSECT, an insect belonging to the order Orthoptera and the family *Phasmidae* and noted for its mimicry. Walking sticks have slender, greatly elongated bodies, much like a stick, with legs resembling twigs. Wings may be absent, but when present are leaflike; hence the name leaf insect is applied to many of the winged forms. The eggs often resemble seeds. One species of walking stick insects, *Palophus titan* is among the largest of living insects, reaching a length of more than a foot. The most common species in the United States is the wingless *Diapheromera femorata*, whose young are pale green, changing to gray and brown as they grow older. They are voracious plant eaters but are seldom abundant enough to cause damage.

Walking Stick Insect

JACK DERMID—NATIONAL AUDUBON SOCIETY

WALLACE, ALFRED RUSSEL, 1823–1913, English naturalist, was born in Usk, Monmouthshire. He left school at 14, and studied surveying and watchmaking. After becoming interested in botany he met the naturalist Henry W. Bates, with whom he went to the Amazon River area to collect specimens, 1848. After returning to England, 1859, Wallace wrote *Travels on the Amazon and Rio Negro* (1853) and *Palm Trees of the Amazon* (1853). In 1854 he went to the Malay Archipelago to study animals. After a visit to Australia, he drew up an imaginary geographic line, named for him, which passed between Borneo and the Celebes and between Bali and Lombok, and separates animals of Australasian (to the east) and Oriental (to the west) origin.

While in the Far East, Wallace thought out—quite independently of Charles Darwin—a theory of natural selection to explain the process of species evolution. He immediately wrote a detailed exposition of his theory and sent it to Darwin, who 16 years earlier had written a lengthy, but still unpublished, manuscript setting forth the same theory. On receiving Wallace's manuscript Darwin generously decided to reveal the younger man's work at the same time he made known his own. As a result, the *Linnean Society's*

Journal published simultaneously the two men's articles on natural selection, 1858. Darwin published *On the Origins of Species . . .* a year later. In developing their theory, both men were indebted to Thomas Malthus' *Essay on the Principle of Population* (1798). While Wallace upheld physical evolution, he believed that man's spiritual nature is supernatural in origin.

Wallace made another major contribution to natural science with his *Geographical Distribution of Animals* (1876), which was the basis of many later zoogeographical studies. In other scientific fields he took unorthodox positions, opposing vaccination and advocating spiritualism and phrenology. He also encouraged large-scale nationalization of land. In addition to the above-mentioned, he wrote *Contributions to the Theory of Natural Selection* (1870), *On Miracles and Modern Spiritualism* (1875; ed. 1896), *Tropical Nature* (1878), *Land Nationalization* (1882), *Darwinism* (1889), *Man's Place in the Universe* (1903), *Social Environment and Moral Progress* (1912), and other works.

WALLACE, EDGAR, full name, Richard Horatio Edgar Wallace, 1875–1932, English writer, was born in Greenwich, the illegitimate son of actors. He left school at 12, worked at odd jobs, served seven years in the army, and was a correspondent in South Africa for Reuter's and the *Daily Mail*, 1899–1902. His *The Four Just Men* (1905) was the first of Wallace's more than 170 amazingly successful suspense novels, many of which featured the detective J. G. Reeder. Wallace also wrote a score of plays (sometimes several played simultaneously in London), 300 or more short stories, and hundreds of columns of dramatic criticism and horse racing news—spending his money as fast as he made it, and sometimes faster. His works include the novels *Sanders of the River* (1911), *Bones* (1915), *The Crimson Circle* (1922), *The Green Archer* (1923), *Mr. Commissioner Saunders* (1930), and *Mr. Reeder Returns* (1932); the plays *The Ringer* (1926), *The Squeaker* (1928), and *On the Spot* (1931); and the scenario for the motion picture *King Kong* (1932).

WALLACE, HENRY AGARD, 1888–1965, U.S. political leader and agriculturalist, was born in Adair County, Iowa, the son of Henry Cantwell Wallace. After graduating from Iowa State College, 1910, he joined the staff of the family-owned magazine, *Wallace's Farmer*, and became its editor, 1924. During this period Wallace worked out ways of forecasting the probable course of the agricultural market (corn-hog ratio) and total corn yields, and developed a high-yield strain of hybrid corn.

Wallace was a Republican until 1928, when he supported the Democratic presidential candidate Al Smith. Wallace also swung Iowa to the support of Franklin Delano Roosevelt in the election of 1932, and was appointed U.S. secretary of agriculture, 1933. In this post Wallace sponsored various New Deal agricultural programs, notably the Agricultural Adjustment Acts (AAA) of 1933 and 1938 (see NEW DEAL). He emphasized national and regional planning, soil conservation, erosion control, and distribution of surplus food products through school lunch and relief programs. He inaugurated crop insurance and set up laboratories to study nutrition comprehensively and to find industrial uses for agricultural products. During his term of office farm income doubled, and U.S. agriculture was put on a basis firm enough to meet the enormous demands placed on it during World War II.

Wallace was vice-president during Roosevelt's third term, 1941–45; but conservative elements in the Democratic party opposed his renomination, 1944, and Harry S. Truman was nominated for the vice-presidency as a compromise candidate. Wallace served as secretary of commerce, 1945–46, but resigned after making a foreign policy speech sharply critical of Truman administration policies. He then served for a year as nominal editor of a liberal weekly magazine, the *New Republic*. As the presidential candidate of the left-wing Progressive party, 1948,

Wallace polled 1,157,172 votes but failed to carry a single state. Wallace later broke with the Progressive party, 1950, over the party's refusal to support the UN police action in Korea.   ROBIN OGGINS

WALLACE, HENRY CANTWELL, 1866–1924, U.S. agriculturist and government official, the father of Henry A. Wallace, was born in Rock Island, Ill., and educated at Iowa State College of Agriculture, where he taught dairying, 1893–95. Part owner and publisher of *Farm and Dairy*, 1894–95, he became associate editor when the magazine was bought by his family and renamed *Wallace's Farmer*, 1895, and succeeded his father as editor, 1916–21. Influential in journalism and farm organizations as a champion of farmers' movements, Wallace was appointed, 1921, secretary of agriculture in the cabinet of Pres. Warren G. Harding, and remained in the same post under Pres. Calvin Coolidge. Wallace wrote *Our Debt and Duty to the Farmer* (1925).

WALLACE, LEWIS, known as Lew Wallace, 1827–1905, U.S. author and soldier, was born in Brookville, Ind. He served in the Mexican and Civil wars and was advanced to the rank of major general for his share in the capture of Fort Donelson, 1862. He fortified Cincinnati, 1863, and saved the city from falling into the hands of Gen. E. Kirby-Smith; and played an important part in the defense of Washington, D.C., July, 1864. After the Civil War, Wallace practiced law in Crawfordsville, Ind. He was governor of the Territory of New Mexico, 1878–81, and U.S. minister to Turkey, 1881–85. His first book, *The Fair God* (1873), a novel about the conquest of Mexico, was followed by *Ben Hur, a Tale of the Christ* (1880). This story of the early days of Christianity was the result of an encounter with the freethinker, Robert G. Ingersoll, whose militant atheism inspired Wallace to define and express his own religious convictions. One of the best sellers of the 1880's, *Ben Hur* remained widely popular for some 40 years, selling more than 2,500,000 copies. It was also successful in a number of stage and screen adaptations, including a version in the late 1950's. Among Wallace's other works are *Life of Gen. Benjamin Harrison* (1888), *The Boyhood of Christ* (1889), *The Prince of India* (1893), *The Wooing of Malkatoon* (verse, 1898), and *Lew Wallace: An Autobiography* (2 vols. 1906).

WALLACE, RHODERICK JOHN, known as "Bobby," 1873–1960, U.S. baseball player, a member of the Baseball Hall of Fame, was born in Pittsburgh, Pa. He played 2,369 games during the years 1894–1918, had a lifetime batting average of .268, and was one of the more versatile infielders in the major leagues. He began his career with the Cleveland National League ball club, 1894–99, played for St. Louis in the National League, 1899–1901, moved to St. Louis in the American League, 1902–16, and finished his career with St. Louis in the National League, 1917–18. Wallace was manager of the American League St. Louis club, 1911–12. He was elected to the Baseball Hall of Fame in 1953.

WALLACE, SIR WILLIAM, 1272?–1305, Scottish hero and patriot, was born probably at Elderslie in Renfrewshire, the second son of Sir Malcolm Wallace (also Walays or Wallensis), a small landowner. William first appears on the historical scene, 1297, as an organizer of the Scottish resistance to Edward I of England. Possessing great strength, undaunted courage, and military skill, and a warm attachment to the interests of his native country, he resolved to free Scotland from the English yoke. Although most of the nobles soon deserted his cause, the people remained firmly behind him. After capturing Aberdeen, Forfar, and other towns, he was engaged in the siege of Dunbar when news came of the advance of a large English army toward Stirling. He immediately marched to meet the enemy and gained a signal victory over them at Stirling Bridge end. Raising a larger army, he drove out numerous English garrisons, then attacked England itself,

ravaging Northumberland, Westmoreland, and Cumberland. Wallace was at once proclaimed governor of Scotland in the absence of King John Baliol, who was then being held captive in England. Edward I, however, then led forth in person an army of 80,000 men, and defeated Wallace at the bloody Battle of Falkirk, March, 1298. Escaping capture, Wallace continued a desultory warfare against the English, while attempting unsuccessfully to win the assistance of Norway, France, and Pope Boniface VIII. Finally, in August, 1305, he was captured, apparently through the treachery of a Scottish nobleman, Sir John Menteith. He was brought to London, tried for treason and convicted at Westminster Hall, dragged by horse first to the Tower of London, and from there to Tyburn, and there was hanged and quartered. His head was subsequently impaled on London Bridge, and his quarters gibbeted at Stirling, Perth, Berwick, and Newcastle-on-Tyne. Wallace's exploits remained a favorite patriotic theme of Scottish poets, and were especially celebrated by Henry the Minstrel, often called Blind Harry.

WALLACE, city, N Idaho, seat of Shoshone County, in the Coeur d'Alene Mountains; on the Coeur d'Alene River, the Union Pacific and the Northern Pacific railroads, and U.S. highway 10; 42 miles ESE of Coeur d'Alene and 13 miles from the Montana state line. Large quantities of silver, lead, gold, and zinc are mined; and timber is cut in the surrounding region. It is the distributing center for a wide area; lumber, minerals, and livestock are shipped. Metal smelting is an important industry. Wallace grew up about a placer mine and was first called Placer Center. Wallace was chartered as a city in 1888. Pop. (1960) 2,412.

WALLACEBURG, town, Canada, S Ontario, in Kent County; on the Sydenham River and the Chesapeake and Ohio Railway; 38 miles NE of Windsor. Wallaceburg has an iron foundry, lumber mills, woodworking plants, brassworks, a die-casting plant, a glass factory, a flour mill, and a beet sugar factory. The town was originally known as The Forks because two branches of the Sydenham River unite there; later, Scottish settlers in the region renamed the town for Sir William Wallace, a Scottish hero. Pop. (1956) 7,892.

WALLACH, OTTO, 1847–1931, Nobel prizewinning German chemist, was born in Königsberg, East Prussia, and was educated at the universities of Berlin and Göttingen. He was lecturer at the University of Bonn from 1873, and professor of chemistry there, 1876–89; then was professor of chemistry and director of the Chemical Institute, University of Göttingen, 1889–1915. Wallach's pioneer researches in the chemistry of terpenes and alicyclic combinations, described in his *Terpene and Camphor* (1909), won him the Nobel prize in chemistry, 1910, "for his initiative work in the field of alicyclic substances." His work was influential in the growth of the perfume and essential oil industry.

WALLACHIA. See WALACHIA.

WALLASEY, county borough, W England, in Cheshire, at the mouth of the river Mersey, across the river from Liverpool. Wallasey was incorporated in 1910, became a county borough in 1913, and a parliamentary borough in 1918. The Birkenhead Docks are located on Wallasey Pool. Textiles, paint, and fertilizer are manufactured. Pop. (1951) 101,331.

WALLA WALLA, city, SE Washington, seat of Walla Walla County; on the Walla Walla River, near the Blue Mountains; on the Northern Pacific, the Union Pacific, and the Walla Walla Valley railroads, and U.S. highway 410; a scheduled airline stop; 110 miles SW of Spokane, near the Oregon border. Walla Walla is the trading and distributing center for a rich valley which produces wheat, prunes, green peas, asparagus, spinach, and nuts. The city has fruit- and vegetable-packing plants and canneries, grain storage plants, dye works, creameries, and vinegar-

and beverage-processing establishments. The first settlement, known as Steptoe, grew up about a Hudson's Bay Company fort; in 1856 the Army built Fort Walla Walla, named from a Nez Percé Indian word designating a rapid stream, for the protection of settlers. The town was laid out and incorporated in 1862. Nearby is the Whitman National Monument. Walla Walla is the site of Whitman College, oldest college in the state, founded as a seminary in 1859. Walla Walla is the birthplace of Gen. Jonathan M. Wainwright. Pop. (1960) 24,536.

WALLA WALLA COLLEGE. See COLLEGES AND UNIVERSITIES.

WALLENSTEIN, BARON ALBRECHT WEN-ZEL EUSEBIUS VON, 1583–1634, Austrian general, was born in Hermanice, Bohemia, and was educated as a Roman Catholic. He served in the army of the Emperor Rudolph II in Hungary, 1604–06, and under Archduke Ferdinand (the future Emperor Ferdinand II) against Venice, 1617. When the Thirty Years' War broke out, 1618, Wallenstein (or Waldstein) added extensively to his already large estates by buying great tracts of land confiscated from Protestants. He offered to raise and maintain an army for Emperor Ferdinand II, 1625, and was rewarded by being created Duke of Friedland. The 50,000-man army Wallenstein raised was devoted to him personally; he followed a policy of paying high wages and of having the army systematically live off the countryside. With this army he defeated the army of Ernst von Mansfeld at the Bridge of Dessau, 1626; and then cleared the Protestants out of Silesia, conquered Holstein with Johann Tilly, and alone subdued Schleswig and Jutland, and expelled the dukes of Mecklenburg, 1627. In the same year he bought the Duchy of Sagan and was made Duke of Mecklenburg. He then sought to expand his conquests farther along the Baltic Coast, but was checked at Stralsund, 1628, where he had to withdraw after an unsuccessful 10-week siege. During this period Wallenstein had alienated the German princes by his dreams of a united Germany under the emperor and by the exactions of his army. In 1630 the princes brought about his dismissal; he resumed his command, 1632, but was defeated by Gustavus Adolphus at the Battle of Lutzen, 1632, although Gustavus was killed.

By this time there was a growing rift between Wallenstein and Ferdinand II. The Spanish party at the imperial court wanted Wallenstein removed. Hoping to free the emperor from the influence of the Spanish party, to bring about peace at the price of religious toleration, and to reorganize the internal structure of the empire, Wallenstein now began secret negotiations with the Swedes and the Saxons. In 1634, however, the emperor removed him from his command and outlawed him. Soon after this Wallenstein was assassinated; while the emperor had not ordered the murder, he rewarded the murderers.

ROBIN OGGINS

WALLER, EDMUND, 1606–87, English poet, was born in Coleshill, Hertfordshire (later Buckinghamshire), was educated at Eton and Cambridge, and became a member of Parliament perhaps as early as 1621. He inherited a fortune from his father, and married an heiress, 1631. In Parliament he sympathized for a time with the growing opposition to King Charles I, but eventually came to support the crown. In 1643 Waller was appointed one of the commissioners to negotiate with the king, who had fled to Oxford. After being implicated in what is called "Waller's plot" (to secure London for the king), Waller revealed the names of his co-conspirators in

CULVER SERVICE
Baron von Wallenstein

order to save his life. He was fined £10,000 and exiled to France, 1644, but was pardoned later, 1651, and returned to England. He was made a commissioner of trade by Oliver Cromwell, whom he eulogized in *A Panegyric to My Lord Protector* (1655), but on the restoration of the monarchy, 1660, he wrote *To the King upon His Majesty's Happy Return* (1660), and sat again in Parliament, 1661–87. Waller's poetry is distinguished by its polished smoothness and restrained metaphor rather than by any great imagination. His mastery of the heroic couplet helped popularize that form. Among his best known lyrics are *On a Girdle*, *Of the Last Verses in the Book*, and *Go, Lovely Rose*. Many of his early poems are addressed to "Sacharissa"—Lady Dorothy Sidney, whom he courted after his first wife's death.

WALLER, FATS, early nickname and professional name of Thomas Waller, 1904–43, U.S. ragtime and jazz piano player, composer, and entertainer, was born in New York City, the son of Edward Martin Waller, pastor of the Abyssinian Baptist Church, and of Adaline Locket Waller, a musician and singer who encouraged Fats in his musical pursuits. Fats studied piano from the age of 6, and took up the pipe organ probably a year or two later; he was playing organ professionally at the age of 10 in church, and from the age of 14 in a motion-picture theater in Harlem. His early piano study under Carl Bohm was largely devoted to the classics. At the age of 16 or 17 he met the greatest of the Harlem ragtime-jazz piano players, James P. Johnson, whose tutelage, within a year or two, transformed Fats into one of the best piano players on the East Coast.

Waller became extremely important as a composer and player of ragtime piano solos, as one of the very best ensemble jazz pianists, and as a writer of innumerable and excellent ballads that lend themselves to jazz performance. He also wrote scores for musical shows such as *Keep Shufflin'* (1928) and *Hot Chocolates* (1929). He attained worldwide fame through his recordings and on European tours, and appeared in several motion pictures. Even by the standards of the concert stage his command of the piano was of a high order, thanks in no small measure to his studies with the famous pianist Leopold Godowsky.

WALLER, SIR WILLIAM, 1597?–1668, English general, was educated at Magdalen Hall, Oxford. A Puritan, he was elected to the Long Parliament, 1640, and became a general in the parliamentary army, 1642. He was victorious at Portsmouth, 1642, suffered reverses at Lansdown and Roundway Down, 1643, defeated royalists at Cheriton, 1644, and lost at Cropredy Bridge, 1644. Because of the Self-denying Ordinance, he resigned his command, 1645, and thereafter became a leader of the Presbyterian party in Parliament. He was imprisoned several times, 1648–59, negotiated with the royalists, and was a member of the Restoration Convention, 1660.

WALLEYE, any of the large, carnivorous, freshwater fishes belonging to the family *Percidae*. The walleyes are yellowish or bluish in color with a dark olive cast. Their bodies are long and slender and their mouths, large. Their size ranges from 2 to 25 pounds. Minnows constitute their diet. Walleyes spawn in early spring, laying a great number of eggs; a 2-pound walleye lays 90,000 eggs. Walleyes are favored as food fish. They have wide distribution throughout the area east of the Mississippi River in the United States, being found most abundantly in the Great Lakes.

WALLFLOWER, a common southern European garden and wall perennial, *Cheiranthus Cheiri*, belonging to the family *Cruciferae*. Its fragrant flowers are usually yellow, borne on long racemes, and its fruits are long, flattened pods. *C. kewensis*, a hybrid between *C. Cheiri* and the Madieran *C. mutabilis*, is prized as a fragrant winter plant grown in greenhouses. The coast wallflower of California, *Erysimum capitatum*, is a member of a closely related genus, and a popular garden plant.

WALLINGFORD, town, S central Connecticut, New Haven County, on the Quinnipiac River, the New Haven Railroad, and U.S. highway 5; 11 miles N of New Haven. The first settlement was made in 1638 and Wallingford was incorporated in 1673. The town has been a center for silverwork since 1835. Choate School for boys, the State Masonic Home, and the Gaylord Farm Sanatorium for the tubercular are there. The town is a trade center for an area in which fruit, vegetables, and livestock are raised. Silverware, brassware, hardware, insulated wire, fireworks, tools, apparel, plastics, and paper boxes are manufactured. Pop. (1960) 29,920.

WALLINGTON, borough, NE New Jersey, Bergen County; on the Passaic River; 9 miles NW of New York City. The borough was incorporated in 1894. Seamless metal tubing, insulated electrical equipment, paper boxes, and handkerchiefs are manufactured. Pop. (1960) 9,261.

WALLIS, JOHN, 1616–1703, English mathematician, was born in Ashford, Kent. He studied at Emmanuel College, Cambridge; was ordained a priest, 1640; deciphered codes for the Parliamentary party during the civil war; and became Savilian professor of geometry at Oxford, 1649. His principal work, *Arithmetica infinitorum* (1655), provided the foundation for the development of integral and differential calculus, and the binomial theorem. Among his other works are *Grammatica linguae anglicanae* (1652), *Mechanica* (1669–71), *Institutio logicae* (1687), and *Sermons* (1791). Wallis introduced the symbol ∞ to represent infinity.

WALLOON, one of a people of southeast Belgium, who speak a dialect of the French language and constitute one of the two main linguistic groups of Belgium (the Germanic Flemings are the other). They are descended from the Belgae of ancient Gaul. Some Walloons are Protestant, others are Roman Catholic. During the Counter Reformation and the Netherlands' struggle for independence from Spain in the late sixteenth and early seventeenth centuries, many Protestant Walloons settled in England and the Dutch Netherlands, where they were known to the Dutch as Huguenots (French Protestants); some of these Huguenots subsequently settled in the Dutch North American colony of New Netherland (New York). The Roman Catholic Walloons remained loyal to Spain, and they subsequently were under foreign rule —Spanish, Austrian, French and Dutch—until 1831, when Belgium became politically independent. See BELGIUM, Social Factors, *Population*, History.

WALLPAPER, colored paper used to decorate broad surfaces within a room—usually the walls, and sometimes the ceiling. Wallpaper may be of either the side-wall or ceiling variety, according to the surface on which it is used; certain designs suitable for use on one variety are not useable on the other. Both sidewall and ceiling papers are, however, normally decorated with a repeated pattern. In addition to these two varieties, certain decorative devices, such as borders, panels and scenics, are made out of wallpaper. Border paper is used to decorate valances, panels, dados, and many other areas where a narrow strip of paper is called for. Panels are one or more strips of paper that together form a single design or mural. Panels are often framed by borders, or may be contained within an area of side-wall paper. Scenics are composed of a series of strips that form a single design when put together; the last strip of a scenic matches the first, so that the design may be repeated over a single surface.

Manufacture of Wallpaper. Hanging paper, the paper base on which a design is printed, is composed of waste paper, ground wood, sulphite, coloring matter, and sizing. Coloring for the design is made of an aluminum hydrate base treated with coal-tar dyes and mixed to produce a desired lake (shade). The lake is mixed with an adhesive such as glue, gum, or a starch preparation, that will hold the color to the paper. Some inks used to decorate wallpaper are made of paste and such materials as bronze powders and finely ground mica.

A coating machine applies a solid background color of china clay, clay with precipitating barium sulphate, or tinted clay to the hanging paper. After drying, the paper is ready to be printed with a design. Designs may be hand- or machine-printed. Block printing, the earliest form of printing, and silk screening, the most popular form of hand printing at midtwentieth century, are especially adaptable to large or irregular designs. The most economical and popular type of commercial printing is by rotary machine. Each color of a design is outlined on a separate roller with strips of sheet brass, raised about $\frac{3}{4}$ of an inch above the surface. Specially prepared felt is stretched between the raised areas when a large area of color is to be filled, or it is fitted to cover only the top of the brass strips when an outline color is desired. The paper is fed into a machine containing a series of these rollers that dip into wells of coloring matter, and print the design on the paper. The paper is then dried and reeled by machine into measured lengths, or submitted to additional treatment, such as overprinting with a screen of pale color, coating with a transparent varnish, or embossing. See CHASING AND EMBOSSING; PAPER; PRINTING.

History. One of the earliest evidences of the use of paper for wall decoration in Europe is an order of 50 sets of painted paper for Louis XI, 1481. Inventories recovered from the years 1595–1690 include lists of "flock" papers, imitations of woven tapestries and fabrics, achieved by a design being printed on paper, which was then spread with glue and heavily sprinkled with chopped silk or wool. Early specimens of flock paper date from ?1425. The French considered domino paper, marble sheets, originally imported from Persia and used for facing book covers or lining boxes, to be the forerunner of wallpaper. Designs, among which were checks, stripes, and lozenges, were painted on large sheets of domino paper, which was then attached to the wall. A fragment of wallpaper that was discovered, 1911, during the restoration of the Masters Lodge of Christ's College at Cambridge, England, was patterned by wood block and letterpress and dates from ?1509. The earliest written record of block-printed paper was made in Holland, 1568. In the same century, also in Holland, a patternless paper coated with metallic paint was produced.

Printing in distemper came into vogue during the latter part of the eighteenth century. Many famous artists of the period created designs for wallpapers printed in this manner. Nicholas Louis Robert, of France, invented a method of preparing wallpaper in continuous rolls, 1799, and the later development of a printing machine, ?1850, facilitated the production of rolls of wallpaper.

Patterns dating from 1780–1820 are considered by many critics to be of particularly high merit; the favored motifs were for the most part classic in inspiration. A period of decorative decadence ensued and lasted until the Gothic revival, late in the nineteenth century.

Chinese Wallpaper. Many critics believe that no wallpaper has ever surpassed in beauty and quality the hand-painted papers made in China. These were brought into Europe by Dutch traders from as early as mid-sixteenth century, and became popular wall decorations during the seventeenth century. The design and execution of these papers strongly influenced later wallpaper design. Usually backed with canvas and mounted on wooden frames, these papers were preserved for centuries. They were sold in sets, and each sheet was unique in pattern. All, however, joined accurately to form a complete design. Typical motifs were scenes from Chinese life, landscapes, and nature scenes.

WALLSEND, municipal borough, NE England, in Northumberland County, on the Tyne River, 5 miles from the North Sea and 4 miles NE of Newcastle, of which it is a residential suburb. Wallsend was incorporated in 1901, and became a parliamentary borough in 1918. The town is a shipbuilding and engineering center. Wallsend takes its name from its location at the eastern terminus of Hadrian's Wall, built in the first century, at the command of the Roman Emperor Publius Hadrian, to prevent Pictish marauders in Scotland from stealing English cattle. Pop. (1951) 48,645.

WALL STREET. See NEW YORK, Economic Factors, *Commerce.*

USDA AND CALIFORNIA WALNUT GROWERS ASSN.
Hard wood from walnut trees, such as this stately black walnut in Monongahela National Forest, W. Va., is used for gunstocks and cabinets; the nuts (inset) are edible.

WALNUT, a tree found throughout the temperate regions of the globe; belonging to the genus *Fuglans*, of the family *Fuglandaceae.* Walnut trees have tall, straight trunks that make them especially suitable as park trees. The long, broad leaves are composed of 7 to 25 leaflets and the fruits are edible nuts. The common English walnut is the fruit of *F. regia*, the Persian or English walnut tree. This tree, native to temperate Asia and southeastern Europe, is cultivated extensively in southern California and southern Europe. The black walnut, *F. nigra*, bears nuts that are usually marketed in the shelled state because the shells are difficult to remove. The nuts of the butternut, or white walnut, *F. cinerea*, are not marketed as extensively as the other varieties. Production of walnuts in the United States is concentrated largely in the states of California and Oregon. Cutting for lumber in the United States amounts to between 30 and 40 million board feet annually.

Black walnut and English walnut have heavy, durable dark wood; butternut wood is softer and lighter. Since walnut wood can be easily worked and takes a high polish it is in great demand for cabinetmaking, gun stocks, and interior finishing.

WALNUT CANYON NATIONAL MONUMENT, N central Arizona, in Coconino County, about six miles E of Flagstaff and 110 miles NNW of Phoenix. The monument comprises an area of 1,880 acres which preserves some 200 small prehistoric cliff dwellings of the Pueblo Indians. The dwellings are located in limestone cliffs which, through erosion, have left a series of ledges and recesses along canyon walls. The dwellings are in the recesses, with the overhanging ledges used as ceilings. Types of pottery found indicate that the cliff dwellings were probably most used from the eleventh to thirteenth centuries. Walnut Canyon was established as a national monument in 1915.

WALNUT RIDGE, city, NE Arkansas, seat of Lawrence County; on the Frisco and the Missouri Pacific railroads, and U.S. highway 63; 80 miles NW of Memphis. The city was incorporated in 1881. It is a trade center for the surrounding agricultural region, in which cotton, corn, and rice are produced. Major industries are sawmilling and cotton ginning. Walnut Ridge is the site of Southern Baptist College. Pop. (1960) 3,547.

WALPOLE, HORACE, 4th **EARL OF ORFORD,** 1717–97, English man of letters, was born in London, the fourth son of Sir Robert Walpole. While a student at Cambridge, Horace (or Horatis) met the poet Thomas Gray, with whom he later traveled on the Continent, 1739–41. After his return to England, Walpole entered Parliament and represented various constituencies until 1767. Obsessed with the memory of his father's achievements, he became a perfunctory parliamentarian, complacently accepting a minor role in an age of little men. An ample fortune enabled him to indulge his sociable and antiquarian tastes, and he bought, 1747, the villa of Strawberry Hill, near Twickenham on the Thames, the adornment of which became the hobby of his life. Setting up a press for fine books, he issued Gray's two Pindaric odes (1757) and various antiquarian works of his own, including *A Catalogue of the Royal and Noble Authors of England* (2 vols. 1758) and *Anecdotes of Painting in England* (4 vols. 1762–71). Notable among his original writings is *The Castle of Otranto* (1764), the first English Gothic novel. Walpole is mainly remembered, however, for his vast correspondence (he is called the "Prince of Letter Writers") with Sir Horace Mann, Madame du Deffand, Madame de Sevigné, and other celebrities of his time. His letters were collected by Paget and Helen Toynbee (19 vols. 1903–25). A projected 50-volume edition of the letters, replies, and miscellaneous Walpoliana was begun by W. S. Lewis and others, 1937.

JOHN W. LUCE CO.
Horace Walpole

BIBLIOG.–Lewis S. Benjamin, *Horace Walpole (1717–1797) A Biographical Study* (1930); Isabel W. V. Chase, *Horace Walpole: Gardenist* (1943); Anna F. De Koven, *Horace Walpole and Madame du Deffand* (1929); Austin Dobson, *Horace Walpole, a Memoir* (1932); Alice D. Greenwood, *Horace Walpole's World: A Sketch of Whig Society Under George III* (1913); Stephen L. Gwynn, *Life of Horace Walpole* (1934); Robert W. Ketton-Cremer, *Horace Walpole: A Biography* (1946); Wilmarth S. Lewis, *Collector's Progress* (1952), *Horace Walpole* (1960); Frank L. Lucas, *Art of Living: Four 18th Century Minds: Hume, Horace Walpole, Burke, Benjamin Franklin* (1959); Kewal K. Mehrotra, *Horace Walpole and the English Novel* (1934); Dorothy M. Stuart, *Horace Walpole* (1927); Montague Summers, *Gothic Quest: A History of the Gothic Novel* (1941); Paul Yvon, *Horace Walpole as a Poet: The Poetical Ideals of a Gentleman Author in the XVIIIth Century* (1924).

WALPOLE, SIR HUGH SEYMOUR, 1884–1941, English novelist and critic, was born in Auckland, New Zealand, the son of a Scottish Episcopal canon who later became Bishop of Edinburgh. He began writing while a student at Cambridge, and after 1909, when *The Wooden Horse* was published, wrote some 50 volumes of fiction, biography, and criticism. Many of his novels form cycles, as in the Rising City trilogy, *The Duchess of Wrexe* (1914), *The Green Mirror* (1917), and *The Captives* (1920); the autobiographical series, *Jeremy* (1919), *Jeremy and Hamlet* (1923), and *Jeremy at Crale* (1921); the swashbuckling Herries series comprising *Rogue Herries* (1930), *Judith Paris* (1931), *The Fortress* (1932), and *Vanessa* (1933); and *The Dark For-*

est (1916) and its sequel, *The Secret City* (1919). Walpole's *Portrait of a Man with Red Hair* (1925) is a masterpiece of the macabre. Among his other works are *Joseph Conrad* (1916), *The English Novel* (1925), *Anthony Trollope* (1928), *The Waverley Pageant* (1932), short stories in *All Souls' Night* (1933), *The Killer and the Slain* (1942), *Katherine Christian* (1943), and *Mr. Huffam, and Other Stories* (1948). Walpole was knighted, 1937, for his services to English literature.

WALPOLE, SIR ROBERT, 1st EARL OF ORFORD, called Robin Bluestring and the Grand Cor

Robert Walpole

rupter, 1676–1745, English statesman, was born in Houghton, Norfolk. He entered Parliament representing Castle Rising, 1701, and then sat for King's Lynn, 1702–12 and 1713–42. Soon recognized as a leading Whig, he became secretary of war, 1708, and treasurer of the navy, 1710, and when the Whigs were defeated, 1710, he became opposition leader in the House of Commons. In 1712, however, the Tories expelled Walpole from Parliament on a questionable charge of corruption while secretary of war, and sent him to the Tower for a short imprisonment.

On the accession of George I, 1714, Walpole became the recognized leader of the House of Commons, and was appointed, 1715, first lord of the treasury and chancellor of the exchequer. Soon, however, jealousies among the Whigs and intrigues by the king's German advisers led Walpole to resign his posts, 1717. As a financier, he worked out a sinking fund to reduce the national debt, 1717; later, he warned against the dangers of speculating in South Sea stock, 1720, and when, later in the year, the South Sea Bubble burst, Walpole was virtually the only Whig politician to survive the crash.

Walpole again became first lord of the treasury and chancellor of the exchequer, 1721, and for more than two decades, 1721–42, dominated British politics—so much so that some have regarded him as Britain's first prime minister. He maintained his position by the judicious use of pensions, patronage, and other forms of bribery (hence one of his nicknames, the Grand Corrupter). He followed a policy of building prosperity at home while avoiding wars abroad. He encouraged commerce by lowering duties and by removing restrictions on colonial trade, thus laying the basis for British free trade. The prosperity that resulted from Walpole's policy did much toward getting England to accept the new Hanoverian Dynasty. Under Walpole the political centers of gravity moved from the House of Lords to the House of Commons and, somewhat, from the king to the prime minister.

From 1737 Walpole's influence diminished as he tried to thwart the popular feeling for a war with Spain. He tried to resign several times, but the king would not allow it. Finally, he was defeated in Parliament, 1742, and he resigned. Shortly thereafter he was created Earl of Orford.   ROBIN OGGINS

BIBLIOG.–Norris A. Brisco, *Economic Policy of Robert Walpole* (1907); Alexander C. Ewald, *Sir Robert Walpole: A Political Biography, 1676–1745* (1878); John Morley, *Life of Walpole* (1929); Milton O. Percival, ed., *Political Ballads: Illustrating the Administration of Sir Robert Walpole* (Oxford History and Literary Studies, vol. 8) (1916); John H. Plumb, *Sir Robert Walpole*, 2 vols. (1956–61); Charles B. Realey, *Early Opposition to Sir Robert Walpole, 1720–1727* (Humanistic Studies, vol. 4, nos. 2-3) (1931); John L. Smith-Dampier, *East Anglican Worthies* (1949); George R. S. Taylor, *Robert Walpole and His Age* (1933).

WALPOLE, town, E Massachusetts, Norfolk County, on the Neponset River and the New Haven Railroad, 15 miles SW of Boston. Machinery, building

papers, shingles, textile products, and hospital supplies are manufactured. Walpole was settled in 1659 and incorporated in 1724. Memorial Park commemorates the town's Revolutionary War soldiers. Pop. (1960) 14,068.

WALPURGIS, SAINT, also Walpurga, Walburga, Vaubourg, and other variations, 710?–?77, English abbess, was born in Devonshire. As did her brothers St. Willibald and St. Winnibald, and her uncle St. Boniface, she went to Germany as a missionary. She lived first at Bischofsheim, and later was abbess of Heidenheim. There she is said to have written a Latin account of the travels of St. Willibald. She is buried in Eichstätt (Eichstadt), and through the stone beneath her tomb flows the so-called Oil of St. Walpurgis (chemically analyzed as water), to which medical cures have been attributed. Her feast is variously observed on February 1 and May 1. According to German folklore, witches gathered in the Harz Mountains on Walpurgis Night, the night before May 1. On May 1 an ancient pagan festival was held that was thought to furnish protection against witchcraft.

ARTHUR W. AMBLER FROM NATL. AUDUBON SOC.

The walrus, seen here in its Atlantic form, is hunted for hide, oil, and tusks. It is a massive, clumsy animal that reaches a length of 12 feet and a weight of 3,000 pounds.

WALRUS, a large fin-footed and tusked carnivore, closely related to the eared seals, belonging to the family *Odobaenidae* and confined to the Arctic regions. There are two species, a Pacific form, *Odobaenus divergens*, found as far south as the Aleutian Islands, and an Atlantic form, *O. rosmarus*, found as far south as Labrador. The walrus is a large, clumsy animal. It reaches a length of 12 feet and a weight of 3,000 pounds. Walruses have no external ears, a point of distinction from the eared seals, and the canines of the upper jaw are greatly enlarged to form the conspicuous projecting tusks. The upper lip is furnished at each side with a number of bristles; otherwise there is practically no hair on the body. The tail is small, the forelimbs nearly as large as the hind, and there are five small claws on both fore and hind feet. The young walrus has short brownish fur covering its wrinkled skin, but this is rubbed off with advancing years, and very old males may be practically furless.

Walruses are usually found living on land or floating ice. They are markedly social, and, except at the breeding season or when attacked, are gentle and inoffensive. It would appear that the females breed only once in three years.

Walruses are hunted for their oil, hides, and the ivory of the tusks. The animals are hunted in the water with harpoons, while on land they are speared or shot.

WALSALL, county borough, central England, in Staffordshire, on the main Birmingham-Manchester highway, 7 miles NW of Birmingham, of which it is a residential and industrial suburb; in the Black Country. Walsall is a manufacturing center in a region where coal and limestone are mined. Iron and steel, machine tools, brass goods, and leather goods are manufactured. Pop. (1962) 119,700.

WALSENBURG, city, S Colorado, seat of Huerfano County; on the Colorado and Southern and the Rio Grande railroads and U.S. highways 85, 87, and 160; about 41 miles S of Pueblo on the Cuchara River. Walsenburg, originally a Spanish village, was visited in the seventeenth century by conquistadores in search of gold. The city is a distributing center for an agricultural area. Timber cutting, coal mining, and the processing of flour, meat, and dairy products are the chief industries. Pop. (1960) 5,071.

WALSH, EDWARD, known as Big Moose, 1881–1959, U.S. baseball player, a member of the Baseball Hall of Fame, was born in Plains, Pa. As a right-handed pitcher—one of the hardest working in major league history—he won 181 games, for an average of .609, while with the American League Chicago team, 1904–16. In 1908 he won 40 games and lost 15, and pitched a total of 464 innings. He played with Boston of the National League, 1916–17.

WALSINGHAM, SIR FRANCIS, 1530?–90, English political leader, was born in either Footscray or Chislehurst, and educated at Kings College, Cambridge, and at Gray's Inn. A Protestant, he lived abroad in the reign of Mary I, but returned to England upon Elizabeth I's accession. He was a member of Parliament, ?1559, 1563–67, and 1574–90; and was sent on diplomatic missions in the service of Lord Burghley as early as 1568. After serving three years, 1570–73, as British representative in France, where he negotiated a defensive alliance, the Treaty of Blois (1572), he was appointed secretary of state, 1573, in which capacity he served until 1590. Walsingham was knighted by Elizabeth, 1577, probably in token of the efficient intelligence service that he had organized at his own expense. He used this system to keep informed on Jesuit and Spanish plots against the queen, and with evidence obtained through it secured the conviction of William Parry, 1585, of Anthony Babington, 1586, and of Mary, Queen of Scots, 1586–87. Walsingham was an advocate of a severe foreign policy with Spain, but was frustrated by Elizabeth in his attempts to put such a policy into effect. He died in debt, having incurred responsibility for the debts of his son-in-law, Sir Philip Sidney.

WALTARI, MIKA TOIMI, 1908– , Finnish novelist, was born in Helsinki, and was graduated from Helsinki University, 1929. He worked as a publisher's assistant, literary critic, and literary reviewer, and served as editor of an illustrated weekly *Soumen Kuvalehti*, 1936–38. He was attached to the state information bureau during the Russo-Finnish War and World War II. Among his novels are *Vieras mies tuli taloon*, 1937 (*A Stranger Came to the Farm*, 1952), *Akhaton* (1937), *Sinuhe, egytilainen*, 1945 (*The Egyptian*, 1949), *Mikael Karvajalka*, 1948 (*The Adventurer*, 1950), and *The Etruscan* (1957).

WALTER, BRUNO, 1876–1962, German conductor, was born Bruno Walter Schlesinger in Berlin, and was educated at the Stern Conservatory. He was assistant to his friend Gustav Mahler at the Vienna Opera, 1901–12; musical director of the Munich Opera, 1913–22, and the Municipal Opera, Berlin, 1925–29; conductor of the Leipzig Gewandhaus, 1929–33, and the Vienna Opera, 1935–36; musical adviser of the New York Philharmonic, 1947–49; and guest conductor of Covent Garden Opera, the Salzburg Festival, the Metropolitan Opera, the New York Philharmonic, and other orchestras. He lived in the United States from 1939, and retired in 1957.

WALTER, JOHN, 1739–1812, English newspaperman and the founder of the *Times*, was probably born in London. Walter began his career as a coal merchant at the age of 16 and built up a successful business; however, he became interested in under-writing, 1781, and soon went bankrupt because of heavy shipping losses, 1782. He then bought a patent for a new printing device, logotypes, fonts of words or segments of words rather than single letters, 1782, printed some books, and began to publish a newspaper, the *Daily Universal Register*, 1785. The *Daily Universal Register* soon became the *Times or Daily Universal Register*, 1788, and a few weeks later, simply the *Times*. He was imprisoned for libel, 1789–91, and retired to Teddington, 1795, handing over direct management of the *Times* to his son, John Walter (1776–1847). Walter was again tried and convicted for libel, 1799, but was not imprisoned.

WALTER, LUCY, also known as Mrs. Barlow, 1630?–1658, English courtesan, was born in Roch Castle near Haverfordwest, Wales. After the destruction of Roch Castle, 1644, by parliamentary forces during the English Civil War, she went first to London and then to The Hague, where she met the exiled Charles II of England, 1648, and was his mistress 1648–51. Charles admitted the paternity of her first child, James Scott, duke of Monmouth (1649–85). In 1651 she gave birth to a daughter Mary, of whom the reputed father was Henry Bennet, earl of Arlington. She was arrested in London as a spy by Oliver Cromwell's men, 1656, but was released and sent abroad.

WALTER, THOMAS USTICK, 1804–87, U.S. architect, was born in Philadelphia, Pa., became an apprentice bricklayer to his father, and studied architecture and engineering with William Strickland. Walter's first major commission, 1881, was for the Philadelphia County Prison (called Moyamensing). Next he built Girard College, Philadelphia, regarded by many as the high point of the Greek Revival style in the United States. In 1857–65 he designed and supervised the addition to the U.S. Capitol of the wings housing the Senate and House of Representatives, and of the dome. In Washington he also added wings to the Patent Office, finished the Treasury Building, and enlarged the Post Office. Walter helped organize the American Institute of Architects, 1857, and was its second president, 1876–87.

WALTERBORO, town, SE South Carolina, seat of Colleton County; on the Atlantic Coast Line Railroad and U.S. highways 15 and 17; 43 miles W of Charleston. Walterboro is a winter resort center, which is noted for fishing and hunting. Its industries include the processing of lumber and naval stores and the manufacturing of chemicals. Pop. (1960) 5,417.

WALTERS, city, SW Oklahoma, seat of Cotton County; on the Rock Island Railroad; 90 miles SW of Oklahoma City. The city is a trade center for an area in which grain, cotton, and livestock are raised. Oil wells are in the vicinity. Cotton ginning, poultry packing, and dairying are leading industries. Pop. (1960) 2,825.

WALTHALL, village, N central Mississippi, seat of Webster County; 105 miles NNE of Jackson. The village is primarily a county administrative center. Cotton and corn are grown in the area. Pop. (1960) 153.

WALTHAM, city, E Massachusetts, Middlesex County, on the Charles River, on the Boston and Maine Railroad and U.S. highway 20; 9 miles W of Boston. Waltham's diversified industries include the manufacturing of watches, knit goods, furniture, enamelware, plumbing supplies, paper, silk goods, shoes, batteries, and oil burners. It is the site of Brandeis University. The site was settled in 1637, and until Waltham became a separate town in 1738 it was a part of Watertown. Waltham was chartered as a city in 1884. Pop. (1960) 55,413.

WALTHAMSTOW, municipal borough, SE England, in Essex County, in the Lea Valley, 7 miles NE of London, of which it is an industrial suburb. Walthamstow is close to Epping Forest, and to the west of the town are several large reservoirs which supply London with water. Walthamstow is the site of the Church of St. Mary (1535), containing collections of brasses and monuments; and almshouses founded in the sixteenth century. William Morris, the poet and artist, was born there, 1834. Pop. (1951) 121,069.

WALTHER VON DER VOGELWEIDE, 1170?–?1230, greatest of the German minnesingers, was born probably in the Austrian Tirol, of noble but impecunious parents. His early years were spent at the Viennese court of Duke Leopold V, where he came under the influence of the well known minnesinger, Reinmar von Hagenau, who initiated him into the techniques of the poetic art. Upon the death of his patron, 1198, Walther became a wandering minstrel, moving from one German and Austrian court to another. During this long period of his life, his poetic productions consisted largely of lyrics celebrating courtly love, nature, social idealism, and the like. Gradually, however, in order to gain the favor of certain of his patrons, he forged his poetry into a political instrument. This instrument—sharp, stinging, often two-edged—was first put into the service of Duke Philip, a Swabian pretender to the imperial Roman throne, and later into the service of two emperors, Otto IV and Frederick II. The latter, in gratitude, gave Walther a small estate near Würzburg, ?1216, and there the great minnesinger spent his last years, without political or financial cares, devoting himself once more to the love lyric. The productions of his later period, including the immortal lyric, *Unter den linden*, took as subject matter the lives and passions of the people, rather than those of the aristocracy, thus transforming the *Minnesang* into a national, rather than a merely aristocratic, possession. Walther is considered by many the greatest German lyric poet before Johann Wolfgang von Goethe. His work had a decisive and lastingly beneficent effect upon the subsequent course of German poetry. See CHIVALRY; MINNESINGER; PROVENÇAL LANGUAGE AND LITERATURE, Literature, *Courtly Love.*

WALTON, BRIAN, or Bryan, 1600?–61, English divine and biblical scholar, was born in Seymour, Yorkshire, and studied at Cambridge. He served as a curate in Suffolk, 1623, and was rector of St. Martin's Orgar in London, 1628–41. Removed from his post on a charge of ritualism, 1641, he was imprisoned for a time, 1642, retired to Oxford, studied Oriental languages, and returned to London, 1647. There he organized a subscription, 1652, for a polyglot Bible. Walton enlisted the aid of several scholars and within a few years published the work: the *London* [or *Walton's*] *Polyglot Bible* (6 vols. 1654–57). Walton was made bishop of Chester, 1660.

WALTON, ERNEST THOMAS SINTON, 1903– , Nobel, prize-winning Irish physicist, was born in Dungarvan, the son of a Methodist minister. He was educated at Methodist College, Belfast; Trinity College, Dublin, and Cambridge University; and in 1927–34 did research in nuclear physics at Oxford University under the direction of Ernest Lord Rutherford. Walton and Sir John Cockcroft collaborated in building one of the first atom-smashing machines, 1932. With it, they accelerated protons to high speed and bombarded atoms of lithium-7 with them, thereby producing alpha particles, or helium nuclei, and energy. By this process they verified Einstein's equation $E = mc^2$ (see ATOMIC ENERGY). Walton joined the faculty of Trinity College, 1934, and became Erasmus Smith professor of natural and experimental philosophy, 1946. He and Cockcroft won the Hughes Medal of the Royal Society of London, 1938, and shared the 1951 Nobel prize in physics for their "pioneer work in the transmutation of atomic nuclei by artificially accelerated atomic particles." Walton wrote many papers on nuclear physics, hydrodynamics, and microwaves. See PHYSICS.

WALTON, GEORGE, 1741–1804, Colonial American lawyer and U.S. political figure, was born near Farmville, Va. He was a member of the Second Continental Congress, 1776–81, and was one of the signers of the Declaration of Independence (1776) and of the Articles of Confederation (1777). He was governor of Georgia, 1779–80 and 1789, and chief justice of Georgia, 1783–89. Three times he served as a judge of the superior court of Georgia, and represented Georgia in the U.S. Senate, 1795–96.

WALTON, IZAAK, 1593–1683, English writer famous for his *The Compleat Angler*, was born Isaac Walton in Stafford. Walton was baptized "Isaac," yet his first name appears as "Isaack" on his marriage license with Rachel Floud, 1626, and he signed the document "Isaak"; the inscription over his grave, in the cathedral at Winchester, gives the first name as "Isaac." From ?1614, Walton was probably an ironmonger—or perhaps, as some authorities insist, a haberdasher—in Fleet Street, London. This was in the parish of John Donne, and Walton struck up a friendship with Donne, and with other men of literary attainments, such as Michael Drayton and Sir Henry Wotton. After the defeat of the Royalists at Marston Moor, 1644, Walton retired from business, lived for a time in the country near Stafford, moved back to London, left it again, and finally lived his last 30 years as the guest of the clergy who were stationed in Winchester (Bishop George Morley and Prebend W. Hawkins).

The Compleat Angler, upon which Walton's fame is based, first appeared in May, 1653. He kept working at it, however, and for the fifth edition, that of 1676, had his friend Charles Cotton—younger than Walton by half a century—contribute some "Instructions how to angle for Trout or Grayling in a Clear Stream." Unique in many ways, *The Compleat Angler* remains not merely the best book on fishing, but also a classic of English literature as (in the judgment of many) the best book on any technical subject. The story is laid in Hertfordshire between Ware and Waltham. Dialogue, verses, song, and discussion alternate in such a way as to make the work a miracle of "contentation" in times of trouble, for the author's gracious prose oozes the inner freedom of an independent man in the stormy days of Oliver Cromwell; significantly, the subtitle of the work is . . . *the Contemplative Man's Recreation.*

After Walton's death the book was largely forgotten until early in the 1750's, when it was revived by the Rev. Moses Browne; subsequently the book was much reprinted, and more than 200 editions are known to exist. A. C. Black published, 1928, a facsimile of the first edition, and an attractive Tricentennial Edition was issued, 1953, under the sponsorship of the Isaak Walton League.

Walton's genius for friendship animates his biographies of Donne (1640), Wotton (1652), Richard Hooker (1662), George Herbert (1670), and Robert Sanderson (1678), which remain models of personal intimacy, simplicity, and sympathy. First collected in 1670, they were reprinted frequently even into the twentieth century. Walton's own life is best told by H. Nicolas, in his 1836 edition of *The Compleat Angler.*

EUGEN ROSENSTOCK-HUESSY

WALTON, SIR WILLIAM TURNER, 1902– , English composer, was born in Oldham, Lancashire. He was educated at Christ Church Cathedral Choir School and at Christ Church, Oxford, but musically he was virtually self-taught. The two works that first made him well known are a string quartet (1922), which was played at Salzburg, 1923; and *Façade* (1922), a musical accompaniment to 26 (later revised to 21) poems by Edith Sitwell. Among Walton's other compositions are the overture *Portsmouth Road* (1925); *Sinfonia concertante* (1927), for piano and orchestra; the oratorio *Belshazzar's Feast* (1931); a symphony (1934–35); the coronation marches *Crown Imperial* (1937) and *Orb and Sceptre* (1953); a violin concerto (1939); scores for motion picture productions of Shakespeare's *Henry V* (1945), *Hamlet* (1948), and *Richard III* (1955); *Te Deum* (1953); the opera *Troilus and Cressida* (1954); a'cello concerto (1956); and Symphony No. 2 (1960). He was knighted in 1951.

WALTZ, an international dance in ¾ time, originated in Europe, probably in Germany, where appeared perhaps the first published description of the new dance, *Etwas über das Waltzen* (1782). The waltz apparently went from Germany to France, ?1790, when a French writer complained about mothers permitting their daughters to dance it. Early in the nineteenth century, the waltz made its way to North America, by way of England. The dance went through different variations in all the countries where it was performed, until it culminated in the beauty of the Viennese waltz, first popularized by Josef Lanner (1801–43) and by Johann Strauss I (1804–49). His son, Johann Strauss, Jr. (1825–99), known as the Waltz King, made the dance a classic by writing hundreds of musical pieces to which it could be danced. In the Viennese waltz there is an overemphasis of the first beat and a corresponding underemphasis of the second, along with the smooth gliding style developed by the advent of the ballroom floor.

CATHERINE P. KEEGAN

WALVIS BAY, or Walfish, an enclave, which is a part of Cape of Good Hope Province of the Union of South Africa, but administered by the territory of South-West Africa, which surrounds it on three sides; on the Atlantic Ocean, about 750 miles NNW of Capetown and 175 miles E of Windhoek. A rail line connects inland to Windhoek, from which an extension passes southward to connect with the main South African lines. The port has a 30-foot-deep channel leading to a 1,500-foot-long wharf equipped with electric cranes. Walvis Bay has cold storage and refrigerating plants. Whaling and fishing remain important occupations. The enclave came into possession of the British Cape Colony in 1884, but the port remained little more than a whaling station until after the British occupation of South-West Africa in World War I. The administration of the enclave was transferred to the government of South-West Africa in 1922. Pop. (1959 est.) 2,400.

WALWORTH, SIR WILLIAM, died 1385, English political figure, was born of a Durham family. After becoming a member of the Fishmongers Guild, he advanced to the position of alderman of Bridge Ward, 1368, became sheriff of London, 1370, and was mayor of London, 1374–77 and 1380–83. He defended London Bridge against Wat Tyler during Tyler's Rebellion, 1381, and is chiefly remembered for having treacherously stabbed Tyler to death at Smithfield, 1381, while King Richard II and Tyler were discussing the demands of the rebels. See TYLER, WAT.

WAMPANOAG, a North American Indian tribe, of the Algonquian linguistic family, which formerly occupied the area east of Narragansett Bay in southern New England, where they were encountered by the Pilgrims of the Plymouth Colony, 1620. At that time the Wampanoag were located in some 30 villages, of which Pokanoket was most important. The chief, Massasoit, was friendly to the settlers, but his son Metacomet, King Philip, led an uprising against the English, 1675–78, in which the tribe inflicted heavy losses on the whites but was itself practically exterminated. The survivors merged with the Narragansett and other tribes. See KING PHILIP'S WAR.

WAMPSVILLE, village, central New York, seat of Madison County; on the New York Central Railroad, and near the New York State Thruway; 24 miles E of Syracuse. Wampsville is a trade center for a dairying area. Pop. (1960) 564.

WAMPUM, a string or belt of shell beads, or some beaded object, worn decoratively and ceremonially by the North American Indians, and used by them as money. The beads were generally of two kinds: white indicated peace, health and prosperity; black (valued at two to one of the white in exchange) signified war, death, sorrow. During the seventeenth century wampum had a standard value as money among the European colonists in New England and New York, and was also used in Virginia, North and South Carolina and on the Pacific Coast. It was frequently counterfeited. Symbolic patterns such as diamonds, squares, parallel lines, peace pipes, animals, and so forth, were woven into belts to convey messages.

WANAMAKER, JOHN, 1838–1922, U.S. merchant, religious worker, and philanthropist, was born in Philadelphia, was educated in common schools, and began his business career as an errand boy. In Philadelphia, Wanamaker and his future brother-in-law, Nathan Brown, established the clothing house of Wanamaker and Brown, 1861; after Brown's death, 1868, Wanamaker founded the house of John Wanamaker and Company, 1868. He opened a department store in Philadelphia, 1876, and added branches in New York City, 1896 and 1906. Active in religious work, he was president of the Philadelphia Young Men's Christian Association, 1870–83. Wanamaker was U.S. postmaster general in Pres. Benjamin Harrison's cabinet, 1889–93.

WANDERING JEW. See SPIDERWORT.

WANDERING JEW, according to medieval legend, a Jew who struck Jesus Christ as the Saviour was on the way to Calvary, and who was condemned to wander throughout the world until His second coming. An early version of the story is ascribed to Matthew Paris (1200–59), who professed to have received the story from an Armenian bishop. According to tradition, the Wandering Jew was a doorkeeper in the palace of Pontius Pilate. The legend was much enlarged by various impostors who appeared in the sixteenth and seventeenth centuries pretending to be the Wandering Jew. A Wandering Jew who appeared in Hamburg, 1547, gave his name as Ahasuerus, and declared that he had been a shoemaker in Jerusalem, and had refused to let Christ rest at his door when He passed by, bearing the Cross. He struck Jesus, who replied, "I will stand here and rest, but thou shalt go on until the last day." Under the names Cartaphilus, Butadeus, and Isaac Laqueden, similar impostors turned up in Brussels, Paris, Moscow, Madrid, and other cities. Among the many modern literary versions of the legend are George Croly's *Salathiel* (1828), Eugène Sue's *Le juif errant* (1844), Edgar Quinet's *Ahasuerus* (1833) and poems by Nikolous Lenau, Herman Heijermans, Friedrick von Schlegel and Adelbert von Chamisso.

WANDFLOWER, a colorful, erect plant belonging to the family *Iridaceae*. Although the wandflower, *Sparaxis tricolor*, is a single species, it is divided into several varieties, depending upon the color and size of the flowers. The plant has simple or slightly branched stems from 6 to 18 inches in height, few flat, swordlike leaves, and spikes of 6-petaled flowers, varying from yellow to bright red. It grows naturally in South Africa, but is cultivated in many countries from bulbs.

WANER, PAUL GLEE, 1903–   , U.S. baseball player known as Big Poison, was born in Harrah, Okla. He was an outfielder with Pittsburgh, 1926–40, Brooklyn, 1941, 1943–44, and Boston, 1941–42, of the National League, and a pinch hitter with New York, 1944–45, of the American League. He was National League batting champion, 1927, 1934, and 1936, and was named the league's most valuable player, 1927. His life-time batting average was .333. Waner was elected to the Baseball Hall of Fame, 1952.

WANHSIEN, city, central China, in Szechwan Province, seat of Wanhsien County, on the Yangtze River, 140 miles NE of Chungking. Wanhsien has an important river port, and is a trade and processing center for the agricultural produce of the Yangtze Valley. Rice, wheat, oranges and other fruits, beans, and sugar cane are the major crops which are packed and processed in the city. Wanhsien has considerable trade in tung oil, medicinal herbs, goat skins, and hog bristles. Pop. (1959 est.) 110,000.

WANNE-EICKEL, city, W Germany, in North Rhine–Westphalia Province, in the Ruhr, a road and railway junction point, 8 miles NE of Essen, and 13 miles WNW of Dortmund. The city forms part of the large industrial belt in the Ruhr coal field, a district which is virtually one 40-mile-long urban area. Coal is mined in the city, and chemicals, mainly oil products, and nitrates, are manufactured. Wanne-Eickel was formed in 1926, with the incorporation of the two towns, Wanne and Eickel. Pop. (1958) 107,521.

WAPAKONETA, city, W central Ohio, seat of Auglaize County; on the Auglaize River, the Baltimore and Ohio and the New York Central railroads, and U.S. highways 25 and 33; 75 miles NW of Columbus. Wapakoneta was the site of an Indian village and according to legend was named for an Indian chief and his wife. In 1831 the Shawnees and Senecas signed a treaty there yielding their lands to the government. Wapakoneta was platted in 1833. The city is a trade center for a diversified agricultural area. Furniture, steel toys, cigars, machine tools, dairy products, and canned goods are manufactured. Pop. (1960) 6,756.

WAPELLO, city, SE Iowa, seat of Louisa County; on the Iowa River; on the Rock Island Railroad, and on U.S. highway 61; 40 miles SW of Davenport. The city is a shipping point for livestock and grain. Wapello, incorporated in 1856, was named in honor of a chief of the Fox Indian tribe. Pop. (1960) 1,745.

CHICAGO NAT. HIST. MUS.

The wapiti, a North American deer of impressive proportions, is found in Yellowstone National Park. A wapiti stag may be a thousand pounds and five and one half feet tall.

WAPITI, a North American deer, belonging to the same group as the Scottish red deer, popularly called elk in western North America. The Wapiti, *Cervis canadensis,* has antlers that are greatly developed and smooth. Its color is dark brown on the head and neck, gray on the back, flanks, and sides, and blackish below, the legs being brown. Its height at the shoulder is about five and a half feet in a full-grown stag, which may weigh as much as 1,000 pounds, making them second only to the moose in size. Today the principal stronghold of the wapiti is in Yellowstone National Park. The Wapiti were at one time found in all northern areas of North America.

WAR, in the traditional legal sense, is a state of affairs that permits two or more hostile groups equally to carry on a conflict by armed force. Its essence is the equal legal status of the states involved—that is, the lack of a legal distinction between aggressors and victims of aggression—and the right of nonparticipating states to be impartial (see NEUTRALITY). The numerous post-World War II treaties that prohibit resorting to hostilities or aggression in the settlement of disputes require that the aggressor be distinguished from the victim in such conflicts. Once this distinction has been made with respect to any war, the participating states are not equal legally. See COURTS, INTERNATIONAL; INTERNATIONAL LAW.

The intensity, frequency, and causes of war in the material sense have varied greatly in history. These variations have depended upon (1) the characteristics of the international political system or organization (see INTERNATIONAL RELATIONS); (2) the rates of political, economic, social, and technological change (see PROGRESS); and (3) differences in the rates of change among these factors in different areas. Among the immediate causes of war have been (1) the rise of an ambitious ruler; (2) the development in a particular country of social, economic, or political institutions favorable to aggression; (3) the invention of a new weapon, tactic, or strategy that seems to promise an easy victory to the power which employs it first; (4) serious political unrest or economic depression in a particular area; and (5) judgmental errors by governments in formulating and pursuing foreign policy.

Peace has been preserved for considerable periods of time—as during much of the second, thirteenth, and nineteenth centuries in Western civilization—when international political institutions have been well adapted to the degree of economic and social contact among the members of the international community (see PEACE). During the twentieth century, the rapid shrinking of the world, as a consequence of technical change, greatly increased international contacts and strains. There was not, however, an equally rapid development of international institutions for dealing with these conditions. Consequently, the twentieth century, like the seventeenth, witnessed unusually severe and frequent wars.

The United Nations represented an attempt to create organs for facilitating a dual program of making aggression unlikely to succeed and of promoting international co-operation. This dual program resembled that of the League of Nations and of other diplomatic and theoretical plans of the previous four centuries for minimizing war. See LEAGUE OF NATIONS; UNITED NATIONS.

The increasing destructiveness and expansiveness of war during the eighteenth, nineteenth, and twentieth centuries led to the gradual development of what was, by mid-twentieth century, a remarkably general and intense opinion that war should be eliminated, and led to study of the problem of war by historians, social scientists, and statesmen. Such studies have generally concluded (1) that war is not an inevitable consequence of human nature; (2) that it has no single cause; (3) that political, economic, ideological, and psychological factors are usually involved in the origin of wars; and (4) that war, being a manmade institution, may be controlled through appropriate modification of human institutions. Probably the most persistent cause of war has been its futility in maintaining the solidarity of states. See ARBITRATION, INTERNATIONAL; BALANCE OF POWER; BELLIGERENCY; DIPLOMACY; DISARMAMENT; IMPERIALISM; INTERNATIONALISM; NATIONALISM; PACIFISM.   QUINCY WRIGHT

WARFARE

Primitive Warfare. Earliest evidences of human life indicate a community existence and a defense of the community against other tribes or races. Some savage or primitive tribes, however, were more warlike than others; and some fought not at all, or rarely. Some, such as the Eskimos of Greenland, the Aurohuacos of Colombia, the Napos of Ecuador, the Lapps, and some African tribes seem to have produced no weapons specifically for warfare. Reasons for primitive war have been given as land, booty, sex, religion, cannibalism, head hunting, human sacrifice, and glory. Presumably stones and clubs were among the first primitive weapons, but the spear, throwing stick, bow and arrow, sword, and knife were developed early in prehistoric times, and with them were developed customs and techniques of warfare. As far as is known, little strategy and almost no tactics were employed; the fighting was largely man-to-man and consisted largely of superior prowess and example. This is illustrated in the stories of such biblical heroes as Gideon, David, Jonathan, and Joshua, of the characters of Homer's *Iliad*, and of chiefs of Indian tribes. Such strategy as was employed took the form of sudden attacks in overwhelming mass, sharp attacks followed by quick retreats, the use of concealment, surprise, and ambush. With advancement into a state of barbarism, these characteristics increased, but seldom could discipline be extended to a degree that permitted economy of force or the employment of reserves. It was usually a principle of primitive and barbaric warfare that all warriors sought the battlefront to attain honors or the other objectives of warfare; there was usually a cult of the warrior. Hence, few were available for security detachments—with the exception, perhaps, of old men who won their honors and retired from active conflict. It may have been by these that battle was directed, the active leaders being more concerned with exhibiting their individual prowess.

Ancient Warfare. The ancient empires of Egypt, Assyria, and Persia had highly developed military systems. The best picture of military organization in this period is found in Xenophon's *Cyropaedia*, which one authority has called "the fountainhead of military thought."

Military service was required of all Persians, who underwent a rigorous 10 years' apprenticeship in which their natural bent for hunting was used to inculcate military ideas. They also served as garrison, guard and police for the state. At the age of 26 or 27 they began active military service, for which they were liable for 25 years. The Persians relied heavily upon cavalry, and used both mounted lancers and mounted archers. The chariot was used at first mainly as a means of conveyance; later, scythes were attached to the wheels to permit deadly charges through enemy ranks. Infantry was armed with short spear and short sword, and shield; little armor was used, except by the wealthier classes, although there is a story of Cyrus distributing armor to all his trained soldiery. The establishment of armories, among other things, suggests that during the period of Persian ascendancy the problem of supply became a factor in warfare, but until late in human history soldiers often provided their own armament.

The wars of the Greeks and Persians saw the beginnings of sea warfare and some advance in tactics and command (see MILITARY STRATEGY AND TACTICS). Epaminondas in the Peloponnesian Wars was the first great military genius, and contributed importantly to tactics—particularly in the oblique order later developed by Frederick the Great—and in strategy. In his final battle of Mantinea, he changed direction of his approach, throwing the rigid battleline of his opponents into confusion. Philip II of Macedon, and his son Alexander the Great contributed the Macedonian Phalanx, the first fixed formation employed in military warfare, and requiring a high degree of discipline. By using spears of different lengths, those in rear ranks extending even with those of the front rank, a solid mass could be put in motion; but could not readily change direction.

The Romans developed a more flexible formation, the legion, broken down into subunits of hundreds and tens, and depending largely upon a short throwing spear and a short sword, and high discipline developed by long training. In the earlier period the aristocracy provided the mounted arm; particularly in later times, the Romans depended upon allies for bowmen. The great success of the legion, however, gradually resulted in Rome becoming dependent upon a professional army, in later times recruited largely from the provinces. The Romans developed siege warfare to high degree, using the catapult, ballista, movable towers (usable as rams), and other structures, and mass formations in which their huge shields were used as protection for sides and overhead as well as front.

The advance in professionalism relieved native Romans from the necessity for military service and brought about a dependence upon conquered peoples that was to be their undoing. An earlier result was the dominance of the Praetorian Guard in Rome, which became a ruling factor and deposed and set up emperors. The most formidable opponent of the Romans in the earlier period was Hannibal of Carthage, whose use of elephants has been compared to modern tank tactics. His victory at Cannae, brought about by a purposely weak center, permitting the surrounding of the Roman forces that penetrated it, has become the classic example of a battle of annihilation. Hannibal's mastery of battle tactics, however, was overcome by the harassing tactics of Fabius who refused to accept battle, and later by the genius of Scipio Africanus, who adopted the indirect approach of cutting off Hannibal's dependencies and sources of supplies, thus forcing him to return to defend Carthage under a considerable disadvantage, and resulting in his defeat. Julius Caesar's Gallic and Civil wars have long been considered models; they illustrate the Roman system at its height, but his original contribution to warfare was slight. In the end the Romans succumbed to their long neglect of cavalry and light forces. At Adrianople, A.D. 378, the Gothic hosts cut the legions to pieces. From then until the invention of firearms, cavalry became a dominant military arm.

Warfare in the Middle Ages. With the downfall of Rome both the professional military force and the theory of universal liability to military service underwent considerable changes. The Germanic hordes that overwhelmed the Roman Empire were tribes in which every member was a warrior, thus leaving the militia theory as a residual legacy. But the preference for cavalry soon gave dominance to the heavily armed and armored knight, who carried an array of equipment that could only be afforded by the wealthy. The knight also needed a few followers to assist him, and for this purpose he employed a team of which he was a champion. As he was usually a noble, he brought in other followers to serve the needs of infantry. War began to be fought on a private basis, although the national fiction was maintained that the noble brought his followers to arms at the command of his overlord, ultimately the king. This fiction was complicated, however, in those cases where the noble owed fealty to opposing lords engaged in warfare against each other, as frequently happened with lords of large holdings, notably the dukes of Burgundy who held fiefs under both the king of France and the Holy Roman Emperor. The story of the Middle Ages, however, is the story of the gradual increase in the power of kings and nations. See FEUDAL SOCIETY, *Influence of Military Development on Feudalism.*

Meanwhile the old nationalistic or tribal idea of universal service produced some infantry that at times upset the dominance of the chivalry. The longbowmen of England, the Genoese crossbowmen, and the pikemen of Switzerland at times successfully opposed the knights in the open field. Castles, however, developed at about the period of the Crusades, proved invulnerable to all but the most sustained and elaborate sieges until the invention of gunpowder.

Siege tactics brought about a return to professionalism and the later Middle Ages saw free companies and the bands of the *Condottieri* that made warfare a highly sporting proposition—so far as their members were concerned—in which maneuver was so exalted that resort to bloodshed was sometimes omitted. Another type of professional, the private persons, scientists, and inventors, who were producing the first artillery, brought about an invasion of the military caste by science comparable to the introduction of the atomic bomb into World War II. The musketeers were at first auxiliary to the pikemen, and the Spanish infantry combining these two elements were the most notable fighters of their time.

Gustavus II Adolphus perfected the tactics of firearms, breaking up the battleline into companies, regiments, and brigades. He also brought artillery to the field of battle.

The Seventeenth and Eighteenth Centuries. The Thirty Years' War was a reversion to barbarism unequaled since primitive times. Tribal war had been marked by the slaughter of prisoners and of conquered peoples; this had been characteristic of the hordes of Attila, Genghis Khan and Tamerlane. But primitive peoples had also adopted prisoners into the tribe, or made slaves of them, and the Romans, not always notable for humanity, had adopted both customs. The Roman Empire was built largely by granting amenities to conquered peoples rather than by peaceful alliances. In the Middle Ages the Roman Catholic church with its Truce of God had done much to mitigate warfare, as had the institution of chivalry. Such conflicts as the Hundred Years' War and the Wars of the Roses affected the population of the countries involved very little, even including those in the direct paths of armies, who might be plundered. But the wars of religion were fought against a background of conflicting ideologies, and it is estimated that during the religious wars of the Reformation and Counter Reformation more than half of the population of the German states perished, while the conditions of life of those who survived were so degraded by ravage and plunder that their development was greatly retarded.

Yet as the religious wars became more and more political there was some return to an age of reason. Grotius and others produced codes of international law. Under the influence of Marshal Vauban with his systems of defense and of sieges, warfare became more scientific and more a matter for armies (see VAUBAN, SÉBASTIEN LE PRESTRE, MARQUIS DE). Sometimes the inhabitants of besieged cities were allowed to leave, while the armies fought it out.

The Duke of Marlborough broke away from siege warfare and returned to maneuver. His devastation of Bavaria added little to the idea of moderation in warfare, but armies in this period were small, casualties were low, and wars had little effect on national populations. It was the custom of this period, also, for armies to go into winter quarters, so that warfare was largely a seasonal occupation. The wars of the eighteenth century were largely carried on in this fashion, the amenities reaching a peak in the somewhat doubtful story of the French offering the British the honor of firing the first volley when they met in the Battle of Fontenoy. But in America in this same period both the French and the British employed the Indians—the French more successfully —and had little success in their probably honest endeavors to restrain the excesses of the red men.

Such defeats as that of Gen. George Braddock in the American wilderness did much to change the formalized tactics of the period, and resulted in the development by Generals Thomas Gage and Sir William Howe and other British leaders of light infantry and of such organizations as Rogers' Rangers, trained to shoot accurately, instead of firing by volleys, and to fight as individual skirmishers, instead of in the fixed formations such as Frederick II used so successfully in his oblique maneuvers.

This tendency was developed further by the American Revolution, which proved on several occasions that accurate rifle fire from defensive or concealed positions, even though from otherwise untrained men, might be effective even against troops highly trained in the tactics of the day. The improvement in the flintlock rifle had made many changes in tactics possible because of its increased accuracy, particularly in the Kentucky rifle which proved deadly in the hands of Gen. Daniel Morgan's riflemen and other frontier troops. General Sir Banastre Tarleton on the British side, and Col. Henry Lee on the American, developed raiding tactics of cavalry on a light horse formula, corresponding somewhat to the light infantry idea. Partisan warfare under Gen. Francis Marion and Gen. Thomas Sumter forecast the guerrilla warfare of the nineteenth century. Despite its occasional excesses and the fact that the war was a rebellion, it was carried on with considerable limitation. Except where Indians were involved, little violence was done to the civilian population, and prisoners were customarily exchanged, although British mistreatment of prisoners on the hulk *Jersey*, in New York Harbor, was met by counter-accusations of American violation of surrender terms in the case of Burgoyne's army.

Armies on both sides were recruited by the volunteer system, the Americans calling out general levies of militia for limited periods, and the British supplementing their forces by hiring mercenaries from the German states of Hesse-Cassel and Baden. Despite American resentment at the Hessians, prisoners were so well treated that many eluded attempts to repatriate them and remained as settlers.

American success undoubtedly affected many features of the French Revolution, which soon followed, particularly the idea of the levy en masse in imitation of the militia system. Again there was present a conflict of ideologies, marked by an increase of excesses on both sides—notable was the French looting of art treasures from conquered lands. Napoleon I used huge mass armies, raised by conscription. He instituted the division system to give greater mobility in maneuver, used masses of artillery and huge cavalry charges. After his defeat of Prussia, the Prussians resorted to conscription and to training successive groups in the small force allotted to them in the peace terms. Karl von Clausewitz translated the policies of August von Gneisenau and Gerhard von Scharnhorst into a theory of absolute war, based on mass armies raised by conscription. Meanwhile technical improvements in arms and transportation brought even greater segments of national economy into absolute war.

The U.S. Civil War. Railroads were used for the first time to transport and supply troops during the Civil War, and many campaigns were fought for the control of railroad lines. The percussion rifle made possible more rapid fire, and the breech-loading repeater was beginning to be used. Rifle fire, backed by masses of artillery, became so heavy that troops were forced into trenches, even on the offensive, in the later stages of the war. By the time of the Franco-Prussian War the needle gun forecast rapid-fire arms, the French mitrailleuse and the U.S. Gatling gun were forerunners of the machine gun, and breech-loading artillery was coming into use. At sea, the *Monitor* and the *Merrimac* of the Civil War had made all wooden navies obsolete, and the application of steam and armor made sea warfare ever more technical. See MONITOR AND MERRIMAC.

But of even more effect on the future was Count Helmuth Karl Bernhard von Molke's quick success based on staff-planned mobilization and war planning. Following the Franco-Prussian War, most nations of Europe hastened to copy German conscription and staff organization.

Despite the effect of mass armies, guerrilla warfare had made some advancement. The word itself derived from the Spanish warfare against Napoleon, of which advantage was taken by the Duke of Wellington to drive the French out of the Peninsula. Giuseppi Garibaldi employed guerrilla tactics successfully in attempts to aid the Franc-Tireurs of the Franco-Prussian War. Similar tactics were employed by American forces, who had long practice in Indian warfare. Especially successful were the Boer commandos of the war against Britain at the close of the century—the word commando being copied by the British for similarly trained troops in World War II.

The Spanish-American War and the Russo-Japanese War followed the more orthodox lines of mass warfare. Barbed wire was first used in the defenses of Santiago, and the siege of Port Arthur forecast the character of World War I. At sea, the submarine and wireless telegraphy were used by the Japanese. The machine gun, the bolt-action repeating rifle, and rapid-fire artillery had begun to change the character of war. Cavalry declined after failure of French charges in 1870. Cavalry divisions were used in the early stages of World War I, but thereafter mounted troops were effective only under exceptional conditions of terrain, as in the Palestine Campaign of World War I or the Polish-Russian War of 1920.

World War I was a continuous trench system built across France and Belgium, which stultified maneuver and strategy. In an attempt to break the deadlock, artillery was increased to a proportion of 20 guns to 1,000 men, whereas 3 guns to 1,000 men had been the highest proportion used in any previous war. Yet defense was increased in depth so that a break-through was rarely attained and none achieved decisive results. The tank, introduced in 1916, was generally employed in such small numbers as to demonstrate potentialities rather than to attain decisive results. The airplane, although in a primitive state, was used from the beginning of the war, at first largely for reconnaissance, but later for bombing, both in direct support of troops and in what later became known as strategic bombing—campaigns against enemy industry. The Germans largely employed Zeppelin dirigibles in bombing raids against London and for long-range transport (see BALLOON, History of Ballooning, *Military Uses*). Their vulnerability, even to normal peace-time hazards, resulted in their gradual abandonment, particularly after the *Hindenburg* disaster of 1937. Motor transport also was used to large extent in World War I. The war was characterized largely by the dominance of the machine gun and rapid-fire artillery, bringing immense weight of fire power to bear against any offensive, so that even when large preponderance of offensive weight was used, a decisive result was seldom attained. See AIR WARFARE; FORTIFICATION, Field Fortifications.

The vast increase in mechanical equipment, including the consumption of ammunition, which reached enormous proportions compared to any previous war, brought much of national effort into the field of warmaking. Conscription was adopted by virtually all the nations at war, and the necessity for exemption of essential workers first became a serious problem. Rationing of critical goods for civilian populations of entire nations was necessary. Warfare now more than ever before affected entire populations.

Absolute war also saw the disappearance of many of the amenities that had marked previous conflicts. Britain widely extended the rule of contraband. Protests from the United States brought the two nations to the verge of war, but the United States became more seriously embroiled with Germany over its failure to observe the old laws of sea warfare in its use of submarines; unrestricted submarine warfare, marked by the sinking of the huge liner *Lusitania* with large loss of life, brought the United States into the war, after which the United States enforced even more rigidly the new British rules of contraband. Blockade was made virtually absolute, and was reduced to an absurdity, reached in self-imposed bans against German art, music, and literature.

Germany had forfeited the good opinion of the neutral world by its violation of treaty guarantee of the neutrality of Belgium at the outset of the war. Stories of alleged German atrocities were highly exaggerated; there was a tendency on both sides to ignore many previous agreements tending to limit the means of warfare. The Germans violated a Hague convention by using poison gas on the battlefield, which in the end was used more effectively against them. Yet much of international law survived, especially in regard to the treatment of prisoners and of conquered populations. Germany's collapse was largely brought about by a collapse of morale just as the Allied victory drive was nearly halted by supply weakness. See CHEMICAL WARFARE; PRISONER OF WAR.

World War II saw the intensification of many of the tendencies and techniques that had been evident in World War I. The tank, developed along the line of big guns and heavy armor, and the airplane restored mobility to the battlefield. The war was less continuous and was fought out in phases resembling the battles and campaigns of former wars—but battles were no longer named for villages, but for nations; the Battle of France, the Battle of Germany, and so on. The tank-airplane combination brought Germany quick victories against Poland, Norway, the Netherlands, Belgium, France, Yugoslavia, and Greece, but the bomber failed to conquer Britain, and the invasion of Russia opened a battle of such vast scale as to restore effect to the defensive. In the east, both sides succeeded in making penetrations, but decisive actions were rare, and the dangers of excessive commitment were illustrated in the Russian counterblow that captured a whole German army at Stalingrad. When the United States entered the war, the problem of reaching a battlefield was vital. In campaigns in Africa, Sicily, and Italy, and against Japan in islands of the Pacific a new amphibious warfare, based upon carefully co-ordinated plans of army, navy, and air forces, was developed. So much did air warfare dominate, however, that much of the fighting was directed toward the capture and development of air bases. Bombing was employed in ever-increasing ratio directed against war industry, culminating in the use of the atomic bomb against Japan.

Total national effort was directed toward winning the war, to an unprecedented degree. Even in the United States, remote from most direct action, much of civilian economy was suspended and the bulk of the nation's industrial potential was directed toward the production of munitions. An entire new navy was virtually created during the course of the war, as well as an air force, the proportions of which seemed fantastic. Germany introduced the pilotless rocket as an agent of destruction.

Not since the Thirty Years' War had civilian populations been subjected to such total involvement in warfare. Entire cities were leveled, and conquered peoples were sometimes used as slave labor. Some hope of future limitation was seen in the formation of the United Nations and in the generally recognized potentialities of atomic warfare. This hope was dimmed by the Soviet refusal to accept U.S. proposals for control of atomic energy, and the subsequent development of atomic and hydrogen weapons by additional nations.

Postwar trends included great advances in jet propulsion, first applied to airplanes by the Germans in World War II; development of extra-long-range bombers; further development of rockets and guided missiles; improvement of the atomic bomb and of a panoply of atomic artillery pieces and other weapons; and development of an even more powerful nuclear device, the hydrogen bomb.

Korean Conflict. Because of political limitations imposed upon United Nations forces, the Korean conflict developed into a battle between land armies. Masses of Communist troops were able to hold their own with the outnumbered but better equipped United Nations troops. Jet-propelled aircraft appeared in limited numbers, as did some new weapons, but both weapons and tactics were largely conventional. See ARMY; NAVY; NAVAL STRATEGY AND TACTICS; AMMUNITION; WORLD WAR I; WORLD WAR II; ARMS; ARMY, U.S.; NAVY, U.S.; REVOLUTION; WAR CRIMES.

BIBLIOG.–Stanislaw Andrzejewski, *Military Organization and Society* (1954); Raymond Aron, *On War* (1959); Roland H. Bainton, *Christian Attitudes Toward War and Peace* (1960); Joseph M. Cameron, *Anatomy of Military Merit* (1960); Karl von Clausewitz, *On War* (1943); Stanton A. Coblentz, *From Arrow to Atom Bomb: The Psychological History of War* (1953); Edward S. Creasy, *Fifteen Decisive Battles of the World* (1955); Arthur G. Enock, *This War Business: A Book for Every Citizen of Every Country* (1952); J. F. C. Fuller, *Military History of the Western World*, 3 vols. (1954–56); Raymond L. Garthoff, *Soviet Image of Future War* (1959); James M. Gavin, *War and Peace in the Space Age* (1959); Jesse G. Gray, *Warriors: Reflections on Men in Battle* (1959); Fritz Grob, *Relativity of War and Peace* (1949); Norman L. Hill and Doniver A. Lund, *If the Churches Want World Peace* (1958); Louise W. Holborn, ed., *War and Peace Aims of the United Nations*, 2 vols. (1943–1948); Irving L. Horowitz, *Idea of War and Peace in Contemporary Philosophy* (1956); Klaus E. Knorr, *War Potential of Nations* (1956); Basil H. Liddell Hart, *Thoughts on War* (1944); C. Wright Mills, *Causes of World War Three* (1959); Ralph L. Moellering, *Modern War and the American Churches* (1957); Lynn Montross, *War Through the Ages* (1960); Paul E. Moyer, *Case for Peace* (1955); William J. Nagle, ed., *Morality and Modern Warfare: The State of the Question* (1960); John U. Nef, *War and Human Progress: An Essay on the Rise of Industrial Civilization* (1951); Tom H. Pear, ed., *Psychological Factors of Peace and War* (1951); Lewis F. Richardson, *Arms and Insecurity: A Mathematical Study of the Causes and Origins of War* (1960); Porter E. Sargent, *War and Education* (1943); *Nature of Peace and War* (1949); Frederick L. Schuman, *Commonwealth of Man: An Inquiry into Power Politics and World Government* (1954); Hans Speier, *Social Order and the Risks of War* (1952); Julius Stone, *Legal Controls of International Conflict* (1959); Alix Strachey, *Unconscious Motives of War* (1957); Franziskus M. Stratmann, *War and Christianity Today* (1957); Alan J. P. Taylor, *Rumours of War* (1953); Arnold J. Toynbee, *War and Civilization* (1950); Robert W. Tucker, *The Just War: A Study in Contemporary Am. Doctrine* (1960); Frederick J. P. Veale, *Advance to Barbarism* (1953); Kenneth N. Waltz, *Man, the State and War: A Theoretical Analysis* (1959); Quincy Wright, *Study of War*, 2 vols. (1942).

WAR, LAW OF. See INTERNATIONAL LAW.

WAR AND PEACE, Russian *Voina i Mir*, a panoramic prose epic of the life of Russian nobility during the Napoleonic Wars, was written, 1862–69, by the novelist Lev Tolstoi (1828–1910), and first appeared serially in the *Russian Messenger*, 1864–69. One of Tolstoi's most important works, the book is a thorough exposition of his well developed, yet ultimately superficial philosophy of history; a serious study of the rigid code of laws and customs, and the corrupt moral atmosphere and the hypocrisy of the age; and a poignant satire of that segment of society to which the author belonged. The novel, which records the lives of the members of four prominent families, has an intricate structure and a multitude of characters. Pierre Bezukhov, typifying the Russian idealist of Tolstoi's time, is forever in doubt as to what is right or wrong, and is unable to answer his own perplexing philosophical questions—questions, it may be added, that Tolstoi himself never answered to his own satisfaction. Prince Andrey Bolkonsky, a man of noble instincts, is unable to defy the tradition in which he has been caught; one of the most poetic love stories in fiction is that of Andrey and Natasha Rostov. The book attained only a slight popularity when first published, but it soon came to be regarded as one of the masterpieces of literature, but a masterpiece more often talked about than read, since its extreme complexity and length make reading it a major exercise in memory, comparable in this respect to Marcel Proust's *The Remembrance of Things Past* and James Joyce's *Finnegans Wake*.

WARANGAL, city, central India, in Andhra Pradesh State, capital of the Warangal District, on the Hyderabad-Vijayavada Railway, 80 miles NE of Hyderabad. Warangal is a trade and processing center for an area in which rice, cotton, oilseed, and peanuts are produced. The city is a cotton-milling center, and is noted for its hand-woven carpets and bookbinding industry. Close to the present city is the old Hindu fortress of Warangal, a name derived from the word *Orakkal*, which means "solitary rock." This fortress was the ancient capital of the Ganpati Dynasty, prior to its capture by the Bahmani, 1424. The city has several old temples, and halls dating from the Moslem period. Pop. (1951) 133,130.

WARBECK, PERKIN, 1474–99, a pretender to the English crown during the reign of Henry VII, was born in Tournai, Flanders (later Belgium), the son of Jehan de Werbecque. He lived in Antwerp, Belgium, Bergen-op-Zoom, Netherlands, and Portugal. In 1491 he sailed to Ireland, where he was mistaken for the son of the Duke of Clarence or a bastard of Richard III. Somewhat supported by the earls of Kildare and Desmond, Perkin was summoned, 1492, to Flanders by Margaret, sister of Edward IV (1442–83), and the principal advocate of the Yorkist cause in exile. Here he was put forth as Richard, duke of York, the son of Edward IV and was accepted as the lawful king of England by the German Emperor Maximilian I, James IV of Scotland, and Charles III of France (who knew, however, that he was an impostor). Perkin failed in an expedition to England in 1495, but was received in Scotland, whose king gave his cousin, Catherine Gordon, in marriage to the pretender. Landing in Cornwall, 1497, Perkin was joined by some people of the country, but fled on the approach of royal troops at Exeter. He was captured, confessed that he was an impostor, and was imprisoned in the Tower; it was said later that he had attempted to escape and had been executed.

WARBLE FLY. See BOTFLY.

WARBLER, a bird belonging either to the family *Compsothlypidae*, or to the family *Sylviidae*. The *Compsothlypidae* are known as the wood warblers or American warblers to distinguish them from the Old World warblers of the *Sylviidae*. Wood warblers occur throughout North, Central, and most of South America. As a rule, they are birds of striking plumage, yellow being the most common color. Approximately 200 species and subspecies are recognized, many of which are confined to

LYNWOOD M. CHACE
Warbler

the tropics. Wood warblers are active birds, almost entirely insectivorous, and mostly arboreal, nesting and feeding among trees and rarely descending to the ground. Despite their name, not all of the warblers are exceptional songsters. Fifty or more migratory species are known in the United States, wintering in the tropics of the Western Hemisphere and returning north to breed in the spring. The eggs, usually four or five in number, are whitish in color with brownish dots on the larger end. ALBERT WOLFSON

WARBURG, JAMES PAUL, 1896–   , U.S. banker and author, was born in Hamburg, Germany, the son of the banker Paul Moritz Warburg (1868–1932). He emigrated to the United States, 1902, and graduated from Harvard University, 1917. He was vice-president, 1921–29, and president, 1931–32, of the International Acceptance Bank, New York City, became a member of Pres. Franklin Roosevelt's so-called Brain Trust and served as financial adviser to the U.S. delegation to the World Economic Conference in London, 1933. He wrote numerous books on international affairs and economic problems, among them, *Last Call for Common Sense* (1949); *Victory Without War* (1951); *West in Crisis* (1959); *Reveille for Rebels* (1960); *Disarmament: The Challenge of the Nineteen Sixties* (1961).

WARBURG, OTTO HEINRICH, 1883–   , Nobel prize-winning German physiologist, biochemist, and physician, was born in Freiburg, Baden. He studied at Berlin and Heidelberg, and received doctorates in both chemistry and medicine. After serving in World War I, he became a professor at the Kaiser Wilhelm Institute, Berlin, and later became its director. Warburg conducted important research in tissue respiration, particularly in the enzymes involved in the fermentation process, and discovered, 1932, the yellow enzyme. His work in tissue respiration proved valuable in the study of cancer. He was awarded the Nobel prize in medicine and physiology, 1931, "for his discovery of the nature and mode of action of the respiratory enzyme." He wrote *Stoffwechsel der Tumoren* (1926), *Katalytische Wirkungen der lebendigen Substanz* (1928), *Schwermetalle als Wirkungsgruppen von Fermenten* (1946), and *Weiterentwicklung der zellphysiologischen Methoden* (1958).

WARBURTON, WILLIAM, 1698–1779, English bishop and author, was born in Newark. Ordained a priest, 1727, he served in various rectories, and became chaplain to the Prince of Wales, 1738. He was named preacher to Lincoln's Inn, 1746, became chaplain to King George II, 1754, dean of Bristol, 1757, and bishop of Gloucester, 1759. Warburton wrote *The Alliance Between Church and State, or the Necessity and Equity of an Established Religion and a Test Law* (1736); *The Divine Legation of Moses, Demonstrated on the Principles of a Religious Deist* (1737–41), an attack on the deists' doctrine of the Old Testament; *Vindication of the Essay on Man* (1739–40), which established a close relationship between Alexander Pope and Warburton; and *Doctrine of Grace* (1762), an attack on Methodism.

WAR CRIMES, actions committed by enemy nationals made subject to punishment by the victorious nation or nations.

Before World War II three types of acts were regarded as war crimes: (1) acts of war committed against a belligerent by noncombatants (persons not in uniform and not acting in accordance with the law of war), and acts committed by inhabitants of territory under military occupation; (2) acts against the law of war, such as the refusal to give quarter, cruel and inhuman treatment of prisoners, misuse of the flag of truce, poisoning of wells and the water supply, bombing of undefended towns, attacks on hospital ships, taking of hostages, ill-treatment of prisoners, pillage, wanton devastation, the imposition of collective penalties, and other acts conditionally forbidden, but subject to the exception of military necessity; (3) acts not forbidden by the law of war, but punishable under International Law, such as Sabotage, Espionage, and Sedition. See INTERNATIONAL LAW.

Only during and after World War II did acts of aggressive warfare, actions against the peace, acts against humanity, and "the common plan or conspiracy" to do such things, come to be regarded as war crimes.

Early Treatment. Offenders against the law of war were primarily responsible to their own national authority, but they might also be legally punished by the offended belligerent in case of capture or apprehension after the war. In practice, such war criminals were seldom punished by their home states except for flagrant acts, and they were not often punished following capture by the enemy because of the danger of reprisals. In wars fought for limited objectives, as opposed to total war having unconditional surrender and military occupation as its objectives, war crimes were forgotten.

After the Battle of Waterloo Napoleon I was sent to St. Helena, but this was a political act. After World War I, despite U.S. opposition to the idea, the Treaty of Versailles declared for the punishment of "offenses against the customs of war and the laws of humanity," even when committed by the heads of states. The Netherlands, however, refused to extradite William II, and Germany refused to surrender the 1,500 alleged war criminals demanded of her by the victors. An agreement was finally reached by which the accused should be tried by a German court at Leipzig. Eventually 12 were tried, of whom 6 were convicted and sentenced to short prison terms. Most of these managed to escape before serving much of their terms.

During World War II the ruthless methods of warfare used by the Axis Powers provoked widespread demands among the Allies (France, Great Britain, the U.S.S.R., and the United States) for the punishment of war criminals after the end of hostilities (see AXIS POWERS). The Moscow Declaration of Nov. 1, 1943, made plans for such action; a United Nations War Crimes Commission was set up in London to draw up a list of accused persons. The declarations of the Yalta and Potsdam conferences reiterated the policy (see POTSDAM CONFERENCE; YALTA CONFERENCE). A four-power agreement of Aug. 8, 1945, set up an international military tribunal for the trial of the major criminals whose offenses had no precise geographical location; the agreement was supplemented by a charter providing the principles under which the court should operate. Four types of war crimes were listed: (1) offenses against the laws and customs of war, a relatively uncontroversial category, although the law of war had become somewhat obsolete; (2) crimes against the peace, involving the planning, preparing, initiating, and waging wars of aggression or wars in violation of international treaties or agreements; (3) crimes against humanity, including the murder, extermination, enslavement, deportation or persecution of persons on political, racial, or religious grounds; and (4) "the common plan or conspiracy to commit any of the foregoing crimes." The traditional view had been that the heads of states and governments were not responsible for "acts of state," and acts done by subordinates on orders from superiors were likewise immune. The four-power agreement invalidated these defenses.

The Nürnberg War Crimes Trial began on Oct. 18, 1945, with the indictment of 24 Nazi leaders: Hermann Goering, Rudolf Hess, Joachim von Ribbentrop, Field Marshal Wilhelm Keitel, Ernst Kaltenbrunner, Alfred Rosenberg, Hans Frank, Wilhelm Frick, Julius Streicher, Walther Funk, Hjalmar Schacht, Grand Admiral Karl Doenitz, Grand Admiral Erich Raeder, Baldur von Schirach, Fritz Sauckel, Field Marshal Alfred Jodl, Franz von Papen, Arthur Seyss-Inquart, Albert Speer, Hans Fritzsche, Robert Ley (who committed suicide before the trial), Gustav Krupp von Bohlen und Halbach (not tried because of senility), Constantin von Neurath, and Martin Bormann (reported dead but tried *in absentia*). The court was composed of four judges, one for each of the four powers. The historic trial ended on Aug. 31, 1946; the decision of the court came on October 1. The following 12 were sentenced to death by hanging: Goering, Ribbentrop, Kaltenbrunner, Keitel, Rosenberg, Frank, Frick, Streicher, Sauckel, Jodl, Seyss-Inquart, and Bormann (*in absentia*). Hess, Funk, and Raeder received life sentences; Schirach and Speer were sentenced to 20 years, Neurath to 15 years, and Doenitz to 10; Von Papen, Schacht, and Fritzsche were acquitted. On Oct. 16, 1946, 10 of the condemned were executed, but Goering cheated the gallows by committing suicide just before the hour of execution. The court also found that the leadership corps of the Nazi party, the Gestapo, the security police (SD), and the elite guard (SS) were all criminal organizations, but the storm troopers (SA), the Reich cabinet, and the general staff and high command of the German armed forces were acquitted of the charge of criminality.

Japanese War Crimes Trials. United States military courts in Manila sentenced Lt. Gen. Masaharu Homma to be shot for ordering the "Bataan death march," and sentenced Lt. Gen. Tomoyuki Yamashita to be hanged for permitting atrocities during the final Philippine campaign. Others were condemned for killing captured fliers, for mistreating prisoners of war, and for cannibalism. Convictions were also made by China, Great Britain, and Australia. Former Japanese Premier Hideki Tojo, and 27 other Japanese leaders were indicted for conventional war crimes, crimes against the peace, and crimes against humanity. Of the 25 who were tried, all were convicted; Tojo and 6 others were sentenced to death, 16 more received life sentences, and 2 received lesser sentences. When the trials ended, 1949, a total of about 4,200 Japanese had been convicted of war crimes, and 720 of those convicted had been executed.

The War Crimes Controversy. Many jurists contend that charges of "crimes against the peace" and "crimes against humanity," as preferred against Axis leaders and others, were either without legal foundation or were based on *ex post facto* law (see EX POST FACTO LAW). Such criticism does not apply to offenses against the "customs" of war, although it is contended that the law of war is both uncertain and obsolete. The proceedings are criticized also as being wholly one-sided (*ex parte*). Some have also denounced the invalidation of the traditional defenses granted to heads of state for "acts of state," and to subordinate officials for actions on superior orders. Moralists have emphasized the one-sided application of the war crimes principle, pointing out that war criminals among the United Nations are seemingly immune from trial; they denounce the whole proceedings as a euphemism for revenge on defeated enemies.

Defenders of the proceedings contend that the various charges of "crimes against the peace" are based on the League of Nations Covenant, the Kellogg-Briand Pact, and other agreements condemning aggressive warfare; and that the "crimes against humanity" are based on the moral condemnation of the civilized world, and are analogous to the Anglo-American common law, developed from case to case and not by prior legislative enactment. They contend that if punishment were limited to offenses against the law of war, and if immunity were granted to heads of state and to subordinate officers acting on superior orders, the guilty would be limited almost entirely to persons of no political and military significance, while the leaders who planned the aggressive war and ordered the great atrocities would go free. Many of the same arguments, pro and con, were raised in connection with the trial of the Nazi "death camp" commandant, Adolf Eichmann, who was tried and convicted by Israel, 1961, on charges of responsibility for the death of some six million Jews during World War II, and hanged in 1962.

WARD, ARTEMAS, 1727–1800, colonial American and U.S. military and political figure, was born in Shrewsbury, Mass., the son of Nahum Ward. He was graduated from Harvard, 1748, served in the provincial militia during the French and Indian War, attaining the rank of lieutenant colonel. He represented Shrewsbury in the Massachusetts legislature (known as the General Court) and was justice of Worcester county court of common pleas, 1762–75. He was a delegate to the provincial council, 1774, and the same year was commissioned a brigadier general. In 1775, he was made a major general by the Continental Congress and had charge of the Siege of Boston until the arrival of Gen. George Washington. Because of poor health, Ward resigned from the army in the spring of 1776 and became chief justice of the court of common pleas for Worcester County. He was a member of the Massachusetts executive council, 1777–80, and of the Massachusetts state legislature, 1782–87, and was its speaker in 1785. He was a Federalist member of the U.S. House of Representatives, 1791–95.

WARD, BARBARA, 1914–   , English journalist and writer, was born in York. She studied at the Lycée Molière and the Sorbonne, Paris, 1929–31, and Somerville College, Oxford, 1932–35. She became a member of the staff, 1939, and foreign editor, 1940, of an English weekly, the *Economist;* joined the staff, 1943, and became a governor, 1946, of the British Broadcasting Corporation. In 1950 she married Robert G. A. Jackson of Australia, a former assistant secretary general of the United Nations. Among her works are *The International Share-out* (1938), *Hitler's*

Route to Bagdad (1939), *Russian Foreign Policy* (1940), *A Christian Basis for the Post-War World* (1942), *Policy for the West* (1951), *Faith and Freedom* (1954), and *Five Ideas that Change the World* (1959).

WARD, EDWARD, known as Ned Ward, 1667–1731, English tavern keeper and prolific author of coarse doggerel verse, was born in Oxfordshire. He wrote *The London Spy* (published in parts, 1687–1709), prose sketches of contemporary social life, particularly in London, and *Hudibras Redivivus* (1705–07), verses burlesquing the Whigs and the Low Church party. His other verses were published from 1691 to 1734. Apart from their other qualities, good and bad, Ward's works are invaluable as records of much of the slang of his time.

WARD, FREDERICK TOWNSEND, 1831–62, U.S. adventurer, was born in Salem, Mass. He received a public school elementary education, and studied at Norwich, Vt., 1846–48. He served as a lieutenant in the French army during the Crimean War, 1853–56, joined William Walker's expedition to Nicaragua, 1855, and in 1859 went to China, where the Taiping Rebellion was in progress. He offered his services to the Chinese government, and organized what was later known as the "ever-victorious army," made up of natives and foreign adventurers. He attained a position of great influence, and was made a mandarin and admiral general by the Chinese government.

WARD, JOHN QUINCY ADAMS, 1830–1910, U.S. sculptor, was born in Urbana, Ohio. He worked for six years in the studio of Henry K. Brown, then opened his own studio in New York, 1861, and was not long in winning public recognition; two years after his arrival in New York, his *Indian Hunter* became the first statue to be placed in Central Park. Ward is best known, however, for his portraits and monuments, which include those of Henry Ward Beecher, in Brooklyn, Gen. George Thomas, in Washington, D.C., and Horace Greeley, in New York City. Ward was one of the founders and president of the National Sculpture Society, one of the founders of the Metropolitan Museum of Art, president of the National Academy of Design, and a trustee of the American Academy at Rome.

WARD, JOSHUA, 1685–1761, English quack doctor, known as "Spot" Ward because of a birthmark, attempted to enter Parliament posing as the member from Marlborough, 1717, but was discovered, and fled to St. Germain, where he lived by peddling a "universal remedy." After being pardoned, 1733, for his attempted fraud in Parliament, Ward returned to London, where he was lionized by his admirers and made a fortune with his remedies.

WARD, MARY AUGUSTA ARNOLD, known as Mrs. Humphry Ward, 1851–1920, English novelist, was born in Tasmania, Australia, but was educated at boarding schools in England. As the daughter of a Spanish Protestant mother and a father who vacillated between Catholicism and the Anglican church, she grew up in an atmosphere of religious confusion and dispute and later, partly as a result of association with such thinkers as T. H. Green, she became a heterodox religionist. In *Robert Elsmere* (1888) she fictionized the strife between modernism and tradition and made a bold plea for a new nonevangelical Christianity. Although its literary merit was brought into question, the book was widely publicized as "controversial" and soon was a best seller on both sides of the Atlantic. Mrs. Ward wrote indefatigably until her death, producing didactic novels and *romans à clef* (novels with characters from life, but with the names changed). Among her later novels are *David Grieve* (1892); *Marcella* (1894); *Helbeck of Bannisdale* (1898); *Lady Rose's Daughter* (1903); *The Case of Richard Meynell* (1911), a sequel to *Robert Elsmere; Delia Blanchflower* (1915); and *Harvest* (1920). She also published a translation of the journals of Henry Frederic Amiel

(1885), and a volume of memoirs, *Recollections of a Writer* (1918). She was active in social and philanthropic work and was a leader of the National League for Opposing Woman Suffrage.

WARD, NATHANIEL, 1578–1652, English colonial clergyman and writer, was born in Haverhill, Suffolk, England, and was graduated from Emmanuel College, Cambridge, 1603. He practiced law for several years, and was rector of Stondon Massey, Essex, 1628–33. Having come into conflict with the Archbishop of Canterbury, William Laud, Ward migrated to the Massachusetts Bay Colony, 1634, and was minister at Agawam (later Ipswich), Mass., 1635–37. At the request of the Massachusetts General Court, he prepared the draft of the Body of Liberties, adopted in 1641, which was the first code of law for Massachusetts. He returned to England, 1646, and was minister at Shenfield, Essex, 1648–52. Under the pseudonym Theodore de la Guard, Ward wrote *The Simple Cobler of Aggawam in America* (1647), a prose satire on the new opinions in his time. He also published sermons and controversial pamphlets.

WARD, WILLIAM GEORGE, nicknamed Ideal Ward, 1812–82, English theologian, the son of the financier William Ward (1787–1849), was born in London and studied at Oxford. He came under the influence of John Henry Newman, 1838, was ordained a priest in the Church of England, 1840, and converted to Roman Catholicism, 1845. In the year before his conversion he had published a controversial Romanist treatise, *The Ideal of a Christian Church*—hence the derisive nickname, Ideal Ward. As editor of the *Dublin Review*, 1863–78, he (in opposition to Newman) supported the doctrine of papal infallibility which during this period was a subject of violent controversy within the church. Ward published numerous controversial theological works, 1852–80.

WARD, a person who is under the age of legal responsibility, or who is regarded as mentally incompetent and has been placed in the legal custody of a guardian or conservator, who manages the property of the ward under the supervision of the proper court. At the termination of the wardship, the guardian or conservator must turn over the property to the ward and render an accounting of the management of the property during the period of the wardship. See GUARDIAN; MINOR.

In U.S. municipal politics, a ward is a territorial subdivision from which one or more aldermen, or members of the city council, are normally elected. In addition, ward boundaries are often used in the determination of larger electoral districts for state or national elections. The administration of city public works is organized on a ward basis in some larger urban areas. See ALDERMAN; CITY GOVERNMENT, *Mayor-Council Form.*

WAR DEBTS, debts incurred by various European countries to the United States during World War I. Prior to the Armistice, the total of all the Allied intergovernmental loans amounted to $16.49 billion; post-Armistice loans totaled $4.28 billion. Nearly half of the total, $10.34 billion, was owed to the United States.

The prevailing opinion in Europe, was that these loans constituted a part of the U.S. contribution toward the common victory, and that they were a substitution for U.S. troops that could not reach the fighting fronts until late in the war. Great Britain proposed universal cancellation. The United States, however, having "borrowed" the money from its people through the Liberty Loans, insisted that the loans must be repaid. Debt-funding agreements were eventually negotiated with all the debtor countries, except the Soviet Union. Under these agreements repayment was to be made over a period of 62 years, but the interest rate varied widely according to the "capacity to pay" of each country; in the case of Great Britain, for example, the rate was to be 3 per cent for the first 10 years, 3½ for the rest of the

period; while for Italy it was ½ per cent for the first 10 years, 2 per cent thereafter. Great Britain and France then made similar agreements with their debtors.

The debtor countries insisted on linking debts and reparations; that is, they insisted that they would pay their debts only to the extent that Germany paid reparations to them. The United States refused to recognize any connection between the two. Besides political difficulties, there were economic obstacles to repayment. Funds raised by debtor countries had to be converted from national currency into foreign exchange. Since the debtor states lacked gold for repayment, they would have to export goods and services, but this was made impossible by high U.S. tariffs. In practice, the European nations made their regular debt payments while at the same time their nationals floated large commercial loans in the United States.

Debt payments were continued until 1931, when Germany declared that she could no longer pay reparations. This led to the Hoover Moratorium, proposed by U.S. Pres. Herbert Hoover, which suspended both reparations and debt payments for one year. At the end of this year, the Lausanne Agreement (July, 1932), practically ended reparations. On Dec. 15, 1932, Great Britain and several other countries made the regular payments, but other states defaulted. A few nations made token payments in 1933 and then went into complete default. Only Finland continued to make the regular payments, but her debt was contracted for postwar rehabilitation, and hence was not properly a war debt. The war debts remained an issue in international diplomacy and American politics until World War II. Then came the lend-lease program, which was followed by the $3.75 billion loan to Great Britain, 1946, and the Marshall Plan, adopted in 1948. See INTERNATIONAL FINANCE; LEND-LEASE ACT; REPARATIONS.

WAR DEPARTMENT, one of the three original departments of the U.S. government. The National Security Act of 1947 reorganized the War Department as the Department of the Army and put it and the other armed services under the National Military Establishment. The National Security Act of 1949 made it one of three "military departments" under the Department of Defense.

Established by act of Congress Aug. 7, 1789, the War Department succeeded a similar department dating from before adoption of the Constitution. The new department exercised many functions later assigned to the Departments of Navy and Interior. The secretary of war ranked next to the secretary of state and secretary of the treasury in the order of succession to the presidency. The first secretary of war was Henry Knox, who served, 1789–95, under Pres. George Washington; the last was Kenneth C. Royall, appointed by Pres. Harry Truman in 1947.

The secretary of war was assisted by an undersecretary of war, an assistant secretary of war and an assistant secretary of war for air. Elevation of the Air Force to equality with the Army and Navy, 1947, removed it from Army control and made the secretaries of the Army, Navy and Air assistants to the secretary of defense without cabinet status.

As formerly constituted, the War Department had control, under the President as commander in chief, of the Army of the United States. The secretary of war was charged with supervision of all military functions, and also had many duties of a civil nature placed upon him by Congress. Among these civil functions were (1) the development, by the Corps of Engineers, of harbors, waterways and navigation and flood control projects; (2) emergency relief of the civil population in case of flood, storm, earthquake, or other disaster too vast in scope for ordinary civilian agencies to handle effectively; (3) preservation of the American Falls of Niagara; (4) defense, maintenance and care of the Panama Canal, and (5) the presidency of the National Forest Reservation Commission. When the department was abolished, all these functions were placed under the secretary of defense. See CABINET.

WARE, HENRY, 1764–1845, U.S. clergyman, was born in Sherborn, Mass. As pastor of the Hingham, Mass., Congregational Church, 1787–1805, he became well known for his liberal or Unitarian views. His appointment as Hollis professor of divinity at Harvard University, 1805, precipitated the Unitarian separation from the Congregationalists and led to the development of the Harvard Divinity School, 1816, where he became professor of theology, 1816. *Letters to Trinitarians and Calvinists* (1820), *Answer to Dr. Woods Reply* (1822), and *Postscript to an Answer* (1823) record Professor Ware's controversies with the Congregationalist theologian Leonard Woods (1774–1854).

WARE, town, central Massachusetts, Hampshire County; on the Ware River, the Boston and Maine and the New York Central railroads; 23 miles W of Worcester. In the late 1930's local residents took over bankrupt mills and set up Ware Industries, Incorporated. Woolen and knit goods, coated paper, and shoes are manufactured. The site was settled about 1720 and was a part of Ware River Parish until 1761 when it was established as a district; in 1775 it was incorporated as a town. Pop. (1960) 7,517.

WAREHAM, town, SE Massachusetts, Plymouth County; on Buzzards Bay, the New Haven Railroad, and U.S. highway 6; 45 miles SSE of Boston. Wareham is a summer resort center and a shipping point for cranberries, oysters, clams, and vegetables. Wareham was settled in 1678 and incorporated in 1739. Early industries were whaling and shipbuilding. Pop. (1960) 9,461.

WAREHOUSING, the activities involved in placing goods in storage. In one sense or another, it is as old as civilization—perhaps older, since primitive man also made use of this type of providence. In his case it was for storage against famine or winter, and the commodity stored usually was dry legumes or grain. Such storage was in jugs, jars, or in cavities chiseled out of stone; or a cavity might be hollowed out of clay earth and its walls hardened by building a fire inside the enclosure. The ancient granaries of Egypt were actually not grain warehouses but immense clay jars and subterranean vaults, strategically situated.

As communal living, with its attendant commerce, developed, the idea of the primitive granaries was applied to the storage of merchandisable commodities. The bazaars of the Orient were adapted to the same purpose; for they were not only selling places but storehouses of the objects for retail trade. In modern times the word *warehouse* came to mean any building, or a part thereof, that is (1) devoted to the storage of merchandisable goods, and (2) strategically placed for trading.

Because of its importance in the economic scheme, warehousing came naturally under government control. As early as 1846 the U.S. government passed "An act to establish a warehousing system." While primarily intended to facilitate commerce in imported goods and to lessen such burdens as demurrage, customs appraisal, and the increasing overhead cost of holding stored goods for market, this act eventually set a pattern for nongovernment controlled warehouses as well.

At Mid-Twentieth Century. The warehouse serves basic as well as specialized industry; it may be used to hold only rod and sheet steel or, at other times, the vast categories of merchandise that await transshipment at railroad or ocean shipping docks. The frozen food industry created its own unique warehouse specialization, but represented only one phase of the immense cold-storage warehouse industry, which includes refrigeration of meats, vegetables, and fruits. The great increase in truck transportation

created a warehouse system entirely different from that required for railroad carloads and ship cargo stowage. Such systems vein the country and have warehouses at strategic distribution points. The storage, moving, and delivery of household goods constitutes a unique warehousing system.

Many of the complicated mechanisms of marketing in the U.S. economy could not function effectively without adequate warehousing. It allows for smoothing out of the diseconomies of seasonal production, particularly notable in the perishable food market. It also serves as a stabilizer to the market by equating short-run supply to demand and thus prevents widespread price fluctuations. It is also to the development of warehousing that the United States owes the growth of nationwide markets for many products and the elimination of the dependence of communities upon local production for their supplies.

WARFIELD, DAVID, 1866–1951, U.S. actor, was born in San Francisco, Calif. He moved to New York, 1890, made his debut in *The Inspector*, and was employed at Weber and Field's Music Hall as a character actor. He attracted the attention of David Belasco, who hired him to play the leading role in *The Auctioneer* (1900–1903). Warfield subsequently starred in other Belasco productions, such as *The Music Master* (1904–07), and *The Return of Peter Grimm* (1911), and became famous as a character actor with a fine sense of comedy and pathos. He played in revivals of *The Music Master*, 1916–20, and gave his last stage preformance as Shylock in Shakespeare's *The Merchant of Venice*, 1923–24.

WARHAM, WILLIAM, 1450?–1532, English churchman, was born in Hampshire. He became master of the rolls, 1494, and Archbishop of Canterbury, 1504, and served as lord chancellor, 1504–15. He officiated at the marriage of King Henry VIII and Catherine of Aragón, 1509, crowned them in the same year, and later played an apparently passive and unwilling role in Henry's suit to have the marriage declared null. Henry insisted that Warham try to persuade the pope to annul the marriage, 1530, and when Warham's influence proved insufficient, attempted unsuccessfully to have Warham named as judge of the suit, 1531. Warham denounced Parliament for its efforts to deny papal supremacy in religious matters, 1532.

WAR HAWKS, in early nineteenth century U.S. history, a small faction in the 12th Congress, 1811–13, which strongly advocated war with Great Britain, ostensibly in retaliation against Britain's practice of kidnaping U.S. mariners into British naval service (see IMPRESSMENT). Most important among the War Hawks were Henry Clay of Kentucky, John C. Calhoun of South Carolina, and Felix Grundy of Tennessee. See WAR OF 1812, *The War Hawks.*

WARM AIR HEATING. See FURNACE, *Space Heating Furnaces;* HEATING.

WARM FRONT, a sloping boundary surface in the troposphere separating two air masses of different densities and temperatures, and one in which warm air replaces horizontally the cold air as the front is displaced by the wind and advances. Ideally the front is regarded as a discontinuity in temperature, although in practice the change in temperature does not occur abruptly but across a zone of finite width known as the transition or frontal zone.

WARM SPRINGS, city, W Georgia, in Meriwether County; at the foot of Pine Mountain, on the Atlantic Coast Line and the Southern railroads, and U.S. highway 27; 60 miles SSW of Atlanta. It is the site of Warm Springs Foundation and the Little White House, where President Franklin D. Roosevelt died in 1945. Pop. (1960) 538.

WARM SPRINGS, town, W Virginia, seat of Bath County; in the Appalachian Mountains, on U.S. highway 220; 130 miles WNW of Richmond. The town is a popular resort center and is noted for its medicinal springs. Pop. about 300.

WARM SPRINGS FOUNDATION. See NA-
TIONAL FOUNDATION.

WARNER, CHARLES DUDLEY, 1829–1900,
U.S. journalist and author, was born in Plainfield,
Mass., and was educated at Hamilton College and at
the University of Pennsylvania. Warner worked as a
surveyor in Missouri, 1853–54, as a lawyer in Chicago,
1858–60, and became editor of the *Evening Press*, 1861,
and then the *Courant*, 1867, in Hartford, Conn. His
most notable works are genial and graceful essays
after the manner of Washington Irving, such as *My
Summer in a Garden* (1870) and *Backlog Studies* (1873).
He also wrote travel books, novels, short stories, and
biographies and collaborated with Mark Twain (see
CLEMENS, SAMUEL LANGHORNE) on the novel *The
Gilded Age* (1873). Warner's fictional trilogy, *A Little
Journey in the World* (1889), *The Golden House* (1894),
and *That Fortune* (1899), traces the accumulation and
loss of a great family fortune, foreshadowing fictional
themes popular in a later period.

WARNER, GLENN SCOBEY, known as Pop,
1871–1954, U.S. football coach, was born in Spring-
ville, N.Y., and graduated from Cornell University.
During his long career, 1895–1940, he was coach at
Georgia, Cornell, Carlisle Indian School, Pittsburgh,
Stanford, Temple, and San Jose State; his 1915–18
Pittsburgh teams and 1927 Stanford team received
top national ranking. Founder of the Warner system,
he developed the single- and double-wing formation
for the offense. He wrote *A Course in Football for
Players and Coaches* (1908).

WARNER, SETH, 1743–84, colonial American
soldier, was born in Woodbury (later Roxbury),
Conn. When about 20 years of age, he settled in
Bennington in the New Hampshire Land Grants
(later Vermont), and with Ethan Allen became one
of the leaders of the armed band called the Green
Mountain Boys, who resisted the attempts of New
York officials to enforce jurisdiction over the land
grants issued by New Hampshire. As did Allen,
Warner became an ardent supporter of the revolutionary cause. He was second in command in the
capture of Ticonderoga, N.Y., May, 1775, and afterward led the expedition that took possession of
Crown Point, N.Y. He was active in the expedition
against Canada, commanded the rear guard of the
army in Arthur St. Claire's retreat from Ticonderoga,
1777, was defeated by Gen. Simon Frazer and Gen.
Friedrich Adolph von Riedesel at Hubbardton, Vt.,
and assisted in forcing the surrender of John Burgoyne, 1777, at the Battle of Bennington. In 1782,
he resigned from the army because of poor health.

WARNER, SYLVIA TOWNSEND, 1893–   ,
English novelist and poet, was born in Harrow-on-
the-Hill, Middlesex, the daughter of a schoolmaster.
She received a private school education, developed
an early interest in music, and became an authority
on fifteenth and sixteenth century music. Among her
works, which are notable for both their subtle humor
and their seriousness, are the poems *The Espalier*
(1925) and *Time Importuned* (1928), and the novels
Lolly Willowes (1926), *The True Heart* (1929), *Elinor
Barley* (1930), *The Cat's Cradle Book* (1940), *The
Corner That Held Them* (1948), and *The Flint Anchor*
(1954).

WAR OF 1812, a war between the United States
and Great Britain, 1812–15, was a phase of the so-
called Napoleonic Wars—a period of general warfare, beginning in the 1790's and ending in 1815,
during which France, under Napoleon Bonaparte,
was at war at one time or other with nearly every
power in Europe.

Origins. Napoleon's victory, 1805, over Austrian
and Russian armies at Austerlitz, Moldavia, made
France supreme on the continent of Europe, but
Adm. Horatio Nelson's victory over the French and
Spanish fleets off Cape Trafalgar, Spain, gave Great
Britain control of the seas. Each side then tried to
strangle the other by blockade and other measures.

In the course of all this, American commercial shipping, which had developed a lucrative trade in areas
dominated by both France and Great Britain, suffered materially (see BLOCKADE, *Paper Blockade*).
Particularly objectionable to U.S. merchants were
two British orders-in-council, 1806, which in effect
placed a blockade on the continent of Europe and
on all other ports under French jurisdiction (see
ORDER-IN-COUNCIL). The situation was complicated
by the British practice of impressment of British seamen serving on foreign vessels. Many U.S. citizens
were among those impressed by the British Navy;
one such incident—the boarding of the U.S. Navy
frigate *Chesapeake* and the seizing of four of its crew,
June 22, 1807—brought the United States to the
brink of war with Great Britain. See CHESAPEAKE.

President Thomas Jefferson was determined, however, to maintain peace, and he endeavored by commercial boycott to force one or both of the belligerents
to recognize U.S. neutrality. The Nonimportation
Act (1806) denied entry into the United States of
certain British manufactured articles, and the Embargo Act (1807) forbade U.S. ships to enter foreign
ports and prohibited all exports from the United
States. A general failure, the embargo was bitterly
opposed by the very shipping interests it was supposed to protect, especially in New England from
where threats of secession were hurled at the President. Finally the embargo was repealed, March,
1809, just before Jefferson left office.

James Madison, who succeeded to the presidency,
initiated the policy of opening U.S. commerce to
the world, except with Great Britain and France
(see NONINTERCOURSE ACT). This policy also failed,
and was succeeded, 1810, by Macon's Bill Number 2,
which reopened trade with France and Great Britain,
but stated that if either nation repealed its decrees
violating neutral commerce, nonintercourse would
be resumed against the other power. Seizing this
opportunity, Napoleon promised to repeal those
edicts of his Continental System that were most
prejudicial to U.S. interests (see BERLIN DECREE;
MILAN DECREE). In accordance with the provisions
of Macon's Bill Number 2, President Madison forbade U.S. shippers to trade with Great Britain.
Believing that the British decrees would not be repealed, Madison, on June 1, 1812, sent a message to
Congress asking for war with Great Britain (although
the French decrees had still not been repealed) and
on June 18, war was declared, on the grounds of
impressment, violations of the three-mile limit, and
violations of U.S. neutral rights. Actually, the British
decrees had been repealed two days before, but word
of this had not yet reached North America. The vote
on the declaration was 79 to 49 in the House and
19 to 13 in the Senate. The New England states, New
Jersey and New York, which together owned three
fourths of American shipping, joined Delaware in
voting against the war, but the southern and western
states were solidly for it.

The War Hawks. The declaration of war, however, was occasioned not solely on the grounds of
British interference with U.S. commerce and seamen,
for on these scores the United States could have
legitimately resorted to war any time from 1807 on.
The congressional elections of 1810–11 had brought
into power a group of young westerners who were
anxious to drive the British from North America.
Believing that Indian uprisings on the frontier were
largely fomented by the British, these congressmen—
called War Hawks—seized upon the shipping controversy as pretext for war with Great Britain and for
subsequent annexation of Canada. Led by Henry
Clay of Kentucky, John C. Calhoun of South Carolina, and Felix Grundy of Tennessee, the War Hawks
gained the support of Madison, who desired the
western vote in the next presidential election, despite
the President's admission that France had seized
more U.S. ships since 1807 than had the British.

Military and Naval Events. So confident was Congress of quick victory that it adjourned without voting war taxes or enlarging the Navy. As a result of this and the skill with which the British regulars and Canadian militia fought against the superior forces advancing against them, the first U.S. attacks on Canada were failures. In August, 1812, U.S. Gen. William Hull, after advancing to Detroit and into Upper Canada (Ontario), abandoned Forts Dearborn and Michilimackinack, fell back on Detroit, and surrendered without firing a shot; other projected invasions of Canada, such as the attack at Queenstown Heights across the Niagara River from Buffalo, N.Y., October 13, also failed, partly because the militia refused to cross into Canada.

At sea, the U.S. Navy fared somewhat better during 1812. The U.S. heavy frigate *Constitution* defeated the British frigates *Guerrière*, August 19, and the *Java*, December 29; the U.S. frigate *United States* captured the British frigate *Macedonian*, October 12; and the U.S. sloop-of-war *Wasp* beat the British brig *Frolic*, October 18. Although U.S. morale value of these victories was great, the military value was slight. Most of the U.S. ships put into harbor during the winter of 1812–13, and for the rest of the war a superior British fleet controlled the seas.

Inland, in 1813, the United States was more successful than in 1812. United States Gen. William Henry Harrison's forces suffered several defeats at the hands of the British and Indians under Gen. Henry A. Proctor, but after Oliver Hazard Perry's victory in the naval battle of Lake Erie, September 10, Harrison turned on Proctor and defeated him in the Battle of the Thames, October 5. In the east, U.S. forces raided York (later Toronto), the capital of Upper Canada, April 27, and burned part of it. They were forced to evacuate the town, however, and a subsequent U.S. invasion of Upper Canada was stopped at Stony Creek, June 6. Two U.S. columns marching on Montreal were turned back at Chateauguay, October 26, and at Chryster's Farm, November 11.

In 1814, Great Britain, Prussia, and Russia succeeded in overthrowing Napoleon, and the British were able to turn more attention to the war in North America. Three invasions of the United States were planned: at Niagara, Lake Champlain, and New Orleans. On the Niagara front, U.S. victories at Chippawa, July 5, and Lundy's Lane, July 25, halted the British advance, and the U.S. naval victory of Commodore Thomas MacDonough on Lake Champlain, September 11, forced the British to withdraw into Canada. Meanwhile, a Creek Indian uprising instigated by the British in Florida, had been put down by U.S. Gen. Andrew Jackson at Horseshoe Bend, Mississippi Territory, March 27.

On the Atlantic Coast, however, a British expeditionary force under Gen. Robert Ross defeated U.S. forces at Bladensburg, Md., and captured Washington, D.C., August 24, where the public buildings were burned in retaliation for the U.S. burning of York. In September, however, a British attack on Baltimore and Fort McHenry failed; it was during this action that Francis Scott Key wrote the lyrics of *The Star-Spangled Banner* (see STAR-SPANGLED BANNER, THE). The invasion of New Orleans also failed when more than 10,000 British regulars were repulsed with heavy losses, Jan. 8, 1815, by militia under Andrew Jackson. See NEW ORLEANS, BATTLE OF, *War of 1812*.

Internal Dissension. Much of New England, especially, was opposed to the war and refused to furnish militia, boycotted the government's war financing, and sent grain and meat to the British armies in Canada. New England discontent culminated in the Hartford Convention, Dec. 15, 1814–Jan. 5, 1815, which proposed measures whose purpose was to give that section a greater voice in national affairs. See HARTFORD CONVENTION.

Peace Negotiations. Almost from the beginning of the war there were efforts to end it. Commissioners from both countries met in the south Netherlands city of Ghent (now in Belgium), August, 1814, and a peace treaty was signed, December 24. The treaty merely ended the war and provided for a return to prewar conditions. No mention was made of impressment, neutral rights, or the right of search. Commissions were set up, however, to settle boundary disputes and commercial relations. See GHENT, TREATY OF.

Results of the War. Although accurate statistics are not available, it is thought unlikely that more than 2,000 U.S. military and naval personnel were killed in the war, and the majority of civilians in the United States and Canada were little disturbed by it. The disruption of maritime commerce led to the establishment of industry in New England, which gradually turned to manufacturing as its primary economic interest rather than shipping. The Federalist party was given its death blow by the stigma of treason attached to it and to the Hartford Convention. In spite of the internal dissension during the war and the failure of the United States to achieve its war aims, the war showed that the country could stand on its own feet; in terms of U.S.–British relations, therefore, the War of 1812 might be said to have been a "second War of Independence."

BIBLIOG.–Henry Adams, *History of the United States of America During the Administration of James Madison*, 2 vols. (1930), *War of 1812* (1944); Francis F. Beirne, *War of 1812* (1949); Alfred LeR. Burt, *United States, Great Britain and British North America, from the Revolution to the Establishment of Peace After the War of 1812* (1940); John P. Cranwell and William B. Crane, *Men of Marque* (1940); Ernest A. Cruikshank, *Political Adventures of John Henry: The Record of an International Imbroglio* (1936); Daniel L. Cushing, *Captain Cushing in the War of 1812* (1944); Cecil S. Forester, *Age of Fighting Sail: The Story of the Naval War of 1812* (Mainstream of Am. Ser.) (1956); Alec R. Gilpin, *War of 1812 in the Old Northwest* (1958); Alfred T. Mahan, *Sea Power in Its Relations to the War of 1812*, 2 vols. (1919); Fletcher Pratt, *Heroic Years: Fourteen Years of the Republic, 1801–1815* (1934); Julius W. Pratt, *Expansionists of 1812* (1949); Charles H. J. Snider] *Under the Red Jack: Privateers of the Maritime Provinces of Canada in the War of 1812* (1928); Neil H. Swanson, *Perilous Fight* (1947); Glenn Tucker, *Poltroons and Patriots: A Popular Account of the War of 1812*, 2 vols. (1954); Frank A. Updyke, *Diplomacy of the War of 1812* (1915).

WAR PRODUCTION BOARD, a federal agency created early in World War II by executive order of Pres. Franklin D. Roosevelt (Jan. 16, 1942) to determine the policies, plans, and methods for producing materials and goods, except food, required for the prosecution of the war, and to limit or prohibit the production of nonessential goods. The War Production Board (WPB) exercised strict control in allocating critical materials to producers; issued orders limiting or prohibiting the use of other materials or the production of specified articles; and devised a system of preferences and priority ratings that indicated the order in which manufacturers were to produce and deliver certain goods. The WPB had the power to compel producers to accept orders and contracts for war production. The board also studied the requirements of the various war agencies, decided which were the most urgent, and then allocated the available supply of goods and materials in such a way as to fill such requirements. An executive order of Oct. 4, 1945, terminated the agency.

WARRANT, a document issued by a judicial authority and directed to a legally competent individual, ordering him to perform a prescribed act. The warrant affords protection to the receiver from liability for damages that might occur in connection with performing the act required by the warrant. Warrants are most frequently issued to a peace officer, such as a sheriff or constable, requiring him to arrest a specified individual and to bring that person into court to be examined, or to answer charges of criminal or civil misconduct. A search warrant directs an officer to search a specified individual or specified premises for stolen property, unlawfully carried

WAR OF 1812

U.S. forces under Gen. Andrew Jackson decisively defeated the British under Sir Edward Pakenham at the Battle of New Orleans, Jan. 8, 1815, two weeks after the Treaty of Ghent was signed ending the War of 1812.

British expeditionary forces burned many public buildings in Washington, D.C., after marching from ships anchored on the Patuxent River.

At the Battle of the Thames, the U.S. forces under Gen. William Henry Harrison won a strategic victory over British troops and Indians on Oct. 5, 1813, thereby securing the northwestern lands.

In the first conflict between the opposing navies, the British ship *Guerriere* was defeated by the U.S. frigate *Constitution* off the Newfoundland Banks in August, 1812.

The U.S. resentment against the British was intensified by the Battle of Tippecanoe in 1811, in which the British were accused of actively encouraging Indian atrocities.

property, or property that is wanted for criminal evidence, and to bring that property before the court. Such a warrant may also include an order to arrest the occupant of the premises containing the seized goods, or the individual on whose person the goods were found.

An officer of the court may receive a warrant ordering the seizure of property of an individual who has been adjudged as bankrupt, and the performance of legal proceedings connected with an act of bankruptcy (see BANKRUPTCY). A warrant may also be issued to give authority to assess and collect taxes and to conduct a sale of the property of individuals who fail to pay their assessment. The holder of a warrant is legally bound to perform his duties only within the limits specified in the warrant.

WARRANT OFFICER, one who holds a military and a naval rank by virtue of a warrant, and who ranks between the highest enlisted grade and the lowest commissioned rank. In the armed services of the United States, warrants are granted by authority of the secretary of the particular service—Army, Navy, or Air Force. In general, the services performed by warrant officers are those of an administrative or technical specialist rather than those associated with command of personnel. Warrant officers wear uniforms identical to those worn by commissioned officers, and rate the salute by subordinate personnel. They are addressed as Mr. or Miss. See NONCOMMISSIONED OFFICER; OFFICER.

WARRANTY, a form of guaranty that is collateral to the main purpose of an agreement or transaction. In the United States, a warranty is generally treated as a condition of a contract allowing a purchaser to reject goods for breach of warranty, or accept them and sue for damages, at his option. See CONTRACT.

At common law, numerous warranties prevailed in the sale of real estate. None of these is in common use in the United States, where common law warranties have been replaced by covenants. The covenant of warranty that is included in most deeds as a matter of fact, is not a common law warranty, but an agreement to defend title as against third persons. It may be either expressed or implied, and in some states it is by statute a part of all transfers of title. See COVENANT; TITLE.

In the United States, in all 37 states that have the Uniform Sales Act, warranties in the sale of personal property are governed by sections 12–16 of that act. In general, implied warranties are: (1) that the seller has title; (2) that the goods are fairly merchantable, or will fairly answer the purpose for which they are known to be bought; (3) that the bulk of goods, sold by sample, corresponds with the sample; and (4) that there are no hidden defects, when the buyer defers to the seller's judgment. A warranty made after a sale is usually not binding unless there was additional consideration for it. No particular words of warranty are necessary for an enforceable warranty to be legally constituted. If a written contract purports to contain all the terms of a transaction, then no oral statements of warranty are of any force or effect. Warranties made in connection with a contract of insurance are material to the risk and are uniformly regarded as conditions, the breach of which relieves the insurer of liability. Warranty of a negotiable instrument, resulting from an endorsement, may be governed by the Uniform Negotiable Instruments Act, which is in effect in all states. See GUARANTY; SALE; VENDOR AND PURCHASER.

WAR RELIEF. See LEND-LEASE ACT; RED CROSS.

WARREN, EARL, 1891–   , U.S. political leader and chief justice of the United States, was born in Los Angeles, Calif., studied at the University of California, and was admitted to the California bar, 1914. After serving in World War I as an infantry lieutenant, 1917–18, he was a captain in the U.S. Infantry Reserve Corps, 1919–35. He resumed the practice of law in Oakland, Calif., and was deputy

city attorney of Oakland, 1919–20, deputy district attorney, 1920–23, chief deputy attorney 1923–25, and district attorney, 1925–38, of Alameda County, Calif. Warren was nominated for the governorship of

Earl Warren   UPI

California by the Republican party, 1942, and missed getting the Democratic nomination by only 100,000 votes; he won the election by a large majority. He won both the Republican and Democratic nominations for the governorship and was re-elected, 1946 and 1950. In 1948 he received the Republican vice-presidential nomination, as the running mate of Thomas E. Dewey, but lost in the election. Warren was an unsuccessful candidate for the 1952 Republican presidential nomination. Appointed chief justice of the United States Supreme Court, 1953, he announced that he was through with politics forever. Under Warren, the Supreme Court assumed a much larger case load than had been usual under Warren's predecessor, and ruled on cases involving controversial constitutional issues (racial segregation, censorship, and so forth) such as the court had sought to avoid hearing during the previous decade. Late in the 1950's and early in the 1960's Warren wrote a number of important dissenting opinions respecting cases in which 5 to 4 split decisions ran counter to his interpretations of the constitutional issues involved.

WARREN, GOUVERNEUR KEMBLE, 1830–82, U.S. soldier, was born in Cold Spring, N.Y., was graduated from West Point, 1850, and became a topographical engineer. During the Civil War he served in the Fifth New York Volunteer Infantry during the Peninsular Campaign, 1862, and participated in the battles of Antietam, Fredericksburg, and Chancellorsville; became chief engineer of the Army of the Potomac, 1863; was instrumental in preventing the capture of Little Round Top at Gettysburg, 1863; and during the final campaign against Robert E. Lee commanded the Fifth Army Corps of the Army of the Potomac. After the Battle of Five Forks, he was removed from command by Gen. Philip H. Sheridan, who charged him with inadequate support, but a court of inquiry rendered a decision largely favorable to Warren. He was later employed in survey work and harbor improvements.

WARREN, JOSEPH, 1741–75, colonial American patriot, was born in Roxbury, Mass., and was graduated from Harvard College, 1759. He then studied medicine under James Lloyd and became a successful physician in Boston, where he rendered valuable services to the community during a smallpox epidemic, 1764. In 1772 and 1775 he was chosen to deliver the anniversary oration in commemoration of the Boston Massacre, 1770. He was an active member of the first Committee of Correspondence of Boston, 1772, and drafted the Suffolk Resolves (1774) calling for the use of force, if necessary, in resisting the unfair colonial policies of England. He was a member of the First, Second, and Third Provincial Congress of Massachusetts, presiding over the Third, and on April 19, 1775, he took part in the Lexington-Concord battle that opened the Revolutionary War. He refused the chief command at the Battle of Bunker Hill, 1775, participated as a volunteer, and was killed.

WARREN, LEONARD, 1911–60, U.S. operatic baritone, was born in the Bronx, New York City, and studied music evenings at the Greenwich House Music School while working as a fur broker with his father during the day. He sang with the Radio City Music Hall Glee Club, 1935–38, and joined the Metropolitan Opera Company, 1938. Warren made his operatic debut, 1939, singing the role of Paolo in

Giuseppe Verdi's *Simon Boccanegra*, and soon achieved world renown for his lead baritone roles. He died on the stage of the Metropolitan Opera House during a performance of *La Forza del Destino* (The Force of Destiny).

WARREN, MERCY, 1728–1814, colonial American and U.S. poet and historian, sister of James Otis and wife of James Warren, Revolutionary patriot, was born Mercy Otis in Barnstable, Mass. Noted for her brilliant intellect, she was frequently consulted by the Massachusetts leaders in the American Revolution. Her dramas, *The Adulator* (1773) and *The Group* (1775), are satires of the Loyalists. She also wrote several tragedies in verse, included in her *Poems, Dramatic and Miscellaneous* (1790). Her *History of the American Revolution* (3 vols. 1805) is a valuable record of current events.

WARREN, ROBERT PENN, 1905– , U.S. writer, was born in Guthrie, Ky., was graduated from Vanderbilt University, and then studied at the University of California, at Yale University, and at Oxford, where he was a Rhodes scholar, 1929–30. He taught at Vanderbilt and other southern schools before becoming professor of English at the University of Minnesota, 1942. He was appointed professor of playwriting, 1951, and of poetry, 1961, at Yale University. With Allen Tate, John Crowe Ransom, and others of the Southern literati, Warren edited and wrote for *The Fugitive*, a magazine that promoted regional attitudes in literature and politics. His novel, *All The King's Men* (1946), a portrait of a Southern demagogue, won a Pulitzer prize for fiction, 1947. Among Warren's other works are *John Brown* (1929); *Pandy Woods and Other Poems* (1930); *Thirty-Six Poems* (1930); *The Circus in the Attic and Other Stories* (1948); *World Enough and Time* (1950); *Brother to Dragons* (1953); *Band of Angels* (1955); *Segregation: The Inner Conflict of the South* (1956); *Promises: Poems 1954–56* (1957), for which he was awarded a Pulitzer prize in 1958; *Selected Essays* (1958); *The Cave* (1959); *You, Emperors, and Others: Poems 1957–60* (1960); *Flood* (1964); and *Who Speaks for the Negro?* (1965).

WARREN, SAMUEL, 1807–77, English lawyer and author, was born near Wrexham. He studied medicine at Edinburgh, 1826–27, then entered the Inner Temple, 1828, and became a barrister, 1837. He wrote a number of legal textbooks, but is chiefly remembered for his novels, *Passages from the Diary of a Late Physician* (1838), and the very popular *Ten Thousand a Year* (1839), a bizarre story of the rise of one Tittlebot Titmouse to wealth.

WARREN, city, SE Michigan, in Macomb County, adjacent to Detroit on the S and 8 miles W of Lake St. Clair. Warren is a major industrial center, producing automotive parts, steel, electrical equipment, tools and dies, plastic moldings, and food products. The General Motors Technical Center is located there as are the Detroit Tank Arsenal, the United States Army Mobility Command, and Macomb County Community College. Organized as Hickory township in 1837, it changed its name to Aba the following year and to Warren shortly thereafter. The village and the township of Warren were incorporated into the city of Warren in 1955. (For population, see Michigan map in Atlas.)

WARREN, city, NE Ohio, seat of Trumbull County; on the Mahoning River, 40 miles SE of Cleveland. The city is an industrial center in which the chief industry is the manufacturing of iron and steel. Lamps, sprinkling systems, automotive cables, steel drums and barrels, furnaces, metal tubing, and tools are also manufactured. Warren was settled in 1798 and became the county seat in 1800. It was incorporated as a village in 1834 and as a city in 1869. (For population, see Ohio map in Atlas.)

WARREN, borough, NW Pennsylvania, seat of Warren County; on the N bank of the Allegheny River; 50 miles SE of Erie. The borough, located in an area that produces oil and natural gas, has many oil wells and refineries. Warren was founded in 1795 on the site of an earlier Seneca Indian village. It was a lumbering center during its early history. Iron and steel products, electronics, furniture, and textiles are manufactured. (For population, see Pennsylvania map in Atlas.)

WARREN, town, E Rhode Island, in Bristol County; on the Warren River, near Narragansett Bay; 10 miles SE of Providence. Cotton textiles are manufactured and the town is a base for oyster gathering. Warren was settled in 1632 and incorporated in 1747. Shipbuilding was an important industry during the eighteenth century. (For population, see Rhode Island map in Atlas.)

WARREN COMMISSION'S REPORT, the official U.S. government account of the events relating to the assassination of Pres. John F. Kennedy on Nov. 22, 1963, in Dallas, Texas. One week after the assassination, Pres. Lyndon B. Johnson appointed a commission to investigate the crime with the admonition to "satisfy itself that the truth is known so far as it can be discovered." The members of the commission were: Chief Justice of the United States Earl Warren (chairman); U.S. Representatives G. R. Ford and T. Hale Boggs; Senators R. B. Russell and J.S. Cooper; Allen Dulles, former head of the Central Intelligence Agency; J. J. McCloy, former disarmament adviser to President Kennedy. J. Lee Rankin, former solicitor general of the United States was general council to the commission. After 10 months of exhaustive investigation, the commission sent its 888-page report to President Johnson and later released 26 volumes of testimony and photographs. Among the commission's findings were: (1) Harvey Lee Oswald fired the shots that killed Kennedy and wounded Texas Governor Tom Connally; (2) this crime and Oswald's subsequent murder by Jack Ruby were no part of a larger political conspiracy; and (3) the Secret Service and the Federal Bureau of Investigation bear some blame for the laxness of the security measures in Dallas. SEE KENNEDY, JOHN FITZGERALD.

WARRENSBURG, city, W Missouri, seat of Johnson County; about 45 miles SE of Kansas City. The chief industrial establishments are the hatcheries, meat-packing plants, and bottling works. Coal mines, blue-sandstone quarries, and clay pits are in the vicinity. Clothing is manufactured. Warrensburg, first settled in 1833, was a training center for both Union and Confederate forces during the Civil War. Warrensburg is the site of the Central Missouri State College. (For population, see Missouri map in Atlas.)

WARRINGTON, county borough, W England, in Lancashire, on the Mersey River, and the Manchester Ship Canal, 15 miles E of Liverpool. Warrington is a manufacturing center, and as such produces machinery, chemicals, soap, glass, and cotton textiles. Warrington is the site of the Church of St. Elphin, containing a Saxon crypt, and its grammar school, which dates from 1526. The town was a religious center in the nineteenth century, and the Independent and Primitive branches of Methodism originated there. Thomas Malthus, the economist noted for his writings on the theory of population growth, attended Warrington Academy. (For population, see England map in Atlas.)

WARSAW, city, N central Indiana, seat of Kosciusko County; on the Tippecanoe River, 95 miles N of Indianapolis. The city is a trade center for a diversified agricultural area. Surgical supplies, toys, canned goods, cut glass, vacuum sweepers, and machinery are manufactured. Warsaw was settled in 1836 and incorporated in 1874. Winona Lake, a summer resort and site of a church camp, is 3 miles east of Warsaw. (For population, see Indiana map in Atlas.)

WARSAW, city, N Kentucky, seat of Gallatin County; on the Ohio River; 40 miles N of Frankfort. Although Warsaw was once a river port, the city is now a trade center for the fringe area of the Blue Grass. Furniture manufacturing and lumber milling are the major industries. Pop. (1960) 981.

WARSAW, city, W central Missouri, seat of Benton County; on the Osage River, and at the head of the Lake of the Ozarks; on U.S. highway 65; 30 miles S of Sedalia. The city is a tourist center, which is noted for hunting and fishing. Pop. (1960) 1,054.

WARSAW, village, W New York, seat of Wyoming County; on the Oatka River, the Baltimore and Ohio and the Erie railroads, and U.S. highway 20; 35 miles E of Buffalo. Warsaw is chiefly an industrial center. Elevators, textiles, canned goods, machinery, paper, and metal products are manufactured. Pop. (1960) 3,653.

WARSAW, town, E Virginia, seat of Richmond County; near the Rappahannock River; on U.S. Highway 360; 45 miles NE of Richmond. The town is a distributing point for sea food, dairy products, and lumber. The courthouse there dates from 1749. Pop. (1960) 549.

WARSAW, Polish Warszawa, province, E Poland, bounded by the provinces of Olsztyn on the N, Białystok on the NE, Lublin on the SE, Kielce on the S, Łódź on the SW, and Bydgoszcz on the NW; area 11,313 sq. mi.; pop. (1959) 2,338,000 (excluding the city of Warsaw). Warsaw lies on Poland's great central plain; it is drained by the Vistula and its tributaries. There are large forests and some marshy areas in the north. The soil is sandy and not very productive. The principal crops are grain, potatoes, sugar beets, and vegetables. The Vistula provides a means of transportation for the manufactures of flour, spirits, sugar, lumber, leather goods, metal goods, and textiles. Warsaw, then called Mazovia, was a principality, which was joined to Poland in 1529. The city of Warsaw is the only large urban center, and lies on the Vistula River.

WARSAW, Polish Warszawa, city, E central Poland, capital of the country; on the Vistula River, 320 miles E of Berlin and 620 miles SW of Leningrad; pop. (1959 est.) 1,095,000.

Setting. Warsaw is the largest city and the major commercial, transportation, and cultural center of Poland. The city lies at an elevation of 440 feet above sea level; its terrain is level to undulating. Its average temperatures are 26°F in January and 66°F in July. Average annual precipitation is 22 inches, with a summer maximum.

Economy. Almost one-fourth of Warsaw's labor force is engaged in government service, although this proportion is decreasing as the number of workers engaged in manufacturing increases. Most manufacturing industries are located in the outlying areas of the city. Wola, to the west, has some 40,000 workers engaged in electrochemical, machine-building, printing, and coke-chemical industries. Kamoniek, east of the Vistula, specializes in clothing, optical instruments, telephonic equipment, and motorcycles. Huta, Zeran, and Sluzewiec are areas developed after World War II. Together with Wola, Kamoniek, and older inner districts such as Praga, east of the Vistula, their output gives Warsaw first rank in Poland for the production of consumer goods. Warsaw's central business district lies in the old city, about 3 square miles in area, on the west bank of the Vistula opposite Praga. There are the national and municipal government offices, and the banks, stores, and commercial offices. Seven railroads and several major highways radiate from Warsaw; the Vistula is navigable by barge.

People. Warsaw's population has fluctuated quite widely; in 1939, 1,295,000 people lived there, but in 1945, at the end of World War II, the population was a mere 162,000. Few European cities were more devastated during World War II than Warsaw; according to official estimates, 85 per cent of the city's buildings were either destroyed or severely damaged. The large Jewish population, about one-third of the

EASTFOTO

Krakówskie Przedmiescie Street, part of the old section of Warsaw, was carefully rebuilt after the war. It is bisected by Royal Castle Square, site of Zygmund August Column.

prewar total, was virtually eliminated during the war. The old city remains the most densely populated part of the capital, in part because of the many large apartment houses built there after the war. The great majority of Warsaw's residents are Roman Catholics; almost all are Poles, as contrasted with the prewar period when there were sizable foreign minorities. Postwar reconstruction permitted improvements of many welfare facilities and utilities in the city, but there are contrasts between the central and outlying districts. In the former, where residential construction advanced more rapidly, most buildings have electricity, water, central heating, and gas; such is not generally the case in the outlying districts.

Features of Interest. In addition to its many new post-World War II buildings, modern Warsaw contains many historic buildings that, although destroyed during the war, were faithfully restored. The Old City (*Stare Miasto*), on a bluff overlooking the valley of the Vistula, contains the reconstructed fourteenth century Cathedral of St. John, the rebuilt Old Town Market Place, and the remains of fourteenth century fortifications such as the Barbican. To the north is the New Town, so-called although it was incorporated in 1408, where there are interesting baroque churches and important business houses. Both old centers have narrow streets that seem bizarre and quaint when contrasted with broad Marszalkówska Street, the city's main north-south artery, which is lined with post-World War II buildings. At the intersection of Marszalkówska and Jerozolimskie streets is the towering Palace of Science and Culture, with its Congress Hall and 3,300 offices and rooms, situated on 120 acres of grounds. North of the inner city lies the Warsaw Citadel, built by Czar Nicholas I when Warsaw was part of Russia. In central Warsaw there are two attractive parks, Kasinski and Saxon (now Victory) parks. On the west side of the Vistula, between the bluff and the river, there are other recreational areas. In the Old City are the University of Warsaw (1816) and numerous research institutions, technical colleges, cultural institutes, and scientific societies. Among the city's several museums and libraries are the State Archaeological Museum (1928), the National Art Museum (1862), the Polish Army Museum (1920), and the National Library (1928), whose holdings total about 1.9 million volumes.

History. Archaeological remains suggest that a settlement existed on the site of Warsaw in very early times. Documentary evidence reveals that Warsaw was already a fortified town in 1413 when it became the capital of Mazovia, one of the provinces of ancient Poland. With the union of Poland and Lithuania in the sixteenth century, Warsaw replaced Kraków as the capital, and subsequently grew rapidly. The city was occupied by Swedish and Prussian troops at various times during the succeeding centuries. It was the capital of French Emperor Napoleon I's Grand

Duchy of Warsaw, 1806–15, and then was occupied by Russia until World War I. Warsaw was occupied by German troops during World War II, 1939–45; in 1943, following an uprising of Warsaw's Jewish population, the Warsaw Ghetto was completely leveled by the Germans. ARTHUR E. MOODIE

WARS OF THE ROSES, the struggle between the houses of Lancaster and York for control of the throne of England during the latter half of the fifteenth century; it was named for the emblems of the two houses—that of Lancaster being a red rose, that of York being a white rose.

Origins. From late in the reign of Edward III, 1327–77, the House of Lancaster had exercised a predominant influence on the throne of England: first in the person of Edward's fourth son, John of Gaunt, duke of Lancaster (1340–99), who exercised great power behind the throne both during his father's declining years, and during the reign of his nephew Richard II, 1377–90; and, after Richard's death, in the persons of Henry IV, 1399–1413, Henry V, 1413–22, and Henry VI, 1422–61, who were respectively the son, grandson, and great-grandson of John of Gaunt. Throughout most of this period England and France were engaged in the Hundred Years' War, 1337–1453, in the course of which England eventually lost most of her possessions on the Continent (see HUNDRED YEARS' WAR). As a result of the territorial losses and the high cost of waging war, the authority of the English crown was substantially weakened at home, especially during the reign of the mentally unbalanced Henry VI, and the country was gradually reduced to a state of near anarchy in which nobles commanding private armies fought one another for control of the realm. One of the most powerful of these was Richard Plantagenet, 3rd duke of York, a descendant of Edward III's fifth son, Edmund of Langley, 1st duke of York through his father, and a descendant of Edward III's third son, Lionel Plantagenet, duke of Clarence, through his mother.

The Wars. During the insanity of Henry VI, 1453–54, Richard of York became protector of the realm. On Henry's recovery, Richard was dismissed from office. Thereupon, Yorkists armed and under Richard Neville, earl of Warwick, defeated the Lancastrians under Edmund Beaufort, 2nd duke of Somerset, at St. Albans, 1455, and Richard of York was reinstated as protector. In 1456, however, Richard was dismissed a second time, and Warwick defeated the Lancastrians at Blore Heath, September, 1459. Fighting continued, and at the battle of Northampton, July, 1460, Warwick captured Henry VI; Parliament attempting to settle the matter, decided that Henry should rule during his lifetime, but should be succeeded by York. In the north, however, the Lancastrians under Henry's queen, Margaret of Anjou, would not yield, and at Wakefield they defeated the Yorkists, and Richard of York was killed. The Lancastrians then marched south, defeated Warwick at the Second Battle of St. Albans, February, 1461, and set Henry VI at liberty.

The Yorkist cause was carried on by Edward of March, the eldest son of Richard of York, who joined Warwick and in February arrived in London, where he was proclaimed king as Edward IV. He at once marched north, and inflicted a decisive defeat on the Lancastrians at Towton, March, 1461. Henry and Margaret continued the war from Scotland. Their forces were defeated by Warwick at Hedgeley Moor and Hexham, 1464. Margaret fled to France, and Henry VI was captured and imprisoned in the Tower of London. Subsequently Edward IV and Warwick quarreled; and the latter fled to France, 1470, where he joined forces with Margaret, returned to England the same year, and restored Henry VI to the throne; Edward IV meanwhile had escaped to the Netherlands. With the support of Charles the Bold, duke of Burgundy, Edward soon returned to England, twice defeated the Lancastrians—at Barnet, where War-

wick was killed, and at Tewkesbury, after which Margaret was imprisoned—and again deposed Henry VI. After the latter's death in the Tower of London, 1471, Edward ruled supreme in England; the only remaining Lancastrian claimant was Henry Tudor, earl of Richmond, who was in France.

Upon the death of Edward IV, 1483, the crown passed to his 13-year-old son, Edward V. He and his younger brother Richard were seized immediately by their uncle, Richard, duke of Gloucester, who claimed the boys were illegitimate and had Parliament proclaim him king as Richard III, 1483. Richard met opposition in England, but suppressed it successfully. In France, however, Henry Tudor marshaled an army, with which he invaded England and defeated Richard's army at Bosworth Field, August, 1485. Richard was killed in the battle, and Tudor was immediately crowned as Henry VII. His marriage with Elizabeth, daughter of Edward IV, 1486, united the houses of Lancaster and York, and gave England peace.

WART. See VERRUCA.

WARTA RIVER, Poland, rises in the Kraków Hills, to the north of the city of Kraków and flows generally NW through the city of Poznań to join the Noteć River 35 miles before its junction with the Oder River at Küstrin. Its length is about 490 miles. The Warta is navigable to Konin, where it is connected with a local canal system. The river also forms part of a canal system upstream from Poznań.

WARTBURG, town, NE central Tennessee, seat of Morgan County; on U.S. highway 21; 135 miles W of Nashville. Coal is mined in the area, and oil refining and lumber processing are leading industries in the town. Wartburg was settled by Swiss and German immigrants in 1845. Pop. (1960) 1,819.

WARTBURG COLLEGE, A private, coeducational, liberal arts college located in Waverly, Iowa. The school, affiliated with the American Lutheran church, was established in 1852; its first instruction at the college level was offered in 1921. Senior students are permitted to take one honor course for achieving a high rank in their major field of study. Preprofessional students transferring at least 32 hours of credit earned at a professional school may earn a degree by completing specified minimum academic requirements at Wartburg. See COLLEGES AND UNIVERSITIES.

WART HOG, a wild swine found in the open plains of Africa. The wart hog, *Chocochoerus aethiopicus*, reaches a height of about two and a half feet, and except for the bristly mane along the back, has no hair. It is characterized by the very large head containing small eyes and two pairs of wartlike growths and by greatly developed tusks, those of the upper jaw being especially large. Its slender tail, tipped with a bush of hair, is held vertically as it trots about. Wart hogs are closely related to pigs.

CHICAGO NAT. HIST. MUS.

The wart hog, the wild swine of the African veldt, has a mammoth head, its body is almost hairless, and from its face grow wartlike protuberances that give it its name.

WARTON, JOSEPH, 1722–1800, English poet and critic, son of Thomas Warton the Elder (1688?–1745) and brother of Thomas Warton the Younger, was born in Dunsfold, Surrey. He studied at his father's school in Basingstoke, at Winchester School, 1735, and at Oriel College, Oxford, 1740–44. He then served as a curate and rector, 1745–55, became second master at Winchester School, 1755, and was headmaster there, 1766–93. Warton was looked upon by the students as a tyrant, and during his term as headmaster there were no less than three student rebellions. In his *Odes on Various Subjects* (1746) and his *Essays on the Genius and Writings of Pope* (1756–86), he took issue with the classicist theory, then popular, that only certain subjects and styles are fit for poetry, and called for a return to the freer literary standards of the Elizabethans and John Milton. He reiterated these views when he edited Alexander Pope's works, 1797.

WARTON, THOMAS, called the Younger, 1728?–90, English poet and critic, son of Thomas Warton the Elder and brother of Joseph Warton, was born in Basingstoke. He received his early education at his father's school in Basingstoke, completed his studies at Trinity College, Oxford, 1750, and taught there as a fellow, 1751–90, professor of poetry, 1757–67, and Camden professor of ancient history, 1785–90. Recognition of Warton's literary talents came with the publication of his poem, *The Triumph of Isis* (1749). He became a fellow of the London Society of Antiquaries, 1771, and a member of Samuel Johnson's Literary Club, 1782. He was named poet laureate, 1785. Warton is chiefly remembered as a critic and historian who influenced the English romantic movement. In his *Observations on the Faerie Queene of Spenser* (1754), Warton asserted that eighteenth century critical theories were not applicable to the work of an unorthodox poet like Edmund Spenser, and that Spenser's subject matter, medieval life and chivalry, was not, as many critics contended, outside the realm of poetry. Warton expanded his critical views in his *History of English Poetry* (3 vols. 1774–81), and called for a revival of interest in medieval literature and life.

WARWICK, RICHARD DE BEAUCHAMP, EARL OF, 1382–1439, English soldier during the Hundred Years' War, father-in-law of Richard Neville (later Earl of Warwick), was born in Worcestershire. He took a prominent part in suppressing Owen Glendower's rebellion, 1403; made a pilgrimage to Rome and Jerusalem; traveled through Europe, 1408–10; and served as lord high steward at the coronation of Henry V, 1413. He was active against the Lollards, 1414, became deputy of Calais, and represented England at the Council of Constance. He had an important command in Normandy during Henry V's French campaign, 1415, and received the surrender of Rouen, 1419, and that of Meaux, 1422. He was entrusted with the education of Henry VI, 1429, and was appointed lieutenant of France and Normandy, 1437.

WARWICK, RICHARD NEVILLE, EARL OF, known as the King Maker, 1428–71, famous English warrior during the Wars of the Roses, was the eldest son of Richard Neville, earl of Salisbury (1400–60). He married Anne, daughter and heiress of Richard de Beauchamp, earl of Warwick, and was himself created earl of Warwick, 1449. In 1455, five powerful Neville peers, with their adherents and vassals, joined the forces of Warwick's uncle, Richard, duke of York, who aspired to overthrow the power of Edmund Beauford, 2nd duke of Somerset (died 1455), the chief adviser of king Henry VI. Warwick's impetuous onslaught contributed greatly to the Yorkist victory in the First Battle of St. Albans, 1454, and in the subsequent period of Yorkist ascendency, Warwick was rewarded with the governorship of Calais and the command of the seas. When civil strife broke out again, 1459, Warwick was with the Yorkist army that was dispersed at Ludford, and

CULVER SERVICE

The King Maker, Richard Neville, earl of Warwick, was killed during the Battle of Barnet, 1471, while attempting to overthrow Edward IV, the Yorkist ruler of England.

he was compelled to retire to Calais. In 1460, however, after the defeat of the Yorkist forces he won the Battle of Northampton, captured Henry VI, and entered London, where Richard, duke of York was proclaimed successor to the throne.

After the disastrous Battle of Wakefield, 1460, in which Richard, duke of York was slain, the leadership of the Yorkist party devolved on Warwick, in behalf of Richard's son, Edward, earl of March. Although defeated at the Second Battle of St. Albans, 1461, Warwick again entered London, always Yorkist in sympathy, and Edward IV was proclaimed king March, 1461.

Warwick was now at the height of his power, for Edward IV appointed him grand chamberlain of England, and warden of the Cinque Ports and of the East and West Marches of Scotland. During the next few years Warwick and his brother John, Lord Montague, subdued the strongholds that were still held by the house of Lancaster, and conducted Henry VI a prisoner to the Tower, June, 1465. From 1464, however, Warwick had misunderstandings with Edward IV, who resented the supremacy of the Nevilles and built up, in opposition, the power of the queen's relatives, the Woodvilles. By 1469 the King Maker was in open revolt against Edward, and an insurrection in Yorkshire and the defeat of the royal forces at Edgecote threw Edward into his hands. The Nevilles' period of power was short, however, and they were declared traitors and forced to flee to France. There, Warwick was reconciled by Louis XI with the Lancastrian Queen Margaret. Subsequently he landed at Plymouth, 1470, at the head of a Lancastrian army. Edward escaped to Holland, and Henry VI was replaced on the throne. But Edward landed on Mar. 14, 1471, at Ravenspur, and gathered an army. In the ensuing Battle of Barnet, 1471, Warwick was slain.

WARWICK, city, E Rhode Island, in Kent County; between Greenwich Cove and Narragansett Bay; 6 miles S of Providence. The city is an industrial center, which is noted primarily for the production of textiles and metal products. It is also noted as a summer resort. Agricultural products of the area include fruit and mushrooms. Warwick was founded in 1642. It was incorporated as a city in 1931. (For population, see Rhode Island map in Atlas.)

WARWICK, municipal borough, central England, capital of Warwickshire, on the River Avon, 19 miles SE of Birmingham. Furniture, gelatin, and agricultural implements are manufactured, and the town has a large livestock market. Warwick has many old and historic buildings, and a medieval wall. It is dominated by its castle, the seat of the Earls of Warwick. Warwick Castle is situated on a high crag, overlooking the river. The present structure was built in the fourteenth century, though one of its towers dates from the eleventh century, and the foundations were laid in 915. The castle contains many valuable works of art. The Church of St. Mary retains twelfth- to fifteenth-century work. The Lord Leicester Hospital was built in the fourteenth century, and was converted into an asylum for the poor by the Earl of Leicester, 1571. Warwick ranked as a borough from the time of Edward the Confessor in the eleventh century. In 1642, during the Parliamentary Civil War, the castle was unsuccessfully attacked by the royalists and withstood a siege. (For population, see England map in Atlas.)

WARWICKSHIRE, county, central England, bounded by the counties of Staffordshire on the NW, Leicestershire on the NE, Northamptonshire on the E, Oxfordshire on the S, Gloucestershire on the SW, and Worcestershire on the W; area of the county, 983 square miles. The River Avon flows from northeast to southwest across the county, which is undulating and well wooded. There is a distinct contrast between the northern and southern sections of the county. The north lies in a coalfield, and is heavily industrialized. The major manufacturing centers are Birmingham, one of the largest cities in England, and Coventry. The southern section of Warwickshire is almost entirely agricultural with wheat, hay, and beans the major crops. Truck farming and orchards are found in the Avon Valley. Well-known towns in the county include Stratford-on-Avon, birthplace of William Shakespeare, and Rugby, famous for its public school. (For population, see England map in Atlas.)

WASATCH MOUNTAINS, a rugged mountain range forming part of the Rocky Mountain System, extending from SE Idaho to central Utah and forming the eastern limits of the Great Basin. The mountains contain deposits of copper, lead, gold, and silver, and the middle slopes are covered with pine forests. The average elevation is about 10,000 feet. Timpanogos Cave National Monument is located on Mount Timpanogos. One of the more noted scenic attractions is Bridal Veil Falls. The cities of Ogden, Salt Lake City, and Provo are on the western slopes of the Wasatch Range. The range is drained by the Weber, Ogden, and Provo rivers.

WASH, THE, an estuary of the North Sea, on the E coast of England, bounded by the counties of Lincolnshire on the N and Norfolk on the S. The rivers Witham, Welland, Nene, and Ouse drain into the estuary, which is about 22 miles long and 15 miles wide. There are numerous sandbanks and mud shoals, which are dry at low water. The shores are low and marshy, at times inundated. The district at the head of the Wash, known as Holland because of its numerous dikes and windmills, forms part of the Fens. See FENS, THE.

WASHBURNE, ELIHU BENJAMIN, 1816–87, U.S. legislator and diplomat, was born in Livermore, Me., and studied at Maine Wesleyan Seminary and Harvard Law School. He established a successful legal practice at Galena, Ill., 1840. He served in the U.S. House of Representatives, 1853–69, as a Whig and later as a Republican, and opposed corruption in legislation, supported Pres. Abraham Lincoln during the Civil War, and became a radical reconstruction-

ist. He was secretary of state for a few days under Pres. Ulysses S. Grant, leaving the post to become minister to France, 1869–77.

WASHINGTON, BOOKER TALIAFERRO, 1856–1915, U.S. educator, son of a mulatto slave woman and a white man, was born near Hale's Ford, Va. After the Civil War, his family moved to Malden, W. Va., where, when he was old enough, Booker worked in the salt furnaces and coal mines. In 1872 he worked his way to the Hampton Normal and Industrial Institute, where he paid his expenses by acting as a janitor. In the fall of 1875 he returned to Malden and taught there for three years. He then attended the Wayland Seminary in Washington, D. C., and in 1879 was appointed an instructor at the Hampton Institute.

Accepting a call to organize and become the principal of a normal school at Tuskegee, Ala., he opened the school on July 4, 1881, in an old church and a dilapidated shanty, with an attendance of 30 students. In advancing the interests of the school, Washington made a great many public addresses both in the North and in the South, and ultimately acquired the reputation of being one of the ablest public speakers in the country. In his educational work he emphasized the importance of the Negro's accumulating property and making himself respected, but he discouraged Negroes from becoming involved in politics. He strongly urged industrial education. He founded the Tuskegee Conference, 1892, and organized the National Negro Business League. He wrote *The Future of the American Negro* (1899), *Up From Slavery* (1901), and *The Man Farthest Down* (1912). At mid-twentieth century many Negroes, particularly younger ones, regarded Washington's example as a poor one to follow: Washington, it was felt, had deferred excessively to the white men's ideas and values, and had accepted favors and concessions when he should have insisted upon his rights.

BIBLIOG.–Hugh Hawkins, ed., *Booker T. Washington and His Critics: The Problem of Negro Leadership* (1962); Basil J. Mathews, *Booker T. Washington: Educator and Interracial Interpreter* (1948); S. R. Spencer, Jr., *Booker T. Washington and the Negro's Place in American Life* (1955).

CULVER

Booker T. Washington

WASHINGTON, BUSHROD, 1762–1829, U.S. jurist, was born in Westmoreland County, Va., was graduated from the College of William and Mary, 1778, and was admitted to the Virginia bar, 1780. He was a member of the Virginia assembly, 1787, and a delegate at the Virginia constitutional convention, in which he supported ratification of the federal Constitution, 1788. He was appointed to the U.S. Supreme Court by Pres. John Adams, 1798. From his uncle, George Washington, Bushrod Washington inherited the Mount Vernon estate and the first president's library and correspondence.

It happened when GEORGE WASHINGTON was president

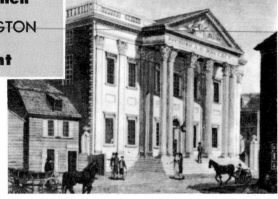

In 1791 the federal government gave both organizational and financial assistance to help start the First Bank of the United States; its principal offices were located in the pioneer city of financial organization, Philadelphia.

BETTMANN ARCHIVE

After the electoral college had unanimously chosen Gen. George Washington as the first President of the United States, he was inaugurated for his first term of office at the Federal Hall in New York City on Apr. 30, 1789

BETTMANN ARCHIVE

For his first cabinet, composed of only four members, President Washington selected men who represented varying, often conflicting, points of view; from left to right are Washington, Knox, Hamilton, Jefferson, and Randolph.

LOSSING'S "OUR COUNTRY"

The American diplomat John Jay was hanged in effigy for his part in the negotiations with Great Britain that resulted in the unpopular Jay's Treaty, concluded in 1794.

PENNSYLVANIA RR.

While Washington was president, construction was begun on the President's Palace, 1792, officially known as the White House by an act of Congress in 1902.

Birthplace: Westmoreland County, Va.
(reconstructed birthplace)

GEORGE WASHINGTON

First President of the United States

1789—1797

WASHINGTON, GEORGE, called the Father of His Country, 1732–99, first president of the United States, was born in Bridges Creek, Westmoreland County, Va., on Feb. 22, 1732. His father was Augustine Washington, a descendant of Lawrence Washington of Sulgrave Manor near Sulgrave, Northamptonshire, England. Augustine Washington was a wealthy landowner who had married twice: his first wife, Jane Butler, had borne him four children; his second wife, Mary Ball, had six children, of whom George was the first.

Little is known of George Washington's childhood, beyond the fact that his early education, such as it was, was gained from his father, from the local sexton, and from a schoolmaster named Williams. The boy learned some Latin, but most of his real education was gained from practical outdoor experience on his father's six plantations, where he learned the principles of estate management, and taught himself mathematics and surveying. The copybook legends about his childhood—his dislike of fighting, his mastery over schoolmates, his misadventure with a cherry tree, and so on—are certainly apocryphal, and are no more than part of the general fund of legend and misinformation perpetuated by the early biography by Mason Locke Weems.

When George Washington was 11 his father died, and subsequently the boy divided his time between the home of his half-brother, Lawrence, his guardian, at Mount Vernon, and his old home, Bridges Farm, where lived Augustine, his other half-brother. Mary Ball Washington, who lived until 1789, is supposed to have had a strong moral influence upon the future statesman's early years.

Washington's brother Lawrence had married into the Fairfax family, whose estate, Belvoir was near Mount Vernon. At Belvoir Washington came into contact with a society where culture and courtly manners were part of the atmosphere, and he responded with appreciation. Here, too, he met Thomas Fairfax, 6th Baron Fairfax, through whom he began his career: in 1748 the Englishman sent a surveying party to his Shenandoah estates, and with this expedition went a young kinsman of his and Washington. The trip, which was a real adventure in hardships for the young men, proved valuable for Washington who, through Lord Fairfax, received the appointment of county surveyor for Culpeper. Both exactitude and endurance were required for the performance of his duties, which took him repeatedly into wild, unsettled country. He gave it up, however, in order to go with his brother to Barbados, 1751; Lawrence had contracted tuberculosis, and died of it the following year. When Lawrence's daughter died a few months later, George Washington inherited the Mount Vernon estate. While in Barbados, it should be mentioned, he contracted smallpox, which left his face deeply pitted.

In the Virginia Militia. In 1752 Edward Dinwiddie (1693–1770), governor of Virginia, appointed Washington district adjutant. This appointment carried the rank of major, and Washington's experience with the Virginia militia interested him more and more in military life. In 1753 he was sent with a mission to protest to the French about their reported encroachments on the Ohio lands of English settlers. The journey was dangerous and arduous, and Washington had to go all the way to Fort Le Boeuf, 20 miles south of Lake Erie, before finding an officer who received his message and replied with a refusal even to consider the English protests. While on this trip, Washington also held a council with the Indians at Logstown, Ohio, but was unable to secure their friendship. Upon his return to civilization, Washington was made a lieutenant colonel to head a regiment under Col. Joshua Fry, and was sent with 150 men to occupy a fort on the Ohio. The French got there first, however, and built Fort Duquesne on the site that is now Pittsburgh. Washington built a temporary fort at Great Meadows, called Fort Necessity; from this base he intercepted a French scouting party, killing the leader, Joseph Coulon, sieur de Jumonville, and several others. The French retaliated by an attack on Great Meadows; they forced Washington to surrender but allowed him to return home. Then, dissatisfied with both the conduct of the war and the British order that colonial officers of whatever rank were inferior to officers appointed by the crown, Washington resigned his commission, 1754.

Early in 1755, however, Gen. Edward Braddock arrived in Virginia as part of a plan for an advance on Fort Duquesne, Niagara, and Crown Point, and Washington accepted an appointment as his aide-de-camp, with the rank of colonel. Braddock soon recognized Washington's energy and ability and, it is thought, was probably guided by his advice when he divided his army in order to make a surprise attack on Fort Duquesne. Washington, although very ill with fever, was with the advance guard when this attack resulted in a bloody defeat, and was responsible for the successful retreat of the men. Braddock, however, was mortally wounded. Washington's bravery and ability on this occasion resulted in his being appointed commander of all the Virginia forces. During the next three years of successfully defending the Virginia frontiers, he found that he was handicapped by continuing friction between colonial and British officers. In 1756 he rode all the way from Winchester to Boston to secure a settlement of this difficulty and succeeded in having his authority upheld. Not until 1758 was Fort Duquesne taken, when the British sent a force of regulars under Gen. John Forbes; Washington, now made brigadier, co-operated. Since the main threat to Virginia's frontiers was now removed, and he was very ill, Washington soon resigned his commission and returned to civil life.

Life at Mount Vernon. As soon as his resignation from the Army had taken effect, Washington was married, 1759, to Martha Dandridge, the wealthy widow of Col. Daniel Parke Custis, by whom she had had two children. Washington added the direction of her estate to his own, and until the outbreak of the revolutionary struggle lived the calm and pleasant life of a wealthy planter, aristocrat, and family man. At Mount Vernon there was scope enough for skill and husbandry, and there was time for the sort of social life that Washington enjoyed: hunting, card playing, horse racing, the theater, and parties were among his amusements. Tobacco was the principal crop, but Washington showed rare sagacity in rotating his crops, and in growing a variety of products so as to provide for the many people supported by the estate. Washington disliked slavery and alleviated its evil features as much as possible by his humane treatment of his slaves and refusal to sell any of them. To Martha Washington's children he was a devoted stepfather; the death of her daughter, Martha Parke (Patsy) Custis, 1773, was a source of grief to him.

The British-Colonial Conflict. Meanwhile, however, he was increasingly conscious of the growing friction between the colonies and the mother country. He was elected to the House of Burgesses, 1758, and he took his seat, 1759. Thus, although not particularly active in politics, he was aware at all times of the course of public events. Furthermore, as the manager of large estates, he was necessarily an importer of goods, and as such he felt the force of the British restrictions on trade. These experiences, superimposed on his unfavorable impressions of the British in the French-Indian campaigns, helped to create a feeling of hostility toward the British that made him from the beginning a strong believer in colonial American independence.

After 1770, if not before, this feeling of hostility had ample justification. The Stamp Act and the British prohibition of colonial paper money imposed tangible grievances. Washington supported the policy of non-importation as a weapon of opposition. When the governor dissolved the Virginia Assembly, 1774, Washington was at the meeting of burgesses at Raleigh Tavern that adopted resolutions to send delegates to the First Continental Congress. He was a leading delegate to the first provincial convention the same summer, and at that time offered to raise a thousand men, pay their expenses, and march with them to relieve Boston. As a result of his militancy he was chosen as one of Virginia's seven delegates to the First Continental Congress. Although opposed to severing relations with the mother country, he was known as a radical because he belonged to the group which believed armed conflict was inevitable. Returning to Virginia, he commanded several militia companies until chosen commander in chief of the colonies' military forces by the Second Continental Congress. This appointment was made not only because Washington's military ability was highly regarded, but as a means of securing southern support for the army, which had been gathered about Boston after the battles of Lexington and Concord. In accepting the command Washington refused all payment except for expenses.

As Commander of the American Army, his task was threefold: to create and train an army; to resist the British; and to persuade a weak, incompetent, and powerless Congress to support the war. To make matters worse, he had at his back subordinates who were constantly conspiring against him. His army, composed of 20,000 men enlisted for short terms, was at times reduced to not more than 2,000. In addition it was supplemented in various campaigns by local militiamen who came and went almost at will. The problem of discipline was acute, particularly as there was a general feeling that in the new democracy military discipline had no place. Training and disciplining the army was the first task of the early months of the war, during which the American forces remained in the country around Boston. Early in 1776 Washington seized Dorchester Heights, a strategic position overlooking the city and the harbor, and periling the British forces both on land and sea. This

led Gen. William Howe to evacuate Boston. A British attack on New York was the next action to be expected, and Washington was charged by Congress with the defense of that city—a difficult, if not impossible, task.

In the first year of the war Washington was hampered by his sense of his own inexperience; instead of taking the conduct of his campaign into his own hands he acted as Congress wished. Meanwhile, a step had been taken that he thoroughly approved: the Declaration of Independence had been signed.

In defending New York, Washington divided his army and placed 9,000 men under Israel Putnam on Brooklyn Heights, Long Island, where they could easily be trapped. Howe, who had encamped on Staten Island, with the assistance of the fleet under his brother, inflicted a crushing defeat on the colonial troops, but failed to prevent their escape across the East River to Manhattan Island. In a leisurely manner Howe's forces compelled the colonial forces to retreat; Washington lost Fort Washington and Fort Lee on the Hudson, then retreated northward from White Plains across the river into New Jersey. Expecting Gen. Charles Lee to bring reinforcements—that arrived only after Lee himself had been captured by the British—Washington continued his retreat across New Jersey toward the Delaware River. Howe, for some reason that has never been explained satisfactorily, did not inflict a crushing defeat on the hardbeset colonial troops, but instead settled his own men in winter quarters and returned to New York. See REVOLUTIONARY WAR.

In one of the most brilliant operations of the war, Washington recrossed the Delaware on Dec. 24, 1776, and struck blows at the British at Trenton and Princeton. In each case he escaped with his forces before reinforcements could arrive. He then took up a strong position at Morristown. These victories heartened the Americans and made possible the continuance of the war. In 1777, British Gen. John Burgoyne, invading the Hudson region from Canada, was forced to surrender at Saratoga to Gen. Horatio Gates; Burgoyne's failure to carry out the British plan of invasion from Canada was the turning point of the war. This was not immediately apparent, however, for Howe had moved his army by sea to Delaware and had defeated Washington at Brandywine, north of Wilmington. The colonial army retreated in good order, but Congress was forced to leave Philadelphia and the city was occupied by the British. After failing to recoup his losses at Germantown, Washington took up winter quarters at Valley Forge, and spent the winter trying to extract from Congress the supplies that his troops so sorely needed. During the severe winter of 1777, the morale of the colonists was probably at its lowest point. Not only did Washington have to endure the indifference of Congress and watch the sufferings of his men, but he became aware that Major General Thomas Conway was fomenting among his officers a plot to supplant him as commander in chief and put General Gates in his place. With this problem Washington dealt quickly and effectively: he wrote a note that brought the matter into the open and produced in Congress a reaction in his favor. The troops at Valley Forge survived the winter and emerged better soldiers and wholly devoted to Washington.

Last Years of the War. Meanwhile, in March, 1778, an alliance with France had been completed. Impressed by the American success at Saratoga and by Washington's considerable resistance at Trenton, Brandywine, and Germantown, the French had decided to add open alliance and force of arms to the money and supplies that they were already giving the colonies. This event apparently frightened the British and gave the Americans a new assurance of victory, but had the unfortunate effect of making many Americans feel that further effort on their part was unnecessary.

Sir Henry Clinton, who became commander of the British forces after Howe's resignation, evacuated

GEORGE WASHINGTON

At Valley Forge, on the Schuylkill River, Washington and Lafayette spent the difficult winter of 1777–78 with a demoralized, ill-fed, and ill-clothed Continental Army.
CULVER SERVICE

Washington executed one of the most brilliant maneuvers of the Revolutionary War on Dec. 24, 1776, when he crossed the icy Delaware River to attack British forces.
CULVER SERVICE

The fact that George Washington had been the president of the Constitutional Convention, 1787, was an important factor in the ultimate adoption of the Constitution.
CULVER SERVICE

CULVER SERVICE

After General Washington's forces had besieged the British position at Yorktown, Pa., for three weeks, the American commander received the surrender of General Cornwallis.

CULVER SERVICE

In 1749 young George Washington was appointed surveyor for Culpeper County, Va. His duties frequently carried him into the wilderness, where he endured many hardships.

Philadelphia and began to march his troops across New Jersey to New York. Washington pursued, and demonstrated his ability as a general at Monmouth, where the two armies met, with the American forces between the British and the coast. Because of Gen. Charles Lee's treachery, Clinton succeeded in retiring to Sandy Hook, and Washington's army took up a position at New Brunswick. Both armies maintained these positions with very little change until 1781.

In 1780 a French army under the Comte de Rochambeau arrived in Rhode Island, but it was decided that an attack on New York would have to wait for a second French force. In 1781, as plans were being made to attack without the expected reinforcement, Comte François Joseph Paul de Grasse arrived with his fleet and indicated his preference for a Southern war theater. Leaving troops to protect the position in New York, Washington marched the main body of his troops to Yorktown, where Gen. Charles Cornwallis, who in 1778 had begun an invasion of the South and taken Charleston and Savannah, was in command. With the assistance of the Virginia militia, French troops brought by De Grasse, and the French fleet, Washington laid siege to Yorktown; and three weeks later Cornwallis surrendered.

Washington's victory at Yorktown was the virtual end of the war, but two years elapsed before an agreement could be reached with Great Britain and the army could be demobilized. Meanwhile there was less need, from the point of view of the colonial government, for keeping the soldiers fed and clothed. Washington was horrified, 1782, to find a plan was afoot in the army to take over the government and make him king. By force of high character and the men's devotion to him he induced them to wait. Eventually they were paid with warrants, of little actual value, as bounty.

Finally, in the spring of 1783, honorable terms of peace, including complete independence, were secured from the British, and on Apr. 19, 1783, the anniversary of the Battle of Lexington, Washington entered the city of New York at the head of his troops. on Christmas Eve of the same year, he resigned his command, turning in a bill for something over £14,000 for expenses, an account of which he had kept meticulously through all the stresses of his campaigns. On the same day he returned to Mount Vernon, hoping to resume the life as a planter which had been interrupted by the war.

The Private Citizen. In 1784 Washington took a horseback journey into the West in connection with his interest in a new route which would connect the Potomac and Ohio rivers and thus open a way from Virginia into the western lands. Through this interest he was brought once more into the public life. His principal concern, however, was his farms and the problems of management entailed by them.

Shays' Rebellion, 1786, made him realize that something must be done to provide a strong central government for the colonies. He reluctantly accepted an assignment as delegate to the Constitutional Convention, 1787, and was chosen as presiding officer of that body. At the actual sessions he said little, but off the convention floor he worked indefatigably for the Constitution, and after the convention he applied the full weight of his influence for its adoption. He recognized that it was not a perfect document, but pointed out that it contained within it machinery for its own amendment, and argued that above all it was necessary at this time to have a foundation upon which a strong central government could be built. After the adoption of the Constitution, it seemed almost a foregone conclusion that Washington would be chosen the first president of the new nation, and he was so chosen unanimously by the electoral college, 1789. With extreme reluctance he accepted the office.

As First President. The work of organization and appointment of officials occupied most of the following year. Washington's appointments were made

CHICAGO HIST. SOC.

From 1759 to 1774, Washington divided his time between his obligations as a legislator and his pleasant life as a gentleman farmer and family man at Mount Vernon, Va.

carefully; for his first cabinet, which comprised only four members, he selected representatives of varying points of view. Secretary of State Thomas Jefferson, for example, was a proponent of the French liberal and democratic ideas that had been so popular during the Revolutionary War, particularly as expressed in the works of Tom Paine. Secretary of the Treasury Alexander Hamilton, on the other hand, believed in a strong central government and in rule by the moneyed classes. During Washington's first administration, two political parties, the Whigs and the Federalists, were formed upon the basis of these opposing philosophies. As a later historian, James Truslow Adams, was to put it, the country accepted the ideas of Jefferson and the social structure imposed by Hamilton.

Friction between the two men grew violent at times, but Washington did his best to reconcile them, believing that they were both necessary to the welfare of the country. He saw that the important problems before him were to establish the nation on a basis of financial stability, and to settle the points still at issue with Great Britain. Because the government had to be strengthened as much as possible in order to achieve those goals, Washington decidedly leaned toward Hamilton's point of view. His support of the financial policies of Hamilton resulted in the establishment of a firm structure of banking and national credit and the imposition of a tariff. When, during the French Revolution, 1789, France was threatened with invasion, he favored England rather than France. As a result, popular feeling ran high, and Washington had to maintain the dignity of the new republic by requesting the recall of the French ambassador, Edmond Genêt. In 1793 Jefferson resigned from the cabinet in protest against this anti-French policy. Another source of popular discontent was the suppression, by armed forces, of the Whisky Insurrection, 1794, although Washington treated the malcontents leniently.

During Washington's second administration, 1793–97, criticism and resentment increased, reaching a high point when the Jay Treaty with Great Britain was signed, 1794. Washington refused to surrender to Congress the state papers dealing with the treaty, thus setting a firm presidential precedent. See JAY'S TREATY.

Despite these points of controversy, there is no doubt that Washington proved himself an able administrator whose policies did much to strengthen the new government and to make it possible for the United States to become a nation. Treaties with Spain and Great Britain settled the points at issue between those countries and the United States; successful campaigns against the Indians made it possible for the states to expand westward. The country was kept at peace, the machinery of government was set in working order, and the national finances were placed on a firm footing.

In 1796, having declined a third term and set a precedent that remained unbroken until 1940, Washington was at last permitted to retire to private life. In so doing he delivered a farewell address that is perhaps the best expression of his basic ideas, his high character, and his practical wisdom. In it he urged upon the U.S. people the importance of unity, non-partisanship, religion, and education and warned them against entering into entangling alliances with foreign powers.

Last Years. Washington was now worn and tired, and felt that he had grown old; but when war with France seemed imminent in 1798, he was asked to undertake the command of the U.S. armed forces. He consented, stipulating only that he should not be asked to take the field until the actual emergency was at hand. Though the scare passed, he was not allowed to enjoy his retirement long: on Dec. 14, 1799, he died of an attack of acute laryngitis, after two days of illness.

Significance. Washington's extraordinary disinterestedness, his devotion to the American cause, his equanimity, and his fortitude, as much as his military ability or qualities as a statesman, resulted in his victory in war and in his greatness as president. He might well be regarded as the epitome of the eighteenth-century gentleman, except that his qualities far transcended that ideal. As a general, he showed his skill not so much in the brilliance of his operations as by his policy of maintaining the war while avoiding pitched engagements which his army would undoubtedly have lost. As a statesman, he placed the interest of his country first, and firmly followed the policies he believed in without regard to popular sentiment. His courage and his faith sustained and unified a divided people as it sustained his own armies.

Bibliog.–Francis F. Bellamy, *Private Life of George Washington* (1951); William A. Bryan, *George Washington in American Literature, 1775–1865* (1952); Gilbert Chinard, ed. and tr., *George Washington as the French Knew Him* (1940); William B. Clark, *George Washington's Navy* (1960); Hugh Cleland, *George Washington in the Ohio Valley* (1956); Marcus Cunliffe, *George Washington: Man and Monument* (1958); Stephen Decatur, *Private Affairs of George Washington from the Records and Accounts of Tobias Lear, His Secretary* (1933); Bernard Fay, *George Washington, Republican Aristocrat* (1931); James T. Flexner, *George Washington*, 2 vols. (1965–68); Douglas S. Freeman, *George Washington: A Biography*, 7 vols. (1948–57); Rupert Hughes, *George Washington*, 3 vols. (1926–30); Clark Kinnaird, *George Washington* (1966); John Marshall, *Life of George Washington*, 5 vols. (1926); Bernard Mayo, *Myths and Men: Patrick Henry, George Washington, Thomas Jefferson* (1959); Louis M. Sears, *George Washington and the French Revolution* (1960); Samuel B. Shirk, *Characterization of George Washington in American Plays Since 1875* (1949); Nathaniel W. Stephenson and Waldo H. Dunn, *George Washington*, 2 vols. (1940); Howard Swiggett, *Great Man: George Washington as a Human Being* (1953); John W. Tebbel, *George Washington's America* (1954); Emily S. Whiteley, *Washington and His Aides-de-Camp* (1936); William E. Woodward, *George Washington: The Image and the Man* (1946).

WASHINGTON, MARTHA DANDRIDGE CUSTIS,

1731–1802, wife of George Washington, was born in New Kent County, Va., daughter of a wealthy planter, Col. John Dandridge. In 1749 she married Daniel Parke Custis. They had four children, two of whom died in infancy. At her husband's death (1757) she was one of the wealthiest women in Virginia. In 1759 she became the bride of George Washington. Though Washington was deeply attached to her children, Martha Parke (Patsy) Custis (died 1773) and John Parke Custis (died 1781), he did not adopt them. However, when John Parke Custis died leaving four children, Washington adopted the two youngest—Eleanor Parke Custis and George Washington Parke Custis. Martha Washington was a gracious hostess, noted for her charm, dignity, and hospitality.

Bibliog.–Alice C. Desmond, *Martha Washington, Our First Lady* (1942); Elswyth Thane, *Washington's Lady: The Life of Martha Washington* (1960).

The state seal of Washington bears the portrait of George Washington, for whom the state was named. The date 1889 beneath the portrait is the date in which the state was admitted to the Union. The seal was adopted in 1889.

BIRD	Willow goldfinch
FLOWER	Rhododendron
TREE	Western hemlock
CAPITAL	Olympia
MOTTO	Alki (By and By)
ENTERED THE UNION	Nov. 11, 1889
ORDER OF ENTRY	42nd

WASHINGTON, state, NW United States, in the Pacific Northwest; bounded on the N by British Columbia, Canada, on the E by Idaho, on the S by Oregon, on the W by the Pacific Ocean, and on the NW by Puget Sound and the straits of Juan de Fuca and Georgia; area 68,192 sq. mi., of which 1,483 sq. mi. are inland water; pop. (1960) 2,853,214. Washington extends 360 miles east-west and 240 miles north-south. It ranks 20th in area and 23rd in population among the states. The state was the 42nd to enter the Union. Washington is nicknamed the "Evergreen State" and its forested and glacier-covered peaks have led many to call it "The Switzerland of America." The state motto is *Alki*, an Indian word meaning *By and By*; the state song is *Washington, My Home*. The willow goldfinch is the state bird, the western hemlock is the state tree, and the western rhododendron is the state flower. Olympia is the capital. See map in Atlas, Vol. 20. For state flag in color, see FLAG.

PHYSICAL FEATURES

Physiography. Mountains and hills cover nearly two thirds of Washington. The Cascade Range extends in a wide belt north to south through the center of the state, its general crest elevation from 4,000 to 7,000 feet above sea level. The lofty, dormant volcanic peaks of the Cascades are among the highest and most conspicuous landmarks in the United States. Most massive of these is Mount Rainier (14,410 ft.), noted for having the country's largest glacial system outside of Alaska. Other high volcanic cones are Mount Adams (12,307 ft.), Mount Baker (10,750 ft.), Glacier Peak (10,436 ft.), and Mount St. Helens (9,671 ft.). Numerous rivers issue from the glaciers of these peaks. Lake Chelan, in a deep and long, glacially cut depression on the eastern slope of the Cascade, is the state's largest body of fresh water.

Elevation Map. White area indicates 0-500 feet above sea level; light gray, 500-2,000 feet; dark gray, 2,000-5,000 feet; black, over 5,000 feet.

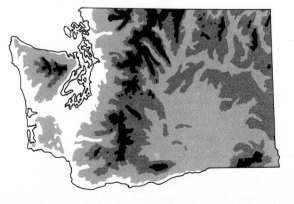

Precipitation Map. White area indicates less than 10 inches annually; light gray, 10-30 inches; dark gray, 30-50 inches; black, over 50 inches.

Population Density Map. White area indicates 1-10 persons per square mile; light gray, 10-25 persons; dark gray, 25-100 persons; black, 100-450 persons.

The densely forested Olympic Mountains, an extension of the Coast Range of Oregon and California, rise abruptly between Puget Sound and the Pacific Ocean in the northwestern corner of the state, or Olympic Peninsula. It is a lofty range, of which glacier-covered Mount Olympus (7,954 ft.) is the highest peak. The Olympics are deeply carved by numerous, swift-flowing rivers that drain off the extremely heavy rainfall and melting snow. To the south, separated from the Olympics by the Chehalis River, are the low Willapa Hills, which rise to about 3,000 feet.

Ranges of the Rocky Mountains, locally called the Okanogans and the Selkirks, extend across northeastern Washington. These highlands are deeply cut by the upper Columbia River and its major tributaries—the Okanogan, the Sanpoil, the Pend Oreille, and the Spokane rivers. One of the country's largest manmade lakes, Franklin D. Roosevelt Lake, the reservoir of Grand Coulee Dam, lies along the Columbia River. The Okanogans and Selkirks are old ranges of metamorphic rocks. Their summit levels are 4,000 to 6,000 feet above sea level. Valley lowlands are narrow and form highway routes into the rough highlands of British Columbia.

The Palouse Hills and the Blue Mountains are on the southeastern border of Washington. The Palouse region is one of rounded loess hills about 2,500 feet in elevation. The Blue Mountains are higher and rockier. The Snake River, the major Columbia River tributary, flows across these highlands through a deep canyon.

The Columbia Plateau covers most of east central Washington. Its major features are extensive rolling plains of wind-deposited soils, tablelands, and spectacular ancient dry river canyons, or coulees. The Columbia River makes a big bend through a gorge-like valley across the plateau, which lies between 2,000 and 3,000 feet above sea level. As a result of the dry climate and the thick beds of hard basaltic lava, erosion features are sharp and precipitous.

The Puget Sound trough, a 30- to 60-mile-wide valley lying between the Cascade and Olympic mountains, is the chief lowland region of the state. Its northern part, primarily an inland sea of islands, peninsulas, inlets, and narrow straits, is often called the Puget Sound basin; among its larger islands are Whidbey, Bainbridge, Camano, and Vashon; its major channels are the Strait of Juan de Fuca, Admiralty Inlet, and the Tacoma Narrows. Puget Sound is in an old glaciated area, and the adjacent land area has a surface of gravelly and sandy prairies, hilly moraines, and numerous bogs and lakes. Numerous, heavy-volume rivers drain from nearby mountains into the sound. They have formed level, alluvial plains such as the valleys of the Puyallup, Duwamish, Snohomish, Stillaguamish, Skagit, and Nooksack rivers.

Climate. Washington has two general types of climate. A marine climate with mild, wet winters and cool, dry summers prevails west of the Cascades, and a continental climate with hot, dry summers and cold, moist winters characterizes eastern Washington. In the west, mild westerly winds from off the Pacific Ocean prevail during most of the winter, moderating temperatures and bringing plentiful moisture. January average temperatures are 38°F at Seattle and 43° at the mouth of the Columbia River. In July the average is 65° at Seattle and 58° on the coast. Extreme heat or cold is unusual; midsummer temperatures seldom exceed 90 degrees and in winter below freezing temperatures are uncommon. The Seattle-Tacoma area has a longer growing season than is usual for points so far north. Precipitation is mainly in the form of drizzle with occasional heavy showers and snows. Precipitation within the area varies mainly according to topography and is extremely heavy on the western, or windward, slopes of the Olympic and Cascade mountains. In some parts of the Olympics it averages more than 140 inches per year, the greatest of any area in the conterminous United States. The Puget Sound area, sheltered by the Olympics, is considerably drier. Sequim averages only 16 inches of precipitation per year; Seattle and Bellingham, 32; and at the mouth of the Columbia, 51. June, July, and August are months of clear and dry weather, while September through May is predominantly cloudy and wet.

Puget Sound, Seattle's vital waterlink with the Pacific, is plied daily by the city's fishing fleet.
BOB AND IRA SPRING

Lumber, the state's greatest single source of wealth, is shipped in raft formations near Tacoma.
PHOTOGRAPH BY CHARLES E. ROTKIN©

PHOTOGRAPH BY CHARLES E. ROTKIN©

Mount Rainier is Washington's highest peak.

PHOTOGRAPH BY CHARLES E. ROTKIN©

Seattle's Space Needle, from 1962 World's Fair

In the east the Cascade barrier blocks the moderating influence of the ocean and sharply reduces the moisture content of the westerly winds. January temperatures average 28°F at Yakima and 27° at Spokane. Summers are warm, July averages being 74° at Yakima and 71° at Spokane. Winter is the wet season and most precipitation is in the form of snow. Yakima, directly in the rain shadow of the Cascades, lies in the state's driest area, averaging only 7 inches annually. Other dry areas are located at Pasco, Richland, Ephrata, and Moses Lake in the central Columbia Plateau. Precipitation increases toward the east, so that Spokane averages 17 inches, Walla Walla 22, and the nearby mountains 30 to 50.

Plants and Animals. Plant and animal life in Washington is diversified and varies largely as a result of elevation and resulting changes in climatic conditions. In western Washington dense coniferous forests of Douglas fir, Western hemlock, Western red cedar, Sitka spruce, and true firs are common up to 3,500 feet. Open, or recently burned-over, areas have deciduous trees such as red alder, broadleafed maple, vine maple, willow, and cottonwood. Covering the forest floor are ferns, mosses, and woody shrubs such as sword fern, salal, huckleberry, and cascara. Rhododendron is a typical flowering shrub.

Animals are abundant. Chinook, king, sockeye, and steelhead salmon are common in the ocean and in the rivers during the spawning season, and halibut, cod, bass, whales, and shrimp are plentiful off shore. There are Dungeness crabs, razor clams, and Willapa and Olympia oysters on the beaches and tidal flats. Rivers and lakes are abundant with rainbow and cutthroat trout, and such valuable fur bearers as beaver, muskrat, mink, otter, and raccoon flourish on the shores. Migratory Canadian geese, snow geese, and mallard, teal, and canvasback ducks thrive in the marshlands during autumn. Upland game animals are numerous over western Washington. Most important are the Olympic elk, Columbia blacktailed deer, black bear, cougar, wildcat, Chinese pheasant, Oregon ruffed grouse, and blue grouse.

In the vast wilderness areas lying between 3,500 feet and 5,000 feet the most common trees are sturdy conifers such as white and alpine firs, mountain hemlock, Western yew, white pine, and lodgepole pine. Animals living in these upland forests include wapiti (elk), mountain goat, cougar, lynx, flying squirrel, pine marten, Pacific fisher marten, bald eagle, and the great horned owl.

In the cold, snow-covered, treeless areas above 5,000 feet, as in the high Olympics and the high Cascades, flowering alpine plants and heather cover the meadows during summer. Mountain goats and elk graze there during summer, and there are animals such as the ermine, snowshoe rabbit, ptarmigan, and snowy owl.

Eastern Washington has desert and semidesert forms of wildlife. Near the eastern foothills of the Cascades, vast areas of sagebrush and bunch grass are the habitat of jack rabbits, coyotes, and rattlesnakes. At higher elevations there are grassland prairies and open forests of ponderosa pine. Characteristic animals are mule deer, elk, porcupine, cougar, and grouse, and other game birds.

SOCIAL FACTORS

Population. Washington's population increased by 474,251, or 19.9 per cent, between 1950 and 1960. This compares with an increase of 37 per cent between 1940 and 1950, when, during World War II, many migrants came to work in defense industries. Foreign-born whites comprised more than 25 per cent of the total population early in the twentieth century. Largest of the immigrant groups who assumed U.S. citizenship in Washington were Canadians, Swedes, Norwegians, British, and Germans. By 1960 foreign-born whites and native whites of foreign and mixed parentage totaled only 633,000, or about 22 per cent.

Nonwhite population is relatively small, numbering about 100,000 or less than 3 per cent. Most of the state's 43,738 Negroes live in Seattle, Tacoma, Spokane, and Yakima. Most immigrants of Asian origin, mainly Japanese, Chinese, and Filipinos, live in the Seattle and Tacoma metropolitan areas or in the irrigated farming valleys of eastern Washington.

Tacoma is surrounded by rich farmland and forests.

PHOTOGRAPH BY CHARLES E. ROTKIN©

PRINCIPAL CITIES

	POPULATION	
	1950 Census	1960 Census
Seattle	467,591	557,087
Spokane	161,721	181,608
Tacoma	109,408	147,979
Yakima	38,486	43,284
Everett	33,849	40,304
Bellingham	34,112	34,688
Vancouver	41,664	32,464
Bremerton	27,678	28,922
Walla Walla	24,102	24,536

There are about 14,000 American Indians living within and outside the 20 reservations in the state. Indian reservation lands comprise about 2.7 million acres, and two of the reservations—the Colville and the Yakima—are among the largest in the United States.

The state's population is about 75 per cent Protestant in religious composition. Largest Protestant denominations are Lutheran, Methodist, Presbyterian, and Baptist. Roman Catholic registered membership includes 228,000 in the Seattle Archdiocese, 62,000 in the Spokane Diocese and 43,000 in the Yakima Diocese. Jewish and Buddhist church groups are localized in Seattle, Spokane, and Tacoma.

Population is unevenly distributed. Western Washington, primarily the densely settled and urbanized Puget Sound basin, has two million inhabitants, as compared with about 800,000 in eastern Washington. Washington's 1960 urban population of 1,948,664 persons was 68.3 per cent of the total. Seattle is the most populous city; other large cities are Spokane and Tacoma.

Education. The largest tax expenditures of the state are for the support of its public schools, colleges, and universities. State law requires that all youths 8 to 15 years of age be enrolled in school. Washington has a department of public instruction, which is administered by an elected superintendent. Each of the state's counties has an elected superintendent. There are local public school districts, each administered by a superintendent and a school board. Boards of regents appointed by the governor oversee the administration of state colleges and universities. By 1960 there were more than 600,000 pupils enrolled in public elementary and secondary schools, and almost 50,000 students in the public colleges and universities.

The largest state institution of higher learning is the University of Washington (1861), in Seattle. Washington State University (1890) is at Pullman, and there are education colleges at Bellingham, Cheney, and Ellensburg. There also are several state-supported junior colleges in Centralia, Vancouver, Pasco, Everett, Aberdeen, Longview, Bremerton, Mount Vernon, Wenatchee, and Yakima.

Private institutions of higher education are Seattle University (1891), Seattle; Gonzaga University (1887), Spokane; St. Martins College (1895), Olympia; Holy Names College (1907), Spokane; St. Edward's Seminary (1931), Kenmore; University of Puget Sound (1888), Tacoma; Pacific Lutheran University (1894), Tacoma; Seattle Pacific College (1891), Seattle; Whitman College (1859), Walla Walla; Walla Walla College (1892), Walla Walla; and Whitworth College (1890), Spokane. Correctional institutions are at Chehalis, Grand Mound, Monroe, and Walla Walla.

Economic Factors

Agriculture is varied and highly specialized in Washington; the total value of all farm products exceeds $600 million annually. In 1960, field and tree crops accounted for $407 million, and livestock, dairy, and poultry products, $236 million. The leading commercial products are wheat, beef cattle, milk, apples, hay, eggs, barley, potatoes, hops, and chickens.

Washington is noted for several specialty crops such as apples, hops, peppermint, peas, and raspberries, in the production of which it generally is the leading state. About half of all U.S. hops production is from Washington.

Eastern Washington is primarily dependent on farming and is the state's main agricultural region, and the Yakima Valley has been called the "Fruit Bowl of the Nation." It is a rich irrigated valley especially noted for its apples, peaches, pears, cherries, grapes, hops, peppermint oil, vegetables, sugar beets, and cattle. Other irrigated valleys famous for apples and other fruit are Wenatchee, Chelan, and Okanogan. A rich grain-producing belt, called the Palouse and Big Bend, extending from Spokane to Walla Walla, produces the state's most valuable farm commodity—an annual spring and winter wheat crop, valued at about $136 million in 1960.

PRODUCTION OF PRINCIPAL CROPS

Crop	Unit	1950-59 Average	1960
Apples	1,000 bushels	24,100	19,500
Apricots	short tons	11,370	10,200
Barley	1,000 bushels	16,683	24,126
Cherries	short tons	18,830	12,100
Grapes	short tons	39,610	38,400
Hops	1,000 lbs.	24,904	26,568
Oats	1,000 bushels	7,614	4,856
Peaches	1,000 bushels	1,456	2,030
Pears	1,000 bushels	5,018	3,130
Peas, dry field	1,000 100-lb. bags	1,737	1,914
Potatoes	1,000 cwt.	8,466	10,075
Prunes	short tons	17,510	10,100
Strawberries	1,000 lbs.	34,343	44,850
Sugar beets	1,000 short tons	654	782
Wheat	1,000 bushels	71,774	65,102

Source: *U.S. Department of Agriculture*

Western Washington is a belt of dairy, poultry, vegetable, and berry farms. The well-watered valleys are intensively farmed to produce peas, market vegetables, strawberries, raspberries, flower bulbs, and holly. Milk is the leading cash product. Livestock producers sell such items as poultry and ranch mink.

Forestry. Forestry is an important occupation in the mountain regions. Nearly half of the state's 19.5 million acres of forests is in national forests and parks. Roads extend into the mountains where numerous logging companies cut much Douglas fir, hemlock, and Ponderosa pine.

Mining. Mineral extraction is relatively minor in the state's economy, even though reserves of soft coal and low-grade ores of lead, silver, copper, gold, zinc, and mercury are extensive. Mines in the Spokane area yield the nation's second largest output of magnesite, and some copper, lead, and zinc. Limestone is quarried near Spokane and at Concrete and Grotto in the western Cascades. Puget Sound basin is noted for clay, sand, and gravel. Total value of Washington's mineral production was $63,894,000 in 1959; $70 million, 1960; and about $66 million, 1961.

Fisheries. Washington is one of the leading fishing states. Seattle, Anacortes, and Bellingham on Puget Sound, Aberdeen on Grays Harbor, and South Bend

PRODUCTION OF PRINCIPAL MINERALS

Mineral	Unit	1959	1960
Coal	1,000 short tons	242	228
Lead	short tons	10,310	7,725
Sand and Gravel	1,000 short tons	21,360	25,297
Stone	1,000 short tons	12,278	13,897
Zinc	short tons	17,111	21,317
Peat	1,000 short tons	32,884	27,770
Clays	1,000 short tons	180	169
Uranium Ore	short tons	152,336	171,255

Source: *U.S. Bureau of Mines*

WASHINGTON

Modern combines expedite the wheat harvest in the agricultural area of the Columbia Basin in southeast Washington.

The rapids of the Skykomish River, as its flows through the forested highlands of the northwestern part of the state of Washington, are near the base of Mount Index.

The concrete Grand Coulee Dam backs the Columbia River into a 151-mile lake extending to the Canadian border.

The Bonneville Dam, situated in the mountains close to the Oregon border, impounds the waters of the Columbia River.

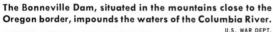

The unique Lake Washington Floating Bridge in Seattle is a four-lane, mile-and-a-quarter-long highway floating on the lake's surface. The Olympic Range is in the background.

on Willapa Bay are the home ports of a large fishing fleet that operates as far north as the Bering Sea off Alaska. The annual value of fish and crustaceans taken averages about $20 million. Salmon, caught by gill-net boats, accounts for more than half this value. Halibut, a bottom fish caught by trawlers, is second in value. Other species include flounders, rockfishes, cod, smelts, Dungeness crabs, Pacific oysters, and razor clams. Oyster farming is practiced in the tidal flats of southern Puget Sound and in Willapa Bay. Fish hatchery work employs several hundred persons.

Manufacturing. Total industrial employment in Washington was about 230,000 in the early 1960's. The leading industry is the manufacture of aircraft and missiles in and near Seattle. The manufacture of wood products, such as lumber, plywood, paper, and shingles, is second in value, and is the main industry in Tacoma, Everett, Bellingham, Longview, Port Angeles, Shelton, and Aberdeen. Washington is one of the leading states in paper and pulp production, and it is second in lumber production. Processing of farm and fishery products, the third-ranking industry, is concentrated in Seattle, Spokane, Yakima, Tacoma, Walla Walla, Vancouver, Wenatchee, Aberdeen, and South Bend. Major exported foods are flour, condensed milk, canned, frozen, and fresh fruit, vegetables, and shellfish. Beet sugar and livestock feeds are a major product of the interior irrigated areas.

A fourth industry is the production of metals and atomic materials. Using cheap electrical energy from Grand Coulee, Bonneville, and other dams in the state, aluminum ingots are produced at Vancouver, Longview, Wenatchee, and Spokane. Copper, lead, and zinc ores are refined at Tacoma, and Seattle has a steel plant. The Hanford atomic plant is at Richland. Other important manufactures are logging machinery, transportation equipment, and merchant and naval ships, at Seattle and Bremerton, and petroleum products, at Ferndale and Anacortes.

Transportation and Commerce. Seattle-Tacoma International Airport is one of the nation's major airline centers. A number of transcontinental and coastwise railways terminate on Puget Sound and the Columbia River: (1) the Great Northern, which passes through an eight-mile tunnel in the Cascades, (2) the Milwaukee, (3) the Northern Pacific, (4) the Union Pacific, and (5) the Southern Pacific. Spokane is a major interior junction of railways and highways. Modern interstate highways are a speedy means for travel and distribution of goods; the principal roads are U.S. highways 2, 10, 410, and 830, from east to west, and U.S. highways 195, 395, 97, 99, and 101, from north to south.

California is Washington's major domestic market, and most goods and raw materials to and from Alaska pass through Seattle and other Puget Sound ports. The most important exports from Washington commercial centers are bulk grain, lumber, plywood, paper, aluminum, cement, apples, beans, peas, and processed farm and fishery products. Leading imports are mineral ores, petroleum, and sulfur from Latin America, the Philippines, and the Gulf Coast; light manufactures and canned foods from Japan; and mineral and fishery products from Alaska.

Tourist Attractions. The varied scenic features and spectacular manmade structures in Washington attract millions of tourists. Their expenditures add more than $150 million per year to the state's economy. Each season Mount Rainier National Park receives more than a million visitors anxious to see its glaciers and alpine wilderness beauty. Similar alpine features and a rugged, primitive coastline attract more than 500,000 to Olympic National Park. Puget Sound, with its combination of ferry cruises, boating, sport fishing, resorts, state parks, and port-city waterfronts, is a major attraction for visitors from the interior of the nation. The beaches along the coast of southwestern Washington are also a

popular tourist attraction. Seattle has an annual midsummer sea fair featured by yachting, hydroplane racing, and other seafaring activities. Camping facilities are provided by the more than 50 state parks, which are located on sea shores, islands, scenic lakes and rivers, wilderness forest sites, and in the mountains. In addition, there are many campgrounds in the national forests of the Cascade, Okanogan, and Blue mountains. Skiing and hunting are popular sports. Grand Coulee Dam, one of the world's largest manmade structures, is visited by hundreds of thousands each year for tours through its power plant and boating on its huge reservoir. Other noted engineering structures are the Tacoma Narrows Bridge across Puget Sound, the Lake Washington Floating Bridge at Seattle, and the Lake Washington Ship Canal in Seattle.

WOODROW R. CLEVINGER

GOVERNMENT

Constitution of Washington was adopted in 1889, preliminary to the admission of the state to the Union. Amendments may be proposed by a two-thirds vote of the elected members of each house of the state legislature, or by a constitutional convention. In either case the amendments proposed are placed before the electorate for ratification by a majority of those voting. Prerequisites for voting are U.S. citizenship; a minimum age of 21; residence in the state one year, in the county 90 days, and in the precinct 30 days; and the ability to read and write English. Washington sends seven congressmen to the U.S. House of Representatives.

State Legislature consists of a house of representatives of not more than 99 members and a senate of not more than 49 members. Reapportionment of the membership of both houses must be considered every 10 years. Representatives are elected for two-year terms, the senators for four-year terms; one-half of the senators are elected every two years. Regular sessions of the legislature, held biennially in odd-numbered years, begin in January and are limited to 60 days.

Executive Officials are the governor, lieutenant governor, secretary of state, treasurer, auditor, attorney general, superintendent of public instruction, commissioner of public lands, and insurance commissioner, all of whom are elected for four years. There are a number of administrative departments headed by officials appointed by the governor to four-year terms. There is no limit on number of terms a governor may serve. The governor has the pardoning power. His veto, which may extend to all legislation except initiated and referred measures, may be overridden by a two-thirds vote of the elected members of each house.

Judicial Power is vested in a supreme court of nine members elected from the state at large for six years, the terms being staggered; in superior courts for the counties, consisting of one or more judges elected for four years; in justices of the peace in the rural precincts, and in such other courts as the legislature may provide.

Local Government. The state is divided into 39 counties, each governed by a commission of three members elected for four years and vested with limited executive and legislative powers. In addition, there are numerous municipal corporations divided into classes according to population.

HISTORY

Exploration. Some authorities suggest that the Spanish under Juan Rodríguez Cabrillo and Bartolomé Ferrilo may have visited the coast of present-day Washington, 1542–44, but this is questionable in light of substantial evidence that they explored the Pacific Coast of North America, only as far north as 42° to 44° N latitude. For the same reason, one may question allegations that the English navigator Sir

Fort Nisqually, founded in 1833 by the Hudson's Bay Company, was for many years the leading port for the Puget Sound and imported and sold supplies to the early settlers. In 1934 the fort was reconstructed on its present site at Point Defiance Park in Tacoma.

WASHINGTON

High Lights of History

Captain Robert Gray was the first white man to discover the Columbia River, which he did in the ship *Columbia* in May, 1792. He named the river in honor of his ship, the first to sail all around the world under the U.S. flag.

Land clearing and lumbering were among the most important activities of early settlers in the Pacific Northwest. To make it possible for the teams of 12 oxen to move the heaviest logs, skid roads were constructed from logs half-embedded in earth and greased with oil.

The first Washington state capitol was built at Olympia in 1860 when Washington was still a territory, and remained the seat of state government until 1893. Elisha Ferry, first governor of the state, took office there in 1889.

Old Fort Colville was erected in 1826 on a fur-trading route at the east bank of the Columbia River, and until 1871 it was the major inland post of the Hudson's Bay Company in Washington Territory. In 1855 the region around the fort was the scene of a gold rush.

On the first day of the season, hundreds of anglers fish in the waters of Blue Lake, in the lower Grand Coulee. Game fish abound in the lakes and rivers of Washington.

Francis Drake reached Washington shores, 1578–79, when he sailed up the western coast of North America, which he named New Albion, as Drake's most northerly landfall was probably in the vicinity of San Francisco Bay (38° N latitude). Juan de Fuca (real name Apostolos Valerianos), a Greek in the service of Spain, claimed he had made a voyage up the western coast, 1592, and of having discovered a strait, which was later named for him. The Spaniard Juan Pérez discovered Nootka Sound and Mount Olympus, 1774, and his fellow countryman Bruno Heceta set foot on the northwest coast at the mouth of the Hoh River, 1775. Capt. James Cook, a British explorer, stopped at Nootka, 1778, thus giving his country a claim to the region. The ensuing dispute over this territory almost led to war between Spain and Great Britain, but the matter was finally settled, 1790, in favor of Great Britain.

Two U.S. ships, the *Washington* and *Columbia*, under John Kendrick, with Robert Gray second in command appeared in the area, 1788, having been sent out by a Boston syndicate interested in the fur trade. Gray returned later on the *Columbia* and discovered the Columbia River, 1792, which he named for his ship. A British explorer, George Vancouver, made extensive explorations in the region, 1792, and it was he who named many of the geographical features there. British claims to this "Oregon Country," based on the explorations of Cook and Vancouver, were strengthened, 1793, by an expedition of the Scottish fur trader Alexander Mackenzie to the British Columbia coast. United States claims, based on Gray's discoveries, were strengthened by the Lewis and Clark Expedition, which sighted the Pacific on Nov. 7, 1805. See LEWIS AND CLARK EXPEDITION.

U.S.–British Controversy over the Oregon Country. Early settlements were made by both British and U.S. fur traders. David Thompson, agent for the British North West Company, established a number of trading posts in the region, 1807–11, including Spokane House near the present-day city of Spokane. John Jacob Astor's Pacific Fur Company established a trading post at Astoria, 1811, and later built smaller inland posts, including at least one within the present state of Washington. During the War of 1812, Astor was compelled to sell his interests to his British rival, but he regained Astoria, 1818. The United States and Great Britain agreed, 1818, on a policy of joint occupation of the Oregon Country for 10 years; they later agreed, 1827, to extend the policy indefinitely, with the proviso that either might terminate it on 12 months' notice. Meanwhile, Spain in 1819, and Russia in 1824, had ceded to the United States their claims to the territory between parallels 42° and 54° 40′ N latitude.

Hudson's Bay Company, which had absorbed the North West Company, 1821, extended its jurisdiction over the Oregon Country, and established Fort Vancouver (on the site of Vancouver, Wash.) as its western headquarters, 1825. John McLoughlin, the company's factor, effectively controlled the region, barring rival traders, but treating U.S. settlers fairly. American exploring expeditions into the region were led by Capt. B. L. E. Bonneville, 1834, Lt. Charles Wilkes of the U.S. Navy, 1841, and Lt. John C. Frémont, 1843; and several U.S. missionary families, under Marcus Whitman, set up a mission near Fort Walla Walla, 1836.

During the 1840's a great tide of U.S. homeseekers migrated over the Oregon Trail into the Pacific Northwest; although the Hudson's Bay Company had exercised its authority fairly, the newcomers in the Williamette Valley, south of the Columbia River, established their own provisional government, 1843.

With expansionist sentiment running strong in the United States, the cry of "Fifty-four Forty or Fight" became an issue in the 1844 presidential campaign. The matter was soon settled peaceably, 1846, when the U.S. boundary was extended to the Pacific along the 49th parallel, but with Great Britain retaining Vancouver Island. See NORTHWEST BOUNDARY DISPUTE; OREGON, History, *Exploration and Settlement*.

Washington Territory. In August, 1848, Oregon Territory was created, with its capital at Oregon City. During the years following many immigrants settled in the region north of the Columbia, and major settlements were established at Olympia, Alki Point (Seattle), and Port Townsend. A movement for division of the territory culminated in the passage of a bill by Congress (approved Mar. 2, 1853) establishing Washington Territory, with an area of more than 193,000 square miles, including parts of present-day Idaho and Montana. In November, 1853, Olympia was proclaimed the territorial capital and Isaac Ingalls Stevens became the governor. When the state of Oregon was formed, 1859, the rest of the Oregon Territory (the region between 42° and 46° N latitude and between Oregon and the Rocky Mountains) was added to Washington. When Idaho Territory was created, 1863, the boundaries of Washington were fixed as they are at present.

A number of Indian tribes, dissatisfied with the reservations assigned to them, went on the warpath, 1855, and perpetrated a series of bloody massacres before being subdued, 1858. Other significant events of territorial history were: the Gold Rush of 1857–58 in the Okanogan and Fraser River districts; the opening of the University of Washington, 1861; the completion of a transcontinental telegraph line, 1864; and the completion of the Northern Pacific to Portland, Ore., 1883.

The Movement for Statehood began in 1861. A constitutional convention was held, 1878, but more than a decade passed before Congress passed the necessary enabling act. Washington was admitted to the Union, Nov. 11, 1889, as the 42nd state.

Statehood. Elisha P. Ferry, who had been territorial governor, became the first state executive. Much significant legislation was enacted in the period after 1900: the direct primary, 1907; female suffrage, 1910; initiative, referendum, and recall, 1912; and Workmen's Compensation, 1911. From the fourth through the sixth decade of the twentieth century the federal government was engaged in the harnessing of Washington's extensive water-power resources. Among the major dams and the dates of their completion were Bonneville, 1937; Grand Coulee, 1941; Rock Island, 1952; McNary, 1953; and Chief Joseph, 1955.

In national and state political affairs, Washington strongly supported the Democratic party, 1932–51. In 1952 the majority of the state's popular votes were cast for the Republican presidential candidate, Dwight D. Eisenhower, and the Republican party gained control of the state's legislature and executive departments, and six of seven seats in the U.S. House of Representatives. By 1956, however, the Democrats had regained control of the state legislature, a position they maintained in 1958 and 1960. However, the state's electoral vote went to the Republican presidential candidate Richard M. Nixon in 1960.

Bibliog.–American Guide Series, *Washington: A Guide to the Evergreen State* (1950); Mary W. Avery, *History and Government of the State of Washington* (1961); Harold E. Barto and Catharine L. Bullard, *History of the State of Washington* (1953); Archie Binns, *Roaring Land* (1942); Howard M. Brier, *Sawdust Empire: The Pacific Northwest* (1958); Frank H. Cass, ed., *Looking Northwest* (1938); Ralph E. Downie, *Pictorial History of the State of Washington* (1937); Charles H. Heffelfinger and George A. Custer, *Evergreen Citizen: A Textbook on the Government of the State of Washington* (1953); Stewart H. Holbrook, *Northwest Corner: Oregon and Washington* (1948); Nard Jones, *Evergreen Land: A Portrait of the State of Washington* (Sovereign State Ser.) (1947); Priscilla M. Kinsman and Others, *Our Washington* (1953); Lucile S. McDonald, *Washington's Yesterdays* (1953); Edmond S. Meany, *History of the State of Washington* (1941); Lancaster Pollard, *History of the State of Washington*, 4 vols. (1938), *History of the State of Washington* (1951); Nancy W. Ross, *Farthest Reach: Oregon and Washington* (1941); Edgar R. Stewart, *Washington: Northwest Frontier* (1957); Edward Thomas, *Washington in Pictures* (1946); Washington (State) University, Bureau of Business Research, *Ocean and Inland Waterborne Foreign Commerce of the State of Washington* (1958); Washington (State) University, Bureau of Governmental Research and Services, *Washington State Government: Administrative Organization and Functions* (Report No. 91) 2 vols. (1948–56); Robert B. Whitebrook, *Coastal Exploration of Washington* (1959); William Wolman, *Development of Manufacturing Industry in the State of Washington* (1958); Sanford C. Yoder, *Horse Trails Along the Desert* (1954).

WASHINGTON, D.C., city, capital of the United States, coextensive with the District of Columbia; on the north bank of the Potomac River, on U.S. highways 1, 29, 50, 211, and 240; 35 miles SW of Baltimore, 210 miles SW of New York City, 900 miles NNE of Miami, Fla., 2,400 miles E of San Francisco, 4,800 miles NNW of Rio de Janeiro, 6,800 miles E of Tokyo, 3,700 miles WSW of London, and 4,900 miles WSW of Moscow. Pop. (1960) 763,956.

Setting. The site of Washington is generally level and low, except in the extreme north where the terrain is hilly, rising to about 400 feet elevation. Some land has been reclaimed from the Potomac River which, at Washington, is at sea level. The over-all area of Washington, D.C., including about 8 square miles of inland water, is 68 square miles. Two streams enter the district from Maryland and flow through the city into the Potomac: the Anacostia River, which widens into an estuary, in the southeast; and Rock Creek, in the northwest. Despite its urban character, the district has more than the usual complement of parks, most of which border the city's three rivers, and there is a wildlife refuge on Rock Creek.

Climate. Washington's climate is of the humid subtropical type. The January average temperature is 34°F and the July average is 77°F. Temperatures are subject to wide fluctuations, however. Summers tend to be quite warm and humid, with temperatures occasionally rising above 100°F. Winters are usually mild, but freezing temperatures are not uncommon, and below-zero temperatures have been recorded, although rarely; some of the worst weather ever experienced in Washington D.C. occurred during the inauguration ceremonies of Pres. John Kennedy in January, 1961. The average annual precipitation in Washington, D.C., is 41 inches, nearly all of it in the form of rain and, but for a slight summer maximum, evenly distributed throughout the year.

Transportation. The Potomac River is crossed by five highway bridges at Washington: from northwest to southeast, they are the Chain, the Arlington Memorial, the Francis Scott Key bridges, the Old Highway, and the East 14th Street. There is also a bridge carrying the southbound lines of the Richmond, Fredericksburg, and Potomac Railroad. The

Pennsylvania and the Baltimore and Ohio railroads enter the city from the north and the west. From the south, the Southern, the Chesapeake and Ohio, and the Seaboard Air Line, enter the city over the tracks of the R, F, and P. These railroads all terminate in Union Station, near the U.S. Capitol. The district is well served by trolley and bus lines. On the Potomac, in Virginia, is Washington National Airport.

Economic Factors. The basic "industry" of Washington, D.C., is the U.S. government and its various agencies, and much of the labor force is engaged in some branch of government service. Catering to the large numbers of tourists who visit the district is also important economically. The small amount of manufacturing activity in Washington is mainly for local use. The production of printed matter is most important, followed by food processing (there is some truck farming within the district), and the making of metal products.

The City Plan. Washington is a planned city, and is laid out around numerous circles and squares connected by straight boulevards. Its original design, considered a masterpiece by many, was prepared by Pierre Charles L'Enfant and was laid out by Andrew Ellicott on a site selected by George Washington. The work was begun, 1791, under L'Enfant's direction, but he was dismissed by Washington, 1792, when he tore down the manor house of Rep. Daniel Carroll (1730–96) of Maryland because the house was in the way. Ellicott, a surveyor, was left to carry on the project as best he could, but not entirely in terms of L'Enfant's plan, which had been lost. His documents were later rediscovered, 1887, and Congress approved, 1901, a further development of the park system as it had been envisaged by L'Enfant insofar as this might be possible in the light of the building that had occurred in the interim 1792–1901. The development was originally directed by a committee whose members included architects Daniel H. Burnham and Charles F. McKim, sculptor Augustus St. Gaudens, and landscape architect Frederick L. Olmsted. Their report, 1902, represented an extension of L'Enfant's original plan and remained the master plan for the municipal development. The development came under the control of the National Commission of Fine Arts, 1910, and the National Capital Park and Planning Commission, 1926. See American Architecture, *Republican Period;* City Planning, *Early Planning in the United States.*

Parks. Many of the numerous parks, monuments, and historic sites of the district are part of the National Capital Parks System. The Mall stretches from the Capitol westward to the Potomac. From the Capitol at its eastern end, or from the Lincoln Memorial near its western end (see Lincoln Memorial), the Mall presents a superb vista, but one that in the early 1960's continued to be marred by the so-called temporary buildings erected during World Wars I and II. The Washington Monument stands at the crossing of the park that extends south from the White House. The largest and most rugged park is Rock Creek, adjacent to which is Zoological Park, commonly called Rock Creek Zoo. Anacostia Park lies along both sides of the Anacostia River. A series of large parks, known collectively as Potomac Park, borders that stream, and contains lakes, pools, and the famous cherry trees, which were given to the city by the mayor of Tokyo, 1912, and whose blooming each spring is one of the more colorful sights of Washington during that season. There are monuments and statues in many of the squares and circles at street intersections. In the early 1960's much of L'Enfant's plan for the city's park system remained unrealized; its projected completion would, it was said, ultimately surround the city with chains of parks and boulevards.

The Capitol Building, the seat of the U.S. government is the dominant architectural structure of Washington. It is centrally located on an elevated site, Capitol Hill, from which radiate streets that divide the city into the four quarters (Northeast, Southeast, Southwest, and Northwest) in terms of which the city's streets are numbered. The cornerstone of the original Capitol building, as planned by William Thornton, was laid by George Washington, Sept. 18, 1793; the still uncompleted building was burned, 1814, by the British during the War of 1812, after which B. H. Latrobe undertook its restoration, completing the president's house by 1817. Latrobe was succeeded, 1818, by Charles Bulfinch, who completed the plans in 1830; the building was completed, 1863, at a cost of $14 million. As subsequently enlarged on several occasions, it covers over three and one-half acres. A major alteration was completed in 1961, at a cost of $17 million. An imposing dome, topped by a statue and illuminated at night, dominates the building. The rotunda under the dome (96 ft. wide, 180 ft. high) contains many historical paintings, as do other parts of the building. Events in U.S. history are depicted on massive bronze doors at the three eastern entrances. Presidents are inaugurated in front of the central entrance.

The White House and Vicinity. The Capitol is flanked by large office buildings for members of the Senate and House of Representatives. The Senate office buildings are two in number; the older of the two was completed in 1909 and enlarged in 1933; the newer Senate Office Building, completed in 1959, is directly to the east of the older one. The original House Office Building dates from 1908; a second one was built in 1933, and a third, the Sam Rayburn House Office Building, was constructed early in the 1960's. To the east is the Library of Congress, established in 1800 (see LIBRARY OF CONGRESS). Just north of the library is the Supreme Court Building (1935), designed by Cass Gilbert and considered one of the finest structures in Washington. The president's residence, known as the White House since the days of Theodore Roosevelt, is the oldest government building in the city (see WHITE HOUSE). Only slightly less venerable is the U.S. Treasury (1836–42), adjoining the White House. On the other side of the White House is the Executive Office Building. In the vicinity of the White House there are numerous other major government buildings; a number of the leading stores and hotels; and other points of interest such as the Pan American Union headquarters; the Corcoran Gallery of Art (1879; west wing added, 1928); Constitution Hall; the U.S. Naval Hospital (1861); Ford Theater (1863), where Pres. Abraham Lincoln was shot, and now a museum, as is the house across the street where Lincoln died; Blair House (c.1810), where Pres. Harry Truman lived, 1948–52, while repairs were being made on the White House; and St. John's Episcopal Church. Farther to the north and northwest of the White House are many of the foreign embassies and legations. Still farther to the northwest are the unfinished Washington Cathedral (officially Cathedral of St. Peter and St. Paul, Protestant Episcopal; construction begun in 1908) and the U.S. Naval Observatory (1893). Also to the northwest is Georgetown, with its many fine, historic buildings. See GEORGETOWN.

Along the Mall that extends west from the Capitol are the National Gallery of Art (1940), containing one of the world's finest art collections; the Freer Gallery of Art (1923); the old and new National Museum buildings; and the Smithsonian Institution (1852), with its Museum of History and Technology (1964). South of the Mall is the great white marble Department of Agriculture Building (1930) and the Bureau of Engraving and Printing (1914; annex added, 1938).

Other Notable Government Buildings are those of the Department of Commerce (1912), which covers an area of about eight acres and is the largest building in Washington; the Department of the Interior (1937); the Department of Justice Building (1934); the National Archives (1935); the new Department of

State Building (1960); the Internal Revenue Building (1935); the Interstate Commerce Commission and the Department of Labor Building (1934); and the Post Office (1934). The Army Medical Center (1923), with its vast Walter Reed General Hospital (1909), stands on the site of old Fort Stevens, a Civil War defense works. (The U.S. Naval Hospital, 1941, is in Bethesda, Md.) At the junction of the Potomac and Anacostia rivers is the Navy Yard, which includes U.S. Marine barracks and a museum. Nearby is an old artillery post, Washington Barracks, and the National War College, which was established there in 1946. Among other features of interest are Bolling Air Force Base, established after World War I and named for Col. Reynal C. Bolling; Anacostia Naval Air Station (1918); a national soldiers' home (1891); the Brookings Institution (1927); and the Carnegie Institution of Washington (1911).

Libraries, Schools, and Research Facilities. Washington is exceptionally well endowed in library facilities. Quite apart from the huge Library of Congress and the many specialized libraries of government departments, there are many others, such as the excellent Washington Public Library, and the Folger Shakespeare Library (1932), which some authorities believe has the finest collection of Shakespearean materials in the world.

Among Washington's many institutions of higher learning are the American University, established in 1893, the Catholic University of America, 1887, Georgetown University, 1789, George Washington University, 1821, Howard University, 1867, National University, 1869, Southeastern University, 1907, Trinity College, 1897, and Washington Missionary College, 1904. There are also teacher-training colleges, a National Training School for Boys and one for girls, and schools for the handicapped. There are also many private and parochial schools in the city.

The World Federation of Educational Associations has its headquarters in Washington, as do the National Academy of Sciences, the Washington Academy of Science, and the American Council of Learned Societies. There are numerous research centers in the city, of which the Brookings Institute and the Carnegie Institution of Washington are probably the most famous.

Religious Buildings. Among the more than 400 churches in the district, the most celebrated are Washington Cathedral (Cathedral of St. Peter and St. Paul) which, although still unfinished in the early 1960's, is one of the largest churches in the world, and the burial place of Pres. Woodrow Wilson; National Shrine of the Immaculate Conception (Roman Catholic), with its lofty campanile; Presbyterian Church of the Pilgrims, overlooking Rock Creek; and Unitarians' All Souls (1924), a Christopher Wren type of building. Among the older churches are St. John's (Episcopal), begun soon after the War of 1812; Foundry Methodist (1904) and Metropolitan Methodist; National Memorial Baptist Church (1933); National City Christian Church (1930); and Universalist National Memorial Church (1930). In northwestern Washington is the principal Moslem Mosque in the United States, built in the 1950's as part of a projected $1.5 million Islamic Center.

Government. Washington's affairs were administered at first by three commissioners, but it was chartered as a city, 1802, the idea being that it would be governed by a mayor appointed by the President and a council elected by the people. Subsequently, however, the structure of the district government was modified again and again until 1874, when the present system was adopted—that of three commissioners appointed by the President and confirmed by the Senate, with the legislative power vested in Congress, each House of which has a committee on the district. Residents of the district have no vote. A joint resolution of Congress was passed, 1960, calling for amendment of the U.S. Constitution to permit residents of the District of Columbia to vote in presidential elections. The Twenty-third Amendment was ratified by the necessary 38 states, March 29, 1961.

History. Early in the history of the United States, Congress met in various cities, among them Philadelphia, Baltimore, and New York. Finally, in July, 1790, Congress appointed a committee to select a location for a permanent capital. Bitter rivalry developed among the partisans of various northern and southern cities and it was soon decided that harmony would best be attained by creating a new city, free from state or sectional loyalties. Maryland and Virginia jointly donated a tract of land, straddling the Potomac River, and approximately 10 miles square. The district was originally made up of the corporations of Washington, Georgetown, and Alexandria, and Washington and Alexandria counties. In 1846, however, Alexandria County was returned to Virginia, leaving only the former Maryland territory in the district. The return of the Virginia land proved to have been a mistake, for even official Washington later spread to the Virginia side of the Potomac, and a great number of persons who work in the district live in Virginia and elsewhere outside of the district. The huge, mazelike Pentagon Building, headquarters of the Department of Defense, is one of many government buildings in Virginia.

The first session of Congress to be held in Washington, D.C., was convened in 1800. Thomas Jefferson was the first President to be inaugurated in Washington, 1801.

In its early years, largely because of the failure to fulfill L'Enfant's plan, Washington was a sprawling, muddy, ugly town. The city was captured and sacked by the British during the War of 1812, and the Capitol, White House, and many other government buildings were burned by the invaders, 1814.

For a long time there was considerable public and official apathy concerning the future development of Washington, a fact that accounts in part for the return of the Virginia portion of the district, 1846. The population of Washington increased enormously, 1800–60. In 1800 it had 3,210 inhabitants; in 1840, 44,000; in 1850, 52,000; and in 1860, 75,000. Rail service to Washington was established, 1835. The telegraph line established between Washington and Baltimore, 1844, was the first telegraph line in the United States. During the Civil War, 1861–65, Washington was threatened by Confederate forces on several occasions—most seriously after the First Battle of Bull Run, 1861, and later, 1864, when Southern forces were within six miles of the city—but remained in Union hands throughout the war.

By 1900 the population had grown to 278,718. During World War II, as in World War I, Washington increased rapidly in population and drastically expanded its office space, and by 1947 the population reached 861,000, as compared to a figure of 663,153 in 1940. By 1950, however, the population had declined to 802,178, and a decade later, in 1960, the population was only 763,956. The metropolitan area, however, which had had 1,464,089 inhabitants in 1950, had 1,967,682 inhabitants in 1960.

After World War II, an extensive building program (including remodeling the Capitol) was initiated and continued into the 1960's.

BIBLIOG.–American Guide Series, *Washington, D.C.* (1942); Russell Baker, *Washington, City on the Potomac* (1959); Morgan Beatty, *Your Nation's Capital* (1956); Claude G. Bowers, *Tragic Era: The Revolution After Lincoln* (1929); Noah Brooks, *Washington in Lincoln's Time* (1958); Mary E. Browning, *Our Nation's Capital: A Portrait in Pictures* (1944); Frank G. Carpenter, *Carp's Washington* (1960); Tristram Coffin, *Your Washington* (1954); Jonathan Daniels, *Frontier on the Potomac* (1946); Deering Davis and Others, *Georgetown Houses of the Federal Period, Washington, D.C., 1780-1830* (1944); Harry L. De Vore, *City on the Potomac* (1946); Eleanor Early, *Washington Holiday* (1955); Harold D. Eberlein and Cortlandt V. D. Hubbard, *Historic Houses of George-Town and Washington City* (1958); Michael Frome, *Washington: A Modern Guide to the Nation's Capital* (1960); Alberta P. Graham, *Washington: The Story of Our Capital* (1953); Alice R. Hager, *Washington, City of Destiny* (1949); Louis J. Halle, *Spring in Washington* (1947); Kilvert Hancock, *City of Sacred Apes* (1957); Edith B. Helm, *Captains and the Kings* (1954); Charles Hurd, *Washington Cavalcade* (Soc. in Am. Ser.) (1948); Lee L. Jensen, *White House and Its Thirty-two Families* (1958); Dorothea Jones, *Washington Is Wonderful* (1956); Stanley P. Kimmel, *Mr. Lincoln's Washington* (1957); Margaret K. Leech, *Reveille in Washington, 1860-1865* (1959); Joseph Leeming, *White House in Picture and Story* (1953); Edward J. Long, *America's National Capital: A Guide in Pictures and Text to Washington, D.C.* (1959); Clara B. MacIntyre, *Introducing Washington* (1948); Joseph W. McGee, *Social and Economic Aspects of the Functional Entity of Washington, D.C.* (Studies in Sociology, vol. 25) (1947); Myrtle M. C. Murdock, *Your Memorials in Washington* (1952), *Your Uncle Sam in Washington* (1952); Frederick H. Newell, ed., *Planning and Building the City of Washington* (1932); Chalmers M. Roberts, *Washington, Past and Present* (1950); Robley D. Stevens, *Your Government Guidebook* (1959); William O. Stevens, *Washington: The Cinderella City* (1943); Jane F. Tompkins and Burt M. McConnell, *White House: A History With Pictures* (1954); Andrew Tully, *When They Burned the White House* (1961); James H. Whyte, *Uncivil War: Washington During the Reconstruction, 1865-1878* (1958).

WASHINGTON, city, NE Georgia, seat of Wilkes County; on the Georgia Railroad, and U.S. highway 78; 85 miles E of Atlanta. The city is a trade center for an area in which dairy products and lumber are produced. Textiles and cottonseed products are manufactured. Pop. (1960) 4,440.

WASHINGTON, city, SW Indiana, seat of Daviess County; on the Baltimore and Ohio and the New York Central railroads, and U.S. highways 50 and 150; 93 miles SW of Indianapolis. The city is a processing center for flour, lumber, dairy products, and canned goods. Shirts are manufactured. Coal mines and oil wells are in the vicinity. Washington was settled in 1805, founded in 1816, and chartered as a city in 1870. Pop. (1960) 10,846.

WASHINGTON, city, SE Iowa, seat of Washington County; on the Rock Island, the Burlington, and the Milwaukee railroads; 98 miles ESE of Des Moines. The city is a trade center for an area in which corn, soybeans, hogs, cattle, and poultry are raised. Farm equipment, radio cabinets, television parts, concrete blocks, and feed are manufactured. Washington was settled in 1838 and incorporated in 1864. Pop. (1960) 6,037.

WASHINGTON, city, N Kansas, seat of Washington County; on the Burlington and the Missouri Pacific railroads; 95 miles NW of Topeka. Washington is a trade and shipping center for an area in which grain and livestock are raised. Dairy products are processed. Pop. (1960) 1,506.

WASHINGTON, city, E. Missouri, in Franklin County; on the Missouri River; on the Missouri Pacific Railroad; 37 miles W of St. Louis. Washington is the site of a plant which manufactures musical instruments, among which is the zither. Shoes, corncob pipes, bone bits, and dairy products are other products manufactured in the city. Washington, settled largely by German immigrants, was platted in 1828 and incorporated in 1895. Pop. (1960) 7,961.

WASHINGTON, city, E North Carolina, seat of Beaufort County; on the Tar River near the head of the Pamlico River estuary; on the Atlantic Coast Line and the Norfolk Southern railroads, and U.S. highways 17 and 264; 90 miles ESE of Raleigh. Washington was founded in 1771, and has many attractive and historic buildings. The city is a market center for tobacco. The chief manufactured products are barrels, foundry products, fertilizer, feed, flour, and work shirts. Tobacco, wheat, and corn are raised, and timber is cut in the area. Pop. (1960) 9,939.

WASHINGTON, city, SW Pennsylvania, seat of Washington County; on the Baltimore and Ohio, the Pennsylvania, and the Waynesburg and Washington railroads, and U.S. highways 19 and 40; 25 miles SW of Pittsburgh. Oil, clay, limestone, sand, and bituminous coal deposits are worked in the area. Glass tableware and food containers, corrugated fiber products, bricks, tin plate, engines, pumps, mold machinery, clay and steel products, chemicals, and beverages are manufactured. Washington was first settled in 1768 on the site of an earlier Delaware Indian village called Catfish's Camp. It was chartered as a city in 1924. Washington is the site of the Washington and Jefferson College (1787). It was incorporated as a borough in 1810 and as a city in 1924. Pop. (1960) 23,545.

WASHINGTON, town, N Virginia, seat of Rappahannock County, on the E slopes of the Blue Ridge Mountains; on U.S. highway 211; 85 miles NNW of Richmond. The town is a shipping center for apples. Washington was named in honor of George Washington, who surveyed and planned the town in 1749. Pop. (1960) 255.

DICK SMITH

A section of the massive Mount Washington, the largest mountain in the Presidential Range and the highest peak in the northeast, is viewed from the top of Mount Adams.

WASHINGTON, MOUNT, N New Hampshire, in the Presidential Range of the White Mountains, the highest mountain of the northeastern United States. Its summit, above the timber line, rises to 6,288 feet. Early explorers, far out at sea, were the first to observe and describe it. The climate can become so forbidding in fall that it makes climbing difficult even for experienced climbers. Temperatures lower than −50°F and winds of velocities higher than 180 miles an hour have been recorded.

In spite of its associations with disasters and near disasters, it has long held an attraction for settlers and travelers. The first known climbing of the mountain occurred in 1642.

WASHINGTON, UNIVERSITY OF, a public, coeducational institution of higher learning, is located in Seattle, Wash. Established as the Territorial University of Washington, 1861, the school offered its first instruction within the year. The name was changed to University of Washington, 1889, when Washington became a state.

Among the university's divisions are arts and sciences, founded in 1861; graduate school, 1884; pharmacy, 1895; education, 1898; engineering, 1899; law, 1899; forestry, 1907; adult education, 1910; business administration, 1917; nursing, 1917; fisheries, 1919; social work, 1934; architecture and urban planning, 1935; dentistry, 1945; and medicine, 1945. Advanced degrees are awarded in most divisions.

The college of fisheries is the only college in the Western Hemisphere that offers degrees in both fisheries technology and fisheries biology. The department of oceanography is the only such department in the United States offering an undergraduate degree in oceanography.

Among the university's publications are *Pacific Northwest Quarterly*, a journal of historical research; *Washington Law Review; Isis*, an international review on the history of science; and *Modern Language Quar-*

terly. See COLLEGES AND UNIVERSITIES.

WASHINGTON AND JEFFERSON COLLEGE, a private, nonsectarian college of liberal arts for men, located in Washington, Pa. The college was formed, 1865, by the merger of Washington College, which had been chartered as Washington Academy, 1787, and Jefferson College, which had been chartered as Jefferson Academy, 1794. In co-operation with Carnegie Institute of Technology, the college offers a five-year combined program of liberal arts and engineering, leading to a bachelor's degree from each institution. The college library contains a collection of early Americana, featuring materials of historical western Pennsylvania. See COLLEGES AND UNIVERSITIES.

WASHINGTON AND LEE UNIVERSITY, a private, nonsectarian institution of higher learning for men, located in Lexington, Va. Founded as Augusta Academy, 1749, the school was known as Liberty Hall from 1776 until 1798, when the name was changed to Washington Academy in honor of a gift of $50,000 from George Washington. The name Washington and Lee University was adopted, 1871, in honor of Gen. Robert E. Lee, who served as president of the school, 1865–70. The university's school of law was established in 1866, and the school of commerce and administration was established in 1906.

An honors program, involving a thesis and a comprehensive examination, is offered in 16 departments. Selected students may be appointed as "scholars of the university," to participate in a fifth year of study following graduation. A co-operative program in engineering is maintained with Carnegie Institute of Technology, Rensselaer Polytechnic Institute, and the Columbia University School of Engineering. Participating students take three years of work at Washington and Lee and two years of engineering at the co-operating institution; upon completion of the program students receive degrees from both schools.

The university library contains special materials on Robert E. Lee, and the Lee Chapel, containing a museum and Lee's mausoleum, is located on the campus. Among the school's publications are *Shenandoah*, a literary magazine issued quarterly, and the *Law Review*, issued in the fall and spring. See COLLEGES AND UNIVERSITIES.

WASHINGTON COLLEGE, a private, coeducational, nonsectarian college of liberal arts, located in Chestertown, Md. The institution, established as Kent County School, 1706, endowed by state land grant, 1723, and chartered by the state of Maryland as Washington College in 1782, the year in which it offered its first instruction at the college level. The school is named for George Washington, who headed the list of its first endowment contributors and served on its first board of directors. Courses of study emphasize individual responsibility for learning. See COLLEGES AND UNIVERSITIES.

WASHINGTON COURT HOUSE, city, SW Ohio, seat of Fayette County; on the Baltimore and Ohio, the Detroit, Toledo and Ironton, and the Pennsylvania railroads and U.S. highways 22, 35, and 62; 39 miles SW of Columbus. The city is a center for livestock marketing. Shoes, gloves, canned vegetables, fertilizer, hog feeders, and store fixtures are manufactured. The town, first called Washington, was founded in 1810 and renamed later in the same year after a court was held there. Washington was incorporated in 1888. Pop. (1960) 12,388.

WASHINGTON MONUMENT NATIONAL MEMORIAL, a marble obelisk, 555 feet high, erected in honor of Pres. George Washington, in Washington, D.C. The Washington National Monument Society began raising funds for the memorial in 1833. Construction began after Congressional authorization in 1848. The monument was built to a height of 153 feet by 1854, but construction was delayed until President Grant approved an act in 1876, which provided that the government would complete the project. The monument was completed in 1884 and dedicated as a national memorial in 1885.

WASHINGTON PARK, village, SW Illinois, in St. Clair County; on the Baltimore and Ohio and the Alton and Southern railroads; a suburb, 3 miles E of St. Louis. The village was incorporated in 1917. Pop. (1960) 6,601.

WASHINGTON STATE UNIVERSITY, a public, coeducational institution of higher learning, is located in Pullman, Wash. The school was chartered, 1890, as Washington State Agricultural College and School of Science, and first offered instruction two years later. The name was changed to the State College of Washington, 1905, and to Washington State University, 1959.

Among the divisions of the university are the colleges of agriculture, engineering, veterinary medicine, home economics, and sciences and arts, all founded in 1917; and the schools of mines, pharmacy, and education, also founded in 1917. The graduate school was founded in 1922, the school of physical education, recreation, and athletics in 1944, and the school of economics and business in 1947. Advanced degrees are offered in all schools and colleges.

The university carries on an honors program, with special courses for honors given in most departments. An advanced placement program, introduced in 1958, enables a student to earn course credit by means of a comprehensive examination. Extensive programs in radio and television broadcasting are offered. The university maintains an audiovisual center that services many far western states. Nuclear research is carried on, utilizing a 100-kilowatt swimming-pool type of reactor located on the campus. See COLLEGES AND UNIVERSITIES.

WASHINGTON UNIVERSITY, a private, coeducational institution of higher learning, is located in St. Louis, Mo. The university was established as Eliot Seminary, 1853, and offered its first instruction the following year. The name was changed to Washington University 1857, when a collegiate department was inaugurated.

Among the university's divisions are liberal arts, founded in 1857; law, 1867; engineering and architecture, 1870; fine arts, 1879; botany, 1885; medicine, 1891; dentistry, 1892; nursing, 1905; business and public administration, 1917; graduate studies, 1922; and social work, 1945. Advanced degrees are awarded in all departments except that of fine arts. The university is affiliated with numerous institutions of medical treatment and research.

Selected students of demonstrated superior ability may be appointed undergraduate Eliot scholars, to pursue individualized programs of study. The university maintains an interdepartmental committee for undergraduate and graduate research in cellular and molecular biology, and a social science institute for the promotion of research and advanced study in the social and behavioral sciences. The headquarters and broadcasting facilities of the St. Louis educational television station are on the university campus.

Among the special collections in the university library are the Pretorius Memorial collection of German language and literature, the W. K. Bixby rare book collection, the Max W. Bryant collection of books on the Romance languages, the John M. Wulfing numismatics library, and the Bryce and Link collections of works on architecture. See COLLEGES AND UNIVERSITIES.

WASHO, one of a North American Indian Tribe, which in itself constitutes a linguistic family—the Washoan. The tribe formerly lived near the shores of Lake Tahoe, on the border of California and Nevada. They were conquered by the Paiute Indians, 1860–62. Subsequently, the Washo tribe of Indians were settled on reservations in Alpine and Mono counties, California, and Douglas, Ormsby, and Washoe counties, Nevada. The entire Washo Indian population was about 700 in 1950.

WASP, a stinging and largely carnivorous insect, belonging to either of two superfamilies, *Vespoidea* or *Sphecoidea*. In both groups the body of the insect is less hairy than in bees, and the hairs are never feathery; the tarsus of the hind leg is formed exclusively for walking, and is not modified into a pollen-carrying organ, as in bees. The abdomen is attached to the thorax by a thin stalk. The *Vespoidea* are either solitary or social. An interesting family of solitary wasps is the *Pompilidae*, whose members prey chiefly upon spiders, especially the poisonous forms. To this family belong the sand wasps, which dig their burrows in sand and stock their nests with insects. Many social wasps belong to the family *Vespidae*, which also includes not only the paper-making wasps but the various types of hornets as well.

In all cases the habits of social wasps are very similar. In the spring a queen wasp emerges from the place where she has spent the winter and proceeds to construct a nest. In the nest eggs are laid, which upon hatching, rapidly develop into worker females who feed the larvae of later eggs. Since wasps are very sensitive to cold, the nest is enveloped in a papery substance, apparently to maintain a high temperature. Fertile males and females are hatched in late summer. They mate when mature; after the matings the males die. The females then seek some suitable form of shelter in which to spend the winter, and they then form new colonies in the spring. The old nest is never used again.

The sting of wasps, and especially of the hornet, is severe, but the insects do not sting unless provoked. Though wasps cause a considerable amount of destruction to fruit, they also destroy a large number of insects.

Wasp's nest, left, is magnified in center view to reveal young wasps. At right are a worker and a queen wasp.

LYNWOOD M. CHACE

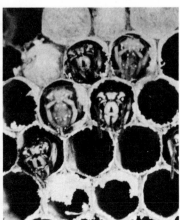

WASP. See WOMEN'S AIRFORCE SERVICE PILOTS.

WASSERMANN, AUGUST VON, 1866–1925, German bacteriologist who devised the Wassermann test for syphilis, was born in Bamberg, and was educated at the universities of Erlangen, Munich, Strasbourg, and Vienna. He began to practice medicine at Strasbourg, 1888, then worked at the Koch Institute of Infectious Diseases, Berlin, where he was director of the experimental therapy and biochemistry department, 1902–13, and became director of experimental therapy at the Kaiser Wilhelm Institute, Berlin, 1913. Wassermann became famous when he applied Jules Bordet's theories to his diagnosis of syphilis, which resulted in the Wassermann test. See SYPHILIS.

WASSERMANN, JAKOB, 1873–1934, German novelist, was born in Furth, Bavaria, left school at the age of 17, and subsequently led a vagabond life until 1896, when he helped found the Munich humor magazine, *Simplicissimus*, and published his first novel, *Die Juden von Zirndorf*, 1896 (*The Jews of Zirndorf*, 1933). Much of his later life was spent on a farm in Styria, where he wrote numerous historical and analytical novels in which he sought to explore the mysterious and complex substrata of human nature. He was a gifted storyteller, but was prone to preach a gospel of transcendental humanitarianism; apart from the merits of his doctrine, his obtrusive use of it lessened the literary effectiveness of his work. Among his novels are *Caspar Hauser*, 1908 (Eng. tr., 1928), *Das Gänsemännschen*, 1915 (*The Goose Man*, 1922), *Christian Wahnschaffe*, 1919 (*The World's Illusion*, 1920); *Der Fall Maurizius*, 1928 (*The Maurizius Case*, 1929), *Etzel Andergast*, 1931 (Eng. tr., 1928), and *Joseph Kerkhoven's dritte Existenz*, 1934 (*Kerkhoven's Third Existence*, 1934). *Mein Weg als Deutscher und Jude*, 1921 (*My Life as German and Jew*, 1933) is autobiographical.

WASSERMANN REACTION. See SYPHILIS.

WASTE, in real estate law, any act of a tenant that lessens the value of real estate, and which he is not entitled to do by virtue of his interest therein. A tenant of agricultural land, for example, is permitted to raise suitable crops and to cut necessary timber; but if he cuts down thrifty fruit trees, or cuts timber trees for the purpose of selling them, it will be deemed waste unless his lease specifically grants him such privileges. Such acts are called voluntary waste. Where a tenant, bound by the terms of his lease to make repairs, fails to do so, the tenant's neglect is called permissive waste. See LANDLORD AND TENANT.

WATAUGA ASSOCIATION, in North American colonial history, the informal and semiautonomous government formed, 1772, by early settlers on the Holston and Watauga rivers in eastern Tennessee, where the effective authority and protection of the established colonies was so slight as to be virtually nonexistent. Under the leadership of James Robertson and John Sevier, the settlers drew up the articles of the Watauga Association, using the laws of Virginia as their guide. This document has been called the first written constitution on the North American continent—the earlier Mayflower Compact, assuming that it may be considered a constitution having been signed prior to the landing of its signers on the continent (see MAYFLOWER COMPACT). During the American Revolution, these western settlements became what one historian called, not implausibly, "the advance guard of civilization"; they took an important part in the war, especially in the Battle of King's Mountain. They later dubbed their region Washington District, and after the war they organized the autonomous state of Franklin, 1784. See FRANKLIN; TENNESSEE, History.

WATCH, a timepiece carried on one's person, particularly worn on a wrist, in a pocket, or attached to the clothing. Watches in general, indicate the time in hours, minutes, and seconds, although some models also show the day of the month through an opening

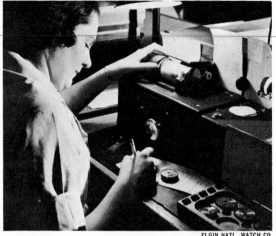

ELGIN NATL. WATCH CO

The timekeeping characteristics of a watch can be ascertained within 15 seconds with this electronic rating machine, an operation that formerly required 24 hours testing.

in the dial. See HOROLOGY, Mechanical Timepieces, *Spring-driven Timepieces.*

The power to drive the hands of a watch is derived from the mainspring, a coiled steel alloy band enclosed in a flat case, called a barrel. The inner end of the spring is attached to an arbor that winds and puts tension on the spring when the watch stem is turned, or, in the automatic self-winding wristwatches, when the natural activity of the wearer of the watch creates such a tension on the spring. A toothed pawl at the winding mechanism prevents the spring from unwinding when under tension. The hour and minute hands are set by the same stem. In early watches, winding was done with a key inserted into the stem.

The hour and minute hands of the watch, circling over the dial or face, operate from separate gear trains, and from separate spindles, one within the other. The second hand operates from a third spindle, the hand circling a separate, small 60-second dial or, if the hand circles the main dial, its spindle is within the hour and minute hand spindles. To provide a uniform rate of movement, the power output of the spring passes through an escapement that is controlled by a balance wheel operating against a spirally coiled hairspring. This precisely balanced wheel consists of two half rims built of different alloys to compensate for temperature variations. The reversing swings of the balance wheel perform the same function as the oscillations of a pendulum of a clock. A metallic watch case and crystal enclose the working unit of a watch.

The hunting case watch has a hinged cover that snaps shut over the crystal. The open-face pocket watch is equipped with a snap-ring over the stem to protect it and act as a chain or fob attachment. Ladies' lapel watches, usually open-face, are attached to the clothing with decorative fastenings.

After World War I the wristwatch became the most popular of this type of timepiece. It is strapped to the wrist by a metal, leather, or fabric band.

Stop watches are equipped with an additional mechanism located under the dial that permits an elapsed time reading to an accuracy of one-fifth of one-tenth of a second. A special stem plunger in the stem starts and stops the timing mechanism and returns the second hand to the zero starting position.

BIBLIOG.–Henry G. Abbott, *Antique Watches and How to Establish Their Age* (c.1897); G. H. Baillie, *Watchmakers and Clockmakers of the World* (1948); M. Gonzalez Benitez, *Questions and Answers for the Student Watchmaker* (1947); Frederick J. Britten, *Watch and Clock Maker's Handbook: Dictionary and Guide* (1955), *Old Clocks and Watches and Their Makers* (1956); Alfred Chapuis and Edmond Droz, *Automata: A Historical and Technological Study* (1958); Alfred Chapuis and

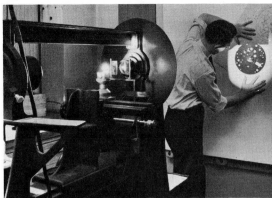

ELGIN NATL. WATCH CO.

A watch manufacturer uses a projection machine to show enlargements of intricate watch parts in order to check all details of finished parts against original drawings.

Eugéne Jaquet, *History of the Self-winding Watch, 1770–1931* (1956); Theodore P. C. Cuss, *Story of Watches* (1952); Donald De Carle, *Clock and Watch Repairing (Including Complicated Watches)* (1959), *Watch and Clock Encyclopedia* (1959); George H. Eckhardt, *United States Clock and Watch Patents, 1790–1890* (1960); D. W. Fletcher, *Watch Repairing as a Hobby* (1947); Henry B. Fried, *Bench Practices for Watch Repairers* (1954), *Watch Escapement: How to Analyze, How to Adjust, How to Repair* (1959); William J. Gazeley, *Watch and Clock Making and Repairing* (1959); Eugéne Jaquet, *Technique and History of the Swiss Watch from its Beginnings to the Present Day* (1953); Hans Jendritzki, *Swiss Watch Repairer's Manual* (1953); Harold C. Kelly, *Watch Repair* (1957); James C. Pellaton, *Watch Escapements* (1949); William R. Pipe, *Automatic Watch* (1952); Joseph W. Player, *Watch Repairing* (1952); Arthur L. Rawlings, *Science of Clocks and Watches* (1948); Emanuel Siebel and Orville R. Hagans, eds. and trs., *Complicated Watches* (1946); James Swinburne, *Mechanism of the Watch* (1951); Arthur G. Thisell, *Science of Watch Repairing Simplified* (1942).

WATER, the most widely distributed compound in nature. Its formula is H$_2$O and its molecular weight is 18.016; it occurs naturally in solid, liquid, and gaseous forms. Great bodies of water cover about five-sevenths of the earth's surface, reaching in some places to depths of more than six miles. Water is essential to plant and animal life, constituting about 70 per cent by weight of the human body and as much as 90 to 95 per cent of the weight of many plants. It is found in fertile soil; in vapor form, it is a variable but important component of the atmosphere from which it condenses in various types of precipitation. It is estimated that often there is as much as 50,000 tons of water vapor present in the atmosphere over a square mile of the earth's surface.

For a long time water was considered to be an element, but in 1781 Henry Lord Cavendish prepared it by burning hydrogen in air. It remained for Antoine Lavoisier, however, to prove that it was a compound of only hydrogen and oxygen.

Physical Properties. At ordinary temperatures water is an odorless and tasteless liquid. It is colorless in thin layers but shows a distinct blue to green color in depth, because the matter suspended in it refracts light. Water boils at 100°C under one atmosphere pressure and freezes at 0°C. Its latent heat of vaporization, or the amount of energy necessary to convert one gram of water at 100°C into steam is 539.7 calories. Its latent heat of fusion, or the amount of energy that must be added to it to transform one gram of ice at 0°C into water at the same temperature, is 79.7 calories. Water has its maximum density 1.000 grams per milliliter at 4°C, or more precisely 3.98°C. The density of water is unique in that it decreases both below and above this temperature of 4°C. The density of ice, which is 0.917 grams per cubic centimeter (milliliter) at 0°C, is less than the density of water, and, therefore, the ice floats on the surface.

There is considerable expansion when water freezes. The specific heat of water is approximately one calorie per gram. This large value gives water a high thermal capacity and accounts for the tempering effects of large bodies of water on the climate of neighboring land areas. Water is almost incompressible and, when pure, is a poor conductor of electricity. Water is an excellent solvent for many inorganic and organic compounds, so much so that it has been called a universal solvent.

Chemical Properties. Water is a highly stable substance and is readily formed from its elements. When heated to temperatures of about 2300°C, it decomposes only to the extent of 2 or 3 per cent. In the presence of a little sulfuric acid, it may be easily electrolyzed, decomposing to form two volumes of hydrogen gas for each volume of oxygen gas released. This is a weight relationship of eight grams of oxygen for every 1.008 grams of hydrogen. Water at ordinary temperatures reacts readily with active metals such as sodium, potassium, and calcium to form the hydroxide of the metal and liberate hydrogen. At higher temperatures, water reacts with the less active metals, such as zinc and iron, to form the oxide of the metal and to release hydrogen.

Water combines with many metallic oxides to form bases and with many nonmetallic oxides to form acids. It unites with many compounds, especially salts, to form hydrates. Cupric sulfate, CuCO$_4$, when crystallized from water solutions, forms blue hydrated crystals having the composition CuSO$_4 \cdot$ 5H$_2$O. Water acts as a catalyst in many cases, causing substances that may be reacting only very slowly to react rapidly, even with explosive violence in some instances. When deuterium, the heavy isotope of hydrogen, is substituted for ordinary hydrogen in water, the water is classified as heavy water. Its formula is D$_2$O.

Natural Waters occur as rain water, surface water, spring and well water, and sea water. The only natural water that is relatively pure is rain water, but even this contains some dissolved gases, such as carbon dioxide, nitrogen, and oxygen, and some dust particles and organic material. Because of the solvent action of water, all natural waters contain substances in solution. Dissolved impurities include, for the most part, the chlorides, sulfates, bicarbonates, and carbonates of calcium, magnesium, iron, sodium, and potassium. The salts of calcium, magnesium, and iron render the water hard, because they hinder soap in forming lather. As much as 3.6 per cent of some ocean waters is dissolved salts, particularly sodium chloride. In land-locked lakes and seas the dissolved solid content may also be high. The Great Salt Lake in Utah contains 23 per cent by weight of dissolved salts.

WATER BEETLE. See DIVING BEETLE.

WATER BUG, any one of a number of insects belonging to the order of true bugs, the Hemiptera. Though all are fairly common insects, probably the most familiar are the giant water bugs. Many species of these flat, oval bugs are found in ponds throughout

AMERICAN MUS. OF NAT. HIST.

The most familiar of the different species of water bugs are giant water bugs which grow to be three and one half inches in length, and usually can be found in ponds.

various parts of the world. Giant water bugs some-times attain a length of three and a half to four inches and are usually of a brownish color. Others are the water boatmen of the family *Corixidae;* the backswimmers, *Notonectidae;* the water scorpions, *Nepidae;* the giant water bugs, *Belostomatidae;* and the creeping water bugs, *Naucoridae.*

WATERBURY, city, SW central Connecticut, seat of New Haven County; on the Naugatuck River, the New Haven Railroad, and U.S. highway 6A; 18 miles SW of Hartford. The city is an industrial center, in which the manufacture of brass products, clocks, and inexpensive watches are the leading in-dustries. Chemicals, copper products, clothing, toys, tools, wire and metal novelties, auto parts, flexible tubing, light fixtures, and foundry and machine shop products are manufactured. Waterbury, settled in 1674 as Mattatuck, was renamed and incorporated in 1686. It was chartered as a city in 1853. Waterbury is the site of the Conservatory of Notre Dame and the Bronson Library. Waterbury developed as a manu-facturing center early in the nineteenth century. The business section was rebuilt after it was destroyed by fire in 1902. Pop. (1960) 107,130.

WATER CHESTNUT, an attractive aquatic plant belonging to the family, *Trapaceae.* The water chest-nut, *Trapa natans,* also called Jesuit's nut, is a hardy plant with small, white flowers and large fruits and is found floating in ponds and lakes. The plant is most significant for its fruits which are similar to chestnuts, although sweeter, and may be eaten either raw or cooked. The fruits are normally hidden in the foliage of the plant until they ripen, at which time they fall to the ground. The water chest-nut is found naturally in Europe.

WATER CLOCK. See CLEPSYDRA.

WATER COLOR, traditionally, the technique of painting with transparent, water-soluble colors that let the background show through. The water colorist (1) sketches in the outlines of his design; (2) covers the paper with a soft wash, and allows it to dry, and (3) colors the outlined objects with a brush, waiting for each color to dry before painting over it with another. In this way several layers of color can be applied one over the other so that each layer influences the color of the next. Some modern water colorists omit the sketched outlines and paint directly over the background, brushing new colors onto ones that have not yet dried, thereby allowing the colors to run together; white spots such as lights and clouds are left dry.

Water-soluble colors, of which there are more than 100 different shades, come in squares, in tiny bowls, or in tubes. They are applied to heavy white (or off-white) paper of high linen content so that it will not become soggy or buckle with wetness.

Gouache Technique, a variation of the traditional water-color method in which the water-soluble colors are rendered opaque (usually by mixing white with them), enables the artist to paint on wood, poster board and other surfaces. Modern water colorists often combine the transparent and opaque methods.

Another technical variation is tempera, in which water-soluble color is combined with casein, egg, or both, to form another type of opaque medium. See TEMPERA.

HISTORY

Water-soluble colors are the oldest painting media known to man. Certain clays and stones, ground to powder and then mixed with water, were used in antiquity and are still used for decorative painting by primitive tribesmen. The people of ancient India, and the ancient Egyptians, Greeks, and Romans used opaque water colors to write and paint on papyrus, cloth, earthenware, stone, and other surfaces.

Chinese water-color technique, which developed from calligraphy, dates from before the time of Christ. The Chinese considered the skillful rendering of their complicated yet graceful writing as worthy an endeavor as the study of painting. Such calligraphy demanded an expertly trained hand and unerring judgment on the part of the writer, who formed the characters with short, deft strokes so as not to let the ink run on the silk or rice paper background. The Chinese actually originated the transparent water-color technique as defined in modern times; they were the first to use washes, and the first to let their colors run into one another, especially in rendering delicate clouds and mists.

Japanese Painting was greatly influenced by the Chinese, and even in the 1960's traditionally oriented Japanese painters were required to master the Chinese alphabet as a way of learning brush control. Japanese water-color, or "diluted ink," painting is a highly disciplined art, requring the painter to work within rigidly fixed limits. He usually kneels before the surface to be painted—often a panel or screen—and then, after much deliberation, makes quick strokes with one or two brushes held in the same hand, creat-ing masterpieces of simplicity and nuance within only a few minutes. He is allowed no preliminary sketching, correction, or erasure. Twentieth century Japanese water colorists have relied heavily on Western influence and have not produced works as beautiful and subtle as those of their forebears.

In India and in the Middle East opaque water color was used in manuscript illumination. The use of rich enamel-like colors with gold foreshadowed later European trends. See CHINESE ART; JAPANESE ART AND ARCHITECTURE; PERSIAN ART AND ARCHITECTURE.

The Middle Ages saw the use of opaque water colors in the illumination of letters, documents, and books; in coloring woodcuts; and, later, in decorating elaborate family escutcheons. Perhaps the earliest true (transparent) water colorist was Albrecht Dürer (1471–1528), who used transparent colors to produce landscapes and nature studies that show him to have been far in advance of his time. Such masters as Andrea Mantegna (1431–1506) and the Hans Holbeins (both father and son), and the Flemish painters used water colors for preliminary sketches (cartoons). In France, water colors were employed to enhance architectural drawings. Except for those of Dürer, however, water colors were not much esteemed during the Renaissance, when a painting could hardly be taken seriously unless done in oils. It remained for the British, in the eighteenth and nine-teenth centuries, to raise the art of the water colorist to eminence.

England. In ?1700 the English Painter Lens introduced the use of ivory as a suitable surface for opaque water coloring of portrait miniatures, of which countless thousands were subsequently exe-cuted in Europe. England boasted such prominent specialists in transparent water color as Alexander Cozens (1700–86), his son John (1752–99), and Paul Sandby (1725–1809), the first to attain real distinc-tion. Thomas Rowlandson (1757?–1827), famed as a caricaturist, achieved remarkable subtlety in his coloring of such works as the *English Review, Vauxhall Gardens.* William Blake (1757–1827) anticipated the dramatic possibilities of the medium in his powerful treatment of religious subjects, such as the *Simoniac Pope.* Two great innovators, Thomas Girtin (1775–1802) and J. M. W. Turner (1775–1851), broke with tradition by relying more on pure color itself and less on color used merely as the finishing touch added to a drawing. In this sense Turner anticipated impressionism and later abstract art. The Society of Water Color Painters was founded, 1804, in London thus establishing the new medium as equal in importance to oils.

The Englishmen Richard Parkes Bonington (1801?–28) and Anthony Vandyke Copley Fielding (1787–1855) strongly influenced the French School. The Frenchmen Jean Louis André Theodore Gericault (1791–1824) and the self-taught Delacroix

(1804–66), belonged to the Romantic school of water colorists, while Gavarni and Constantin Guys (1802–92) used them in depicting French social life. In Germany, the fine draftsman Adolph Friedrich Erdmann von Menzel (1815–1905) also worked in water colors, as did the Viennese Rudolf von Alt (1812–1905) and Franz von Alt (1821–1914).

United States. The first significant U.S. water colorist was John James Audubon (1785–1851) whose illustrations for *Birds of America* show him to have been a skilled craftsman. Until the advent of Winslow Homer (1836–1910), however, water color was not considered comparable to oil painting in the United States. Homer devised a technique of applying one coat of heavy color instead of superimposing successive light washes as the English had done. His method gave Homer's works an impact and freedom that often led critics to denounce them as unfinished. He was followed by the modernist Maurice B. Pendergast (1861–1924), and John Marin (1870–1953), who eschewed formalism and worked toward abstract concepts.

Twentieth Century Water Colorists became increasingly experimental. The Russian-born Wassily Kandinsky (1866–1944) painted one of the first, if not the first, truly abstract compositions in water color, 1910. Mark Tobey (1890–   ) turned to Oriental sources for his opaque "white writing" style. George Grosz (1893–1959) worked in Germany with the colored-drawing method and later in the United States with a wet-on-wet technique combining all kinds of tools and methods. The younger artists seemed to prefer oil painting on a grandiose scale to the more intimate water-color technique, which requires a more disciplined hand.

Martin O. Grosz

Bibliog.–Leonard Brooks, *Watercolor, a Challenge* (1957); Chris Choate, *Architectural Presentation in Opaque Watercolor* (1961); Leonard A. Doust, *Watercolour Drawing* (1960); Paul Duval, *Canadian Water Colour Painting* (1955); Alois Fabry, Jr., *Water-color Painting is Fun* (1960); Francis M. R. Flint, *Water Colour Out of Doors* (1959); Lloyd Goodrich, *American Watercolour and Winslow Homer* (1945); Arthur L. Guptill, *Watercolor Painting Step-by-Step* (1957); Adrian K. G. Hill, *On the Mastery of Water-colour Painting* (1957), *Beginner's Book of Water-colour Painting* (1959); Barbara A. Jones, *Water-color Painting* (1960); Norman Kent, ed., *Watercolor Methods* (1955); Claude Muncaster, *Landscape and Marine Painting* (1958); John B. Musacchia and Others, *Course in Beginning Watercolor* (1956); Herb V. Olson, *Painting the Figure in Watercolor* (1958), *Painting Children in Watercolor* (1960); Leonard Richmond, *From the Sketch to the Finished Picture: Water-colour Painting* (1954), *Technique of Water-Colour Painting* (1955); William B. Schimmel, *Water Color: The Happy Medium* (1958); Jacob G. Smith, *Watercolor Painting for the Beginner* (1957); Edgar A. Whitney, *Watercolor: The Hows and Whys* (1958); Paul Wyeth, *How to Paint in Water-colours* (1958).

WATER-COOLING SYSTEM. See Automobile, The Automobile Engine; Condenser, *Surface Condensers;* Internal Combustion Engine, *Lubricating and Cooling.*

WATERCOURSE, a stream usually flowing in a particular direction, along a definite channel, and discharging into some other body of water. In law, persons owning the land constituting the banks of the stream are known as the riparian owners and their rights and obligations with respect to the water in the watercourse are well fixed by customary law. They have no property right in the water itself, but simply a right to use it (*usufruct*). See Riparian Right.

WATER CRESS, a European aquatic plant naturalized in North America, *Roripa nasturtium-aquaticum,* belonging to the family *Cruciferae.* The plant has roundish leaves, white flowers, and trailing roots that rest in water or mud. It is usually found in ditches, ponds, or at the edge of streams. Water cress grows perennially, being planted either with its seeds or with segments of its roots. Because of its pungent leaves, water cress is widely used in salads.

WATER CYCLE. See Hydrologic Cycle.

NEW YORK STATE DEPT. OF COMMERCE

With its spectacular 215-foot drop, Taughannock Falls in New York's Taughannock Falls State Park is the highest single waterfall situated east of the Rocky Mountains.

WATERFALL, the flow of a stream of water over a vertical or steeply inclined wall. Waterfalls contribute to scenic attractions, and are often harnessed to form an important source of power.

They are most commonly caused by a stream eroding its bed across varying rock structures. When a band of soft rock, such as shale, is found underlying a more resistant rock, such as dolomite, the soft layer is often eroded from beneath the hard layer, causing a projecting ledge. This ledge may eventually break away, causing the fall to move upstream. Niagara Falls was formed by this type of action, and is moving upstream toward Buffalo, N.Y., at the rate of four to five feet per year. At the base of a fall of this kind potholes are common features. These are small, deep pools with steep sides, which have been drilled into the rock by the grinding action of pebbles whirled about by the turbulent water.

In the deep gorges of young streams, waterfalls often alternate with rapids. Tributary streams bring down large boulders, which pile up in the main stream near the mouths of the tributaries and act as barriers to the water. This can cause a fall. Where the main stream is cutting its valley more rapidly than its tributaries are cutting theirs, the tributary streams are said to form hanging valleys. The streams frequently discharge their water into the main stream over steep walls, and form spectacular waterfalls. In the gorge cut by the Columbia River through the Cascade Range, the famous Multnomah and

U.S.G.S.—DARTON

New York's Trenton Falls on West Canada Creek are useful as well as beautiful. Their several waterfalls supply electric power to Utica, N. Y., 12 miles distant.

Latourelle falls have been produced in this way. Hanging valleys have frequently been caused by differential glacial erosion. Falls on the walls of fiords have usually been formed in this way, and Yosemite Falls in California was similarly caused by a glacial hanging valley.

Where streams flow over a bedrock which has many joints crossing the bed of the stream, falls may occur as a result of the underlying rock wearing away block by block rather than gradually, and the stream falls over the perpendicular face of a joint. If the bedrock has easily separated bedding planes in addition to a distinct pattern of joints, "stairway falls," or a cascade may result. This particular geological pattern is seen in the falls which are located on the Potomac River in the Fall Zone.

NOTED WATERFALLS OF THE WORLD

Fall	Est. Height (in feet)	River	Location
NORTH AMERICA			
Yosemite	2,425	Yosemite	California
Ribbon	1,612	Ribbon	California
Takakkaw	1,600	Yoho	British Columbia
Silver Strand	1,170	Meadow	California
Grand	1,038	Hamilton	Labrador
Multnomah	850	Columbia	Oregon
Bridalveil	620	Bridalveil	California
Nevada	594	Merced	California
Illilouette	370	Illilouette	California
Vernal	317	Merced	California
Virginia	316	South Nahanni	Northwest Territories
Lower Yellowstone	308	Yellowstone	Wyoming
Sluiskin	300	Paradise	Washington
Montmorency	275	Montmorency	Québec
Snoqualmie	270	Snoqualmie	Washington
Seven	266	South Cheyenne	Colorado
Taughannock	215	Taughannock	New York
Shoshone	210	Snake	Idaho
Palouse	198	Palouse	Washington
Narada	168	Paradise	Washington
Niagara	167	Niagara	New York–Ontario
Manitou	165	Black	Wisconsin
Tower	132	Yellowstone	Wyoming
Upper Yellowstone	109	Yellowstone	Wyoming
Upper Mesa	106	Snake	Idaho
SOUTH AMERICA			
Angel	5,000	Caroní	Venezuela
Kukenaam	2,000	Kukenaam	Venezuela
King George VI	1,600	Mazaruni	Guyana
King Edward VIII	840	Mazaruni	Guyana
Kaieteur	741	Potaro	Guyana
Marina	500	Potaro	Guyana
Tequendama	482	Bogotá	Colombia
Paulo Afonso	275	São Francisco	Brazil
Iguaçu	210	Iguaçu	Argentina–Brazil
Guaíra	100	Paraná	Brazil–Paraguay
EUROPE			
Gavarnie	1,385	Gave de Pau	France
Krimml	1,250	Krimml	Austria
Giessbach	980	Giessbach	Switzerland
Rjukanfoss	980	Mana	Norway
Staubbach	980	Staubbach	Switzerland
Trümmelbach	950	Trümmelbach	Switzerland
Vettisfoss	856	Mörkedola	Norway
Voringfoss	535	Bjoreia	Norway
Cascata delle Marmore	525	Velino	Italy
Skjeggedalsfoss	525	Tyssaa	Norway
Toce	500	Toce	Italy
Glomach	370	Elchaig	Scotland
Reichenbach (upper fall)	300	Reichenbach	Switzerland
AFRICA			
Kalambo	3,000	Kalambo	Zambia
Tugela	2,800	Tugela	Republic of South Africa
Maletsunyane	630	Orange	Lesotho
Aughrabies (King George's)	480	Orange	Republic of South Africa
Baratieri	460	Ganale Dorya	Ethiopia
Murchison	400	Victoria Nile	Uganda
Howick	364	Umgeni	Republic of South Africa
Karkloof	350	Umgeni	Republic of South Africa
Victoria	350	Zambezi	Rhodesia
AUSTRALIA and NEW ZEALAND			
Sutherland	1,904	Arthur	New Zealand
Wollomombie	1,700	Macleay	Australia
ASIA			
Gersoppa	830	Sharavati	India
Kegon	350	Daiya	Japan
Cauvery	320	Cauvery	India

Occasionally falls are caused by an igneous dike crossing the path of a stream. The greater resistance of the igneous rock makes it a barrier to erosion, while the bedrock around it can be worn away fairly readily by the stream, and a step is formed. Yellowstone Falls is an example of this type of fall.

Waterfalls of any considerable height and volume are valuable sources of power. Part or all of the stream may be diverted from its course and made to turn a turbine, thus furnishing energy for the generation of electric power. Falls were formerly used to turn water wheels. The manufacturing cities of Lowell, Lawrence, Fall River, and Holyoke in Massachusetts, Rochester in New York, and Minneapolis in Minnesota, originally grew up around falls.

WATER FLEA, any of the minute free-swimming arthropods belonging to the class Crustacea. Water fleas are classified in the order Cladocera which contains several genera: *Alona; Leptodora;* and *Daphnia.* One species, *Daphnia pulex,* has water flea as its common name. It has a small, oval body that is covered by a transparent bivalved shell. It measures approximately 1/10 inch in length. It swims about in a jerking fashion due to the movements of its second pair of antennae.

WATERFORD, county, S Ireland, in the province of Munster, bordered S by the Atlantic Ocean, W by Cork, N by Tipperary and Kilkenny, and separated from Wexford on the E by Waterford Harbor; area 710 sq. mi.; pop. (1956) 74,031. Waterford is mountainous in the north and northeast. The coast line, in some places rugged, has several indentations, the chief of which are the estuary of the Suir River, forming Waterford Harbor, Dungarvin Bay, and Youghal Bay. The county has more pastures than cultivated land, and dairying and pig raising are important; the chief crops are oats, wheat, potatoes, and vegetables. Marble is quarried. The offshore and salmon river fisheries are important in the economic life. The chief towns are the capital, Waterford, and Dungarvin, both port towns.

WATERFORD, town, S Ireland in county Waterford, on a tidal estuary fed by the Suir, Barrow, and Nore rivers, some 8 miles from the sea and 84 miles SSW of Dublin. Waterford has an important port, and a headquarters for salmon and sea fishing; it is a trade center for cattle, sheep, pigs, and agricultural produce. There are breweries, salt works, foundries, flour mills, and shipyards in Waterford. Waterford has both Roman Catholic and Anglican cathedrals. Its ancient name was *Cuan-na-groith,* but it first came to importance under the Danes, in the ninth century. King Henry II of England landed nearby in the twelfth century, and Waterford became a chartered town under King John, who also established a mint there. During the eighteenth century Waterford was a well known glassmaking center, but the industry died out. Waterford remained under the British crown until the formation of the Irish Republic, 1919. Its Gaelic name is Phort Láirge. Pop. (1956) 28,691.

WATER GAS. See Gas Manufacture.

WATER GLASS, a solution of disodium silicate, Na_2SiO_3, or sodium metasilicate of varying concentration, in water. It may be prepared by fusing silicon dioxide with sodium hydroxide or sodium carbonate

$$SiO_2 + Na_2CO_3 \rightarrow Na_2SiO_3 + CO_2 \uparrow$$

The glassy disodium silicate remaining may be brought into solution by the application of live steam. Water glass is salt of a strong base and a very weak acid; hence, its water solution is very alkaline because of hydrolysis. The compound finds use as a waterproofing agent, a fireproofing agent for textiles, and an adhesive and stiffener for corrugated paper and cardboard. It has been used as an egg preservative, as the solution fills the pores of the eggshell, preventing the penetration of air and bacteria.

WATER HEMLOCK. See Hemlock.

WATER HEN. See Coot.

WATER HOREHOUND. See Horehound.

WATER HYACINTH, a tropical aquatic herb belonging to the family *Pontederiaceae.* The water hyacinth, *Eichhornia crassipes,* remains afloat because its petioles, or leaf stalks, are inflated with air, forming buoyant bladders. Its flower stalk is one foot in height, bearing six-petaled flowers that are pale violet and are found in a series of eight to each spike. When the plant is ready to flower it sends out roots that attach the plants to a muddy bottom; it usually thrives in one foot of water. The plant is native to the tropics of the Western Hemisphere and Florida in the United States. It has on occasion posed navigational problems on Florida rivers where dense accumulations of the water hyacinth formed obstructions.

WATER LILY, any one of various water plants of the family *Nymphaceae,* particularly the genus *Nymphaea.* There are more than 40 species with numerous varieties and hybrids. The water lilies are perennial herbs characterized by oval-shaped, floating leaves that range from two inches to two feet in diameter. Their flowers are quite conspicuous, usually in shades of white, blue, yellow, or red. The largest species in size found in the United States is *N. tuberosa* having pure-white flowers. The common white water lily, *N. odorata,* is found in many American lakes and slow moving streams.

WATERLOO, city, SE Illinois, seat of Monroe County; on the Gulf, Mobile and Ohio Railroad; 20 miles SSE of St. Louis. The city is a trade center for an area in which grain, poultry and livestock are raised. Pop. (1960) 3,739.

WATERLOO, city, NE Iowa, seat of Black Hawk County, on the Cedar River, the Great Western, the Rock Island, the Illinois Central, and the Waterloo, Cedar Falls, and Northern railroads, and U.S. highways 20, 63, and 218; 87 miles NW of Des Moines. Waterloo is a trade center for a diversified agricultural area. Farm supplies and machinery, clothing, and engines are manufactured, and soybean oil and meat products are processed. Waterloo was founded as Prairie Rapids in 1845 and, with the establishment of the post office in 1851, was renamed Waterloo. The town was laid out in 1854 and was chartered as a city in 1868. Pioneer Park, along the river, has recreational facilities and several reproductions of pioneer structures. The exhibits of the Dairy Cattle Congress and the National Belgian Horse Show are held there each year. Sinclair Lewis, who became a Nobel prize-winning author, worked for a daily newspaper in Waterloo in 1908-09. Pop. (1960) 71,755.

WATERLOO, town, W central New York, one of the two seats of Seneca County; on the Seneca River, on the Lehigh Valley and the New York Central railroads, and U.S. highway 20; about 35 miles WSW of Syracuse. Auto bodies, canned foods, condiments, and stove products are manufactured. It is a popular summer resort for the Finger Lakes region. Pop. (1960) 5,098.

WATERLOO, town, Canada, Québec, seat of Shefford County; on the Canadian National and the Canadian Pacific railways; about 54 miles ESE of Montreal. Waterloo has sawmills, toy and furniture factories, a wire-goods factory, and feed mills. The town developed around a mission in 1796 and was incorporated in 1890. Pop. (1956) 4,266.

WATERLOO, city, Canada, S Ontario, in Waterloo County; on the Canadian National and the Canadian Pacific railways; a NW suburb of Kitchener; 55 miles WSW of Toronto. The city is an industrial center. Distilling, flour milling and the manufacture of agricultural implements, furniture, shoes, upholstery fabrics, brooms, and clothing are the leading industries. Waterloo was established in a farming region, which was settled during the nineteenth century by Mennonites from Pennsylvania. Pop. (1956) 16,373.

WATERLOO, BATTLE OF, the final battle of the Napoleonic Wars, was fought June 18, 1815, near the village of Waterloo, 12 miles S of Brussels, Belgium (then a part of the Kingdom of the Netherlands). The upshot of the battle was that British, Prussian, and Dutch forces commanded by Arthur Wellesley, 1st duke of Wellington, and Gebhard Leberecht von Blücher defeated the French forces of Emperor Napoleon I, thereby ending the emperor's power forever.

After his abdication, 1814, Napoleon had been exiled to Elba. He escaped in February, 1815, however, and regained control of France. Alarmed at the return of the man who had kept Europe in a condition of turmoil for almost 20 years, the Allies paid no attention to his professions of peace, suspended their negotiations at Vienna (see VIENNA, CONGRESS OF), and gathered their forces to invade France. Napoleon had available about 198,000 men but used only 124,000 in the campaign. Opposed to these were more than 600,000 Allied troops, including armies of at least 400,000 men under Russian and Austrian command, which advanced westward from the Rhineland and northern Italy, and two armies under Wellington (93,000 men) and Blücher (117,000 men), which advanced southward from the Netherlands. The Allied strategy was for all of these forces to strike at Napoleon simultaneously. Napoleon, however, planned to intercept and destroy the armies of Wellington and Blücher, before Austrians and Russians could concentrate on the eastern border of France.

Moving with his accustomed swiftness, Napoleon marched his forces into Belgium early in June, and interposed them between Wellington and Blücher. Skirmishing began on June 15, and on the following day, while the French Marshal Michel Ney engaged in an inconclusive fight with Dutch and British troops at Quatre Bras, the other wing of the French army defeated the Prussians at Ligny. Blücher was wounded, and Napoleon, who thought the Prussians had been routed, assuming that they would retreat eastward toward Namur, detached Marshal Emmanuel de Grouchy with 33,000 men to pursue and defeat them. Actually, however, Blücher marched northward toward Wavre to join Wellington who, after the Prussian defeat, had fallen back to Waterloo and taken up a strong position there.

The main French army, numbering about 70,000 men, advanced on Wellington's position and arrived there on June 17, late in the day. Wellington's forces, numbering 67,000 men in the field, were concentrated directly to the north, across the Brussels-Charleroi road. The first French attack, late on the morning of June 18, hit the British right (west) flank, and was unsuccessful. The main attack, against Wellington's center, routed a Dutch outpost brigade, but was repulsed by British troops behind the ridge. A French attack against a Prussian vanguard on the French right (east) met with some success, but the French cavalry failed in numerous assaults on the British right center. Just before sunset, Napoleon massed the remaining Imperial Guard for a final attack on Wellington's battered center; the attack was repulsed with heavy losses and the guard forced back in disorder. At about 7:30 in the evening, Blücher's forces began to arrive, whereupon Wellington advanced his lines, and the French began a retreat that soon became a rout: although the guard resisted to the last, the rest of the French army was speedily dispersed. The French losses in killed, wounded, and missing have been estimated at more than 30,000, while the Allies reported 22,000 casualties.

Napoleon's defeat was largely the result of his inadequate supervision of his wing and corps commanders; Grouchy's failure to prevent the Prussians from joining Wellington; and Wellington's skillful dispositions and stubborn resistance. Finally, the arrival of the Prussians turned the French failure at Waterloo into a disaster. Following the battle, Napoleon went directly to Paris, where he abdicated, June 22. See NAPOLEON I, *Napoleonic Europe, 1803–15.*

WATERMAN, MARCUS, 1834–1914, U.S. figure and genre painter, was born in Providence, R.I., and was educated at Brown University in that city. He then studied in New York City and in Boston, where he settled, 1874. His pictures, chiefly Oriental scenes, are notable for their brilliant sunlight effects. Among the best known are *The Roc's Egg, The Merchant and the Genius, The Arab Country House, Citron Seller, Street in Algiers,* and *In the Alhambra.* He also painted forest scenes and New England landscapes.

WATERMARK. See PAPER.

WATERMELON, the fruit of the trailing vine *Citrullus vulgaris,* a plant native to Africa, but now widely cultivated throughout the world. It is of great commercial importance in the United States. There are many cultivated varieties of watermelon. Some hard-rinded, rather solid, white-fleshed varieties, known as citrons, are used for preserves, and are not edible raw. Other large, coarse kinds, known as stock or pie melons, are grown to a limited extent for stock food. The bulk of the crop is grown for dessert purposes. Good commercial melons weigh from 10 to 25 pounds each. The rind is green, mottled with a lighter tint; while the ripe flesh is usually red in color, very watery, and permeated with seeds. About 2.5 per cent of the juice is sugar. Texas, Florida, Georgia, Indiana, Mississippi, and California are the leading states in watermelon cultivation. Only the smaller varieties are grown in the North.

WATER METER. See FLUID METER.

WATER MOCCASIN. See MOCCASIN.

WATER MOLD. See MOLD.

WATER MOTOR. See HYDRAULIC MACHINERY.

WATER OUZEL. See DIPPER.

WATER PLANT. See AQUATIC PLANTS.

WATER POLO, a ball game played in a swimming pool by seven-man teams of swimmers. The game has undergone many rule changes since ?1870,

CHICAGO SUN

Great endurance, as well as swimming skill, are needed to play water polo well. Here a player attempts to score a goal as a member of the opposing team tries to block it.

when it was first played. The changes have been designed to make the game less rough and dangerous, but it is still a strenuous game, calling for great endurance, swimming skill, and considerable courage. Essentially the game is basketball played by swimmers. The first standardized rules were adopted in 1897. Originally the game was played with a soft, partially inflated rubber ball that players could grip in one hand and carry under water while swimming. Such softball water polo is still played in Europe, but in the United States has been supplanted, as too rough, by hard-ball polo.

The players having lined up on their respective sides of the center line, the referee puts the ball in play by tossing it into the center of the pool. Players may swim with the ball in one hand, but may not hold it with both hands. It may be passed from player to player as in basketball, but may not be carried under water. A net is suspended above the surface of the water at each end of the pool. The object of the game is to toss the ball into the net. The team making the most goals wins. The game is divided into two playing periods, with a five-minute rest period between.

WATER POWER, one of two natural sources of power that man has used since remote antiquity, the other being wind power. Of the two, water power eventually outstripped wind power in its importance to the human race, because of its value in generating electricity.

The first use of water power came through the water wheel. Water moving along the bed of a stream was used to turn a water wheel. The power of the moving wheel in turn was transmitted to the stones of a mill for grinding flour or used to operate another wheel which would raise water from the stream and send it into higher channels where it would be used for irrigation.

No one knows exactly when the first water wheels were developed, but their origins are found early in the history of man. Up to the eighteenth century, water and wind power, plus the power produced by animals and human muscles, were the only sources of power known to man. Subsequently, the steam engine, the gasoline engine, the hydroelectric generator —itself a form of water power—and the atomic reactor gave man enormously improved sources of energy for doing the world's work.

The Water Wheel. There are three main types of water wheel. Perhaps the simplest type is the undershot wheel, in which water moves against vanes on the bottom of a wheel inserted in a stream; since the only power moving against the wheel is the strength of the current itself, this type of water wheel is relatively inefficient. The most efficient type is the overshot wheel, in which water is channeled to the top of the wheel, strikes vanes on the wheel, and moves it in the reverse direction from the undershot wheel. This wheel makes more direct use of falling water itself, and was a relatively late development.

The third type, the breast wheel, operates when a stream of water strikes the wheel on the upstream side, about two-thirds of the way up, and makes it rotate in the same direction as the undershot wheel.

Water wheels and hydroelectric turbines alike depend upon the force exerted by water falling through a given distance—called the head—in performing work. Every cubic foot of water can exert a force of over sixty pounds when it strikes a water wheel. The higher the head, the greater the force exerted by the water.

Power for Factories. The first factories in the United States were built along rivers so that water power might be used to drive machinery. Even before the advent of the steam engine and electricity, this kind of water power was an important source of industrial power. When Eli Whitney was inventing the cotton gin, a single water wheel could provide most of the power for the factories in which Whitney developed the principles of mass production. The textile factories and metal-working factories of New England, which developed along the many rivers of that area, had batteries of tools connected to their water wheels. A belt or gearing carried the power from the water wheel to a shaft which revolved continuously. Belts from this shaft ran out to the individual loom and lathe. The machines were started or stopped by slipping the belt on or off the drums connected to the machines. The drive shaft could also be disconnected for a general shut-down, but the water wheel itself ran continuously. Water wheels also provided the power to run sawmills, sugar mills, grist mills, and nearly all the factories well into the nineteenth century.

In their day, considerable ingenuity was applied to the design of the wheels to get the maximum return on the potential power, and in devising channels and chutes for controlling the flow of water. However, after the coming of the steam engine, steam rapidly supplanted water wheels as the motive power for factories.

Turbine Power. The old water wheel was, in a sense, a forerunner of the modern turbine, which also uses the power of falling water, mathematically expressed in the weight of the water times the height from which it falls to provide power. This power, however, is produced in the form of electricity. Unlike the water wheel, which revolved vertically, the modern turbine revolves horizontally. It stems from the year 1827, when a 25-year-old Frenchman named Benoit Fourneyron (1802–67) won a prize in the design of a water wheel which received the water internally, instead of being acted upon externally. From that time, the turbine for the production of hydroelectric power has been steadily improved, notably by Uriah A. Boyden (1804–79), and by James B. Francis (1815–92).

Water Power Resources, Actual and Potential. It is estimated that the United States has developed about 10 per cent of its total water power resources. Not all of these resources can be developed, however, because of engineering or cost difficulties. In an ordinary year, about 35 per cent of the total electricity sold to the public in the United States is produced from water power, and 30 per cent of electric generating installations use water power.

It is estimated that about 54 million kilowatts of generating capacity could be derived from water power in the United States. This involves using the somewhat under 50 per cent of our total water power potential which is capable of development from an economic and engineering standpoint. If all installations were built that could be built practically, the production of hydroelectric power in the United States would increase six times or more.

In the northeastern United States, utilizing what water power could practically be harnessed, these hydroelectric installations would produce only about 30 per cent of the total electric power consumed in the area. All feasible water power sites east of the Rocky Mountains would provide only 60 per cent of the electricity generated in this area in 1950.

Potential water power resources in the United States are greatest in the Far West, and 60 per cent of the practical potential water power resources lie in the 11 states of the Pacific Coast and the Rocky Mountains. The greatest potentialities lie in the Pacific Northwest, where 40 per cent of our total national practical water power resources are found.

In most areas, full development of water power resources would require a co-ordination of water power requirements with those of water supply, irrigation, and flood prevention. Typical of such co-ordinated use of water power is the Tennessee Valley Authority, whose work, in addition to building dams which will produce an eventual capacity of 2.85 million kilowatts of electricity, also provides a navigation channel for shipping from the Ohio River to Knoxville, Tenn., a plan for reducing flood waters at Cairo, Ill., by three feet, and an area-wide program of erosion control, reforestation, and rural electrification. See TENNESSEE VALLEY AUTHORITY.

The 11 proposed dams of the Columbia River system, of which 3 have been built, will provide a capacity of over 3 million kilowatts. In addition, the dams will provide irrigation for several million acres of farm land. The Columbia River will also provide navigation for oceangoing boats almost 200 miles inland. Other extensive sources of water power that had still to be adequately developed in the early 1960's were those in the Central Valley of California, in the St. Lawrence River, the Missouri Valley, and the Colorado Valley.

The over-all value of water power steadily increased in the twentieth century, although the relative importance of water power was not appreciably altered. However, water power is an important force for social development, particularly in view of the fact that the water power future of the United States lies in the Far West, where large deposits of coal are not available for the production of electricity. For 1929, the index of water power in the United States has been estimated at 74. In 1940, the index had risen to 100, and during the peak of wartime consumption it reached 153.

The main advantages of water power stem from the fact that it is not a destroyer of natural resources, as the production of power from the burning of coal or oil has been shown to be. The chief disadvantage of water as a source of power is that there is not enough water. See CONSERVATION, *Care of Individual Resources;* DAM; HYDRAULIC MACHINERY; HYDROELECTRIC POWER; HYDROKINETICS; HYDROSTATICS; NATURAL RESOURCES; POWER, *Water Power;* POWER PLANT; RESERVOIR.

WATERPROOFING, any method or material used to render an otherwise pervious material relatively impervious to water, or to protect any surface from the effects of contact with moisture.

WATERPROOFING IN CONSTRUCTION

Waterproofing is used in new and old construction to prevent penetration of water into or through walls, floors, roofs, ceilings, foundations, and other construction components. There are four types of waterproofing in general use in construction: integral waterproofing, surface coating, waterproofing with adhesive membranes, and independent sheathing.

Integral Waterproofing is sometimes used in the manufacture of concrete, plaster, mortar, and other self-hardening products. Its purpose is to fill the pores of the finished material with an active, inert or water-repellent substance. Integral compounds are of little

Textile fabrics are waterproofed by applying the waterproofing material, usually a compound of rubber, to one side, both sides, or through the fabric's warp and woof.
HERCULES POWDER CO.

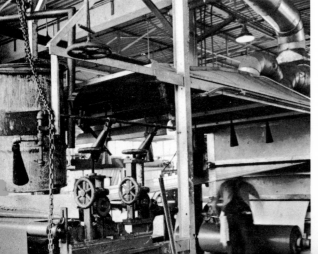

use, however, in preventing leakage through cracks which may develop after the surface has hardened.

Surface Coatings are liquid applications of a waterproofing material which may be applied by pouring, dipping, brushing, spraying, or troweling. The object is to form a continuous adhesive or penetrating coat or film that will prevent the passage of water from either direction. The surface coating is usually applied to the side most likely to be subject to contact with water. Paints, oils, varnishes, shellac, gums, rubber, wax, tars, asphalts, and resins are excellent examples of surface coatings used for waterproofing. The success of any surface coating depends upon the continuity of the waterproofing layer.

Adhesive Membranes consist of a continuous or overlapping layer of paper, fabric, or composition material cemented in sheet form to the surface to be waterproofed, with additional waterproofing usually applied to the outer surface of the fabric. Often several alternate layers of waterproof cement and paper or fabric are used to obtain strength and added protection.

Independent Sheath or Shell. An independent, watertight shell of some durable material such as copper, lead, or stainless steel is often used in important underground construction and in other places where absolute watertightness is a prime essential. In such work, all joints and corners are soldered, crimped, or welded to insure a complete seal.

WATERPROOFING OF TEXTILES

In the waterproofing of fabrics, one usual requirement is that the material, after waterproofing, be easily flexible. Application of waterproofing material to fabrics may result in the complete penetration of the interstices of the fabric; in the formation of a waterproof surface layer, as in oilcloth; or in adhesion to the threads of a tightly knit fabric of water-repellent particles sprayed into place. Various compounds of natural or synthetic rubber are the materials most commonly used.

OTHER WATERPROOFING

In machine and metalwork, various waterproofing methods, which are more properly anticorrosion treatments, are employed primarily to prevent contact with moisture present in the atmosphere. These methods include oiling, painting, galvanizing, nickel, chromium, and copperplating.

During World War II methods were developed to permit operation of motor-driven vehicles under water for short periods by sealing vital parts with a temporary adhesive membrane of plastic, waterproof material which could be removed when the vehicle reached dry land again. Also, the U.S. Navy developed a method of "mothballing" inactive ships by covering all important surfaces including guns, engines, instruments and machinery with a plastic film from within which most of the air had been exhausted.

WATER SKIING, a sports activity in which one rides over water on one or two skis. A rope secured to a boat and held by the skier tows him across the water. Water skis are at least 4 feet long and from 4 to 8 inches wide. The boat towing the skier travels at a speed of about 30 to 35 miles per hour.

Competitive water skiing is divided into three events: slalom, jumping, and tricks. In slalom competition, the skier is required to follow a course marked with buoys without riding over or straddling the obstacles. Each contestant of the jumping event is judged by the distance and form of his jump from a ramp 20 to 22 feet long, approximately 6 feet wide, and from 5 to 6 feet high. The jumper ascends the ramp while being towed, and uses the forward motion gained from the towing to propel himself through the jump. No standard form of skiing is required for the trick skiing event; contestants are judged on their form and the types of tricks they

WATER—
TREASURE WE IGNORE

A DROP OF DEW, runoff rivulets from supersaturated moss, and the billowing sea are all links in the hydrologic cycle. This is the constant movement of water from ocean back to ocean by means of evaporation, condensation, rain, and runoff—a circular process that washes and nourishes all life on earth. A man's weight is 70 per cent water. A blade of grass is 90 to 95 per cent water. Water covers three fourths of the earth, as river, lake, swamp, sea, icecap. The Bible tells us we are survivors of a flood. Today's scientists concur that all life began in the oceans and that, though certain creatures have succeeded in living out of water, none we know has or will succeed in living without it.

VAN BUCHER, PHOTO RESEARCHERS

JAVA can feed its enormous population because its hot, humid weather and rich, volcanic soil are ideal for the growing of rice. Low-lying clouds keep the warm moisture near to the ground, and rainfall throughout the year is very heavy. This unusual climate permits several rice crops per year. The workers who are transplanting seedlings in the paddy in the foreground are surrounded by rice fields at several different stages of cultivation.

A BUCKET OF WATER from this Tunisian well is not so heavy as to need a camel to draw it; rather, the well is so deep the man would tire himself out cranking the bucket up.

LIKE THE PREHISTORIC Swiss lake dwellers, some Filipinos live in bamboo houses on stilts. These are safe from floods and from falling trees in storms, and stand directly over food and transportation.

HARRISON FORMAN

COLD WATER IN CANALS fixes the colors in printed silk fabrics, a very old manufacture of Japan.

KATO, FPG

MUCH OF THE SALT WE EAT is obtained by letting sea water evaporate and gathering the residue. These salt flats are in southern Spain.

NED HAINES, RAPHO-GUILLUMETTE

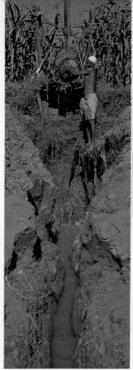

SAHARA FARMERS buy water and channel it in ditches from a dam to their crops. It is measured out through a water comb.

A WATER WHEEL, common throughout North Africa, is a continuous device for drawing water from a well and emptying it into a trough.

A NILE FARMER lifts water from ditches to crops by a counterweighted sweep.

MAN AND WATER IN NATURE

FOR THOSE OF US whose concerns over water extend no further than to the kitchen tap or the shower stall, it is hard to imagine that people on every continent are coping right now with water as nature provides it where they are—too much or too little of it, muddy, salty, stagnant, turbulent, or frozen. In many areas of Asia, the Middle East, Africa, and Latin America, economic and social progress is slowed by antiquated ways of using water and by widespread disease resulting from water pollution.

IN DRY, DUSTY TIMBUKTU (Mali) vendors sell gourds of water from a tied-shut pigskin.

WATER IS PLENTIFUL in Indonesia, but safe drinking water is not. Villagers must go to a community spring for water to cook with. While they're there, they do what washing is needed.

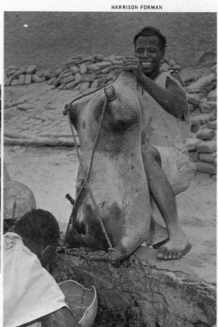

IRRIGATION, the miracle-worker in making arid land green, can be expensive of water. In the sun, the shallow irrigation channels lose great quantities of water by evaporation.

MODERN WATER TECHNOLOGY

IN MANY PARTS OF THE WORLD, man's basic water needs are met better than ever before. Regular disasters of the sort that gave the name China's Sorrow to the Yellow River are avoided where government sponsorship has allowed the building of vast flood control and conservation projects. But the developing technology that makes this possible has created new problems. Each year huge amounts of industrial wastes are dumped into the world's waters. Each year more people waste more water. The future of water in the balance of nature is of grave concern; it and the future of man are inextricably linked.

ONE IRONICAL RESULT of making water easy to get is that it is often thoughtlessly wasted.

BEFORE THE TVA TAMED IT, the Tennessee River system periodically ravaged seven states.

IN INDIA, the Damodar Valley development project includes eight large-scale dams to provide flood control, power, and irrigation.

F.S.N.B.

Water skiing became popular as a competitive sport in the United States during the late 1940's; by 1953 there were water skiing clubs in almost every state in the Union.

F.S.N.B

Water skiing, an exciting and popular warm-weather sport, requires the participants to have unusual agility and coordination; many water skiers are very good snow skiers.

perform. The first recorded U.S. water skiing competition was held, 1936, at Massapequa, N.Y. The American Water Ski Association was organized and held its first annual national tournament in 1939.

WATER SNAKE, a semiaquatic, nonpoisonous snake found in both the Eastern and Western hemispheres. Ten species have been identified in North America, the majority of them east of the Mississippi. The common water snake, *Natrix sipedon*, is found from Canada to North Carolina and westward to Kansas. It is pale reddish brown above, banded with dark brown stripes, the lower parts being yellow or white blotched with red. It measures about three feet in length and one and a half inches in diameter. Water snakes frequent the borders of rivers, streams, and ponds, or make their homes in swamps, taking to water for protection if disturbed. Their food consists of frogs, toads, and fish. Though vicious when attacked, they are quite harmless.

U.S. FISH AND WILDLIFE SERVICE

The water snake, a nonpoisonous reptile common to regions of North America east of the Mississippi River, usually is harmless, but can react viciously when it is attacked.

WATER SOFTENING. See HARD WATER, *Water Softening;* ION EXCHANGE.

WATER SPANIEL, a sporting water dog used in retrieving game birds and represented by two breeds, the Irish water spaniel and the American water spaniel. The Irish water spaniel developed from an ancient stock of water dogs in the southern regions of Ireland. The dog is the tallest representative of the spaniels and is noted for its exceptional loyalty to its owner. It has a topknot of hair on its head and a curled growth of hair between its eyes, giving it a unique appearance. Its coat sheds water naturally, thus making the dog highly sought for as a water game retriever. A category in competitive dog breeding was first provided for this variety in 1859.

The origin of the American water spaniel appears to be a mystery. It is thought that it may have derived from the Irish water spaniel and a variety of a group of retrievers. The dog is highly regarded by hunters because of its ability to swim and its keen sense of smell.

FRASIE STUDIO

The Irish Water Spaniel, which is renowned for its ability as a hunting dog, has a curly-haired, almost waterproof coat, which helps it to retrieve game from water easily.

WATERSPOUT, a small, whirling funnel-shaped cloud that appears over oceans or inland waters, and extends from the surface of the water to the base of an overhead cloud. Waterspouts occur in tropical waters generally, and their rotation is usually counterclockwise, as in a cyclone.

Waterspouts may precede a squall, in which case the vortex is formed in the clouds by the action of air currents flowing in opposite directions. They may also originate just above the surface of the water in strongly convective air currents, building upward, similar to whirlpools of dust and sand seen above deserts. Waterspouts vary in height from a few hundred to several thousand feet, and are rarely destructive.

WATER SUPPLY, the treatment and delivery of water from its natural location to the point of its consumption. Water is one of the important elements upon which man depends for his continued existence and progress. The first and most vital problem encountered by the builders of cities, and by those who located and developed industries, was that of obtaining an adequate and an unfailing supply of fresh water.

Water Consumption. Rates of water consumption are influenced by various factors, such as size of the community; amount of industry in the area; standards of living; pressure on the system; the cost of water to the ultimate consumer; and the extent of the use of metering. The rate of water consumption is greatly affected by climate. Cities located in areas having extreme variations in temperature and precipitation will show a higher per capita rate than cities located in areas where the temperature and precipitation are more uniform. The per capita rate of consumption in the United States is in general higher than that in other countries.

Source of Supply. Evaporation from the surfaces of all bodies of water takes place continuously. The water rises in the form of vapor until it reaches such a height and such a temperature that it is condensed into cloud formations. At this point it is distilled water, practically free from all solids and chemicals. From the clouds the vapor is returned to earth as rain. The rain eventually finds its way into rivers or lakes, percolates into the ground, soaks into vegetation, or evaporates. The part that flows into rivers and lakes, or percolates into the soil, can be made available for water supplies. Water supplies are designated as surface supplies when taken from rivers or lakes, and ground water supplies when taken from underground facilities, such as wells or springs.

Water Supply Systems. A water supply system is made up of the structures, equipment and appurtenances required for collecting, treating, and distributing water. Works for the collection of water include wells, galleries, intakes in rivers and lakes, impounding reservoirs, and aqueducts or pipelines. Works for the treatment of water include settling basins, filtration plants, softening plants, aerators, ozone, and chlorinating equipment. Works for the distribution of water include pumping stations, underground pipelines, and distributing or equalizing reservoirs.

Water Treatment. A satisfactory public water supply does not contain organisms that cause disease, such as typhoid, cholera or amebic dysentery; must be free from objectionable tastes, odors, gases, and minerals; and must be clear and colorless and reasonably soft. Because of the solvent power of water and the distribution of finely divided soluble matter in the atmosphere, on the earth's surface, and in the ground, pure water is seldom, if ever, found in nature. Surface water is generally contaminated and therefore unsafe and unsatisfactory for consumption, unless treated in some manner. Underground waters passing through the soil and the underlying rock formation may dissolve compounds causing the water to be highly mineralized and hard. Calcium and magnesium compounds are objectionable in that they cause hardness; iron and manganese because they stain everything with which they come in contact; hydrogen sulfide by reason of its disagreeable taste and odor. In general, it is possible through various treatment processes to change the quality of natural waters and make them safe and satisfactory for public use.

Purification by Storage. Purification by prolonged storage and settlement requires the retention of the water in a basin for such a period that the suspended solids may settle. This treatment is satisfactory as a purification process only for relatively pure waters containing large quantities of suspended solids.

Rapid Sand Filtration. In a rapid sand filtration plant certain chemicals, called coagulants, are added to incoming raw water. The coagulants generally used are ferrous sulfate, ferric chloride, ferric sulfate, aluminum sulfate, sodium aluminate, and lime. These compounds do not, of course, remain in the water, but are precipitated and removed by settling of filtration. The addition of the coagulant to the water, followed by mixing or agitation, results in the formation of a precipitate that entangles the mud, bacteria, and suspended matter into clumps readily removed by settling. After thorough mixing, the water passes into settling basins where it passes along at a slow rate. The solids settle out in the form of sludge. This sludge is periodically removed without interrupting the operation of the plant. From the settling basin, the clarified water passes on to the filter beds.

The filter is a basin with a strainer system in the bottom, containing 18 to 24 inches of graded gravel and, above this, 24 to 30 inches of filter sand. The coagulated and settled water filters down through sand and gravel and passes on to a filtered water reservoir, and from here on to the ultimate consumer. When the rate of flow through the filter becomes less, due to the sand being clogged, the sand is washed by forcing filtered water upward from the strainer system. The sand is lifted and agitated in the rising stream of clean water and the finely divided and suspended matter at the surface is carried away in wash water troughs and wasted to the sewer. This filter washing operation requires only a short period; the filter is then ready for service again.

Sterilization with Chlorine. Water that has been treated efficiently in a rapid sand filtration plant should be practically free of harmful bacteria. Complete removal of pathogenic bacteria is most frequently assured by the application of chlorine to the incoming raw water and also to the filter effluent. Chlorination does not take the place of filtration, since it removes no foreign matter from the water and does not improve the physical characteristics of the water.

Aeration. Aeration is sometimes used as a purification process, either separately or preliminary to filtration. In connection with surface supplies aeration may be used to remove offensive tastes and odors due to dissolved gases. In connection with ground water supplies aeration reduces the carbon dioxide content, eliminates hydrogen sulfide, and oxidizes the iron. The oxidized iron precipitates as an insoluble compound which can be filtered. Aeration is accomplished by allowing the water to flow over cascades or steps, by spraying from nozzles, or by trickling through trays filled with coke.

By rigid control of watersheds and sources of supply and efficient scientific treatment of water supplies, the toll of water-borne diseases in U.S. and Canadian municipalities has been reduced to an extremely low figure. See HARD WATER; ION EXCHANGE.

BIBLIOG.—Edward A. Ackerman and Others, *Technology in American Water Development* (1959); American Society for Testing Materials, *Manual on Industrial Water and Industrial Waste Water* (1960); Edwin P. Anderson, *Audels Domestic Water Supply and Sewage Disposal Guide* (1960); Harold E. Babbitt and James J. Doland, *Water Supply Engineering* (1955); Nelson M. Blake, *Water for the Cities: A History of the Urban Water Supply Problem in the United States* (1956); John Bowman, *Water Supply To-day* (Pageant of Progress Ser., no. 20) (1950); Arthur H. Carhart, *Water—Or Your Life* (1951); Dudley T. Dougherty, *Water Problem, a Solution* (1957); Gordon M. Fair and John C. Geyer, *Elements of Water Supply and Waste-water Disposal* (1958); Cyril S. Fox, *Geology of Water Supply* (1953); William A. Hardenbergh and Edward R. Rodie, *Water Supply and Waste Disposal* (1961); Jack Hirshleifer and Others, *Water Supply: Economics, Technology and Policy* (1960); Charles P. Hoover, *Water Supply and Treatment* (1957); Walter B. Langbein and William G. Hoyt, *Water Facts for the Nation's Future* (1959); Daniel W. Mead, *Hydrology* (1950); Ben Moreell, *Our Nation's Water Resources, Policies and Politics* (1956); Elmer T. Peterson, *Big Dam Foolishness: The Problem of Modern Flood Control and Water Storage* (1954); Kenneth L. Roberts, *Water Unlimited* (1957); Michael H. Salzman, *New Water for a Thirsty World* (1960); Yang-ch'Eng Shih, *American Water Resources Administration*, 2 vols. (1956); Ernest W. Steel, *Water Supply and Sewerage* (1960); Robert J. Sweitzer, *Basic Water Works Manual* (1958); John C. Thresh and Others, *Examination of Waters and Water Supplies* (1958); Thomas H. P. Veal, *Supply of Water* (1953); Chester O. Wisler and Ernest F. Brater, *Hydrology* (1959); John C. Wooley and R. P. Beasley, *Farm Water Management* (1950); Forrest B. Wright, *Rural Water Supply and Sanitation* (1956).

WATERTON, CHARLES, 1782–1865, English naturalist, was born near Wakefield, Yorkshire. His travels took him to Spain, Rome, the United States, and the West Indies; he made a number of visits to British Guiana, where his exploits included riding an alligator, 1920. Waterton developed **a** method for preserving his animal specimens without the use of internal stuffing. He wrote a number of essays and an account of his travels, *Wanderings* (1825).

WATERTON LAKES NATIONAL PARK, W Canada, in SW Alberta Province; at the U.S.

CANADIAN CONSULATE GENERAL, CHICAGO

Beautiful Cameron Lake is characteristic of the spectacular and rugged mountain and wilderness scenery of the Waterton Lakes National Park in Alberta, Canada.

boundary, adjoining Glacier National Park in Montana, with which it forms the Glacier-Waterton Lakes International Peace Park, created in 1932 by joint action of the Canadian and United States governments. Set aside in 1895, Waterton Lakes National Park has spectacular mountain scenery. The outstanding feature is Upper Waterton Lake, which lies in a deep trench between two high mountain ranges and is crossed by the international boundary line. The region was explored late in the 1850's by Lt. Thomas Blakeston, and it is believed that he named the lakes in honor of Charles Waterton, an English naturalist. The park offers excellent fishing, golf, trails, motor drives, and tourist accommodations.

WATERTOWN, town, W central Connecticut, Litchfield County; on the New Haven Railroad and U.S. highway 6; 5 miles NW of Waterbury. The city is an industrial center in which silk and rayon goods, agricultural machinery, and hardware are manufactured. Watertown was settled in 1677 and was separated from Waterbury and incorporated in 1780. John Trumbull, the lawyer and poet, was born there, 1750. Pop. (1960) 14,837.

WATERTOWN, town, E Massachusetts, Middlesex County; at the head of tidewater on the Charles River; on the Boston and Maine Railroad and U.S. highway 20; a residential suburb, six miles W of Boston. Textiles, clothing, electrical equipment, and many small consumer goods are manufactured. Watertown was founded in 1630. In 1775 the Provincial Congress met in the First Parish Church in Watertown. Watertown has a number of well preserved old houses. A U.S. Arsenal was established there in 1816. Pop. (1960) 39,092.

WATERTOWN, city, N New York, seat of Jefferson County; on the Black River, the New York Central Railroad, and U.S. highway 11; 64 miles N of Syracuse and 10 miles E of Lake Ontario. The city is a trade and processing center for a dairying region. Machinery, tools, plumbing equipment, boats, and clothing are manufactured. Watertown is a summer resort center for the Thousand Islands State Park. It was settled in 1800 by New England pioneers and was incorporated as a city in 1869. A papermaking industry, which reached its peak in the 1890's, was established, utilizing power from the Black River Falls. Pop. (1960) 33,306.

WATERTOWN, city, NE South Dakota, seat of Codington County; on the Big Sioux River near Lake Kampeska; on the North Western, the Great Northern, and the Minneapolis and St. Louis railroads, and U.S. highways 81 and 212; 95 miles NNW of Sioux Falls. Watertown is a trade and processing center for an area in which wheat and livestock are raised. The

city has grain elevators, flour mills, machine shops, and meat-packing plants. Watertown was founded in 1878 on a treeless prairie at the terminus of the railroad and was named for Watertown, N.Y., the home of some of the early settlers. Pop. (1960) 16,077.

WATERTOWN, city, SE Wisconsin, in Dodge and Jefferson counties; on the Rock River, the North Western and the Milwaukee railroads, and U.S. highway 16; 42 miles WNW of Milwaukee. Watertown is a trade and industrial center for a region in which corn, dairy cattle, and poultry are raised. The city has a market for geese, which are a specialty of the area. Apiary supplies, cutlery, rubber goods, furnaces and boiler equipment, tools, and electrical equipment are manufactured. Watertown was founded in 1836 by New Englanders. These settlers were joined in 1848 by German political refugees among whom was Carl Schurz, a journalist and reformer, whose wife established one of the first kindergartens in the United States there in 1856. Watertown is the seat of Northwestern College (1865). Pop. (1960) 13,943.

WATER-TUBE BOILER. See BOILER, *Water-Tube Boilers.*

WATER VALLEY, city, N Mississippi, one of the two seats of Yalobusha County; on the Illinois Central Railroad; 130 miles NNE of Jackson. The city is a trade center for an area in which cotton, watermelons and livestock are raised; clothing is manufactured. Water Valley was incorporated in 1858. Pop. (1960) 3,206.

WATERVILLE, city, S Maine, Kennebec County; on the Kennebec River, the Maine Central Railroad, and U.S. highway 201; 19 miles NNE of Augusta. The city is located at the site of Ticonic Falls, which are harnessed for hydroelectric power. Waterville is a trade and processing center for an area of dairy and truck farms. The city has pulp and paper mills, and textiles are manufactured. Colby College was founded there in 1813 as Waterville College. The Redington Museum has a number of pioneer and historical relics. Waterville was settled in 1754 as part of the adjacent settlement of Winslow. It was incorporated as a separate town in 1802. Pop. (1960) 18,695.

WATERVILLE, town, central Washington, seat of Douglas County; on U.S. highway 2; 105 miles E of Seattle. The city is a trade center for an agricultural area in the Columbia Basin, in which grain and livestock are raised. Waterville was founded in 1886. Pop. (1960) 1,013.

WATERVLIET, city, E New York, in Albany County; on the Hudson River, the Delaware and Hudson Railroad, and U.S. highway 4; opposite Troy and 5 miles NNE of Albany. Watervliet is an industrial center in which steel castings, abrasives, construction materials, furniture, and textiles are manufactured. Watervliet comes from a Dutch word meaning flowing stream. The city was incorporated in 1896. Ann Lee founded the first colony of the Shaker Society, a religious sect, there in 1776. The city is the site of an arsenal, which was established in 1813. Pop. (1960) 13,917.

WATERWAYS, INLAND, rivers, lakes, and canals, which are used for the transporting of goods and people. Rivers such as the Nile, Rhine, Danube, Volga, Amazon, Mississippi, and Yangtze have long histories as arteries of traffic. Other rivers, while not navigable, have been important economically for the floating of timber. At first the use of rivers and lakes was a simple regional matter with crude canals being built around natural obstructions. It was not until technological advances were made during the eighteenth and nineteenth centuries that canals were built to extend, and join, river systems. During this time, complex patterns of inland waterways were developed in Europe, and water-borne traffic became the major means of transporting cargo. During the twentieth century the waterways have declined in relative importance as a result of the introduction of the gasoline engine and the growth of railway and

INLAND WATERWAYS

St. Louis is a focal point for Mississippi barge traffic.

Ocean-going freighters connect with Great Lakes ports through the St. Lawrence Seaway. A London trade ship, above, leaves the Eisenhower Lock near Massena, N. Y.

The Intracoastal Canal is a boon to Texas' Gulf shipping.

The Mississippi River has enabled New Orleans, La., to become a major inland port for shallow-draft shipping.

A tug pushes cargo on the Mohawk River, New York State, which is part of the state barge canal that, with the Hudson River, connects the Great Lakes with the Atlantic.

highway systems. Waterways, however, still form an important means of transportation.

Economics of Waterways. The major inland waterways have developed where rivers and lakes flow in the same direction as trade. Water carriers can transport bulky commodities at a lower cost per unit ton than any other conveyance, where time is not a factor. As a result the main products moved by water are nonperishable, bulky goods, such as iron ore, coal, lumber, and grain.

Distribution. Inland waterways are most conspicuous in the European landscape. France, northern Germany, and England in particular have highly developed waterway systems. In Africa the Congo River is the only major waterway, as the fall line is too close to the coast for full utilization of the other rivers. In Asia many of the long navigable rivers flow into the Arctic Ocean, away from the trade routes, and are therefore of limited use. Rivers flowing south and east, such as the Yellow and the Yangtze, have long been used for transportation. In South America there are two outstanding inland waterways. The Amazon River system forms virtually the only means of transportation for a vast area in the north, and the Paraná-Paraguay system is the major outlet for products from the inland country of Paraguay. The Murray River in Australia is the only waterway of importance, and canals have not been developed. In North America the two outstanding waterways are the Mississippi System and the St. Lawrence Seaway.

The Development of Inland Waterways in North America. In North America rivers were channels of colonization. From 1600 to 1700 river craft and canoes moved upstream as far as the fall line. A canal-building period, inaugurated about 1776, lasted through 1850. One of the first lock-operated canals was built by the Potomac Company around the falls at Harpers Ferry in the 1780's. Traffic on the Mississippi River was heavy at this time with cargoes of raw materials moving south to the port of New Orleans. The Erie Canal, built between 1817 and 1825, from Albany to Buffalo, united the agricultural Midwest with its logical market, the industrial East. By 1829 the steamboat era on the Mississippi had begun, and from that time until the Civil War inland waterways were most important. About 1850 the railroads began to take over some of the traffic, and their effect was felt everywhere except the lower Mississippi.

The present movement has reversed the historical trend on the Mississippi System, where most of the water-borne trade consists of movement of raw materials upstream to the industrial centers. The New York Barge Canal continues to carry goods into New York City even though the railroad parallels its course, and the Ohio River continues to be the main artery within the Pittsburgh district, carrying coal, iron, gasoline, and gravel. On the Great Lakes bulk freighters have been constructed to handle the cargoes, and many are self-loading and interchangeable carriers. Special steel barges carry such commodities as ore, grain, coke, pulp, lumber, sand, and gravel. The development of the St. Lawrence Seaway has enabled ocean ships to utilize the Great Lakes. After about 1930, there was a rebirth of the amount of traffic carried on inland waterways in North America. The opening of the St. Lawrence Seaway in 1959 was an important aspect of this new development. In addition there has been improvement on the Atlantic Intracoastal Waterway, which is a sheltered passage from Cape Cod to the tip of Florida, and the Gulf Intracoastal Waterway from Carrabelle, Fla., to Brownsville, Tex. The Illinois Waterway connects the Great Lakes ports with the Mississippi and Gulf of Mexico.

WATFORD, municipal borough, SE England, in Hertfordshire; on the River Gade; a residential suburb, 18 miles NW of London. Paper, paint, and food products are manufactured. The borough has the churches of St. Mary, which is Early English style, and St. James, which contains examples of Early English sculpture. Pop. (1961) 75,700.

WATFORD CITY, village, W North Dakota, seat of McKenzie County; on the Great Northern Railroad and U.S. highway 85; 115 miles WNW of Bismarck. The city is a trade center for an area of coal mines and wheat and livestock farmers. Watford City was incorporated in 1934. Pop. (1960) 1,865.

WATKINS GLEN, village, W central New York, seat of Schuyler County; in the Finger Lakes region, at the S end of Seneca Lake; on the Erie, the New York Central, and the Pennsylvania railroads; 64 miles SSE of Rochester. Watkins Glen is a popular tourist resort, and has an important salt-producing industry. Watkins Glen State Park, adjacent to the village, is a narrow gorge through which a stream falls about 700 feet in a series of cascades in a distance of two miles. The site was settled in 1788 and was called Salubria after the mineral springs found there. The settlement was incorporated as Jefferson in 1842, and renamed Watkins Glen in 1852. Pop. (1960) 2,813.

WATKINSVILLE, town, NE Georgia, seat of Oconee County; on the Central of Georgia Railroad and U.S. highways 129 and 441; 55 miles E of Atlanta. The city is a trade center for an area in which cotton, wheat, and corn are grown. Pop. (1960) 758.

WATLING STREET, an ancient Roman highway in Great Britain. It began in Dover, passed through Canterbury and Rochester to London; from there it extended by way of St. Albans and Wroxeter to Chester, where it connected with roads to northern Britain. A branch of Watling Street ran southward from Chester to Caerleon, near the mouth of the Severn River. Traces of the road are still to be found along many parts of its course, and in some sectors it is still an important highway. A street in London retains its name, which probably is derived from the name of an ancient tribe.

WATONGA, city, W central Oklahoma, seat of Blaine County; on the Rock Island Railroad and U.S. highways 270 and 281; 55 miles WNW of Oklahoma City. The city is a cotton ginning and milling center. Watonga was settled in 1892. Pop. (1960) 3,252.

WATROUS, HARRY WILSON, 1857–1940, U.S. genre painter, was born in San Francisco. He studied art at the Atelier Bonnât and the Académie Julian in Paris. In the period 1894–1935 his works, characterized by careful attention to details in small figures, won many important prizes in U.S. exhibitions. Among his canvases are *Passing of Summer*, in the Metropolitan Museum, New York City; *A Study in Black*, in the St. Louis Museum; *The Drop Sinister; Who Cares;* and *The Line of Love.*

WATSEKA, city, E Illinois, seat of Iroquois County; on the Iroquois River, the Chicago and Eastern Illinois and the Toledo, Peoria and Western railroads, and U.S. highway 24; 73 miles S of Chicago. The city is a trade center for an area in which corn, wheat, and livestock are raised. Dairy products, batteries, and soft drinks are manufactured. Watseka was incorporated in 1867. Pop. (1960) 5,219.

WATSON, JOHN, pseudonym Ian Maclaren, 1850–1907, Scottish author and clergyman, was born in Manningtree, Essex, England. He was graduated from Edinburgh University, 1870, studied for the ministry at New College, Edinburgh, and Tübingen University in Germany, and became a Free Church minister in 1874. He held several posts at churches in Scotland and was assigned, 1880, to a Presbyterian church in Liverpool. There his eloquence as a preacher brought him widespread fame. He built a church and was one of the founders of Liverpool University. During the first of three lecture tours in the United States, he gave the Lyman Beecher lectures at Yale University, 1896. The public response to his lectures was enthusiastic; Watson returned to the United States in 1899 and in 1907. On the last tour he died at Mount

Pleasant, Iowa. His *Beside the Bonnie Brier Bush* (1894) is a series of brief character sketches depicting the humorous and pathetic aspects of life in the little village of Drumtochty. Other works in the same vein are *Days of Auld Lang Syne* (1895) and *Kate Carnegie* (1897). His Yale lectures were published as *The Cure of Souls* (1896).

WATSON, JOHN BROADUS, 1878–1958, U.S. behaviorist psychologist, was born in Greenville, S.C. He was graduated from Furman University, Greenville, 1900, and the University of Chicago, 1903, and was a member of the experimental psychology staff of the latter institution, 1903–08. In 1908 he was appointed professor of experimental and comparative psychology and director of the psychology laboratory at Johns Hopkins University, where he taught until 1920, when he entered the advertising business. Watson was the founder, in 1913, of the school of psychology known as behaviorism, and was the author of: *Animal Education* (1903), *Behavior* (1914), *Suggestions of Modern Science Concerning Education* (1917), *Psychology from the Standpoint of a Behaviorist* (1919), *Behaviorism* (1925), *Ways of Behaviorism* (1928), and *Psychological Care of Infant and Child* (1928). He was editor of the *Psychological Review* (1908–15), and of the *Journal of Experimental Psychology* (1915–27).

WATSON, JOHN SELBY, 1804–84, English author and murderer, studied at Trinity College, Dublin, and served as curate in Somerset, 1839–41, and schoolmaster in Stockwell, a suburb of London, 1844–70. He edited a number of classical texts and translations and compiled a biography of the English scholar Richard Porson (1759–1808). Watson's scholarly career was cut short when he murdered his wife and was condemned to prison for life, 1871.

WATSON, MARK SKINNER, 1887– , U.S. journalist, was born in Plattsburg, N.Y., and studied at Union College, Schenectady. He was a reporter and traveling correspondent for the Chicago *Tribune*, 1909–14, held editorial posts with the Baltimore *Sun*, 1920–41, and became a military correspondent at the beginning of World War II. He was awarded a Pulitzer prize for international correspondence, 1945, and received the U.S. Army Medal of Freedom, 1946.

WATSON, THOMAS, 1557?–92, English poet and musicologist, was born in London. Little is known of his life, but it is thought that he was a man of independent means and that literature and music were mere hobbies with him. It is known that he visited Paris, 1581, and there met the English statesman, Sir Francis Walsingham, who became his patron. Watson's pastoral and love poetry was written more often in Latin than in English. His Latin poetry was published in *Hecatompathia* (1582), his English verse in *The Tears of Fancie, or Love Disdained* (1593). He wrote a number of songs, compiled *The First Sette of Italian Madrigalls Englished* (1590), and translated Sophocles' *Antigone* from Greek to Latin.

WATSON, THOMAS EDWARD, 1856–1922, U.S. political leader and author, was born in Columbia County, Ga., and studied at Mercer University. He was admitted to the Georgia bar, 1875, and became a champion of the Southern agrarian movement. He was a Democratic member of the Georgia legislature, 1882–83, and a Populist leader in Congress, 1891–93, where he introduced the first legislation providing for rural free delivery of mail. He was the Populist vice-presidential candidate, 1896, the Populist presidential candidate, 1904 and 1908, and was elected to the U.S. Senate, 1920. Watson founded *Watson's* magazine (1905), *The Weekly Jeffersonian*, and *Watson's Jeffersonian* magazine (1906). Among his writings are *The Story of France* (1899), *The Roman Catholic Hierarchy* (1910), and biographies of Thomas Jefferson, Napoleon I, and Andrew Jackson.

WATSON, SIR WILLIAM, 1858–1935, English poet, was born in Burley-in-Wharfedale, Yorkshire, and reared in Liverpool. He published *The Prince's Quest*, his first long poem, 1880, and gained critical recognition for *Wordsworth's Grave* (1890). His verse is dignified rather than ardent, showing more the influence of Matthew Arnold than that of Alfred Lord Tennyson. He also wrote epigrams and political verse. He was knighted in 1917. Among his works are *Excursions in Criticism* (1893), *Lacrymae Musarum* (1893), *The Eloping Angels* (1893), and *The Purple East* (1896).

WATSON-GORDON, SIR JOHN, 1788–1864, Scottish portrait painter, was born in Edinburgh. He exhibited from 1826 at the Royal Institution, Edinburgh, became a member of the Royal Scottish Academy, 1829, exhibiting there from 1830; became president of the Scottish Academy, 1850, was elected to the Royal Academy, 1851, and was knighted in the same year. His portraits of *David Cox* (Birmingham Art Gallery), *Sir Walter Scott* (National Gallery of Scotland), *Sir David Brewster*, and *De Quincey* (National Portrait Gallery) are among his most characteristic.

WATSONVILLE, city, W central California, in Santa Cruz County; on the San Benito River and the Southern Pacific Railroad; 70 miles SSE of San Francisco and 5 miles E of Monterey Bay of the Pacific Ocean. Watsonville is a trade and processing center for a fruit-growing area. Vinegar, pectin, spray chemicals, boxes, and crates are manufactured. The city was founded in 1851 and was chartered in 1903. Pop. (1960) 13,293.

WATT, JAMES, 1736–1819, Scottish inventor, was born in Greenock. After a year apprenticed to an instrument maker in London, Watt became mathematical instrument maker to the University of Glasgow, 1757. He became interested in improving Thomas Newcomen's steam engine, and began experiments, ?1761; later, while repairing a model of the Newcomen engine for the university, he conceived the idea of separating the condenser from the cylinder, 1764. Watt's condensing engine was patented, 1769; the original patent was extended later by act of Parliament until 1800, and further improvements to increase efficiency were patented in 1781–84. Watt's engine was financed by Matthew Boulton and later by John Roebuck, and it rapidly replaced other engines. Watt retired from business in 1800, leaving his sons, James (1769–1848) and Gregory (died 1804) in charge.

WATT, SIR ROBERT ALEXANDER WATSON, 1892– , Scottish physicist, was born in Brechin, Scotland. He attended Dundee University College and worked in the Meteorological Office of the Department of Science and Industrial Research, 1915–36. He headed Bowdsey Research Station for the air ministry, 1936–38, and was primarily responsible for the development of radar in Great Britain. He was knighted for this work in 1942.

WATT, a unit of power equal to the consumption or conversion of one joule of work in one second. In the meter-kilogram-second system of units, the unit of power is the newton-meter per second and is equivalent to one watt. The watt is named in honor of James Watt, who invented the steam engine. In the practical system of electrical units, the watt is the unit of power and is equal to the rate at which energy is expended in an electrical circuit by a current of one ampere flowing under a potential difference of one volt. If P be the power in watts, I, the current in amperes, and V, the potential difference in volts, then $P = VI$. Useful conversions include the following: 1 horsepower $= 746$ watts; 1 watt $= 10^7$ ergs/sec $= 0.239$ calories/second $= 0.000948$ British Thermal Units/sec.

WATTEAU, ANTOINE, 1684–1721, French painter of Flemish extraction, was born Jean Antoine Watteau at Valenciennes, the son of a roof slater. He studied with Claude Gillot at Paris, 1702, and later with Claude Audran. Since he had quit the parental home without funds, his initial period in Paris was one of extreme hardship, and for a time he even worked in a "painting factory" where house painters were employed to do piecemeal work on pictures. Watteau came to be the quintessential painter of his age. Disdainful of the vast canvases of the previous decades, Watteau chose to paint small-scale pictures for intimate rooms and boudoirs. In the characteristic and well known *Embarkation for Cythera* (1717; now in the Louvre, Paris), for example, the exquisite figures are scarcely a foot high. His costumed figures scintillate in flashes of green, yellow, blue and lavender, in brilliant contrast to the somber browns of his predecessors.

Watteau glorified in his works a refined and aristocratic society whose members were primarily interested in cultivating their rococo pleasures. Love, both sensual and emotional, is expressed in the gestures, the postures, the whole atmosphere of his pictures. Lovers of all types disport in the midst of a perfectly groomed Nature, where the trees seem like examples of the hairdresser's art and the earth a downy couch: for Watteau, "Nature" was literally the Luxembourg Gardens. Perhaps inevitably, there is an over-all note of sadness in his works—of *tristesse*, or longing, which, once satisfied, simply becomes further longing. Even the colors of Watteau's paintings are erotic and play upon the nerve ends of the imagination, although the sentiments are more of the spirit than of the heart. The dominant mood is a graceful playfulness that seems bound to end in excruciating melancholy. Watteau's own name for this genre was *peinture de fêtes galantes*.

Watteau's famous portrait of *Gilles* (in the Louvre), the melancholy clown, is a literary commentary on the nature of sophisticated humor. On a more purely painterly level, however, his pictures are fine studies of texture: silk and satins, misty vistas through the woods, tapestry-like vegetation were all drawn with a fine line and painted with an exquisite brush. Above all, however, Watteau was a poet—there was no poet to compare with him in the literature of his time—and lyric poetry flowed from his brush. His stylized shepherds and shepherdesses, his *fêtes champêtres*, his rustic dances are all literature. And even fashion followed his lead, so that the style of a sacque with loose pleats hanging from the shoulders, derived from figures in his paintings, was long known as the "Watteau." Among his most famous works is his last, *Enseigne de Gersaint* (Berlin), which he painted in eight days, in a feverish state of ill-health. This work is an exquisitely composed interior study, a painting of paintings being displayed, with a view of a group of people so fluidly and harmoniously presented that they seem figures in a ballet.

Watteau suffered always from an undermined constitution, and he was carried off by "pulmonary consumption" (probably tuberculosis) in Nogent-sur-Marne. For such a short life his output was prodigious. The Louvre has 10 of his canvases, but there are many examples throughout the world. His posthumous influence was widespread, and eventually almost 600 engravings of his works were made by various masters. He was a member of the Academy from 1717.   ANTHONY KERRIGAN

WATTERSON, HENRY, 1840–1921, U.S. journalist, was born in Washington, D.C. Although he admired Abraham Lincoln and disapproved of the secession of the Southern states from the Union, during the Civil War Watterson joined the Confederate army out of sheer loyalty to Tennessee, and served as editor of the *Rebel*, the Confederate army newspaper. As editor from 1868 of the Louisville *Courier-Journal*, he advocated home rule for the South, together with full legal and civil rights for Southern Negroes. He campaigned for Horace Greeley, 1872, and Samuel Jones Tilden, 1876, and was Democratic representative in Congress, 1876–77. His paper received a Pulitzer prize, 1918, for his editorials approving U.S. entrance into World War I. He resigned from the *Courier-Journal* in the same year. Among his books are *Abraham Lincoln* (1890), *The Compromises of*

Life (1903), "*Marse Henry*": *An Autobiography* (2 vols., 1919), and *The Editorials of Henry Watterson* (1923).

WATTLE. See ACACIA.

WATTMETER, an electrical instrument that measures electric power. In direct current circuits, the measurement of power is almost always made from separate determinations of voltage and current. The measurement of power in an alternating current circuit makes use of a dynamometer type of instrument consisting of a current coil and a voltage coil that turns in the magnetic field of the current coil. The deflection of the moving coil can be shown to be directly proportional to the power; hence, the scale over which the deflections are indicated is calibrated to read directly in watts.

WATTS, GEORGE FREDERICK, 1817–1904, English allegorical painter and sculptor, was born in London. He studied at the Royal Academy, and there he exhibited, 1837, his first works: two portraits of women and a picture of a wounded hero. In the competition for the decoration of the new Houses of Parliament, 1842, he was rewarded with the prize of £300 for his *Caractacus Being Led in Triumph Through the Streets of Rome*, which enabled him to spend the next two years in Florence. Upon his return to London, 1846, he entered a second competition; his cartoon, *King Alfred Inciting the Saxons to Meet and Resist the Danes at Sea*, was awarded a prize, and the artist was commissioned by the government to paint the *St. George and the Dragon* fresco in the Hall of Poets, Westminster Abbey.

At about this time Watts turned to the symbolic work that forms his message to the age—the power of love and the fallacy of the fear of death, the danger of riches, and the cruelty of greed. The most notable of this group are *Faith, Hope, and Charity, Love and Life* (1885), *Love and Death* (1877–96), *Love Triumphant* (1898), and the trilogy of *Eve*. He executed numerous portraits of the most distinguished men of his day. Although Watts' sculpture includes only some half-dozen pieces, these works are characterized by greatness of conception, nobility of style, and boldness and breadth of execution. He was elected Royal Academician in 1867.

WATTS, ISAAC, 1674–1748, English clergyman and hymn writer, was born in Southampton, and educated at the Stoke Newington Nonconformist Academy in London. After a few years as a tutor, he became assistant pastor of a Nonconformist chapel in Mark Lane, London, and served as pastor from 1702 until his retirement, 1712. Watts wrote a number of famous English hymns, including *O God, Our Help in Ages Past* and *When I Survey the Wondrous Cross.* Among his works are *Horae Lyricae* (1706), *Hymns* (1707), *The Psalms of David* (1719), *Divine and Moral Songs for Children* (1720) and *Scripture History* (1732).

WATTS-DUNTON, WALTER THEODORE, 1832–1914, English critic and poet, was born in St. Ives, Huntingdonshire, was privately educated, then studied law and was admitted to the bar. He soon turned his attention to literature, however, and joined, 1874, the staff of the *Examiner;* he began to contribute to the *Athenaeum*, 1875, for which, over a 20-year period, he wrote some of his best work. Like his friend, George Borrow, he was interested in gypsy lore, and both his unconventional poems, *The Coming of Love* (1897), and his novel, *Aylwin* (1898), deal with Romany life. He is chiefly remembered as a nurse-maid to the genius of Dante Gabriel Rossetti and Algernon Swinburne. Rossetti died despite his ministrations, but Swinburne, whom he kept in seclusion for 30 years at his estate, The Pines, Putney, was transformed—for better or worse—from a dope-addict, an alcoholic, and a notorious rake into a quiet, bookish country squire, who had exchanged the romantic liberalism of his youth for jingoism and tory imperialism.

WAUCHULA, city, W central Florida, seat of Hardee County; on the Atlantic Coast Line Railroad and U.S. highway 17; 49 miles ESE of Tampa. The city is a shipping center for truck crops, strawberries, and citrus fruits. Fruit canning is the chief industry. Wauchula was settled in the 1830's during the Second Seminole War. (For population, see Florida map in Atlas.)

WAUGH, EVELYN ARTHUR ST. JOHN, 1903–66, English writer, born in London, son of a London publisher, educated at Lancing and Oxford (Hertford College). He was the author of 28 books—including the biographies *Rosetti* (1928), the prize-winning *Edmund Campion* (1935), and *The Life of the Right Reverend Ronald Knox* (1959)—and several travel books; but it was his novels that made him a great figure in modern English literature and, according to Edmund Wilson, "the only first-rate comic genius that has appeared in England since Bernard Shaw." His first novel, *Decline and Fall* (1928), describes the adventures of a simple theology student victimized and exploited in hilarious if sometimes gruesome fashion by socially privileged and morally decadent people. A similar theme appears in later novels, especially *A Handful of Dust* (1934), in which the protagonist finds himself the captive of an eccentric illiterate in a South American jungle who will give him food only so long as he reads Dickens aloud. Waugh's satires are hilarious, fanciful, sometimes macabre. In *Vile Bodies* (1930) he mocked the "bright young things" of English society in the 1920's; in *Black Mischief* (1932) and *Scoop* (1938) his subjects were devious politics in an African state and the foolishness of the press and public opinion. During World War II he served in the Commandos and was with the partisans in Yugoslavia when the proofs of his most famous novel were dropped to him by parachute. This novel was *Brideshead Revisited* (1945), the story of the decline of an aristocratic Roman Catholic family, with brilliant humorous scenes and sharp critical judgements of life and art but, in the last analysis, a truly tragic novel. The decline of aristocratic English Catholicism was also a major theme in Waugh's World War II trilogy, *Men at Arms* (1952), *Officers and Gentlemen* (1955), and *Unconditional Surrender* (1961). Among his other novels are *Put Out More Flags* (1942), *Scott-King's Modern Europe* (1949), a satire of Californian mores, *The Loved One* (1948), the historical novel *Helena* (1950), the enigmatic *The Ordeal of Gilbert Pinfold* (1957), and his last novel, *Basil Seal Rides Again* (1963).

Waugh's intelligence and humor were combined with a genius for English prose. He never wrote an awkward sentence. A convert to Roman Catholicism, he was a deeply conservative man who would not drive a car and disliked the telephone. He had a low opinion of mankind as a whole while enjoying the devotion of many friends. He was married twice and had six children. One son, Auberon, wrote novels somewhat in his father's manner.

WAUGH, ALEC RABAN, 1898–   , English writer, born in Hampstead, brother of Evelyn Waugh. He was educated for the army at Sandhurst and served in both world wars. He wrote over 40 books, mainly novels, beginning with the (then) sensational *The Loom of Youth* (1917) and including the popular *Island in the Sun* (1956). The latter was set in the West Indies, where Alec Waugh lived for many years. Among several other books concerned with that region is a history, *A Family of Islands* (1963).

WAUKEGAN, city, NE Illinois, seat of Lake County; on the North Shore of Lake Michigan. It is an industrial center in which asbestos and metal goods, outboard motors, lacquers, tools, and pharmaceutical products are manufactured. The city was first settled in 1835 and was known as Little Fort. The name was changed to Waukegan, a Pottawattomie Indian word meaning Little Fort, in 1849. Waukegan was char-

tered as a city in 1859. (For population, see Illinois map in Atlas.)

WAUKESHA, city, SE Wisconsin, seat of Waukesha County, 16 miles W of Milwaukee. It is an industrial center in which motors, steel products, tile and enamel goods, and malted food products are manufactured. During the last part of the nineteenth century Waukesha was a popular resort center, which was noted for its springs. The settlement was first known as Prairieville, but was later renamed Waukesha. The city is the site of Carroll College and of Mount St. Paul College. (For population, see Wisconsin map in Atlas.)

WAUPUN, city, SE Wisconsin, in Dodge and Fond du Lac counties; 58 miles NW of Milwaukee. Dairy cattle and vegetables are raised in the surrounding area. Waupun has a milk condensery and a vegetable cannery. The Wisconsin State Prison is located there. Waupun was founded in 1838. The name is from an Indian word meaning "early day." (For population, see Wisconsin map in Atlas.)

WAUSAU, city, N central Wisconsin, seat of Marathon County; about 130 miles N of Madison. Wausau is the headquarters of an insurance firm and the commercial hub of an agricultural region in which dairying is important. The city has woodworking industries, and manufactures of batteries, chemicals, and snowplows. A major point of interest is Rib Mountain State Park, located on Rib Mountain (1,940 ft.), the highest point in Wisconsin. Wausau is a winter sports center. Wausau was originally a lumbering center, which was known as Big Bull. The settlement was renamed Wausau in 1850. (For population, see Wisconsin map in Atlas.)

WAUWATOSA, city, SE Wisconsin, in Milwaukee County; on the Menomonee River, 5 miles W of Milwaukee. Wauwatosa is a residential and industrial suburb of Milwaukee. Castings, screws, bolts, and construction materials are manufactured. Wauwatosa was established as a village in 1892, and became a city in 1897. (For population, see Wisconsin map in Atlas.)

WAVE. A physical periodic disturbance by means of which energy is transmitted from one point in space to another point. The disturbance may be a very simple one such as the ripples produced on a calm and undisturbed pond by dropping a pebble into it, or it may be very complex, such as a shock wave associated with an explosion. It is customary to associate with a wave motion some sort of medium to serve as a carrier of the motion, although there may be some difficulty about the medium in certain kinds of waves.

Any simple periodic wave train exhibits certain properties by which it can be identified: speed, reflection, refraction, interference, diffraction, and for transverse waves, polarization is a distinguishing property as well. Interference and diffraction are unique in indicating a wave motion.

As a simple approach to the subject, one may consider simple harmonic motion. The up and down undamped motion of a small mass attached to the end of a flexible spring is a fair approximation to such a motion. In this type of vibratory motion the changing

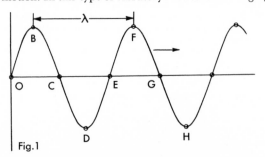

Fig. 1

Sine, or Harmonic Transverse Wave

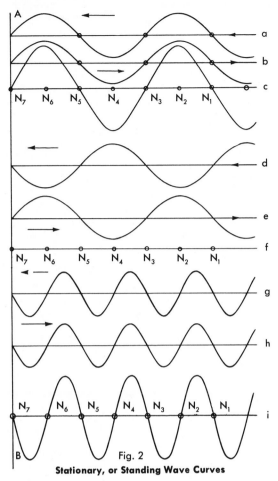

Fig. 2
Stationary, or Standing Wave Curves

where A is the maximum value for the displacement above or below the line x. The maximum displacement is defined as the amplitude.

While what already has been said applies to a transverse wave, that type of wave in which the displacement of propagation by the medium is at right angles to the direction of travel, it also applies to waves in which the vibration or displacement is parallel to the direction in which the wave is traveling. Such waves are known as longitudinal waves, of which sound waves in air are typical.

Transverse Waves in a String. One of the simplest of wave problems for analysis is the wave motion set up in a perfectly flexible string under tension. If the string such as a piano string is plucked, the disturbance is transmitted simultaneously in opposite directions toward its fixed ends from which reflection takes place. The result of the superposition of the two waves traveling in opposite directions with equal speeds will be a stationary wave. The interference is such that nodes will exist at the ends, and at intermediate points the vibration of segments of the string will take place at right angles to the direction of travel. The maximum displacement at the center is called an antinode, assuming the string vibrates in only one segment or loop. The speed of travel v of the wave, the tension F of the string and the mass per unit length m of the string are related in the following manner

$$v = \sqrt{\frac{F}{m}}$$

Since the distance, L, between two nodes is ½ a wave length, then

$$v = \frac{\lambda}{T} = \frac{2L}{T} = 2Lf$$

where f is the frequency of the oscillation. Combining the two equations

$$f = \frac{1}{2L} \sqrt{\frac{T}{m}}$$

This is the law of vibrating strings obtained experimentally. In the case of sound, f is the frequency of the tone emitted by the string.

In the preceding discussion it was assumed that the disturbance was of the simple harmonic type. A wave may also be a composite of a number of simple harmonic oscillations. The wave form is no longer sinusoidal. In extreme cases it may approximate a square-topped wave, one which rises suddenly to its maximum displacement which it retains for a half period before suddenly dropping to a maximum in the opposite direction.

J. Fourier in 1807 discovered that any periodic disturbance could be expressed in terms of a number of sine or cosine functions, resolving the complicated wave form into a series of simple ones. Component waves comprising the complete wave form are known as harmonics or overtones. A string may vibrate emitting sounds which are multiples of the frequency of the fundamental. The number of overtones and their amplitude of vibration determine the quality or timbre of a musical tone.

Huyghens' Principle. When one passes to the problem of the spatial distribution of wave disturbances, Huyghens' principle becomes effective in both the mathematical and the graphical analysis of such wave problems. Suppose that a wave is advancing outward from some vibrating source. At any given distance from the source all points in the disturbance may be in the same phase. A surface passing through these vibrating particles in the same phase of vibration is known as a wave front, and it moves onward from the source with the same speed in all directions in an isotropic medium. Huyghens indicated that at any instant all points in a wave front could serve as secondary sources of new disturbances traveling onward. At any instant the surface tangent to all of the wavelets constitutes the new wave front. At large distances from a point-vibrating source in an isotropic medium the wave fronts may be sensibly considered

acceleration, a, of the moving particle is proportioned to its displacement, y, from its rest or equilibrium position as is indicated mathematically in the following expression

$$a = -4\pi^2 y / T^2 = -4\pi^2 f^2 y.$$

Here, T is the period or time of a round trip of the vibrating mass and f is its frequency and thus the reciprocal of the period. If, while the mass is vibrating up and down, the system is moved at a uniform speed in a horizontal direction, the mass will follow a sinusoidal path (Fig. 1) typical of the advancement of a simple transverse wave. Such a wave form is designated as a sine wave, and since each particle in it executes simple harmonic motion, the wave is said to be a harmonic wave, or a progressive wave. The distance of a point in the wave from the origin O in the horizontal direction determines its phase and is expressed in terms of the period T or in terms of radians. The time required for the crest at B to travel to its position at F is the period T; the distance between the two crests is the wave length λ. The two points B and F are said to be in the same phase of vibration. Other pairs of points in the wave form may be in the same phase such as O and E, the distance between which is again a wave length. The two points O and B are said to be a quarter of a period $(T/4)$ or $\pi/2$ radians out of phase, while O and C are a half period or π radians out of phase. The crest moves onward with a speed v which is related to the period, T, frequency, f, and wave length, λ, in the following manner: $v = \lambda / T = f\lambda$

The general equation for the displacement y at any instant, t, at a distance x from the origin O for a wave traveling to the right is

$$y = A \sin 2\pi \left(\frac{t}{T} - \frac{x}{\lambda} \right)$$

to be no longer spherical, but plane-wave fronts. The solutions of refraction, interference, and diffraction problems are aided by the use of this principle.

Stationary or Standing Waves. When one wave front is advancing in a direction at right angles to another wave front, and then is reflected, it sets up what are known as stationary or standing waves. The medium is agitated by two sets of waves traveling in opposite directions. When the speeds, amplitudes, and frequencies are the same, as in the case of total reflection, regions of no disturbance, known as nodes, and regions of maximum disturbance, known as antinodes or loops, may be observed.

Referring to figure 2, let AB represent a reflecting surface. Let a and b represent the incident and reflected wave at a particular instant, say $t = 0$. Adding the ordinates of both waves, one obtains the resultant wave c. It is observed that at the points N_1, N_3, and N_5 and N_7, there is no disturbance. These points are called nodes. Curves d and e represent the incident and reflected waves at an instant a quarter of a period later, when $t = T/4$. Curve f depicts the addition of the ordinates resulting in zero disturbance all along the line. The curves g, h, i represent the situation another quarter of a period later, $t = T/2$. The position of the nodes has not changed, whereas the medium between the nodes oscillates up and down. The wave resulting from two such trains of waves of equal amplitude and frequency and traveling in opposite directions with equal speeds is known as a stationary or standing wave. These waves are so called because the nodes do not advance in space, neither do the antinodes or loops. The same reasoning may be applied to the longitudinal wave, where the medium oscillates to and fro in the line in which the incident and reflected waves are traveling. The stationary wave plays an important role in the behavior of light and sound waves.

Beats. Stationary waves are a manifestation of interference. Another type of interference results when two wave trains of equal amplitude but of different frequencies agitate a medium simultaneously. When two tuning forks of slightly different frequency are sounded simultaneously, pulsations or variations in the intensity of the sound are heard. These variations in the intensity are known as beats. The number of beats per second is equal to the difference in the frequencies of the two sounds. When the frequency of the beats increases beyond a certain minimum, the beats merge into tone known as a beat tone. Beat tones play an important role in the consonance and dissonance resulting from several frequencies sounded simultaneously. The variations in intensity due to the combination of waves of different frequency are not confined to sound waves. They occur in all kinds of wave motion where the described conditions prevail.

The Doppler Effect is observed when there is relative motion between the source of waves and their recipient. If a sounding whistle approaches a stationary listener, it is obvious that more sound waves will be intercepted per second than if the source is at rest. The result is an apparent increase of the pitch in an approaching source and a decrease in pitch when the source is receding. See DOPPLER EFFECT.

Water Waves. Water waves are of two types, the one in which gravitational force plays the important role, the other in which surface tension is the controlling factor.

In deep water waves controlled by gravitational force, the paths of the individual particles of water during the passage of the wave are circles. It may be shown that the speed, v, of a deep water wave depends upon the acceleration of gravity, g, and the period of the wave, T, in the following manner:

$$v = gT/2\pi$$

or since $v = \lambda/T$, $v = \sqrt{g\lambda/2\pi}$. The longer the wave, the greater is its speed of travel. A wave 10,000 ft. long would travel about 153 miles per hour.

If the wave is moving in shallow water, the depth, d, plays its role in the following expression for the speed, namely, $v = \sqrt{dg}$, obviously the speed of a wave rolling up on a beach becomes retarded.

Capillary Waves. When water waves have a length less than 3 mm, surface tension is the controlling force in their propagation. Analysis shows that the speed of propagation depends upon the surface tension, σ, the density, ρ, of the medium, and the wave length, λ, in the following manner

$$v = \sqrt{2\pi\sigma/\lambda\rho}$$

For wave lengths in water longer than about 10 cm the surface tension effect is negligible, whereas for wave lengths less than 3 mm the gravity effect is negligible. For waves in which both gravity and surface tension are important, the velocity of propagation of such surface waves is given by

$$v = \frac{g\lambda}{2\pi} + \frac{2\pi\sigma}{\lambda\rho}$$

Thus, the shorter the wave, the greater its speed of travel. For uncontaminated water the ripple speed of a wave 1 millimeter long approximates 16 miles per hour. By measuring the wave length and speed of the ripples, Lord Rayleigh measured the surface tension of some liquids.

Longitudinal Waves in Liquids. Liquids in general require very large pressures (forces per unit area) to produce small volume changes. However, their compressibility is sufficient to allow the propagation of longitudinal waves or compression waves. Newton showed that the speed of propagation of such a wave depended only on the compressional elasticity or bulk modulus, E, and the density, ρ, as follows

$$v = \sqrt{E/\rho}$$

It is interesting to note that the speed does not depend on the wave length. In water the speed of the longitudinal waves at 20°C is 1,450 meters per second or 3,300 miles per hour. High or supersonic frequencies have been used for depth sounding and also submarine detection. On land the propagation of longitudinal waves has been used for detecting oil pockets and ore deposits.

Wave Mechanics. The dual character of light resulting from attempts to explain optical phenomena in terms of mechanical models indicates that the photon exhibits wave properties as well as mass properties namely inertia and momentum (Compton effect). De Broglie of France in 1924 made the startling suggestion that inasmuch as the photon possessed momentum, moving particles such as electrons might also exhibit wave properties. The Compton effect indicated that the momentum of a photon was

$$mv = h/\lambda = hf/c$$

where h is Planck's constant, and is equal to 6.62×10^{-27} ergs, f the frequency associated with the photon, and c the speed of light. De Broglie reasoned from the same relationship that the wave length of the moving particle might have a wave length

$$\lambda = h/mv$$

where m is the mass of the particle and v the speed with which it is traveling.

In 1927 Davisson and Germer projected a beam of moving electrons (particles) on a nickel crystal which served as a diffraction grating. The reflected beam gave rise to a pattern which was interpreted as a diffraction pattern. The projected electrons had an energy of 54 electron volts or 8.64×10^{-11} ergs. The diffracted beam was at such an angle that the wave length corresponded to 1.65×10^{-8} cm or 1.68 Ångstrom units. The computation from the De Broglie equation gave a wave length of 1.67×10^{-8} cm. Almost simultaneously G. P. Thomson in England, projecting a beam of electrons through a thin foil obtained a beautiful series of concentric rings as a diffraction pattern with a result in agreement with the De Broglie hypothesis.

Generalizing somewhat it is concluded that every moving particle has waves associated with it. The waves are very short, too short to be detected except in special cases.

In the hands of Schrödinger, Heisenberg, and others the development of the particle wave idea formed a new branch of physics now called wave or quantum mechanics.

The principles of quantum mechanics lead to a wave equation formulated by Schrödinger which must be satisfied by an electron in an atom subject to specific boundary conditions. The Bohr theory of the atom postulated that the electron rotated in a definite orbit about the nucleus and that its momentum was $nh/2\pi$ where n is an integer. Wave mechanics regards the electron as a wave moving in a circular orbit about the nucleus. The solution of the wave equation indicated that the waves in the orbit must be an integral number corresponding to the integer, n, in the momentum equation. The wave length of the electron is then given in wave mechanics as

$$\lambda = h/mv$$

where v is its speed in the orbit. The wave length in the path is

$$\lambda = 2\pi r/n$$

where r is the radius of the orbit. Hence,

$$2\pi r = nh/2\pi \text{ or } mvr = nh/2\pi$$

mvr is the angular momentum which is quantized as an integral multiple of $h/2\pi$ in conformity with the Bohr postulate.

Wave mechanics appears to have placed the theory of atomic structure on firm ground. All theories have the advantage of stimulating further progress and point new directions in which to advance over present knowledge.

WAVELLITE, a rare mineral of secondary origin that is a hydrous aluminum phosphate, $Al_3(OH)_3(PO_4)_2 \cdot 5H_2O$. Although of orthorhombic crystalline structure, crystals are rare. Wavellite is found in small quantities, associated with aluminous, metamorphic rocks, and in deposits of limonite and phosphorite. It is translucent, may be white, yellow, brown, or green, and has a hardness of 3.5 to 4, with a specific gravity of 2.3 (see HARDNESS.) It is infusible and insoluble in water.

WAVELL OF CYRENAICA AND OF WINCHESTER, ARCHIBALD PERCIVAL WAVELL, 1st **VISCOUNT,** 1883–1950, British field marshal, was educated at Winchester College, the Royal Military College at Sandhurst, and the Staff College at Camberley. After serving in the South African War and on the Indian frontier, 1908, he fought in France, 1914–16, during World War I, losing his left eye. Wavell continued in the army in various posts, commanding at Aldershot the 6th Infantry Brigade, 1930–34, and the 2nd Division, 1935–37. Wavell became major general, 1933, lieutenant general, 1938, and general, 1940. He was named commander in chief in the Middle East, 1939, and when World War II began in Africa, his small army, pressed by an Italian force led by Marshal Rodolfo Graziani, retreated into Egypt. Beginning in December, 1940, however, Wavell started a successful drive to force the Italians back. He used land, air, and sea forces effectively, taking Tobruk in the Cyrenaica Campaign, but was defeated by the Italian-German army under Gen. Erwin Rommel. Next, Wavell served as commander in chief in India from 1941 to 1943, except for a short time in 1942, when he was supreme allied commander in the Southwest Pacific. In 1943 he was created both field marshal and viscount. He was viceroy and governor general of India, 1943–47. Wavell wrote *The Palestine Campaigns* (1928), *Allenby: a Study in Greatness* (1940), *Generals and Generalship* (1941), *Allenby in Egypt* (1943), and *Speaking Generally* (1946).

WAVEMETER, also known as a frequency meter, is an instrument used to determine the frequency, and thereby also the wave length, of a source of radio frequency power. The wavemeter consists essentially of a coil and a variable capacitor calibrated in terms of the frequency at which it resonates with the coil. When such an instrument is brought near a source of radio frequency power, the capacitor is then adjusted for a maximum reading. Resonance is indicated by a maximum reading on a meter or by a small electric lamp.

WAVERLY, city, NE Iowa, seat of Bremer County; on the Cedar River, the Chicago Great Western and the Illinois Central railroads, and U.S. highway 218; 100 miles NNE of Des Moines. The city is a processing center for an area of poultry and dairy farms. Farm machinery and pharmaceuticals are manufactured. Waverly was incorporated in 1859. Pop. (1960) 6,357.

WAVERLY, village, S New York, in Tioga County; on the Lackawanna, the Erie, and the Lehigh Valley railroads; 75 miles SSW of Syracuse, and at the Pennsylvania border. Waverly is a processing center for a region in which truck farming and the raising of dairy cattle and poultry are leading activities. Furniture, paint, gloves, and silk ribbon are manufactured. Waverly was incorporated in 1853. Pop. (1960) 5,950.

WAVERLY, village, S Ohio, seat of Pike County; on the Scioto River, the Detroit, Toledo and Ironton and the Norfolk and Western railroads, and U.S. highway 23; 58 miles S of Columbus. The village is a lake resort and a market center for an area in which lumbering is important. Waverly was founded as Uniontown in 1829. Pop. (1960) 3,830.

WAVERLY, town, W central Tennessee, seat of Humphreys County; on the Louisville and Nashville Railroad and U.S. highway 70; 56 miles W of Nashville. The town is a trade center for a region in which peanuts and livestock are raised. Clothes, concrete blocks, and wood products are manufactured. Waverly was laid out in 1836. Pop. (1960) 2,891.

WAVES. See WOMEN OF THE U.S. NAVY.

WAX, a system of organic compounds which are, in general, esters of long chain or high molecular-weight monohydroxy alcohols and high molecular-weight carboxylic acids. In this respect they differ chemically from fats and oils, which are esters of the polyhydroxy alcohol glycerine. Waxes differ physiologically from fats and oils since they are not digestible. Waxes have certain physical properties in common, although they are mixtures and therefore are not chemically pure compounds. All have a slippery feeling, are insoluble in water, and have relatively low melting points.

Waxes may be classified as animal, insect, vegetable, and mineral waxes. A common animal wax is spermaceti, a crystalline wax obtained from sperm oil taken from the blubber and head cavity of the sperm whale. This wax is largely cetyl palmitate, $C_{15}H_{31}COOC_{16}H_{33}$, and has a solidification point of about 45°C. Beeswax is a typical insect wax. It is a mixture of cerotic acid, $C_{25}H_{51}COOH$, and myricyl palmitate, $C_{15}H_{31}COOC_{31}H_{63}$, and has a solidification point of 62° to 66°C. Carnauba wax is a vegetable wax found as a coating on the leaves of certain species of Brazilian palm trees. Carnauba wax contains some myricyl alcohol, $C_{31}H_{63}OH$, some cerotic acid, $C_{25}H_{51}COOH$, and the ester, myricyl cerotate, $C_{25}H_{51}COOC_{31}H_{63}$. This wax has a high solidification point of about 89°C and thus can remain solid in warm weather. It also can be polished to a high luster.

Although mineral waxes have the characteristic properties of other waxes, they are not true waxes in the chemical sense, since they are not esters. Ozokerite, or earth wax, is often found near the surface of the ground in petroleum wells. The material is a complex compound of solid paraffin hydrocarbons and is thought to have been formed by the evaporation of shallow deposits of petroleum. Ozokerite may be refined by treatment with sulfuric acid followed by washing with water and alkali.

The refined material, which has a solidification point of 56° to 83°C, is known as ceresin and is used as a substitute for beeswax.

Paraffin wax, which is obtained from the higher boiling portions of the fractional distillation of petroleum, is a mixture of hydrocarbons of high molecular-weight that have a composition approximating $C_{20}H_{42}$ to $C_{24}H_{50}$. This waxlike substance has a solidification point of 51° to 55°C.

Uses. Waxes find extensive use in the fabrication of candles and waxed paper, and the production of home-canned foods and waterproofed fabrics, coverings for electrical insulators, and polishes. Because of its relative hardness and its ability to be polished to a very high luster carnauba wax finds extensive use in floor and automobile polishes. Petroleum type of waxes, however, constitute 90 per cent of the industrial waxes.

WAXAHACHIE, city, NE Texas, seat of Ellis County; on the Rock Island, the Southern Pacific, the Fort Worth and Denver, the Missouri-Kansas-Texas railroads, and U.S. highways 75 and 287; 28 miles S of Dallas. Waxahachie is a trade and processing center for an agricultural region. The city has a cotton market, and plants and vegetables are shipped. Cottonseed oil, furniture, and textiles are manufactured. Waxahachie is an Indian word meaning "cow town," referring to the large number of cattle which once were raised in the vicinity. Pop. (1960) 12,749.

WAXHAWS, BATTLE OF, an engagement of the Revolutionary War, was fought May 29, 1780, in the Catawba River region of South Carolina, near the North Carolina border, and ended in a massacre of the colonial American force. The engagement came about when some 350 Virginians, under Col. Abraham Buford, while enroute to the defense of Charleston, were overtaken by a force of British cavalry under Col. Banastre Tarleton. The Virginians surrendered almost at once, but the British commander attacked the unarmed men; more than 100 were slain outright, 150 were severely wounded and abandoned on the field, and only 53 were spared to become British prisoners. Colonel Buford and a few of his men escaped, however, and thus details of Tarleton's atrocity became known. Bitterness engendered by what was called "Tarleton's quarter" so stirred the colonials' will to fight as to be a significant factor in their victories in the battles of King's Mountain and Cowpens.

WAX MYRTLE. See CANDLEBERRY; MYRICA.

WAXWING, a bird belonging to the family *Bombycillidae* and the subfamily *Bombycillinae*, which consists of a single genus and three species. The bird is so named because in the typical species several of the secondary feathers of the wing, and in some cases some of the tail feathers, have red waxlike tips at the shaft. Waxwings are tree-nesting birds from 7 to 7½ inches in length. They have soft grayish brown plumage and black markings on the head and chin. The wings are slate colored, and across the tail is a large yellow band. A notable feature is the mobile crest upon the bird's head, which is erected when the bird becomes excited. Waxwings feed on insects and small fruits. The largest and handsomest species is the Bohemian waxwing, *Bombycilla garrula*, found in the northern parts of the Northern Hemisphere. The

RONALD AUSTING FROM
NATL. AUDUBON SOC.
Cedar Waxwings

cedar waxwing, cedar bird, or cherry bird, *B. cedrorum*, is common throughout temperate North America. The third species is the Japanese waxwing, *B. japonicus*, found in Japan and other parts of Asia.

WAYCROSS, city, SE Georgia, seat of Ware County; N of Okefenokee Swamp on the Atlantic Coastal Plain; on the Atlantic Coast Line Railroad and U.S. highways 1, 23, 82, and 84; 90 miles SW of Savannah. Waycross is a trade and processing center for lumber, honey, alligator hides, pecan nuts, and vegetables produced in the area. It is a railroad junction and machine shops of the Atlantic Coast Line Railroad are located there. Waycross was founded early in the 1870's. Pop. (1960) 20,944.

WAYLAND, FRANCIS, called the First Citizen of Rhode Island, 1796–1865, U.S. educator, was born in New York City, and was educated at Union College and Andover Theological Seminary. As president of Brown University, 1827–55, he expanded the school's equipment, introduced the elective system, and gave increased emphasis to scientific studies. He was a prominent advocate of temperance, abolition, prison reform, and the free school system.

WAYLAND THE SMITH, hero in legends of both England and Germany. After learning the art of forging weapons, Wayland (or Wieland) went to the trolls, who taught him smelting and the secrets of the mixture of metals. He fell into the power of King Nidung, who mutilated his feet. After avenging himself by killing Nidung's two sons and violating his daughter, Wayland made himself a pair of wings and flew to Valhalla. He is said to have resided for a time in England, and "his" cave is shown to tourists at Ashdown, Berkshire. The story is related to the Greek Myth of Daedalus.

WAYNE, ANTHONY, nicknamed Mad Anthony, 1745–96, colonial American revolutionist, was born in Chester County, Pa. He worked as a surveyor, and then he took charge of his father's tannery. He participated in the patriot movement, 1775, became a member of the Provincial Assembly, was appointed colonel of a Chester County regiment in the Continental service, 1776, and led the American attack at Three Rivers, Canada, covering the retreat from Three Rivers (Trois Riviéres) to Ticonderoga. He was commander at Fort Ticonderoga, 1776–77. Appointed brigadier general, 1777, he commanded the Pennsylvania line at Morristown and was prominent

CHICAGO HIST. SOC.
Anthony Wayne

in the Battle of Brandywine. He was acquitted of negligence after a defeat at Paoli, and recovered his prestige with a daring attack on Germantown. After spending the winter of 1777–78 at Valley Forge, he commanded the advance attack on Monmouth, 1778, and, having been transferred to the command of a corps of light infantry, led a successful surprise attack at Stony Point, 1779, an action which won him a congressional medal. He prevented a British occupation of West Point, 1780, assisted Lafayette in the Yorktown campaign, 1781, and served under Nathanael Greene in Georgia. He retired with a major general's brevet, 1783.

Wayne was a Pennsylvania assemblyman, 1784–85, and was a delegate to the Pennsylvania convention that ratified the U.S. Constitution. In 1791–92 he served in the U.S. House of Representatives for a Georgia district. Wayne was made major general of the U.S. army which was fighting Indians in the Northwest Territory, 1791; he defeated the Indians at Fallen Timbers, 1794, and negotiated the Greenville Treaty, 1795.

BIBLIOG.–James Barnes, *Hero of Stony Point, Anthony Wayne* (1916); Thomas Boyd, *Mad Anthony Wayne* (1929); Rupert

S. Holland, *Mad Anthony: The Story of Anthony Wayne* (1931); Richard C. Knopf, ed., *Anthony Wayne: A Name in Arms* (1960); Fletcher Pratt, *Eleven Generals: Studies in American Command* (1949); John H. Preston, *Gentleman Rebel: Mad Anthony Wayne* (1934); Harry E. Wildes, *Anthony Wayne, Trouble Shooter of the American Revolution* (1941).

WAYNE, JAMES MOORE, 1790?–1867, U.S. jurist, was born in Savannah, Ga., and was graduated from the College of New Jersey (later Princeton University), 1808. He practiced law, served as an officer of Georgia Hussars in the War of 1812, and was elected to the legislature, 1815, after opposing a law for the suspension of the collection of debts. He became judge of the Georgia superior court, 1824. As a member of Congress, 1829–35, he supported Pres. Andrew Jackson, and was appointed associate justice of the U.S. Supreme Court, 1835. Wayne opposed the rechartering of the United States Bank, and remained loyal to the Union in the Civil War.

WAYNE, city, NE Nebraska, seat of Wayne County; on the North Western Railway; 87 miles NE of Omaha. Wayne is a processing center for an area in which stock raising and the production of grain are leading activities. Nebraska State Teachers College at Wayne was founded in 1921. Wayne was platted in 1881, and named for Gen. Anthony Wayne, an American Revolutionary War officer. Pop. (1960) 4,217.

WAYNE, town, W West Virginia, seat of Wayne County; on Twelvepole Creek and U.S. highway 52; 45 miles WSW of Charleston. The town is a trade center for an area of diversified farms and coal mines. Glass is manufactured. Pop. (1960) 1,274.

WAYNESBORO, city, E Georgia, seat of Burke County; on the Central of Georgia and the Savannah and Atlanta railroads, and U.S. highway 25; 145 miles ESE of Atlanta. The city is a trade center for an area in which cotton is grown. Clothing, canned foods and metal products are manufactured. Waynesboro was laid out in 1783. Pop. (1960) 5,359.

WAYNESBORO, town, SE Mississippi, seat of Wayne County; on the Gulf, Mobile and Ohio Railroad, and U.S. highways 45 and 84; 100 miles SE of Jackson. The town is a processing center for an area in which cotton and livestock are raised. Cotton ginning and lumbering are leading industries. Pop. (1960) 3,892.

WAYNESBORO, borough, S Pennsylvania, in Franklin County, on the Pennsylvania and Western Maryland railroads; 52 miles SW of Harrisburg. Waynesboro is a trade and industrial center for a fruit-growing region. Machine tools, metal products, and clothing are manufactured. Waynesboro was founded in 1797 and named for Gen. Anthony Wayne, an American Revolutionary War officer. It was captured by Confederate forces in 1863 during the Civil War. Pop. (1960) 10,427.

WAYNESBORO, city, S Tennessee, seat of Wayne County; on U.S. highway 64; 80 miles SW of Nashville. The city is a trade center for an area of diversified farms. Pop. (1960) 1,343.

WAYNESBORO, independent city, W central Virginia, on the South River, the Chesapeake and Ohio and the Norfolk and Western railroads, and U.S. highways 250 and 340; 97 miles NW of Richmond, in the Blue Ridge Mountains. The city is a trade and industrial center in a region of apple growing, and dairy farming. Furniture, wood products, stoves, synthetic textiles, pencils, and pipe-organ parts are manufactured. During the Civil War, a Union force defeated a Confederate force near there. Waynesboro was settled in 1700, and incorporated as a city in 1948 when it separated from Augusta County. Pop. (1960) 15,694.

WAYNESBURG, borough, SW Pennsylvania, seat of Greene County; on Tenmile Creek, near the Monongahela River, the Pennsylvania and the Monongahela railroads, and U.S. highway 19; 40 miles SSW of Pittsburgh. The borough is a trade and processing center for an area in which livestock are raised, and coal and gas are produced. Stone quarrying and lumbering are leading industries, and wood products, bricks, and flour are manufactured. Waynesburg is the site of Waynesburg College (1850). Waynesburg was incorporated in 1816. Pop. (1960) 5,188.

WAYNESBURG COLLEGE, a coeducational, private institution of higher learning, located in Waynesburg, Pa. An extension center at Uniontown, Pa., offers two years of college study. The college, associated with the United Presbyterian church, was established and offered its first instruction in 1849. The college library contains the Trans-Appalachian Library and Readings, a collection of materials on the westward movement across the Appalachian Mountains and into the area of the Monongahela, Allegheny, and Ohio rivers. See COLLEGES AND UNIVERSITIES.

WAYNE STATE UNIVERSITY, a coeducational, public institution of higher learning, located in Detroit, Mich. Originally the Colleges of the City of Detroit, a loose federation formed, 1933, and operated by the Detroit board of education, it was placed under municipal control and its name was changed to Wayne University, 1934. The university was jointly supported and controlled by the city and state governments, from 1956 to 1959, when an amendment to the state constitution placed the institution completely under the supervision of the state. At that time its name was changed to Wayne State University.

Among the various divisions of the school are liberal arts, education, business administration, engineering, law, medicine, nursing, pharmacy, and social work. Programs of graduate study are offered in most departments. See COLLEGES AND UNIVERSITIES.

WAYNESVILLE, town, central Missouri, seat of Pulaski County; in the Ozark Mountains, 49 miles S of Jefferson City. The town is a trade center for a diversified farming area. Waynesville was platted in 1839. Pop. (1960) 2,377.

WAYNESVILLE, town, W North Carolina, seat of Haywood County; on the Southern Railway and U.S. highways 19 and 23; 63 miles SE of Knoxville. The town is a resort center near the Great Smoky Mountain National Park. Shoes are manufactured. Waynesville was incorporated in 1871. Pop. (1960) 6,159.

WAYNFLETE, WILLIAM OF, 1395?–1486, English clergyman was born William Patyn in Wainfleet, Lincolnshire, and studied at Oxford. As headmaster of Winchester College, 1429–40, Waynflete (or Wainfleet) became a protégé of Henry VI, who appointed him provost of Eton College, 1443–47, and bishop of Winchester, 1447–86, and made him a royal emissary in dealing with Jack Cade, 1450. Waynflete was a privy councilor, 1454–60, and lord chancellor of England, 1456–60, during the Duke of York's regency. Although a Lancastrian, and an ally of Henry VI in the coup d'état of 1470, William continued as bishop of Winchester under the Yorkist kings Edward IV and Richard III. Waynflete founded Magdalen College, Oxford, 1458 (completed 1480), and a free grammar school at Waynflete, 1484. See WARS OF THE ROSES.

WEA, one of a North American Indian tribe of the Algonquian linguistic stock, closely related to the Miami and the Piankashaw, first mentioned by French missionaries as living in eastern Wisconsin, later on the site of Chicago, 1673, and still later along the banks of the Wabash River in Indiana. Toward the end of the eighteenth century they joined the Miami in warfare against settlers and the U.S. Army until the Indians were defeated by Maj. Gen. Anthony Wayne at the Battle of Fallen Timbers, near the site of Toledo, Ohio, Aug. 20, 1794. On Aug. 3, 1795, members of the tribe took part in the signing of the Treaty of Greenville, which put a temporary end to the Indian-white war in the Northwest Territory.

They sold their last lands in Indiana, 1820, and moved to Illinois and Missouri; they were moved again, 1832, this time to the Kansas country; and were moved from there, 1868, to Indian Territory (Oklahoma) where they consolidated with the Piankashaws, Kaskaskias, and Peorias on lands called the Peoria and Miami Reservation. There were more than 700 Indians living on this reservation in 1950.

WEAKFISH, a salt water food fish *Cynoscion regalis*. The weakfish, often called the grey squeteague, has an average length of about 3 feet and a weight of approximately 12 pounds. Its coloration is silvery with a yellow hue in its fins. The characteristic feature of its mouth is a protruding lower jaw and two large canine teeth in its upper jaw. The flesh around its mouth is easily torn when the fish is hooked; its common name was given because of this feature. The male weakfish is capable of producing sounds that resemble croakings. This noise is intensified during the spawning seasons. The weakfish lays its eggs from May until September; usually spawning occurs at sea but the fish have been known to spawn within inland bays. Because of the excellent flavor of its meat, the weakfish is commercially fished. It is found in the coastal waters from Massachusetts to Florida. The spotted squeteague, *C. nebulosus*, is found in the coastal waters from Virginia to Texas. It is quite similar to *C. regalis* but is slightly smaller and has conspicuous black spots on its body.

WEALD, THE, a region of SE England; lying in the counties of Surrey, Kent, and Sussex; bounded by the North Downs on the N, the English Channel on the SE, and the South Downs on the SW; area about 400 sq. mi. The Weald is an eroded anticline, rimmed by the Chalk Downs, and with sandstone hills in the center. Between these two highland areas is a low plain, formed mainly on clay, which is chiefly productive agricultural land. The Chalk Hills are used mainly for the grazing of sheep, while the sandstone areas are frequently forested.

MASLOWSKI & GOODPASTER FROM NATIONAL AUDUBON SOC.

The least, or pygmy, weasel is the smallest of the weasel family, with a body only six inches long. It inhabits the northern countries, and feeds principally on field mice.

WEASEL, a small carnivorous mammal of the family *Mustelidae*. Weasels have a slim head and neck, a slender body, and long tail, males being much larger in body than females. The animal's coat is usually brown, with white chin, throat, and belly. When the weasel is found in northern regions its fur becomes white in winter and is known as ermine. The change is effected by an autumnal molt. Early in spring the fur again changes to brown. The tail tip, however, remains black throughout the year. Contrary to general belief, the weasel is not a blood sucker. It feeds on rats, mice, rabbits, and other small mammals, birds, frogs, and insects. The weasel is an inveterate enemy of the western ground squirrel and in this respect is a genuine asset to the farmer. The animal gives birth to six to eight young at one time.

The common weasel, *Mustela cicognani*, is widely distributed over the United States. Males have a total length of 11 inches, females 9 inches. The long-tailed bridled weasel, *M. frenata*, found in Mexico and Texas, may reach a length of 19 inches.

W. J. HAMILTON, JR.

WEATHER, the state of the atmosphere as determined by the measurement of air temperature, barometric pressure changes, wind velocity, humidity, cloud formations, and precipitation. The weather may be described by referring to one or more of these meteorological elements. Thus the weather is said to be warm or cold, dry or humid, clear or cloudy, or calm or windy. Weather also denotes the direction from which the wind is blowing, in speaking of the weather side, as contrasted with the lee, or sheltered side. See ATMOSPHERE; CLIMATE; METEOROLOGY; RAIN; WEATHER BUREAU, U.S.; WEATHER FORECASTING; WIND.

WEATHER BUREAU, U.S., a bureau of the Department of Commerce that collects, records, and disseminates data pertaining to weather conditions for the purposes of current information, forecasting, and for their statistical value.

A national weather service was established by a congressional act in 1870 under the Signal Corps of the Army, but the U.S. Weather Bureau was not organized until 1890, when Congress placed the bureau under the Department of Agriculture, transferring the weather services from the Signal Corps. Subsequent legislation and executive decisions greatly increased the responsibilities, especially in providing weather data for civil aviation. Finally in 1940 the bureau was transferred to the Department of Commerce.

In 1960 the Weather Bureau maintained about 300 offices, manned by full-time personnel, at cities and airports throughout the United States, in Puerto Rico, and some of the islands of the Pacific Ocean. In addition, weather reports were made at about 675 other locations by such agencies as the Federal Aviation Agency, state and municipal groups, and by private citizens. The Weather Bureau also had approximately 12,700 substations providing less complex reports and observations. In co-operation with the U.S. Coast Guard, Navy, and certain maritime interests the Weather Bureau maintains ocean weather stations in the Atlantic, the Pacific, the Gulf of Mexico, and in the Arctic.

Weather Services. The 300 local Weather Bureau offices operate radar for weather surveillance; make surface and upper air measurements required for forecasting; make records and transmit reports; and issue forecasts and warnings. Approximately 4,000 of the substations make reports of local current weather conditions by telephone or telegraph, primarily for agricultural services; and issue flood, hurricane, and severe storm warnings. About 500 stations located on waterways display storm warning signals for the benefit of shipping.

A national meteorological center is maintained by the Bureau at Suitland, Md., which analyzes weather conditions over the Northern Hemisphere, prepares guidance prognostic material, and disseminates it by way of rapid communication media to civil and military locations to support their own weather activities. A severe local storm forecasting center at Kansas City, Mo., issues timely warnings for the protection of life and property if severe storms and tornadoes are indicated.

The field stations of the Weather Bureau issue daily bulletins, forecasts, warnings, and advice for the benefit of agriculture, business, transportation, and industry. Forecasts are regularly available four times daily to cover the ensuing 36 to 48 hours. In critical situations warnings of storms and cold waves are issued as warranted without regard to regular schedules.

Weather bulletins and forecasts are published by nearly every daily newspaper, and broadcast by commercial radio and television stations. More than

750 such stations maintain microphones in Weather Bureau stations. In 11 major cities automatic telephone forecast repeaters averaged about 51,000 weather calls per day per installation in 1960, and reached a peak of 407,000 calls in one day at one location.

The Aviation Weather Service operated by the Federal Aviation Agency operates 24 hours a day to supply information and weather forecasts for air operations in the United States and over transoceanic routes. It consists of about 240 airport stations connected by teletypewriter circuits that collect and exchange detailed hourly reports of current weather information. By international agreement the U.S. Weather Bureau provides forecasts for many overseas air routes.

Another service of the U.S. Weather Bureau is a specialized horticultural protection service in those states where raising fruit and vegetables is a major activity. In a similar manner, the Weather Bureau assists the U.S. Forest Service by providing current data and forecasts of humidity, wind, and thunderstorm conditions in the forested regions of the country in which forest fires are a hazard.

The Weather Bureau collects weather information from ships at sea by radio, and supplies bulletins of reports, forecasts, and storm warnings to ships on the oceans and the Great Lakes. Closely akin to the marine meteorological service is the hurricane warning service that gives storm warnings and advice in the hurricane belt during the critical storm seasons.

Climatological Services. The U.S. Weather Bureau operates a climatological field service, staffed by area and state climatologists who supervise and co-ordinate projects in applied climatology, with the co-operation of state universities, chambers of commerce, and other state offices. The field staff investigates severe storms and prepares weekly reports for state and national weather and crop summaries. The Climatological Service also collects, analyzes, summarizes and publishes data obtained from the 300 regular Weather Bureau stations, and some 11,000 substations manned by unpaid co-operative observers. The data is useful to agriculture, commerce, and transportation.

There are three weather recording centers, located at San Francisco, Calif., Kansas City, Mo., and Chattanooga, Tenn., for the collection of climatological data. The major portion of the analytical work is done at the National Weather Records Center at Asheville, N.C., which is also the repository of all U.S. weather records, as well as some foreign and oceanographic weather data. This center is equipped with electronic computers for the mass of data processing involved. Monthly and annual climatological reports emanate from the Asheville center.

Research results are published in technical journals, and in *Weather Bureau Technical Papers.* Interpretive reports appear in the *Weekly Weather and Crop National Summary*, the *Mariner's Weather Log* and maps for the *National Atlas Series.*

Hydrologic Services. The Weather Bureau operates a river and flood forecasting service in 89 districts covering all of the principal rivers and tributaries in the United States. In the system there are 10 river forecasting centers, each responsible for a major river basin and each furnishing reports to the district offices within the basin. River stages are observed and reported daily from about 1,300 stations. Daily forecasts, good for 24 to 72 hours are made from many stations on the larger rivers. The date is of value for purposes of navigation, water utilization, and flood control.

Further activities of the Weather Bureau include collaboration with the Army Corps of Engineers in collecting and publishing precipitation data, of use in flood control work; snowfall and run-off data for use by the Department of Agriculture in connection with watershed and irrigation projects.

Research and Development. The Weather Bureau conducts basic and applied meteorological research in its own laboratories, and under contract at universities and other institutions to expand the knowledge of the science of the atmosphere, and to improve the services of the Weather Bureau. The many research programs include the study of the intepretation of surface and upper air data, hurricane and tornado characteristics, instrumentation, and, in particular, co-operation with the National Aeronautical and Space Administration, NASA, in the study of the collection, processing, and analysis of meteorological data developed from the use of satellite instrumentation. See WEATHER FORECASTING; CLIMATE; METEOROLOGY.

WEATHERFORD, WILLIAM, 1780?–1824, Creek Indian chief, was the son of a white man and a half-breed. He led the attack and ensuing massacre at Fort Mims, 1813, but was defeated at the Battle of the Holy Ground later in the year, and narrowly escaped capture. After the final defeat of the Creeks at Horseshoe Bend, 1814, Weatherford surrendered to Gen. Andrew Jackson, and was well treated by him. He afterward settled on a plantation at Little River, Ala. So far as is known, his subsequent relations with the whites were amicable.

WEATHERFORD, city, N central Texas, seat of Parker County; on the Texas and Pacific, and the Weatherford, Mineral Wells, and Northwestern railways, and U.S. highways 80 and 180; 60 miles W of Dallas. The city is a market and shipping center for an area in which fruit, truck crops, cotton, grain, pecans, peanuts, and cattle are raised. The chief industries are peanut-oil milling, and the manufacturing of oil-field equipment. Weatherford was established in 1850 and incorporated late in the decade. Pop. (1960) 9,759.

WEATHER FORECASTING, the prediction of forthcoming atmospheric activity for a definite period of time in a defined area; based on various current and past meteorological observations. Weather forecasting is the principal practical application of the science of meteorology (see METEOROLOGY).

Weather forecasting is based, essentially, on making observations of such data as temperature; relative humidity, or dew point; barometric pressure; wind direction and velocity; cloud types and their estimated height and speed and direction of movement; the amount of clear sky; horizontal visibility; weather conditions of precipitation, fog, or other phenomena at the time of observation; the amount of precipitation since the previous observation; and the range of temperatures and barometric pressures since that last obervation.

HISTORY

Forecasts based on such crude observations were, at best, reliable for only a few hours ahead, and no substantial progress was made for longer range forecasts until the fact was firmly established that weather conditions move from place to place. This phenomena was first noted in 1743 when Benjamin Franklin traced the movement of a storm from Philadelphia to Boston by weather reports he received through the mail. However, it was not until after the invention of the telegraph that the dream of rapidly collecting current weather reports from many different locations could be realized. Daily charting of weather information from a number of reporting stations was begun by the Smithsonian Institution in 1850. France set up a similar service in 1863. An act of Congress in 1870 established a national weather service under the Signal Corps of the Army and this agency later became the U.S. Weather Bureau.

WEATHER OBSERVATIONS

To serve their purpose in forecasting, observations are made from a given location at the same prearranged times of each day, in order that previous recordings may be compared on an equal basis. An exception is made if a sudden drastic weather change, such as a severe storm or intense temperature change is noted. In such a case observations may be made and reported without regard to time schedules. Also for purposes of equal comparison the location and exposure of instruments must not be changed.

Temperatures for surface readings are made from a reliable thermometer that should be suspended in a louvered box that permits free air circulation but protects the thermometer from direct sun's rays and strong winds. Government weather and forecasting stations also use recording thermometers, or thermographs, whereby a continuous record of temperatures is made by a stylus on a 24-hour or 7-day chart. High-altitude temperature readings are obtained from the radiosonde. See RADIOSONDE.

Humidity. The amount of moisture in the air, or the humidity, is another important element in weather forecasting. The forecaster expresses this amount of moisture in terms of relative humidity, which is the percentage of water vapor in the air in relation to the maximum amount of vapor the air can hold at a given temperature, without changing into visible moisture. Closely associated with relative humidity is the dew point temperature, which is the temperature at which vapor changes into visible moisture in the form of dew, frost, fog, or clouds. Determination of relative humidity and dew point is made by use of a psychrometer, which consists of a dry-bulb and a wet-bulb thermometer mounted together. The temperature readings of both thermometers are made simultaneously. If the relative humidity is less than 100 per cent, the reading of the wet-bulb thermometer will be less than that of the dry-bulb, because of the evaporation that affects the wet bulb. The difference between the two readings is known as the depression of the wet bulb, and, from standard formulas, or, more often, from U.S. Weather Bureau tables, the dew point or relative humidity may be read directly. For upper air humidity data, the weather forecaster uses radiosonde coded information. Other instruments used in determining humidity are hygrometers, both direct reading and recording.

Pressure readings at any surface weather forecasting location are obtained from barometers of one type or another (see BAROMETER). Continuous recordings of barometric pressures are made on the barograph. Predictions of weather to come are not dependent upon isolated barometer readings, but rather on the comparison of readings taken over some time interval. If the current reading shows a lower pressure than one taken several hours previously a falling barometer is indicated, which, combined with other factors, may point to an oncoming storm.

Wind. Wind direction and velocity, and a record of each extending several hours prior to the current reading, are of importance to the weather forecaster. Wind direction is shown on a weather vane, and is expressed as the compass point or number of degrees from north on a circle from which the wind is blowing. In the weather forecasting station this information is shown visually on a direct-reading dial in the station; and it is also recorded on a chart. The velocity of the wind is obtained from one of several types of anemometers, and is read on land in miles per hour, and, on the sea in knots. Recordings of wind velocity are also shown in direct-reading dials in the weather station, and recorded, often on the same chart as that used for wind direction. Upper altitude wind data is obtained by observation of the direction and speed of movement of the radiosonde at various high altitudes. Several systems of standardizing the measurement of wind velocities have been devised for convenience in weather reporting. One of these is the Beaufort Scale. See BEAUFORT SCALE.

Clouds. The weather observer and forecaster obtains some of his most important data from the types of clouds he observes, their height, direction, and speed of movement. These observations are significant in an appraisal of the condition of the weather for the immediate future, and, often, for several hours to come. In 1894 the International Meteorological Congress in Munich adapted a classification of clouds based upon their appearance and the altitude at which they are observed. Each classification of clouds has its significance with reference to the weather at the time of the observation, and for the relatively immediate future. See CLOUD. Height and speed of cloud formations are best determined by observation of the movement of weather balloons, and from the telemetering instruments, known as dropsondes, parachuted from balloons. The U.S. Weather Bureau maintains approximately 150 weather balloon observation locations. In addition to noting all of the data pertaining to the clouds, it is important that the forecaster observe the relative amount of clear sky in the forecasting area, expressed as a percentage of cloud coverage in the sky hemisphere.

Visibility. Since the days of commercial aviation weather forecasting has included the element of visibility. Briefly, this is defined by the Weather Bureau as the mean distance, taken toward the horizon, at which prominent objects may be seen and identified by the unaided eye. It is usually expressed in miles and fractions thereof, although in conditions of rain, sleet, snow, and fog it may be given in feet.

Precipitation. The ever continuing hydrologic cycle consists of evaporation of water, condensation, precipitation, and run-off. Of these, all but run-off are of interest to the weather forecaster. Evaporation, particularly from the surface of the ocean, supplies most of the water that condenses to form clouds, and is subsequently precipitated to the earth in the form of fog, rain, sleet, hail, or snow. Although both evaporation and condensation have a bearing on the weather, their measurement is highly technical, and principally a matter of concern to the advanced meteorologist. The condition of precipitation at the time of the weather observation and a measure of its amount in the immediate past reports furnishes a basis for predicting the nature of the precipitation in the weather period ahead, tempered by conditions that exist in neighboring reporting areas. Precipitation is measured, usually in hundredths of inches in a standard rain gauge. The gauge may be either the direct-reading or the recording type. The U.S. Weather Bureau standard rain gauge consists of a metal cylinder, 8 inches in diameter and about 24 inches deep. The precipitation entering the gauge passes through a funnel into a measuring tube that has one-tenth the area of the 8-inch cylinder, so that the depth of the water in the tube is 10 times greater than the amount that has actually fallen. The measuring tube is graduated into tenths of inches, which permits an accuracy of measurement of one-one-hundredth of an inch of actual precipitation. Roughly, a measurement of one inch of snow is the equivalent of one-tenth of an inch of rain. When measuring snow the measuring tube is removed, and direct readings are taken on the gauge cylinder. To record precipitation, the U.S. Weather Bureau uses a similar 8-inch cylinder, but the precipitation is caught in a bucket, weighed, and translated into inches of water, and recorded on a continuous chart. Radar measurement of precipitation was started during the 1950's, based upon the volume and intensity of radar echoes.

FORECASTING AND MAPPING

Weather forecasting is based upon some knowledge of meteorology coupled with skill and experience in interpreting the data supplied from current observations, locally and elsewhere. If the prediction is to cover a span of 12, 24, or 36 hours, it becomes necessary to know and evaluate the effects of observations taken at locations for many miles around, and particularly from those stations lying westerly of the point

WEATHER FORECASTING

Weather observations are analyzed before issuing forecast.

A weather balloon carries an electronic stratometer aloft to measure the atmospheric conditions at high altitudes.

U.S. servicemen take instrument readings for weather data.

U.S. Army Signal Corps men demonstrate the use of equipment at weather forecasting station, Fort Monmouth, N.J.

As a U.S. Navy plane flies into the eye of a hurricane an observer and a photographer get data to track its course.

of observation, since, in general, the movement of weather is from the west to the east. The weather maps, as compiled by the U.S. Weather Bureau, and reproduced in many of the daily newspapers throughout the country are essential to all but immediate or spot forecasts, as they indicate all conditions, and particularly the frontal movements of air masses.

Mapping. In the United States and Canada, and in many other countries, weather observations are made four times daily. Observations of both surface and upper-atmosphere conditions are made and recorded, and the information is sent to collecting centers by radio and teletype. The information is decoded and entered on weather maps. The forecaster making up the map studies the reports of surface and upper-air conditions, and from them identifies the speed and direction of all air masses, sketches in all apparent frontal movements, and identifies the fronts as to warm, cold, or occluded.

From the observations of pressures, the weather mapper draws lines through points of equal pressures, the lines being known as isobars (see Isobar). In a similar way, lines drawn through points of equal temperatures are called isotherms. The U.S. Weather Bureau, in conjunction with international meteorological organizations, standardized a great number of symbols that indicate both the character and magnitude of all factors that have a relation to the weather. The weather map that illustrates this article employs many of the several hundred symbols used in constructing weather maps. From the data collected and charted on weather maps, the forecaster is enabled to make a prediction of probable weather for the ensuing 24 to 36 hours. In the event of sudden, drastic storm or temperature changes that might adversely affect commerce, agriculture, or human safety, interim reports are issued.

Weather Satellites and Rockets. In 1960 the National Aeronautical and Space Administration (NASA) sent its first weather satellite Tiros I into orbit. The satellite sent thousands of televised pictures back to earth showing cloud formations over many sections of the globe, which were valuable for forecasting weather activity. In 1961 NASA's Tiros III was the first satellite to detect a hurricane. Other uses for weather satellites included the determination of the relationship of radiation balance between the Earth, Sun, and outer space; and a measurement of the radiation entering the Earth's atmosphere. Rocketry was employed to study temperatures, winds, pressures, and air densities in atmospheric stratas from 10 to 100 miles above the earth's surface.

In 1962 United States and Soviet scientists agreed on a proposal to establish a world weather watch consisting of a network of regional forecasting centers linked by meteorological satellites. The agreement developed from a United Nations General Assembly resolution, calling for peaceful cooperation in space, and messages exchanged between Pres. John F. Kennedy and Premier Nikita Khrushchev concerning specific space projects. The plan called for expanding and improving global observation of weather by both conventional means and weather satellites. World and regional centers would collect, analyze and disseminate weather information. While political details were being settled, the United States continued to launch the Tiros series of weather satellites and prepared for the more advanced Nimbus late in 1962.

Bibliog.–Irving Adler, *Weather in Your Life* (1959); American Meteorological Society, *Forecasting in Middle Latitudes* (1952); William M. Bergman, III, *Experiences with the Weather* (1958); David I. Blumenstock, *Ocean of Air* (1959); Joe Bolton, *Wind and the Weather* (1957); John A. Day and Fred W. Decker, *Rudiments of Weather* (1958); Robert M. Fisher, *How About the Weather?* (1958); Frank H. Forrester, *1001 Questions Answered About the Weather* (1957); Joseph J. George, *Weather Forecasting for Aeronautics* (1960); Carl L. S. Godske and Others, *Dynamic Meteorology and Weather Fore-* *casting* (1957); Denys J. Holland, *Weather Inference for Beginners Made Clear in a Series of Actual Examples* (1953); Ernest B. Koeppe and George C. Long, *Weather and Climate* (1959); Charles Laird and Ruth Laird, *Weathercasting* (1955); Paul E. Lehr and Others, *Weather: Air Masses, Clouds, Rainfall, Storms, Weather Maps, Climate* (1957); Thomas M. Longstreth, *Understanding the Weather* (1953); Sverre Petterssen, *Weather Analysis and Forecasting*, 2 vols. (1956); *Weather Forecaster* (1955); Athelstan F. Spilhaus, *Weathercraft* (1951); Ivan R. Tannehill, *Hurricane Hunters* (1955).

WEAVERBIRD, a member of the family *Ploceidae*, noted for its intricately woven nests. Weaverbirds are small, with short bills similar to those of finches, to which they are related. Most species live in the warmer parts of the Orient. The English sparrow and European tree sparrow are weavers that have migrated to the United States.

WEAVERVILLE, village, N California, seat of Trinity County; on U.S. highway 299; 205 miles N of San Francisco. The village is a trade center for an area in which livestock is raised and timber is cut. Weaverville was settled in 1850. Pop. (1960) 1,736.

WEAVING, the art of interlacing yarn threads or other filaments by means of a loom, so as to form a web of cloth or other woven fabric.

Warp and Woof. In this process two sets of threads are made to traverse the web at right angles to each other. The threads that extend from end to end of the web in parallel lines are called the warp; the other threads, which cross and interlace with the warp from side to side of the web, are called the weft or the woof.

In all forms of weaving the warp threads are set up in the loom first; the weft threads are then worked into the warp, to and fro, by means of a shuttle. It was by this fundamental process of interlacing two sets of thread in looms of simple mechanism that the mummy cloths of Egypt, the fine damasks and tapestries of the Greeks and Romans, the Indian muslins, the shawls of Cashmere, and the famed textile fabrics of Italy and the Netherlands were produced. From the last-named countries weaving by means of a hand loom was introduced into England.

The Basic Hand Loom consists of a frame of four upright posts braced together by cross beams. The center beam at the back is the warp beam; the beam in front is that on which the web is wound; and the beam just below this, in front, is the breast beam, for the support of the weaver at his work.

At the top of the loom is an apparatus by which the heddles are lifted or lowered by means of treadles under the foot of the weaver. These heddles consist of two frames, from which depend cords attached by a loop or eye to each thread in the warp. These threads are attached to the frames alternately so that when one heddle is raised every second thread in the warp is also raised, while the remaining threads are depressed; this is called shedding the warp.

When the warp threads are shedded (parted), there is left a small opening (a shed) between the threads. Through this opening the weaver drives his shuttle from side to side. The shuttle, which is hollow in the middle, contains the weft thread wound round a bobbin, or pirn; and as the shuttle is shot across the web this weft thread unwinds itself. Once a weft thread has been thus introduced, it is then necessary to bring it to its final place in the fabric. This is accomplished by means of the lay, or batten, which is suspended from the top of the loom, and works to and fro like a pendulum by an attachment of vertical rods (called swords) at each side. Attached to the lay is the reed, an instrument similar to a comb having a tooth raised between every two threads of the warp. By driving up the lay after a weft thread has been introduced, the weaver strikes home that thread to its place in the cloth.

Improved Hand Looms. A great improvement was made on the hand loom when John Kay invented, ?1740, the fly shuttle, so called. This enabled the weaver to drive the shuttle both ways with the right hand by means of a cord attached to a box, or trough. Each jerk of the cord, which was placed at each end of the shuttle race, impelled the shuttle to and fro.

Joseph Jacquard of Lyons, in 1801, invented an apparatus by which the most intricate patterns could be woven as readily as plain cloth. This is accomplished by an ingenious arrangement of hooks and wires, by means of which the warp threads are lifted in any order and to any extent necessary to make one shedding required by the pattern. The order in which these hooks and wires are successively lifted and lowered is determined by means of a series of pasteboard cards punctured with holes; the holes correspond to a certain pattern and, as the cards pass successively over a cylinder or drum, the hooked wires pass through the holes and lift the warp threads in an order that insures the arranged pattern being woven into the fabric. When the pattern is extensive, the machine may be provided with as many as 1,000 hooks and wires.

The Power Loom. Another development was made in the art of weaving by the invention, 1784, of the power loom by the Rev. Edmund Cartwright. In the power loom, which was gradually improved and eventually adapted to electric power, the principal motions of the old method of weaving, such as shedding the warp threads, throwing the shuttle, and beating up the thread, are still retained. Although the principle of the loom is the same in all kinds of weaving, there are numberless modifications for the production of special fabrics. The lappet loom is one suitable for weaving either plain or gauze cloths, and also for putting in representations of flowers, birds, or the like.

Types of Weave. Cross weaving is a process in which, as in gauze weaving, the warp threads, instead of lying constantly parallel, cross over or twist around one another, thus forming a plexus or interlacing independent of that produced by the weft. Double weaving consists in weaving two webs simultaneously one above the other, and interweaving the two at intervals so as to form a double cloth. Kidderminster or Scotch carpeting is the chief example of this process. Pile weaving is the process by which fabrics such as velvets and corduroys are produced. In the weaving of these fabrics, besides the ordinary warp and weft, there is what is called the pile warp, the threads of which are left in loops above the surface until cut, and the cutting of which constitutes the pile. See TEXTILES; INDUSTRIAL REVOLUTION; LOOM.

BIBLIOG.—Mary M. Atwater, *Shuttle-craft Book of American Hand-weaving* (1951), *Byways in Hand-weaving* (1954); Elizabeth C. Baity, *Man is a Weaver* (1942); Lotte Becher, *Hand-weaving: Designs and Instructions* (How to do it Ser.) (1955); Mary E. Black, *New Key to Weaving: A Textbook of Hand Weaving for the Beginning Weaver* (1957); Lili Blumenau, *Art and Craft of Hand Weaving* (1955); Harriette J. Brown, *Hand Weaving for Pleasure and Profit* (1954); Eve Cherry, *Teach Your self Handweaving* (1957); Ulla Cyrus, *Manual of Swedish Hand Weaving* (1957); Marguerite P. Davison, ed., *Hand-weaver's Source Book* (1953); Josephine E. Estes, *Original Miniature Patterns for Handweaving* (1960); Berta Frey, *Designing and Drafting for Handweavers* (1958); Osma P. C. Gallinger, *Joy of Hand Weaving: The Complete Step-by-Step Book of Weaving* (1950); Gertrude G. Greer, *Adventures in Weaving* (1951); Sen Gupta, *Weaving Calculations* (1959); Alice Hindson, *Designer's Drawloom* (1958); Ruth Overman and Lula E. Smith, *Contemporary Handweaving* (1955); Helvi Pyysalo and Viivi Merisalo, *Hand Weaving Patterns from Finland* (1961); Malin Selander, *Weaving Patterns* (1956), *Swedish Handweaving* (1959); Lillian E. B. Simpson and Marjorie Weir, *Weaver's Craft* (1957); Heather G. Thorpe, *Handweaver's Workbook* (1956); Harriet Tidball, *The Double Weave Plain and Patterned* (1960); Kate Van Cleve, *Hand Loom Weave for Amateurs* (1948); Alice V. White, *Weaving is Fun* (1959); Stanislaw A. Zielinski, *Encyclopaedia of Hand-weaving* (1959).

WEBB, ALEXANDER STEWART, 1835–1911, U.S. soldier and educator, son of James Watson Webb, was born in New York City. He was graduated from the U.S. Military Academy, 1855, served against the Seminoles in Florida, 1856, and was assistant professor of mathematics at West Point, 1857–61. He served in the Civil War, and was brevetted major general in the regular army, 1865, for his services. He resigned from the service, 1870, and was president of the College of the City of New York, 1869–1902. He wrote *The Peninsula: McClellan's Campaign of 1862* (1881).

WEBB, SIR ASTON, 1849–1930, English architect, was born in London. He designed many notable buildings, among them the Britannia Royal Naval College, Dartmouth, the architectural surroundings for the Victoria Memorial, and the French Protestant church, Soho; with D. Ingress as a partner he supplied the designs for the Royal United Service Institution, the new Christ's Hospital, and Birmingham University. He was knighted, 1904, was royal gold medalist (architecture), England, 1905, and received the gold medal of the American Institute of Architects, 1907. In 1912 his design was chosen for the new front of Buckingham Palace. He was president of the Royal Academy, 1919–25.

WEBB, BEATRICE, 1858–1943, British Socialist writer, wife and collaborator of Sidney Webb, was born Beatrice Potter in Gloucester, of a wealthy timber-merchant family, and was privately educated. At the age of 25 she was, as she put it, "a rather hard and learned woman with a clear and analytical mind," yet deep and pervasive religious feeling led her to take part in Charles Booth's colossal 17-volume *Life and Labour of the People in London*, to which she made her first contribution in 1887. By 1890, when her *The Lords and the Sweating System* appeared, she had outgrown the current economic slogans and "was confirmed in her faith in the application of the scientific method to social organization." She met Sidney Webb, 1890, and after finishing her book on *The Co-operative Movement in Great Britain* (1891), was married to him, 1892. From that time on, their work became one, and most of her subsequent publications were in collaboration with her husband. Two major works she wrote herself: the reminiscences, *My Apprenticeship* (1926), dedicated to "The Other One"; and *Men's and Women's Wages: Should They Be Equal?* (1919). Beatrice Webb never used her title, Lady Passfield. She died in Passfield Corner, Liphook, Hampshire.   EUGEN ROSENSTOCK-HUESSY

WEBB, CHARLES HENRY, pseudonym John Paul, 1834–1905, U.S. journalist, was born in Rouses Point, N.Y. Inspired by the newly published *Moby-Dick*, he shipped aboard a whaler at the age of 17. Subsequently, after working at a variety of occupations, he founded the *Californian*, 1864, in which he printed early works by Bret Harte and Mark Twain. He returned to New York, 1866, where he published Mark Twain's first book, *The Celebrated Jumping Frog of Calaveras County* (1867). He is most famous for his *John Paul's Book* (1874), a collection of letters first written for the New York *Tribune*. He also wrote the parodies *St. Twel'mo, or the Cuneiform Cyclopedist of Chattanooga* (1868), a satire on the pompously moralistic romance *St. Elmo* (1867), by Augusta Jane Evans, and *Sea-Weed and What We Seed* (1876); and *Vagrom Verses* (1889).

WEBB, JAMES WATSON, 1802–84, U.S. editor and diplomat, was born in Claverack, N.Y. He served as an officer in the U.S. Army, 1819–27, founded the New York *Morning Courier*, 1827, and two years later merged it with the *Enquirer*. He was U.S. minister to Brazil, 1861–69. In 1865 he arranged by secret treaty with Napoleon III for the withdrawal of French troops from Mexico.

WEBB, PHILIP SPEAKMAN, 1831–1915, English architect, was born in Oxford, and studied at Aynho, Northamptonshire. He entered the architectural office of G. E. Street, where he met William Morris and became an enthusiastic supporter of Morris' arts and crafts movement. Morris' famous Red House, Upton (1859), was designed by Webb as his first commission, and two years later he became a member of Morris' decorating firm. He was the creator, with R. N. Shaw, of the so-called Queen Anne style. With Morris, Webb founded the Society for the Protection of Ancient Buildings, 1877, in which work use was made of a method, invented by Webb, for strengthening the walls of old buildings by filling in with new material.

WEBB, SIDNEY JAMES, 1st BARON PASS-FIELD, 1859–1947, British political leader, founder of the Fabian Society, and partner in a famous marriage (see WEBB, BEATRICE), was born in London, received the most significant part of his education in Switzerland and Germany, and then entered the British civil service, 1878. He left the civil service, 1891, and subsequently stood for the London County Council in the elections of 1892, 1895, 1898, 1901 and 1905; served on the Royal Commission on Trade Union Law, 1903–06; and was a professor of political economy in the School of Economics of the University of London (the London School of Economics), from 1913. A member of the executive committe of the Labour party from 1915, Webb was elected to Parliament, 1922; was president of the Board of Trade in Ramsay MacDonald's first cabinet, 1922–1923, and secretary of the colonies and dominions in his second; and was created Baron Passfield, 1929. Later, however, when MacDonald formed his Union cabinet in August, 1931, Webb opposed him. Webb wrote *Socialism in England* (1890), *London Education*; *Grants in Aid* (1920), and many other works, most of them, as the following, with his wife Beatrice: *The History of Trade Unionism* (1894); *Industrial Democracy* (1897); *Problems of Modern Industry* (1898); *English Local Government* (10 vols., 1906–29); *The Break-up of the Poor Law* (1920); *The State and the Doctor* (1910); *A Constitution for the Socialist Commonwealth of Great Britain* (1920); *The Consumer's Co-operative Movement* (1920); *Methods of Social Study*, (1932), which contains an exposition of the methods of investigation used by the authors and an examination of the place of sociology among the sciences; and *Soviet Communism, A New Civilization?* (2 vols., 1936), called by the Webb's a "work of Supererogation."

EUGEN ROSENSTOCK-HUESSY

WEBB CITY, city, SW Missouri, in Jasper County; on the Missouri Pacific and the Frisco railroads, and U.S. highways 66 and 71; 160 miles SW of Jefferson City. It is in the Tri-State lead- and zinc-mining region. The city is a processing center for an area of dairy farms. Shoes, clothing and explosives are manufactured. The quarrying of sand and gravel pits in the vicinity is important, but lead and zinc deposits are nearly exhausted. Webb City was platted in 1875, at the beginning of the greatest mining era in the history of Missouri. Pop. (1960) 6,740.

WEBER, KARL MARIA FRIEDRICH ERNST VON, 1786–1826, German composer, founder of the Romantic opera in Germany, was born in Eutin,

CULVER SERVICE
Karl Maria von Weber

near Lübeck, the son of a theatrical impresario. He studied under Abbé Georg Joseph Vogler, through whom he became *Kapellmeister* of the Breslau municipal theater, 1804–06. After leaving Breslau he served for a time as musical director to Duke Eugen of Württemberg, and was in Stuttgart, 1807–10, as private secretary to Duke Ludwig, brother of the king of Württemberg. He became involved in the corrupt court life of Stuttgart, however, was accused of embezzlement, and was banished from the city. Subsequently he was director of the opera in Prague, 1813–16, and director of the German opera in Dresden from 1817 until his death. He died in

London, where he had gone to direct the production of *Oberon*. His first success was the Romantic opera, *Der Freischütz* (1820), probably the earliest example of German musical nationalism. Among his other dramatic works, are *Euryanthe* (1823), *Oberon* (1826), and incidental music for Wolff's *Preciosa* (1821). Von Weber's other productions comprise choral and symphonic works, concertos, songs, and many compositions for the piano, including the popular rondo, *Invitation to the Dance* (1819). His exoticism, purposeful exaggeration, and brilliant orchestral coloring strongly influenced the art of Hector Berlioz and Richard Wagner.

WEBER. MAX, 1864–1920, German sociologist, was born in Erfurt. After studying the history of law under the famous Levin Goldschmidt in Berlin, he broadened his interests to include agrarian history (*Romanische Agrargeschichte*, 1891), and began to teach economics in Freiburg, 1894. Called to the more comprehensive chair of political economy in Heidelberg University, 1897, he became a leader of the Neo-Kantian school there and for the first time applied the principles of this school of thought to the social sciences. Taking his cue from the natural sciences, Weber accepted the rigid methodological limitations inherent in atheism; that is, the scientist and his objects are held to be totally separated, and the values of human beings are assumed to have no power over the scientist's mind. He differed from the natural scientists, however, in stressing the uniqueness of each social fact—a uniqueness that renders the usual quantitative methods of physics inapplicable to the social sciences.

Using this method, Weber wrote the essay on *The Protestant Ethic and the Spirit of Capitalism* (Eng. Tr. by Talcott Parsons, 1930), which made him famous and which was never to be long out of print. The essay had a significant influence on many scholars, notably Richard H. Tawney, who built on Weber's thesis in his *Religion and the Rise of Capitalism* (2nd ed. 1929). The thesis is important in the fact that it seeks to explain modern capitalism and technological production without recourse to the materialistic tenets of liberalism and of Marxism. Thus, he held that the Calvinistic laity, in a parallel to the medieval asceticism of the body, trained their minds to an "inner-worldly asceticism" and recognized their "calling" for developing wealth, not for selfish enjoyment, but for its own sake and according to its own laws of accumulation. Weber taught that everyone chooses his own value arbitrarily from among a multitude of possible and available values, and that the social world is governed by "chance" (one of Weber's most frequently used terms); and that in fulfilling one's own value one becomes the ideal "type" of this chosen path—as, for instance, "religious man," "economic man," "patriotic man," and so forth. Even Jesus himself was generalized by Weber into the "charismatic type," and Weber's close friend, Ernst Troeltsch, in regard to "this solution of heroic despair," called him the "modern Machiavelli." Weber saw his own calling in the austere service of his "value-god," the Nation; that is, his ultimate value was the survival of the nation of which, quite by chance, he happened to be born a citizen. Weber embodied the end of the era of Darwinian nationalism which led to two World Wars; his was an immense intellect incapable or unwilling in its intellectualizing to grant the slightest concession to any future of mankind—to the faith that enables an individual to escape from the bonds of his "type" and to change and be changed creatively.

In 1900 Weber suffered what was reported to be a "nervous breakdown." Still seriously ill in 1903, he resigned his professorship. A year or two later his condition was improved, but not sufficiently for him to resume an official university position. Thus for more than a decade he lived in Heidelberg as a private scholar. When the German Empire collapsed in defeat, 1918, Weber declined a call to teach in Vienna, served in his nation's delegation to the Peace Conference of Versailles, began to teach in Munich, 1919, and soon died.

Most of the extensive research done during Weber's illness only reached the public after his death. Especially important among the many works are *Gesammelte Politische Schriften* (1921), *Wirtschaftsgeschichte* (edit. by S. Hellman and M. Palyi, 1923), *Gesammelte Aufsätze zur Soziologie und Sozialpolitik* (1924), and *Gesammelte Aufsätze zur Religionssoziologie* (3 vols., 1920–21). Many of his writings are available in English translation. EUGEN ROSENSTOCK-HUESSY

WEBER, WILHELM EDUARD, 1804–91, German physicist, was born in Wittenberg, was educated at the universities of Halle and Göttingen, and was professor of physics at Göttingen from 1831, except for a period of political exile. Weber worked with Karl Friedrich Gauss in a study of terrestrial magnetism and in the invention of an electromagnetic telegraph. He originated the absolute system of electrical units, based on Gauss's system of magnetic units. He collaborated with his elder brother, Ernst Heinrich Weber, in a study of wave motion, and with his younger brother, Eduard Friedrich Weber, in a study of the physiology of walking. The weber, a unit of magnetic flux, was named after Wilhelm Weber.

WEBERN, ANTON VON, 1883–1945, Austrian composer and musician, was born in Vienna and attended the University of Vienna, where he studied under Arnold Schönberg. After graduation, 1906, he conducted many theater orchestras throughout Germany and Austria. He returned to Vienna, aided Schönberg with the formation of the *Verein fur Musikalische Privataufführungen* (Society for Private Musical Performances), 1918, and superintended the performance of many advanced modern works. He became the conductor of the Vienna Workers' Symphony Concerts and formed an amateur choir, the *Kimststelle*. During World War II, Webern music was banned and Webern himself was persecuted, although not imprisoned. In the closing days of the war he was mistakenly shot and killed at Mittersill, Austria, by a soldier of the invading allied army.

His works are noted for their extreme concentration and precision; many of them are brief, exquisite miniatures. He wrote chamber and orchestral music, and composed a number of songs and choral works, among the best known being his Opus 15, *Five Sacred Songs* (1917–22). Among his works on music theory are an essay in the symposium *Arnold Schönberg* (1912) and *Der Weg zur Neuen Musik* (1933).

WEBSTER, DANIEL, 1782–1852, U.S. lawyer, orator, and political leader who wanted, perhaps above all else, to become president, was born in Salisbury (now Franklin), N.H. His father Ebenezer, the fourth Ebenezer in a line that had lived in North America from about 1635, had been a soldier under Gen. Jeffery Amherst in Canada during a phase of the French and Indian War; had later served as a captain in the American Revolution; and had subsequently, despite his meager education, attained considerable political influence in his state. He sent the delicate Daniel to Phillips Exeter Academy and to Dartmouth College so that the son might have a better start than the father. (It may be noted that sending Daniel away to school was something of a financial hardship for the father, although Daniel's four years at Dartmouth cost less than $200 out-of-pocket.) Having been graduated, 1801, young Webster taught for a short time in Fryeburg, Me., and during this period, if not before, was nicknamed "All Eyes" in reference to his piercing eyes, with which, throughout his life, he could intimidate the most courageous witness or opponent. He subsequently read law under an eminent Bostonian, Christopher Gore, and was admitted to the bar, 1805. So that he might live near his father, who was seriously ill, Webster set up his office in Boscawen, N.H.

Daniel Webster

Not long after Ebenezer Webster's death, Daniel moved to Portsmouth, N.H., and there founded a successful law practice and married, 1808, a clergyman's daughter, Grace Fletcher (died 1828). Two sons were born of this happy marriage; Edward died of illness in the Mexican War (a war that Webster had opposed), while the other son, Fletcher, fell while commanding the Twelfth Massachusetts in the Second Battle of Bull Run, 1862. On Dec. 12, 1829, about a year after Grace Webster's death, Webster married Caroline Le Roy (born 1799) of New York; there was no issue, but Webster later dedicated one volume of his *Works* to her.

A Convinced Federalist, Webster first drew national attention to himself as a politician at a meeting in Rockingham County, 1812. His *Rockingham Memorial*, as his address there is called, protested against U.S. intervention in the Napoleonic Wars, brought his name before the whole country, and particularly endeared him to New Englanders, most of whom were opposed to U.S. war against Great Britain (see WAR OF 1812). Elected to the thirteenth Congress, 1813, Webster was immediately made a member of the committee on foreign relations and from June 10, 1813, embarrassed the administration by his exposure of the French lies (see MADISON, JAMES). On Jan. 14, 1814, he delivered the first of his "great" speeches, a fulmination against the conduct of the war that was "so furious that it was suppressed for a hundred years" (Charles Beard).

Private Law Practice and Fame as an Orator. Webster retired from Congress, 1817, to lay more solid foundations for his law practice in Boston— "the capital of New England," as Webster characterized the place. In his first year there, his income rose tenfold. Webster specialized in federal Supreme Court cases, participated in more than 1,000 of them, and swayed the highest tribunal in a number of decisions of great purport. In the Dartmouth College Case (1818), for example, the principle was established that a charter granted by a state cannot be invalidated by later legislation of the grantor state. It was a blemish on his professional honor that Webster had first accepted a fee from the state's party and later prevaricated, but his victory, and such stirring utterances as the famous "It is a small college; and yet there are those who love it," led people then, as in many other cases, to forgive and often to forget his opportunism and the wide latitude he permitted himself (see DARTMOUTH COLLEGE CASE).

During this period Webster blossomed as an orator. The same speaker who at Exeter had not had the courage to rise in class for declamation exercises, now rose to unequaled fame with three resounding orations: that on the "Pilgrim Fathers and the Settlement of New England" (Dec. 22, 1820); that delivered at the laying of the cornerstone of the Bunker Hill Monument (1825); and that eulogizing John Adams and Thomas Jefferson (1826), who had both passed away on the fiftieth anniversary of the Declaration of Independence. "Godlike Webster," as he came to be called, had a voice of extraordinary volume, flexibility, and musicality; this, and his strict subordination of rhetoric to content, and his great effervescence of good will and humor, combined to attract vast crowds. In 1840, before radio and television, 15,000 persons climbed lonely Mount Stratton, Vt., for the privilege of hearing him; the same privilege at his last speech in New York, 1852, cost everyone in the audience $100 hard money.

Return to Politics. By 1822 Webster could afford to re-enter politics and promptly did so, first as a representative from Massachusetts, 1823–27, and then as a senator, 1827–41 and 1845–50. The Crimes Act of 1825 was largely Webster's work and bears his name. With Henry Clay and John C. Calhoun, Webster formed a great triumvirate. Embracing the industrial interests of the North, he turned against the threats of Southerners who wished to invalidate the high duties of the new tariff. In his famous "Reply to Hayne" (Jan. 26 and 27, 1830) Webster convinced reponsible men throughout the nation that the states form a true Union, and thereby made it certain that when South Carolina came out, 1832, for the alleged right of nullification, this was recognized for what it was—a sectarian doctrine and nothing more. Much later, in the Civil War, Webster's vision of the great destiny of a united country was shown to have captured the whole nation. See CALHOUN, JOHN CALDWELL, *States' Rights;* NULLIFICATION.

Ambition. The remainder of Webster's life was dominated by an unceasing and never successful quest for the presidency. His parliamentary triumphs stood in his way in a country that had never given its highest office to an athlete of eloquence. Webster joined the Whigs, but in 1833, in 1836, and in 1840, he failed to become their candidate. In 1840, President Harrison appointed him secretary of state. After one month, Harrison died and the new President Tyler received the dutiful resignations of Harrison's cabinet members, with the exception of Webster's, for he claimed to be indispensable in the negotiations with England over the Maine boundary. After the Webster-Ashburton Treaty (1842) was signed—he had used secret service money to put it over—Webster tried to heal the breach with his party by resigning, May, 8, 1843.

Back in the Senate from 1845, he supported ("not as a Massachusetts man, nor as a Northern man, but as an American") Clay's Compromise of 1850 and scolded the North for its resistance to the claims of the South to win back their fugitive slaves. This speech, delivered Mar. 7, 1850, filled the Rotunda of the Capitol and the avenues of the city with crowds waiting "for the only man who could draw such an assembly." Of this speech, in which Webster sought "to beat down the Northern and the Southern follies, now raging in equal extremes," it may be said to have prolonged the peace for 10 years, but it also earned him the vitriolic attack *Ichabod* from the pen of the abolitionist poet John Greenleaf Whittier, who wrote that "The glory has departed from Israel."

Becoming secretary of state once more, July 22, 1850, in the cabinet of Pres. Millard Fillmore, Webster entered, December 20, upon the famous Hülsemann correspondence with the Austrian charge d'affaires which sounds as if written in the 1960's. In it, Webster vindicated the right of the United States to sympathize with, and to recognize, revolutionary governments (specifically, at that time, the Hun-

garian). Webster saved the Hapsburg refugees in Turkey and also invited the Hungarian revolutionary hero Lajos Kossuth to America.

In 1852, as in previous presidential election years, Webster tried again for the Whig nomination to the presidency. When he failed, he repudiated the Whig choice, Gen. Winfield Scott, and sided with Pierce, the man agreeable to the South.

Significance. Despite such lapses, despite his dogged chase after the presidency, despite the financial chaos of his affairs and his dependence on "loans" and gifts from the manufacturers, the Christian enthusiasm of Webster-the-man was certainly genuine, and as a patriot he cemented the nation with his large vision of its great future-in-unity as very few had done before or were to do later. Upon his death, in his "ocean-mansion" at Marshfield, Mass., there was an outburst of deep mourning throughout the country that was to remain virtually unique in its scope and in its intensity. The various eulogies of the day, by Rufus Choate, Edward Everett, and others, are an important source for gauging Webster's position in the hearts of the people.

Webster's Works were edited and published in his lifetime by Edward Everett (6 vols. 1851); more complete is the National Edition, edited by J. W. McIntyre: *The Writings and Speeches of Daniel Webster* (18 vols. 1903). The best bibliography of Websteriana is in Volume II of the *Cambridge History of American Literature* (1918). There are extensive biographies by George C. Curtis (1870) and Claude M. Fuess (1930), and short ones by A. L. Benson (1929), S. H. Adams (1930), G. W. Johnson (1939), J. B. McMaster (1939), and M. T. Carroll (1945). New documents appear in H. A. Bradley and J. A. Winans, *Daniel Webster and the Salem Murder Case* (1956). Nathaniel Hawthorne's *The Great Stone Face* and Stephen Vincent Benét's *The Devil and Daniel Webster* are notable among the various poetical evocations of Webster. In the latter he takes on the Devil himself in a property case tried before a judge and jury of traitors, pirates, and murderers all prejudiced in the Devil's favor—and wins the case.

EUGEN ROSENSTOCK-HUESSY

BIBLIOG.–Samuel Hopkins Adams, *Godlike Daniel* (1930); Holmes M. Alexander, *Famous Five.* (1958); Allan L. Benson, *Daniel Webster* (1929); Robert L. Carey, *Daniel Webster as an Economist* (1929); Helen S. N. Cournos, (Sybil Norton, pseud.), *Candidate for Truth: The Story of Daniel Webster* (1953); Richard N. Current, *Daniel Webster and the Rise of National Conservatism* (Lib. of Am. biography) (1955); Claude M. Fuess, *Daniel Webster,* 2 vols. (1930); Gerald W. Johnson, *America's Silver Age: The Statecraft of Clay-Webster-Calhoun* (1939); John B. McMaster, *Daniel Webster* (1939); Bertha Rothe, ed., *Daniel Webster Reader* (1956); John B. Rust, *Daniel Webster: A Character Sketch* (1927?); Caroline LeR. Webster, *Mr. W & I* (1949).

WEBSTER, JOHN, 1580?–?1625, English dramatist, born probably in London, was the son of a tailor and was himself a member of the Merchant Taylors' company. Practically nothing is known of his life. His first plays were written in collaboration with other dramatists, particularly Thomas Dekker. *The Famous History of Sir Thomas Wyat* and the comedies *West-Ward Hoe* and *North-Ward Hoe* were published in 1607 under Webster's and Dekker's names. Webster's two great tragedies *The White Divil* (produced ?1611, published 1612) and *The Dutchesse of Malfy* (produced ?1614, published 1623) are both memorable for their grim terror and their vivid characterizations. Among his later works are *The Devils Law-case* (published 1623), *Appius and Virginia* (produced ?1639, published 1654), and *A Cure for a Cuckold* (produced ?1625, published 1661).

WEBSTER, NOAH, 1758–1843, U.S. lexicographer, was born in West Hartford, Conn., and was educated at Yale College. He was admitted to the bar, 1781, but did not take up the practice of law, turning instead to teaching and writing. In 1783 he began publishing *A Grammatical Institute of the English*

Language, a work which was to influence American education for a hundred years. The first volume, later called *The American Spelling Book*, was supplemented by a grammar (1784) and a reader, *An American Selection of Lessons in Reading and Speaking* (1785). Throughout the nineteenth century "Webster's blue-back speller" was the basic American textbook; by 1890 it had sold more than 60,000,000 copies.

Following the publication of the speller, Webster began agitating in behalf of copyright legislation, and became active in Federalist propaganda. In October, 1787, he published a timely pamphlet advocating adoption of the proposed U.S. Constitution. After editing the unsuccessful *American Magazine* in New York, 1787, he spent several years in Hartford, then returned to New York to edit two Federalist organs, the *Herald* and the *Minerva*. His *Dissertations on the English Language* (1789) was followed by a number of scientific and political works, including *A Brief History of Epidemic and Pestilential Diseases* (1799), *Ten Letters to Dr. Joseph Priestley* (1800), and *Experiments Respecting Dew* (written in 1790; published in 1809).

Noah Webster

He retired from journalism in 1803 to devote himself to lexicography, and in 1806 published his *Compendious Dictionary of the English Language*, remarkable for its inclusion of 5,000 words not listed in earlier works. This led the way for his great work, *An American Dictionary of the English Language* (2 vols., 1828), which he finished during a residence in Cambridge, England.

Webster compromised with classical orthography, and within the limits of the modified classical system rationalized between American and British usage, and introduced many Americanisms. Another advantage of his dictionary was its logical definitions. His weakest point was etymology; he is said to have learned 20 languages, but his knowledge of at least some of them must have been superficial, for he derived such words as *preach* and *establish* from Hebrew. After his death, the dictionary was improved and enlarged as the *International Dictionary*. Many revisions and abridgments were published.

WEBSTER, PELATIAH, 1726–95, colonial American political economist, was born in Lebanon, Conn., and was graduated from Yale College, 1746. He became a merchant in Philadelphia, wrote a series of conservative essays on finance, and published *A Dissertation on the Political Union and Constitution of the Thirteen United States of North-America* (1783), advocating a stronger union.

WEBSTER, town, S Massachusetts, Worcester County; on the New York Central and the New Haven railroads; 15 miles S of Worcester and 2 miles N of the Connecticut border. Webster is a trade and manufacturing center for a region in which dairy products and fruit are produced. Textiles, woolen goods, and optical products are manufactured. Webster was first settled in 1713 and the town adopted its present name in 1811. Within the town area is Lake Chaubunagungamaug (area 2 sq. mi.), which is a resort center. Pop. (1960) 13,680.

WEBSTER, city, NE South Dakota, seat of Day County; on the Milwaukee Railroad and U.S. highway 12; 150 miles NE of Pierre. The city is a lake resort and a processing center for an area in which wheat and livestock are raised. Webster was platted in 1880. Pop. (1960) 2,409.

WEBSTER-ASHBURTON TREATY, a treaty negotiated between the United States and Great Britain, 1842, by Secretary of State Daniel Webster and the special British Commissioner Alexander Baring, 1st Baron Ashburton, for the settlement of various issues, especially the long-disputed boundary between Maine and Canada. Relations between the two countries had been disturbed by the Caroline affair, the McLeod case, and the Aroostook War in the disputed region. All the issues were satisfactorily settled by the treaty and by accompanying exchanges of notes. The United States obtained about 7,000 of the disputed 12,000 square miles; the boundary in the Lake Huron and Lake of the Woods region was rectified; and agreements were made regarding extradition, free navigation of the St. John River, and the slave trade.

WEBSTER CITY, city, central Iowa, seat of Hamilton County, on the Boone River, the North Western, the Fort Dodge, Des Moines, and Southern, and the Illinois Central railroads, and U.S. highway 20; 60 miles N of Des Moines. The city is a trade center for a diversified farming area. The town has a hatchery and a meat-packing plant, and is a center for livestock marketing. Washing machines and metal products are manufactured. Webster City was settled in 1856. Pop. (1960) 8,520.

WEBSTER GROVES, city, E Missouri, in St. Louis County; on the Missouri Pacific and the Frisco railroads, and U.S. highways 50, 66, and 67; about 10 miles SW of St. Louis, of which it is a residential suburb. Webster Groves was chartered as a city in 1914. The city is the site of Webster College (1916) and Eden Theological Seminary (1848). Pop. (1960) 28,990.

WEBSTER SPRINGS, or Addison, town, central West Virginia, seat of Webster County; on the Elk River and the Western Maryland Railroad; 65 miles ENE of Charleston. Coal is mined in the vicinity. Webster Springs was incorporated in 1892. Pop. (1960) 1,132.

WEDDELL SEA, a wide projection of the Atlantic Ocean into the Antarctic Continent; bounded by the South Orkney Islands on the N, the Atlantic Ocean on the E, Antarctica on the S, and Palmer Peninsula of Antarctica on the W. The southern section of Weddell Sea is covered by the Filchner Ice Shelf. The northern section of the Weddell Sea is an important whaling area.

WEDDING ANNIVERSARY, an annual marking of the date on which a wedding took place. Each anniversary is commonly associated with a type of gift considered appropriate for the year being celebrated. The most common classification is as follows:

First	Paper
Second	Cotton
Third	Leather
Fourth	Fruit and Flowers, or Silk
Fifth	Wood
Sixth	Sugar and Candy, or Iron
Seventh	Wool or Copper
Eighth	Bronze or Pottery
Ninth	Willow or Pottery
Tenth	Tin or Aluminum
Eleventh	Steel
Twelfth	Silk or Linen
Thirteenth	Lace
Fourteenth	Ivory
Fifteenth	Crystal
Twentieth	China
Twenty-fifth	Silver
Thirtieth	Pearl
Thirty-fifth	Coral
Fortieth	Ruby
Forty-fifth	Sapphire
Fiftieth	Golden
Fifty-fifth	Emerald
Sixtieth	Diamond
Seventy-fifth	Diamond

WEDDING DANCE, a painting by Pieter Brueghel the Elder, dated 1566. This painting, a gay crowd scene full of color and life, though unsigned, bears the obvious imprint of the Flemish master. The influence of Hieronymus Bosch, whose grotesque figures had affected Brueghel's early work, is not pervasive in *Wedding Dance*, although the painting has something of Bosch's vitality and love of color. To the casual observer it appears to be nothing more than a simple peasant scene, but some critics have said that the painting depicts lust under the disguise of an innocent wedding celebration; the bagpipes played in the picture, for example, appear in other works by Brueghel (and by Bosch) as symbols of vice. The full beauty of Brueghel's workmanship was obscured by rubbing and repainting, and dirt; a careful restoration of the work was effected late in the 1940's at the Detroit Museum of the Arts, which owned the painting at mid-twentieth century; many hitherto unrecognizable details were revealed, including the fact that a good deal of the repainting had been done, probably in Victorian times, with the idea of making the scene less bawdy and abandoned. As late as 1961 the unbowdlerized *Wedding Dance* had yet to be reproduced in any generally available art books in the United States, but it could be seen on public display in the Detroit Museum.

WEDDLE'S RULE. See NUMERICAL INTEGRATION.

WEDEKIND, ERIKA, 1868–1944, German soprano, the sister of the writer Frank Wedekind, was born in Hanover. From 1891 to 1894 she studied with the Hungarian soprano Aglaia Orgeni (1841–1926). She joined the Dresden Court Opera, 1894, and sang with that troupe until 1909; during this period she also toured extensively, gaining a reputation for her skillful execution of such lyric roles as Madame Butterfly, Rosina in *The Barber of Seville*, Violetta in *La Traviata*, and Mimi in *La Bohème*.

WEDEKIND, FRANK, 1864–1918, German playwright and poet, was born in Hanover, and studied law, soon decided for a career in journalism, and then

turned to acting, 1897. His first play, *Frühlings Erwachen* (Spring's Awakening), 1891, is a satire on bourgeois sexuality and hypocrisy. While he was on the staff of *Simplicissimus*, the German satirical magazine, from 1896, his antimonarchical satires cost him a term in jail, 1899, but after his release he resumed writing poems, and satirical songs that he sang in artist cabarets, and plays. His work sharply attacked conventional morality, but in his later years he developed a *Moral der Schönheit* (morality of beauty) that equated physical fitness and beauty. Among his other plays, each full of Expressionist symbolism and sensuality, are *Erdgeist* (Spirit of the Earth), 1895, *Die Büchse der Pandora* (Pandora's Box), 1901, and *Totentanz* (Dance of Death), 1906.   MARTIN GROSZ

CULVER SERVICE
Frank Wedekind

WEDEMEYER, ALBERT COADY, 1897– , U.S. army officer, was born in Omaha, Neb., and was graduated from West Point, 1918. He became major general, temporary, 1943, and lieutenant general, temporary, 1945. He served on the War Department General Staff, 1941–43, was deputy chief of staff, Southeast Asia Command, 1943, and became commander of U.S. Forces in the China Theater and chief of staff to Generalissimo Chiang Kai-shek, 1944. Wedemeyer was made commander of the 6th Army, 1949. He retired, 1951, and became an airplane manufacturing executive.

WEDGE, a mechanical device, once considered to be one of the six simple machines, consisting of a material such as wood or steel that tapers to a fine edge. Mechanically, a wedge is a double inclined plane. A substantial mechanical advantage can be realized by the use of a wedge which, disregarding the element of friction, depends upon the ratio of the length of the wedge to its thickness. Thus, a wedge that is long in proportion to its thickness has the more

favorable mechanical advantage. Wedges are used to lift heavy objects short distances, and to separate two contiguous surfaces.

WEDGWOOD, JOSIAH, 1730–95, the most famous of English potters, was born in Burslem, Staffordshire, and from 1759 had his own pottery business there. His first achievement was an improvement of a cream-colored ware that had been manufactured in English potteries from 1725. He presented a service of the improved ware to Queen Charlotte, 1762, and was appointed potter to the queen, 1763, whereupon his creation was dubbed Queen's Ware. Wedgwood perfected his Jasper ware, 1775–79, which was the result of long experimentation to improve the white

CULVER SERVICE
Josiah Wedgwood

salt-glaze pottery base to one that would rival porcelain biscuit. His creaton was hard enough to polish on a wheel of jasper and would take metallic stains evenly through the mass and on the surface by washes. This made possible a wide range of shades in different colors, among them Wedgwood's famous blue, lilac, sage green, olive green, yellow, and rich black. In 1775 Wedgwood engaged the English scuptor-designer John Flaxman, who did cameo reliefs that are marvels of microscopic detail.

Vases, plaques for jewelry and furniture, mantel insets, and wall decorations were made in Jasper ware. Probably the most renowned examples of Wedgwood's work are his reproductions of the Barberini or Portland vase. He made 50 copies of the vase and sold them to subscribers at 50 guineas apiece. He was elected to the Royal Society, 1783.

WEDGWOOD, THOMAS, 1771–1805, English physicist and philanthropist, was born in Staffordshire, the third son of Josiah Wedgwood, the potter. He attended Edinburgh University, 1787–1789. Wedgwood discovered a process by which nitrate and chloride of silver could be used to make photographs on glass, and published a paper (1802) on this subject in the *Journal of the Royal Institute of Great Britain*. He is also remembered for his philanthropies, especially toward Samuel Taylor Coleridge.

WEDNESDAY. See WEEK.

WEDOWEE, town, E Alabama, seat of Randolph County; on U.S. highway 431; 77 miles ESE of Birmingham. The town is a ginning center for an area of cotton farming. Clothing is manufactured. Pop. (1960) 917.

WEED, THURLOW, 1797–1882, U.S. journalist and political leader, was born in Greene County, N.Y. He became a printer's apprentice after meager education. He worked on several newspapers and bought the Rochester *Telegraph*, 1825. Weed became active in politics, 1824, supporting De Witt Clinton in New York and John Quincy Adams for the presidency. He was an Anti-Mason from that party's beginning until it merged with the Whigs, 1834. His efforts were centered around the advancement of William H. Seward. His astute management was largely responsible for Seward's election as governor, 1838, and as senator, 1848 and 1854. Weed edited the Albany *Evening Journal*, 1830–62. When Seward was elected to the Senate, Weed became a Republican and worked assiduously for his favorite's nomination for the presidency, 1860. As Seward's manager at the Chicago Convention, Weed was bitterly disappointed at Abraham Lincoln's nomination. Although he was consulted by Lincoln and was a member of an unofficial mission in Europe, 1861, Weed's influence declined as the Radical Republican movement emerged. After 1863 he lived in New York City, where he edited the *Commercial Advertiser* from 1867.   DONALD RIDDLE

A well known poison weed is poison sumac, often confused with other forms of sumac; shown here (left to right) are smooth sumac, staghorn sumac, dwarf sumac, poison sumac.

Plantain is one of the many common yard weeds; although most weeds have little value to man, and are enemies to plants, some have important medicinal and food values.

WEED, an unwanted plant that belongs to any of various families and that competes with cultivated plants for life and is otherwise obnoxious to man. Weeds are structurally and physiologically similar to other plants. Ragweed is a weed, not only because of its crowding habit of growth, but because its pollen induces hay fever; the tree of heaven is considered a weed in some regions because of its rank growth and the unpleasant odor of its leaves.

Plants may be considered weeds in one but not another region. Sunflowers are weeds in many parts of the Middle West, but in some areas are cultivated for their seeds, from which a useful oil may be expressed, or as ornamental plants.

Some weeds may have beneficial effects. When plowed under they add to the organic matter of soils. Dense growths of some weeds effectively control soil erosion. Some plants commonly regarded as weeds are occasionally used as food for human beings; among these are dandelion and wild mustard. Others, such as horehound, have medicinal properties.

Control

Preventive Control centers upon the prevention of weed dissemination. Such control is achieved by the use of clean agricultural seed, the thorough cleaning of agricultural machinery which is to be transported from one area to another, and the maintenance of plant quarantine stations at national borders to prevent the introduction of foreign plants which might assume weedy characteristics in a new land.

Mechanical Control involves the destruction of weeds by mechanical means. These include the pulling, cutting, or hoeing out of annual weeds before seed production, and of the roots and underground stems of perennial weeds; burning of weed-infested areas; the use of mulches, such as straw, paper, and dead leaves, which, placed around the stems of garden plants, inhibit the growth of weeds; and by drainage, which causes the disappearance of water-loving weeds.

Biological Control uses other living organisms to combat weeds. Biological control is of several types: the use of smother crops, such as alfalfa, sweet clovers, soybeans, sunflowers, and others which compete successfully with weeds for water, light, and nutrients and which thus smother the weeds; the use of fungi which cause diseases of weeds; the use of animals, such as pigs, that root in freshly plowed soil and eat the underground parts of such weeds as bindweeds.

Chemical Control includes the spraying of weeds and soils with chemical agents poisonous or otherwise injurious to weeds. Among the chemicals thus used are ferrous sulfate, copper sulfate, sodium and other chlorates, arsenical compounds, zinc sulfate, ammonium thiocyanate, carbon bisulfide, sodium chloride, petroleum oils. 2,4-dichlorophenoxyacetic acid (2,4-D), 2,4,5-trichlorophenoxyacetic acid (2,4,5-T), ammonium sulfamate (Ammate), and trichloroacetate (TCA). Some of these are general, killing many types of weeds, as well as garden and field plants. Sodium chloride or common salt, petroleum oils, ammonium thiocyanate, arsenical compounds, and sulfuric acid are of this type. Some chemical weed killers attack certain weeds but do not harm other plants. Iron sulfate, for example, is especially toxic to

CHEMICAL SPECIALTIES CO.

Poison ivy is a type of poison weed that contains an oily substance which upon contact with the skin of an animal usually causes a painful irritation and water blisters.

wild mustards; zinc sulfate kills weeds in coniferous seedbeds without harming the conifer seedlings.

Caution must be used in certain types of weed control. Harrowing and plowing may actually spread weeds by cutting their rhizomes into small pieces, each of which grows into a new plant as shown by quack grass and bindweed. The introduction of disease-producing fungi must be done with extreme caution so that the fungi do not attack valuable plants. Chemical weed killers must be handled in such fashion that they do not poison the soil or injure desirable plants.   HARRY J. FULLER

WEEK, the interval of seven days now in almost universal use as a division of the calendar. It is not based on any periodicity in nature as are the day, month, and year. It may have been suggested, however, by the roughly similar intervals between the quarters of the moon, but it is not commensurable with the lunar month. The origin of the week has been attributed to the Hebrews, to the Chaldeans, and also to the Egyptians.

The Ptolemaic arrangement of the heavenly bodies according to their distance from the earth was in the following order, beginning with the most distant: Saturn, Jupiter, Mars, the Sun, Venus, Mercury, and the Moon. According to ancient astrology these bodies presided in this succession over the hours of the day. If the first hour is assigned to Saturn, the 25th, or first hour of the second day, falls to the Sun; the 49th, or first hour of the third day, to the Moon; and so on until the seven bodies are accounted for.

From the Anglo-Saxon designations of the planets, among which the ancients included the Sun and Moon, the modern names of the days of the week have been formed: Saturday (Saturn, or Saeterdaeg); Sunday (Sun, or Sunnandaeg); Monday (Moon, or Mōnandaeg); Tuesday (Mars, or Tíwesdaeg); Wednesday (Mercury, or Wōdnesdaeg); Thursday (Jupiter, or Thuresdaeg); Friday (Venus, or Frīgedaeg). The Latin equivalents are Dies Saturni, Solis, Lunae, Martis, Mercurii, Jovis, and Veneris.

WEEKS, JOHN WINGATE, 1860–1926, U.S. public official, was born near Lancaster, N.H., and was graduated from Annapolis, 1881. Weeks was a U.S. congressman, 1905–13, and a U.S. senator, 1913–19. He was Secretary of War in the cabinets of Presidents Warren G. Harding and Calvin Coolidge, 1921–25.

WEEKS, SINCLAIR, 1893–   , U.S. industrialist and cabinet official, was born in West Newton, Mass. In February, 1944, he was named U.S. senator from Massachusetts to fill a vacancy and served until December. He was treasurer of the Republican National Committee, 1941–44; and was secretary of commerce in Pres. Dwight D. Eisenhower's cabinet, 1953–58.

WEEMS, MASON LOCKE, 1759–1825, U.S. clergyman and writer, was born in Dumfries, Va. He was educated for the Protestant Episcopal ministry and was ordained, 1784. He became a wandering preacher and wrote a number of biographies and religious tracts. He is remembered for his *Life of Washington*, first published in 1800. The fifth edition (1806) was greatly expanded and it was in this edition that the cherry tree anecdote and others equally apocryphal first appeared.

WEEVIL, any of a large number of beetles belonging chiefly to the suborder Rhyncophora. They are characterized by the prolongation of the anterior part of the head into a snout or proboscis, which is generally used by the female as an ovipositor and by both sexes for boring. The body is solid and compact, and the antennae, arising from either side of the snout, are angularly bent. The larvae of the weevil are white, footless grubs.

Several families are distinguished, the *Curculionidae* being the most important. Familiar forms of this group are the chestnut weevil, *Curculio auriger,* the large chestnut weevil, *C. probascideus,* and the pecan

or hickory nut weevil, *C. caryae.* The adult insects bore into nuts and deposit their eggs within. Here they hatch and the grub matures, ready to eat its way out when the nuts fall.

Weevils destructive to fruit are also included in this family. Strawberries are attacked by the strawberry weevil, *Anthonomus signatus,* for example. Other important varieties of *Curculionidae* are the notorious cotton boll weevil, several kinds of clover leaf weevil, and the alfalfa leaf weevil.

JENNIE LEA KNIGHT
FROM NATL. AUDUBON SOC.
Clover Leaf Weevil

A subfamily of the *Curculionidae,* the *Colendrinae,* includes the various forms which infest stored grains. The most widely distributed are the granary weevil, *Sitophilus granavia,* and the rice weevil, *S. oryza,* small brown beetles which deposit their eggs in the interior of the grain kernel. In addition to the Rhynocophora, some beetles of the family *Mylabridae* are commonly called weevils. These include the bean, cowpea, and pea weevils.

Insecticidal sprays and dusts for control of various weevils contain DDT, lindane, calcium arsenate, and toxaphene.

WEGENER, ALFRED LOTHAR, 1880–1930, German geophysicist, born in Berlin, and educated at the universities of Heidelberg, Innsbruck, and Berlin. He taught meteorology at the University of Marburg, 1908–12, and meteorology and geophysics at the University of Graz, 1924–29. He was a member of expeditions to Greenland, 1906–08, 1912–17, 1929, and was in command of a German expedition to central Greenland, 1930, in which he lost his life. In *Die Entstehung der Kontinente und Ozeane,* 1915 (*The Origin of Continents and Oceans,* 1924), he put forth the Wegener Theory of Continental Drift, in which the present world continents are presumed to have evolved from a single primordial continent, and to have changed their positions by gradual drifting over a semiliquid layer. See GEODESY, *Continental Drift.*

WEIDMAN, JEROME, 1913–   , U.S. Pulitzer prize-winning writer, was born in New York City, studied at City College of New York and New York University law school, and was admitted to the bar, 1937. His first successful work of fiction was the novel *I Can Get It for You Wholesale* (1937), a bitter and cynical commentary on American life as lived in the microcosm of the Garment District in New York City. He shared a 1960 Pulitzer prize for his part in the writing of *Fiorello!* (1959), a musical comedy. Other works are *What's In It for Me?* (1938), *Letter of Credit* (1940), *I'll Never Go There Any More* (1941), *The Lights Around the Shore* (1943), *The Third Angel* (1953), and *Your Daughter Iris* (1955).

WEIGHING MACHINE, a device for determining the force with which a body or mass is attracted to the earth. In the English system of weights, the standard unit used in weighing machines is the pound; in the metric system, it is the gram.

The beam balance, pivoted in the center, was used in the days before the building of the Egyptian pyramids, and the Old Testament has many references to the use of weights and balances. The steelyard, with its favorable mechanical advantage made possible by placing the pivot nearer one end of the beam, was another early modification of the balance. (See BALANCE.) Many refinements of the beam type of balance so increased its weighing accuracy that it became an invaluable adjunct to the chemical and scientific laboratory by the mid-nineteenth century.

The first platform scale was invented in 1830 by Thaddeus Fairbanks at St. Johnsbury, Vt. It consisted of a series of multiplying levers connected so that the weight required to counterbalance the mass being weighed was negligible. A sliding weight, used with or without additional counterpoise weights, balanced the load being weighed, and the correct weight was read directly on the calibrated slide, or was readily computed by adding the counterpoise weights. In 1857 the E. and T. Fairbanks Company of St. Johnsbury applied a similar principle to produce the first railroad scale.

With the improvements in steels and metallurgical processing of the middle and late nineteenth century weighing machines that depended upon the elasticity of springs became important. In general, they were easier and faster to read than the beam balance, which led to their wide usage in food and bulk product markets.

In 1895 the Computing Scale Company of Dayton, Ohio, introduced the first computing scale that gave readings for both weight and price of an article. Shortly thereafter, in 1899, the company that was later to become the Toledo Scale Company developed new dial and fan type scales for weighing products ranging from a fraction of a pound to a semi-trailer load of steel.

Specialized types of scales developed in the twentieth century included those that record weights of materials moving on conveyor belts; the automatic control of weights during packaging; counting pieces for the purposes of cost, processing, or production control; and the linking of automatic weighing devices with electronic computers.

WEIGHT LIFTING, the gymnastic sport of lifting weights in a prescribed manner. Individuals may engage in weight lifting in order to increase their strength, to improve their athletic performance, or to enhance their physical appearance; or they may compete against one another in weight-lifting contests.

The modern sport of weight lifting developed in England, and soon became popular in many countries, most notably Germany, France, Austria, Switzerland, Egypt, and Japan. The organized sport derived, however, from the informal activity, practiced since ancient times, of pitting one's ability to perform feats of strength, such as lifting heavy objects, against the similar ability of others. Weight-lifting exhibitions were numerous in the United States during the nineteenth century, and formal weight-lifting competition gained popularity in the early years of the twentieth century. The first participation of a U.S. athlete in international weight-lifting competition occurred in 1930.

The three major types of lifts included in official competition are (1) the two-handed, or military, press, (2) the snatch, and (3) the clean and jerk. In the military press, the lifter uses both hands to raise a weight from the floor to rest on his chest, shoulders, or neck. He then lifts the weight until his arms are fully extended above his head. While bringing the weight to this locked-arm position, the contestant is required to maintain an erect position, thereby necessitating maximum utilization of the arm and shoulder muscles. In a snatch lift, one or both hands bring the weight

from the floor to the locked overhead position in a continuous movement. Since he is permitted to assume a squatting or split position while lifting, the contestant is thus able to use the muscles of the legs as well as those of the arms and shoulders. In the clean and jerk lift, the weight is hoisted with one or two hands from the floor to rest on the chest, and then to an overhead position; the contestant is permitted to assume a squatting or split position while lifting the weight. In all types of lift, contestants are judged by the total number of pounds lifted in three trials.

Competitive weight lifting is divided into seven classes according to the body weight of contestants. The various classes and the upper limits for the weight of lifters performing in these classes are as follows: bantamweight, 123¼ lbs.; featherweight, 132¼ lbs.; lightweight, 148 ¾ lbs.; middleweight, 165 lbs.; light heavyweight, 181 lbs.; middle heavyweight, 198 lbs.; and heavyweight, unlimited. In competition at mid-twentieth century, average totals for the three lifts ranged from about 700 pounds for bantamweights to about 1,100 pounds for heavyweights.

WEIGHTS AND MEASURES. All measurements consist in determining how many times an unknown quantity contains some known quantity of the same kind. Any measurement therefore is essentially a comparison between the unknown magnitude and the accepted standard. The abstract quantity, in terms of which the measurement is expressed, is called a unit. A concrete representation of a universally accepted unit is called a standard. For example, the common unit of length in Great Britain is the yard, and the standard yard of that country is the distance between two lines crossing two gold studs set in a certain bar of platinum kept in London, the measurement being made when the temperature is 62°F, and the barometric pressure 30 inches. The international standard of length is the International Prototype Meter, preserved at the International Bureau of Weights and Measures at Sèvres, France. Until recently its length was expressed as 1,553,164.13 times the wave length of the red cadimum line in air (760 mm pressure, 15°C). A U.S. scientist at the invitation of the French government first made the determination of the standard meter in terms of the wave length of the red cadmium line. However, at the eleventh convention on weights and measures in Paris during October, 1960, the new standard for the meter was defined in terms of an orange-red spectral line of the gas krypton-86 and is 1,650,763.73 times the wave length of this line. Krypton-86 was chosen because its spectral line is easily produced, is very stable, and possesses a high degree of definition. The accuracy in this measurement is now of the order of one part in one hundred millions. A copy possessed by the federal government is the official standard of length in the United States, the U.S. yard being defined since 1895 as 3600/3937 meter. The yard is an example of a simple or fundamental unit; the square and cubic yards, obtained from it, are derived units.

The subjoined tables show the principal units of length, volume, and weight established in the United

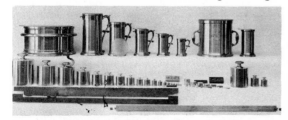 

U.S. standards of capacity, mass, and length as kept in the National Bureau of Standards are shown, upper left; at upper right is Kilogram No. 20, national standard of mass; and below, Prototype Meter No. 27, standard of length.

States, although numerous local divergencies exist, since state laws and the usages of commerce do not always strictly adhere to national usage.

Common Linear Measure

12 inches	= 1 foot
3 feet	= 1 yard
5½ yards	= 1 rod, pole, or perch
40 rods	= 1 furlong
8 furlongs	= 1,760 yards
	= 5,280 feet
	= (statute) mile
3 miles	= 1 (land) league
1,760 yards	= 1 mile
5,280 feet	= 1 (statute) mile

Special linear units are the hand, which is used in measuring horses, and which equals 4 inches; the fathom, which is used in measuring ropes, soundings, and so forth, and which equals 6 feet; the chain, which equals 100 links or 66 feet, used in surveying; the nautical mile, 6,080.27 ft. (U.S.) or 6,080 ft. (British). See MILE; KNOT.

Square or Land Measure

144 square inches	= 1 square foot
9 square feet	= 1 square yard
30¼ square yards	= 1 square rod
40 square rods	= 1 rood
4 roods	= 1 acre
640 acres	= 1 square mile
10 square chains	= 1 acre

Cubic or Solid Measure

1,728 cubic inches	= 1 cubic or solid foot
27 cubic feet	= 1 cubic or solid yard
128 cubic feet	= 1 cord

Dry Measure

2 pints	= 1 quart
4 quarts	= 1 gallon
2 gallons	= 1 peck
4 pecks	= 1 bushel

The U.S. bushel is 2,150.42 cubic inches; the British bushel is 2,218.192 cubic inches.

Liquid Measure

4 gills	= 1 pint
2 pints	= 1 quart
4 quarts	= 1 gallon
63 gallons	= 1 hogshead
2 hogsheads	= 1 pipe or butt
2 pipes	= 1 tun

The U.S. Standard liquid gallon is 231 cubic inches, the British imperial gallon 277.274 cubic inches. The legal barrel in most states of the United States is 31½ gallons; in some, 32 gallons.

Avoirdupois Weight

27.34375 grains	= 1 dram
16 drams	= 1 ounce
16 ounces	= 1 pound
28 pounds	= 1 quarter
4 quarters	= 1 hundredweight (cwt.)
20 cwt.	= 1 ton (long)

The long ton (2,240 lbs.) is generally used only for coal and minerals in the United States; the commercial ton is 2,000 pounds. In Great Britain the long ton is always used.

Troy Weight

24 grams	= 1 pennyweight (dwt.)
20 pennyweight	= 1 ounce
12 ounces	= 1 pound

Troy weight is now restricted to gold, silver, and jewels, except pearls and diamonds, which are weighed in carats (1 carat = 3.0865 grains troy).

Apothecaries' Weight

20 grains or minims	= 1 scruple
3 scruples	= 1 dram
8 drams	= 1 ounce
12 ounces	= 1 pound

Apothecaries' Fluid Measure

60 minims	= 1 fluid dram (ʒ i)
8 fluid drams	= 1 fluid ounce (℥ i)
16 fluid ounces	= 1 pint (O i)
8 pints	= 1 gallon (C i)

Approximately, 1 minim = 1 drop; 1 dram = 1 teaspoonful; a fluid ounce = 2 tablespoonfuls; 2 ounces = 1 wineglassful.

WEIHAI, port city, E China; on the N coast of Shantung Peninsula, at Weihai Bay on the Yellow Sea; 140 miles NE of Tsingtao, 370 miles SE of Peking. Until 1949, when the name was changed to its present form, the town and port were named Weihaiwei ("awe-inspiring sea fort"), perhaps in reference to a fort which stood on this site during the Ming dynasty. The city of Weihai is a commercial center of Shantung Province. The leading industries are cotton and silk weaving, oilseed milling, and the manufacture of rubber goods, matches, and soap. During the Sino-Japanese War, 1895, Japan captured the important Chinese naval base at Weihaiwei but was persuaded by France, Germany, and Russia to relinquish it in exchange for an indemnity. The indemnity was paid by China with funds obtained from Great Britain. In return, the British in 1898 were granted the right to use the port, which they utilized as a naval coaling station ("Port Edward") until 1930, when it was returned to the Chinese. The port was occupied by the Japanese, 1938–45. Pop. (1962 est.) 200,000.

WEIL, SIMONE, 1909–43, French mystical writer, was born in Paris, the daughter of a physician. Although of middle class Jewish background, she manifested an early desire to share the sufferings of the working classes. She taught in a secondary school at Le Puy, 1931–34, and became interested in, but did not join, the Communist party. She went to Spain, 1936, and aided the Loyalists in the Civil War, spending several weeks at the Catalonian front. She manifested a strong interest in Roman Catholicism, but never joined the Church. During World War II, she went to America, 1942, and then to England, where she refused to eat more than was allowed to her countrymen in Nazi-occupied France, and soon died of what was described as "voluntary starvation." Her principal work is *Waiting for God* (1950).

WEILL, KURT, 1900–50, German-American composer, was born in Dessau, Germany, and educated at the Berlin High School of Music. He was

CULVER SERVICE
Kurt Weill

trained for serious music, studied under the esoteric Busoni, and wrote several works for orchestra and chamber groups. While still a student, however, he played popular tunes in beer halls and conducted small theater orchestras. In his first opera, *Der Protagonist* (1924), as in subsequent works, he embraced the concept of what he termed "functional music" —music hall ballads, tango, shimmy, and blues rhythms as adapted to the theater stage. In *The Royal Palace* (1927) he interpolated movie films into the live stage action, and in the very popular *The Czar Has Himself Photographed* he used jazzy music to good effect. With Bertold Brecht he wrote his most famous work, *Die Dreigroschenoper* (The Three-Penny Opera), 1928, whose plot and characters are based largely on those of the eighteenth-century *The Beggar's Opera* of John Gay. In this "song-play," with melodies the public could hum and with lyrics in the argot of the streets, Weill achieved his masterpiece. It was a great popular success and made a star of Lotte Lenya, whom Weill later married.

Despite his popularity, Weill was persuaded to flee Germany for Paris after the burning of the Reichstag, 1933. The film version of *Die Dreigroschenoper*, directed by G. W. Pabst, and starring Lotte Lenya, was destroyed—so it was thought—by the Nazis as "degenerate art"; late in the 1950's, however, a complete version was reassembled from bits and pieces and the film restored to life. In the meantime, in an English version by Marc Blitzstein, *The Three-Penny Opera*, enjoyed a long run on the off-Broadway stage in New York City during the 1950's and early 1960's.

Weill emigrated to the United States, 1935, studied English, and wrote the score for *Johnny Johnson* (1936). His *Knickerbocker Holiday* (1938), with libretto by Maxwell Anderson, established Weill's reputation on Broadway, and introduced his hit tune "September Song." Among his other Broadway musicals were *Lady in the Dark* (1941), *One Touch of Venus* (1943), *Street Scene* (1947), and *Lost in the Stars* (1949), the last with Maxwell Anderson.

MARTIN GROSZ

WEIL'S DISEASE, or infectious jaundice, an infectious disease caused by the spirochete, *Leptospira icterohaemorrhagic*. It is characterized by the sudden appearance of a headache, backache, muscular pain, nausea, vomiting, chills and fever, and in many cases the development of jaundice. In severe cases, lesions in the kidneys, liver, capillaries, and skeletal muscles may give rise to kidney dysfunction and hemorrhage. Drinking water and stagnant water contaminated by excreta of wild rats is the most common source of human infection. The chief portal of entry is the gastrointestinal tract, but other routes may be the respiratory tract, mucous membranes of the eye, and even skin cuts and abrasions. Men are affected more often than women, chiefly because exposure occurs more frequently as a result of work in rat-infested areas.

Treatment includes bed rest and adequate administration of fluid. Bismuth preparations have been used with some success. The mortality and severity of the disease has been lessened by the use of specific antiserum. Convalescent serum may be substituted in certain cases when antiserum is not available. Antibiotics have proved helpful, also.

WEIMAR, city, central Germany, in the East German district of Erfurt, in Thuringia; on the Ilm River, 15 miles E of Erfurt and 135 miles SW of Berlin. Weimar has textile and publishing industries. Electrical equipment and musical instruments are manufactured. The city is important for its historical and literary associations. During the nineteenth century Weimar was the cultural center of Germany. Under the patronage of Duke Charles Augustus of Saxe-Weimar, Johann Wolfgang von Goethe and Johann Christoph von Schiller, both German poets and playwrights, lived and worked in Weimar. They are both buried in the grand ducal vault in the city. The Goethe-Schiller Archives is a building in which manuscripts of these two poets and those of several others are retained. Franz Liszt, the composer, was a musical director in Weimar from 1848 to 1859. Weimar was known as early as the ninth century. It was long the capital of the Saxe-Weimar-Eisenach grand duchy. In July, 1919, following German defeat in World War I, the constitution for the German Republic was adopted there by the national assembly. This republic, which expired with Hitler's advent to power, was often called the Weimar Republic. In 1919, Weimar was the scene of the ratification of the Treaty of Versailles. Following World War II Weimar became part of Soviet-occupied Germany. Pop. (1959) 63,800.

FRASIE STUDIO

The Weimaraner, originally called the Weimar Pointer, is the result of selective breeding of German hunting dogs. It was not introduced into the United States until 1929.

WEIMARANER, a gray sporting dog noted for its speed. It was first bred by the dukes of Weimar, Germany, in the early 1700's. Its ancestor was the Red Schweisshund, a type of bloodhound. It is extremely intelligent, makes an excellent hunting dog, and because of its sensitive nose rivals the bloodhound as a trailing dog. It stands about 26 inches high at the shoulder and weighs about 75 pounds. The head is like a pointer's, long and slim, with tapered muzzle. The tail is cropped, and the body is strong and clean, with muscular legs and firm feet. It was first used to hunt bear, deer, and wolves, and later used to retrieve birds. The dog's soft mouth makes it an ideal bird retriever. Breeding is controlled in Germany, where only the best puppies are raised to maturity. First brought to the United States in 1929, they were exhibited in 1941 at American Kennel Club obedience trials and registered in 1943. Weimaraners do not adjust to kennel life and are usually happiest in domestic surroundings.

WEINBERGER, JAROMIR, 1896–   , Czech composer, was born in Prague, studied music there and in Leipzig, and then spent four years in the United States, 1922–26, teaching composition at Ithaca Conservatory. He left his homeland and in 1939 settled in New York City. His genius for orchestral arrangements of old rounds and folk tunes is best represented in the rollicking *Polka and Fugue* from his opera, *Schwanda the Bagpiper* (1927), and in his set of variations, *Under the Spreading Chestnut Tree* (1938). Among his other works are the operas *The Beloved Voice* (1930) and *Outcasts of Poker Flat* (1932); and *Lincoln Symphony* (1941).

EASTFOTO

The Castle Museum in Weimar is a remnant of the palace constructed, 1790 to 1803, under the direction of Duke Charles Augustus of Saxe-Weimar and Johann von Goethe.

WEINGARTNER, PAUL FELIX EDLER VON MÜNZBERG, 1863–1942, Austrian conductor and composer, was born in Zara, Austria (later Zadar, Yugoslavia). He studied under W. A. Rémy at Graz and won the Mozart prize at Leipzig, 1881. He was the conductor of the Royal Symphonic concerts in Berlin, 1891–98, and of the Boston Opera Company, 1912. In 1927 he was appointed director of the Academy and Music Society in Basle, Switzerland. Among his musical compositions are the operas *Sakuntala* (1884), *Genesis* (1892), and *Kain und Abel* (1914). Among his literary works are *Symphony Since Beethoven* (1904) and *Buffets and Rewards* (1937).

WEINMAN, ADOLPH ALEXANDER, 1870–1952, U.S. sculptor, was born in Karlsruhe, Germany, but was brought to the United States at the age of 10. He studied at Cooper Union and the Art Students' League, New York City, and was a pupil of Philip Martiny and Augustus Saint-Gaudens. Among his works are the General Macomb monument in Detroit and the Soldiers' and Sailors' monument in Baltimore. He designed the United States dime and half-dollar issued in 1916.

WEIR, JULIAN ALDEN, 1852–1919, U.S. painter, was born in West Point, N.Y., the son of the artist Robert Walter Weir. He studied with his father and with Jean Léon Gérôme in Paris, and received a citation at the Paris Salon, 1881. Weir was one of the founders of the Society of American Artists and was one of the 10 who seceded from the society in 1898. He was a disciple of Jules Bastien-Lepage, and in his early painting he adopted the subdued palette of that French realist. His later, more characteristic work, such as *Portrait of a Young Girl* (Luxembourg) and *Idle Hours* (Metropolitan Museum), is in an intimate, lyric vein, and reflects the influence of the Impressionists.

WEIR, ROBERT STANLEY, 1856–1926, Canadian lawyer and poet, was born in Hamilton, Ontario. He attended McGill University, practiced law in Montreal, Québec, and became a judge of the exchequer court of Canada. His poetry was collected in *After Ypres* (1917) and *Poems, Early and Late* (1923). He composed the words to the popular song *O, Canada!*

WEIR, a sharp-edged retaining barrier over which water flows, and which is so constructed as to measure the quantity of that flow; also a spillway type of dam used to contain or raise a stream or river level; also a bank or levee used to hold a river to its bed or to divert the flow to a new bed.

Weirs are widely used by hydraulic engineers in measuring the flow of water in a channel, and from such measurements to determine the potential use of the available water for purposes of power development, irrigation, flood control, and navigation. The quantity of water flowing over a weir is expressed by the formula: $Q = KLH^{3/2}$ where Q is the volume of the water discharged; K is an empirical constant, depending upon the velocity of the water approaching the weir, and the height of the weir; L is the effective length of the weir; and H is the height of the water above the weir.

WEI RIVER, N central China, rises in the mountains of central Kansu Province and flows E for about 450 miles, across Shensi Province, to join the Yellow River at the border of Shansi Province. The Wei is one of the chief tributaries of the Yellow River. The Wei River has cut a deep valley through loess deposits in its lower course. Its comparatively level valley is densely populated, and is intensively cultivated. The fortress city of Tungkuan stands close to the confluence of the Wei and Yellow rivers. Sian is the most important city in the Wei Valley.

The region along the Wei River is of historic importance, as apparently early migrations passed through this corridor from central Asia into what is now China. The valley is recognized as the birthplace of Chinese civilization.

WEIRTON, city, N West Virginia, in Brooke and Hancock counties, on the Ohio River, the Pennsylvania Railroad, and U.S. highway 22, 30 miles W of Pittsburgh. Weirton is an industrial center in a coal-mining region. The city has steel mills and plants which specialize in tin- and zinc-plating. Construction materials and chemicals are manufactured. Weirton was for many years an unincorporated company town. It was incorporated as a city in 1947. Pop. (1960) 28,201.

WEISER, JOHANN CONRAD, 1696–1760, colonial American Indian agent, was born in Württemberg, Germany, and came to North America in the wave of Palatine emigration, 1710. He learned the Indian language and customs during his boyhood spent in the Mohawk country, and later used this knowledge to promote friendly relations between the Indians and the provincial government, to do Christian mission work, and to prevent alliance of the Iroquois with France. He was one of the commissioners who laid out Reading, Pa., 1755.

ALFRED DE GRAZIA

WEISER, city W Idaho; seat of Washington County; at the junction of the Weiser and Snake rivers; on the Union Pacific Railroad and U.S. highways 30 and 95; 65 miles NW of Boise, at the Oregon border. Weiser is the commercial center for the irrigated Weiser Valley, in which fruit and wheat are grown. The city has a flour mill, a creamery, and metal working plants. Weiser was founded in 1863. The city is a center for tourist boats passing through Hell's Canyon of the Snake River, to the north. Pop. (1960) 4,208.

WEISMANN, AUGUST, 1834–1914, German biologist, was born in Frankfurt-am-Main, studied at the University of Göttingen, and served as professor of zoology at the University of Freiburg, 1866–1912. His early researches were devoted to zoology. In 1892 he developed a theory of heredity based on the immortality of the germ plasm. According to this theory the germ plasm is the primordial substance around which new body cells are developed, and as it is formed by the union (amphimixis) of the sperm and the ovum it serves as an unbroken continuity between the generations. Among his writings are *Studien zur Descendenztheorie*, 2 vols. 1875–76 (*Studies in the Theory of Descent*, 1882), and *Das Keimplasma*, 1892 (*The Germ-Plasm, a Theory of Heredity*, 1893). A number of his shorter works were collected in English translation in *Essays upon Heredity and Kindred Biological Problems* (2 vols. 1889–92).

WEISSE ELSTER RIVER, E central Germany, rises in W Czechoslovakia, 4 miles SE of Aš near the German-Czechoslovakian border. The stream flows generally north through Saxony to the Saale River, 4 miles south of Halle. Total length is more than 140 miles.

WEISSENFELS, city, central Germany, in the East German district of Halle, in Saxony; on the Saale River, 20 miles SW of Leipzig. Weissenfels is a highway and railroad junction. The city is in a lignite-mining region, and forms part of an industrial belt centered in Leipzig. Chemicals, shoes and machinery are manufactured. The seventeenth century Augustburg Castle is on a hill near the city. Following World War II, the city became part of the zone which was occupied by armed forces of the Soviet. Pop. (1958) 46,900.

WEISSMULLER, JOHN, 1905– , U.S. swimmer, was born in Winbar, Pa. He is considered one of the greatest short-distance swimmers and was named swimmer of the half-century in 1951. He won three Olympic championships: the 100 and 400 meter free style in 1924 and the 100 meter free style in 1928. He later turned professional and was featured in many motion pictures as Tarzan. See BURROUGHS, EDGAR RICE.

WEIZMANN, CHAIM, 1874–1952, British Zionist leader and chemist, was born in Grodno Province, Russia, and studied at the universities of Berlin and

Freiburg. He taught at the University of Manchester 1904–16, and became a naturalized Briton, 1910. During World War I he was director of the Admiralty Laboratories, 1916–19. Weizmann became active in the World Zionist Organization, and was its president 1920–31. At the same time he served as president of the Jewish Agency for Palestine, 1929–31 and 1935–46. He became chairman of the board of governors of the Hebrew University, Jerusalem, and director of the Daniel Sieff Research Institute, Palestine, 1932. When the new Jewish state of Israel was set up, 1948, Weizmann was elected its first president. His *Trial and Error*, (1949) is autobiographical. See ACETONE.

WIDE WORLD
Chaim Weizmann

WEIZSÄCKER, FREIHERR VIKTOR VON, 1886–1957, pioneer German physician and psychiatrist, was born in Stuttgart, but lived most of his life in Heidelberg, 1910–41 (except for the period of his World War I service), and from 1945 until his death. Members of the family distinguished themselves in various ways: His father, many years prime minister of Württemberg, was made a baron (*Freiherr*); his grandfather, Karl Heinrich von Weizsäcker (1822–99), produced a translation of the New Testament that was still well known at mid-twentieth century; his brother, Freiherr Ernst von Weizsäcker (1882–(1951), was a diplomat from 1920, and during the Nazi period after 1933, and was convicted and sent to prison by the Nürnberg Tribunal after World War II; and his nephew, Karl Friedrich von Weizsäcker (1912–), became one of Germany's most important physicists and "historians of nature" (*Die Geschichte der Natur*, 1949; rev. ed. 1956).

Viktor von Weizsäcker studied under the physiologist Johannes von Kries (1853–1928) and the internist Ludolf von Krehl (1861–1937) investigating the heart as a "heat-producing machine," and for 10 years his researches were largely oriented to their strictly mechanistic point of view. In the meantime, however, Weizsäcker's own life experience gradually forced him to modify his scientific tenets radically. Among the experiences that contributed to this transformation were his service in a field hospital during World War II; his friendship with members of the Patmos Group—scholars, of diverse backgrounds, who from 1915 or before shared the conviction that the war represented an all-but-total breakdown of prewar standards and attitudes, and that new ways of life and thought would have to be discovered if the lessons of the war were to be learned and acted upon fully; and, most significantly, the impression made upon Weizsäcker by Sigmund Freud. Thus, although he seriously damaged his standing among physicians who practiced medicine according to abstractions in school books, and later endangered his very existence after the Nazis took power, 1932, Weizsäcker chivalrously recognized and acknowledged Freud as the great ram against the walls of stultifying verbal and conceptual abstractions of the prevailing mechanistic Cartesian medicine, according to which body and mind are totally separate. See DESCARTES, RENÉ.

Fundamental among the abstractions opposed by Weizsäcker were those of the "case," and of "illness per se," according to which (1) any given disease is assumed to be an independent entity that is essentially the same in its every occurrence and, therefore, (2) anyone with the disease is not a person but a "case" to be "handled." For Weizsäcker, however, the discoveries of Freud and others demonstrated that each person's way of being healthy or sick is original and unique, and must be responded to accordingly by the

physician, who must acknowledge that the body has its wisdom, that arbitrary conceptual judgments lead to folly, and that the physician is as mortal as his patient. In his *Soziale Krankheit und soziale Gesundung* (1930), Weizsäcker attacked socialistic sickness insurance on the ground that so long as socialism simply takes over the principles of liberal mechanistic medicine, neuroses are bound to breed whose very bases are the insurance payments themselves. Mechanistic science-medicine and capitalism are two sides of one coin, Weizsäcker believed; and the Soviets, by seeking to retain mechanistic science, are obliged for this very reason also to uphold capitalism, although in the degenerated form of "state-capitalism."

In reality, according to the viewpoint of Weizsäcker and others of his school (see UNCONSCIOUS, THE, *Existentialism and Existential Psychoanalysis*), the sick person cannot be met by the scientist as an object, but must be approached biographically. The physician must in some way identify his own life-and-death with that of the person and with the person's hopes and fears for the future; thus may the physician hope to assist the person's *own* strategy for overcoming sickness and regaining health. Much of Weizsäcker's doctrine anticipated many later developments in psychosomatic medicine, but most psychosomaticists, while recognizing the interplay of mind and body in the patient, generally fail in practice to enter the decisive crisis of their "patients." They practice "medicine before the crisis," as Weizsäcker put it, rather than a "medicine after the crisis," a truly biographical medicine such as that espoused by Weizsäcker. This biographical medicine Weizsäcker taught to a group of devoted friends, among whom Wilhelm Kütemeyer was most important, and later made the guiding principle of the Otfried Förster Institute, Breslau, which he headed during four years of World War II.

During most of his career, Weizsäcker was barely tolerated by the powerful leaders of "official" medicine. Deprived of speech and motion for the last years of his life, he was, for the sake of reconciling the profession, bowdlerized as just another philosopher and physician as, for instance, in the misleading posthumous volume, Weizsäcker-Wyss, *Zur Medizin und Philosophie*. Weizsäcker's remarkable *Hipokrates und Paracelsus, Helfen und Heilen*, in *Die Schildgenossen* (1926), the clearest statement of his position, seemed to have been forgotten or suppressed making it all the more difficult to see that Weizsäcker represented a complete rejection of centuries of Cartesian science. He was an original thinker, a founder of a new scientific attitude in which the Cartesian concept of "objective" Nature is replaced by awareness of Reality as "Creation" such that the scientist himself can no longer try to stand outside of, and aloof from, his "subject," but must return into the common fold as a creature, listening to and speaking with other "creatures." In this light, Weizsäcker is best understood in the context of his editorship of *Die Kreatur* (1926–30), with Joseph Wittig and Martin Buber. An incomplete bibliography of Weizsäcker's many writings appears in the *Festschrift, Freundesgabe für Viktor von Weizsäcker* (1956). His *Körpergeschehen und Neurose* (1933), *Menschenführung* (1955), and *Pathosophie* (1956) are fundamental works.

EUGEN ROSENSTOCK-HUESSY

WELCH, WILLIAM HENRY, 1850–1934, U.S. pathologist, was born in Norfolk, Conn., and studied at Yale University; at the College of Physicians and Surgeons, Columbia University; and abroad. He introduced European pathology techniques at Bellevue Hospital Medical College, 1878–83. He was professor of pathology at Johns Hopkins University, 1884–1916, director of Johns Hopkins School of Hygiene and Public Health, 1916–26, and professor of the history of medicine there, 1926–31. Welch did research in animal diseases, and in diphtheria and pneumonia, and discovered the bacillus that causes "gas gangrene." He served as U.S. Army surgeon general during World War I.

WELCH, city, S West Virginia, seat of McDowell County; on the Tug River, the Norfolk and Western Railway, and U.S. highway 52; 64 miles S of Charleston. The city is a trade and mining center in the Pocahontas coal field. Lumbering is a leading activity and beverages are manufactured. Welch was settled in 1885, and incorporated in 1892. A state hospital for miners is there. Pop. (1960) 5,313.

WELD, THEODORE DWIGHT, 1803–1895, U.S. abolitionist, was born in Hampton, Conn. In 1825 he came under the influence of Charles G. Finney (1792–1875), a Presbyterian evangelist, and became a member of Finney's group. He preached in New York for two years, and studied theology at Oneida Institute. He became interested in the anti-slavery movement, 1830, and joined the newly formed American Anti-Slavery Society, 1831. He wrote *The Bible Against Slavery* (1837) and *American Slavery As It Is* (1839), both of which influenced Harriet Beecher Stowe.

WELDING, a method or procedure for joining metals by the application of pressure or heat, or by a combination of the two.

PRESSURE WELDING

The only true pressure welds that are made without the aid of heat are the cold welds that are used to unite the surfaces of a few ductile, nonferrous metals. In order to produce successful cold welds, the surfaces to be joined must be absolutely clean. The two metal components are usually placed between dies that cover the exact area to be welded, and sufficient pressure, either in the form of a sudden impact or a slow squeeze, is exerted.

Forge Welding is a combination of pressure and fusion welding. It is the oldest form of welding. The pieces of metal to be joined are heated until they are in a plastic condition, then superimposed upon each other and joined by hammering or other pressure. Forge welding, as practiced by the blacksmith, was the first method known by which man joined one metal molecularly with another.

FUSION WELDING

Fusion welding is accomplished by melting the metal in the area of juncture by means of gas, electricity, or some other form of heat. Sometimes, filler metal in the form of welding rods are added to the area to compensate for the metal that is burned away or to assure strength in the weld area by the addition of metal.

Gas Welding. The first commercially successful application of gas welding occurred in 1906 when the French engineer, Eugene Bournonville, developed a torch that mixed oxygen and acetylene under pressure, and which, when united in the correct proportions and ignited, produced temperatures as high as 6300°F, substantially higher than the melting points of commonly used metals. The use of oxy-acetylene gas welding grew rapidly after that and the gas was also applied to the flame cutting of metals. In addition to oxygen and acetylene, it was soon discovered

that the combination of oxygen and hydrogen, other fuel gases and oxygen, and air and acetylene, mixed in the right proportion and fed under pressure through a blowpipe or torch, would produce a sufficiently hot flame for metallic welding and cutting.

The gases used in oxy-acetylene and other gas welding is supplied in pressurized containers, each fitted with a release valve. Tubes or hoses lead from each gas container to a regulator in which the correct proportion of each gas may be regulated to give the correct mixture at the torch nozzle. The mixed gases are piped to the torch and they are ignited by a spark or flame. The temperatures of the different parts of the welding flame are shown in the accompanying drawing of the oxy-acetylene flame.

Electric Welding. The most extensively used welding procedures are those that employ electric welding, which may be divided into two major classifications: arc welding and resistance welding.

Arc welding includes such methods as bare and shielded carbon and metal arc welding, submerged arc welding, inert gas welding, and atomic hydrogen welding. Resistance welding includes spot welding, seam welding, and projection welding.

Arc welding, as commonly practiced, necessitates the use of a welding machine, or generator, to supply the electric power to produce the arc; a lead to the electrode holder that holds either a carbon or a metallic rod; and a lead that is attached to the work to be welded (which must be grounded). In most welding, the lead to the electrode is from the negative pole of the generator, and that to the work, positive; however, in some cases, where coated metal electrodes are used, reverse polarity is necessary. Welding heat is provided by the electric arc produced at the electrode terminal (see ELECTRIC ARC). Heats of approximately 6500°F are achieved.

Carbon-arc welding employs a carbon rod as the negative electrode in making the arc at the weld, in much the same manner as the arc in an arc lamp. The heat of the arc melts a pool of metal on the surface of the work. If additional metal is required it is supplied by melting metallic welding rod into the weld.

Metal-arc welding is similar to the carbon-arc except that the electrode consists of a metal rod or wire that is fed and melted into the weld, thereby acting as its own filler metal. The composition of the metal electrode is usually equal to, or of a richer alloy analysis than the metal being welded.

Bare, shielded-arc, and inert gas welding are adaptations of arc-welding procedures, used when oxidation of metals at welding temperatures must be considered. The natural affinity of most metals for the oxygen and nitrogen in the air causes the metals to oxidize, with increased rapidity as temperatures increase. If such oxidation of metals being welded is not detrimental to the welded structure, it is not necessary to guard against oxidation and the electrodes, either carbon or metal, may be used bare without treating the electrodes or introducing nonoxidizing gases. If, however, oxidation is detrimental to the welded structure, an inert gas must be introduced that will suppress the formation of oxides.

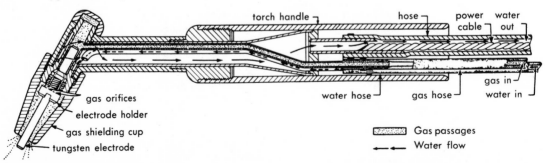

Sectional View of a Torch Used for Inert Gas, Shielded Arc Welding

This is accomplished by coating the electrodes with a material that, when heated, will give off an inert gas such as helium or argon, in sufficient amount to prevent the association of the metal with oxygen or nitrogen. In the inert gas-welding method, shielding is accomplished by introducing a flow of inert gas (usually helium) at the weld, and using a semi-permanent electrode, such as one made of tungsten, and using filler metal in the weld. The most common form of inert gas welding is known under the trade name of Heliarc welding. Submerged arc welding is another form of shielded welding, wherein oxidation is prevented by covering the weld area with a granular flux, and the arc welds are made under the protective flux.

Atomic-hydrogen welding maintains an arc between two tungsten electrodes, around which flows a stream of hydrogen gas. The heat of the arc transforms the molecular hydrogen to atomic hydrogen with higher temperatures resulting than obtained by the metal-arc method, plus perfect shielding at the weld.

Resistance Welding. In the resistance welding process, two or more pieces of metal are welded together by the combination of heat and pressure. The weld is effected by passing a low voltage current between two opposing electrodes at the location of the weld. Pressure between the electrodes and the amount of current determine the nature of the weld. Resistance welding lends itself well to fast-production welding through the use of continuous welding machines for each type of resistance weld being produced. The most common forms of resistance welds are spot welds, which use small circular electrodes above and below the work to produce a series of small weld spots; and seam welds, in which the work is automatically fed through the welder and welds are produced at close intervals, similar to the stitches of a sewing machine.

Thermit Welding is a fusion method whereby welding occurs when finely divided aluminum and iron oxide particles in a molten state are poured or channeled around the elements to be welded. Temperatures in excess of 5000°F are achieved in the thermit process. Thermit welding is well adapted for repairing massive broken parts around which a container may be filled to receive the molten thermit. See THERMIT.

TYPES OF WELDS

The most common types of welds that may be made by either pressure or fusion welding, and by gas or electric arc methods are: lap welds, wherein one piece of metal to be welded is placed over another, and a fillet weld is made at the top or under side of the lapped pieces; butt welds that are made when two edges are butted together (usually with a small gap separating them) and a weld bead is run at the juncture; and corner welds, where the edges of two pieces of metal are placed together to form an angle, and weld metal is deposited on one or both sides of the angles so formed. See FLAME CUTTING.

BIBLIOG.: Andrew D. Althouse and Others, *Modern Welding Practice* (1958); American Welding Society, *Welding Handbook*, 3 vols. (1957-60); Cecil G. Bainbridge, *Practical Welding Repairs* (1960); Orville T. Barnett, *Filler Metals for Joining* (1959); Walter H. Bruckner, *Metallurgy of Welding* (1954); Harry L. Campbell, *Working, Heat Treating, and Welding of Steel* (1940); Harry D. Churchill and John B. Austin, *Weld Design* (1949); Arthur C. Davies, *Science and Practice of Welding* (1956); Rollen H. Drake, *Aircraft Welding* (Drake's Aircraft Mechanic Ser.) (1951); Joseph W. Giachino and Others, *Welding skills and Practices* (1960); Frank D. Graham, *Audels Welders Guide: Questions and Answers* (1959); George Haim and J. A. Neumann, *Manual for Plastic Welding: Polyethylene* (Welding of Plastics Ser.) (1954); Heating, Piping and Air Conditioning Contractors National Association, *Standard Manual on Pipe Welding* (1951); Bain R. Hilton, *Welding Design and Processes* (1953); Theodore B. Jefferson and Gorham Woods, *Metals and How to Weld Them* (1954); Franz Koenigsberger, *Design for Welding in Mechanical Engineering* (1949); Joe L. Morris, *Welding Principles for Engineers* (1951), *Welding Processes and Procedures* (1954); J. Alex Neumann and Frank J. Bockhoff, *Welding of Plastics* (1959); Marvin M. Parker, *Farm Welding: Arc and Oxyacetylene Welding* (McGraw-Hill Rural Activities Ser.) (1958); Popular Mechanics Magazine, *Welding, Brazing and Soldering: How to Build Your Own Welding Equipment and Use it Effectively* (1950); Herbert P. Rigsby, *Welding Fundamentals* (1948); Herbert P. Rigsby and Chris H. Groneman, *Elementary and Applied Welding* (1948); Boniface E. Rossi, *Welding Engineering* (1954); Robert E. Smith, *Forging and Welding* (1956); Wallace A. Stanley, *Resistance Welding* (1950); Emanuele Stieri, *Basic Welding Principles* (Prentice-Hall Technical-Industrial-Vocational Ser.) (1953); Robert D. Stout and William D. Doty, *Weldability of Steels* (1953); Harry Udin and Others, *Welding for Engineers* (1954); Howard R. Voorhees and James W. Freeman, *Elevated-temperature Properties of Weld-deposited Metal and Weldments* (1958); *Welding Encyclopedia* (1951); Edward G. West, *Welding of Non-ferrous Metals* (1952).

WELFARE WORK. See CHARITY; PHILANTHROPY; PUBLIC WELFARE; SOCIAL SERVICE.

WELHAVEN, JOHAN SEBASTIAN CAMMERMEYER, 1807–73, Norwegian author, was born in Bergen. From 1830 he was involved in a literary feud with his brilliant contemporary, Henrik Wergeland, which led to the founding, by Welhaven and his friends, of *Vidor*, 1832, the first Norwegian journal of literary criticism. He became lecturer, 1842, and professor of philosophy, 1846, at the University of Christiania. Of his poetical works the most important are *Digte* (1839), *Nyere Digte* (1845), *Halvhundrede Digte* (1848), *En Digtsamling* (1859), all remarkable for deep feeling and a classical purity of style.

WELL. See ARTESIAN WELL; NATURAL GAS; PETROLEUM, Recovery and Transportation, *Drilling and Wells;* WATER SUPPLY.

WELLAND, city, Canada, SE Ontario; seat of Welland County; on the Welland River and the Welland Ship Canal, and the Canadian National, the New York Central, the Wabash, and the Toronto, Hamilton and Buffalo railroads; 39 miles SE of Hamilton. Welland is a railway junction and a commercial and manufacturing center. Niagara Falls provides hydroelectric power for numerous industrial establishments such as foundries, steel plants, cotton mills, cordage factories, sawmills and planing mills, carbide works, and fertilizer plants. The city was founded in 1849 and incorporated in 1917. Pop. (1956) 16,405.

WELLAND CANAL, Canada, in Ontario, crosses the Niagara Peninsula, skirting Niagara Falls, and connects Port Weller, on Lake Ontario, with Port Colburne, on Lake Erie. The canal is 27.6 miles long, 310 feet wide, and its depth averages 30 feet. The first canal around the falls was completed in 1839; it was enlarged and improved in 1845 and in 1887; the present canal was under construction from 1913 to 1933. Eight locks are needed to lift vessels 326.5 feet, the height of the rise between Lakes Ontario and Erie. It requires seven to nine hours to complete passage. The Welland Ship Canal forms part of the St. Lawrence Seaway.

WELLES, GIDEON, 1802–78, U.S. political leader, was born in Glastonbury, Conn. After education at the academies at Cheshire, Conn., and Norwich, Vt., Welles studied law. His career, however, was in politics. In 1826 he became part owner and editor of the Hartford *Times.* He served in the Connecticut legislature, 1827–35, was comptroller of public accounts, 1835, 1842–43, and was appointed postmaster of Hartford by Andrew Jackson, 1836–41. He was defeated as candidate for Congress, 1834, and for the Senate, 1850. His antipathy to slavery led Welles to join the Republican party in 1854. He established the

MESERVE COLLECTION
Gideon Welles

Hartford *Evening Press* as a Republican organ, 1856, and became a member of the Republican National Committee and its executive committee and was an unsuccessful candidate for governor of Connecticut the same year. He was a member of the Chicago convention that nominated Abraham Lincoln, 1860, but did not share its enthusiasm for Lincoln.

President Lincoln's appointment of Welles as secretary of the navy was particularly fortunate. His counsel was sound and his administration was honest and efficient. With the able assistance of Gustavus Fox, Welles transformed the small and ineffective Navy into an efficient and powerful force. Resisting political pressure, he was farsighted in the development of ironclads, improved ordnance and gunnery, assisted energetically in the production of John Ericsson's *Monitor* and co-operated in joint naval and land operations. His support of Lincoln in the cabinet was invaluable, especially as Radical Republican opposition emerged. Accepting Lincoln's reconstruction policy, Welles loyally co-operated with Andrew Johnson as Lincoln's successor. Remaining in the cabinet until 1869, Welles supported the conservative movement in the Republican party in 1866 and returned to the Democratic party in 1868.

After his retirement Welles voted the Democratic-Liberal Republican ticket, 1872, and for Samuel Tilden, 1876. He published important articles in the *Galaxy*, 1869–78, and wrote *Lincoln and Seward* (1874). His published diary (3 vols. 1911) became a major historical source for investigation of the war and reconstruction periods, although its reliability was later questioned.   DONALD RIDDLE

WELLES, ORSON, 1915–   , U.S. actor and director, was born George Orson Welles in Kenosha, Wis. His Dublin debut at the age of 16 was followed

CULVER SERVICE
Orson Welles

by appearances in the United States with Katherine Cornell. In 1937 he founded the Mercury Theater, in New York City. Among his stage productions were *Macbeth* (1937), a modern-dress *Julius Caesar* (1937), *The Cradle Will Rock* (1937), and *Shoemakers' Holiday* (1938). He worked for a number of years as a radio director and actor, and his *Mercury Theater of the Air* presented some of the best drama ever to be presented on U.S. radio; Welles' version, 1938, of H. G. Wells' *War of the Worlds* was so realistic that it produced a temporary but widespread panic along the eastern seaboard, where many people feared that the United States was being invaded by monsters from Mars. As a film director, Welles was famous for his originality and bizarre effects, particularly in his use of light and shadow. Among his films are *Citizen Kane* (1940), *The Magnificent Ambersons* (1941), *Journey into Fear* (1942), *Macbeth* (1950), *Othello* (1955), and *The Trial* (1963). In 1962 he wrote a blank verse adaptation of *Moby Dick* for the stage.

WELLES, SUMNER, 1892–1961, U.S. diplomat, was born in New York City and was graduated from Harvard University. After serving as secretary in the U.S. embassy in Tokyo, 1915–17, and in Buenos Aires, 1917–20, he became chief of Latin-American affairs, 1921–22, U.S. commissioner to the Dominican Republic, 1922, and in 1924 was commissioned to offer mediation in the Honduras Revolution. His appointment as assistant secretary of state, 1933, was interrupted by an ambassadorship to Cuba, but was resumed later in the same year. In 1937 Welles became undersecretary of state; he conferred with European leaders on the international situation, 1940, led the U.S. delegation to the Pan American Conference at Rio de Janeiro, 1942, and resigned, 1943.

WELLESLEY, RICHARD COLLEY WELLESLEY, MARQUIS, 1760–1842, British political figure, was born in Dublin. He studied at Eton and Oxford, and, after a parliamentary career, was selected by William Pitt the Younger, to be governor general of India. He was raised to the British peerage as Baron Wellesley, 1797. In seven years of vigorous administration he secured results unparalleled in the annals of the East India Company: he foiled the machinations of Tipu Sahib, sultan of Mysore, he thwarted French dreams of dominion in India, and he doubled the revenue of the company, whose grateful directors awarded him an annuity of $25,000. Resolutions condemning him for abuse of power in India were moved in both Lords and Commons, but were defeated. He undertook an unsuccessful mission as ambassador to Spain, 1809, but a few months later returned to England to become foreign minister in the Spencer Perceval cabinet. Retiring from that post, 1812, he thereafter identified himself with the cause of the Irish Catholics and with Roman Catholic emancipation. See WELLINGTON, ARTHUR WELLESLEY, 1st DUKE OF.

WELLESLEY, town, E Massachusetts, in Norfolk County; on the New York Central Railroad; about 14 miles WSW of Boston. Wellesley is a residential suburb of Boston. Textiles and shoes are manufactured. Wellesley is noted as the site of Wellesley College (1870) and the Babson Institute (1919). The town has a junior college and several preparatory schools. The area was first settled around 1660, and Wellesley was incorporated and separated from Needham in 1881. Pop. (1960) 26,071.

WELLESLEY COLLEGE, a private, nonsectarian, liberal arts college for women, located in Wellesley, Mass. Chartered in 1870, the college offered its first instruction in 1875.

Divisions of the college include art, physical science, economics, education, language, history, philosophy, political science, physical education, sociology, anthropology, and psychology. Master's degrees are offered in many departments.

Students in their junior and senior years may participate in a summer internship program in government agency work, held in Washington, D.C. A year of study abroad at approved institutions in Paris, Munich, Florence, Geneva, or Madrid is offered to students entering their junior year.

Special library collections include the Plimpton Collection of Italian books and manuscripts, collections of early and rare editions of English poetry, and the Mayling Soong Foundation Collection of works on the Far East. See COLLEGES AND UNIVERSITIES.

WELLESZ, EGON, 1885–   , Austrian composer, was born in Vienna and studied at Vienna University, where, with Anton von Webern, he became a pupil of Arnold Schonberg, 1906. His work shows the influence of Gustav Mahler and Claude Debussy, and he is noted for his studies of Byzantine music. Among his orchestral works are a symphonic poem, *Vorfrühling* (1912), and two symphonies, Opus 62 (1945) and Opus 65 (1948).

WELLINGTON, ARTHUR WELLESLEY, 1st **DUKE OF,** 1769–1852, British military and political leader, was born in Dublin, or in Meath, Ireland; attended Eton and a military academy at Angers, France; and entered the British army as an ensign, 1787. Through the influence of his elder brother, Richard Colley Wellesley, then Lord Mornington, Arthur Wellesley rose rapidly in the army. He served in the Netherlands, 1794–95, was promoted to colonel, 1796, and was sent with his regiment to India.

After his brother became governor-general of India, 1797, Colonel Wellesley was given successively more important commands; he became supreme military and civil commander of Mysore, 1800, and was promoted to major-general, 1802. He defeated the Maratha army at the battles of Assaye and Argaum, 1803, then returned to England, 1805, and entered Parliament, 1806. This was a period when the ambitions of Napoleon I seemed a threat to all of Christendom, however, and Wellington's military ability was sorely needed in the field. He led an expedition against Copenhagen, 1807, and commanded an army sent to the relief of Portugal, 1808, returned to England briefly, then went back to Portugal, 1809, and in the next five years drove the French out of the Iberian Peninsula (see PENINSULAR WAR). During this period he became successively Earl and Marquis of Wellington, 1812, field marshal, 1813, and Duke of Wellington, 1814.

After his return to England, 1814, Wellington was sent as ambassador to Paris. He then took Castlereagh's place at the Congress of Vienna, 1815, and after Napoleon's escape from Elba, took command of the allied forces against the new Bonapartist threat. On June 16, Marshal Michel Ney attacked Wellington's army at Quatre-Bras, causing the latter to fall back to Waterloo; Wellington held firm there, June 18, against repeated French charges, until the Prussian army under Gebhard von Blücher could come up, whereupon the united armies routed the French. See WATERLOO, BATTLE OF.

CHICAGO HIST. SOC.
Wellington

Wellington remained in France until 1818 as commander of the allied army of occupation. After his return to England, he served in the cabinet as master general of the ordnance, 1818–27, was commander-in-chief of the British army, 1827–28, and reluctantly became prime minister, 1828. During his term in office he repealed the Test and Corporation acts, 1828, and, acting against his own opinions, brought about Roman Catholic emancipation, 1829. In 1830 he resigned rather than grant Parliamentary reform.

His opposition to reform made him unpopular during the reform agitation of 1831–32. Wellington served as foreign secretary in Robert Peel's short-lived ministry, 1834–35, then was leader of the Opposition in the house of lords, 1835–41. As a member of the cabinet without office in Peel's second government, 1841–46, he did not favor Peel's repeal of the Corn Laws, 1846, but nevertheless insured the bill's passage through the house of lords. When Peel fell, 1846, Wellington retired from active politics. He was made commander in chief for life, 1842, and in 1848, at the time of the Chartist troubles, he was called in to organize London's various military forces of that day.

During the latter part of his career Wellington strongly opposed changes in the army and was substantially able to protect the army from large-scale changes. The result, after his death, was the debacle of the Crimean War, which showed that a modern army could not operate efficiently under the system of military organization—with purchase of commissions, and so forth—that had prevailed during the Napoleonic Wars.

Significance. Wellington is regarded more highly as a military organizer and tactician than as a strategist; still, there is no doubt that he was one of Britain's greatest soldiers. He made an important contribution to British politics, as well, by supporting Roman Catholic emancipation and Peel's repeal of the Corn Laws. Although personally opposed to both measures, he supported them from a sense of duty, and there is no doubt that without this support neither measure could have passed the house of lords. His action at these times prevented possible crises in which the house of lords would have obstructed the will of the people. By so acting, Wellington may well have helped prevent in England the kind of middle class revolution that occurred in so many European countries during his lifetime.   ROBIN OGGINS

BIBLIOG.: Richard Aldington, *Wellington* (1953); Finlay C. Beatson, *Wellington: The Bidassoa and Nivella* (1931); Douglas H. Bell, *Wellington's Officers* (1940); Oliver Brett, Wellington (1928); Susan C. Buchan, *Sword of the State: Wellington After Waterloo* (1931); Charles R.M.F. Cruttwell, *Wellington* (Great Lives, 67) (1936); Godfrey Davies, *Wellington and His Army* (1954); William H. Fitchett, *Great Duke*, 2 vols. (1911); John W. Fortescue, *Wellington* (1961); George R. Gleig, *Life of the Duke of Wellington* (Everyman's Library. Biography no. 431) (1942); Philip Guedalla, *Wellington* (1935); Charles O. Head, *Napoleon and Wellington* (1939); George Hooper, *Life of Wellington* (1890); William O. Morris, *Wellington, Soldier and Statesman, and the Revival of the Military Power of England* (Heroes of the Nations) (1904); Charles W. C. Oman, *Wellington's Army 1809-1814* (1912); Charles A. Petrie, *Wellington, a Re-assessment* (1956); Philip H. Stanhope, *Notes of Conversations with the Duke of Wellington, 1831-1851* (1940); Frederick W. Tickner, *Wellington* (Children's Heroes Ser.) (1941); Gerald Wellesley and John Steegmann, *Iconography of the First Duke of Wellington* (1935); Muriel Wellesley, *Wellington in Civil Life: Through the Eyes of Those Who Knew Him* (1939).

WELLINGTON, city, S Kansas, seat of Sumner County; on the Santa Fe and the Rock Island railroads, and U.S. highways 81 and 160; 30 miles S of Wichita. The city is a trade and processing center for an area in which wheat is grown. In the 1930's, oil fields were developed in the vicinity. Wellington was founded in 1871. Pop. (1960) 8,809.

WELLINGTON, city, NW central Texas, seat of Collingsworth County; on the Fort Worth and Denver Railway and U.S. highway 83; 350 miles NW of Austin. The city is a trade, processing, and shipping center for an area in which grain, cotton, and livestock are raised. Wellington was incorporated in 1909. Pop. (1960) 3,137.

WELLINGTON, city, capital of New Zealand, at the S end of North Island; on Port Nicholson Bay of Cook Strait; about 300 miles S of Auckland. The city is built on the lower slopes of the Tinakori Hills and on a peninsula jutting into the bay. Much of the business and industrial areas are on land reclaimed from the harbor. Wellington, with its excellent natural harbor, vies with Auckland as the principal import and export point of New Zealand. The city is a major commercial center, but has few industries. Industrial production is centered in Lower Hutt, formerly a suburb of Wellington, but now a separate city. Wellington is the site of the governor-general's residence, the houses of Parliament, and many administrative buildings. A rail line connects the capital with Auckland and other important centers of North

Wellington is viewed from the top of Mount Victoria, one of the many hills on which the residential area is built. Most of the business section lies along Lambton Harbour.

Island; regular ferry service across Cook Strait is maintained with South Island points such as Christchurch. There is air service to all parts of the country and overseas. Among the buildings of interest are the National Art Gallery, the Dominion Museum, the Roman Catholic cathedral (seat of an archbishop), and the Anglican cathedral. Victoria University (1897), a constituent of the University of New Zealand, is in Wellington. Wellington was the first settlement of the New Zealand colonists in 1840. The settlement was named after Arthur Wellesley, 1st Duke of Wellington. The capital was transferred there from Auckland in 1865. Pop. (1959) 143,200.

WELLS, DAVID AMES, 1828–98, U.S. economist, was born in Springfield, Mass., and studied at Williams College and Lawrence Scientific School, Harvard. After some years as a publisher, he turned to economics. His pamphlet *Our Burden and Our Strength* (1864) helped restore foreign credit to the United States by emphasizing the future of Northern industrialism. Wells was special U.S. commissioner of revenue, 1866–70, but lost the position because of his conversion to the principles of free trade. He became chairman of the New York tax commission on local taxation, 1871, was adviser to Garfield and Cleveland on tariff problems, and was president of the American Social Science Association, 1877. Among his writings are *Robinson Crusoe's Money* (1876), *The Silver Question* (1877), *A Primer of Tariff Reform* (1884), *Practical Economics* (1885), and *The Theory and Practice of Taxation* (1900).

WELLS, HERBERT GEORGE, 1866–1946, English writer, was born over his father's hardware and sporting-goods store in Bromley, Kent. His mother took him out of school, 1880, and tried to make a shop assistant of him, but he resisted stubbornly, resumed his education, 1883, and won a scholarship to the Normal School of Science, South Kensington, 1884. While there he took a biology course with Charles Darwin's associate, Thomas Henry Huxley, and in his free time went to Kelmscott House in Hammersmith to hear William Morris and the young George Bernard Shaw lecture on socialist ideas. Wells failed in his third year and was flung on the world without a degree.

After a short tenure as a teacher he collapsed with lung trouble and, while convalescing, wrote his first novel, *Lady Falkland's Companion* (unpublished), and a first version of *The Time Machine*. Wells went back to teaching, 1888, first in a private school and then in a cramming establishment, where he taught others and also prepared for his own finals, catching up and graduating from London University with first-class honors in zoology, 1890. In 1891 he married his cousin Isabel Mary Wells. In 1893 his health collapsed again and during his long convalescence he began writing to make ends meet, contributing short articles to *The Saturday Review*, then under the brilliant editorship of Frank Harris, and to *The Pall Mall Gazette*. His first marriage ended in divorce, 1895, and he married Amy Catherine Robbins, by whom he had two sons, George Philip, 1901, and Frank Richard, 1903.

Wells' *The Time Machine* (1895) was the first work to exploit his gift for transforming speculation about the social implications of scientific developments into exciting and plausible fiction. In this vein he wrote *The Island of Dr. Moreau* (1896), *The Invisible Man* (1897), *When the Sleeper Wakes* (1899), *The First Men in the Moon* (1901), and *The Food of the Gods* (1904). This cycle overlaps another that consists of semi-autobiographical novels of social conflicts in English life: *Love and Mr. Lewisham* (1900), *Kipps* (1905), *Tono Bungay* (1909), and *Mr. Polly* (1910). A less successful group of novels deals with the clash between instinctual and socially acceptable behavior patterns; *Ann Veronica* (1909) is the first and best of these, but in *The Passionate Friends* (1913) and *The Wife of Sir Isaac Harmon* (1914) a sharp decline of concentration

and interest is evident. His later novels tend to be diffuse and didactic, although the light-hearted satires, *The Autocracy of Mr. Parham* (1930) and *Apropos of Dolores* (1936), have much of the spirit of his best work.

In *Boon* (1916), a satirical pamphlet, Wells expressed his impatience with the aesthetic approach to writing and came out for a utilitarian literature with defined social aims, the chief of which should be the prevention of such events as World War I, which was then raging. Wells felt that the lesson of that conflict was that, unless men combined in some world organization to make creative use of their gifts, national rivalries would annihilate mankind in a series of increasingly destructive wars. Much of his writing urging this view is mere hasty journalism, and his tendency to underestimate the practical difficulties won him an undeserved reputation for facile optimism. Some of his propaganda was unquestionably brilliant. The *Outline of History* (1920), for example, was designed to undermine the narrowness of nationalism by fostering a world view of a common human heritage. *The Science of Life* (1930) was intended to introduce to the common reader the scientists' conception of man's place in the natural order. Wells considered a general acceptance of the scientific outlook essential to the rational conduct of human affairs. He belongs in the tradition of English Liberal Humanitarianism, and all his virtues and defects are evident in his interesting *Experiment in Autobiography* (1934).

In addition to his many books, Wells wrote a large number of vividly imagined stories, *The Plattner Story* (1897) and *The Country of the Blind* (1911) being typical collections. He also wrote a great number of influential speculative essays on social questions, beginning with *Anticipations* (1901).   ANTHONY WEST

WELLS, HORACE, 1815–48, U.S. dental surgeon, the first to demonstrate the usefulness of nitrous oxide gas—"laughing gas"—and to employ it in dental and surgical operations, was born in Hartford, Vt. He studied dentistry in Boston, where he started his dental practice, later moved back to Hartford, and finally settled in New York City. Having attended a public demonstration of "laughing gas," Dec. 10, 1844, and observed that people felt no pain while the gas was in effect, he conceived the idea of using it for surgical anesthesia, and the following day, while under the influence of the gas, had one of his teeth extracted painlessly. After experimenting successfully in his office he arranged for a demonstration in the Massachusetts General Hospital, Boston, January, 1845. Not enough gas was given and the patient felt pain; thus Wells was denounced as a failure. He spent the remainder of his life in a vain effort to prove his work.   FLORIS VAN MINDEN, D.D.S.

WELLS, municipal borough, SW England, in Somersetshire, at the foot of the Mendip Hills; 18 miles S of Bristol. Wells is a cathedral town, and a marketing center. The cathedral, one of the finest in England, is believed to have been founded in 704, but was built principally in the twelfth and thirteenth centuries. Also notable is St. Cuthbert Church, and the Bishop's Palace, a thirteenth century moated building with a fourteenth century gatehouse. St. Andrew's Wells, from which the town takes its name, were famous in the Middle Ages and were thought to have a curative effect. Wells became the seat of a bishop in 909. Pop. (1951) 5,835.

WELLSBURG, city, extreme N West Virginia, seat of Brooke County; on the Ohio River and the Pennsylvania Railroad; 34 miles WSW of Pittsburgh, in a coal mining region. The city is a mining and industrial center in which paper products, glass, and cement are manufactured. Wellsburg was platted in 1790 and founded as Charles Town in 1791. It was renamed Wellsburg in 1816. A flood-control project was started late in the 1820's. Pop. (1960) 5,514.

WELLS COLLEGE. See COLLEGES AND UNIVERSITIES.

WELLS, FARGO AND COMPANY, was founded, 1852, by Henry Wells (1805–78) and William George Fargo (1818–81) to provide banking facilities and an express route for California gold miners. The company is survived by the Wells, Fargo Bank and Union Trust Company, San Francisco.

The express idea originated in the custom of sending parcels to addressees "in care of" coach drivers or the captains of sailing vessels. With the expansion of railroads westward, express business also expanded, and when gold was discovered on the West Coast, 1848, a need arose for quick transcontinental express and (later) passenger service to settled areas.

The first overland stages—23 days from San Francisco to Tipton, Mo.—were launched in 1858. Until the completion of the Union Pacific Railroad, the Overland Mail Company carried all U.S. mails between the Missouri River and the Pacific Coast; clamor for even swifter mail-transport brought the romantic but short-lived Pony Express, 1860–61.

During the Civil War, when the express was recognized as much safer than the mails, Wells, Fargo and Company was pre-eminent among several companies that kept communication alive between soldiers in the field and civilians at home. In 1916, Wells, Fargo and Company was one of eight express companies still extant, operating over 107,529 miles.

At the outbreak of World War I, it was decided that all express matter should be handled by one concern; American Railway Express Company was selected and was recognized as a public utility. It purchased the tangible property of Wells, Fargo and Company, and other lines; it was eventually, 1929, superseded by the Railway Express Agency. See EXPRESS COMPANY; OVERLAND MAIL; PONY EXPRESS. JAMES COLVIN

WELLSTON, city, S Ohio, in Jackson County, on the Baltimore and Ohio and the Chesapeake and Ohio railroads, and U.S. highway 35; 60 miles ESE of Columbus. The city is a trade center for an area in which truck farming is a leading activity. Machinery, clothing, and tools are manufactured. Wellston was founded in 1874, and chartered as a city in 1876. Pop. (1960) 5,728.

WELLSVILLE, village, SW New York, in Allegany County; on the Genesee River and the Erie railroad; 70 miles SE of Buffalo. The village is a trade and processing center for an oil-producing area. Oil well supplies, turbines, and aircraft parts are manufactured. Wellsville was settled in 1795. It was incorporated as Genesee in 1871 and as Wellsville in 1873. Pop. (1960) 5,967.

WELLSVILLE, city, E Ohio, in Columbiana County; on the Ohio River and the Pennsylvania Railroad; 81 miles SE of Cleveland. The city is an industrial center in an area which has clay mines and oil and gas wells. Pottery, chinaware, firebrick, and clay-working machinery are manufactured. Wellsville was founded in 1797, and was chartered as a city in 1890. Pop. (1960) 7,117.

WELSBACH, BARON CARL AUER VON, 1858–1929, Austrian chemist, was born in Vienna, was graduated from the Vienna Polytechnic, and then studied under Robert Wilhelm von Bunsen in Heidelberg. While doing reserach in rare earths, he succeeded, 1885, in splitting didymium into praseodymium and neodymium, and about 1907 separated ytterbium into two elements, identical with ytterbium and lutetium discovered by Georges Urbain (1872–1938). He invented the Welsbach gas mantle and burner, 1885, and an automatic gas lighter based on the pyrophoric alloy known as Auer metal. See GAS LIGHTING, *Gas Mantle.*

WELSH CORGI, any of two cattle-scattering breeds of working dog bred in the British Isles. The Cardigan Welsh Corgi was brought to Wales by Celtic migrators about 1200 B.C. The dog has been trained by its tenant-farmer owners to scatter and drive away trespassing cattle. It performs this task by

FRASIE STUDIO

Of the two breeds of Welsh Corgi, the Cardigan and the Pembroke (shown here), the Pembroke is higher and shorter. Both breeds are intelligent, watchful dogs for the home.

quickly nipping at the hocks of the cattle and then dropping to the ground to avoid the kicking heels. It is a highly intelligent animal, performing its work and returning to its home through whistle commands given by its owner. It is a small, swift dog with short legs and a long back capable of springlike power. It has a long tail and its ears are rounded.

The Pembroke Welsh Corgi was transported to Wales in the early twelfth century from Belgium. Also a cattle-working dog, it is contrasted with the Cardigan breed by having a higher body with shorter back and legs that are straighter and slimmer in structure. Both breeds were interbred at the beginning of the twentieth century but this practice has been discontinued and each is now independently bred.

WELSH LANGUAGE AND LITERATURE. Welsh belongs to the Celtic branch of the Indo-European languages, forming, with Breton and the extinct Cornish, the Brythonic or "p" group of Celtic (see CELTS). The three main dialects are Gwynedd (Anglesey and Carnarvonshire), the Powysian of Mid-Wales, and the southern, including Gwentian and Dimetian. The relative isolation and independence of the Welsh have kept the language lively and tenacious; it is the sole language of about 190,000 Welshmen, and some 800,000 speak both Welsh and English.

Literature. With a few important exceptions, the chief original works of Welsh literature are in poetry. The oldest specimen is a series of stanzas in the Juvencus Codex of the University College, Cambridge, belonging to the ninth century. The early thirteenth century *Book of Aneirin* preserves in part the orthography of the manuscript from which it was copied, and gives specimens of poetry that may date from the eighth or ninth century. There are poems of the same cycle in the *Book of Taliesin* (thirteenth century). Two chief language zones existed for this poetry: Gwynedd and Powys. The *Book of Aneirin* and the oldest nucleus of the *Book of Taliesin*, together with certain poems of the *Black Book of Carmarthen* (twelfth century), belong to the Gwynedd; while other poems of the *Black Book* and most of the Llywarch Hen poems of the *Red Book of Hergest* belong to the Powysian. In the *Taliesin* literature, and sporadically in other books, there is a great deal of poetry that reflects the monastic studies of the early Middle Ages. Welsh poetry from the period 1100–1300 is represented mainly by the compositions of the court poets Meilir, Gwalchmai, Cynddelw, Dafydd Benfras, Llywarch ap Llywelyn, Gruffydd ap yr Ynad Coch, and others whose poems generally exhibit great vigor and terseness of expression, and highly developed technical skill. Dafydd ap Gwilym (1340?–1400) brought erotic verse to a high degree of perfection, but the chief characteristic of his work is a consummate blending of the themes of love and nature. In this regard he was frequently imitated by later poets. The more ascetic side of Welsh life was expressed by Siôn Cent (fourteenth century). Iolo Goch (1320–98), Gutto'r Glyn, Lewis Glyn Cothi, and Ieuwan Deulwyn linked poetry with political movements.

Tudur Aled, writing early in the sixteenth century, was the last pre-Reformation Welsh poet of distinction. His chief successor in the Tudor period was William Lleyn. During the English Civil War and the Commonwealth the leading figure was Hugh Morris, a writer of love poetry.

Toward the middle of the eighteenth century a great revival of Welsh poetry took place through the efforts of writers such as Goronwy Owen (1723–69) who had studied at the English universities and were familiar with classical models. From that time a large number of poets were to give striking expression to various phases of Welsh life.

In prose the chief medieval work is the volume of legends called the *Mabinogion*. There are also extant many manuscripts containing translations from French and Latin, notably stories of the Charlemagne cycle. The whole Bible was translated into Welsh, 1588, by William Morgan, and revised by Richard Parry and John Davies, 1620. The translation of the Bible was followed by a succession of devotional and theological works. One of the most remarkable prose works of the seventeenth century is the *Book of the Three Birds*, by Morgan Lloyd (1619–59), a prominent Welsh Puritan and a follower of Jakob Böhme. The chief development of Welsh prose, however, began in the nineteenth century, when a large number of excellent works on theology, biography, general literature, and politics, as well as works of fiction were published. The twentieth century saw a notable renascence of Welsh literature in all forms.
EDWARD ANWYL

The Twentieth Century saw a remarkable renaissance in all fields of literature. Of particular influence in the first decades of the century were the literary critics Sir Owen Morgan Edwards (1858–1920), Sir John Morris-Jones (1864–1929), and Emrys ap Iwan (1851–96).

The poet Thomas Gwynn Jones (1871–1949) experimented with many old forms, achieving great technical virtuosity; he frequently drew upon traditional Celtic materials.William John Gruffydd (1881–1954) rebelled against the poetic traditions of the nineteenth century. Robert Williams Parry (1884–1956) wrote with power in the bardic tradition. David Gwenallt Jones (1899–   ) used many verse forms, exploring the relation of Christian spirituality to sensuous experience.

Saunders Lewis (1893–   ), distinguished for his historical and political studies, also wrote poetry, drama, and fiction. Edward Tegla Davies (1880–   ) wrote short stories and essays, often in a satiric vein. Thomas Rowland Hughes (1903–49) was the author of a number of realistic novels set in the quarrying districts. Also writing in the realistic manner, Kate Roberts (1891–   ) brought the short story to importance in Welsh literature.

BIBLIOG. John T. Bowen and Thomas J. R. Jones, *Teach Yourself Welsh* (1960); Llewelyn W. Griffith, *Voice of Wales: Music and Literature* (Arts in Britain Ser., no. 9) (1947); Myrddin Jenkins, *Welsh Tutor* (1959); John M. Jones, *Welsh Grammar* (1954); David M. Lloyd and Elizabeth M. Lloyd, eds., *Book of Wales* (1954); Cecile O'Rahilly, *Ireland and Wales: Their Historical and Literary Relations* (1924); Thomas Parry, *History of Welsh Literature* (1955); W. O. Thomas and H. Meurig Evans, *Complete Welsh-English, English-Welsh Dictionary* (1958); Gwyn Williams, ed., *Presenting Welsh Poetry* (1959).

WELSH SPRINGER SPANIEL, a sporting dog found principally in Wales and western England. The color of the breed is a deep red and white; the color does not vary. It has a strong, muscular body well adapted for the grueling paces of game scenting. Its flat, thick coat with soft undermatting allows the dog to work in thicket areas and provides excellent insulation for climatic changes. Its ears hang close to its cheek and gradually narrow to the tip.

The keen sense of smell possessed by the dog can be of disadvantage for without training the dog will often leave its master and hunt alone. Once disciplined, the dog is considered to have few peers in detecting most types of game. The dog also has a gentle disposition and is at ease in the company of children, making it a pleasant domestic pet. The Welsh springer spaniel is more adapted to work as a hunting dog, however, and is at its best form when not restricted to the confines of the city.

TOPLIGHT TEMPLATE OF TWIN PONDS
For more than 100 years the Welsh Terrier has been used in Wales as an excellent hunting dog, and is renowned for its ability to track down such game as otter and badger.

WELSH TERRIER, a sporting dog native to Wales and noted for ease of handling. The color of the breed is black and tan, leading to its once-common name of the black and tan wire-haired terrier. It stands about 15 inches high and usually weighs about 20 pounds. Its skull is flattened and its eyes are set far apart; the jaws are square and elongated. It has a thick, wiry coat on a muscular, short-backed body. The Welsh terrier has been used as a hunting dog for more than 100 years in Wales and was usually accustomed to track the otter, fox, and badger. The dog was first entered in a show class of its own in England in 1884. It was brought to the United States in 1888 but did not receive popularity as a competitive and hunting dog until the early 1900's. The breed is characteristically well mannered and intelligent.

WEMBLEY, municipal borough, SE England, in Middlesex; a residential and industrial suburb, seven miles NW of London. Electrical equipment, pharmaceutical products, and machinery are manufactured. Wembley is the site of a large sports stadium, used for many international events, including the 1948 Olympic Games. Wembley was incorporated in 1937. Pop. (1951) 131,369.

WENATCHEE, city, central Washington, seat of Chelan County; on the Columbia River, the Great Northern Railway, and U.S. highways 2 and 97; 98 miles ESE of Seattle. Wenatchee is the shipping center for orchards in the Entiat River, Lake Chelan, Methow, and Okanogan valleys, which produce more than 50 per cent of Washington's apple crop. Some apricots, peaches, and cherries also are shipped. The city has fruit-packing plants; cold storage, drying, and freezing plants; canneries, and plants handling apple by-products. In 1951 the city became the site of a new aluminum plant. Other manufactures are lumber, boxes, concrete, flour, and dairy products. Wenatchee was founded in 1888, relocated on the banks of the Columbia River in 1892, and incorporated in 1901. Pop. (1960) 16,726.

WENCESLAUS, SAINT, 908?–935, patron saint of Bohemia, was born in Alt-Bunzlau, Bohemia, the son of a Christian father and a heathen mother. Wenceslaus was converted to Christianity by his grandmother, St. Ludmilla. Against his mother's wishes, as Duke of Bohemia he promoted Christianity in his country by the introduction of German priests. Hoping to re-establish paganism, Wenceslaus' mother and brother murdered him, Sept. 28, 935. The carol *Good King Wenceslaus*, which celebrates his legend, was written in the nineteenth century to a tune dating from the thirteenth century. Roman Catholics celebrate St. Wenceslaus' feast on September 28.

WENCESLAUS, also Wenzel, Wenzeslaus, or Vaclav, the name of four medieval kings of Bohemia, the fourth of whom was also king of Germany and Holy Roman Emperor.

Wenceslaus I, died 1253, the son of Ottokar I, was King of Bohemia from 1230 until his death. An enthusiastic patron of the arts, he welcomed to his court many of the scholars and minnesingers of his day. He was himself a poet of some merit. He was succeeded by his son, Ottokar II.

Wenceslaus II, 1271–1305, the son of Ottokar II, was King of Bohemia from 1278 until his death, but did not assume power until 1290; in the interim the country was ruled by a German regency. At the invitation, 1291, of a group of Polish nobles, Wenceslaus extended his domain to the Kraków area, and he was crowned King of Poland, 1300. The following year he accepted the crown of Hungary for his son, Wenceslaus III. His growing power and increasing dominions incurred the envy and enmity of the German princes, who demanded that he surrender his new territories and forebear from seeking additional ones. Wenceslaus refused, and war ensued. He repulsed a German invasion, 1304, and was gathering his forces to resist a second attack at the time of his death. He was succeeded to the Bohemian throne by his son, Wenceslaus III.

Wenceslaus III, 1289–1306, was King of Hungary, 1301–04, and King of Bohemia, 1305–06. His rule was never more than nominal. Within a year of his father's death, the Bohemian Empire collapsed. The young Wenceslaus III was assassinated by the victorious German coalition.

Wenceslaus IV, 1361–1419, was born in Nürnberg, the son of Holy Roman Emperor Charles IV. He succeeded to the Bohemian crown as Wenceslaus IV, 1363, and to the crowns of Germany and the Holy Roman Empire as Wenceslaus, 1378. Within a short time he proved himself a drunken, ineffectual ruler, easily manipulated by others for their own benefit. Conspiracies of Bohemian nobles, 1394, and of German princes, 1400, deprived him of nearly all temporal power. He was several times imprisoned by various factions, but was in each instance released as being harmless. His titles, and what little power went with them, passed on to his brother Sigismund.

WENCHOW, or Yungkia, city, E China, in Chekiang Province; on the Wu River, about 20 miles from the East China Sea, and about 225 miles S of Shanghai. The city is a commercial center; bamboo products, silk goods, and food products are manufactured. The port at Wenchow has considerable trade in timber. Wenchow was one of the Chinese ports opened to foreign trade by the Chefoo Convention of 1876, and was an important tea exporting port in the nineteenth century. Since that time the city has lost importance because of the lack of railroad service, and because the Wu River is not easily navigable for modern ships. Pop. (1953) 157,000.

WEND, one of a Western Slavic people living chiefly in the Lusatia region of East Germany and Poland (see LUSATIA). They formerly occupied nearly the whole of the Elbe Basin. They call themselves Serbs or Sorbs. Their language, of which there are two marked dialects, Saxon and Prussian, with numerous local and half-Germanized varieties, holds an intermediate position between Polish and Czech (Bohemian); it was first reduced to written form in the sixteenth century.

WENDELL, BARRETT, 1855–1921, U.S. writer and educator, was born in Boston. He was graduated from Harvard, 1877, and returned three years later to enter the department of English. He became a full professor, 1898, and did much to foster systematic and critical study of U.S. literature. Wendell delivered the Clark lectures at Cambridge University, 1902–03, and lectured at French universities, 1904–05. His *France of Today* (1907) was translated into French and German, and long ranked as a minor classic on the Continent. Notable among his other works are *Cotton Mather* (1891), *William Shakespere* (1894), *A Literary History of America* (1900), *The Privileged Classes* (1908), and *The Mystery of Education and Other Academic Performances* (1909).

WENDT, GERALD, 1891– , U.S. scientist, was born Gerald Louis Wendt in Davenport, Iowa, and attended Harvard University, 1906–16. He was instructor of chemistry at the University of Chicago, 1917–18, and was appointed dean of the School of Chemistry and Physics, Pennsylvania State College, 1925. Among his works are *Matter and Energy* (1930) and *Atomic Energy and the Hydrogen Bomb* (1950).

WENTWORTH, BENNING, 1696–1770, colonial American governor, was born in Portsmouth, N.H., was graduated from Harvard College, 1715, settled as a merchant in Portsmouth, and was royal governor of New Hampshire, 1741–67. Several years after entering upon the office, he began making grants of land in what is now Vermont, with the result that a long controversy sprang up with New York, which also claimed the territory on the strength of a charter that had been issued, 1674, by Charles II to his brother, the Duke of York. By exacting heavy fees for land grants and by other means Wentworth accumulated a fortune large for the times, erected a splendid mansion, and surrounded his authority with much pomp and circumstance. Finally, having alienated many of his friends in the colony and in England, he found it expedient to resign, 1767. He later gave 500 acres of land to Dartmouth College.

WENTWORTH, SIR JOHN, 1737–1820, British colonial governor in North America, a nephew of Benning Wentworth, was born in Portsmouth, N.H., and was graduated from Harvard College, 1755. When sent by New Hampshire to England to ask for repeal of the Stamp Act, 1765, he was appointed governor of New Hampshire and surveyor of the king's woods in North America, 1766–76. He gradually lost popularity as he adhered, more and more, to British policies; exiled by the state of New Hampshire, 1778, he returned to England. In Nova Scotia he served as surveyor of the king's woods, 1783–92, and was lieutenant governor, 1792–1808.

WENTWORTH, WILLIAM CHARLES, 1793–1872, Australian lawyer and patriot, was born in New South Wales, Australia, the son of a government surgeon. He went to England and was admitted to the bar, 1822, than studied briefly at Peterhouse, Cambridge, 1823, before returning to Australia. He practiced law in Sydney, and was a co-founder of a newspaper, the *Australian*, 1824. He advocated Australian self-government and is given a large share of credit for the Constitution Act of 1842, which granted limited self-government to Australia. He founded the University of Sydney, 1852, and after another visit to England became president of the new legislative council of Australia, 1861.

WENTWORTH, village, N North Carolina, seat of Rockingham County; 75 miles NW of Raleigh. The Troublesome Iron Works, which was built in the village in 1770, was probably the first industry of that type in the state. Pop. (1959 est.) 125.

WERDNIG-HOFFMAN PARALYSIS, a rare hereditary disease characterized by degeneration of certain nerve cells in the spinal cord and a wasting away of the muscles. Most of the cases are thought to originate from a recessive gene. The disease is normally expressed at the sixth month after birth. The child shows difficulty sitting up, and its equilibrium is so affected that it has difficulty learning to walk. Muscles in the body trunk, neck, and limbs cannot remain contracted for long periods of time and the head cannot be held up. Power loss usually begins in the muscular areas of joints close to the center of the body and as the disease progresses, areas extended to the ends of the limbs become affected. The disease increasingly immobilizes the child until about the fifth year, when the paralysis results in death.

Both sexes may be equally affected; intellectual development is not impaired. The anterior horn cells in the spinal cord, which are essential in the reflex arc, are progressively destroyed in the disease. See NERVOUS SYSTEM, Conduction of Nerve Impulses, *Reflexes*.

WEREWOLF, according to ancient legends and popular superstition, a human being capable of transforming himself, or of being transformed involuntarily, into a wolf who hunts and devours human beings by night. Werewolves appear in the work of Herodotus, in medieval literature, and in the folklore of almost all peoples. In lands where no wolves exist the uncanny men assume the shapes of whatever beast is considered the most fierce. In parts of Africa, for example, men are believed to become leopards or crocodiles. Both the process of transforming oneself or being transformed into a wolf and the psychosis in which one imagines oneself to be a wolf are known technically as lycanthropy.

WERFEL, FRANZ, 1890–1945, German-Czech poet, playwright, and novelist, was born in Prague of wealthy Jewish parents, attended Prague and Leipzig universities, served in the Austrian army in World War I, and married, 1918, Alma Marie Schindler, the widow of the composer Gustav Mahler. He left Austria at the time of the Nazi occupation, and in 1940 came to the United States, where he spent his last years. Werfel was first known as a poet (*Einander*, 1915) and an Expressionist dramatist (*Goat Song*, 1921), he turned to prose fiction in *Verdi* (1924). In his subsequent works Werfel gave increasing prominence to the theme of self-realization through religious faith; and his own quest for spiritual certitude ended in a renewal of his Judaism. Notable among his other works are *The Man Who Conquered Death* (1927), *Class Reunion* (1929), *The Pure in Heart* (1929), *The Pascarella Family* (1932), *The Forty Days of Musa Dagh* (1933), *Embezzled Heaven* (1940), *The Song of Bernadette* (1941), *Jacobowsky and the Colonel* (1944), and *Star of the Unborn* (1946).

WERGELAND, HENRIK ARNOLD, 1808–45, Norwegian lyric poet, editor, and national leader was born in Christiana, the son of Nicolai Wergeland, a prominent clergyman who played a significant role in the Eidsvoll constituent assembly, 1814. Having been tutored at the parsonage with the understanding that he would study theology, Henrik attended the Cathedral School in Oslo from 1819, and then matriculated, 1825, at the national university.

Under the spell of romantic emotion and an exceptionally deep passion for nature, he wrote the monumental *Creation, Man, and Messiah* (1830), a cosmological interpretation in the [John] Miltonic vein. As a student leader, he was a deep-dyed patriot who believed that the emerging national culture must stem from the rugged fiord and valley communities; yet he greatly admired the sophisticated champions of the French Revolution and the Enlightenment. Fired by the events in Paris during the July, 1830, uprising, he made a hurried visit to France and England, and returned to Norway aflame with enthusiasm for the new day of democracy.

Neither his doctrine nor his behavior was strictly orthodox, with the result that after his graduation from the university Wergeland failed to get the usual appointment in the state church. He had no certain livelihood until 1841, when he took a position in the National Archives. During the 1830's, he edited papers and wrote untiringly, producing sensitive lyric poems and articles in the interest of a general cultural education. His pen was often dipped in acid, and he in turn was the object of vituperation, but during the last decade of his life, he won the hearts of his people in sheaf after sheaf of extraordinary lyrics, among the best known of which are *To Spring*, *To My Golden Flower*, and *Jan van Huysum's Blossoms*.

Wergeland is known especially for his imaginativeness, for the freshness of his lyric moods, for the intense passion he experienced in the presence of nature, and for the sentiment of democratic charity evoked in all his works. He died in his modest Oslo home after a lingering illness. Subsequently he came to be recognized as the undisputed genius of the Norwegian national renaissance of the early nineteenth century.   THEODORE JORGENSON

WERNER, ALFRED, 1866–1919, Nobel prize-winning Swiss chemist, was born in Mulhouse, Alsace-Lorraine, and educated at Karlsruhe, Zürich, and Paris. He taught at Zürich Polytechnic, 1889, and became professor of organic chemistry at the University of Zürich, 1895. His first important scientific work was in the stereochemistry of nitrogenous compounds. In 1893 he announced the coordination theory of valency, a classification method that brought about the discovery of isomers of numerous metallic combinations. Werner was awarded the 1913 Nobel prize in chemistry in "recognition of his work on the linkage of atoms in molecules, by which he has thrown fresh light on old problems and opened up new fields of research, particularly in inorganic chemistry." Among his writings are *A Manual of Stereo-Chemistry* (1904) and *New Opinions in the Field of Inorganic Chemistry* (1905).

WERTHAM, FREDRIC, 1895– , U.S. psychologist and author, was born in Germany, and studied neurology and psychiatry in Munich, Vienna, Paris, and London. He immigrated to the United States, 1921, worked at Johns Hopkins Hospital, and organized his own clinic, 1932. Among his works are *The Brain as an Organ* (1934); a novelistic case history of a young murderer, *The Dark Legend* (1941); a study of the poet Ezra Pound, *The Road to Rapallo* (1949); a denunciation of comic magazines as a major cause of juvenile crime, *Seduction of the Innocent* (1954); and another treatise on the causes of juvenile delinquency, *Circle of Guilt* (1956).

WESCOTT, GLENWAY, 1901– , U.S. novelist, was born in Kewaskum, Wis., and attended the University of Chicago, 1917–19. During the 1920's, as many of his contemporaries, he lived a bohemian existence in Paris and on the French Riviera, and traveled extensively through Europe. He published his first novel *The Apple of the Eye* (1924) during this period, and followed it with the successful *The Grandmothers—A Family Portrait* (1927), which won the Harper prize. He was originally interested in becoming a poet, and a flair for the poetic is apparent in his novels, particularly in his rhythmic, lyrical prose. Among Wescott's works are *A Calendar of Saints for Unbelievers* (1932), *The Pilgrim Hawk* (1940), and *Apartment in Athens* (1945). His stories are collected in *Good-Bye Wisconsin* (1928), his essays in *In Fear and Trembling* (1932).

WESER RIVER, Germany, is formed by the junction of the Werra and Fulda rivers at Münden and flows generally NNW, for a distance of about 300 miles, to the North Sea. The river flows through a hilly upland to Minden, and then flows across the North German Plain to Bremen, the most important city on its banks. North of Bremen the Weser is broad, and has several islands. It enters the North Sea at

Bremerhaven. The Weser River is navigable throughout its length, and it is connected with the Elbe River by the Weser and Mittelland canals. The flow of water in the river is controlled by a system of dams on its tributaries.

WESLACO, city, extreme S Texas, in Hidalgo County; on the Missouri Pacific Railroad and U.S. highway 83; 230 miles ESE of San Antonio. The city is a shipping and processing center for an area in which citrus fruit, vegetables, and cotton are grown by irrigation. The processing of feed, fertilizer, and the production of boxes are leading industries. Weslaco was incorporated in 1921, and requires that all new buildings be in the Spanish style of architecture. Pop. (1960) 15,649.

WESLEY, CHARLES, 1707–88, English Methodist clergyman and hymn writer, was born in Epworth, Lincolnshire. While at Christ Church College, Oxford, 1726–32, he and his brother, John Wesley, were leaders of the Holy Club, whose members were derisively dubbed Methodists because of their emphasis on method in conduct. After serving briefly and not very successfully as a missionary in Georgia, 1735–36, and as unlicensed curate at Saint Mary's, Islington, 1738–39, he spent 17 years traveling extensively as an itinerant preacher. In 1756 he settled in Bristol to continue his work, but in 1771 he moved to London. He was always closely associated with his brother John, although the two differed on certain doctrinal points. Charles Wesley's hymns—it is said he wrote over 6,500 songs—played an important role in the Methodist movement; some attained a wide and lasting popularity, especially *Jesus, Lover of My Soul; O for a Thousand Tongues to Sing; Hark, the Herald Angels Sing!* and *Love Divine, All Loves Excelling.* See METHODISM.

WESLEY, JOHN, 1705?–91 English evangelist, founder of Christian Methodism, but not of the Methodist church, was born in the Manse of Epworth, England, the fifteenth child of Samuel and Susannah Wesley, both of whom took a formative hand in his religious upbringing. He was educated in Charter House School, London, and in Oxford at Christ Church College and Lincoln College (M.A. 1727). After the first of what was to be a series of many unfinished courtships—under the classic name "Cyrus" he corresponded with "Varanese," who, in plain English, was Sarah Kirkham—he was ordained deacon and made a fellow of Lincoln. In Lincoln, he formed the Holy Club, so called, whose strict rules and schedules for pieties and readings procured for its members the nickname of "methodists," and thus the Father of Methodism was christened with a Platonic and Aristotelian, and totally nonscriptural name. Later, regular visits to prisoners and to sick enlarged their "method."

When James Edward Oglethorpe needed two clergymen for his North American venture, John and his younger brother Charles Wesley (1707–88) were sent to Oglethorpe's new colony of Georgia, 1735, and the life-long partnership of the two brothers began in earnest. John's most significant positive experience in America, the Georgia ministry having proved a failure, was meeting the Moravian Brethren of Count Nikolaus Ludwig von Zinzendorf and being told, to his surprise, that Christ could not be found "in general."

Conversion. Landing in England, 1738, Wesley again met a legate of Count Zinzendorf, Peter Böhler, and once more was asked if he knew that no ecclesiastical grandeur or sacraments would help him unless he realized that Christ had died for *him.* Wesley's idea of religion had previously been dominated by the social and historical setting of his life; family, university, and country had seen to that: you were a visible Christian in a visible church or you were not a Christian at all. Wesley's "Aldersgate Street Experience"—during his attendance of a meeting of Moravian Brethren—at 8:45 P.M. on May 24, 1738,

changed all this. Wesley now acknowledged that God cannot create a free soul unless this soul faces God's death as a personal communication to her (the soul) made for her sake, creating a bond that remains forever invisible to everybody else in the world, and only shines forth into the visible world through this soul's perpetual witness in the form of new and resourceful acts inspired by this invisible source.

The experience of May 24, called "conversion" by Wesley, helped him later to discover his future, original path. But before this, he went to Zinzerdorf's estate and Moravian center at Herrnhut itself. Finding the group there not active enough to suit him, Wesley decided to steer an independent course and responded to his own conversion by adopting the open field and the open road under the open sky as his invisible church in the midst of the visible Established Church of England. Yet, as he wrote in his *Journal,* "I hardly could reconcile myself to this baroque way of preaching because I so firmly was attached to every point of ecclesiastical observance and ritual that I nearly deemed it a sacrilege to save souls except inside a church-building."

For some 50 years, then, Wesley persisted in this conservative policy of not actually breaking away from the visible church, but of planting within it centers of sanctifying spiritual revival. In fanning the fires of living faith in the masses—masses much abused by the brazen and impudent victors of the Glorious Revolution, the British gentry, in England, Ireland, and in the colonies—Wesley markedly changed the moral temper of these territories and made over their inhabitants. For more than 50 years he rode annually from about 5,000 to 8,000 miles, with Bristol, London, Newcastle, and Dublin (Ireland) his starting points; he crossed the Irish Channel no less than 42 times. Those patrons of the Established church who acceded to his preaching, themselves were to receive the benefits of this revival; but, through no fault of Wesley, most patrons of the Established church frustrated, ridiculed, and hated his method.

Throughout his life, Wesley remained satisfied with the barest minimum of an organization. In 1744, however, he called a conference of his ministers for the first time; their subsequent annual meetings remained the one formal aspect of the Methodist movement. Otherwise, for 45 years, the saintliness, magnetism, and incisive good judgment and common sense of Wesley had to suffice and did suffice in supplementing the thousands of letters and the hundred thousands of miles. By 1784, however, the changed status of the North American lands made it imperative to act across the ocean independently from the Anglican church, which had forfeited its established hold on the new United States. Wesley accordingly appointed a superintendent, Francis Asbury, and gave him the competence of ordaining bishops in America. Thus, after years of infinite patience with the Established church, and infinite perseverance in his circuit-rider mission, it was the pressure of new conditions that made Wesley act with the incisiveness of a statesman. Subsequently the logic of events led to the independence of the Methodists as a church visible around the invisible church that had gathered during John Wesley's apostolic pilgrimage. See METHODISM.

Personal Life. In his private affairs, Wesley fared unluckily. He definitely tried to marry a Miss Grace Murray, but brother Charles made this impossible by a rudeness and meanness of action that one can only excuse by assuming it to have resulted from some unconscious jealousy: he could not forgive John that he, Charles, had not been taken into his confidence. The detestable result was that Grace married somebody else, and John rushed in to such an ill-chosen marriage that the wife soon became his mortal enemy and they separated. The religious division of labor of the two brothers, in which Charles had cultivated their ties with the official church, thereafter was seriously impaired; thus did the personal life do harm to the work. In retrospect, it is important to remember that "methodism" was not a term chosen for the final traits of the Aldersgate Street experience, but a purely accidental nickname dating from the adolescence of John Wesley before his conversion. Wesley's saintliness alone tied the two periods of his life together.

Works. John Wesley personally edited his *Works*, which appeared in Bristol (32 vols. 1771–74); later editions were issued in London, 1829–31 and 1868–72. The famous *Journals* edited by N. Curnock (8 vols. 1909–10), cover the years 1743–90. Wesley's *Letters* (8 vols. 1931) were edited by J. Telford. The *Works* include, among other things, histories of Rome and England; an ecclesciastical history; educational treatises; biblical commentaries; many hymns; and translations from several languages.

EUGEN ROSENSTOCK-HUESSY

BIBLIOG. Eric W. Baker, *Herald of the Evangelical Revival* (New World Lib., no 1) (1948); Evelyn D. Bebb, *Wesley: A Man with a Concern* (1950); Mabel R. Brailsford, *Tale of Two Brothers: John and Charles Wesley* (1954); John W. Bready, *England: Before and After Wesley* (1938); William R. Cannon, *Theology of John Wesley* (1946); George C. Cell, *Rediscovery of John Wesley* (1935); Edwin B. Chappell, *Studies in the Life of John Wesley* (1929); Leslie F. Church, *Knight of the Burning Heart: The Story of John Wesley* (1953); Frank W. Collier, *John Wesley Among the Scientists* (1928); John W. Deschner, *Wesley's Christology* (1960); William L. Doughty, *John Wesley, Preacher* (1955); George Eayres, *John Wesley: Christian Philosopher and Church Founder* (1926); Maldwyn L. Edwards, *Astonishing Youth: A Study of John Wesley as Men Saw Him* (1959); Grace E. S. Harrison, *Son to Susanna: The Private Life of John Wesley* (1938); Paul L. Higgins, *John Wesley: Spiritual Witness* (1960); Franz Hildebrandt, *From Luther to Wesley*, (1952); Alfred W. Hill, *John Wesley Among the Physicians: A Study of Eighteenth Century Medicine* (1958); William H. Hutton, *John Wesley* (Great English Churchmen Ser.) (1927); Thomas R. Jeffrey, *John Wesley's Religious Quest* (1960); Harry H. Kroll, *Long Quest: The Story of John Wesley* (1954); Umphrey Lee, *Lord's Horseman: John Wesley the Man* (1954); Abram Lipsky, *John Wesley: A Portrait* (1928); Gabrielle M. V. Long (Marjorie Bowen, George Preedy, pseuds.), *Wrestling Jacob: A Study of the Life of John Wesley and Some Members of the Family* (1937); Kathleen W. MacArthur, *Economic Ethics of John Wesley* (1936); Francis J. McConnell, *John Wesley* (1961); Maximin Piette, *John Wesley in the Evolution of Protestantism* (1937); William E. Sangster, *Path to Perfection* (1957); John Telford, *Life of John Wesley* (1930); John M. Todd (John Fox, pseud.), *John Wesley and the Catholic Church* (1958); Colwyn E. Vulliamy (Anthony Rolls, pseud.), *John Wesley* (1954); John D. Wade, *John Wesley* (1930); John H. Whiteley, *Wesley's England* (1938); Colin W. Williams, *John Wesley's Theology Today* (1960); Caleb T. Winchester, *Life of John Wesley* (1906).

WESLEYAN COLLEGE, a private institution of higher learning for women, associated with the Methodist church, and located at Macon, Ga. Men are admitted on a limited basis. Established as the Georgia Female College, 1836, the school offered its first liberal arts instruction in 1839. The name was changed to Wesleyan Female College, 1843, and to Wesleyan College, 1919. The school of fine arts was added in 1924.

The college sponsors an internship program for teachers, a master's program in music, a junior year of study at selected universities abroad, and the Junaluska Summer Music School. Among the college library's special collections are the McGregor Collection of rare Americana, the Park Collection of rare Georgiana, art books, musical recordings. See COLLEGES AND UNIVERSITIES.

WESLEYAN METHODIST CHURCH. See METHODISM.

WESLEYAN UNIVERSITY, a private, nonsectarian institution of higher learning for men, located at Middletown, Conn. The school was founded as a college of liberal arts, 1831, under the auspices of the Methodist Episcopal Church, and offered its first instruction the same year.

Programs of graduate study leading to a master's degree are offered in most departments; women are admitted to the graduate school. The university conducts an honors college for superior students in their junior and senior year, and a co-operative study program with California Institute of Technology and Columbia University's School of Engineering. Courses designed to increase reading comprehension and speed are offered. The school also maintains an electronics laboratory for special development in language ability.

Among the special collections in the university library are the Davison Collection of rare books, the Johnston Collection of early Atlases, and the Barney Collection of poetry works. The Department of School Services and Publications issues the *Weekly Reader*, *Our Times*, and *Current Events*, all of which are used by students in elementary and secondary schools. See COLLEGES AND UNIVERSITIES.

WESSEL, JOHANN, sometimes called Gansfort or Goesvort, 1420?–?1489, Dutch theologian and reformer, was born in Groningen, and brought up by the Brethren of the Common Life in Zwolle. He was educated at Cologne, Heidelberg, and Paris and spent a short time in Rome. He spent the latter part of his life mostly in retirement in the place of his birth. He was called Lux Mundi (Light of the World) by his friends, but because of his strenuous opposition to the prevalent Scholastic philosophy his enemies dubbed him *Magister Contradictionum* (Master of Contradictions). He regarded Christianity as entirely spiritual and denied that indulgences could apply to other than ecclesiastical penalties.

WESSELY, NAPHTALI HERZ, 1725–1805, German Hebrew poet and essayist, was born in Hamburg. He studied at Copenhagen and participated in the Jewish Enlightenment movement which, under the leadership of Moses Mendelssohn, was designed to bring Jews into closer harmony with European intellectual and cultural affairs. He devoted the last 20 years of his life to completing an epic poem about the prophet Moses, *Shire Lif'ereth* (published in six parts, 1789–1829). He also wrote on ethics and on Hebrew grammar, and composed a commentary on Leviticus.

WESSEX, an Anglo-Saxon kingdom in southern Britain. In 494, Cerdic (died 534) landed on Southampton Water, and after years of warfare became king of the West Saxons (Old English *West seaxe*), 519. Following the Battle of Deorham, 577, the West Saxons secured access to the Bristol Channel, and won Cirencester, Gloucester, and Bath. The Welsh of Wales were thus cut off from the Welsh in Somerset, Devon, and Cornwall. As Northumbria, Mercia, and Wessex struggled for supremacy, 613–825, Cenwealh (643–72) and his successors, Caedwalla and Ine, gradually extended the borders of Wessex. Somerset was conquered; London recognized the West Saxon power; and laws were issued. Wessex was Christianized, nominally at least, in the seventh century. It was not, however, until the time of Egbert (802–39), whose youth had been spent in the court of Charlemagne, that the supremacy of Wessex over Northumbria and Mercia was in any sense assured. The union of England under Egbert was premature, however, and it required the later Danish invasion to force the men of Northumbria and Mercia to recognize the overlordship of Wessex.

It was not till after the Treaty of Wedmore (878), between the Danish king Guthrum and Alfred the Great (849–901), that the latter was able to begin his great work of reconquering England from the Danes. Alfred's successors, Edward the Elder, Athelstan, Edmund, Edred, and Edgar, continued this endeavor, and in Edgar "the royal power reached its highest point," as it has been said. The shire system originated in Wessex. From the death of Edgar, 975, to the accession of Canute, 1016, Wessex passed through evil days owing to the attacks of the Danes, who succeeded in placing a Danish dynasty on the throne. For 800 years following the Norman Conquest, 1066, Wessex did not exist even as an informal geographical term.

In the nineteenth century, however, the novelist Thomas Hardy revived the term, but not the entity, in his *Far From the Madding Crowd* (1874) and subsequent novels; Hardy's "Wessex," insofar as it is a real place, is often identified as the county of Dorsetshire.

WESSINGTON SPRINGS, city, SE central South Dakota, seat of Jerauld County; on the Milwaukee Railroad; 89 miles ESE of Pierre. The city is a trade and shipping center for an area in which grain and livestock are raised. Wessington Springs was founded in 1880. Pop. (1960) 1,488.

WEST, ANTHONY PANTHER, 1914– , English critic and novelist, was born in Hunstanton, Norfolk, son of the writers H. G. Wells and Rebecca West. He began contributing reviews to the *New Statesman and Nation* (later the *New Statesman*), 1937, and later, barred from service during World War II because of a history of tuberculosis, joined the staff of the British Broadcasting Company, 1943. He emigrated to the United States, 1950, and became associated with the *New Yorker* magazine in the same year. Among his works are *On a Dark Night*, 1949 (in the United States, *The Vintage*, 1950), *Another Kind* (1951), *D. H. Lawrence* (1951), *Heritage* (1955), and *Principles and Persuasion* (1956).

WEST, BENJAMIN, 1738–1820, colonial American and British historical painter and portraitist, was born in Springfield, Pa., the son of Quaker parents who did nothing to encourage him in artistic pursuits, yet by the age of seven he was already painting, using paints made of leaves, berries, and the like, and brushes manufactured from the hairs of a cat. Thus largely self-taught, at the age of 16 he was a practicing portraitist in the vicinity of Philadelphia, but not yet in the big city itself. His first historical painting, *The Death of Socrates*, was painted for a gunsmith during this period. Finally, at the age of 18 he was painting portraits in Philadelphia itself, and subsequently he dared move to New York to carry out the same activity. Aided by some New York merchants, 1760, he went to Italy to study, remained there for three years, and was an official success in the sense that he was elected to the academies of Parma, Florence, and Bologna. Among the paintings dating from these years are *Cimon and Iphigenia* and *Angelica and Medora*.

At the end of his studies West stopped off for a visit in England, and remained there for the rest of his life; he married and established himself in expatriation. Despite his backwoods origin, he not only attracted the attention of George III, but gained the king's friendship as well. For the next 40 years he enjoyed the royal patronage, and sketched or painted some 400 pictures, most of them large. He helped found the Royal Academy, and succeeded Sir Joshua Reynolds as its president, 1792.

West effected a minor revolution in historical painting by clothing his figures in the costumes of the period being depicted rather than on the costumes of the ancients. His *Death of General Wolfe* (Grosvenor House, London), done shortly after his appointment as court historical painter, 1712, initiated and exemplified the new practice. Such innovations were superficial, however, and in the end West contributed nothing really new to the art of painting; his pictures were large, but his inspiration was not. Lord Byron qualified him as "that dotard West, Europe's worst daub, poor England's best." Personally, however, he was a man of great generosity, and the encouragement he gave to American painters away from home was probably more important ultimately to art than his paintings; his home and studio were long a center for American artists who had come to London to study.

Among West's more notable paintings are *Christ Healing the Sick* (National Gallery, London), *Death on the Pale Horse* (Pennsylvania Academy), *Alexander the Great and His Physicians*, *The Black Prince at Poictiers*, and *Penn's Treaty with the Indians*. Hampton Court, near London, has much of his work. ANTHONY KERRIGAN

WEST, JESSAMYN, 1907– , U.S. author, was born in Indiana; her family moved to California when she was six, and she attended Whittier College in southern California. Her first book, *The Friendly Persuasion* (1945), was a collection of sketches concerning the life of a Quaker family. Among her other works are a macabre novel, *The Witch Diggers* (1951); a collection of stories of adolescent life, *Cress Delabanty* (1953); and an account of the development of one of her novels into a motion picture, *To See the Dream* (1957).

WEST, NATHANAEL, 1902–1940, U.S. novelist, was born Nathan Weinstein, and was graduated from Brown University, 1924. His first novel, *The Dream Life of Balso Snell* (1931), marked him as a writer of unusual talent, an impression fully confirmed by *Miss Lonelyhearts* (1933), a surrealistic satire on the inner sufferings of a newspaperman who writes an advice-to-the-lovelorn column and makes the fatal error of empathizing excessively with the tragic-comic dilemmas of the people who ask advice of "Miss Lonelihearts." West went to Hollywood, 1935, to translate his second novel into a screen play, and remained there writing scenarios, most of them undistinguished, until his death in an auto accident near El Centro, Calif. Other works are *A Cool Million* (1934) and a celebrated novel on Hollywood decadence, *The Day of the Locust* (1939).

WEST, REBECCA, real name Cicily Fairfield Andrews, 1892– , English writer, was born in Ireland and educated at George Watson's Ladies' College in Edinburgh, Scotland. She left a stage career to become a political writer for English and U.S. periodicals, a critic (*Henry James*, 1916; *D. H. Lawrence*, 1928), and a novelist (*The Return of the Soldier*, 1918; *The Judge*, 1922; *The Thinking Reed*, 1936). Among her other works are *Black Lamb and Grey Falcon* (1941), a Balkan travel book; *The Meaning of Treason* (1947), a character study of some men considered to be traitors; and *A Train of Powder* (1955). She was the mother of the critic and novelist, Anthony West. See WELLS, HERBERT GEORGE.

WEST, ROY OWEN, 1868–1958, U.S. cabinet officer, was born in Georgetown, Ill., studied at DePauw University, and was admitted to the bar, 1890. He served as secretary of the Republican National Committee, 1924–28, and as secretary of the interior in the cabinet of Pres. Calvin Coolidge, 1928–29. As special assistant to the U.S. attorney general, 1941–53, he heard the cases of conscientious objectors to military service.

WEST, THE, as a region in the United States, has no definite boundaries, but is generally considered to comprise the eight Rocky Mountain States and the three Pacific Coast States. So defined, the West comprises one-third of the area and contains one-sixth of the population of the conterminous United States.

The West is predominantly an area of mountainous terrain, consisting of north to south trending mountain ranges, which reach heights of over 12,000 feet. Intermediate in elevation are the broad areas of the Columbia Plateau, Colorado Plateau, and the Great Basin. Contrasting with these higher areas, are the lower valleys, and especially the Great Valley of California and the Willamette-Puget Sound lowlands. Important rivers crossing the region are the Columbia and Snake Rivers in the north, and the Sacramento and San Joaquin rivers in central California.

Climatically, the area is one of great diversity although characterized by general aridity. Except for the westward facing slopes of the Coast Ranges and Sierra Nevada, the average annual rainfall is only about 15 inches. This figure is even smaller in the south where true desert conditions are found in Arizona and Southern California. Temperatures differ widely from one part to another.

Population is sparse in most of the region, but there are three major areas of density, which are concentrated in the Puget Sound area; the Bay area around San Francisco; and in Southern California around Los Angeles. Denver and Salt Lake City are also major centers of population density.

Agriculture and forestry dominate the economy over most of the region. Farming is restricted in area by a lack of adequate water supply, and is characterized by intensive cultivation of river valleys. Vegetables, rice, grapes, citrus fruits, and cotton are most important in the south. In the northern, less diversified valleys, beans, potatoes, sugar beets, and wheat are produced. In the uplands, dense stands of timber and grazing areas for cattle and sheep are economically important. The Palouse District of Columbia Plateau is one of the leading wheat-producing areas of the United States.

The region is well endowed with scattered mineral deposits—lead, zinc, iron ore, gold, silver, petroleum, and copper, of which the last is perhaps the most important economically. Manufacturing in the urban areas is diversified, and benefits greatly from the proximity of mineral raw materials and rich timber resources. Seattle and Southern California are noted for the manufacture of aircraft.

History of the North American West

In U.S. history, the West has been essentially a sociopolitical concept rather than a specific geographical area Thus, until 1803 the area between the Alleghenies and the Mississippi River was considered the West. With the purchase of the Louisiana Territory, and the annexation of Texas, the West became the territory west of the Great Plains: the Great Basin of Utah, northwest Nevada, and southern Idaho; California; and the Oregon country. Later, as the continent was settled and new states added to the Union, the Far West so called, came to be defined as the Rocky Mountain and the Pacific States, designated as the Rocky Mountains Division and the Pacific Division by the Bureau of the Census. Still later, with the admission of Hawaii as a state, it became the westernmost part of the country; for cultural reasons, however, Hawaii could hardly be regarded as part of the West in the ordinary sense. The significance of the concept of the West in U.S. history is best understood in terms of Frederick J. Turner's studies of the frontier psychology in American cultural development. See Frontier.

The West came into the possession of the United States by the purchase of Louisiana Territory from France, 1803; the annexation of Texas (including the state of Texas and parts of New Mexico, Colorado, Wyoming, Kansas, and Oklahoma), 1845; the cession by Mexico, 1848, of California and New Mexico (including what is now those two states, Arizona, Nevada, and Utah); the Gadsden Purchase (territory now in the southern part of Arizona and New Mexico); and by the Oregon Treaty (1846) with England, by which the Pacific Northwest was divided at the 49th parallel (the present states of Oregon and Washington, and parts of Idaho and Wyoming).

The Fur Trade. Except for the settlement of Texas, migration into the West was delayed by the popular misapprehension that the Great Plains area was unsuitable for agriculture and habitation. This was the discouraging estimate of the central and southern parts of the western territory reported by earlier government expeditions, especially those of Zebulon Pike, 1806–07, and Stephen Long, 1819–20. Hence fur trading rather than agriculture occasioned the first economic exploitation of the West. It followed established lines of penetration: the Santa Fe Trail to the Gila River area, the Arkansas River route into Colorado, and the Missouri River gateway into the Rocky Mountains. So profitable was the northern fur trade that rendezvous—predetermined periodic meetings for the exchange of pelts and supplies—were held in many of the valleys of the Rocky Mountain country, and trading posts established. Proceeding from these points, practicable ways were found to the Columbia River, and into California.

Missionary Activity. While the fur trade was burgeoning, Christian missionary work with the Indians was begun, and colonization was initiated by such "pioneers of the pioneers" as Wyeth, Whitman, Lee, and De Smet. Wyeth, a New England trader, became interested in the commercial potentialities of the West through the Boston teacher Hall J. Kelley, who talked of organizing an "Oregon Colonization Society." Kelley's talk came to nothing, but Wyeth, a man of action when there was money involved, made two expeditions, 1832–33 and 1834, into what later became Oregon Territory. The expeditions failed commercially, owing to the courteous but implacable opposition of Hudson's Bay Company, and Wyeth returned to New England. Some of his companions remained in the West, however, among them the Rev. Jason Lee, whose Methodist mission furthered agricultural and educational development. Lee and Wyeth journeyed to Oregon by sailing around Cape Horn; the two expeditions of the Presbyterian missionary Dr. Marcus Whitman were overland from St. Louis. On the first, 1835, Whitman and the Rev. Samuel Parker surveyed the need for Presbyterianism in Oregon. Whitman returned, 1836, with his bride, Narcissa, and the Rev. and Mrs. H. H. Spalding, to set up a medical mission near the confluence of the Walla Walla and Columbia rivers. Whitman's party was the first including women to cross the Rockies and the first, coincidentally, to expose the Cayuse Indians to epidemic measles. Whitman's medicines did not help the Indian victims of the disease and the Cayuse, thinking the medicine to be poison, massacred the missionaries, 1847. Roman Catholic missionaries were active in the area by 1838; the work of Father Pierre-Jean De Smet among the Flatheads in Montana and Idaho was especially important.

Settlement. The celebrity of Capt. John Frémont's two expeditions, 1842 and 1843–44, contributed to "the Oregon disease" of the 1840's. Although Frémont was dubbed "the Pathfinder" by the public, his routes had long been known to the fur traders. Frémont's published reports did, however, serve as useful guides for many settlers. Small parties reached Oregon and California in 1841–42, but migration on a large scale began in 1843, when some 1,000 persons, with 120 wagons and 1,500 cattle, began new lives in the Oregon country. In 1845 a single wagon train for Oregon included 3,000 people. And in 1847, following settlement of the Oregon boundary dispute, some 4,000 to 5,000 new settlers came into the area.

The raising of cattle is still important in the West, but it is not at all uncommon now for the cowboy to be riding in a helicopter instead of on a horse.
STANDARD OIL CO. (N.J.)

The Mormon emigration to Utah, 1846, was a major achievement in the settlement of the West. After leaving Nauvoo, Ill., those persecuted people not only reached their destination after incredible hardships, but ventured to settle where irrigation was necessary for the success of their agriculture. What they learned of irrigation methods was of the highest value in the development of irrigation generally.

By 1848 the United States was in possession of the entire West contained in its present borders with the exception of the Gadsden Purchase—and, of course, Alaska and Hawaii. As settlers followed the explorers and fur traders, it appeared that agriculture, already dominant in Oregon and Utah, would be the pattern of economic exploitation, although the fur trade continued in diminished proportion. But the discovery of gold in California and the ensuing Gold Rush, 1849, changed the situation: gold became and continued as a major economic factor in many places of the West—in California, Montana, Colorado, and elsewhere. Silver succeeded gold as the miner's quest and was in turn followed by copper, which became especially profitable after the flotation process of separating the mineral from earth and rock was developed.

Development. The mineral wealth of the West heightened the already apparent necessity for transcontinental railroads to connect West and East. The transcontinental extension of railroads had been discussed from 1845, but differences of judgment as to routes delayed construction. A system whereby the federal government aided railroad financing through land grants from the public domain had been worked out, and its effectiveness demonstrated, as early as 1856 by the construction of the Illinois Central Railroad, largely as a result of the leadership of Stephen A. Douglas. In view of the possible need for a southern route, the Gadsden Purchase was made, 1853. The strategic necessity of transcontinental railroads was demonstrated by the Civil War, during the early years of which the required legislation was adopted by Congress, 1862, and construction begun, 1863. The junction of the Central and the Union Pacific at Promontory Point, Utah, 1869, formed the first railway link of the West with the East; it was followed by the lines that ultimately formed the Santa Fe, the Southern Pacific, the Northern Pacific, and the Great Northern railroads.

As the railroads reached the Great Plains the development of the cattle industry furnished the basis for a growth that reached a considerable part of the West; Montana and Wyoming soon shared with the Great Plains in what became a major economic enterprise.

The Homestead Act of 1862 led to a marked increase in the population of the West after the Civil War. Mastery of the techniques of dry farming and the extension of irrigation furthered agriculture; the range cattle industry was followed by sheep raising; mining was extended; lumbering and fisheries became important in the Pacific Northwest; and shipping from West Coast ports extended transcontinental rail traffic.

Admission to the Union. The earliest political organization of the West antedated the political development in the regions of the Great Plains. California was admitted as a state, 1850, without having passed through a territorial period, and Oregon, after only a brief time as a territory, was admitted in 1859. Although Kansas was admitted as a state in 1861, Nevada, 1864, preceded Nebraska, 1867. Colorado became the "Centennial State," 1876, Washington and Montana entered the Union, 1889, under the same legislation that admitted North and South Dakota of the Great Plains; Idaho and Wyoming soon followed, 1890. Utah, which in number of inhabitants had long since been qualified for statehood, was denied admission to the Union until 1896 because of the practice of polygamy by the Mormons. Owing to their sparsity of population and the limita-

tions of mining as an economic basis for settlement, Arizona and New Mexico were not admitted to statehood until 1912.   DONALD W. RIDDLE

BIBLIOG.–Ed Ellsworth Bartholomew, *Biographical Album of Western Gunfighters* (1958); Lucius M. Beebe and Charles M. Clegg, *American West: The Pictorial Epic of a Continent* (1955); Ray A. Billington, *Far Western Frontier, 1830–1860* (New Am. Nation Ser.) (1956); Ray A. Billington and James B. Hedges, *Westward Expansion: A History of the Am. Frontier* (1960); William Brandon, *Men and the Mountain: Frémont's Fourth Expedition* (1955); Dee Brown, *Trail Driving Days* (1952); Raymond Carlson, ed., *Gallery of Western Paintings* (1951); Dan E. Clark, *West in American History* (1937); Myra Cooley, *Meet Me on the Green: The Saga of Beads and Buckskins* (1960); Harrison C. Dale, ed., *Ashley-Smith Explorations and the Discovery of a Central Route to the Pacific, 1822–1829* (1941); Harry E. Danford, *Builders of the West* (1959); Bernard A. De Voto (John August, pseud.), *Across the Wide Missouri* (1948); Howard R. Driggs, *Westward America* (1942), *Old West Speaks* (1959); John C. Frémont, *Narratives of Exploration and Adventure* (1956); Dorothy Gardiner, *West of the River* (1941); Gilbert J. Garraghan, *Chapters in Frontier History* (Science and Culture Ser.) (1934); Edmund W. Gilbert, *Exploration of Western America, 1800–1850* (1933); William H. Goetzmann, *Army Exploration in the American West, 1803–1863* (Yale Univ. Yale Publications in Am. Studies 4) (1960); Jacob R. Gregg, *History of the Oregon Trail, Santa Fe Trail, and Other Trails* (1955); LeRoy R. Hafen and Carl C. Rister, *Western America: The Exploration, Settlement, and Development of the Region Beyond the Mississippi* (1950); William F. Harris, *Look of the Old West* (1955); Gwinn H. Heap, *Central Route to the Pacific* (Far West and the Rockies Hist. Ser., vol. 7) (1957); James D. Horan, *Great American West: A Pictorial History from Coronado to the Last Frontier* (1959); Robert W. Howard, ed., *This Is the West* (1957); Bliss Isely, *Blazing the Way West* (1939); Agnes C. Laut, *Pathfinders of the West* (1937); John Leakey, *West that Was: From Texas to Montana* (1958); Lloyd Lewis and Stanley M. Pargellis, eds., *Granger Country: A Pictorial Social History of the Burlington Railroad* (1949); Lloyd McFarling, ed., *Exploring the Northern Plains, 1804–1876* (1955); James Monaghan, *Overland Trail* (Am. Trail Ser.) (1947); Nell Murbarger, *Sovereigns of the Sage* (1958); Charles Neider, ed., *Great West* (1958); Allan Nevins, *Frémont: Pathmaker of the West* (1939); John C. Parish, *Persistence of the Westward Movement, and Other Essays* (1944); Frederick L. Paxson, *History of the American Frontier, 1763–1893* (1924), *Last American Frontier* (1937); Earl S. Pomeroy, *In Search of the Golden West: The Tourist in Western America* (1957); Charles Preuss, *Exploring with Frémont* (Okla. Univ. Am. Exploration and Travel Ser., no. 26) (1958); Glenn C. Quiett, *They Built the West: An Epic of Rails and Cities* (1934); Fred Reinfeld, *Trappers of the West* (1957); Robert E. Riegel, *America Moves West* (1956); Martin F. Schmitt and Dee A. Brown, *Settlers' West* (1955); Glenn Shirley, *Buckskin and Spurs: A Gallery of Frontier Rogues and Heroes* (1958); Henry N. Smith, *Virgin Land: The American West as a Symbol and Myth* (1950); Edith A. Tucker, *Adventuring Westward* (1950); Frederick J. Turner, *Frontier in American History* (1950); Edward S. Wallace, *Great Reconnaissance: Soldiers, Artists and Scientists on the Frontier, 1848–1861* (1955); Walter P. Webb, *Great Plains* (1944); Paul I. Wellman, *Indian Wars of the West* (1954); Carl I. Wheat, *Mapping the American West, 1540–1857* (1954).

WEST AFRICA, SPANISH. See SPANISH SAHARA.

WEST ALLIS, city, SE Wisconsin, in Milwaukee County; on the North Western, the Milwaukee, and the Soo Line railroads; a residential and industrial suburb, 3 miles WSW of Milwaukee. Machinery, electrical milling machines, power shovels, trucks, tractors, wheelbarrows, transformers, steel containers and cylinders, and gasoline motors are manufactured. West Allis was incorporated in 1906. Pop. (1960) 68,157.

WEST BEND, city, SE Wisconsin, seat of Washington County; on the North Western Railway and U.S. highway 45; 30 miles NNW of Milwaukee. The city is a trade and industrial center for an area in which dairying and truck farming are leading activities. The city has a vegetable cannery, and aluminum utensils, automobile accessories, leather goods, and agricultural tools are manufactured. West Bend was founded in 1845 and incorporated in 1885. A large majority of the present population consists of descendants of the city's early German settlers. Pop. (1960) 9,969.

WEST BENGAL, state, E India, bounded by Sikkim and Bhutan on the N, Assam on the NE, East

PRESS INFORMATION BUR. GOVT. OF INDIA

Chowringhee Street, one of the chief commercial thorough-fares of Calcutta, borders a large park. Calcutta is the capital of West Bengal, and one of India's major ports.

Pakistan on the E, the Bay of Bengal on the S, Orissa on the SW, Bihar on the W, and Nepal on the NW; area 34,945 sq. mi., pop. (1951) 26,301,992. The irregularly shaped state extends from the foothills of the Himalayan Mountains in the north, across the Ganges River plains to the Bay of Bengal. In the south West Bengal extends from the Ganges Delta to the dissected rim of the central Indian Plateau. West Bengal is an important agricultural state, and supports a very dense rural population. In the Darjeeling District in the north, tea, tobacco, and oranges are important crops, and there are valuable timber stands of teak, oak, and bamboo. Farther south in the alluvial plains, rice, the major subsistence crop, is supplemented by millet, cotton, sugar cane, oilseeds, and barley. The delta region produces almost half of India's jute crop. West Bengal is one of the major industrial states in India. There are two main centers of industrial production; the area along the Hooghly River, centered on Calcutta, and the towns along the Damodar Valley in the west. The Damodar Valley produces about one-third of India's coking coal, and there are large steel mills at Dungapur. Rural industries include the milling of jute and cotton. Calcutta, the largest city in India, is the capital. The greater part of the population is Hindu, but about 20 per cent is Moslem. West Bengal was created in 1947 from part of the former Bengal Province. In 1950 the territory of Cooch-Behar was merged with West Bengal, and in 1954 the former French possession of Chandernagore was added. In 1956 portions of Bihar State were transferred to West Bengal.

WESTBORO, or Westborough, town, E central Massachusetts, Worcester County; on the New York Central Railroad; 9 miles E of Worcester. The town is a trade center for a diversified agricultural area. Abrasives, shoes, underwear, leather goods, paper boxes, and tape are manufactured. Westboro was settled about 1675 and was first known as Marlborough. It was incorporated in 1717. Eli Whitney, inventor of the cotton gin, was born there. Westboro has a state hospital for the insane. Pop. (1960) 9,599.

WESTBRANCH, city, N central Michigan, seat of Ogemaw County; on the New York Central Railroad; 144 miles NNW of Detroit. Westbranch is a processing center for a region in which potatoes, fruit, dairy cattle, and poultry are raised. There are oil wells in the vicinity. The city is a popular sports center for hunting and fishing. Pop. (1960) 2,025.

WEST BROMWICH, county borough, central England, in Staffordshire, six miles NW of Birmingham. It is a part of the Birmingham industrial area. Steel and machinery are manufactured. A leading

point of interest is the sixteenth century Oak House, which was opened as a museum and art gallery in 1898. Pop. (1951) 87,985.

WESTBROOK, city, SW Maine, Cumberland County; on the Presumpscot River, the Boston and Maine, the Maine Central, and the Sanford and Eastern railroads, and U.S. highway 202; 6 miles W of Portland. The city is an industrial center in which paper, textiles, and machinery are manufactured. A large number of the inhabitants are French-Canadian. Westbrook was called Saccarrappa until renamed in 1815. The city was incorporated in 1889. Pop. (1960) 13,820.

WESTBURY, village, SE New York, in Nassau County, on Long Island and the Long Island Railroad; a residential suburb, 22 miles E of New York City. Clothing and machinery are manufactured. Westbury was settled in 1650, and incorporated as a village in 1932. Pop. (1960) 14,757.

WEST CHESTER, borough, SE Pennsylvania, seat of Chester County; on the Pennsylvania Railroad and U.S. highways 202 and 322; about 25 miles W of Philadelphia. Primarily an agricultural trade center, West Chester has tree nurseries and food-canning plants, and mushrooms are grown. Shipping tags, air compressors, generators, springs, auto radiators and heaters, wheels, pumps, dairy equipment, dog food, hosiery, and crayons are manufactured. West Chester was founded in 1788 and was incorporated in 1799. A state teachers college is there. Pop. (1960) 15,705.

WESTCLIFFE, town, S central Colorado, seat of Custer County; and 110 miles SSW of Denver. The town lies between the Sangre de Cristo and the Wet Mountain ranges of the Rocky Mountains, at an altitude of about 7,800 feet above sea level. Silver and lead are mined in the vicinity. Oats, hay, and dairy cattle are raised. Pop. (1960) 306.

WESTCOTT, EDWARD NOYES, 1846–98, U.S. banker and novelist, was born in Syracuse, N.Y. He was educated in the public schools and early entered the banking business, meeting with considerable success and becoming an expert on finance. He was also known as a singer and composer of ability. In 1895, when tuberculosis compelled his retirement from business, he devoted himself to writing *Davia Harum.* After numerous rejections it was accepted, 1897, and on its publication, 1898, six months after the author's death, enjoyed widespread popularity. As a play starring William Crane (1845–1928), it enjoyed a long life, and a motion picture version, with Will Rogers, was very successful.

WESTERLY, town, SW Rhode Island, in Washington County; on the east bank of the Pawcatuck River, opposite Connecticut, on the New Haven Railroad and U.S. highway 1; 40 miles SW of Providence. Principal industrial activities include the making of textiles and printing presses. Granite quarrying, dairying, and truck gardening are conducted in the vicinity. The town was formerly a shipbuilding center. Westerly was settled in 1648 and incorporated in 1669. A naval training station was established at Westerly during World War II. Pop. (1960) 14,267.

WESTERMARCK, EDWARD ALEXANDER, 1862–1939, Finnish anthropologist and author, was born in Helsinki. He was professor of philosophy at the Academy of Åbo, Finland, and professor of sociology at the University of London, 1907–30. During 1898–1902 he traveled in Morocco, studying the modes and manners of primitive peoples. Among his works are *The History of Human Marriage* (1891), *The Origin and Development of the Moral Ideas* (1906–08), *The Belief in Spirits in Morocco* (1920), *A Short History of Marriage* (1926), *Memories of My Life* (1927), *Wit and Wisdom in Morocco* (1930), and *Ethical Relativity* (1932).

WESTERN AUSTRALIA, state, Australia; bounded by the Timor Sea on the N, Northern Territory and South Australia on the E, the Great Australian Bight on the SE, and the Indian Ocean on

AUSTRALIAN NEWS & INFORMATION BUR.

The capital and commercial center of Western Australia, Perth, with its ornate buildings and broad, tree-lined streets, is among the most beautiful cities of Australia.

the S, W, and NW; area 975,920 sq. mi.; pop. (1954) 639,771.

Physical Factors. Western Australia consists of a large plateau lying at an elevation of 1,000 to 2,000 feet above sea level. Above this surface isolated groups of block mountains rise to heights of 3,000 to 4,000 feet, notably in the Kimberley Plateau in the northeast, and the Hamersley Range in the northwest. Two large areas of low-lying plain are the basin of the Great Sandy Desert in the north, and the level Nullarbor Plain in the south, which extends into the state of South Australia. There is a narrow discontinuous coastal plain in the west.

The coast north of the Kimberley Plateau is deeply dissected, and the numerous off-shore islands form the Bonaparte Archipelago. Similarly north of the Hamersley Range the coast has many islands. Between these two areas is a long, low coastal region known as the Eighty Mile Beach.

Western Australia's most important stream is the Swan River which rises in the Darling Range in the southwest and flows north, then southwest to the coast at Perth. Other rivers are for the most part seasonal. The numerous salt flats in the interior, which is known in Australia as the outback, become lakes after infrequent rains.

Rainfall is deficient in most of Western Australia. The north coastal section is tropical, and receives rain during the summer months, November to April, but many parts of the area are subject to drought. The northern flanks of the Kimberley Plateau receive an annual rainfall of about 60 inches. Port Hedland on the western section of the north coast has an average annual rainfall of 10 to 15 inches, which occasionally falls in two or three days, followed by a long period of drought. Rainfall in the southwest, which averages 25 to 30 inches annually, occurs chiefly in the winter months, between May and September. A broad stretch of desert extends across the country from the Great Sandy Desert in the north to the Gibson Desert, the Great Victoria Desert, and the Nullarbor Plain in the South. Temperatures in Western Australia vary from a mean annual of 84°F in the north, to 60°F in the south but the diurnal range, especially in the desert area, is much larger. Forests are generally limited to the southwest, where there are valuable stands of karri and jarra, which are types of eucalyptus trees.

Economic Factors. Economic activity is concentrated south of Perth on the Swan River. Stock raising is important in the Kimberley Plateau.

Agriculture occupies a belt some 250 miles wide, extending from the coast in the west, and from the Swan River in the north. In this area the coastal plain is irrigated, and dairying and the growing of fruit and vegetables are important. Further inland is a mixed farming belt, where wheat, oats and clover are grown, and beef cattle and sheep are raised. To the east of this is a highly mechanized area of wheat farms, in which sheep, largely Merino which are raised for wool, form a secondary income. The raising of sheep on the uplands of the central and northwestern sections is the only other major agricultural activity of Western Australia.

Western Australia has valuable mineral deposits, of which the most important is gold. Gold is mined in a large section of the Western Plateau. The most productive is the Coolgardie Field, with its center of Kalgoorlie. Iron ore is mined north of the Kimberley Plateau, and is shipped to New South Wales. Other important mineral deposits are asbestos, coal, silver, manganese, and lead.

Manufacturing industries are not highly developed in the state. Most industrial production is concentrated near Perth, and there are steel mills, which were established 1956, at Kwinana south of Perth. Perth is the capital and major city, and Freemantle is the chief port.

Social Factors. Most of the state's population is concentrated in the vicinity of Perth and is largely of British origin. Aborigines number about 11,000. Education is free at all levels, and compulsory at the primary level. There is no state church.

Government. The state's governor is appointed by the crown, but is invariably a citizen of Western Australia. Parliament is made up of two houses, a legislative council composed of 30 members elected for six-year terms, and a legislative assembly composed of 50 members elected for three-year terms. Voting is compulsory.

History. The first settlement was attempted in 1826 with 20 convicts and a detachment of soldiers, which were sent from New South Wales. In 1829 a settlement was founded on the Swan River on the present site of Perth and Freemantle. These early settlers were given large land grants, and principally engaged in pastoral and some agricultural pursuits. The colony did not prosper, however, and in 1850 the settlers asked that it be granted a penal settlement. Convicts continued to be transported to the colony until 1868. The discovery of gold in 1892 and 1893 in the Kalgoorlie area resulted in an influx of settlers. In 1901 Western Australia became an original state of the Commonwealth of Australia.

WESTERN COLLEGE FOR WOMEN. See COLLEGES AND UNIVERSITIES.

WESTERN ELECTRIC COMPANY, an important manufacturer of electrical and electronic materials. Western Electric was the outgrowth of a company, Gray and Barton, founded in Cleveland, 1869, to manufacture telegraph printing equipment. Western Union joined, 1872, in organizing the $150,000 successor company, Western Electric Manufacturing Company, in Chicago. The new company continued to construct Morse code transmitters and Gray printers; officers of the company helped launch the first commercial typewriter and manufacture Thomas Alva Edison's electric equipment.

In the 1870's, competition from the telephone induced Western Electric to enter the telephone manufacturing field. Eventually, however, a compromise in a Western Union–Bell Telephone patent suit removed the telegraph company entirely from the telephone field, and Western Electric, lacking a license to manufacture Bell phones, stood to lose all its telephone manufacturing business. By competing with other Bell manufacturing licensees, Western Electric convinced Bell officials that it should be the logical manufacturing unit for the Bell System, and the Bell organization arranged to purchase Western Union's interest in Western Electric, 1881.

At that time there were about 70,000 telephones in the United States. By 1905 Western Electric was the world's largest electric manufacturing and distributing organization, and the U.S. telephone census numbered 4 million instruments.

During World War I, in co-operation with the Navy, the company established a nationwide communications network, and manufactured the first ship-shore radio equipment and the first plane-ground equipment.

In 1922 a complete separation was effected between organizations handling the company's Bell Telephone business and its electrical supply business, with the former becoming its full-time task.

As an outgrowth of telephone research, the company developed, 1926, the first commercially feasible sound motion pictures. In 1930, to insure an adequate supply of direct printing telegraph instruments, it purchased the Teletype Corporation.

During World War II, Western Electric manufactured all types of communications equipment for the armed forces, including radar equipment, radio communication transmitters and receivers, carrier telephone equipment, gun directors, and underwater warfare devices.

Total sales of Western Electric Company in 1961 amounted to about $2.61 billion. About 75 per cent of total sales were made to the Bell Telephone companies, and of the remainder, the U.S. government was the principal sales outlet.   JAMES COLVIN

WESTERN EUROPEAN UNION, established in 1948 by Great Britain, France, Belgium, West Germany, Italy, Luxembourg, and the Netherlands, was designed to further economic and cultural exchange and to strengthen collective defense. To some extent it replaced the European Defense Community, rejected by France in August 1954, in which national forces were to serve under a supranational command. Western European Union (WEU), however, remained intergovernmental. The chief premise for the establishment of WEU was the necessity of consolidating the defense of Western Europe. The WEU defense organization has been closely merged with NATO, and its social and cultural activities were transferred to the Council of Europe in June 1960.

WESTERN FEDERATION OF MINERS, a U.S. labor union, founded at Butte, Mont., 1893, and organized to include all employees of metal mines and smelters. In addition to being an aggressive labor organization, it was politically important because of the pressure of the mine owners themselves, who wished miner support for William Jennings Bryan's famous 16–1 plan of coinage ratio for silver and gold. This projected the union into the public arena as an organization that had not only a labor platform but decided economic views as well. The union developed ambitious hopes to become a national union, and to this end it affiliated with the American Federation of Labor (A.F. of L.) in 1896. From the outset this was an unfortunate uniting of forces, for there was an incompatibility of structure as well as conflict arising from the miners' goal of becoming a dominant national labor group. It split from the A.F. of L. two years later, and established a rival national organization named Western American Labor Union which existed only by grace of its Western Federation of Miners (W.F. of M.) membership.

The strike history of the W.F. of M. was the worst in United States labor history up to that time. Between its date of founding and 1904, the W.F. of M. had tied up mines in Colorado, Utah, Idaho, and Nebraska and almost precipitated civil war. After a protracted strike in the Cripple Creek district of Colorado, the W.F. of M. was all but wiped out by vigilantes hired by, or in sympathy with, the Mine Owners Federation, 1904. Charles Moyer, president of the W.F. of M., and William Haywood, its secretary and treasurer, realized that a change of strategy was demanded. Together with G. Pettibone, they had been acquitted some years earlier of the murder of former Governor Steunenberg of Idaho, and this added to the antilabor feeling of the country. They

decided survival required affiliation with another group. Together with the Western American Labor Union, the Socialist Labor party, and other labor groups, they formed the Industrial Workers of the World (I.W.W.) at Chicago, 1905. See INDUSTRIAL WORKERS OF THE WORLD.

The I.W.W. was dominated by the W.F. of M., and mistakenly gained a reputation for anarchism when it was fundamentally formed for labor union survival. A conservative faction gained control of the W.F. of M., 1907, bringing about its withdrawal from the I.W.W. The W.F. of M. again became affiliated with the A.F. of L. and the United Mine Workers of America, 1911. In October, 1916, the W.F. of M. was reorganized under a new name, International Union of Mine, Mill and Smelter Workers, and received a charter from the A.F. of L. This union became, 1935, one of the original members of the Committee for Industrial Organization, a constitutionless body that had separated from the A.F. of L. See AMERICAN FEDERATION OF LABOR AND CONGRESS OF INDUSTRIAL ORGANIZATIONS; LABOR MOVEMENT.

WESTERN ILLINOIS UNIVERSITY, a public, coeducational, institution of higher learning, located in Macomb, Ill. The school was founded, 1899, as Western Illinois Normal School; its first instruction was offered in 1902. The name was changed to Western Illinois State Teachers College in 1921; Western Illinois State College in 1947; and to its present form in 1957.

A reorganization of academic departments, 1959, resulted in the establishment of three divisions: education, arts and sciences, and graduate studies. Masters' degrees are offered in biological sciences, business education, chemistry, education and psychology, English, geography, mathematics, physics, and social science. Summer study tours are conducted throughout the United States and abroad. The school sponsors a summer music camp annually. See COLLEGES AND UNIVERSITIES.

WESTERN KENTUCKY STATE COLLEGE, a public, coeducational institution of higher learning, located in Bowling Green, Ky. The present institution is the product of a merger, in 1907, of Southern Normal School and Western Kentucky State Normal School into Western Kentucky State Normal School and Teachers College. The name was changed to Western Kentucky State Teachers College, 1930, and to its present form, 1948.

The school is composed of two divisions, a college of liberal arts and a teachers college for the training of teachers, administrators, and supervisors for state schools. Additional programs are offered in medical technology and forestry. A summer institute is conducted for science teachers and a government-sponsored summer program in science and mathematics is conducted for selected high school juniors. There is also a summer art education workshop. Masters' degrees in education are offered. See COLLEGES AND UNIVERSITIES.

WESTERN MICHIGAN UNIVERSITY, a public, coeducational institution of higher learning located in Kalamazoo, Mich. Established, 1903, as Western State Normal School, instruction was first offered in 1904. The name was changed to Western State Teachers College, 1927; Western Michigan College of Education, 1941; Western Michigan College, 1955; and to its present form ,1957.

A reorganization of the school's departments, 1956, established five academic divisions: education, liberal arts and sciences, business, applied arts and sciences, and graduate studies. A special honors program is conducted for selected freshman and sophomores. Co-operative work-study programs are offered to students of petroleum distribution, food distribution, retailing, secretarial arts, foundry technology, and drafting technology. See COLLEGES AND UNIVERSITIES.

WESTERN ONTARIO, UNIVERSITY OF, a public institution of higher education, located in

London, Ont., Canada. Incorporated, 1878, as the Western University of London, Ont., affiliated with the Church of England, the school was placed under supervision of provincial and municipal governments by legislative acts of 1908, 1923, and 1955.

The university's divisions are arts and sciences, graduate studies, law, medicine, nursing, and business administration. Among the institutions affiliated with the university are St. Peter's Seminary and Christ the King College of Arts, Ursuline College of Arts, and Huron College of Arts, all at London, Ont., and Waterloo College of Arts, Waterloo, Ont. The university operates the J. B. Collip Medical Research Laboratory and eight teaching hospitals. Summer school is conducted at the English-French Summer School in Trois-Pistoles, Que.

Various publications are issued, among them, *Folio*, a student literary magazine, *The Business Quarterly; Medical Journal; University Gazette;* and *Occidentalia*. The library contains more than 240,000 volumes, including the Barnett collection of rare items of North American history.

WESTERN RESERVE, a historical region in NE Ohio, comprising more than three million acres south of Lake Erie, reserved by Connecticut after the state had ceded the rest of its western lands to the United States, 1786. Connecticut's claim was based on the old colonial charter, which granted lands all the way to the South Sea (Pacific Ocean). Connecticut assigned, 1792, half a million acres to some of its citizens who had suffered from British raids during the Revolution; and sold, 1795, the remainder to the Connecticut Land Company. Many settlers went from Connecticut to the western territory; the chief settlement established was Cleveland. Since the region was within the boundaries of the Northwest Territory, there was confusion in political jurisdiction; later, however, Connecticut made an agreement with the federal government whereby the Western Reserve should become part of the newly organized Ohio Territory, 1800. The region gave its name to Western Reserve University, founded in 1826. See CLEVELAND, MOSES; NORTHWEST TERRITORY.

WESTERN RESERVE UNIVERSITY, a private, nonsectarian institution of higher learning, located in Cleveland, Ohio. The existing university is the product of a merger, in 1882, of Western Reserve College and Adelbert College, both founded, 1826, forming Adelbert College of Western Reserve University. The present name was adopted in 1884.

Among the university's various divisions are Adelbert College, a liberal arts college for men founded 1826; the school of medicine, 1843; Flora Stone Mather College, a liberal arts college for women, 1888; Franklin Thomas Backus School of law, 1892; the schools of dentistry, 1892, library science, 1904, and applied social sciences, 1916; Frances Payne Bolton School of Nursing, 1923; Cleveland College, a liberal arts college for part-time and adult students in continuing education, 1925; the graduate school, 1926; the school of architecture, 1929, integrated into the department of art and architecture, 1953; and the graduate school of business, 1952.

Notable research studies are conducted in housing for the aged, medical education, metabolic diseases, documentation theory, mental development, and social work. See COLLEGES AND UNIVERSITIES.

WESTERN SAMOA, an independent nation, S Pacific Ocean, consisting of two large islands, Savaii (660 sq. mi.) and Upolu (430 sq. mi.), and two smaller islands, Manono and Apolima; about 2,500 miles NE of Sydney, 2,250 miles SSW of Honolulu, and 1,600 miles NE of Auckland, New Zealand. Pop. (1961) 114,000.

The climate is tropical, with a mean daily temperature of about 80° F. and an average annual rainfall of more than 110 inches. The islands are fringed by coral reefs and consist of the summits of a partially submerged volcanic range. Apia, located on the

UNITED NATIONS

Imports, which consist primarily of sugar and manufactured goods, are brought by steamer to the harbor of Apia, where they are transferred to lighters.

northern coast of Upolu, is the capital and only town.

Western Samoa's economy is based on agriculture. The islanders are largely self-sufficient, producing yams, taro, breadfruit, and pawpaws for their own consumption; and copra, cocoa, and bananas largely for export. The predominantly vegetable diet is supplemented by pork, poultry, and fish. Although Western Samoa was once well forested, most of the best timber has been cut. A dense blanket of ferns and shrubs, however, covers the mountains and helps prevent erosion. There are no known minerals of economic importance and very few manufacturing industries. Few land animals are native to Western Samoa. Land and sea birds are common, and there are a few snakes and lizards. Fish and other sea animals, including large sea turtles, are found in the lagoons inside the reefs.

The population is predominantly Polynesian, with about 6,000 Europeans or persons of mixed Caucasian-Samoan ancestry. The Samoans live in small coastal villages or in Apia. They have retained their ancient social structure, which is based on the extended family group and is headed by a *matai*, or chief, who is an elected official.

History. Samoa's first contact with Europeans came in 1722 with the arrival of the Dutch Admiral Jacob Roggeveen. Other explorers visited the islands before 1800, but European influence was relatively minor until the arrival in 1830 of the London Missionary Society which, along with Roman Catholic and Wesleyan missionaries, successfully converted the Samoans to Christianity. By 1861, Great Britain, Germany, and the United States had established agencies in Apia. For the next 37 years, native rivalries and conflicting imperial interests characterized Samoan conditions. A peace settlement, providing for a legislature and two chiefs as joint kings, was signed in 1873, but after a few years the new government collapsed and dissension continued. A three-power conference in 1889 guaranteed Samoan independence, selected a single Samoan ruler, and granted the three Western powers authority to supervise the Apia Municipal Council. In 1899, however, the kingdom was dissolved, and Germany and the United States renewed their claims to the islands. Germany annexed the western islands (which now constitute Western Samoa), the United States took the eastern islands, and Britain renounced its claim in return for recognition of British priority in other Pacific islands. Western Samoa remained under German rule until 1914, when it was captured by New Zealand and Australian forces. In 1920 New Zealand assumed the administration of Western Samoa under a League of Nations mandate and continued administration under a UN trusteeship in 1946. A 1954 conference provided for the independence of Western Samoa, and on January 1, 1962, Western Samoa became the first independent Polynesian state.

Government. Western Samoa is governed by a legislative assembly which, early in 1962, consisted of 46 members serving three-year terms. A prime minister, assisted by eight cabinet members, heads the administrative branch. Two *fautua*, or native kings, serve as joint heads of state. After their deaths they will be replaced by a single head of state, elected for a five-year term by the legislative assembly. The seat of government is Apia.

WESTERN UNION TELEGRAPH COMPANY, the world's largest telegraph and cable company, is the outgrowth of the invention of the telegraph by Samuel F. B. Morse, and the construction of the first wire, from Baltimore to Washington, under a congressional appropriation, 1843.

By 1851 over 50 telegraph companies were operating in the United States. Most of them were Morse licensees, but others used other devices, such as the House printing telegraph, which printed and received letters instead of dots and dashes. Among companies using the House method was the New York and Mississippi Valley Printing Telegraph Company, organized in 1851, by Hiram Sibley and Samuel L. Selden; in 1856 it consolidated the 14 companies north of the Ohio River to form the Western Union Telegraph Company. This company ultimately absorbed 540 independent companies. Included among these companies was Postal Telegraph, Inc., the second largest U.S. telegraph company, purchased by Western Union in 1943.

The first transcontinental telegraph line was begun immediately after the beginning of the Civil War, and was finished in 3 months and 20 days. With the Civil War scarcely over, a world-girdling overland line to Europe was begun, by way of the Pacific Northwest, and planned to pass through Alaska and cross the Bering Strait, reaching Europe via Siberia. Cyrus W. Field's laying of the first successful Atlantic cable, 1866, halted these plans, but as a result of the negotiations for right of way, Alaska was purchased by the United States from Russia.

By 1960 Western Union operated approximately 72,000 miles of pole line, 660,000 miles of cable, 4.65 million telegraph channels, and over 9,300 telegraph and cable offices. Virtually all of its messages are transmitted by automatic machine.

Automatic relays, automatic repeaters, teleprinter-multiplex repeaters, printers, and carrier circuits have made possible new operating methods. One new development, Telefax, makes it possible for the customer to send his own telegram by dropping it into a slot, where the message is automatically scanned and transmitted. A receiving machine reproduces the message in facsimile form. See FACSIMILE; TELEGRAPHY.   JAMES COLVIN

WESTERN WASHINGTON COLLEGE OF EDUCATION, a public, coeducational, institution of higher learning, located in Bellingham, Wash. The college was chartered as Washington State Normal School in Bellingham, 1893, and its first instruction was offered six years later. The name was changed to its present form in 1937.

The school's curriculum emphasizes the study of general education, and includes a National Science Foundation program for the improvement of secondary mathematics teaching, and a preparatory program for teaching foreign languages in elementary schools. Masters' degrees in education are offered. See COLLEGES AND UNIVERSITIES.

WESTFIELD, city, SW Massachusetts, Hampden County; on the Westfield River, the New York Central and the New Haven railroads, and U.S. highways 20 and 202; 8 miles W of Springfield. Boilers, bicycles, textile machinery, paper products, abrasives, women's dresses, gas pumps, hardware, and novelties are manufactured. The site was first settled and called Woronoco in 1640. It was incorporated and renamed Westfield in 1669, and chartered as a city in 1920. It is the site of a state teachers college, which was founded as Westfield State Normal School in 1839. Pop. (1960) 26,302.

WESTFIELD, town, NE New Jersey, in Union County; on the Jersey Central Railroad; about 10 miles SW of Elizabeth. Paint, toys, and cinder and concrete products are manufactured. Many of the residents commute to larger cities in northeastern New Jersey and to New York City. A noted point of interest is the Scudder House, which served as the headquarters of William Alexander, American Revolutionary War general. Pop. (1960) 31,447.

WEST FLANDERS, province, W Belgium; bounded by the North Sea on the N and NW, by Netherlands on the NE, by the Belgian provinces of East Flanders and Hainaut on the SE, and by France on the SW and W; area 1,248 sq. mi.; pop. (1960) 1,066,000. The surface is generally level, and the well cultivated sandy soil produces flax, hops, and barley. Livestock are raised. The principal industries are the manufacturing of linens and lace, which is largely concentrated in Bruges, the capital. The principal seaport is Ostend.

WEST FRANKFORT, city, S Illinois, in Franklin County; on the Illinois Central Railroad; 85 miles SE of St. Louis. The city is a trade center for an area in which coal mining is a leading activity. The city's loss in population from 1950 to 1960 can be attributed partly to a decline in coal production. West Frankfort was incorporated in 1905. Pop. (1960) 9,027.

WEST HAM, parliamentary and county borough, SE England, in Essex, on the Thames river, an E suburb of London. West Ham has large railway works and shipbuilding yards. Other industries include the manufacturing of silk textiles, paving stones, and chemicals. It has an interesting Norman and Perpendicular church. Pop. (1961) 157,000.

WEST HARTFORD, town, central Connecticut, in Hartford County; on U.S. highways 5, 6, and 44; a residential and industrial suburb, 3 miles W of Hartford. Steel balls, burial vaults, tools and dies, screws, and chemical products are manufactured. The area was settled in 1679 but did not become a separate community until 1854. Noah Webster was born there. The city is the site of the American School for the Deaf (1817), the first permanent American school for the deaf. Pop. (1960) 62,382.

WEST HARTLEPOOL, county borough, NE England, in Durham County; on the North Sea, 26 miles S of Newcastle. West Hartlepool has an important port, which is one of the chief outlets for coal from the area. Timber, for use as pit props, is imported. The town has shipyards, and machinery and asbestos products are manufactured. West Hartlepool was founded in 1844. Pop. (1961) 77,000.

WEST HAVEN, town, S Connecticut, in New Haven County; on Long Island Sound, the New Haven Railroad, and the Connecticut Turnpike; a residential suburb, 2 miles SW of New Haven. The chief manufactures are aircraft parts, tools, gun parts, webbing, auto tires and tubes, fertilizer, velvets, perfumes, elastic fabrics, pipe organs, rock drills, glazed paper, and beer. West Haven was settled by colonists from New Haven in 1648; it was chartered as an independent town in 1921. Pop. (1960) 43,002.

WEST HAZLETON, borough, E central Pennsylvania, in Luzerne County; on Big Black Creek and the Lehigh Valley Railroad; 30 miles SSW of Scranton. The chief industry is the manufacturing of paper boxes. Anthracite coal is mined in the vicinity. West Hazleton, which was incorporated in 1889, is primarily a suburb of Hazleton. Pop. (1960) 6,278.

BWI AIRWAYS PHOTO

Like most other islands of the West Indies, St. Lucia has many miles of beaches for recreation. In the background an inactive volcano dominates the skyline.

WEST HELENA, city, E Arkansas, in Phillips County; 95 miles ESE of Little Rock. The major industry is the manufacture of wood products. West Helena was incorporated in 1917 and has a mayor-council form of government. Pop. (1960) 8,385.

WEST HIGHLAND WHITE TERRIER, a small domestic dog native to Scotland. The color of the breed is usually pure white. The West Highland white terrier averages about a foot in height, has short, muscular legs, and a straight tail that measures about six inches. Its sharply pointed ears are held erect on its head, which is of medium width. Its weight varies from 13 to 19 pounds.

The breed is thought to have originated at Poltallock, Scotland in the early part of the nineteenth century. It is highly probable that the lineage goes back to the fourteenth century. Today, the dog maintains many of its hunting traits but it is primarily a pet. The West Highland white terrier is a hardy dog and has been imported as a pet and a competitive show animal in the United States.

WEST INDIES, an archipelago in the Caribbean Sea, extending in a rough arc from Florida in the N to Venezuela in the S, and separating the Caribbean Sea and the Gulf of Mexico from the Atlantic Ocean; area about 90,000 sq. mi.; pop. about 20,000,000. The islands are divided into three main groups: the Bahama Islands, the Greater Antilles, and the Lesser Antilles. See the entries on the separate islands.

History. The West Indies were so named by Columbus, who landed at San Salvador in October 1492 convinced that he had found a route to India. The Antilles he supposed to be the legendary country of Antilia. Early in the sixteenth century, Spain established several settlements on the islands, and British, French, Dutch, and Danish colonization followed. West Indian possessions proved exceedingly valuable to the colonizing nations of Europe in the seventeenth and eighteenth centuries, particularly for their production of sugar, grown on plantations worked by slave labor. Their prosperity made the islands attractive to the numerous pirates and smug-

glers of the late seventeenth and early eighteenth centuries. They were primarily from Spain, France, and England, a source of contention. The claims of England in 1670 and of France in 1697 were recognized by Spain. As a result of the Treaty of Paris, 1763, Great Britain gained dominance in the area. In 1804 Haiti gained independence from France, and Santo Domingo (Dominican Republic) broke away from Spain in 1844. As a result of the Spanish-American War in 1898, Puerto Rico was ceded to the United States. Cuba became independent from Spain and remained under U.S. suzerainty until 1934.

The Federation of the West Indies, formed in January 1958, consisted of 10 British possessions: 9 territories of the Lesser Antilles including Trinidad, together with Jamaica and its former dependencies. A federal constitution was established providing for a governor general as representative of the British Crown and a bicameral legislature, with the seat of government in Trinidad. The first federal elections were held in March 1958, and internal self-government was granted in August 1960. The larger islands possessed internal autonomy within the Federation. In October 1961, as a result of an island-wide referendum, Jamaica voted to leave the Federation and assume full independence in August 1962. This decision on the part of its largest and most powerful member inevitably jeopardized the existence of the Federation, and the withdrawal of Trinidad and Tobago in January 1962 led to its dissolution in May 1962. The remaining territories—Antigua, Barbados, Dominica, Granada, Montserrat, St. Kitts-Nevis-Anguilla, St. Lucia and St. Vincent—agreed in the same month to form a new West Indies Federation, to be established in 1964. An advisory council of ministers from the eight territories, which by then possessed almost complete internal autonomy, was set up in London to discuss details of a proposed constitution. The chief problem facing the new Federation is that of economic viability. It was the belief that they were supporting more than their fair share of the economic burden of the first federation and that they had more to lose than gain from their association with the smaller islands that prompted Jamaica and Trinidad to secede. The people of Barbados, the Leeward Islands, and the Windward Islands, which make up the new Federation, are still almost entirely dependent upon agriculture for their

PRINCIPAL ISLANDS OF THE WEST INDIES

Island	Area (sq. mi.)	Pop. (1960)
	(in thousands)	
Bahama Islands (Br.)	4,404	105
Turks and Caicos Islands (Br.)	166	6
GREATER ANTILLES		
Cuba	44,206	6,797
Dominican Republic	18,700	2,994
Haiti	10,700	3,505
Jamaica	4,411	1,621
Puerto Rico (U.S.)	3,423	2,361
LESSER ANTILLES		
Virgin Islands (U.S.)	132	33
Virgin Islands (Br.)	67	7
Leeward Islands		
Antigua and Barbuda (Br.)	171	62
Guadeloupe (Fr.)	583	270
Martinique (Fr.)	427	277
Montserrat (Br.)	33	12
St. Kitts-Nevis-Anguilla (Br.)	168	59
Windward Islands		
Dominica (Br.)	305	60
Grenada and the Grenadines (Br.)	133	89
St. Lucia (Br.)	238	94
St. Vincent (Br.)	150	80
Barbados (Br.)	166	232
Trinidad and Tobago	1,980	844
Netherlands Antilles	341	190

livelihood. Sugar is the dominant export crop, but fruit, vegetables, copra and cotton are also vital in some areas. It is expected that with continued British aid, industrial activities will be developed. At present, although many small plants exist for the processing of local agricultural products, there is no heavy industry in the West Indies Federation. The tourist industry forms an important source of income in Barbados, Antigua, and Grenada and is expected to become more important throughout the area.

BIBLIOG.—A. P. Newton, *European Nations in the West Indies, 1493-1688* (1933); Charles Schuchert, *Historical Geology of the Antillean-Caribbean Region* (1935); Eric Williams, *Capitalism and Slavery* (1944); Alan Burns, *History of the British West Indies* (1954); Mary Proudfoot, *Britain and the United States in the Caribbean* (1954); John H. Parry and Philip M. Sherlock, *Short History of the West Indies* (1956); F. R. Augier and others, *Making of the West Indies* (1960); John Wilhelm, *Guide to the Caribbean Islands* (1960); Daniel Guérin, *West Indies and Their Future* (1961); David Lowenthal, ed., *West Indies Federation* (1961).

WESTINGHOUSE, GEORGE, 1846–1914, U.S. inventor and manufacturer, was born in Central Bridge, N.Y. He studied engineering at Union College, Schenectady, and joined his father's manufacturing business in that city. He patented the air brake, 1869, and followed this with other devices for improved railroad safety. Other important Westinghouse inventions were electrically controlled railroad switches and signals, apparatus for transmitting natural gas by a pressure system, and improved alternating current transformers. Westinghouse directed the commercial development of his inventions, founding works in the United States, Canada, and Europe, and incorporating the Westinghouse Electric Company in 1886. His great contribution was recognized by his election in 1955 to the Hall of Fame.

WESTINGHOUSE ELECTRIC CORPORATION, founded as Westinghouse Electric Company in 1886 by George Westinghouse. Its major function is the manufacture and sale of electrical apparatus and appliances for the generation, transmission, utilization and control of electricity. It also manufactures and sells steam and gas turbines and related equipment. Its products include practically all electrical and related mechanical equipment required by electric power companies, electrified railways, city transit systems and industrial plants, as well as propulsion equipment for the marine industry and electrical equipment used in aviation. Its consumer goods include many types of farm and household electrical appliances. Profits from more than $1.91 billion of sales for the year ending Dec. 31, 1961, exceeded $45.45 million.

WEST IRIAN, the western half of the island of New Guinea in the SW Pacific Ocean, formerly part of the Dutch East Indies. See NEW GUINEA.

In October, 1962, West Irian was transferred to the temporary administration of the UN, and later to Indonesia. The agreement between Dutch and Indonesians provided that the people of West Irian should decide their final political status by a plebiscite to be held in 1969. Once in control President Sukarno of Indonesia announced that West Irian was an integral part of Indonesia.

WEST KAZAKHSTAN, region, U.S.S.R., W Kazakh Soviet Socialist Republic, bounded by the Kazakh regions of Aktyubinsk on the E, and Guryev on the SE, and by the Russian Soviet Federated Socialist Republic regions of Astrakhan on the SW, Volgograd on the W, Saratov on the NW, Kuybyshev on the N, and Orenburg on the NE; area of the region totals 60,900 square miles. The Ural River flows north to south through the central part of the arid region, which generally has a steppe type of climate. Wheat, millet, mustard seed, and livestock are raised in the north, and cattle, sheep, and camels are grazed in the south. Industry is largely undeveloped except at Uralsk, the capital and largest city, which is a meat-packing center.

WEST LAFAYETTE, city, W central Indiana, in Tippecanoe County; on the Wabash River, opposite Lafayette, on U.S. highways 52 and 231; 60 miles NW of Indianapolis. The city was incorporated in 1924. West Lafayette is the site of Purdue University. Pop. (1960) 12,680.

WESTLAND, provincial district, New Zealand, W South Island; bounded by the provincial districts of Nelson on the NE, Canterbury on the SE, and Otago on the SW, and by the Tasman Sea on the NW; area 4,880 sq. mi.; pop. (1960) 18,700. The terrain of Westland rises steeply from a narrow coastal plain in the northwest to the Southern Alps in the southwest, where Mount Cook rises to 12,349 feet, the highest part of New Zealand. Precipitation averages more than 100 inches annually. There is some dairying, and gold and coal are mined in the north. Much of the district is forested and lumbering is an important industry. The major towns are Greymouth and Hokitika, the capital.

WEST LIBERTY STATE COLLEGE, a public, coeducational college of liberal arts and education, located in West Liberty, W. Va., with a branch for adult education in Wheeling, W. Va. The school was chartered as West Liberty Academy, 1837; the name was changed to West Liberty State Normal School, 1870, the year in which college-level instruction was first offered. The name was changed to West Liberty State Teachers College, 1931, and to its present form in 1943. The school's divisions are education, founded 1870; dental hygiene, 1938; business, 1938; and liberal arts, 1943. See COLLEGES AND UNIVERSITIES.

WEST LONG BRANCH, borough, E New Jersey, in Monmouth County; 30 miles SSE of Newark. The borough is chiefly residential and was once the summer residence of Woodrow Wilson. Monmouth College (1956) was founded there as a junior college in 1933. West Long Branch was incorporated in 1908. Pop. (1960) 5,337.

WEST LOTHIAN, county, SE Scotland; bounded by the Firth of Forth on the N, by Midlothian on the SE, by Lanarkshire on the SW, and by Stirlingshire on the NW; area 120 sq. mi.; pop. (1961) 93,000. From lowlands along the Firth of Forth the surface rises gradually to a hilly region in the south where there are heights of 1,000 feet. There are moorland and rocky areas in the south and southeast. About two thirds of the county is under cultivation. Dairy farming is the most important activity. Coal and oil-bearing shales are worked; iron ore is mined; and there is some manufacturing of steel. Deposits of limestone, sandstone, and fire clay are also worked. The principal towns are Linlithgow, Bathgate, Bo'ness, and Armadale. Traces of Antonine's Wall, a Roman rampart dating from 143 A.D., and ancient castles reflect the county's historic associations.

WESTMEATH, county, Ireland, in Leinster Province; bounded by Cavan on the N, by Meath on the E, by Offaly on the S, by Longford on the NW, separated from Roscommon on the W by the Shannon River and the Lough Ree; area about 680 sq. mi.; pop. (1961) 52,800. The surface is gently undulating, with no height rising to more than 500 feet. Bogs take up some area, as do the numerous lakes. The capital, Mullingar, is connected by canal with Dublin. The other town of importance is Athlone. The county was separated from Meath in 1543.

WESTMINSTER, city, N Maryland, seat of Carroll County, on the Western Maryland Railway and U.S. highway 140; 29 miles NW of Baltimore. The manufacturing of shoes, liquor, and canned goods are the leading industries. Westminster was settled in 1764 and incorporated in 1837. Frequent Civil War skirmishes occurred in the area, and during the Gettysburg Campaign, Westminster was an important supply depot for Federal forces. The city is the site of Western Maryland College, founded in 1860, and of the Methodist affiliated Westminster Theological Seminary. Pop. (1960) 6,123.

WESTMINSTER, municipal borough, or the City of Westminster, SE England, one of the metropolitan boroughs of London; on the N bank of the River Thames, W of the City of London. Westminster is the seat of the British monarch and the British Parliament. Within the city are many important public buildings. The House of Commons, with its clock tower Big Ben, and the House of Lords are situated beside the River Thames. Westminster Abbey, seat of an Anglican bishop, and Westminster Cathedral, seat of a Roman Catholic arch-bishop, are within the city. Two royal palaces still exist in Westminster: St. James's Palace, built by Henry VIII in 1532; and the comparatively modern Buckingham Palace, which is the home of the reigning sovereign. Government buildings, which are grouped in the area of Whitehall, include the Admiralty, the War Office, the Home Office, the Treasury, the Foreign Office, and Scotland Yard, which is the headquarters of the police force.

Some of the finest examples of British art are contained in the Tate Gallery, the National Gallery, and the National Portrait Gallery. Westminster has many famous theaters, notably Covent Garden, and the Theatre Royal in Drury Lane, which was founded in 1663. The district of Soho has numerous restaurants and places of entertainment. Mayfair and Belgravia are exclusive residential districts. Among the famous streets in Westminster are Downing Street, in which the home of the British prime minister is located; and the fashionable shopping centers on Picadilly and Regent Street.

The Saxon King Sebert built a monastery there during the sixth century. During the eleventh century, King Canute began the construction of the Palace of Westminster, in which the sovereigns of England held their court for 500 years. Edward the Confessor (1042–66) rebuilt Sebert's monastery and called the church West Minster, from which the City of Westminster has taken its name. The church, which has since been rebuilt, is known as Westminster Abbey. See LONDON.

WESTMINSTER ABBEY, the most famous British church, in which British sovereigns are crowned, married, and buried, and where there are memorials to many great Englishmen. Officially, as from the time of Elizabeth I, the abbey is the Collegiate Church of St. Peter, Westminster. It is a magnificent Gothic building standing on low ground on the left bank of the Thames in the district of Westminster, London, and adjoining the houses of Parliament.

History. According to legend, the site of Westminster Abbey formerly was that of a temple of Apollo, which was displaced by a church built by the "first Christian king," Lucius, in the second century. It is doubtful that either Lucius or his church actually existed, but there is some slight evidence for the story that an Anglo-Saxon church occupied the site of Westminster Abbey as early as 616, when it was built by Sebert, the "first Christian king" of the East Saxons; there is less evidence for the claim that this building was consecrated by the Apostle St. Peter, who rematerialized on earth for just this purpose. In any case, this church, for which a charter was issued, 785, by Offa of Mearcia, was destroyed by the Danes, but was rebuilt, 925. A large abbey, or house for monks, was built there, 1049–65, but the present building is really a church, not an abbey. Begun in the latter part of the thirteenth century at the order of Henry III, it was subsequently altered and enlarged repeatedly. The Chapel of Henry VII, erected, 1503–19, at the order of that king, was designed by William and Robert Vertue. The two western towers were designed by Sir Christopher Wren, 1714. Fragments of a Romanesque church built on the site by Edward the Confessor in the eleventh century are said to be contained in the present building.

The church has the form of a Latin cross. Including Henry VII Chapel, the church's extreme length is

BRITISH INFORMATION SERVICES
The Coronation Chair, in which English monarchs are crowned, is in Westminster Abbey. Beneath is the Stone of Scone on which the Scottish kings were crowned until 1297.

530 feet 9 inches, its width, 220 feet. The nave is 154 feet long, 105 feet high. The body of the church is 105 feet high; the height of the towers is 225 feet. The transept is 200 feet long, 80 feet wide. There are more than 20 stained-glass windows, and a number of pieces of fine old tapestry and Venetian glass mosaics. The interior is finished chiefly in rich marble.

Beyond the transept, in a semicircle about the choir, there is a series of eight chapels. The most interesting is that of Henry VII, which forms the extreme eastern part of the abbey. This chapel is a very beautiful structure, with glass-covered gates decorated with roses in allusion to the joining of the houses of York and Lancaster in the marriage of Henry VII and Elizabeth. The chapel is in itself larger than many a cathedral. It contains over 1,000 statues and figures. Carved choir stalls of dark oak line either wall. Each stall is assigned to a knight of the Order of Bath. Each seat is marked with armorial bearings in brass, and the sword and banner of the occupant are suspended above the seat. The distinguishing glory of this chapel is a suspended ceiling of fine tracery. Especially remarkable architecturally is the absence of ribs in the fan vault, whose constituent parts are fitted together with extreme precision.

In the choir is the Coronation Chair of English sovereigns. Beneath it the famous Stone of Scone, the sacred stone of the ancient Scottish sovereigns, which Edward I brought originally to Westminster, where it remained thereafter except for a short time, 1950, when it was stolen by schoolboys and returned to Scotland.

Memorials. Services are held in the abbey, but it is celebrated chiefly for the royal burial vaults and innumerable monuments to celebrated men. It is regarded by Englishmen as the national Valhalla or Temple of Fame. There are many memorials on the walls, and statues of prominent men, but the presence of a memorial is not necessarily an indication of burial in the abbey. Some of the most famous names are William Pitt, Lord Chatham; Canning and Palmerston, noted statesmen; Lord Mansfield, the statesman judge; Sir Robert Peel, the parliamentary reformer; Sir Eyre Coot, commander of the British forces in India; Warren Hastings, the subject of Macaulay's famous essay; Cobden, the free trader; Wilberforce, the emancipator of slaves; Sir Isaac Newton, the student of physics; Charles Darwin, the eminent naturalist; Fox and the younger Pitt, side by side; and Rowland Hill, the advocate of cheap postage. The sarcophagus of Major André, who conspired with Benedict Arnold to deliver West Point to the British during the American Revolution, may be seen in the south aisle. David Livingstone, the African explorer, and Robert Stevenson, the engineer, lie in the nave.

The Chapel of Henry VII is particularly the burial ground of royalty: Lady Margaret Douglas; Mary, Queen of Scots; Charles II; William and Mary; Queen Anne; Henry VII and his wife; Queen Elizabeth I; James I and George II—all rest here.

The portion of the south transept known as the Poets' Corner is of especial interest. Here are the remains of the historians Grote and Macaulay; the great poets Chaucer and Spenser; of Goldsmith, Gray, and Addison; of Thomson, Southey, and Campbell; of Dickens and Thackeray; of Butler, Johnson, and Dryden. Georg Friedrich Händel and David Garrick are buried here, and Wordsworth, Watts, and John Wesley are not far away. Shakespeare lies in the church of Stratford, and Robert Louis Stevenson in far off Samoa, but their memorials are here, together with a bust of Henry Wadsworth Longfellow, the only U.S. poet represented.

WESTMINSTER COLLEGE, a private liberal arts college for men, located at Fulton, Mo. The school, affiliated with the Presbyterian church, was established as Fulton College, 1851; its first instruction was offered the same year. Two years later, the name was changed to Westminster College, and a charter was obtained from the state.

In addition to its four-year liberal arts program, Westminster offers a special six-year engineering program in connection with Stanford University. Participants in the program follow a course of study that leads to an A.B. degree from Westminster, and an M.S. degree from Stanford.

It was during a speech delivered at Westminster College in 1946, that the British statesman Winston Churchill first used the term Iron Curtain to describe the barrier that had developed between the Soviet Union and the Western nations. See COLLEGES AND UNIVERSITIES.

WEST MONROE, city, N Louisiana, in Ouachita Parish; on the Ouachita River, opposite Monroe; on the Illinois Central Railroad and U.S. highway 80; 155 miles NNW of Baton Rouge. Paper, soap, clothing, and chemicals are manufactured. Pop. (1960) 15,215.

WESTMORELAND, city, NE Kansas, seat of Pottawatomie County; 45 miles NW of Topeka. Westmoreland is a trade and processing center for an area in which corn, wheat, and oats are grown, and cattle are raised. Pop. (1960) 460.

WESTMORLAND, county, N England, bounded by Cumberland on the NW and N, by Durham and Yorkshire on the E, and by Lancashire and Morecombe Bay of the Irish Sea on the S and W; area about 789 sq. mi.; pop. (1951) 67,383. The county is generally mountainous and forms part of the Lake District. The northeast and north have some tracts of moorland. The chief rivers are the Eden in the north and the Lune and Kent in the south. Cattle and sheep are pastured, and considerable amounts of dairy products are produced. Gypsum, granite, slate, and limestone are quarried and some lead is mined. The few industrial products include woolen goods, paper, and explosives. Prehistoric stone implements have been found in the county, and there are vestiges of old Roman roads and camps. Westmorland was established as an administrative county in 1131.

WEST NEW YORK, town, NE New Jersey, in Hudson County; on the W bank of the Hudson River; in the New York City metropolitan area, about 5 miles NE of Jersey City. West New York is a shipping center, which is equipped with docks and grain elevators. Textiles, rubber goods, cottonseed oil, and buttons are manufactured. The town was incorporated in 1898. Pop. (1960) 35,547.

WESTON, EDWARD, 1850–1936, U.S. electrical engineer, was born and educated in England, and came to the United States, 1870. He invented improved nickel-plating and electroplating machinery; his cadmium cell, 1891, was adopted by the United States, Great Britain, and Germany as the official standard of electromotive force, 1908.

WESTON, EDWARD PAYSON, 1839–1929, indefatigable U.S. pedestrian, was born in Providence, R.I. He accomplished his first feat of note by walking from Boston to Washington to attend Lincoln's inauguration, 1861. In 1867 he walked from Portland, Me., to Chicago (1,326 miles) in 26 days. In 1879, by covering in England a distance of 550 miles in 141 hours 41 minutes, he brought to the United States the Astley Belt, the token of the world's championship. He crossed the United States twice, 1909–10, first from New York to San Francisco, and then from Los Angeles to New York. At the age of 75 he walked a distance of 1,546 miles in 51 days. From 1867 up to his death he is said to have walked the equivalent of the circumference of the earth three times.

WESTON, city, N central West Virginia, seat of Lewis County; on the Monongahela River, the Baltimore and Ohio Railroad, and U.S. highways 19, 33, and 119; about 75 miles NW of Charleston. Glassware, lumber, bricks, and window shades are manufactured, and there are oil and gas wells in the vicinity. Weston, originally named Preston and later Flesherville, was settled in 1784; it was incorporated in 1818 and chartered as a city in 1847. Pop. (1960) 8,754.

WESTON, town, Canada, SE Ontario, in York County; on the Canadian National and the Canadian Pacific railways; an industrial suburb, about 3 miles NW of Toronto. Skates, bicycles, stoves, electric ranges, toiletware, and wood products are manufactured. Weston was incorporated in 1881. Pop. (1956) 9,543.

WESTON-SUPER-MARE, municipal borough, SW England, in Somersetshire, on the Bristol Channel, at the base of Worlebury Hill; 20 miles SW of Bristol. The borough is chiefly a resort center. It has a fine view of the coast of Wales opposite and the usual seaside recreational facilities. It became a municipal borough in 1937. Pop. (1951) 40,165.

WEST ORANGE, town, NE New Jersey, in Essex County; on the Erie Railroad, in the New York City metropolitan area, about 2 miles NW of Newark and 10 miles W of New York City. The town is the center of the manufacturing and laboratory activities of the Edison Plant. Thomas A. Edison moved his laboratory from Menlo Park to West Orange in 1887. Pop. (1960) 39,895.

WEST PALM BEACH, city, SE Florida, seat of Palm Beach County; on Lake Worth, the Florida East Coast and the Seaboard Air Line railroads; scheduled air line stop; connected with Palm Beach by three bridges and a ferry across Lake Worth; about 60 miles N of Miami. West Palm Beach is the commercial center for Palm Beach and is also a prominent resort. The site was settled in 1880 by Irving R. Henry, who sold the holding in 1893 to Henry Flagler, the railroad builder and developer of Palm Beach. Pop. (1960) 36,208.

WESTPHALIA, German Westfalen (western plain), former Prussian province, W Germany, now a part of the state of North Rhine–Westphalia of the German Federal Republic; area of Westphalia as such, about 7,805 sq. mi.; area of North Rhine–Westphalia, 13,139 sq. mi.; pop. of the combined state (1950) 13,147,066.

The greater part of the surface is hilly, with the Weser Mountains and the Teutoburger Forest in the east and the Sauerland Mountains and the Westerwald in the south; the rest belongs to the North German Plain. The province lies generally on the watersheds between the Weser, Ems, and Rhine rivers. It possesses vast deposits of coal in the Ruhr District and elsewhere, and is Germany's largest producer of iron and iron pyrites; zinc, lead, copper, antimony, and quicksilver are also mined. Heavy iron and steel industries of vast proportions are concentrated in and around the cities of Bochum and Dortmund. The other important cities are Münster, Bielefeld, and Paderborn, the first of which is the capital. Other products are linens, leather, glass, cottons, paper, chemicals, sugar, pottery, and tobacco. Wheat, barley and potatoes are important crops; horses, cattle, sheep, and pigs are raised. One of Europe's great canals, the Rhine-Ems, extends from Dortmund to the middle of the Ems; and the area has well developed highway and rail systems.

History. The Prussian province of Westphalia (area 7,805 sq. mi.) was created, 1815, at the end of the Napoleonic Wars and became part of the new German Empire, 1871. The term *Westfalen*, however, dates from the eleventh century or before (as early as 755, by some accounts), when Westphalia was part of the old duchy of Saxony, whose other principal portion was known as the *Ostfalen* (eastern plain). The Holy Roman Emperor Frederick I Barbarossa separated Westphalia from Saxony, 1180, and gave it to the Archbishop of Cologne, whose successors ruled the duchy until 1803, when it was divided between Hesse-Darmstadt and Prussia. Then, in 1807 (Peace of Tilsit), Napoleon I created the so-called Kingdom of Westphalia for his brother Jerome. It embraced a large part of Low Germany between the Elbe and the Rhine—that is, the area to the northwest of a line drawn from the Main to the Havel—and included an area of 14,625 square miles and a population of about two million persons. Its capital was Cassel. It was enlarged by the addition of Hanover (another 9,950 square miles and 650,000 inhabitants), but later the whole of the northern region from the Elbe near Lüneberg to Wesel on the Rhine was incorporated within France, 1812, thus reducing the area to 17,535 square miles and its population to 2,066,000 persons. The kingdom went out of existence with the fall of Napoleon, after which the area was assigned to Prussia and part of it constituted as the province of Westphalia.

After World War I part of the province was occupied by French troops until 1925. The province suffered bombing and was all but devastated during World War II, after which it was put under British military occupation. The reorganized state of North Rhine–Westphalia (including the old state of Lippe and the districts of Köln, Aachen, and Düsseldorf) entered the West German federation, 1949.

WESTPHALIA, PEACE OF, the treaty, or the treaties, by which the Thirty Years' War was ended, 1648, whose provisions influenced political and religious affairs in Germany for a century and a half (see THIRTY YEARS' WAR). Every Christian nation of Europe, except England and Poland and the Archduchy of Muscovy, was represented at the peace conferences, which lasted for several years.

To the religious and political difficulties of the Holy Roman Empire, which were largely responsible for the war, the following measures were applied: (1) Calvinists as well as Lutherans were to receive the benefits of the religious Peace of Augsburg (1555), by which each ruler was to determine the religion of his state; (2) the Edict of Restitution (1629) was nullified and Protestant princes were confirmed in the possession of land they had held in 1624; (3) the independence of the states of the empire, already practically complete, was given official recognition by imperial sanction of their treaty-making power. Thus, the political and religious fragmentation of Germany was legalized and made permanent: any serious attempt to unify all or part of the area would almost certainly be a violation of the peace.

International complications were adjusted (1) by the cession of Western Pomerania and the mouths of the Oder, Elbe, and Weser, as fiefs of the empire, to Sweden, which was thenceforth to have three votes in the Imperial Diet; (2) by the cession to France of the bishoprics of Metz, Toul, and Verdun, and of the emperor's rights throughout Alsace, except the city of Strasbourg; and (3) by the recognition of the independence of the Netherlands and Switzerland. These provisions formed the foundation of international law until the French Revolution.

WEST PITTSTON, borough, NE Pennsylvania, in Luzerne County, on the W bank of the Susquehanna River, opposite Pittston; on the Lehigh Valley, the West Pittston–Exeter, and the Lackawanna railroads, and U.S. highway 11; about 10 miles SW of Scranton. Silk mills are the chief industrial establishments of West Pittston. The borough is built on the site of Jenkins Fort, a small stockade which, in 1778, was burned by the British. The town was known as Jenkins Fort until it was renamed, 1859. Pop. (1960) 6,998.

WEST PLAINS, city, S Missouri, seat of Howell County; on the Frisco Railroad, and U.S. highways 63 and 160; 160 miles SSW of St. Louis. West Plains is a processing center in the Ozark Mountains. Baseball bats and shoes are manufactured, and fruit and dairy products are processed. West Plains has a livestock market and feed mills. Pop. (1960) 5,836.

WEST POINT, city, E Mississippi, seat of Clay County; on the Columbus and Greenville, the Gulf, Mobile and Ohio, and the Illinois Central railroads; about 20 miles NW of Columbus. Cottonseed oil, textile products, caskets, dairy products, candy, poultry and meat products, and farm implements are manufactured. Pop. (1960) 8,550.

WEST POINT, city, E Nebraska, seat of Cuming County; on the North Western Railway, and U.S. highway 275; 55 miles NW of Omaha. West Point is a shipping point for the grain, livestock, and dairy products of the region. Livestock feed and butter are processed, and veterinary supplies are manufactured. The city was incorporated in 1858. Pop. (1960) 2,921.

WEST POINT, a United States military reservation, SE New York, in Orange County; situated on the W bank of the Hudson River, and on the New York Central Railroad; about 50 miles N of New York City. The site was occupied as a military post during the Revolution. The U.S. Military Academy was formally opened at West Point in 1802, located on 1,770 acres of land purchased by the government in 1790. By 1960, through purchases and gifts the reservation consisted of 16,011 acres. The reservation is situated on a plateau high above the Hudson River and commands a superb view of the river valley. See MILITARY ACADEMY, U.S.

WESTPORT, town, SW Connecticut, in Fairfield County, near the mouth of the Saugatuck River; on the New Haven Railroad and U.S. highway 1; 25 miles SW of New Haven. Westport is a summer resort and a center for artists and writers. Liquid soap, embalming fluid, electrical goods, chemical products, cordage, and toys are manufactured. Pop. (1960) 20,995.

WEST PRUSSIA, a former province of Prussia, was bordered on the W by Pomerania and on the E by East Prussia; its capital was Danzig. West Prussia consisted of the land northward from the border of Russia, and of Posen north of the river Netze, to the Gulf of Danzig. Before the first partition of Poland, 1772, most of the land of West Prussia belonged to the Poles, and most of the inhabitants of West Prussia speak Slavonic, except in Danzig and a few other places. After World War I, the territory was divided. See PRUSSIA; POLAND.

WEST READING, borough, SE Pennsylvania, in Berks County; on the Schuylkill River and U.S. highway 422, opposite Reading, of which it is a residential and industrial suburb. The borough has a paper mill and large textile plants. It was incorporated in 1907. Pop. (1960) 4,938.

WEST ST. PAUL, city, SE Minnesota, in Dakota County; adjacent to and S of Saint Paul, of which it is a residential suburb. The processing of dairy products is the leading industry. West St. Paul was incorporated in 1889. Pop. (1960) 13,101.

WEST SPRINGFIELD, town, S Massachusetts, in Hampden County; on the Connecticut and the Westfield rivers, opposite Springfield; on the New York Central Railroad and U.S. highways 5 and 20. West Springfield is an industrial center in which paper, chemicals, and machinery are manufactured. The town was settled about 1660 but it remained part of Springfield until it was separated and incorporated as West Springfield in 1774. During the French and Indian War and the American Revolution, the village common was used as a camp site by several forces. Pop. (1960) 24,924.

WEST TERRE HAUTE, city, W Indiana, Vigo County; on the Pennsylvania Railroad and U.S. highways 40 and 150; 2 miles W of Terre Haute. The city was incorporated in 1933. Pop. (1960) 3,006.

WEST TEXAS STATE COLLEGE, a public, coeducational institution of higher learning located in Canyon, Tex. Amarillo Center, the college's evening school for part-time students, is located in Amarillo, Tex. The college was established as West Texas State Normal College, 1919; its first instruction was offered the same year. The name was changed to West Texas State Teachers College in 1923, and to its present form in 1949. The undergraduate college was reorganized, 1951, into four academic divisions: humanities, sciences, social sciences, and the professional and vocational group. The graduate division was founded in 1930. The college conducts National Science Foundation summer institutes in chemistry, mathematics, and physics. Educational tours throughout the United States are also conducted during the summer. See COLLEGES AND UNIVERSITIES.

WEST UNION, village, S Ohio, seat of Adams County; 5 miles N of the Ohio River, and 53 miles SE of Cincinnati. West Union is a processing center for the tobacco, corn, and wheat which are grown in the area. The village was platted in 1804. Pop. (1960) 1,762.

WEST UNION, town, N central West Virginia, seat of Doddridge County; on the Baltimore and Ohio Railroad and U.S. highway 50; 80 miles NNE of Charleston. West Union is a trade and processing center for a region in which fruit, potatoes, and tobacco are grown. The town has sawmills, and there are gas and oil wells in the vicinity. Pop. (1960) 1,186.

WEST UNIVERSITY PLACE, city, SE Texas, in Harris County; near U.S. highway 59; a residential suburb, within the city of Houston, 3 miles SW of the business district. Rice University is one half mile east of the city. Pop. (1960) 14,628.

WEST VIEW, borough, SW Pennsylvania, in Allegheny County; on U.S. highway 19; five miles NNW of Pittsburgh, of which it is a residential suburb. West View was incorporated in 1905. Pop. (1960) 8,079.

WESTVILLE, city, E Illinois, Vermilion County; on the Chicago and Eastern Illinois and the New York Central railroads, and U.S. highway 150; 6 miles S of Danville and 128 miles S of Chicago. The city is a trade center for an agricultural area. Textiles are manufactured. Westville was laid out in 1873 and incorporated in 1896. Pop. (1960) 3,497.

WESTVILLE, town, Canada, N central Nova Scotia, in Pictou County; on the Canadian National Railway; about 75 miles NE of Halifax. The mining of coal and iron is the leading economic activity of the area. Pop. (1956) 4,247.

WEST VIRGINIA IND. AND PUB. COMM.

WEST VIRGINIA

West Virginia, first in the production of coal, has a mountain-dominated landscape.

WEST VIRGINIA, state, E central United States, bounded by Ohio, Pennsylvania and Maryland on the N, by Maryland and Virginia on the E, by Virginia on the S, by Kentucky on the SW, and by Ohio on the W; area 24,181 sq. mi., including 101 sq. mi. of inland water; pop. (1960) 1,860,421.

West Virginia is irregular in shape—roughly oval with two narrow extensions, one to the north between Ohio and Pennsylvania, and another to the east between Maryland and Virginia. Its extreme dimensions are about 245 miles north-south and 275 miles east-west. Because of its two narrow territorial appendages, which can be taken to resemble panhandles, West Virginia came to be known as the "Panhandle State." By reason of its generally hilly terrain West Virginia has been popularly called the Mountain State, and the unofficial state song is *West Virginia Hills* (music by H. E. Engle, words by Ellen King). West Virginia ranks 41st in area and 30th in population among the states. The state's motto is *Montani semper liberi* (Mountaineers Are Always Freemen). The state flower is the rhododendron, the state bird is the cardinal, and the state tree is the sugar maple. Charleston is the state capital. See map in Atlas, Vol. 20. For state flag in color, see FLAG.

PHYSICAL FACTORS

Topography. The terrain of West Virginia is generally hilly or, less generally, mountainous. Its average elevation of about 1,500 feet is the highest of any eastern state. About 90 per cent of the state lies in the Appalachian Plateau region of the Appalachian Mountains (see APPALACHIAN MOUNTAINS, *Structure*). The eastern panhandle and the eastern and southeastern margins of the state form part of another component of the Appalachian Mountains: the Newer, or Folded, Appalachians, also known as the Ridge and Valley section. (See FOLD). Separating these two regions, the Appalachian Plateau and the Newer Appalachians, is the Allegheny Front, which forms a distinct, if irregular, escarpment that extends irregularly from Bluefield, on the West Virginia-Virginia line, northeastward to Keyser, on the West Virginia-Maryland border.

The Appalachian Plateau consists essentially of maturely dissected, horizontal-lying sedimentary strata. From a geomorphological point of view, the Appalachian Plateau is indeed a plateau, but it does not have the level surface characteristic of many plateaus: erosion has cut numerous deep valleys and most of the surface is sloping, some very steeply. In the eastern and southern part of the Appalachian Plateau of West Virginia, the land surface is so rugged that it can aptly be called mountainous; many such areas are locally, but imprecisely, called mountains, as are, for example, the Allegheny Mountains. Most of the peaks in these and other mountains, so called, are from 2,500 to 3,500 feet above sea level, and trend from northeast to southwest. Spruce Knob (4,680 ft.),

WEST VIRGINIA

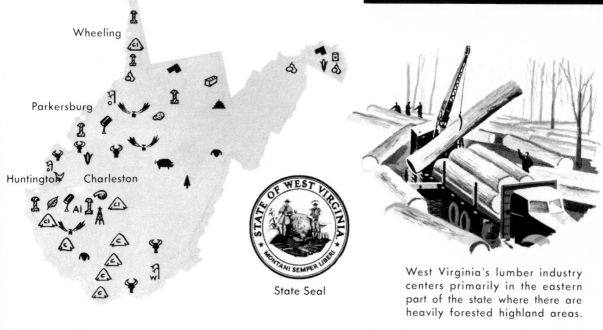

Wheeling

Parkersburg

Huntington   Charleston

State Seal

State Seal

West Virginia's lumber industry centers primarily in the eastern part of the state where there are heavily forested highland areas.

PRINCIPAL RESOURCES, INDUSTRIES, AND PRODUCTS

Al	Aluminum		Limestone
	Canning		Natural gas
	Cattle		Oats
	Cement		Petroleum
	Chemicals		Potatoes
	Clay		Poultry
	Coal		Salt
	Corn		Sheep
	Fruit		Stone
	Hay		Timber
	Hogs		Tobacco
	Iron and steel		Wheat

State Flower
Big Rhododendron

State Bird—Cardinal

In 1760, the western part of the state was settled by families of German descent.

Many black bears inhabit the wooded mountain areas of eastern West Virginia.

The aluminum industry is important in Charleston, the capital of the state.

in the Allegheny Mountains, is the highest point in the state. Elevations in the Appalachian Plateau generally decline to the west so that elevations in the center, which generally vary between 1,000 and 2,500 feet, fall to about 500 feet near the Ohio River.

East of the Allegheny Front, along the extreme eastern and southeastern edges of the state, is part of the Newer Appalachians, also known as the Ridge and Valley section. This rugged area, difficult of access, consists of parallel ridges and valleys, running northeast-southwest, that were apparently formed by complex and excessive geological folding. In this area, along the valley of the Potomac River, is West Virginia's lowest elevation: 240 feet above sea level.

As in other states, the Allegheny Front forms a distinct drainage divide, separating runoff destined for the Ohio River system from that destined for the Potomac. Most of the streams on the Appalachian Plateau drain generally to the northwest, toward the Ohio River by way of the Monongahela, Little Kanawha, Kanawha, and Guyandot river systems. East of the Allegheny Front, drainage is mainly to the northeast, toward the Potomac River. Many of West Virginia's rivers flow down steep gradients through deep, narrow valleys that have great scenic charm by reason of the rushing streams, waterfalls, and steep, wooded slopes. Because of the irregular terrain, most of the roads and towns are located in river valleys. Often the towns and villages are strung out along valley slopes. West Virginia contains neither large natural lakes nor large reservoirs; there are, however, a great many mineral springs. Berkeley Springs and White Sulphur Springs are most important.

Climate. West Virginia, whose climate is of the humid continental type, has generally hot summers, cool winters, and abundant precipitation. The climate varies considerably from place to place, however, in large measure by reason of differences in elevation. The January mean temperature, for example, is 37.9°F at Charleston and 32.6°F at Clarksburg. The July mean temperatures for these places are 76.9°F and 73.8°F, respectively. The average annual precipitation at Charleston is 45.8 inches, that at Clarksburg 42.06 inches. Precipitation is distributed throughout the year, with the maximum occurring in summer. During a typical winter, several feet of snow will fall at the higher elevations. The wettest sections of the state (the mountains) average 60 inches of precipitation a year; the driest sections average 30 inches.

WILDLIFE

Plants. Because West Virginia's diversified terrain offers a variety of plant habitats, the flora is highly varied. The predominant vegetation consists of trees, most of them of the broadleaved deciduous type. Evergreens mantle the mountain peaks and slopes; beech, hemlock, maple, oak, and hickory are plentiful at lower elevations; and sugar maple, willow, sycamore, and river maple are the principal trees of the valleys. Red cedar, yellow poplar, black walnut, hickory, ash, cottonwood, buckeye, pitch pine, aspen, butternut, chinquapin, and gum trees grow here and there throughout the state. Rhododendron, laurel, crab apple, hawthorn, dogwood, redbud, and pussy willow grow in the mountains.

West Virginia has a seasonal succession of beautiful flowers—white bloodroot, violet, hepatica, buttercup, wakerobin, golden ragwort, trailing arbutus, trillium, geranium, columbine, jack-in-the-pulpit, crested iris, pink lady's slipper, black-eyed Susan, daisy, field lily, wild rose, goldenrod, morning glory, and aster, among others. There are more than 60 kinds of fern to be found in the state. Blackberries, raspberries, huckleberries, and cranberries can be gathered in many localities.

Animals. The largest wild animal of West Virginia is the black bear, most specimens of which are to be encountered in the more remote sections of the Al-

legheny Mountains. Other animals are the white-tailed deer, lynx, raccoon, mink, skunk, woodchuck, opossum, beaver, and otter. Among the numerous smaller animals are squirrels, mice, moles, shrews, rabbits, and hares.

West Virginia's rivers and ponds have many and varied species of water birds, among them grebes, loons, migratory ducks and geese, herons, bitterns, and occasional gulls, terns, and cormorants. Snipe and sandpiper live in the marshland; plover, quail, and woodcock, in wooded areas. Among the more common songbirds are the whippoorwill, Baltimore oriole, bobolink, purple finch, scarlet tanager, indigo bunting, cardinal, vireo, mocking bird, bluebird, robin, warbler, and thrush. There are predatory birds, too, such as owls, hawks, falcons, osprey, buzzards, the bald eagle, and the rare golden eagle.

West Virginia's streams contain several kinds of game fish, of which the most significant are brook, rainbow, and Loch Leven trout; muskellunge, walleyed pike; and smallmouthed and largemouthed bass. Among other fish to be found in the state are carp, rock bass, catfish, perch, sunfish, blue gills, suckers, eels, and gar.

SOCIAL FACTORS

Population. According to the federal census of 1960, the population of West Virginia was 1,860,421, a decrease of 145,131, or 07.2 per cent, from the official 1950 population of 2,005,552. Of the 1960 total, 38.2 per cent (711,101 persons) was classified as urban population. On the average, there were 77 persons per square mile in 1960. The most populous sections are in the north and west; the least populous in the south and east. About 5 per cent of the 1960 population was Negro. According to the 1960 census, the largest city of West Virginia is the capital, Charleston; other major cities, in descending order of population, are Huntington (largest in 1950), Wheeling, Parkersburg, Weirton, Clarksburg, Fairmont, and Morgantown. The most prominent religious denominations in the state are the Methodist, Baptist, and Roman Catholic.

Education. Attendance in public schools is compulsory for all children age 7 through 16, and is free for all between 6 and 21 years of age. Among the institutions for higher learning are West Virginia University (founded in 1867), in Morgantown; Alderson-Broaddus College (1871), Philippi; Bethany College (1840), Bethany; Bluefield State College (1895), Bluefield; Concord College (1872), Athens; Davis and Elkins College (1904), Elkins; Fairmont State College (1867), Fairmont; Glenville State College (1872), Glenville; Marshall University (1837), Huntington; Morris Harvey College (1888), Charleston; Salem College (1888), Salem; Shepherd College (1871), Shepherdstown; West Liberty State College (1837), West Liberty; West Virginia Institute of Technology (1895), Montgomery; West Virginia State College (1891), Institute; West Virginia Wesleyan College (1890), Buckhannon; and Wheeling College (1954), Wheeling.

Public Welfare. West Virginia's state department of welfare and state board of control administer hospitals, and correctional and penal institutions. A

PRINCIPAL CITIES

City	Population	
	1950 Census	1960 Census
Charleston	73,501	85,796
Huntington	86,353	83,627
Wheeling	58,891	53,400
Parkersburg	29,684	44,797
Weirton	24,005	28,201
Clarksburg	32,014	28,112
Fairmont	29,346	27,477
Morgantown	25,525	22,487

WEST VIRGINIA
High Lights of History

The Indian fighter Maj. Samuel McCulloch escaped capture, 1777, by driving his horse over a precipice.

Legend has it that "Elizabeth Zane's dash" to get gunpowder to defend Fort Henry against Indian attack helped win this "last battle of the Revolution."

The President's Cottage, White Sulphur Springs, served as a summer home for Presidents Martin Van Buren, John Tyler, and Millard Fillmore. It is now a museum.

Lord Dunmore's War ended with the decisive defeat of the Indians at the Battle of Point Pleasant, Oct. 10, 1774.

John Brown's raiding party took refuge in the engine house of the Harper's Ferry armory when all escape routes were cut off after their famous raid, 1859. Their position was successfully stormed by 90 Marines led by Robert E. Lee.

state board of children's guardians has control and custody over dependent and neglected children. Among West Virginia's welfare institutions are children's homes at Elkins and Huntington; a home for mentally defective children at St. Mary's; and several homes for the aged and infirm. Among the state's correctional institutions are industrial schools at Salem, Huntington, Pruntytown, and Lakin; the West Virginia Penitentiary, Moundsville; and the medium security prison, Huttonville.

Among the state-operated hospitals are emergency hospitals at Fairmount and Welch. Berkeley Springs Sanitarium, owned by the state, is leased to private operators. There are state-operated mental institutions at Huntington, Spencer, Lakin, Weston, and Barbourville, and tuberculosis sanatoriums at Hopemont, Beckley, and Denmar. There are also special schools for handicapped children.

ECONOMIC FACTORS

Agriculture in West Virginia is handicapped by the prevalance of hilly or mountainous terrain. The most important branch of agriculture in the state is livestock raising, especially cattle, sheep, and hogs, which are raised on the extensive hill pastures. Dairying and poultry raising are also important. Livestock raising is best developed in the bluegrass region of the southeastern part of the state.

PRINCIPAL CROPS

Crop	Unit	1947–1956 Average	1957	1958
		thousands		
Apples	bushel	4,030	5,000	5,200
Corn	bushel	9,355	6,216	8,305
Hay	ton	984	903	1,026
Peaches	bushel	612	470	840
Tobacco	pound	4,144	3,278	3,047

Besides hay, the principal crops raised in West Virginia are corn, deciduous fruits, wheat, potatoes, and oats. The eastern panhandle is noted for fruit growing, particularly for apples and peaches. Tobacco is grown in the Huntington vicinity.

The most flourishing farming sections of West Virginia are along the Ohio Valley and in the eastern panhandle. The average farm is slightly over 100 acres in size, and there is a high proportion of very small farms.

Forestry and Fisheries. West Virginia became an important source of forest products in the eighteenth century, and in the 1950's, although virgin forests were virtually nonexistent, the state was still about 60 per cent forested and continued to support important forest industries. Production of hardwood lumber is most important particularly in the eastern section of the Appalachian Plateau. Major commercial species are oak, walnut, chestnut, yellow poplar, maple, and ash. Softwoods are also produced. The state maintains a vigorous program to restore and conserve its forest resources for commercial and recreational uses.

The extensive freshwater fisheries of West Virginia are important only for recreational purposes.

Mining. Mining is a major industry in West Virginia, which ranks close to the top of the list of states in value of mineral production. Coal, natural gas, petroleum, and natural gasoline are the principal mineral products. About 70 per cent of the state is underlaid by coal in the Appalachian coal field. The coal is of the bituminous or semibituminous quality, much of it of coking quality; and West Virginia ranks as the leading producer of bituminous coal in the United States. The rugged terrain precludes use of stripping methods, and most coal production is done in mines. Major coal producing counties are Logan,

MINERAL PRODUCTION

Mineral	Unit	1958	1959
Clays	short ton	509,806	595,724
Coal	short ton	119,467,697	119,692,129
Natural Gas	million cu. ft.	204,581	215,000
Natural gas liquids:			
Natural gasoline	gallon	27,917,000	29,242,000
LP-Gases	gallon	235,524,000	308,316,000
Petroleum (crude)	42-gal. bbl.	2,186,000	2,177,000
Salt	short ton	626,709	810,914
Sand and Gravel	short ton	5,252,586	4,854,052
Stone	short ton	5,598,623	5,922,993

McDowell, Raleigh, Fayette, and Marion, but coal is also produced in many other counties, and the state contains vast reserves of this fuel. Natural gas is produced mainly in the southern and western sections of the state. Other minerals produced in West Virginia are sand, gravel, stone, clays, salt, lime, magnesium compounds, and cement.

Manufacturing. In the post-World War I period manufacturing occupied an increasingly important position in the economy of West Virginia, which has many advantages for manufacturing: vast fuel deposits, water power, lumber, and easy access to many other raw materials. Most important is the iron and and steel industry, most of it in the northern panhandle where it forms part of the Pittsburgh, Pa., iron and steel area. Charleston, Clarksburg, Huntington, Morgantown, and Parkersburg are the main iron and steel centers. There are a large number of metal-working plants in the state, whose major principal metal products are mining machinery, construction machinery, agricultural and construction implements, railroad equipment, and hardware.

The extensive salt deposits of the Kanawha Valley support a large chemical industry. And the abundance of silica sand and natural gas have made West Virginia a center of glassmaking, principally at Moundsville, Charleston, Clarksburg, and Fairmont. Clay products are made in the northern panhandle. Among other things manufactured are synthetic fibers, explosives, electrical equipment, paper products, printed matter, food products, rubber products, leather goods, and construction materials.

Transportation. The rugged terrain, and particularly the many deep valleys, make transportation in West Virginia more difficult than in most areas of the eastern United States. The navigable rivers of the state—especially the Kanawha, Monongahela, and Ohio rivers—are very important in the transportation of coal and other bulk cargo. Huntington, Parkersburg, Pleasant Point, and Wheeling are the main river ports on the Ohio.

The state is served by several railroads, principally the Chesapeake and Ohio and the Baltimore and Ohio. The highway system comprises some 40,000 miles of roads of various types. Among the major routes are U.S. highways 40, 50, and 60 running east-west, and 19, 21, 119, and 220 running north-south. Of 50 or so airports in the state, more than half are available for public use. Charleston, Clarksburg, Morgantown, Parkersburg, and Elkins are the major commercial airports. Eastern, American, and United airlines provide the principal air services.

Tourist Attractions in West Virginia are many and varied; tree-covered uplands, numerous historic relics and sites, mineral springs, and hunting and fishing areas are among the most popular. Particularly attractive are views from the mountain roads that give the motorist access to all but the most rugged sections of the state. Among many notable tourist centers are the resorts at White Sulphur Springs and Berkeley Springs. Not far away, also in the eastern panhandle, is historic Harpers Ferry, where three states converge (see HARPERS FERRY). Across the state, on Blennerhasset Island in the Ohio

WEST VIRGINIA

A popular vacation area for tourists who like relaxation is the sylvan 7,000-acre Greenbrier Estate, located in Greenbrier County.

Away from the state's urban and industrial areas many close-knit agricultural families reside in the foothills of the mountains.

Blain Island in Charleston is an example of the industrial progress that has taken place in the state. The Great Kanawha River flows by.
CHESAPEAKE & OHIO RY.

West Virginia spruce trees are felled in the winter, cut into four-foot lengths, and sent to paper mills in the spring.
WEST VIRGINIA PULP & PAPER CO.

The dam on the Elk River near Sutton is made of concrete, has a height of 220 feet, and drains an area of 537 square miles.
WEST VIRGINIA INDUSTRIAL & PUBLICITY COMM.

River, is the site of the mansion where Harman Blennerhasset and Aaron Burr laid plans to create an empire for themselves in the southwest. A state 4-H camp is located on the childhood home of Thomas Jonathan "Stonewall" Jackson, at Jackson's Mill, near Clarksburg. Moundsville is so named for a huge conical Indian burial mound. Rehoboth Church (1784), in Monroe County, is a historic log church. Throughout the state, the sites of numerous frontier forts are marked.

West Virginia has a comprehensive system of state parks, with well equipped recreational facilities. Among these, Watogo State Park is the largest; but Blackwater Falls, Babcock, Cacapon, Hawk's Nest State, Grandview State, Holly River, Tomlinson Run, and Pinnacle Rock parks are also noteworthy. Civil War battlefields are preserved in Droop Mountain Battlefield Park and Carnifex Ferry Battleground. In addition, there are over a million and a half acres of forested uplands in the Monongahela National Forest, and extensive recreational facilities in state forests.   KENNETH THOMPSON

PAUL'S PHOTOS

West Virginia's Canaan Valley in Tucker County is typical of the rolling tree-covered highlands penetrating all of the state, rimmed on the east by the Allegheny Mountains.

GOVERNMENT

The Constitution of West Virginia is that adopted in 1872, as since amended. Amendments must be approved by two-thirds of all members of each house of the state legislature, and then ratified by a majority of the electors. A constitutional convention may be called by a majority of the elected members of each house of the legislature if a majority of the state's voters are in favor of it. The proposed amendments must then be ratified by the majority of the electors voting. Any United States citizen who has been a resident 1 year in the state and 60 days in the county may vote after registration.

The Executive Officials are the governor, secretary of state, treasurer, auditor, attorney general, and commissioner of agriculture, all elected for four years; the governor is not eligible to succeed himself. There is no lieutenant-governor; in case of a vacancy in the governorship the office devolves upon the president of the senate. The governor's veto, which extends to all bills passed by the legislature, may be overridden by a majority of the elected members of each house.

The Legislature is composed of a senate of 32 members elected for four years and a house of delegates of 100 members elected for two years with at least one delegate from each county. Both houses of the legislature are apportioned according to population and are reapportioned every 10 years. Regular sessions convene annually in the second week of January. Legislators are paid for 60 days only during regular sessions; special sessions may be called upon petition of two-thirds of the legislature's members; there are no remunerative limitations on the length of special sessions.

The Judicial Power is vested in a supreme court of appeals comprising five judges elected by popular vote for 12 years; in 24 circuit courts, with judges elected for 8 years; in courts of limited jurisdiction established by legislative enactments; and in justice of the peace courts.

HISTORY

Settlement. John Lederer, a German surgeon who had been sent out on a westward exploring expedition by Gov. William Berkeley of Virginia, reached a point near Harpers Ferry, 1669–70. Two years later Thomas Batts and Robert Fallam explored the West Virginia region as far west as Kanawha Falls. A fur trader, Abraham Wood, who had discovered the Great Kanawha, 1671, and his agents Gabriel Arthur and James Needham, made contact with Cherokee Indians in the area, 1673, and competed with the Spanish in trading with them. Although it is possible that there may have been white settlers near the site of Shepherdstown as early as 1719, Morgan Morgan is credited with being the first to

build a permanent home in the state: in 1726–27, or perhaps a few years later, he built a log cabin near Bunker Hill in Berkeley County. After 1730 many settlers came into the region, principally from Pennsylvania and Maryland rather than from the old section of Virginia; the first permanent settlement was probably that of Stephan Sewell and Jacob Marlin, 1749. The isolated settlements suffered severely from Indian attacks during the French and Indian Wars, 1754–63, after which a royal proclamation forbade settlement in the trans-Allegheny region; many home seekers disregarded the law, however, and settlement continued. A proposal was made to create a new colony, to be called Vandalia; this project received royal approval, but was never carried out because of the outbreak of the American Revolution.

In 1775 the population of this section of Virginia was estimated at 30,000. During Dunmore's War, 1774, against the Indians, the Battle of Point Pleasant was fought at the mouth of the Great Kanawha, in which the whites won a decisive victory. During the Revolution, the settlements of Western Virginia suffered severely from Indian attacks instigated by the British.

Prior to the Civil War, 1861–65, West Virginia was a part of the state of Virginia. The first federal census, 1790, enumerated 55,873 persons in the West Virginia region; by 1800 the population had increased to 78,592. The opening of the Mississippi to navigation stimulated commercial activity; and from 1811 there were steamboats on the Ohio River, the state's most important waterway. The region was also greatly benefited by the construction of the National Road, which reached Wheeling in 1818; the Baltimore and Ohio Railroad reached Wheeling in 1852. Throughout this period the people of western Virginia were becoming increasingly irritated at the discrimination against them; they complained of inequality in taxation, underrepresentation in the legislature, and unequal distribution of funds for public works.

West Virginia Becomes a State. On April 17, 1861, despite the protests of delegates from the western portion of the state, Virginia seceded from the Union. On May 13 representatives from 26 western counties met in convention at Wheeling, repudiated the Ordinance of Secession, and summoned a "Virginia State Convention" to meet at Wheeling, June 11. This second convention, with representatives of 40 counties in attendance, declared the state offices vacant and organized a provisional government. A third convention, in which 47 counties were represented, at Wheeling, November 26, drew up a constitution for the "Restored Government of Virginia" that was ratified, May 3, 1862, by a vote of 18,862 to 514. Pres. Abraham Lincoln signed the Act of

Admission, Dec. 31, 1862; finally, on June 19, 1863, West Virginia was admitted to the Union as the 35th state. Arthur I. Boreman was the first governor.

Civil War. In the early stages of the war, minor skirmishes were fought in what is now West Virginia. Several Confederate raids were made later, but eventually the Federals, under Generals George B. McClellan and William Starke Rosecrans, gained complete control of the region. West Virginia contributed about 36,530 soldiers (or 32,068, according to some authorities) to the Union Army, and about 7,000 to that of the Confederacy. Slavery was abolished on Feb. 3, 1865, prior to the adoption of the Thirteenth Amendment to the U.S. Constitution.

Post-Civil War. The original constitution was amended, 1866 and 1871, and a new constitution adopted, 1872. The capital, first located in Wheeling, was moved to Charleston, 1870, returned to Wheeling, 1875, and moved to Charleston again, 1885. The old capitol was destroyed by fire, 1921; the new capitol was dedicated on June 20, 1932.

During the first three decades of the twentieth century, West Virginia was the scene of a long and bloody struggle over the right of coal miners to organize. In World War I the state furnished 68,924 men to the Armed Forces. In World War II it had about 223,000 men and women in service; death casualties were about 5,825. In June, 1950, flash floods swept north central West Virginia, taking over 30 lives. At Farmington in 1954 an explosion killed 16, the worst mine disaster in a decade.

The Democratic party was dominant in West Virginia, 1872–92. From 1896, however, the Republicans were generally dominant in the state, although Woodrow Wilson received the state's electoral votes in the presidential election of 1912, and a Democrat was elected governor in 1916. The Democrats were again dominant from 1932 until 1956, when the state's electoral votes went to Pres. Dwight D. Eisenhower. In 1960, however, the state supported the Democratic party candidate, John F. Kennedy. In 1960 West Virginia sent six congressmen to the U.S. House of Representatives.

Bibliog.—Charles H. Ambler, *Francis H. Pierpont, Union War Governor of Virginia and Father of West Virginia* (1937); Charles H. Ambler and Festus P. Summers, *West Virginia: The Mountain State* (1958); American Guide Series, *West Virginia: A Guide to the Mountain State* (1946); James M. Callahan, *History of West Virginia, Old and New*, 3 vols. (1923); Philip M. Conley and Boyd B. Stutler, *West Virginia Yesterday and Today* (1952); John P. Hale, *Trans-Allegheny Pioneers* (1931); Josiah Hughes, *Pioneer West Virginia* (1932); Oscar D. Lambert, *West Virginia and Its Government* (1951), *West Virginia, Its People and Its Progress*, 3 vols. (1958); Virgil A. Lewis, *History and Government of West Virginia* (State Government Ser.) (1922); William A. MacCorkle, *Recollections of Fifty Years of West Virginia* (1928); James C. McGregor, *Disruption of Virginia* (1922); Lucullus V. McWhorter, *Border Settlers of Northwestern Virginia from 1768 to 1795* (1915;) Maude A. Rucker, comp., *West Virginia: Her Land, Her People, Her Traditions, Her Resources* (1930); Morris P. Shawkey, *West Virginia, in History, Life, Literature and Industry*, 5 vols. (1928).

WEST VIRGINIA STATE COLLEGE, a public, coeducational institution of higher learning, located in Institute, W. Va. It was established as an educational institute by legislative act, 1891; its name was changed to West Virginia Collegiate Institute, 1915, the year in which it was authorized to offer college-level instruction; the present name was adopted in 1929. The school's departments are agriculture, art, biology, business administration, chemistry, drama, economics, education, English, German, physical education, history, home economics, mathematics, military science, music, philosophy, physics, psychology, political science, Romance languages, sociology, and technical science. Co-operative programs in engineering and agriculture are conducted with West Virginia University and West Virginia Institute of Technology. See COLLEGES AND UNIVERSITIES.

WEST VIRGINIA UNIVERSITY, a coeducational, public institution of higher learning, located in Morgantown, W. Va. It was established as the Agricultural College of West Virginia, 1867, and instruction was offered the same year. The name was changed to West Virginia University in 1868.

Among the divisions of the university are agriculture, arts and sciences, engineering, and law, all founded, 1895; music, 1897, medicine as a two-year school, 1900, and as a four-year school, 1960; military science, 1911; education, 1927; physical education, 1928; graduate school, and mines, 1930; pharmacy, 1936; journalism, 1939; commerce, 1951; and dentistry, 1953. The university conducts a co-operative work-study program in civil engineering with the State Road Commission of West Virginia, and the Kanawha Valley Graduate Center of Science and Engineering, Institute, W. Va. A conservation workshop is sponsored jointly by the university and the state conservation commission. The West Virginia University Council on Economic Education conducts an annual summer education conference in co-operation with the National Council on Economic Education.

The university library has collections of materials on West Virginia history, the Southern Appalachians, coal mining, and Shakespeare. Publications include *West Virginia Law Review* and *West Virginia Fourth Estatesman.* See COLLEGES AND UNIVERSITIES.

WEST VIRGINIA WESLEYAN COLLEGE, a private, coeducational, liberal arts college affiliated with the Methodist church, and located in Buckhannon, W. Va. The school was established, 1890, as West Virginia Conference Seminary and instruction was offered the same year; the name was changed to its present form in 1904. Co-operative programs in engineering are conducted with the University of Pittsburgh, University of Pennsylvania, and Bucknell University; in forestry with Duke University; and in nursing with several near-by hospitals. The college library has collections of materials on Methodist history and Abraham Lincoln. An alumni magazine, *Sundial,* is published monthly. See COLLEGES AND UNIVERSITIES.

WESTWARD MOVEMENT. See FRONTIER; OVERLAND TRAILS; PIONEER LIFE; PUBLIC LAND.

WEST WARWICK, town, central Rhode Island, in Kent County; W of Greenwich Bay, on the Pawtuxet and Flat rivers and the New Haven Railroad; 12 miles SSW of Providence. A wide variety of textile products are manufactured in the town. West Warwick was separated from Warwick and incorporated in 1913. Pop. (1960) 21,414.

WESTWEGO, town, SE Louisiana, in Jefferson Parish; on the Missouri Pacific, the Texas and Pacific, and the Texas Pacific-Missouri Pacific Terminal Railroad of New Orleans railroads; on the west bank of the Mississippi River, opposite New Orleans. Westwego has port facilities and is a processing center for sea food. Ships, fabricated metal products, wood preservatives, alcohol, and chemicals are manufactured. Pop. (1960) 9,815.

WESTWOOD, borough, NE New Jersey, in Bergen County; on the New Jersey and New York Railroad; 17 miles NNW of New York City, of which it is a residential suburb. The growing of vegetables is a leading occupation of the area. Pop. (1960) 9,046.

WEST YORK, borough, SE Pennsylvania, in York County; on the Western Maryland Railway and U.S. highway 30; adjacent to York and about 25 miles SE of Harrisburg. Pottery, hosiery, furniture, and machinery are manufactured. West York was incorporated in 1905. Pop. (1960) 5,526.

WETASKIWIN, city, Canada, S central Alberta; on the Canadian Pacific Railway; about 42 miles S of Edmonton. The city is a trade center for an area in which there are livestock, dairy, and poultry farms; timber stands; and oil wells. It has grain elevators, a flour mill, and creameries and is an important livestock-shipping point. Wetaskiwin was incorporated as a city in 1906. (For population, see Alberta map in Atlas.)

WETHERSFIELD, town, central Connecticut, Hartford County; located 5 miles S of Hartford, of which it is a residential suburb. The town was first settled in 1634. Wethersfield is the site of the Connecticut state prison. (For population, see Connecticut map in Atlas.)

WETTING AGENT, a substance that appreciably reduces the surface tension of water. Such substances are known as soaps or detergents. Many synthetic chemicals have the ability to lower the surface tension of water and thus permit the solution to more effectively wet surfaces and penetrate crevices, and thus function as a better cleansing agent. Sodium lauryl sulfate, $C_{12}H_{25}OSO_3Na$, and other sulfonated fatty acids, substituted naphthalenes, pyridine bases, and cresol preparations function in this way. They are sold under various trade names as detergents.

Detergents find use in the dye industry to help in the uniform and deeper penetration of the dye into fabrics, and in the paint industry to increase spreading qualities. They permit cleansing in hard waters, because their calcium salts are soluble, whereas those of common soaps are not. See SURFACE TENSION.

WEXFORD, county, SE Ireland, in Leinster Province; bounded by St. George's Channel on the E and S, and by the counties of Wicklow on the N, Waterford on the SW, Kilkenny on the W, and Carlow on the NW; total area, about 907 square miles. The county is hilly in the north and west, with Mount Leinster reaching 2,610 feet and Black Stairs 2,409 feet. The principal streams are the Slaney, which widens into an estuary called Wexford Harbor, and the Barrow, which flows south between Wexford on the east and Kilkenny and Waterford on the west, and widens into Waterford Harbor in its lower course. Sandbars endanger shipping, especially off the east shore. Wexford Harbor is inaccessible during low tides, and Rosslare was made into an artificial harbor (1906). There is considerable farming and stock raising. The town of Wexford has little industry and is chiefly a center for fishing. (For population, see table in Ireland article.)

WEXFORD, city, SE Ireland, capital of Wexford county, on the S shore of the Slaney River estuary; about 72 miles S of Dublin. A sand bar obstructs entrance to the estuary for ships drawing more than 12 feet, and an artificial harbor was constructed at Rosslare, six miles south, in 1906. The chief exports are whisky, livestock, and agricultural produce. Wexford has shipbuilding yards, tanneries, breweries, distilleries, iron foundries, flour mills, and a factory manufacturing agricultural implements. Noted points of interest are the ruins of the twelfth century Selski Abbey, the churches of St. Patrick and St. Peter, and the old Bull Ring. Wexford was founded by the Danes in the ninth century, and later it was one of the first landing places for the English invaders. (For population, see Ireland map in Atlas.)

WEYBURN, city, Canada, SE Saskatchewan; on the Souris River, approximately 70 miles SE of Regina. Wheat, oats, and dairy products are marketed in Weyburn. The city has grain elevators, a flour mill, creameries, a sash and door factory, machine shops, an oil refinery, and coachworks. Wire and cable are manufactured. Weyburn was incorporated as a city in 1913. (For population, see Saskatchewan map in Atlas.)

WEYDEN, ROGIER VAN DER, also known as Roger de la Pasture, 1400?–64, Flemish painter, was born in Tournai, Belgium, and was probably a goldsmith before being apprenticed to the painter Robert Campin, a fellow townsman. By 1435, when he moved to Brussels, he was already famous enough to be named painter to the municipality. He painted four important compositions for the Brussels town hall, but these later disappeared. When he was about 50, he

METROPOLITAN MUSEUM OF ART
Detail from *The Annunciation*—a spiritually serene masterpiece by the Flemish painter Rogier van der Weyden.

visited the great cities of Italy; his fame had preceded him, and he was awarded commissions by patrons and honored by native artists. His masterpiece, *Descent from the Cross*, hangs in the Prado, Spain, along with eight other works attributed to him. Rogier's artistic career was marked by success after success, both at home and abroad. He died in Brussels.

Of all the masters of the Flemish school, Rogier was the most deeply spiritual. His glazed color and luminosity was typically Flemish, but the figures in his dramatic compositions are rent by religious emotion and expiatory suffering. He excelled in depicting the intense and restless drama of Christianity, but could also paint portraits in the serene manner of his predecessors, the Van Eycks, or of his Italian contemporaries, as exemplified by the portrait of Francesco d'Este in the Metropolitan Museum, New York City. Also in the Metropolitan is an impressive and typical work, *Christ Appearing to His Mother*, originally one wing of a triptych whose other two panels are in the cathedral of Granada, Spain. The Colegio del Patriarca, Valencia, has an exquisite small triptych. Influences of his Italian voyage are visible in his later work; he, in turn, influenced the Italians, as well as the contemporary Germans, and the Spanish during the sixteenth century.   ANTHONY KERRIGAN

BIBLIOG.–M. J. Friedländer, *From Van Eyck to Brueghel* (1956); Erwin Panofsky, *Early Netherlandish Painting*, etc. (1954).

WEYGAND, MAXIME, 1867–1965, French general and colonial administrator, was born Louis Maxime Weygand in Brussels, Belgium. He was educated at St. Cyr Military Academy and the Saumur Cavalry School, became a hussar officer, and served in World War I as chief of staff to General Ferdinand Foch. He was inspector in chief of the French army, 1931–35, and at the beginning of World War II, 1939, was commander of the French forces in Syria. During the German invasion of France, he replaced General Maurice Gamelin as Allied commander, 1940; he made a desperate attempt to halt the Nazi advance but after the collapse of the Maginot Line he advocated an armistice. In the puppet Vichy regime Weygand served as minister of defense and as governor general of Algeria. He was a prisoner of the Germans, 1942–45. After the liberation of France, 1945, he was arrested and charged with collaboration with the Germans, but he was exonerated and his rights were restored, 1948. His memoirs of World War II are called *Recalled to Service* (1952).

WEYLER Y NICOLAU, VALERIANO, MARQUIS OF TENERIFE, 1839–1930, Spanish general, was born in Palma de Mallorca. He was military attaché of the Spanish legation in Washington during the U.S. Civil War. He conducted successful campaigns in Cuba, 1868–72; against the Carlists in Northern Spain, 1875–76; and in Mindanao, Philippine Islands, 1889. In 1896 he was sent to Cuba, where his methods of repressing Cuban nationalists caused widespread unrest and caused U.S.–Spanish tension. He was recalled, 1897, and made captain-general of Madrid. He became chief of staff of the Spanish army, 1920.

WEYMOUTH, town, E Massachusetts, Norfolk County; on the Weymouth Fore River and the New Haven Railroad; 11 miles SE of Boston. The production of electric power for Boston and the manufacturing of shoes are the principal industries. Granite quarries are in the vicinity. Weymouth, which was established in 1622, was the second Massachusetts settlement. In 1635 it was incorporated as a town, and was the first Massachusetts town to adopt the town-meeting system. Pop. (1960) 48,177.

WHALE, any of about 100 species of large marine mammals belonging to the order Cetacea. Its external appearance is fishlike. It is almost hairless and has no visible neck, ears, or hindlimbs. Its forelimbs are modified to form paddle-like flippers. It has a strong tail with a broad horizontal fluke, and is perhaps the strongest marine swimmer. Yet it is a true mammal, having warm blood, lungs, and mammary glands. A thick layer of blubber under the skin conserves its body heat. Its nostrils open by a blow hole on top of its head, and its lungs are built to resist great pressures. The characteristic spout of water issued by surfaced holes results from the condensation of warm, moist, expired air by the cooler air found near the ocean surface. The cow whale gives birth to a live calf, which it nuzzles to the surface for its first breath of air.

Whalebone Whales. The characteristic of the whalebone whale of the suborder Mysticeti is the mouth plates of baleen, popularly called whalebone. This is not bone, however, but a very flexible and elastic substance similar to horn. The many flattened plates hang down into the mouth cavity, and strain from the water the small organisms upon which the whale feeds. Whalebone whales are further characterized by the loose attachment of their ribs to the backbone, permitting them to take in a large supply of air. This permits the whale to remain under water for long periods. Genera are *Balaena*, including the right whale; *Balaenopiera*, including the fin whales or rorquals; *Magaptera*, including the humpback whale; *Rhachianectes*, including the gray whale of the Pacific; and *Neobalaena*, including the rare pigmy whale of southern seas, whose whalebone is very valuable.

The Toothed Whales of the suborder Mysticeti are characterized by a lack of whalebone, the presence of teeth, and several other anatomical differences. Important species include cachalot, or sperm whale; bottle-nosed whale; beluga; narwhal; dolphin; and porpoise. Others are the grampus, the killer whale,

Whalers exercise a skilled effort in maneuvering the carcass of a whale to the beach where trimming is conducted. Bladders surrounding the whale aid in keeping it afloat.

and the rare beaked whales. Many are hunted for their oil.

From the point of view of the whaler, the blue whale, or sulfur-bottom whale, *Sibboldus musculus*, is the most important. This whale is the largest living animal. It has been known to reach a length of 113 feet and weight of more than 170 tons. An average animal measures more than 70 feet. The finbacks reach a length of 55 to 60 feet, and a weight of 50 tons. The humpback is much smaller, weighing about 27 tons. The bowhead is one of the most valuable whales, but is found only among the ice floes of the Arctic. The cachalot is rarely found out of tropical waters, where it goes in schools of hundreds.

WHALING

The pursuit and capture of whales for food, oil, and other products has been practiced for not less than a thousand years. As an industry, it is believed to have begun about 1550. The English, Russians, Danes, Norwegians, and Dutch entered the field before, or soon after 1600, when whales were discovered in great abundance in the waters off northern and northwestern Europe. Whaling was practiced by U.S. sailors during the nineteenth century, resulting in nearly 800 American whalers on the sea during the peak year of 1846.

Whaling is now carried on with specially built steamships of high speed and easy maneuverability, designed to permit processing of captured whales at sea. A gun mounted in the bow fires a barbed harpoon with explosives in its head. The bomb explodes inside the whale's body and kills the animal instantly. To prevent loss of the whale by sinking and to permit the ship to pursue other whales in the vicinity, the body is drawn alongside the ship, air is pumped into the body to keep it buoyant, the kill is marked with a buoy or flag to identify the ship to which it belongs, and the chase continues until the school is scattered and lost.

WHALEBONE. See RIGHT WHALE; WHALE.

WHALE OIL, the oil which is extracted from all whales except the sperm whale. Whale oil is extracted from the blubber or fat by boiling and steaming. Much oil is also yielded from the meat and bones, particularly from the larger whales. The yield of oil from a large whale, such as the blue whale, may be up to 180 barrels. Whale oil varies in color from pale yellow to almost water-white in the finer grades, to pale brown or darker in the more crude varieties. It has an odor that is characteristic of fish oil. The specific gravity is 0.917 to 0.924, the saponification number is 160 to 202, and the iodine number is 90 to 146. The oil is solidified at 0 to 2°C. Whale oil is used in soap manufacture, as an illuminant, for leather dressing, as a lubricant for screw-cutting machines, for quenching steel in tempering opera-

After a whale has been taken in, cutting operations occur either on a specially outfitted whaling vessel or on the land. The oil-rich blubber is sliced off for processing.

WHALE

Smoke billows from the harpoon gun of a Canadian whaleboat as the harpoon is shot toward a 50-ton humpback whale in the whaling grounds off the coast of British Columbia.

NATL. FILM BOARD OF CANADA

CONSULATE GENERAL OF JAPAN

Japanese fishermen cut up a whale on the deck of a modern whaling boat off the Japanese coast. The two most valuable commercial products of the whale are its oils and bones.

CONSULATE GENERAL OF JAPAN

Sperm whales, belonging to the toothed variety of whales, are most valued for oil found in a cavity in their heads.

A British survey ship, the SS *Eagle*, shown on a mission in the rich whaling waters of the South Shetland Islands.
BRITISH INFORMATION SERVICES

NATL. FILM BOARD OF CANADA

A humpback whale is towed up on a seaplane ramp at Coal Harbour, British Columbia, where it is being "flensed," or peeled of its skin, before being cut up for blubber.

tions, and as a constituent in oleomargarine and plant insecticides.

BIBLIOG.–Glover M. Allen, *Whalebone Whales of New England* (Memoirs, vol. 8, no. 2) (1916); American Guide Series, *Whaling Masters* (1938); Roy C. Andrews, *Whale Hunting With Gun and Camera* (1935); Clifford W. Ashley, *Whaleships of New Bedford* (1929), *Yankee Whaler* (1942); Frank E. Beddard, *Book of Whales* (1900); Georges Blond, *Great Story of Whales* (1955); Karl Brandt, *Whale Oil: An Economic Analysis* (Fats and Oil Studies, no. 7) (1940); Paul Budker, *Whales and Whaling* (1959); John Chrisp, *South of Cape Horn: A Story of Antarctic Whaling* (1958); Lars Christensen, *Such is the Antarctic* (1935); Albert C. Church, *Whale Ships and Whaling* (1960); Ross Cockrill, *Antarctic Hazard* (1957); Erich Dautert, *Big Game in Antarctica* (1937); Everett J. Edwards and Jeanette E. Rattray, *Whale Off!! The Story of American Shore Whaling* (1956); Joseph Gomes, *Captain Joe: Whaleman From New Bedford* (1960); Chester C. Howland, *Thar She Blows!* (1951), *Whale Hunters Aboard the Grey Gold* (1957); Michael Hyde, *Arctic Whaling Adventures* (1957); Harry R. Lillie, *Path Through Penguin City* (1955); Alfred B. Lubbock, *Arctic Whalers* (1937); Edgar L. McCormick and Edward G. McGehee, eds., *Life on a Whaler* (1960); Hakon Mielche, *Thar She Blows!* (1952); John R. Norman, *Field Book of Giant Fishes* (1949); Robert B. Robertson, *Of Whales and Men* (1954); Frances D. Robotti, *Whaling and Old Salem: A Chronicle of the Sea* (1950); Ivan T. Sanderson, *Follow the Whale* (1958); Edouard A. Stackpole, *Sea-hunters: The New England Whalemen During Two Centuries, 1635–1853* (1953); Whales Research Report, *Scientific Reports*, 5 vols. (1948-51); Addison B. C. Whipple, *Yankee Whalers in the South Seas* (1954).

WHALLEY, EDWARD, 1616?–?1675, English regicide, was a woolen draper by trade. He served as colonel in the parliamentary forces in the English Civil War and fought at Marston Moor, 1644, and in other important battles. As a member of the court that tried Charles I, he signed the death warrant, 1649. On the accession of Charles II, 1660, Whalley wisely fled to New England and remained in hiding until his death.

WHANGPOO RIVER, or Hwangpoo, river, E central China, mostly in Kiangsu, flowing about 75 miles from Tai Lake complex E and then N through the Yangtze Delta region into the mouth of the Yangtze River. Its chief tributary, the Soochow River also rises in the lake area and flows about 65 miles E into the Whangpoo. The Whangpoo River in 25 miles of its lower course provides the harbor for China's metropolis and chief port, Shanghai. A wide network of canals and small streams connects the Whangpoo and Soochow with Shanghai's agricultural hinterland, neighboring cities, and the Grand Canal and Yangtze Estuary. The Whangpoo is a tidal river, its depth changing with the ocean tides reaching it through the Yangtze Estuary. The river is dredged of silt annually to provide a channel about 30 feet deep at low tide.

WHARTON, EDITH NEWBOLD JONES, 1862–1937, U.S. novelist, was born in New York City. A member of an old and wealthy family, she was educated privately and traveled widely through Europe. After her marriage, 1885, to Edward Wharton, a Boston banker, she spent much of her life in Paris. A collection of her early short stories, *The Greater Inclination* (1899) was followed by *The Valley of Decision* (1902), a story of eighteenth century Italy. *The House of Mirth* (1905) is the first of her many novels dealing with the efforts of tradition-bound characters to surmount social barriers. Her most characteristic works are stories of fashionable life in Europe and the United States, but *Ethan Frome* (1911), the simplest and most powerful of her tragic narratives, is a tale of frustrated love on a New England farm. As a disciple of Henry James, she was deeply concerned with moral values, and character, not situation, as the basic factor in her tragedies; she was fond of contrasting the cultures of different periods, classes, and countries. Notable among her works in this vein are *Madame de Treymes* (1907), *The Custom of the Country* (1913), *The Age of Innocence* (1920, Pulitzer prize), *Hudson River Bracketed* (1929), and *The Gods Arrive* (1932). Collections of her later short stories are *Xingu and Other Stories* (1916), *Certain People* (1930), and *Ghosts* (1937). Among her other works are *The Fruit of the Tree* (1907), *Fighting France* (1915), *Glimpses of the Moon* (1922), *The Old Maid* (1924), *Twelve Poems* (1926), *Twilight Sleep* (1927), *The Children* (1928), and *A Backward Glance* (autobiography, 1934).

WHARTON, city, SE Texas, seat of Wharton County; on the Colorado River, the Santa Fe and the Southern Pacific railroads, and U.S. highway 59; about 60 miles SW of Houston. The city is a trade and processing center for an area in which rice and cotton are grown. Cottonseed oil and dairy and meat products are processed. Oil wells and sulfur mines are in the vicinity. Pop. (1960) 5,734.

WHEAT, a cereal grain of the grass family *Gramineae*, and the genus *Triticum*. Wheat is a major food crop of countries in the temperate regions and is second only to rice as a source of food on a world basis. Wheat is grown on more of the world's acreage than any other crop and is adaptable to a wide range of soils and climate. Eight species of wheat grown under cultivation are common wheat, club wheat, durum wheat, poulard wheat, Polish wheat, emmer, spelt, and einkorn.

Within the species there are numerous varieties adapted to a wide range of climatic conditions. Winter varieties, which comprise a major portion of the wheat grown in the United States, are sown in the fall and harvested the following summer. Spring varieties are sown in the spring and harvested in the fall.

About 95 per cent of all wheat grown in the United States is common wheat, *T. vulgare*. The remaining acreage consists principally of durum wheat, *T. durum*, and club wheat, *T. compactum*. Common wheat produces slender spikes; the kernels are either red or white and may be either soft or hard, depending on the variety. Durum wheat, a spring variety, has narrow, compact spikes and very hard kernels. Club wheat, of which there are both spring and winter varieties, has short spikes.

Market Classes of Wheat. Wheat grown in the United States is divided into seven market classes according to the botanical type, the area where it is grown, or the major use. These classes are hard red winter, soft red winter, hard red spring, white, durum, red durum, and mixed. Production is confined largely to the first five of these classes.

Over half of the wheat produced in the United States is of the hard red winter variety, which is used primarily for bread flour. It is grown extensively in areas of limited rainfall in the states of Kansas, Nebraska, Oklahoma, Texas, and Colorado. The soft red winter variety, which accounts for about 15 per cent of the wheat grown in the United States, is used primarily for pastry, cracker, biscuit, and cake flour. It flourishes in areas of abundant rainfall in many states east of the Mississippi River, most notably, Ohio, Indiana, Illinois, Missouri, and Pennsylvania. Hard red spring wheat comprises about 15 per cent of the total annual production in the United States. Most of this wheat, also used primarily for bread flour, is grown in North Dakota, South Dakota, Montana, and Minnesota.

White wheat totals about 15 per cent of all wheat produced in the United States and is grown principally in Washington, Oregon, California, Idaho, Michigan, and New York. White wheat includes spring and fall varieties of common and club wheats and is used principally for the same purposes as soft red winter wheat. Durum wheat provides less than 3 per cent of the wheat grown in the United States. A granular meal, semolina, is made from durum wheat and used in manufacturing macaroni, spaghetti, and related products. Production is centered chiefly in North Dakota and neighboring states.

Description. A kernel, or grain, of wheat consists of an outer bran coat; an aleurone layer; an endosperm, which constitutes the bulk of the kernel and consists largely of starch and some gluten or protein; and a germ, or embryo plant.

When a wheat seed germinates, or sprouts, portions of the embryo emerge as roots and foliage. As the plant grows, the root system develops into a fibrous network that usually penetrates to a depth of from three to five feet in the soil. The developing stem is similar to that of other grasses, with nodes, or joints, and internodes. The stem is hollow, except in some durum and poulard wheats. Leaves typical of the grass type emerge at the nodes. The spike, or head, is formed at the top of the stem, and bears 15 or more fertile spikelets. Several flowers form in each spikelet. In nature the flowers are self pollinated, but cross pollination may be done to produce new varieties. Awns or beards are produced on the heads of some varieties. Each plant usually produces two or more stems at the crown, a characteristic known as tillering, or stooling. See PLANT PHYSIOLOGY.

Origin and Distribution. The origin of wheat is obscure, but it is one of the oldest crops grown by man. There is evidence that wheat may have been grown first in southeastern Asia, perhaps in the region of Afghanistan. Since earliest historical times, wheat has been an important source of food. Some forms of wheat were probably cultivated before 4000 B.C., and some grains of wheat, perhaps wild, have been found in Egyptian tombs dating from before 5000 B.C.

Wheat was introduced to North America by the colonists early in the seventeenth century. The chief areas of wheat production shifted westward, along with the settlers' westward migration, but wheat is grown in 42 states of the United States and in most Canadian provinces.

Most of the world wheat crop is produced in temperate zones, the main wheat belt generally lying between latitudes of 30 to 55 degrees in the North Temperate Zone and 25 to 40 degrees in the South Temperate Zone. Throughout the area of greatest wheat cultivation the rainfall generally averages between 12 and 45 inches annually.

Wheat is produced in some 50 different countries, but the United States, the U.S.S.R., and China are the largest producers; other major wheat-producing countries are Canada, France, Italy, India, Turkey, Argentina, Australia, and Spain. About one-fourth of the world wheat crop is produced in North America.

The United States has two major wheat-producing areas: the central and southern Great Plains, where the main production is hard red winter wheat; and the northern Great Plains, where the main production is hard red spring wheat.

The two principal wheat-producing states are Kansas and North Dakota. Other leading states are Oklahoma, Montana, Washington, Nebraska, Texas, Colorado, Idaho, Illinois, Michigan, and Ohio.

CULTIVATION

Yields of wheat can be increased through the use of improved varieties and more efficient production practices. In the early 1960's average yields were estimated at more than 20 bushels per acre, but many wheat growers secured considerably better yields. Wherever it can survive the winters, winter wheat yields considerably more than spring wheat.

Selecting the Variety. The selection of the variety of wheat suitable for growth in each area is dependent upon soil and climatic conditions in the area and upon certain qualities of the wheat itself, such as its resistance to certain diseases, its hardiness, and its yielding ability. Plant breeders use cross breeding, or hybridization, followed by careful selection of the most desirable lines thus produced, in developing new varieties suitable for cultivation in specific areas.

Preparing the Soil. Production methods for wheat grown in humid areas differ somewhat from those used under dryer conditions. In growing the hard red spring wheats in some parts of the northern Great Plains, the rainfall is insufficient to grow a crop every year. In these areas, a common practice is to fallow the soil in alternate years, cultivating the soil, without a crop being grown. This has the effect of conserving much of the moisture and holding it in the soil, thus making much of the rainfall from two years available in growing one crop. In many of these areas, in order to reduce wind erosion, the land is divided into alternate strips of fallowed land and land seeded to wheat. Wind erosion may be further reduced by cultivating with implements that leave the soil in a roughened condition, or which leave the stubble from the preceding crop on the surface of the soil.

In more humid areas, wheat is often grown in rotation with other crops. Winter wheat is planted early in the fall, after the migration of the Hessian fly, a destructive insect pest. Recommended dates of seeding are commonly called fly-free dates. Where varieties of wheat resistant to this insect are used, the fly-free dates are disregarded. Most winter wheats are planted in September, but may be planted as late as October in southern regions. Spring wheat is seeded as early as the soil is in condition for making a good seed bed, frequently in March or April.

Wheat grows best in a firm, mellow seed bed with sufficient moisture for germination of the seeds and growth of the plants. In preparing a seed bed, the land is plowed, and then cultivated by discing and harrowing. If the planting follows a cultivated crop removed in early fall, plowing may not be necessary.

Planting. The average rate of planting is five to eight pecks per acre in humid areas, and about three to four pecks per acre in dry country. Wheat may be seeded with a special machine called a drill, which places the seeds in rows a few inches apart and at a desired depth. Where moisture is abundant, the usual depth is one to one and one-half inches; in drier areas the recommended depth is two to three inches. In humid areas, especially, commercial fertilizers may be applied with the drill at the time of seeding, in accordance with soil needs. In many areas, nitrogen fertilizer is applied in the spring to fall-planted wheat. This practice is known as top dressing.

Harvesting. Most wheat grown in North America is harvested with tractor-operated combines that cut and thresh the grain in one operation. Until mid-twentieth century wheat, in the humid regions, frequently was cut with a reaper, which bound the grain into bundles. The bundles were then placed in shocks and the grain was later separated from the straw with threshing machines. Combines, however, replaced this process almost entirely. See FARM MACHINERY.

Storing. To minimize spoilage of wheat in storage, its moisture content should be 14 per cent or less. In areas of low humidity, the moisture content reaches this level naturally before harvest. In humid areas, however, where drying is slow, and where losses may occur in the fields if harvesting is delayed, driers are frequently used on farms or in elevators to reduce the moisture content in the harvested grain to a safe level. In major wheat areas, much harvested grain is hauled directly to elevators or central storage buildings. In other areas some of the grain is stored on the farms where it is produced.

Diseases and Insect Pests. Among the serious diseases of wheat are smuts, stem rusts, leaf rusts, scab, and mosaic. Insects that damage wheat include the Hessian fly, jointworm, sawfly, chinch bug, grasshopper, and aphid. The diseases are controlled by using disease-resistant varieties of wheat, by treating the seed with chemicals, and by crop rotation and other cultivation practices.

The most serious insect pest of winter wheat, the Hessian fly, is a tiny fly that emerges late in summer and lays eggs on the leaves of the small plants. These eggs hatch into maggots that suck juices from the base of the stems. Control consists of planting at a time that delays the appearance of the young wheat plants until after the flies have emerged and died. The soil may be treated with certain chemicals that act as systemic insecticides in the growing plants (see INSECTICIDE). Some varieties of wheat resistant to damage caused by this insect are suitable for growth in certain areas. In the early 1960's, plant breeders in agricultural colleges and in the U.S. Department of Agriculture were attempting to develop disease-resistant varieties of improved quality wheat.

CONSUMPTION

About 80 per cent of the wheat used in the United States is consumed in food products. About 10 per cent is used for seed, slightly less than 10 per cent is used for feed for livestock, and a small fraction is manufactured into miscellaneous products.

The estimated annual per capita consumption of cereal grains in the United States at mid-twentieth century included approximately 120 pounds of wheat as compared to about 26 pounds of corn, 5 pounds of rice, 3 pounds of oats, 1 pound of rye, and 1 pound of barley. At that time, however, the per capita consumption figure for wheat was decreasing gradually.

Food Products. Most wheat used for human consumption is made into flour; small amounts are used for breakfast foods and miscellaneous food products. Flour is made from the endosperm, the central and major portion of the wheat kernel. Between 70 and 75 pounds of flour are commonly obtained from 100 pounds of wheat. The outer portions of the kernel and the wheat germ yield bran and middlings, or shorts, which are used primarily as livestock feeds. Some bran and wheat germ are also used as food for humans.

Most of the flour used in making bread is manufactured from the hard red wheats, which are high in gluten. Buffalo, Kansas City, and Minneapolis are the leading U.S. flour-producing centers, although flour mills are located in many other cities in the United States. See FLOUR.

Exports. Wheat is one of the United States' most important agricultural exports. At mid-twentieth century, it was not uncommon for as much as 45 per cent of a year's crop to be exported, and special government programs for subsidizing the disposal of surpluses abroad seemed likely to be a major factor in increasing wheat exports still more. Under these programs, wheat was being exported under special price concessions or payment plans, or was being given as relief grants to underdeveloped countries. Increasing amounts of export wheat were being transported through the Saint Lawrence Seaway in ships loaded at Great Lakes ports. See GRAIN TRADE.

Production Statistics. A mid-twentieth century decline in per capita use of wheat in the United States was somewhat offset by population increase so that domestic consumption of wheat for food remained fairly constant.

At mid-twentieth century, the average annual production of wheat in the United States exceeded one billion bushels. At the same time, average annual domestic consumption for all purposes was about 600 million bushels; almost 500 million bushels per year were exported.

Although the total harvested acres of wheat in the United States generally decreased during the years following World War II, increased yields per acre served to maintain production at a high level and the serious surpluses that resulted sometimes totalled more than an average year's crop. Some surplus, or carryover, is desirable for security reasons, but high amounts entail burdensome storage costs. Wheat production was placed under an acreage control and price support program shortly after World War II in order to prevent prices from decreasing to levels ruinously low for wheat farmers. Government price-supported loans and purchases by the Federal Commodity Credit Corporation aided the wheat farmer, but a wheat-production program that would decrease surpluses and provide fair returns to wheat producers had yet to be formulated early in the 1960's. See AGRICULTURAL ENGINEERING; AGRICULTURE; AGRICULTURE IN THE UNITED STATES.

GEORGE P. DEYOE

BIBLIOG.—Joseph S. Davis and others, *Wheat in the World Economy: A Guide to Wheat Studies of the Food Research Institute* (1945); Marvin C. Dubbé, *Grains of Wheat* (1934); Edgars Dunsdorfs, *Australian Wheat-growing Industry, 1788–1948* (1957); Vernon C. Fowke, *National Policy and the Wheat Economy* (1957); Naum Jasny, *Wheats of Classical Antiquity* (1944).

WHEATLAND, town, SE Wyoming, seat of Platte County; near the Chugwater River; on the Colorado and Southern Railway and U.S. highway 87; 64 miles N of Cheyenne. Wheatland is the trade and processing center for an irrigated region in which sugar beets, wheat, poultry, and livestock are raised. Mica quarries are in the vicinity. Pop. (1960) 2,350.

WHEATLEY, PHYLLIS, 1753?–84, American Negro poet, was born in Africa, but was brought to America, ?1761, and sold as a slave to a Boston merchant, who educated her and encouraged her natural poetic bent. She enjoyed a considerable vogue as a literary prodigy in America, and in England, 1773. She published *An Elegiac Poem on the Death of George Whitefield* (1770) and *Poems on Various Subjects, Religious and Moral* (1773).

WHEATON, HENRY, 1785–1848, U.S. jurist, diplomat, and historian, was born in Providence, R.I., was graduated from Brown University, 1802, studied law, and was admitted to the bar, 1805. In New York from 1812, he edited the *National Advocate,* 1812–15, and was judge of the marine court of New York City, 1815–19. He was a member of the state assembly, 1823, chargé d'affaires to Denmark, 1827–35, and minister to Prussia, 1837–46. His best known work is *Elements of International Law* (1836).

WHEATON, city, NE Illinois, seat of Du Page County; on the North Western Railway and U.S. highway 30; 25 miles W of Chicago, of which it is a residential suburb. Wheaton was founded in 1837, platted in 1852, and incorporated in 1859; it became the county seat in 1867. The city is the site of Wheaton College (1853). Pop. (1960) 24,312.

WHEATON, village, W Minnesota, seat of Traverse County, on the Mustinka River, the Milwaukee Railroad, and U.S. highway 75; 175 miles WNW of St. Paul. Wheaton is a shipping point for grain, poultry, and livestock. Butter and poultry products are processed. The village was settled in 1884. Pop. (1960) 2,102.

WHEATON COLLEGE. See COLLEGES AND UNIVERSITIES.

WHEATSTONE, SIR CHARLES, 1802–75, English inventor, pioneer in telegraph invention, was born in Gloucester, studied at King's College, London, and was knighted, 1868. He made experiments in sound and light, 1823?–'35, worked with William Fothergill Cooke in the field of telegraphy, and improved telegraphs, 1837 and 1845. Wheatstone's Bridge, a device for measuring electrical resistance of conductors, and his method for measuring the velocity of electricity in a conductor are enduring contributions to the science of electricity. He invented the concertina, 1829. Among his other activities were cryptography, and doing experiments in the fields of acoustics and color perception.

WHEATSTONE BRIDGE, an instrument used in electrical measurements for the rapid determination of unknown resistances. The bridge appears in many forms, from the inexpensive slide-wire type to expensive laboratory equipment. In the illustration, a wire of uniform cross-section and composition, that is, one of uniform resistance, is stretched over a meter stick so that the distances K and L are easily

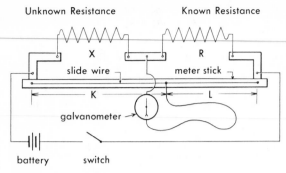

Unknown Resistance   Known Resistance

X   R

slide wire   meter stick

K   L

galvanometer

battery   switch

A Wheatstone Bridge is used to test electrical resistance.

measured. The known resistance, R, the unknown resistance, X, the galvanometer, and battery are connected in circuit by means of heavy copper straps of very small resistance. In operation the battery current will divide, one portion flowing through the slide wire and the other through the resistances R and X. If the loose contact wire is moved along the slide wire to a point where the galvanometer indicates "no current," the bridge is then said to be balanced and the voltage drop through X is equal to that along the wire of length K. Similarly the drop through R is equal to that along the wire of length L. If the current through R and X is l_1 and that through K and L is l_2, then the voltage drops are

$$l_1X = l_2K$$
$$l_1R = l_2L.$$

From these two equations it follows that

$$\frac{X}{R} = \frac{K}{L} \text{ or } X = R\frac{K}{L}$$

and the unknown resistance X is determined in terms of R, a known resistance, and two measured lengths K and L. Although the instrument is named for Sir Charles Wheatstone who called attention to the network in 1843, it was S. H. Christie who first described the bridge some ten years earlier in 1833.

WHEEL, a circular frame or solid disk which can rotate on an axis. The ability of the wheel to modify and transmit motion makes it one of the most essential devices in machinery. When the wheel was invented is not known. Evidence indicates that prehistoric man utilized the principle of the wheel more than 10,000 years ago. The chief advantage of the wheel depends upon the fact that rolling friction is considerably less than sliding friction (see FRICTION). For example, much of the force required to slide a heavy load over a rough surface is needed simply to overcome friction. If wheels are placed under the load, the friction is greatly diminished, and a much smaller force is needed to keep the load in motion at constant speed. When a wheel is rigidly attached to an axle, it functions as one of the six simple machines (see MACHINE). Its mechanical advantage lies in the fact that a force applied to the outer rim of a wheel is multiplied by the distance through which it acts, or the radius of the wheel The steering wheel of a car illustrates this advantage. To attempt to steer the car by the driving shaft would admittedly be very difficult, but a small force easily directs the car if a large steering wheel is attached to the shaft.

WHEELER, BURTON KENDALL, 1882–   , U.S. political leader, was born in Hudson, Mass., and educated at the University of Michigan Law School. Wheeler practiced law in Montana, served in the state legislature, 1911–13, was U.S. district attorney, 1913–18; and entered the U.S. Senate as a Democrat, 1923. He was vice-presidential candidate on the Robert La Follette ticket, 1924. Wheeler remained in the Senate until 1947; he supported New Deal labor legislation, but opposed Pres. Franklin D. Roosevelt's policies in foreign affairs.

WHEELER, JOSEPH, nicknamed Fighting Joe, 1836–1906, Confederate cavalry officer and U.S.

political and military figure, was born near Augusta, Ga. He was graduated from West Point, 1859, but resigned from the U.S. Army when Georgia seceded from the Union, and became a Confederate officer. He was given command of the cavalry in the Army of the Mississippi, 1862, and later of Tennessee. He showed unusual daring and ability in charge of the cavalry covering Braxton Bragg's retreat from Kentucky, 1862, at Chickamauga and around Chattanooga, 1863, and (now a lieutenant general) in the unsuccessful campaign to resist William T. Sherman's march through Georgia and South Carolina, 1864–65. As a U.S. representative from Alabama, 1883 and 1885–1900, he was an advocate of North-South conciliation. He resigned from Congress, 1898, to become U.S. major general of volunteers in the Spanish-American War; he led the cavalry at Las Guasimas, San Juan Hill, and Santiago, then served briefly in the Philippines. He retired from the Army, 1900, with the rank of brigadier general. He wrote *Cavalry Tactics* (1863) and *The Santiago Campaign* (1898).

WHEELER, WAYNE BIDWELL, 1869–1927, U.S. prohibitionist, was born near Brookfield, Ohio, and worked his way through Oberlin College. He joined the Anti-Saloon League of Ohio, 1893, and took a law degree at Western Reserve University, 1898, the better to give legal advice to the league. He was attorney for the National Anti-Saloon League from 1915. He prosecuted over 2,000 saloon cases, defeated a "wet" candidate for the Ohio senate with a "dry" candidate of his own, and was active in lobbying for a Prohibition Act in Congress during World War I.   ALFRED DE GRAZIA

WHEELER, WILLIAM ALMON, 1819–87, vice-president of the United States during the administration of Pres. Rutherford B. Hayes, 1877–81, was born in Malone, Franklin County, N.Y. He studied at the University of Vermont, was admitted to the bar, 1845, was a member of the federal House of Representatives, 1861–63, 1869–77. Nominated by the Republicans as their candidate for the vice-presidency, 1876, he was ultimately declared elected by a majority of one vote. See TILDEN, SAMUEL JONES.

WHEELER, town, N Texas, seat of Wheeler County; on U.S. highway 83; 16 miles west of the Oklahoma border, and 275 miles NW of Dallas. Wheeler is a trade center for an area in which cotton, fruit, and cattle are raised. There are natural gas wells in the vicinity. Pop. (1960) 1,174.

WHEELER-LEA ACT, 1938. See MARKETING.

WHEELING, city, in the N panhandle of West Virginia, seat of Ohio county; on the Ohio River, the Baltimore and Ohio, the Pennsylvania, and the Nickel Plate railroads, and U.S. highway 40; scheduled airline stop; about 45 miles SW of Pittsburgh, Pa. The city lies in an important industrial center near extensive natural gas and coal deposits. Wheeling, which is known for its large iron and steel industries, is a center for the manufacturing of cans, toys, electrical equipment, tubes, enamelware, glassware, vitrified china, calico, proprietary medicines, tooth paste, and tobacco and food products. It is connected by bridges with Bridgeport, Martin's Ferry, and Bellaire, Ohio. The Wheeling area was settled, 1769, by the Zane family; the town was established, 1795, incorporated, 1806, and chartered as a city, 1836. In 1818 the National Road was opened in Wheeling. Wheeling was the center of the Unionist sympathy that caused the separation of West Virginia from Virginia. The city served as the state capital from 1875 to 1885. Wheeling began to flourish industrially with the establishment of glass factories in 1821. In 1830 a local paper industry began, soon followed by the establishment of the first iron works; the local tobacco industry was founded in 1879. In March, 1936, Wheeling suffered extensive destruction from floodwaters of the Ohio River and Wheeling Creek. Pop. (1960) 53,400.

WHEEL LOCK. See FIREARMS.

WHEELOCK, ELEAZAR, 1711–79, colonial American educator, founder and first president of Dartmouth College, was born in Windham, Conn. His ancestors had first settled in Massachusetts in 1637. He was graduated from Yale, 1733, and then, from 1735, as Congregationalist pastor at Lebanon, Conn., during the Great Awakening, he proved to be a popular and emotional preacher (see AWAKENING, *The Great Awakening*). To augment his small income he tutored men for college. Among these was the Mohegan Indian, Samson Occom, who later raised money from English and Scottish sources for Moor's Charity School, Lebanon, for Indians and poor whites (founded 1754). Wheelock soon decided to start a school for the education and conversion of Indians. After a charter (1769) had been granted by Gov. John Wentworth, Wheelock founded his school in Dresden (now Hanover), N.H. This school was named after William Legge, the second Earl of Dartmouth, who had been a generous contributor. Wheelock was more of an administrator than scholar or writer, but he did write *A Brief Narrative of the Indian Charity School, in Lebanon, Connecticut* (1763). During the American Revolution Wheelock showed strong character and determination in keeping his school open without interruption.

John Wheelock, 1754–1817, Eleazar's eldest son by his second marriage, was born in Lebanon, and went to Yale for three years, but got his degree at Dartmouth, 1771. During the Revolution he rose to the rank of lieutenant colonel in command of some New Hampshire companies. As the second president of Dartmouth College, from 1779, the son constructed new buildings, established salaried professorships, and founded, 1798, the Dartmouth Medical School. His battle with the trustees, which resulted ultimately in the famous Dartmouth College case, clouded his last years; the case was settled by the Supreme Court, 1819, in favor of the position Wheelock had held.   HERBERT FAULKNER WEST

WHEELWRIGHT, JOHN, 1592?–1679, colonial American clergyman, was born in Lincolnshire, England, studied at Cambridge, 1611–18, immigrated to the Puritan colony of Massachusetts Bay, 1636, where he became pastor of the Church of Mount Wollaston (later Braintree). He sympathized with the Antinomian views of his sister-in-law, Anne Hutchinson (see HUTCHINSON, ANNE MARBURY), and was banished, 1637. With several persons who sympathized with him, he founded the town of Exeter, N.H., 1638, and moved to what is now Wells, Me., 1643. The sentence of banishment was revoked, 1644, and he returned to Massachusetts, where he served as pastor of the Church of Hampton for about six years. He lived in England, 1657–62, and, after returning to the colonies, was made pastor at Salisbury, N.H.

WHETSTONE, an abrasive stone used for the final sharpening, or whetting of edged tools. Whetstones are fashioned from relatively fine abrasives, such as chalcedony silica, sandstone, and carborundum. The finest-grained whetstones are most effective when used with oil, and are known as oilstones. Whetstones are cut in various shapes for convenience in sharpening such tools as knives, plane blades, sickles, and scythes.

WHICHER, GEORGE FRISBIE, 1889–1954, U.S. educator and author, was born in Lawrenceville, N.J., and studied at Amherst College and Columbia University. He taught English at the University of Illinois, 1913–15, and at Amherst, 1915, where he became a professor in 1922. He wrote *This Was a Poet* (1938), *Alas, All's Vanity* (1942), and *Walden Revisited* (1945). See LONGFELLOW, HENRY WADSWORTH; LOWELL, JAMES RUSSELL; METAPHOR; POETRY; REALISM; TRANSCENDENTALISM; WHITTIER, JOHN GREENLEAF.

WHIDBEY ISLAND, a long, irregularly shaped island at the entrance to Puget Sound, NW Washington, in Island County; east of the Strait of Juan de Fuca. One of the largest islands within the conterminous United States, it has an area of 225 sq. mi., of which 19 sq. mi. are inland water. Whidbey Island is linked by Deception Pass Bridge to Fidalgo, and thence to the mainland, and also by ferry at the island's southern tip to Everett. Agriculture is the chief industry on the island. Poultry, dairy cattle, wheat, bulbs, seeds, and berries are raised. The principal towns on Whidbey Island are Oak Harbor, which is near a naval air station, Langley, and Coupeville, the county seat. The island's first settlement grew from a Catholic mission that was established in 1840. Pop. (1960) 18,245.

WHIG, a former English political type, traditionally opposed to the Tories. Like many political names, whig was first applied in derision; it is a shortened form of "Whigamore," a term applied to the Covenanting men of the southwest of Scotland, and variously derived from *whig*, sour whey, and *whiggam*, a sound made by drivers to urge on their horses. The word seems to have been generally applied after the Restoration, 1660, to the whole Presbyterian party in Scotland, and later in England to all who were suspected of opposition to the king, or of sympathy with the nonconformists. See TORY.

WHIG PARTY, a conservative U.S. political party, 1834–?56. Following the election of Thomas Jefferson as president, 1800, the Federalist party declined in influence and numbers until there was practically but one party, the Republican or Democratic-Republican (not to be confused with Republican party organized in 1856); finally during the Andrew Jackson administration, 1828–36, various elements of opposition coalesced and the Whigs emerged to contest with what had become the Democratic party.

The presidential candidates of 1824—Jackson, John Quincy Adams, William Harris Crawford, and Henry Clay—ran without party organizations. Since no candidate received an electoral majority, Adams was elected by the House of Representatives. During his administration the supporters of Jackson formed the Democratic party. Its first opponent was the National Republican party whose candidates were Adams, 1828, and Clay, 1832. Anti-Masonry became a national political party in 1832 (see ANTIMASONIC PARTY). The attempt of South Carolina to nullify the tariff law, 1832, precipitated a crisis in which many advocates of States' Rights joined the opposition to Jackson (see NULLIFICATION). Although the Federalist party had ceased to exist, there were, especially in New England, a considerable number who maintained its principles; these, led by Daniel Webster, formed part of the inchoate opposition. Finally, in 1834, National Republicans, Anti-Masons, certain States' Rights men, and the remaining Federalists, joined in forming the Whig party.

As an opposition party with several divided elements, the Whigs did not develop consistent party principles, except that they supported propertied, business, and financial interests through protective tariff schedules. Lacking in clear-cut political ideas, they nevertheless had able leaders, among whom Clay, Webster, and Abraham Lincoln were the most celebrated. Whig party membership, unequally distributed, was strongest in New England and the South. Only two Whig presidents were elected: William Henry Harrison, 1840, and Zachary Taylor, 1848.

Because the New England Whigs and the southern Whigs differed strongly on the slavery question, the party disintegrated when slavery became a political issue. Although three-fourths of the slaves were owned by Whigs, abolition of slavery became a tenet of some of the Whig group in the North, with the result that from 1852 the demise of the party was certain. Always susceptible to the propaganda of native Americanism, many Whigs joined the Know-Nothing party. Finally, in 1856 and after, the abolitionist and protective tariff elements of the Whigs joined the Republican party, while in the South and in the southern parts of the Northwest the majority of the Whigs returned to the Democratic fold.

DONALD W. RIDDLE

WHIPPET, a swift English sporting dog, noted for its ability as a racer. The animal measures about two feet in height and weighs approximately 20 pounds. Its head and muzzle are slender and long and its nose is black. Keen, intelligent eyes, usually dark hazel in color, show the general alertness of the dog. Its back is long and powerful; the line of its chest is deep in the forequarters, curving in a concave manner near the hindquarters. A highly streamlined body, a smooth coat, and strong legs account for the dog's swiftness; it is capable of speeds up to 35 miles per hour. The whippet is a hardy dog and merits highly as a rabbit chaser.

The whippet was developed as a breed during the mid-nineteenth century. The breed resulted from crossed matings of English greyhounds and a variety of terriers. Later, the breed was mated with Italian greyhounds, resulting in many of the characteristic qualities of the whippet. It was given official recognition in England in 1891. Today the dog is usually raced in circular tracks employing the use of electric rabbits, which act as an incentive for the dogs to run.

WHIPPING. See CORPORAL PUNISHMENT.

WHIPPLE, GEORGE HOYT, 1878–   , U.S. pathologist, was born in Ashland, N.H., and educated at Yale University and Johns Hopkins Medical School. After serving as pathologist at Johns Hopkins Hospital, 1910–14, he became professor at the University of California Medical School, 1914, and professor of pathology and dean of the school of medicine at the University of Rochester, 1921. Conducting much of his research in the study of anemia in animals, he discovered the beneficial effect of liver in the regeneration of the blood, 1920. This discovery was applied to human anemics, 1926, by George Minot and William Parry Murphy. All of the three men shared the 1934 Nobel prize for physiology and medicine "for their discovery of the liver therapy of anemia."

WHIPPLE, WILLIAM, 1730–85, colonial American soldier and political figure, was born in Kittery, Me. He was elected to the Continental Congress, 1776–79, and was a signer of the Declaration of Independence. In the Revolutionary War he commanded a brigade in the campaign against Gen. John Burgoyne, 1777, and, with Gen. John Sullivan, fought against the British in Rhode Island, 1778. He served as a judge of the New Hampshire superior court, 1782–85.

WHIPPLE'S DISEASE, an intestinal disorder giving rise to a gradual loss of weight and strength. The symptoms are an intermittent fever, a chronic cough, a low blood pressure, and anemia. Occasionally the disease begins with arthritis of many body joints. Granules of fatty matter occur in the lymph nodules of the intestinal mesenteries, and large, foamy ameboid cells occur in the mucous lining of the small intestine. The cause of the disease is thought to arise from a breakdown in the mechanisms of fat metabolism (see METABOLISM). Males between the ages of 30 and 65 years are predominantly afflicted. The disease may perhaps be transmitted genetically. Treatment is directed toward ridding the patient of each symptom. Corticotropin and corticosterones appear to be the most effective therapeutic agents (see STEROID; ACTH). Without effective treatment, the disease ends in death after about five years.

WHIPPOORWILL, a North American goatsucker of the family *Caprimulgidae*, receiving its name from its cry, which is loud and clear, and heard only at night. The whippoorwill, *Caprimulgus vociferus*, is about 10 inches long and in appearance and habits resembles the other goatsuckers. It is a mixture of black, brown, and gray above, buffy with black spots below. The

NATL. AUDUBON SOC.
Whippoorwill

bristles at the base of the bill are an inch long and very stiff, and there is a narrow white collar. The lateral feathers of the rounded tail are largely white. It is found in the northern regions of North America. Farther to the south the whippoorwill is replaced by a larger species called chuck-will's-widow, *C. carolinensis*.

WHIP SCORPION, a tropical scorpion-like animal belonging to the order Pedipalpida. Whip scorpions receive their name from the long, whiplike tail of some species. They vary in length from a half inch to about six inches. The whip scorpion does not possess a poison gland or stinging organ. It has pincered grasping limbs called pedipalpi that are used to capture the insects of its diet. It is a burrowing arachnid found in tropical areas and the southern regions of the United States.

ROBERT C. HERMES FROM NATL. AUDUBON SOC.
The Whip scorpion is so named because of its long whiplike tail, and is found in tropical areas and in the southern United States. It lives in burrows and feeds on insects.

WHIPWORM. See THREADWORM.

WHIRLWIND, a mass of air which is much higher than it is long and which rotates rapidly around a more or less vertical axis. It is a purely local phenomenon and does not last long. Whirlwinds vary in intensity from the dust whirl in the street to the hurricane. Desert whirlwinds are not uncommon, and usually spring up about 10 or 11 o'clock in the morning, when the ground has been warmed by the sun's rays. The lower air begins to ascend. As the inflowing currents move through a limited space, and as the irregularity of their flow prevents them from meeting at a common center, they deviate a little to one side or the other, and a small gyrating column is developed. This may rise eventually to a height of several hundred or even a thousand feet. At this elevation it spreads out laterally, the supply of warm air is soon exhausted, and the whirl quickly disappears.

WHISKEY, or whisky, an intoxicating beverage distilled from barley, wheat, rye, corn or oats. First produced in the British Isles in the sixteenth century, it took its name, originally *whiskybae*, from the Anglo-Irish *usquebaugh* (from Gaelic *uisge-beatha*), meaning "water of life" (compare French *eau-de-vie*, Latin, *aqua vitae*, both meaning brandy). In the United States the spelling "whiskey" is given to native products, and "whisky" is reserved almost exclusively for imported varieties. There are four main varieties of whiskey: rye; corn, or Bourbon; Irish; and Scotch. Fruit juices are used in blended whiskies.

Irish, made from barley, oats, and malt, is brewed in large pot stills. For the preparation of the brew, or wort, the grain is mashed and then mixed with malt, to which yeast is added to hasten fermentation. The resulting beer is triple distilled to produce a liquor very high in alcoholic content.

Scotch is produced in the same way as Irish, but is made primarily from barley, and the final distillate is not as strong. The product of the district of Islay, in Scotland, is made with malt which has been baked over a peat fire; it is often used in blending and accounts for the characteristic smoky flavor of Scotch. Both Scotch and Irish are blended whiskies, and may not be designated as "straight."

Bourbon and Rye. Bourbon, or corn whiskey, a distinctive product of the United States, and rye whiskey, manufactured chiefly in Canada, are made from a mixture of grains and malt, but less malt is used than in Scotch and Irish. Distillation produces a liquor of 160 proof (80 per cent alcohol) or less. The straight whiskey is reduced with water to a strength of 100 to 103 proof and is stored in a bonded warehouse. Aging in barrels of charred white oak permits water to evaporate, increasing the concentration of ethyl alcohol and acid; this acts to increase esters and higher alcohols. American whiskies stored in new barrels mature in four years or less. The old cooperage used for Scotch and Irish requires an aging period of from seven to eight years.

Most whiskies are reduced and blended before bottling. According to Federal regulations, bottled whisky must be at least 80 proof (40 per cent alcohol) and not more than 110 proof (55 per cent alcohol). Scotch and blended Bourbons are commonly bottled at proof strengths ranging from 80 to 90, and rye is commonly bottled at 100 proof. Practically colorless when freshly distilled, whiskey takes on an amber color during the aging process. The color may be darkened by the addition of caramel or of Pedro Ximenez, a blending sherry used to reduce the sharpness of young whiskies. See DISTILLING INDUSTRY.

WHISKEY REBELLION, an uprising in western Pennsylvania against the federal Excise Law of 1791, which laid a heavy tax on whiskey, the most important marketable product of the western region. The strongly egalitarian folk of the back country, already upset by the aristocratic tendencies of the new federal government, viewed the whiskey tax as confirmation of their worst fears. Meeting informally in Brownsville, 1791, and in convention at Pittsburgh, 1792, they adopted violent resolutions against the Federalist "tyranny." Tax collectors, meanwhile, risked life and limb when venturing into the area. Opposition continued despite a placative modification of the law, 1792, and in the face of a warning proclamation by Pres. George Washington. In 1794, after all conciliatory efforts had failed, the President ordered a militia force of about 15,000 men into the region, whereupon the leaders of the insurrection disappeared without offering even token resistance. More than 20 prisoners were taken and sent to Philadelphia to be tried for treason; several were convicted, but were pardoned by Washington, whose decisive action had done much to establish the authority of the new federal government.

WHISKEY RING, in post-Civil War U.S. history, a gang of corrupt distillers, politicians, and internal revenue officers who defrauded the federal government of large sums of revenue money. The ring originated in St. Louis, but was soon operating in Chicago, Milwaukee, and other cities. Because of the collusion of many local and even national officials, the ring was considered impregnable for a time. In 1874, however, with the aid of George Fishback of the St. Louis *Democrat* and others, Secretary of the Treasury B. H. Bristow gathered sufficient evidence for the indictment of more than 200 persons, including Col. O. E. Babcock, Pres. U.S. Grant's secretary.

WHIST, a card game, similar to bridge, for four persons, who play as two teams of two players each. Whist, known to date from the year 1500 or before,

was most popular in the period 1700–1900. A 52-card deck is used.

WHISTLER, JAMES ABBOTT McNEILL, 1834–1903, U.S. painter, etcher, and lithographer, born in Lowell, Mass. He was an outstanding personality in later nineteenth-century art. His works, though varying in quality, include a select few that are among the most original products of the period. They represent a purely aesthetic aim: the pursuit of beauty in design, tone, and color, independent of subject matter or story. This is implied in the titles he used— *Arrangement, Nocturne, Harmony, Symphony*—and was further asserted in his writings and in the polemics in which he became involved. Active intelligence and sharp-edged wit made him a formidable controversialist and an influence on ideas of art; he is a link between the nineteenth-century conception of art for art's sake and the abstract trends of more recent times.

Whistler spent only some years of his youth in the United States, and his expatriate life helps to explain his somewhat isolated position as an artist. The son of Maj. George Washington Whistler, by his second wife, Anna Matilda McNeill, he was taken to St. Petersburg (the modern Leningrad) at the age of 9, his father being consultant engineer in the construction of the St. Petersburg–Moscow railroad. He had his first drawing lessons at the Imperial Academy of Science. When the family returned to America, he became a cadet at West Point (1851–54) but failed to qualify for the U.S. Army, and after a few months as draftsman in the U.S. Coastal Survey, he went to Paris in 1855 to study art.

A Bohemian student at the academic atelier of Gleyre, he made friends with a number of French painters, among them Fantin-Latour, who introduced him to Courbet. The realism of Courbet and his circle was reflected in Whistler's early oil paintings and his French Set of etchings (1858). Possibly in the hope of gaining wealthy Victorian clients, he moved in 1859 to London, henceforward his headquarters. His reception was not unfavorable. Refused at the Salon of 1858, his painting *At the Piano* (Cincinnati Art Museum) was exhibited at the Royal Academy in 1860 and highly praised. He was made welcome in the Pre-Raphaelite circle of Dante Gabriel Rossetti, and something of the latter's manner appears in Whistler's figure paintings of the 1860's, e.g., in *The White Girl* (1863) and *Little White Girl* (1864). He still maintained close contact with Paris, however, and *The White Girl* (National Gallery, Washington), later known as *Symphony in White, No. 1*, placed him with the French avant-garde, and in the company of Manet, in the Salon des Refusés of 1863.

In this decade, Whistler turned away from realism. His series of dockland etchings, the Thames Set, realistically elaborate masterpieces begun in 1859, were followed by paintings of the Thames at Chelsea that showed a more poetic appreciation of the river atmosphere. Japanese prints and the Chinese porcelain that he vied with Rossetti in collecting introduced a new element of design into his work. It appears in *La Princesse du Pays de la Porcelaine* (*Rose and Silver*, 1863–64), now to be seen in the setting Whistler later designed for it (1876–77), the famous Peacock Room of the Freer Gallery of Art, Washington. An unexplained visit to Valparaiso in 1866 produced seascapes in dim evening light that herald the beautiful nocturnes of the 1870's.

His most creative period was the 1870's. Superbly composed portraits, with an expressive simplicity of silhouette owing something to Velázquez, include the portrait of his mother, *Arrangement in Grey and Black* (1872, Louvre); of Carlyle, a companion piece in style (1873–74, Glasgow Art Gallery); of Miss Cicely Alexander, *Harmony in Grey and Green* (1873, Tate Gallery). His nocturnes show a blending of Eastern and Western design of a unique kind. A fine decorative sense, which extended to a nicety of placing of the butterfly monogram he evolved from his initials, now also appeared in interior schemes. In his view, a picture was part of an ensemble, and a room should be complete as a work of art. To the dismay of his patron, F. R. Leyland, Whistler employed this approach in the dining room (now known as the Peacock Room) of Leyland's London house. Leyland's architect Jeckyll designed the interior scheme. When the room was completed, however, Whistler, in Leyland's absence, and without his permission, covered over the Cordova leather of the walls with his peacock pattern of blue and gold.

A ferocious diatribe of the critic John Ruskin on the nocturnes exhibited at the Grosvenor Galleries in 1877—the magnificently abstract *Nocturne in Black and Gold–The Falling Rocket* (c. 1874, Detroit Institute of Arts) being the main object of attack—led to a disastrous lawsuit in 1878. Ruskin had accused Whistler of "flinging a pot of paint in the public's face," and Whistler instigated a £1,000 libel suit against Ruskin. A technical victor, awarded a farthing damages but no costs, Whistler was left bankrupt and embittered and with some loss of confidence and direction. Later productions include delicate etchings of Venice (1880–86) and Holland (1884) and numerous lithographs, pastels and water colors, and portraits, always elegant but less original than those of the 1870's, e.g., *Sarasate* (1884, Carnegie Institute, Pittsburgh). In the papers collected in *The Gentle Art of Making Enemies* (1890), he waged a one-man war against British critics, academicians, and Philistines. It includes the brilliant "Ten O'Clock" lecture of 1885, asserting the lonely eminence of the master, "in no relation to the moment at which he occurs." His retrospective exhibition of 1902 again placed him high in esteem.

Sometimes called impressionist, Whistler was not so in realistic aim or technical method. He belongs to no school though he is necessarily included in accounts of British art. An unconventional president of the Royal Society of British Artists, he was compelled to resign in 1888—with the remark that "the artists went out and the British remained." In this century his work has been overshadowed by postimpressionist and later developments, but the permanent value of the best of it has never been seriously questioned.　　　　　　　　　WILLIAM GAUNT

BIBLIOG.–Theodore Duret, *Histoire de J. McN. Whistler et de son oeuvre* (1904); William Gaunt, *The Aesthetic Adventure* (1945); James Laver, *Whistler* (1930); E. R. and J. Pennell, *The Life of James McNeill Whistler* (1908); Denys Sutton, *Nocturne* (1963).

WHITBY, town, Canada, SE Ontario, seat of Ontario County. It has an excellent harbor. Chief industries include foundries, machine shops, and tanneries. Founded in 1836, the settlement was known as Perry's Corners until it was renamed for an English seaport. (For population, see southern Ontario map in Atlas.)

WHITBY, urban district, in the North Riding of Yorkshire, NE England, at the mouth of the Esk River; 57 miles NE of York. Whitby is the base of a fishing fleet, and is a popular resort center. Whitby was formerly a jet-mining center; and is noted for its jet ornaments. The ruins of the Whitby Abbey, originally founded in 658, destroyed by the Danes in the ninth century, and rebuilt soon after the Conquest, overlook the town. The seventh century English poet Caedmon lived in the monastery at Whitby. James Cook, the explorer, sailed from Whitby at the start of the voyage in which he reached the eastern coast of Australia in 1770. (For population, see England map in Atlas.)

WHITE, ANDREW DICKSON, 1832–1918, U.S. educator and diplomat, was born in Homer, N.Y., was graduated from Yale, 1853, spent three years in Europe, and then returned to teach history at the University of Michigan, 1857–64. Elected in absentia to the New York senate, 1863, he became chairman of the committee on education and worked with Sen. Ezra Cornell to secure legislation for the establishment of Cornell University, of which White was first president, 1868–85. He was U.S. minister to Germany, 1879–81, and Russia, 1892–94, and ambassador to Germany, 1897–1902. In 1899 he was president of the American delegation at the first International Peace Conference at The Hague. Among his writings are *History of the Warfare of Science with Theology in Christendom* (2 vols., 1896), *Autobiography* (2 vols., 1905), and *Seven Great Statesmen in the Warfare of Humanity with Unreason* (1910).

WHITE, BYRON RAYMOND, 1917–　, U.S. jurist, was born in Fort Collins, Colo., and grew up in nearby Wellington. He was educated at the universities of Colorado, Oxford (on a Rhodes scholarship), and Yale. During World War II, he served in U.S. Naval Intelligence. An outstanding athlete, "Whizzer" White paid his way through law school by playing professional football for the Detroit Lions. He was clerk to the Chief Justice of the Supreme Court from 1946 to 1947, after which he practiced law in Denver. During the 1960 presidential campaign, White led the Colorado Kennedy Committee and later acted as chairman of the National Citizens for Kennedy movement. In 1961, he was named as Deputy Attorney General and in March, 1962, on the retirement of Justice Charles Evans Whittaker, he was appointed an associate justice of the U.S. Supreme Court.

WHITE, EDWARD DOUGLASS, 1845–1921, U.S. jurist, was born in Lafourche Parish, La., and studied at the Jesuit College, New Orleans, and Georgetown College. He was admitted to the Louisiana bar in 1868. He was judge of the state supreme court, 1879–88, and U.S. senator, 1891–94. Pres. Grover Cleveland appointed him an associate justice of the U.S. Supreme Court, 1894, and Pres. William Howard Taft appointed him chief justice, 1910. White is best known for his "rule of reason" criterion, which was important to his interpretation of the Sherman Antitrust Act, and for his opinion supporting the Adamson Act, which set an eight-hour day for railroad workers, 1916.

WHITE, ELWYN BROOKS, 1899–　, U.S. poet, essayist, and humorist, was born in Mount Vernon, N.Y., and was graduated from Cornell University, 1921. He joined the staff of the *New Yorker* as a contributing editor, and wrote articles for *Harper's* magazine, 1938–43. White's essays, like those of his friend James Thurber, are characterized by their gentle humor and their graceful, distinctly American prose style. Among his works are *The Lady Is Cold* (1929), *Is Sex Necessary?* (with James Thurber, 1929), *One Man's Meat* (1943), *Here Is New York* (1949), *Charlotte's Web* (1952), and *The Second Tree from the Corner* (1954). To a revised edition (1959) of *The Elements of Style* (1918) by William Strunk, Jr., White added an introduction and a new chapter, "An Approach to Style."

WHITE, HENRY, 1850–1927, U.S. diplomat, was born in Baltimore, Md., and educated in the United States and France. He held various diplomatic posts, 1883–1905, then became ambassador to Italy, 1905. He was the senior U.S. representative at the Moroccan Conference of Algeciras, 1906, ambassador to France, 1907–09, chairman of the U.S. delegation to the fourth Pan-American Conference, 1910, and a member of the U.S. Peace Commission, 1918.

WHITE, JOSEPH BLANCO, 1775–1841, British Protestant apologist, was born José Blanco in Seville, Spain, and was ordained a Roman Catholic priest, 1800. He went to England, 1810, became an Anglican priest, 1814, and was later converted to Unitarianism. He became associated with the members of the Oxford Movement, and they learned much about Catholic dogma from him.

WHITE, PATRICK, 1912–　, Australian novelist, was born in London, England. The years of his youth were divided between Australia and England, and he studied at Cambridge, 1932–35. He served with the Royal Air Force during World War II and then settled near Sydney, Australia. His novels are in the tradition of James Joyce and Gertrude Stein. Among his novels are *Happy Valley* (1939), *The Living and the Dead* (1941), *The Aunt's Story* (1948), *The Tree of Man* (1955), *Voss* (1957), *Riders in the Chariot* (1961), and *The Solid Mandala* (1966). White also wrote plays, including *The Ham Funeral* (1947), *The Season at Sarsaparilla* (1961), *A Cheery Soul* (1962), and *Night on Bald Mountain* (1962).

WHITE, PEREGRINE, 1620–1704, the first child born of English parents in New England, was born on the *Mayflower* in a Cape Cod harbor, Nov. 20, 1620. In "consideration of his birth" he received 200 acres of land. He later held civil and military offices.

WHITE, STANFORD, 1853–1906, U.S. architect. He studied in Europe, 1878–79, and became associated with Charles F. McKim and William R. Mead, 1879. White's talent as an architect was chiefly decorative. He had the faculty of adapting European artistic effects to New World conditions; thus the Giralda Tower, Seville, served as a model for that of Madison Square Garden, New York City. Among architectural works with which he was associated are the New York University buildings, Washington Arch, Century and Metropolitan Club buildings, and the Madison Square Presbyterian Church, all in New York City, and the University of Virginia buildings. The building of the Gorham Manufacturing Company, New York City, has been called his best work. He was shot to death on June 25, 1906, by Harry K. Thaw while attending a theatrical performance on the roof of Madison Square Garden.

WHITE, STEWART EDWARD, 1873–1946, U.S. novelist, was born in Grand Rapids, Mich., and was educated at the University of Michigan and at Columbia Law School. His first book was *The Westerners* (1901), an adventure novel originally written for *Munsey's* magazine. It was followed by *The Blazed Trail* (1902), *Conjuror's House* (1903), and *The Silent Places* (1904)—fruits of a sojourn in the Hudson Bay country—and by many action yarns set in Old California. Among the best of his western tales are the trilogy *Story of California* (1927) and the cycle of novels collected as *The Saga of Andy Burnett* (1947).

WHITE, TERENCE HANBURY, 1906–64, English novelist, was born in Bombay, India, and was graduated from Oxford, 1928. Among the best-known of his romantic fantasies are *The Sword and the Stone* (1938), *Once and Future King* (1939), *The Witch in the Wood* (1939), *Mistress Masham's Repose* (1946), *The Scandalmonger* (1952), and *The Master* (1957).

WHITE, THEODORE HAROLD, 1915– , U.S. journalist and author, born in Boston. After graduating from Harvard College in 1938, he went to China, where he became the Far Eastern correspondent of *Time* magazine. He was in China during much of World War II, covering the Chungking government. In 1946 he returned to the United States, where, with Annalee Jacoby, he published *Thunder out of China*, a highly acclaimed account of the turmoil engulfing China at that time. After 1948 White spent much time in Europe as a correspondent for the Overseas News Agency and the *Reporter*. From this period came *Fire in the Ashes* (1953), which dealt with the regeneration of Western Europe after World War II. In 1958 White published a novel, *Mountain Road*, set in China during the last years of the war. *The Making of the President, 1960* (1961) and *The Making of the President, 1964* (1965) were White's next major works. They provided penetrating accounts of the presidential campaigns of 1960 (John F. Kennedy vs. Richard Nixon) and 1964 (Lyndon B. Johnson vs. Barry Goldwater).

WHITE, WILLIAM, 1748–1836, colonial American and U.S. Episcopal bishop, was born in Philadelphia. He was appointed chaplain to the Continental Congress, 1777, and held that position while the Congress met in Philadelphia. In 1787 he was consecrated in London the first bishop of the diocese of Pennsylvania.

WHITE, WILLIAM ALLEN, 1868–1944, U.S. author and journalist, was born in Emporia, Kans., and was educated at the University of Kansas. As owner and editor of the Emporia *Gazette* from 1895, he became one of the most articulate spokesmen for small-town, middle-class America, and was known as the Sage of Emporia. One of his first notable editorials was "What's the Matter with Kansas?" (1896), attacking the Populists; he later supported the Bull Moose party of Theodore Roosevelt. Although he held no public office, he played an important behind-the-scenes role in the state and national politics of the Republican party, and in 1920, 1928, and 1936 he was a member of the National Convention. He joined the Committee to Defend America by Aiding the Allies, 1940, and served briefly as its chairman. He won a Pulitzer prize, 1923, for an editorial on freedom of speech, written after he had been arrested for having expressed sympathy with striking railroad workers. Among his works are volumes of short stories depicting the mild vicissitudes of small-town life in the Middle West, such as *The Real Issue* (1896); *The Court of Boyville* (1899); *Stratagems and Spoils* (1901); and *In Our Town* (1906); *A Certain Rich Man* (1909); *In The Heart of a Fool* (1918); *Woodrow Wilson* (1924); *Calvin Coolidge* (1925); a collection of his editorials, *Forty Years on Main Street* (1937); *A Puritan in Babylon: The Story of Calvin Coolidge* (1938); *The Changing West* (1939); and *Autobiography* (1946, Pulitzer prize).

WHITE BASS, a fresh-water game fish belonging to the family Serranidae. The white bass, *Lepibema chrysops*, has a deep, silver-colored body, a divided dorsal fin, longitudinal stripes above its midline, and a golden hue on its undersides. In length it may reach 18 inches, and its weight ranges from one to two pounds. It inhabits the deep, cold lakes and rivers in the Mississippi Valley and Great Lakes regions.

WHITE FATHERS, members of the Society of Missionaries of Africa (W.F.), known also as the *Patres Albi* (P.A.). The order was founded in 1868 at Algiers by Cardinal Charles-Martial Lavigerie for the purpose of Christianizing the Muslims and pagans of Africa. The White Fathers live "as Arabs among Arabs"; their white habit—consisting of a robe and burnoose, a *chechia* (red fezlike hat), and a rosary worn about the neck instead of the 99 beads of Muhammad worn by Muslims—is an adaptation of Arab dress. Houses of the society outside Africa are used exclusively for training missionaries. There are about 4,000 White Fathers.

WHITEFIELD, GEORGE, 1714–70, English evangelist, early leader of Methodism, was born in Gloucester, came under the influence of John and Charles Wesley at Oxford, and experienced a "new birth," 1735. In 1738 he sailed for North America to join the largely unsuccessful Wesley mission in the colony of Georgia, but he returned to England in the next year, to collect funds for a projected orphanage in Georgia, the support and development of which became one of the great objects of his life. Whitefield made six other visits to America. Since the main body of the clergy denied him the use of their pulpits, he held services in the open air. Going to Scotland, 1741, on the invitation of Ebenezer Erskine (1680–1754), he traveled through the country preaching. A second tour in Scotland, 1742, resulted in a remarkable revival at Cambuslang, Lanarkshire. Early in 1741 a breach occurred between Wesley and Whitefield, the latter holding the Calvinistic doctrine of predestination, and Wesley the Arminian view.

WHITEFISH, any fish of the genus *Coregonus* and allied genera that inhabit the rivers and lakes of North America and are especially abundant and important as food fishes in the Great Lakes region. *C. clupeaformis*, the lake whitefish, occurs in the Great Lakes and their tributaries. It averages about four pounds in weight, and nearly two feet in length. It is shaped much like a salmon, has rather large scales, and is dusky bluish on the back and silvery white on the sides and belly. There is an adipose fin behind the dorsal one, and the tail is deeply forked. It is a powerful swimmer and lives most of the time in deep water, eating crustaceans, mollusks, and insects. It spawns during the fall in deep water.

WHITEFISH BAY, village, SE Wisconsin, in Milwaukee County; on Lake Michigan; 7 miles N of Milwaukee. Whitefish Bay, established, 1892, is located between the villages of Shorewood and Fox Point; all three are residential suburbs of Milwaukee. (For population, see Wisconsin map in Atlas.)

WHITEHALL, town, E New York, in Washington County; at the S end of Lake Champlain and the N terminus of the Champlain Canal; about 65 miles NE of Albany, near the Vermont border. Whitehall has silk mills. The town was founded in 1759 by Maj. Philip Skene of the British army. During the Revolutionary War, this settlement, then called Skenesborough, gave aid to General Burgoyne during his invasion of New York. (For population, see New York map in Atlas.)

WHITEHALL, city, Ohio, in Franklin County; 7 miles E of Columbus, of which it is a residential suburb. Whitehall was a village of less than 5,000 in 1950. In six years, it quadrupled in size and in 1956 was incorporated as a city. It was exemplary of a nationwide trend in large cities to spread population outward. (For population, see Ohio map in Atlas.)

WHITEHALL, borough, SW Pennsylvania, in Allegheny County, a suburb of Pittsburgh. It was created in 1947 by the joining of the townships of Baldwin and Bethel. (For population, see Pennsylvania map in Atlas.)

WHITEHEAD, ALFRED NORTH, 1861–1947, British philosopher and mathematician, born in Ramsgate, Kent. His father was headmaster of a private school and later a clergyman. At the age of 14, Whitehead was sent to the Sherborne School in Dorsetshire, and in 1880 he earned a scholarship to Trinity College, Cambridge, where he remained as a student and then as a fellow until 1910. In 1890 he married Evelyn Wade. They reared three children: North (b. 1891), Jessie (b. 1893), and Eric (b. 1898).

Whitehead's first book, published in 1898, was *A Treatise on Universal Algebra, With Applications*, which dealt mainly with symbolic logic. The book was acclaimed, and Whitehead was shortly elected to the Royal Society. As a teacher he enjoyed wide popularity. With his most famous pupil, Bertrand Russell, he collaborated for ten years on a three volume classic in mathematical logic, *Principia Mathematica*, published between 1910 and 1913. In this work, the two men extended the ideas of the Italian logician, Guiseppe Peano, and attempted to prove that mathematics is a part of logic.

In 1910 Whitehead left Cambridge and in 1911 began to teach at the University of London. Three years later he became professor of applied mathematics at the Imperial College of Science and Technology in Kensington. During this period he wrote *Introduction to Mathematics*, a popular and successful primer. Gradually, Whitehead's interests turned from mathematics to physical theory, and this in turn brought him to problems of perception and the philosophy of science. In 1919 he published *An Enquiry Concerning the Principles of Natural Knowledge*, and in the following year, *The Concept of Nature*, a collection of lectures.

In 1924, Whitehead left England to teach at Harvard as professor of philosophy. He remained there until his retirement in 1937 and continued to live in Cambridge, Mass., until his death.

In 1925, his Lowell Lectures were published as *Science and the Modern World*, a study of the development of modern science, its place and influence in Western culture. He then turned from the philosophy

Alfred North Whitehead

CULVER

of science to the study of cosmology and metaphysics. The climax of his thought appeared in *Process and Reality*, consisting of the Gifford Lectures at the University of Edinburgh (1927–8). Here, Whitehead presented his mature "philosophy of organism." *Adventures of Ideas* (1933) further elaborated his philosophy.

Philosophy. Whitehead is one of the most comprehensive and complex of twentieth-century philosophers. His views developed as his work proceeded from mathematics to the speculative philosophy of *Process and Reality*, which he defines as ". . . the endeavor to frame a coherent, logical, necessary system of general ideas in terms of which every element of our experience can be interpreted." (*Process and Reality*, Part I, Chapter I).

As a speculative philosopher, Whitehead sought an alternative to the "scientific materialism" that he believed to be presupposed by the classical physics of the modern period. "Scientific materialism" is the view that the ultimate constituents of the universe are bits of matter which are senseless, valueless, and purposeless, the motions of which are entirely subject to mechanical laws, and which lack any kind of creativity or spontaneity. Whitehead's philosophy of organism takes events rather than bits of matter as the ultimate constituents of the universe. Each event, no matter how purely physical it may appear to be, is basically creative, and possesses a mental as well as a physical pole.

The key term in Whitehead's philosophy is "process," his name for the flow of *events*, that is, chains and webs of occurrences that make up the whole of reality. A single pulse in the life of a fundamental physical particle is an event. So is the history of a nation. Events are composed of smaller events (smaller in space and time), and these of still smaller ones. At bottom there is the least event, "the limiting type of event, having but one member." This minimal building block, the smallest unit of process, is an *actual occasion*. Complex clusters of actual occasions form *enduring objects*, like electrons, chairs, bodies, and so on. These complex enduring objects maintain their identity while changing, by the persistence of stable, gradually altering patterns inherited and modified from previous events. No physical part of a man's blue eyes remains identical with those of his childhood, but there has been an unbroken continuity of pattern of blue eyes, for all the material replacement in between.

Every event has both a mental and a physical pole. As an evolutionist Whitehead realized that mentality could not evolve from inanimate objects unless in some sense it were already present in inanimate objects. The minimal building blocks, or actual occasions, are "drops of experience, complex and interdependent." (*Process and Reality*).

Events on the mental side *prehend eternal objects* like red, pentagon, humanity, anything that can "be again." Eternal objects are not specific in time or space, as events are. They are possibilities which are actualized only through being prehended by actual events. Unlike Plato's universals, eternal objects are not independently real. Space-time, like eternal objects, is abstracted from concrete process and has no independent reality. Although it comes into being in the context of a past that is given, an actual occasion is self-creating. An actual occasion composes itself as a harmony of eternal objects that have previously been concreted in actual occasions. In creating itself, the actual occasion selects from many possible patterns of harmony which abide in the *Primordial Nature of God*. The completed actual occasion *perishes* and becomes *objectively immortal*. That is, it loses its subjective aspect or *presentational immediacy*, and continues to exist only as it is prehended by other actual occasions. The actual occasion which has thus become objectively immortal takes up its status in the actual world, which the *Consequent Nature of God* constantly strives to persuade toward more complex harmonies and higher creativity. In His latter aspect, God strives to bring about the satisfaction of all actual occasions making up the universe, but He is limited by the creativity of all the other actual occasions. Thus, Whitehead's God is not omnipotent.

NATHANIEL LAWRENCE

BIBLIOG.–Nathaniel Lawrence, *Whitehead's Philosophical Development* (1956); Ivor Leclerc, *Whitehead's Metaphysics* (1958); Victor Lowe, *Understanding Whitehead* (1962).

WHITEHEAD, CHARLES, 1804–62, English author, was born in London. His first book of poems, *The Solitary* (1831), brought him critical recognition. He then wrote the celebrated *Autobiography of Jack Ketch: Lives of an English Highwayman* (1834). He was a friend of Charles Dickens and William M. Thackeray. He moved to Australia in 1857.

WHITEHEAD, ROBERT, 1823–1905, English inventor, was born in Bolton-le-Moors, Lancashire, and became an engineer, working on the Continent 1844–1905. At Fiume he invented the Whitehead torpedo, 1866, a self-propelling cylindrical projectile. His eldest son, John (died 1902), worked with him in improving the weapon.

WHITEHEAD, WILLIAM, 1715–85, English poet laureate, born in Cambridge. Through the influence of the earl of Jersey, to whose son he was tutor, Whitehead was appointed to succeed Colley Cibber as poet laureate in 1745. The poetry he wrote to fulfill the obligations of his post is competent but undistinguished. He also wrote plays.

WHITEHORSE, city, Canada, S Yukon Territory; on the Yukon River and the Alaska Highway; the northern terminus of the White Pass and Yukon Railway from Skagway, Alaska. Whitehorse was made the capital of the Yukon Territory in 1951, replacing Dawson which had been the territorial capital since its establishment in 1898. Whitehorse is the import and export center of the Yukon Territory. It was an important trading center during the Klondike Gold Rush of 1898, and became a tourist center with the completion of the Alaska Highway in 1946. The city was named for the Whitehorse Rapids of the Yukon River. (For population, see Yukon map in Atlas.)

WHITE HOUSE, 1600 Pennsylvania Avenue, Washington, D.C., is the official residence of the President of the United States. It is the oldest public building in the national capital. Among the world's great residences of state it is surpassed by none in simple charm and dignity. Designed during the first administration of George Washington, the White House is an epitome of the history of the Republic and a symbol of the traditions of the nation.

The building was originally called the President's Palace, but during the period of Jeffersonian simplicity was referred to as the President's House. The origin of the name White House is uncertain. It was formerly supposed that the name was applied after the War of 1812 because of the white paint that was used to cover up smoke marks on the reconstructed building; later research revealed, however, that the name had been used informally in 1813 and perhaps before. The house was officially designated the Executive Mansion, 1818, but the popular name White House was more commonly used. At the suggestion of Pres. Theodore Roosevelt, Congress made the name White House official in 1902.

Early History. The White House was designed, 1792, by James Hoban (1762?–1831) who planned it a gentleman's house in the late eighteenth century Renaissance style, to be built at a cost of $400,000—a figure considered exorbitant by many at the time. The subsequent cumulative investment of public money in the building amounted to more than $16 million by 1960. The cornerstone was laid on Oct. 16, 1792, at the place selected by Maj. Charles L'Enfant and Pres. George Washington. The 18-acre site, purchased for $1,212.70 (1960 value was about $20 million), was an eminence facing the Potomac, and about a mile and a half from the eminence selected for the capitol. The building was first occupied late in November, 1800, but it was still far from finished. During the War of 1812 the British captured the capital and destroyed the White House, Aug. 24, 1814. After the war, Hoban superintended the reconstruction, making use of the original sandstone walls and adhering to his original plans. The house was reoccupied by Pres. James Monroe in the fall of 1817, but the work was not completed until 1829. Water was piped into the building from a spring, replacing the old pumps, 1833; water from the city system was introduced in 1853. Gas lighting, installed in 1848, was replaced by electricity during Pres. Benjamin Harrison's administration, 1889–93. Central heating was added in 1853. Bathrooms were introduced during the administration of Rutherford B. Hayes, 1877–81, and the first telephone line was brought into the building at about the same time. During the first Administration of Pres. Franklin D. Roosevelt a swimming pool was added beneath the west terrace.

Additions and Repairs. By 1900 the combination of executive offices and family residence had made living conditions almost intolerable for the members of the president's household. When Pres. Theodore Roosevelt moved his family of growing children into the White House a drastic alteration of the interior seemed imperative. The interior was completely rebuilt, 1902, but the architecture of the original building was reverently preserved. Two wings were added: the Executive Office Building at the end of the west terrace and a building at the end of the east terrace to provide an entrance to the White House for the general public. These wings were enlarged several times, and extensive repairs were made on the main building in 1927, 1935, and 1949–52.

In 1948 it was reported that the White House was in danger of collapse. In 1949 it was closed for occupancy and Congress voted $5.4 million to pay for interior rebuilding and refurbishment—earlier proposals that the White House be replaced having been rejected in the face of public horror at such a prospect; ultimately the renovation cost about $6.5 million. The original design and exterior were retained, but several new features were added, among them an impressive state stairway in the entrance hall to replace the old, half-hidden staircase, and a two-story basement. The hipped roof was eliminated to allow more room on the attic floor. The renovated mansion, completed in 1952, has 77 rooms, 8 more than before repairs began.

General Description. Not including the terraced galleries on the sides, the White House is 170 feet long, 85 feet wide, and 58 feet high. Although it appears as a building of two stories, it has a basement at ground level and an attic concealed by the crowning balustrade. The north front, facing Pennsylvania Avenue, has an impressive colonial portico with four Ionic columns, forming a porte-cochère and a porch. At each side of the portico are symmetrical rows of windows. The south front has a semicircular columned portico with a second-story porch, added by Pres. Harry S. Truman, 1948, that looks out over lawn and gardens to the Presidential Ellipse—a circular recreational area with baseball diamonds, and football and hockey fields. The east gallery extends 215 feet from the main building, while the west gallery reaches out only 165 feet; each is 35 feet wide; they are almost indiscernible since they scarcely rise above the crest of the surrounding ground. The Executive Office Building, connected with the White House by a corridor under the west terrace, is about 140 feet long and 100 feet wide.

The principal rooms on the main floor of the White House are the East Room, the "great hall" used for major state gatherings; the Green Room, used for informal receptions; the Blue Room, used for state receptions; the Red Room, a reception room for smaller dinners; the State Dining Room; the Diplomatic Reception Room; and the Library. The second floor, open only to members of the President's household and guests, can be reached from the east end of the central corridor by means of a wide stone stairway or by an elevator. There are seven bedroom suites; the Monroe Drawing Room; and the Oval Room, or President's Study. The attic floor has 14 rooms, including storerooms and servants' quarters. The American colonial and European Renaissance schools are well harmonized in the furnishings. Beginning in the 1960's, an effort was made by the wives of the presidents to decorate the White House with authentic American art and furniture.

The grounds comprise a fenced and wooded park of 18 acres, divided by the White House into the North and South Grounds. The South Grounds are the president's private gardens. They were formerly open to the public during the annual Easter Monday "egg rolling," but this custom was discontinued in 1949. Over 80 types of trees are on the grounds, many with interesting histories. Official visitors enter the Executive Office Building from West Executive Avenue; on visiting days the public may inspect the main floor of the White House.

BIBLIOG.—Amy L. Jensen, *The White House and Its Thirty-four Families* (1965); J. F. T. and B. M. McConnell, *The White House* (1954); White House Historical Association, *The White House, A Historic Guide* (1966 ed.).

WHITE LEAD, a basic carbonate of lead used as a white pigment and surface coating in paints. White lead, $Pb(OH)_2 \cdot 2PbCO_3$, claims about 3 per cent of all lead manufactured in the United States. Formerly the leading white pigment, white lead has been displaced by titanium dioxide and other substances.

In the older Dutch process, lead disks, or buckles, are placed in earthenware pots stacked over dilute acetic acid and surrounded by decomposing tanbark. Acid vapor and carbon dioxide turn the buckles to basic lead carbonate of fine quality in three to four months. Other processes use cheaper lead and are faster. The Carter process, which uses atomized lead, acetic acid, and carbon dioxide, takes about one week, and the French process, which involves precipitation from a solution of litharge, one to two days. The Sperry process is electrolytic.

White lead is used as a basis for putty, and in ceramic glazes, lubricating greases, and special adhesives. Sublimed white lead is basic lead sulfate, $2PbSO_4 \cdot PbO$, and is an excellent pigment. One of the whitest lead pigments is supersublimed white lead, made from atomized lead and sulfur dioxide. Another pigment is basic white lead silicate, $2PbSiO_3 \cdot Pb(OH)_2$.

WHITEMAN, PAUL, 1891–1967, popular U.S. orchestra leader and promoter, was born in Denver, Colo. At 16 he was playing the violin with the city's symphony orchestra; at 17 he was first violinist. He left Denver a few years later to play with the San Francisco People's Symphony Orchestra and the Minetti String Quartet. During World War I "jass" (later spelled jazz) became the musical rage, and Whiteman soon organized his own jazz orchestra, 1919. Classically trained, he decided that his destiny was, as he put it, to "make a lady out of jazz." On Feb. 12, 1924, he played a jazz concert in Aeolian Hall, New York, for which Victor Herbert wrote a suite of serenades and George Gershwin and Ferde Grofé composed *Rhapsody in Blue*. Even earlier, however, he had dubbed his music "symphonic jazz" and himself the "King of Jazz." Actually his music, whatever it may have been, was never closely related to true jazz. Whiteman continued as an orchestra leader until early in World War II, and then became a radio executive and disc jockey.

WHITE MOUNTAINS, a group of mountains in central New Hampshire and W Maine, a part of the Appalachian System. They contain the highest elevations in New England. The mountains of this group occupy an area of 1,270 square miles, and extend from Squam Lake, in the south, to the Androscoggin and Upper Ammonoosuc Valley in the north. The mountains represent remnants of a former very high plateau. Some peaks tower more than one mile above the surrounding lowlands. The group is divided by

D. JORDAN WILSON—PIX

The United States presidential residence since 1800, when Pres. John Adams moved in, the White House has undergone many changes, reflecting both the changing temperament of the country and the personal tastes of presidents and first ladies. The familiar north portico with its stately pillars graces Pennsylvania Avenue.

Crawford Notch into the Presidential Range on the east and the Franconia Mountains on the west. The eastern portion contains the highest peaks in the group including Mount Washington, 6,288 feet; Mount Madison, 5,363 feet; Mount Adams, 5,805 feet; Mount Jefferson, 5,785 feet; Mount Monroe, 5,390 feet. The highest peak of the Franconia Mountains is Mount Lafayette 5,249 feet.

The White Mountain region is a famous summer-resort area, offering a ruggedness of scenery hardly equaled elsewhere east of the Rocky Mountains. Among the most interesting peaks is Profile Mountain, the rock formations of which compose the "Old Man of the Mountains." Most of the mountain group lies within the White Mountains National Forest. The region's main towns are Conway, Plymouth, Gorham, Berlin, and Lancaster, all in New Hampshire.

WHITE OAK SWAMP, BATTLE OF, an engagement of the Seven Days' Battle of the U.S. Civil War, was fought June 30, 1862, near the Chickahominy River, 20 miles east of Richmond, Va. When its Peninsular Campaign to capture Richmond was stopped only seven miles from the Confederate capital, the Union Army of the Potomac had begun a general retreat toward Chesapeake Bay. Pursuing Confederate forces had been repulsed at Mechanicsville, June 26; Gaines Mill, June 27; and Savage Station, June 29. At White Oak Swamp the Confederates attempted to force a passage at the bridge crossing the swamp in order to turn the Union right (north) flank, and cut off its escape. Part of the Union rear guard held the bridge while part repulsed Confederate attacks at Frayser's Farm, and the main Union force retreated safely to Malvern Hill. See SEVEN DAYS' BATTLE.

WHITE PASS, a routeway through the Coastal Range on the border between SE Alaska and NW British Columbia, elevation 2,888 feet, 14 miles NE of Skagway. The White Pass and Yukon Railway between Skagway and Whitehorse follows this route. In 1897 during the Klondike Gold Rush, White Pass was used as an alternate route to the more difficult Chilkoot Pass to the northwest.

WHITE PERCH, an Atlantic coastal game fish belonging to the bass family *Serranidae*. The white perch, *Morone americana*, is a small fish weighing an average of one pound and measuring about eight inches in length. It is whitish in color with a thin yellow band at its midline. Its divided dorsal fin characterizes the fish as being a bass. The fish is highly adaptable to varied habitats. It appears to flourish equally well in fresh and salt water. Predominantly found along the Atlantic Coast from Nova Scotia to South Carolina, it often invades the fresh inland rivers of New York, Pennsylvania, and Virginia. The white perch spawns in shallow water in the spring from April until June.

WHITE PLAINS, city, SE New York, seat of Westchester County; on the Bronx and Mamaroneck rivers and the New York Central Railroad; about 21 miles NE of New York. Valves, fittings, plumbing and heating materials, wire, cable, concrete pipe, and tile roofing are among the products manufactured. White Plains was first settled in 1683 by emigrants from Connecticut; it was incorporated in 1866, and chartered as a city in 1916. White Plains was named for the abundance of white balsam growing in that section of the state. On July 9, 1776, the Provincial Congress, which had moved to White Plains, ratified the Declaration of Independence. Chatterton Hill, in White Plains, was the scene of the Battle of White Plains (Oct. 28, 1776). Pop. (1960) 50,485.

WHITE PLAINS, BATTLE OF, an engagement of the Revolutionary War, was fought Oct. 28, 1776, in White Plains, N.Y., between a part of the Continental army commanded by Gen. George Washington and a part of the British army commanded by Sir William Howe. Driven from Long Island and Manhattan Island by the numerically superior Brit-

ish, Washington had retreated to White Plains, October 23. Howe pursued him, and with a force of more than 4,000 succeeded in dislodging 1,600 Continentals from their position at White Plains. The British lost 230 men, the Americans about 130. During the night of October 31, Washington retired to a strong position nearby, and Howe returned the bulk of his force to New York City. Subsequently, however, Washington abandoned southern New York, crossed his small army to the west side of the Hudson River, and established headquarters at Hackensack, N.J.

WHITE RIVER, NW Arkansas and SW Missouri, rises in the Ozark Plateau in Arkansas and flows NE into Missouri, then E and SE across Arkansas to empty into the Mississippi River in SE Arkansas. The Black River is the leading tributary. Bull Shoals Reservoir is on its upper course. The length of the river is about 690 miles.

WHITE RUSSIA. See BYELORUSSIAN SOVIET SOCIALIST REPUBLIC.

WHITE SANDS NATIONAL MONUMENT, S New Mexico, in Otero and Dona Ana counties, in the Tularosa Valley, about 12 miles SW of Alamogordo and 155 miles S of Albuquerque. Established in 1933, the park encloses 140,247.04 acres of white gypsum sands and features shifting dunes, which vary in height from 10 to 60 feet. Vegetation is scanty and unique in adaptation to some regions of nitrogen-free soil; animal life is limited to small rodents and insects of protective white or light coloring. The White Sands Proving Ground, created by the federal government in 1945 for Army and Navy testing of guided missiles, is concentrated southwest of the monument.

WHITESBURG, city, SE Kentucky, seat of Letcher County, in the Cumberland Mountains; on the Louisville and Nashville Railroad and U.S. highway 119; 112 miles SE of Lexington. Whitesburg is a mining center for the coal, clay, sand, and gravel deposits in the vicinity. Beverages and timber products are processed. The city was settled in 1840, and incorporated in 1872. Pop. (1960) 1,774.

WHITE SEA, a large, almost triangular gulf extending SW from the Arctic Ocean; bounded by Arkhangelsk Region on the SE, the Karelian Autonomous Soviet Socialist Republic on the W, and the Murmansk Region on the N. The outer portion, between the Kanin and Kola peninsulas, is 150 by 75 miles; the inner portion, which includes the bays of Kandalakshskaya, Onezhskaya, and Dvinskaya, is 150 by 250 miles; and the two portions are connected by a strait 100 miles long and 35 miles wide. The total length from northwest to southeast is 300 miles; area is about 36,500 square miles. The Dvina, Onega, and Mezen are the principal rivers which flow into the White Sea. The sea is frozen from October to May, but icebreakers keep the main port, Arkhangelsk, ice-free. The main products shipped are grain and lumber. The sea is connected with the Baltic Sea and the interior river systems by Lake Onega and the Baltic–White Sea Canal, which is open to small vessels.

WHITE SULPHUR SPRINGS, city, SE West Virginia, in Greenbrier County; on the Chesapeake and Ohio Railway and U.S. highways 60 and 219; about 80 miles SE of Charleston and 4 miles from the Virginia boundary. The city is a resort center in which the leading attractions are mountain scenery and medicinal springs. The resort, one of the most luxurious in the United States, has golf courses and extensive recreational features. The area was settled in about 1750, and by the 1830's was a noted resort. Old White, a noted hotel of that period, was used as a hospital during the Civil War. Pop. (1960) 2,676.

WHITETHROAT, one of the common sparrows, also known as the white-throated sparrow, and Peabody bird. The whitethroat, *Zonotrichia albicollis*, can be indentified by its varied colors. Its head is widely striped with black and white. Its brown body is set off with a white throat, white abdomen, and grayish breast. A yellow patch occurs anterior to the eye. The bird usually builds its nest on or near the ground. It breeds in eastern North America from Canada southward to Massachusetts and westward to Montana. It winters in southern Texas and Florida.

LYNWOOD M. CHACE
The Whitethroat, a Sparrow.

WHITEVILLE, town, SE North Carolina; seat of Columbus County; on the Atlantic Coast Line Railroad and U.S. highways 74, 76, and 701; 14 miles NE of the South Carolina border, and 95 miles S of Raleigh. Whiteville is a trade and processing center for an area in which tobacco and corn are grown. Textiles, wood products, and fertilizer are manufactured. Pop. (1960) 4,683.

WHITEWATER, city, SE Wisconsin, in Walworth County; on Whitewater Creek, the Milwaukee Railroad, and U.S. highway 12; about 45 miles WSW of Milwaukee, in a region in which vegetable farming and dairying are leading activities. Hardware specialties, farm equipment, and fences are the principal manufactured products. The city grew up around a mill built there in 1839. Whitewater is the site of a state teachers college. Pop. (1960) 6,380.

WHITGIFT, JOHN, 1530?–1604, English prelate, was born in Great Grimsby, Lincolnshire. He became Lady Margaret professor of divinity, 1563; master of Pembroke College, Cambridge; a queen's chaplain; regius professor of divinity, and master of Trinity, 1567; dean of Lincoln, 1571; bishop of Worcester, 1577; archbishop of Canterbury, 1583; and a privy councilor, 1586. He enjoyed the favor of Queen Elizabeth I, who upheld him in the severity of his policy toward the Puritans and Roman Catholics.

WHITING, WILLIAM FAIRFIELD, 1864–1936, U.S. cabinet member and industrialist, was born in Holyoke, Mass. He was president of a large paper-manufacturing firm in Holyoke and, in 1928, succeeded Herbert Hoover as U.S. secretary of commerce in Pres. Calvin Coolidge's cabinet.

WHITING, city, NW Indiana, in Lake County; on Lake Michigan, the Baltimore and Ohio, the Baltimore and Ohio Chicago Terminal, the Chicago Short Line, the Elgin, Joliet and Eastern, the Indiana Harbor Belt, the New York Central, and the Pennsylvania railroads, and U.S. highways 12 and 20; 17 miles SE of Chicago, of which it is an industrial suburb. The city formed as the result of the building of oil-refining plants there in 1889. In addition to oil products, chemicals, metals, and roofing materials are manufactured. Pop. (1960) 8,137.

WHITLEY CITY, town, S Kentucky, seat of McCreary County; on U.S. highway 27 and the Southern Railway; 90 miles S of Lexington, and 9 miles N of the Tennessee border. Whitley City is a coal-mining center in the Cumberland Mountains. Cumberland Falls State Park is near the town. Pop. (1960) 1,034.

WHITLOCK, BRAND, 1869–1934, U.S. author and diplomat, was born in Urbana, Ohio. He worked as a reporter and correspondent for the Toledo *Blade,* 1887–90, and the Chicago *Herald,* 1890–93, was admitted to the bar, clerked in the office of the Illinois secretary of state 1893–97, practiced law in Toledo, and was mayor of Toledo, 1905–13, declining a fifth term to become U.S. minister to Belgium. As a writer Whitlock was best known for his realistic novels of crime and machine politics, such as *The Thirteenth District* (1902), *The Turn of the Balance* (1907), and *Big Matt* (1928). Among his other works are an autobiography, *Forty Years of It* (1914), *Belgium: A Personal Record* (1919), *La Fayette* (1929), and *The Stranger on the Island* (1933).

WHITMAN, MARCUS, 1802–47, U.S. missionary and pioneer responsible for creating the interest that led to early settlement of the Pacific Northwest, was born in Rushville, N.Y. He was graduated from the Berkshire Medical Institute, Pittsfield, Mass., and practiced medicine in Canada and in Wheeler, N.Y. In 1834 he offered himself to the American Board of Commissioners for Foreign Missions, and was assigned to the Oregon Territory. He, his wife, and three other missionaries traveled to the West, taking with them the first wagon ever to cross the Rocky Mountains. They reached Fort Walla Walla, an English trading post, Sept. 1, 1836, and soon established a mission about 25 miles from the fort. Whitman paid a visit to Washington, D.C., 1843, and, according to some historians, interviewed Pres. John Tyler and other government officials in an effort to prevent the cession to England of the Oregon claim (see NORTHWEST BOUNDARY DISPUTE). Other scholars believe that the visit was made in order to dissuade the Board of Commissioners from abolishing his mission. On Nov. 29, 1847, his mission was attacked by Cayuse Indians, and Whitman, his wife, and 12 others were killed; the rest were taken prisoner.

WHITMAN, SARAH HELEN POWER, 1803–78, U.S. poetess, was born Sarah Helen Power in Providence, R.I. In 1828 she married John W. Whitman, a lawyer of Boston. After his death, 1838, she returned to Providence and engaged in literary pursuits. She entered into a conditional engagement with Edgar Allan Poe, 1848, and after his death she published a work defending his character: *Edgar Poe and His Critics* (1860). Her collected poems were published in 1879.

WHITMAN, WALT, 1819–92, U.S. poet known for such unforgettable poems as *Pioneers O Pioneers, Drumbeats,* and *Come Lovely and Soothing Death,* was born

CHICAGO HIST. SOC.
Walt Whitman

Walter Whitman in Paumanok (now West Hills), Long Island, N.Y. Many of the facts of his ancestry and much of his own life remain obscured by legends, mostly of Whitman's own making. Thus the father, a carpenter of small means, had come from English stock, but the family had not, as the poet later claimed, been in the New World from the days of the Pilgrim Fathers. The mother, Louisa van Velsor, of Dutch and Welsh extraction, was the one great and enduring power over the son's soul, and he was later to write such sentences as "The best of every man is his mother"—a striking contradiction to his otherwise individualistic teachings. His greatest work, *Leaves of Grass* (seven distinctly different editions in Whitman's lifetime: 1855, 1856, 1860, 1867, 1871, 1881, 1891)—significantly not called blooms or fruits, but leaves—Whitman described as the activated flowering of his mother's temperament. With this mother-worship was coupled a definite hostility toward the father. Beyond anyone else, however, Whitman loved himself. There is not the slightest evidence that he ever loved, or even associated intimately with a woman, although a year before his death he suddenly and irrelevantly claimed to have had seven illegitimate children; yet in the Calamus poems of the 1860 edition of *Leaves of Grass,* later suppressed, he had demanded in no uncertain terms that the physical love between males should be recognized as *the* normal thing. See CARPENTER, EDWARD.

Of his childhood, Whitman remembered having once heard the Quaker preacher Elias Hicks; from this he deduced his alleged spiritual heritage from Quakerism. In May, 1823, the family moved to Brooklyn. The very next year a hero of the Revolu-

Walt Whitman is pictured as he looked in 1855, when the first edition of *Leaves of Grass* was published. In the background are depicted Brooklyn in the 1850's, when he edited the *Freeman*, and Jamaica, one of the Long Island towns in which he taught school.

tion, Lafayette, came through town and, in passing, is said to have kissed the young Whitman; in telling this story later, Whitman asserted that he had thus undergone a spiritual baptism as the singer of American liberty. Genuine poet that he was, Whitman may well be believed that the waves of the ocean taught him "always to see beyond the things on hand as the ocean always points beyond the waves of the moment."

Three Main Periods are discernible in Whitman's life. During the first, up to about 1850, he developed as a journeyman of letters—a man whose livelihood depended upon the skill with which he manipulated the written word. After 1850 and into the 1870's, however, he lived the life of the poet who saw himself as the Bard of America, and was so viewed by some, at least, of his contemporaries. During the third phase of his life, from 1873, he lived in retrospect, cultivating the legend of his ancestry and of his own past life, and ultimately building, in Camden, N.J., a granite tomb for himself, designed after a sketch of William Blake and fit for a hero.

The First Phase of Whitman's Life. His adolescence was trivial and hard. After a few years of schooling, he went to work at the age of 11, began learning the printing trade at 13, and by his late teens had already done a considerable amount of writing for various newspapers, and had taught school in seven different towns on Long Island. His was a rather bohemian existence, and when at 19 he boldly founded a magazine, *The Long Islander*, its publication was so irregular that it soon expired. His first book, *Franklin Evans; or The Inebriate* (1842), a sentimental prohibitionist novel, paid him well, and Whitman was encouraged in the idea of making writing his profession. A year later, in an antislavery text, he used for the first time the *vers libre*, the free rhythm, for which most of his later work was to be known. His free versification was later glorified as an emancipation from "feudal poetry"; at the time, however, it was chosen because it was easy (see FREE VERSE; PROSODY). Apart from this technical feature, nothing of the Whitman who was to be called the Bard of America and The Good Gray Poet was evident in his early articles and verses. His own way of life as the easy comrade of the "Open Road" was not evinced in these texts: he had not yet begun to live it. Indeed, it took a road block to develop in Whitman the admirable singleness of purpose that led him to mold his life uniquely: from 1846 he had been editor of the Brooklyn *Eagle*, but antislavery views such as Whitman's were unpopular in New York, and he was fired, 1848.

Second Phase of Whitman's Life. He now decided to travel. That he was in a mental and spiritual turmoil may be inferred from his choice of destination: the city of New Orleans, in the heart of the slave country. He later spoke of having done some literary work there (as a newspaper writer), and of a mysterious love affair, but he cannot have worked for more than two months in New Orleans, and in terms of his later development the more fruitful part of the trip was his return journey to New York by way of Wisconsin's new pioneer settlements and Niagara Falls. For now he saw his country, "America the beautiful," for the first time.

The journey resulted in a real change: the earning of his livelihood and his future as a poet parted company. While earning bread and butter by working with his father helping build cheap houses in Brooklyn, the future poet joined the literary clique who met at Pfaff's Beer Cellar on Broadway, and read voraciously in the models whose work he was sure to surpass: Homer, the Bible, Shakespeare, Heine, Scott, and Ossian, and the up-to-date French literature of social reform and social revolution. In one such French book, George Sand's *Duchess of Rudolfstadt*, Whitman found the "singer of democracy" eloquently described and predicted. It is not known whether this prescription—which he tried so hard to conceal that it was not discovered for decades after his death—determined his subsequent development, or if he already had decided on his new course before stumbling on the French inspiration. What can be said with certainty is that after 1850 he ceased to be the journeyman of letters. From 1850 until 1873, he was the self-styled Bard of America.

The author of the *Leaves of Grass*, who personally set the type of the first edition of about 800 copies, 1855, sang of himself as the representative of America; and his "Song of Myself" is the first poem that comes to mind when one wishes to envisage the poet's new note: "Myself I sing." The tone was too new to be listened to by many in America, but the Sage of Concord, Ralph Waldo Emerson, recognized Whitman's discipleship, and wrote a fateful letter without which Whitman might never have become known. Part of it was printed in the second, enlarged edition of *Leaves of Grass* (1856). "I greet you at the beginning of a great career," Emerson wrote. "I find it [*Leaves of Grass*] the most extraordinary piece of wit and wisdom that America has yet produced. I find incomparable things, said incomparably well, as they must be." Emerson went on to praise the book as a compound of the Hindu Bhagavadgita and the New York *Herald*. In a letter to a friend he said that "Americans who are abroad, can now return: unto us a man is born." Americanism was the magic of these poems to such a degree that foreigners extolled it before the people back home took much notice; as someone said, "it was unnecessary to be so American in America." Many Europeans, however, anxious to throw off their romantic and feudal sentimentalities, were obliged to make a clear-cut decision between a volume on their own poet Nikolaus Lenau, *Tired of America* (1855) by Ferdinand Kürnberger, and the *Leaves of Grass*.

The first country to decide in favor of Whitman was England. Whitman's "These States conceal an enormous beauty, which native bards, not rhymers manipulating syllables and emotions imported from Europe, should justify by their songs, tallying themselves to the immensity of the continent, to the fecundity of its people, to the appetite of a proud race fluent and free," was echoed when W. M. Rossetti brought him before the British, 1868; two years later Anne Gilchrist came forward for the women. On the Continent itself the Socialist workers took up Whitman's songs as songs of their own liberation: "Comrades, unite and liberate yourself of everything that hinders the human spirit," Whitman cried. Willingly did they admire "Not a dilettante democrat, [but] a man who adores streets, loves docks, loves to talk with free men, loves to be called by his given name and does not care that any one calls him Mister." They could appreciate the fact that he "would quit no matter what time a party of elegant people to find the people who love noise, vagrants, to receive their caresses and their welcome, listen to their rows, their oaths, their ribaldry, their loquacity, their laughing, their replies—and knows perfectly how to preserve his personality among them and those of his kind."

Before these new sounds could make headway in the still-colonial soil of the United States, the spiritual desert of the Civil War decade had to be crossed. This conflict took all intellectual America by surprise. Whitman, too, had still actually to live belatedly the kind of life that would authorize him to sing his song of the common man. The common man, after all, was no bohemian loafer, especially in wartime. While Whitman did not enlist, his brother George did, and late in 1862 lingered wounded in a hospital. News of this set the poet moving: and after visiting with his brother and other wounded in a field hospital in Virginia, he went on to Washington and there, most of the time until 1873, held jobs in various departments of the government. He was fired from one of them, however, for having written "an immoral book,"—the 1860 edition of *Leaves of Grass*—whereupon William Douglas O'Connor denounced Interior Secretary James Harlan in a pamphlet, *The Good Gray Poet: A Vindication* (1866). Apart from all this, Whitman's heart was with the wounded and suffering youngsters in the hospitals, and he went to them often—entertaining, caressing, assisting them; in telling of it later, promoting his own legend, he claimed to have nursed 80,000 or more patients.

Whitman suffered a serious illness in 1864; and a paralytic stroke, 1873, made him look 20 years older than his actual age, and forced him to leave his government clerkship and to go to his brother's house in Camden. But he had already achieved the task of translating the *Leaves of Grass* message into prose in his *Democratic Vistas* (1871). Emerson, by this time, was repelled by Whitman's coarse catalogue style, and Whitman, for his part, bluntly denied any debt to Emerson; in this very work, however, he used Emerson's essay form, just as Friedrich Nietzsche was doing in Europe (see EMERSON, RALPH WALDO, *Incoherence Made a Virtue*). In restating his egalitarian creed, Whitman now made room, in hours of peril, for the poet-prophet—that is, for the Bard himself—who alone would retain the right to have personality while others would be absorbed into the solidarity of the mass of men. For Whitman, Solidarity and Personality were to be the eternal dual of the social order.

Third Phase of Whitman's Life. In his own physical breakdown, Whitman shared something of the death of his mother; it was like a double death. The remaining decades were lived in retrospect. The letters to his mother were published as a part of *Specimen Days and Collect* (1882). He remained most of the time in his brother's house, but partial recoveries of his health enabled him to travel, 1879 and 1880. A trickle of visitors, most of them from England but other s from elsewhere in the United States, entertained the cripple. Again, as in 1848, seeming misfortune helped him, for when the Society for the Suppression of Vice attacked his verses as immoral, sales soared; a house could be bought, 1884, and some earthly riches collected, so that his visiting benefactors were amazed. In his last years he wrote some serene poems about death and continued his never-ending revisions of *Leaves of Grass*, producing the so called Deathbed Edition of 1891. Publication of a 13-volume definitive edition of Whitman's complete works was begun early in the 1960's with volume one of his *Letters* (Edit. by Edwin H. Miller, 1961). To be inclued in the project was the first variorum edition of *Leaves of Grass*, edited by Sculley Bradley and Harold W. Blodgett, and to include the variations in the extant manuscript sources, as well as those in published editions. See AMERICAN LITERATURE, *Transcendentalism*.   EUGEN ROSENSTOCK-HUESSY

BIBLIOG.—Gay W. Allen, *Solitary Singer: A Critical Biography of Walt Whitman* (1959); Roger Asselineau, *Evolution of Walt Whitman*, 2 vols. (1960); Clara Barrus, *Whitman and Burroughs, Comrades* (1931); William E. Barton, *Abraham Lincoln and Walt Whitman* (1928); Joseph Beaver, *Walt Whitman—Poet of Science* (1951); Arthur E. Briggs, *Walt Whitman, Thinker and Artist* (1952); Van Wyck Brooks, *Times of Melville and Whitman* (Everyman's Lib., New Am. ed.) (1953); Henry S. Canby, *Walt Whitman, an American: A Study in Biography* (1943); Richard V. Chase, *Walt Whitman Reconsidered* (1955); Leadie Mae Clark, *Walt Whitman's Concept of the Common Man* (1955); Babette Deutsch, *Walt Whitman, Builder for America* (1941); Robert D. Faner, *Walt Whitman & Opera* (1951); Hugh I'A. Fausset, *Walt Whitman: Poet of Democracy* (1942); Florence B. Freedman, ed., *Walt Whitman Look at the Schools* (1950); Emory Holloway, *Free and Lonesome Heart: The Secret of Walt Whitman* (1960); Haniel Long, *Walt Whitman and the Springs of Courage* (1938); Leo Marx, *The Americanness of Walt Whitman* (1960); Edgar Lee Masters, *Whitman* (1937); Sydney Musgrove, *T. S. Eliot and Walt Whitman* (1953); Jerome Nathanson, *Forerunners of Freedom: The Re-creation of the American Spirit* (1941); Nathan Resnick, *Walt Whitman and the Authorship of the Good Gray Poet* (1948); Frederik Schyberg, *Walt Whitman* (1951); Horace Traubel, *With Walt Whitman in Camden*, 4 vols. (1908–1959); Perry D. Westbrook, *Greatness of Man: An Essay on Dostoyevsky and Whitman* (1961); Charles B. Willard, *Whitman's American Fame* (Studies, vol. 12: Americana Ser. no. 3) (1950); Frances Winwar, *American Giant: Walt Whitman and His Times* (1941).

WHITMAN, town, SE Massachusetts, in Plymouth County, on the New Haven Railroad; about 15 miles SSE of Boston. It is located in a poultry-raising district. The manufacturing of shoes is the leading industry. The area was settled about 1670; in 1875 the town was separated from Abington and East Bridgewater and was known as South Abington until 1886, when the present name was assumed. Pop. (1960) 10,485.

WHITMAN COLLEGE, a private, nonsectarian, coeducational college of liberal arts located at Walla Walla, Wash. The school was established in 1859, and offered its first college-level instruction in 1882. Whitman sponsors co-operative study programs in engineering with Columbia University and California Institute of Technology, and in medical technology with St. Luke's School of Medical Technology, Spokane, Wash., and the School of Medical Technology at the Children's Orthopedic Hospital, Seattle, Wash. The college library contains the Eells collection of materials on the history of the Northwest. The *Whitman Alumnus* is published four times a year. See COLLEGES AND UNIVERSITIES.

WHITMAN NATIONAL MONUMENT, SE Washington; on the Walla Walla River and U.S. highway 410; near Walla Walla. The monument commemorates a landmark on the Oregon Trail where, in 1836, Marcus and Narissa Whitman established the Waiilatpu Mission for religious work among the Indians. In 1847, the Whitmans and other white settlers were massacred by the Indians. The 96-acre monument was established in 1936.

WHITNEY, ELI, 1765–1825, U.S. inventor, was born in Westboro, Mass., and worked his way through Yale, from which he was graduated in 1792. Going to Georgia as a teacher, he found a generous patron in Gen. Nathanael Greene's widow, on whose estate he resided, and studied law. His patron and a group of cotton planters suggested that he devise a machine that would separate the seeds from short strand cotton more quickly than this could be done by hand, and thus make green seed cotton a profitable crop. He obligingly invented the cotton gin, which increased production two hundredfold, made the South rich, and roused a storm of unprincipled greed in its beneficiaries. His shop was rifled, and the machinery stolen and pirated. Two states confiscated the process outright, on the pretexts that it was not new, was injurious, and was so important that no one should have a monopoly on it; one gave him five years' royalties; another allowed $50,000, which was eaten up in lawsuits to collect it; and all forced Congress to refuse patent renewal. In despair Whitney relinquished a partnership to manufacture the gin in New Haven, turned to inventions in firearms, and was the first to make interchangeable parts. Government contracts beginning in 1798 enabled him to found a successful business at Whit-

CHICAGO HIST. SOC.
Eli Whitney

neyville that took advantage of his interchangeable parts idea and of division of labor.

WHITNEY, GERTRUDE VANDERBILT, 1877?–1942, U.S. sculptor, was born Gertrude Vanderbilt, the daughter of Cornelius Vanderbilt, in New York City. She studied under James Fraser, at the Art Students' League, and in Paris. She married Harry Payne Whitney, 1896. Her works include the Aztec Fountain (1910) and the Titanic Memorial (1914), Washington, D.C.; the Peter Stuyvesant Memorial (1936), New York, and the Columbus Memorial, Palos, Spain. She founded the Whitney Museum of American Art, 1931, which was consolidated with the Metropolitan Museum of Art, 1943.

WHITNEY, JOSIAH DWIGHT, 1819–96, U.S. geologist for whom Mount Whitney was named, brother of the philologist William D. Whitney, was born in Northampton, Mass., was graduated from Yale College, 1839, and studied in Paris, Berlin, and Giessen, 1842–47. In Iowa, Whitney was state chemist and a professor at the state university, 1855–58, then became the first state geologist of California, 1860, and conducted an extensive geological and topographical survey of that state and of the Rocky Mountains, 1860–74. From 1874 he taught geology at Harvard University.

WHITNEY, WILLIAM COLLINS, 1841–1904, U.S. financier and public official, was born in Conway, Mass. He was graduated from Yale, 1863, and from the Harvard law school, 1864, and was admitted to the New York bar, 1865. He took a prominent part in the movement against the Tweed Ring, and was corporation counsel of New York City, 1875–82. He was secretary of the Navy, 1885–89, and helped secure Grover Cleveland's nomination in 1892.

WHITNEY, MOUNT, the highest peak in the United States, outside of Alaska, is situated in the Sierra Nevada, California, in Tulare and Inyo counties, about 70 miles E of Fresno. Its height is 14,495 feet. The mountain was named for Prof. Josiah Dwight Whitney, head of the California Geological Survey, which first measured the height in 1864. Its summit, a challenge to mountain climbers, is a nearly level snow field. The peak was first scaled, 1873, by a three-man team of climbers.

WHITSUNDAY. See PENTECOST.

WHITTIER, JOHN GREENLEAF, 1807–92, U.S. poet, newspaper editor, and antislavery agitator, was born near Haverhill, Mass., in the farmhouse built by his ancestor Thomas Whittier, who had come to New England from Wiltshire, 1638. The Whittiers were plain Yankee farmers little different from their Merrimack Valley neighbors, except that for several generations the Whittiers had been professed Quakers. The children of John and Abigail Hussey Whittier were reared to a life of hard physical labor and stern frugality, mitigated only by cheerfulness and mutual affection. Young Greenleaf, as he was called, received little education until he was able to earn a couple of terms at Haverhill Academy by binding shoes. Earlier, however, he had been an eager reader of the few

books that came into his possession, including notably a volume of Robert Burns's poems.

A sample of his rhyming, sent to the country paper by his sister, brought young Whittier to the attention of the hardly less youthful editor, William Lloyd Garrison, who interested himself in his contributor's education and eventually helped him to secure the editorship of the *American Manufacturer* in Boston, the first of several such positions that Whittier successfully filled between 1829 and 1832. Meanwhile he was producing a large amount of fluent rhetorical verse that gained him a local reputation as a newspaper poet of merit, but no prospect of a livelihood. Several publications of this period, such as *Legends of New England* (1831), the poet regretted in later life. In addition to ill health and literary discouragement, Whittier suffered at least one, and perhaps more, disappointment in love. He was never married.

Crusading Abolitionist. Early in the 1830's he turned decisively from poetry to the service of the un-

CHICAGO HIST. SOC.
John Greenleaf Whittier

popular antislavery cause. After announcing his position in the pamphlet *Justice and Expediency* (1833), he attended the organization meeting of the Antislavery Society in Philadelphia, and was a signer of its declaration of principles. For the next 20 years and more he devoted his time and energy to promoting Abolitionist gospel, proving himself as a skillful politician and lobbyist, a shrewd arguer both in print and on the platform, and a vigorous editor of crusading papers, notably of the *Pennsylvania Freeman*, 1838–40.

He was hardly daunted when a proslavery mob burned, 1838, the new Pennsylvania Hall where his office was situated. Ultimately Whittier's most effective contribution to antislavery propaganda consisted of poems that bluntly rebuked the general tendency to condone the national crime of chattel slavery. In addition to the collection called *Voices of Freedom* (1846), he composed verse editorials on the progress of abolitionism down to the Civil War. Most famous of these political poems was his withering denunciation of Daniel Webster in the restrained invective poem *Ichabod.*

The Rustic Balladist. In 1842 Whittier's frail health forced him to retire to the home that he shared with his mother and sister at Amesbury, Mass. He turned increasingly to his early preoccupation with local scenes and the folklore, which he now embodied in some of his best known ballads and idyls, such as *Skipper Ireson's Ride, Maud Muller, The Barefoot Boy,* and *Telling the Bees.* His *Leaves from Margaret Smith's Journal* (1849), is a charming prose narrative of early colonial days. Much of his later literary work appeared in the *Atlantic Monthly.* During the Civil War, out of which Whittier expected nothing good except emancipation of the slaves, he wrote the stirring lines of *Barbara Frietchie* as a tribute to a legendary instance of patriotism. But the high moment for him came with the passage of the constitutional amendment forbidding slavery, commemorated in his *Laus Deo.*

For nearly 30 years after the war, Whittier enjoyed a long Indian summer of life and produced much of his maturest work. The longest and best of his Yankee pastorals, *Snow-Bound* (1866), consists of detailed and tender reminiscences of his boyhood on an isolated farm. It was matched by the warmer idyl of German immigration, *The Pennsylvania Pilgrim* (1872), a sympathetic record of a nearly realized Utopia. During his last decades Whittier wrote many of the searching personal and religious lyrics that testify to his touching reliance on the Eternal Goodness. After a brief period of illness he died in his 85th

The renowned poet John Green-leaf Whittier is portrayed at left as he appeared in the early 1850's. In center panel appears a scene from his long pastoral, *Snowbound*. At right is Whittier's birthplace, located at East Haverhill, Mass.

year, while on a visit to friends in Hampton Falls, N.H.

In the *Proem* written for a new edition of his poems (1847), Whittier minimized his literary powers, but claimed that his works breathed an ardor for human freedom, for tolerance, and for social justice that needed no apology. The most homespun of the New England poets of his day, he was respected and be-loved for the high integrity of his character and the sincerity of his religious fervor—qualities beyond the reach of literary skill.   GEORGE FRISBIE WHICHER

BIBLIOG.–George W. Arms, *Fields Were Green* (1953); Whitman Bennett, *Whittier, Bard of Freedom* (1941); Thomas W. Higginson, *John Greenleaf Whittier: His Personal Qualities* (1924); Elizabeth L. Howell, *Elizabeth Lloyd and the Whittiers* (1939); William S. Kennedy, *John G. Whittier: The Poet of Freedom* (American Reformer Ser., vol. 9) (1892); Samuel T. Pickard, *Life and Letters of John Greenleaf Whittier*, 2 vols. (1904), *Whittier Land: A Handbook of North Essex* (1956); John A. Pollard, *John Greenleaf Whittier, Friend of Man* (1949); Arthur Rowntree, *Whittier: Crusader and Prophet* (1946); Fredrika S. Smith, *John Greenleaf Whittier, Friend and Defender of Freedom* (1948).

WHITTIER, city, S California, in Los Angeles County; on the Pacific Electric and the Union Pacific railroads; 13 miles SE of Los Angeles, in an area of fruit and dairy farms, and oil and gas wells. The main economic activities are the manufacturing of oil-well tools, welding rods, steel-alloy products, metal polish, gas and oil furnaces, spray chemicals, and tile. Pack-ing houses handle citrus fruits, avocados, mushrooms, and walnuts. Whittier, primarily a residential suburb of Los Angeles, was founded by Quakers, 1887, and was named for John Greenleaf Whittier; it was in-corporated as a city in 1898. A state school for delinquent boys and Whittier College (1901) are located there. Pop. (1960) 33,663.

WHITTIER COLLEGE. See COLLEGES AND UNI-VERSITIES.

WHITTINGTON, RICHARD, 1358?–1423, Eng-lish merchant, was the son of a Gloucestershire knight. Of his early life nothing is known, but by 1380 he was a substantial city mercer who had lent large sums of money to Richard II, Henry IV, and Henry V. He was lord mayor, 1397, 1406, and 1419, and was member of Parliament for London, 1416. His bene-factions aided St. Bartholomew's Hospital, Greyfriars Library, and the Guildhall. He is the hero of the folkloric romance of Dick Whittington and His Cat.

WHITTLE, SIR FRANK, 1907–   , English aero-nautical inventor, was born in Coventry, entered the Royal Air Force at the age of 16, and studied at the Royal Air Force College, the Central Flying School, and the R.A.F. School of Aeronautical Engineering. He worked with Power Jets Limited to perfect a gas engine that uses jet propulsion, 1937–46, and in 1941 the first flights with the Whittle engine in a jet-pro-pelled airplane were made. He became technical adviser on engine design and production to the ministry of supply, 1946, and was made temporary air commodore. He was knighted in 1948. He was a technical adviser for British Overseas Airways Cor-poration, 1948–52.

WHITTLESEY, WILLIAM, died 1374, English prelate, studied at Oxford. Whittlesey (or Wittlesey)

was made Archdeacon of Huntingdon, 1337, and Bishop of Rochester, 1360. As Archbishop of Canter-bury, 1368–74, he proved ineffective in dealing with the state-church controversy during the reign of Edward III.

WHITWORTH, SIR JOSEPH, 1803–87, English engineer and philanthropist, was born in Stockport. While working in London, 1825–33, he discovered a method of constructing a truly plane surface. He set up as a toolmaker in Manchester, 1833, and gradually developed his system of standard measures and gauges; the present screw gauge of Great Britain is known by his name. During the Crimean War, 1854, he began to make experiments with rifles, and later with cannon, and devised a method of obtaining sound castings from compressed steel. He was elected to the Royal Society, 1857, and was created a baronet, 1869. Whitworth endowed 30 scholarships in me-chanics, and at his death left over $3 million to education and charity.

WHOLESALING, a stage of the marketing process covering the transfer of goods from producers to re-tailers. A wholesaler is the first intermediary between producer and consumer; the second intermediary is the dealer or retailer. Another term for wholesaler is jobber, although there are certain distinctions between the two.

There are different types of wholesalers, and each type was originated to serve the complex economics of modern civilized life. A general wholesaler is one who buys and assembles merchandise from wide areas and sells it in appropriate lots to dealers. A specialty wholesaler, unlike the general wholesaler, handles only a limited variety of merchandise. The catalogue wholesaler is a merchandiser who sells from a catalogue, without recourse to salesmen or dealers; some catalogue wholesalers sell only to other whole-salers. A co-operative wholesaler merchandises only to retail co-operatives.

The wholesaler and jobber are differentiated inas-much as sometimes a jobber is merely a broker deal-ing in large lots, but not handling it through his own warehouse, or taking actual ownership of the goods. A wholesaler has a greater overhead than a jobber, must maintain a greater sales force, and as a rule carries a greater asset of good will. Critics of the com-petitive system of distribution frequently claim that the function of the wholesaler is nonproductive and increases the expense of modern marketing unduly. In the organization of widespread, complex markets that handle thousands of consumer commodities, however, the wholesaler provides an indispensable service to the producer and retailer, and enjoys the economies of specialization of service and facilities. See MARKETING; WAREHOUSING; CO-OPERATIVE; RE-TAILING.

WHOOPING COUGH or pertussis, an acute contagious upper respiratory disease, caused by the bacillus *Hemophilus pertussis*, and transmitted by the secretions of the mouth and nose. The incubation period lasts about 7 to 14 days, after which the usual signs of a head cold appear, accompanied by a slight rise of body temperature and general discomfort. Whooping cough is characterized by frequent series of spasmodic coughs followed by a sudden convulsive inspiration, the whoop. If severe, it often ends in vomiting. The typical case lasts about six weeks. However, complications may occur, such as broncho-pneumonia, pleurisy, infection of the middle ear, or hemorrhage caused by blood congestion brought on by the severe coughing.

Although whooping cough occurs at all ages, about 85 per cent of the cases are in children under 7 years old. More than 40 per cent occur in infants less than 2 years and the highest mortality rate is in infants under 6 months of age. Effective immunization includes vaccination between the ages of 6 and 12 months. Diagnosis is difficult in atypical cases and in the early stage before the intense coughing spells, but is confirmed when laboratory tests show that *H. pertussis* is present.

Treatment of the disease begins with warmth and bed rest. Sedation is often given to calm the patient and control the convulsive coughing. The antibiotics chloromycetin, streptomycin, and aureomycin have been found effective in whooping cough.

WHOOPING CRANE, a large North American marsh bird, of the family *Gruidae*, noted for its size and loud cry, and now rapidly becoming extinct. The whooping crane, *Grus americana*, is nearly 5 feet long and has a wingspread of about 7½ feet. Its plumage is white; its bill is slender, sharp, and long. The bird constructs its nest of grasses and reed stems on the ground and lays two eggs that are olive in color with brown spots. Its habit of eating corn has caused its near extinction. Farmers, fearing ruin of their crop, killed the birds in great numbers and so now they occur only in northern Saskatchewan and the southwestern regions of the Northwest Territory in Canada. They are very wary of humans and avoid them rigorously.

WHYMPER, EDWARD, 1840–1911, English traveler and explorer, was born in London. He was educated privately, and in 1860 was sent by a London firm to make sketches of Alpine peaks. He ascended Mont Blanc, 1864, the Matterhorn, 1865, and made trips to Greenland, 1867 and 1872. He visited the Ecuadorean Andes, 1879–80, was the first to reach the summit of Chimborazo, 1880, and collected specimens of South American plants and fossils. Among his works are *Scrambles Among the Alps* (1871), *Travels Among the Great Andes of the Equator* (1892), *Chamonix and Mont Blanc* (1896), and *Zermatt and the Matterhorn* (1897).

WIARTON, town, Canada, S Ontario, in Bruce County; on Colpoy Bay, an indentation of Georgian Bay of Lake Huron; on the Canadian National Railway; 115 miles NW of Toronto. The town is a trade center for a region in which lumbering, fishing, and farming are leading activities. Furniture and dairy products are manufactured. Wiarton was first settled in the mid-1860's. Pop. (1960) 1,954.

WIBAUX, town, E Montana, seat of Wibaux County; on the Beaver River, the Northern Pacific Railway, and U.S. highway 10; 7 miles W of the North Dakota border, and 215 miles NW of Billings. Wibaux is a shipping point for the sheep, cattle, and grain which are produced in the area. The town has a grain elevator and a machine shop. Pop. (1960) 766.

WICHITA, a North American Indian tribe belonging to a confederacy of Caddoan-speaking tribes (see CADDOAN). The Wichita were closely related linguistically to the Pawnee, with whom they were closely associated in their early history. Their original range is believed to have extended from the Arkansas River in Kansas south into Texas. The Spanish explorer Francisco Vasquez de Coronado encountered them, 1541, in what is now the state of Kansas, during his search for Quivera, a legendary city of treasure. The Wichita were agriculturalists, and they traded corn and pumpkins to the wandering Indians in return for game. In 1801 their number was greatly reduced by smallpox. After the Civil War, the U.S. government settled the Wichita on a reservation in Indian Territory (modern Caddo County, Okla.). In 1950 there were 460 Wichita Indians living on this reservation. CLARK WISSLER

WICHITA, city, S central Kansas, seat of Sedgwick County; at the confluence of the Arkansas and Little Arkansas rivers; on the Santa Fe, the Rock Island, the Frisco, the Midland Valley, and the Missouri Pacific railroads, and U.S. highways 54 and 81; a scheduled airline stop; 130 miles SW of Topeka. The city is the industrial, commercial, and banking center for southern Kansas and northern Oklahoma. In addition to flour mills, petroleum refineries, and airplane factories, Wichita has large stockyards and meat-packing plants, grain elevators, and factories which manufacture textiles, leather goods, building materials, food products, farm machinery, tools and dies, and oil-well drilling and field equipment.

The site was settled by the Wichita Indians in 1863; after the Civil War the Wichita were removed to Indian Territory, and white settlers came. Cattle were driven along the Chisholm Trail through Wichita to Abilene, the railhead. The Santa Fe Railway reached the city in 1872, and Wichita then became the railhead at the end of the Chisholm Trail. The settlers, however, soon fenced off the land blocking the path of the Chisholm Trail, and enabling Dodge City to replace Wichita as a cattle market. The resultant economic lag was offset, somewhat, by the product of the new grain farmers of the prairie, who made Wichita the fourth largest milling center of the country. Shortly after World War I, oil was discovered in the Wichita area and in the city itself, and the wells and refineries became sources of a large part of the city's wealth.

The city is the site of several institutions of higher learning, among them Carmel Academy, founded as All Hallows College (1888); Fairmount College founded, 1892 and renamed University of Wichita in 1957; and Friends University (1898) known as Garfield, which was founded by the Society of Friends. The University of Wichita is noted for its police school.

Notable attractions in the city are the Roman Catholic Immaculate Conception Cathedral (1912), the Municipal Forum (1910), the Wichita Art Museum (1935), Riverside Park, the Wichita Horse and Mule Market, which is attended by buyers from all over the world, and Lawrence Stadium, where the national semipro baseball tournament is held each year. Pop. (1960) 254,698.

WICHITA, UNIVERSITY OF. See COLLEGES AND UNIVERSITIES.

WICHITA FALLS, city, N Texas, seat of Wichita County, on the Wichita River, the Fort Worth and Denver City, and Missouri-Kansas-Texas railroads, and U.S. highways 82, 277, 281, and 287; a scheduled airline stop; about 105 miles NW of Fort Worth and 12 miles from the Oklahoma line. Wichita Falls is an industrial city, a large oil center, and a wholesale and retail distributing point for northern Texas and southern Oklahoma. Oil refineries, foundries, textile-processing plants, a cottonseed-oil mill, grain elevators, cold-storage plants, and factories manufacturing air-conditioning equipment, frozen-food lockers, shoes and leather goods, and dairy products are located in the city. The city began as a trading post, grew as a cattle market, and flourished with the arrival of railroads and the discovery of oil. The first permanent settlers arrived in the region in 1861. Wichita Falls is the site of a state hospital and Hardin Junior College (1937). Sheppard Field, an Air Force base, is nearby. Pop. (1960) 101,724.

WICKARD, CLAUDE RAYMOND, 1893–   , U.S. public official, was born near Camden, Ind., and was educated at Purdue University. A successful farmer, he joined the Agricultural Adjustment Administration, 1933, becoming director of the North Central Division, 1937–40. In 1940 he was appointed undersecretary of agriculture and later the same year secretary of agriculture in the cabinet of Franklin D. Roosevelt. During World War II he had a major role in the national food program and in the lend-lease shipment of food abroad. Under Pres. Harry S. Truman, 1945–53, he served as director of the Rural Electrification Administration. He was elected to the U.S. Senate, 1956.

WICKERSHAM, GEORGE WOODWARD, 1858–1936, U.S. lawyer and public official, was born in Pittsburgh, Pa., and studied at Lehigh University and at the University of Pennsylvania law school, graduating in 1880. He went to New York, 1882, where he soon acquired an extensive practice, especially in corporation cases. He was attorney general in Pres. William Howard Taft's cabinet, 1909–13, chairman of the National Commission of Law Observance and Enforcement, 1929–32, and president of the International Arbitral Tribunal under the Young Plan treaties, 1932–36.

WICKHAM, ANNA, 1884–   , English poetess, was born in Wimbledon, Surrey, lived and studied in Australia from the age of six, then returned to England, 1905. Among her volumes of poetry are *Songs of John Oland* (1918), *Contemplative Quarry* (1920), *The Man with a Hammer* (1921), and *The Little Old House* (1922).

WICKLIFFE, CHARLES ANDERSON, 1788–1869, U.S. political figure, was born in Springfield, Ky., studied law at Bardstown, Ky., and was admitted to the bar, 1809. He was a U.S. congressman, 1823–33; became lieutenant governor, 1836, and governor, 1839, of Kentucky; and served as U.S. postmaster general in the cabinet of Pres. John Tyler, 1841–45.

WICKLIFFE, city, NW Kentucky, seat of Ballard County; on the Mississippi River, four miles south of its junction with the Ohio River; on the Gulf, Mobile and Ohio and the Illinois Central railroads, and U.S. highways 51 and 60; 205 miles SW of Louisville. Wickliffe is a shipping point for an area in which tobacco, corn, and potatoes are grown. Pottery is manufactured. A buried Indian village in the vicinity has yielded valuable archaeological artifacts. Pop. (1960) 917.

WICKLOW, county, SE Ireland, in Leinster Province; bounded by St. George's Channel on the E, and by the counties of Dublin on the N, Wexford on the S, and Carlow and Kildare on the W; area 781 sq. mi.; pop. (1956) 59,906. The center of the county is traversed north to south by the Wicklow Mountains, the highest point being Lugnaquilla (3,039 ft.) in the central part. Principal streams are the Slaney, which rises in the west and flows south into Carlow; the Avoca, which rises in the north central part and enters the sea at Arklow. Considerable stock raising and some farming are practiced. Lead, copper, and sulfur are mined and some stone is quarried. The capital and chief port is Wicklow, which has only a small harbor.

WICKRAM, JÖRG, died ?1562, German novelist, called the father of the German novel, and prose writer, was probably born in Colmar. He became town clerk of Burghim in 1555. His novels include *Rittes Galmy* (1539), *Der Knabenspiegel* (1554), and *Der Goldfaden* (1557). Of several plays, the most popular is *Der verlorne Sohn* (1540). His *Das Rollwagenbüchlein* (1555) is a collection of witty tales.

WIDENER, PETER ARRELL BROWN, 1834–1915, U.S. financier and philanthropist, was born in Philadelphia. He was in the meat business many years, became a power in local Republican politics, and with the profits made on a government meat contract during the Civil War, invested in Philadelphia street railways and helped organize the United States Steel Corporation.

WIDGEON, any duck measuring 8 to 21 inches in length and belonging to the genus *Mareca*. The European widgeon, *M. penelope*, has a cinnamon-red head and neck, white coloration at the top of its head, brownish-gray upper plumage, and brownish-red and white undersides. It makes its nest on marshy ground and lays from 8 to 18 pale-buff eggs. It occurs in the northern regions of the Eastern Hemisphere. The baldpate or American widgeon, *M. americana*, is similar to its European counterpart except that its head has a patch of green running from its eyes to the base of its neck. The rest of its neck is white with intermingled dark spots.

WIDNES, municipal borough, NW England, in SW Lancashire, on the Mersey River and the Manchester Ship Canal, 11 miles ESE of Liverpool. Chemicals, pharmaceuticals, grease, paint, and copper and steel products are manufactured. Widnes developed as an industrial center in the nineteenth century and was incorporated in 1892. Pop. (1951) 48,795.

WIECHERT, ERNST EMIL, 1887–1950, German novelist, was born in Kleinorth, East Prussia, went to school at Königsberg, and taught in secondary schools. The Nazi government imprisoned him for a time, 1938, but he was allowed to continue his work during World War II; his *Der Totenwald*, 1945 (*The Forest of the Dead*, 1947), deals with life in a concentration camp. Among other works are *Die Flucht* (The Escape), 1916, *Jedermann* (Everyman), 1931, *Die Majorin*, 1934 (*The Baroness*, 1936), and *Missa sine nomine* (Mass Without a Name), 1950.

WIELAND, CHRISTOPHER MARTIN, 1733–1813, German man of letters was born near the Free Imperial City of Biberach, Suevia, the son of a pastor, and was brought up in Kloster Bergen (Elbe), Tübingen, and Switzerland. From 1760 he served as a counselor in Biberach, and the Count Stadion became the patron under whose guidance the "naturally benevolent" (Madame de Staël), Wieland put aside the pietism and Platonism that had dominated him before and gave free reign to the admirable fairness and joy-in-others that enabled him to create in the *Der teutsche Mercur* (1733–1810), which he founded (after the model of the *Mercure de France*) and edited until 1789 as a forum for all German literature and poetry. His *Der goldene Spiegel* (The Golden Mirror), 1772, so impressed the widowed Duchess Amalia that she had him come to Weimar as educator of the princes, and became his lifelong friend. At Weimar, he welcomed Johann Wolfgang von Goethe, 1775, in some immortal verses that are perhaps, Wieland's best claim to fame. Also much reprinted is his *Augustus and Horace*, originally written as an introduction to his translation of Horace. Attracted to the plays of Shakespeare by their romantic and fairyland qualities, Wieland translated 22 of the plays into German prose. His own masterpiece is *Oberon* (1780), a long poem whose subject matter is taken from *Huon de Bordeaux*, an old French tale. That Wieland produced a tremendous quantity of writing is evident in the fact that when the first collection of his complete works was issued, under his own supervision, 1794–1805, it filled 43 large volumes. As to Wieland's significance, Goethe wrote: "The German nation owes Wieland her style. From him, she has learned to express herself adequately, and this is not a small matter."   EUGEN ROSENSTOCK-HUESSY

WIELAND, HEINRICH OTTO, 1877–1957, Nobel prize-winning German chemist, was born in Pforzheim, and was educated at the universities of Berlin, Munich, and Stuttgart. After teaching at various universities in Germany, he served as professor of chemistry at the University of Munich, 1925–52. Wieland was awarded a 1927 Nobel prize "for his research on bile acids and analogous substances." He also did research on the organic nitrogen compounds and the alkaloids.

WIEN, WILHELM, 1864–1928, Nobel prize-winning German physicist, was born in Gaffken, East Prussia. He studied at the universities of Göttingen, Heidelberg, and Berlin. He was professor of physics at the University of Würzburg, 1900–20, and at the University of Munich, 1920–28. He conducted research in thermodynamics, radiation, cathode rays, canal rays, and X rays. Wien was awarded the 1911 Nobel prize in physics "for his discoveries concerning the laws of heat radiation." His formula for the relation between energy and wave length of radiation contributed to the development of the modern quantum theory.

WIENER, NORBERT, 1894–1964, U.S. mathematician, a founder of cybernetics, was born in Columbia, Mo., and studied at Tufts College, Cornell, Harvard, Cambridge, Göttingen and Columbia universities. He joined the faculty of the Massachusetts Institute of Technology, 1919, and became professor of mathematical logic, 1932. His *Cybernetics* (1948, rev. ed. 1961), a study of control and communication in the animal and machine, is a classic work on the subject. Among his other works are *The Fourier Integral and Certain of Its Applications* (1933), *Human Use of Human Beings* (1950), *I Am a Mathematician* (1956), *Nonlinear Problems in Random Theory* (1958), and *Tempter* (1959).

WIENER NEUSTADT, city, E Austria, Lower Austria Province; 30 miles SW of Vienna. A canal used in transporting coal and timber extends from the city to Vienna. Wiener Neustadt has rail yards and machine shops, and plants manufacturing textiles, leather goods, machinery, sugar, paper, and pottery. A twelfth-century castle was converted by Maria Theresa to a military school in 1752 and in 1919 was made a school for young boys. The thirteenth-century Liebfrauen Church is Romanesque in style, but has fifteenth century additions. Notable is the fifteenth-century Cistercian Abbey. The city was founded in 1192. Allied bombing heavily damaged the city during World War II. (For population, see Austria map in Atlas.)

WIENIAWSKI, HENRI, 1835–80, Polish violinist and composer, was born in Lublin, studied at the Paris Conservatory, 1843–48, began to tour at the age of 11, and within a few years had an almost unrivaled reputation as a violinist throughout Europe and America. He was solo violinist to the tsar of Russia, 1860–72, professor at St. Petersburg Conservatory, 1862–67, and at Brussels, 1874–77. Among his compositions are two concertos for the violin; the second, his Concerto in D minor, Opus 22 (1870), is considered the best of his creative work.

WIERTZ, ANTOINE JOSEPH, 1806–65, Belgian painter of historical subjects and portraits, was born in Dinant, studied art at Antwerp Academy, and won the academy's grand prize, 1832, which enabled him to study in Rome. He settled at Liège, 1836, but moved to Brussels, 1848, where a studio, later known as the Musée Wiertz, was built for him by the Belgian government. Early in his career he came under the influence of Michelangelo; Peter Paul Rubens was a later influence. All of Wiertz' art evinces the workings of a grotesque and fantastic imagination. Wiertz invented a method of painting styled *peinture mate,* in which fresco and oil painting are combined. He concentrated on academic subjects such as *Greeks and Trojans Contending for the Body of Patroclus* (1848) and *Death of Dionysius* (1848), but his handling of them was never merely academic. He wrote a *Eulogy on Rubens* (1840) and *Characteristics of Flemish Painting* (1863).

WIESBADEN, city, W Germany, in the West German state of Hesse, located at the foot of the Taunus Range; 20 miles W of Frankfurt-am-Main. Wiesbaden has been noted since Roman times for its hot springs. It has luxurious hotels and modern thermal establishments that draw health seekers from all parts of the world. The nearby countryside is dotted with orchards and vineyards. Wiesbaden has a large trade in wine; surgical instruments, chocolate, furniture, cement, and fertilizers are manufactured. Since World War II, Wiesbaden has expanded rapidly and is now a fine modern city, strongly American in character, with many cultural associations (including book-publishing and film-making). An international drama festival is held each May. The Romans called it Aquae Mattiacorum and fortified it in 12 B.C. From 1806 to 1866 it was the capital of the Duchy of Nassau. American troops captured the town in the early spring of 1945. (For population, see Germany map in Atlas.)

WIG, an artificial headdress of hair used by actors and actresses, by legal officials in several countries, and formerly, according to the dictates of fashion, by all classes of private persons. Wigs have been found on Egyptian mummies, and were also used by the Persians and the ancient Greeks, and Romans. According to Livy, Hannibal wore one as a disguise, and the Emperors Otho, Domitian, and Caracalla used wigs to cover their baldness. The Roman wig was a kind of skullcap fringed with hair; more artistic, no doubt, were the blond wigs for the ladies, alluded to by Ovid and Martial. The early Church Fathers, such as Tertullian, denounced wigs as "of the devil," but in the seventeenth century they were part of a proper churchman's professional attire. Wig wearing by men was made fashionable in France by Louis XIII, 1610–43, although, in the fourteenth century, false tresses (*coifs à templettes*) had been worn by ladies. Louis XIV (1638–1715) raised the wig to its highest degree of size and fashion. Toward the end of the eighteenth century the wig began to give place to the powdered queue. Louis XV (1710–74) reduced its dimensions, and Benjamin Franklin stood wigless before Louis XVI (1754–93). The French Revolution abolished wigs, but the patriots introduced the "Brutus" type. Queen Anne's reign, 1702–14, saw the apotheosis of the English wig. In the reign of George III, 1760–1820, wigs ceased to be generally fashionable. During the twentieth century, however, women's rapidly changing hair styles forced fashionable ladies to rely on wigs from time to time.

WIGAN, county borough, NW England, in S central Lancashire; 17 miles NE of Liverpool. There are canal and railroad connections with Liverpool and Manchester. Wigan is an industrial center, and coal is mined in the vicinity. The manufacture of cotton textiles, metal products, chemicals, and the distilling of oil are leading industries. Wigan was formerly an important center for the manufacture of bells and pottery. Perhaps because of the bluntness of its name, Wigan has acquired some humorous notoriety as a sort of archetypal provincial industrial town, bleak, grimy, and utterly dull.

WIGGIN, KATE DOUGLAS, 1856–1923, U.S. author, was born Kate Douglas Smith in Philadelphia. After graduating from Abbott Academy, Andover, Mass., she lived in California for several years, where she organized in San Francisco the first free kindergarten on the Pacific Coast. Her first husband, 1881–89, was Samuel B. Wiggin, a San Francisco lawyer. Among her most popular publications are *The Birds' Christmas Carol* (1887), *Timothy's Quest* (1890), *A Cathedral Courtship* (1893), the *Penelope* books (3 vols. 1893–1901), *Marm Lisa* (1896), *The Diary of a Goose Girl* (1902), *Rebecca of Sunnybrook Farm* (1903), *Rose o' the River* (1905), *New Chronicles of Rebecca* (1907), *The Old Peabody Pew* (1907), *Susanna and Sue* (1909), *Mother Carey's Chickens* (1911), *The Story of Waitstill Baxter* (1913), *Penelope's Postscripts* (1915), *Ladies in Waiting* (1918), and *Homespun Tales* (1920).

WIGGLESWORTH, MICHAEL, 1631–1705, colonial American clergyman and poet, who believed that the floors of Hell are paved with the skulls of unbaptized infants, was born in England (probably in Yorkshire), and was taken to North America, 1638, where the family settled in New Haven. He was graduated from Harvard, 1651, and was pastor of the church at Malden, Mass., from 1656. His most important poem, *The Day of Doom; or, A Poetical Description of the Great and Last Judgment* (1662), gave rather morbid expression to some of the theological beliefs of the early New England Congregationalists, and was an extraordinary best seller in its day. He went to Bermuda for his health, 1663, and for the same reason declined the presidency of Harvard, 1684. He also wrote *Meat Out of the Eater or Meditations Concerning the Necessity, End and Usefulness of Afflictions Unto God's Children* (1669).

BRITISH INFORMATION SERVICES

Within these Norman walls of Barbican Gate, Carisbrooke Castle, built on Isle of Wight in the English Channel, Charles I was imprisoned before he was beheaded in 1649.

WIGHT, ISLE OF, island, separated from S England by the Solent (NW) and Spithead (NE) channels; an administrative county forming part of Hampshire; extends 23 miles from E to W and 14 miles from N to S; area 147 sq. mi.; pop. (1951) 95,594. The surface is hilly, especially in the central part which comprises a row of chalk downs traversing the island from east to west; and soils are generally poor. The Medina is the chief stream. Oats and barley are grown, and sheep are raised on the higher chalk downs. Wool, flour, and sand are exported. The manufacture of yachts and small craft is the major industry. The island is a summer resort noted for its picturesque scenery. Ventnor, Ryde, Cowes, Yarmouth, and Shanklin are resort towns. Newport is the capital. The Isle of Wight was purchased by the crown during the reign of Edward I (1272–1307). It was a residence of Queen Victoria. The island was known as Vectis or Ictis during Roman times.

WIGTOWNSHIRE, county, extreme SW Scotland, bounded by Ayrshire on the N, Kirkcudbrightshire on the E, the Irish Sea on the S, and by the North Channel on the W and NW; area 488 sq. mi.; pop. (1951) 31,625. Wigtownshire forms part of the region of Galloway. The county, which has a deeply indented coast, can be divided into three sections. In the north is a highland area, which is a noted sheep-raising area. In the south is a broad peninsula, between Wigtown and Luce Bay, known as The Machers. The Machers is generally a plain on which hay, oats, and barley are grown, and dairy cattle and pigs are raised. In the west, a narrow strip of land connects The Machers with a northwest-southeast trending peninsula, The Rhinns of Galloway. Wigtown is the capital. Stranraer, the largest town and chief port, has boat connections with Ireland.

WIGWAM, an Abnaki word for "their dwelling," variously transliterated *wigouam, wikwam,* and *wigiwam,* was adopted by the North American colonists to describe an Indian dome-shaped house, covered with bark or mats. Among the Menominee, this type of house was called a *wikiop;* among the Sac (or Sauk), as a *kickapoo;* among the Fox, as a *wikiyap* or *w̆ikiyapi;* among the Ojibway, as a *wigiwam;* and among the Lanape, as a *wikwam.* The word was sometimes incorrectly used for any kind of Indian house. Most of the Algonquian-speaking tribes used this form of house in winter, but some preferred the more portable tepee as a summer residence.

In U.S. Political History, the headquarters of Tammany Hall, New York City, were known as the wigwam from 1810. Later, various buildings, usually temporary structures used for political conventions, were called wigwams as, for example, the Chicago Wigwam, where Abraham Lincoln was nominated for the presidency.

WILBER, city, SE Nebraska, seat of Saline County; on the Big Blue River, and the Burlington Railroad; 27 miles SW of Lincoln. Wilber is a trade and processing center for an area in which wheat, corn, dairy cattle, and hogs are raised. Sausage is manufactured. Wilber was platted in 1873, and incorporated in 1879. Pop. (1960) 1,358.

WILBERFORCE, WILLIAM, 1759–1833, English philanthropist and crusader against slavery, was born in Hull, was educated at Cambridge University, and entered Parliament as member for Hull when only 21 years old. He became parliamentary leader of a committee of philanthropists pledged to the abolition of slavery, 1787, and from this time he exerted all his energies in the support of the movement. Owing to his efforts, but aided by the influence of William Pitt, the Younger, resolutions condemning the slave trade were passed by the House of Commons, 1789, 1792, and 1804, but it was not until 1807 that a bill abolishing the slave trade became law. Wilberforce's energies were then transferred to the cause of emancipation of those already in bondage, and shortly before his death the bill for the total abolition of slavery passed its second reading. Declining health caused his retirement from Parliament, 1825. He published *Practical View of the Prevailing Religious System of Professed Christians in the Higher and Middle Classes of this Country, Contrasted with Real Christianity* (1797).

WILBUR, CURTIS DWIGHT, 1867–1954, U.S. jurist and public official, was born in Boonesboro, Iowa, the brother of Ray L. Wilbur. He resigned from the Navy after graduating from the U.S. Naval Academy, 1888, and began to practice law in Los Angeles, Calif., 1890. He was judge of the county superior court, 1903–18, and associate justice, 1919–22, and chief justice, 1922–24, of the state supreme court. He served as secretary of the Navy in Pres. Calvin Coolidge's cabinet, 1924–29. He was made judge of the Ninth U.S. Circuit Court of Appeals, 1929, became senior judge, 1931, and retired, 1945. He was responsible for the organization of the juvenile court of Los Angeles and was influential in the passage of California juvenile court law.

WILBUR, RAY LYMAN, 1875–1949, U.S. physician, educator, and public official, was born in Boonesboro, Iowa, the brother of Curtis D. Wilbur. He studied at Stanford University, Cooper Medical College, and abroad at Frankfurt-am-Main, London, and Munich. He joined the faculty of Stanford University, 1900, was professor of medicine, 1909–16, dean of the medical school, 1911–16, and became president of the university, 1916. Granted a leave of absence, Wilbur served as secretary of the interior in Pres. Herbert Hoover's cabinet, 1929–33. He returned to Stanford as president and in 1943 became chancellor for life. He served on the California war council, 1917, 1941–46.

WILBUR, RICHARD PURDY, 1921–   , U.S. poet, was born in New York City, and studied at Amherst College and Harvard University. He taught English at Harvard, 1950–57, Wellesley College, 1955–57, and became a professor of English at Wesleyan University, 1957. Wilbur returned to the use of traditional verse forms, and was particularly interested in nature, which he dealt with in his poetry in a mild, restrained manner. Among his works are *The Beautiful Changes* (1946), *Ceremony* (1950), and *Things of This World* (1956), for which he received the National Book Award and a Pulitzer prize in 1957.

WILBURTON, city, SE Oklahoma, seat of Latimer County; near the Ouachita Mountains, on the Rock Island Railroad and U.S. highway 270; about 130 miles ESE of Oklahoma City. Lumber mills, coal mines, and gas wells are in the vicinity. Located near by is Robber's Cave State Park, one of the largest recreational areas of the state. Wilburton is the site of the Eastern Oklahoma Agricultural and Mechanical College. Pop. (1960) 1,772.

WILCOX, ELLA WHEELER, 1850–1919, U.S. poet, was born in Johnstown Center, Wis., and studied at the University of Wisconsin. Her first book was a volume of temperance poems, *Drops of Water* (1872), but she first became widely known when her quasi-erotic *Poems of Passion* (1883) was rejected as immoral by the Chicago publishers Jansen and McClurg. After a long career as a lyricist of purple passion and platitudinous optimism ("Laugh and the world laughs with you") she became absorbed in spiritualism and theosophy. During World War I she toured U.S. Army camps in France, reciting her poems and lecturing on sexology, but collapsed from overexertion, and died shortly after her return to the United States. Among her other works are *Mal Moulée* (1885), *An Erring Woman's Love* (1892), *The Story of a Literary Career* (1905), *The Art of Being Alive* (1914), and *The Worlds and I* (1918).

WILD, JONATHAN, 1682?–1725, English criminal, subject of Henry Fielding's satirical *History of the Life of the late Mr. Jonathan Wild the Great* (1743), was the head of an elaborate organization of London thieves. He acted as an agent for returning stolen goods to their owners at a price, and informed on such thieves as he could not control. For a time his activities were tolerated by the authorities, but he was eventually imprisoned for causing a riot, and hanged at Tyburn for selling some stolen lace.

WILD BOAR. See PIG.

WILDCAT, a wild feline of moderate size. In the United States the term usually applies to either of two large cats, the lynx or the bobcat. Both are characterized by a ferocious disposition, a blunt tail or "bobtail," and a weight ranging from 15 to 40 pounds, with the lynx being the heavier of the two. It is usually impossible to domesticate these animals. The term is also applied to the Old World wildcat, *Felis sylvestris*, measuring only several feet and found in Scotland and central Europe.

WILDE, OSCAR FINGAL O'FLAHERTIE WILLS, 1854–1900, Irish dramatist, poet, and dandy, was born in Dublin. Wilde's mother was a writer and had a literary salon in Dublin so that Wilde was brought up in a world of wit and affectation. He distinguished himself as a scholar, wit, and "aesthete" almost immediately upon his arrival at Oxford, 1874, and was a national figure, a subject for caricature in *Punch* and in Gilbert and Sullivan's *Patience*, by the time he arrived in London, 1878. He had already published a volume of verse when, in 1882, he made a fantastic tour of the United States, lecturing in silk knee breeches on the aesthetic cult and scattering witticisms as pearls before provincial swine; thus, for example, to a conventional young honeymooner's

observation on the wonder of Niagara Falls, Wilde replied that it would be more wonderful if it went the other way.

In 1884 Wilde married Constance Lloyd (died 1898), and a period of intensive literary production ensued, beginning with his fairy tales, *The Happy Prince and Other Tales* (1888) which was followed by *The Picture of Dorian Gray* (1891), a novel written in imitation of Joris Karl Huysman's *À rebours*. After issuing a volume of essays Wilde began a short but brilliant career as a dramatist. His first comedy, *Lady Windermere's Fan*, was produced in 1892; in 1893, after it had been refused a license in London, he published his play *Salomé* in French. It was finally produced by Sarah Bernhardt in Paris, 1896, and was translated into English, 1894, by Lord Alfred Douglas (1870–1945). *An Ideal Husband* and *The Importance of Being Earnest* were both produced in 1895 and were both playing when Wilde was accused by the 8th Marquis of Queensberry of homosexual activities. Wilde countered by suing Queensberry for criminal libel. He lost his suit and was immediately brought to trial and convicted for offenses under the Criminal Law Amendment Act. He spent two years at hard labor and was ruined financially as well as in reputation by this train of events, which he had himself put in motion. After his release from jail, he lived in France as an outcast from England, rejected by most of his former friends, except for a few such as Frank Harris and George Bernard Shaw. The single literary product of this period was the sincere but excessively rhetorical and maudlin *Ballad of Reading Gaol* (1898). He died a Roman Catholic.

With the exception of the last, Wilde's plays are a curious mixture of brilliant dramatic invention and hackneyed imitation of the "well made" problem comedies, which were the dramatic staple of his period; and they are, in their intentions, similarly a mixture of brilliantly witty, fundamentally serious skirmishes against stupid conventionality and stereotype sentimental themes. The mixture is characteristic of Wilde's whole career. At his brilliant best, as in *The Importance of Being Earnest*, he could produce an irrepressibly witty and formidably shrewd commentary on the society of his time.   ARTHUR MIZENER

BIBLIOG.–Boris L. Brasol, *Oscar Wilde, the Man, the Artist, the Martyr* (1938); Charlie L. Broad, *Friendships and Follies of Oscar Wilde* (1955); Patrick Byrne, *Wildes of Merrion Square: The Family of Oscar Wilde* (1953); Alfred B. Douglas, *Oscar Wilde, a Summing Up* (1950); St. John G. Ervine, *Oscar Wilde: A Present Appraisal* (1952); André P. G. Gide, *Oscar Wilde* (1951); Vyvyan B. Holland, *Oscar Wilde: A Pictorial Biography* (1961); Lloyd Lewis and Henry J. Smith, *Oscar Wilde Discovers America, 1882* (1936); Vincent O'Sullivan, *Aspects of Wilde: With an Opinion by Bernard Shaw* (1938); Hesketh Pearson, *Oscar Wilde: His Life and Wit* (1956); Edouard Roditi, *Oscar Wilde* (Makers of Modern Lit. Ser.) (1947); Frances Winwar, *Oscar Wilde and the Yellow Nineties* (1958); George Woodcock, *Paradox of Oscar Wilde* (1950).

WILDE, PERCIVAL, 1887–1953, U.S. dramatist, was born in New York City, and was graduated from Columbia University, 1906. He was the author of many plays for the Little Theater movement. Among his works are *Dawn and Other One Act Plays of Today* (1915), *Confessional and Other American Plays* (1916), and *Eight Comedies for Little Theaters* (1922).

WILDEBEEST. See GNU.

WILDER, THORNTON NIVEN, 1897–   , U.S. playwright and novelist, was born in Madison, Wis., but grew up in China, where his father held consular appointments. He was graduated from Yale, 1920, studied at the American Academy in Rome, and lectured on literature at the University of Chicago, 1930–36. His first novel was *The Cabala* (1926). *The Bridge of San Luis Rey* (1927) won a 1928 Pulitzer prize; in this story of eighteenth century Peru, a Franciscan monk traces the lives of five victims of a catastrophe to show that their death was providential. *Heaven's My Destination* (1935) is an ironic satire on a contemporary theme, but *The Woman of Andros* (1930) and *Ides of March* (1948) reflect his interest in classical subjects. *Our Town* (1938), a drama of simple New England life, and *The Skin of Our Teeth* (1942), a rollicking semi-experimental pageant, both won Pulitzer prizes. Among his other plays are *The Trumpet Shall Sound* (1926), *The Long Christmas Dinner* (1931), and *The Matchmaker* (1954). During the 1960's, he was at work on a cycle of 14 short plays on the seven ages of man and the seven deadly sins.

PETRELLE HARPER & BROTHERS
Thornton Wilder

WILDERNESS CAMPAIGN, in U.S. Civil War, the early phase of the Union Army strategic offensive that eventually destroyed General Robert E. Lee's Confederate Army of Northern Virginia and captured the Confederate capital, Richmond. The offensive campaign began with several bloody but inconclusive battles, fought May 5–6, 1864, in a thick forest just south of the Rapidan River, E central Virginia, 50 to 55 miles NNW of Richmond. Advancing southward on Richmond, the Union commander, Gen. U. S. Grant, had at his disposal the Army of the Potomac, numbering nearly 120,000 troops commanded by Gen. George G. Meade. Between this force and Richmond was Lee's army of about 70,000 men. Grant ordered Meade to cross the Rapidan, and turn Lee's right (east) flank. Meade crossed the river without difficulty, May 4, but Lee, foreseeing Grant's plan, had in the meantime reinforced his own right, retaining sufficient forces on his left (west) flank to attack the weakened Union right (west). The Confederates attacked the Union right, May 5, and fighting raged through May 6 with neither side gaining a decided advantage. Meanwhile, the Union advance against Lee's left had been checked by the Confederates; in the course of this fighting many wounded men on both sides burned to death in a forest and brush fire, set ablaze by artillery. Moving nearer Richmond, Grant unsuccessfully attacked Lee at Spotsylvania Court House on May 8–12 and completed the campaign with the Battle of Cold Harbor, June 1–3. The Union lost about 50,000 men as compared with Confederate losses of about 32,000, but the three battles had drained Confederate resources and the Union emerged with an advantage.

WILDERNESS ROAD, an emigrant trail, which at its greatest extent led from Harpers Ferry, Va., through the Appalachian Mountains to the Falls of the Ohio (site of Louisville, Ky.), and which, together with the Ohio River, was a main route to the West before 1800. The trail was first marked by Daniel Boone, who guided a party of settlers to Transylvania Company lands in the Kentucky River valley, March, 1775. The Boone party followed an extension of the Virginia Path—which led from Pennsylvania through the Shenandoah Valley southward into the Carolinas—from a point near present-day Wytheville, Va., southwestward to the Watauga settlement in eastern Tennessee (see WATAUGA ASSOCIATION). From there Boone blazed a trail westward along the Virginia-Tennessee boundary, through the Cumberland Gap, then northward about 50 miles along an Indian trail called Warriors Path, and finally northwestward along several small rivers to the site on the Kentucky River where the outpost of Boonesboro was constructed. A branch from this trail led northwestward from Rockcastle River to the Falls of the Ohio. The Virginia legislature provided, 1779, for the improvement of the Wilderness Road in order to prevent the western settlements from falling under British influence. After Kentucky became a state, 1792, other improvements were authorized, and sections were leased to contractors who were permitted to collect tolls for compensation. Traffic on the Wilderness Road declined after the National Road, started in 1811, was completed north of the Ohio River. The route of the old road is followed by U.S. Route 25 from Middlesborough, Ky., to Richmond, Ky. See OVERLAND TRAILS, *Eastern Trails*.

BIBLIOG.–Henry A. B. Bruce, *Daniel Boone and the Wilderness Road* (1922); Katharine Clugston and Richard Stevenson, *Wilderness Road* (1941); Andrew Davidson, *Wilderness Road* (1960); Archer B. Hulbert, *Boone's Wilderness Road* (1903); Robert L. Kincaid, *Wilderness Road* (1955).

WILDLIFE CONSERVATION, the art of restoring, conserving, and managing wild animal species. Its objective is to achieve the greatest possible yield consistent with other uses of the land. This yield may be in the form of meat, fur, or other benefits, in human health or pleasure obtained while hunting, in education or pleasure derived from merely studying or observing the animals in their homes, or in such intangible values as the preservation of rare species which may be of interest chiefly to scientists.

Original Abundance. When Europeans first arrived in America, they found the animal life enormously abundant. Because it was not evenly distributed, some exploring parties starved. Vast areas, however, teemed with game birds and large mammals. Sixty million buffaloes and perhaps as many as 100 million antelopes grazed over the prairies. Many other species of both game and prey animals existed in countless numbers.

The Decline. For centuries the hordes of game had served as food for Indians and for other far more numerous predatory enemies. Still they continued in undiminished numbers. The coming of the white men, however, had catastrophic results. Animals were slaughtered, forests were cut and burned, and the earth was plowed. Swamps and marshes—the homes of great flocks of waterfowl and countless beavers, muskrats, mink, and other animals—were drained. Increasingly vast numbers of domestic animals—cattle, sheep and horses—were turned out on the ranges to graze. Thus, the food and the homes of many wild animals were permanently destroyed.

In 1838, market hunters killed 300 tons of passenger pigeons in Michigan. Millions of buffaloes were shot on the plains to feed travelers, settlers, and the construction gangs of the transcontinental railroads. Many more were killed for their hides. Still others were slaughtered for sport, and the carcasses left to rot. By 1895 no more than 600 individuals had survived, and the myriads of passenger pigeons were completely wiped out to the last bird, 1910. Other species that were exterminated were the great auk of the Labrador region, the heath hen of northeastern United States, and the Labrador duck of the far north. Many other birds and mammals were extirpated over large areas.

Public Conscience Awakening. By 1900 an aroused public demanded that something be done. Closed hunting seasons were declared to permit the animals to rear their young undisturbed and so to repopulate the ranges. The females of some species were protected throughout the year. The fashionable use of bird plumage for women's hats was stopped by law. By degrees the states took action to do away with commercial dealings in game within their borders. Refuges were established where the animals could breed and from which the increase could spread to the surrounding region. Forest and range fires were reduced to a minimum to protect habitats and food supply, and to protect wildlife from burning to death or from eventual starvation. Game farms were established where some species were reared and then liberated in the wild. Treaties were concluded with Canada and Mexico to protect migratory birds.

Many Species Restored. In general, this program succeeded admirably. Some species even became too numerous for their own good. This was often partly due to the extermination of their natural enemies which originally had done much to hold them in check. Some of the large browsing mammals, including white-tail deer, mule deer, and elk, became so abundant in places that they devoured all available winter food and seriously impaired the ability of the shrubs and trees to produce more.

Conservation Agencies. State conservation of wildlife is effected through the fish and game departments and legislatures. Several agencies of the federal government also play a vital part. The Fish and Wildlife Service, formed in 1940 from the Bureau of Biological Survey and Bureau of Fisheries, administers federal conservation laws, protects and regulates the hunting of migratory waterfowl, pursues research in wildlife habits, diseases and economic relations, and administers the system of approximately 275 national wildlife refuges totaling almost 18 million acres. The Forest Service makes provision for the increase and cropping of wildlife on the 180 million acres of national forests. The National Park Service administers the more than 22 million acres of national parks and national monuments, which are sanctuaries for all kinds of wildlife. Hunting is never permitted there. The Soil Conservation Service makes provision for wildlife and its habitats in planning for control of erosion and for soil and cover restoration on the Soil Conservation districts throughout the country.

Probably the largest, most vigorous, and best known of the private organizations for wildlife conservation is the National Audubon Society. Another important group is the International Committee for Wild Life Protection. Its efforts to secure the enactment of protective legislation extend far beyond the borders of the United States.   VICTOR H. CAHALANE

BIBLIOG.–Durward L. Allen, *Our Wildlife Legacy* (1954); John D. Black, *Biological Conservation: With Particular Emphasis on Wildlife* (1954); Willis C. Bumgarner, *Guidebook for Wildlife Protectors* (N.C. Univ. Guidebook Ser.) (1955); Devereux Butcher, *Seeing America's Wildlife* (1955); Garth Christian, *Place for Animals: A Plea for the Preservation of Wildlife and the Establishment of Nature Sanctuaries* (1958); Anthony Cullen and Sydney Downey, *Saving the Game* (1960); Frank F. Darling, *Wildlife in an African Territory* (1960); James W. Day, *Poison on the Land: The War on Wild Life, and Some Remedies* (1957); Earl Denman, *Animal Africa* (1957); Ira N. Gabrielson, *Wildlife Management* (1951), *Wildlife Conservation* (1959); Edward H. Graham and William R. Van Dersal, *Wildlife for America: The Story of Wildlife Conservation* (1949); Wallace B. Grange, *Way to Game Abundance* (1949); Dorothy C. Hogner, *Conservation in America* (1958); Charles Lagus, *Operation Noah* (1960); Aldo S. Leopold and Frank F. Darling, *Wildlife in Alaska: An Ecological Reconnaissance* (1953); Walter J. C. Murray, *Sanctuary Planted* (1953); Edward M. Nicholson, *Britain's Nature Reserves* (1957); William A. Peters, *Feathers Preferred: A Sportsman's Soliloquy* (1951); Eric Robbins and Ronald Legge, *Animal Dunkirk* (1959); William F. Sigler, *Wildlife Law Enforcement* (1956); Reuben E. Trippensee, *Wildlife Management*, (2 vols. (1948–1953); Jay Williams, *Fall of the Sparrow* (1951); Leonard W. Wing, *Practice of Wildlife Conservation* (1951); Hugh M. Worcester, *Hunting the Lawless* (1955).

WILD RICE, a tall aquatic grass belonging to the genus *Zizania* and the family *Gramineae*. The grass is cultivated for its grain, which is narrower than the grain of rice, and for ornamental purposes. It is usually best grown in pools up to 3 feet deep, but can prosper at the edge of pools and marshes. *Z. aquatica*, the North American species, often called water rice, grows to a height of 10 feet. Its leaves range from 12 to 18 inches in length and are about 2 inches wide. The Asian species, *Z. palustris*, is similar to the North American species but it has narrower leaves.

WILDWOOD, city, S New Jersey, in Cape May County; on the Pennsylvania-Reading Seashore Lines Railroad; about 40 miles S of Atlantic City. The city is in a resort and ocean-fishing region on the Atlantic Ocean. Cement blocks and fertilizer are manufactured and the city is a market center for grain and fruit which are grown in the area. Wildwood was founded in 1888. Pop. (1960) 4,690.

WILEY, HARVEY WASHINGTON, 1844–1930, U.S. chemist and agitator for pure food, was born in Kent, Ind., and studied at Hanover College and Indiana Medical College. He was professor of chemistry at Purdue University, 1874–83, and Indiana state chemist, 1881–83. He was appointed chief chemist of the U.S. Department of Agriculture, 1883; his work culminated in the passage of the Food and Drugs Act, 1906. His administration of the law roused such a storm of protest that the Remsen Referee Board was appointed. Cleared of charges that a member of his department had received greater recompense than was legal, Wiley nevertheless resigned, 1912. He was professor of agricultural chemistry at George Washington University, 1899–1914, and was director of the food, sanitation, and health bureau of *Good Housekeeping* magazine from 1912. Among his writings are *Foods and Their Adulteration* (1907), *Health Reader* (1916), *Beverages and Their Adulteration* (1919), *History of Crime Against the Food Law* (1929), an autobiography (1930), about 60 government pamphlets, and hundreds of scientific papers.

WILFRID, SAINT, or Wilfrith, 634?–709, English ecclesiastic, was born in Northumbria. At the Synod of Whitby, 664, Wilfrid was instrumental in establishing Roman Catholic ascendancy over the Celtic, or Columbite, church. He was made Archbishop of York, 665, but had considerable difficulty in establishing authority over his see. A journey to Rome for renewed papal authority resulted in a victory for Wilfrid over those who opposed his bishopric. St. Wilfrid is remembered for the establishment of numerous churches whose architectural splendor was one of the prides of medieval England.

WILHELM, German name of two Prussian kings, William I and William II.

WILHELM, CROWN PRINCE, in full Friedrich Wilhelm Viktor August Ernst von Hohenzollern, 1882–1951, crown prince of Germany, eldest child of William II, was born at Potsdam, and attended the University of Bonn. He commanded the Fifth Army in the West during World War I and was nominally in charge of German operations against Verdun. He fled with his father to Holland after the defeat of Germany, and renounced his rights of succession to the crown. He returned to Germany, 1923, but declared he would take no part in politics. His memoirs were published in English under the title, *I Seek the Truth* (1926).   ALFRED DE GRAZIA

WILHELMINA, full name Wilhelmina Helena Pauline Maria, 1880–1962, queen of the Netherlands, was born at The Hague, only child of William III and Emma of Waldeck-Pyrmont. She succeeded her father, 1890, but the queen mother governed as regent until the queen came of age, Aug. 31, 1898. Wilhelmina married Heinrich, duke of Mecklenburg-Schwerin (1876–1934), 1901. The only child of this union was a daughter, Juliana, born on April 30, 1909. When the Germans invaded Holland, 1940, Queen Wilhelmina fled to England, and established a government-in-exile. The crown princess and her children preceded her and eventually took refuge in Canada at Ottawa. In 1948 Wilhelmina resigned her authority, believing that a younger person could better perform the royal duties. Her daughter became queen, and Wilhelmina retired from public life.

WILHELMSHAVEN, city, NW Germany in the West German state of Lower Saxony, on the W shore of Jade Bay; 42 miles NW of Bremen. The city is a bathing resort and has one of the most important harbors in Germany. Wilhelmshaven has three large basins and several smaller ones, including one used by a shipbuilding yard. The harbor has three locks and six dry docks. The Ems-Jade Canal enters the commercial harbor. The principal exports are farm products; the chief imports are coal and lumber. The Wilhelmshaven site was purchased by Prussia from the Grand Duchy of Oldenburg in 1853 at the time of the building of the Prussian navy. Construction of the town and harbor was begun in 1855, and the harbor was completed in 1869. In 1918 the crews of two German battleships mutinied here, a prelude to Germany's subsequent capitulation. During World War II the city was a center for the building of submarines; it was heavily bombed by Allied planes throughout the war. Pop. (1958 est.) 99,900.

WILKES, CHARLES, 1798–1877, U. S. naval officer and explorer, was born in New York City. He entered the U. S. Navy, 1818. He commanded the U. S. (Wilkes) expedition that explored the Antarctic continent, about 280 Pacific islands, and the Pacific Coast of North America, 1838–42. He was a captain at the beginning of the Civil War, and was in command of the *San Jacinto* when, on Nov. 8, 1861, it intercepted the British mail steamer *Trent* in the Bahama Channel and captured James M. Mason and John Slidell, the Confederate commissioners to Britain. Wilkes was temporarily disgraced for insubordination, 1864, but was placed on the retired list as a rear admiral, 1866. See TRENT AFFAIR.

WILKES, JOHN, 1727–97, English political leader, was born in London. As a young man he led a dissolute life, and joined the Medmenham Monks, otherwise known as the Hell-Fire Club of Sir Francis Dashwood. In 1757 he entered Parliament. In 1762 Wilkes and Charles Churchill founded *The North Briton*, a paper bitter in its abuse of the prime minister, Lord Bute (see BUTE, JOHN STUART, 3rd EARL OF; CHURCHILL, CHARLES); after Bute's fall, 1763, the paper continued to attack the government, and in No. 45, Wilkes even attacked statements made in a speech by George III. The king took offense, and proceedings were launched against Wilkes, who was arrested under the terms of a general warrant (one that did not name the people to be arrested). Wilkes claimed parliamentary privilege, and was soon released; but the case raised an important constitutional point and gave rise to a judgment (*Wilkes v. Wood*, 1763) that writs of this sort were illegal—an important landmark in the protection of the liberties of the English subject.

The government made a further attempt to discredit Wilkes by denouncing, 1764, an obscene poem, *Essay on Woman*, that he had printed for private circulation. At the same time the House of Commons voted that parliamentary privilege did not cover the charge of seditious libel. Wilkes fled to France. While he was abroad, he was expelled from Parliament, convicted of libel, and outlawed.

Wilkes returned to England, 1768, and was elected to Parliament for Middlesex; he then surrendered to the authorities and was committed to prison. His outlawry was soon reversed; but in February, 1769, he was once more expelled from Parliament for libel. Immediately re-elected to his Middlesex seat, he was expelled again. Re-elected again, he was expelled a third time. On the occasion of his third re-election, his defeated opponent was seated in his place. The government looked silly throughout the affair, and knew it, and obviously had responded to royal pressure. The affair helped discredit the king's role in politics and provided the Opposition with a cause to rally around. In 1769 the Society of Supporters of the Bill of Rights was founded to support Wilkes' Middlesex campaign; later it advanced a program calling for various reforms of Parliament and thus became the first reform society.

The indefatigable Wilkes was again elected to Parliament for Middlesex, 1774, and at long last was allowed to take his seat, which he held until 1790. He was also elected Lord Mayor of London, 1774, and from 1779 to his death he was city chamberlain. During the American Revolution he supported the colonials. He helped crush the Gordon Riots in 1780 In 1782 the record of his explusions was expunged from the journal of the House of Commons.

ROBIN OGGINS

WILKES-BARRE, city, NE Pennsylvania, seat of Luzerne County; on the E bank of the Susquehanna

GREATER WILKES-BARRE C. OF C.

On the banks of the Susquehanna River, Wilkes-Barre is an important manufacturing hub in eastern Pennsylvania. It was originally founded as the city of Wyoming, 1796.

River; on the Delaware and Hudson, the Jersey Central, the Lackawanna and Wyoming Valley, the Lehigh Valley, and the Pennsylvania railroads, and U.S. highways 11 and 309; scheduled airline stop; about 18 miles SW of Scranton, in the center of the Wyoming Valley anthracite coal region. The principal manufactured products are rayon, shirts, textiles, lace, window shades, tobacco products, biscuits, beer, wire rope, insulated wire, cables, radio parts, tinware, fabricated metal products, and locomotives. Wilkes-Barre, founded in 1769, was originally called Wyoming and later renamed for John Wilkes and Col. Isaac Barre, two members of the British Parliament; it was incorporated as a town, 1806, and chartered as a city, 1871. Wilkes-Barre flourished with the discovery of anthracite coal in the 1760's; the anthracite industry began in the Wyoming Valley. Among the features of interest in Wilkes-Barre are a landscaped park marking the site of Fort Wilkes-Barre (1776) and a park along the Susquehanna River marking the site of Fort Wyoming (1771). An airport serving both Wilkes-Barre and Scranton is located at nearby Awoca. Pop. (1960) 63,551.

WILKESBORO, town, NW North Carolina, seat of Wilkes County; on the Yadkin River, the Southern Railway, and U.S. highway 421; 50 miles W of Winston-Salem. Wilkesboro is a shipping point for timber and dairy products. The town was settled in the 1770's and incorporated late in the 1880's. Pop. (1960) 1,568.

WILKIE, SIR DAVID, 1785–1841, Scottish painter and etcher, among the foremost of British historical genre painters (the Scottish Teniers), was born in Cults, Fifeshire, and entered the Royal Academy schools at Edinburgh at the age of 14. He was elected painter in ordinary to George IV, 1830, and knighted, 1836. During the latter part of his career he painted many portraits, among others *Sir Walter Scott and Family* at Abbotsford (1817). In 1840 he went to Istanbul, the Holy Land, and Egypt, and, dying on the homeward journey, was buried at sea. Among other works are *Pitlessie Fair* (1804), *The Blind Fiddler* (1806), *Rent Day* (1808), and *The Chelsea Pensioners* (1821).

WILKINS, SIR GEORGE HUBERT, 1888–1958, Australian polar explorer and aviator, was born in Mount Bryan East, South Australia. During the Balkan War, 1912–13, he was photographic correspondent with the Turkish troops and he went with the Vilhjalmur Stefansson Canadian Arctic Expedition, 1913–17. During World War I he was official photographer with the Australian Imperial Forces in France. He was second in command of the British Imperial Antarctic Expedition, 1920; naturalist with the Ernest Shackleton Expedition, 1921; leader of the British Museum Expedition to Australia, 1923–25, and of two Arctic expeditions, 1926–27, 1928, and of an Antarctic one, 1928–29. Observations during his 1928 flight with Carl Ben Eilson from Alaska to Green Harbor, Spitsbergen, proved that there is no land between Alaska and the Pole. He tried in vain to reach the North Pole by submarine, 1931, and managed the Lincoln Ellsworth Trans-Antarctic Expedition 1933–39. Wilkins was knighted in 1928. He wrote *Flying the Arctic* (1928), *Undiscovered Australia* (1928), and *Under the North Pole* (1931).

WILKINS, MARY ELEANOR, better known by her married name, Mary E. Wilkins Freeman, 1852–1930, U.S. short-story writer and novelist, was born in Randolph, Mass. Except for a year at Mount Holyoke Seminary she had little schooling, but gained much knowledge while acting as secretary to Oliver Wendell Holmes. The best of her 230 or so short stories about rural life in New England are collected in *A Humble Romance* (1887) and *A New England Nun* (1891), and tell of the decadence of the moldering, time-forgotten villages of eastern Massachusetts. Among her other works are a play, *Giles Corey* (1893); a novel, *Pembroke* (1894); *The Portion of Labor* (1901); and *Edgewater People* (1918).

WILKINS, WILLIAM, 1779–1865, U.S. political figure, was born in Carlisle, Pa., and studied at Dickinson College in Carlisle. Wilkins served in the U.S. Senate, 1831–34, and as secretary of war, 1844–45, in Pres. John Tyler's cabinet.

WILKINSBURG, borough, SW Pennsylvania, in Allegheny County; on the Pennsylvania Railroad and at the junction of U.S. highways 22 and 30; an industrial suburb, 5 miles E of Pittsburgh. Pumps, machine tools, lubricating equipment, and brick tiles are manufactured. Wilkinsburg was settled late in the eighteenth century. Pop. (1960) 30,066.

WILKINSON, JAMES, 1757–1825, colonial American and U.S. soldier and adventurer, was born near Benedict, Md. He entered the Continental army, 1775, and served nearly three years. As aide-de-camp and adjutant general to Gen. Horatio Gates he was made the official messenger to Congress to report the surrender of John Burgoyne at Saratoga, a mission he was tardy in fulfilling. He was forced to retire from the Army, 1778, because of his involvement in the (Gen. Thomas) Conway Cabal. He was clothier general of the Army, 1779–81, retired when irregularities were found in his accounts, and emigrated

CULVER SERVICE
James Wilkinson

to Kentucky, 1784, where he soon found opportunities for intrigue and perhaps treason. He took an oath of allegiance to the Spanish king and received an annual pension; he was deeply involved in the Spanish Conspiracy, a plot to make the trans-Allegheny area (present-day Kentucky) a Spanish protectorate. He re-entered the U.S. Army, 1791, served in the Indian War under Gen. Anthony Wayne, and succeeded to the command of the Army on Wayne's death, 1796. As governor of Louisiana Territory from 1805, he entered into the Aaron Burr Conspiracy, which he eventually revealed to the government when the project seemed likely to fail. Although he was the chief witness in the Burr treason trial, he remained under suspicion himself; he was tried by court-martial, 1811, but finally acquitted.

During the War of 1812, as a major general, he was given command of the Northern Department, where he proved so inefficient that he was soon removed—this in a period when the U.S. Army was among the most inefficient in the world. He was brought before a military court of inquiry, but was acquitted and honorably discharged, 1815. He went to Mexico, 1821, and died there. Wilkinson's *Memoirs* (3 vols. 1816) are interesting enough, but are so self-serving and omit so many significant documents that they cannot properly be relied upon uncritically.

WILL, considered philosophically, is that faculty of soul or that function of mind that is concerned with decision and choice. Since choice is, ultimately, either for good or for evil, the problem of the Will has usually been taken to be one of ethics.

Has man free choice, and if so, in what does it consist? To the rational Greek and practical Roman mind, free choice is not a major issue, for it was assumed that a man's Will must, if he is sane, follow the dictates of either his reason or his destiny. Thus Socrates, according to Plato, regarded the performance of good as a matter of knowledge: if one knows the good, one will act accordingly—it is inconceivable that one who knows the good should willfully do evil. The Stoics deprecated the Will and advised the apathetic endurance of the inevitable.

With the coming of Christianity and the idea of sin, the question of will acquired an enlarged significance and received a radically different answer. That a man is responsible for his sins presupposes, according to Thomas Aquinas, that he is free to choose between good and evil; the implication is, contrary to the Socratic doctrine, that one may know the difference between good and evil, and yet choose evil. "The proper act of free choice is," according to Aquinas, "election, for we say that we have a free choice because we can take one thing while refusing another; and this is to elect." Whether this act of election is due primarily to Will or to Intellect was much debated during the Middle Ages. To the Thomists, it seemed that Intellect must be nobler (and hence primary) because it possesses its object by mental assimilation, whereas the object of Will is always in some sense external. To the Scotists, on the other hand (see DUNS SCOTUS, JOHANNES), the recognition of the supreme object of Will as the good must imply the primacy of Will, for to love God, they were sure, is nobler than simply to know Him.

In Modern Philosophy the notion of Will-as-function tended to replace the scholastic idea of Will-as-faculty. Thomas Hobbes argued that Mind is only Matter-in-motion; and that Will, accordingly, is but a material appetite. Arthur Schopenhauer regarded Will as a primal force, one that is to be conquered by Mind. Friedrich Nietzsche saw Will as the passion of the superman for power (self-conquest).

In the twentieth century the problem of the Will seemed of less and less interest to most philosophers. To those—probably the majority—convinced that everything is accomplished by the inexorable operation of the laws of Nature, the problem of man's Will is meaningless. For most others the problem remained an unresolved enigma.   ROBERT WHITTEMORE

WILL, a legal document by which a person gives directions for the disposal of his property after his death. The law of wills, in the United States, has been greatly influenced by the common law of England, the English Statute of Frauds (see FRAUD, Statute of Frauds), and the English Statute of Wills (1837). Wills of real and personal property were recognized even before the Norman Conquest, 1066–71. With the coming of the Normans and the feudal system, wherein land was allotted in return for military service to the king, there came a restriction on the disposal of realty by wills. The first Statute of Wills (1540) was aimed at removing some of the common law restrictions on devices of realty. The disposal of personalty was never restricted to so great an extent as was the disposal of realty. The Statute of Frauds, throwing safeguards about the execution of devices of land, did not equally safeguard the disposal of personalty by wills.

Modern statutes, however, have gone far to place the disposal of both kinds of property on a parity.

Although the basis of the acts pertaining to wills in most of the states within the United States is in English law, the modern statutes differ in the various jurisdictions and their construction produces a lack of uniformity in court decisions. The general requirements, execution, and revocation of wills are practically the same in all states. Other statutory requirements vary. In each case, the particular statutes and the decisions construing them are the controlling factors.

General Legal Principles. The right to dispose of property is not regarded as an absolute property right but a right given by statute. The state has the power and authority to prescribe rules for the disposal of property by will. Generally, all real and personal property, both legal and equitable, contingent and vested, to which an owner may have title at his death, may be disposed of by will. This property, however, is always subject to the payment of the testator's debts or other encumbrances. In general, also, the property is subject to payment of expenses of administration of the estate and for allowances to the widow and minor children during the settlement of the estate. Homestead and dower rights are also usually reserved.

As a general rule, any person of full age, of sound mind and memory, and not under legal restraint, who has property or an interest therein, may devise and bequeath it by will. Testamentary capacity to make a will exists when the testator has sufficient mind and memory (1), to understand the nature of the business in which he is engaged; (2), to comprehend generally the nature and extent of his property; (3), to hold in his mind the names and identity of those who have natural claims upon his bounty; (4), to be able to appreciate his relationship to the members of his family.

Wills may be vitiated by fraud or undue influence practiced on the testator. Fraud consists of a misrepresentation of a material fact made with an intention to deceive and resulting in leading another to rely upon the existence of the fact to his detriment. Undue influence is described as that degree of importunity that deprives a testator of his free agency and leaves him too weak to resist, and which will render the instrument not his free and unconstrained act. See UNDUE INFLUENCE.

The statutory requirements relating to the manner in which wills are to be executed are mandatory and for this reason it is extremely important in the drawing of a will that the local statutes be consulted. A will disposing of personal property should be executed in accordance with the law of the domicile of the testator. A will of real property should be executed according to the law of the state where the property is located. Subject to the statutory provisions pertaining to unwritten wills and to the wills of soldiers and sailors, it is a general requirement that all wills be expressed in writing. It is essential that the testator knows and understands the contents and meaning of a will in order for it to be valid. In general, it is necessary that any written will be signed by the testator at the end of the document and be witnessed by one or more witnesses, who must sign their names in the presence of the testator and of each other. Generally, a witness should be a person who has no beneficial interest in the will. An addition or correction may be made to a will, or any devise or bequest therein may be revoked, by a codicil, which must be executed with the same formality as the will. A will may be revoked by an express clause in another will; by destroying or canceling the document with intent to revoke it; or by a new will containing provisions inconsistent with those of the first one.

Types of Wills. In general, wills are of two kinds: written and oral. The oral will is known as nuncupative; it is made before witnesses and later reduced to writing. In most states that recognize the validity of nuncupative wills, their operation is restricted to the disposition of personal property. The law supposes such a will to be made during the last sickness of the deceased, which prevented him from executing a more formal instrument. Nuncupative wills may also be made by soldiers and sailors on active duty, who are allowed to make such wills because of general inability to secure the proper execution of a written will. A holographic will is written by the testator entirely in his own handwriting and shows his testamentory intent and disposition without being formally executed as is required of ordinary wills. Joint wills are two or more wills, written on one document, that dispose of the property held by the various testators. Mutual wills are reciprocal; the property of each testator is devised or bequeathed to the other or in accordance with the other's wishes. Wills are both joint and mutual when they are executed jointly and have reciprocal provisions. A conditional or contingent will depends upon a future uncertain event, the happening of which is a condition precedent to the existence and operation of the will. In cases where there is no will (see INTESTACY) the laws of descent and distribution will operate. See CURTESY; DESCENT AND DISTRIBUTION; DOWER; LEGACY; INHERITANCE; PROBATE.

CHESTER R. DAVIS

BIBLIOG.–Thomas E. Atkinson, *Handbook of the Law of Wills and other Principles of Succession* (Hornbook Ser.) (1953); Stanley J. Bailey, *Law of Wills, Including Intestacy and Administration of Assets* (1957); Nathan R. Caine, *Your Family Without You* (1957); Forrest Cool, *Wills* (Law Review) (1948); William J. Grange and Others, *Wills, Executors, and Trustees* (1950); Bruce S. Ker, *Wills, Probate and Administration: A Manual of the Law* (1959); Earl S. MacNeil, *What Women Want to Know About Wills* (1959); Richard R. B. Powell, *Cases and Materials on Trusts and Wills* (Amer. Casebook Ser.) (1960); Max Rheinstein, *Law of Decedents' Estates* (1955); Esmond Schapiro, *Everyone Needs a Will* (1957); Robert J. Schwartz, *Write Your Own Will* (1951); Terence Sheard, *Canadian Forms of Wills (Annotated)* (1960); Gilbert T. Stephenson, *Drafting Wills and Trust Agreements* (1954).

WILLAERT, ADRIAN, 1480?–1562, Flemish musician, founder of the Venetian school of musical composers, was born in Bruges, Belgium. He was employed by the Duke of Ferrara and the Archbishop of Milan, 1522, and appointed, 1527, singing master of St. Mark's, Venice, where he established a school. He was a prolific composer of motets and madrigals, and is regarded as the creator of the madrigal and the double chorus. Among his published works are five Masses (1536), a volume of hymns (1542), and *Musica nova* (1557).

WILLAMETTE RIVER, W Oregon, rises in two streams in the Cascade Mountains, unites in Lane County, and flows for 250 miles in a northerly direction to its confluence with the Columbia River NW of Portland. Among the river's tributaries are the McKenzie, the Santiam, and the Clackamas. The river, which is partly navigable, supplies considerable water power for industry. Its valley, sheltered by high mountains, is an important fruit-growing region. The cities of Portland, Salem, and Eugene are on the Willamette.

The first settlers in the Willamette Valley were French-Canadian representatives of Hudson's Bay Company, who came about 1830. In 1834 the Rev. Jason Lee established a Methodist mission in the region, and later his influence was a factor in establishing U.S. sovereignty in the Oregon country. United States settlers set up a provisional government with their own constitution in 1845. Two years later there were about 6,000 people in the valley; the census of 1850 showed that it had a population of 11,631 out of 13,294 for the entire Oregon Territory.

WILLAMETTE UNIVERSITY. See COLLEGES AND UNIVERSITIES.

WILLARD, EMMA HART, 1787–1870, U.S. educator, was born in Berlin, Conn., and educated at Berlin and Hartford academies. She married Dr. John Willard of Middlebury, 1809. In 1814 she opened the Middlebury Female Seminary in their home, introducing successfully to American women the "unfeminine" subjects, mathematics and philosophy. She opened a new seminary at Waterford, N.Y., 1819, but when it failed to receive state appropriations, she moved to Troy, N.Y., 1821, where a building was provided by the city. The Troy Female Seminary (later the Emma Willard School), which became a model for later women's high schools, graduated teachers trained in history, philosophy, and the sciences. In addition to teaching there, Mrs. Willard was in full charge from the time of her husband's death, 1825, until 1838, when she married Dr. Christopher Yates, whom she divorced in 1843. She became active in the common school reform movement, 1838, assisting in particular Henry Barnard of Connecticut. She was elected to the Hall of Fame, 1905. Among her works are the poem, *Rocked in the Cradle of the Deep* (1830), *Advancement of Female Education* (1833), *Journal and Letters from France and Great Britain* (1833), and numerous textbooks.

WILLARD, FRANCES ELIZABETH CAROLINE, 1839–98, U.S. reformer, was born in Churchville, N.Y., but while still very young moved with her parents to Wisconsin, where she was graduated from the Northwestern Female College, 1859. She taught for several years in New York and Illinois, and then became president of the Ladies' College, Evanston, Ill.; when this institution became the Woman's College of Northwestern University she was made dean and professor of aesthetics. She resigned, 1874, and became president of the Chicago branch of the Woman's Christian Temperance Union (W.C.T.U.), an organization then in its infancy. She also served as corresponding secretary for the national organization. In 1876 she began speaking for woman's suffrage. She was temporarily editor of the Chicago *Post and Mail*, 1878. She became president of the W.C.T.U., 1879, and was re-elected every year until her death. In 1887 she was chosen president of the World's Woman's Christian Temperance Union. She traveled in Europe, Asia, and Africa, 1868–71, and in England, 1892. She was assistant editor of *Our Day*, and for many years was editor in chief of the W.C.T.U. organ, *Union Signal*. Among her works are *Nineteen Beautiful Years* (1868), *Woman and Temperance* (1883), and *A Classic Town* (1892).

WILLARD, JESS, 1883– , U.S. heavyweight boxer, was born in Pottawatomie, Kan. He won the world's heavyweight championship from Jack Johnson in 1915 and lost it to Jack Dempsey in 1919.

WILLEMITE, a zinc silicate mineral having the usual formula $Zn_2(SiO_4)$, but frequently one in which manganese takes the place of the zinc. Willemite has a hexagonal, rhombohedral crystallography, usually occuring in massive to granular form, rather than as crystals (see CRYSTALLOGRAPHY). It has a specific gravity of approximately 4, and a hardness of 5½ (see HARDNESS). It is white when pure, but as found it may be reddish, yellow-green, or brown, and is translucent to transparent. Willemite is found in limestone deposits, principally in Franklin, N. J., in association with franklinite and zincite. It is a valuable ore of zinc.

WILLEMSTAD, city, capital of the Netherlands West Indies; on the S coast of the island of Curaçao; 170 miles NW of Caracas, Venezuela. Willemstad has large oil refineries, for which it imports crude oil from the Venezuelan oilfields. The city has an important port, and is the commercial center for the island. Willemstad also has an extensive tourist industry. The city is located on one of the finest harbors of the West Indies, consisting of the long channel of St. Anna Bay, which opens into an expansive inner bay, known as Schottegat; both are deep enough for ocean liners. A floating bridge across the harbor connects the main part of the city with Otrabanda, "The Other Side." Among the principal points of interest are Wilhelmina Park; the Town Hall; and, in the vicinity, the historical Jewish Cemetery, which was established in 1650. Pop. (1958) 44,062.

WILLESDEN, municipal borough, SE England, in Middlesex, a residential suburb to the NW of London. The borough has important railroad shops. Willesden was incorporated in 1933. Pop. (1951) 179,647.

WILLETT, WILLIAM, 1856–1915, English builder and the originator of daylight-saving time, was born in Farnham, Surrey. Willett conceived the idea of daylight-saving time in 1907 and wrote *The Waste of Daylight* (19 editions, 1907–12). See TIME.

WILLIAM I, variously called the Conqueror, the Norman, and the Bastard, 1027?–87, king of England,

CULVER SERVICE
William I

was born in Falaise in Normandy, the natural son of Duke Robert II (the Devil) of Normandy and his mistress, Arlette, the daughter of a tanner. William succeeded his father as Duke of Normandy, 1035, but was not firmly established in power until 1047. In 1051, he visited his cousin, the King of England, Edward the Confessor, who allegedly promised him the succession to the English throne. In 1064, the powerful Harold of Wessex, himself a pretender to the English throne, was forced to acknowledge William's priority.

When Edward the Confessor died, however, Harold seized the vacated throne. William thereupon invaded England, and defeated and slew Harold at the Battle of Hastings (or Senlac), Sept. 28, 1066—probably the most important single date in English history, and certainly the most remembered. William then laid waste the English countryside, battled his way into London, and had himself crowned king, Dec. 25, 1066. He spent the next few years suppressing uprisings of the English, and in driving back the ambitious Malcolm III of Scotland. After he had thoroughly devastated the north of England; had induced Hereward the Wake, who had held out on the Fens, near Ely, to make peace; and had forced Malcolm III to submit at Abernethy, 1072, William at last was able to regard his conquest of England as completed. The conquest had to be maintained, however, and to this end he suppressed the power of the nobles; reduced the temporal authority of the church; and put down numerous uprisings, including two led by his son Robert, 1080 and 1082. Wars on the Continent took William away from England on several occasions.

William authorized the compilation of the Domesday Book, 1085. He established the Norman feudal system in England, 1086. Ultimately, after a tempestuous reign of 21 years, he died ingloriously at Rouen from injuries sustained falling off his horse. He was succeeded by his son William II.

WILLIAM II, called Rufus, 1056?–1100, king of England, succeeded his father William the Conqueror, 1087. A new invasion of England by Malcolm III of Scotland prompted William to invade Scotland and annex Cumberland, which he peopled with English and Flemings. An insurrection aimed at usurping his crown in favor of his brother Robert was quelled through lying promises and stratagem. In 1093, he appointed the unwilling Anselm, archbishop of Canterbury, but soon had reason to regret it: a long and bitter quarrel, resolved only by William's death, arose between the two over recognition of the pope's authority and the power of the Roman Catholic church in England (see ANSELM, SAINT). William was killed by an arrow, probably accidentally, while on a hunting trip in the New Forest. Tradition records his unwitting slayer as one Walter Tirel, a Norman. William was succeeded on the throne by his younger brother, Henry I Beauclerc.

WILLIAM III, 1650–1702, king of England, was born in The Hague, the posthumous son of William

II of Orange, ruler of the United Netherlands. In 1677, he was married to Mary, the daughter of James, duke of York, who became king of England as James II, 1785. After the Glorious Revolution, 1688, a number of English nobles, both Tories and Whigs, asked William to accept the English crown. He readily did so and soon landed at Torbay with an army of 15,000 men. Most of the leaders and populace rallied to the cause of the newcomer, not so much out of affection for him as out of hatred for the tyrannical James II, who was forced to take refuge in France under the protection of Louis XIV. Parliament declared the throne vacated, 1689, and shortly thereafter William and Mary were crowned king and queen of England. James II, having rallied his forces, was defeated by William in the Battle of Boyne, 1690. The surrender of Limerick to William's forces, 1691, ended James's hopes of regaining the crown and secured the accession of William and Mary.

William then took the field against his enemy, Louis XIV. His designs were thwarted, however, and he reluctantly signed the Peace of Ryswick (1697). His further attempts to unite Europe against France failed, and important domestic issues directed his energies away from the Continent and back to England.

William's reign marked the transition from the personal government of the Stuarts to the parliamentary rule of the Hanoverians: control of the army was transferred to Parliament; a better system of finance was introduced and the Bank of England was established; the constitutional rights of the people were set on a firmer basis. Yet William remained unpopular with both Parliament and the people: his foreign birth, his unfamiliarity with English customs, and his reserved temperament all served to alienate him from the affection of the nation. During his later years the king's measures were almost invariably opposed by Parliament. The death of Queen Mary, 1694, aggravated his difficulties. His death, occasioned by a fall from his horse, aroused little grief among the populace. Later historians, however, were to treat him more generously than did his contemporaries, for in ridding England of the tyranny of James II, and in reforming the nation's political and financial institutions, William accomplished far more for the welfare of the English people than had most of his native-born predecessors.

WILLIAM IV, 1765–1837, king of England and of Hanover, 1830–37, was born in Windsor, the third son of George III. He spent his early years as a naval officer, and later was called "The Sailor King" by admirers; his detractors, however, called him "Silly Billy." He became heir to the English throne, 1827, and succeeded his brother George IV, 1830. He was popular with the nation because of his genial and simple character and his sympathy with liberal principles. During his reign, the great Reform Bill of 1832 was passed, as were such related measures as the abolition of colonial slavery, 1833; the reform of the poor laws, 1834; and the Municipal Reform Act, 1835. His niece, Victoria, succeeded him on the English throne.

WILLIAM I, German name Wilhelm Friedrich Ludwig, 1797–1888, king of Prussia and German emperor, was born in Berlin, the son of Frederick William III of Prussia. He served in the war against Napoleon I, 1814–15, and received the Iron Cross for gallantry. At the accession of his brother King Frederick William IV of Prussia, 1840, Wilhelm became Prince of Prussia. His reactionary sympathies at the time of the Revolution of 1848 in Berlin made him extremely unpopular, and he was forced to take refuge in England. When King Frederick William IV went insane, 1858, Prince William became regent; he succeeded to the Prussian throne, 1861. He made Otto von Bismarck his chancellor, 1862, and fully supported his policy of solving German problems by "Blood and Iron" rather than by parliamentary

procedure and diplomacy. With William's consent, Bismarck set about to establish complete Prussian ascendancy in Germany. The Schleswig-Holstein War, 1864, the Austro-Prussian War, 1866, and the Franco-Prussian War, 1870–71, were all fought and won to this end, and William, having eliminated all serious opposition to his ambitions, was crowned Emperor of Germany, Jan. 18, 1871. He spent his remaining years consolidating his power, persecuting minority groups, and forming alliances with other imperialist powers. He was succeeded to the Prussian and imperial German thrones by his son Frederick III.

WILLIAM II, Friedrich Wilhelm Viktor Albert, 1859–1941, king of Prussia and emperor of Germany, was born in Berlin, the son of Frederick III of Prussia

CULVER SERVICE
William II

and Princess Victoria (princess royal) of England. Called to the throne by the death of his father, 1888, William immediately proclaimed his divinely given right to rule and soon made it evident that he was to be no puppet king; in all the departments of imperial government, foreign relations, and military affairs he demonstrated an irrepressible and exuberant energy. He called for the resignation of the extremely powerful Bismarck, 1890, and thenceforth kept the office of chancellor subservient to himself. By temper and tradition a thorough autocrat, he startled Europe by speeches in which he indicated an exalted notion of his imperial responsibility, and intimated his firm resolve to maintain the high monarchial traditions of the House of Hohenzollern.

Anxious to extend the power of Germany and to secure for her a dominant role in world politics, he entered enthusiastically into the already tempestuous arena of colonial expansion. By cultivating friendly relations with Turkey, he furthered German commercial and financial interests in the Near East; by maintaining close personal relations with his army and by creating a powerful navy, he secured formidable means of defending and advancing his own imperial and imperialist interests.

Within Germany, he made every effort to speed the transition from an agricultural to an industrial economy. The growing power of the Socialist movement within his own empire constituted an ever present menace to his imperial ambitions. Despite his immense influence, he was on several occasions forced, because of Socialist opposition, to withdraw or see defeated his more reactionary schemes.

World War I overshadowed the later years of William's reign. The emperor's dealings with the radical Socialist party during the war and the armed merchantmen controversy with the United States, resulting finally in the entrance of the United States into the conflict, stand out among other great events of an eventful reign.

With the defeat of German arms, autumn, 1918, and the spread of revolutionary propaganda, the emperor's position became untenable. On Nov. 9, 1918, he abdicated the throne and fled to Holland, where he later purchased an estate at Doorn. Here the empress, who prior to her marriage, 1881, had been Princess Augusta Victoria of Schleswig-Holstein-Sonderburg-Augustenburg, died in 1921. A year later, the former emperor married Hermine of Schönaich-Carolath, princess of Reuss (1887–1947). By his first marriage William II had six sons and one daughter. He wrote *My Early Life* (1926), *My Ancestors* (1929), *Recollections of Three Kaisers* (1929).

BIBLIOG.—Maurice Baumont, *Fall of the Kaiser* (1931); Jacques D. Chamier, *Fabulous Monster* [*A Biography of the ex-Kaiser*] (1934); Joachim von Kürenburg, *Kaiser: A Life of*

Wilhelm II, Last Emperor of Germany (1955); Emil Ludwig, *Wilhelm Hohenzollern: Kaiser Wilhelm II* (1934); Karl F. Nowak, *Kaiser and the Chancellor: The Opening Years of the Reign of Kaiser Wilhelm II, Germany's Road to Ruin: The Middle Years of the Reign of the Emperor William II* (1932); George S. Viereck (George F. Corners, pseud.), *Kaiser on Trial* (1937); René Viviani, *As We See It* (1923); Wallscourt H. H. Waters, *Potsdam and Doorn* (1935); Robert Graf von Zedlitz-Trützschler, *Twelve Years of the Imperial German Court* (1924).

WILLIAM I, Willem Frederik, 1772–1843, king of the Netherlands, was born in The Hague, the son of William V, the last hereditary stadholder of Holland. He commanded the Dutch army against France, 1793–95. Defeated, he joined the Prussian army and served as general until captured by the French at Jena, 1806. Released, he joined the Austrian army and served with distinction at the Battle of Wagram, 1809. After the fall of Napoleon I, the Congress of Vienna created the new Kingdom of the Netherlands out of Belgium and Holland, and elected William as its first king. His years on the throne, 1815–40, were troubled by Belgium's desire for independence, a desire fulfilled in 1839. He abdicated in 1840.

WILLIAM II, Willem Frederik George Lodewijk, 1792–1849, king of the Netherlands, was the son of William I. He fought with the Duke of Wellington in Spain during the Napoleonic Wars, and commanded the Dutch army at the Battle of Waterloo. He was caught between the Belgian desire for independence from the Netherlands and his father's desire to maintain unity. He approved of the Belgian revolt, 1830, but fought against them, 1832, only to be defeated by French forces. Becoming king after his father's abdication, 1840, William instituted financial improvements, granted a constitution to his subjects, and created a bicameral Parliament. He was succeeded by his son William III.

WILLIAM III, Willem Alexander Paul Frederik Lodewijk, 1817–90, king of the Netherlands, the son of William II, succeeded his father in 1849 and ruled until 1890. Although opposed to political liberalism, he was a constitutional monarch and, in the main, on good terms with the Netherlands Parliament. He gave a parliamentary constitution to his Luxembourg subjects, and used his large personal fortune to further social reform. He was married to Princess Sophia of Württemberg, 1839, and to Princess Emma of Waldeck-Pyrmont, 1879. The sons of his first marriage died unmarried, and his throne passed to the daughter of his second marriage, Wilhelmina I.

WILLIAM II, 1154–89, king of Sicily, was the son of Margaret of Navarre and of William I the Bad of Sicily. Ascending the throne, 1166, he ruled nominally for several years under the regency of his mother. As king, William supported the papacy and leagued with the Lombard cities. He was constantly on bad terms with Emperor Frederick I, and engaged in an unsuccessful war against Egypt. Sympathetic to the motives of the Third Crusade, he permitted the Crusaders to pass through his territory and forced the Egyptian Sultan Saladin to retreat from a position before Tripoli.

WILLIAM II, PRINCE OF ORANGE, 1626–50, Dutch stadholder, was the son of Frederik Henry and the grandson of William the Silent. At the age of 14, he was married to Princess Mary, the eldest daughter of Charles I of England. Upon his accession to power, 1647, he opposed ratification of the newly signed Treaty of Münster between Spain and the United Netherlands because he hoped for the further enlargement of Dutch territory. To the same end he negotiated a military-aid treaty with France. The states of Holland, however, were opposed to further conflict. William triumphed in the ensuing struggle for power, but only after imprisoning the leading members of his opposition. Shortly after resumption of negotiations with France, William succumbed suddenly to the pox. His posthumously born son became William III of England.

WILLIAM AND MARY, COLLEGE OF, a public, coeducational institution of higher learning, located in Williamsburg, Va. Affiliate institutions are the Richmond Professional Institute, at Richmond, Va., and the Norfolk Division, at Norfolk, Va.

The College of William and Mary is the second oldest college in the United States. It received its name from the English monarchs who signed its first charter. In 1617 an institution, to be known as the University of Henrico, was about to be founded at Williamsburg, but was not because of an Indian massacre. Through the efforts of the Rev. James Blair, the Bishop of London's commissary in Virginia, a royal charter was obtained, 1691, the royal grant including the quitrents from 20,000 acres of land in Virginia. For these concessions, the college was to pay two books of Latin verse annually as rent. The Rev. James Blair also raised £3,000 for the college through pledges by London merchants, and an additional £300 from pirates whom he had aided in obtaining pardons.

The college conducts a co-operative program with various higher educational institutions throughout the state, leading to a master's degree in education. It also offers masters' degrees in aquatic biology, education, English, history, law and taxation, physical education, psychology, and physics. The school library has collections of materials on Virginia, early American history, dogs and hunting, horticulture and early gardening, and the history of war. Publications include the *Alumni Gazette*, and *William and Mary Quarterly.*

Among the notable buildings on the campus are the Sir Christopher Wren building (1697), which was used as a hospital by the French army during the Yorktown campaign; the Brafferton Building (1723), the college's original Indian school; and the President's House (1732), which was occupied by Lord Cornwallis, 1781, and, after the Battle of Yorktown, by French soldiers who accidentally burned it—after which it was restored by King Louis XVI of France. See COLLEGES AND UNIVERSITIES.

WILLIAM JEWELL COLLEGE, a private, coeducational, liberal arts college, affiliated with the Baptist Church, and located at Liberty, Mo. The school offered its first instruction in 1850 and was chartered nine years later. The school's departments are ancient languages, modern languages, economics, business administration, chemistry, education, English, history, mathematics, astronomy, music, philosophy, physical education, physics, political science, psychology, religion, and sociology. See COLLEGES AND UNIVERSITIES.

WILLIAM OCKAM, not William "of" Ockam, 1285?–?1349, radical English Franciscan thinker, was born probably in Ockam (Ockham, or Occam), south of London, and became a Franciscan monk, and a student and then a magister in theology in Oxford. By 1322 he had been advanced to the position of inceptor; this meant that he had already taught for a number of years and had seemingly fulfilled the requirements for the doctorate up to the ceremony of promotion. In any case, he and his party were strong enough to remove from office the chancellor of the university, John Lutterell (died 1335). As it happened, this event became the turning point in William's life, for Lutterell went immediately to Avignon, France, and there sought to convince the Papal Court that William was a heretic. William was summoned to Avignon, 1323, and had to remain during the examination of this question, which lasted until 1328. Finally, some 51 articles in William's works on logic, physics, and the Eucharist were declared "pestilential" and heretical; in large measure this finding was based on hearsay in the lecture notes of William's students. In the spring of 1328, William fled from Avignon, via Aigues Mortes and Genoa, to the Holy Roman emperor's camp near Pisa, and to Ludwig [Louis] IV the Bavarian: "Sire, defend me with thy sword: I shall defend thee with my pen." William kept his word on this score to the end of his life.

Together with two other Franciscan fugitives, William was excommunicated, June 8, 1328, and stayed so, but in the Franciscan Order he never lost his standing; he was its vicar from 1342, and he retained the Great Seal of the Order until just before his death. The Franciscans, in William's days, were trying to save their ideal of poverty in the face of papal opposition; there is extant one eloquent letter by William to his Order on this problem; others among his pamphlets attack the popes as having fallen into heresy themselves. William followed the emperor to Munich, 1330, and later he took a hand in the election of Ludwig's successor, Charles IV, 1348. At this time, his Order tried to reconcile him with the church; the outcome of their effort is unknown. April 10 is given as the day of William's death, but the year—probably 1349 or 1350—remains uncertain; the cause was the Black Plague.

Up to the time of his trial in Avignon, William tried, as a good Franciscan, to prevent the intrusion of pagan philosophical doctrines into Christian theology, and stressed the omnipotence and lasting freedom of the living God against the naïve Greek systematization of God's qualities. Thus he wrote that "God can change sin into virtue. Now, he asks us to praise his name; but tomorrow he may command us to hate his name." William's character is further revealed by this proud declaration: "I never want to be defeated by the mass. The talk of so many that one never should oppose the mass, I consider rank heresy. The multitude, as a rule, is in error; and very often the solitary man may put all the rest to flight. This is what Biblical tradition teaches."

On the other hand, modern scholars have probably attributed too much to William in suggesting that Copernicus, Luther, and Descartes (among others) were all his direct descendants. In the main, William was a medieval logician who identified soul with mind, defended Aristotle insofar as he understood him, and protected God's Trinity against rationalists. In a negative sense, however, he did open the gates to later scientific investigation by his radical "Nominalism," for which he soon became so famous that his title, the Venerable Inceptor, was often misconstrued to "Inceptor [that is, Founder] of Nominalism." In the centennial debate over the Universals, William taught that man's general concepts are purely cerebral ("nominal") and have no external reality; only the particular and individual has concrete existence. To illustrate the distinction: since antiquity respect for the heavens had led to the assumption that the stars must be composed of a special matter qualitatively different from that of which the earth is composed. William was first to teach that there is no reason to assume such a heavenly matter in general, as this is an unnecessary and arbitrary general concept. William's sentence *"entia non multiplicanda sunt praeter necessitatem"* (Entities should not be multiplied beyond necessity) became famous as "Ockam's Razor," the law of parsimony by which all unnecessary whiskers of thought are to be shaved off. As applied to Movement, Time, and Space, it meant that William denied the "thingness" of all three. With respect to movement, it is enough, he wrote, to say that something moves from one place to another. Time is nothing by itself. When we perceive change or movement from one place to another, we call this Time. In this belittling of Time as a mere by-product, William was indeed the ancestor of Descartes. See ABÉLARD, PIERRE; CONCEPTUALISM; CONCORDANCE; DESCARTES, RENÉ; NOMINALISM; REALISM, *In Philosophy and Theology;* UNIVERSAL.

In his polemics against the papacy, William, as a true Franciscan, was not so much concerned with furthering the interests of the secular state as he was in purging the church of her depraved practices. It is in this connection that his highly important doctrine of popular sovereignty of the church must be understood. In a civil emergency, William taught, a people, a community, a body of men can legislate for themselves; hence the church, too, with a recalcitrant leadership at the top, might be reformed from the bottom up. To this end, he proposed, all believers in each parish should choose delegates to an electoral assembly of their diocese, principality, or kingdom. By these assemblies, the delegates to a universal council could be chosen. And in such a council, even though no pope had convened it or presided over it, the church could be embodied. This doctrine, heeded more or less by the more conciliatory churchmen of the next centuries, and later applied by the North American colonists in their revolution, reveals the radical "spatialisation" engendered by Nominalism. God now was separated from His church, for the church now had been moved over to the realm of Space; therefore the church could be organized from the bottom upward.

Many of William Ockam's works had yet to be published in the 1960's, and most of those that had been remained largely inaccessible to the general reader. Stephen Chak Tornay's brief *Ockham: Studies and Selections* (1938) may be used with caution, but a better guide to William's work in theology is Robert Guelluy's *Philosophie et Théologie chez Guillaume d'Ockham* (1947). For William's life see Philotheus Boehner's *Study on the Life and Works of Ockham* (Franciscan Institute Publications No. 1, 1944).

EUGEN ROSENSTOCK-HUESSY

WILLIAM OF CHAMPEAUX, French Guillaume de Champeaux 1070?–1121 or 1122, French theologian, was born in Champeaux (near Melun); studied in Paris under Manegold of Lautenbach, in Laon under Anselm, and in Compiégne; and then taught from 1103 in Paris, where his student Pierre Abélard (Abailard) debated with him so impressively that Champeaux modified his doctrine. In 1108, he crossed over to the left bank of the Seine and instituted the mystical tradition of the Monastery of St. Victor. He was Bishop of Châlons-sur-Marne from 1113, and as such gave his moral support to the Cistercian Bernard de Clairvaux, who wished to found a new monastery, 1115. In regard to the problem of universals, Champeaux recognized that men, through their linguistic generalizations, enter upon the plan of Creation itself, that concepts are formed within the historical process and are thus "time-nourished," and that articulate speech must at any historical moment bear witness to the plan of Creation by distinguishing the essential from the accidental (see ABÉLARD, PIERRE; CONCEPTUALISM; REALISM, *Realism in Philosophy;* UNIVERSAL). In the same vein, he held to the doctrine of "Creationism" for each soul; that is, one's soul is created immediately as one enters upon the earthly pilgrimage. Champeaux' book on the Eucharist furnishes valuable details about contemporary practices. He contributed significantly to the development of the literary form of *quaestio*, in which two justifiable theses are opposed to each other so that two equally authorized thinkers can enter upon a disputation in a mutual effort to discover truth, in contrast to the pre-Christian method of the solitary thinker. The *quaestio*, which was the prime methodological advance of the Middle Ages over pagan antiquity, had great ramifications in many realms of endeavor. The medieval universities were founded on this method of disputation, in contrast to the pre-Christian academies, in which only the one, official point of view was represented. See CONCORDANCE; SCHOLASTICISM; UNIVERSITY.

EUGEN ROSENSTOCK-HUESSY

WILLIAM OF MALMESBURY, 1090?–?1143, Anglo-Norman chronicler, was born in Somersetshire and studied at Malmesbury Abbey, where he became a monk and later served as librarian and precentor. His principal works are *Gesta regum anglorum* (Acts of the English Kings), ?1125, a history of the

English kings after the Norman Conquest, 1066, and *Historia novella* (Modern History), 1142, a continuation of the history. Although some scholars find William's chronology faulty, it is generally admitted that his works present a lively and accurate portrait of the times. Among his other works are the *Gesta pontificum anglorum* (Acts of the English Prelates), 1125, and *De antiquitate glastoniensis ecclesiae* (History of the Church at Glastonbury), 1129–39.

WILLIAM OF NEWBURGH, 1136?–98, English historian, was born in Yorkshire, but spent the greater part of his adult life at the Augustinian monastery of Newburgh. William is remembered chiefly as the author of the *Historia rerum anglicarum*, probably the best contemporary account of English life in the twelfth century. The *Historia* is a well written, if somewhat loosely structured, chronicle of the years 1066–1198, and is especially important as a corrective to Geoffrey of Monmouth's fabulous *Historia britonum*.

WILLIAM OF NORWICH, 1132?–44, traditional English child martyr, was a tanner's apprentice. Of no particular note during his short lifetime, he achieved considerable posthumous fame because of the supposed cause of his death. On Easter Day, 1144, he was found dead, murdered under mysterious circumstances. Unjustified rumors were soon circulating to the effect that William had been a victim of so-called Jewish ritual murders. The credulity, ignorance, and avarice of the local populace overpowered their reason, and the deceased young William was in time awarded the status of a martyr. No reputable historian credits the popular contemporary interpretation of William's demise.

WILLIAM OF WIED, PRINCE, 1876–1945, King of Albania, born in Neuwied, Prussia, the son of William, prince of Wied, and the cousin of Emperor William II. He was for some years a military officer. In 1912, Albania was proclaimed independent, and the international control commission of six powers which directed the new nation selected William, the following year, to rule it. His reign lasted six months. He did not speak Albanian, nor was he familiar with the country, nor did he appoint ministers who could serve him well. In September, 1914, without sufficient friends or funds to rule effectively, he was forced to leave the country, but refused to abdicate. Any chance of his return ended with the coming to power of Ahmed Bey Zogu (later King Zog I) in the 1920's. William died in Rumania. His wife was Sophie, princess of Schoenburg-Waldenburg; they had two children. See ALBANIA.

WILLIAMS, CHARLES WALTER STANSBY, 1886–1945, English novelist, poet, and critic, was born in London and studied at St. Alban's School, London University, and Workingmen's College. Williams worked for the Oxford University Press, 1908–45, first as reader, later as an editor. He wrote books of poetry, biography, criticism, and theology, and edited anthologies, wrote prefaces, and did translations, but is best known for his remarkable novels in which theological and occult matters are treated in terms of penny-dreadful adventure yarns, among which the best known are *War in Heaven* (1930), *Descent into Hell* (1937), and *All Hallows' Eve* (1945).

WILLIAMS, ELEAZAR, 1789?–1858, U.S. missionary and pretender to the throne of France, was born in Caughnawaga, N.Y. Williams is thought to have been the grandson of Eunice Williams. During the War of 1812 he served as U.S. secret agent among the Canadian Indians; after the war, having taken orders in the Episcopal church, did missionary work among the Oneida Indians in Green Bay, Wis., 1822–50. In about 1840 he began to assert that he was the "lost dauphin," son of Louis XVI and Marie Antoinette, claiming to have been taken from a revolutionary prison by an agent of the royal family, and brought to New York. Although he received a brief visit from Prince de Joinville, son of King Louis Philippe, at his home in Green Bay, Wis., 1841, Williams' claims never received serious attention. He translated the prayer book into Iroquois, 1853, and wrote *A Life of Te-ho-ra-gwa-ne-gen* (Thomas Williams).

WILLIAMS, EMLYN, 1905– , Welsh playwright and actor, was born in Mostyn, Flintshire, Wales, and studied at Christ Church, Oxford. His most successful dramas were *Night Must Fall* (1935) and *The Corn Is Green* (1938). He also achieved great success with his evenings of readings from Dickens. His autobiography, *George*, appeared in 1961.

WILLIAMS, SIR GEORGE, 1821–1905, English philanthropist, was born in Dulverton, Somersetshire. He was the originator, 1844, treasurer, 1863–85, and president, 1885, of the Young Men's Christian Association. He was knighted in 1904.

WILLIAMS, GEORGE HENRY, 1820–1910, U.S. jurist and public official, was born in New Lebanon, N.Y. He was admitted to the bar, 1844, began practice in Iowa and was a district judge, 1847–52. He was chief justice of the Oregon Territory, 1853–57, U.S. senator from Oregon, 1865–71, and supported the Radical Republicans in their opposition to Pres. Andrew Johnson's reconstruction policy. He was a member of the Joint High Commission that negotiated the Treaty of Washington with England, 1871, and U.S. attorney general, 1871–75. In 1873 he was nominated by Pres. Ulysses S. Grant as chief justice of the United States, but failed to receive Senate confirmation. He was mayor of Portland, Ore., 1902–05.

WILLIAMS, JOHN, 1664–1729, colonial American clergyman, was born in Roxbury, Mass., was graduated from Harvard, 1683, was ordained a minister, 1688, and was made pastor of a church in Deerfield. On Feb. 29, 1704, a party of French and Indians under Hertel de Ronville surprised the town, killed many of the inhabitants, among them two of Williams' children, and captured about 300 others, including Williams, his wife, and his remaining children except one absent son. On the second day's march toward Canada Mrs. Williams became exhausted, and was tomahawked. Williams and the children reached Canada in safety, however, and there, after about a year's captivity, Williams and his son Stephen were bought by the French governor, 1706, and returned to Massachusetts, 1707. The daughter Eunice who was eight years old when captured, was retained by the Indians, adopted their language and customs, married an Indian brave, and could not be persuaded to give up her savage life. She is thought to have been the grandmother of Eleazar Williams, who claimed to be the lost dauphin. John Williams published an account of his captivity, *The Redeemed Captive Returning to Zion* (1707).

WILLIAMS, OSCAR, 1900–64, U.S. poet and anthologist, began writing poetry when he was 17 years old. He edited a poetry magazine, *Rhythmus*, 1923. Much of Williams' poetry deals with the problems of man in a mechanized world. Among his poetical works are *The Golden Darkness* (1921), *In Gossamer Grey* (1921), *The Man Coming Toward You* (1940), *That's All That Matters* (1945), and *Selected Poems* (1947). Among his anthologies are *A Little Treasury of Modern Poetry* (1946) and *Immortal Poems of the English Language* (1952).

WILLIAMS, ROGER, 1604?–83, colonial American religious leader, the founder of Rhode Island, was born in London, England. Through the patronage of Sir Edward Coke, Williams attended Charter House School and Pembroke College, Cambridge, which awarded him a degree, 1627. He then took religious orders and for a time served as chaplain in the Essex household of Sir William Masham. By this time Williams had become a Puritan, however, and as such he sailed for New England, 1630, and became assistant at the church of Salem, Mass., 1631. He had already objected, however, to the failure of the Puritan church of Massachusetts to separate formally from the Church of England, and to the amount of control over the individual conscience exercised by the Boston church. This created a good deal of opposition, and Williams soon resigned his Salem post and retired to Plymouth Colony. However, he returned to the church at Salem in 1633 and became its pastor in 1634. In addition to his earlier charges, Williams now claimed that the royal charter gave settlers to the New World no valid title to land, and insisted that the land should be purchased from the Indians. He denied the power of the magistrates to exact oaths of civil obedience and declared that the civil authorities should not punish violations of the first four Commandments. For these views he was formally banished from the Massachusetts Bay Colony, October, 1635. In January, 1636, however, he fled to the territory of the Narragansett Indians and there, in June of 1636, he founded Providence, the first settlement in what was to be Rhode Island, according to a principle that at that time was so revolutionary as to be virtually unthinkable—the principle of absolute religious toleration.

Williams farmed for a living, and in his trading with the Narragansett so won their confidence that he was able to keep them neutral during the Pequot War of 1637. He founded the first Baptist church in North America, 1639, but he soon changed his views, and recognized no one true church. Returning to England, 1643, he passed the time during the long voyage writing his *Key into the Language of America*, on the speech of the New England Indians. Once in England, he obtained a charter (1644) from Parliament that united several settlements into the colony of Rhode Island, guaranteed its independence, and secured its boundaries against encroachments by its orthodox neighbors, Massachusetts and Connecticut. While in England, Williams entered the revolutionary controversy, and wrote several pamphlets, of which the most notable is *The Bloudy Tenent of Persecution, for Cause of Conscience* (1644), which advocates absolute liberty of conscience in religious matters. Returning to Rhode Island, Williams served as its governor, 1644–47. Back in England, 1651, he successfully secured the dismissal of William Coddington, who had been appointed governor of Aquidneck Island, an integral part of the colony. While in London, Williams published *The Bloudy Tenent Yet More Bloudy* (1652) and *The Hireling Ministry None of Christ's* (1652), the latter an argument against an established church and a tax-supported clergy.

Williams returned to Rhode Island once again, and was its "president," 1654–58, during which time he secured toleration for Quakers. Thereafter he served the colony in various capacities before dying in poverty. ROBIN OGGINS

BIBLIOG.–Perry Miller, *Roger Williams, His Contribution to American Thought* (1953); Ola Elizabeth Winslow, *Master Roger Williams* (1957).

WILLIAMS, TENNESSEE, 1914– , U.S. playwright, was born Thomas Lanier Williams in Columbus, Miss., and studied at the universities of Missouri and Iowa, and Washington University in St. Louis. His first Broadway success was *The Glass Menagerie* (1944), which deals with the frustrations of a family whose mother refuses to abandon her dreams of regaining a life of gentility. In this and in *A Streetcar Named Desire* (1947; Pulitzer prize), Williams displayed a craftsmanship and poetic vision that marked him as one of the outstanding talents in the contemporary U.S. theater. His plays are basically character studies, often depressing, sometimes disgusting, frequently about neurotic individuals shut off from

CULVER SERVICE
Tennessee Williams

the world and tormented by the unfeeling people they find around them. With his genius for theater language, however, Williams manages over and over again to give these sad souls the power at least to explain themselves in clear, honest, and poignant terms. Other works include two volumes of one-act plays, *American Blues* (1939) and *27 Wagons Full of Cotton* (1946); *Summer and Smoke* (1948); a novel, *The Roman Spring of Mrs. Stone* (1950); *The Rose Tattoo* (1951); *Camino Real* (1953); *Cat on a Hot Tin Roof* (1955; Pulitzer prize); *Orpheus Descending* (1957); *Sweet Bird of Youth* (1959); *Period of Adjustment* (1960); *Night of the Iguana* (1961); and *The Milk Train Doesn't Stop Here Anymore* (1963).

WILLIAMS, WILLIAM, 1731–1811, U.S. patriot, was born in Lebanon, Conn., studied at Harvard College, and during the French and Indian War served on the staff of Col. Ephraim Williams (1714–55) and took part in the Lake George Expedition, 1755. He served in the Continental Congress, 1776–78, 1783–84. Williams was a member of the committee that drew up the Articles of Confederation, and was a signer of the Declaration of Independence.

WILLIAMS, WILLIAM CARLOS, 1883–1963, U.S. poet, dramatist, and writer of fiction and critical prose. Though he excelled all others of his craft in helping his countrymen to realize their roots, he himself was the son of immigrants (an English father and a Puerto Rican mother, who before her marriage had been an art student in France), a fact influential in Williams' approach to poetry. It is striking that his paternal grandmother's maiden name was Emily Dickinson. Like the poet Emily Dickinson, Williams chose one American city—in his case, Rutherford, New Jersey—from which to observe the world. Indeed, his lyrics are synechdochic letters written to people all over that world who found joy in his special insights into his homeland—insights recorded on the prescription pads that replaced the eighteen copybooks of verse he had been so proud of as a student.

After an education at Horace Mann High School (New York City), in Switzerland, at the University of Pennsylvania (class of 1906), and as intern both in New York City and Leipzig, Dr. Williams went back to Rutherford to marry Florence Herman, establish their home, and begin his career as pediatrician. Outgoing by nature, he had been lucky in his early friends, one of whom, Ezra Pound, influenced his diction and metrics right up through Williams' last volume, *Pictures from Brueghel and Other Poems.* Another intimate was the painter Charles Demuth, whose illustration of the lyric "The Great Figure," now in the Metropolitan Museum of Art in New York, embodies the clarity of image (semiabstraction would perhaps be a better description) that linked Williams to two contemporary movements: the Objectivists in poetry and the "Immaculates" in painting. This last group numbered among its adherents a third friend, Charles Sheeler. *Spring and All* (1923) is dedicated to Demuth. Although they did not know each other personally, the painter John Marin and William Carlos Williams were fellow citizens of Rutherford and shared a fascination for the place, as the doctor-poet indicated in his introductory note to a Marin catalogue. References to the Old Masters in Williams' final volume of poetry completed in framework fashion his interest in painting.

Though for many readers Williams is at his best in brief lyrics (collections of these came out in 1950 and 1951, as well as in the reprinted section of *Breughel*), for others he is primarily the author of *Paterson*, the five books of which appeared between 1946 and 1958. For reasons of symbolism and of aesthetic distance, he selected as focal metaphor this New Jersey city near his native Rutherford. The largest silk-producing center in the United States, it serves (if taken from one aspect) as a cocoon composed of interwoven natural fibers, out of which emerges that metamorphic emblem, the butterfly, representative of the human imagination.

Paterson the city is both hero and heroine—the human race. It offers the poet a way to incarnate his ideas in the things apart from which, he believes, they have no existence. In mosaic technique, he achieves an epic study in sources, as in his impressionistic history *In the American Grain* (1925). Water, rock, and fire are its three leading types of "metamorphosis," the noun he uses in the epigraph to *Paterson* to define the poem. Like other novelists and poets of the twentieth century, Williams sees failure of communication as central to man's imprisonment, though he keeps faith in art as a liberating principle. His entire work is a testament of perpetual change, and his power to effect change both in poetry and in its serious readers did not end on March 4, 1963, when he died in his sleep of a cerebral hemorrhage.

SISTER M. BERNETTA QUINN, O.S.F.

BIBLIOG.—Among other books published by Williams are his play *Many Loves* (1958); three collections of short stories (*The Knife of the Times and Other Stories*, 1932; *Life Along the Passaic River*, 1938; *Make Light of It*, 1950); four novels (*A Voyage to Pagany*, 1928; *White Mule*, 1937; *In the Money*, 1940; *The Build-Up*, 1952); his autobiography (1951); and *Selected Essays* (1954). Vivienne Koch's full-length work on him appeared in 1950; Linda Wagner published a second in 1964. John C. Thirlwall edited his letters in 1957 and wrote an excellent article on *Paterson* in *New Directions 17.*

WILLIAMS, WILLIAM SHERLEY, called Old Bill, 1787–1849, U.S. trapper, explorer, and guide, was born in Rutherford (now Polk) County, N.C., but settled with his family on a farm near St. Louis, Mo. At the age of 15 Williams ran away and joined the Osage Indians in Southwestern Missouri, with whom he lived until 1825, when he became emissary and interpreter for a U.S. government expedition to survey the road from the mouth of the Kansas River to Santa Fe, N.M. From his arrival in New Mexico until the end of his adventurous life Williams roamed all over the great West—from the Mississippi to the Pacific, from the Columbia to the lower Rio Grande. In the winter of 1848–49, he reluctantly undertook to guide Col. John C. Frémont's fourth expedition from Pueblo, Colo., to California, but in attempting to cross La Garita Mountains, north of the Rio Grande, the party lost 11 of its 33 men, all its 120 animals, and most of its equipment in a blizzard.

FREDERIC E. VOELKER

WILLIAMSBURG, independent city, SE Virginia, seat of James City County; on a peninsula between the York and James River estuaries; about 45 miles SE of Richmond. The city is chiefly noted as a historical and cultural center. It was the colonial capital of Virginia, and is the site of William and Mary College (1693), second oldest college in the United States. The site was first settled in 1633 as Middle Plantation, an outpost of Jamestown. When the statehouse at Jamestown was burned in 1699,

Colonial Williamsburg (above, the capitol) was recreated through donations made by the Rockefeller family.

COLONIAL WILLIAMSBURG

Williamsburg was laid out and named in honor of William III of England. The colonial capital was removed to the new city and remained there until 1780. The city charter, granted in 1722, is the oldest in the state.

The restoring of the colonial appearance of Williamsburg began in the late 1920's. Colonial buildings were restored, existing buildings of modern type were torn down and replaced by others of colonial design to preserve the colonial atmosphere. Among the restored or reconstructed buildings are the Governor's Palace; the famous Raleigh Tavern, where Phi Beta Kappa is said to have been founded; the Capitol, where Patrick Henry made his famous "treason" speech in 1765; and the oldest academic building in English America, a unit of the college designed by Sir Christopher Wren. (For population, see Virginia map in Atlas.)

WILLIAMS COLLEGE, a private, nonsectarian, liberal arts college for men, located in Williamstown, Mass. The school, which was chartered and offered its first instruction in 1793, was named for Col. Ephraim Williams, an early, major contributor to its establishment. The college library has collections of materials on Samuel Butler, William Cullen Bryant, Edwin Arlington Robinson, and the Shakers, as well as the Chapin Library of rare books. See COLLEGES AND UNIVERSITIES.

WILLIAMSPORT, city, NE central Pennsylvania, seat of Lycoming County; located about 75 miles N of Harrisburg. The chief manufactured products of Williamsport are wire rope; leather products; boilers; valves; fire hydrants; auto, airplane, and marine motors; radio tubes; wood products; veneer; paper; glue; shoes; shirts; and silk. Williamsport, originally the site of an Indian village called French Margaret's Town, was settled in 1795. It was incorporated as a borough in 1806, and chartered as a city in 1866. Williamsport was one of the leading cities in the output of sawed lumber in the late 1860's. The Negro Slave Refuge (1838), a station of the Underground Railroad, is a leading point of interest. (For population, see Pennsylvania map in Atlas.)

WILLIAMSTOWN, town, NW Massachusetts, Berkshire County; at the base of the Taconic Mountains. The town is a summer-resort center. Williamstown was laid out in 1747 as West Hoosac. Under the terms of the will of Col. Ephraim Williams, who was killed in the Battle of Lake George, Sept. 8, 1755, a bequest was left for a free school if the town's name should be changed to Williamstown. The town is the site of Williams College. (For population, see Massachusetts map in Atlas.)

WILLIAM THE LION, 1143–1214, king of Scotland, succeeded his brother Malcolm IV, 1165, beginning what was to be the longest reign in Scottish history. William initiated the long friendship between Scotland and France with a formal alliance. He was later held in custody in Normandy, 1174–89, for taking part in the rebellion of the sons of Henry II of England against their father. William finally signed the Treaty of Falaise (1189), which made him Henry's Scotch vassal and provided for the subjugation of the Scotch church to the Church of England; later, however, he bought an abrogation of this treaty from Richard I, thus re-establishing the independence of the Scotch church. He spent the last decades of his long reign in the improvement of Scotland's internal affairs.

WILLIAM THE SILENT, PRINCE OF ORANGE, 1533–84, founder of the Dutch Republic, was born in the castle of Dillenburg, Nassau, the son of William, count of Nassau, and Juliana of Stolberg. Although born a Lutheran, he was educated in the Roman Catholic faith at the court of Emperor Charles V (King Charles I of Spain). He became Prince of Orange, 1544, and Count of Nassau, 1559. In 1555, Charles appointed him commander of troops in the Netherlands and governor of Holland, Zeeland, Utrecht, and West Friesland. Upon the accession of Philip II to the Spanish throne, 1556, William served in the war against Henry II of France, and was instrumental in negotiating the Peace of Cateau-Cambrésis (1559). But when Philip attempted to crush Protestantism in the Low Countries as a preliminary to gaining complete control there, William severed his allegiance to Spain and by 1561 he was the leader of opposition to Philip in the Netherlands.

William proclaimed his renewed adherence to the Protestant faith, 1568, and organized two armies to oppose Philip. One was destroyed by Alva, the governor of Spain; the other proved ineffective because of lack of funds, and was finally disbanded. William's cause suffered another defeat, 1568, when an army organized by him and Archduke Matthias was defeated by Spanish troops at Gembloux. William founded, 1579, the league of seven northern provinces that later became the Dutch Republic. Philip II put a price on his head, 1581, and three years later William was murdered at Delft by Balthasar Gérard, a French Roman Catholic fanatic.

William was one of the most forceful and idealistic personalities of his time. To his patience, perseverance, and skill the Dutch Republic owed its political unity and independence.

WILLIMANTIC, city, E central Connecticut, seat of Windham County; at the junction of the Natchaug and Willimantic rivers where the Shetucket is formed; on the New Haven and the Central Vermont railroads, and U.S. highway 6; 19 miles E of Hartford, in an area of vegetable farms. The manufacturing of thread is the main industry. Other manufactures include velvet, silks, rayon, braid, yarn, foundry products, paper-mill machinery, and construction supplies. Willimantic was settled in 1822, incorporated as a borough in 1833, and chartered as a city in 1893. It was the site of the first cotton-thread plant in the United States. Pop. (1960) 13,881.

WILLING, THOMAS, 1731–1821, U.S. lawyer, merchant, and financier, was born in Philadelphia, and studied law in England. He returned to America and established, with Robert Morris, the banking firm of Willing and Morris, which, during the American Revolution, was the financial agent for the Continental Congress. He became mayor of Philadelphia, 1763, and was associate justice of the Pennsylvania supreme court, 1766–74. He was active in prerevolutionary movements, and was a delegate to Congress, 1775–76. Feeling that it was premature, he voted against the Declaration of Independence. He was active in raising a fund to prevent the threatened dissolution of the American army, 1780. He was a founder of the Pennsylvania Bank and of the Bank of North America, and was the first president of the Bank of the United States, 1791.

WILLIS, NATHANIEL PARKER, 1806–67, U.S. author and journalist, was born in Portland, Me. He was graduated from Yale, 1827, edited several annuals for S. G. Goodrich, then founded and edited the *American Monthly Magazine*, 1829–31. He was foreign correspondent, 1831–36, for the New York *Mirror* and was later associated with the *Corsair*, the *New Mirror*, the *Evening Mirror*, and the *Home Journal*. He traveled in Europe and the Middle East, and published several volumes of frothy sketches and gossipy travel letters. He was esteemed in fashionable circles for his light verse and society chitchat. Other works are the poems *Sketches* (1827); two tragedies in blank verse, *Bianca Visconti* (1837) and *Tortesa the Usurer* (1839); a volume of short stories remarkable for their surprise endings, *Dashes at Life with a Free Pencil* (1845); and a novel, *Paul Fane* (1857).

WILLIS, THOMAS, 1621–75, English anatomist, was born in Great Bedwyn, Wiltshire, and studied at Christ Church College, Oxford. He became Sedleian professor of natural philosophy at Oxford and founded the Royal Society of London, 1660, and was physician to Charles II, 1662. He was made a fellow of the Royal College of Physicians, 1664, and began to practice medicine in London, 1666. Willis is credited with being the first to distinguish *diabetes mellitus* from *diabetes insipidus* and other forms of the disease. In *Cerebri anatome nervorumque descriptio et usus*, 1664 (*Of the Anatomy of the Brain*, 1681), he described a part of the brain later called the circle of Willis.

WILLISTON, city, NW North Dakota, seat of Williams County; on the Missouri River at the head of Garrison Reservoir; on the Great Northern Railway and U.S. highways 2 and 85; 165 miles NW of Bismarck. Williston is a trade center and shipping point for an agricultural area in which poultry, wheat, and livestock are raised. It is in the Williston Basin oil and gas field. Flour and butter are manufactured. The area was settled largely by homesteaders early in the 1900's. Williston was named by James J. Hill, railroad president, for a New York stockholder, S. Willis James. Pop. (1960) 11,866.

WILLISTON PARK, village, SE New York, in Nassau County; W central Long Island; 15 miles E of New York City, of which it is a residential suburb. Williston Park was incorporated in 1926. Pop. (1960) 8,255.

WILLKIE, WENDELL LEWIS, 1892–1944, U.S. political figure, was born in Elwood, Ind., studied at Indiana University, and was admitted to the bar, 1916. He became president of the Commonwealth and Southern Corporation, a utility holding company, 1933; when this position involved him in a controversy with the Tennessee Valley Authority he became such a severe critic of the New Deal that he switched his political affiliation from Democratic to Republican. As unsuccessful Republican candidate for president, 1940, he attacked Pres. Franklin D. Roosevelt's New Deal but supported his foreign policy. He went as Roosevelt's unofficial emissary to England, 1941, and the Middle East, U.S.S.R., and China, 1942. His book, *One World* (1943), was an eloquent plea for international co-operation. See NEW DEAL; TENNESSEE VALLEY AUTHORITY.

WILLMAR, city, W central Minnesota, seat of Kandiyohi County; on the Great Northern Railway and U.S. highways 12 and 71; about 90 miles WNW of Minneapolis, in a lake region. The city is the commercial center and shipping point for an area in which grain and livestock are raised. Machine shops; sash-and-door, soft-drink, and dairy plants; and hatcheries are the chief industrial establishments. Willmar, a divisional point for the Great Northern Railway, was founded in 1869. Willmar was incorporated in 1874. Pop. (1960) 10,417.

WILL-O'-THE-WISP, a natural atmospheric phenomenon, *ignis fatuus*, demonstrated by the appearance at night of a pale flame, generally of a bluish color, over marshes. The cause of the phenomenon is not apparent, but it is believed to be due to the spontaneous combustion of marsh gas produced from decaying vegetable or animal matter. The flame appears to flicker and move about.

WILLOW, any of a number of species of trees included in the genus *Salix* of the family *Salicaceae*. Willows are characterized by their smooth, polished bark; by their long, slightly notched leaves; and by their silky, erect, barren catkins. They grow readily and rapidly from cuttings. The branches of some droop to the ground giving the tree a "weeping" character as Napoleon's willow, *S. babylonica*. The black willow, *S. nigra*, is a large-growing species, with flaky bark, reaching to 40 feet in height. The yellow willow, *S. vitellina*, also very large, is abundant in eastern North America. Willows thrive in moist ground, especially by the sides of rivers or ponds where they effectively prevent banks from washing away. The supple twigs of some species are used in basketry.

U.S. FOREST SERVICE

The weeping willow, one of several species of willows, is best known for its graceful, drooping branches. It grows best in moist ground, close to river banks or ponds.

WILLOWS, city, N central California, seat of Glenn County; on the Southern Pacific Railroad and U.S. highway 99; 78 miles N of Sacramento. The city is a trade and processing center for an irrigated area in which rice and cattle are raised. Willows was incorporated in 1886. Pop. (1960) 4,139.

WILLS, HELEN NEWINGTON, 1906– , U.S. tennis player, was born in Centerville, Calif., and studied at the University of California. She was U.S. women's singles tennis champion, 1923–25, 1927–29, and 1931, and won the championship of France four times and of England eight times. She is considered one of the greatest women tennis players of all times.

WILLSTÄTTER, RICHARD, 1872–1942, German chemist, was born in Karlsruhe, Baden, and was graduated from the University of Munich, 1894, where he taught organic chemistry, 1902–05, 1915–25. He was professor at Zürich Polytechnic, 1905–12, and at the University of Berlin, 1912–15, and director of the Kaiser Wilhelm Institute, 1912–15. He received the Nobel prize in chemistry in 1915 "for research on coloring matter in the vegetable kingdom, principally on chlorophyll."

WILMERDING, borough, SW Pennsylvania, in Allegheny County; on the Pennsylvania Railroad, in an industrial area; 10 miles SE of Pittsburgh. The borough's chief industry is the manufacturing of airbrake equipment and tools. Pop. (1960) 4,349.

WILMETTE, village, NE Illinois, in Cook County; on Lake Michigan, the North Western Railway, and U.S. highway 41; 14 miles N of Chicago, of which it is a residential suburb. A noted point of interest is the Baha'i House of Worship, a nine-sided structure, which is the center of the Baha'ism religion in the United States. Wilmette was founded in 1869 and incorporated in 1872. Pop. (1960) 28,268.

WILMINGTON, city, NE Delaware, seat of New Castle County; on the W bank of the Delaware River at the mouth of the Christina, which is joined by the Brandywine within the city limits; on the Baltimore and Ohio, the Pennsylvania, and the Reading railroads, U.S. highways 301, 40, and 202, and steamship, bus, and truck lines; 27 miles SW of Philadelphia. Pop. (1960) 95,827.

Wilmington, the state's only city of more than 12,000 population, includes almost one fourth of Delaware's population; its industries produce a majority of the state's products, and its banks hold a majority of the state's deposits. Because of favorable state tax provisions, the city is one of the largest centers for the incorporation of businesses in the United States. Built on a low strip of land backed by low rolling hills that overlook the Delaware River, Wilmington covers an area of 11.26 square miles, rising from tideland to a height of 260 feet. The business center is in the area near the confluence of the Christina and the Brandywine rivers.

Economic Factors. Since its early days, Wilmington has been an important manufacturing center. It has large hard-rubber hose, dyeing, and cotton-textiles plants, and is a center for glazed kid production. Its chief commodities are chemicals, iron and steel products, leather, food, textiles, machinery, paper, canned fruits and vegetables, apparel, bakery products, hosiery, fiber cans, petroleum and coal products, and nonferrous metal products. Poultry dressing and packing is also important. Piers and wharves extend along the Christina for two miles, and a marine terminal was constructed in 1923. There are important ship building and repair yards.

Features of Interest. Rodney Square, a sunken garden, is the civic center, about which are grouped the city's administrative, cultural, and business activities. The site of Fort Christina at The Rocks, where the first Swedish expedition landed, is preserved in a state park. Also of interest are the Delaware Academy of Medicine, 1816, and Old Town Hall, 1798, a historical museum. Among the city's historic churches are Holy Trinity Church, known as Old Swedes Church, 1698; Asbury Methodist Church, dedicated by Bishop Francis Asbury, 1789; and Friends' Meeting House, 1816. The city is the seat of Tower Hill School. Two Wilmington neighborhoods, Brandywine Village, and Rockford Village, a century-old mill workers' community, are of special interest. The public street market is a characteristic Wilmington institution. Near the city are several estates of the Du Pont family, the Du Pont Experimental Laboratories, and the Alfred I. Du Pont Memorial Carillon Tower.

History. The settlement of Wilmington goes back to the days of New Sweden (see NEW SWEDEN). In 1638 the first Swedish expedition landed at The Rocks and established Fort Christina. Five years later Gov. Johan Printz moved the seat of authority to Tinicum, near the site of what was later to be Philadelphia, but in 1654 his successor, Johan Rising, moved it back to Christina. In 1655 New Sweden was conquered by the Dutch and made part of New Netherland; in 1664 it came under English sovereignty. About 1730 Andrew Justison drew up a plan for the town, which was at first called Willingtown for Justison's son-in-law. It was incorporated as a borough in 1739, and in 1745 the name was changed to honor the Earl of Wilmington. It was chartered as a city in 1832. Wilmington was a strong antislavery center and was a station on the Underground Railroad during the Civil War period.

WILMINGTON, city, SE North Carolina, seat of New Hanover County; located at the head of the estuary of the Cape Fear River, near the Atlantic Ocean; on the Atlantic Coast Line and the Seaboard Airline railroads, and U.S. highways 17, 76, 74, 117, and 421; scheduled airline stop; 135 miles SSE of Raleigh. Cotton, tobacco, peanuts, lumber, and naval stores are exported from Wilmington Harbor. The chief manufactured products of the city are fertilizer, lumber, creosoting materials, cotton goods, and bromine. In 1665 the first settlers, from Barbados, arrived at the site of Wilmington, and by 1725 permanent plantations had been established. Originally named New Liverpool, Wilmington was renamed for Spencer Compton, earl of Wilmington, in 1739; it was incorporated in 1760, and chartered as a city in 1866. Cornwallis occupied Wilmington in 1781 before starting his march to Yorktown; during the Civil War the town was the chief port of entry for Confederate blockade runners. (For population, see North Carolina map in Atlas.)

WILMINGTON, city, SW Ohio, seat of Clinton County; 45 miles NE of Cincinnati; in a fine agricultural area. Among manufactures are tubing and valves for jet motors, air and hydraulic controls, tools and dies, concrete, furnaces, and seed graders. Flour and canned goods are also produced. (For population, see Ohio map in Atlas.)

WILMOT PROVISO, a proposed amendment to appropriations bills in the U.S. Congress during the Mexican War (1846–48) which would have prohibited slavery in territories acquired from Mexico as a result of the war. Rep. David Wilmot, a Pennsylvania Democrat, introduced his amendment on Aug. 8, 1846, to a $2,000,000 appropriations bill requested by Pres. James K. Polk to purchase disputed land from Mexico. Adopted by the House, the Wilmot Proviso (as it came to be called) was not acted on by the Senate. The next year Congress rejected the Wilmot Proviso after an acrimonious debate, and on Feb. 2, 1848, the United States acquired California and New Mexico in the Treaty of Guadalupe Hidalgo. Although never enacted, the Wilmot Proviso had a permanent effect on the developing sectional conflict. The Proviso intensified the controversy over the extension of slavery into the territories, including the nettlesome constitutional question over Congressional powers in this area. It also defined the slavery issue in terms adopted by the Free Soil Party in 1848 and the Republican Party in the mid-1850's.   DAVID BRODY

WILSON, ALEXANDER, 1766–1813, Scottish-U.S. ornithologist and poet, was born in Paisley, Renfrewshire, Scotland, and was a weaver's apprentice, 1779–89. While working as a peddler, 1789–94, he composed numerous dialect poems and published anonymously a penny chapbook *Watty and Meg* (1792), which sold over 100,000 copies. He emigrated to New York City, 1794, and while teaching school in Pennsylvania and New Jersey became acquainted with the naturalist William Bartham, and the engraver Alexander Lawson, who encouraged him in his study of North American birds. He continued writing poetry; *The Foresters* (1805) is a metrical account of his journey through the wilderness to Niagara Falls, 1804. He became the assistant editor of Abraham Rees's *Cyclopaedia*, 1807, and published the first seven volumes of his nine-volume *American Ornithology* (1808–13).

WILSON, ANGUS, 1913– , British author, was born Angus Frank Johnstone-Wilson in Bexhill-on-Sea, Sussex, the son of William Johnstone-Wilson, and studied at Westminster School and Merton College, Oxford. He worked in the department of printed books, British Museum, and during World War II served in the foreign office, 1942–46. He was deputy superintendent of the reading room, British Museum, 1949–55. Among his fiction and criticism: *The Wrong Set* (1949), *Emile Zola* (1952), *For Whom the Cloche Tolls: A Scrapbook of the Twenties* (1954), *A Bit Off the Map* (1957), *The Old Men at the Zoo* (1961), and *Late Call* (1964); plays: *The Mulberry Bush* (1957) and *After the Show* (1959).

WILSON, CHARLES ERWIN, 1890–1961, U.S. business executive and government official, was born in Minerva, Ohio, and studied at the Carnegie Institute of Technology. After working for Westinghouse Electric and Manufacturing Company he became sales manager and chief engineer of Delco Remy Company, 1919, a General Motors subsidiary, and was made General Motors vice-president, 1928, and president, 1941. He served as secretary of defense in the cabinet of Pres. Dwight D. Eisenhower, 1952–57.

WILSON, CHARLES THOMSON REES, 1869–1959, Nobel prize-winning Scottish physicist and inventor of the cloud chamber, born in Midlothian, and educated at Cambridge, 1888–92. He taught physics at Cambridge from 1900, and was appointed observer at the Observatory for Solar Research, 1913, lecturer, 1918, and professor of natural philosophy, 1925–34. He conducted his major investigations in the field of atmospheric electricity, and received the 1927 Nobel prize in physics, with Arthur Holly Compton "for his discovery of the vapor condensation method of rendering visible the paths of electrically charged particles," in 1911.

WILSON, EDMUND, 1895– , U.S. literary and social critic, was born in Red Bank, N.J., and was graduated from Princeton University, where he

Edmund Wilson

studied under Christian Gauss (1876–1946), and began a lifelong friendship with F. Scott Fitzgerald. After serving in World War I, Wilson held editorial positions with the magazines *Vanity Fair*, 1920–21, and the *New Republic*, 1926–31. He was literary critic of *The New Yorker*, 1944–48. In his analysis of the literary works of his time he blended elements of historical and social criticism with his own personal agnostic fervor. He was one of the first to recognize the merit of Ernest Hemingway's works, and wrote with great perception on the poetry of T. S. Eliot and the novels of Evelyn Waugh. His most famous work is *Axel's Castle* (1931), a study of symbolism in contemporary literature. Among other works of criticism are *The Triple Thinkers* (1938), *The Wound and the Bow* (1941), *Classics and Commercials* (1950), *The Shores of Light* (1952), *Patriotic Gore: Studies in the Literature of the American Civil War* (1962), and *O Canada: An American's Notes on Canadian Culture* (1965). Among his sociological and historical works are *To the Finland Station* (1940), *The Scrolls From the Dead Sea* (1955), *The American Earthquake* (1958), and *Apologies to the Iroquois* (1959).

WILSON, HARRY LEON, 1867–1939, U.S. novelist, was born in Oregon, Ill. He became a writer for the comic weekly *Puck*, 1892, and was editor, 1896–1902. In 1912 he settled in Carmel, Calif., where he began writing the light humorous novels for which he was best known, among them, *Bunker Bean* (1912), *Ruggles of Red Gap* (1914), *The Wrong Twin* (1921), *Merton of the Movies* (1922), and *Two Black Sheep* (1931).

WILSON, (JAMES) HAROLD, 1916– , British prime minister, born in Huddersfield, educated at Oxford, where he later taught economics. He was a Socialist from early days. He entered Parliament in the Labour sweep of 1945 and sat in the cabinet as President of the Board of Trade—one of the youngest cabinet ministers of the century. Wilson was generally associated with the intellectual left wing of the party during the years of Labour opposition, 1945–64. After his election as leader of the party in 1963 he necessarily took a position nearer the middle of the road. In October, 1964, the Labour party won the general election and Wilson became prime minister. His parliamentary majority was dangerously slight, and Britain's economy was lagging, yet Wilson confounded pessimists by remaining in power while improving the economic situation.

WILSON, HENRY, 1812–75, U.S. political figure, was born Jeremiah Jones Colbath in Farmington, N.H., and changed his name at the age of 21. He established a shoe-making business in Natick, Mass., and was elected to the state legislature in 1841. An Abolitionist, he left the Whigs for the Free Soil party, and joined the new Republican party, 1856. He was a U.S. senator, 1855–72, and vice-president of the United States, 1873–75, under Pres. Ulysses S. Grant. Wilson wrote a *History of the Rise and Fall of the Slave Power in America* (3 vols. 1872–75).

WILSON, SIR HENRY HUGHES, 1864–1922, British soldier, was born in Ireland. He studied at Sandhurst Military College and entered the army in 1884; he saw service in Burma, 1885–89, and in South Africa, 1899–1901. At the outbreak of World War I he accompanied the first expeditionary force as assistant chief of staff to Sir John Denton French, and later became a corps commander and acted as liaison officer with the French field headquarters. He was British representative in the Supreme War Council at Versailles, 1917, chief of the Imperial General Staff, 1918, and advocated unity of command on the Western Front. He was created both a baronet and a field marshal in 1919, and he was elected to Parliament for North Down, Ireland, in 1922. He was murdered later in the year, however, by certain persons who were members of the Irish Republican army.

WILSON, JAMES, 1742–98, U.S. legislator and jurist, was born in St. Andrews, Scotland, and educated at St. Andrews, Glasgow, and Edinburgh universities. He emigrated to America, 1765, and became a tutor at the College of Philadelphia, where he was later trustee and professor of law. After reading law under John Dickinson, he was admitted to the bar, 1767. He became a leader in the Pennsylvania patriot movement, and wrote the influential pamphlet, *Considerations on the Nature and Extent of the Legislative Authority of the British Parliament* (1774), a legal argument for the American cause. He was a member of the Continental Congress, 1775–77, and was one of the signers of the Declaration of Independence. He returned to legal practice, and was again elected to the Continental Congress, 1782–83, 1785–87. Wilson was an important member of the U.S. Constitutional Convention, 1787, in general supporting Federalist policies, but advocating popular election of the president and of both houses of legislature. He helped persuade the Pennsylvania delegation to ratify the new Constitution, 1787, and then later he also was one of those who helped to write the Pennsylvania state constitution, 1790. Within this same time and later as well, 1789–98, he also served as an associate justice of the U.S. Supreme Court.

WILSON, JAMES, 1836–1920, U.S. public official, was born in Ayrshire, Scotland. He migrated to the United States, 1851, studied at Grinnell College, and served in the Iowa legislature, 1868–73. He was a U.S. Congressman, 1873-77, 1883-85. Later, 1891–97, he became not only professor of agriculture but also served as the head of the state Agriculture Experimental Station at Iowa Agricultural College. As U.S. secretary of agriculture, a post which he held from 1897 to 1913, he greatly expanded and modernized the Department of Agriculture.

WILSON, JAMES HARRISON, 1837–1925, U.S. soldier, was born near Shawneetown, Ill., and studied at the U.S. Military Academy at West Point. During the Civil War he served on the Union side and won distinction at Fort Pulaski, Chattanooga, the Wilderness Campaign, and Nashville. After commanding the Third Division of Gen. Philip H. Sheridan's cavalry with the Army of the Potomac, he became chief of cavalry of the Military Division of the Mississippi, 1864. Wilson led cavalry raids, during which he was responsible for taking various towns in Alabama and Georgia. He was also responsible for the capture of Jefferson Davis, 1865. He retired from the Army, 1870, but volunteered in the Spanish-American War. He served with distinction in this war. He was second in command of the force sent to China during the Boxer Rebellion, 1900. Wilson retired again from the Army in 1901.

WILSON, JOHN, pen name Christopher North, 1785–1854, Scottish author and educator, was born in Paisley. He was graduated from Magdalen College, Oxford, 1810, and associated with the literary colony in the Lake District for five years. He lost his patrimony through the speculations of his uncle and was admitted to the Scottish bar, 1815. He settled in Edinburgh, where, in 1817, he began writing for *Blackwood's Edinburgh Magazine*. His most important contribution was the *Noctes Ambrosianae*, transcribing his table talk with his bibulous cronies, James Hogg, William Maginn, John Gibson Lockhart, and others. Of the 71 *Noctes Ambrosianae*, 1822–35, Wilson is attributed 41, the rest being written in collaboration. His fame rests entirely on the sprightly erudition and wild, Gaelic humor which these papers so eloquently display. In his own time, however, he had a reputation as a thinker and not at all as a wit, and was professor of moral philosophy at Edinburgh University, 1820–51. Among his other works were *The Isle of Palms* (1812), *The City of the Plague* (1816), *Lights and Shadows of Scottish Life* (1822), *The Trials of Margaret Lyndsay* (1823), and *The Recreations of Christopher North* (1842).

WILSON, MARGARET, 1882–   , U.S. novelist, was born in Traer, Iowa, and was educated at the University of Chicago. She did missionary work in India and she also taught school in Chicago. Then, in 1923, she settled permanently in England. Among her works are a story of pioneer life in Iowa, *The Able McLaughlins* (1923; Pulitzer prize, 1924), *The Kenworthys* (1925), *Daughters of India* (1928), *The Crime of Punishment* (1931), *One Came Out* (1932), *The Valiant Wife* (1933), *The Law and the McLaughlins* (1936), and *The Devon Treasure Mystery* (1939).

WILSON, RICHARD, 1714–82, Welsh landscape painter, was born in Penegoes, Montgomeryshire, and began his career as a portrait artist. With the money he acquired from portraiture he fulfilled his desire of visiting Italy to study landscape painting in Rome, where he was influenced by the work of Claude Lorrain and Francesco Zuccarelli (1702–88), and developed a pseudo-Italian style, a tendency to paint Greek temples and ruins into his landscapes. He returned to Great Britain, 1755. His success with *Niobe* (1760) was but short-lived, although it did serve to establish him as the first British landscape painter, and it was only in the centuries following his death that Wilson's work was recognized and truly appreciated for what it actually was. He was one of the original members of the Royal Academy. Among his other works are *The Lake of Nemi* (1761), and *View of Rome from the Villa Madonna* (1765).

WILSON, WILLIAM BAUCHOP, 1862–1934, U.S. labor leader and public official, was born in Blantyre, Scotland. In 1870 he was taken by his family to Pennsylvania, where he worked from childhood in the coal mines, became a union organizer, and was president of the district union, 1888–90. In 1890 he helped found the United Mine Workers of America and was international secretary-treasurer of the union, 1900–08. He served in the U.S. House of Representatives from 1907 to 1913. For part of this time, 1911–13, Wilson headed the labor committee and was influential in organizing the U.S. Bureau of Mines. Under Pres. Woodrow Wilson he was the first U.S. secretary of labor. 1913–21. He presided over the International Labor Conference, 1919.

WILSON, WILLIAM LYNE, 1843–1900, U.S. public official and educator, was born in Middleway, Va. (later W. Va.), and educated at Columbian College (later George Washington University) and the University of Virginia. He served in the Confederate army during the U.S. Civil War. He became assistant professor of ancient languages at Columbian College, 1865–71, was admitted to the bar, 1869, and practiced law in Charleston, W.Va., 1871–82. He was president of West Virginia University, 1882–83. He was a member of the U.S. House of Representatives 1883–95, and as Democratic floor leader secured passage of a bill (1893) repealing the Sherman Silver Purchase Act. Wilson was U.S. postmaster general in the cabinet of Pres. Grover Cleveland from 1895 to 1897, and during this time and later, 1897–1900, Wilson also served as president of Washington and Lee University.

UNDERWOOD & UNDERWOOD

The 19th Amendment to the Constitution, granting suffrage to women, was passed by Congress in 1919 and ratified by the states in time for women to vote in the 1920 national elections.

BROWN BROTHERS

The Big Four (left to right), Vittorio Orlando, David Lloyd George, Georges Clemenceau, and Woodrow Wilson, represented the great Allied powers in signing the Versailles Treaty at the end of World War I.

The *Lusitania,* a British liner, was torpedoed without warning in 1915, killing 124 Americans and arousing much U.S. feeling against Germany.

CULVER SERVICE

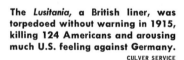

CULVER SERVICE

In April, 1917, hoping to make the world "safe for democracy," the United States entered World War I. It proved to be more bloody and more expensive than any previous war.

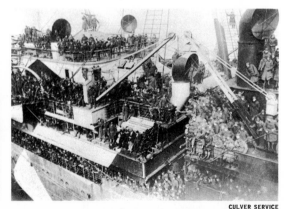

CULVER SERVICE

A wave of relief and optimism spread across the nation as jubilant U.S. soldiers returned from Europe, marking the end of a war that most people hoped would "end all war."

Birthplace: Staunton, Va.

WOODROW WILSON
28th President of the United States
1913—1921

WILSON, WOODROW, 1856–1924, 28th President of the United States, was born Thomas Woodrow Wilson in Staunton, Va., on Dec. 28, 1856, where his birthplace is maintained as a state museum. He was brought up in the South, where his father, Joseph Ruggles Wilson, served as Presbyterian pastor in Augusta, Ga., Columbia, S.C., and Wilmington, N.C. The influence of his father was important in his early religious and intellectual development, and it proved to be lifelong. After a year at Davidson College in North Carolina, he entered Princeton, 1875, and was graduated in the class of 1879. He was serious and studious, but gave over much of his time to various special and independent interests and therefore did not attain particularly high grades. After a year at the University of Virginia Law School and a brief attempt at practice in Atlanta, he turned to studies in political science, 1883, entering the graduate school of the Johns Hopkins University, where he received a doctorate, 1886, with a brilliant thesis entitled *Congressional Government.*

He began teaching at Bryn Mawr College, 1885, went to Wesleyan University, 1888, and to Princeton, 1890, as professor of jurisprudence and political economy. Within a short time he established himself as an outstanding lecturer and a leader among the faculty. His essays and his public addresses won for him a high reputation outside academic circles. He was chosen, 1896, to make the chief address at the sesquicentennial celebration of the university, and his exposition of the theme "Princeton in the Nation's Service" outlined the policy that was to be followed during the succeeding half-century. It assured his position of leadership and after the resignation of Francis L. Patton (1843–1932), he was unanimously elected to the university presidency, June 9, 1902.

College President. Wilson began his administration with the prestige of a great teacher and the enthusiastic support of faculty and trustees. Without loss of time he matured plans of vigorous development. In 1905 he called to the faculty a group of 47 young scholars to inaugurate the preceptorial system for student guidance that was destined to invigorate the academic life of Princeton and to set an example for sister institutions. More revolutionary was his plan for a social reorganization that would group the undergraduates in residential quadrangles, bring them into closer touch with the faculty, and eliminate the upperclass "eating clubs," which Wilson regarded as undemocratic. The plan was later adopted in principle by Yale and Harvard, but at Princeton it aroused bitter opposition among alumni, trustees, and faculty, and was given up, 1907. This rebuff to the president's policy was followed by an acrid quarrel with Andrew F. West (1853–1943) dean of the graduate school, in the course of which the plans of the latter were approved by a majority of the trustees—whereupon Wilson gave serious thought to the possibility of resignation.

Governor. That decision was hastened, perhaps determined, when the New Jersey governorship was offered to him by leaders of the Democratic political machine. Wilson accepted this opportunity to enter public life and was elected, Nov. 8, 1911. His two years of service in Trenton were marked by vigorous and successful leadership in reform legislation, despite the opposition of the very bosses who had naïvely considered him a harmless idealist, and by his emergence in the national political arena. When the Democratic Convention met in Baltimore, June, 1912, Wilson was one of four outstanding aspirants for the presidential nomination, among whom Champ Clark of Missouri held the lead. As the deadlock persisted, Wilson's strength increased, with the support of William Jennings Bryan, who was alienated from Clark because of Clark's equivocal attitude toward the conflict between progressive elements in the party and Tammany Hall's machine politicians, Wilson secured the necessary two-thirds vote on the 46th ballot. The Republicans were split between progressives and regulars and Wilson was elected President, Nov. 5, 1912, securing 435 electoral votes as against 88 for Theodore Roosevelt and 8 for Pres. William Howard Taft.

President. Wilson entered the White House with only two years of experience in practical politics, but with a background of intensive study of government, outstanding ability as a public speaker, and above all the capacity for personal leadership. It was primarily the last quality that enabled him to push through Congress in the earlier sessions of his administration, important reform legislation designed to liberalize the industrial system of the nation and to reduce special privilege. Lowered tariff schedules and a federal income tax were provided by the Underwood Tariff Act (1913). The Federal Reserve Act, enacted in the same year, stimulated the flow of capital. Creation of the Federal Trade Commission, 1914, and the provisions of the Clayton Antitrust Act were designed to combat monopoly, and to assure the freedom of labor organization. The outstanding success of Wilson's legislative program was facilitated by the invaluable support in Congress of Bryan, whom he had appointed secretary of state, and by the shrewd counsel of the president's unofficial adviser, Col. Edward M. House.

Foreign affairs early demanded the attention of the new President. At the outset of revolutionary strife in Mexico, Wilson refused to recognize Gen. Victoriano Huerta as legal ruler of that country. When Huerta had some U.S. sailors arrested and refused to apologize for the incident, Wilson ordered Marines to land at Veracruz. Formal war with Mexico was averted by the timely offer of mediation by the ABC powers (Argentina, Brazil, and Chile), Apr. 25, 1914. But the continuation of the Mexican War and constant threats to the U.S. border maintained an atmosphere of diplomatic uneasiness until the end of Wilson's administration.

The Outbreak of World War I, in the summer of 1914, initiated a long series of foreign problems that culminated in U.S. intervention. Wilson was determined upon a policy of strict neutrality, despite his personal sympathy with the Allied cause. That neutrality was irksome to both sides. Methods of British maritime control constituted what Wilson regarded as flagrant interference with U.S. rights under international law. The German threat to sink merchant ships without warning constituted, in Wilson's opinion, an attack not merely upon legal rights but upon human rights. To Germany, Wilson expressed the gravest of warnings; on Feb. 11, 1915, he declared that in the event of the destruction of U.S. shipping or lives the United States would be constrained to hold the German government "to a strict accountability."

Wilson soon found himself in a dilemma because of his policies. Powerful mercantile interests on the eastern seaboard felt that he was too neutral. Secretary of State Bryan, on the other hand, felt that Wilson was not neutral enough, and that his policy tended to favor England and would lead to war with Germany (this conflict eventually led to Bryan's resignation, June 8, 1915). The sinking of the *Lusitania*, May 7, 1915, with the loss of many American lives, was followed by lengthy negotiations with Germany. After the sinking of the *Sussex*, March, 1916, and Wilson's threat to break diplomatic relations, Germany promised that submarines would not attack merchant ships without giving warning. In the meantime, the President searched for means of mediation that might end the war. Acting on his behalf, Colonel House conducted long but fruitless negotiations, 1915–16, pointing toward a compromise peace between Germans and British. Popular confirmation of Wilson's policy, which combined patience with invariable insistence upon U.S. rights, was given in the presidential election of 1916, in which Republican majorities of the East were wiped out by returns from the Middle West and West. The President was re-elected by 277 electoral votes as against the 254 electoral votes which were cast for his Republican opponent, Charles Evans Hughes.

Wilson, still hoping for a compromise settlement, demanded that the belligerents state their war aims; and, on Jan. 22, 1917, in a speech before the Senate he insisted that there must be a "peace without victory." But Germany had already decided to resume unrestricted submarine warfare; when that decision was announced publicly, Wilson broke off diplomatic relations and, following the sinking of some American ships, he appeared before Congress, Apr. 2, 1917, to ask for a declaration that a state of war existed with Germany. The declaration was voted by overwhelming majorities on April 6.

Wilson's Capacity for Leadership was nowhere more clearly expressed than in his conduct of the war. He inspired the sense of a great national endeavor in which every citizen played his part and made his sacrifice. He gave unmitigated support to the industrial and military leaders responsible for the mobilization of U.S. economic and military power. He expressed U.S. war aims in a series of well-timed and deeply impressive addresses that culminated in his 14-point peace program, Jan. 8, 1918 (see FOURTEEN POINTS). His speeches stressed the necessity of international organization for the protection of all free and peace-loving nations. For the assurance of such a regime he proposed a League of Nations. See LEAGUE OF NATIONS.

Facing defeat in the early autumn of 1918, the Germans turned to Wilson and proposed peace upon the basis of his Fourteen Points. The French and British, however, were suspicious of any premature armistice that would not permit satisfaction of their war aims, which were not those that Wilson had propounded. After conferences with Colonel House, who represented the President in Paris, they finally agreed to peace on the basis of the Fourteen Points, but with minor reservations. The German and Allied delegates signed the Armistice, Nov. 11, 1918.

Wilson was determined to attend the peace conference in Paris. He was deeply and correctly suspicious of the purposes of the victorious French and British, and eager to replace the old European system with one more expressive of the will of free peoples and capable, he believed, of assuring their peace and liberty by means of a League of Nations. He arrived in France, Dec. 13, 1918, and a month later the peace conference convened. He was hailed as a savior by the peoples of Europe and despite an unfavorable diplomatic atmosphere in Paris, he was able to force approval of the Covenant of the League of Nations. After a brief visit in Washington, he returned to Paris, March, 1919, and thereafter found himself caught in the wrangles that attended the settlement of territorial and economic problems; much of his influence was dissipated by the fact that he was personally involved in these aspects of the treaties. With deep misgiving he accepted various compromises, which finally resulted in the unworkable Treaty of Versailles, which was signed by the Germans, the Allies, and the United States, June 28, 1919. He received the Nobel peace prize for 1919.

Defeated. Despite his disappointment at various aspects of the settlement, Wilson returned to the United States convinced that the essence of his program was embodied in the treaty and that it would be approved at home. Public opinion generally seemed to favor the league, which was warmly advocated by such Republicans as William Howard Taft and Elihu Root; but the Democrats had lost control of the Senate and Henry Cabot Lodge, chairman of its Foreign Relations Committee, mobilized all political and personal opponents of the President against him. Wilson himself played into their hands by refusing to make any compromise. In an effort to arouse public opinion he embarked upon a countrywide tour of speeches, but his health, undermined by his Paris experience, now gave way completely and he had to return to Washington, his tour unfinished, physically and nervously exhausted. On Oct. 2, 1919, he suffered nervous and physical collapse from which he never entirely recovered.

Deprived of their leader, the Democrats and the pro-league Republicans in the Senate were unable to achieve a vote of ratification for the treaty and the league. It would not have been difficult to secure a compromise, but Wilson, physically helpless, emotionally affected in his judgment, lacking the day-by-day counsel of his former adviser and friend, Colonel House, would yield nothing short of unconditional ratification. His insistence that his followers vote against any resolution that contained reservations brought them paradoxically to the aid of the bitter-end opponents of the treaty. It failed of passage by seven votes.

The remaining year of Wilson's administration, a pathetic anticlimax, was concluded in routine administration, over which the President, a semi-invalid, exercised a distant control at best. The presidential election of 1920, to which he looked forward as a national plebiscite endorsing his policies, brought the Republicans into office. For three years Wilson led a life of retirement in Washington, mourning the collapse of the idealistic crusade that he had led, but dignified in his refusal to indulge in public recrimination or complaint. He died at the age of 67, Feb. 3, 1924.

Personal Qualities. Throughout his life Wilson was dependent upon the affection and sympathy of those close to him, in early years his father, later his immediate family and a few intimate friends. He was married, June 24, 1885, to Ellen Louise Axson (1860–1914), who exerted an important influence upon his personal happiness and the success of his career. Her death at about the time of the outbreak of World War I, in August, 1914, deprived him of his greatest support at the time he needed it most. Three daughters were born of this marriage; Margaret;

Jessie, who married Francis B. Sayre; and Eleanor, who married William G. McAdoo. On Dec. 18, 1915, Wilson was married to Edith Bolling Galt (1872–1961).

The power of Wilson's personality was admitted by all except the most prejudiced of his enemies. Among his intimate associates his magnetism, his geniality, his consideration of others found free expression; but he could not project these qualities to influence those whom he did not like or trust, or into general political associations. His adherence to his principles was inflexible; but this virtue passed easily into the vice of intolerance when he met disagreement or criticism. Two of his dearest friendships, with Princeton Prof. John G. Hibben (1861–1933), and Colonel House, were destroyed because of this trait.

His leadership was most effective when he was dealing with a group rather than with an individual, as may be seen in his influence over the student body and faculty at Princeton, and in the effect of his public addresses, not merely in the United States but throughout Europe. His idealism was so lofty, however, and he was so impatient of opposition to it, that he could not maintain the level of support which he demanded. Both as president of Princeton and of the United States he achieved astounding success in the first phases of his administration, only to go down to defeat in the end.

Wilson's Published Writings are extremely numerous. Among the more important are *Congressional Government, A Study in American Politics* (1885), *The State: Elements of Historical and Practical Politics* (1889), *Divisions and Reunion, 1829–1889* (1893), *An Old Master and Other Essays* (1896), *George Washington* (1896), *A History of the American People* (5 vols. 1902), and *Constitutional Government in the United States* (1908). The finest expression of Wilson's literary quality and political philosophy is to be found in his speeches and state papers. They have been collected in the edition published by Ray Stannard Baker and William E. Dodd: *The Public Papers of Woodrow Wilson* (6 vols. 1925–27). In these papers is to be found the explanation of his great popular influence, his genius for simplification of complex issues, and his mastery of the phrase that makes the idea attractive.

CHARLES W. SEYMOUR

BIBLIOG.—Em B. Alsop, ed., *Greatness of Woodrow Wilson, 1856–1956* (1956); Thomas A. Bailey, *Wilson and the Peacemakers* (1947); Ray S. Baker (David Grayson, pseud.), *Woodrow Wilson: Life and Letters*, 7 vols. (1946), *Woodrow Wilson and World Settlement*, 3 vols. (1960); Herbert C. F. Bell, *Woodrow Wilson and the People* (1945); John M. Blum, *Woodrow Wilson and the Politics of Morality* (1956); Edward H. Buehrig, ed., *Woodrow Wilson and the Balance of Power* (1955), *Wilson's Foreign Policy in Perspective* (1957); Ruth Cranston (Anne Warwick, pseud.), *Story of Woodrow Wilson* (1945); Roy W. Curry, *Woodrow Wilson and Far Eastern Policy, 1913–1921* (Bookman Monograph Ser. no. 1) (1957); Josephus Daniels, *Wilson Era*, 2 vols. (1944–1946); Arthur P. Dudden, ed., *Woodrow Wilson and the World of Today* (1957); John A. Garraty, *Woodrow Wilson: A Great Life in Brief* (1956); Cary T. Grayson, *Woodrow Wilson: An Intimate Memoir* (1960); Herbert C. Hoover, *Ordeal of Woodrow Wilson* (1958); Edward M. Hugh-Jones, *Woodrow Wilson and American Liberalism* (1948); Frank K. Kelly, *Fight for the White House: The Story of 1912* (1961); Earl Latham, ed., *Philosophy and Politics of Woodrow Wilson* (1958); Arthur S. Link, *Road to the White House* (1947), *Woodrow Wilson and the Progressive Era: 1910–1917* (1954), *New Freedom* (1956), *Wilson the Diplomatist: A Look at His Major Foreign Policies* (1957), *Struggle for Neutrality, 1914–1915* (1960); David G. Loth, *Woodrow Wilson, the Fifteenth Point* (1941); Silas B. McKinley, *Woodrow Wilson: A Biography* (1957); Laurence W. Martin, *Peace Without Victory: Woodrow Wilson and the British Liberals* (1958); George B. Noble, *Policies and Opinions at Paris, 1919* (1935); Armin Rappaport, *British Press and Wilsonian Neutrality* (Stanford Univ. Publications; Univ. Ser. Hist., and Political Science, vol. 7, no. 1) (1951); Edwin C. Rozwenz, ed., *Roosevelt, Wilson and the Trusts* (1950); George S. Viereck (George F. Corners, pseud.), *Strangest Friendship in History: Woodrow Wilson and Colonel House* (1932); Arthur C. Walworth, *Woodrow Wilson*, 2 vols. (1958).

WILSON, city, E central North Carolina, seat of Wilson County; on the Atlantic Coast Line and the Norfolk Southern railroads, and U.S. highways 117, 264, and 301; about 48 miles E of Raleigh. Wilson is one of the largest bright-leaf tobacco markets in the world. The city is the site of the Atlantic Christian College (1902). The chief industries of Wilson are cottonseed-oil milling, lumbering, tobacco stemming, and soft-drink bottling. Wagons, trucks, fertilizer, and dental supplies are manufactured. Pop. (1960) 28,753.

WILSON, borough, E Pennsylvania, in Northampton County; near the Delaware River, on U.S. highway 22; a residential and industrial suburb, bordering on Easton; 52 miles N of Philadelphia. Machinery, textiles, and paper cups are manufactured. Pop. (1960) 8,465.

WILSON TARIFF ACT. See TARIFF.

WILTON, town, S England, in Wiltshire; 4 miles W of Salisbury, and about 90 miles WSW of London. Wilton is a market town which is noted for the manufacture of carpets, particularly of the Wilton carpet. It was the capital of the Saxon Kingdom of Wessex, and the seat of a bishop until 1050. Wilton's September Sheep Fair is known throughout England. Pop. (1951) 2,857.

WILTSHIRE, county, S England, bounded NW and N by Gloucestershire, NE by Berkshire, E and SE by Hampshire, S by Dorsetshire, and W by Somersetshire; area 1,345 sq. mi.; pop. (1951) 387,379. For the most part the county is an undulating upland. In the south is the Salisbury Plain, which is formed from chalk and has an elevation of about 400 feet. The plain is separated from the Marlborough Downs and the White Horse Hills to the north by the narrow Vale of Pewsey. The principal streams are the Bristol Avon and Salisbury Avon. Dairy farming predominates in the north while sheep and beef cattle are raised in the chalk regions to the south. Wheat, turnips, and fodder crops are grown. The county was formerly noted for its woolen-cloth production, particularly during the fifteenth and sixteenth centuries. Wiltshire is noted for its antiquarian remains: the Druidic circles of Stonehenge and Avebury, earthworks of Wansdyke, ancient camps and barrows, the monastic remains of Malmesbury and Laycock, and the Devizes and Old Sarum castles. Salisbury is the county seat and largest town.

WIMBLEDON, municipal borough, SE England, in Surrey; a residential suburb, eight miles SW of London. International tennis tournaments are held at Wimbledon each year. The town was incorporated in 1905. Pop. (1951) 58,158.

WINCHENDON, town, N Massachusetts, Worcester County; on the Boston and Maine and the New York Central railroads, and U.S. highway 202; near the New Hampshire border, about 36 miles NNW of Worcester. Toys, woodenware, cotton fabrics, woodworking machinery, and furniture are manufactured. The site was settled in 1752, and was first known as Ipswich Canada; upon incorporation in 1764, the name was changed to Winchendon. Pop. (1960) 6,237.

WINCHESTER, city, E Indiana, seat of Randolph County; on the New York Central and the Pennsylvania railroads, and U.S. highway 27; 25 miles E of Muncie. The city is a trade center and shipping point for an area in which grain and livestock are raised. Glass, furniture, and gloves are manufactured. Winchester was settled about 1816 and was incorporated in 1890. Indian burial mounds are found in the vicinity. Pop. (1960) 5,742.

WINCHESTER, city, NE central Kentucky, seat of Clark County; in the Blue Grass Region; on the Chesapeake and Ohio and the Louisville and Nashville railroads, and U.S. highways 60 and 227; about 18 miles E of Lexington. The city is a market center for an area in which tobacco and livestock are raised. Bluegrass-seed stripping, limestone quarrying, and the manufacturing of children's clothing, seed harvesters, bricks, lumber, and beverages are the leading industries. Winchester, which was named for Winchester, Va., was founded in 1792 and incorporated in 1793. Pop. (1960) 10,187.

WINCHESTER, town, NE Massachusetts, in Middlesex County; on the Boston and Maine Railroad; eight miles NNW of Boston, of which it is a residential and industrial suburb. Watch hands, felt, leather goods, and chemicals are manufactured. The site was settled in 1638, and was called successively Woburn Gates, South Woburn, and Black Horse Village; when separately incorporated with parts of Lexington, Cambridge, Medford, and Stoneham in 1850, it was renamed Winchester. Pop. (1960) 19,376.

WINCHESTER, town, S Tennessee, seat of Franklin County; near the Elk River, on the Louisville and Nashville Railroad and U.S. highways 41 and 64; 45 miles SE of Nashville. The town is a trade center for an area producing livestock, dairy cattle, poultry, potatoes, hay, and tobacco. Winchester's principal commodities are dairy products, clothing, rayon goods, silk straw hats, wood products, and medicines. The town was founded in 1814. Pop. (1960) 4,760.

WINCHESTER, independent city, N Virginia, seat of Frederick County; near the N entrance to the Shenandoah Valley; on the Baltimore and Ohio, the Pennsylvania, and the Winchester and Western railroads, and U.S. highways 11, 50, 340, and 522; about 70 miles WNW of Washington, D.C., in an important apple-growing region. Large warehouses for apples are there and apple products, fruit-grading equipment, barrels, textiles, rubber soles and heels, flour, and dairy products are manufactured. The city is the site of Shenandoah Valley Military Academy (1764). An Apple Blossom Festival is held there annually in May. Originally known as Fredericktown, the city was laid out in 1744; it was enlarged in 1752 and named for Winchester, England. Winchester was incorporated as a town in 1779 and chartered as a city in 1874. Fort Loudoun, an outpost of the French and Indian War, was built there in 1756 by George Washington. Pop. (1960) 15,110.

WINCHESTER, city and municipal borough, S England, seat of Hampshire; 12 miles NNE of Southampton and 60 miles SW of London. Winchester is a market town for a large region of diversified farms. Aircraft and pharmaceutical products are manufactured. The city was significant in the early development of the country. It was known as Caer Gwent by the ancient Britons, and Venta Belgarum by the Romans. The city became capital of the Kingdom of Wessex in 519, and during the last three Saxon and the first two Norman centuries it disputed London's claim as the capital of England. Winchester was made the seat of a bishop in the seventh century. The city has many important historic buildings. Winchester Cathedral, founded in the eleventh century, is one of the largest in England. Hyde Abbey was the burial place of King Alfred and several Saxon kings. Winchester Castle was built by the Normans, and was the birthplace of Henry III. Winchester College, founded in 1387 by William of Wykeham, is one of the earliest English schools. Pop. (1951) 25,710.

WINCKELMANN, JOHANN JOACHIM, 1717–68, German archaeologist, founder of the history of art as an independent discipline, was born in Stendal, in the Altmark of Brandenburg. Although his family was poor, Winckelmann had from early youth a rare singleness of purpose: he was going to study the art of the ancients and all the handicaps of his origin were not going to stop him. Lacking adequate schooling, he overcame this by hard study; lacking social contacts, he found his way into the house of the Count Bünau, as the count's librarian, 1748–54, and there met influential people. Although born a Protestant, he became a Roman Catholic, 1754, on the advice of the papal nuncio in nearby Dresden, who said that as

a Catholic, Winckelmann would meet with fewer obstacles in Italy. In 1755, Winckelmann's preparations bore fruit and he made Rome his home, where Cardinal Albani became his protector, 1758, the painter Raffaello Mengs, his friend. From 1763 he was inspector of antiquities in Rome. His first book (1760), published in French, is a description of a private collection in precious gems, done in the traditional manner, in which art was treated as the amusement of collectors and art "history" as a series of anecdotes or, at best, brief biographies of artists. With his *Geschichte der Kunst des Altertums* (1764), however, Winckelmann treated art on a level with great poetry, as one of the necessities of the human spirit: art unfolds historically in a lawful order and triumphs over human whims or wishes; civilizations "speak" in the terms of art as much as they speak through their religion or literature. By setting this new standard for the study of antiquity, Winckelmann also set the pace for other branches of the history of art (medieval, comparative, modern, and so forth), but he himself was not to be able to apply the new method to all periods of art: on a journey to Vienna, 1768, he was honored by the Empress Maria Theresa and then, while on his return journey to Rome, he was murdered by a burglar in a Trieste inn. News of his premature death was received with mourning throughout Europe; the Winckelmann-Programs of the German Archaeological Society are an attempt to perpetuate his spirit.

English translations of his history appeared in London (1850) and in Boston (1872); the collected works were published in Donaueschingen (12 vols. 1825–29), and his letters were published in Berlin (4 vols. 1952–57). The definitive study of Winckelmann is K. Justi's *Winckelmann und seine Zeitgenossen* (3 vols. 1866–72; 5th ed. 1956). Eugen Rosenstock-Huessy

WIND, natural motion of the air in relation to earth's surface without regard to direction or velocity. In meteorology wind is the component of air motion parallel to the surface of the earth, the direction being determined by a wind cone or weather vane. An anemometer registers the speed. Any other component of air motion than that parallel to the earth's surface is termed an air current. See Anemometer; Anticyclone; Atmosphere; Beaufort Scale; Chinook; Cyclone; Gale; Hurricane; Meteorology; Monsoon; Trade Wind; Tornado; Typhoon; Weather Forecasting; Whirlwind.

WINDAUS, ADOLF, 1876–1959, German chemist, was born in Berlin, and educated in medicine and chemistry at Berlin and Freiburg. He was professor at the Univeristy of Innsbruck, 1913–15, and became professor and head of the Chemical Institute at the University of Göttingen, 1915. He received the 1928 Nobel prize for chemistry "for his studies on the constitution of the sterols and their connection with the vitamins." In 1931 he extracted crystalline Vitamin D by irradiating ergosterol; this was the first vitamin to be extracted in its pure form.

WINDBER, borough, SW Pennsylvania, in Somerset County; on the Pennsylvania Railroad; in a bituminous coal-mining region in the Allegheny Mountains; 73 miles SE of Pittsburgh. The Berwind-White Coal Company developed the borough as a residential area for its employees in 1897, inverting the syllables of the company name for the town's name. Pop. (1960) 6,994.

WIND CAVE NATIONAL PARK, an area of about 27,000 acres in the Black Hills of SW South Dakota; about 10 miles N of Hot Springs. The feature is Wind Cave, which is noted for its many limestone formations, resembling large honeycombs. The cave was discovered in 1881 by Tom Bingham, a Black Hills pioneer, who was attracted by a strange whistling sound that was caused by a strong draft of air rushing from a 10-inch opening in a rock. This is the only natural opening ever discovered; the present manmade opening was accomplished by digging down about six feet to a long fissure leading to the cave's corridors and galleries. The cave takes its name from the strong blasts of air blowing outward from the entrance when the barometer is falling, and blowing inward when the barometer is rising. Bands of antelope, elk, deer, and one of the largest buffalo herds in the United States are protected within the fenced park area.

WINDER, city, N central Georgia, seat of Barrow County; on the Seaboard Air Line Railroad and U.S. highway 29; 40 miles NE of Atlanta. Winder is a textile manufacturing center. The city was incorporated in 1893. Pop. (1960) 5,555.

WINDERMERE, LAKE, NW England, in Cumberland; the largest lake in England, extends 10½ miles from N to S and is about 1 mile wide, with a maximum depth of 219 feet. Lake Windermere is in the English Lake District, a popular resort area. There are several wooded islets in the lake, which is drained by the Leven to Morecambe Bay.

WINDFLOWER. See ANEMONE.

WINDHOEK, city, capital of South-West Africa, situated in the Auas Mountains; 170 miles E of Walvis Bay, the country's chief port. The town is located in a highland district that lies between the Namib and the Kalahari deserts. Windhoek is the commercial center of a region in which grapes, figs, and citrus fruits are grown, and sheep and goats are raised. There is a railroad and highway connection with Walvis Bay. Another railway runs south to connect with the main South African system. During World War I Windhoek was occupied by forces of the Union of South Africa, to which country South-West Africa was mandated by the League of Nations after the war. Pop. (1951) 29,717.

WINDISCH-GRÄTZ, ALFRED CANDIDUS FERDINAND, PRINCE ZU, 1787–1862, Austrian general, was born in Brussels, and entered the Austrian army, 1804. He served during the Napoleonic Wars and became lieutenant field marshal and division commander, 1833. He commanded forces in Bohemia, 1840, and rigorously suppressed the insurrection at Prague, June, 1848, after his wife and son were killed in rioting; when an insurrection broke out in Vienna later in the year, he declared a state of siege and took the city by storm. With his brother-in-law, Prince Felix von Schwarzenberg (1800–52), he persuaded the Austrian emperor, Ferdinand I, to abdicate in favor of his nephew, Francis Joseph I, 1848. He led an army into Hungary and took Budapest, 1849, but was recalled. He was governor of Mainz under the Diet of the German Confederation, 1859.

WINDMILL, a mechanical device designed to capture the energy of air currents through sails, sweeps, or vanes radiating from a shaft and to convert that energy into useful work. The principle of operation is very similar to that of the water wheel or steam turbine. The sails or vanes are set at an angle to the wind direction, so that the plane in which the sails rotate is approximately at right angles to the direction in which the wind is blowing. Since the wind direction is variable, provision must be made to rotate the sail-mounting structure so that the sails will face into the wind.

In modern windmills, instead of large sails or sweeps there are a considerable number of thin, sheet-metal blades arranged radially about a shaft and forming a wheel. This wheel is mounted on a shaft with a rudder or tail vane which, with any change of wind direction, will permit the wheel to run into the wind, or, when wind velocity is excessive, will turn the wheel slightly out of the wind. The blades of the wheel are slightly concave on the windward side and are so set that they revolve at a peripheral speed about 2.5 times that of the wind.

Windmills are very commonly used in rural areas throughout the world to operate water pumps and generators for home electric-light and power systems. In the United States, however, the gasoline engine

and the extension of rural electric power lines have replaced the windmill.

WINDOM, city, SW Minnesota, seat of Cottonwood County; on West Des Moines River, the North Western Railway, and U.S. highway 71; 75 miles SW of Minneapolis. The city is a trade center for an agricultural area producing poultry, corn, oats, and flax. Windom manufactures farm machinery, tile, and butter. The area was first platted in 1870 and became a city in 1920. Pop. (1960) 3,691.

WINDOW, an opening in the wall or roof of a building or vehicle, designed to admit light, air, or both. The disposition of windows in a building is known as fenestration. So far as is known, the earliest windows to play an important part in architectural construction were the clerestory lights in the great temples and palaces of Egypt, as at Karnak and Thebes, and in the Assyrian and Persian palaces, where large roof windows were formed with timber in the manner of modern deck lights, as at Korsabad and Persepolis (later Iran); these, of course, were open to the elements. Historians dispute the amounts and sources of light in Grecian and Roman temples; there is little doubt, however, but that some of these temples had openings in the roof, and it has been suggested that some were lighted by openings in the ceiling only, the roof above being of thin marble slabs which allowed a diffused light to penetrate the cella—the space enclosed by the walls. There are windows in one wall of the Erechtheum on the Acropolis, however, and the great temple at Agrigentum in Sicily had windows in the walls of the side aisles. In Roman houses the atrium, or principal hall, was open to the roof, while the rooms entering off the same were lighted only by the doors. They later had windows protected by shutters, and a transparent material, probably mica, was used for glazing until, in the second century, horn came into general use for this purpose. In the Middle Ages cloth seems to have been used.

Windows are sometimes built up as separate architectural features in the roof. These are called dormer windows, from the fact that dormitories in old monasteries were often in the roof. Such windows are common in French Renaissance buildings. When a window projects from the face of the wall and is supported on corbels (weight-sustaining projections of wood or stone), it is called an oriel window; these were common in English houses of the fifteenth century. Lattice windows are frames divided into small panes with astragals or lozenges; French or casement windows open like doors.

WINDPIPE. See TRACHEA.

WIND RIVER RANGE, W central Wyoming, one of the highest and most massive ranges of the Rocky Mountains. The Wind River Mountains are composed of igneous and metamorphic rocks; the general summit level, at 12,000 feet, is the surface of an ancient peneplain. Monadnocks such as Gannett (13,785 ft.) and Fremont (13,730 ft.) rise above the snow line. The range rises from surrounding basins, which are about 7,000 feet above sea level. At the southern edge is South Pass, a valley 25 miles wide, through which the Oregon Trail passed. Lumbering is the most important activity. Lodgepole, white, yellow, and whitebark pine cover the slopes to 10,000 feet; above the timber line, buttercups, lupine, gentians, and grasses thrive during the short growing season.

WINDSOR, town, N central Connecticut, in Hartford County; on the Farmington River and the New Haven Railroad; six miles N of Hartford. The town is a trade center for a tobacco-growing area. Tomatoes and squash are other important crops. The canning of vegetables is a leading industry. Windsor was settled by colonists from Plymouth in 1633; and it was called Plymouth until 1637, when it was renamed by settlers from Dorchester. Windsor formed a part of the original Connecticut Colony which was founded in 1639. Pop. (1960) 19,467.

WINDSOR, village, E Vermont, in Windsor County; approximately 30 mi. SE of Rutland. Brass, bronze, and aluminum castings; rubber soles and heels; and screw machines are manufactured. The Vermont State Prison is located there. Windsor was settled in 1764, and the state constitution was formed there in 1777. The meeting place, now a museum of colonial relics, was used by the general assembly of Vermont until Montpelier became the permanent capital in 1805. (For population, see Vermont map in Atlas.)

WINDSOR, town, Canada, W central Nova Scotia; seat of Hants County; on the Avon River and the Canadian Pacific Railway; about 35 miles NW of Halifax. Windsor is a commercial center and shipping point for an area in which apple growing, lumbering, and fishing are leading activities. Gold, manganese, antimony, barite, gypsum, limestone, and marble deposits are in the vicinity. Windsor has textile mills, and plaster, fertilizer, and woodworking plants. The settlement, which grew up around a French fort, was incorporated in 1878. From 1789 to 1923, Windsor was the seat of King's College, the oldest university in Canada, which was moved to Halifax and affiliated with Dalhousie University following a disastrous fire. (For population, see Atlantic Provinces map in Atlas.)

WINDSOR, city, SE Canada, in the S part of the province of Ontario, seat of Essex County; on the shore of the Detroit River, here spanned by the Ambassador Bridge and the Detroit-Windsor Tunnel to Detroit, Michigan, which is about 2 miles to the northwest.

Windsor is an important industrial center, and has a considerable shipping trade. Its port receives hundreds of vessels in foreign and coasting services. Principal manufactures are transportation equipment, pharmaceuticals, tools and cutlery, textiles, food products, concrete products, brass and copper products, carbonated beverages, paints and varnishes, electrical machinery, and clothing.

The Windsor region, known as South Side, was settled by French farmers in the 1740's. The village established there was called successively The Ferry, Richmond, and South Detroit until, in 1836, it was renamed Windsor, for Windsor, England. The city was incorporated in 1892; in 1935, Windsor annexed the border cities of East Windsor, Sandwich, and Walkerville. During the War of 1812, British General Brock's headquarters were located in Windsor. Activities of the Fenian Raid were centered here in 1837 (see FENIANISM). During the Civil War, Windsor was a destination point for slaves escaping from the United States via the Underground Railroad. Windsor is the seat of Assumption University. (For population, see southern Ontario map in Atlas.)

WINDSOR, town, Canada, S Québec, in Richmond County; on the St. Francis River; approximately 80 miles E of Montreal. The manufacturing of pulp and paper is the chief industry. First settled about 1803 when sawmills and grist mills were established, the town was known for more than a century as Windsor Mills. However, Windsor did not become incorporated until 1899. (For population, see southern Quebec map in Atlas.)

WINDSOR, officially New Windsor, municipal borough, SE England, in Berkshire, on the River Thames; about 22 miles W of London. Windsor is a market town for a region of diversified farms. The present borough replaced an older one, now represented by the village of Old Windsor, about two miles to the east. Windsor Castle is a residence of the British sovereign. The castle was built for William the Conqueror during the eleventh century, and now contains many valuable art works. St. George's Chapel in Windsor Castle is the official church of the Knights of the Garter. Other public buildings include the Guildhall and the Masonic Hall, both designed by Sir Christopher Wren, a late seventeenth-century architect. (For population, see England map in Atlas.)

WINDSOR, the name of the ruling family of Great Britain since 1917. The original dynastic name of the Windsor family was Saxe-Coburg-Gotha, derived from the filial lineage of Edward VII, the eldest son of Queen Victoria. The family name, of German origin, was Wettin. During World War I, George V, caught up in a wave of anti-German sentiment, decided to change the name of Britain's royal house from the Teutonic Saxe-Coburg-Gotha to Windsor, from Windsor Castle, the principal residence of British royalty from the time of William the Conqueror. His official proclamation of the change took place on July 17, 1917.

George V, successor to Edward VII, ruled 1910–36. The next successor to the throne was Edward VIII, George V's eldest son, who ruled briefly from January to December of 1936. Upon his decision to abdicate (see EDWARD VIII), the crown devolved upon his brother George VI, who reigned 1936–52, and died without male heirs. He was succeeded by his daughter Elizabeth II, whose reign began in 1952. In 1960 Elizabeth II proclaimed that subsequent generations of the direct royal line, except for princes and princesses, would be officially designated members of the house of Mountbatten-Windsor. This change was made in honor of her husband, Philip Mountbatten.

WINDSOR CASTLE, the chief residence of the British royal family, stands on an eminence near the Thames, in Windsor, Berkshire. The buildings and immediate grounds cover an area of 12 acres. A terrace surrounds the castle on the north, east, and south sides; below, on the east, is the sunken garden, opposite the private apartments; and on the north are the ornamental pleasure grounds, known as the "slopes." St. George's Chapel, built chiefly by Edward IV, is a cruciform edifice; in the choir are the stalls of the sovereign and of the knights companions of the Order of the Garter; beneath it is the royal vault where Henry VI, Edward IV and his queen, Henry VIII and Jane Seymour, Charles I, George III and his queen, George IV, William IV and his queen, Edward VII and Queen Alexandra, George V, George VI, and other members of the royal families are buried. Opposite the choir is the Albert Memorial Chapel. The Great Park (about 1,800 acres) is traversed for three miles by a magnificent avenue, the Long Walk. Terminating the Walk is Snow Hill, an eminence surmounted by a statue of George II; at its side is the royal palace and mausoleum of Frogmore, in the latter of which rest the re-

Windsor Castle

PAN AMERICAN WORLD AIRWAYS

mains of Prince Albert and Queen Victoria. Virginia Water, a large ornamental lake, lies in the south of the park.

A fortress was built on the site of Windsor Castle by William the Conqueror, who made it the chief seat of government in England. Henry I made extensive additions to the fortress, converting it into a palace. Henry III strengthened its fortifications. Edward III was born here, and after his accession rebuilt and greatly enlarged the palace, especially the Round Tower, that it might better serve as a meeting place for members of the Order of the Garter, established about 1346. James II and William of Orange added fine collections of paintings. During the reigns of George III and George IV more than $5 million of public money was spent for further additions and improvements. New stables were built during the early part of Queen Victoria's reign.

WINDTHORST, LUDWIG, 1812–91, German statesman. He was the leader of the Roman Catholic Centre party in the German Reichstag during Otto von Bismarck's anti-church Kulturkampf. Although an opponent of Bismarck, he supported the latter's economic policies.

WINDWARD ISLANDS, a group of islands in the West Indies; forming an arc between the Leeward Islands on the N, and Venezuela on the S; bounded by the Caribbean Sea on the W, and the Atlantic Ocean on the E; area about 1,250 sq. mi.; pop. (1966 est.) 644,000. The Windward Islands include the British possessions of Dominica, St. Lucia, St. Vincent, Grenada, and the Grenadines, the administration of which is split between St. Vincent and Grenada, and the French island of Martinique. See individual islands.

WINDWARD PASSAGE, a channel, 55 miles wide, connecting the Atlantic Ocean on the NE with the Caribbean Sea on the SW, and separating the West Indies islands of Cuba and Hispaniola.

WINE, the fermented juice of the wine grape. The term may also be applied to fermented juices of other fruits, including peach, elderberry, and date. Man's use of wine antedates written records. Wine vessels are found in pre-historic diggings, while wine's part in religious rites, festivals, and the daily life of early man is depicted in countless carvings, hieroglyphics, and cave paintings.

Botanically, the wine grape is of the genus *Vitis*, species *vinifera*, from the Latin meaning "wine producer." It is believed to have originated on the slopes of the Caucasus Mountains and from there spread westward, carried by successive waves of Cimmerians, Phoenicians, Greeks, Romans, and others throughout Europe. *V. vinifera*, with its 30-odd varieties, includes those grapes from which the vast bulk of the world's wine comes, whether from Europe, Asia, Africa, South America, or California. The exceptions are improved North American species of native origin— *V. labrusca, riparia, rupestris,* and others, and hybrids of these with *vinifera*—grown mainly in the United States and Canada east of the Rockies.

Winemaking. Crushing of the ripe grapes is usually done today by rollers with special resilient knobby surfaces that break the skins without crushing the seeds, which would impart a bitterness. In certain areas grapes are traditionally squeezed by treading with the carefully pre-washed bare feet of workers, which accomplishes the same end.

When the grapes are crushed, the fermentation process may begin. Fermentation is essentially a reduction, under the action of yeast, of a watery sugar solution to ethyl alcohol, with accompanying release of carbon dioxide gas. In fruit juices, this can proceed spontaneously from microscopic yeast cells present in the air, but modern winemakers control and improve the fermentation with special yeasts of their own.

After fermentation, the juice remaining is wine. In a complete wine fermentation, all the sugar has been changed to alcohol and carbon dioxide gas (which escapes) and the wine is a "dry" wine—that is to say, without sweetness. From this point on, winemaking is basically a matter of aging, storing, temperature control, and avoidance of contact with air.

Wine Classification. Wines may be classified as still, sparkling, and fortified. Of these, still wines represent the overwhelming bulk of the wine consumed in wine-drinking countries. In these areas, it is regarded as a part of the daily diet and consumption figures are huge—some 40 gallons per capita annually in France, for example. In some newer wine-growing countries, where wine has little or no tradition of common use, such as Australia, South Africa, and the United States, per capita annual consumption is still below a half a gallon. In most Latin American countries, home-grown wine enjoys wide popularity.

Sparkling wines, such as champagne, are made by a special process, under which the gas of a secondary fermentation is imprisoned within the bottle, accounting for the pressure, released in effervescence, built up within the container.

Fortified wines, including port, sherry and such specially flavored wines as vermouth, are made with the addition of grape spirits, which raises their natural alcohol content to 18 or 20 per cent by volume. They serve mainly as dessert wines or as apéritifs.

Wine Names. From earliest times wines took their names from geographical designations: regions, hills, rivers, towns, and villages. Wines from certain areas gained distinction, due to local conditions of climate and soil. Thus arose the fame of Chablis (a village), Burgundy (a province), Moselle (a river), and so forth. Later, these and other names came to be used by growers in newer wine areas. This tendency has lately been challenged and resisted by the older wine countries, notably France, which claim that the names designate specific wines from specific districts and are not generic in meaning. Some of the best United States producers now drop the use of so-called generic names—Sauternes and Burgundy, for example —feeling they suggest imitations of the European originals. Instead, U.S. producers identify their best wines by the name of the grape variety wholly or predominantly used—for example, California Pinot Chardonnay, and Cabernet Sauvignon; and New York State Delaware.

Wine is currently produced commercially in about 27 states of the United States. The four leading wine-growing states, in order, are California, New York, Ohio, and Michigan. The 14 leading wine-producing countries of the world are France-Italy (first place, with about a billion seven hundred thousand gallons annually; varies from one year to another), followed in descending order by Spain, Algeria, Portugal, Argentina, the U.S.S.R., the United States, Yugoslavia, Germany, Rumania, Greece, Hungary, and Chile.

Experts judge wine by color, clarity, aroma (or bouquet), flavor, and taste. As standards, they have only remembered impressions, based on hundreds of past tastings. For beginners, it is well to remember that wine's sole reason for existence is aesthetic pleasure, both of the wine itself and of the food which accompanies it. All the so-called rules about wines are only aids to greater appreciation of a meal-time drink.   TOM MARVEL

BIBLIOG.–Herbert W. Allen, *History of Wine* (1962); Tom Marvel, *A Pocket Dictionary of Wines* (1963); Frank Schoonmaker, *Encyclopedia of Wine* (1964); Greyton H. Taylor, *Treasury of Wine and Wine Cookery* (1963).

WINEBRENNER, JOHN, 1797–1860, U.S. clergyman, was born near Walkersville, Frederick County, Md. He was ordained to the ministry of the German Reformed Church, 1820, but soon fell out of favor with more conservative members of his congregation because of his revivalist method. After being dismissed from his church in Harrisburg, Pa., Winebrenner spent several years as an itinerant preacher.

In 1830 he founded the General Eldership of the Church of God, whose members were known as Winebrennerians.

WINFIELD, city, S Kansas, seat of Cowley County; on the Walnut River, the Santa Fe, the Frisco, and the Missouri Pacific railroads, and U.S. highways 77 and 160; 17 miles N of the Oklahoma border and 39 miles SSE of Wichita. The city is a commercial center for an area which is important for the production of oil and gas. Agriculture in the vicinity is diversified. Part of the city's income is derived from municipally owned oil wells. Flour milling, produce packing, alfalfa milling, and the manufacturing of gas burners and water cans are leading industries. The city is the site of Southwestern College (1885) and St. John's Lutheran College (1893). Winfield was settled in 1870 and incorporated in 1871. Pop. (1960) 4,117.

WINFIELD, town, West Virginia, seat of Putnam County; on the Kanawha River; 20 miles NW of Charleston. The town is a trading center for an area in which coal mining is the leading activity. Corn, potatoes, and tobacco are grown. Pop. (1960) 318.

WINGATE, ORDE CHARLES, 1903–44, British army officer, was born in Naini Tal, India, and was educated in England, entering Woolwich Military Academy, 1921. In Palestine, 1938, he led night patrols that stopped Arab raids, and then he went to the Sudan, 1940, to organize a revolt in Ethiopia by which Emperor Haile Selassie was restored to the throne. As brigadier he went to India, 1942, to organize a force known as Chindits or Wingate's Raiders, which traveled a thousand miles in enemy-held Burma, destroying Japanese outposts and supply bases. He was promoted to major general, 1944.

WINGED VICTORY OF SAMOTHRACE. See NIKE.

WINKELRIED, ARNOLD VON, died 1386, a knight of the Swiss canton of Unterwalden, a hero in the struggle for Swiss independence. According to tradition, at the decisive Battle of Sempach, near Luzern, 1386, the Austrians presented a dense front of spears, which the utmost efforts of the Swiss failed to penetrate. At last Winkelried rushed forward, grasped as many of the Austrian spears as he could, and bore them to the ground by sheer weight, thus making a path for his comrades over his pierced body.

WINKLER, CLEMENS ALEXANDER, 1838–1904, German chemist, was born in Freiberg. He was educated at the Freiberg School of Mines, and served as professor of chemical technology and analytical chemistry there, 1873–1902. Winkler investigated the properties of gases and of the metal indium, and isolated a new element from argyrodite, 1886, and named it germanium.

WINNEBAGO, one of a North American Indian tribe belonging to the Siouan linguistic family (see SIOUX). They first became known to white men, 1634, when the French explorer Jean Nicolet found them living in the Green Bay region of present-day Wisconsin. The Winnebagos were surrounded by Algonquian tribes and had absorbed many cultural traits from these neighbors, particularly from the Menominee. They lived in lodges of bark, reeds, skins, and wood, and carried on some agriculture to supplement their hunting, fishing, and gathering of wild rice. The Winnebago were friendly to the French and, after 1763, to the British, but after the Revolutionary War they resisted American settlement in the Northwestern Territory, and allied themselves with Great Britain against the United States during the War of 1812. During the 1820's and 1830's, however, they ceded all their Wisconsin lands to the United States; some of the tribe moved to Minnesota (then part of Iowa Territory), some remained in Wisconsin. After the Sioux War in Minnesota, 1862, about 1,000 Winnebago were transferred to Omaha Indian lands in Nebraska Territory. In 1950 there were 1,481 Winnebago living on the

Winnebago Reservation in Nebraska and about 1,500 on public domain allotments in Wisconsin.

WINNEBAGO, LAKE, E central Wisconsin, the largest of the state's many lakes; about 30 miles long and from 5 to 10 miles wide; area 215 sq. mi. Its major tributary and outlet is the Fox River, which enters it at Oshkosh and leaves it at Menasha and Neenah. The lake, named for the Winnebago Indian tribe, was formerly an important shipping route used by the lumber industry.

WINNEMUCCA, city, N Nevada, seat of Humboldt County; on the Humboldt River, the Southern Pacific and the Western Pacific railroads, and U.S. highways 40 and 95; 150 miles NE of Reno. The city is situated in a mining area in which gold, silver, copper, and tungsten are produced. Smelting and bottling plants are leading industrial establishments. Winnemucca is a shipping point for cattle and sheep. A trading post was established in 1850. The city was incorporated in 1917. Pop. (1960) 3,453.

WINNER, city, S South Dakota, seat of Tripp County; on the North Western Railway, and U.S. highways 18 and 183; 35 miles SSE of Pierre. The city is a trade center for a poultry, dairy, and grain region, and its chief commodities are dairy products and soap. Winner was founded chiefly by homesteaders, early in the 1900's. Pop. (1960) 3,705.

WINNETKA, village, NE Illinois, in Cook County; on Lake Michigan and the North Western Railway; 16 miles N of Chicago, of which it is a residential suburb. The village has two lake-front parks, a golf course, and is noted for its public school system. Winnetka was incorporated in 1869. Pop. (1960) 13,368.

WINNFIELD, town, N central Louisiana, seat of Winn Parish; on the Rock Island, the Louisiana and Arkansas, and the Illinois Central railroads, and U.S. highways 84 and 167; 135 miles NW of Baton Rouge. Limestone and gypsum quarrying, salt mining, and the manufacturing of concrete and wood products are the leading industries. It is the birthplace of Huey P. Long. Pop. (1960) 7,022.

WINNIBIGOSHISH, LAKE, N central Minnesota, situated in the Chippewa National Forest, in Cass and Itasca counties; forms a part of the headwaters of the Mississippi River; maximum width is about 12 miles. The size of the lake was increased to about 180 square miles after the construction of a dam at its eastern outlet. It is a resort center and there are facilities for boating, fishing, and swimming.

WINNIPEG, city, S central Canada, capital of Manitoba; at the junction of the Assiniboine and the Red rivers; on the Canadian National, the Canadian Pacific, the Great Northern, the Midland of Manitoba, and the Northern Pacific railways; about 60 miles N of the North Dakota boundary and 40 miles S of Lake Winnipeg from which the city takes its name. Pop. (1956) 255,093. Greater Winnipeg, pop. (1956) 409,000, includes St. Boniface, St. James, St. Vital, and other suburbs. Winnipeg is a supply point for the expanding central Canadian mining area, an important wholesale and a retail mail-order distributing center, and a gateway to a vast fishing and hunting region. Through Winnipeg pass most of the exports of Canada's agricultural West, making it one of the largest grain markets in the world, and an important livestock and fur market.

Principal Features. Winnipeg was platted with wide streets and tree-shaded boulevards. Two large parks, Assiniboine and Kildonan, and 47 other public parks and 15 golf courses provide recreation areas. Among the city's outstanding buildings are the Parliament Building, the Provincial Law Courts, the Federal Building, and the Civic Auditorium. Winnipeg is the seat of the University of Manitoba and its four affiliated colleges: St. John's, United, St. Paul's, and St. Boniface.

Inexpensive and abundant electric power from the Winnipeg River has encouraged the development of a

CANADIAN NATL. RY.

Panoramic view of Winnipeg shows the meandering junction of the Red and Assiniboine Rivers, below. The Canadian city's name means "murky water" in Cree Indian tongue.

large number of manufacturing industries. Slaughtering and meat packing, flour and feed mills, dairy-product processing, printing and publishing, and the manufacturing of paper, railway rolling stock, iron and steel, mining equipment and supplies, chemical products, cotton and jute bags, clothing, and bakery products are leading industries. The city has railway shops and an automobile assembly plant.

Government and History. The government of Winnipeg is administered by a council composed of a mayor and 18 aldermen. The mayor is elected for a two-year term by popular vote; three aldermen are elected annually from each of the city's three wards and they hold office for two years.

The site of Winnipeg was originally occupied by the Hudson's Bay trading post known as Fort Garry (now a national park), built, 1822, near the mouth of the Assiniboine. The fort was replaced, 1835, by a larger structure, and a colony of settlers was established outside the walls of the fort. The settlement was given a Cree Indian name taken from the words *win* (murky) and *nipiy* (water). In 1870, after Manitoba became a part of Canada, the Hudson's Bay Company transferred the territory to the Canadian government, and in 1873, Winnipeg was incorporated as a city. With the arrival of the railroad in 1885, Winnipeg became western Canada's main distributing center.

In 1950, the swollen waters of the Red, Assiniboine, and Seine rivers flooded the city, causing serious damage and leaving thousands homeless.

A metropolitan system of government for Winnipeg and 16 surrounding municipalities was initiated in 1960.

WINNIPEG, LAKE, Canada, in Manitoba, N of the city of Winnipeg. The lake has an irregular elongated shape; it is about 250 miles long, and 40 to 55 miles wide; area is about 9,400 sq. mi. It receives the Berens and the Winnipeg rivers from the east, the Red River from the south, the Dauphin, or Little Saskatchewan, from the west, and drains northward by the Nelson River to Hudson Bay. The lake lies in the great level plain formerly occupied by glacial Lake Agassiz. It was discovered by Pierre Gaultier de Varennes, sieur de la Vérendrye, early in the 1730's.

WINNIPEGOSIS, LAKE, Canada, in Manitoba, W of Lake Winnipeg and NW of Lake Manitoba, lying in the ancient lake plain formed by glacial Lake Agassiz, area about 2,100 sq. mi. Its length is about 125 miles and its width varies from 10 to 20 miles. It is navigable and is connected with Lake Winnipeg by Lake St. Martin and the Dauphin River. Lake Winnipegosis is noted for pike fishing.

WINNIPESAUKEE, LAKE, E central New Hampshire, in Belknap and Carroll counties, and between the Ossipee and Belknap Mountains; maxi-

mum length about 20 miles, width varies from 5 to 12 miles. Winnipesaukee is New Hampshire's largest lake. The lake is the center of a noted resort area. It has an irregular shore line and many islands dot the surface. An annual regatta is held and excursions are made around the lake in the summer months. There is good fishing for chinook, landlocked salmon, trout, perch, smelt, and bass during summer and winter seasons.

WINNSBORO, town, NE Louisiana, seat of Franklin Parish; on the Missouri Pacific Railroad; 60 miles ESE of Shreveport. Winnsboro is situated in a rich agricultural area producing cotton, yams, hay, fruit, livestock, and grain. The town manufactures cotton gins and compresses, wood products, and bricks, and has oil and gas wells. Winnsboro was founded around 1844 and was incorporated in 1902. Pop. (1960) 4,437.

WINNSBORO, city, N central South Carolina, seat of Fairfield County; on the Southern Railway, and near U.S. highway 321; 32 miles N of Columbia. The city is a trade center for an area producing corn, cotton, beef, lumber, and granite. There is a granite works; textiles and tire cord are made at adjacent Winnsboro Mills. The area was settled in 1755 and was incorporated in 1785. Pop. (1960) 3,479.

WINONA, city, SE Minnesota, seat of Winona County; on the Mississippi River, the Burlington, the North Western, Chicago Great Western, the Milwaukee, and the Green Bay and Western railroads, and U.S. highways 14 and 61; 100 miles SE of St. Paul. Winona, a trade and industrial center, manufactures flour, dairy products, candy, malt beverages, feed, patent medicines, clothing, fur garments, gloves, wood products, feed-mill equipment, auto chains and accessories, metalware, bricks, and rock-drilling equipment. The city's name comes from a Sioux Indian word meaning firstborn daughter. Winona was founded in 1851 and was chartered as a city in 1857. The city became an important dairy and meat-packing center, a large producer of sauerkraut, and one of the largest hay and clover-seed markets in the country. Winona is the seat of the Winona State College, founded, 1860; College of St. Teresa, a women's college founded, 1893, and originally called the Winona Seminary; and St. Mary's College, a liberal arts college for men, founded, 1913. The Mississippi Wildlife and Fish Refuge is located at Winona. Pop. (1960) 24,895.

WINONA, city, N Mississippi, seat of Montgomery County; on the Illinois Central and Columbus and Greenville railroads, and U.S. highways 51 and 82; 45 miles ENE of Jackson. The city is a trade center for a livestock, dairy, poultry, cotton, and timber region. Winona manufactures cottonseed products, chemicals, dairy products, cotton goods, and picture frames. Pop. (1960) 4,282.

WINOOSKI, city, NW Vermont, in Chittenden County; on the Winooski River, the Central Vermont Railway, and U.S. highways 2 and 7; 2 miles NE of Burlington, of which it is an industrial suburb. Woolen textile milling is the chief industry. Screens, lime, and dairy products are manufactured. Winooski is the seat of St. Michael's College (1904). It was settled in 1772 and incorporated in 1888. Its name is an Indian word meaning beautiful river. Winooski is situated on the site of Fort Frederick, one of the earliest military structures in the region. The development of manufacturing began in 1835 with the establishment of a woolen mill at the river falls. Pop. (1960) 7,420.

WINSLOW, EDWARD, 1595–1655, American colonist, was born in Droitwich, England. In 1617 he joined the English Puritans in Leiden, and sailed, 1620, on the *Mayflower* to the New World. He was agent for Plymouth in negotiating with the Indian leader Massasoit, 1621–22, and represented the colony on several diplomatic and commercial missions to England, becoming agent in 1629. He was governor of Plymouth 1633, 1636, and 1644, a founder of the New England Confederation, 1643, and was active in setting up trading posts along the New England coast. After a final sojourn in England, 1649–54, he was appointed head of a British commission sent to take the West Indies from the Spanish; he took Jamaica, and died of fever on the return voyage. Winslow wrote the earliest accounts of life in the Plymouth Colony, *A Relation or Iournall of the beginning and proceedings of the English Plantation setled at Plimoth in New England* (1622); *Good News from New England* (1624); *The Glorious Progress of the Gospel among the Indians in New England* (1649).

WINSLOW, JOHN ANCRUM, 1811–73, U.S. naval officer, was born in Wilmington, N.C. He entered the Navy, 1827, as a midshipman, served in the Mexican War, and attained the rank of commander, 1855. During the U.S. Civil War he was attached to the Mississippi flotilla of gunboats, 1861, and then was promoted captain, 1862, put in command of the *Kearsarge*, and sent in pursuit of Confederate cruisers. He engaged in battle with the *Alabama*, June 19, 1864, off Cherbourg, France, and sank her after a brief engagement, for which he was commended by Congress and made commodore. He was promoted to rear admiral, 1870, and was commander in chief of the Pacific squadron, 1870–72.

WINSLOW, city, E central Arizona, in Navajo County; on the Santa Fe Railway and U.S. highway 66; scheduled airline stop; situated at an elevation of 4,856 feet, 150 miles NE of Phoenix. Winslow is the commercial center and shipping point for an area in which the grazing of cattle and sheep are the leading activities. Wool is shipped, and a number of Indians are engaged in handicraft industries. Winslow is a tourist center, which is noted for its dry and cool climate and its desert scenery. Winslow was established in 1881 as a division terminal for the railroad. Pop. (1960) 8,862.

WINSOR, JUSTIN, 1831–97, U.S. librarian and historian, was born in Boston, Mass., and educated at Harvard and abroad. He was superintendent of the Boston Public Library, 1868–77, and librarian of Harvard University, 1877–97. He took part in the founding of the American Library Association, 1876, and served as its president, 1876–85, 1897. Among his works are *A History of the Town of Duxbury* (1849), *The Reader's Handbook of the American Revolution* (1880), *The Mississippi Basin* (1895), and *The Westward Movement* (1897). He edited *The Memorial History of Boston* (4 vols. 1880–81) and *A Narrative and Critical History of America* (8 vols. 1884–89).

WINSTANLEY, GERARD, 1609–1652, English political and religious leader, was a prominent member of the Levelers and the leader of the Diggers, a group that advocated the right of the common people to cultivate and live on land, rent free, and that attempted to cultivate the wastelands of St. George's Hill, Walton-on-Thames, Surrey. He was considered by Thomas Comber, dean of Durham (1645–99), to have been the real founder of the Quaker sect. Among his writings were *New Law of Righteousness* (1649) and *Law of Freedom* (1651). See LEVELERS.

WINSTED, city, NW Connecticut, in Litchfield County; on the New Haven Railroad, and U.S. highway 44; 17 miles NW of Hartford. The chief manufactures are clocks, hosiery, underwear, sweaters, electric appliances, pins, edged tools, enamel wire, hat felts, cutlery, and fishing tackle. Dairy and poultry farming are leading activities in the vicinity. Winsted was settled in 1756 and first incorporated in 1771; it became a borough in 1858 and was chartered as a city in 1917. Pop. (1960) 8,136.

WINSTON-SALEM, city, NW North Carolina, seat of Forsyth County; in the Piedmont section of the state; on the Norfolk and Western, the Southern, and the Winston-Salem Southbound railroads, and U.S. highways 52, 158, 311, and 421; scheduled airline stop; 67 miles NNE of Charlotte. Winston-Salem, a

WINSTON-SALEM C. OF C.

Winston-Salem is one of the main tobacco markets in North Carolina. The city received its name in 1913 when the two adjoining towns of Winston and Salem were combined.

tobacco-products manufacturing center and a leading bright-leaf tobacco market, began its tobacco industry in 1812 with the opening of the first tobacco factory and market. Among the city's chief commercial products are hosiery, underwear, bathing suits, yarn, cotton goods, furniture, boxes, caskets, fertilizers, paints, batteries, air-conditioning machinery, and conveying machinery. The city is the seat of a women's school, Salem College, founded, 1772; Wake Forest College, founded, 1833, and the Winston-Salem Teachers College, founded, 1895, as the Slater Industrial and State Normal School. Winston-Salem was created, 1913, from the consolidation of two towns, Winston and Salem. Salem was first settled, 1766, by German-speaking Moravians; the town's name is an approximate transliteration of the Hebrew word for peace, *shalom*. Winston was founded, 1849, and was named for a Revolutionary War soldier. Interesting buildings in Old Salem are the Wachovia Museum, 1794; the John Vogler House, 1818, Salem Tavern, 1784; and the Lick-Boner House, 1787. Pop. (1960) 111,135.

WINTER, FRITZ, 1905–   , German painter, was born in Allenbrögge. He worked in the Westphalian coal mines, 1921–27, and studied at the Bauhaus School in Dessau under Paul Klee, Wassily Kandinsky, and Oskar Schlemmer, 1927–30. He was forced into exile by the Nazis, 1933, who considered his works degenerate; he moved to Bavaria, married, lived on a farm, and worked as a craftsman until he was drafted into the German army, 1939. During World War II he completed over 500 sketches; they were displayed in Germany, 1945–49, during which time he was a prisoner of war in Siberia. When he returned to Germany, 1949, he was acknowledged as the foremost German painter of his day. In 1954 he became a professor at Kassel Werkakademie.

WINTER, the coldest season of the year that begins in the Northern Hemisphere on December 22, when the sun reaches its farthest southern declination, or southern solstice. On this day the Northern Hemisphere has the least hours of daylight in the year; and in the Southern Hemisphere, the most daylight hours. In the Northern Hemisphere winter endures until the vernal equinox.

WINTERGREEN, an aromatic, low-growing shrub, *Gaultheira procumbens*, with bell-shaped flowers, scarlet berries, and leather-like foliage. Both berries and foliage persist through the winter, and are the source of the pungent flavoring called wintergreen. It is known also as boxberry and teaberry. The aromatic oil present in the leaves of the plant is called oil of wintergreen. Chemically, it is methyl salicylate, $C_8H_8O_3$ and is used medically as a counterirritant.

WINTER HAVEN, city, central Florida, in Polk County; on the Atlantic Coast Line and the Seaboard Air Line railroads, and U.S. highway 17; 46 miles

E of Tampa, in an area of small lakes. The city is a packing center and shipping point for an area in which oranges, grapefruit, tangerines, pineapple, papayas, tomatoes, and strawberries are grown. Canning of fruits is the chief industry. Florida maintains a citrus-inspection bureau there, and there is a federal citrus products station. The Florida Orange Festival is held every January. Pop. (1960) 16,277.

WINTER PARK, city, E central Florida, in Orange County; on the Atlantic Coast Line and the Seaboard Air Line railroads and U.S. highways 17 and 92; four miles N of Orlando, of which it is a residential suburb. The city is built around three small lakes. It was founded in 1858 as Lakeview; renamed Osceola in 1870, and Winter Park in 1881. The city is the site of Rollins College (1885). Pop (1960) 17,162.

WINTERSET, city, S central Iowa, seat of Madison County; on the Rock Island Railroad, and U.S. highway 169; 28 miles SW of Des Moines. The city is a trade center for an area producing fruit, grain, hybrid seed corn, feed, and limestone. Winterset manufactures stock and poultry remedies and floor clips; it also has a stone-polishing works. The city was founded, 1846, and incorporated, 1876. The original Delicious apple tree was discovered here, 1872. Pop. (1960) 3,639.

WINTERTHUR, city, Switzerland, in the canton of Zürich; on the Töss River, 17 miles NE of the city of Zürich. Winterthur is a railroad junction and an industrial town. Textiles, locomotives, machinery, and food products are manufactured. The Roman settlement, Vitudurum, now known as Ober Winterthur, lies to the northeast. Winterthur was founded in 1180 by a count of Kyburg. For two centuries the town was ruled by the Hapsburgs. Pop. (1958 est.) 77,400.

WINTHROP, JOHN, 1588–1649, colonial American political leader, first governor of the Massachusetts Bay Colony, was born in Edwardstone, Suffolk, England, of a prominent Puritan family. He studied at Trinity College, Cambridge, was admitted at Gray's Inn, 1613, and to the Inner Temple, 1628. Financial difficulties, plus the troubles of suiting a Puritan conscience to the atmosphere of Cavalier England, led Winthrop to join the newly chartered Massachusetts Bay Company, 1629. He was elected governor of the company and of the colony, 1629, and landed with some 700 colonists in Massachusetts, 1630, settling first at Charlestown, and soon afterward at Boston. They were soon joined by some 1,200 others. He was re-elected annually until 1634, when he became deputy governor, 1634–37. In 1636 an investigating committee led by the Rev. John Cotton rebuked Winthrop for leniency in disciplinary decisions, and won from him a promise of a more severe policy in the future. Increasingly theocratic in his later career, Winthrop, succeeding Sir Henry Vane as governor, 1637–40, 1642–44, was active in the banishment of Anne Hutchinson and her followers, and in the movement that increased the power of the colonial magistrates over the members of the colony. During this period he became a founder of the New England Confederation, and its first president. He was deputy governor again, 1644–46, and governor, 1646–49. Winthrop was the author of one of the most valuable source books on the history of colonial New England, a diary, appearing as *The History of New England 1630 to 1649* (2 vols. 1825–26).

WINTHROP, JOHN, 1606–76, colonial American governor of Connecticut, was born at Groton Manor, Suffolk, England, the son of John Winthrop, the first governor of the Massachusetts Bay Colony, and Mary Forth. He studied at Trinity College, Cambridge, and the Inner Temple, London. He went to Massachusetts, 1631, took part in the settlement of Ipswich, 1633, went to England, 1634, and returned with a commission from Lord Say and Sele, and Lord Brook, authorizing him to build a fort at the mouth of the Connecticut River, and to act as governor or commander for a year. This fort, called Saybrook, cut off the Dutch from the control of the river. He was governor of Connecticut, 1657–58, 1659–76. In England, 1661–63, he was instrumental in securing from Charles II the extremely liberal charter of 1662, which united the colony of New Haven with Connecticut and gave the inhabitants the rights of Englishmen.

WINTHROP, JOHN, 1714–79, colonial American astronomer and physicist, was born in Boston, Mass., a descendant of John Winthrop, the first governor of the Massachusetts Bay Colony. He was educated at Harvard, was professor of mathematics and natural philosophy there, 1738–79, and received Harvard's first honorary LL.D. degree, 1773. Winthrop founded the first American laboratory of experimental physics at Harvard, 1746. He made an extensive study of sunspots, 1739, observed the transits of Mercury in 1740, 1743, and 1769, and studied the transits of Venus in 1761 and 1769. He was also a pioneer in American seismology, and wrote *Lecture on Earthquakes* (1755), a study of the New England earthquake of that year. He supported the theories of Benjamin Franklin in the field of electricity.

WINTHROP, town, E Massachusetts, in Suffolk County; on a peninsula jutting into Boston Bay; four miles ENE of Boston, of which it is a residential suburb. Winthrop is a summer-resort center. It is connected with Boston by bus line. Winthrop was settled in 1635 and was separated from North Chelsea in 1852. Pop. (1960) 20,303.

WINTON, town, NE North Carolina, seat of Hertford County; on the Chowan River, and U.S. highways 13 and 158; 60 miles ENE of Raleigh. The town is a trade center and has a sawmill. Winton was established, 1766, and was burned in the Civil War. Pop. (1960) 835.

WINTON, borough, NE Pennsylvania, in Lackawanna County; on the Delaware and Hudson and the Lackawanna railroads; about 8 miles NE of Scranton. Coal mining and the manufacturing of textiles are the chief industries. The borough was settled in 1849 and previously named Saymour and Mount Vernon. It was renamed Winton in 1874 and was incorporated as a borough in 1877. Pop. (1960) 5,456.

WINWOOD, SIR RALPH, 1563?–1617, English political figure, was born in Aynhoe, Northamptonshire. He succeeded Sir Henry Neville as England's ambassador to France, 1601, went to The Hague as agent to the States-General of the United Provinces, 1603, and was appointed secretary of state in England, 1614. He urged Sir Walter Raleigh to attack the Spanish fleet and Spanish settlements in South America and as a member of Parliament, 1614, defended the king's right to levy taxes.

WIRE, a thin metal in the form of a thread or slender rod. It is usually made by drawing the metal through dies. In cross section, wire is usually circular. For making wire the most suitable metals are steel, copper, zinc, aluminum, nickel, tungsten, chromium, platinum, and their alloys.

The process of making wire is similar for almost all metals. Metal ingots are heated to a softening temperature and rolled into billets, then into rods. Through successive rolling the rod is reduced to a diameter of ¼ to ½ inch and reeled onto a coil. The oxide scale formed during these operations is removed by immersion in acid baths. The wire is dried by baking.

One end of the coil is inserted in a swedging machine which hammers the end of the wire into a small enough diameter to permit it to pass through the hole of the first die. The die consists of a block of steel, diamond, or similarly hard material. The wire is pulled through the die by winding on a rotating drum. This process is repeated with dies of increasingly smaller holes. Because repeated drawing tends to produce hardness, it is often necessary to resort to intermediate annealing. Steel wire often needs a protective coating to retard corrosion. For this purpose a thin layer of zinc, copper, cadmium, aluminum, or enamel is applied.

Wire Gauges. Wires are drawn to standard sizes, or gauges. Steel wire is usually reckoned by the steel wire gauge. Nonferrous wires are reckoned by the American wire gauge. The Birmingham or Stubbs gauge and British Imperial Standard gauge are also used to some extent in the United States. Those gauges serve to classify wires from approximately 0.625 inches in diameter down to 0.000878 inches.

Materials. The most commonly used material for wire of great strength is steel. By great amounts of drafting and by various heat treatments, it is possible to obtain tensile strengths of approximately 400,000 pounds per square inch. Wire of this class is used in pianos, springs, and wire cables, and must not only conform to high standards of tensile strength but also have high endurance, or "fatigue strength."

Uses. Steel wire is used for such products as springs, wire rope, control cables, and steel wool. Aluminum wire is used primarily for electrical conductors of the high-tension type and is usually combined with one or more steel wires for greater strength. Copper wire is commonly used for carrying electrical current and is also combined with steel wire where great strength is needed. Silver wire is used for electrical wiring and in the field of surgery.

Wire rope resembles in appearance the more common hemp rope. Most wire ropes are made of steel. There are many types used in construction, each having been developed for varying degrees of tensile strength, stretch, abrasive wear, fatigue, resistance to corrosion and safety factors, according to need.

There are two basic patterns, or lays, used in making wire rope: the regular, and the Lang lay. The regular lay is the more common. Wires are twisted in one direction to form the strands, and the strands, in turn, are twisted in the opposite direction to form the ropes. The outer layers are approximately parallel to the longitudinal axis of the rope.

In rope of the Lang lay, the wires in the strands and the strands in the rope are twisted in the same direction. The outer wires run diagonally across the longitudinal axis of the rope and are thus more exposed. These ropes are very resistant to abrasion and are highly flexible, but regular lay ropes are less likely to kink or untwist and are generally easier to handle in most applications.   J. C. LITTLE

WIRT, WILLIAM, 1772–1834, U.S. political figure and author, was born in Bladensburg, Md. He was admitted to the bar, 1792, practiced law in Virginia, and was a prosecution counsel at the treason trial of Aaron Burr, 1807. Wirt held various offices in Virginia from 1799 and was U. S. attorney for Richmond, 1816. As U. S. attorney general in the cabinets of James Monroe and John Quincy Adams, Wirt figured in such important cases as *McCulloch* v. *Maryland* and *Gibbons* v. *Ogden.* He was the Anti-Masonic party's candidate for the U. S. presidency in 1832. Wirt wrote *The Letters of a British Spy* (1803).

WIRTZ, WILLIAM WILLARD, 1912– , U. S. public official, was born in DeKalb, Ill., and was graduated from Beloit College, 1933, and from Harvard Law School, 1937. He taught at the University of Iowa, 1937–39, and in the School of Law, Northwestern University, from 1939 until 1942, when he became assistant general counsel of the U. S. Board of Economic Warfare. He was with the War Labor Board, 1943–45, and was chairman of the National Wage Stabilization Board, 1946. He was a full professor of labor law at Northwestern from 1946, and developed an extensive private practice from 1955. As under secretary of labor, 1961–62, Wirtz repeatedly demonstrated that his reputation as an effective labor-management arbitrator was deserved. When Arthur J. Goldberg was appointed to the U.S. Supreme Court, 1962, Wirtz was named U.S. secretary of labor.

WISCONSIN

ALLISON-LIGHTHALL

A leader in dairy goods, this Great Lakes state is popular among outdoor enthusiasts.

WISCONSIN, state, NE central United States, bounded on the N and NE by Lake Superior and the Upper Peninsula of Michigan, on the E by Lake Michigan, on the S by Illinois, and on the W by Iowa and Minnesota; area 56,154 sq. mi., including 1,449 sq. mi. of inland water; pop. (1960) 3,951,777.

Wisconsin is shaped something like a mitten whose thumb, Door Peninsula, extends into Lake Michigan. Its maximum dimensions are about 295 miles E–W, 315 miles N–S. Among the 50 states, Wisconsin ranks 26th in size, 15th in population. The name of the state derives from the French *Ouisconsing,* which itself was derived from one or more of the Sac (Sauk) Indian words *Ouiskonsing, Ouiskousing, Miskounsing, Miskousing,* or *Wis-Kansin* (meeting of the waters); or from the Menominee Indian word for "living place"; or from the Ojibway word *Wishkonsing* (place of the muskrat's hole). The state's popular name, "Badger State," is an allusion to early prospectors in the Wisconsin lead-mining region who, like badgers, burrowed in caves on the hillsides. "Forward" is the state motto; unofficially, the sugar maple is the state tree, the robin is the state bird, and the violet is the state flower. Madison is the capital. For map see Atlas, Vol. 20. For state flag in color, see FLAG.

PHYSICAL FACTORS

Topography. The state may be divided into five physiographic regions: the Lake Superior Lowland, the Northern Highland, the Central Plain, the Western Upland, and the Eastern Ridges and Lowlands.

The Lake Superior Lowland is composed of two low-lying areas, which are separated by the northeast to southeast oriented Douglas Range and the high Bayfield Peninsula. The Apostle Island group is an extension of the peninsula. Streams, flowing northward, form falls and rapids as they descend the southern margin at each segment of the lowland. The stream valleys have cut from 50 to 100 feet into the otherwise relatively even surface of the Lake Superior Lowland along their way to Lake Superior. As a result of the slow tilting of the Lake Superior Basin in the course of several centuries, the streams as they enter the lake have widened, "drowned" mouths, often partially blocked by wave-built sand bars. Largest of these estuary mouths is that of the St. Louis River, blocked by a 9-mile-long bar extending across the bay from Wisconsin to Minnesota, forming a natural breakwater for the harbor at Duluth-Superior.

The Northern Highland is the broad upland of northern Wisconsin, which is underlaid by ancient igneous and metamorphosed crystalline rocks, an extension into the United States of the so-called

The Wisconsin state seal shows a quartered shield on which are a plow, a pick and shovel, an arm and hammer, and an anchor. The shield is held by a sailor with a rope coil and a yeoman with a pick. Above are a badger and the state motto.

BIRD	Robin
FLOWER	Wood violet
TREE	Sugar maple
CAPITAL	Madison
MOTTO	Forward
ENTERED THE UNION	May 29, 1848
ORDER OF ENTRY	30th

ROTKIN—P.F.I.

Wisconsin's state capitol at Madison is in a tree-filled square near the shores of Lake Mendota.

Canadian or Laurentian Shield. Averaging 1,000 to 2,000 feet above sea level, the surface is undulating with an occasional rounded ridge or hill. One of these, the Penokee, or Gogebic, Range in Iron and Ashland counties, is one of the active iron-ore mining areas of the Lake Superior region. Another, Timms (or Tim's) Hill in Price County, rises 1,952 feet above sea level and is considered the highest point in the state.

Originating in the higher portion to the north, clear streams radiate toward the southeast, south, and southwest. These include the headwaters of the Wisconsin, the Chippewa, the St. Croix, the Wolf, and the Menominee, all major rivers of the state. Numerous small falls and rapids enhance the attractiveness of the forest scenery, and in places they have been harnessed for hydroelectricity. There are thousands of swamps and lakes.

The Central Plain, shaped something like a boomerang, borders the southern or lower outer margin of the Northern Highland. Rivers originating in the Northern Highland flow across the Central Plain in

flattened gradients. The northeastward-extending arm and the upper portion of the northwestward one have uneven surfaces with numerous small lakes and swamps; the western portion of the central area has thousands of acres of low marshy land. Steep-sided, flat-topped buttes rise abruptly above this flat lowland surface in the nonglaciated portion.

The Western Upland in the southwest rises 300 feet above the Central Plain, and is glaciated only in the northern and southeastern extremities. Most of the region is characterized by ridges and deeply cut valleys. The deep, wide gorges of the Mississippi and Wisconsin rivers are partly filled with thick deposits of glacial material, gravel, and sand. Other streams such as the Chippewa, the Black, the La Crosse, and the Kickapoo, along with numerous tributaries, create a dense network of valleys. The Baraboo Range, an old, worn-down mountain range of quartzite rock, rises to more than 1,600 feet, about 700 feet above the surrounding area.

The Eastern Ridges and Lowlands area, bordering Lake Michigan, is composed of three parallel ridges of resistant limestone which are separated by broad shallow lowlands of several miles' width. The easternmost ridge projects northeastward into Lake Mich-

In Racine, Frank Lloyd Wright's Johnson Wax Research Tower rises 153 feet over a base that is only 13 feet in diameter at its narrowest point. It was constructed in 1950.

JOHNSON WAX

Population Density Map of Wisconsin. White areas, 5–25 inhabitants per square mile; light gray areas, 25–50 inhabitants; dark gray areas, 50–150 inhabitants; black areas, over 150 inhabitants.

Precipitation Map. White areas, 24–28 inches of precipitation annually; light gray areas, 28–32 inches; dark gray areas, 32–36 inches; black areas, 36–40 inches.

With over two million milk cows, Wisconsin produces more milk and cheese than any other state.

igan as Door Peninsula. Its western edge diverts the drainage of the lowland immediately to the west—the lower Fox River northward through broad, shallow Lake Winnebago to Green Bay, and the Rock River southward through Horicon Marsh to Illinois and the Mississippi River.

South of Lake Winnebago is one of the world's largest concentrations of drumlins—linear hills shaped like whalebacks and arranged in roughly parallel alignment. In the southeast, oriented north-south parallel to Lake Michigan, is the so-called Kettle Moraine, a jumbled assemblage of steeply sloping gravelly knobs and ridges randomly interspersed with deep, enclosed basins, or "kettles." Portions of this Kettle Moraine country have been set aside as state forests and recreational areas.

Drainage. The bulk of Wisconsin's runoff goes to the Gulf of Mexico by way of the Mississippi, but the waters of the Fox River and its main tributary the Wolf drain into Green Bay.

Wisconsin has nearly 9,000 lakes, ranging in size from 10 acres to 137,708 acres (Lake Winnebago, the largest). Total area of inland lakes is 1,449 square miles. The greatest concentration of lakes is in the northwest from Polk to Sawyer County and in the north in the Vilas-Oneida counties section. In addition to the inland lakes, Wisconsin's boundaries include approximately 670 miles of Lake Michigan and Lake Superior shoreline.

Climate is of the humid continental type. The state heats rapidly in summer and cools as readily in winter. Absence of high mountains in the north allows cold outsurges of wintry arctic air to move across the state; in summer, importations of warm air from the southwest and south also help to widen the gap between winter and summer averages. In July the warmest area is in the southwest, with the averages above 72°F; the coolest sections are in the most northerly and highest parts of the state, in the

Hops, which give beer its distinctive taste, are added to a boiling mixture in large brew kettles at a brewery in Milwaukee. The city has long been one of the world's most important centers of beer production.

Vilas County area and along Lake Superior, where the July average is below 66°F. In January the warmest part of the state is in the southeast along the Lake Michigan shore. January averages range from 22°F here to 10°F in the Northern Highland. Precipitation averages about 30 inches per year in the state as a whole; it is heaviest, over 32 inches, in the southwest, and in the Eau Claire, Chippewa, Clark, and Taylor counties area, and lightest near the Great Lakes, with less than 28 inches near Lake Superior. The southern part of the state has about 30 inches of snowfall annually, while the north has approximately 55 to 60 inches.

Plant Wildlife. About 45 per cent of the state is forested, although originally more than 80 per cent of Wisconsin was covered by trees. Over much of northern Wisconsin and the Central Plain a second growth forest of small timber covers thousands of square miles. Hardwoods far outnumber evergreens. Aspen, once a minor member of the original forest, is now the most abundant tree. Maples, white spruce, red pines, and jackpines are widespread; balsam fir is common, particularly in the northwest. White cedar, black spruce, and tamarack grow in the glacial bogs. There are small groves and wooded areas in southern Wisconsin, and in the rougher sections of the Western Upland and the Kettle Moraine country there are commercial quantities of oaks and hard maples. In the marshlands of the Central Plain, sedge growth, sphagnum moss, and the rare pitcher plant are found. Blueberries are common in the sandy barrens of the north, and huckleberry, thimbleberry, blackberry, wild raspberry, and wild strawberry are widespread. Common wildflowers are violet (the state flower), trillium, spring beauty, lady-slipper, Indian paint brush, daisies, chicory, goldenrod, and aster.

Animal Wildlife. Big game animals are the whitetail deer and black bear, found in the northern and western forested areas. A few wolves and bobcats

BORDEN, INC.
Process cheese is made in Plymouth. Food processing is one of the state's most valuable industries.

are to be encountered in the north; coyotes, in the northern and central areas. Red fox, gray fox, beaver, otter, muskrat, mink, skunk, and raccoon are common smaller animals. Among the other small animals are rabbit, gray and red squirrel, and woodchuck. Badgers are rare, even though Wisconsin is called the Badger State.

The ring-necked pheasant and Hungarian partridge, introduced from Europe, are found in the agricultural areas, quail occur in the southwest, and the ruffed grouse is abundant in the northern forested regions. The sharp-tailed grouse and the prairie chicken live in the diminishing open areas in the central and northern parts of the state. Ducks, geese, and coots pass through Wisconsin in spring and fall.

A truck made in Oshkosh is loaded aboard an ocean vessel berthed at a Milwaukee cargo terminal.
MILWAUKEE SENTINEL PHOTO

Iron is shipped to Midwestern industrial cities by carrier from Superior, a major Great Lakes port.
ROTKIN—P.F.I.

Horicon Marsh, a wildlife refuge, is a favorite stopping-off place for Canada geese.

The muskellunge, or musky, and northern pike, are common game fish. Among other game fish are sturgeon; walleye; largemouthed and smallmouthed bass; and brook, brown, rainbow, and lake trout. Pan fish, such as the yellow perch, bullheads, blue gills, pumpkin seeds, rock bass, and crappies are called the bread-and-butter fish of Wisconin anglers. Minnows are taken for bait, and such "rough fish" as the carp, drum, suckers, redhorse and sheepshead are an important source of low-cost animal food.

SOCIAL FACTORS

Population. The population of Wisconsin increased by 517,202, or 15.1 per cent, between 1950 and 1960, a rate slightly smaller than the national average. Population density for the state averaged 72 persons per square mile. Milwaukee County, the most densely settled county with 4,300 persons per square mile, contained 20 per cent of the state's population. Most of northern Wisconsin is sparsely settled. Density was less than 10 per square mile in Forest County. More than 60 per cent of the population was classified as urban. Populations of 46 cities were in excess of 10,000, in 1960. The 10 largest cities were Milwaukee, Madison, Racine, West Allis, Kenosha, Green Bay, Wauwatosa, Appleton, La Crosse, and Sheboygan. The people are principally of north European origin. Fewer than 2.5 per cent of the inhabitants were classified as nonwhite. Protestants, of which almost two-thirds were Lutherans, made up 52 per cent of the church membership, and 46 per cent were Roman Catholics.

PRINCIPAL CITIES

	Population	
	1950 Census	1960 Census
Milwaukee..................	637,372	741,324
Madison (capital)..........	96,056	126,706
Racine....................	71,193	89,144
West Allis.................	42,959	68,157
Kenosha...................	54,368	67,899
Green Bay.................	52,735	62,888
Wauwatosa................	33,324	56,923
Appleton..................	34,010	48,411
La Crosse.................	47,535	47,575
Sheboygan................	42,365	45,747
Oshkosh..................	41,084	45,110

Education. General administration of public schools is under a superintendent of public instruction elected for four years. Schools not under municipal jurisdiction are supervised by an elected county superintendent. School attendance is compulsory for most children from the age of 7 to 16.

The major institution of higher education is the University of Wisconsin (1848), at Madison with a division, the University of Wisconsin at Milwaukee, in Milwaukee; eight University Extension Centers, offering the first two years of university work, are located in Kenosha, Racine, Sheboygan, Manitowoc, Menasha, Green Bay, Marinette, and Wausau. Teacher training is given at seven Wisconsin state colleges at Eau Claire (1916), LaCrosse (1909), Oshkosh (1871), River Falls (1874), Stevens Point (1894), Superior (1896), Whitewater (1868); Wisconsin State College and Institute of Technology (1866), at Platteville, and Stout State College (1903), at Menomonie; and at 22 two-year county colleges for the training of rural elementary teachers. Among Wisconsin's private colleges and universities are Alverno College (1887), at Milwaukee; Beloit College (1846), at Beloit; Carroll College (1840), at Waukesha; Lawrence College (1847), at Appleton; Marquette University (1874), at Milwaukee; Milwaukee-Downer College (1848), at Milwaukee; Northland College (1892), at Ashland; Ripon College (1851), at Ripon; and St. Norbert College (1893), at DePere.

Public Welfare. The State Department of Public Welfare consists of a board of nine members and a director with his staff. The department operates state institutions such as the diagnostic center at Madison; three hospitals for the mentally ill—Mendota State Hospital, Madison; Central State Hospital, Waupun; and Winnebago State Hospital near Oshkosh; the Child Center, Sparta; seven correctional centers—the Northern Colony and Training School, Chippewa Falls; the Southern Colony and Training Center, Union Grove; the Wisconsin State Prison, Waupun; the Home for Women, Taycheedah; the School for Boys, Waukesha; the School for Girls, Oregon; and the State Reformatory, Green Bay; and the Workshop for the Blind, Milwaukee. Among welfare institutions operated by other state agencies are the School for the Deaf, Delavan, under the Department of Public Instruction; and the State Tuberculosis Sanatorium, Wales, and Lake Tomahawk State Camp, both under the State Board of Health.

ECONOMIC FACTORS

General Characteristics. Manufacturing is the major wealth-producing economic activity. Value added to raw materials, by processing, amounts to about $4 billion annually, and manufacturing employs about 30 per cent of the labor force. Following in decreasing order as producers of wealth are agriculture, the recreation industry, mining, forestry, and fishing.

Agriculture. Wisconsin's farmland is located mainly in the southeast, the south, and the southwest. The Eastern Ridges and Lowlands Region had the greatest acreage of the more productive farm land. Nearly seven-eighths of Wisconsin farm income derives from the sale of livestock and livestock products, but cash crops are important in localized areas. As the nation's major dairying state, Wisconsin usually ranks first in milk and cheese production, and first or second in butter production.

Three-fifths of the land area in Wisconsin is farm land, of which nearly half is used for crops, among which hay, corn, and oats—feed crops for dairy cattle and other animals—require 93 per cent of total crop land. These three important crops do not thrive equally well everywhere; thus where summers are cooler, as in the environs of Lake Michigan and toward the north, oats and hay acreages are greater. Corn growing is more important in southern and western Wisconsin. Alfalfa is the outstanding hay crop, and Wisconsin is the country's leading producer; in the acid soils to the north, where alfalfa does not thrive, clover and timothy are grown instead.

The beef cattle industry was increasingly emphasized in the post-World War II period. Hogs are raised in greatest numbers in the south central and southwestern areas, where most corn is grown for grain rather than for silage. Sheep are produced in the Western Upland and in the south central part of the state. Poultry raising is a sideline on many farms, with particular emphasis on turkeys in the post-World War II period.

PRODUCTION OF PRINCIPAL CROPS

Crop	Unit	1950-59 Average	1960
		(in thousands)	
Corn for grain..........	bushels	94,671	108,500
Corn for canning.......	tons	300,880	262,900
Cranberries............	barrels	297,300	379,000
Lima beans............	pounds	10,560	11,160
Oats.................	bushels	135,184	103,917
Sweet peas............	pounds	265,740	212,000
Tobacco...............	pounds	22,165	20,845

SOURCE: *U.S. Department of Agriculture*

WISCONSIN CONSERVATION DEPT.

Wisconsin's thousands of lakes provide ample opportunity for those interested in fishing. Here fishermen calmly wait in a rowboat for muskelunge to strike their lines.

Cash crops have great local importance. Wisconsin leads in the production of canning peas, sweet corn, and beets, all three grown mainly in the southeast. Large quantities of cucumbers for pickles, cabbages for kraut, snap beans, and lima beans are also raised. Wisconsin ranks second among the states producing cranberries, which are grown on marshy lands of the Central Plain and in parts of the Northern Highland. Production of cherries is concentrated in Door Peninsula. Apples are also important there as well as in the southwest. Cigar tobacco is raised in the south central portion in eastern Dane and northern Rock counties and in and around Vernon County in the southwest.

Forestry. Pulpwood (from aspen and other species) rather than lumber is the principal forest product, along with an ever increasing harvest of Christmas trees. In 1960 Wisconsin was producing over 50 per cent of the pulpwood used by its paper mills, and it was expected that within a few years this would rise to 65 or 70 per cent. Some of the hardwoods—hard maple, yellow birch, and oak—provide veneer for furniture and wood for interior trim and flooring.

Fisheries. Commercial fishing is not a major economic activity. The value of the annual catch ranges from between $2 million to $3 million. The Wisconsin catch of 16,805,713 pounds in 1959, three fourths of it from Lake Michigan, represented about 25 per cent of that taken from the Great Lakes by U.S. fishermen. The more highly prized species, however, lake trout and whitefish, come almost exclusively from Lake Superior, since by 1960 the devastations of the parasitic lamprey eel (sea lamprey) had eliminated the lake trout as a commercial fish in Lake Michigan, and almost abolished the whitefish. Chubs, herring, smelt, and perch are also important commercial fish caught in the Great Lakes. Carp, buffalo, catfish, and sheepshead account for about nine tenths of the total caught in the Mississippi River.

Mining. Wisconsin produced minerals valued at $77,171,000 in 1960, an increase over $71,959,000 in 1959. The state stood second in production of abrasive stone and third in production of sand and gravel. The value of nonmetallic minerals produced is about twice that of the metallic. Limestone and sandstone are quarried as building stone; sandstone is crushed for molding sand for foundry use; granite supplies monumental stone; and quartzite is used for

PRODUCTION OF PRINCIPAL MINERALS

Mineral	Unit	1959	1960
Iron Ore (usable)...	1,000 short tons	701	1,502
Sand and Gravel....	1,000 short tons	41,999	35,681
Stone..............	1,000 short tons	13,522	16,486
Zinc (recoverable)...	short ton	11,635	18,410

abrasive and refractory purposes. Metallic mineral production is small. Wisconsin usually ranks sixth in iron ore mined, but produces only about 1.5 per cent of the country's total. The ore is high grade, mainly hematite, and contains above 50 per cent iron content. Zinc and lead (19,575 short tons in 1960) are mined in Lafayette, Grant, and Iowa counties.

Manufacturing. Manufacturing, the state's major economic activity, employs nearly one third of the labor force, provides almost 40 per cent of the income, and accounts for three fourths of the basic wealth in goods produced. Wisconsin is eleventh among the 50 states in value added to raw materials through manufacturing. Slightly more than half of manufacturing employees are engaged in processing metals, one fifth process agricultural raw materials, and one fifth work with forest raw materials. Machinery is the most important manufactured product, followed by processed foods, mainly dairy products and canned vegetables, and then by paper and paper products. The state ranks first in production of engines and turbines, dairy products and paper products, and second in automobiles and farm machinery, including tractors.

Manufacturing is concentrated in seven major regions. The southeast lake shore, the Milwaukee region, which employs more than half the total labor force, turns out machinery, electrical apparatus, metal goods, and beer. The lower Fox River valley, with 10 per cent of the workers, concentrates on paper manufacture. The Rock River valley, with 10 per cent of the workers, produces transportation equipment, machinery, and metal goods. Other leading industrial areas are the upper Lake Michigan shore, the upper Wisconsin River valley, Eau Claire, and La Crosse.

Transportation. The state has a dense network of railroads with the densest concentration in the southeast around Milwaukee.

The pattern of major highways, like that of the railroads, is extremely dense in the southeast in the Milwaukee area and throughout the Eastern Ridges and Lowlands region. From the southeast, main highways lead west, northwest, and north. The Western Upland also has a closely spaced road grid. Throughout the rest of the state the net is more open with several extensive roadless areas in the Northern Highland and part of the Central Plain. In the 1960's the main through roads were being transformed into dual highways, or freeways, some of which were to form a part of the new interstate system. Numerous bus and truck lines crisscross the state. A unique feature is the milk pick-up system in which fleets of tank trucks visit the dairy farms each day to haul the milk to market.

Four major airlines provide interstate service, and two smaller lines serve numerous cities within the state and beyond into Minnesota, Michigan, and Illinois. The state has a total of 161 airfields.

Most of the state's streams, navigable for small boats only, are used mainly by pleasure craft, but two streams, the Mississippi and the lower Fox, are used for commercial navigation. The federal government maintains a nine-foot-minimum channel in the Mississippi, and barge trains carrying petroleum products, coal, and other bulk cargo visit Wisconsin river ports. By virtue of locks around its falls and rapids, the Fox River is navigable into Lake Winnebago for vessels drawing no more than six feet. Coal barges come upstream from Green Bay to Oshkosh on the west shore of Lake Winnebago.

Commerce. Wisconsin's chief export items are iron ore, originating largely in Minnesota, shipped from the ports of Superior and Ashland to the iron and steel manufacturing centers of the lower Great Lakes; and machinery, engines, cars, metal goods, processed dairy products, paper, grain, and beer. Major imports are pulpwood from Minnesota, Michigan, and Ontario; coal from Illinois and the Appalachian coal field; petroleum products; iron and steel; barley; limestone and cement; and natural gas via pipelines from Texas, Oklahoma, and Canada.

Wisconsin's principal ports are Duluth-Superior, Milwaukee, Ashland, Green Bay, Manitowoc, Port Washington, Kewaunee, Menominee-Marinette, Sheboygan, and Racine.

Communications. There were 37 daily newspapers and 283 weeklies published in Wisconsin in 1960. In addition, 15 television stations and 100 AM and FM radio stations were in operation within the state.

Recreational Resources and Tourist Attractions. The state's chief tourist attractions are the lakes and streams, for fishing, swimming, and boating; forests of pines, hemlock, and hardwoods; wildlife, which include deer and bear and numerous smaller types; and an uneven topography.

Major tourist centers in the southeast are in the lake sections of the wooded Kettle Moraine country near Lake Geneva and Oconomowoc, slightly farther north at Wisconsin Dells on the Wisconsin River and at Green Lake, and in east central Wisconsin around the Waupaca chain of lakes. Door Peninsula is unique with its double coastline—rocky bluffs along Green Bay and sandy beaches on Lake Michigan. In the far north are the two great concentrations of lakes, in Vilas and Oneida counties, and again farther west, from Sawyer to Burnett to Polk counties. Summer is the chief tourist season, but hunting and fishing are popular in winter.

Some notable points of interest are The Dells, a picturesque gorge cut into cross-bedded sandstone by the Wisconsin River; Devils Lake, in a state park in the Baraboo Range in Sauk County; Little Norway, rural museum in a valley near Blue Mound; Cave of the Mounds and Lost River Cave, in dolomitic limestone in the vicinity of Blue Mound; Tower Hill State Park, in Iowa County overlooking the Wisconsin River; First Capitol State Park, a frame building that served as Wisconsin's territorial capitol. Other major attractions are the parks of Pattison, Copper Falls, and Interstate in the northwest; Brunet Island and Rib Mountain in the central part; Peninsula and Potawatomi on Door Peninsula in the northeast; Big Foot Beach in the southeast; and Menick, Penot, Wildcat Mountain, and Wyalusing in the southwest.

ROBERT W. FINLEY

GOVERNMENT

Constitution. Wisconsin is governed under its original constitution (1848), as amended. Proposed amendments may originate in the legislature or in a constitutional convention. Amendments proposed in the legislature must be approved by most elected members of each house in two successive sessions, and ratified by a majority of the voters. A constitutional convention may be called by majority vote of both houses of the legislature; amendments proposed by the convention must then be approved by a majority of the voters. Any U.S. citizen 21 years of age or over may register to vote in Wisconsin for presidential and vice-presidential electors, but residency in the state one year and in the precinct for 10 days must be established in order to vote for congressional and state officers.

The Legislature consists of an assembly whose membership may not be less than 54 or more than 100, and of a senate whose membership must total not less than one-fourth and not more than one-third that of the assembly; thus, there cannot be more than 33⅓ senators—33 for all practical purposes. Senators are elected for four years, assemblymen for two years. There is no constitutional provision for voter legislation by initiative or referendum. Regular sessions are held biennially in January of odd-numbered years; there is no constitutional limit on the length of legislative sessions.

The Executive Officials are the governor, lieutenant governor, secretary of state, treasurer, and attorney general, elected for two years; and the superintendent of public instruction, elected for four years. There is no constitutional limitation on successive re-election to the governorship. The governor appoints state administrative officers. His veto, which is applicable to all legislation, may be overridden by two-thirds vote of the members present in each house of the legislature.

The Judicial Authority is vested in a supreme court of seven justices, elected for 10-year terms; in circuit courts, each with one judge elected for six years; in county courts, each with one judge elected for six years; in superior courts; and in justice of the peace courts.

HISTORY

Exploration. The early European exploration of the Wisconsin area was made by the French from their settlements in New France (Canada). The explorer Jean Nicolet, first white man known to have entered the region, visited the Winnebago Indians at the mouth of the Fox River, 1634. The fur traders Pierre Esprit Radisson and Medart Chouart, sieur de Groseilliers, traveled extensively through the area, 1658–59; and the Jesuit priest Claude Jean Allouez, who worked among Indians on the shores of Lake Superior and Lake Michigan, established several missions, of which the most important one was St. Francis Xavier Mission, on the site of present day De Pere. Extensive explorations around the Great Lakes and in the region of the Mississippi River valley by Louis Jolliet, Father Jacques Marquette, Daniel Greysolon Duluth, Robert Cavelier, sieur de La Salle, Brother Louis Hennepin, and others, later provided a basis for France's claim to the region. An important geographical factor that directed French interest to the country was the waterway between Lake Michigan and the Mississippi River provided by the Fox and the Wisconsin rivers—the Wisconsin was called the Oviesconsing by the French—with a two-mile portage between the two streams. Subsequently, forts were built: La Baye at *Vert Baie* (Green Bay), the oldest permanent white settlement on the western shore of Lake Michigan, 1684; La Pointe on Lake Superior, 1718; and at several sites on the upper Mississippi such as Prairie du Chien, 1685. Early in the eighteenth century the Fox Indians went on the warpath and gave the French considerable trouble before being subdued, 1738. At the end of the French and Indian War, 1763, all of New France was given to the victorious British, but French language and customs persisted in the Wisconsin region.

British Influence. Although British sovereignty in Wisconsin theoretically ended, 1783, when the Treaty of Paris gave to the United States all former British territory south of Canada and east of the Mississippi River (except for Florida, which was ceded to Spain), Great Britain exercised considerable influence there until after the War of 1812. Relying chiefly on their French-Canadian employees to deal with the Indians, British fur traders developed a flourishing business in the region, and not until after Jay's Treaty (1794) were British military trading posts in northwestern United States abandoned. Even later, British fur traders maintained their dominance in the region (see NORTHWEST TERRITORY). During the War of 1812 the western Indians fought as allies of the British; in combatting them a U.S. expedition built Fort Shelby at Prairie du Chien, 1814, and for the first time the U.S. flag was raised over Wisconsin. Within a month this fort was taken by the British, however, who held the region until the war ended, 1815.

Territorial Period. In the meantime, the Wisconsin area had been a part of Indiana Territory, 1800–09, and Illinois Territory, 1809–18. Military rule, established by the U.S. government during the war, came to an end when Wisconsin became part of Michigan Territory, 1818. The fur trade continued to be the basis of the economy, but John Jacob Astor's American Fur Company supplanted the British. The region suffered from Indian hostilities in 1827, and during the Black Hawk War, 1831–32. Rapid white settlement followed, mainly by native-born Americans. The Territory of Wisconsin, created in 1836, included present-day Wisconsin, Iowa, Minnesota, and parts of the Dakotas. The capital was established at a new townsite, Madison, which was surveyed and platted in 1837. A movement for statehood, soon under way, was complicated by Wisconsin's protests against the federal government for awarding to Illinois a strip of her southernmost territory, extending directly west from the southern tip of Lake Michigan to the Mississippi, and to Michigan her northeasternmost territory, the Upper Peninsula—in the first instance to give Illinois an outlet on Lake Michigan, in the second instance to compensate Michigan for territory that it had lost to Ohio (see TOLEDO, *History*). Eventually, however, Congress passed the Enabling Act of 1846, and Wisconsin was admitted to the Union, May 29, 1848, as the 30th state.

Wisconsin As a State. During the Civil War more than 90,000 men from Wisconsin served in the Union's armed forces. In the meanwhile a large number of foreign born, mainly Germans and Irish, had settled in Wisconsin. After the war there was large-scale immigration from Germany and Scandinavia, and later from Polish Russia. There was a great industrial development, 1880–90, especially in dairying, lumbering, and iron mining. In the late nineteenth century liberal political movements such as The Grange and the Wisconsin State Federation of Labor gained considerable support in the state. Robert M. La Follette, a liberal Republican elected governor in 1900, initiated a period of extensive political and social change in Wisconsin; after his death, 1925, his Progressive tradition was continued by his two sons Robert M. La Follette, Jr., and Philip F. La Follette. Among measures adopted by the state as part of the senior La Follette's "Wisconsin Idea" were income tax (1911), mothers' pensions (1913), and unemployment compensation (1932). See PROGRESSIVE PARTIES, *La Follette Progressives*.

Post-World War II Developments. The Wisconsin Centennial Exposition was held in Madison in 1948. The U.S. Supreme Court declared invalid, 1951, a Wisconsin state law prohibiting public utility strikes. A strike by members of a United Auto Workers and Congress of Industrial Organizations local union, employed by a plumbing fixture plant at Kohler, April, 1954–September, 1960, was the longest major strike in U.S. history. Except for the influence of the Progressive party, Wisconsin politics through the sixth decade were generally dominated by conservative elements, reflecting the influence of the state's rural population. After the Democratic party landslide for Franklin D. Roosevelt, 1932, Republicans were regularly elected to the state's governorship until Gaylord A. Nelson, a Democrat, was elected to that office, 1958. In the same year Wisconsin voters re-elected William E. Proxmire to the U.S. Senate; this was the first time in more than 100 years that the state had re-elected a Democrat to that office. The state's 12 electoral votes were cast for the Republican party presidential candidates in 1952, 1956, and 1960. In 1960 Wisconsin sent 10 congressmen to the U.S. House of Representatives.

BIBLIOG.–American Guide Series, *Wisconsin: A Guide to the Badger State* (1954); H. Russell Austin, *Wisconsin Story: The Building of a Vanguard State* (1957); Theodore C. Blegen, *Land Lies Open* (1949); Susan B. Davis, *Old Forts and Real Folks* (1939); August W. Derleth (Tally Mason, pseud.), *Wisconsin, River of a Thousand Isles* (1942); Leon D. Epstein, *Politics in Wisconsin* (1958); Frederick L. Holmes, *Old World Wisconsin: Around Europe in the Badger State* (1944); Side Roads: Excursions into Wisconsin's Past* (1949); Robert S. Hunt, *Law and Locomotives: The Impact of the Railroad on Wisc. Law in the 19th Century* (1958); Meridel Le Sueur, *North Star Country* (1945); Morleigh (pseud.), *Merry Britain in Pioneer Wisconsin* (1950); William F. Raney, *Wisconsin: A Story of Progress* (1940); Harvey A. Uber, *Environmental Factors in the Development of Wisconsin* (1937); Bertha K. Whyte, *Wisconsin Heritage* (1954); *Wisconsin: Stability, Progress, Beauty*, 5 vols. (1946).

WISCONSIN, UNIVERSITY OF, a public, coeducational institution of higher learning, located in Madison, Wis. The first movement toward the founding of the institution took place, 1836, when Wisconsin was still a territory; Congress provided two townships of public land for the university, 1839, legislation necessary for the opening of the institution was passed, 1848, and instruction offered, 1849.

The university operates a division at Milwaukee and extension centers at Green Bay, Kenosha, Manitowoc, Marinette, Menasha, Racine, Sheboygan, and Wausau. Students may receive the equivalent of the first two years of instruction at an extension center; the junior and senior years may be taken at the Madison or Milwaukee campus.

Among the various divisions of the university are: law, founded 1868; engineering, 1871; agriculture, 1888; graduate studies, 1889; music, 1895; commerce, 1900; medicine, 1907; library science, 1910; journalism, 1913; nursing, 1924; education, 1930; pharmacy, 1950; and home economics, 1951. The extension division was founded in 1916.

The university conducts an institute for research in the humanities, and maintains special programs in Indian studies, adult education, and nuclear engineering. Numerous institutes, clinics, schools, and workshops are held each year. A library of educational films is maintained for use by schools throughout the state. The museum of the state historical society is located on the Madison campus.

The university library has collections of materials on the history of science, Scandinavian literature, Russian history, bees, German philology, and the history of pharmacy. Numerous publications are issued, among them, the *Wisconsin Alumnus*, an alumni bulletin that is supplemented by a newspaper, the *Badger Report;* a series designed to aid secondary school teachers in curriculum planning; bulletins and annual reports of the Agricultural Experiment Stations; reports from the Washburn Observatory; the *Journal of Land Economics;* and *Monatshefte fuer Deutschen Unterricht*, a monthly bulletin for teachers of German. The University of Wisconsin Press publishes books of a scholarly nature on a wide variety of subjects. See COLLEGES AND UNIVERSITIES; WISCONSIN AT MILWAUKEE, UNIVERSITY OF.

WISCONSIN AT MILWAUKEE, UNIVERSITY OF, an extension division of the University of Wisconsin, located in Milwaukee, Wis. The Milwaukee division resulted from a merger, in 1956, of Wisconsin State College at Milwaukee and the Extension Division of the University of Wisconsin, which had been established in 1908. The school comprises a college of letters and science, with a special honors course for talented students; school of education, which maintains a laboratory elementary school; department of military science and tactics; and department of home economics, all located at the Kenwood campus, and the divisions of commerce, engineering, and pharmacy, and the evening school, all located at the downtown campus. Master's degrees are offered in business administration, education, engineering, mathematics, political science, and social work. See COLLEGES AND UNIVERSITIES.

WISCONSIN RAPIDS, city, central Wisconsin, seat of Wood County; on the Wisconsin River, the North Western, the Milwaukee, the Soo Line, and the Green Bay and Western railroads; 94 miles NNW of Madison. The city is a shipping point and processing center for an area in which lumbering, and the raising of cranberries, dairy cattle, hay, and oats are leading activities. Pulp, paper, and paper products, stoves, paints, flour, and dairy and meat products are manufactured. In the vicinity are extensive forest nurseries for the reforestation of the state and to furnish pulpwood for the paper industry. The city was established in 1900 by the union of Grand Rapids and Centralia; it was known as Grand Rapids until 1920, when the name was changed to avoid confusion with Grand Rapids, Mich. Pop. (1960) 15,042.

WISCONSIN RIVER, rises in N Wisconsin, in the lake region near the Michigan-Wisconsin border, and flows S through the Wisconsin Dells, E and S around Baraboo Range, and then flows W, north of Military Ridge, to its junction with the Mississippi River, 4 miles S of Prairie du Chien. Its length is about 430 miles. The upper channel of the Wisconsin is interrupted by rapids which have been developed for hydroelectric power. A major scenic attraction is the Wisconsin Dells, where the river cuts a gorge through a sandstone layer. Lower course of the river is navigable for small boats to Portage, where a canal crosses the 2-mile-wide divide to the Fox River, thus connecting the Mississippi and the Great Lakes. Major reservoirs impounded behind dams are Wisconsin, Castle Rock, Petenwell, Du Bay, and Spirit.

WISDOM, BOOK OF, or Wisdom of Solomon, a Jewish Deuterocanonical book, once ascribed to Solomon but now believed to have been written by an Alexandrian Jew, or Jews, between the second century B.C., and A.D. 40. It was accepted, 1546, by the Roman Catholic Council of Trent as canonical and as part of the Bible, but was rejected by Protestants and placed by them in the Apocrypha. The book is divided into three sections: Chapters 1–5, in which wisdom is glorified as the source of temporal and eternal happiness; Chapters 6–9, in which the nature and origin of wisdom are described; and Chapters 10–19, in which Jewish history is retold to show the power of wisdom. See APOCRYPHA; BIBLE; DEUTEROCANONICAL BOOKS; OLD TESTAMENT.

WISE, HENRY ALEXANDER, 1806–76, U.S. political figure, was born in Drummondtown, Va. He was graduated from Washington College, Pa., 1825, and was admitted to the bar about two years later. He was a member of Congress, 1833–44, first as a Democrat, and later as a Whig, minister to Brazil, 1844–47, and as governor of Virginia, 1856–60, signed the death warrant of abolitionist John Brown, 1859. He opposed secession, but when Virginia seceded he accepted a commission in the Confederate army and served throughout the Civil War. After the war he practiced law.

WISE, JOHN, 1652–1725, colonial American Congregational clergyman, was born in Roxbury, Mass. He was graduated from Harvard College, 1673, and became pastor of Chebacco, in Ipswich, Mass., 1680. He was fined and deposed from the ministry for a few weeks by Gov. Edmund Andros, 1687, for encouraging his townsmen to resist a tax that Andros had imposed. He was a deputy to the legislature from Ipswich, 1689. He opposed the plan of Increase Mather to place the churches under the jurisdiction of an ecclesiastical council in *The Churches' Quarrel Espoused* and *A Vindication of the Government of New England Churches.*

WISE, THOMAS JAMES, 1859–1937, English bibliographer and forger, was born in Gravesend, Kent. He began collecting books at the age of 17 and by 1912 had acquired such a reputation for discernment that he was frequently consulted by those interested in purchasing books purported to be rare. It would appear that his own excellent collection of rare works, known as the Ashley Library, and sold upon his death to the British Museum, was financed in part by advising those who came to him to buy books that he had forged and placed in the hands of auctioneers. He compiled important bibliographies of the works of Alfred Tennyson, Samuel Taylor Coleridge, William Wordsworth, and others.

WISE, town, SW Virginia, seat of Wise County; on U.S. highway 23; 150 miles WSW of Roanoke. The town is a trade center for an area in which bituminous coal is mined. There is some agricultural production in the narrow valleys. Wise was damaged by Union troops during the Civil War. Pop. (1960) 2,614.

WISEMAN, NICHOLAS PATRICK STEPHEN, 1802–65, Irish-English Roman Catholic prelate, was born in Seville, Spain. At 16 he entered the English College at Rome, where he later was rector, 1828–40. He became known as an able lecturer. In conjunction with Daniel O'Connell, he established, 1836, the Dublin *Review*, to which he was a regular contributor. He was made vicar-apostolic of the central division of the Roman Catholic Church in England, 1840, with the title of bishop, and became president of St. Mary's College at Oscott. He was transferred to London, 1846. When the Roman Catholic hierarchy was restored in England, 1850, he was made archbishop of Westminster and cardinal.

WISHART, GEORGE, 1513?–1546, Scottish reformer, was born probably in Pittarrow, Forfarshire. Charged with heresy, 1538, for teaching the Greek Testament, he fled to England. After travels in England and Europe, he returned to Scotland, 1543, where he was arrested, tried and condemned for heresy, and burned at St. Andrews, 1546. His preaching and martyrdom inspired John Knox, who led the Reformation in Scotland.

WISMAR, city, N Germany, in the East German district of Rostock; on Wismar Bay; 125 miles NW of Berlin. The chief industries are fishing and shipbuilding, and the manufacture of sugar, paper, machinery, and food products. During medieval times Wismar was a port of the Hanseatic League. Wismar was held by Sweden from 1648 until 1803, when it was ceded to Mecklenburg. Pop. (1959 est.) 54,800.

WISSEMBOURG, German Weissenburg, town, NE France, department of Bas-Rhin; on the Lauter River at the German border; 35 miles NNE of Strasbourg. The chief industrial products are processed foods and furniture. Wissembourg became a city in 1255. Located in the disputed region of Alsace-Lorraine, Wissembourg has alternately passed from German to French sovereignty. In 1870, during the Franco-Prussian War, the Germans won their first important victory over the French at Wissembourg. Pop. (1959 est.) 4,940.

WISSLER, CLARK, 1870–1947, U.S. anthropologist, was born in Wayne County, Ind., and studied at Indiana and Columbia universities. He was curator of ethnology, 1905–07, curator of anthropology, 1907–42, and editor of the anthropological publications for the American Museum of Natural History, 1907–42. He was professor at the Institute of Human Relations at Yale University, 1924–40. Wissler conducted research on the culture of the American Indian and made anthropometric studies. Among Wissler's writings are *Man and Culture* (1922), *The American Indian* (1922, ed. 1938), *An Introduction to Social Anthropology* (1929), and *Indians of the United States* (1940).

WISTARIA, a genus of hardy climbing shrubs belonging to the family *Leguminosae.* Although originally named for Professor Caspar Wistar (1761–1818), a famous American anatomist, the spelling of wisteria had been given in the original description of the genus and still finds wide usage. Wistarias bear odd-pinnate leaves with entire leaflets, and usually racemes of bluish or violet flowers, followed by long pods. They thrive in rich, well drained soil, reaching a length of over 30 feet, and make excellent wall or trellis plants. The species most com-

J. HORACE MCFARLAND CO.
Wistaria

monly grown is *W. floribunda*, the Japanese wistaria, a hardy climber and an ornate shrub with drooping clusters of purplish flowers. *W. frutescens* is the American wistaria with shorter, darker flowering racemes.

WISTER, OWEN, 1860–1938, U.S. writer, was born in Philadelphia, a grandson of the actress Fanny Kemble. He began writing music at an early age, and after being graduated from Harvard, 1882, spent two years studying and composing in Paris. He received encouragement from Franz Liszt, who auditioned his *Merlin and Vivien*, but soon abandoned the idea of a musical career as impractical, took a course in law at Harvard, and began practicing in Philadelphia, 1889. During trips to Wyoming for his health, he developed an enthusiasm for frontier life and began, 1891, writing romantic stories of the old West. His most notable achievement in this vein was *The Virginian: A Horseman of the Plains* (1902), in which the hero, replying to the foul-mouthed villain's unspeakable aspersion, utters the classic challenge, "When you call me that, *smile.*" Among Wister's other works are *The Dragon of Wantley* (1892), *Red Men and White* (1896), *Lin McLean* (1898), *Ulysses S. Grant* (1900), *Philosophy 4* (1903), *The Seven Ages of Washington* (1907), *When West Was West* (1928), *Roosevelt—The Story of a Friendship* (1930).

WITAN. See WITENAGEMOT.

WITCHCRAFT, the practice of black magic, especially by persons who have gained supernatural power by selling their souls to the Devil (see MAGIC). Instances of witchcraft appear throughout history and in all civilizations, but it seems to flourish most whenever orthodox religion is in a period of ferment, and especially of decline or transition. Witchcraft is a form of religious dualism whose adepts, accepting the supremacy of an evil principle or being, draw their followers mainly from among ignorant or confused members of orthodoxy; and the excesses of those opposing supposed witchcraft are in part attributable to fear, confusion, and over-zealousness in enforcing the threatened orthodoxy.

Some scholars, such as Margaret Murray, believe that witchcraft is a continuing development of an old religion (specifically the Mithraic cult of antiquity) that is forced to go underground when a new faith becomes predominant. Others contend that, during the Christian Era at least, witchcraft has generally been associated with the rites and doctrines of various Manichaean heresies, such as those of the Bogomiles, Cathari, and Albigenses. It is virtually impossible to prove or disprove such theories, however. Witches, condemned and persecuted by ecclesiastical and often civil authority, have always operated clandestinely, and literature on their activities is almost entirely prejudiced (court records of witchcraft trials) or sensational (broadsides, chapbooks, pamphlets, and under-the-counter "occulta").

Folklore of Witchcraft. As described in folkloric literature, the power of witches is always devoted to malignant ends: witches may dry up the milk of cows, blight crops, and bring on bad weather; they may bedevil whole communities and prepare loathsome phylacteries and love philters; they may bring on disease and death by constructing a wax image of the intended victim and piercing it with pins, or melting it. Conventionally spoken of as "she," the witch is usually but not always depicted a woman; her male counterpart, a warlock or wizard, is usually a devotee of alchemy and astrology and the study of things that mere mortals obviously are not supposed to tamper with (see FRANKENSTEIN). Her constant companion is a servant in the form of a dog or cat given to her by the Devil, or which is perhaps the Devil himself; and she revels with demons who aid her in corrupting the innocent. She is usually unable to cry; but in the most dire circumstances she can shed three tears, no more. Somewhere on her body there is a "Devil's Mark"—a small blue spot on the skin that is insensitive to pain. She is often credited with the ability to change humans into any kind of beast. She generally has power over all other creatures through her knowledge of charms and spells. One of the most potent of her powers is usually that of her "evil eye," by which she can inflict any sort of evil upon humans and beasts. If she is cast into a pond or stream, she will not sink, but will be buoyed up by the Devil's power; this "ducking" process was long one of the favorite methods of detecting witches—if the accused sank and drowned, she was adjudged innocent and buried in sanctified ground.

Rites and Rituals. It is difficult, if not impossible, to demonstrate or describe the continuity of witchcraft as a cult over long periods (more than 100 years, or so), yet there is little doubt but that at certain times large numbers of witches banded together in disciplined organizations. In England the basic unit of the cult was a coven comprising 13 members. The central rite was a diabolical revel known as the Sabbat, which was generally held on Thursdays, Fridays, or great feasts of the church. Meeting at midnight in lonely rendezvous, the devotees performed lewd dances and sang bawdy songs while the Devil, presiding in the form of a dog, ape, or "black man," piped their accompaniment. The English sabbat was presided over by a vicar of the Devil, called the Master, and probably the regional leader of the cult. Formal dedication to the Devil and renunciation of Christianity was followed by the "infernal round," in which the witches, straddling broomsticks, coursed around their minister. The sensation of flying, described by some participants, was produced by a magic ointment, of which the active ingredient was aconite, which they rubbed into their skin. The revel ended in orgies and cannibalistic feasts until, with the rising of the morning star, the witches dispersed. The Sabbat figures in numerous works of art and literature, notably in paintings by Teniers, Queverdo, Breughel, and Bosch; and in Goethe's *Faust* and Robert Burns's *Tam O' Shanter*.

On the Continent, there were sporadic outbursts of Satanism in which the liturgy of the Mass was perverted with diabolical intention. These began with folk practices such as the Feast of Fools and the legendary Mass of St. Secaire, and culminated in the Black Mass, which rewarded jaded sensation seekers with sophisticated debauchery; a vivid, if somewhat mannered, description appears in J. K. Huysmans' novel, *Là bas* (Down There).

Witch Hunts. Professedly antisocial and antireligious, witches have always been prosecuted by church and state, at least nominally; it is known, however, that in some periods persons high in government (Madame de Montespan and Catherine de Médicis are among the more notorious examples) condemned witchcraft publicly yet practiced it themselves. And by definition, celebration of the Black Mass required a defrocked priest who, although excommunicate, was still in possession of his supernatural powers and would be until death and damnation. Some witches, such as the Witch of Endor, were occasionally tolerated among the Jews, but the Old Testament definitely declares that "Thou shalt not suffer a witch to live" (Exodus 22:18). Necromancers and soothsayers were banished from Rome by the triumvirate, 42 B.C., and by Claudius and Tiberius, and were executed by Vitellius. Malicious spells were forbidden, fifth century B.C., in the Law of the Twelve Tables. The first known witch hunt in the modern sense, however, began under Valens, A.D. 367. Blackmail, politics, prejudice, and the persecution of innocent old crones and "wise women" played an important part in this hunt, as in most later ones. By the time of Pope Alexander IV, witchcraft had become identified with heresy, and in 1258 and after, suspected witches were investigated by the Holy Inquisition. Of the countless thousands whom the Holy Office delivered to the secular authorities for punishment many, such as Joan of Arc, were undoubtedly victims of political intrigue or were otherwise guiltless; others, such as the infamous Gilles de Retz, were admittedly guilty of ritual murder, sodomy, and other abominations. In France, particularly, witchcraft was during certain periods associated with mass poisonings and illegal midwifery. A bull (1484) of Pope Innocent VIII, although primarily directed against witchcraft in Germany, brought on bloody hunts throughout Europe, especially after the publication of an influential manual of demonology, *Malleus maleficarum* (Hammer of Witches), 1486, by two German Dominicans, Jakob Sprenger (1436–95), dean of Cologne University, and Prior Heinrich Kramer (1430?–1505). This work was long accepted by Protestant witch hunters as definitive authority, even after many Roman Catholic authorities had rejected it and its conclusions.

Witchcraft hysteria was especially prevalent in England during the Civil War. During six months of 1645, for example, no less than 150 supposed witches were executed. In the same year the fever hit New England, where a number of citizens of Springfield were said to be possessed of the Devil. The children of a Salem minister, aroused by voodoo tales of an old Negro slave, became hysterical and accused various people of bewitching them, 1692. A terrible witch hunt followed, during which 19 persons were hanged and many imprisoned. The Puritan divines, Increase and Cotton Mather, who were avid students of demonology, were partly responsible for this outburst of fanaticism.

The first legal measure against witchcraft was passed in Scotland in 1563 and the last victims in England were executed in 1716. In Britain witches were generally hanged, but on the Continent the prescribed method of execution was burning at the stake. In 1770 two Negroes were burned at Kaskaskia, Ill., and in 1877 five alleged witches were burned by a mob in Mexico. Belief in witchcraft generally languished in the twentieth century, but charges of "hexing," "overlooking," and casting the "evil eye" were not uncommon. In some rural areas any old woman who lives alone, collects herbs, and is mildly eccentric is likely to be known as a witch; and the manufacturers of grigri charms have little difficulty in finding a wide market for their products.

Most modern authorities assume that persons convicted of witchcraft in earlier times actually were not witches as charged: since there is no Devil, the argument runs, it would have been impossible for anyone to have been in league with the Devil. At least one twentieth century historian, however, Montague Summers, contended (1) that the Devil exists, (2) that most persons convicted of being in league with him were entirely guilty as charged, and (3) that such alliances continue to be entered into by witches in the twentieth century. And in his works *Witchcraft Today* (1954) and *The Meaning of Witchcraft* (1959) Gerald Brosseau Gardner, director of The Museum of Magic and Witchcraft, Castletown, Isle of Man, described himself proudly as a "member of one of the ancient covens of the Witch Cult which still survive in England." See DEVIL; EXORCISM; LEA, HENRY CHARLES; SUMMERS, MONTAGUE.

BIBLIOG.–George L. Burr, ed., *Narratives of the Witchcraft Cases, 1648–1706* (1914); Alphonse L. Constant (Eliphas Levi, pseud.), *Transcendental Magic: Its Doctrine and Ritual* (1958); Thomas D. Davidson, comp., *Rowan Tree and Red Thread* (1950); Reginald T. Davies, *Four Centuries of Witch-Beliefs* (1947); Samuel G. Drake, ed., *Annals of Witchcraft in New England and Elsewhere in the United States from Their First Settlement* (1869); Lawrence G. Green, *These Wonders to Behold* (1959); Christina Hole, ed., *Witchcraft in England* (1947); *Mirror of Witchcraft* (1957); Pennethorne Hughes, *Witchcraft* (1952); Frederick Kaigh, *Witchcraft and Magic of Africa* (1947); George L. Kittredge, *Witchcraft in Old and New England* (1958); Henry C. Lea, comp., *Materials Toward a History of Witchcraft*, 3 vols. (1957); David Levin, ed., *What Happened in Salem?* (1960); Charles Low, *Great Asiatic Mysteries* (1937); Cotton Mather, *On, Witchcraft* (1956); Jules Michelet, *Satanism and Witchcraft: A Study in Medieval Superstition* (1955); Mario N. Pavia, *Drama of the Siglo de Oro: A Study of Magic, Witchcraft, and Other Occult Beliefs* (1959); Rossell H. Robbins, *Encyclopedia of Witchcraft and Demonology* (1959); St. John D. Seymour, *Irish Witchcraft and Demonology* (1913); Montague Summers, *Geography of Witchcraft* (1958); *Witchcraft and Black Magic* (1961); Joseph Turmel (Father Louis Coulange, André Lagarde, pseuds.), *Life of the Devil* (1930); Charles W. Upham, *Salem Witchcraft*, 2 vols. (1959); Harry E. Wedeck, *Treasury of Witchcraft* (1961); Robert H. West, *Invisible World* (1939); Charles Williams (Peter Stanhope, pseud.), *Witchcraft* (1944); John W. Williams, *Voodoos and Obeahs: Phases of West India Witchcraft* (1932).

WITCH HAZEL, a genus of winter-flowering shrubs native to the Orient and to eastern North America belonging to the family *Hamamelidaceae*. The best known species of the genus, *Hamamelis*, is the common witch hazel, *H. virginiana*. It is the source of an extract used medically for the reduction of inflammation and is also frequently planted as an ornamental shrub. Its flowers are yellow in color with four narrow petals and occur in small clusters. The shrubs are favored because their flowers bloom in late autumn. The species prospers in shady areas. The Japanese and Chinese species, *H. japonica* and *H. mollis*, flower in mid-winter. The fragrant Ozark witch hazel, *H. vernalis*, is a sun-preferring species native to a small area in Missouri and Oklahoma.

WITENAGEMOT, Anglo-Saxon *witena gemōt* (*witan*, sages or councilors; *gemōt*, assembly or court), the council of the Anglo-Saxon kings (see HEPTARCHY). The witenagemot, composed of church officials and nobles, nominally had considerable power, including the authority to elect the king, depose him when it saw fit, and to advise him in matters of importance. In practice, however, it often had little influence, unless the king actually sought its advice. After the Norman Conquest, 1066, the witenagemot ceased to be significant in Britain. The Normans subsequently introduced their *Curie Regis* (king's council), an advisory and judicial body, from which evolved the British Parliament. There appears to have been no relationship between the Anglo-Saxon and the Norman councils, and a theory that the witenagemot was a direct antecedent of Parliament has been rejected by most historians.

WITHER, GEORGE, 1588–1667, English poet, was born in Bentworth, Hampshire. He settled in London about 1610, and in the congenial fellowship of William Browne and Michael Drayton he began to write. Certain political allusions in his satirical *Abuses Stript and Whipt* (1613) brought him to the Marshalsea Prison for a few months in 1613. He served against the Scottish Covenanters, 1639, and on the outbreak of the English Civil War raised a troop of horse for the Parliament; he was captured by Royalists, but his life was spared—it was said—at the intervention of the poet Sir John Denham (1615–69), who felt that as long as Wither was alive he (Denham) could not be considered England's worst poet. At the Restoration of the monarchy, 1660, Wither was arrested and imprisoned for three years. His later productions are generally regarded as either tediously satiric or tediously pietistic. Among his other works are *Prince Henrie's Obsequies* (1612), *Epithalamia* (1612), *Fidelia* (1617), *Shepherds Hunting* (1615), *Wither's Motto* (1621), *Faire-Virtue, the Mistress of Philarete* (1622), *Hymns and Songs of the Church* (1623), *Britain's Remembrancer* (1628), and *Hallelujah* (1641).

WITHERITE, a somewhat rare barium carbonate mineral, $BaCO_3$, found in association with galena. Witherite has an orthorhombic, dipyramidal crystallography, with poor cleavage (see CRYSTALLOGRAPHY). It is translucent, white to gray; has a specific gravity of 4.3, and a hardness of $3\frac{1}{2}$. It is found in Northumberland and Cumberland in England, in Salzburg, and near Lexington, Ky., Yosemite Park, Calif., and at Thunder Bay, Ontario. Witherite is a minor source of barium. It was named for its discoverer, D. W. Withering (1741–1799).

WITHERSPOON, JOHN, 1723–94, Scottish-American clergyman and educator, was born in Gifford, Lothian, and studied at the University of Edinburgh. He was pastor of Beith, 1745–57, and of Paisley, 1757–67. He became president of the College of New Jersey (later Princeton University), 1767, and supported the colonists in disputes with England. He was a delegate from New Jersey to the Continental Congress, 1776–79 and 1780–82, and was the only clergyman to sign the Declaration of Independence.

WITNESS. See EVIDENCE.

WITTE, SERGEI YULIEVICH, COUNT, 1849–1915, Russian public official, was born in Tiflis. As finance minister, 1893–1903, Witte advocated the development of home industries by reasonable protection and the introduction of foreign capital. He extended railroads and stopped extreme fluctuations in the value of paper currency. He was president of the committee of ministers, 1903–05, and used this office to develop administrative reforms. He negotiated the Treaty of Portsmouth, which ended the Russo-Japanese War, and became president of the ministry in the new constitutional regime, 1905, but resigned, 1906.

WITTENBERG, city, E Germany, in the East German District of Halle; on the Elbe River; 55 miles SW of Berlin. Cloth, hosiery, leather, beer, and machinery are manufactured. Martin Luther was a professor in the university that was founded at Wittenberg, 1502, and was merged with the university at Halle, 1815. The castle church, restored, 1892, contains the tombs of Luther, Melanchthon, Frederick the Wise, and John the Steadfast. On its doors Luther nailed his 95 theses against indulgences, 1517. Luther's house is preserved, and his statue stands in the market place. Wittenberg was the capital of the Duchy of Saxe-Wittenberg. It was occupied by the French, 1806, and by the Prussians, 1814. Pop. (1959 est.) 48,100.

WITTENBERG UNIVERSITY, a private, co-educational institution of higher learning in Springfield, Ohio, is associated with the United Lutheran church. Chartered as Wittenberg College, 1845, it offered its first instruction the same year; its name was changed to the present form in 1959. Divisions of the university are: divinity school, founded 1845; arts and sciences, 1845; graduate studies, 1883; music, 1887; community education, 1923; and professional studies, 1957. A combined engineering program is conducted with Case Institute of Technology, Cleveland, and Columbia University, New York City.

WITTGENSTEIN, LUDWIG JOSEF JOHANN, 1889–1951, Anglo-Austrian logician, was born in Vienna. He received the most important part of his education at Cambridge University in England, and for a time studied mathematical logic with Bertrand Russell, who later introduced Wittgenstein's most important published work to the world of logicians and positivists. Of Wittgenstein's system, as expounded in *Tractatus Logico-Philosophicus* (1922), Russell said admiringly that he could find nothing wrong with it and that "to have constructed a theory of logic which is not at any point obviously wrong is to have achieved a work of extraordinary difficulty and importance," but that this did not of itself prove Wittgenstein's theory correct.

Wittgenstein's approach to philosophy, which is in terms of the theoretical aspects of language and mathematics, excludes from consideration the actual truth or falsity of any statement; that is, the truth or falsity of a statement is determinable solely in terms of the logical system (the "language") within which the thinker thinks. Further, the things that are likely to be of greatest interest to living human beings in time—those that require decisions and action—are outside the scope of logic and linguistic analysis except insofar as statements are made about them, in which case the statements alone may properly and meaningfully be considered in the abstract.

Thus the whole realm of life as actually lived is left to accident, to habit, to the power of church or state, or—as in Wittgenstein's case—to a type of mysticism. For Wittgenstein, philosophy is no more and no less than the analysis of statements in terms of other statements; what a living person does or should do about any statement is not the province of philosophy as conceived by Wittgenstein and the various schools of logical positivism and linguistic analysis that were to be so decisively influenced by him.

Language in this context is considered nominalistically; that is, words and other symbols are arbitrary, neutral objects to be manipulated at will. The idea that words and other symbols have a reality of their own, or that they are, or can be, active and actuating powers that derive from, preserve, foster, and even make human history—that may bring people together or plunge them into war—is not acceptable to Wittgenstein, Russell, and others of like mind; but that words do have such power is acknowledged backhandedly in their irritated concern with linguistic "disease"—the fact that people persist in responding actively to sacred and historically revered names (God, Abraham Lincoln, and so forth) despite "irrefutable proofs" that such behavior is logically absurd. Opponents of positivism have pointed out that the positivists' expressions of irritation are, in terms of logic, entirely absurd, since the fact that logicians and rationalists become angry at what they regard as illogic and unreason suggests that logicians and rationalists, as living persons, respond illogically and unreasonably to at least the "sacred names" of Logic and Reason.

Wittgenstein's endeavors paralleled those of Edmund Husserl, whose phenomenological method is essentially a way of clarifying and manipulating ideas and images in the mind without reference to their truth or falsity, or to their implications for the world of action—except insofar as these implications themselves become ideas in the mind. Both approaches were formidably challenged by various existentialists, who acknowledged the usefulness of Wittgenstein and Husserl and their schools in the perfection of scientific method (in the natural sciences), and their value in countering the excesses of Idealism, but who recognized that the total neutrality of Logic and Phenomenology leads one ultimately to embrace an Absolute Relativism that is as much in error as the Absolute Idealism of Hegel and his followers. See EXISTENTIALISM; GENERAL SEMANTICS; IDEALISM; LOGIC; NOMINALISM; PHENOMENOLOGY; POSITIVISM; SEMANTICS.

WITTIG, JOSEPH, 1879–1949, German prelate and writer who in his life and works sought to heal the breach between Roman, Greek, and Protestant Christianity, and who was the central figure in a notorious miscarriage of ecclesiastical justice, was born in the strongly Roman Catholic village of Neusorge, in Silesia, the sixth child of a carpenter. He was ordained a priest, 1903, studied Christian archaeology in Rome, 1904–06, and then was lecturer, 1909–11, and professor, 1911–26, of *Kirchengeschichte* (Church History) at the University of Breslau. He continued the Rauschen *Grundriss der Patrologie* (Handbook of Patristics), 1921 and 1926 (in English, 1959, ed. by Altaner) and published scholarly studies on the Ambrosiaster and other subjects. He also wrote many popular essays of which one, "*Die Erlösten*" (The Redeemed)—published first, 1922, in his friend Karl Muth's distinguished periodical *Hochland*, and reprinted in Wittig's *Meine Erlösten in Busse, Kampf und Wehr* (1923)—prompted a Jesuit to attack the author as "Luther Redivivus." Actually, Wittig exemplified and sought to revive the people's faith of the Christian centuries before any schism or heresy; and a quarter of a century later Pope Pius XII said of the essay that "he [had] never read anything more beautiful." Still later, on Nov. 18, 1959, Pope John XXIII, in instructing the ecclesiastical censors, described the rules in a way precisely in accordance with Wittig's understanding of them in 1926.

In the meantime, however, Wittig's main work, *Leben Jesu in Schlesien Palästina und anderswo* (2 vols. 1925; ed. 1958), fell under the accusation of modernism—an accusation the basis for which remained quite incomprehensible to all save those who made it. Wittig had tried to resist the words spoken at his ordination, "*segregatus a populo*" (separated from the people), for his concern was not for the intellectual Modernists, but for the faithful whose simple faith Wittig sought to defend against the arrogance of rationalism and scientism (see MODERNISM; RATIONALISM). Wittig's position in the matter is set forth in great detail in his and Eugen Rosenstock's *Das Alter der Kirche* (3 vols. 1927–28), in whose third volume documents and correspondence related to the case are given in full. By this time, however, Wittig had already been excommunicated for having refused to repudiate his books, the books had been put on the Index, and Wittig had been "retired" from his university chair by the republic.

Together with the Israelite Martin Buber and the Protestant Viktor von Weizsäcker, Wittig edited and published the unique periodical *Die Kreatur* (1926–30). He married and returned to his native village, where he lived in a house built by his own hands; it was there, in March, 1946, that he received a telegram from the Vatican saying: "Wittig liberated from his excommunication." This was in response to a request from the new bishop of Breslau, the Polish Cardinal Hlond, who had asked Pius XII for it as a favor for his German diocesans. Ecclesiastical bureaucrats in Germany sought to conceal the papal action, but ultimately without success. Meanwhile, the Poles had expelled Wittig from his home. Later, while making his way slowly to a new home in the West, he died in Göhrde, Lüneburger Heide, leaving posterity a prophecy of "an age of non-conceptualized sufferings" ("*Vorstellungslose Leiden*"). *Das Joseph Wittig Buch* (edited by Paul M. Laskowsky, 1949) is a memorial anthology of Wittig's writings.

EUGEN ROSENSTOCK-HUESSY

WITU, a former sultanate in what is now Kenya. The Sultanate was established in mid-nineteenth century as a tributary of the Sultan of Zanzibar; it was a narrow strip of land (about 1,200 sq. mi. in area) extending northward along the Indian Ocean coast from the N branch of the Tana River; its capital city was Witu. The inhabitants were mostly Swahilis, many of whom were slaves. Witu came under German protection, 1885; and under British rule following the division of East Africa into British and German spheres, 1890. Slavery was abolished, and early in the 1900's Witu ceased to exist as a political entity.

WITWATERSRAND, (White Waters Ridge) colloquially the Rand region, Republic of South Africa; in Transvaal Province. The Rand is a low range of hills extending east and west from the city of Johannesburg. The ridge contains rich gold seams, and the region is the largest gold producing area in the world. The Rand region is densely populated; the major town is Johannesburg. See TRANSVAAL.

WLOCLAWEK, city, central Poland, in Bydgoszcz Province; on the Vistula River; 87 miles WNW of Warsaw. There are granaries, breweries, ironworks, a pottery works, and a food-processing factory. The town was heavily damaged early in World War II. (For population, see Poland map in Atlas.)

WOBURN, city, E Massachusetts, in Middlesex County; on the Boston and Maine Railroad; 10 miles NNW of Boston. Shoes, leather products, chemicals, glue, foundry products, and machine-shop products are the chief manufactures. Woburn was settled in 1640, incorporated in 1642, and chartered as a city in 1888. Pop. (1960) 31,214.

WOBURN, town, S central England, in Bedfordshire; 40 miles NNW of London. Woburn is a market center for an area of diversified farms. Woburn Abbey, the principal seat of the Duke of Bedford, occupies the site of a Cistercian abbey founded in 1145. The present mansion, built in the eighteenth century, contains a notable collection of portraits and other works of art.

WODEHOUSE, PELHAM GRENVILLE, 1881– , English humorous writer, was born in Guildford and studied at Dulwich College. His frothy stories about young English wastrels had a long vogue, both in England and the United States. While in France, 1940, he was arrested by the Nazi police. He received much adverse publicity by making a radio address under the auspices of the Nazi Propaganda Ministry in which he facetiously praised his captors; after the liberation of France, Wodehouse was held in preventive detention until March, 1945. Among his works are *The Pothunters* (1902); *A Gentleman of Leisure* (1910); *A Damsel in Distress* (1919); *Leave it to Psmith* (1923); *The Inevitable Jeeves* (1924); *Blandings Castle* (1935); *Uncle Fred in the Springtime* (1939); *Mating Season* (1949); *Nothing Serious* (1950); *Jeeves and the Feudal Spirit* (1954); *French Leave* (1956); an autobiography, *Over Seventy* (1957); *Carry On Jeeves* (1960); *The Ice in the Bedroom* (1961); and *Author, Author!* (1962).

WOHLER, FRIEDRICH, 1800–82, German chemist, was born in Eschersheim, near Frankfurt-am-Main. After studying medicine at Marburg and Heidelberg he spent a year studying chemistry under Jöns Jakob Berzelius in Stockholm, and became a professor of chemistry at the University of Berlin, 1825–31, Kassel, 1831–36, and Göttingen, 1836–82. Wöhler opened up the field of organic chemistry by synthesizing the organic compound urea, 1828; he also contributed greatly to the knowledge of isomerism. Equally famous for his analysis of minerals, Wöhler isolated beryllium, 1828, and yttrium, 1828; he prepared an impure form of aluminum, 1827, isolated the pure substance, 1845, and was the first scientist to describe its properties.

WOKING, town and urban district, SE England, in Surrey; on the Basingstoke Canal; 24 miles SW of London. Electrical equipment and soap are manufactured. A Muslim mosque, and an Oriental institute are in the district. (For population, see England map in Atlas.)

WOLCOTT, OLIVER, 1726–97, colonial American patriot, a signer of the Declaration of Independence, was born in Windsor, Conn., the son of Roger Wolcott, and was graduated from Yale, 1747. He was a delegate to the Continental Congress, 1775–78 and 1780–84; lieutenant governor of Connecticut, 1786–96, and governor, 1796–97. During the Revolutionary War he served in the defense of New York, 1776, and in the Saratoga Campaign.

WOLCOTT, OLIVER, 1760–1833, U.S. public official, was born in Litchfield, Conn., the son of Oliver Wolcott, and was graduated from Yale College. He served in the Revolutionary War, qualified for the bar, 1781, and became Connecticut comptroller of public accounts, 1788–89. He was appointed by Pres. George Washington as auditor, 1789–91, and comptroller, 1791–95, of the U.S. Treasury and succeeded Alexander Hamilton as secretary of the treasury, 1795–1800. He resigned from Pres. John Adam's cabinet after becoming involved in Hamilton's machinations against the President, and was a judge of the Second U.S. Circuit Court, 1801–02, president of the Bank of America, 1812–14, and governor of Connecticut, 1817–27.

WOLCOTT, ROGER, 1679–1767, colonial American governor, was born in Windsor, Conn. He was second in command of the expedition that captured Louisburg from the French, 1745. He served as deputy governor, 1741–50, and governor, 1750–54, of Connecticut. He wrote *Poetical Meditations* (1725).

WOLF, FRIEDRICH AUGUST, 1759–1824, German philologist, was born in Hagenrode, near Nordhausen, was a schoolmaster, 1779–83, and then served as professor of classical philology in Halle from

1783 until 1806, when he fled from the French occupation to Berlin. He became a member of the Academy of the Sciences, 1807, and in 1810 a professor in the newly-founded University of Berlin. Advised later to go to the south of France for his health, he did so, but died along the way at Marseilles.

Wolf's fame, as "destroyer" of Homer as a poet, rests on his *Prolegomena ad Homerum* (1795), the thesis of which is that the ancient epic poems of Homer, the *Iliad* and the *Odyssey*, are not what they seem, but a series of independent chansons that were thrown together in Athens not before 555 B.C. (see GREEK ALPHABET; GREEK LANGUAGE AND LITERATURE, Literature; HOMER). This thesis gave impetus to the many applications of the Higher Criticism, as it was called, to the Bible, the Avesta, the Nibelungen, and other ancient works. The bardic theory of James MacPherson (1736–96), supported by the Ossianic poems forged by MacPherson himself, lent plausibility to the rampant skepticism.

The Homeric Question, as the dispute over the authenticity of Homer's works came to be called, was of more than merely literary significance, for Homer had been of prime importance for the whole of the Greek tradition, and thus of the Western tradition generally, one of whose prime fundaments was rejected by Wolf and others who denied the integrity of the *Iliad* and the *Odyssey* and even the actual existence of any poet named Homer. It was of more than antiquarian interest, therefore, that in the period after World War I many students of the matter— beginning outside of Germany with John A. Scott (*The Unity of Homer*, 1921)—challenged Wolf's thesis. Yet Wolf's principal argument—that Homer could not read or write since there had been no written Greek language in his time—remained; and it seemed almost unthinkable that poems of such great length could have been composed without the use of pen and ink. Finally, however, this most telling of anti-Homer arguments was deprived of all force by the discovery, 1952, that the Greeks had had a written language no less than 500 years before Homer lived. For an account of this, see VENTRIS, MICHAEL GEORGE FRANCIS.   EUGEN ROSENSTOCK-HUESSY

WOLF, HUGO, 1860–1903, Austrian composer, was born in Windischgraz, Styria (later Slovenjgradec, Yugoslavia), the fourth son of Philipp Wolf, a leather merchant. He attended various schools in Graz, St. Paul in the Lavant-Tal, and Marburg on the Drave, 1865–75, and studied music at the Vienna Conservatory, 1875–77. After 1877 he continued his musical education by self-instruction and in order to earn a living gave piano lessons and was a music critic for the Vienna journal *Wiener Salonblatt*, 1884– 87. From 1888 he worked exclusively at musical compositions, writing instrumental, choral, and stage works and over 250 songs. In 1898, however, he was committed to the Lower Austrian Asylum in Vienna. Among his works are the songs *Die Spinnerin* (1878), *Zur Ruh, zur Ruh* (1883), *Eichendorff-Lieder* (1880–88), *Mörike-Lieder* (1888–89), *Goethe Lieder* (1888–90), *Spanisches Liederbuch* (1889–90), and *Italienisches Liederbuch* (Vol. II, 1896); the instrumental work, *Penthesilea* (1883); and the unfinished opera *Manuel Venegas* (begun 1897).

WOLF, any of the wild, carnivorous mammals belonging to the family *Canida*. The European wolf, *Canis lupus lupus*, is about three and a half feet long, excluding the tail. The color is generally yellowish gray above, with some black, and the underparts whitish; wholly black races occur in some localities. The wolf has long legs, a lank body, erect ears, and a bushy tail which hangs downward between the haunches. Twenty-four subspecies occur in North America, including the Great Plains wolf, *C. lupus nubilus*, predominantly gray, over five feet long; the Alaskan tundra wolf, *C. lupus tundrarum*; the Eastern wolf, *C. lupus lycaon*. The Texan red wolf, *C. niger rufus*, is found in the southern United States.

NEW YORK ZOOLOGICAL SOC.
The timber wolf, a large wolf found in the eastern and northern parts of the North American continent, ranges in color from black to white, but is most commonly gray.

Wolves are usually nocturnal in their habits, spending the day in the den, which may be a cave, a hollow tree, or even a burrow. Wolves usually live in small packs. The pack is normally composed of parent wolves, pups, and relatives. Almost any kind of animal food, fresh or in state of carrion, is eaten. The wolf's intelligence and power of learning by experience are great. The young, born in the spring, number from 3 to 13 in a litter. The wolf's howl is long and loud, but captured wolves soon learn to bark.

WOLFE, JAMES, 1727–59, English general, was born in Westerham, Kent, England. He entered the British army as a second lieutenant, 1741, and served in Flanders, Germany, and Scotland, 1742–53, and was quartermaster general in Ireland, 1757–58, and at Rochefort, 1758. During the French and Indian War he commanded a brigade at Louisburg, 1758, where he gave brilliant support to Jeffrey Amherst in the siege and capture of the fort. He was made major general and commander of the British expedition sent to Canada to wrest the power from the French, 1759.

CULVER SERVICE
James Wolfe

After months of futile attempts to dislodge the forces of the Marquis de Montcalm from the well fortified city of Québec, Wolfe landed his army at night on the Heights of Abraham above the city, Sept. 12–13, 1759, and engaged the French in the battle which gave the English supremacy in Canada. Wolfe and Montcalm were both killed in the battle.

WOLFE, THOMAS CLAYTON, 1900–38, U.S. novelist, was born in Asheville, N.C., son of a stonecutter addicted to poetry, in which he instructed the son. His mother, by her own admission, tended to baby Wolfe as the youngest of her eight children; all biographers agree that her pathological possessiveness and domination had a profound effect on Wolfe's life, but there is no complete agreement as to the precise nature of the effect. In any event, just before his sixteenth birthday, Wolfe matriculated in the University of North Carolina, Chapel Hill; while there he began writing plays, the first of which, *The Return of Buck Gavin*, was performed by the Carolina Players, with Wolfe himself in the title role. Accepted at Harvard University, 1920, Wolfe enrolled in

George Pierce Baker's famous 47 Workshop and continued trying to become a playwright. Upon leaving Harvard, 1924, Wolfe accepted a teaching position at New York University's Washington Square College, in which he continued off and on during the next six years. He returned, 1925, from the first of several European journeys, with the script of a play, *Mannerhouse;* after a year of unsuccessful efforts to get it produced, Wolfe concluded that he was not to be a dramatist. Through his efforts to sell the play, however, he met Aline Bernstein, a stage designer; their relationship was an important factor in Wolfe's life for a number of years.

Wolfe established a reputation as a serious writer with the publication of *Look Homeward, Angel* (1929). The book was obviously autobiographical—as his later works were to be—and created something of a scandal in his home town of Asheville; but Wolfe was in New York. It was through this work that Wolfe first became associated with Scribners' great editor, Maxwell Perkins, who was to guide not only Wolfe's literary efforts but nearly every aspect of his life. His sensitive appreciation of Wolfe's work and his ability to transform huge masses of uncontrolled prose into somewhat more readable form led some critics to look upon him as virtually co-author of Wolfe's novels.

Wolfe resigned his teaching post, 1930, and returned to Europe armed with a Guggenheim Fellowship. Except for the *Portrait of Bascome Hawke* (1932), Wolfe published no significant work until 1935, when *Of Time and the River* and a collection of shorter pieces, *From Death to Morning,* appeared.

Wolfe continued to be strongly rebuked by many critics for the verbosity of his style and for the apparent formlessness of his work; such criticism, whether justified or not, pained Wolfe deeply, and his admirers even more. The vividness of his imagery, the intensity of his feeling, and the commanding, Whitmanesque sweep of his prose are among the undeniable virtues of his work, and helped to establish him as a major writer whose work continued to be cherished by many and remained an influence in American letters. His *The Story of a Novel* (1936) gives an account of Wolfe's literary methods as understood by Wolfe himself.

Already weakened by overwork and dissipation, Wolfe contracted pneumonia, 1938, and within the year died of "cerebral complications." His "editor," however, had more than one million words of unpublished manuscript on hand, and set himself to the task of editing the legacy. *The Web and the Rock* (1939), *You Can't Go Home Again* (1940) and *The Hills Beyond* (1941), the last a collection of shorter pieces and chapters of an unfinished novel, were the result. They were followed by Wolfe's *Letters to his Mother* (1943) and *Selected Letters* (1956).

WOLFF, CHRISTIAN, BARON VON, 1679–1754, German philosopher, was born in Breslau, educated at the University of Jena, and on the recommendation of his friend and mentor, G. W. Leibniz (1646–1716), was appointed professor of mathematics and natural philosophy at Halle, 1706. Wolff's system, derived in large part from Leibniz, constitutes an extension of that thinker's extreme rationalism to all departments of thought. Wolff believed that reason, subject only to limitations imposed by the laws of logical thought, is capable of encompassing all Reality, even including the Divine. Building a system on the foundation of his faith in the efficacy of mind, Wolff elaborated its principles in a dozen large tomes covering ontology, cosmology, logic, ethics, and rational theology. They enjoyed a wide circulation, and his reputation outside of Halle grew rapidly. Inside it was another matter, however, for Halle at that time was dominated by an anti-intellectualist clergy who considered no one entitled to speak of truth who had not experienced a religious conversion. Having been expelled from Halle, 1731, the apostle of reason took refuge at Marburg, where he found a sympathetic audience for his viewpoint, and soon all Germany was debating his philosophy. Cognizant of this fame, and determined to make amends for the action of his predecessor, Frederick II of Prussia recalled Wolff to Halle in triumph, 1740. Elected chancellor, 1743, and ennobled, Wolff lived to see his system adopted throughout the state; he died not knowing that his system would be annihilated a generation later by Immanuel Kant (1724–1804).   ROBERT WHITTEMORE

WOLF-FERRARI, ERMANNO, 1876–1948, Italian operatic composer, was born in Venice, the son of the German painter, August Wolf, and Emilia Ferrari. He studied under Joseph Gabriel von Rheinberger in Munich, 1893–95, remained in Germany until 1899, and was director of the Liceo Benedetto Marcello in Venice, 1901–?07. His most popular works were *Il segreto di Susanna* (The Secret of Suzanne), 1909, a comic opera about a young wife whose attempt to conceal her innocent vice of smoking cigarettes leads her husband to think she has a lover; and the tragic *I gioielli della Madonna* (The Jewels of the Madonna), 1911, whose fickle heroine, Maliella, tempts a would-be suitor to steal the gems from a sacred image. Among his other works are *Cenerentola* (1900); *Idomeneo* (1931), a revision of an opera by Wolfgang Amadeus Mozart; and *Le dama boba* (1939).

WOLF POINT, city, NE Montana, seat of Roosevelt County; on the Missouri River, the Great Northern Railway, and U.S. highway 2; scheduled airline stop; 270 miles ENE of Great Falls. It is situated in a region in which there are diversified farms, coal mines, and oil wells. Wolf Point is an important wheat-shipping center. The city has a flour mill and a creamery. Settlement began in 1878 and the city was incorporated in 1915. Pop. (1960) 3,585.

WOLFRAM. See TUNGSTEN.

WOLFRAMITE, a mineral composed of ferrous manganous tungstate, $(Fe, Mn)WO_4$, usually found in quartz veins and pegmatite dikes, and often associated with pyrite, sphalerite, galena, scheelite, and other minerals. Wolframite is the principal ore of tungsten. Its color and streak are black to brown, the luster is submetallic to resinous, and the crystals are prismatic. It has a specific gravity of 7 to $7\frac{1}{2}$, and a hardness of 4 to $4\frac{1}{2}$ (see HARDNESS). China furnishes nearly one half of the world's supply of wolframite. Other important deposits are in Bolivia, England, New South Wales, Burma, and in the United States in the Black Hills, South Dakota.

WOLFRAM VON ESCHENBACH, 1170?–1219 or 1225, the most prominent German minnesinger, hailed from Franconia, and had a small fief near Ansbach (name changed, 1917, to Wolframs-Eschenbach). As an impecunious knight, Wolfram lived (as depicted in Richard Wagner's opera *Tannhäuser*) at the court of the landgrave of Thuringia, 1203–16. Wolfram wrote the *Parzival* (16 books; 24,810 lines in rhymed couplets), which Richard Wagner used for his opera of this name; a fragmentary epic, *Titurel;* and the *Willehalm* (9 books; 13,988 lines in rhymed couplets). In each case, he borrowed his themes from French models, especially Chrétien de Troyes, but Wolfram's strong religious temper led him to change the material in a very free way; his sense of one humanity made him so stress catholicity that in one work even a Moslem is made the Christian hero's brother under God. In his passionate search for the meaning of life, Wolfram transcended the social limitations of the courtier's existence. Of his lyrics, the *Tagelieder* rank with the finest poems of German literature. There are many complete or partial editions of his works in German, but no adequate English translations except for one of the *Parzival* (Tr. by Helen M. Mustard and Charles E. Passage, 1961). See CHRÉTIEN DE TROYES; MINNESINGER; PERCEVAL; ROMANCE.

EUGEN ROSENSTOCK-HUESSY

WOLFSBANE. See ACONITE.

WOLFVILLE, town, SE Canada, in King's County, Nova Scotia; at the mouth of the Cornwallis River, on Minas Basin, an arm of the Bay of Fundy; on the Dominion Atlantic and the Canadian Pacific railways; 45 miles NW of Halifax. A creamery, woodworking plant, and fruit-drying plant are the town's chief industrial establishments. The town was known as Mud Creek until 1831. Wolfville is the seat of Acadia University. Pop. (1956) 2,497.

WOLLASTON, WILLIAM HYDE, 1766–1828, English chemist and physicist, was born in East Dereham, Suffolk, educated in medicine at Caius College, Cambridge, and first practiced at Bury St. Edmunds, then in London. He retired from medicine, 1800, to devote himself to empirical science, and developed, in the early 1800's, a method for making platinum more malleable. He was the discoverer of the elements palladium and rhodium, 1803, and did research on columbium, tantalum, and titanium. In the field of optics, he discovered the dark lines in the sun's spectrum, 1802, and invented the camera lucida, the reflecting goniometer, and improved lenses and prisms. He established the Geological Society's annual Wollaston medal.

WOLLASTONITE, a calcium silicate mineral found extensively in metamorphic contact with crystalline limestone in association with such minerals as calcite, calcium feldspars, and tremolite. It has a chemical formula $Ca(SiO_3)$, a specific gravity of 2.9, and a hardness of 5 to $5\frac{1}{2}$ (see HARDNESS). It is white or gray, translucent, has a vitreous luster, and triclinic crystals (see CRYSTALLOGRAPHY). Wollastonite is mined in many parts of the United States, Mexico, and Europe in formations where it is a major part of the rock mass. It is used in making floor and wall tile, coatings for welding electrodes, and as a constituent of mineral wool.

WOLSELEY, GARNET JOSEPH WOLSELEY, 1st VISCOUNT, 1833–1913, British military leader, was born in Golden Bridge, county Dublin, Ireland. He served with the British army in the second Burma War, 1852–53, in the Crimea, 1854–56, in the Sepoy Mutiny in India, 1857–59, in China, 1860, and in Canada, 1861–71, commanding the Red River Expedition against the rebel Louis Riel, 1870. He was in charge of the expedition against the King of Ashanti, 1873–74, in Natal, 1875, completed the subjugation of the Zulus, 1879–80, and conquered Arabi Pasha in Egypt, 1882. He was created viscount, 1885, for his attempt to rescue Gen. Charles George ("Chinese") Gordon at Khartoum; he became field marshal, 1894, and was commander in chief of the British army, 1895–1900. Wolseley wrote *The Soldier's Pocket-book for Field Service* (1869), *The Life of the Duke of Marlborough* (1894), *The Decline and Fall of Napoleon* (1895), and *The Story of a Soldier's Life* (1903).

WOLSEY, THOMAS, 1475?–1530, English cardinal and statesman, was born in Ipswich. He studied and taught at Magdalen College, Oxford, and in 1500 was appointed rector of Lymington. Henry VII employed him as his personal chaplain and sent him on several diplomatic missions. Henry VIII made him a member of the king's council. He became Bishop of Lincoln, 1514, and later the same year Archbishop of York. The year 1515 saw him rise to power as perhaps the most influential person in the kingdom. In that year he was made a cardinal by Pope Leo X, and was appointed lord chancellor by Henry VIII. Wolsey now endeavored to secure for his country the position of arbiter between Francis I of France and Holy Roman Emperor Charles V. In the inevitable war, which broke out in 1521, England sided with Charles.

Thomas Wolsey

Wolsey hoped by the aid of the emperor to secure his fondest ambition—the papacy. The invasions of France, 1522 and 1523, by the English proved failures, however, and the friendship between England and the emperor cooled. Charles's victory at Pavia, 1525, alienated the English, and was followed by an alliance between England and France, 1527.

During these years Wolsey had shown his zeal for reform and for learning by his foundation of Cardinal (afterward Christ Church) College, Oxford, and of a college at Ipswich. His further designs were checked however, by the divorce question. Henry VIII wished to divorce Catherine of Aragon in order to marry Anne Boleyn, and Wolsey endeavored to induce the papacy to declare the king's marriage invalid; but he failed, 1529. His many enemies, reinforced by the indignant Anne Boleyn, had been long waiting the opportunity to bring about his ruin. Their success was almost complete. He was stripped of all his offices except the archbishopric of York, and was forced to retire humbly to his see. His detractors, however, had no intention of allowing him a peaceful retirement, and it seems unlikely that Wolsey himself had any intention of maintaining one. On a charge of high treason, to which he had imprudently given color by his own intrigues, he was summoned to London, 1530. He died at Leicester Abbey on his way there.

WOLVERHAMPTON, county and borough, W central England, in Staffordshire; 13 miles NW of Birmingham. Wolverhampton is part of the Birmingham industrial district. Among its manufactured products are locks, machinery, tools, bicycles, steel goods, chemicals, and enameled ware. The Church of St. Peter is chiefly of thirteenth and fourteenth century construction. Wolverhampton's annual Wednesday Market Day was granted, 1258, by Henry II. Wolverhampton sent its first representative to Parliament in 1832. Pop. (1959 est.) 146,100.

CHICAGO NAT. HIST. MUS.

The wolverine, which belongs to the same family as minks, weasels, otters, and skunks, is characterized by a long black coat having yellowish white bands along both sides.

WOLVERINE, a North American carnivore belonging to the family *Mustelidae*, which also includes weasels, minks, otters, skunks, martens, and badgers. Though rarely seen, the wolverine, *Gulo luscus*, is widely distributed from northern United States to the Arctic Ocean. Its stance and strong body resemble that of a bear and it has a long black coat with a yellowish white band along each side. Males measure about 41 inches in total length. Largest of the weasel family, wolverines are aggressive, cunning animals, often stealing bait from the hunter's trap. They prey upon birds, squirrels, and even deer.

WOLVERINE STATE, a popular name for the state of Michigan, deriving from the large number of wolverines, which at one time existed in the state.

WOMAN'S CHRISTIAN TEMPERANCE UNION, NATIONAL. See NATIONAL WOMAN'S CHRISTIAN TEMPERANCE UNION.

WOMAN SUFFRAGE. See SUFFRAGE, *Woman Suffrage.*

WOMBAT, a marsupial belonging to the family *Phascolomidae*, distinguished by having only one incisor on each side of the upper jaw. The common

CHICAGO NAT. HIST. MUS.

The wombat, a bearlike marsupial that is usually about 40 inches long, sleeps during the day and feeds at night. It lives in burrows, in holes among rocks, or on the ground.

wombat, *Phascolomis mitchelli*, measuring 40 inches from tip of snout to root of tail, is confined to Australia. The wombats have massive, clumsy bodies; short, thick legs; tails; and five toes on each foot. They resemble small bears and their claws are capable of excavating burrows.

WOMEN IN THE AIR FORCE, or (WAF), the women's component of the U.S. Air Force, organized as part of the regular Air Force and the Air Force Reserve by the Women's Armed Services Integration Act (June 12, 1948). WAF, which includes all women in the Air Force except members of the Nurses' Corps and the Medical Specialist Corps, performs many administrative and technical occupations at Air Force establishments in the United States and overseas. WAFs may not be assigned to combat aircraft or other hazardous duty. The WAF basic training center and officers candidate school are at Lackland Air Force Base near San Antonio, Tex.

Until the act of June 12, 1948, Air Force women were members of the Women's Army Corps (WAC), a reserve component of the U.S. Army (see WOMEN'S ARMY CORPS, U.S.). During World War II more than 40,000 WACs served with the U.S. Army Air Forces. When the U.S. Air Force was established as a separate armed service, September, 1947, postwar demobilization had reduced the number of air WACs to less than 6,000 officers and enlisted women. Many of them subsequently transferred to the new service. During the late 1950's and the early 1960's WAF maintained a peacetime strength of about 6,000 officers and enlisted women.

WOMEN MARINES, the women's component of the U.S. Marine Corps. Marine women perform a large variety of administrative and technical jobs, and hold ranks and grades identical to Marine men— up to the rank of colonel. Enlisted women receive basic training at Parris Island, S.C., officers and officer candidates attend schools at Quantico, Va.

During World War I the Marine Corps enlisted women to perform administrative and clerical duties. In February, 1943, a Marine Corps Women's Reserve, authorized at 18,000 officers and enlisted women, was established to perform administrative and technical duties at Marine Corps establishments in the United States during World War II. The Women's Armed Services Integration Act (June 12, 1948) established the Women Marines as a regular part of the Marine Corps. In 1960 there were about 1,600 Women Marines on active duty.

WOMEN OF THE U.S. NAVY, or WAVES, the women's component of the U.S. Navy. WAVES hold the same enlisted grades and commissioned ranks as Navy men through the rank of commander, although the woman assistant to the chief of naval personnel holds the temporary rank of captain. WAVES are employed at many administrative and technical jobs, mainly on shore establishments in the United States and overseas, and thereby release Navy men for sea duty. Enlisted WAVES receive

basic training at Bainbridge, Md.; officer candidates are trained at Newport, R.I.

During World War I more than 11,000 women, classified as yeoman (F) were enlisted by the Navy to perform clerical and technical jobs. Yeoman (F) was disbanded in 1919. In World War II, the Congress established the Women's Reserve of the United States Naval Reserve, July 30, 1942, and by war's end, Sept. 2, 1945, more than 86,000 WAVES were on active duty in the United States, Alaska, and Hawaii. Postwar demobilization had reduced the number of WAVES on active duty to less than 2,000 at the time the Women's Armed Services Integration Act (June 12, 1948) established the enlistment and appointment of women in the regular Navy and its reserve component on a permanent basis. In 1960 WAVES on active duty constituted about 2 per cent of Regular Navy personnel.

WOMEN'S AIR FORCE SERVICE PILOTS, or WASP, a corps of women civilian pilots under the jurisdiction of the United States Army Air Forces, organized, 1942, for ferrying aircraft, making meteorological, administrative, and test flights, breaking in engines with slow-time flying, and towing targets. First known as Women's Auxiliary Ferrying Squadrons (WAFS), the organization name was changed in 1943. The WASP was inactivated in December, 1944.

WOMEN'S ARMY CORPS, U.S., or WAC, a basic branch of the U.S. Army services that in peace time provides a cadre of women trained in a wide variety of noncombat military occupations which in time of war or national emergency women generally could take over, releasing men for more hazardous duties (see ARMY, U.S., Organization of the Army, *Basic Branches*). WACs hold rank and grade identical to Army men—up to the rank of colonel. Enlisted women receive basic training at Fort McClellan, Ala. (the permanent WAC Center); officers and officer candidates attend schools at Fort Lee, Va.

The WAC came into being shortly after the United States entered World War II when the Women's Army Auxiliary Corps (WAAC) was established, May 14, 1942; it was made an integral part of the wartime Army of the United States, and was renamed Women's Army Corps, Sept. 1, 1943. By early in 1945 more than 100,000 WACs were on active duty in the United States and overseas. The WAC was made a part of the Regular Army by the Women's Armed Services Integration Act (June 12, 1948). More than 14,000 WACs saw active duty during the Korean conflict, 1950-53. In 1957 the corps was renamed the United States Women's Army Corps. In 1960 there were more than 7,000 WACs on active duty.

WOMEN'S CLUBS, GENERAL FEDERATION OF. See GENERAL FEDERATION OF WOMEN'S CLUBS.

WOMEN'S COLLEGES. See COEDUCATION; COLLEGES AND UNIVERSITIES; EDUCATION.

WOMEN'S RESERVE OF THE COAST GUARD RESERVE, or SPARS, a component of the U.S. Coast Guard established, November, 1942, to provide for the recruitment of women into the service to perform administrative shore duties. The first SPARS to serve outside the continental United States were landed in Hawaii, January, 1945; in May a group was sent to Alaska. Demobilized, 1945-46, SPARS was reactivated, 1951, with eligibility limited to former members.

WOMEN'S RIGHTS, the protections guaranteed to women, by law and by custom, which enable them to participate on an equal status with men, in the political, legal, social, and economic institutions of a society (see SUFFRAGE). The legal rights of women can be more arbitrarily limited to those covering property rights, rights over children, and position under the criminal law. The status of women in the field of economic activity has been subject to action to remove sex discrimination, but more particularly it has been governed by protective legislation, which is in substance a portion of the more comprehensive field of social legislation.

LEGAL RIGHTS

In the laws of every nation with a written legal system, there are enactments and provisions dealing especially with women, as distinguished from all of the people—including women—owing obedience to these laws. Without exception there has been no system of jurisprudence that applied equally to men and women alike.

Development of English Law. The English law, from which that of the United States derives, has a long history relating to the position and rights of women. Prior to the accession of William the Conqueror, 1066, Anglo-Saxon laws were an admixture of Germanic tribal customs and mores, decrees of the Saxon kings, and probably some Roman law. Anglo-Saxon women could both inherit and dispose of property, gain custody of children upon the death of their husbands, and be protected from ill-treatment in marriage. Women could be divorced for adultery, but could not divorce their husbands for the same reason, but by mutual consent husband and wife could separate. Women were not specifically mentioned in regard to the criminal law, but historians assumed it applied to both men and women alike.

After 1066, English law comprised the common law, the statute law, and the civil and canon law; but the common law, except where expressly overridden by the statutes, was the law of the land. The property rights of women during the feudal period were complicated by the varieties of serf, freeman, and lord status. Originally the female tenant was excluded as a landholder because she could not fulfill the military obligations of tenure, but later it became customary for the lands of a male tenant to pass to his female children if there were no males to inherit. There were, however, various exceptions to this right. On the other hand, unmarried women could acquire and inherit personal property in the same way as men, and widows were entitled to one-third of the husband's goods upon the event of his death. Under the criminal law severe punishment supplanted the fines and penance of the old Saxon law for both men and women, and frequently the punishment was unusually harsh if the defendant was a woman. The wife's relation to her husband was judged to be similar to that of a serf to his lord; hence, any act of a wife against her husband was *petit treason* and was cause for an exceptionally severe penalty and, in many cases, the death penalty. This same relationship gave the wife certain advantages, however; she could, for example, obtain clemency or acquittal if it appeared that she had committed a crime at the direction of her husband. During this period a married woman had practically no direct property rights. Her husband or others, however, could leave property to a trustee for the use and benefit of a married woman, and equity would prevent a husband's dealing with the property in a manner to her detriment. She also had no independent right to engage in contracts except when so authorized for the benefit of a third person. Upon her husband's death a widow received one-third of his goods, and she might claim one-third of his lands for use during her lifetime.

After the Reformation, changes occurred in the law with respect to women's rights. No longer did one-third of a husband's goods automatically pass to his wife upon his death; he could, in fact, will his entire estate to a stranger. The jurisdiction of the ecclesiastical courts over laymen was abolished by Act of Parliament, 1640, and many offenses that had been considered as sins under the church became criminal or civil misdeeds under the jurisdiction of the state. Punishments inflicted upon women under the criminal law increased in severity during the next century, and

women convicted as witches were subject to especially brutal execution.

Reformation of the marriage laws during the eighteenth century somewhat modified the wife's subjection to her husband, and during the nineteenth century there was a substantial change in the legal status of women in England. Previously the legislature rarely discussed the needs of women or attempted to remedy injustices to which they were subjected. Most of the changes during this period were related to the extension of political rights to women, and to their protection as wage earners. Punishments under the criminal law were greatly modified; the death penalty was abolished in many instances, for example, and the courts frequently exercised clemency when the defendant was a woman. Married women acquired additional property rights under the Married Woman's Property acts of 1870 and 1882. The act of 1882 stated that a wife could acquire, hold, and dispose of property in the same way as a single woman, thereby taking away all rights of a husband over his wife's holdings. In general, whereas the common law held that a woman was—as were children and the mentally unsound—a legally incapable person, new statutes gave her rights and responsibilities in relation to property, crime, and her children, that in most respects were equal to those of her husband.

Legal Rights in the United States. Women's legal position is complicated by the lack of uniformity of the laws among the many states. In general, U.S. statutory law followed the English example of broadening women's rights, but it was not until 1908 that a state court of appeals, in New York, upheld a woman's right to contract directly with her husband for voluntary separation instead of through a third person, or trustee. This case set a precedent in allowing women to make independent contracts and thus accelerated changes in the social and economic status of women. Further enactment of legislation removing the civil and legal disabilities of women continued throughout the first half of the century. By mid-twentieth century, remaining inequities to women were few in number and minor in importance when compared with the extent of law reform that had been accomplished for women during the years since 1900. See MARRIAGE; HUSBAND AND WIFE; DIVORCE.

WOMEN IN INDUSTRY

Prior to the Industrial Revolution, early in the nineteenth century, women's labor was largely confined to the home. The women of the European peasant and working classes had for centuries been occupied in productive labor in addition to their domestic activities. This labor was chiefly agricultural work, spinning, and sewing, and was carried on in the home or in the adjacent fields and gardens worked by the family. Apart from scattered instances of their employment in factories of the textile trade in England as early as the sixteenth and seventeenth centuries, the most important occupation of women outside of their homes was domestic service. In the early period of U.S. history, women rarely worked outside of their homes, but many of their domestic duties actually comprised productive tasks that were later to be transferred to organized industry. In the United States during the first half of the nineteenth century young women were employed to some extent in the eastern textile factories, and throughout the nineteenth century many women, especially newly arrived immigrants, formed a sizable domestic servant class. It was not until the Civil War period, however, that U.S. women began to follow occupations that had been formerly held only by men.

Problems in the Employment of Women. Many of the social and economic problems that arose from the employment of women during the early years of the Industrial Revolution came as a result of the general changes in social patterns imposed by the growth of towns and cities and the expansion of mechanized laissez-faire industry, rather than because of any actual enhancement of their position as productive laborers. The first developments in machine operation and the establishment of factories took place in occupations, such as spinning and carding, that were traditionally performed by women and children. The ease and simplicity of the newly mechanized processes encouraged women to follow the work to the factory. But long working hours, low wages, and night work, associated with the beginnings of competitive enterprise, soon had a deleterious effect upon the health of many women so employed. Often, the family life of mothers working long hours disintegrated, and standards of domestic comfort and welfare deteriorated. These changes were concomitant with the rapid expansion of factory towns, the sanitary conditions of which were notoriously bad, the homes and tenements jerry-built and crowded, and limited recreation facilities.

During the early years of the factory system the employment of women, both in England and the eastern states of the United States, tended to depress over-all wage scales because women underbid men in the labor market in order to increase the family income. In particular areas their employment resulted in unemployment among adult males. Evidence indicates, however, that the employment of women has not in the long run encroached upon the employment of men, but that primarily the increase in the number of women workers has resulted from the inability of the male population of working age to meet the increased demand for labor.

The consequent social and economic changes caused in the nineteenth century by the withdrawal of many women of the working classes from their traditional place and influence in the home, stimulated consideration of remedial legislation to limit working hours, fix minimum wages, and prohibit women from certain occupations. Early regulatory laws of this type soon came into conflict with the increasing legal, political, and economic independence of women; in some respects this conflict still existed in the United States, and to a much greater extent in other countries, at mid-twentieth century.

Extent and Characteristics of the Employment of Women. During the years 1850–1950, the development of machinery, increase in job specialization, and readiness of women to make use of opportunities for economic as well as political independence contributed to increased employment of women. The Civil War and World Wars I and II exercised powerful influences in the same direction, for during each of these periods the increased demand for labor and the loss of male workers to the Armed Forces brought women into occupations in which they had never before been employed. The fact of national need and patriotic service at these times removed many of the social disabilities previously incurred by working women.

The invention of office equipment and machinery after the Civil War provided an important stimulus to the employment of women. In 1870, 11,000 U.S. women were working in clerical occupations; by 1900 the number was 395,000; during World War I, they were performing 90 per cent of all such work; and in 1960 approximately 6.7 million women filled clerical positions in the United States. After World War I women were employed in almost every gainful occupation classified by the federal census, with certain definite occupational trends appearing. The proportion of women in agriculture, extraction of minerals, manufacturing, and domestic service decreased, and the percentage in trade, professional services, transportation, communication, and clerical occupations, increased. During World War II women entered many heavy industries and occupations previously entirely dominated by men. They constituted 11 per

cent of the workers in iron and steel plants in 1942 and 20 per cent of the labor force in metalworking plants. Approximately 200,000 women served in the Armed Forces, and 25 per cent of Civil Service jobs were filled by women. In total, women comprised 36 per cent of the civilian labor force.

In general, the age trends for both men and women were the same between 1900 and 1960, with the median age rising. Between 1940 and 1950 alone, the median age of employed women increased from 31.9 years to 36 years.

Although many women terminated their paid employment at the end of World War II, a larger percentage of women continued in business and industry than in any previous peacetime period of the United States. In 1960, 33 per cent of the U.S. labor force was composed of women, and only about 6 per cent of working women were in agricultural occupations. Almost half of the women workers were married and living with their husbands, and working mothers constituted more than 20 per cent of all mothers of children under 18. The total labor force of the United States more than doubled between 1900 and 1960, but the number of working women more than tripled in the same period.

BIBLIOG.—Montague F. Ashley-Montague, *Natural Superiority of Women* (1953); Simone de Beauvoir, *Second Sex* (1953); Elizabeth Bragdon, ed., *Women Today* (1953); Vera Brittain, *Lady into Woman: A History of Women from Victoria to Elizabeth II* (1953); Constance B. Burnett, *Five for Freedom* (1953); Eric J. Dingwall, *American Woman: A Historical Study* (1957); Maurice Duverger, *Policial Role of Women* (1955); Eva Firkel, *Woman in the Modern World* (1956); Edith L. Fisch and Mortimer D. Schwartz, eds., *State Laws on the Employment of Women* (1953); Valborg Fletty, *Public Services of Women's Organizations* (1951); Aylesa Forsee, *American Women Who Scored Firsts* (1958); Mary W. Godwin, *Rights of Women* (1955); Oliver O. Jensen, *Revolt of American Women* (1952); Mirra Komarovsky, *Women in the Modern World: Their Education and Their Dilemmas* (1953); Esther C. P. Lovejoy, *Women Doctors of the World* (1957); Fru Alva R. Myrdal and Viola Klein, *Women's Two Roles: Home and Work* (1956); Maud W. Park, *Front Door Lobby* (1960); Eleanor Roosevelt and Lorena A. Hickok, *Ladies of Courage* (1954); Charles T. Seltman, *Women in Antiquity* (1957); Domingo A. Songalia, *Women's Rights* (1958).

WOMEN'S TRADE UNION LEAGUE OF AMERICA, NATIONAL, a fraternal organization, 1903-50, of wage-earning women that attempted to obtain better working conditions for women, fought to reduce discrimination in jobs for reasons of race or sex, and worked for improved social legislation. The national league was dissolved, 1950, but individual leagues that had been organized in Chicago, New York, and Milwaukee continued to operate; their objectives remained the same as those of the national league had been.

WONSAN, or Genzan, city, E North Korea, on the shore of East Korea Bay; 90 miles E of the North Korean capital, Pyŏngyang. Wŏnsan has an excellent harbor, and is a commercial center for a region in which rice, soybeans, and millet are grown. Cattle are raised, and fishing is a major industry. Gold is mined in the vicinity. Wŏnsan is a rail and highway junction, connected with Vladivostok in the U.S.S.R., as well as with principal Korean centers. Pop. (1959 est.) 112,952.

WOOD, ANTHONY, 1632-95, English antiquary and biographer, was born in Oxford and studied at Oxford. He wrote the *Historia et Antiquitates Universitatis Oxoniensis* (1674) and *Athenae Oxonienses, an Exact History of All the Writers and Bishops Who have had Their Education in the University of Oxford from 1500-1690* (2 vols., 1691-92; vol. 3,1721). Other works are *The Ancient and Present State of the City of Oxford* (1773) and *A Survey of the Antiquities of the City of Oxford* (ed. by A. Clark, 1889-1899).

WOOD, GEORGE BACON, 1797–1879, U.S. physician, was born in Greenwich, N.J., and studied medicine at the University of Pennsylvania. He was professor of chemistry, 1822–31, and of materia medica, 1831–35, at the Philadelphia College of Pharmacy, and professor of materia medica and pharmacy, 1835–50, and of the theory and practice of medicine, 1850–60, at the University of Pennsylvania. His most important work was the compilation of *The Dispensatory of the United States* (with Franklin Bache, 1833).

WOOD, GRANT, 1892–1942, U.S. artist, was born on a farm near Anamosa, Iowa. His education, interrupted by World War I service, included study at the University of Iowa, the Chicago Art Institute, and the Académie Julian in Paris. Wood's most important paintings delineate with painstaking realism the life of the rural Iowa he had known from his childhood. Characteristic even of Wood's most realistic work is his ability to evoke formal completeness and symbolic force. Among his best known paintings are *American Gothic* (1930), *Woman with Plants, Daughters of the Revolution, Dinner for Threshers,* and *Parson Weem's Fable.*

WOOD, JOHN, known as Wood of Bath, 1705?– 1754, English architect, was born probably in Yorkshire and settled in Bath, 1727. He laid out a number of streets, terraces, and groups of houses in Bath, among them Queen's Square, the Royal Crescent, and the North and South Parade, establishing the Palladian style as characteristic of the town and leading the way toward more progressive city planning. Many of his later architectural designs, such as the royal private baths, were completed by his son John Wood (died 1782).

WOOD, LEONARD, 1860–1927, U.S. physician, army officer, and administrator, was born in Winchester, N.H., and was graduated from Harvard Medical School, 1884. He joined the U.S. Army, 1886, and served as a medical and line officer in the expedition against the Apache Indian warrior Geronimo. In 1897–98 Wood helped his friend Theodore Roosevelt recruit the 1st U.S. Volunteer Cavalry— the so-called Rough Riders—for service in the Spanish-American War. As colonel of the regiment, he took a conspicuous part in the Santiago campaign, particularly at Las Guasimas. He was promoted major general of volunteers, 1898, and served as military governor of Santiago, 1898–99, and of Cuba, 1899–1902. The efficiency of his Cuban administration won him promotion to major general, 1903, and appointment as military governor of Moro Province, P.I., 1903–06, and commander of the military division of the Philippines, 1906–08. He became chief of staff of the U.S. Army, 1910–14. An early advocate of military preparedness, he started civilian training camps, 1913; his wise emphasis on preparedness irked Pres. Woodrow Wilson, with the result that Wood, although the ranking officer, was not appointed to supreme U.S. command in World War I; in World War II this precedent was cited when Dwight D. Eisenhower, rather than Douglas MacArthur, was appointed as supreme commander.

Wood commanded the Department of the East, 1914–17, the Southeastern Department, 1917–19, and the Central Department, 1919–21. Having failed to gain the Republican presidential nomination, 1920, he became governor general of the Philippine Islands, 1921–27. His administration was efficient, but obnoxious to leaders of the Filipino independence movement. Wood wrote *The Military Obligation of Citizenship* (1915), *Our Military History* (1916), *National Defense* (1917), *Universal Military Training* (1917), and *Report of the Special Mission to the Philippines* (with W. Cameron Forbes, 1921).

WOOD, the hard, fibrous inner substance found under the bark of trees, shrubs, and other plants. In popular usage, wood is practically synonymous with lumber (see LUMBERING). Botanically, wood is the vascular tissue, xylem, found not only in trees and shrubs, but in all members of the phylum Tracheophyta (see TRACHEOPHYTA). The various species of trees are divided into two groups: hardwoods, or angiosperms, which have broad leaves, and softwoods,

or gymnosperms, which have needle-like leaves. Wood, through its various uses, can provide man with several of his basic needs, such as fuel, shelter, clothing, and food.

Composition. The constituents of wood are found in the fibrovascular bundles that form the circulatory system in all higher plants. These bundles are composed primarily of xylem, which conveys water and dissolved mineral salts from the roots to the leaves, and phloem, through which food manufactured in the leaves passes in dissolved form to other parts of the plant (see TREE). The elements of xylem essential in conduction are the vessels, arising from fusion of longitudinal rows of cells, and the tracheids, developed from single cells. In both cases the cell protoplasm has disappeared and the walls have become thickened by the deposition of lignin, which gives the wood its hardness.

Growth. In the first year of growth these bundles are arranged around the central pith at some distance from one another. In the second year the cambium layer is differentiated from embryonic tissue between the phloem and xylem, stretching from bundle to bundle. The cambium divides internally and externally, the internal cells becoming additional xylem, the external cells becoming additional phloem. In this manner the xylem, or wood, expands yearly, carrying the cambium ring farther from the center with continued growth. Only the most recent phloem growth remains functional, however; the older cells are crushed in the continual expansion of the trunk.

There is a marked difference between wood formed in the spring and that formed in autumn. The walls of the vessels of spring wood are thin, and consequently the passages are large; the lignification of the walls of autumn wood diminishes the size of the passages. The autumn wood with its closer grain bounds the ring of any given year. These annual rings are useful in determining the age of stems. See ANNUAL RINGS.

The cells of the oldest annual rings eventually become blocked by tyloses, intrusions of protoplasmic substance, and cease functioning. These rings comprise the dark central portion of the stems of old trees, the heartwood. The outer, lighter portion is the sapwood, which continues functioning. The annual rings increase in thickness until the tree attains maturity; there is then a stationary period, followed by a decline in the amount of woody material laid down each year.

Use. Wood, the use of which was formerly restricted to lumber, pulp for paper, distillation of alcohol, and a few isolated special products, is of importance as a plastic material. Wider usage has been delayed for several reasons: wood dries slowly and splits and warps while doing so; it catches fire easily; it is subject to rotting and attack by insects; it fluctuates in its physical properties with changes in temperature or moisture; it is weak across the grain; and it is frequently too soft. Under the leadership of the Forest Products Laboratory of the U.S. Department of Agriculture at Madison, Wis., these problems have been attacked vigorously and, to a great extent, successfully solved. Strength of wood has been increased by compression and resin impregnation, more efficient methods of kiln-drying have been developed, chemical treatment has reduced warping, and means have been found to make wood fireproof, rotproof, and insect resistant. See FORESTRY.

WOOD ALCOHOL. See METHYL ALCOHOL.

WOODBINE, city, SE Georgia, seat of Camden County; on the Satilla River, the Seaboard Air Line Railroad, and U.S. highway 17. Woodbine is a fishing and sawmilling center. Boxes are manufactured. The city was incorporated in 1893. Pop. (1960) 845.

WOODBINE, any of a number of species of vines. All of them are characterized by their ability to climb fixed objects by means of tendrils, which are slender and often coiled extensions of leaves or stems that cling to fixed objects for support. The vines are cultivated primarily for their extensive and beautiful foliage. A common woodbine found in the United States is the Virginia creeper, *Parthenocissus quinquefolia*, which is found in the New England area south to Florida and westward into Mexico. Another common woodbine is the honeysuckle, *Lonicera canadensis*, which is found from Canada into the northeastern United States.

WOODBRIDGE, township, NE New Jersey, in Middlesex County; on the Jersey Central, the Pennsylvania, and the Reading railroads; about 23 miles SW of New York. Woodbridge is a center for brick, tile, and ceramics industries; chemicals and metal goods are also manufactured. The area was settled, 1665, by a group of colonists from New England. Woodbridge was the site of the first New Jersey press, established, 1751. Pop. (1960) 78,846.

WOODBURY, LEVI, 1789–1851, U.S. public official and jurist, was born in Francestown, N.H., was graduated from Dartmouth College, 1809, and practiced law at Francestown and Portsmouth, N.H. He was judge of the state superior court, 1817–23, governor of New Hampshire, 1823–24, state legislator, and speaker of the house, 1825, and U.S. senator, 1825–31, 1841–45. In Pres. Andrew Jackson's cabinet, he served as secretary of the navy, 1831–34, and secretary of the treasury, a post he also held under Pres. Martin Van Buren, 1834–41. He was an associate justice of the U.S. Supreme Court, 1846–51.

WOODBURY, city, SW New Jersey, seat of Gloucester County; on the Pennsylvania-Reading Seashore Lines Railroad; 9 miles S of Philadelphia. Woodbury is chiefly a residential city but has several industries, among which are hosiery, dress, handbag, and patent medicine manufacturing, and lumber processing. Truck-garden products of the surrounding farms are marketed at Woodbury. Pop. (1960) 12,453.

WOODBURY, town, central Tennessee, seat of Cannon County; on Stones River and U.S. highway 70; 40 miles SE of Nashville. Woodbury is a trade center for an area of diversified farms. Cheese, shirts, and corrugated boxes are manufactured. Pop. (1960) 1,562.

WOOD CARVING, the ornamentation or sculpture of wood with tools of various types, and the objects produced by such means (see SCULPTURE). In its classic form, the art dates probably from early Egyptian times; and among the ancient Greeks, certainly, it was among the oldest forms of sculpture, and perhaps the oldest.

In the Orient the art dates at least from the eighth century, where ornamentation for temples of worship largely assumed the form of masks and small figurines. Little use was made of wood carving for domestic decoration until mid-sixteenth century, when it came into limited use in the embellishment of palaces of the Japanese shoguns. The Chinese sometimes utilized carved wood for pillars and beams in home construction, but the finest Chinese wood carvings are to be found in the Confucian, Buddhist, and Taoist temples. Many of the Chinese examples are finished with lacquer, but Japanese wood carvers usually employed natural wood. Some of the finest Japanese wood carving appears in the ornamental buttons known as *netsukes*.

African Wood Carvings fall into two principal categories: those created by the fetish-worshiping Negro tribes, and those produced in the Moslem areas bordering the Mediterranean Sea. None of the fetishistic art has been applied to architectural design. In the main it has been limited to idols, drinking cups, headrests, and masks used in tribal rites and dances (see AFRICAN NEGRO SCULPTURE; NEGRO, In Africa, *African Negro Art and Music*). Moslem wood carving, conversely, achieved a finesse rarely encountered. See MOSLEM ART AND ARCHITECTURE.

Europe. In the Scandinavian countries interior decoration of sills, beams, and heavy furniture in bas-relief was common in the ninth century and perhaps earlier. During the Norman period in England, from 1066, wood carving was chiefly confined to church and tomb decoration, little of it of enduring merit. During part of the same period, however, outstanding work was being done by Catalan artisans on both sides of the Pyrenees; extant Catalan polychrome carvings depicting religious themes are among the finest artistic expressions of the twelfth and thirteenth centuries. The best of early English Gothic wood carving was attained in the decoration of fifteenth century English cathedrals; outstanding features of this era were intricacy of design, and a slight flattening of relief carving. French Gothic carving of the same period was outstanding in its lacelike detail; German Gothic was equally outstanding in its high relief, shadow, and forceful outlines. See GOTHIC ART AND ARCHITECTURE.

By the end of the sixteenth century the influence of the Italian Renaissance had wrought a major transformation in most of European wood carving. In France, one of the first nations to feel the Italian influence, elaboration and attention to detail, tempered by traces of Gothic, stamped wood carving of that period as distinctly individualistic; particular attention was given to preserving the natural beauty of the wood, chiefly walnut. Flemish, English, and German wood carvings of the period were elaborated by strapwork, scrolls, and figures in high relief. Some of the outstanding examples of Flemish work were designed for church decoration.

High point of the Baroque in wooden sculpture was perhaps achieved in the dozens of remarkable figures in the Valladolid Museum dating from the sixteenth and seventeenth centuries. These are among the most fluid, the most expressive and emotional art of all time. Several representations of saints, of crucified virgins, and of tortuous processional groups form one of the great summations of Western art (see BAROQUE). With the diminution of the effect of the Renaissance during the eighteenth century, French Rococo, symbolic and expressive of the pomp and elaboration of the reigns of Louis XIV and Louis XV, came into being. See FRENCH ART AND ARCHITECTURE.

The Twentieth Century saw a revival of interest in wood carving based on an artistic utilization of the essential qualities of the wood used, in contrast to the earlier approach in which these qualities were generally ignored, or even fought, by artisans whose prime concern was the idea to be suggested, the figure to be represented, or the area to be decorated. Modern concern with grain, texture, ,sinuosities, knots, and the like was analogous to the interest of many painters in the peculiarities of their painting materials as such. The Constructivists used wood along with other material in the fabrication of their images, but other sculptors confined themselves to wood alone as their principal medium. One such was the U.S. sculptress Louise Nevelson who constructed wooden sculpture that is cut, nailed, glued, and joined, thus superseding the limits of wood carving as such; this type of construction was, of course, inspired by the Cubist wood constructions that Pablo Picasso and others had created during World War I. Carved and polished wood was used by the English sculptor Henry Moore, as in his *String Figure, No. 3* (1938), where convex and concave forms are visually joined by a play of strings. An earlier masterpiece of the century is Ossip Zadkine's masterful totem in the Grand Palais, Paris.   ANTHONY KERRIGAN

BIBLIOG.–Doris Aller, *Sunset Wood Carving Book* (1951); Herbert S. Anderson, *How to Carve Characters in Wood* (1953); Al Ball, *Wood Carving for Fun and Profit* (1960); Enid Bell, *Practical Wood-carving Projects* (1951); Ralph E. Byers, *Wood Carving with Power Tools* (1959); Erwin O. Christensen, *Early American Wood Carving* (1952); Alan L. Durst, *Wood Carving* (How to do it Ser.) (1959); Herbert H. Grimwood and Frederick Goodyear, *Introduction to Decorative Woodwork* (1936); Walter B. Hunt, *Whittling with Ben Hunt* (1959); John L. Lacey, *Book of Woodcarving* (1953); A. W. Lewis, *Wood Decoration with V-tool and Gouge* (1953); Peter Morton,

Carver's Companion: A Guide to Carving in Wood and Stone (1959); Percival E. Norman, *Sculpture in Wood* (How to do It Ser.) (1954); Elmer J. Tangerman, *Whittling and Woodcarving* (1937), *Design and Figure Carving* (1940); Leon Underwood, *Figures in Wood of West Africa* (Chapters in Art Ser.) (1948).

WOODCHUCK, or groundhog, a North American marmot familiar throughout the country from Hudson Bay southward to South Carolina and westward to Nebraska. It is between 16 and 19 inches long, and a reddish or grayish grizzle in color. It burrows deeply in field, hillside, or woods, remaining secluded during the day, and seeking its food, consisting of green vegetation, at night and early morning. It hibernates during the winter.

WOODCOCK, a wading bird closely related to the snipe belonging to the family *Scolopacidae.* The coloring is a combination of brown, gray, and buff, with black markings, and there are two transverse buff stripes at the back of the head. The birds frequent marshy woods, and feed upon worms, insects, and mollusks. During the breeding season the cocks have a habit of following certain tracks in the woods, called cock roads, and while traveling these they utter whistling notes. The nest is a depression lined with dry leaves, in which four eggs are laid. The woodcock of the United States, *Philohela minor*, is 11 inches in length, and is found only east of the Mississippi and south of the Canadian forests; it migrates slowly in autumn from the more northern districts to the southern states. The European woodcock, *Scolopax rusticola*, is 3 inches larger and of similar habits.

WOODCUT, a medium for the reproduction of illustrative material, is the oldest known form of printing. In essence the method is simple, but only highly skilled artisans can produce good work by means of it. A woodcut is no more than an engraved wood block. On one smoothed surface of a carefully selected slab of close grained wood the subject to be reproduced is drawn or photographed. Skilled craftsmen cut away the background from this drawing, leaving untouched the original surface of lines that are part of the drawing. When this surface is properly inked, covered with a sheet of paper and subjected to sufficient pressure, it yields an impression on the paper of the original drawing. Each transcription of the original design is called an impression; the pattern or picture common to all impressions from the same printing surface is called the print. Strictly speaking, wood engraving is slightly different from the making of woodcuts, in that in the former the grain of the wood runs at right angles to the surface of the block, and the cutting is done with a special tool, called a graver or burin, which can be used as a drawing tool. Woodcuts and wood engravings are printed in the same way.

History. The Chinese produced block-printed books in the third century B.C., if not before, but books made by similar methods did not appear in Europe until the fifteenth century. These block books, so called, consisted of pictures and brief texts, all of which were cut on wood printing blocks and hand printed by the method described above. The earliest extant example is the *Biblia pauperum* (Poor Bible). These books antedated the invention of printing by movable type, of course, and contributed to its development, in a sense, since printing by movable type was essentially an elaboration of the adjustments that printers had long been making when certain of the engraved letters in texts cut underneath wood-block pictures became broken and had to be separately recut.

A single printed sheet showing St. Christopher, and dated 1423, is the earliest extant European woodcut print. In the early days, all the printed visual reports or reproductions of pictures, sculpture, architecture, and so forth were the work of artisan print makers. These reproductions were not original works of art, and the craft of woodcutting, with rare exceptions (Albrecht Dürer and Hans Holbein) was the work of technicians rather than artists. For 350 years after its introduction, wood engraving was the only method by which picture-printing plates could be used along with type. Titian was one of the first to use the woodcut for an original work of art. His *Pharaoh's Army Submerged in the Red Sea* (1549) was drawn freely in open lines and roughly printed; thus there was no need for meticulous mechanical work by an artisan-copyist. The total liberation of the woodcut from a purely technical role was not accomplished until the nineteenth century, when artists such as Paul Gauguin, as in his *Women at the River* (1892; Metropolitan Museum, New York), abandoned traditional copying techniques and worked the blocks as if they were sculpturing. Graphic art was revitalized by this new approach.

RALPH FLETCHER SEYMOUR; ANTHONY KERRIGAN

BIBLIOG.–R. John Beedham, *Wood Engraving* (1938); John R. Biggs, *Woodcuts: Wood-engravings, Linocuts and Prints by Related Methods of Relief Print Making* (1959); Douglas C. Bliss, *History of Wood-engraving* (1928); Willy Boller, *Masterpieces of the Japanese Color Woodcut* (1957); Pearl S. Buck, comp., *China in Black and White* (1945); Chinese Woodcutters Association, *Woodcuts of Wartime China, 1937–1945* (1946); Margaret S. Dobson, *Block-cutting and Print-Making by Hand* (1928); Len A. Doust, *Manual on Wood Engraving* (1934); Albrecht Dürer, *Complete Woodcuts* (1946); Helen S. N. Estabrook, comp., *Old Testament Stories in Woodcut* (1947); Shizuya Fujikake, *Japanese Wood-block Prints* (Tourist Lib. New Ser., no. 10) (1949); Herbert E. A. Furst (Tis, pseud.), *Modern Woodcut: A Story of the Evolution of the Craft* (1924); Basil Gray, *Japanese Woodcuts* (1957); Lubor Hájek, *Osaka Woodcuts* (1959); Jack R. Hillier, *Japanese Masters of the Colour Print* (1954), *Japanese Print: A New Approach* (1960); Arthur M. Hind, *Introduction to a History of Woodcut* (2 vols.) (1935); Owen E. Holloway, *Graphic Art of Japan: The Classical School* (Chapters in Art Ser., vol. 28) (1957); F. W. H. Hollstein, *German Engravings, Etchings, and Woodcuts, ca. 1450–1700* (1954), *Dutch and Flemish Etchings, Engravings and Woodcuts, ca. 1450–1700* (1954); Julius J. Lankes, *Woodcut Manual* (1932); Clare V. H. Leighton, *Wood-engraving and Woodcuts* (How to do It Ser., no. 2) (1932); Iain Macnab, *Student's Book of Wood-Engraving* (1938); Hans A. Mueller, *Woodcuts & Wood Engravings: How I Make Them* (1939); Raymond W. Perry, *Block Printing Craft* (1938); John Edgar Platt, *Colour Woodcuts: A Book of Reproductions and a Handbook of Method* (1938); Gwendolen M. D. Raverat, *Wood Engravings* (1959); Imre Reiner, *Woodcut/Wood Engraving: A Contribution to a History of the Art* (1947); Graham Reynolds, *Thomas Bewick: A Résumé of his Life and Work* (1950); Bernard Sleigh, *Wood Engraving Since Eighteen-Ninety* (1932); Lawrence C. Wroth and Marion W. Adams, *American Woodcuts and Engravings, 1670–1800* (1946); Hiroshi Yoshida, *Japanese Wood-block Printing* (1939); Carl Zigrosser, *Book of Fine Prints* (1956).

WOOD DISTILLATION, the heating of wood in a closed retort or oven to a temperature of 160° to 450°C in the absence of oxygen. This process breaks the wood down into simpler substances and is more generally known as the destructive distillation of wood. Ordinarily dried hardwoods, such as beech, hickory, maple, and oak, are decomposed by this procedure, yielding gaseous fuel products, charcoal, and a liquid aqueous condensate called pyroligneous acid. From this pyroligneous acid, which is composed of approximately 65 per cent methyl alcohol, 15 per cent acetone, 10 per cent methyl acetate, and some tars, components may be removed by a process of fractional distillation. Commercial methyl alcohol, or wood alcohol, and acetone were formerly prepared by this method. However, synthetic organic methods for the preparation of wood alcohol and acetone have almost entirely replaced this procedure. Some charcoal is prepared by wood distillation, however, because this method yields an especially pure product. A cord of dry hardwood can yield about 1,000 pounds of charcoal.

WOODIN, WILLIAM HARTMAN, 1868–1934, U.S. political figure, was born in Berwick, Pa., and studied at Columbia University. He was a close personal friend of Franklin Delano Roosevelt, and became a member of the inner circle of Roosevelt's advisers and secretary of the treasury in Roosevelt's first cabinet, 1933. Demands were made for his resignation after his name appeared on a preferred list of House of Morgan customers, but Roosevelt refused to let him resign, even for reasons of health, until a few months before Woodin's death.

WOODLAND, city, central California, seat of Yolo County; on the Sacramento Northern and the Southern Pacific railroads and U.S. highways 40 and 99; 20 miles NW of Sacramento. Woodland is in a fertile, irrigated area where sugar beets, walnuts, almonds, and rice are grown. The chief industries are rice and olive oil milling, and the production of almond hullers, dairy goods, concrete pipe, and wine. Pop. (1960) 13,524.

WOODMEN OF THE WORLD. See MUTUAL BENEFIT SOCIETY; FRATERNAL ORGANIZATION.

WOODPECKER, any bird that belongs to the large family *Picidae,* which is usually regarded as including two subfamilies, the woodpeckers and the soft-tailed wrynecks. The woodpeckers are climbing birds, the feet having two anterior and two posterior toes. The head is large, the neck very muscular, and the tongue extremely long and wormlike, with a barbed and horny tip. It can be greatly extended and the sticky substance that coats it traps the insects upon which the bird feeds. When in search of food, the woodpeckers climb trees, clinging closely with the claws and in many cases being supported by the very stiff, pointed quills of the tail. With the powerful chisel-like beak, the bird chips off loose bark or digs into the decayed wood in which the eggs or larvae of insects have been hidden, and its habits are more valuable in the destruction of woodborers than they are harmful to the trees. At the breeding season, the woodpecker excavates a hole in the stem of a tree, at first horizontal, then downward to the depth of a foot or more and in this hole the eggs are laid.

Woodpeckers are numerously represented in all parts of the Northern Hemisphere where trees grow. In the United States and Canada two small black and white species, the downy and the hairy woodpeckers, are familiar almost everywhere. Other common species are the flicker, the red-headed woodpecker, and the yellow-bellied sapsucker.

WOOD PEWEE, a small songbird belonging to the flycatcher family *Tyrannidae.* The bird, measuring about 6 inches in length, has olive-colored upperparts and grayish to yellowish-white underparts. Its folded wings are margined with pale gray and white coloration. The wood pewee's food largely consists of insects and particularly weevils. It builds its nest well off of the ground in trees; two to four creamy white eggs with a darker ring at the large end are laid. The bird breeds in North America and migrates to South America in the winter.

WOOD PIGEON, a large European pigeon belonging to the family *Columbidae.* Its color is glossy green and purple at the neck with a white patch on each side. Its most characteristic feature is a wide band of white across its wings that is seen while the bird is in flight. The bird normally reaches a length of 16 inches. The wood pigeon, *Columba palumbus,* is found in almost all of the treed areas of Europe. It builds its nest in trees and hedges or occupies old nests of other birds.

WOOD PRESERVATION, protection of wood, usually by means of chemical treatment, against destructive agents such as sunlight, water, and insects. The primary purpose of preservative treatment is to increase the life of the wood in service, thereby decreasing repair costs and eliminating frequent replacement.

Decay of wood is caused by the action of fungi. Favorable temperatures, air, moisture, and food are necessary to fungous growth. Wood will not rot if completely dry, or if submerged in water. Decay is most likely where timber is in contact with earth, masonry, or other timber. Moisture, collecting at these points, favors fungous growth. To deprive the fungi of the necessary elements for growth, chemicals are injected to "poison" the food supply—the wood. Effective treatment requires good penetration of the preservative.

The heartwood of some woods, such as cedar, catalpa, osage orange, black locust, cypress, and redwood, is long-lived even when untreated. Others, such as douglas fir, tamarack, longleaf pine, walnut, and white oak, are moderately durable, and others such as red oak, red gum, elm, beech, hemlock, shortleaf pine, and spruce, are relatively short-lived.

Coal-tar creosote is a standard preservative that is most effective and generally useful. It is an amber black or brownish oil derived from distillation of coal tar and is used to preserve wood used in docks, bridges, railway ties, pilings, and posts. It is satisfactory for all uses where the wood is not to be painted and where a faint odor is permissible. Salt preservatives are used for interiors or wood that may be painted. They are not recommended for wood that is in contact with or near the ground, or in water. The standard salt preservatives are chromated zinc chloride, which is 80 per cent chloride and 20 per cent sodium dichromate, and Wolman salts, which are 25 per cent sodium fluoride, 25 per cent sodium arsenate, $37\frac{1}{2}$ per cent sodium chromate, and $12\frac{1}{2}$ per cent dinitrophenol.

The wood to be treated is run into a large cylinder, or retort, 6 to 9 feet in diameter and up to 175 feet in length. The cylinder is filled with preservative and pressure up to 200 pounds per square inch is applied until the required quantity of preservative has been injected into the wood. Wood is treated by either a full cell or empty cell process.

In the full cell process, the seasoned wood is first subjected to a partial vacuum so as to remove some of the entrapped air inside the wood, and the preservative is then applied. A cubic foot of wood of some species will absorb from 6 to 25 pounds of creosote by this process. This method is used chiefly for piles to be set in waters where marine borers are very destructive. In the empty cell process, commonly used for the treatment of most woods, lumber is treated without a preliminary vacuum; in some cases, compressed air is admitted to the cylinder before the treating solution is poured in. After treatment, a final vacuum and the air still entrapped in the wood help in removal of surplus preservative. It is customary to use from 8 to 12 pounds of creosote per cubic foot and about ¾ of a pound of chromated zinc chloride or 0.35 of a pound of Wolman salts.

Where pressure treated wood is not available, an open tank process is sometimes used with either creosote or the preservative salts. The wood is immersed in the liquid, which is kept at about 200° F. for several hours, then quickly immersed in a cold bath of the preservative for several hours more, or left in the hot solution until it cools. In cooling, contraction of trapped air in the wood creates a partial vacuum that soaks some of the preserving liquid into the wood. Penetration is limited, however, and timber so treated will not be as well preserved as that treated by pressure processes.

Creosoted railway ties usually last from 30 to 35 years if not destroyed by other means. Creosoted bridge timbers, poles, and posts remain sound for from 35 to 50 years. Wood treated with creosote or the chemical salts resists decay, termites, and other destructive insects.

Various other preservatives, particularly mercuric chloride, have been used in the past, but have been superseded by the other materials. Use of mercuric chloride was abandoned chiefly because it is a poison.

WOOD PULP, pulverized and chemically treated wood that is used in the manufacture of paper and other products. The pulp is made from the wood of most common species of trees, including softwoods, such as pine, spruce, hemlock, and fir, and hardwoods, such as oak, aspen, maple, and gum.

Wood to be made into pulp for paper products must first have its bark removed. This may be accomplished mechanically in the forests, after the trees have been felled, or at the mills; or the bark may also be removed chemically while the tree is still living. The cut wood is taken to the mills, and the wood fibers are then separated either mechanically or chemically. Pulp prepared by grinding the wood under water is of inferior grade, its fibers short and easily discolored. Superior quality wood pulp is prepared from wood that is cut and boiled under pressure with a solution of caustic soda, sodium sulfide, or calcium bisulfite. The product is then pressed, washed, and bleached. See PAPER.

Wood pulp may be chemically treated so as to remove most of its components except the cellulose, which is used in the manufacture of such products as plastics, rayon, explosives, and cellophane.

WOOD-RIDGE, borough, NE New Jersey, in Bergen County; on the Passaic River, the New Jersey and New York Railroad, and U.S. highway 46; 8 miles N of Newark. Chemical manufacturing, the reclaiming of motion-picture films, the operation of greenhouses, and truck gardening are among the leading industries. Wood-Ridge was settled in the mid-eighteenth century. Pop. (1960) 7,964.

WOODRING, HARRY HINES, 1890–   , U.S. banker and government official, was born in Elk City, Kans., of which state he was governor, 1931–33, before serving as assistant secretary of war, 1933–36, and secretary of war, 1936–40, in Pres. Franklin D. Roosevelt's cabinet.

WOOD RIVER, city, SW Illinois, in Madison County; on the Mississippi River, the Gulf, Mobile, and Ohio, the Illinois Terminal, and the New York Central railroads, and U.S. highway 67; in the St. Louis metropolitan area, 10 miles N of East St. Louis. The city is chiefly an oil-refining center. Wood River was founded by an oil company in 1907. Pop. (1960) 11,694.

WOODRUFF, any of about 80 species of the genus *Asperula,* which occurs naturally in Europe and Asia. Woodruffs are small, hardy herbs with small, fragrant, four-petaled flowers. They rarely grow over two feet. The commonest woodruff is the sweet woodruff, *A. odorata,* with white flowers and erect stems. The leaves of this plant are used in preparing May wine. Woodruffs usually favor a moist soil and are cultivated for garden bordering or to enhance the appearance of cut bouquets.

WOODSFIELD, village, E Ohio, seat of Monroe County; 94 miles E of Columbus. Woodsfield is a trade center for an area in which corn, wheat, and oats are grown. There are oil and gas wells and timber in the vicinity. Dairy products, vaults, and tools are manufactured. Pop. (1960) 2,956.

WOODS HOLE, village, SE Massachusetts, in Barnstable County; on the New Haven Railroad and on a peninsula between Vineyard Sound and Buzzards Bay. A U.S. Bureau of Fisheries station, an oceanographic institute, and a marine biological laboratory are in Woods Hole. Pop. about 1,300.

WOOD SORREL, any of about 500 species of light-sensitive herbs belonging to the genus *Oxalis.* Most of the species have clover-like leaves. Their flowers are usually solitary with colors ranging from white and yellow to pink and red. The tubers of some species have been used as food, while the leaves of others have been placed in salads. The common wood sorrel of North America and Europe, *O. Acetosella,* is stemless with three notched leaflets; it is often called shamrock. Most of the other species occur in Africa and South America.

WOODSTOCK, city, NE Illinois, seat of McHenry County; on the North Western Railway and U.S. highway 14; 51 miles NW of Chicago. The city is a trade center for a diversified farming area. Typewriters, beds, and foundry and machine-shop products are manufactured. Woodstock was settled in the 1830's by pioneers from Vermont. The county seat was moved there from McHenry in 1844. Pop. (1960) 8,897.

WOODSTOCK, town, N Virginia, seat of Shenandoah County; on the Southern Railway and U.S. highway 11; 80 miles W of Washington, D.C. The town is a trade center for an area in which apples, dairy products, and poultry are produced. Food packing equipment and textiles are manufactured. Woodstock was incorporated in 1872. Pop. (1960) 2,083.

WOODSTOCK, town, Canada, W New Brunswick, seat of Carleton County; on the St. John River and the Canadian National and the Canadian Pacific railways; about 45 miles NW of Fredericton. Woodstock is an important market center for potatoes. A lumber mill and factories producing hardwood products, farm machinery, and foundry items are the major industrial establishments. United Empire Loyalists settled in the vicinity in 1784. Woodstock was incorporated in 1856. Pop. (1956) 4,308.

WOODSTOCK, city, Canada, S Ontario, seat of Oxford County; on the Thames River, the Canadian National and the Canadian Pacific railways; about 77 miles SW of Toronto. The city is a trade and industrial center for an area in which dairying is important. Textiles, hosiery, fire engines and apparatus, trucks, stoves, machine parts, pipe organs, concrete pipe, paper boxes, ornamental ceramics, and powdered milk are manufactured. The city grew up about a tavern founded there in 1834 and was named for Woodstock, England. It was incorporated as a city in 1901. Pop. (1956) 18,347.

WOODSTOCK COLLEGE. See COLLEGES AND UNIVERSITIES.

WOODSVILLE, village, NW New Hampshire; seat of Grafton County, at the junction of the Ammonoosuc and Connecticut rivers, on the Boston and Maine Railroad and U.S. highway 302; 70 miles NNW of Concord. Woodsville is a trade center for an area in which dairy products, poultry, and timber are produced. Pop. (1960) 1,596.

WOOD TAR. See WOOD DISTILLATION; TAR.

WOODVILLE, town, SE Mississippi, seat of Wilkinson County; on the Illinois Central Railroad and U.S. highway 61; 35 miles SE of Natchez. The town is a trade center for an area of diversified farms. Sawmilling is a leading industry. Pop. (1960) 1,856.

WOODVILLE, town, E Texas, seat of Tyler County; near Neches River; on the Southern Pacific Railroad and U.S. highways 69, 190, and 287; 85 miles NE of Houston. The town has lumber mills, cotton gins, and a ceramic-tile plant. Woodville was settled in 1847 and incorporated in 1929. Pop. (1960) 1,920.

WOODWARD, city, NW Oklahoma, seat of Woodward County; on the North Canadian River, the Santa Fe and the Missouri-Kansas-Texas railroads, and U.S. highways 183 and 270; about 125 miles NW of Oklahoma City. The city is a trade center for an area in which livestock, grain, and poultry are raised. A poultry-packing plant, a bottling works, and a hatchery are there. Woodward is the seat of the Woodward Junior College. The United States Great Plains Field and Experiment Station is in the vicinity. The city was incorporated in 1906. Pop. (1960) 7,747.

WOODWORTH, SAMUEL, 1784–1842, U.S. poet and journalist, was born in Scituate, Mass. During the War of 1812 he published a newspaper in New York City, *The War,* but he is best remembered as author of the song *The Old Oaken Bucket* (1817).

WOOL, the fleecy hair of sheep and certain other animals, most notably the camel, llama, and certain species of goats. It is distinguished from other types of animal hair by the waviness and scaly covering of the fibers, both of which cause the wool to mat together. Wool fibers also have greater elasticity than ordinary hair. Known and used from prehistoric times, wool was long one of the most important fibers used by man. No known wild animal of any period has exactly resembled the wool-bearing sheep. In the supposed progenitors of the sheep, hair or fur formed the outer coat, with a fine, soft wool or fur next to the skin. Through many centuries of breeding, selection, feeding, protection and careful handling, the wool has been cultivated and the hair largely eliminated. This development was accompanied by continuing improvement in the fineness of the wool, the average length of the bulk of its fibers, known as the staple, and the adaptability of the wool.

The principal wool-producing countries of the world are Australia, the U.S.S.R., New Zealand, Argentina, the Union of South Africa, and the United States. Total world production of wool in 1958 was about 5.3 billion pounds. See SHEEP.

Types. Wool is classified into three general types: carding, or clothing, wools; combing, or worsted, wools; and miscellaneous, or carpet or blanket, wools. This classification is based on the length, fineness, and felting qualities of the staple.

The finest wools, such as that produced by the Merino sheep, have a staple that is only one or two inches long; the wool of the Lincoln sheep, in contrast, is eight inches or more long, and in some breeds the wool may exceed a foot in length. The finer, short staple wools interlock, or felt, more readily; in carding and spinning, the scales of the curly filaments form a thread that does not untwist. Longer, less wavy, staple wools are better suited to combing and to making nonfelting worsteds; they are also more lustrous than the carding wools. Modern combing machinery, however, permits combing of the Merinos with long-wooled types, producing a fiber that combines fineness and suppleness with length of staple and luster. The coarse, long-stapled wools are used in making blankets, carpets, and coarse clothing.

Quality. There is a fairly direct relationship between waviness, fineness, and the number of the scales on the shaft of the hair. Finer wool is more wavy and contains a larger number of scales than coarser wool. Because the number of waves to the inch can be easily counted with the naked eye, it makes an excellent basis for judging wool. Elasticity is important to wool quality. Fiber breakage, one of the most common wool defects, is caused by weak spots in the fiber that make it unfit for combing.

All unwashed wool contains some fatty or greasy matter called yolk, or suint. This material is secreted by the skin of the wool-bearing animal, and prevents the fibers from matting together, except at the ends, where dust adheres to the yolk. The covering protects the fleece from dust and grit which would injure it, and accounts for the wool's cloture, the closed or open condition of the fleece. Before the wool is processed, the yolk must be removed to improve felting qualities and enable the fibers to absorb dyes.

Wool from different parts of the body of an animal varies in fineness, length of staple, hairiness, and softness. The shoulder wool is the finest and most even; breech, or buttocks, wool is the coarsest. The average yield of fleece for all breeds is about 7 pounds, but in the American Merino it often amounts to 15 to 20 pounds for rams, and 12 to 15 pounds for ewes. Machine shearing, which produces more wool because the shearing is closer, has almost entirely replaced hand shearing on the larger ranges in North America.

WOOLEN TEXTILES

Woolen textiles are of two main types, woolens and worsteds, according to the character of the fiber used and the treatment to which it is subjected The raw materials consist of (1) wools; (2) noil, the short fibers removed from the wools in the combing operation; (3) remanufactured materials, chiefly shoddy or mungo; and (4) cotton or cotton sweepings, which act as a binding around which other materials center to form a compact thread. Shoddy is prepared

by tearing up other fabrics or by use of waste from woolen and worsted manufacture.

Process of Manufacture. Raw wool is first thoroughly cleansed by passing it through machines charged with soap, alkali, and rinsing solutions, and then is dried. The quality of the yarn to be made is determined by blending some or all of the materials mentioned above. The various materials are placed in superimposed layers, each of which is lightly oiled to make the fibers more plastic. This stack is then beaten, often with the aid of air blasts, to effect a thorough mixture of the fibers. The blend is passed through revolving, spoked drums that mix the fibers more finely.

The next major step, carding, involves separating and mixing the individual fibers of a blend so as to produce a uniform sliver of wool, perhaps 60 to 80 inches wide and ⅛ inch thick; this is broken up into 60 to 80 slivers which are spun into threads on a mule. The mule draws out the condensed sliver, twisting it to prevent breaking and to make a compact yarn; the spun yarn is then wound on the spindles. See YARN.

Spun yarn is passed through a loom (see WEAVING). First a warp is laid; this consists of the threads running the length of a fabric. The warp is divided into two parts, between which the shuttle can lay the filling. At each passage of the shuttle there is a change of the threads depressed and raised. Each successive pick, or filling thread, is pressed close against the previous one to give the cloth a firm texture, and the cloth as produced is wound on a drum, or beam.

Finishing. Woolen fabric as it leaves the loom is rough, harsh, and unattractive. Typical woolen cloths are submitted to several treatments to give them the needed finish. Among these are (1) burling and mending, to correct weaving faults; (2) scouring, to cleanse the fabric; (3) fulling, or milling, to produce the desired finish; (4) additional scouring to remove the fulling agents; (5) tentering, to set the cloth at the desired width and straighten it; (6) raising, to produce the necessary pile; (7) shearing, to leave a fiber pile of uniform height; and (8) pressing, to secure the desired gloss.

Worsted. Both long and short wool fibers are used for worsteds. The long wool is combed, to remove the short fibers, then finished, or put into a more or less parallel condition. It is then ready for the drawing and spinning operations. Short wool is carded before combing.

Drawing and Spinning consists in passing the slivers through various machines to produce yarns and in twisting them to produce firm threads. For the warp, two single threads are normally twisted together. Filling yarns are usually single, but in some better quality fabrics double yarns are used for this purpose also.

Woolen textiles are almost invariably dyed before being used. See FELT; FLANNEL; TEXTILES; TWEED.

BIBLIOG.–Peter Alexander, *Wool: Its Chemistry and Physics* (1954); Barclays Bank, Limited, *Wool* (1960); Charles L. Bird, *Theory and Practice of Wool Dyeing* (1951); Alston H. Garside, *Wool and the Wool Trade* (1955); Giles E. Hopkins, *Wool as an Apparel Fiber* (1953); International Correspondence Schools, *Wool Preparation* (1949); Ernest R. Kaswell, *Textile Fibers, Yarns, and Fabrics: A Comparative Survey of their Behavior with Special Reference to Wool* (1953); Samuel Kershaw, *Wool: From the Raw Material to the Finished Product* (1953); William F. Leggett, *Story of Wool* (1947); Pablo Link, *Wool Glossary* (1954); Arthur V. May, *Story of Wool* (Commodity Ser. no. 2) (1947); Robert W. Moncrieff, *Wool Shrinkage and Its Prevention* (1954); Werner Von Bergen and Walter Krauss, *American Wool Handbook* (1948); Percival A. Wells, *Wool* (How Things are Obtained Ser.) (1957).

WOOLF, VIRGINIA STEPHEN, 1882–1941, English novelist and essayist, was born in London, the daughter of Sir Leslie Stephen. In 1912 she married the political writer Leonard Woolf (1880–   ), founded with him the Hogarth Press, 1917, and published books by Katherine Mansfield, T. S. Eliot, and

E. M. Forster, and English translations of many of Sigmund Freud's essays. Her first novel, *The Voyage Out* (1915), shows Forster's influence. In her short stories, *Monday or Tuesday* (1921), she experimented with subtle, indirect methods of characterization; in her later novels, such as *Jacob's Room* (1922), *Mrs. Dalloway* (1925), and *To The Lighthouse* (1927), she developed a stream-of-consciousness technique resembling that of James Joyce, but perhaps less coherent and more mannered. Eventually, fearful that she was becoming insane, Mrs. Woolf drowned herself. Among her other works are *The Common Reader* (1925), *Orlando* (1928), *A Room of One's Own* (1929), *The Waves* (1931), *Flush* (1933), *Roger Fry* (1940), and *The Death of the Moth and Other Essays* (1942).

BIBLIOG.–Joan Bennett, *Virginia Woolf* (1945); David Daiches, *Virginia Woolf* (1963); Ralph Freedman, *The Lyrical Novel: Hermann Hesse, André Gide, and Virginia Woolf* (1963).

WOOLLCOTT, ALEXANDER, 1887–1943, U.S. author and journalist, was born in Phalanx, N.J., and was educated at Hamilton College. He was drama critic of the New York *Times*, 1914–22, *Herald*, 1922, and *World*, 1925–28, edited the *New Yorker's* "Shouts and Murmurs" department, and conducted a weekly radio program, *The Town Crier*, 1929–40. He was eccentric and exhibitionistic in personal life, and he displayed an odd mixture of cantankerous wit and sentimentality in his writing. In 1941 he went on the stage with a road show production of George Kaufman's *The Man Who Came to Dinner*, playing the part of the outrageous Sheridan Whiteside—Woollcott himself. Among his works are *Mrs. Fiske* (1917), *Shouts and Murmurs* (1923), *Going to Pieces* (1928), *While Rome Burns* (1934), and *Long, Long Ago* (1943).

WOOLLEY, SIR CHARLES LEONARD, 1880–1960, British archaeologist, studied at New College, Oxford. He conducted excavations in Corbridge, England, 1906–07, in the Nubian Desert, 1907–11, in Carchemish (later Karkamis), Turkey, 1912–14, 1919; and in 1914 he accompanied Col. Thomas E. Lawrence ("Lawrence of Arabia") in a survey of the Mount Sinai country, described in Woolley's *Wilderness of Zin* (1936). He conducted extensive excavations at the Chaldean city of Ur in Mesopotamia, 1922–34, and in Atchana, Hatay, Turkey, 1937–39 and 1946–49. Among his publications are *The Development of Sumerian Art* (1935), *A Forgotten Kingdom* (1953), and *History Unearthed* (1958).

WOOLMAN, JOHN, 1720–72, colonial American Quaker minister, was born in Ancocas (later Rancocas), N.J., near Mount Holly, was educated at the local Quaker school, and established a successful tailoring business, doing occasional notarizing, surveying, and teaching as well. Having decided to become a Quaker minister, 1743, he thenceforth went on annual journeys to testify at Quaker meetings in the Northern and Southern colonies and along the frontier. He opposed slavery as inconsistent with Christian teachings, wrote one of the earliest North American abolitionist treatises in America, *Essay on Some Considerations on the Keeping of Negroes* (2 parts, 1754–62), and refused to use products of slave labor. His simple, semi-mystical faith and indignation at social injustice are evident in his famous *Journal* (1774; ed. 1922) and in the essays *Considerations on Pure Wisdom and Human Policy* (1758) and *A Plea for the Poor* (1763; eds. 1837 and 1898).

WOOLNER, THOMAS, 1825–92, English sculptor and poet, was born in Hadleigh, Suffolk. He was one of the original members of the Pre-Raphaelite Brotherhood, and contributed poetry to *The Germ*. After two unprofitable years in the Australian gold fields, 1852–54, Woolner returned to England and established himself as a sculptor. Most notable among his busts are those of Alfred Tennyson, John Henry Newman, Charles Darwin, Charles Dickens, and William Gladstone.

WOOLWICH, metropolitan borough, London, England, on the south side of the River Thames, about 10 miles SW of the City of London. It is an industrial center for engineering, electronics, and other industries. Early in the sixteenth century Woolwich became the chief shipbuilding town for England's growing fleet; ships were built there until the mid-nineteenth century. Still standing is the royal arsenal, which was built in the seventeenth century as a fortification against the Dutch fleet.

WOOLWORTH, FRANK WINFIELD, 1852–1919, U.S. merchant, founder of the Woolworth store chain, was born in Rodman, N.Y. After some experience as a clerk-salesman whose salary ranged from nothing to $10 per week, he opened the first successful 5-cent store at Lancaster, Pa., 1879, soon converting it into a 5-and-10-cent store. With two other men, Woolworth opened stores all over the East, and gradually throughout the United States and Canada; he incorporated the chain as F. W. Woolworth Company, 1912. He erected, 1913, the Woolworth Building, New York City, 792 feet high and the world's tallest building at that time.

WOONSOCKET, city, N Rhode Island, in Providence County; 14 miles NNW of Providence. The city is an important industrial center. Textiles, rubber goods, machine tools, plastics, wearing apparel, and electronic equipment are manufactured. Woonsocket was founded in 1666, incorporated in 1867, and chartered as a city in 1888. Industrialization of the city began in 1810 with the organization of the textile industry; in 1840 the spinning and weaving of wool became important, soon followed by the manufacturing of machinery and tools. (For population, see Rhode Island map in Atlas.)

WOOSTER, city, NE Ohio, seat of Wayne County; it lies on U.S. highways 30 and 250 about 30 miles SW of Akron. The chief manufactures are mill machinery, aluminumware, brushes, paints and varnishes, roofing materials, bricks, fire-fighting equipment, ladders, truck bodies, and oil- and gaswell tools. Wooster was settled in 1807, incorporated in 1817, and chartered as a city in 1869. The city is the seat of the College of Wooster (1866) and the Ohio Agricultural Experimental Station. (For population, see Ohio map in Atlas.)

WOOTTON, RICHENS LACY, called Dick, 1816–93, U.S. trapper, fur trader, scout, and pioneer settler, was born in Mecklenburg County, Va. He had an adventurous career in the Rocky Mountains and on the Santa Fe Trail, and built the first good road over the difficult Raton Pass from Colorado to New Mexico.   FREDERIC E. VOELKER

WORCESTER, EDWARD SOMERSET, 6th **EARL OF** and 2nd **MARQUIS OF,** 1601–67, English soldier and inventor, was born in London. During the period of the English Civil War, Somerset supported Charles I in South Wales, 1643, was created Earl of Glamorgan, 1644, and assigned to raise royalist troops in Ireland, 1645–46, but lost royal favor because of a treaty that he signed there. He succeeded to his father's titles, 1646, was exiled on the Continent, 1648–52, and returned to England, where he eventually won back most of his lands and honors. An amateur inventor, Worcester wrote *A Century of Inventions* (1663), in which he described a steam engine that raised a column of water 40 feet.

WORCESTER, JOHN TIPTOFT, EARL OF, 1427?–1470, English Yorkist leader in the Wars of the Roses, was made Earl of Worcester, 1449, and treasurer of the exchequer, 1452. For his cruelty as constable of England, 1462–67 and 1470, he was called the Butcher of England. He was responsible for the execution of the Earl of Oxford, Sir Ralph Grey, and many Lancastrians. When Edward IV fled, Worcester was found in hiding, tried, and killed. He had some fame as a scholar.

WORCESTER, JOSEPH EMERSON, 1784–1865, U.S. lexicographer, was born in Bedford, N.H. He was graduated from Yale College, 1811, and for five years taught school in Salem, Mass., where

Nathaniel Hawthorne was among his pupils. His earliest lexicographical work is [Samuel] *Johnson's English Dictionary, as Improved by Todd and Abridged by Chalmers, with Walker's Pronouncing Dictionary, Combined* (1827). He was employed, 1829, to abridge Noah Webster's *An American Dictionary of the English Language* (2 vols. 1828), and soon published his own *Comprehensive Pronouncing and Explanatory Dictionary of the English Language* (1830). Other works are *Universal and Critical Dictionary of the English Language* (1846) and the illustrated quarto *A Dictionary of the English Language* (1860), the latter his most important work.

WORCESTER, THOMAS PERCY, EARL OF, 1344–1403, English soldier, became admiral of the fleet of the north, 1378, took part in expeditions to Brittany, 1380, against Spain, 1386, and was chief ambassador to France, 1392. When Richard II was deposed, 1399, Worcester was named admiral by Henry IV. Joining with his brother and nephew in rebellion against Henry IV, 1403, he was captured and beheaded.

WORCESTER, city, central Massachusetts, one of the seats of Worcester County; on the Blackstone River, the Boston and Maine, the New York Central, and the New Haven railroads and U.S. highway 20; about 40 miles W of Boston. The city is an industrial and educational center and a wholesale distributing point. Worcester is the location of the home offices of several large insurance firms and of numerous manufacturing companies. Machine tools and mill machinery, wire and wire products, abrasives, leather goods, shoes, textiles and clothing, airplane and automotive parts, firearms, woodworking products, paper and paper products, electrical goods, lubricants, roller skates, plastics, rugs and carpets, sheet metal products, trolley and railroad cars and buses, and turbines are manufactured. An annual event, the Worcester Music Festival, was instituted shortly after the Civil War. The Worcester Art Museum was founded in 1898. Other cultural establishments are contained in the museums and libraries of the American Antiquarian Society, the Worcester Historical Society, and the Worcester Natural History Society. The Memorial Auditorium was opened in 1933. Among Worcester's educational institutions are Clark University (1887), College of the Holy Cross (1843), Worcester Polytechnic Institute (1868), Assumption College (1910), a state normal school (1871), and Worcester Academy (1832). The site was settled in 1713. Worcester became a town in 1722 and was chartered as a city in 1848. It was early a transportation center, beginning with the opening of a stage line to Boston in 1783. Power for early manufactures was provided by damming Mill Brook and other small streams. Among the early products were potash, textiles, paper, carpets, and church bells. Pop. (1960) 186,587.

WORCESTER AREA C. OF C.
Worcester is one of the primary industrial and cultural centers of Massachusetts. In the middle of the city, above, are museums, churches, frame homes, and factories.

WORCESTER, municipal borough, W England, capital of Worcestershire; on the river Severn; 105 miles NW of London. Gloves, boots and shoes, porcelain, wines, sauce, and vinegar are manufactured. The cathedral is on the site of one built by St. Wulfstan in the eleventh century. Other notable buildings are the Guildhall, Market Hall, the Commandery, St. Oswald's Hospital, and the Royal Porcelain Works. The Battle of Worcester was fought there in 1651, during the English Civil War, between forces of Charles II and Oliver Cromwell. Pop. (1951) 59,700.

WORCESTER POLYTECHNIC INSTITUTE. See COLLEGES AND UNIVERSITIES.

WORCESTERSHIRE, county, central England, bounded by the counties of Staffordshire on the N, Warwickshire on the E, Gloucestershire on the S, Herefordshire on the W, and Shropshire on the NW; area 699 sq. mi.; pop. (1951) 522,974. The terrain of the county is generally undulating. Two hilly areas are Wyre Forest in the northwest, and the Clent Hills in the northeast. The rivers Severn and Avon drain the county to the southwest. In the southeast is the Vale of Evesham, where apples, pears, plums, and hops are grown. Coal is mined in the north near Dudley, and in the Severn Valley in the northwest. Carpets are manufactured at Kidderminster, and fireclay at Stourbridge. Other industrial towns are Dudley, noted for glassware, and Redditch where needles are manufactured. The capital is the cathedral city of Worcester.

WORDEN, JOHN LORIMER, 1818–97, U.S. naval officer, was born in Westchester County, N.Y. In 1835 he entered the Navy as a midshipman. In January, 1862, during the Civil War, he was given command of the famous ironclad *Monitor* and superintended the last stages of its construction. He took the vessel to Hampton Roads, Va., where on March 9 he engaged in battle with the Confederate ironclad *Merrimac* (see MONITOR AND MERRIMAC). He received the thanks of Congress and was promoted to commander. In 1863, commanding the monitor *Montauk*, he destroyed the privateer *Nashville* under the guns of Fort McAllister, and participated in the bombardment of Charleston on April 7. He attained the rank of rear admiral, 1872, and retired in 1886.

WORD GAMES AND PUZZLES, forms of mental and verbal recreation involving the use of words, are among the most ancient means of entertainment; they probably grew out of magic spells and charms, the words of which were supposed to possess magical powers. Thus, one might be able to free oneself from a spell by saying the words of the spell backwards, thereby unwinding it; and perhaps the oldest word game of all, the riddle, once had a deadly serious purpose—he who could not answer the riddle remained forever in the riddler's thrall.

A favorite game of the ancient Greeks and Romans was the creation of palindromes, which are, in effect, spells that can not be unwound. A palindrome is a word or sentence that reads the same backward or forward, as, the first man's supposed first words to his new mate: "Madam, I'm Adam." Another example of a palindromic sentence is Napoleon's imaginary lament, "Able was I ere I saw Elba." Probably the most famous palindrome is the ancient Latin, *Sator Arepo tenet opera rotas* (The sower Arepo held the wheels at work). This palindrome is remarkable in that it can also form a palindromic square that can be read four ways:

```
S A T O R
A R E P O
T E N E T
O P E R A
R O T A S
```

Riddles appear in ancient Egyptian literature, in the Bible, and in the earliest Greek literature. The famous riddle of the Sphinx was, according to legend, answered correctly by Oedipus; he thereby freed

Thebes from the hold of the Sphinx, which was so vexed at having the riddle solved that it killed itself. One of the more elegant phrasings of this riddle is this: "What goes on four feet, on two feet, and three; but the more feet it goes on, the weaker it be?" The answer was, "Man, who crawls as a baby, then walks upright, then uses a cane."

In the Middle Ages riddles were often philosophical or religious in tone as: "Three is one and one is three; believe it not and Hell you'll see" (The Trinity). During the eighteenth century, riddle-making, usually in verse form, became a game, and one who had a reputation as a brilliant riddler was much envied.

In modern times riddles became longer and less elegant, often depending less on the "wisdom" of the one tested than on his cleverness with puns. Many modern riddles take the form of complex mathematical problems (see MATHEMATICS FOR RECREATION). Others are exercises in logic and semantics, such as the following: An explorer is visiting an island inhabited by two rival tribes; the members of the one tribe always tell the truth; the members of the other invariably lie. While making his way to a village, the explorer comes to a fork in the road; a native happens by, but the explorer has no way of telling to which tribe he belongs. What single question can elicit a reply that will tell him which road to take whether the native is a truth-teller or a liar? The explorer points to one of the roads and asks, "If I were to ask you if this road leads to the village, would you answer 'Yes'?" If he is pointing to the wrong road the answer will be "No" whether the native is a liar or a truth teller. The explorer is actually making two inquiries in one, and the liar naturally lies in reply to both. To the query, "Is this the road to the village?" the liar would answer "Yes"—since it is not. To the explorer's real question, "Would you answer 'Yes'?" the native must lie and say "No." A truth-teller would naturally answer "Yes" to both questions. If the road pointed to was the right road, a native of either tribe would be forced to answer "Yes."

Puzzles. One of the oldest and most popular word puzzles is the anagram. An anagram is made by transposing the letters of a word or phrase to form another word or phrase. A good anagram should relate to the original word: "merchandise—nice red hams;" or "penitentiary—nay, I repent it." The origin of anagrams is obscure, but they reached their height of popularity at the French court prior to the Revolution. Louis XIII had a royal anagrammist in his retinue. See ANAGRAM.

Another form of word puzzle is the acrostic, a poem in which the first letter of each line, when read from top to bottom, forms a word. The word acrostic was first used by the Greeks in reference to the utterances of the sibyls, who sometimes wrote each line of a prophecy on a separate sheet of paper. The first letter of the first word on each sheet spelled the name of the person to whom the prophecy was directed (see ACROSTIC). During the twentieth century the double-acrostic supplanted the simpler form. The double-acrostic has two "uprights" formed by the first and last letters of words (called "lights") found by clues, which may be given in verse form. The uprights give the answer to the puzzle. An example of a simple double-acrostic: Puzzle: He would be most likely to sing "God Save the King."

Clues: 1. A vertical piece of wood forming the side of an opening.
2. Russian Secret Service (initials).
3. High land.
4. Character in Dickens: "Little_____."

Solution: 1. J A M B
2. O G P U
3. H I L L
4. N E L L

The uprights form the name "John Bull."

The rebus, another word puzzle of ancient origin, is closely related to hieroglyphics. In a simple rebus, pictures stand for letters or words; when the pictures are properly identified and "read," the letters form a word or the words form a sentence.

Probably the most popular twentieth century puzzle, especially in the United States, is the crossword puzzle. See CROSSWORD PUZZLE.

WORDSWORTH, WILLIAM, 1770–1850, English poet, was born in Cockermouth, Cumberland, in northwest England. His father was an attorney; his mother, Anne Cookson, was the daughter of a merchant in nearby Penrith. He had three brothers and a sister, Dorothy, who became his lifelong confidante. Both parents were dead before Wordsworth was 17; they left an involved estate and the orphaned family was largely dependent on unsympathetic relatives.

Political Enthusiasms. Wordsworth attended Hawkshead Grammar School, 1778–87, near his home; and St. John's College, Cambridge, 1787–91. He considered the instruction in St. John's mediocre and his associates were rather a bore, but during his vacations he took long journeys through regions of natural beauty; most important was a walking tour through France to the Alps, 1790. The mountains awed him, and the progress of the French Revolution excited his political passions. On graduation, January, 1791, he moved to London, but declined to adopt a profession and in November returned to France, where he became involved in an affair of the heart with a young lady of Blois, Annette Vallon, who gave birth, 1792, to Wordsworth's daughter, Caroline, whom he was not to see until 1802. Partly through the influence of Michel Beaupuy, a soldier idealist who reminded him of the noblest republicanism of ancient Rome, Wordsworth's devotion to the revolution was intensified and he became an enthusiastic Girondin and associated with members of the party in Paris. The outbreak of war between France and England was a shock to him; back in his own country he felt a painful separation from the feelings of his countrymen. In the vain hope of making money by his verse, he brought out in 1793 *An Evening Walk* and *Descriptive Sketches*, in which his responses to nature were clouded by the poetic diction of the time. He responded to the political and ethical ideas of William Godwin, and under their influence, 1795–96, wrote *Guilt and Sorrow* and a grim poetic drama, *The Borderers*.

Friendship with Coleridge. Aided by a convenient bequest he took a cottage at Racedown, Dorsetshire, and lived there, 1795–97, with his sister Dorothy, who went with him to Alfoxden, Somersetshire, near Bristol, so that they might have daily association with Samuel Taylor Coleridge, who was living at Nether Stowey. The friendship between Wordsworth and Coleridge was fruitful to both, for each suggested subjects and modes of treatment to the other, and Wordsworth even wrote a few lines that were to remain in the text of Coleridge's *The Rime of the Ancient Mariner*; but Coleridge's more theoretic mind had a much more effective impact upon Wordsworth's. In the *Lyrical Ballads* (1798), the "Ancient Mariner" appeared between the same covers with Wordsworth's "Tintern Abbey." In the unconventional simplicity of the language and in the choice of realistic situations from common rural life, the collection challenged established standards of poetry. For a long time Wordsworth and Coleridge were to be pursued by the hue-and-cry that began over *Lyrical Ballads*; and it was to explain and justify his unconventionality that Wordsworth wrote his most famous prose composition, the "Preface" to the second edition of the *Ballads* (1800).

Autobiography in Blank Verse. By 1798 Wordsworth's enthusiasm for the revolutionary cause had waned. Of many reasons for this change of heart, the decisive one appears to have been the aggressiveness of French foreign policy, as shown in the invasion of Switzerland. Wordsworth surveyed the development of his character and opinions in *The Prelude* (1850), a very long (14 books) autobiographical poem in blank verse, which contains much of his best writing. It was begun before 1800 and he had a complete draft by 1805, but he rewrote it completely at least four times and was constantly revising the successive drafts; the final draft, set down in 1839, was published posthumously in 1850. As a poetic work the final draft is perhaps superior to the draft of 1805, but this earliest draft is more precious as a revelation of the poet's mind and inner being, and is more dependable, forthright, and candid.

A Lyrical Stamp Agent. In 1799 he moved with Dorothy to the Lake Country in which he had grown up, and established a simple household at Grasmere. In 1802 he married Mary Hutchinson, the daughter of a tobacco importer in Penrith, and a friend of his youth. In 1813 he moved to a larger house at Rydal Mount, his final home. In the same year he was given the distributorship of stamps for Westmoreland (and later for Cumberland, too), and in this moderately paid and undemanding office he was able to maintain his family after the Spartan fashion desired by himself and his wife, without having to do hackwork. Dorothy remained part of the household, of course, a source of bother and sorrow after 1835 when her mind began to give way.

The Classic Odes. The *Poems* (1807) mark an intellectual advance on the *Lyrical Ballads*, especially in such pieces as the odes to "Duty" and on the "Intimations of Immortality," which have a grandeur of form and thought matched only by the Tintern Abbey lines—if there. Another admirable collection, *The White Doe of Rylstone* (1815) contains the austere and stoical "Laodamia." In 1814 Wordsworth had brought out *The Excursion*, a poem in blank verse, twice as long as *The Prelude*. Long as it is, *The Excursion* was but a third of Wordsworth's original project, which was to be called *The Recluse*. The first part of the project, *The Prelude*, he described as the "antechapel"; *The Excursion* as the "gothic church"; and many of his shorter pieces as "little cells and oratories." Only the first book of the third part was completed, and it remained unpublished until 1888. *The Excursion* is undeniably central to Wordsworth's conception of his work, and an understanding of it indispensable for the study of his thought—of which it offers the most comprehensive and perfectly articulated expression; it is seldom read, however, and in poetic quality and general interest is in the main far inferior to *The Prelude*.

It is commonly believed that the poems written after 1815, when Wordsworth turned 45, add little to his achievement. Admittedly, they are seldom quite "new," many are prosaic, and some are extremely tedious. Yet to the very end of his life Wordsworth occasionally produced sonnets and lyrics of unalloyed beauty.

Fame. After 1820, and markedly after 1830, Wordsworth's poetry became exceedingly popular. There were many collected editions. Younger poets learned from him. Official respect was shown, 1843, when he was named to succeed Robert Southey as poet laureate.

Shortly after putting the finishing touches on a new six-volume edition of his poems, Wordsworth died at Rydal Mount. He was buried at Grasmere. C. H. Patton assembled a bibliography, *Amherst Wordsworth Collection* (1936); Cornell University Library compiled a *Bibliography of The Wordsworth Collection* (1939); E. De Selincourt edited his *Letters: The Later Years* (1939).   EDWARD KILLORAN BROWN

BIBLIOG.–Lascelles Abercrombie, *Art of Wordsworth* (1952); Frederick W. Bateson, *Wordsworth: A Re-interpretation* (1954); Arthur Beatty, *William Wordsworth: His Doctrine and Art in Their Hist. Relations* (1961); Frances M. B. Blanshard, *Portraits of Wordsworth* (1959); Peter Burra, *Wordsworth* (Great Lives Ser.) (1957); Charles N. Coe, *Wordsworth and the Literature of Travel* (1953); John F. Danby, *Simple Wordsworth: Studies in the Poems, 1797–1807* (1960); Helen Darbishire, *Poet Wordsworth* (1950); Ernest De Sélincourt, *Wordsworthian, and other Studies* (1947); Henry C. Duffin, *Way of Happiness: A Reading of Wordsworth* (1948); Malcolm Elwin, *First Romantics* (1948); David Ferry, *Limits of Mortality: An Essay on Wordsworth's Major Poems* (1959); George M. Harper, *William Wordsworth: His Life, Works and Influence* (2 vols.) (1960); Raymond D. Havens, *Mind of a Poet* (1941); John Jones, *Egotistical Sublime: A History of Wordsworth's Imagination* (1957); Norman Lacey, *Wordsworth's View of Nature, and Its Ethical Consequences* (1948); Catherine M. Maclean, *Dorothy and William Wordsworth* (1927); Florence Marsh, *Wordsworth's Imagery* (1952); Marian Mead, *Studies in Wordsworth* (1929); George W. Meyer, *Wordsworth's Formative Years* (1943); David Perkins, *Quest for Permanence: The Symbolism of Wordsworth, Shelley and Keats* (1959); Herbert E. Read, *Wordsworth* (1949); Henry Crabb Robinson, *Correspondence with the Wordsworth Circle (1808–1866)* (2 vols.) (1927); Elsie Smith, ed., *Estimate of William Wordsworth by His Contemporaries, 1793–1822* (1932); James C. Smith, *Study of Wordsworth* (1946); Newton P. Stallknecht, *Strange Seas of Thought: Studies in William Wordsworth's Philosophy of Man and Nature* (1958); Frances Winwar, *Farewell the Banner . . . Three Persons and One Soul . . . Coleridge, Wordsworth and Dorothy* (1938).

WORK, HENRY CLAY, 1832–84, U.S. song writer, was born in Middletown, Conn., and was a printer by trade. Besides his *Marching Through Georgia* (1865), one of the best-known songs of the Civil War, he wrote *Kingdom Coming;* the temperance song long associated with the play *Ten Nights in a Barroom, Come Home, Father; Grandfather's Clock;* and *Lily Dale.*

WORK, HUBERT, 1860–1942, U.S. physician and public official, was born in Marion Center, Pa. He studied medicine at the University of Pennsylvania and went into practice in Colorado, where he founded the Woodcroft Hospital for Mental and Nervous Diseases, 1896. He was U.S. postmaster general, 1922–23, and U.S. secretary of the interior, 1923–28.

WORK, the transference of energy that results when a force is applied to a body in order to move it against some resistance. Thus, work is the displacement of a body by a force. If an accelerating force changes the speed of motion of a body, the force does work against inertia and produces a change in the kinetic energy of the body (see INERTIA; KINETIC ENERGY). To keep a car in steady motion along a road, work is done against the frictional resistance of the air, road, and moving parts of the engine. Such work is transformed into heat. When a body is lifted, the work done against gravity is stored up as potential energy in the body (see ENERGY; HEAT; POTENTIAL ENERGY).

The amount of work done is the product of the force and the distance through which the force acts, provided both force and motion are in the same direction. No work is done on a body by a force that does not move the body, nor on a moving body on which no force is acting to change its speed or direction. A unit of work is the product of a unit of force acting through a unit of distance. So-called absolute units of work are the erg, or dyne-centimeter, in the CGS system; the joule (equal to 10^7 ergs), in the MKS system; and the foot-poundal, in the English FPS system (see CENTIMETER-GRAM-SECOND SYSTEM; ELECTRICAL AND MAGNETIC UNITS; FOOT-POUND-SECOND SYSTEM). Among gravitational, or engineering units of work are the gram-centimeter, the foot-pound, and the ton-mile. The rate at which work is done is called power, and is measured in such units as horsepower and kilowatts.

WORKMAN, WILLIAM HUNTER, 1847–1937, U.S. explorer, was born in Worcester, Mass.; was graduated from Yale 1869, and from the Harvard Medical School, 1872; and practiced medicine in Worcester, 1874–89. His exploring expeditions took him to Europe and Algeria, 1892–96, Ceylon and Java, 1897–99, and to the glaciers and loftier summits of the Himalayas and Karakoram Range, where he reached elevations of more than 23,000 feet, 1892–1912. His wife, Fanny Bullock Workman, accompanied him on most of his ascents and was co-author of *Algerian Memories* (1895), *In the Ice World of Himalaya* (1900), *Through Town and Jungle* (1904), *Ice-Bound Heights of the Mustagh* (1908), *Peaks and Glaciers of Nun Kun* (1909), *The Call of Snowy Hispar* (1910), and other books.

WORKMEN'S COMPENSATION, payments made by employers to industrial employees who have been temporarily or permanently disabled by occupational accidents or illnesses. The amount of compensation is normally established by the state or federal workmen's compensation laws, varying in scope and liberality, that were enacted during the first half of the twentieth century by every state of the United States and by the federal government. Most other industrial nations also passed similar legislation during this period, or had done so earlier.

History. As mechanization of industrial production increased in the nineteenth century, the number of injuries and fatalities resulting from industrial accidents increased alarmingly. English common law, as applied in England and the United States, proved inadequate in meeting this problem, because it left the major share of the burden of such disabilities on the injured workers themselves.

Under common law an injured worker or the survivors of a worker killed on the job could collect no damages unless negligence by the employer could be proved in court. In practice this was difficult, because the employer could usually command superior legal counsel and had an easier time securing witnesses in his behalf. Moreover, under the common law doctrine of contributory negligence, the employer had only to prove that the worker's own negligence had contributed to the accident to be wholly absolved of liability. According to the fellow-servant rule, an employer had no liability if he could prove that the accident was partly attributable to a fellow employee of the injured or deceased party. Finally, the assumption-of-risk doctrine absolved the employer of liability if he could prove that the worker took the job with knowledge of its inherent risks.

Late in the nineteenth century steps were taken to provide a more equitable sharing of industrial employment risks. In England an employers' liability law was passed, 1880; similar laws were passed in the United States by several states and the federal government during the next 30 years. The injured worker was still required to prove negligence on the part of the employer, but the employer's common law defenses were either eliminated or modified. The procedure was still very costly and time-consuming, however, because of the need for court action to establish an employer's liability.

Workmen's compensation laws were enacted in Germany, 1884, Austria, 1887, Hungary, 1891, Norway, 1894, Finland, 1895, and England, 1897; by 1910 all European nations and Russia had such laws. In the United States, Maryland enacted a workmen's compensation law, 1902, but the U.S. Supreme Court soon declared it to be unconstitutional. Attempts by several of the states to pass and retain such legislation continued to fail until 1910, when New York became the first state to enact successful legislation of this type. By 1921, 42 states and 3 territories had enacted workmen's compensation laws; Mississippi was the last state to do so, 1948.

The new philosophy embodied in the workmen's compensation laws held (1) that the price of a finished product should cover all costs of production, including a major proportion of the costs of industrial accidents; (2) that the employer is in a position both to pass the cost of industrial accidents on to the consumer and to bring about a safer work environment, and should therefore pay the initial costs of workmen's compensation insurance, with the hope that employers would tend to eliminate conditions that might result in accidents in order to lower insurance costs; and (3) that labor relations in general, as well as injured workmen, in particular, would benefit if compensation could be collected without having to establish specific incidents of negligence on the part of either employer or employee.

The manner in which workmen's compensation has developed has made it difficult to determine where the final resting place for the cost of the compensation really is. It is thought by some economists that a large portion of the cost may still rest with industrial workers. Even if this is true, however, it is generally believed that the cost is spread over a broader base than it was when it fell almost entirely on the injured workers and their families. It is also thought that the system has provided some limited incentive for the employer to correct the conditions that might result in accidents. Most observers agree that two definite advantages have stemmed from the workmen's compensation system: the two parties spend much less time in court with much less money being taken up in court costs; and the injured worker can collect compensation as a matter of right under the existing legislation without the fear of jeopardizing his employment.

Typical Provisions. In all states some types of employment are not covered. Agricultural workers, casual workers, domestic help, railway employees

WORKMEN'S COMPENSATION ACTS IN THE VARIOUS STATES

Jurisdiction	Type	Second Injury Fund	Occupational Disease Coverage
Alabama	Elective	Yes	Schedule
Alaska	Compulsory	Yes	Full
Arizona	Compulsory	Yes	Schedule
Arkansas	Compulsory	Yes	Schedule
California	Compulsory	Yes	Full
Colorado	Elective	Yes	Schedule
Connecticut	Elective	Yes	Full
Delaware	Compulsory	Yes	Full
District of Columbia	Compulsory	Yes	Full
Florida	Elective	Yes	Full
Georgia	Elective	No	Schedule
Hawaii	Compulsory	Yes	Full
Idaho	Compulsory	Yes	Schedule
Illinois	Compulsory	Yes	Full
Indiana	Elective	Yes	Full
Iowa	Elective	Yes	Schedule
Kansas	Elective	Yes	Schedule
Kentucky	Elective	Yes	Full
Louisiana	Elective	No	Schedule
Maine	Elective	Yes	Schedule
Maryland	Compulsory	Yes	Full
Massachusetts	Compulsory	Yes	Full
Michigan	Compulsory	Yes	Full
Minnesota	Compulsory	Yes	Full
Mississippi	Compulsory	Yes	None
Missouri	Elective	Yes	Full
Montana	Elective	Yes	Schedule
Nebraska	Elective	Yes	Full
Nevada	Compulsory	No	Full
New Hampshire	Compulsory	Yes	Schedule
New Jersey	Elective	Yes	Full
New Mexico	Elective	No	Schedule
New York	Compulsory	Yes	Full
North Carolina	Elective	Yes	Schedule
North Dakota	Compulsory	Yes	Full
Ohio	Compulsory	Yes	Full
Oklahoma	Compulsory	Yes	Schedule
Oregon	Elective	Yes	Full
Pennsylvania	Elective	Yes	Full
Rhode Island	Elective	Yes	Full
South Carolina	Elective	Yes	Full
South Dakota	Elective	Yes	Schedule
Tennessee	Elective	Yes	Schedule
Texas	Elective	Yes	Schedule
Utah	Compulsory	Yes	Full
Vermont	Elective	Yes	Schedule
Virginia	Compulsory	No	Full
Washington	Compulsory	Yes	Full
West Virginia	Elective	Yes	Full
Wisconsin	Compulsory	Yes	Full
Wyoming	Compulsory	Yes	None

engaged in interstate commerce and employees in non-profit organizations or agencies are commonly excluded. Although about half the states permit employers to choose not to come under the jurisdiction of the law, most employers elect to participate because their nonparticipation makes them liable to court action under which they are denied their former common law defenses. Early in the 1960's, probably over half the gainfully employed workers in the United States were covered by workmen's compensation laws. Most of those not covered, with the exception of farm workers, were employed in relatively nonhazardous jobs.

Many states exempt employers from compensation law coverage if they employ fewer than a stipulated number of workers, usually from three to five. The majority of state laws provide compulsory coverage for at least some public employees; in most of these states elected public officials are not covered.

Benefits paid to injured workmen usually depend on three factors: the rate, or percentage of the base pay, stipulated by law; the term, or period of payment; and the fixed, maximum weekly total payment allowed by law. At mid-twentieth century the last factor was all important for most workers because the maximum weekly benefits authorized by many states had not been advanced to keep pace with rising wages; consequently the injured worker reached the ceiling established by the maximum weekly amount before the rate factor could be fully utilized. Maximum weekly benefits in 1958 ranged from $25.00 to slightly over $40.00 and were less than 50 per cent of the average manufacturing worker's weekly wage at that time. Most state laws also limit death benefits to a maximum of $8,000 to $10,000. Death benefits are normally paid in weekly installments that end when a widow remarries or when surviving children attain a specified age.

There are four classes of disability payments: permanent total; permanent partial; temporary total; and temporary partial. The last class is the most common. Benefits decline with a decline in the permanence and extent of the disability. Most state laws provide for medical and hospital benefits, crutches, artificial limbs, and other appliances where needed.

Payments for superficial injuries are eliminated by requiring a waiting period before compensation begins. The most common length of waiting period is seven days. Benefits covering this period are usually paid after the worker has been incapacitated for a specified period of time.

The payment of benefits is secured in most state laws by requiring the employer to insure his liabilities either through a private casualty insurance company or through a state-sponsored fund. In many states employers may also act as self-insurers, subject to approval by the compensation system's administrative agency.

After 1936 almost all states included coverage for occupational diseases in their legislation. The state may provide either schedule coverage, or coverage limited to certain diseases listed in their laws, or blanket coverage of all diseases whose origin is job-associated.

In order to remove the employers' reluctance to hire a person who has suffered a serious, compensable injury, most states maintain second-injury funds. Thus, if an employee is disabled as a result of a second injury, his present employer is liable only for the approximate cost of the last injury; the balance of the benefits comes out of the state's second-injury fund. Some states place in the second-injury fund any death benefits awarded in cases where there are no survivors. Other states endow the fund through general tax receipts.

All workmen's compensation laws cover legally employed minors; some state laws provide extraordinary benefits if illegally employed minors are injured. A few states allow illegally employed minors to sue for damages in addition to the benefits provided by law.

All but five states administer their legislation through a workmen's compensation commission or board whose decisions may be appealed to the courts. Alabama, Louisiana, New Mexico, Tennessee, and Wyoming administer their legislation completely through the courts.

Federal Laws. The federal government has three workmen's compensation laws. The federal Employers' Liability Law (1908) covers interstate railway employees and seamen. The federal Employees' Compensation Act (1916) covers all civil employees of the federal government. The Longshoremen's and Harbor Workers' Compensation Act (1927) applies to workers in the noted industries as well as to employees of private industry in the District of Columbia and employees of private firms engaged in construction work for the federal government outside the United States. In general, federal benefits are more liberal than state benefits.

Weaknesses. Workmen's compensation has been criticized on several points. In the opinion of some observers, chief among these criticisms are: incomplete coverage of occupational diseases; inadequate rehabilitation of injured workers; inadequate maximum benefits; inefficient administration of the program, and inadequate coverage of hazardous employment. See EMPLOYERS' LIABILITY.   CHESTER A. MORGAN

WORKS PROJECTS ADMINISTRATION, known as WPA, 1935–44, the national work relief agency of the New Deal administration of U.S. President Franklin D. Roosevelt, was organized, May, 1935, as the Works Progress Administration, and reorganized by the president's Reorganization Plan No. 1, 1939, as the Works Projects Administration. The purpose of the WPA was to provide work for needy unemployed persons through a program of public work projects in co-operation with federal, state, and local sponsors.

By the end of 1935 the WPA had established regional offices to supervise and administer the work relief program in each state, and to review projects suggested by local, state, and federal agencies. A project having been approved, the WPA employed, supervised, and paid the workers, all of whom, with the exception of certain specialists, had to hold eligibility certificates issued by the Federal Emergency Relief Administration (FERA) and the U.S. Employment Service. An unemployed person who refused to accept a job in private industry would be refused a certificate or, if already employed by the WPA, would lose his certification. After 1939 local sponsors of a WPA project were required to pay 25 per cent of its cost. As a part of a general reorganization of the executive departments, 1939, the Works Projects Administration was incorporated in the Federal Works Agency. WPA activities were gradually co-ordinated with the national defense program from its beginnings in 1940, but not until after the Japanese attack on Pearl Harbor, Dec. 7, 1941, were all nondefense projects terminated; thereafter only war service and community health and welfare projects were continued. In December, 1942, Congress authorized the liquidation of WPA, and on June 30, 1944, it came to an end.

The Primary Purpose of WPA was to provide work relief to those needing it. The law required that 95 per cent of all persons hired must hold FERA certificates; so that specialists and technicians who might not be available on the relief rolls could be hired when necessary, the law permitted the hiring of 5 per cent uncertified personnel. Only one person in a family could be employed by the WPA; the minimum age for eligible workers was 18. Every six months the FERA sought to determine whether a person continued to be needy and unemployed. In order to emphasize the temporary nature of the work, Congress provided, 1939, that no person could be employed on a project for more than 18 consecutive months; persons dropped as a result of this 18-month rule might, however, be recertified after a month and re-employed immediately.

Wages and Hours. The WPA security wages were well above the scale of direct relief but substantially below the wages paid in private industry. At the project's beginning, the wages varied from $19 to $94 monthly, according to skill, prevailing wages in the community, and the local level of the cost of living. The wage scale was raised in 1938, and in 1939. The law of 1939 provided for the payment of a prevailing hourly wage; each worker then had to work the number of hours necessary to give him his security wage. The result was a very wide variation in the working hours, even within one project. In 1939, against strong union opposition, the prevailing hourly wage provision was abrogated; the law set up instead an 8-hour day, a 40-hour week, and a 130-hour month for all WPA workers.

WPA ACTIVITIES

From July 1, 1935, until June 30, 1943, a total of $10.75 billion of WPA funds was expended; project sponsors made $2.84 billion available for the activities of the program. More than 8.5 million persons were given employment. The number of workers on WPA rolls varied from month to month as well as year to year. The highest number employed in any one month was 3.24 million, in November, 1938.

The laws provided that WPA projects should be socially useful and not competitive with private enterprise. In addition, certain types of projects were specifically banned by Congress and others were specifically recommended. An attempt was made to avoid merely "makework" projects such as those of the Civil Works Administration, an earlier federal work relief agency. An effort was made to take care of all occupational groups found on the relief rolls, among which were industrial workers, technicians, clerks and other white-collar workers, professional men and women, writers, musicians, and artists.

Construction Projects were most numerous in the WPA program. The agency's workers built or improved more than 651,000 miles of roads and streets; constructed about 78,000 new bridges and reconstructed about 46,000 others; built 353 new airplane landing fields, more than 4.76 million feet of new runways, and improved other airport facilities; erected about 35,000 new buildings and renovated about 90,000 old ones; installed or improved almost 28,000 miles of storm and sanitary sewers and nearly 20,000 miles of water mains; constructed or improved about 4,000 water or sewage treatment plants, pumping stations and other utility plants; and constructed or improved more than 8,000 parks, 1,000 new swimming and wading pools, 10,000 tennis courts, and several thousand playgrounds and athletic fields.

The Federal Writers Project, organized by states, published excellent guidebooks for each of the conterminous 48 states and for many cities and regions, and in addition made collections of materials dealing with local folklore and traditions. Although out of date in many respects by 1960, for many states the WPA guides remained the best single-volume reference source. The WPA Historical Records Survey, also organized by states, published hundreds of volumes giving inventories of public records especially of counties, but also of other governmental units and agencies. Libraries, museums, and archives were helped in cleaning and improving their facilities.

WPA Artists painted numerous murals in post offices and other public buildings. Theater projects in many large cities presented plays that attracted large audiences, and WPA orchestras were operated in some of the large cities. Projects were also set up for other professional groups.

Other Activities. WPA workers made 383 million garments and 118 million other household articles for distribution to needy families and public institutions. They conducted more than 32 million visits to families in need of housekeeping assistance, and served more than 1.2 million lunches to school children. The recreational and educational projects served millions of persons; thousands of illiterates learned to read and write and many foreign-born persons studied English and citizenship with WPA assistance. The National Youth Administration, organized within the WPA, gave part-time employment to youths aged 16 to 24, enabling hundreds of thousands of young people to continue in school and to gain work experience.

FRANK L. ESTERQUEST

WORLAND, city, N central Wyoming, seat of Washakie County; on the Big Horn River, the Burlington Railroad, and U.S. highways 16 and 20; about 118 miles NW of Casper. The city is a trade and processing center for an irrigated agricultural area. Livestock is fed there during the winter. Grain and bean elevators, beet-sugar factories, and oil refineries are there. Pop. (1960) 5,806.

WORLD BANK. See BANK FOR RECONSTRUCTION AND DEVELOPMENT, INTERNATIONAL.

WORLD COUNCIL OF CHURCHES, an ecumenical fellowship of Christian denominations, organized officially in 1948, with headquarters in Geneva, Switzerland (see ECUMENICAL MOVEMENT). Beginning with the modern ecumenical movement at the Edinburgh Conference, 1910, the World Council of Churches was first proposed in 1937 and organized provisionally at Utrecht, the Netherlands, 1938, with Archbishop William Temple of Canterbury as its first president. According to the constitution that was drawn up in the same year, its purposes are (1) "to carry on the work of the two world movements of Faith and Order and Life and Work; (2) to facilitate common action by the churches; (3) to promote co-operation in study; (4) to promote the growth of ecumenical consciousness in the members of all churches; (5) to establish relations with denominational federations of worldwide scope and with other ecumenical movements; and (6) to call world conferences on specific subjects as occasion may require, such conferences being empowered to publish their own findings." In furtherance of these goals the council publishes several periodicals. World Assemblies were held in Amsterdam, Netherlands, 1948; in Evanston, Ill., 1954; and in New Delhi, India, 1961. In 1959, there were 172 affiliated denominations, chiefly Protestant and Orthodox, comprising more than 150 million members in 50 or more countries.

WORLD COURT. See COURTS, INTERNATIONAL.

WORLD GOVERNMENT, a theoretical international system in which some or all governmental powers formerly held by sovereign states would be held by an international authority. Plans for achieving world government range from the strengthening of economic and political ties between and among nations to the formal establishment of a constitutional order with final authority over all political and economic matters.

Before World War I, such thinkers as William Penn and Immanuel Kant proposed utopian plans for international political systems. Subsequently, two conferences at The Hague, Netherlands, 1899 and 1907, attempted to codify existing international law and establish a world court to settle disputed international legal questions; however, the court had no effective means of enforcing its decisions. The League of Nations, founded in 1919, was the first international agency that was to regulate national conflicts actively, but the league's power depended on the voluntary co-operation of member states; lacking the full support of the major world powers, most notably the United States, the league was unable to cope with German, Italian, and Japanese military aggression during the 1930's (see LEAGUE OF NATIONS). During World War II plans for a United Nations (UN) organization were formulated and approved by the major Allied powers, and the United Nations came into being, 1945. The UN Charter established a Security Council empowered to enforce UN decisions by force if necessary, but the council's actions required agreement between the major powers, and when the Western powers and the Soviet Union became estranged (the Cold War, so-called), the Security Council's ability to act effectively was vitiated. See UNITED NATIONS.

During the 1950's many advocates of world government viewed regional confederations as first steps toward an international political system. In West Europe progress was made toward co-ordination of national economic and military policies, and some political co-operation was achieved as a result. International agencies, such as the European Coal and Steel Community and the European Atomic Energy Community, were given power to make binding decisions for member states. In addition, two rival trading blocs—the six-member European Economic Community and the seven-member European Free Trade Association—were committed to the establishment of uniform external tariffs and free interchange of peoples and goods between their own member nations. See INTERNATIONALISM; INTERNATIONAL LAW; INTERNATIONAL ORGANIZATION; SOVEREIGNTY.

WORLD HEALTH ORGANIZATION. See UNITED NATIONS, Specialized Agencies, *The World Health Organization (WHO)*.

WORLD PEACE FOUNDATION, a nonprofit organization founded, 1910, by Edwin Ginn, U.S. educational publisher, for the purpose of promoting peace, justice, and good will among nations. The organization seeks to increase public understanding of international problems by an objective presentation of the facts of international relations through its publications and by the maintenance of a documents library and a reference library, which furnish information on current international problems. Among its publications are *International Organization*, a quarterly journal dealing with various aspects of international co-operation, and *Documents on American Foreign Relations*, an annual covering United States foreign policy.

The documents library, located at Boston, Mass., is famous for its League of Nations collection. The library was expanded after World War II to contain the complete documentation of such international organizations as the United Nations, the Food and Agriculture Organization, the International Bank for Reconstruction and Development, the International Civil Aviation Organization, the International Labor Organization, the International Monetary Fund, the World Health Organization, the Pan American Union, the Far Eastern Commission, and the United Nations Relief and Rehabilitation Administration. It also has extensive documentation of such organizations as the International Telecommunications Union, the International Refugee Organization, the International Trade Organization, and the International Commission for Air Navigation.

WORLD SERIES. See BASEBALL.

WORLD'S FAIR. See EXPOSITION.

The global scale of World War I set a new pattern for combat in the twentieth century.

WORLD WAR I, 1914–18, also called the Great War and the European War, was fought on three continents and the oceans at a cost of about 10 million dead, 20 million wounded, and nearly $200 billion spent directly in furtherance of the war. On one side were the Allies, a coalition of more than 25 nations and associated countries, the chief of whom were France; the United Kingdom and the British Empire; Russia; the United States; Italy; and Japan. On the other side were the Central Powers consisting of Germany; Austria-Hungary; the Ottoman Empire (Turkey); and Bulgaria. The Allies were ultimately the victors, and dictated the several peace treaties, concluded 1919–20, formally ending hostilities.

Origins of the War. The outbreak of war in Europe, July 28, 1914, came about largely as a result of power relationships, under development from 1871, if not before, that were manifested formally in the Triple Alliance of Germany, Austria-Hungary, and Italy, and the Triple Entente of Great Britain, France, and Russia (see TRIPLE ALLIANCE; TRIPLE ENTENTE). As the offspring of efforts by the various powers to secure economic and military advantages over other powers, these alignments had, by early twentieth century, involved their members in a complexity of military commitments and in arms-building programs from which, as events proved, war was to result.

Symptomatic of the mounting tension that culminated in World War I were the two Balkan Wars, 1912 and 1913, in the course of which several Balkan countries wrested territory from the Ottoman Empire. These wars, which saw the rise of Serbia as a significant power, were encouraged by czarist Russia, which sought to enhance its position in southeastern Europe as champion of the Slavs. Austria, whose hold over a large Slavic population was insecure, had wanted to intervene on behalf of the Ottoman Empire and attack Serbia, but had been stopped by Germany, which was committed to support Austria under the Triple Alliance but wished that there be no general war at that time (see BALKAN WARS). Thus, the assassination, June 28, 1914, of Archduke Francis Ferdinand, heir-apparent to the Austro-Hungarian throne, and his wife, by a Serbian terrorist at Sarajevo, Bosnia, provided Austria with a fairly plausible excuse to strike down Serbia and thus protect the empire against Slav nationalism (see SLAVS, *Pan-Slavism*). Although there was no proof that Serbia was directly implicated in the assassination plot, Austria sent Serbia an ultimatum, July 23, demanding concessions so stringent that it was expected Serbia would reject it, and thus give Austria an excuse to attack. Serbia's reply, delivered two minutes before the 48-hour deadline expired, July 25, was conciliatory but ambiguous; on the basis of the ambiguity, Austria declared war on Serbia, July 28. Russia, meanwhile, had promised to give military aid to Serbia in the event of an attack; France had assured Russia of its support; Great Britain had proposed mediation of the crisis; and Germany had warned each of the Entente Powers not to interfere.

Upon learning of Austria's declaration of war against Serbia, Russia mobilized. There ensued a flurry of diplomatic exchanges between the Great Powers. Germany demanded a halt to mobilization by Russia and France; Germany promised Great Britain that it would not attack France if the former would pledge France's neutrality; Great Britain requested that Germany respect the neutrality of Belgium, in the event Germany should decide to attack France. These negotiations proved to be futile. Germany declared war on Russia, August 1, and on France, August 3—having invaded Belgium, August 2, en route to France. Great Britain now had no choice but to declare war on Germany, and did so on August 4. See EUROPE, History, *The Triple Entente Versus the Triple Alliance*, *The Near East and the Balkans*, and *World War I*.

The German Plan. Germany planned to strike rapidly against France and then, with France crushed, to deal with the proverbially "slow" Russians. Since the strong fortress system along the French frontier might prove to be a time-consuming obstacle, the Germans invaded France by way of Belgium. This plan had been adopted, 1905, by Count Alfred von Schlieffen, then chief of the German general staff, on the theory that its military advantages outweighed other considerations, including the practical danger of British hostility. Schlieffen's plan concentrated the

WORLD WAR I

"We are saving you, YOU save FOOD"

Well fed Soldiers WILL WIN the WAR

Americans and Canadians were urged to speed production and conserve food through nationwide poster campaigns.

NATL. ARCHIVES

"No Man's Land," the unoccupied land between hostile front-line trenches, was a desolate area of ruin and death.

NATL. ARCHIVES

The foot soldier performed the major role in World War I. Here, German troops move to the front in France, 1918.

ACME

General Pershing (right) arrived in Boulogne, June 13, 1917. With him is one-armed French General Pelletier.

At a time of crisis, Parisian taxicabs took French troops to the front during the First Battle of the Marne, 1914.

After overcoming stalwart resistance in Belgium, the victorious German forces carried the offensive into France, crossing the southern border of Belgium, August, 1914.

mass of the German forces on the right (western) wing for a gigantic wheel through Belgium and northern France. If the French forces took the offensive against the German left wing, its very weakness would be an asset. Like a revolving door, the more heavily the French pressed on one side, the more forcefully would the other side swing round behind them. From a German point of view, the French war plan was ideal, for most French theorists were intoxicated with the belief that all virtue and wisdom lay in the offensive, and had from 1912 molded French military policy accordingly. Since they themselves relied only on their active-service troops, the French included only German regulars in their calculations; in fact, the Germans made good use of reservists in their striking force.

WESTERN FRONT, 1914

Invasion of France. Having taken the forts and city of Liège, the Germans poured rapidly into the Belgian plain, swept forward, and reached the French frontier on schedule. Had the French reinforced Belgian resistance, the Germans might have been held up on the line Namur-Antwerp, but the French were intent on their own dream-offensive; thus, while the Germans swept easily through Belgium, the French hurled their two right wing armies across the Lorraine frontier of Germany, Aug. 14, 1914, into a trap from which they recoiled in disorder. They were able to regain their fortified frontier, however, and rallied in its shelter. Marshal Joseph Joffre's right hand blow in Lorraine having failed, he struck a left hand blow at the supposedly weak German center in Belgian Luxembourg, August 21. Blundering forward into the wooded Ardennes, the two French armies ran slantwise into the advancing Germans and suffered a fresh defeat.

The Germans failed to realize or exploit this opportunity, but in western Belgium, beyond the Meuse, three German armies rapidly closed in upon the French Fifth Army on the extreme left, and the little British Expeditionary Force alongside it. With these forces Joffre had intended to envelop the German right wing; instead, they were outflanked and outnumbered and fell back just in time to escape disaster. With all of his armies in retreat, Joffre at last sensed that all was not going well. Resolutely, he drew troops from his right wing to create a new striking force on his left that he could use against the enemy's marching flank. But this new plan soon collapsed, and the newly formed Sixth Army fell back to shelter within the fortified zone of Paris.

German Errors. The impression in the German camp that victory had virtually been won coincided with news of an emergency on the Russian front, and Gen. Helmuth von Moltke sent several corps to deal with it. He further weakened his right wing by detailing many troops to guard his communications through Belgium. Thus, in the decisive test on the

Marne, the German right flank was greatly outnumbered. In addition, German supply lines were strained by the Belgians' destruction of the bridges over the Meuse. It also became impossible for the Germans to reinforce their right wing with troops from their left. The German generals, especially Gen. Alexander von Kluck, increased the weakness of their own situation by outrunning such supplies as they had, so that troops, already exhausted from forced marches in August heat, had also to forage for food. And finally, the French telegraph system having been destroyed by German cavalry, Moltke lost touch with his army commanders.

The Battle of the Marne. Thinking it impossible to make a stand on the Marne, on Sept. 1, 1914, Joffre had ordered the retreat to be continued to a line south of the Seine. The governor of Paris, Joseph Gallieni, having learned, September 3, that the Germans had changed direction in their advance on Paris and were moving across his front, urged Joffre by telephone to sanction a counteroffensive. Joffre hesitated for some hours, decided to continue the retreat, then hesitated again; at this point there was another phone call from Gallieni, who insisted on speaking to Joffre personally. Joffre detested telephones, but Gallieni had proposed Joffre as commander in chief while foregoing it himself from a scruple of honor; Joffre took the call. What passed between them will never be known with certainty. According to his staff and secretaries, Gallieni vehemently urged Joffre to take the counteroffensive and by the force of his arguments gained Joffre's assent. Joffre, according to his own account, told Gallieni that he had already made up his mind to take the counteroffensive in accordance with Gallieni's proposals of that morning. Most authorities hold that Joffre was decisively influenced by "his master's voice."

Although Gallieni's orders to the Sixth Army were issued at 8:30 P.M., Joffre's were not sent out until several hours later and did not reach the armies until early September 5. Both Gen. Louis Franchet d'Esperey, commander of the Fifth Army, and the British felt that it was too late to make a change and their armies continued the retreat for another day. Meanwhile, the Sixth Army moved against the enemy's flank and temporarily unhinged the German right wing; Kluck pulled back half his army to meet the flank threat, and then drew off the rest in the hope of winning a local victory—thereby leaving a gap of 30 miles. The British columns, having turned back to the north, September 6, began moving into the gap, September 9, at a moment when the German leaders were already alarmed by false rumors that large British and Russian forces were disembarking

Improvement of long-range weapons and mechanical transportation during World War I gradually ended the use of horses in warfare. Here, British cavalry go into action.

on the Belgian coast in their rear (in reality these were the 3,000 marines sent as a bluff by Winston Churchill, the first lord of the admiralty); the fresh shock was too much and with German high command approval, the armies of Marshal Karl von Bülow and Kluck fell back in hasty retreat.

The Allies might have converted the retreat into a serious defeat, but moved so cautiously that the Germans were able to reknit their right wing on the Aisne. And now the machine gun began to reveal its full significance, cementing the line into an impenetrable barrier (see GUN, Machine Guns). Tardy as usual in awakening to reality, Joffre wasted several days before he began to grope for an open flank. His northwestward maneuvers, the "race to the sea," were easily forestalled by the Germans, and by October the entrenched front stretched from the Swiss frontier to the English Channel. See MARNE, BATTLES OF THE.

The Struggle at Ypres. Sensitive to the danger of the Belgian army at Antwerp, the Germans initiated a bombardment of Antwerp, September 28. On Churchill's initiative, the British sent belated reinforcements—not enough to prevent the fall of Antwerp, but enough to help the Belgian army to slip safely away down the coast, where, having wisely rejected Joffre's suggestion that the Belgians march inland to join his imagined decisive wing, the Belgians were able to thwart Gen. Erich von Falkenhayn's planned "grand sweep" down the coast following the fall of Antwerp, October 10, by opening the locks and letting in a flood from the sea. This forced the Germans to throw all their weight inland, in the Ypres sector, where the Allied defense had been formed fortuitously by the arrival of the main British army which had just arrived there as part of the left tip of Joffre's latest ineffectual outflanking maneuver. As Gen. Douglas Haig's corps advanced from Ypres it was thrown on the defensive by a German offensive. From October 29, a series of heavy blows crashed on the thin British line, while Foch and Marshal John French, sublimely disregarding reality, went on issuing orders to "continue the advance" although their troops were barely holding the ground. Haig's center was broken on the third day, but the Germans did not exploit their success and in confusion were tumbled back by a local British counterattack; French reserves arrived in growing numbers and took over the southern flank before the German offensive swelled afresh, reaching its climax, November 11.

The storm now at last subsided. Defense had triumphed over attack—the kind of attack upon which, before the war, all the general staffs had assumed success depended. To the German troops it seemed that from "every bush, hedge and fragment of wall" there was "a machine gun rattling out bullets." In fact, however, the British, having started the war with few machine guns, and reduced to still fewer by the time they arrived in Flanders, had depended on their rifle shooting with which, after the lesson given them by the Boers, they had been trained to produce "15 rounds rapid" per minute. But the poverty of their resources and the delusions of the Allied chiefs had increased the strain on the desperately thin line "of tired, haggard and unshaven men, unwashed, plastered with mud, many in little more than rags" that stood between the Germans and their goal. After the first month there was little left of the original British Expeditionary Force. Back home, however, a million volunteers had already come forward, and the new British armies were allowed time to grow during a period of deadlock on the Western Front.

THE RUSSIAN FRONT, 1914

On the Russian front, there was a similar, if less firmly established, deadlock. Marshal Conrad (Count Franz Conrad von Hotzendorff), the Austrian chief,

ARMY WAR COLLEGE
During World War I the artillery was used more effectively and more intensively than in any previous war in history. Here a British howitzer is prepared for firing.

had desired to cut off the Russian forces in the protruding Polish "tongue," by a combined offensive of the Germans from the north side and the Austrians from the south. His allies were disinclined to move until they had settled with France and finally, August 20, the Austrian took the offensive alone. Soon he collided with half of the main Russian forces, who were also advancing southward, and other Russian armies, advancing westward, crashed into his weak flank near Lemberg. Conrad's forces, sorely tried, would probably have been cut off but for the folly of the Russians, whose unciphered wireless orders revealed to Conrad that the Russians were closing on his line of retreat. Just in time, his badly mauled forces fell back 150 miles. Within a month Conrad had lost the province of Galicia and 350,000 of his 900,000 men.

On the Baltic side of Poland, there was disaster for the Russians. To meet the urgent clamor of the French, the Russians had hastened their invasion of East Prussia. One army, under Gen. Pavel Rennenkampf, advanced westward and was met near the frontier by the bulk of the German forces in the east. The issue hovered in the balance and Rennenkampf was about to retreat when he found that the Germans were already retreating to evade another Russian army, under Gen. Aleksandr Samsonov, which had crossed the southern border and threatened the Germans' rear. Gen. Max von Prittwitz, the German commander, telephoned to Moltke to announce that he was about to make a precipitous retreat, and was promptly superseded by Gen. Erich von Ludendorff, who had just won laurels at Liège, but was comparatively junior in rank, and had to be provided with a titular chief—a retired general, Paul von Hindenburg: deference was paid to seniority, but Ludendorff was to be in charge. While Moltke was weakening his right by sending troops to help on the Russian front, one of Prittwitz' staff, Lt. Col. Max Hoffmann, had already initiated a series of moves by which Samsonov's army was to be caught and crushed at Tannenberg (later Stebark, Poland), while Rennenkampf toiled forward with no enemy in front of him, the German forces having been rushed back to strike at Samsonov's flank. Again the swift German moves were made sure by the Russian commanders' habit of sending out unciphered wireless orders that could be easily intercepted and read; in addition, there was no co-ordination of the two Russian armies by the higher command, and the two commanders disliked each other. A total of 90,000 Russian prisoners were taken at Tannenberg, and there would have been more if Ludendorff had not interfered with a contradictory series of orders. The legend of "Tannenberg" made a national hero of the senile Hindenburg, and Ludendorff's military reputation swelled proportionately.

The Austrian disasters soon compelled the Germans to send forces southward, and in October Russia deployed seven armies for a "steamroller" advance through Poland towards Berlin; Allied hopes rose, but Ludendorff dislocated the Russian advance by switching his forces round the northern flank and driving a wedge into the joint near Lódź: the Russians were pushed back toward Warsaw, and the two sides settled down in trench lines astride long-suffering Poland.

THE WAR AT SEA

As the war became a gigantic siege, sea power assumed its historic importance. The German high seas fleet stayed in its harbors waiting, while the British grand fleet in its northern bases exerted a largely invisible domination of the sea. Germany was stripped of her colonies, and her commerce was swept from the sea routes, which remained open for the passage of the merchant ships and transports of Britain and her allies. A New Zealand expedition occupied Samoa, an Australian expedition took New Guinea, and Japan took Tsingtao on the coast of China. In Africa, Togoland was taken in August, 1914; the Cameroons, although a harder obstacle, was conquered by Gen. Louis Botha's expedition; German East Africa, the largest and richest of Germany's colonies, eventually fell to Gen. Jan Christiaan Smuts' expedition, 1915, although the German Gen. Paul von Lettow-Vorbeck continued to wage guerrilla warfare until the end of the war.

Command of the sea meant more to Britain than the capture of German colonies: if the security of sea routes were endangered, Britain's power to sustain the struggle would be paralyzed. The Germans' naval preparations had been concentrated on building battleships for a battle they would not risk. In direct attack on Britain's trade routes, Germany's few cruisers gave much trouble in proportion to their numbers, enough to show what might have been done; but by the end of 1914 the outer seas had been swept clear of German warships, the main German fleet was bottled in the North Sea, and it seemed that the British had definitely achieved command of the sea by which to exert economic pressure on Germany.

Submarine Warfare. In the submarine, however, the Germans had a weapon with which, despite the enemy's surface superiority, they could operate against the approaches to her home ports. In February, 1915, the Germans initiated a submarine campaign against commerce, proclaiming the waters round the British Isles a war zone in which all ships, enemy or neutral, would be sunk on sight. Britain retorted by claiming the right to intercept all ships suspected of carrying goods to Germany, and to bring them into British ports for search. The British thus irked neutral nations, the United States especially, but Germany eased the friction by torpedoing the great liner Lusitania, May 7, 1915: the drowning of 1,100 civilians was more of a shock to U.S. opinion than even the desolation of Belgium, and led the U.S. government to recognize the possibility of participation in the war. The immediate tension was relieved, however, by Germany's promise to modify her submarine action. From that time, however, Anglo-U.S. tension caused by the blockade was to be relieved repeatedly by some fresh German act at sea. Meanwhile, the economic pressure on Germany was gradually tightened, although it was not yet a stranglehold.

WESTERN FRONT, 1915

With the repulse of the German attempt to break through at Ypres the trench barrier was consolidated from the Swiss frontier to the English Channel. Modern defense had triumphed over direct attack, and stalemate ensued. Germany might well have sought peace, helped by the bargaining assets she possessed in her occupation of others' territory, but her military leaders were drugged by Carl von Clausewitz' maxim: "To introduce into the philosophy of war a principle of moderation would be an absurdity. War is an act of violence pushed to its utmost bounds." The maxims of Clausewitz had as tight a grip on the opposing armies, and French leaders particularly were obsessed with the desire to recover lost territory. On both sides leaders, intent on "concentrating superior force at the decisive spot," ignored the awkward fact that the more they concentrated their own forces the easier it was for the enemy to concentrate against them. Thinking of "force" in terms of numbers, the armies neglected the possibilities of mechanical power and in appreciating its effect on their theories. The tale of the obstruction which each new weapon met from those who, as exponents of superior force, had most cause to welcome it, would be incredible were it not established fact.

The military leaders, except for Marshal Horatio Kitchener, remained confident of early victory despite continual disproof. False confidence strengthened the soldiers' unwillingness to modify their creed of concentration against the main enemy, to seek a way round the trench barrier that faced them along the Western Front; it strengthened their resistance to untried instruments, thus hindering the adoption of new means to overcome the trench barrier. Thus, when the first armored trench-crossing machine, the tank, was demonstrated to Kitchener, he called it "a pretty mechanical toy."

Trench Warfare in the West. Throughout 1915, lured on by the mirage of early victory, the French hurled themselves again and again on the entrenched front; each time Joffre found that the defenses had grown stronger and was amazed. At the end of the year he had blunted the sword of France: the total of casualties had risen from 850,000 in 1914 to nearly 2.5 million. "Nibbling" 500 yards into the German defenses in Champagne cost 50,000 men in February-March; the offensive "was none the less fecund in results," Joffre reported. In April, 60,000 men were lost in the St. Mihiel fiasco. The Germans retorted, April 22, with a more effective salient cut at the other end of the Western Front. During the previous weeks prisoners taken by the French near Ypres had disclosed that the Germans were preparing to use poison gas; the local French commander was impressed, but his superiors were incredulous, so that French troops were defenseless against the strange mist that crept forward from the German trenches against the left of the Ypres salient, April 22. Those who were not suffocated, fled, leaving a gap four miles wide in the front (see CHEMICAL WARFARE). But the Germans themselves had been skeptical of the new weapon, and had allotted no fresh reserves or extra ammunition for the attack. The resistance

German submarines sank hundreds of Allied ships in 1917, threatening to cut off the lines of supply to the British Isles. This U-boat surrendered to the U.S.S. *Fanning.*

LIBRARY OF CONGRESS

Because of the increased use of rapid-fire arms, trench warfare reached its height in World War I. Here, troops on the Western Front are entrenched beside a machine gun.

of the Canadians on the flank of the breach, and the arrival of English and Indian reinforcements, saved the situation, whereupon Foch, anxious to regain the "lost ground, " launched a series of abortive counter attacks in which the British troops served merely as an easy target for German artillery practice.

On May 9, Joffre's postponed offensive was launched, near Arras, with Foch in charge. Joffre predicted that it would be "the beginning of the end," and spoke of "the war being over in three months." The idea of surprise was abandoned in favor of a six-days' bombardment. A force of 18 divisions, with 1,250 guns, was concentrated against a 12-mile sector held by four German divisions. When the futile effort was at last suspended, French losses totaled 102,000; the British, attacking toward Aubers Ridge, had even less success and proportionately higher casualties. See ARRAS, *World War I.*

It was reported to the president that "no single general, not even excepting Foch, has any more faith in an offensive proving successful," but those generals were helpless to save their men from the fatal delusions of the general-in-chief: plans for a fresh offensive went forward. By their adherence to the theoretical ideal of destroying the main army of the main enemy, the allied chiefs eventually encouraged Bulgaria to join the enemy alliance, allowed their own ally Serbia to be overrun, let slip the chance of probing Austria's weakness, and caused hundreds of thousands of unnecessary casualties.

THE MEDITERRANEAN

Turkey's Entry into the War. Following the revolution of Young Turks, 1909, German instructors had permeated the Turkish army, whose chief, Enver Pasha, had been military attaché in Berlin. News of Britain's entry into the war, however, caused so sharp a shock as to produce from Turkey—long Britain's friend—the astonishing offer of an alliance with Russia, Turkey's traditional enemy. Such an alliance did not suit Russia's long-standing aim of annexing Constantinople (later Istanbul), however, and the British admiralty's action in taking over two Turkish battleships, which were being built in British shipyards, tilted the scales additionally in Germany's favor. At the end of October, 1915, the German admiral, with Enver's connivance, led the Turkish fleet in a raid against the Russian ports in the Black Sea. Next, under German dictation, and Enver's ambition for glory, Turkey lost her only efficient force in a December stroke against the Caucasus. Her next venture, to cut the Suez Canal artery to Britain's power in the East, also failed.

For Germay, however, Turkey's entry was desirable as a distraction to British Empire forces, and bolted the Black Sea back gate. Turkey's participation in the war also provided the Allies with an alternative idea for their strategy—that of lopping off Germany's "limbs" before attacking the trunk. Its advocates argued that the enemy alliance should be viewed as

a whole, pointing out that a stroke in some other theater of war would enable Britain to exploit hitherto neglected sea power advantages. Lt. Col. Maurice Hankey, Churchill, the Secretary of the War Council, David Lloyd George, and Kitchener, recognized the futility of the trench war in France. Just as there was a chance of proper investigation of alternative strategies, there came an appeal from Russia for a demonstration to relieve the Turkish pressure on her forces in the Caucasus. Having no troops yet available, Kitchener suggested that a naval demonstration against the Dardanelles might help. Churchill seized upon the suggestion and there ensued the officially "disastrous" Dardanelles Campaign which actually, however, did have important and beneficial effects for the Allies. Throughout the Allied headquarters in France the generals were united in opposing any plan that might take away even a fraction of the troops dedicated to the dream of early victory in the West. Their opposition delayed, and finally strangled, the alternative schemes for a coordinated land-sea endeavor in the soft underbelly of Europe. Only when it appeared that Bulgaria was about to enter the war on the German side were troops made available. Meanwile, the naval attack on the Dardanelles went forward, and no one suggested that it might be withheld until a combined stroke could be delivered by surprise. In February, 1915, the bombardment of the outer forts began; after they had been evacuated by the Turks, demolition parties were landed. The Turkish government made ready to abandon Constantinople; Bulgaria repented her inclination toward the German side; Italy and Greece made fresh moves toward joining the other side. The naval advance continued, but in a desultory way. Under the spur of a telegram from the admiralty, a general fleet attack was launched on March 18. In the interval the Turks had laid mines in a bay where earlier the Allied fleet had freely maneuvered. The forts had been practically silenced and the minesweepers sent in to clear the main passage, when a French battleship struck the unsuspected row of mines and sank in less than two minutes with nearly all hands; two hours later a couple of British battleships struck mines almost simultaneously, and were badly damaged. The admiralty telegraphed that five more battleships were being sent out, and that "it was important not . . . to encourage the enemy by an apparent suspension of the operations." Yet British Adm. John de Robeck decided that he "could not get through" without the help of the army, and in the months that followed made no further attempt to do so, despite much prompting. At the moment that De Robeck had signaled the order for a hasty retirement, however, the Turkish defenders of the straits had been on the verge of collapse: they had no reserve of mines, were short of ammunition, and the gun crews were demoralized. German as well as Turkish officers felt they had little hope of resisting any renewal of the naval attack.

The military attack began under heavy handicaps, the worst being lack of organization. At the War Office not a single preparatory step had been taken. When Sir Ian Hamilton was hurried out to the Dardanelles on a day's notice, the sum of his information comprised a prewar handbook on the Turkish Army, a prewar report on the forts, and an inaccurate map. He found, moreover, that his troops had been so chaotically distributed in their transports that they had to be sent to Alexandria for redistribution, which entailed several weeks' further delay. Meanwhile the Turks were sending in reinforcements. Hamilton's landing was made on April 25, at a number of points in the area. The dispersion of the landing places mystified the enemy so completely that 48 hours passed before they began to concentrate their forces. The opportunity so created went begging, however: many of the troops were inexperienced, and in any case they were outnumbered and insufficiently equipped. Two months passed before the government, under Churchill's vehement prompting, decided to raise Hamilton's force to a total of 12 divisions. By the time these reinforcements arrived, the Turkish strength had risen to 15 divisions. Hamilton's subsequent efforts, through no fault of his, failed to make much headway. At home, the government had lost faith and was anxious to withdraw, but delayed the decision for fear of harming morale, and also of the loss that might be suffered in the process of evacuation. When Ian Hamilton declared in favor of continuing, he was replaced by Sir Charles Monro, commander of an army in France. Asked to report on the Dardanelles situation, Monro visited several beachheads in a single morning, without going farther, while his chief of staff, still on board ship, was already drafting Monro's recommendation for evacuation. Kitchener refused to sanction the withdrawal at first, and hurried out to investigate; but adverse gusts of opinion at home were developing into a gale and reluctantly he consented to the evacuation, which was carried out late in December, and early in January, 1916. As the last craft moved off from Helles, January 8, the dark sky was suddenly reddened with the glare of blazing dumps. Thus ended a farsighted venture that had been wrecked by a chain of errors hardly rivaled in history.

Even though it failed, the Gallipoli expedition had upset the whole war plan of the Germans for 1915. The menace to Austria, quivering under the pressure from Russia and Serbia, became obvious when the Dardanelles attack opened. Falkenhayn felt that he must cut out the Serbian ulcer from Austria's side before it was swollen by Allied reinforcements. But before he could even do this the Russians must be pushed back to a safe distance. See DARDANELLES, *World Wars I and II;* SALONIKA CAMPAIGNS.

EASTERN FRONT, 1915

The early months of 1915 saw the Russians pushing back the Austrians in southern Poland. The long-invested fortress of Przemysl, with 120,000 men, fell into the Russians' hands, March 23, and they gained the passes of the Carpathians, threatening to pour into the plains of Hungary. Deciding that he must help the Austrians to drive back the Russians before even cutting a route to Turkey through Serbia, Falkenhayn accepted Conrad's plan for a flank stroke on the north of the Carpathians in the Görlitz-Tarnow sector. The thrust easily pierced the shallow Russian front, May 3, and by May 14 an 80-mile advance, to the San, had been achieved. Falkenhayn's armies broke through the newly knit front and the Russian armies relapsed into a prolonged retreat, abandoning a 400-mile stretch of territory and leaving 400,000 prisoners in the enemy's hands. Rejecting Ludendorff's misgivings, Falkenhayn sanctioned an offensive northward to cut off the Russian forces in the Polish salient, with the aid of a converging attack from East Prussia. The Russians extricated themselves from the Polish salient, but lost 750,000 prisoners. The failure of the British at the Dardanelles having encouraged Bulgaria to join Germany, Falkenhayn at last was able to turn against Serbia.

Serbia Overrun. Austria's attempted invasions of Serbia, August-September, and November, 1914, had been brusquely repulsed. The Serbian infantry were fine fighters, but the lack of modern equipment hampered them in following up their successes. Throughout the first nine months of 1915 they stood idle, it never having occurred to the French and British to provide them with technical troops and matériel.

On Aug. 6, 1915, the Austro-German striking force under Marshal August von Mackensen crossed the Danube, and a week later the Bulgarian armies struck westward into southern Serbia across the defenders' rear. Isolated and hard-pressed, the Serbians were driven west through Albania; those who sur-

Huge German Zeppelins having a range of more than 6,000 miles and top speeds exceeding 70 miles per hour crossed the English Channel on bombing raids during World War I.

vived the retreat over the mountains joined the forces of the Entente at Salonika. Eventually these forces included many British, Italian, and Russian contingents as well as the rebuilt Serbian Army, but these troops did little fighting and the Germans sarcastically termed Salonika their "largest internment camp."

WESTERN OFFENSIVE, AUTUMN, 1915

On September 25, Joffre launched in France the great offensive for which so much had been sacrificed. Joffre's plan was to strike a two-handed blow against the sides of the huge salient formed by the German line in northern France. Gen. Édouard de Curières de Castelnau's army was to strike in Champagne; Foch was to strike near Arras with the British co-operating on his left, toward Loos. Joffre declared that he was "confident of a great and possibly complete victory."

The assault was preceded by a bombardment of four days. The German commanders drew back their main strength to their second position, a method that foreshadowed Pétain's "elastic" defense of 1918. The French, after overrunning the first position in Champagne, failed to make any real impression on the second despite three days of assaults. Joffre pushed the harder here, because in the final plan he had made it his main stroke. The comparative reduction of Foch's effort, reacted unfavorably on the British attack. Foch's troops made little progress; the fighting commanders, having lost faith in his dreams through prolonged experience, seem to have nullified his vehement orders by gentle evasion. The British offensive was delivered six hours before Foch's. Counting on Sir John French's reserve of 3 divisions to back him up, Haig launched his 6 divisions in the first assault against four German regiments. Haig's hopes had been raised by the possibility of using cloud gas, but the wind played him false; and when a divisional commander overruled his gas expert's objection by the order that "the programme must be carried out whatever the conditions," he gassed his own men. The attack was partially effective on the right, however, and the 15th Division almost broke through, causing a panic in the German Command. Whatever chance there was of exploiting this narrow penetration vanished because Sir John French failed to deliver the reserves in time, and the attack broke down.

German counterattacks and bad weather imposed a long delay, yet Joffre, French, and Haig were united in their determination to continue the offensive. The official history comments that it "brought nothing but useless slaughter of infantry." Haig ascribed the failure entirely to French's refusal to move up the reserves; French was removed and Haig was appointed to succeed him.

Italy Enters the War. In May, Italy had definitely thrown off the artificial ties of the old Triple Alliance and declared war on Austria, her hereditary foe. Militarily, however, her aid seemed unlikely greatly to affect the situation; this proved to be the case. By August, 1917, the Italians had fought 11 "Battles of the Isonzo," had suffered hundreds of thousands of casualities, and were still on the Isonzo.

THE WEST IN 1916: VERDUN AND THE SOMME

That the Allies should concentrate on gaining the decision in France was generally accepted as the only feasible course in 1916. It was not for want of men that the effort failed, for the Allies had a total of 139 divisions in France, against 117 German divisions of smaller man power. But Joffre was still barren of new ideas: more heavy guns, more shells, more men—such was his sole recipe for success. Even in this he was forestalled. In February, Falkenhayn, more subtle than Joffre, planned to attack a point—Verdun—that the French pride would be loath to give up, and thereby hoped to draw their reserves into the maw of his artillery. Unfortunately, his conventionally minded executive subordinates so misapplied his intentions as to spoil the aim. The French played into Falkenhayn's hands, at first, so intent were they on their own offensive schemes that early warning of German plans fell on deaf ears. The German bombardment began on a front of 15 miles, early February 21; nine hours later a thin chain of German infantry advanced, to feel out the strength of the French resistance before the mass of the infantry was launched (a method which economized life). The attack developed more widely February 22, and thereafter the defenders' line gave way. Joffre, typically slow to realize the gravity of any situation, thought the attack to be merely a feint. Castelnau, however, greatly daring, managed to obtain Joffre's authority to go to Verdun to discover the true situation and to take necessary action. Appalled at what he found, Castelnau ordered that the line be held at all costs, entrusted the defense to Gen. Henri Pétain, and thus the immediate danger to Verdun was checked. During the ensuing lull the British replaced the French on the Arras front, the Italians made another attack (the fifth) on the Isonzo front, and the Russians hurled untrained masses on the German front at Lake Narocz near Vilna, gallantly sacrificing their troops to help their Allies. But these diversionary efforts did not prevent Falkenhayn from pursuing his attrition offensive at Verdun.

At the end of March, Falkenhayn had to give in to royal pressure for a return to sweeping old fashioned methods—"the employment of men, not merely . . . machines and munitions." As a result, German casualties increased. So did those of the French, for Joffre removed the restraining hand of Pétain and put Gen. Robert Nivelle in charge at Verdun with orders to retake Fort Douaumont. The Germans introduced a new kind of diphosgene gas shell, June 20, and reached the Belleville Heights, the last outwork of Verdun. But in Russia, meanwhile, a sudden attack by Gen. Aleksei Brusilov's armies and a catastrophic Austrian collapse forced Falkenhayn to withdraw troops from the Western Front at a time when a British offensive was forthcoming. By early July Falkenhayn's "mincing machine" had slowed and stopped. It had devoured some 315,000 Frenchmen (compared to a German loss of 281,000) and depleted French reserves slated for Joffre's long-planned Somme offensive. From this time the British assumed the main burden of the French campaign.

The Somme Offensive. Haig entrusted his main attack on the Somme to Gen. Henry Rawlinson's Fourth Army. Eleven divisions were to lead the assault, on a 14-mile front, with 5 more up in close support. This gave the British a 6 to 1 superiority over the Germans in that sector. Marshal Edmund Allenby's army would help with a subsidiary attack near Gommecourt. An atmosphere of false confidence

In the midst of the devastation caused by a hard-fought battle, soldiers of the German army stand on a pontoon bridge hastily constructed across a mud flat in Flanders.

encouraged Haig to gamble on a quick breakthrough but Rawlinson desired a long bombardment and a short advance. He was granted the bombardment but Haig insisted that he should take both the German first and second position at a single bite. The element of surprise was ignored. The heavy artillery was spread evenly along the front, its fire so dispersed that many strong points were never touched. The assault, launched after sunrise so as to insure good visibility for the attackers' artillery, gave the same advantage to the enemy. Success depended on whether the hard-pressed British infantry could cross No-Man's-Land before the barrage lifted, but this race was lost before it started, and the battle soon after. The barrage went on, the infantry fell behind, and reinforcements were pushed in at the wrong points and at the wrong times. In the tactical plan no latitude had been allowed for initiative in exploiting local advantages, or in adjusting the artillery arrangements. In the end, 60,000 men were lost—the heaviest day's loss that a British army had ever suffered.

A fresh opportunity was created, July 14, by Rawlinson's initiative in attempting to storm the Germans' second position by a night approach across an exposed area, followed by an assault in the first faint gleam of dawn. The novelty proved brilliantly successful, but was inadequately exploited.

After this fresh disappointment Haig played for smaller stakes, carrying out a series of local attacks until ready for a further large effort. Propaganda encouraged a false faith in this attrition program, but Haig was soon reduced to gambling again on a breakthrough, utilizing a new weapon, the tank. Although it was obviously important to wait until the tank was perfected mechanically and available in sufficient numbers to gain the full effect of surprise, the desire for anything that might redeem the fading prospects of the Somme offensive led to its premature use. A handful of the new machines helped, despite their mechanical defects, toward the partial successes obtained September 15 and 25, but the Somme offensive eventually foundered in the November mud. Both armies had lost vast numbers of men who in quality could never be replaced; the Allies lost over 600,000 men 420,000 British), the Germans more than 440,000 largely in counterattacks.

RUSSIAN AND BALKAN FRONTS, 1916

After 1915 the most that was expected of Russia was that she pin down enough German forces to enable the French and British to gain superiority in the West. In the spring she was holding 46 German and 40 Austrian divisions on her front, and was preparing for a July offensive. In May, however, Conrad weakened his front against Russia by drawing off some of his best divisions for a stroke in the Trentino–Alto Adige—the first part of a plan to put Italy out of the war. The bulk of the Italian reserves were switched from the Isonzo and Conrad's plan failed. In the meantime, Russia came to Italy's aid with an offensive in Galicia. Unconventionally Brusilov made preparations at more than a score of different places, lulling the Austrians into a false security; when Brusilov's troops suddenly advanced, June 4, the hostile front collapsed, and in three weeks Brusilov took some 250,000 prisoners. But reserves to back up Brusilov were slow in arriving, the Germans sent in reinforcements, and the belated Russian attack was a disaster, with a million casualties, that hastened the revolt against martial massacre that culminated in the end of czarist government in Russia.

Nevertheless, the indirect efforts abroad had been large, for the Russians' dramatic achievement had emboldened Rumania to enter the war, August 27, in common course with the Entente.

The Conquest of Rumania. Prompted by her own ambitions and Russian advice, Rumania's main armies advanced westward over the Carpathians into Transylvania. Their excessive caution enabled the Austro-German command to prepare a counter-offensive. While the Rumanian columns crept westward, Bulgarians under August von Mackensen invaded the Dobruja, Rumania's "backyard" on the Black Sea. The Rumanian reserves chased after him, thus exposing their southern frontier and weakening their western offensive, whereupon Falkenhayn, who had just been replaced in supreme command by Hindenburg and put in charge of the Transylvania counteroffensive, struck at the paralyzed Rumanian masses and threw them back on the Carpathians; he failed to cut them off, however, and was delayed at the mountain passes. In mid-November, just before the winter snows sealed the passes, he succeeded in breaking through and pursued his invasion eastward through the plains toward Bucharest, while Mackensen switched his forces back from the Dobruja, November 23, and crossed the Danube at Svishtov, southwest of Bucharest, and attacked the forces opposing Falkenhayn. Under this double pressure Rumanian resistance collapsed and the capital fell into German hands, December 6. Soon they won possession of the greater part of Rumania, with its much needed wheat and oil. Having cleared another piece off the board, the Germans were better able to resist the French and British in the West.

The Middle East, 1916

From 1915 British forces had been engaged in various military actions in "Mespot" (Mesopotamia) but after the loss of Kut to the Turks, Dec. 8, 1915, the chief of the imperial general staff, Sir William Robertson, had stopped all operations in Mesopotamia until the forces there might be reorganized and their communications improved. In August, 1916, Sir Frederick Maude was sent to take command. Like most commanders, he was susceptible to his immediate horizon, and by subtle if unconscious steps he changed Robertson's defensive policy into one of advance upon Baghdad. In December Maude began a series of small attacks to loosen the Turks' position on the west bank of the Tigris, and by February, 1917, he was well placed for an attempt to cut off the retreat of their main forces on the east bank. His attempt to do so failed, but he had made a strategic gain and was given permission to press on to Baghdad, which the Turks abandoned to him, March 10.

Meanwhile, command of British troops in Egypt had been assumed by Sir Archibald Murray. Encouraged by news of the revolt of the Sherif of Mecca, who in June had thrown off the Turkish yoke, Murray gave thought to the idea of advancing to Palestine. By autumn the Arab rising seemed about to collapse, but a brilliant and unconventional young archaeologist and temporary soldier, Col. T. E. Lawrence, succeeded in combining the spasmodic and irregular efforts of the Arabs so that the flame of revolt was

spread eventually through a thousand miles of the desert, consuming the resources of the Turks as they strove to protect their railway lifeline from the raids he guided or inspired. In December, upon completion of a railway and a pipeline across the desert, the British occupied Magdhaba and Rafah. They attacked Gaza, the gateway to Palestine, March 26, but withdrew just as the garrison was about to surrender. Murray had reported the affair in terms of a victory, however, and was thus spurred in April to attempt a fresh attack—one that proved a costlier failure against defenses now strengthened. Murray was replaced forthwith by Sir Edmund Allenby.

The War on the Seas, 1916

British naval strategy had held that maintenance of sea supremacy was more vital than defeat of the German fleet. German naval strategy had been to avoid a decisive action until the British fleet had been weakened by means of mines and torpedoes, the fear of which had intensified the normal prudence of British sea strategists. In April, 1916, however, in the face of a virtual ultimatum from Pres. Woodrow Wilson, Germany abandoned her unrestricted campaign of submarine warfare. Deprived of this weapon, the German navy was goaded to its first, and last, attempt to carry out its initial plan. Thus, the German high sea fleet under Adm. Reinhard von Scheer, put to sea, May 31, hoping to destroy some isolated portion of the British fleet. The British grand fleet, under Adm. John Jellicoe, had put to sea the day before. The Battle of Jutland, so-called, ensued the same day. The British won the battle in the sense that they retained control of the seas, but British losses actually were greater than those of the Germans. A decisive naval victory might have shortened the slow and costly process of exhaustive slaughter on land, but this one naval battle of World War I was, as a battle, negligible. It ended with the German fleet back in harbor and the grand fleet victoriously at sea, but the Germans could console themselves with the fact that they had scored more points than a foe of much superior strength and of immense prestige, at whose hands they might well have expected annihilation. The German fleet ventured out again some three months later and even sailed within close reach of the English coast, but was not brought to battle by the grand fleet, which ran into a submarine ambush. The grand fleet was subsequently debarred by its own orders from venturing into the southern half of the North Sea.

After Jutland, Scheer reported to the Kaiser, July 4, that a German victory "at not too distant a date" required the "crushing of English economic life through U-boat action against English commerce." German statesmen opposed this argument, which

Britain succeeded in confining the German offensive to the continent with its powerful fleet until Germany abandoned surface warfare for systematic submarine attacks.

World War I

prevailed in the German admiralty, and some believed that it would be to Germany's interest to seize a favorable moment for negotiating peace. Vigorous military and naval propaganda was employed to counteract such "defeatism." When Hindenburg and Ludendorff took over the supreme command, a conference was assembled at Pszczyna early in September, 1916. The chief of the naval staff, Adm. Henning von Holtzendorff, pressed his case for unrestricted submarine warfare in which all ships would be sunk without warning, thus avoiding the risks entailed by the "visit and search" rule. The foreign minister, Gottlieb von Jagow, warned that "Germany will be treated like a mad dog against which everybody combines," and Chancellor Theobald von Bethmann-Hollweg obtained the Kaiser's permission to make a peace move in the United States. The military and naval leaders remained united in their determination to obstruct such a diplomatic step, however, and when told by the Kaiser that the idea of resuming unrestricted submarine warfare must be postponed, Holtzendorff easily persuaded the general staff to join in a campaign against the chancellor's authority.

A few days after the dispatch of the discreetly vague German peace note, and almost simultaneously with President Wilson's offer to mediate, Hindenburg and Ludendorff decided to force the chancellor's hand and frustrate his peace plans by launching an unrestricted submarine campaign forthwith. The possibility that it would invite U.S. intervention had been weighed, but discounted, and the unrestricted campaign was duly proclaimed, Feb. 1, 1916.

NEW LEADERSHIP, 1916

In Germany the military power was paramount, but among the opposing peoples there were signs of an opposite tendency. In France, there was a series of governments curiously subservient to the military power; Joffre stayed on, sacrificing his assistants to postpone his end. This came late in 1916 when a jaded people, thirsting for a leader who promised something better than interminable attrition, chose Gen. Robert Nivelle to be Joffre's successor. The British had already tried a change of command, and the Somme catastrophe did not suggest that doing just this was a quick and certain remedy. Their government had been reshuffled in May, 1915, when the Liberal Prime Minister Herbert Asquith stilled public dissatisfaction by forming a coalition government in which the Conservative element acquired a preponderant voice. As time passed, public frustration was increasingly identified with the continued presence of the original prime minister—the man whose reply "wait and see" to a criticism was remembered against him. Ultimately, after considerable political maneuvering, David Lloyd George succeeded in forming a government. He replaced the traditional large cabinet with a small war cabinet of ministers free from departmental cares and able to give their whole attention to the war. Besides the prime minister, the five original members were Andrew Bonar Law, Lord George Curzon, Lord Alfred Milner, and Arthur Henderson. The war cabinet system came close to being dictatorship within democracy—fulfilling the needs of efficiency without sacrificing the right to discussion. Owing to internal political factors, however, Lloyd George's position was weaker than it appeared on the surface, and he was forced to seek his ends by increasingly devious, time-consuming means.

Grand Strategy, 1917. Early in the year the Allied leaders conferred in Rome. France no longer had sufficient men of military age to replace her losses; in these circumstances, the Italian leader Conte Luigi Cadorna suggested the French and British might find it profitable to join with Italy in a campaign to remove Austria from the war. Lloyd George thought this a sound proposal, but French

Complex networks of fortified trenches, covered and camouflaged, were constructed when lines of defense became stabilized in the middle and late phases of World War I.

Prime Minister Aristide Briand, assured by Nivelle that it was possible to break through the Western front, urged the importance of not unsettling military plans already far advanced. Nivelle, it seems, had succeeded not only to Joffre's place but also to illusions Joffre had gradually shed; confident of achieving a decisive stroke, Nivelle desired that France should play the leading role in it. The French army, therefore, would deliver the main blow, in Champagne. Haig appreciated the fact that Nivelle's plan promised a stronger effort by the French, which released British troops for his own planned offensive in Flanders. But when Nivelle asked him to take over more of the French front so as to release French troops for the Champagne attack, Haig saw his Flanders plan threatened. Ordered to relieve the French south of the Somme, Haig did so, but the French soldiers complained of Haig's obstructiveness, and the British of Nivelle's high-handedness. As a result of subsequent heated arguments and compromises— during which Lloyd George, in his desire for unity of direction and his impatience with time-wasting wrangles, accepted arrangements that horrified Haig and Robertson—a compromise was reached by which Haig agreed to act under Nivelle's strategic direction during the forthcoming offensive, but with the right of appeal. The Germans then proceeded to upset the very foundations of Nivelle's plan.

While waiting to see whether the submarine campaign would be decisive, Ludendorff had put his time to use reorganizing the German war machine. Anticipating a renewal of the Allied offensive on the Somme, he fell back to a new and immensely strong line of defense, that was rapidly constructed across the base of the great salient formed by the German front between Arras and Reims. To make his strategic retirement the more effective, he presented the Allies with a desert: roads were mined, houses were demolished and the ruins strewn with explosive booby traps. The main withdrawal, March 16, dislocated Nivelle's plan, and astounded the Allied chiefs, who could hardly believe that any soldier would willingly abandon occupied ground, however valueless.

Nivelle's Offensive, 1917. The British attack on Arras, April 9, began well, thanks to improved artillery methods and a new gas shell that paralyzed hostile artillery. Vimy Ridge fell to the Canadian corps, but the success was not effectively exploited, largely because of inadequate logistics. As the British butted at a hardening resistance, their losses increased without compensating profit.

Nivelle's efforts in Champagne, April 16, were a tragic fiasco, in which the attacking troops were trapped in a web of machine-gun fire, and French Senegalese troops broke and fled. Nivelle had expected to advance six miles by evening; the actual advance was about 600 yards. The only Allied gain was the elimination of Nivelle: after some face-saving delay, during which a mutiny broke out, May 3, and spread through 16 army corps, Henri Pétain succeeded him, May 15. Pétain restored tranquility by meeting the just grievances of the troops; he restored confidence by his reputation for sober judgment and for avoiding reckless attacks. But the military strength of France was never to be fully restored: Nivelle had completed Joffre's work too well.

Pétain held that the only rational strategy was to keep on the defensive while waiting "for the Americans and the tanks." The new emphasis on tanks showed a dawning recognition that machine warfare had superseded mass warfare. Reinforcement from America had become a certainty when the United States entered the war against Germany on Apr. 6, 1917—some days before Nivelle's disastrous offensive.

U.S. Involvement in the War

For two and a half years Pres. Woodrow Wilson had held to a policy of neutrality while striving to find a basis of peace upon which the warring countries might agree. The President's efforts to persuade the Allies were hindered by the fact that, in carrying neutrality into the realm of moral judgment, he seemed unwilling to distinguish between aggressors and victims; in Germany, meanwhile, those who were in a mood to talk peace were ever more helplessly in the grip of militarists who scorned concessions not won by conquest. Wilson's tendency to classify all belligerents alike as naughty boys seemed confirmed by rebuffs to his good intentions, but he remained confident that peace would ultimately be secured by mediation. The declaration of the German submarine campaign, despite the pledges formerly given to him, dimmed his confidence, and he at once severed diplomatic relations, while still hoping that Germany's actions would stay short of her threats. The sinking of several U.S. ships dimmed this hope, and then a telegram was intercepted and deciphered that showed that Germany planned to incite Mexico to action against the United States. More ships were sunk, and at length the President conquered his hesitations, and the United States entered the war.

The news was a great moral tonic to the Allies, but the country was not prepared for war and for a long time U.S. aid remained a promissory note, except in the economic sphere. Congress was aghast at the appeals for loans that soon came from Europe, and tried to restrict the flow, but during the first three months of war the U.S. government made advances totaling $1.145 billion (£229 million pounds, £1 = $5), all to be used to pay for supplies bought in the United States, and Britain had added $965 million (£193 million) to her loans, without any such restriction. Overriding British fears that British credit would be damaged thereby, the U.S. Treasury authorized long advances to the Allies up to $2.5 billion (£500 million) a month. Simultaneously the economic grip on Germany could at last be tightened with strangling effect, regardless of protests from remaining neutrals, as the United States enforced and extended the very blockade measures against which it had formerly protested.

The Submarine Problem, 1917

In April, 1917, one ship in every four that left the British Isles was sunk by German submarine action. The Allies lost nearly a million tons of shipping (60 per cent of it British) during that month, when the sinkings reached their peak. The starvation of Britain and the collapse of her armed effort might have ensued but for the courage of British merchant seamen. The government expanded shipbuilding, rationed food, and increased home production of goods, yet the situation worsened. In vain, the navy multiplied existing means of combating the submarine, but the

ACME

On April 2, 1917, Pres. Woodrow Wilson asked Congress to declare that a state of war existed with Germany. The declaration of war was overwhelmingly approved, April 6.

most obvious method of all—bringing the ships to port in convoy—was rejected by most admiralty professionals as theoretically unsound. Even after the United States entered the war, First Sea Lord Jellicoe opposed the idea of convoys. It was Lloyd George who made the decisive intervention, visiting the admiralty and warning them beforehand that he intended to consult any officers he wished, irrespective of rank; many younger officers were known to favor the convoy idea. He found the board was now suddenly willing to try the experiment. The first convoy left Gibraltar on May 10; by September over-all British shipping losses had fallen to 200,000 tons a month, while the loss in the convoys was reduced to a bare 1 per cent. Meanwhile, special submarine chasers, aircraft, and the new horned mines exacted an ever-rising toll of submarines, whose menace was largely subdued by the end of the year.

Continental Action, 1917

Preliminaries. Upon superseding the discredited Nivelle, Pétain at once manifested his intention of staying on the defensive until U.S. forces arrived. Haig, however, no longer forced to conform to French plans, was eager to fulfill his long-cherished desire for an offensive in Flanders, which he believed would bring a victory so decisive as to end the war. In fact it brought disaster. Years later Haig claimed that his dominant reason for that offensive had been to take pressure off his Allies: "the possibility of the French Army breaking up *compelled me to go on attacking.*" There is no evidence for the existence of such a thought at the time, however, and his letters show clearly that he was filled with the idea that it was possible for the British army to defeat the Germans single-handed "at an early date," and that he believed the French to be entirely capable of holding their own throughout.

A preliminary siege-war attack on the Messines Ridge, June 7, proved an almost complete success within its well defined limits, and had the unfortunate effect of inspiring the higher command with happy confidence in the greater effort that was to follow. Haig counted on an early breakthrough, and said that "opportunities for the employment of cavalry in masses are likely to offer." Yet general headquarters knew that the Ypres area, as reclaimed marshland, was bound to revert to swamp if the drainage system were to be destroyed by prolonged bombardment; and that "in Flanders the weather broke early each August with the regularity of the Indian monsoon." Haig chose not to mention such facts to the war cabinet when seeking approval of his plans in London. Emphasizing the presumed "exhaustion" and declining morale of the German army, he assured the cabinet that he had "no intention of entering into a tremendous offensive involving heavy losses." As the cabinet hesitated, Jellicoe intervened in favor of Haig's plan, predicting that unless the army captured the submarine bases on the Belgian coast Britain's whole war effort might soon collapse. Thus Haig won his case and preparations went forward on both sides of the battle front, the German commanders having agreed that a British offensive at Ypres was certain, and predicted its exact pattern with perfect accuracy. For an early breakthrough, surprise would be of vital importance, but Haig chose to attack in the bare Flanders plain so that his immense preparations were displayed to the eyes of the German observers; a fortnight of bombardment gave them further warning.

Passchendaele. The offensive was launched, July 31, after over 3,000 guns had poured 4.5 million shells on the German defenses. This bombardment did not suffice to silence enemy machine guns, many of them ensconced in concrete pillboxes. On the left the full objective was reached, but on the crucial right wing the attack was a total failure; Haig reported to the war office that the results were "most satisfactory." On August 4, Haig's intelligence chief wrote in his dairy that "Every brook is swollen and the ground is a quagmire." Thus the next big effort had to be postponed until August 16. It failed, but Haig remained confident and reported, August 21, that the end of the German reserves was in sight, although the struggle might still be severe "for some weeks." The prime minister went to Flanders to see for himself, and Haig called attention to the poor physique of the prisoners then being taken as proof that his offensive was bringing the German army to the point of exhaustion. All able-bodied prisoners having been removed from the corps cages before his arrival, the prime minister had to admit that the prisoners were a "weedy lot."

Late in September there was a temporary improvement in both the weather and the British situation, and Haig decided, September 28, that the enemy must be on the point of collapse, and that tanks and cavalry could be pushed through; and reported that German losses exceeded the British "not improbably by a hundred per cent" (actually they were much less than the British). Even as the weather deteriorated and the mud became worse, Haig remained optimistic, and his aides tried to

NATL. ARCHIVES RECORD GROUP III

In a narrow protective trench, May 4, 1918, a contingent of the 369th Infantry, 93rd Division of the American Expeditionary Force, awaits an advance by German troops.

believe in his reassurances. There was talk of winning the war before Christmas. But the attack of October 12 ended with the attacking troops, save those who had perished in the mud, back on their starting line. Several fresh efforts later in the month made little or no progress, but on November 6, the troops advanced the few hundrd yards necessary to occupy the site of what had been the village of Passchendaele, whereupon Haig, his honor satisfied, at last called a halt. In a practical sense he was no nearer reaching the ports that had been his goal than when he had started. Despite his pledge that he would not commit the country to "heavy losses," his doomed dream of a decisive victory in Flanders fields had cost the British 400,000 men.

Breakdown in Italy. Each autumn the Germans demolished one of the weaker allies. In 1917 it was to be Italy's turn, the idea being to ease the pressure on war-weary Austria. Ludendorff could spare only six divisions, but a soft spot on the Italian front was found in the Caporetto sector, which was attacked, October 24, by the six German divisions and nine Austrian divisions. A breakthrough was at once achieved, was quickly widened, and soon the Italian front collapsed. Cadorna saved the wreckage of his army by a hasty retreat to the Tagliamento, and thence to the Piave, leaving more than 250,000 prisoners in the enemy's hands. He was replaced by Gen. Armando Diaz, who played a Pétain-like role in restoring confidence. Fortunately for the Italians, the enemy, surprised by the extent of their own success, tried to push on with inadequate materièl and communications. Thus the Italians were able to reknit, and hold their line, on the Piave, although they had lost 600,000 men.

Russia's Breakaway. The disappearance of Russia from the war followed the Italian disaster. With revolution in the air, the czar was forced to abdicate March, 1917. Long-repressed hatred of a corrupt and inefficient regime, combined with disgust which the war produced, allowed for little hope that the moderate parties that first took over the government could sustain themselves, much less a war effort. In May, another, more leftist government, headed by Aleksandr Kerenski, combined a cry of peace with platform appeals to the troops to carry on the war. The Russian reactionaries attempted a counterrevolution, thus providing an opportunity for the Bolsheviks of the extreme left to overthrow Kerenski in October. Under Lenin and Trotsky, the Bolsheviks concluded an armistice with Germany in December; the peace negotiations were then prolonged until March, but an unopposed invasion forced acceptance of Ger-

This camouflaged steel and concrete "pillbox" faced the no-man's land in France between the lines of the American Expeditionary Force and those of the German forces.
NATL. ARCHIVES

The tank, exemplified here by U.S. models, was developed during World War I to break the stalemate produced on the Western Front by trench warfare and the machine gun.

many's drastic terms. Large numbers of German troops were now available for the Western front.

Cambrai. As early as August 3 it had been suggested that with the Flanders offensive bogged down, a diversionary action might be attempted—a great tank raid in the dry downland near Cambrai. The idea appealed to British Gen. Julian Byng, but was dropped as the Flanders offensive resumed. In mid-October the plan was revived, however, and Byng threw all of his forces into its prosecution. On November 20, 380 tanks rolled forward before a gun had opened fire. Six divisions joined in the attack, on a six-mile front. Absence of the customary bombardment took the Germans by surprise, and the deep trenches of the Hindenburg Line were quickly breached. Three defense lines had been overrun, and only a half-finished line separated the British from open country, but the tanks had all been used, the infantry were unable to make progress without them, and the cavalry were easily stopped by a few machine guns. Thus time was gained for German reserves to cement the breach and prepare a counterstroke. By the end of the month the British lost much of what they had gained in territory, but not the invaluable experience in the application of a new method of warfare—the "Cambrai Key," as it came to be called.

Jerusalem. Lloyd George, anxious to retrieve Murray's spring failure in Palestine, replaced Murray with Allenby who took to the field against the Turks late in October. Under cover of a feint against Gaza, Beersheba was seized. A week later Allenby broke through the enemy's weakened center and the ensuing Turkish retreat was steadily followed up. By November 14, Jaffa was Allenby's. He next wheeled to the right for an advance inland on Jerusalem, which was occupied December 9.

ALLIED PLANS, 1918

Call for Unity. In August, 1917, Paul Painlevé, prompted by Foch, urged on the British government the necessity of forming an inter-Allied general staff. In accord with the principle, but opposed to an organ of an exclusively military nature, Lloyd George sounded out President Wilson on the idea of an "Allied Joint Council with permanent military and probably naval and economic staffs attached to work out plans for the Allies." Late in 1917 a Supreme War Council was formed, composed of the principal statesmen of the different countries, together with permanent military representatives. In the economic sphere, establishment of the council led to an improvement in the combination of munition, shipping, and food resources. The powers disagreed, however, as to how much executive power the military committee should have, with the English holding, against the others, that it should have little or none. The

World War I

problem was complicated by the fact that Pétain was simultaneously urging that the British ought to take over a larger share of the front. In time the French became more insistent on a readjustment of shares, and the new prime minister, Georges Clemenceau, insisted that Haig should take over an additional 55 miles, and threatened to resign if his demands were not met; Haig retorted that he would resign if they were met. Pétain and Haig were agreed to a 25-mile extension, and the Supreme War Council swallowed its dignity and accepted this private settlement.

The dispute gave impetus to the movement toward co-ordination, and soon the military advisory committee was developed into an executive board, with Foch as chairman, which should control an inter-Allied general reserve of 30 divisions. Immediately there was a furor in London, and Lloyd George had to remove Robertson, who objected to the changes; Henry Wilson now became chief of the general staff.

This reshuffle did not remove the main obstacle to the inter-Allied reserve; Haig, when called upon to contribute his share (nine divisions), replied that he had made his dispositions to meet the coming offensive and could spare none. In desperation Foch appealed to the Supreme War Council, but Haig had gained Clemenceau's support and Lloyd George hesitated to risk a fresh political crisis. Haig preferred to rely on a personal arrangement he had made with Pétain for mutual support. In making his dispositions, Haig placed the bulk of his strength in the north.

GERMAN OFFENSIVES

Disappointed by the results of the submarine campaign, Ludendorff had decided on a bid for victory by attack on land. Profiting by the lesson of the Allies' abortive efforts, 1915–17, he insisted that the guiding principle must be to strike "where the enemy is weak" and that "all means must be applied to achieving the first essential of success, namely, surprise." Ludendorff decided to attempt his initial breakthrough in the Cambrai–St. Quentin sector.

The Germans had been even slower than the Allies to recognize the value of the tank. For lack of such a master key to surprise, Ludendorff had to depend on familiar means; stealth of preparation, so that the assaulting divisions came up by night; masses of artillery that opened fire without disclosing their presence by previous "registration"; a brief but intense bombardment, largely of gas shell; infiltration tactics by which the leading infantry acted as probing fingers, while those who followed pushed in wherever the defense was weakening.

March Breakthrough. The bombardment, by over 6,000 guns on the 60-mile front, began early March 21. Six or less hours later the German infantry began their infiltration, aided by a thick fog. The British forward zone was quickly overrun, and by nightfall the battle zone had been breached in several places. March 22 was also foggy and the British were forced back 10 miles to the Somme. On March 23, again under cover of fog, the river line was forced. The British front now sagged badly, and had become disjointed as it was pushed back and back through open country, yet reserves were slow in arriving. On the Third Army front, Byng's belated withdrawal from the Flesquières salient became disjointed, producing a state of confusion that nullified the success of the reserves farther north in stabilizing the line, and contributed to a break between the Fifth and Third armies. The British command considered falling back "northwestward to cover the Channel Ports," thus abandoning touch with the French, but Pétain was quick to detect this inclination and met with Haig, March 24, warning him that if the British gave way further the French would fall back southwestward in order to cover Paris. This intimation was a shock to Haig, who had expected the French to fill the breach. Haig sought a means of overruling Pétain and even telegraphed to London; having opposed the idea of an inter-Allied chief when there was a risk of his reserves being taken away, Haig felt differently when he needed French reserves. At a conference at Doullens, March 26, Foch was appointed to co-ordinate the operations on the Western front. While his determination and confidence did much to restore morale behind the front, and news that someone fresh had taken charge had a similar effect in the British fighting line, his appointment actually made little difference to the flow of reinforcements. Foch became Commander in Chief of the Allied Armies, April 14, but he confessed later that he had been "no more than conductor of an orchestra. . . ." Haig, Pershing, and Pétain, fortified by the right of appeal to their own governments, would not brook interference nor accede to his desires more than their own judgment allowed. Foch could coax, but not control.

By March 27 the German tide had reached Montdidier, but thenceforth it made little progress, thanks to the dogged resistance of countless small packets of British soldiers, and subsequently to the arrival of French reserves in greater number, and sooner, than Pétain had promised. But the Germans contributed at least as much to their own frustration; for most officers, at all levels, had yet to grasp adequately the full implications of their own new tactics. Even Ludendorff dissipated his reserves trying to redeem tactical failures, and failed at times to exploit lines of least resistance. The German advance also suffered a check from the retreating enemy's abandonment of their stores; the troops could not resist the time-consuming temptation to pillage. Ludendorff took 80,000 prisoners and crippled the Fifth Army, but he missed the strategic decision on which he had staked so much, continued his effort past the point when difficulties exceeded the prospects, and depleted his own resources.

The April Breakthrough. His bid for victory at one blow having clearly failed, Ludendorff decided to launch a diversionary offensive in the north, toward the important railway junction of Hazebrouck. Most of his reserves, however, were now occupied in holding the huge salient that he had driven into the Allied front near Amiens. Late to make up his mind, Ludendorff was too quick to act; on April 1 he decided to launch the stroke on April 9, although only 11 fresh divisions could be moved there in time. Fate was kind to him, however, in providing obtuse opponents, an unexpectedly soft spot at which to strike, and another cloak of fog. From April 1 a general northward movement of the German reserves and artillery was known to Haig, but he remained convinced that the enemy's next attack would be opposite Arras because that was where he would have attacked if he had been Ludendorff—for Arras, Haig's strongest point, was the theoretically "correct" aim for the enemy. Haig's "Passchendaele" assumption that the Germans would go on trying despite previous failures was shared by the army commander on the actually threatened sector, who rejected proposals from his subordinates for rearward preparations to meet the danger of a breakthrough toward Hazebrouck, and left a Portuguese division, in which morale was known to be poor, to hold a large sector of the line for a few days longer. On April 9, with the front wrapped in fog, nine German divisions were launched against three brigades on an 11-mile front. The Portuguese were swept away, and the breach was rapidly widened northward; by the second night it was 30 miles wide, but only 5 miles deep, since lack of reserves and difficulties of supply hindered the Germans in exploiting their initial success.

Ludendorff, lured by the hope that what had been intended as a mere diversion might become a victorious offensive, sent more divisions, although still in a

In September, 1918, U.S. artillerymen fire on the German lines opposite Baleycourt Woods, Meuse, France, destroying two German army corps headquarters 19 miles away.

piecemeal way. But his intention of delivering a converging attack against the Ypres salient was forestalled when the British retreated there and used reserves thus released to repel the German attempt to carry the dominating height of Kemmel, near Ploegsteert. By April 18 the Germans had penetrated 10 miles, but were 5 miles short of Hazebrouck. But for the British withdrawal from Passchendaele, the danger could hardly have been averted, for Foch had been reluctant to send French reserves northward because of his preconceived idea that the enemy's "correct" course was to continue their attack toward Amiens. Tardy French reinforcements did arrive in time to meet a resumption of the German offensive, April 25, but not in time to consolidate their defensive position; they were thrown off Kemmel Hill and the Germans might have broken through had not Ludendorff hesitated and only sanctioned a fresh effort, April 29, when it was too late. Once again he had violated two fundamental lessons of war experience—never to check momentum once attained, and never to resume mere pushings.

The May Breakthrough. Ludendorff now became obsessed with the idea of redeeming his lost opportunity and of striking a decisive blow at the British in Flanders. The first step was to draw the French reserves back to their front. Shrewdly, he chose a sector so strong naturally that it was weakly held—the Chemin-des-Dames Ridge north of the Aisne, which was the sector nearest Paris so that the French reserves might be drawn there the more easily. The preparations for this diversionary offensive against the Chemin-des-Dames exemplify German military technique at its highest level. Elaborate precautions were taken to conceal assembly of the forces: every artillery wheel had wool wired onto its tire; every axle was wired with a leather covering; every horse's hoof was muffled in rags; every chain, ring, shield, or ladder was wrapped in straw. The attacking divisions were brought up by nightly stages, hiding in woods by day. The 3,700-gun bombardment opened May 27, on a 30-mile front, between Reims and Soissons, on a system intended to produce maximum confusion in the defense. Several hours later, at 3:30 A.M., the barrage moved on; it consisted of a "hurricane of gas shells in front followed by a sheet of shrapnel paving the way for the infantry advance." A wave of 14 German divisions struck 5 Allied divisions—or rather the dazed survivors—which were swiftly overwhelmed. The defenders had 5 divisions in reserve, but these too were engulfed in the advancing flood, which swept on to the unguarded bridges of the Aisne. By nightfall the Germans had reached the Vesle, a penetration 12 miles deep.

Foch had been taken completely by surprise, although prior to the attack U.S. intelligence, studying the situation in detachment, had by deductive reasoning concluded that the next German offensive would be against the Chemin-des-Dames sector, late in May; French intelligence had been impressed, but the operations branch had disagreed, encouraged in its incredulity by the fact that air reconnaissances had failed to detect signs of German preparations. Early on May 26, two Germans had been taken prisoner and under cross-examination had disclosed the plan. It was too late to prepare an adequate defense, but the French commanders in the area could not bring themselves to abandon such hallowed ground; they decided to stay rather than withdraw strategically, and thus lost their troops as well as the ground.

Once again Ludendorff was ensnared by the unforeseen measure of his own success. Having intended only a diversion, he had limited the objective to the high ground south of the Vesle, and there the Germans halted, May 28. But the situation was so tempting that Ludendorff decided to push on, postponing his intended blow in Flanders. During the pause, however, the wine cellars of Champagne fought for France, and with "drunken soldiers lying all over the road" subsequent German progress was slow despite slight opposition. The German center reached the Marne, 15 miles beyond the Vesle, May 30, but Pétain had rushed reserves to the scene, where they formed a formidable obstacle. Ludendorff's attempt to expand the flanks of the new breach was frustrated by Pétain's new dam; and its failure was signalized by the appearance of U.S. troops in the battle line, and by their counterattack at Château-Thierry on the Marne. A hastily prepared, ill-concealed German attack against the Noyon-Montdidier sector, June 9, was quickly brought to a standstill.

German Exhaustion. For three years, 1915–17, French and British military chiefs had talked confidently of the early exhaustion of the German army under the attrition of Allied attacks; such optimism had been wholly contrary to fact. The German offensive, however, did greatly reduce German strength and morale; this trend was to continue, with ever-growing momentum, and made all the worse because stomachs were empty. The Allied blockade was truly a stranglehold: food and other necessities were scarce; sickness became rampant and many men in the ranks, if not sick enough to be hospitalized, were not fit enough to fight. Pitiful letters from home told of even worse conditions. While German strength waned, that of the Allies waxed as U.S. forces poured into France in numbers that more than compensated for the huge losses the British and French had sustained in resisting the German offensive.

PERSHING AND HIS ALL-AMERICAN ARMY

Upon entering the war the United States lacked an army adequate to be of any help in Europe. That an army of millions was required was obvious, and conscription was adopted within a few weeks. According to Gen. John J. Pershing, however, "it was . . . practically six months before the training of our army was under way." He blamed this on a delay in the building of cantonments to house the newly raised troops; but according to Gen. Peyton March, U.S. Army chief of staff in 1918, Pershing himself was responsible for needless and almost disastrous delay in using U.S. troops even after their arrival in France.

Pershing was determined to build an all-American army independent of the Allies, although he was forced to depend upon them for much of his "independent" army's equipment. In his stand for national sentiment he was, of course, following the bad example of French and British commanders, yet he perhaps carried it further in a time of crisis, to the point that he in fact imperiled the Allied cause. As his memoirs show, he was the main and often the sole, obstacle in the way of giving the Allied armies early reinforcement. President Wilson was willing to

U.S. ARMY

Members of the U.S. infantry, with bayonets fixed on the ends of their rifles, scramble over the edge of a sand-bag trench to lead a charge on the German lines, 1918.

respond to their urgent appeals, but Pershing stood firm, and even when he was forced to yield something on paper, he was quick to recover it in practice.

When the storm broke over the Allied front, Mar. 21, 1918, there were 300,000 U.S. troops in France, of which only two divisions were in the line. During the crisis on the Somme, March 28, Pershing declared that the U.S. troops were at Foch's disposal for use wherever required, but two months passed before more than four U.S. divisions were actually made available to help hold the line, and not until May 25, coincidently with the third German offensive, did the 1st Division strike the first U.S. blow in a local attack at Cantigny, near Montdidier. During those two dangerous months, the French and British governments made ceaseless and frantic efforts to hasten the intervention of U.S. forces. Foch bluntly told Pershing, April 25, that "the American Army may arrive to find the British pushed into the sea and the French driven back behind the Loire, while it tries in vain to organize on lost battlefields over the graves of Allied soldiers." Pershing declared indifferently that he was willing to take that risk. Seemingly nothing could shake his objection to using U.S. troops to fill gaps in the Allied ranks. "I thought that the best and quickest way to help the Allies would be to build up an American Army," he wrote later. How it could be the "quickest" was an argument that historians have found hard to understand. Early in May, meeting with Pershing at Abbeville, Lloyd George, Clemenceau, and Italian Prime Minister Vittorio Orlando pointed out that the war might be lost if Pershing continued to withhold support, "whereupon," Pershing wrote later, "I struck the table with my fist and said with the greatest possible emphasis, 'Gentlemen, I have thought this program over very deliberately and will not be coerced.' " Since the war was not lost, Pershing was proved "correct," but disaster was averted by a margin so narrow that the Allies had to sacrifice additional lives and incur excessive expenses to help the general prove his point.

There can be little question, however, but that the entry of U.S. forces, however belated, was a major factor in enabling depleted Franco-British forces to take advantage of the German exhaustion. After Pershing had achieved a bargain wholly advantageous to his plan of building a self-contained U.S. force, 300,000 troops arrived every month until, in mid-July, there were 21 complete U.S. divisions in France.

SECOND BATTLE OF THE MARNE

After devoting a month or more gathering reserves for a further effort, and learning that "the enemy in Flanders was still so strong that the German army could not attack there yet," Ludendorff decided to

German prisoners are led under guard through streets of Verdun, 1918. Verdun and its surrounding hills were the scene of some of the bloodiest battles of World War I.

create yet another diversion by an attack on either side of Reims.

But this sector was no longer a weak one, and the French had been forewarned as early as July 5, fully 10 days before the attack came. Moreover, Pétain now adopted a recoiling buffer method of defense, absorbing the initial impetus of the attack by a lightly held forward position and awaiting the attackers on a strong position in the rear. The attack east of Reims proved a costly failure from the start; west of Reims, along the Marne, the Germans had more success at first, but the attack collapsed, July 16.

Prior to Ludendorff's Reims adventure, Foch had postponed a planned French offensive and had assembled an army under Gen. Charles Mangin on the west side of the Marne salient. Foch intended to launch this before the expected German attack, but Pétain persuaded him to let the enemy strike first. Mangin's attack, launched July 18, employed the "Cambrai Key": without any artillery preparation, several hundred small tanks suddenly emerged from the woods and quickly broke through the German line, followed by the infantry. After a bound of four miles on the first day, however, the attack came to a standstill, the Allies having not yet acquired the ability to exploit a success. Other armies around the salient joined in the offensive, July 20, but accomplished little. U.S. divisions took part, but they lacked the experience necessary to overcome the German resistance; the French, by contrast, suffered from too much experience. The Germans evaded them all and established themselves on a shortened line along the Vesle, where Ludendorff at last prepared for his Flanders stroke. See MARNE, BATTLES OF THE.

The "Black Day." On August 8 the Cambrai Key was used again, and this time the nerve of the German troops broke with repercussions that shook the supreme command. As part of Foch's program of sustained pressure on the enemy, Haig was to launch an attack aimed at disengaging Amiens. British preparations for this operation proved that the British had at long last learned both the necessity and the art of surprise; 13 divisions, over 2,000 guns, and 456 tanks were smuggled into the area undetected. The main blow was delivered by the Australian and Canadian corps. Under a cloak of fog the tanks overran the enemy's flimsy defenses and the day's objective was easily gained. Thereafter the attack came to a standstill, but the first shock had made a deep impression. The Kaiser announced that "The war must be ended," and Ludendorff agreed. His ultimate verdict was that "August 8th was the black day of the German Army in the history of the war."

The Ebb. Foch urged Haig to push hard, but Haig had at last become aware of the folly of continued hammering at hardening resistance. Since Foch had already arranged that the offensive should be ex-

tended to neighboring sectors, Haig pointed out, perhaps application of this indirect leverage was the better way to loosen the resistance. Foch gave way, and no less than four major advances were launched at various fronts on the line, August 21–26, whereupon Ludendorff sanctioned a general withdrawal to the Hindenburg Line, thus abandoning almost all the ground he had gained.

On September 12, Pershing erased the St. Mihiel salient on the far side of Verdun. The withdrawing Germans were overtaken and badly hustled by the swiftness of the U.S. onrush before reaching the shelter of the Michel Line across the base of the salient. Pershing's intention had been to push on, past Metz, toward the Germans' main lateral railway, which ran only 20 miles behind the Michel Line; this would have endangered the whole German position on the Western front, if it could have been achieved; but Gen. Hunter Liggett, who played the chief part in the St. Mihiel stroke, doubted that it could have been, considering the inexperience of the U.S. troops. Pershing, however, remained sure that a great opportunity had been missed.

Allied Offensive. Foch now was filled with the vision of a decisive victory through a simultaneous general offensive in which the British and U.S. pincers should close on and cut off the main German armies. He proposed that the St. Mihiel attack be limited; that the main U.S. attack be delivered in a northwesterly, instead of a northerly, direction; and that Pershing's army should attack west of the Argonne, while a mixed U.S.–French army, under a French commander, should attack over the more difficult ground between the Argonne Forest and the Meuse. A violent argument ensued, the upshot of which was that Pershing gave up his own strategic plan for a share in Foch's, while Foch yielded to Pershing's insistence that U.S. forces would fight as a separate whole, free from any French control or advice. Pershing chose the more difficult sector east of the Argonne, and made his task still harder by rejecting Foch's suggestion that he give up the St. Mihiel attack. As a result raw U.S. divisions had to be used in the greater effort.

The great salient formed by the German front between Verdun and Ypres was to be crushed between a giant pair of pincers. The right pincer, the U.S. Army in the Meuse-Argonne sector, was to strike first, September 26, thus (it was hoped) drawing off some of the forces facing the left pincer—the First, Third, and Fourth British armies on the Cambrai–St. Quentin sector—where the defenses were strongest and the enemy most heavily massed. Each pincer would be supported by the French armies on their inner flanks. Finally, as a supplementary lever, a combined Anglo-Belgian force was to strike from Ypres, September 28. Pershing's untried troops were expected to break through the enemy's three successive positions in the first day, to exploit the success during the night, and to be halfway to Sedan and the lateral railway by the next morning.

After three hours' intense bombardment by 2,700 guns, the U.S. attack was launched on a 20-mile front. The Germans damped the shock by adopting the spring-buffer method of defense, holding the main resistance some miles in the rear where the nonexpectant U.S. troops, their initial impetus lost, blundered into a cunningly woven belt of fire. The attack never regained momentum, the enemy had time to bring up reinforcements, and congestion and confusion on the roads behind helped to retard the U.S. advance. By mid-October Pershing was forced to suspend operations in order to reorganize, having covered only a third of the distance to the main lateral railway. Some 18,000 prisoners had been captured, but U.S. casualties exceeded 100,000, plus perhaps an equal number of stragglers.

The left pincer proved the more effective. Byng's left and Gen. Henry Horne's right assaulted the

On Nov. 11, 1918, the German delegates met with Allied military commanders in a railroad carriage in the Forest of Compiègne, and there accepted Allied armistice terms.

Canal du Nord, September 21, penetrated on a narrow sector, then spread out fanwise, and reached the outskirts of Cambrai on the next evening.

On General Rawlinson's front meanwhile, 1,600 guns had been smothering the defenses for 56 hours (the first 8 hours with gas), forcing the defenders to take refuge in their deepest shelters. Rawlinson's assault was to be launched on a 9-mile front, spearheaded by one British and two U.S. divisions. One of the U.S. divisions made a preliminary attack to clear three enemy advanced posts, and reported success, but doubt then arose whether the posts were occupied by U.S. or German troops. The ill-consequence was that the artillery put down the barrage half a mile in front of the infantry starting line, September 29, while the questionable posts, actually still in German hands, lay precisely within the half-mile interval; the advancing U.S. infantrymen were mowed down in swaths, and the other U.S. division was handicapped the more. Nevertheless, its men reached and breached the forward edge of the Hindenburg Line—only to be taken in the rear by Germans who emerged from dugouts. The day was partially redeemed by the success of the 46th British Division, whose men had gained the St. Quentin Canal and swarmed across before the Germans realized the situation. Another division then carried the advance beyond the rear of the Hindenburg Line, creating a leverage helpful to the efforts of Australian troops to widen the breach.

By October 5, the British had driven their way through the German defense system into open country, and had taken 36,000 prisoners, yet the British were unable to advance fast enough to produce general collapse of the German front. One cause was the difficulty of keeping the British force supplied; another was the fact that the force had suffered heavy casualties: many of the enemy were surrendering freely, but not the machine gunners, whose delaying power was a continuing problem.

In Flanders, the attackers had swept forward 8 miles in 2 days, and captured 10,000 prisoners, but were then held up by the mud.

The Fatal Stroke. Ludendorff had hoped to hold fast in his strong lines in France, perhaps withdrawing gradually, so as to give German statesmen time to negotiate a favorable peace. On September 15, however, Allied forces in Salonika, spearheaded by Serbs skilled in mountain warfare, struck at a weak point on the Bulgarian front. Soon the whole line west of the Vardar collapsed under the converging pressure of the Serbs and French, whose pursuit drove on toward Skopje. A British attack east of the Vardar failed, but helped to pin the enemy's reserves. British aircraft caught the retreating Bulgarians in the Kosturino Pass, turning retreat into rout. The Bulgarians sought an armistice, which was signed on September 29; in Ludendorff's judgment at the

time, this "sealed the fate of the Quadruple Alliance," all the more because on that very day he had received disquieting reports of the French "grand offensive" against the Hindenburg Line. That evening, Ludendorff took the precipitate decision to appeal for an armistice. Prince Max of Baden, of pacific reputation, was made chancellor. To help in negotiating peace without confessing defeat, the prince asked for a breathing space of a few days, but Hindenburg insisted that a "peace offer to our enemies be issued at once," and Ludendorff plaintively reiterated, "I want to save my army." The appeal for an immediate armistice, sent to President Wilson, October 3, was a confession of defeat for all to see. Within a few days the German command became more optimistic, and Ludendorff saw some hope of a secure withdrawal to a shortened defensive line on the frontier. But his earlier despair was already known throughout Germany, and was dissipating the will to resist.

Collapse of Turkey. During spring and summer, 1918, Allenby's situation in Palestine had remained relatively stable. The late summer, however, brought plans for a new offensive. During the final days of preparation, Arab raiders distracted the enemy by cutting the railways from Deraa, focal point of enemy communications. Allenby's powerful attack along the Mediterranean coast, September 19, then swept the dazed defenders aside. Some Turkish forces tried to escape over the Jordan, but were caught by British aircraft. Damascus was occupied October 1, and Turkey capitulated, October 31. Some 75,000 prisoners had been taken at a cost of less than 5,000 casualties.

Collapse of Austria. The Italian front remained comparatively quiet until June, 1918, when the Austrians attacked the Italian line on the Piave; had some early success, but then were forced to withdraw in disorder, with a loss of over 100,000 men—enough to bankrupt Austria's military power. By mid-October the Italians felt able to take the offensive which began October 24 with an unsuccessful attack in the Grappa region. Italian and British forces managed subsequently to gain a footing on the far side of the Piave, October 27, and the Austrian army command ordered a general retreat of its already mutinous troops, October 28. On October 29, with Austrian troops a fugitive rabble, Austria begged for an armistice.

Collapse of Germany. Revolution broke out in Germany, November 4, and spread rapidly over a country in which a mood of hopelessness prevailed. The fleet mutinied when its leaders tried to send it out against the British fleet. The Kaiser could not bring himself to believe, however, that there was any widespread wish that he abdicate.

When, on November 6, German delegates left Berlin to treat for an armistice, Allied leaders had already been debating for a month what they should demand before consenting to suspend their advance. President Wilson's ill-considered belief that determination of armistice conditions must be left to the military advisers enabled Foch to make Allied military terms subservient to French political aims. "If France intends to separate the Rhineland from Prussia," he remarked to Clemenceau, "there is no time to be lost in stopping the armistice accordingly," and took care to insert the occupation of Rhine bridges in his draft terms. In addition, the enemy must surrender a third of their guns, half their machine guns, and a large part of their railway material.

When the draft terms were discussed by the statesmen, November 1, Foch admitted that the Allied armies could not prevent the Germans from withdrawing to a new and shorter line, since they were then retreating faster than they could be followed by the British. However, there were now 2 million U.S. troops in France, and the U.S. advance, with Liggett in executive charge in the Meuse-Argonne, was resumed, November 1. The fortnight's pause had been well spent on reorganization, for the new U.S. advance went forward smoothly and reached Sedan and the railway within a week.

While Foch prepared for a new offensive to begin on November 14, Germany underwent a political revolution, and the Kaiser was forced to abdicate and flee the country, November 9. The Germans were now incapable of further resistance. At 5 A.M., November 11, the German delegates accepted the terms dictated to them in Foch's railway carriage in the Forest of Compiègne. The last shots of World War I were fired six hours later.

B. H. LIDDELL HART

The Armistice was virtually an unconditional surrender by Germany (see ARMISTICE, *Armistice Terms and Specific Armistices*). Formal peace between Germany and all of the Allies (except Russia of course) was concluded at Versailles, Jan. 18–June 28, 1919 (see VERSAILLES, TREATY OF). For discussion of peace treaties between the Allies and others of the Central Powers see NEUILLY, TREATY OF (Bulgaria); ST. GERMAIN, TREATY OF (Austria); SÈVRES, TREATY OF (Turkey); TRIANON, TREATY OF (Hungary). See also articles on persons, places, battles, campaigns, and weapons mentioned.

BIBLIOGRAPHY

BACKGROUND: Harry E. Barnes, *Genesis of the World War* (1927); Frank P. Chambers, *War Behind the War, 1914–1918: A History of the Political and Civilian Fronts* (1939); John S. Ewart, *Roots and Causes of the Wars (1914–1918)* 2 vols. (1925); Sidney B. Fay, *Origins of the World War*, 2 vols. in 1(1948); George P. Gooch, *Before the War*, 2 vols. (1936); Wolfram W. Gottlieb, *Studies in Secret Diplomacy During the First World War* (1957); Arno J. Mayer, *Political Origins of the New Diplomacy, 1917–1918* (1959); Walter Millis, *Road to War: America, 1914–1917* (1935); Pierre Renouvin, *Immediate Origins of the War (28th June—4th August 1914)* (1928).

GENERAL HISTORIES: John Buchan, *History of the Great War*, 4 vols. (1922); Cyril B. Falls, *Great War* (1959); Irvin S. Guernsey, *Reference History of the War* (1920); Francis W. Halsey, comp., *Literary Digest History of the World War*, 10 vols. (1919); Sir John A. Hammerton, *World War (Pictorial History of the Great War, 1914–1918)* 2 vols. (1935); Basil H. Liddell Hart, *Real War, 1914–1918* (1930), *History of the World War, 1914–1918* (1934); Carlton J. H. Hayes, *Brief History of the Great War* (1943); Charles F. Horne and Walter F. Austin, eds., *Source Records of the Great War*, 7 vols. (1923); Francis J. Reynolds, ed., *Story of the Great War*, 8 vols. (1916–1920); Frank H. Simonds, *History of the World War*, 5 vols. (1917–1920).

CAMPAIGNS: Sir Charles E. Callwell, *Dardanelles* (1919); Sir James E. Edmonds, *Military Operations, France and Belgium*, 5 vols. (1922–32); Philip H. Gibbs, *Battle of the Somme* (1917); T. E. Lawrence, *Seven Pillars of Wisdom* (1947); Hunter Liggett, *A. E. F., Ten Years Ago in France* (1928); Alan Moorehead, *Gallipoli* (1956); Frederick Palmer, *Our Greatest Battle (the Meuse-Argonne)* (1919); Henri P. B. O. Pétain, *Verdun* (1930); Edward A. Powell, *Italy at War and the Allies in the West* (1919); Marion C. Siney, *Allied Blockade of Germany, 1914–1916* (1957); Frederick E. Whitton, *Marne Campaign* (1917).

ARMS AND SERVICES: Josephus Daniels, *Our Navy at War* (1922); Thomas G. Frothingham, *Guide to the Military History of the World War, 1914–1918* (1920), *Naval History of the World War*, 3 vols. (1926); John R. Jellicoe, *Grand Fleet, 1914–1916: Its Creation, Development and Work* (1919); Douglas W. Johnson, *Topography and Strategy in the War* (1917); David Masters, *Submarine War* (1935); Sir Henry J. Newbolt, *Naval Operations* (Official History of the Great War, vol. 5) (1931); Sir Walter A. Raleigh, *War in the Air*, 6 vols. (1922–37); Reinhard Scheer, *Germany's High Sea Fleet in the World War* (1934); Owen G. Thetford and Edwin J. Riding, comps., *Aircraft of the 1914–1918 War* (1954); Edwin T. Woodhall, *Spies of the Great War* (1932).

MEMOIRS AND BIOGRAPHIES: Arminius, pseud., *From Sarajevo to the Rhine: Generals of the Great War* (1933); Georges Clemenceau, *Grandeur and Misery of Victory* (1930); Charles G. Dawes, *Journal of the Great War*, 2 vols. (1921); Ferdinand Foch, *Memoirs* (1931); David Lloyd George, *War Memoirs*, 6 vols. (1933–37); James W. Gerard, *My Four Years in Germany* (1917); Paul von Hindenburg, *Out of My Life* (1920); Edward M. House, *Intimate Papers* (1926–1928); John J. Pershing, *My Experiences in the World War*, 2 vols. (1931).

A war sparked in Europe spread to involve 57 nations in a worldwide conflagration.

WORLD WAR II, 1939–45, a war fought on three continents (and Oceania) and three oceans, and involving 57 nations. On one side were the Allies— later known as the United Nations, chief of whom were the United States; the United Kingdom, and the British Empire and Commonwealth; the U.S.S.R., France, and China. On the other side were the Axis nations, chiefly Germany, Italy, and Japan. The conflict began with an unfolding series of Axis aggressions —against Poland, 1939, which led Britain and France to declare war; against the U.S.S.R., June, 1941; and against the United States, December, 1941. The war was fought in two theaters: Europe, including North Africa, from 1939 to May, 1945; and the Pacific, from late 1941 to September, 1945, and including the last phases of the Chinese-Japanese conflict, that had begun in 1937. See articles on places, battles, campaigns, and persons mentioned.

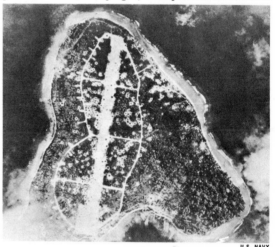

U.S. NAVY
Navy air bombardments were essential to the Allied victory in World War II. Here bombing has pockmarked a Japanese airbase on Ballale Island, one of the Solomon Islands.

Background. World War II began on Sept. 1, 1939, when Germany invaded Poland, but the war had been in the making from the time of Adolf Hitler's coming to power in Germany, January, 1933. Nazi foreign policy was based in part on principles laid down in *Mein Kampf*, an autobiography written by Adolf Hitler in 1923, and on a refusal to accept the losses of territory and population imposed by the Treaty of Versailles, 1919. This policy sought the reunion of all Germans in a single state, and the securing of 'living space' for German expansion, through the domination of eastern Europe including the Ukraine. As a step toward these goals, it was thought necessary to make Italy an ally, to assure the neutrality of Great Britain, to destroy French power, to bring Austria, Czechoslovakia, and Poland under subjection, and to reduce Soviet objections to German expansion by forming a Nazi-Soviet alliance.

Hitler first worked to restore Germany's military strength. The Treaty of Versailles had abolished Germany's air force, restricted her navy, limited her army to a long-term force of 100,000 men, and forbidden her to build fortifications in the Rhineland or within 50 kilometers east of the Rhine. In addition, Germany had joined the League of Nations, and was taking part in the world disarmament conference that had opened in February, 1932. Hitler soon withdrew from both the disarmament conference and the league. When Italy invaded Ethiopia, 1935, a crisis was created during which Hitler was able to throw over the restrictions on Germany's armaments, to announce that an air force had been created, and to introduce conscription so as to expand the army. An agreement with Britain followed, which allowed Germany to expand her navy and to begin building submarines. In 1936, Hitler sent troops into the Rhineland.

In 1936 Germany and Italy intervened in Spain to secure the triumph of Gen. Francisco Franco and to test out new weapons. This partnership, known as the Rome-Berlin Axis, combined with the democracies' reluctance to risk war, allowed Germany to risk even bolder strokes. In March, 1938, Germany invaded and annexed Austria. In September, after a crisis which brought Europe to the brink of war, the Munich Agreement gave Germany the Sudeten region of Czechoslovakia. In March, 1939, Hitler sent troops to occupy Prague, assumed a protectorate over Bohemia and Moravia, set up Slovakia as a puppet state, and demanded Danzig and a road across the Polish Corridor. In spring, 1939, Italy seized Albania and then signed a military alliance with Germany.

Throughout this period, Britain and France felt they could only lose by war and pursued a policy of appeasement even at the expense of their solemn pledges; but each new crisis ended with the two democracies at an increased disadvantage in the European balance of power. The turning point was Hitler's occupation of Prague. He had promised that the Sudetenland was his last territorial demand. In March, 1939, he broke this promise with the annexation of Czechoslovakia, and his demands on Poland showed that new aggression was being prepared. Britain and France now had to decide either to oppose any further advance or surrender Europe to Nazi Germany. France already had an alliance with Poland; and in April, 1939, Britain promised to support Poland if its existence were threatened. Neither state, however, could give direct help in case of attack. The situation hinged on the Soviet Union, but it also wanted to avoid war, and when Germany offered a nonaggression pact, the U.S.S.R. accepted it. The German-Soviet Pact (Aug. 21, 1939) freed Hitler from the threat of a war on two fronts, and led to the German invasion of Poland, September 1, and to British and French declarations of war on Germany, September 3.

The Polish Campaign. Poland was exposed to German attack from three directions. The German armies were vastly superior in numbers, equipment, and organization. Only partly mobilized when war broke out, Poland brought into action 40 infantry divisions, 10 cavalry brigades, and a motorized brigade. Against Poland the Germans massed 70 divisions, 14 of them motorized or mechanized, and an air force outnumbering Poland's by more than 8 to 1.

The campaign took the form of a series of attacks designed to encircle the Polish forces. In the north, two armies struck from Pomerania and East Prussia at the Polish Corridor, while a force from East Prussia drove south toward Warsaw. Along the Silesian frontier, Gen. Karl Rudolf Gerd von Rundstedt's army group thrust prongs toward Łódź and Kielce, while his forces in Slovakia advanced on Kraców. Within two days the frontier defenses had given way and the Poles were in retreat. On September 5 the Germans joined hands across the corridor. Two German prongs now converged on the Polish forces west of Warsaw. The advance on Warsaw from the north struck heavy going, and a German tank force which reached the city on September 9 was beaten back. But a new encircling movement threatened the capital. The German forces thrust east of Warsaw toward Brest-Litovsk while, on the southern wing, tank columns reached the San River by September 12 and headed in the direction of Lvov.

The Poles now tried to form a defense line with Warsaw as its pivot, with one front running eastward

to halt the German drive from East Prussia, and another extending southward along the line of the Vistula. A Polish counterattack checked the southern German spearhead. The northern front was more difficult to establish, and Warsaw was virtually surrounded, September 16; The U.S.S.R. sent troops across the frontier and announced the occupation of eastern Poland, September 17; and the Soviets and Germans partitioned Poland, September 29.

Lull in the West. Germany was able to throw the bulk of her forces into Poland because Britain and France were not ready to embark on a major offensive against the fortifications of the Westwall. They preferred to remain in fortified positions and force Germany to batter her armies against them, wearing down her strength; whereupon they would crush the weary Germans with a decisive counterattack. By strangling Germany in the grip of sea power, they hoped to sap her resources. Germany would be driven to the gamble of an assault on the Maginot Line or a drive through the Low Countries; and in either case the Allies believed that their defensive strategy would insure her defeat. Meanwhile the main task was to bring to bear the superior potential resources which the Allies believed they possessed. French manpower was mobilized, a British expeditionary force was transported to the Continent, and war production was stepped up in an effort to overtake Germany's superiority in such modern weapons as tanks and planes.

Germany's economy was regulated for war purposes, and facilities for producing synthetic and substitute materials had been extensively developed. The U.S.S.R.'s neutrality added to German sources of supplies from abroad. But overseas trade was still important to Germany, and the task of checking this fell on the British and French navies. Their superiority in surface strength let them clamp a close control over neutral commerce and maintain constant watch on the sea approaches to Germany. Even so, merchant ships slipped through their net, and British and French sea supply lines were attacked by German submarines and surface raiders—particularly pocket battleships, two of which were at sea in the closing months of 1939. On December 13 the British cruiser *Exeter* and two British light cruisers caught up with the *Graf Spee* off the Uruguayan coast. The lighter ships so damaged the *Graf Spee* that she fled to the neutral port of Montevideo. The German captain, ordered to leave port or be interned, and unwilling to fight his way clear, moved out of the harbor and scuttled his ship.

The Northern Flank. The first winter of the war saw land operations at a standstill. It was a period marked by Germany's attempts to consolidate her political position in southern and eastern Europe, by Russia's advance in the Baltic area and her winter war with Finland, and by Allied efforts to increase economic pressure on Germany.

The Soviet invasion of Finland aroused indignation in Allied countries, which planned military help to the smaller country; thus the Allies came close to becoming embroiled with the Soviet Union and driving her into the arms of Germany. The conclusion of peace between the U.S.S.R. and Finland, March, 1940, ended the plan; but the crisis increased Germany's fear of danger from Scandinavia and her determination to secure her northern flank.

On April 9, 1940, German troops occupied Denmark. Simultaneously the Germans struck from the sea at six Norwegian ports along the coast from Oslo to Narvik; within a few hours the Germans controlled the chief centers of Norway. The Norwegians rallied, but successful resistance depended on Allied help. The first Allied troops landed, April 16, but lacked heavy equipment or adequate antiaircraft guns. German superiority in the air could not be challenged, and the growing superiority of German infantry and tank forces, in numbers and equipment, enabled them to

WORLD WAR II

Although hard hit by the attack on Pearl Harbor, the U.S. Navy had thwarted the Japanese in the Pacific by mid-1942 and by late 1943 had taken the offensive against the enemy.

The jungle islands of the Pacific were outposts of terror where the men of both sides fought against thick tropical foliage and the insufferable climate as well as the enemy.

House-to-house fighting was prevalent in the last phase of World War II, as Allied forces moved into the Nazi homeland and destroyed the remaining pockets of German resistance.

The Allies used highly mechanized units against Rommel's Panzer forces during the North African Campaign, 1941–43. Here, an Allied tank destroyer moves over the desert roads.

Camouflage was used effectively during winter months by the Soviets. Here, troops in white mop up remnants of the German infantry in a village on the central front, 1943.

take the offensive. Within two weeks the Allied situation had become hopeless, and by June the Germans were in undisputed possession of Norway.

Invasion of the Low Countries. The outcome of the Norwegian campaign greatly increased the uneasiness of Allied public opinion about the conduct of the war. In March, this resulted in a change of government in France, where Paul Reynaud came to power. In Great Britain the Neville Chamberlain government was replaced by a coalition under Winston Churchill. These political changes had no immediate effect on Allied strategy; military leaders were content to await Hitler's next move. Finally, on May 10, came the long-expected invasion of Belgium and the Netherlands.

Two French armies and the British Expeditionary Force, with a total of 25 divisions, swung into position from Mesières to Louvain, with the Belgian army on their left; another French army dashed toward Holland to strengthen Dutch resistance. The five German armies whose assault these forces had to meet were greatly preponderant in armor; and their air support vastly exceeded anything available to the Allies. On May 15 the Dutch capitulated and Holland was out of the war. In Belgium, the landing of glider troops inside the fort of Eben Emael forced its surrender and tore a gap in the frontier defenses that had been expected to delay the German advance.

Farther south, the Germans struck their decisive blow just above the Maginot Line at Sedan. This area was covered by the Ardennes Forest, which the French had supposed impenetrable; but the Germans penetrated it in three days, and their armored spearheads fell upon the slender French forces holding the line of the Meuse. The Germans crossed at Sedan and at two points farther north, May 13, pouring in reinforcements to exploit the foothold; they broke through completely, May 17, and raced westward toward the coast. By May 20 the Allied forces in Belgium were cut off and threatened with encirclement. The Allies fell back behind Brussels, while in the rear the Germans threatened Allied supply lines as they drove up the coast. The Germans launched a heavy attack on the Belgian army, May 24; this army surrendered, May 28, exposing the Allied left wing, and apparently sealing the doom of the French and British forces.

The one hope that remained was escape by sea before the outlet at Dunkerque was closed. French and British fell back toward the coast and, while rear-guard actions provided the time so desperately needed, the British navy and thousands of small craft of all kinds, aided in the final stages by French ships, carried out the evacuation. The royal air force, though inferior in numbers, controlled the air over Dunkerque, covering the withdrawal. When the operation ended, June 2, over 330,000 troops had been taken off the beaches, of whom 122,000 were French or Belgian.

The Fall of France. If Hitler had been able to follow up Dunkerque by an immediate invasion of England, that island probably would have fallen. But the Germans lacked the necessary barges and other craft to transport an army across the English Channel, and men trained for landing operations. The British navy controlled the seas, and to offset this factor by air power meant that the royal air force must first be destroyed. A crushing blow against France while she was still reeling was dictated; and with France out of the war, it was not inconceivable that the British might make peace.

The French, meanwhile, strove desperately to organize an effective defense. Along the line of the Somme they improvised the Weygand Line, adapting their methods to the lessons of German armored tactics. Unhappily they lacked both time and resources. They had fewer than 50 divisions against double that number. The German offensive was launched, June 5; the French fell back to the Seine,

BRITISH OFFICIAL PHOTO

The German attempt to annihilate Britain in the Blitz of 1940 was bravely foiled by the R.A.F., but nightly raids by the German Luftwaffe brought the tragedy of war to London.

June 8; the government left Paris, June 10; and the Germans crossed both the Seine and the Marne, June 12. To prevent the destruction of Paris, it was declared an open city, and on June 14 the Germans marched unopposed into the capital. Italy, avid for gains without effort, declared war on June 10. By this time the French army had been cut into three main segments, and the duty of resistance was increasingly falling on isolated units.

Within the French government, one faction was for continuing the fight, but another, led by Pierre Laval and including both Marshal Henri Philippe Pétain and Gen. Maxime Weygand, whose military prestige carried great weight, felt that surrender was unavoidable. On June 16, by a vote of 14 to 10, the French cabinet decided to ask for an armistice; and on June 22 the terms were signed with Germany and Italy. France was out of the war, with most of her territory under German occupation, the rest nominally ruled from Vichy by a government formally headed by Pétain but in which Laval was the moving spirit and the agent of German control.

The Battle of Britain. With the fall of France, Britain and the Dominions stood alone against the Axis forces. The Atlantic Coast from Norway to the Pyrenees was in German hands and, in the channel ports, troops were massing for the invasion of England. German plans called for the landing of 22 divisions, with 17 more in reserve, as well as airborne troops. For operations on this scale, in the face of the British navy, the Nazis felt they must command the air. There were raids on British ports and shipping during July, 1940; and then the Germans began a sustained effort to knock out Britain's air defenses, August 8.

The royal air force had at this stage around 1,000 fighter pilots, and some 640 planes. Though greatly inferior to the enemy in numbers, this force was high in quality and morale, and was aided by the radar screen which gave warning of approaching bombers. Its Spitfires and Hurricanes were the finest fighter planes of the time. The defenders had to battle raiding forces of 500 or 600 planes day after day. In the most intensive period, from August 24 to September 6, the British lost 103 pilots killed and 128 wounded. Plane losses by this time were nearly 500, and losses exceeded replacements. They were still lower than German losses, which went as high as 73 planes downed on the single day of August 15. A switch in German tactics eased the pressure, when the Germans turned from the airfields to concentrate their attack on London, September 7. For a month London took terrible punishment from the air; but after the first week in October, the intensity of the assault declined, and by the end of the month the attempt to attain quick victory by daylight bombing had been abandoned. German losses of at least 2,375 planes were too high to be continued, and German bombers turned to less accurate, but also less costly, night raids. This meant that invasion was indefinitely postponed.

The Battle of the Atlantic. The adoption of night bombing by the Germans was followed by a broadening of objectives to all Britain's ports and industrial cities. The new phase began with a mass raid on Coventry, November 14. During the following winter and spring, the Germans made a sustained attempt to destroy Britain's war production and to wreck the ports taking in vital supplies from overseas.

The whole task of guarding the seas now fell on the shoulders of the hard-pressed British navy. During the winter of 1940 it looked like a losing battle. British naval resources were inadequate to maintain an effective convoy system against wolf packs of submarines seeking to starve Britain into surrender. The transfer by the United States to Britain of 50 overage destroyers, and Canada's production of frigates and corvettes designed for convoy work, offered some relief but did not redress the balance. Shipping losses ran far beyond replacements, and the chief hope was that expanding shipbuilding in the United States and Canada would close the gap before it was too late.

Nonetheless, Britain not only held out against the assault from air and sea, but struck back as well. Her planes hunted down German submarines. Her fleet kept watch over the German-occupied coast. When the new German battleship *Bismarck* appeared in the North Atlantic, May, 1941, she was promptly intercepted, and on May 27 she was caught and sunk. By the spring of 1941 a counteroffensive had begun in the air. Night raids on the Ruhr and Rhineland and on German oil installations grew in weight and frequency. When German strength shifted to the east for the Soviet offensive, the blitz against England subsided and released the air power that at the moment was Britain's chief offense weapon.

Libya and East Africa. In Africa, Italy faced a depleted British fleet and a small force guarding Suez. British Somaliland was overrun in August, 1940, and in September an Italian force advanced into Egypt from Libya as far as Sidi Barrani. The British did not give up without argument. At sea, British squadrons swept the Mediterranean almost unchallenged. A raid on Taranto, Nov. 11, 1940, crippled three Italian battleships. On Jan. 10, 1941, British warships bombarded Genoa. On March 28 an Italian squadron near Crete was attacked by carrier aircraft, and in a night action British warships met the enemy off Cape Matapan, sinking three cruisers and two destroyers and severely damaging the battleship *Vittorio Veneto*.

Land operations were equally disastrous for Italy. In Egypt a force of 30,000 under Gen. Archibald P. Wavell confronted Marshal Rodolfo Graziani's army of 260,000 at Sidi Barrani. While Graziani was engaged in cautious preparations, Wavell struck. The Italian forces were driven across Cyrenaica. When Wavell reached El Agheila, February 5, he had shattered Graziani's army and taken over 133,000 prisoners. Simultaneously a British force of 70,000 invaded Italian East Africa with its garrison of 300,000. On April 6, 1941, Addis Ababa was liberated, and by the end of November Italian East Africa was in British hands. Meanwhile, however, Germany had come to the aid of her ally: The German Afrika Korps, under Gen. Erwin Rommel, and the Italians were able to launch a drive, March, 1941, which in three weeks recovered Cyrenaica except for the port of Tobruk, to which the British clung. An attempt by Wavell to stage a counteroffensive in June was unsuccessful; and Britain's position was threatened further by the loss of Greece.

Greece and Crete. During autumn and winter, 1940, Hungary, Rumania, and Bulgaria were pressed into agreements which made them economic and military satellites of the Axis. On Oct. 28, 1940, Italian troops in Albania invaded Greece. But Greek forces checked the Italian drive and even advanced

U.S. NAVY
The depth charge became a more effective antisubmarine weapon after improved launching devices, more powerful explosives, and sonar were developed during World War II.

into Albania. Then on Apr. 6, 1941, German troops invaded Yugoslavia and Greece. Organized resistance in Yugoslavia was crushed in two weeks. British forces were sent to Greece, but were unable to halt the German armored columns, and Germany's command of the air was a paramount factor. The British forces were forced into a retreat to the sea. On April 23 the Greeks capitulated, and by May 1 the British forces had withdrawn to Crete with a loss of 14,000 men. On May 20 an air-sea attack was launched against the island. Parachute and glider troops captured a foothold and, under cover of air power, rapidly built up strength. On May 29 Crete was evacuated with a loss of 13,000 troops.

The Invasion of the U.S.S.R. The Soviet Union had sought to offset Germany's eastward penetration by pushing her own control westward. The annexation of the Baltic States, the seizure of eastern Poland, and the attack on Finland were all part of a pattern. Her uneasiness over Germany's advance down the Danube was shown by her insistence on securing Bessarabia when the Axis forced a readjustment of Rumania's frontiers, 1940. Both states were maneuvering for the impending clash.

By 1941 Hitler had decided to attack. The progress of Soviet preparations made it desirable to strike before these were complete. The need to devote German military strength to watching the U.S.S.R. hampered the campaign against Britain and was blamed for its failure. There was hope that, by launching a crusade against Bolshevism, Hitler might find a basis for peace in the west, and Rudolf Hess flew to Britain with hopes of persuading the British to withdraw from the war.

On June 22, 1941, nearly 200 divisions were hurled against the tremendous front from the Baltic to the Black Sea, supported by the bulk of the German air force. At first their success was spectacular. By the end of the month the main defenses had been pushed back to the Berezina. To the north a column thrust through the Baltic States toward Leningrad. In the south the western Ukraine was overrun and Lvov fell by the end of June. However, the Russians showed themselves able to slow down the tank spearheads and prevent a complete breakthrough. Their refusal to surrender when cut off gave the main armies time to re-form after each retreat. While the

Russian armies remained intact, territorial gains were not decisive. Many factories were moved far to the east, and supplies from Britain and the United States were soon on the way.

In the south the Germans swept over the Ukraine, closed on Kiev and thrust a spearhead beyond the isolated Crimea to Rostov. In the center and the north the Germans found rough going. By September they had battered their way to the gates of Leningrad, beginning a siege which was not finally lifted until January, 1944. The German advance on Moscow was bitterly opposed in the battles for Smolensk and Kaluga: though both these points were in German hands by September, the drive was temporarily exhausted while still short of its goal. The effort was renewed in October. The Russians were pressed back along an arc whose main points were Vyazma and Bryansk and Orel. A state of siege was proclaimed in Moscow itself, but the defenses held. In a last effort the Germans launched a fresh assault in mid-November. The spearheads pressed perilously close, and a tank column broke through one of Moscow's suburbs. But the first week of December saw the Germans halted. Rostov was retaken, November 29, and the Russians embarked on a counteroffensive, December 6, to relieve Moscow against exhausted German armies with overburdened supply lines and equipment inadequate against the Russian cold. By January, 1942, the Moscow front had been driven back 50 miles from the capital. The Germans still clung to strong points, and their offensive strength was unimpaired; but the counteroffensive was a bright spot in a period which saw setbacks for the Allies in Africa, Asia, and the Pacific.

Pearl Harbor. In the Far East, Japan occupied Indochina after the fall of France. A treaty between Japan, Germany, and Italy promised mutual support in case the United States should enter the war. A neutrality agreement between the U.S.S.R. and Japan, April, 1941, followed by the German invasion of the U.S.S.R., removed any immediate danger from the U.S.S.R. Britain and the United States moved toward a stiffer policy, but this made Japan determined to strike while her chances were most favorable. An envoy was sent to Washington to spin out discussions while Japan completed preparations for the gamble on which she had decided.

The blow fell on Pearl Harbor on Dec. 7, 1941. Over 300 planes from a Japanese task force struck at the U.S. base, taking it by surprise. The defending air forces, caught on the ground, were virtually wiped out. Of eight battleships in the harbor, five were put out of action, crippling U.S. naval power in the Pacific. Simultaneously, Japanese forces struck at Midway Island, landed on Wake, Guam, and Luzon, and invaded Malaya. Germany and Italy supported Japan by declaring war on the United States, December 11.

U.S. ARMY

After Japan disrupted China's access to Indochina and the sea, supplies had either to be flown into China or taken there in trucks via the tortuous Burma Road.

The next few months saw spectacular progress by Japan. The British warships *Prince of Wales* and *Repulse* were sunk attempting to intercept the Malayan expedition. Luzon fell, April, 1942, after a gallant stand by U.S. and Philippine forces on Bataan, and the rest of the Philippines were soon overrun. Singapore fell, February 15. Borneo and New Guinea were invaded, and an Allied force of cruisers and destroyers was annihilated in the Java Sea at the end of February. Java was conquered early in March; Burma had fallen by the end of April; and the Japanese stood at the borders of India and almost within striking distance of Australia.

The Crisis in Africa. By November, 1941, both sides in Africa were preparing for an offensive. The newly formed British Eighth Army struck on November 18. The XXX Corps swept around the southern flank of the defenses along the Egyptian border and headed for Tobruk. Farther north, the XIII Corps strove to join other British columns in a crushing blow at the remaining Axis forces. Rommel, taken by surprise, rallied and struck back. The German tanks, fewer in number than those of the British, were heavier in armor and fire power, and Rommel used them in deadly concentrations against the more dispersed British forces. British determination to fight it out turned the tide: the first corridor thrust through to Tobruk was broken by Rommel's armor, but a more solid junction was made, December 4. Rommel retreated westward, and by early January he had fallen back to El Agheila. But reinforcements were on the way to him; British supply lines were strained, and it was to Rommel's advantage to strike before British reinforcements could come up. On Jan. 22, 1942, he struck the exposed British forces, which were forced to retreat to a line from El Gazala to Bir Hachèim. There, in mid-February, Rommel was again brought to a halt.

Both sides prepared for a new effort. This time Rommel struck first. On May 27, 1942, his armor swung around Bir Hachèim from the south and drove toward Tobruk. The thrust was halted by British concentrations around Knightsbridge, and for several days the battle raged. Then a concentrated Axis assault obliged the Free French garrison at Bir Hachèim to withdraw on June 10, and a tank battle on June 13 resulted in heavy British losses. A swift attack broke the defenses of Tobruk before they were fully organized and forced the surrender of its garrison of 25,000. It was largely the royal air force's command of the air that saved the retreating Eighth Army. Rear-guard actions held off pursuit while British forces withdrew to the defensive position of El Alamein, Egypt. There on June 30 the Axis advance was brought to a halt 70 miles from Alexandria. The Eighth Army had lost 80,000 men and the bulk of its tanks in the course of the fighting.

Stalingrad and the Caucasus. The Russian winter offensive, while it relieved Moscow, failed to wrest the initiative permanently from the hands of the Germans. On June 28 the Germans launched their main offensive in the Ukraine; and on July 1, after a siege of eight months, the Germans gained possession of Sevastopol. The immediate German objective was the conquest of the industrial and food-producing areas of the Ukraine and the oil fields of the Caucasus. Tied to this was the objective of securing the lower Volga and thence launching a wide outflanking movement which, co-ordinated with a drive in the north, would encircle Moscow.

World War II

The first blow was struck from Kursk toward the Don at Voronezh. A force of 80 divisions crashed through the Russian defenses. At the end of July Rostov fell, and the southern arm of the German offensive reached the foothills of the Caucasus by the beginning of September. The advance to the Volga encountered greater obstacles. On the northern flank the Russians clung to Voronezh. Between Voronezh and the bend of the Don the Germans were unable to establish substantial footholds across the river. Within the Don bend the Russians fought a delaying battle, and not until August 22 did the Germans cross the river. They faced even harder going between the Don and the Volga; but gradually their forces pushed up to the Volga. By September 12 their columns had reached Stalingrad, which now became the focus of the struggle and its symbol. Every house became a defense point. German bombs and shells reduced the city to ruins, but the Russians fought amid the wreckage. For two months the siege continued. Gradually the Germans reduced the defenders to pockets along the river bank. By the first week in November the German fury was spent, and conditions were set for the counterattack that turned the tide.

The Battle of Supply. For over a year, virtually the whole weight of Germany and her satellites had been thrown against the Soviet Union. The U.S.S.R. could not endure the strain indefinitely. It was urgently desirable that the other Allies draw off substantial German forces, and an invasion of western Europe was most certain to do this.

But first the problem of supply had to be solved. In 1942 Allied war production was still inadequate to meet the demands upon it. Britain's manpower was almost at its peak of mobilization. United States factories turned out 50,000 planes, 1942, and by early 1943 were producing 2,000 tanks and 7,000 planes a month. A U.S. Army of 9 million men was being trained and equipped. But urgent demands in the Mediterranean and the Pacific impeded the massing of necessary forces and equipment for an invasion of Europe. There was also the problem of getting supplies to the battle areas. Over 8 million tons of shipping were sunk by German submarines in 1942, and at one stage losses were almost equal to the amount being turned out by U.S. shipyards. The submarine had to be mastered before a major effort against Europe could be undertaken.

The Bombing Offensive, steadily growing in scale, linked the campaign against German submarines with the attempt to wreck German war potential. Coastal bases were repeatedly attacked, and raids were directed against major shipping and naval centers, along with centers of transportation and heavy industry. By summer, 1942, U.S. bombers had begun daylight raids on points from the Baltic to southern Germany. On May 30, 1942, more than 1,100 British bombers struck at Cologne and the thousand-plane raid was soon followed by the thousand-ton raid as the standard for a major attack. See AIR WARFARE, *World War II, 1939–45.*

To the extent that German production was reduced and German transport disrupted, the Russians shared in the benefits of these raids; but the effect as yet was imperceptible. It was only by engaging at least 50 German divisions that the Allies could satisfy the U.S.S.R. demand for substantial relief; but when all factors were considered, it was decided that a major assault on Europe must wait for at least another year. The risks of an invasion of France were illustrated by the Dieppe raid, Aug. 19, 1942, during which a force succeeded in landing and maintaining a foothold for several hours; but the attack had little success in penetrating Dieppe, and the force of 5,000 lost over 3,300 men. Thus it was decided to embark on the conquest of North Africa.

Victory at Alamein. The first step was to dispose of the Axis threat to Egypt and the Suez Canal. In

PAUL'S PHOTOS
Nürnberg, a production center for machinery, planes, and tank engines, was heavily stormed by the Allies. Survivors in the ruined city lived in huts and washed in the streets.

the race to build up strength, the advantage now swung to the British. During the summer the British gained sea and air supremacy in the Mediterranean and harried Axis supply lines. Fresh divisions reached the Eighth Army; a new command team of Sir Harold Alexander and Sir Bernard Montgomery took over; supplies of the newest U.S. tank, the Sherman, helped overcome the earlier inferiority in weight of armor; and the ascendancy of the R.A.F. over the battlefield was an incalculable advantage.

Rommel made a strenuous effort to strike before the growing Allied strength could be brought into play. On August 30 he attacked the southern end of the line at the Qattara Depression, but he was unable to break through. The British assault was launched on the night of October 23, striking the northern sector some 10 to 12 miles inland from the coast. A bulge was driven into the German defenses and on November 1 the Eighth Army broke through. In a battle around El Aqqaqir, November 2, Rommel's armor was shattered, and his forces began a full retreat, November 4. By mid-February, after a pursuit of 1,400 miles, the Eighth Army stood before the Mareth Line, where Rommel turned to make a stand.

The Conquest of North Africa. After the fall of France, French North Africa was nominally neutral under Vichy. Its occupation by the Allies would provide bases for control of the Mediterranean and for invasion of southern Europe.

The invasion of North Africa took place Nov. 8, 1943. Convoyed by a powerful naval force, the largest invasion armada yet employed in warfare moved on Casablanca, Oran, and Algiers. The whole enterprise was commanded by Gen. Dwight D. Eisenhower. The hope that the French would welcome the invasion without resistance was frustrated, and although fighting was half-hearted, ending after only three days, it had important consequences: in Europe it gave Hitler an excuse to occupy the whole of France; and in Tunisia it gave the Axis a chance to pour in men and equipment before the Allies could occupy that country, which prolonged the battle in Africa until the following spring.

The first thrusts were made toward Tunis and Bizerte. However the Germans had forestalled the Allies. The first Allied thrusts were thrown back. The Axis forces held the main ports and the heights commanding the coastal plain, and the Allies settled down on a mountain line parallel to the coast some 50 miles inland. This was the situation when Rommel's forces arrived in Tunisia. In mid-February Rommel struck against the American sector in the south, drove the defenders back 55 miles to seize the Kasserine Pass, and threatened the Allied communication and supply system behind the Tunisian front. These gains were of little permanent advantage. The

Germans were checked, and Rommel withdrew to the Mareth Line. In March the Axis garrison launched an attack on the Eighth Army. It failed with serious losses in tanks. The Eighth Army in its turn attacked on the night of March 20, and by March 28 the main defenses of southern Tunisia had fallen to the Allies.

By mid-April the Afrika Korps had merged with forces under Marshal von Arnim for a last-ditch defense of the northeast corner of Tunisia. The final assault opened on April 19. United States forces captured Mateur on May 3 and opened the way for an advance on Bizerta. To the south the British massed tanks and planes for an all-out effort along a route from Medjez-el-Bab to Tunis. On May 6 they blasted their way through the Axis positions. On May 12 the last resistance was subdued, and North Africa was firmly in Allied hands.

The Stalingrad Offensive. At Stalingrad the Russians had been preparing a great counteroffensive. It was launched on November 19. One army group in the north broke out from a bridgehead across the Don at Serafimovitch. Another struck at Kalach, cutting off the German Sixth Army which lay between that town and Stalingrad. The encircled Germans made no effort to fight clear: Field Marshal Hermann Goering had promised to keep them supplied from the air, and Hitler had ordered them to hold fast. A German tank force tried to break through from the southwest, but was thrown back, and the Sixth Army was doomed; by February 2 resistance was crushed and a German force of 330,000 had been liquidated. Meanwhile, attacks were launched along the Don. The third week in December saw Russian thrusts in the direction of Kharkov, while the progress of the Russians along the lower Don threatened Rostov and the more than 35 German divisions in the Caucasus. An attack on this latter force, in January, was the signal for a German withdrawal, and on February 14 the Germans were forced from Rostov. Kursk fell, February 8, and Kharkov was taken, February 16; in three months the U.S.S.R. had advanced some 400 miles. The Germans, thrown back on their bases, launched a counterdrive, however, and regained Kharkov, March 14. By the end of March a deadlock had set in, with the U.S.S.R. holding a salient westward from Kursk and the Germans clinging to a salient eastward from Orel. Meanwhile in the north, the capture of Schlüsselburg (renamed Petrokrepost, 1944) enabled the Russians to drive a corridor through to Leningrad; and the capture of Rzhev, March 3, dislodged the Germans from one of their main strongholds on the Moscow sector. The Russian offensive was the first major setback administered to the Germans in Europe.

Turn of the Tide in the Pacific. In the Pacific, the U.S. Navy had so far recovered from its losses at Pearl Harbor by summer, 1942, that it was in a position to oppose further Japanese efforts to extend conquests.

The first major defensive action was fought in May, 1942. Early in the month, a new Japanese move was in preparation against the supply lines linking the United States and Australia. An Allied carrier task force was sent to intercept the enemy. On May 7 its planes located one section of the Japanese force in the Coral Sea and attacked it, sinking a carrier. Contact was made with a second force, May 8, and such damage was inflicted on the Japanese fleet that it turned in retreat. A still more decisive battle followed this check to Japanese sea power. The Japanese launched an expedition against Midway. United States naval forces moved to meet it. Battle was joined on June 4 and again fought by carrier planes, assisted on the U.S. side by land-based bombers from Midway. By the end of the day the Japanese force had been compelled to retreat. Land and carrier-based planes harried the enemy for two more days. The Japanese lost 10 warships, including

U.S. ARMY SIGNAL CORPS

Troops and jeeps moved to the front on a highway in Angaur carved out of jungle. U.S. forces took this island in the Palau group only after fierce opposition by the Japanese.

4 carriers. The nature of the action, in which the major surface units never came to grips with each other, emphasized the importance of the air arm.

Midway marked the end of Japanese possession of the initiative in the Pacific. However, the Japanese were still pressing through New Guinea toward Port Moresby and the approaches to Australia; and establishment of a Japanese garrison and air base on Guadalcanal in the Solomons indicated an intention to strike at the main supply route to Australia. To forestall this, it was felt necessary to take Guadalcanal. On Aug. 7, 1942, a force of U.S. Marines landed on Guadalcanal, seized the airfield, and clung on against efforts to dislodge them. The next four months saw a costly naval campaign as the Japanese sought to destroy the U.S. invaders and their covering forces. An attack on August 8 brought the loss of one Australian and three U.S. cruisers. On August 24, a carrier task force intercepted a Japanese transport group and turned it back with heavy losses. Another group was checked off Cape Esperance, October 11. Two weeks later, a Japanese force was defeated near Santa Cruz Islands. The climax came with the Battle of Guadalcanal. It opened on the night of November 13 when a heavy Japanese force was intercepted near Savo Island and turned back. In the next two days a Japanese transport group was virtually destroyed. The Japanese lost two battleships and eight cruisers, in addition to lighter craft. A further Japanese attempt to land reinforcements was broken up off Lunga Point on November 30. United States losses in this series of engagements included two carriers and six cruisers. At one stage the Pacific fleet had only one battleship and one carrier fit for action. But new major units were added to the fleet by autumn, 1942, and Japanese losses, almost double those of the United States, turned the preponderance of strength to the U.S. fleet.

The establishment of U.S. naval ascendancy doomed Japanese efforts to hold Guadalcanal. The arrival of U.S. reinforcements in November, coupled with the check to the Japanese naval effort, decided the issue. On Feb. 7, 1943, the Japanese garrison was withdrawn. Guadalcanal now became a base for operations against the remaining Solomons. New

During a lull in the fighting, members of the U.S. Marine Corps assault forces in the Bougainville jungles listen to a sermon given by their chaplain in a front-line chapel.

Georgia was invaded on July 2; landings were made on Vella Lavella on August 15 and on Bougainville on Nov. 1, 1943; and neutralization of these islands carried the United States on the first stride along the island road that led to Japan.

New Guinea. Simultaneously a drive under Gen. Douglas MacArthur was under way in New Guinea. The check of the Japanese above Port Moresby in the autumn of 1942 was followed by a counterdrive which captured Buna and Gona in December. Naval skirmishing around New Guinea resulted in deterioration of Japanese destroyer strength. Heavy air blows at convoys and escorts approaching New Guinea reached a high on Mar. 3, 1943, when 12 transports and 10 escorting warships were destroyed in the Bismarck Sea. The bases of Salamaua and Lae fell in September, 1943. The extremities of the Japanese penetration were being lopped off, and footholds had been gained for a further advance in New Guinea and the central Pacific.

Sicily and Italy. At the Casablanca Conference, January, 1943, it was decided to invade Sicily. During spring and early summer a sustained air assault was carried out. Allied naval forces imposed a blockade. On June 11, the island of Pantelleria capitulated, clearing the passage across the channel between Tunisia and Sicily. On the night of July 9, 1943, parachute and glider troops descended on Sicily, and at dawn the next day the invading forces landed on the southeast tip of the island. The U.S. Seventh Army went ashore in the vicinity of Licata and Gela. The British Eighth Army landed on the east coast from Cape Passero to Avola. The island held an Axis garrison of 400,000, but the Italians who made up the bulk of its strength put up feeble resistance, and its defense fell on a German force of between three and four divisions. No serious effort was made to defend the whole island. The Germans concentrated on holding a mountain line covering the approaches to Messina, with its center curving around Mount Etna. The Eighth Army was checked in its attempt to advance up the east coast, and Montgomery shifted his weight to his left flank with an assault on the center of the Etna Line. Meanwhile U.S. forces swung into line and joined the assault on the main Axis positions. By August 6 the Etna Line had been split and the Germans were in retreat. Messina was occupied, August 17, and the island was in Allied hands.

The invasion of Italian soil was fatal to Dictator-Premier Benito Mussolini's regime. The king dismissed Mussolini, July 25, and appointed Marshal Pietro Badoglio in his place. By mid-August Badoglio was convinced that there was no alternative to surrender. Secret negotiations began which led to the signing of an armistice on September 3. The terms were virtually unconditional surrender—the formula adopted at Casablanca—and the announcement was held up until a full-scale invasion had been launched against the Italian mainland.

On Sept. 3, 1943, the advance guard of the Eighth Army crossed the Straits of Messina and drove inland against light resistance. Five days later an amphibious force seized Taranto; and on September 9 the U.S. Fifth Army landed on the beaches of Salerno. The Germans concentrated against this last force. While the Allied landing in southern Italy was met by only rear-guard action, the landing at Salerno was hotly opposed by German troops gathered in anticipation of such a move. Air and naval support helped contain German counterattacks, however, and the rapid progress of the Eighth Army up the peninsula threatened the German rear. On September 17 the Eighth and Fifth armies met, and the Germans retired to a line covering Naples from the south. There was a six-day battle for the Sorrento Ridge, but a breach was effected, September 28, and Naples fell to the Allies, October 1.

On the left flank, the Fifth Army broke the Volturno Line, October 13, and the Germans fell back to their "winter line" along the Garigliano (lower Liri River) and the Sangro rivers. The Eighth Army forced the Sangro in the latter part of November; the Moro River was crossed in the second week in December. With the capture of Ortona, the drive came to a halt, and attention turned back to the west coast. Here the Germans had organized their defenses with Cassino as a pivot. A series of assaults carried the outlying strong points but failed to take Cassino itself. On Jan. 22, 1944, the Allies staged a new coastal landing at Anzio in the rear of the German defenses, hoping that this would draw off enough German strength to make possible a breakthrough; but the German commander relied primarily on his reserves to meet the new threat. A fresh drive on Cassino failed; the Anzio beachhead was strongly assailed and the area of the landing was narrowly contained, although it remained a potential threat to the German position. A further effort to break through at Cassino was made, March 15, when a massive air bombardment was directed against the town; but the ground attack followed too slowly, and the Italian front remained deadlocked throughout the winter and spring. The Allies thus found themselves unable to reap the full fruits of Italy's surrender, but the Mediterranean was completely freed, and the invasion of Italy was an initial step toward drawing off some of the German forces available for the Russian front.

Advance to the Dnepr. In the U.S.S.R., the summer of 1943 saw the last serious effort by the Germans to regain the initiative. They launched an attack against the Kursk salient, July 5, and gained

Military cemeteries erected on many of the Pacific Islands during the Solomon Islands campaign are testimony to the high price in lives paid during the hard-fought landings.

some ground, but the main Russian positions held, and after 12 days the German drive stopped. The U.S.S.R. launched an offensive of its own. On July 13 it opened a drive against the German-held salient around Orel. By August 5 the U.S.S.R. had seized Orel and Belgorod. The area of attack expanded into the Ukraine, and a pincers operation was set in motion against Kharkov, which fell on August 23. The offensive was extended to the Donets Basin and the Black Sea coast. Capture of Taganrog, August 30, broke the German defenses in the south, and by September 25 the Soviet armies had reached the bend of the Dnepr.

On the central front the capture of Orel was followed by pressure toward Bryansk and by attacks farther north which threatened Smolensk, the main German base on the central sector. The Desna Line broke in mid-September, and Bryansk fell, September 17. On September 25 Smolensk fell into Russian hands. In three months the U.S.S.R. had advanced 250 miles.

The forces that reached the Dnepr bend established bridgeheads across the river early in October, and from the Dnepr bend to the Black Sea the U.S.S.R. launched attacks, widening their footholds beyond the river. Melitopol fell on October 23, and Kherson fell on November 4, giving the U.S.S.R. command of the east bank of the lower Dnepr. From the bridgehead beyond Krememchug the U.S.S.R. broke out, October 17, to capture Dnepropetrovsk, October 25. A new thrust in mid-November linked the main bridgehead with others farther west, giving the U.S.S.R. command of a 200-mile stretch of the Dnepr and a foothold that extended to a depth of 75 miles. Farther north, Kiev had fallen on November 6.

The Recovery of the Ukraine. On December 13, the U.S.S.R. launched a new offensive against Vitebsk and in heavy fighting encircled it except for a narrow corridor. On December 24, the U.S.S.R. attacked around Kiev, taking the vital rail junction of Zhitomir, December 31; the junction of Berdichev fell, Jan. 5, 1944; and to the south, the Russians threatened the flank of the German forces in the southern Ukraine. These forces were assailed in their turn. Kirovograd was captured, January 8, and on it, with Belaya Tserkov (taken four days previously), was pivoted an enveloping movement against Germans in the intervening area. In the third week of January, Gen. Ivan Konev attacked the eastern base of this salient; a companion thrust was launched from the west by Gen. Nikolai Vatutin; and on February 3 the two Russian columns joined hands to isolate the remnants of 10 German divisions. By the third week of February the trapped Germans had been liquidated. By that date, major operations in the south were temporarily stalled, and the U.S.S.R. shifted its main effort to the area of Leningrad.

Leningrad. For two years only minor action had been seen in this sector. The Germans had consolidated their positions, and the siege lines around Leningrad were a system of fortifications 20 miles deep. The assault was launched, Jan. 14, 1944, by two columns, one from a pocket opposite Kronshtadt and the other from Leningrad itself. In a week of fighting the Leningrad columns broke through the German ring, joined to isolate the German forces between them, and fanned out south and west. Novgorod fell on January 20. Other thrusts developed to force the Germans into general retreat. Staraya Russa fell on February 18; Kholm was taken three days later. By the first week in March the Germans had been driven almost to the border of Latvia and Esthonia; Leningrad was free, and in the north the U.S.S.R. had almost reached its 1939 frontiers.

End of the Ukrainian Campaign. On March 4, in the south, a massive drive under Marshal Georgi Zhukov was launched from west of Zhitomir. Two days later Konev struck in the center of the front toward Uman and Gen. Rodion Malinovsky opened a drive from Krivoy Rog. The German line crumbled. Konev broke through the center and drove to the Bug, while Malinovsky pressed the Germans farther east toward Odessa. By the end of the third week in March, Zhukov had broken through east of Tarnopol, Konev had swept across the Bug and the Dnestr into Bessarabia, and the Germans farther east were pulling out to avoid encirclement. The Prut was reached, March 26, and the U.S.S.R. drove across the border into Rumania. On April 10 Odessa fell to the U.S.S.R. Two days earlier an offensive had been launched against the Crimea. By April 18 the U.S.S.R. stood before Sevastopol; and on May 19 the Germans were driven out. Since the start of the winter drive the U.S.S.R. had captured over 150,000 square miles of territory, killed or captured more than half a million of the enemy.

The Pacific Offensive. At the first Québec Conference, August, 1943, the decision was taken to press a vigorous offensive in the Pacific. The key to the situation was U.S. naval ascendancy. A fast and powerful carrier force was organized as a striking arm to soften up Japanese bases and provide long-range cover for invasion operations. By establishing footholds at key points and using these as bases from which sea and air power could command the surrounding area, it was possible to bypass Japanese garrisons, leaving them in harmless isolation as the advance swept westward.

The main line of the offensive lay through the central Pacific. The Gilbert Islands were the first objective. Carrier strikes were directed at this group; and on Nov. 20, 1943, Army units landed on Makin and a Marine division assaulted Tarawa. Makin was secured on November 22, but Tarawa was subdued only after three days, at a cost of over 3,700 casualties. The toughness of the defenses on Tarawa and the tenacity of Japanese opposition provided lessons in dealing with the Marshall Islands. A more prolonged bombardment preceded the attack on February 2. The main fighting took place on Kwajalein. On February 5 U.S. control was complete. Ten days later a landing was made on Eniwetok, and with its capture on February 20 all the Marshalls were under U.S. control.

Ahead lay the Marianas, where the Japanese were strongly posted on Saipan and Guam. Again long-range naval and air attacks were undertaken, and the great Japanese naval base on the intervening island of Truk was neutralized by successive attacks. On June 10, 1944, the Navy opened a four-day bombardment of Saipan; on June 14 an invading force landed on the island. The Japanese resisted fiercely. At sea, the Japanese threw into action their long-hoarded naval strength to destroy the invading force. From Japanese carriers over 500 planes were launched, June 19, against the beachhead and supporting ships. Japanese planes were kept from landing and refueling

Aerial bombing, intensive naval bombardment, and three days of some of the bloodiest fighting of World War II occurred on Tarawa between U.S. and Japanese forces.

U.S. MARINE CORPS

During World War II, casualties of the U.S. Marine Corps received immediate medical attention at aid stations such as this one located on the island battlefield of Iwo Jima.

on Guam, and Japanese carriers were thus stripped of their protecting planes and left vulnerable to pursuit. Two carriers were sunk before they could escape and damages inflicted on three others, on a battleship, and on lesser craft. This repulse of Japanese sea power sealed the fate of the Marianas. Guam now came under naval bombardment, and a force of more than two divisions landed July 21. The battle was similar to that on Saipan. The last organized resistance was broken, August 10, but small bands protracted mop-up operations for months. The island of Tinian was invaded, July 24, and subdued by August 8, and the Marianas were effectively occupied.

In New Guinea, Salamaua and Lae were taken in September, 1943. In February, 1944, command of the Huon Peninsula was attained. Rabaul was nullified as a naval base by air-sea bombardment. A landing on the southwest end of New Britain on December 26 gave the Allies command of Vitiaz Strait and threatened Rabaul by land. In February, seizure of Green Island and the Admiralty Islands isolated Rabaul. On April 22, landings in the Hollandia area and near Aitape isolated Japanese garrisons farther east. Occupation of Wakde Islands and the coastal area opposite it began on May 17; Biak Island was invaded 10 days later; and a landing on the Vogelkop Peninsula, July 30, virtually completed Allied control of New Guinea. The drives in the central and southwest Pacific were converging. With the attack on the Palau Islands, September 15, the two operations merged and U.S. forces stood on the threshold of the Philippines.

Prelude to D-Day. During 1943 and early 1944, activity in the West was directed toward the coming invasion of Europe. The battle was still largely one of supply, with the Allies striving to clear the sea lanes and disrupt German production and transportation by a sustained air offensive.

A critical achievement was defeat of the German U-boats. Production of corvettes for convoy work made more protection for shipping available. By agreement with Portugal in October, 1943, the Allies occupied the Azores, closing one of the last gaps in the Atlantic. As a result, shipping losses began to decline in April, and by June, the Allies were sinking U-boats at the rate of one a day. The Battle of the Atlantic ended in decisive victory for the Allies.

In the bombing assault on Germany, this period saw adoption of the "saturation raid," in which a maximum blow was delivered in a minimum space of time. In April, 1943, a sustained campaign began against heavy industry in the Ruhr. On July 24, Hamburg was hit by the first of eight raids which left it virtually paralyzed. In August, heavy raids hit Berlin; but not until November was Berlin assailed in a sustained campaign. Then night raids

continuing into January, followed by day raids, March, 1944, seriously damaged the capital's industries and railway network.

The campaign now moved into the pre-invasion period. Destruction of German air power was of primary importance. A concentrated assault on German aircraft factories began with a raid on Leipzig Feb. 19, 1944. In the next six days bombers struck factories from Braunschweig (Brunswick) to Steyr with 18,000 tons of bombs. Attacks were continued throughout March. The result was a serious reduction in the production of German fighter craft, weakening the power of the German air force to oppose the coming invasion.

Also of vital importance was the crippling of German transport. Here the chief targets were railways and oil refineries. Oil was one of Germany's weak spots; and Allied air bases in Italy made it possible to hit German sources of oil with a succession of damaging raids on Ploesti in Rumania. Throughout the spring there were attacks on the German railway network, particularly in western Europe. On the eve of the invasion an attempt was made to cut the Loire and Seine crossings and isolate the invasion area from outside support. By D-Day virtually every bridge over those two rivers had been wrecked, and German supplies and reinforcements had to be detoured through the Orléans gap.

In June, 1944, Hitler launched the V-1 flying bomb against London. In a week 8,000 bombs killed 5,500 Londoners. In August, the V-2 rocket came into use, and in eight months took almost as many lives as the 1940 blitz.

The Fall of Rome. In Italy, the Allies launched a new offensive in the spring of 1944. The British Eighth Army shifted to the Cassino sector, while the U.S. Fifth Army concentrated on the coastal flank. On May 11, 1944, a drive was launched along the whole front. In a week the main strong points were carried and Cassino was captured on May 18.

The Germans had organized another defense line, but by the time Cassino fell, the line had been penetrated, and on May 23 it came under full-scale assault. On the same day, the forces in the Anzio beachhead took the offensive, and the converging attacks threatened the whole German position. The Germans avoided being trapped by a strong rearguard defense and by establishment of a new line along the Alban Hills. When the chief positions in the Alban Hills were captured, June 2, it was the signal for a full retreat. Rome had already been declared an open city, and on June 4 the Allies occupied the capital.

At Orvieto the Germans made the first of a series of delaying stands. Stronger opposition was met in the Arno Valley, and not until August 12 was Florence taken. By that time the Germans organized

Strong German resistance threatened an Allied attempt to establish the Anzio beachhead early in 1944. Artillery and air support aided the 5th Army in holding the position.

U.S. ARMY

With the Normandy beachhead well established after the initial D-Day landings in June, 1944, troops consolidated the lodgment area and advanced inland to capture Paris.

the Gothic Line covering the approaches to Bologna and Ravenna, and the Allies again faced strong mountain positions. Nevertheless, Rimini was taken, September 2; Forlì, November 10; Ravenna, December 15; but by the end of the year the drive was stalled along the Senio River, and the Italian front settled down to a winter of deadlock.

The Invasion of Normandy. By August, 1943, the outline plans for Operation Overlord had been approved at the Québec Conference, and by the end of the year supreme command had been entrusted to Gen. Dwight D. Eisenhower, with Air Marshal Arthur W. Tedder as his deputy and General Montgomery as field commander of the invasion force. The operation was directed against a strongly garrisoned coast. The beaches were guarded by underwater obstacles and by wire, mine fields, and numerous strong points on the high ground commanding them. New types of weapons and special landing craft had to be provided, and air command over the invasion area as well as naval mastery of the channel were necessary to insure success. The vital matter of supply raised difficult problems: it would take time to capture ports of any size, and their facilities were almost sure to be wrecked by the Germans. Prefabricated harbors were devised, towed across the channel in the days following the invasion, and set up at Arromanches. Immense quantities of fuel had to be provided; this problem was solved by laying flexible pipeline across the channel.

The weather forced postponement of the invasion by one day. That night the air force attacked coastal defenses and communications to soften up the invasion area. On June 6, shortly after midnight, airborne troops dropped inland to seize key points and block roads by which German reinforcements might arrive. Shortly after dawn five divisions from the U.S. First and British Second armies landed on the Normandy coast from Caen to the base of the Cotentin Peninsula. A foothold was quickly attained. The greatest opposition was encountered on Omaha Beach in the U.S. sector, where the attack was pinned down for several hours; but within 24 hours the coastal wall was breached, a quarter of a million men had landed, and troops were driving inland.

The Germans were unable to drive back the Allies. By July 18, when they had raised their force to 27 divisions, the Allies had 30 divisions in Normandy as well as complete supremacy. The German field commander Marshal Rommel was therefore reduced to using his forces piecemeal at the greatest point of danger. He concentrated on the defense of Caen, where a breakthrough would open a direct road to Paris. By June 10 the beachheads were linked in a continuous front. United States forces cut off the Cotentin Peninsula, June 18, capturing Cherbourg, on June 27 and St.-Lô, July 18.

The Battle of Normandy. Throughout these weeks, British and Canadian forces battered at Caen. By the last week in June the Germans had gathered seven tank and four infantry divisions in this area trying to halt the advance. In spite of this the defense was gradually undermined, and on July 9 the Germans were forced out of Caen. On July 25 an offensive was launched from St.-Lô while a supporting thrust pinned down the Germans below Caen. By the second day the German line was breached, and the U.S. Third Army under Gen. George Patton drove through and swept south to Brittany. The Germans tried to cut off the armored spearheads by striking at the coastal corridor around Avranches. The attack was beaten off, August 7, and while U.S. forces overran Brittany, Patton's tanks swung around the rear of the main German armies toward a junction with the Canadians who had opened a new drive from Caen. The Canadians were checked at Falaise, but the Germans were caught in a bulge with only a narrow exit, and although some of the trapped forces were withdrawn, it was at the price of heavy losses as Allied guns and planes hammered at the traffic through the gap. The ring was sealed around the remnant on August 20. By the end of August the German forces that had crossed the Seine were fleeing to the north. The Germans in Normandy lost over 400,000 casualties and had been shattered as a fighting force.

The U.S. Seventh Army landed in the south of France, August 15, and advanced up the Rhône, effecting a junction with the main Allied front early in September. The Germans retreated to the frontiers of France. Paris was liberated, August 25. The U.S. First Army drove through Amiens to Sedan and Liège, and by September 11 its spearheads had crossed the German border near Trier. The British Second Army took Brussels, September 3, and Antwerp, the next day. Along the coast, the Canadian First Army captured Le Havre and Dieppe, Boulogne and Calais, and laid siege to other channel ports.

By mid-September supply facilities had been outrun by the advance, and the Germans were rallying behind the Siegfried Line. To effect a breach, the Allies struck at the route around the flank of the Westwall to the North German Plain. On September 17, airborne troops were dropped at Arnhem to seize the Rhine crossing and effect a junction. The corridor driven through by the ground troops was cut by the Germans, and the spearhead was checked five miles short of its goal. The airborne troops at Arnhem were rapidly reduced by German attacks, and the ground column could not break through to them. On September 25 the remnant was withdrawn, and the Allies settled down to the winter battle of the frontiers of Germany.

The Russian Summer Offensive, 1944. By summer, 1944, the Germans were committed to major efforts on two fronts, in addition to the struggle in

Five U.S. soldiers prepare to blow up a series of concrete pyramids called "Dragon Teeth," which formed part of the tank barrier defenses of the Siegfried Line in Germany.
U.S. ARMY SIGNAL CORPS

Italy and the task of occupying most of Europe from Norway to Greece, with the Russian front absorbing two-thirds of Germany's military strength. Creation of a second front in the west left Germany incapable of stemming the Russian offensive launched during the Battle of Normandy.

The first blow was struck against Finland, which had joined in the German attack on the U.S.S.R. in 1941, recovered the territory lost in 1940, and aided in closing the ring on Leningrad. Ten days after the offensive was opened, July 10, the Russians had broken the Mannerheim Line, overrun the Karelian Isthmus, captured Vyborg (Viipuri), and cleared the railway between Leningrad and Murmansk.

The drive on the central front opened on June 23. Vitebsk was taken, June 26. The Russian armies thrust westward with such speed that on July 3 Minsk was in Russian hands. In the north a drive was launched against the Baltic States, July 11. Vilnius (Vilna) fell to the central armies, July 13. The Baltic forces captured Pskov, July 23. Daugavpils (Dvinsk) fell, July 27, and by August 1 the Russians had thrust a spearhead to the Gulf of Riga and temporarily cut off the German forces in Latvia and Estonia. On the southern flank a drive was launched from the Ukraine, July 16. By July 27, it had captured Lvov. The upper Vistula was crossed, August 2, and a strong bridgehead established. The central armies, which captured Brest-Litovsk, July 28, reached the Vistula in their turn and by the beginning of August were battling for Praga, the east-bank suburb of Warsaw. Within Warsaw a rising by Polish underground forces sought to expel the German garrison, only to be suppressed after a protracted struggle.

By the beginning of August the Russians had driven 400 miles from the Dnepr to the Vistula, and faced the problems of extended supply lines and stiffening German resistance. Counterattacks forced the Russians back from Warsaw and restored communications with the German forces in the Baltic States. A renewed Russian drive in the Baltic area once more cut off the German garrisons, October 10, captured Riga, October 13, and compressed the remnants of 30 German divisions into the peninsula west of the Gulf of Riga. But attacks toward Warsaw were thrown back. With the halting of the offensive on a line along the Vistula and Narew rivers, the Russians turned to the valley of the Danube and the Nazi satellite states.

The Balkans and the Danube. Rumania and Hungary, tempted by territorial gains, had sent troops to take active part in the Russian campaigns. Bulgaria had managed to maintain ostensible neutrality against the U.S.S.R., although she had declared war on the other Allies; but she had lent substantial material aid to Germany, allowed German troops to occupy the country, and shared in the spoils from Yugoslavia and Greece. On August 20, the Russians struck into Rumania; on August 23, the king announced Rumania's withdrawal from the war. Bulgaria was brought to terms by a Russian invasion of the country. In December, the Russians set up a provisional government on captured Hungarian territory. Armistices were signed with Rumania, September 12; Bulgaria, October 28; and Hungary, Jan. 20, 1945. In the far north, Finland had agreed to an armistice on September 4.

The collapse of Rumania enabled the Soviet armies to occupy the line of the Carpathian Mountains and to reach the Iron Gate on the Danube early in September. By the end of the month the Russians were pressing into Transylvania. A thrust across the Danube linked up with Yugoslav resistance forces to capture Belgrade, October 20. Meanwhile a westward drive had been launched, October 6, with its northern flank protected by armies advancing in Czechoslovakia and forming a link with the main front in Poland. On October 21, a Russian spearhead had reached the Danube at a point 86 miles below Buda-

While a Marine sentry attempts to get a few moments of rest in a foxhole on the beach of Iwo Jima, his dog, a member of the famed K-9 Corps, remains alert and watchful.

pest, and the main front had reached the Tisza River. The German forces covering the approaches to Budapest were pushed back, and by the second week in December, Pest, on the east bank of the Danube, was encircled and the Russians began to crush the German garrison. Buda on the west bank was also in danger. At the end of November a drive across the Danube struck up the west bank. The corridor between Balaton Lake and the Danube was forced, and the Russians closed on Buda from the south, while the forces north of the city drove to the Danube and linked up with the southern column. By December 27 Buda was under assault. The Germans struck the Russian positions north of Balaton Lake early in January, 1945, drove to the Danube, and attacked the lines ringing Budapest. But the ring held firm; and after a month of fighting the Russians gained part of the lost ground. Meanwhile, Pest was subdued, Jan. 18, 1945, and the last resistance in Buda was crushed, February 13.

Advance to the Oder. On the main front, the offensive opened, January 12. In the north an army group under Gen. Ivan Chernyakovsky drove on East Prussia toward Königsberg (renamed Kaliningrad, 1946). In the south, Konev drove toward Kraców. Two other army groups attacked in the center. Gen. Konstantin Rokossovski drove on East Prussia from the south, while Zhukov attacked along a broad front on either side of Warsaw. Zhukov set the pace. In a double thrust he outflanked and enveloped Warsaw, which fell on January 17. Kraców and Łodź fell, January 19. Toruń was encircled, January 27, and a ring was closed around Poznań to the west. Konev reached the upper Oder, January 22, and in the next week his forces overran the industrial area of Silesia. In the center the defenses of the "Oder quadrilateral" before Küstrin (Kostrzyń) were overwhelmed, and by February Zhukov was established along a broad stretch of the Oder.

The drive on East Prussia was meanwhile making steady progress. On January 25, Rokossovski's spearhead reached the Baltic east of Danzig (Gdańsk), cutting off the Germans in East Prussia. Contact between the two Russian forces was established, January 27, with the capture of Rastenburg (Ketrzyn Mazowiecki). The Germans in East Prussia were compressed into a pocket along the Baltic coast.

By the beginning of February the Russians had cleared almost the whole of Poland and thrust a wedge into Germany. On February 4 Zhukov crossed the upper Oder, encircled Breslau, February 16, and reached the Neisse River to bring his front into line with that of Konev. On February 24 Rokossovski struck west of Danzig; and a parallel drive was launched by Zhukov, March 1. The twin thrust pierced the German lines and drove to the Baltic,

U.S. ARMY SIGNAL CORPS

Pontoon bridges, often quickly erected under screens of smoke, carried the Allies across the Rhine into the heart of Germany for the final thrusts in the European theater.

March 4. Zhukov then turned westward to clear the right bank of the lower Oder and bring the front opposite Stettin. Rokossovski fought eastward along the Baltic coast, converging on Danzig, which fell on March 30. The siege of Königsberg ended with its capture, April 9; and the only German forces left east of the Oder were the divisions cut off in the Baltic States.

In March, a new offensive swept westward below the Danube while the forces north of the river began a parallel advance. The drive closed on Vienna, and on April 7 the Russians drove into the city. German resistance was crushed on April 13. The front was pushed westward some 50 miles before the drive came to a halt.

The Battle for the Rhineland. On the Western Front the Allied advance had been halted at the frontiers, and behind the fortifications of the Westwall the Germans were regrouping and raising Home Guard levies to bolster the defense. The Allies in their turn were forced to halt and regroup in preparation for a major offensive effort. The question of supply was now more acute than ever. For the new operations, Antwerp was vitally necessary. The port had been captured intact but the approaches had to be cleared of Germans before Antwerp would be usable. It took a month of fighting, beginning on October 6, to drive the Germans from positions in the flooded countryside. During this period British and Canadian forces cleared the Germans from the area south of the lower Rhine and gave the Allies command of the left bank from Arnhem to the sea. Meanwhile U.S. forces captured Aachen, October 21. November saw the development of a general offensive along the whole front. Metz was attacked on November 8 and fell on November 22. In the next two weeks the U.S. Third Army pushed forward to the Saar Valley and battered at the Siegfried Line. In Alsace, U.S. and French forces drove to the Rhine, capturing Belfort, November 22, and Strasbourg, November 23. On the left (north) flank, U.S. forces drove from Aachen toward the Rhine. By the second week in December the Germans had been driven across the Roer River, and preparations were under way for a decisive push.

Ardennes Counteroffensive. To forestall the assault Von Rundstedt launched a counteroffensive, December 16, against the lightly held Ardennes sector. The Germans effected a breach, but its sides were contained by troops from the U.S. First and Third armies. A force cut off at Bastogne delayed the advance by holding out for eight days until a corridor was pushed through to their relief; and on December 24 the German spearhead halted four miles short of the Meuse. The bulge was contained, and the Allies gradually reduced the salient. By mid-January the Allies again controlled the situation. The Germans had delayed Allied offensive plans by

six weeks, but at the cost of 120,000 casualties and serious losses in tanks and heavy equipment. See ARDENNES, *Battle of the Bulge in World War II.*

Final Campaign in Rhineland. The Allied drive on the Rhineland opened, February 8. Canadians and British attacked the north flank of the Westwall. The Roer assault was delayed when the Germans opened the dams, but by February 23 the floods had subsided. United States forces drove across the Roer and reached the Rhine, March 2. The First Army captured Cologne, March 6, and turned south to meet the Third Army, which had taken Trier, March 2, and which reached the Rhine north of Coblenz, March 7. The Third crossed the Moselle while the Seventh made a frontal assault on the Westwall. On March 8 the First Army seized the Remagen Bridge across the Rhine, and established a bridgehead on the east bank which greatly aided the main crossing. By March 25 the whole Rhineland was cleared, and the five German armies in that area had been almost shattered. The main drive on the Rhine, launched on the night of March 23, included a British–U.S. airborne and amphibious crossing near Wesel, and by next morning bridgeheads had been established across the river from Remagen to near the Netherlands border. From there one spearhead drove north of the Ruhr, while another struck south from the Remagen bridgehead. Their junction, April 1, trapped 21 German divisions, and when the Ruhr pocket was reduced, April 19, it had yielded 325,000 prisoners. Practically no organized force now stood between the Allies and Berlin. In the center their forces swept forward to the Elbe and the Mulde. On the northern flank the British and some U.S. units drove to the lower Elbe, besieged Bremen and Hamburg, which fell, April 26, and May 3, crossed the Elbe, occupying Mecklenburg and Schleswig-Holstein, while the Canadians cut off the Netherlands. In the south the U.S. and French swept through Bavaria and the Black Forest down toward the Danube and along the border of Czechoslovakia.

In mid-April the Russian offensive opened. Crossing the Oder, Zhukov made a frontal assault on Berlin. Simultaneously Konev drove toward Berlin from both south and west. By April 21 the attack had battered its way into Berlin itself. On May 2 the last defenders surrendered. Meanwhile the Russians reached the upper Elbe, where they met U.S. forces near Torgau, April 25.

In Italy the Allies opened a new drive on April 9. On April 19 the British Eighth Army broke through and swept into the Po Valley. Northern Italy was swiftly occupied. Mussolini was captured by Italian partisans and put to death on April 28. On April 29 an agreement was signed surrendering German forces in Italy, effective May 2.

Other surrenders quickly followed. In the north the Germans tried to secure a free hand against the Russians by making terms with the British. Montgomery rejected their overtures and demanded surrender of all forces in northwest Germany, the Netherlands, and Denmark. On May 4 Montgomery's terms were accepted. Next day the German Fifth and Nineteenth armies in the south laid down their arms. The only remaining resistance was in Bohemia and Moravia where the Russians were battling toward Prague. Military disintegration was accompanied by political collapse. Hitler was reported to have committed suicide, April 30. A new government was formed with Adm. Karl Doenitz at its head, and after futile efforts to split the western Allies from Russia, overtures were made for cessation of hostilities. Early on May 7 German representatives at Reims signed a document providing for unconditional surrender; and on May 8 the heads of the three German armed services signed a similar instrument in Berlin to close the war in Europe officially.

The Philippines and Burma. Autumn, 1944, found the United States poised for invasion of the

After heavy preliminary bombardment, columns of smoke rise in the sky over Leyte, the scene of the initial invasion of the Philippines by the United States on Oct. 21, 1944.

Philippines. On October 20 forces commanded by General MacArthur landed on Leyte. The Japanese struck with what was left of their fleet to destroy the American transports and isolate the invading force. On the night of October 24, one force entered Surigao Strait south of Leyte, while a stronger force rounded the island through San Bernardino Strait to the north. Simultaneously a third group came down from north of Luzon. The first two forces were destroyed in the Battle of Leyte Gulf. The southern force was ambushed in Surigao Strait. The second force took a light U.S. force by surprise and for a time threatened the beachhead area. The main U.S. fleet had been drawn off by the northern force but turned to meet the new danger, and the Japanese retreated. It was a crippling defeat for Japan. It cost her 3 battleships, 4 carriers, 10 cruisers, and 9 destroyers, against U.S. losses of 3 small carriers and 3 destroyers. Another battleship was sunk in November; Japan's last modern battleship, the *Yamato*, was sunk by carrier planes in the following April; and the rest of the Japanese fleet was driven into home ports.

With command of the sea secure, the United States proceeded to reconquer the Philippines. Organized resistance on Leyte was broken by December 25. A landing was made on Mindanao, December 19, and on Jan. 9, 1945, two corps landed on the shores of Lingayen Gulf and drove toward Manila. By March 4, U.S. control of the city was complete. Control over southern Luzon was achieved by April. Conquest of the northern half of the island involved a campaign against mountain defenses and lasted until the end of June.

During this period the Japanese were also retreating on the mainland of Asia. Their conquest of Burma had completed their blockade of China, except for air transport "over the hump." Gen. Joseph W. Stilwell advocated an attempt to reopen land communications with China through northern Burma. Gen. Orde Wingate conducted a protracted raid into Burma, depending on air supplies. It was decided to use this method to support an expedition to clear the way for a road from India through Ledo to the Chinese border. In March, 1944, an airborne force was set down in the jungle of northern Burma to begin a drive against the Japanese base of Myitkyina, while British and Indian troops undertook a diversionary offensive toward Akyab in Arakan. Myitkyina was encircled in May; but the Arakan drive was halted, and the Japanese launched a counterdrive across the Indian border. Air power helped check the Japanese and relieve the Indian force in Arakan; and by spring, 1944, the Japanese were cleared from India.

From Myitkyina, which was captured in August, columns struck down toward Bhamo and Mandalay. Mandalay fell, March 20; an armored thrust on Feb-ruary 27 seized the railway town of Meiktila; and when the spearheads from Mandalay and Meiktila joined, March 30, the British controlled the central plain. Operations were also in progress along the west coast. Rangoon was captured, May 3, the Ledo Road to China had been opened, January 22, and, by May, Burma was under Allied control.

The Capture of Okinawa. With the conquest of the Philippines, few important stepping stones lay between those islands and Japan. In the Ryukyus, the island of Okinawa would provide useful harbors and air bases, and Iwo Jima in the Volcano group provided facilities for Japanese interception of bombing raids which had to be eliminated. The attack was launched on Iwo Jima, Feb. 19, 1945. It was hoped that six weeks' bombardment would batter the defenders into submission, but caves and fortified positions survived, and the attackers had to advance almost without cover. The Japanese force of 20,000 fought to the death, and conquest of the island's eight square miles took 26 days and cost 20,000 American casualties.

On Okinawa, the Japanese offered the same fanatical resistance. The landing forces easily secured a foothold, April 1, only to find that the Japanese had concentrated their forces in hill positions in the southern part of the island. These Japanese positions had to be taken by frontal assault, and not until June 21 could the island be regarded as conquered.

The Air Assault on Japan. The war was now carried to Japan. United States air power had a new weapon for long-range assault—the B-29 or Superfortress. In the summer and autumn of 1944 these planes, operating from bases in western China, had raided Japanese cities. Occupation of Saipan and Guam provided bases for a more sustained campaign. On Nov. 24, 1944, Tokyo was raided in daylight by 111 bombers. For nearly four months attacks were chiefly directed against aircraft factories. By March, 1945, however, new facilities made possible night raids at low level against Japan's leading cities. By mid-April, 35 square miles of Tokyo had been laid waste in three fire raids, and Nagoya, Osaka, and Kobe had all been hard hit. On May 14, a campaign began to wipe out Japanese war production. Within a month, Japan's five leading industrial centers had been virtually eliminated as productive centers. By mid-August, 60 places had been hit, 110 square miles of Tokyo lay in ruins, and Japanese targets were being hit by as much as 6,600 tons of bombs a night.

Japan was being devastated from the air and strangled from the sea. By summer, 1945, Japan's merchant marine had been wiped out and her communications with the mainland cut. On July 26, during the Potsdam Conference, a declaration was issued calling on Japan to surrender or risk annihilation. What lay behind this was revealed with terrible clarity, August 6, when a single atomic bomb was

Two New Zealander sharpshooters take cover behind trees while attempting to pick off occupants of a Japanese pillbox fortification on Guam, largest of the Marianas Islands.

U.S. Marines prepare to attack a heavily reinforced concrete pillbox occupied by the Japanese forces located on Tarawa, one of the Gilbert Islands in the central Pacific.

dropped on Hiroshima, over half of which was destroyed by the blast. Three days later, August 9, another bomb was dropped on Nagasaki with equally devastating results. While Japan was reeling from these blows, the U.S.S.R. declared war, August 8, and launched her armies against Japanese forces in Manchuria. On August 14, Japan accepted the Potsdam Declaration calling for unconditional surrender. On September 2 the formal instrument was signed on board the battleship U.S.S. *Missouri* to bring World War II to a close.

The Price of Victory. The war had lasted six years and a day. The combatants had mobilized 100 million men and women in their armed services and lost some 16 million of them. Russian military death casualties were estimated at over 6 million. German losses were 3.5 million. The United States lost 300,000 in killed and missing; the British Commonwealth lost 440,000. Even these losses were overshadowed by the toll of civilian lives. The Germans were charged with the deaths of 10 million civilians in occupied regions or in concentration camps, and total civilian deaths caused by the war in Europe and Asia probably exceeded 20 million.

Material losses were equally staggering. United States expenditures exceeded $350 billion; Britain spent $300 billion, Germany $280 billion. Almost all of southeast Asia and Indonesia had been overrun by Japan. Germany's path of conquest stretched from the Arctic Ocean to the Aegean Sea and from the Netherlands to the Caucasus. The ravages of Russian land and cities involved a loss of over $100 billion. Some 20 million displaced persons had been torn from their homes, and whole areas had been reduced below the starvation level by deliberate action of the Axis nations. With depleted resources and exhausted peoples, the world faced the task of rebuilding after its ordeal.

The Home Front. The major belligerents of World War II threw all productive resources into their war efforts. In every country people accepted rationing and shortages. In the United States, for example, automobile tires, gasoline, sugar, coffee, canned foods, meat, fats and oils, butter, cheese, and shoes were rationed. In many areas housing shortages led to rent control. Strategic war materials were allocated wherever they were most needed. Workers were frozen in their jobs. The federal budget rose from $9 billion in 1941 to $98.4 billion in 1945—$81 billion of which was spent on national security. In six years the United States produced 17 million rifles and pistols, 2.5 million trucks, 300,000 planes and 53 million tons of shipping. United States lend-lease aid to Allies, from March, 1941, to September, 1946, amounted to $50 billion (see LEND-LEASE ACT). The other warring nations not only had to expand national effort but had to replace productive facilities

damaged or destroyed by the enemy. In every country mobilization of manpower was virtually complete. In 1943, of some 16 million British men of working age, 15 million were in the armed forces, civil defense, or war industry. In Germany, compulsory labor was instituted for men aged 16 to 65 and women aged 17 to 45. In countries within the combat zones, including Great Britain, civilian deaths caused by the war exceeded military deaths. World War II was rightly called a total war in the sense that virtually all the people of the warring nations took part in it.

Postwar World. Despite the devastation caused by World War II, recovery was swift. The peoples of the world were aided in their efforts toward recovery by programs such as the Marshall Plan.

One terrible aspect of World War II involved crimes committed by Axis nations, ranging from the Bataan death march and the sack of Nanking to genocide—the systematic extermination of whole peoples, especially Slavs, Gypsies, and Jews. The magnitude of these crimes became more fully known during the war crimes trials at Nürnberg after the war. Nineteen top Nazi leaders were convicted at Nürnberg, 1946, and 25 Japanese war leaders were found guilty in war crimes trials in Tokyo, 1948. Over 2,000 separate trials of lesser war criminals took place. The 1960's began with a grim reminder of the horrors of World War II, when former Gestapo officer Adolf Eichmann stood trial in Israel and was found guilty of supervising the extermination of 6 million European Jews. Eichmann was hanged in 1962. Perhaps the most poignant reminder of these horrors, however, was the diary of Anne Frank, a 15-year-old Jewish girl who hid from the Nazis for two years, was discovered, and died in a concentration camp.

Politically, the location of troops in Europe at the end of the war set the pattern of postwar alignment. Except for Austria, all nations occupied by Russian troops fell into the Communist orbit. Peace treaties were signed in Paris for Italy, Rumania, Bulgaria, Hungary, and Finland, 1947, and these countries were admitted to the United Nations, 1955. A Japanese treaty was signed, 1951, and Japan became a UN member, 1956. Germany was partitioned into four occupation zones after the war, but the United States, Britain and France merged zones, 1949, thus establishing the West German Republic. The Russians, in turn, declared their zone a country, 1949, and gave it full sovereignty, 1957. Early in the 1960's there were still two Germanys. Moreover, the threat of a new war in Europe again became imminent as tensions increased over the massive refugee flow into West Germany from East Germany via the Western sector of Berlin. The problem was further complicated by Russian intentions to sign a separate peace treaty with East Germany and turn over control of Western access to Berlin. Matters became critical in August 1961 when a wall dividing the two sectors of the city was erected by East Germans in an attempt to stop the refugees from fleeing their communist government. Military forces from each side massed at the border. Although negotiations between Eastern and Western diplomats later eased tensions, both wall and troops were still part of the Berlin landscape in 1962.

Military technology continued to develop in the postwar period. At the end of the 1950's hydrogen bombs 50 times more powerful than the Hiroshima bomb, and intercontinental guided missiles were in the arsenals of the Soviet and U.S. forces. In 1960 an atomic-powered submarine made a round-the-world voyage submerged throughout. Other weapons were equally transformed or, in some cases, were discarded. By 1958 the last battleship had been retired from the U.S. Navy. At the end of World War II it was believed that manned aircraft could not possibly fly faster than the speed of sound; in 1961 a test pilot flew at over four times the speed of sound. In the postwar period the major powers

U.S. NAVY

The signing of the instrument of surrender by the Japanese foreign minister aboard the battleship, U.S.S. *Missouri*, on Sept. 2, 1945, formally ended fighting in World War II.

developed biological and chemical weapons of great destructive potential.

At the end of World War II nuclear weapons were a U.S. monopoly. By 1967 they were in the possession of the U.S.S.R., Great Britain, France, and China, with other nations about to join the so-called atomic club. Moreover, new techniques had made atomic weapons financially feasible for poorer nations, raising the possibility that all nations might in time become atomic powers. Thus, within little more than two decades, the chief problem facing the world had changed from rebuilding after one war to preventing the occurrence of another. See articles on places, battles, campaigns, and persons mentioned.

EDGAR McINNIS

BIBLIOGRAPHY

BACKGROUND: Joseph W. Alsop and Robert Kintner, *American White Paper* (1940); Gilbert W. Beebe and Michael E. De Bakey, *Battle Casualties* (1952); Burton H. Klein, *Germany's Economic Preparations for War* (Harvard Economic Studies, v. 109) (1959); Amelia C. Leiss and Raymond Dennett, eds., *European Peace Treaties after World War II* (1954); M. J. Proudfoot, *European Refugees: 1939-52* (1956); Edward J. Rozek, *Allied Wartime Diplomacy* (1958); Shigenori Togo, *Cause of Japan* (1956); John W. Wheeler-Bennett, *Nemesis of Power: The German Army in Politics, 1918-1945* (1954).

HISTORIES: Sir Winston L. S. Churchill, *Second World War*, 6 vols. (1948-53); Herbert Feis, *Churchill, Roosevelt, Stalin: The War They Waged and the Peace They Sought* (1957); Walter Görlitz, *History of the German General Staff, 1657-1945* (1960); Edgar McInnis, *War*, 6 vols. (1940-46); *Pictorial History of the Second World War*, 10 vols. (1944-49); William L. Shirer, *Rise and Fall of the Third Reich* (1960); Louis L. Snyder, *War: A Concise History, 1939-1945* (1960); Peter Young, *World War 1939-45: A Short History* (1966).

BATTLES AND CAMPAIGNS: Wladyslaw Anders, *Hitler's Defeat in Russia* (1953); Walter Ansel, *Hitler Confronts England* (1960); Jack Barnard, *Hump: The Greatest Untold Story of the War* (1960); Correlli Barnett, *Desert Generals* (1960); Raymond de Belot, *Struggle for the Mediterranean, 1939-1945* (1951); Ewan Butler and J. Selby Bradford, *Story of Dunkirk* (1955); Gilbert Cant, *Great Pacific Victory: From the Solomons to Tokyo* (1946); Peter Fleming, *Operation Sea Lion* (1957); Adolphe Goutard, *Battle of France, 1940* (1959); David A. Howarth, *D Day: The 6th of June, 1944* (1959); Walter Lord, *Day of Infamy* (1957); Friedrich W. von Mellenthin, *Panzer Battles, 1939-1945* (1956); Vivian Rowe, *Great Wall of France: The Triumph of the Maginot Line* (1959); Heinz Schröter, *Stalingrad* (1958); Telford Taylor, *March of Conquest: The German Victories in Western Europe, 1940* (1958); John Toland, *Battle: The Story of the Bulge* (1959).

ARMS AND SERVICES: Gladeon M. Barnes, *Weapons of World War II* (1947); Lionel E. O. Charlton, *Royal Air Force, from September 1939 to September 1945*, 5 vols. (1941-47); Ladislas Farago, *War of Wits: The Anatomy of Espionage and Intelligence* (1954); Frank O. Hough, *Island War: The U.S. Marine Corps in the Pacific* (1947); Rikihei Inoguchi and Others, *Divine Wind: Japan's Kami Kaze Force in World War II* (1958); Gerald Pawle, *Secret War, 1939-1945* (1956); Henry Salomon and Richard Hanser, *Victory at Sea* (1959).

BIOGRAPHIES AND MEMOIRS: Henry H. Arnold, *Global Mission* (1949); Omar N. Bradley, *Soldier's Story* (1951); Harvey A. De Weerd, *Great Soldiers of World War II* (1944); Karl Dönitz, *Memoirs: 10 Years and 20 Days* (1959); Charles A. J. M. de Gaulle, *War Memoirs*, 3 vols. (1960); William F. Halsey and Joseph Bryan, *Admiral Halsey's Story* (1947); Hastings L. Ismay, *Memoirs* (1960); Albert Kesselring, *Kesselring: A Soldier's Record* (1954); Ernest J. King and Walter M. Whitehill, *Fleet Admiral King, A Naval Record* (1952); Bernard L. M. Montgomery of Alamein, *Memoirs* (1958); Louis Mountbatten, *Report to the Combined Chiefs of Staff by the Supreme Allied Commander, Southeast Asia, 1943-1945* (1951); Elmer B. Potter and Chester W. Nimitz, eds., *Great Sea War* (1960); Erwin Rommel, *Rommel Papers* (1953); Milton Viorst, *Hostile Allies: FDR and Charles de Gaulle* (1965); Jonathan M. Wainwright, *General Wainwright's Story* (1946); *War Reports of George C. Marshall, H. H. Arnold and Ernest J. King* (1947).

WORM, any of several invertebrates including the flatworms of the phylum Platyhelminthes, the roundworms of the phylum Nemathelminthes, the proboscis worms of the phylum Nemertea, the hairworm of the phylum Nematomorpha, the arrowworms or Chaetognatha, the segmented worms of the phylum Annelida and the spiny-headed worms, Acanthocephala. See ACANTHOCEPHALA; ANNELIDA; ARROWWORM; FLATWORM; HAIRWORM; ROUNDWORM.

WORMS, city, W Germany, in West German state of Rhineland-Palatinate; on the Rhine River; 36 miles SSW of Frankfurt-am-Main. Patent leather, machinery, woolen goods, soap, amber wares, cork, furniture, chemicals, paints, and Liebfraumilch wine are manufactured in the city. The Romanesque cathedral dates from the eighth century. Other features of interest are the Church of St. Paul, the Liebfrauen and St. Martin churches, the ancient Jewish synagogue and the monument to Luther (1856). Worms, originally the Celtic *Borbetomagus*, was a Roman town until the fifth century, when it was made the capital of the Burgundian kingdom. In 1122 the Concordat of Worms was concluded there, and in the first part of the following century Worms became an early free imperial city. It was occasionally the residence of the Frankish kings, and numerous diets (legislative assemblies) were held there. The most famous of these was the Imperial Diet of 1521, before which Martin Luther, German leader of the Reformation, made his noted defense. Worms suffered from French aggression in 1689 and 1792, passed into French hands for a 13-year period beginning in 1801, and was occupied by French forces after both World War I and World War II. (For population, see Germany map in Atlas.)

WORMS, DIET OF, held in 1521, was convened by the Holy Roman Emperor Charles V for the purpose of examining and passing upon the religious doctrines of Martin Luther. Having been assured of safe conduct, Luther obeyed the emperor's summons to appear at Worms. When asked whether he would withdraw those of his teachings that had been condemned by the pope, Luther refused to do so, and persisted in his refusal against the arguments of various theologians who tried to argue with him. After 10 days of this, the emperor realized the futility of further dispute and ordered Luther to leave Worms. The Diet of Worms played a significant role in the history of Protestantism by demonstrating that Roman Catholic and Lutheran doctrines could not be reconciled easily, if at all. See LUTHER, MARTIN; REFORMATION.

WORSAAE, JENS JACOB ASMUNSSEN, 1821-85, Danish archaeologist, born in Vejle. He spent several years researching abroad, returning in 1847 to become inspector of Danish prehistoric and historic monuments. Among his greatest discoveries were Denmark's neolithic kitchen middens. He was one of the first full-time professional archaeologists, and is credited with founding the modern science of prehistoric archaeology.

WORTHING, municipal borough, S England, in Sussex, on the English Channel; 61 miles SSW of London. The town is a popular seaside resort. Hot-houses, in which flowers, fruit, and vegetables are grown, are on the coastal plain in the vicinity. Pop. (1951) 69,375.

WORTHINGTON, city, SW Minnesota, seat of Nobles County; on Lake Okabena, the Rock Island and the North Western railroads, and U.S. highways 16 and 59; 145 miles WSW of Minneapolis. The city is noted for the Okabena apple, which was developed in orchards on the southern shores of Lake Okabena. The chief industries of Worthington are creameries, elevators, and a rendering plant. Worthington was established in 1871 under the name Okabena. Pop. (1960) 9,015.

WOTTEN, SIR HENRY, 1568–1639, English diplomat and poet, was born in Boughton Malherbe, Kent, studied at Oxford University where he became a close friend of John Donne. While in Florence, 1602, Wotten heard of a plot to assassinate James VI of Scotland, and traveled to Scotland to warn the king. When the grateful monarch became James I of England, 1603, Wotten was knighted. He was James's ambassador to Venice, 1604–12, 1616–19, and 1621–24. Wotten is credited with defining an ambassador as an "honest man sent to lie abroad for the good of his country."

WOUK, HERMAN, 1915–   , U.S. novelist and playwright, was born in New York City, studied at Columbia University, and served during World War II in the U.S. Navy. His novel *The Caine Mutiny* (1951), a moralistic, self-righteous tale of mutiny aboard a U.S. Navy destroyer-minesweeper during World War II, was awarded a 1952 Pulitzer prize. Among his other works are the novels *Aurora Dawn* (1947), *The City Boy* (1948), and *Marjorie Morningstar* (1955), and a superficial but deeply felt study of the Jewish religion, *This Is My God* (1959).

WOUND, an injury to tissue wherein the skin is broken. The process of healing is fundamentally the same in all wounds, but its activity is dependent upon the amount of tissue destroyed and whether or not infection is present. Some types of tissue, such as nervous tissue, are unable to reproduce themselves. Other types, such as liver, have remarkable powers of regeneration. The connective tissue regenerates most perfectly.

If a wound is inflicted by a sharp clean object, such as a knife in a surgical operation, and the edges brought together by stitches, there is almost no loss of tissue, and very little space in which blood and lymph may collect. By the end of 12 hours, connective tissue cells, called fibroblasts, begin to grow from either side of the wound into the small lymph- and blood-filled space of the wound. They then lay down so-called collagen fibers, which act as a cementing substance, as they fasten the two surfaces of the wound together and form the wavy bundles of scar tissue. Later the collagen fibers shorten and contract, causing the scar to raise. Blood vessels grow into the wound space along with the fibroblasts and form branching networks of capillaries supplying nourishment to the rapidly growing cells. This abundant blood supply causes the scar to be red, but as the collagen fibers contract, the blood vessels disappear, the scar becomes white, and epithelium grows over the wound. Infection in this type of wound prevents this simplified type of healing and results in larger scars.

If there has been a considerable loss of tissue so that the edges of the wound cannot be sewed together by fibercytes, then the gap is filled up from below, a process known as healing by granulation. The wound is first filled with a mixture of coagulated blood, lymph, and connective tissue cells. The fibroblasts commence growing into this exudate along with the blood vessel capillaries and form the so-called granulations. White blood cells wander to the surface of the granulation and serve as scavengers, keeping the growing surface relatively free of infection that might halt the repair process. Near the surface of the wound the fibroblasts are at right angles to the surface, while deeper they are parallel to it. As the wound fills in with this new tissue, the fibroblasts all become arranged parallel to the surface of the wound. Within two or three days from the time the wound occurred, the epithelium grows in from the edges of the wound to cover it.　HERMAN S. WIGODSKY, M.D.

WOUWERMAN, PHILIPS, 1619–68, Dutch artist, was born in Haarlem. He began his career by painting religious pictures, but later turned to portraying battle charges and scenes in which horses could be shown to good advantage. The horses appearing in his first work of this type are clumsy and awkward, but gradually he endowed them with graceful movement. He produced more than 800 works.

WRANGELL, BARON FERDINAND PETROVICH, VON, 1794–1870, Russian explorer, was born in Pskov. He made a voyage around the world, 1817–19, explored the Arctic regions, 1820–23, and circumnavigated the world a second time, 1825–27. He was governor general of Russian colonies in Alaska, 1829–34 and became a vice-admiral, 1849. Wrangell Island, discovered by T. Long, a U.S. whaler, 1867, was named in Wrangell's honor.

WRANGELL, town, SE Alaska, at the northern tip of Wrangell Island, which lies between Eastern Passage and Zimovia Strait, 155 miles SSE of Juneau. In 1936 a mooring basin and breakwater were completed at a cost of $81,000. The principal industries are lumbering and fur farming; salmon fishing centers are in the vicinity. Pop. (1960) 1,315.

WRANGELL ISLAND, or Wrangel, one of the Alexander Islands, SE Alaska, between Zimovia Strait on the W and Eastern Passage on the E; pop. about 1,500. Wrangell Island is part of the Tongass National Forest. Fort Wrangell was erected in 1867 and abandoned in 1877. Later a settlement on the site of the fort was an outfitting point during the Klondike Gold Rush. Leading economic activities are fishing, fish processing, and fur farming. A vocational boarding school for the Indians of southeastern Alaska is there.

WRASSE, any of several species of beautifully colored fishes found in warm, tropical seas. Wrasses have a characteristic continuous dorsal fin, a small mouth with large teeth, and fused bones in the neck accompanied by secondary teeth in the throat that aid in breaking the shells of mollusks, which are the fishes' food. The wrasses rarely exceed one foot in length. They occur along the southern coast of California and along the coast of South Carolina and Florida.

WRAY, town, NE Colorado; seat of Yuma County, on the North Fork Republican River, the Burlington Railroad, and U.S. highways 34 and 385; 140 miles ENE of Denver. Wray is a trade center for an area in which wheat, corn, sorghums, and dairy cattle are raised. Pop. (1960) 2,082.

WREN, SIR CHRISTOPHER, 1632–1723, English architect, was born in East Knoyle, Wiltshire, and studied at Wadham College, Oxford, 1646–50. He was appointed professor of astronomy at Gresham College, London, 1657, and Savilian professor of mathematics at Oxford, 1660. He was appointed, 1661, by Charles II assistant to Sir John Denham, surveyor general of the royal buildings; was commissioned, 1663, to survey and report upon St. Paul's Cathedral, with a view to its restoration; and was engaged on the Sheldonian Theatre, Oxford, and Trinity College, Cambridge, 1663. After the great fire of London, 1666, he made a survey of the ruins, and

CULVER SERVICE
Sir Christopher Wren

proposed a plan for laying out the area, with wide and commodious streets and squares, and with a line of convenient quays along the Thames, but the owners of the sites involved objected to the plan and it was not used. Among the other buildings designed or rebuilt by Wren are the Royal Exchange, Chelsea Hospital, the Custom House, Temple Bar, Greenwich Hospital, Hampton Court Palace, Winchester Palace, Marlborough House, Ashmolean Museum, and part of Windsor Castle. Wren designed more than 50 churches in London. The first stone of St. Paul's from Wren's designs was laid on June 21, 1675, the last in 1710; the choir was opened for divine service in 1697 (see St. Paul's Cathedral). He was one of the original members of the Royal Society, and became president in 1680. He was knighted in 1673.

WREN, PERCIVAL CHRISTOPHER, 1885–1941, popular English novelist and adventurer, was born in Devonshire. He served with the French Foreign Legion in North Africa, and presented a romantic view of the legion in *Beau Geste* (1924), best known of his many novels, and in its sequels—*Beau Sabreur* (1926), *Beau Ideal* (1928), and *The Good Gestes* (1929)—each one a colonialist tract on the absolute rightness of European control of African affairs, and each one full of interesting and curious details of life among the Arabs, the legionnaires, and the post-World War I British upper classes. There are at least three motion picture versions of *Beau Geste*, and hundreds of other films were obviously inspired in part by the Wren books.

WREN, any member of one of the large and widely distributed families of perching birds, the *Troglodytidae*. Wrens are found in both hemispheres, a large number occurring in the New World. Of 350 or more known species, only 30 occur in the Old World. Most of the birds are in the tropics, but about 10 species reach eastern North America. Wrens are birds of medium size, plain colored. The predominant colors are brown or gray, usually with darker barring; the underparts are white, gray, buffy, tawny, or reddish. Their bills are long, slender, and curved downward at the tip.

AMERICAN MUS. OF NAT. HIST.
Wren

Wrens live near the ground, inhabiting shrubbery rather than trees, or the reeds of marshes, patches of cactus, or piles of rocks. Their nests are large and bulky, containing from 6 to 11 eggs, which are laid twice yearly. Wrens usually seek insects for their food.

One of the commonest songbirds in America is the house wren, *Troglodytes aedon aedon*. The adults are cinnamon brown above with red coloration in the area of the tail, and grayish white below. The back is indistinctly barred, wings and tail finely barred. The nest is made of twigs, lined with grasses, and placed in a birdhouse, in a cavity of a tree, or in a crevice. Those species which breed in the northern part of eastern North America migrate southward to southern United States and Mexico for the winter.

WRESTLING, the sport of hand-to-hand combat between two unarmed opponents, each of whom attempts to force the other to the ground and on his back, and to pin his shoulders in an immobile position there. Wrestling is one of the oldest of sports, and probably was originated by primitive man as an exercise of the physical skills needed for survival in his battles against men and animals. The existence of a cast bronze figurine (?3000 B.C.) of two wrestlers, each holding on to his opponent's hips, testifies to the ancient origin of wrestling as a sport. Wrestling was

extremely popular among the ancient Greeks, Romans, and Japanese, but was practiced in some form by most of the peoples of the world throughout history. National and international matches were held during the Middle Ages; many championship bouts were staged exclusively for royalty and the court, but others were sponsored by the rulers as public spectacles. In medieval Japan, as in Greece and Rome, wrestling was a national sport patronized by the ruling house.

WREXHAM, Welsh Gwrecsam, municipal borough, NE Wales, in Denbighshire; 25 miles S of Liverpool. The borough is in a coal-mining area, and has tanneries and textile mills. The Church of St. Giles (1472) contains the tomb of Elihu Yale, the first donor of Yale University. Pop. (1951) 30,962.

WRIGHT, FRANCES, known as Fanny, 1795–1852, U.S. reformer, was born in Dundee, Scotland. While visiting the United States, 1824, she discussed the problem of Negro slavery with Thomas Jefferson and James Madison, and gained their approval of her plan for emancipation, which was to buy a tract of land, purchase slaves, and let them earn their freedom. She invested a large part of her sizable inheritance in land in western Tennessee, 1825, and established a colony of freed slaves in Haiti, 1830. As a public speaker, she embraced many controversial causes, such as birth control, women's emancipation, and free unions rather than marriage.

WRIGHT, FRANK LLOYD, 1869–1959, U.S. architect, was born in Richland Center, Wis. In 1884 he entered the Department of Civil Engineering at the University of Wisconsin, but, rebelling against the academic approach to architecture, he went to Chicago, 1887, and became a member of Louis Sullivan's staff, assisting Sullivan in such Chicago projects as the Auditorium Building, 1889, and the Transportation Building, 1893, for the World's Columbian Exposition. When Wright opened his own architectural firm six years later, Sullivan's influence was strongly apparent in his designs.

Wright's early private dwellings, built in and around Chicago, exemplify the basic principle of his architectural philosophy: analysis of the nature of the building materials, and of the climate, surroundings, and function of the building. His houses seem to be part of the landscape, rather than imposed upon it. Wright's so-called Prairie Houses, such as the Heurtley House (1902), Oak Park, Ill.; Robie House (1906), Chicago; and Coonley House (1908), Riverside, Ill., are low and flat-roofed, with broad overhangs. The Hill, or Mountain Houses, such as his residence, Taliesin (1914; rebuilt 1932), Spring Green, Wis., and Falling Water (1937), Bear Run, Pa., seem almost to be part of the hills on which they are built. Holding that each climate requires its own form of architecture, Wright used locally available materials as much as possible. Thus, for his houses in California, where relatively little brick, stone, or wood was available, he devised a decorated concrete block, poured at the building site; in the rocky deserts of Arizona, however, he made walls of piled up rocks. Inside his houses, brick or stone piers are never plastered over and the grain of wood is used decoratively. He revolutionized the architectural use of glass by transforming the window from a hole in the wall to a continuous band or wall of glass extending to the ceiling, and further enhanced the sense of interior spaciousness by using moving screen partitions, second story rooms with railings instead of an interior wall, and different ceiling heights.

In Wright's commercial and institutional structures he was much concerned with the architectural problems posed by the uses to which a building is to be put. His first important commercial structure, the Larkin Building (1904), Buffalo, N.Y., was distinguished for its simplicity of exterior design and revolutionary use of materials. It was the first completely air-conditioned office building, and the first in which plate-glass doors and metal furniture, designed by Wright, were used. Unity Church (1906), Oak Park, Ill., the world's first poured concrete building, went virtually unnoticed in the United States but was hailed by European architects as the birthplace of a new architecture. The Imperial Hotel (1922), Tokyo, Japan, dramatically brought Wright international fame when its radical floating foundations and canti-levered floors enabled it to withstand the disastrous earthquake of 1923; late in the 1950's and early in the 1960's, however, there were indications that the Wright building, long subordinated to a "modern-istic" annex, would be torn down by the owners of the hotel, who said they could make better use of the space with a taller building with lower ceilings and the like. The Johnson Laboratory (1939), Racine, Wis., is a tube of glass; the floors are cantilevered from a central shaft enclosing the "mechanics" of the building. The Guggenheim Museum (1959), New York City, is essentially a spiral ramp, along which the paintings seem to float in space.

Among Wright's published works are his lively *Autobiography* (1932; rev. ed. 1943); *Organic Architecture* (1939); *When Democracy Builds* (1945); an analysis of the work of Louis Sullivan, *Genius and the Mobocracy* (1949); *A Testament* (1957); and a magnificent collection of *Drawings for a Living Architecture* (1959).

MARYA LILIEN

Wright's philosophy of architecture is in complete opposition to that of those who make up the so-called Bauhaus School—Mies van der Rohe, Walter Gropius, Le Corbusier, and their followers—builders of "machines for living" that were derided as "egg crates" by Wright. He himself called his architecture "organic"—that is, growing out of the landscape rather than imposed upon it. The material below is excerpted from articles written by Frank Lloyd Wright for editions of THE AMERICAN PEOPLES ENCYCLOPEDIA YEARBOOK.

ORGANIC ARCHITECTURE

Architecture is the basic endeavor of mankind— the Mother art. Architecture *presents* man; literature tells you about him; painting pictures him to you; you can listen and hear him. But if you want to realize him and experience him, go into his buildings! That is where you will find him as he is. In our build-ings you see that, in spite of the fact that we have lived a long time as an independent civilization, we have done very little to create a culture of our own; and there is no true culture that is not indigenous culture. We cannot claim to have a culture until we have an indigenous architecture, rather than a con-glomerate of borrowings and restatements of other, genuine cultures, until we understand what it means to live in that indigenous architecture, and until we know the difference between a good building and a bad one and know what makes the one good and the other inferior.

We have what we call modern architecture. But most of it is not new. When new materials such as glass and steel came to hand, there were no architec-tural forms suited to their use with nobility, inspira-tion, or even intelligence. In most modern architec-ture we have mere novelty, the old steel frames with the new glass effects, shoddy sensationalism, new-fangled inventions and superficial beautifications but little or no architecture truly appropriate to the new materials and techniques. We must search for the natural way to build with them—to build in a way appropriate to the unprecedented life to be lived in them. Breaking with the past, we must struggle to grasp the present; that will enable a greater splendor of life to be ours than any known to Greek, Roman, Goth, or Moor.

Organic building is natural building, and so Or-ganic architecture is the answer. When I speak of architecture as Organic I mean the great art of struc-ture coming back to its early integrity; I mean be-

ginning again at the beginning: building the right kind of building in the right way for the right man. The space to be lived in is the core, the reality of any building, and we must find the new forms in terms of that space. In Organic architecture, construction proceeds harmoniously from the core, the planned, organized inside, outward to a consistent outside. The exterior is neither a convenient shell wrapped around the core, nor an inflexible frame into which the core is stuffed; the exterior is, rather, a natural extension of the core. Thomas Jefferson didn't live long enough to become aware of Organic architec-ture, but he prophesied it when he built that little four-inch wall on a curve so that a four-inch-thick wall would stand. Davy Crockett had something of it when he tied the tail of a coon to the back of his coonskin cap.

Architecture always has been and always will be a great indigenous idea; its beauty is the beauty of integrity.

Architecture has been dead for 500 years, as far as any true vitality is concerned. It is now coming alive again, and I believe that new meanings and new ways will enable us to act again with courage and thus provide ourselves with a living culture worthy of our freedom.

FRANK LLOYD WRIGHT

WRIGHT, GEORGE, 1847–1937, U.S. baseball player, a member of the Baseball Hall of Fame from 1937, was born in New York City. He was a member of the first professional baseball team, the Cincinnati Red Stockings, 1869–70, and played with Boston in the National Association, 1871–75, Boston in the Na-tional League, 1876–78, 1880–81, and Providence in the National League, 1879, 1882.

WRIGHT, HAROLD BELL, 1872–1944, U.S. novelist, was born in Rome, N.Y. He was a minister of the Christian church, 1897–1908. His best known novels are simple, sentimental tales of life in the Ozarks such as *The Shepherd of the Hills* (1907), and in the Great American West, such as *The Winning of Barbara Worth* (1911). Among his other works are *The Mine with the Iron Door* (1923), *God and the Groceryman* (1927), *Ma Cinderella* (1932), and *The Man Who Went Away* (1942). Although marked by a strong sermon-istic tone, Wright's works are better written than most popular novels. *The Winning of Barbara Worth* has a certain nonliterary significance in the fact that it was through his performance in a silent motion picture version of this novel that the Hollywood star Gary Cooper first caught the public fancy.

WRIGHT, LUKE EDWARD, 1846–1922, U.S. public official, was born in Giles County, Tenn. He became a member of the Philippine Commission, 1900, was vice-governor, 1901–04, governor, 1904, and governor general, 1905, of the Philippine Islands. Under Pres. Theodore Roosevelt, Wright served as U.S. ambassador to Japan, 1906–07, and U.S. Secre-tary of War, 1908–09.

WRIGHT, PATIENCE LOVELL, 1725–86, the first colonial American sculptor, was born in Borden-town, N.J. She executed wax portraits of colonial American leaders and of English royalty. In 1772 she settled in London, where she later acted as a spy for the American revolutionist Benjamin Franklin.

Joseph Wright, 1756–93, Patience Wright's son and also a sculptor, was born in Bordentown, N.J., but moved to England with his mother at the age of 16. During a stay in France, 1782, he became a friend of Franklin and through him executed the portrait, life mask, and small bust of George Wash-ington the next year in America. Washington ap-pointed him first diesinker and engraver of the United States Mint, 1792.

WRIGHT, QUINCY, 1890–   , U.S. educator, was born in Medford, Mass., and studied at Lombard College, Galesburg, Ill., and at the University of Illinois. He was a professor of political science, 1923–31, and of international law, 1931–56, at the Univer-sity of Chicago, and became a professor of international law at the University of Virginia, 1958. He was a consultant to the U.S. Foreign Economic Administration and the U.S. Department of State, 1943–44, to UNESCO, 1949, and to the U.S. High Commissioner in Germany, 1949–50. Among his writings are *The Cause of War and Conditions of Peace* (1935), *The Study of War* (2 vols. 1942), and *International Law and the United Nations* (1956). See BOYCOTT, Boycott in International Relations; BUFFER STATE; WAR.

WRIGHT, RICHARD, 1908–60, U.S. novelist and short story writer, was born near Natchez, Miss. He educated himself by reading, worked at odd jobs in Memphis and elsewhere, and came to Chicago, 1934, where he worked on the Federal Writers' Project of the Works Project Administration (WPA). In 1937 he moved to New York, wrote *Guide to Harlem* for the Writers' Project, and became a contributing editor of the Communist *New Masses.* His first book, *Uncle Tom's Children* (1938), consists of four vitriolic novelettes about racial discrimination in the South. In his first notable success, *Native Son* (1940), the murder of a white girl by a Chicago Negro is viewed as the end product of segregation and sordid environment. Among his other works are *Twelve Million Black Voices* (1941); an autobiographical novel, *Black Boy* (1945); *The Outsider* (1953); *White Man, Listen* (1957); *The Long Dream* (1958); and *Eight Men* (1961).

WRIGHT, SILAS, 1795–1847, U.S. political leader, was born in Amherst, Mass., was graduated from Middlebury College, Vermont, 1815, and was admitted to the bar, 1819. He served as a member of the U.S. House of Representatives, 1827–29, U.S. senator, 1833–34, and was the governor of New York, 1844–46. He was a leader of the Democratic party in northern New York, and an influential member of the Albany Regency, which controlled the New York Democratic party.

WRIGHT, WILLARD HUNTINGTON, pseudonym S. S. Van Dine, 1888–1939, U.S. art critic, novelist, and journalist, was born in Charlottesville, Va., and studied at Pomona College and Harvard University. He became literary editor of the Los Angeles *Times,* 1907, and was successively editor of the *Smart Set,* art critic of *Forum,* literary editor of the New York *Evening Mail,* music and art editor of the San Francisco *Bulletin,* and art critic of *Hearst's International* magazine. While convalescing from an illness, 1925, he wrote *The Benson Murder Case,* first of what was to remain a popular series of detective novels featuring Philo Vance, an impossibly and insufferably urbane and scholarly master sleuth. Among Wright's earlier books are *Europe After 8:15* (with H.L. Mencken and George Jean Nathan, 1913), *Modern Painting* (1915), *The Man of Promise* (1916), *The Future of Painting* (1923). Among his other detective novels, all written under the pseudonym S. S. Van Dine, are *The Canary Murder Case* (1927), *The Greene Murder Case* (1928), *The Scarab Murder Case* (1930), and *The Winter Murder Case* (1939). Of somewhat special interest is Wright's *Misinforming a Nation* (1917), an essay on the *Encyclopaedia Britannica.*

WRIGHT BROTHERS, U.S. inventors prominent in the early twentieth century, were pioneers in the field of aeronautics and aerodynamics. Wilbur Wright, 1867–1912, born in Millville, Ind., and his brother Orville Wright, 1871–1948, born in Dayton, Ohio, were raised in Dayton, where they became partners in the Wright Cycle Company, 1896. From childhood they were interested in the possibility of devices by means of which man might be able to fly, and began experimenting with kites and gliders,

BROWN BROS.
Wilbur Wright

1896. They found the work of Otto Lilienthal, Samuel P. Langley, Octave Chanute, and Sir Hiram Maxim inadequate, and conducted pioneer researches in

BROWN BROS.
Orville Wright

aerodynamics. In 1900 Orville built the first aeronautical wind tunnel for their tests (see AERONAUTICS). By 1902 they had produced a biplane that incorporated such new principles as the aileron, the horizontal elevator, the vertical rudder, and the single set of controls. This machine was tested at Kitty Hawk, N.C., Dec. 17, 1903, before a handful of skeptical natives. Four flights were made—the first flights ever achieved by man in a motor-driven, heavier-than-air machine. In the first flight Orville kept the machine off the ground for 12 seconds; in the fourth flight, Wilbur achieved a record of 59 seconds, and covered some 852 feet in the air. The Wright Brothers received their first patent in 1906; three years later they tested their machine successfully for the U.S. Army. Wilbur Wright also made demonstration flights in France, 1908, and New York, 1909. They were the founders of the American Wright Company, 1909, of which Wilbur was the first president until his death; Orville was president from 1912 until 1915, when he sold his interest in the company. During World War I, Orville Wright served with the U.S. Signal Corps Aviation Service as a major, and following the war spent most of his time as director of the Wright Aeronautical Laboratory in Dayton. Orville Wright was the inventor of the split wing flap (patented 1924) that was used on dive bombers in World War II.

WRIGHT BROTHERS NATIONAL MEMORIAL, NE North Carolina, in Dare County on a barrier beach, between the Atlantic Ocean and Kittyhawk Bay; 35 miles W of Elizabeth City, area 324 acres. The memorial, authorized in 1927; is at Kill Devil Hill. In this area of sand hills, Orville and Wilbur Wright, pioneer aviators, conducted their gliding experiments from 1900 to 1902, and powered-flight tests in 1903. The principal feature is the Wright Memorial Shaft, a 60-foot granite pylon, situated on a hill.

WRIGHTSVILLE, city, central Georgia, seat of Johnson County; on the Wrightsville and Tenille Railroad, and U.S. highway 319; 115 miles SE of Atlanta. The city has a textile mill and a cannery. Pop. (1960) 2,056.

WRIOTHESLEY, HENRY, 3rd **EARL OF SOUTHAMPTON,** 1573–1624, English patron of arts, was born near Midhurst, Sussex, and was educated at Cambridge. He was the patron of several poets, among them William Shakespeare, who dedicated *Venus and Adonis* and *The Rape of Lucrece* to him. He is supposed by some to be the patron and friend addressed by Shakespeare in the *Sonnets.* He was condemned to death for participating in the conspiracy of Robert Devereux, earl of Essex, 1601, but the sentence was commuted, and he was released and restored to court favor by James I, 1603. He helped to outfit the Virginia expedition of 1605, and served on the council of the Virginia Company, 1609–24.

WRIT, a written order issued by a court, in the name of the sovereign or state, to an officer of the law (or, rarely, to a private citizen) requiring the recipient to perform or refrain from performing a specific act. Many writs demand that the officer report to a specified authority at a specified date on his success or failure to fulfill the order. Writs were of great importance in the development of the English common law in that the early kings sought to have all wrongs righted by their agents or courts instead of by the church and they accomplished this by the issuance of writs that defined enforceable rights. In time these congealed into formal inflexible procedures, so that it was said that there was no right or justice without a writ. This was remedied by the Statute of Westminster 2d (1285) by which the king's chancellor was permitted to vary the forms of writs to meet new situations. Many of the old common law writs survived into the twentieth century, among them writs of assistance, debt, detinue, ejectment, error, habeas corpus, mandamus, and trespass. Generally, however, codes of procedure have eliminated many of these and substituted a simple form of process. See PROCESS; PROCEDURE; LAW.

WRITING, in the widest sense, is a system of human intercommunication by means of visible markings used conventionally. In a narrower, more precise sense, writing is a device for expressing notions of linguistic value, and corresponds to what is commonly called "written language." The history of fully developed systems of writing can be traced no more than 5,000 years, but the antecedents and forerunners of writing have a much longer history. See CALLIGRAPHY; COMMUNICATIONS; LANGUAGE.

The Significance of Writing in Human Affairs. In order to communicate thoughts and feelings there must be a conventional system of signs or symbols. Communication normally requires the presence of at least two people, the one who emits and the one who receives the communication. Visual communication can be achieved by means of gesture and mimicry, and by means of signals made with fire, smoke, light, and so forth. Auditory communication ranges from such simple media as whistling with the intention of calling someone, through more sophisticated artificial means such as drums, whistles, or trumpets used as acoustic signals, to the most important system of auditory communication—spoken language. Language is seemingly universal, in that within the span of human knowledge there has never existed a group of men who have not possessed a fully developed language. Simple ways of communicating feeling by the sense of touch are, for instance, the handclasp or the backslap. A fully developed system of communication by handstroking is used among blind deaf-mutes, for which the best known example is provided by the case of the U.S. writer and educator Helen Keller.

Such means of communication share two limitations. First, they are restricted temporally: once a word is uttered or a gesture made, it is gone and cannot be revived except by repetition. Secondly, they are restricted spatially; they can be used only by persons more or less in proximity to each other. The need for a way to convey thoughts and feelings in a form not limited by time or space led, early in human history, to the development of methods of communication by means of objects and markings on objects.

PRIMITIVE METHODS

Object Writing. Systems of mnemonic signs to keep accounts by means of objects are known throughout the world. The simplest and the most common are the so-called counting sticks for keeping records of cattle. These are simple wooden sticks with carved notches corresponding to the number of cattle under the custody of a herdsman. Another simple device is keeping livestock accounts with the help of little pebbles in a sack. A more complicated mnemonic system was the so-called quipu writing of the Peruvian Incas, in which accounts concerning objects and beings were recorded by means of strings and knots of various length and color. The wampum of the North American Indians, consisting of strings of shell beads, frequently tied together in belts, served as money, ornaments, and also as a means of communication.

Markings. Such object writing is very limited in comparison with the system of markings on objects, executed by the hands in drawing, painting, scratch-

ing, or incising. Probably the most natural way of communicating ideas by means of visible markings is by the use of pictures. Among primitive peoples pictures served, however crudely and imprecisely, the needs served in later times by writing. In the course of time the picture developed in two directions: (1) pictorial art, in which pictures continued to reproduce more or less faithfully the objects and events of the surrounding world in a form independent of language; and (2) writing, in which signs, whether retaining their pictorial form or not, became ultimately secondary symbols for notions of linguistic value.

Primitive Drawings. If defined as a device for expressing linguistic elements by means of conventional visible marks, then writing has a history of no more than 5,000 years. But in the earliest times man felt the urge to draw or paint pictures on the walls of his primitive dwelling or on the rocks in his surroundings—just as a child no sooner learns to crawl than he begins to scribble on the wallpaper or to draw crude pictures in the sand. Throughout the world there are traces of primitive man's imaginative powers in drawings on rocks dating from the oldest Paleolithic down to modern times (see CAVE ART; ART, PRIMITIVE, *Paleolithic Art*). These drawings are called petrograms if they are drawn or painted, petroglyphs if incised or carved. They usually depict man and animal in various relations to each other. Best known are the faithful reproductions of animal figures left by Paleolithic man in Europe and the graceful painting of the South African Bushmen. An immense number of rock drawings and carvings has been found in North America, especially in the mountainous regions. In most cases it is difficult if not impossible to ascertain the purpose or the urge that prompted man to draw or incise a picture, since the circumstances that led to its execution are unknown. The picture might be a manifestation of magical, or religious, or aesthetic expression, or a combination of these. No one can say with certainty whether a particular picture was drawn for the purpose of insuring good hunting or as an expression of the artistic impulse. It is probable that several factors were involved. When a hunter returned from a successful chase, or a warrior from a military expedition, he perhaps felt the desire to record his experiences in a picture. The picture may have been drawn as the result of his artistic urge, yet also served to commemorate past experiences. It could also have had the magic purpose of securing another good hunt or a successful raid in the future. Because they did not form part of a conventional system of signs and could be understood only by the man who drew them or by his family and close friends who had heard of the event, such pictures were not writing in any meaningful sense of the term.

FORERUNNERS OF WRITING

Pictorial Communication. The most widespread of the forerunners of writing was that generally called pictographic, or ideographic, writing, which is exemplified in a simple communication "no thoroughfare" found in New Mexico on a rock placed near a precipitous trail. The design shows a mountain goat standing upright and a man on a horse upside-down; thus were roving Indians warned that a mountain goat could climb up the rocky trail, but a horse would fall. Such a picture or series of pictures describes to the eye what the eye sees in a way parallel to that achieved by a picture originated under the artistic-aesthetic urge, but these drawings attempted to communicate a certain message in such a way that it could be understood by the people for whom the message was intended, and did not primarily serve the purpose of artistic-aesthetic expression. Moreover, the differences between pictures and the drawings in question lie not only in the divergent aims, but also in the form of execution. Like all drawings for the purpose of communication, these are characterized by stereotyped execution as well as by omission of all details (grass, mountains, and so forth) not necessary for the expression of the communication. In short, these drawings lack all the embellishment, the artistic effect, evident in pictures representative of artistic purposes. Hence, this forerunner of writing can be regarded as of the descriptive or representational stage or type by reason of the close connection between the technique of expression in art and in writing.

Mnemonic Devices, among the forerunners of writing, are well exemplified by a drawing of a panther on a shield found in Africa. This drawing may originally have had the magic purpose of transmitting the qualities of the panther to the man who owned the shield, but in the course of time the drawing became also a symbol that communicated to everyone the fact that the shield was owned by a certain person. While in this instance the symbol of the panther became a property mark, whose aim was that of utilitarian writing, it was not in itself writing; even though it stood for a personal name and may have been habitually associated with one certain person, it was not part of a well established conventional system. Nevertheless it was an important step in the direction of writing. The identifying method of recording proper names includes also the various ways by which American Indians designate personal and tribal names. Of mnemonic character are drawings made by the Ojibwa Indians for the purpose of recording songs, or by the Ewe Negroes of Togo to record proverbs, as exemplified by a picture of the needle with thread to represent the proverb "the thread follows the needle" (not vice versa), resembling in meaning the English saying "a chip off the old block" or "like father, like son." See NAME; PLACE NAME.

Transition to Written Words. While in the descriptive-representational device the communication was achieved by means of drawings describing an event in a form quite similar to that achieved in a drawing resulting from an artistic-aesthetic urge, the aim of the identifying-mnemonic device was not to describe an event, but to help to remember or identify an object, a being, or a story. Thus a complete correspondence was established and gradually conventionalized between certain symbols, on the one hand, and certain objects of the surrounding world, on the other. Since these objects had names in the spoken language, a further correspondence was established between the written symbols and their spoken counterparts, and it was from such correspondence that full writing evolved.

WORDS, SYLLABLES, AND ALPHABETS

Logography, or word writing, is a system in which a sign normally stands for one or more words of the language. The Sumerians of Mesopotamia took this important step toward a fully developed writing (see SUMERIAN LANGUAGE AND LITERATURE). The organization of the Sumerian state and economy made it imperative that records be kept of goods transferred from the country to the city and vice versa. Such records were kept in a concise ledger form, of the type "five sheep" or "10 bows plus personal name." In this system, "five sheep" was written by means of two signs corresponding to two words in the language, instead of by five separate pictures of sheep such as were needed to express the idea of "five sheep" in the various pictographic systems. The difference can be further illustrated by the way in which such a sentence as "man killed lion" was expressed in the two systems. This sentence had been expressed by a drawing of a man, spear in hand, in the process of killing a lion; in logography this sentence of three words was written by means of three conventional signs representing man, killing (spear), and lion.

Theoretically, a device in which individual signs can express individual words should naturally lead toward a development of a complete system of word signs. However, such a complete system never existed, either in antiquity or in more modern times, for to create and memorize thousands of signs for thousands of words and names existing in a language and to invent new signs for newly acquired words and names was as impracticable then as now. A logographic writing might continue to be used as a limited system only, or it had to find ways to overcome the difficulties in order to develop into a useful system. Experience with the Micmac and Cherokee word writings, created artificially in modern times for the use of American Indians, has demonstrated the impracticability of such limited systems. A primitive logographic writing can develop into a full system only if it succeeds in attaching to a sign a phonetic value independent of the meaning which this sign has as a word. This "phonetization" was unquestionably the most important single step in the history of writing. In modern usage this device is called rebus writing. It is exemplified in the drawing of an eye and of a saw to express the phrase "I saw," or in that of a man and a date to express the word "mandate." With the introduction of phonetization and its subsequent systematization, complete systems of writing developed which made it possible to express any linguistic form by means of symbols with conventional syllabic values. See PHONETICS.

Word-Syllabic Systems. Seven fully developed word-syllabic systems arose in the ancient Orient. The earliest was Sumerian, attested in southern Mesopotamia from ?3100 B.C. to A.D. 50. The others are the Proto-Elamite writing around Susa in southern Persia, attested ?3000 B.C.; the Proto-Indic writing in the Indus Valley, attested ?2200 B.C.; the Chinese writing attested from ?1300 B.C. to the present; the Egyptian system from ?3000 B.C. to A.D. 400, then the Cretan systems in Crete, Greece, and the Aegean region generally from ?2000 to 1200 B.C.; and finally hieroglyphic Hittite in Anatolia and Syria from ?1500 to 700 B.C. Of these seven writings, Proto-Elamite and Proto-Indic remain undeciphered, while the successful decipherment of Cretan was begun only in 1953 with the brilliant work of Michael Ventris. Outside of the Orient, there remains only the Maya writing in Central America, which may have to be included among the word-syllabic systems; however, the claim of the Russian, J. V. Knorozov, to have deciphered the Maya writing had not been fully substantiated at mid-twentieth century.

All word-syllabic systems are alike in having preserved throughout their long history a mixture of logographic and syllabic spellings. Thus the words "Gudea the king went" are written in Sumerian as *Gu-de-a* LUGAL *i*-GIN, showing words written logographically, such as LUGAL (king) and GIN (to go), and syllabically, such as *Gu-de-a* and the verbal prefix *i*-. The word-syllabic systems differ greatly in the typology of the syllabic usage. The Sumerian and the derived Assyro-Babylonian systems have signs for monosyllables ending in a vowel or consonant, such as *ta, at, tam*, and very rarely for dissyllables such as *ata*, or *tama*. Egyptian has signs for monosyllables and dissyllables ending in a vowel, such as t^x or t^xm^x; x stands for any vowel, which is not specified, as in t^x functioning for *ta, te, ti, tu,* or *to*. The Hittite and Cretan systems have signs only for monosyllables ending in a vowel, such as *ta, te,* and so forth. Chinese uses signs for monosyllables ending in a vowel, or consonant, such as *ta, at, tam.*

Syllabic Systems. Out of the word-syllabic systems four types of syllabic systems developed: Elamite, Hurrian, and other cuneiform syllabaries from the Sumerian (Mesopotamian); West Semitic syllabaries, such as Phoenician, Old Hebrew, and others from the Egyptian; Aegan syllabaries, such as Linear B and Cypriote, from the Cretan; and the Japanese syllabary from the Chinese. Only two of the four types employed syllabic signs exclusively, namely the West Semitic and some Aegean writings. A very limited number of logograms was used in the derived cuneiform systems and some of the Aegean writings, while the Japanese syllabic system, called *kana*, can be used side by side with a logographic system, called *kanji*.

Alphabetic Systems. Several attempts were made during the second millennium B.C. to find a way to indicate vowels in the syllabaries of the Egyptian-West Semitic type, but no full vocalic system was developed. The usual way was to add phonetic indicators as helps in reading the vowels unspecified in the syllabic signs, as in the case of m^x-l^x-la^x-t^x-y^x (I ruled) where the syllabic sign y^x added to t^x assures that the sign t^x would be read as *ti*, and not, for example, as *ta*, *tu*, or the like. But while the Egyptians and West Semites used these so-called *matres lectionis* sparingly, the Greeks used them systematically after each syllabic sign. Thus the Greeks, having fully accepted the forms of the West Semitic syllabary, evolved a system of vowel signs which, when attached to the syllabic signs, reduced the value of these syllabic signs to simple consonants, and thereby created the first full alphabetic system of writing (see GREEK ALPHABET; GREEK LANGUAGE AND LITERATURE; WOLF, FRIEDRICH AUGUST; VENTRIS, MICHAEL GEORGE FRANCIS). Having learned the systematic use of vowel marks from the Greeks, the Semites subsequently developed their own alphabets. Thus, with the exception of the group of writings derived from China and a small group of writings developed in modern times among the so-called primitive societies, all the systems of writing in use at mid-twentieth century, though differing in outer form, were founded upon principles of writing developed in the Semito-Greek area. See ALPHABET; CHINESE LANGUAGE AND LITERATURE; JAPANESE LANGUAGE AND LITERATURE; SANSKRIT LANGUAGE AND LITERATURE; SEMITIC LANGUAGES.   I. J. GELB

WRIT OF ASSISTANCE. See ASSISTANCE, WRIT OF.

WROCŁAW, province, SW Poland; bounded by Posnań on the N, Łódź on the NE, Opole on the E, and by Czechoslovakia on the S and Germany on the W; area 9,550 sq. mi.; pop. (1959 est.) 1,750,000. The terrain rises gradually from the Oder River in the northeast to the Sudeten Mountains in the southwest, which rise to 5,255 feet at Sněžka on the Czechoslovakian border. The province is drained to the north by the Oder, Bóbr, and Kwisa rivers. Metalworking, glass manufacturing, and textile and paper milling are concentrated in the cities of Breslau, Wałbrzych, Jelenia Góra, and Legnica. Coal is mined in the southeast. The principal crops are rye, potatoes, oats, wheat, barley, and flax. Breslau (Wrocław) is the capital.

WROCKŁAW. See BRESLAU.

WROUGHT IRON, a two-component metal, consisting of highly refined metallic iron mixed with

CHICAGO ART INSTITUTE

A handsome brazier, with its gracefully stylized foliage and skillfully executed human figures, is an example of wrought-iron work done in Italy during the Renaissance.

minute and uniformly distributed particles of silicate slag. It is called a two-component metal because there is no chemical combination between the iron and slag. Slag is made of iron oxide and silica.

No other ferrous material contains this glasslike slag, which aids in resisting atmospheric and aqueous corrosion and increases the ductility and malleability of wrought iron. Between 200,000 and 250,000 fibers of slag per square inch are threaded through the pure iron. Good quality wrought iron should have less than 0.10 per cent carbon content. If not alloyed with nickel, its tensile strength is approximately 47,000 pounds per square inch; its yield point, 30,000 pounds per square inch, with an elongation in 8 inches of about 35 percent, and a reduction in area of 48 percent.

The use of wrought iron antedates the Pyramids. Because of its unique properties, wrought iron, both flat-rolled and as pipe, is used for many applications that necessitate a material resistant to corrosion, abrasion, and shock, and one with superior forming and welding qualities. A few of the uses include ornamental ironwork, smokestacks, steam pipes, drain lines, and boiler stay bolts for locomotives and railroad cars, brine lines, condenser tubing, bridges, marine craft, roofing and siding, and radiant heating and snow-melting lines. In the last two applications, wrought-iron pipe provides high heat emission, ease of fabrication, almost identical thermal expansion coefficients with concrete, and

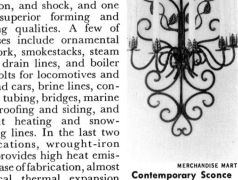

MERCHANDISE MART
Contemporary Sconce

Wrought iron was frequently used for decorative purposes during the Middle Ages. These wrought-iron wall hangings were made by European artisans of the thirteenth century.

high corrosion resistance, which are essential when heating pipes are to be imbedded within floors, walls, or outside driveways and walks.

Until 1930, wrought iron was produced almost entirely by hand in puddling furnaces. Molten pig iron was stirred with a long-handled tool, a rabble, to refine it by oxidation and other chemical reaction of carbon, silicon, sulfur, phosphorus, and manganese. As the metal became purified in the presence of the refining slag, the mixture became spongy and plastic. Masses of this conglomeration, weighing between 200 and 300 pounds, were removed from the furnace and squeezed into sections known as blooms.

Under a process developed in 1927, molten refined iron is poured in a thin stream into a ladle filled with molten slag. As the iron plunges into the cooler slag, gases trapped in the liquid iron are liberated with such force that the metal particles are shattered. Each particle of iron picks up some of the silica slag and settles to the bottom, collecting together to form a "sponge" weighing about 8,000 pounds. The sponge is pressed into a bloom and later rolled into desired shapes and sections.

WRYNECK, an Old World bird related to the woodpeckers, but differing from them in the soft tail that does not have spiny shafts, and the absence of bristles round the nostrils, which are partially covered by a membrane. The plumage is curiously mottled with black, brown, gray, and white. The common wryneck, *Fynx torquilla*, is found in England during the summer, but it does not usually extend to the north. This species is widely spread over Europe and Asia, while the other three species are African.

WRYNECK. See TORTICOLLIS.

WUCHANG, city, central China, capital of Hupei Province; on the S bank of the Yangtze River; opposite the cities of Hankow and Hanyang, which are separated by the Han River; 290 miles W of Nanking and 420 miles SW of Shanghai. Wuchang, Hankow, and Hanyang are called the Han cities and form the joint tri-city municipality of Wuhan. Wuchang is primarily the administrative and cultural center of the municipality. It is the seat of the Hupei provincial government, has a mint, and is the seat of Wuhan University. Residential and business sections are situated within the old city wall. Industrial plants and the water front are outside the city walls. Industrial establishments include cotton, silk, and paper mills; railroad repair shops; and a shipyard. Fishing is important, especially for the kweiyu (mandarin fish). Wuchang is the north terminus of a trunk railroad, which connects the city with Hengyang and Canton in the south. The city is connected by ferry to a railroad linking Hankow with Peking in the north. Among the points of interest is the noted seven-story pagoda of the ancient Pautung Temple. Wuchang is an ancient city. It is known to have been the seat of the San-miao aborigines, and under the Chow Dynasty belonged to the Kingchow and Chu states. In the Three Kingdoms era (third century), it was the capital of Wu. The city maintained its importance through the Tang, Mongol, Ming, and Manchu eras, and was held by the Taiping rebels in the nineteenth century. In 1911, Wuchang was the scene of the military revolt that overthrew the Manchu Empire. It was occupied by the Japanese, 1937–45. Pop. (1955 est.) 400,000.

WUCHOW, or Tsangwu, city, S China, in Kwangsi Province; on the Hsi River; 115 miles W of Canton. Wuchow is a river port, which handles most of the Hsi Basin's products, primarily tung oil and timber. Industries are shipbuilding, glass manufacturing, cotton spinning, and weaving. Pop. (1959 est.) 207,000.

WUHAN. See HANKOW; HANYANG; WUCHANG.

WUHU, city, E China, in Anhwei Province; on the Yangtze River; 55 miles SSW of Nanking. Wuhu is a distributing center for rice, wheat, cotton, tea, and silk. Traffic on the Yangtze River is supplemented by canals and highways. There are power and light plants and cotton-spinning factories. The Fanchang iron-ore deposits are in the vicinity. The Japanese took Wuhu in 1937 to exploit its coal and iron-ore deposits. Pop. (1959 est.) 204,000.

WULFENITE, a lead molybdate found in oxidized portions of lead veins as a secondary mineral. Wulfenite has the chemical composition, $PbMoO_4$. In some deposits calcium may replace some of the lead. Wulfenite has a tetragonal crystalline structure (see CRYSTALLOGRAPHY), a specific gravity of approximately 6.8, and a hardness of 3 (see HARDNESS). It is usually orange-red in color, with a vitreous to adamantine luster. It is a minor source of molybdenum, and is found principally in Arizona, Utah, and New Mexico.

WULFSTAN, SAINT, or Wolstan, or Wulstan, 1010?–95, English ecclesiastic, was born in Long Itchington, Warwickshire. After receiving Holy Orders, he spent 25 years in a Benedictine monastery, where he was esteemed for his piety, humility, and ascetic way of life. He accepted the bishopric of Worcester reluctantly, 1062, but proved to be an efficient administrator. Upon William the Conqueror's triumph, 1066, Wulfstan submitted to Norman authority and was allowed to retain his see; in return, he helped William subjugate the powerful English barons. Wulfstan helped to stop slave trade between England and Ireland. He was canonized in 1203. His feast day is January 19.

WULFSTAN, died 1023, English prelate, was Archbishop of York, 1003–23, and Bishop of Worcester, 1003–16. Wulfstan's alliterative prose homily, *Sermo ad Anglos*, dealing with the ruinous Danish raids on England, 1010–11, combines excellent descriptive passages with polished moral discourse. Of more than 50 works once ascribed to Wulfstan, only 4 or 5 are considered authentic by scholars.

WUNDT, WILHELM MAX, 1832–1920, German physiologist, encyclopedic thinker, and father of experimental psychology, was born in Neckarsau, in

CULVER SERVICE
Wilhelm Wundt

Baden, near Heidelberg, at whose university he studied and taught physiology from 1857, having earlier studied in Tübingen and Berlin. He taught in Zürich for one year, 1874, then was called to the chair of philosophy in Leipzig, 1875, at a time when philosophy was in such disrepute that there seemed nothing improper in appointing a physiologist to the chair in that subject. Wundt, however, did not disparage philosophy, and he continued its systematic teaching throughout his life; yet his fame is based on his having started, 1879, the first Institute of Experimental Psychology, a field in which his *Grundzüge* (Principles) were to be dominant for 30 years or more; a whole school published in the Institute's volumes.

In the study of *Völkerpsychologie* (Psychology of Nations), however, Wundt's achievement was distinctly more personal. With incredible energy he examined customs, myths, and languages, in order to discover the laws of their hold on man. His most important discovery, one whose implications had not yet been fully explored in the early 1960's, has to do with the relation of word and sentence; logically and historically, he found, sentences precede words, which means that a complete spiritual act is presupposed by all its parts. Wundt acknowledged the need for myth; even scientists need their myth, he admitted, as do capitalists and families, because they all must be steeped in some vital identification with previous lives and generations. At this point, however, Wundt failed to recognize that a man's foreknowledge of his mortality makes him into a spiritual, "unnatural" being. That is, Wundt restricted his philosophy to the natural world view and to an ethics that abstracts *from* man's foreknowledge of death, and thus deprives man of its full impact and significance. Hence, he was seemingly content to leave the future of groups and peoples to accident. Indeed, his astounding work *Logik* (1880–83; 3rd ed. 1906–08) omits all consideration of any aims of mankind, or of individual men. In this work, which is a unique embodiment of the scientific mind, the methods of physics, chemistry, biology, psychology, history, social science, political science, jurisprudence, economics, demography, anthropology, and philology are all digested and embodied as the living logic of the giant "Science." Truly, scientific positivism, in its replacing the future of nations by the future of science, had its most thorough representative in Wundt.

Wundt's bibliography is very large, but relatively few works are available in English translation. His *Völkerpsychologie* (2 vols. 1900; 1905–06) was translated under the misleading title, *Folk-psychology* (1916). His *Grundzüge der physiologischen Psychologie* (1874) became *Principles of Physiological Psychology* (1904); and his *Grundriss der Psychologie* (1896) became *Outlines of Psychology* (1907). These and the few other English translations do not, of course, take into account revisions in later editions of the German works.

EUGEN ROSENSTOCK-HUESSY

WUPATKI NATIONAL MONUMENT, N central Arizona, in Coconino County, about 28 miles NE of Flagstaff, on the west bank of the Little Colorado River; area 35,693 acres. The park is composed chiefly of a group of pueblo ruins probably built and inhabited in the twelfth century by the ancestors of the modern Hopi. Architectural features utilized by these farming Indians include T-shaped doors, employment of outside wall ventilators, an inexplicable circular pit topped by high walls and a surrounding bench, and the clever adaptation of the natural red sandstone walls to the structure. The Museum of Northern Arizona undertook the excavation of five rooms of the Nalakihu ruins and the restoration of two of them in 1933. The park was established in 1924.

WUPPERTAL, city, W Germany, in the West German state of North Rhine–Westphalia, on the Wupper River, a tributary of the Rhine; 16 miles SSE of Essen. Wuppertal incorporates the former cities of Barmen, Elberfeld, and four smaller towns, and extends for 8 miles along the narrow valley of the Wupper. The city is an important manufacturing center producing steel goods, textiles, lace, chemicals, buttons, organs, pianos, paper, and canned foods. Barmen, mentioned in various chronicles as early as the eleventh century, was not incorporated until 1808. Elberfeld assumed importance as a manufacturing center in the nineteenth century. Wuppertal has a number of technical and other schools. The city is served by a pioneer monorail, rapid-transit system. Pop. (1958 est.) 416,050.

WU RIVER, or Wu Kiang, S central China, in Kweichow and Szechwan provinces, a tributary of the Yangtze River. It rises in two branches, the Liuchung and Sancho in western Kweichow, and flows about 500 miles NE, N, and NW through Szechwan to the Yangtze River about 50 miles below Chungking. The river descends some 3,000 feet in its course, and is navigable only in its lower reaches. There are rice fields in the lower valley.

WÜRTTEMBERG, historical region and former kingdom, republic, and state, S Germany; bounded on the NE and E by Bavaria, on the SW by Hohenzollern, on the W and NW by Baden, and on the SE by Switzerland; area 7,530 sq. mi. Until the thirteenth century the history of Württemberg was that of Swabia, of which Württemberg formed the north central part. Upon the division of Swabia into several small states, 1254, the territory came under the counts of Württemberg, owing allegiance to the House of Hapsburg—later to rule Austria and dominate the Holy Roman Empire—and was made a duchy, 1495. Württemberg was a Protestant stronghold early in the Reformation, and as a result was

at odds with the Holy Roman Emperors during the religious wars of the sixteenth and seventeenth centuries. As an ally of France against Austria during the Napoleonic Wars, Württemberg was rewarded with cessions of Hapsburg territory and was made a kingdom, 1805. It became a member of Napoleon I's Confederation of the Rhine, 1806, but supported the Allies (Austria, Great Britain, Prussia, and Russia) against France in the Waterloo Campaign, 1815. Württemberg joined the Zollverein, 1834, a German customs union headed by Prussia. It sided with Austria against Prussia in the Seven Weeks' War, 1866, in which Prussia proved herself to be the most powerful state of Germany. Although not a member of Prussia's North German Confederation, Württemberg was allied with Prussia by secret treaty, sided with Prussia in war with France, 1870–71, and was admitted to the German Empire, 1871. See NORTH GERMAN CONFEDERATION.

After World War I, Württemberg became a republic of the German Weimar Republic, 1918, but under the National Socialist (Nazi) government, 1933–45, it was reduced to an administrative unit. At the end of World War II, 1945, Württemberg was divided between the U.S. and French zones of occupation. The northern halves of Württemberg and Baden were later combined to form the state (*Land*) of Württemberg-Baden with Stuttgart as capital, 1946, and southern Württemberg was merged with the former Prussian district of Hohenzollern to form the state of Württemberg-Hohenzollern, with Tübingen as capital. Both states joined the West German Republic, 1949, and both merged with what remained of Baden to form the new state, Baden-Württemberg, 1952.

WURTZ, CHARLES ADOLPHE, 1817–84, French chemist, was born in Wolfisheim, near Strasbourg. He became professor of chemistry at the Sorbonne, 1853, and was dean of the Sorbonne medical faculty, 1866–75. Wurtz discovered the methyl and ethyl amines, as well as the synthesis of hydrocarbons from alkyl iodides and sodium. He also did valuable research on the oxidation products of the glycols. He was the author of the monumental *Dictionnaire de chimie pure et appliquée*, first published in 1869.

WÜRZBURG, city, S central Germany, in the West German state of Bavaria; on the Main River; 60 miles SE of Frankfurt-am-Main. The city is a railroad junction and an industrial center. Tobacco products, pianos, furniture, precision instruments, machinery, railroad cars, bricks, sugar, malt, beer, wine, vinegar, and chocolate are manufactured there. The Romanesque cathedral was founded in the ninth century. The Marienberg Fortress, long the residence of a bishop, stands on a hill overlooking the Main River. A new episcopal palace was built between 1719 and 1744. Leading educational institutions include Würzburg University (1403) and a music school. In 1859 Würzburg was the scene of a meeting to promote the union of small German states. Pop. (1958 est.) 111,246.

WYANDOT, a North American Indian tribe, of Iroquoian linguistic stock, comprising the remnants of several independent tribes, which were broken up by the Iroquois tribes south of the St. Lawrence River in the seventeenth century (see HURON). The Wyandot were found in Ontario, western New York, Pennsylvania, southern Michigan, and northern Ohio. They lived in bark lodges, and subsisted chiefly by agriculture. Most of them sold their Ohio lands and moved to Kansas, 1842, from where they were removed to Indian Territory (Oklahoma), 1867. In 1950 there were about 900 Wyandot Indians on a reservation in Oklahoma.

WYANDOTTE, city, SE Michigan, in Wayne County; on the Detroit River, the Detroit and Toledo Shore Line, the Detroit, Toledo, and Ironton, the New York Central, the Wyandotte Terminal, and the Wyandotte Southern railroads; 12 miles SW of

Detroit. The chief manufactures of Wyandotte are chemicals, soda, metal toys and novelties, trunks, compression gaskets, brass pipe fittings, beverages, and dairy products. Wyandotte was settled in 1818 and incorporated as a city in 1867. By 1862 Wyandotte had the first steel-analysis laboratory in the United States, and in 1864 the first Bessemer steel in the United States was manufactured there. In 1891 a saltworks was established. Pop. (1960) 43,519.

WYANT, ALEXANDER HELWIG, 1836–92, U.S. landscape painter, was born in Evans Creek, Tuscarawas County, Ohio. His paintings are notable for their delicacy and refinement. Among his works are *Looking Toward the Sea* and *Broad, Silent Valley.*

WYATT, SIR FRANCIS, 1575?–1644, British colonial governor in America, was the grandson of the poet Sir Thomas Wyatt. He was knighted, 1603, and was chosen governor of Virginia to succeed Sir George Yeardley, 1620. He arrived in the colony in October, 1621, bringing with him a new constitution. When the Virginia Company was dissolved, 1624, he was appointed royal governor, a post he held until 1626, when he returned to England. He was governor again, 1639–42.

WYATT, JAMES, 1746–1813, English architect, was born in Staffordshire. He went to Rome to study, 1760, returned to England, 1766, and soon attained success as a designer in the Greco-Italian style. He later was a leader of the Gothic revival. His infelicitous restorations of cathedrals earned and justified his nickname—The Destroyer.

WYATT, SIR MATTHEW DIGBY, 1820–77, English architect and art critic, was the first Slade professor of fine arts at Cambridge University, 1869. He assisted in designing the Crystal Palace and was architect for the East India Company, 1855, but is best known for his writings on art, among which are *Geometric Mosaics of the Middle Ages* (1848), *Industrial Arts of the 19th Century* (1851), and *Art Treasures of the United Kingdom* (1857).

WYATT, SIR THOMAS, 1503?–42, English poet and diplomat, was born in Allington Castle, Kent, and studied at Cambridge. He took part in diplomatic missions to France and Italy, and was appointed privy councilor, 1533. He was believed to have been the lover of Anne Boleyn and was imprisoned for a few weeks at the time of her disgrace, 1536, but the exact reason for this action is uncertain. After his release he helped suppress a Lincolnshire uprising and was knighted, 1537. He was an ardent student of the Italian popularizer of the sonnet, Petrarch, and is credited, with Henry Howard, earl of Surrey, with introducing the sonnet into English literature. Among Wyatt's works are a translation from Plutarch, *Quyete of the Mynde* (1528); a metric translation of the seven penitential Psalms, *Certayen Psalmes* (1549); and the sonnets, rondeaux, and satiric couplets that were first published in Richard Tottel's *Miscellany* (1557).

Sir Thomas Wyatt, the Younger, 1521?–54, son of the poet Sir Thomas Wyatt, led the insurrection known as Wyatt's Rebellion, 1554, in an effort to prevent the marriage of Queen Mary to Philip of Spain. He gained some initial victories outside London, and his own followers were joined by many of the queen's. His force was stopped, however, in the streets of London, and Wyatt was captured and executed.

WYCHERLEY, WILLIAM, 1640?–1716, English dramatist, was born in Clive, near Shrewsbury, and was educated in France, where he was converted to Roman Catholicism—a faith he later embraced or disembraced as the political weather changed. He was educated at Queen's College, Oxford, and then began to study law in the Inner Temple, but he remained more interested in literature and in the licentious pleasures offered by Restoration social life than in law. After the success of his first play *Love in a Wood* (written ?1659; produced 1671), he became

a favorite of the Duchess of Cleveland, mistress of Charles II. *Love in a Wood*, a frivolous, lively, witty comedy in the style of Sir George Etherege, was followed by *The Gentleman Dancing-Master* (produced ?1672; published 1673), based on Pedro Calderón de la Barca's *El maestro de danzar* (the Dancing Master), and *The Country Wife* (produced ?1673; published 1675). In title, theme, and dialogue, *The Country Wife* ranks as one of the coarsest and most indecent plays in the English language, but Wycherley's satiric characterizations may indicate a tendency (perhaps intentional) to criticize the ambiguous moral standards of the period. *The Plain Dealer* (produced ?1674; published 1677), borrowed in part from Molière's *Le misanthrope*, is also marked by obscenity, but seems in effect a bold, powerful satire of vice and hypocrisy, a masterwork of an authentic moralist, or of an ambitious playwright who wanted both to please his fellow libertines and to pacify the increasingly numerous critics of theatrical bawdiness. Among Wycherley's other works are *Hero and Leander, in Burlesque* (1669), *Epistles to the King and Duke* (1683), *Miscellany Poems* (1704), *The Idleness of Business: A Satyr* (1705), and *On His Grace the Duke of Marlborough* (1707). His marriage to the Countess of Drogheda lost him his favor at court and a post as royal tutor. After her death he was bankrupted by the expense of litigation to secure her estate, and spent seven years in debtors' prison. James II, who admired *The Plain Dealer*, finally released him and gave him an annual pension of £200.

WYCLIFFE, JOHN, surname also spelled Wyclif, Wyclef, and Wickliffe (among other variants), 1330?–84, English ecclesiastical reformer, was born in the hamlet of Ipreswell (later Hipswell), Yorkshire, into a family whose name derived from that of the nearby village of Wycliffe-on-Tees. His birth may have occurred as early as 1320. In any case, he was educated at Balliol College, Oxford, where he became a Master, ?1360 and a Doctor of Divinity, 1370 or before. During these university years he also held several positions as parish priest, the last of which was in Lutterworth, Leicestershire, 1374–84.

Church and State. Wycliffe early accepted the teachings of the archbishop of Armagh, Richard Fitz Ralph (died 1360), on the relation between Church and State—a relation that was becoming ever more ambiguous in the course of the Avignon Captivity, 1309–77, when the popes resided in Avignon, and papal and French interest became too closely identified for British tastes. The British Parliament secured Wycliffe's services after 1366, when he endorsed its effort to abolish the tribute to the papacy. In his books on "Dominion," of which one of the first was perhaps *Determinatio quaedem de dominio* (?1366, but more probably in the early 1370's), Wycliffe made his own Fitz Ralph's doctrines on God's overlordship over Church as well as State. Against the papal domination of Church and State, which had been claimed by Boniface VIII, 1302, Wycliffe assumed God's dominion over all men, laity as well as clergy, thereby stressing the priesthood of all the believers; he considered all men equal in holding service of God. "The faithful man hath the whole world of richess, but the unfaithful hath not even a farthing," he wrote in *De civili dominio* (I, 7, 12). "Sin is nothing, and men when they sin, become nothing. If, then, sinners are nothing, it is evident that they can possess nothing."

Popularization of Doctrine. In line with his emphasis on the priesthood of all believers, Wycliffe took part in the efforts of the English to replace Latin and French by their native tongue in the affairs of church and state. Thus, the Latin Bible was translated into English 1360?–?82—partly by Wycliffe, partly by his disciples, especially Nicholas of Hereford—not, as was to be the case 150 years later, in an attempt to refute the scholastic interpretation of Scripture by going back to the Hebrew and Greek original, but for the purpose of popularizing religious knowledge among the laity. These translations were passionately suppressed by the authorities; a measure of their popularity, however, is the fact that more than 150 manuscripts are extant, despite the destruction of many. An original organization was set up for spreading this religious education. So-called Poor Preachers—"poor" only in the sense that they held no church offices—carried manuscripts of the text through the country and read them to the laity. Thus they anticipated by 400 years something of the technique of John Wesley and created a disquiet among the regular clergy just as later Methodism was to do—for the mass of the people now took an immediate part in the movement of ideas at Oxford. As the suspicions of the episcopate grew, 18 conclusions drawn from Wycliffe's writings were declared to be wrong, May, 1377, but Parliament and Lancastrians stood by "their" theologian, and the proceedings against Wycliffe were stopped. Later, at a meeting in Lambeth Palace, London, 1378, the citizenry even rioted to protect Wycliffe from being convicted and sentenced as a heretic.

Crisis. Later in 1378 there began the Great Schism that was to divide the Papacy for decades to come, 1378–1408. This event seems to have impressed Wycliffe as a premonition of a world crisis; at least, his teachings soon became far more radical than Fitz Ralph's. Wycliffe now attacked the clerical privilege connected with the Eucharist, ?1381. In particular, he took offense to the then routine expression to the effect that the priest, at Mass, was "making the Lord's Body." If the priest by himself could work the miracle, Wycliffe reasoned, then the equality of layman and cleric was not genuine. In so attacking the doctrine, be it noted, Wycliffe did not deny the miraculous and true presence of God in the Host. Yet by applying his leveling doctrines not merely to the fringe (the earthly possessions of the church) but to the very center of the Visible Church, Wycliffe lost the active support of his Lancastrian patrons, and the Begging Monks—Dominicans and Franciscans—became the irreconcilable opponents of Wycliffe and his rank heresy. They succeeded in silencing his four foremost disciples at Oxford, but Wycliffe himself, stricken by a series of strokes, was not molested while he lingered on at Lutterworth. When he died on St. Sylvester's Day, Dec. 31, 1384, his enemies exultantly saw in this date of his death the revenge of Sylvester I, the pope who was then believed to have received the worldly possessions of the Roman Catholic Church from the Emperor Constantine the Great, 314. See DONATION OF CONSTANTINE.

Influence. Since Wycliffe's Poor Preachers, together with Gerhard Groot's Brethren of the Common Life, formed the visible soldiery of the Movement for Reform, Wycliffe's fate did not end with his death. His manuscripts were carried off to Bohemia where they impressed John Huss. Hence, Wycliffe's good name, unsullied officially in his lifetime, was attacked at the Council of Constance, 1415, by which he was named a heretic; and in 1428 the Church felt strong enough to order his bones unearthed, burned, and the ashes strewn into the River Swift, a contributory of the Avon. Yet the Church was not always to be so secure, for ultimately Wycliffe was to be called the Morning Star of the Reformation. See LOLLARDS.

Wycliffe's many works are available in the publications of the British Wyclif Society (1883 and after). Wycliffe's basic convictions are summarized in his *Trialogus* (after 1382).　EUGEN ROSENSTOCK-HUESSY

WYE, river, Wales and England, rising on the eastern slope of Plynlimmon, in Wales, near the source of the Severn River. It flows 130 miles in a winding course southeast and then south to the estuary of the Severn. The valley of the Wye is celebrated for its beauty, particularly the part that forms the Monmonthshire-Gloucestershire border, in the vicinity of the ruined Tintern Abbey.

WYETH, ANDREW NEWELL, 1917– , U.S. painter, born in Chadds Ford, Pa. He received his training from his father, the noted illustrator N. C. Wyeth, and began to exhibit at the age of 20. Working primarily in water color and tempera, Wyeth won wide recognition for his intensely personal and uniquely realistic style. In his most characteristic works–meticulous depictions of the land and people of Maine and Pennsylvania–striking effects of light and unusual perspective combine to produce mystic overtones of solitude and loneliness. Among his best-known works are "Christina's World" (1948) and "Chambered Nautilus" (1956).

WYETH, NATHANIEL JARVIS, 1802–56, U.S. trader and promoter, was born in Cambridge, Mass. He led settlers to Oregon, 1832 and 1834, and stimulated popular and official interest in Oregon long before it definitely became U.S. territory. Wyeth established what later became the famous Fort Hall on the Oregon-California Trail, 1834.

FREDERICK E. VOELKER

WYKEHAM, WILLIAM OF, 1324–1404, English ecclesiastic and statesman, born at Wickham, Hampshire. Educated in Winchester, he entered the service of Edward III about 1347. In 1356 he began a long career as supervisor of royal building operations at Windsor and elsewhere, and in 1364 he was appointed keeper of the privy seal, becoming very influential in government circles. For his services he received benefices valued in 1365 at over £870. In 1367 he was promoted to the rich bishopric of Winchester and in the same year became chancellor of England. Four years later he was driven from office in an outburst of anti-clericalism, and in 1376, on quarreling with John of Gaunt, suffered a heavy fine and the seizure of his estates for alleged malversation in office. He was pardoned by Richard II in 1377 and acted as Chancellor to the new king from 1389 until 1391, when he retired to his diocese.

Much of Wykeham's wealth was spent on the foundation of a school at Winchester (1378–94) and a college, known as New College, in Oxford (1380). The former contained the beginnings of the public school system in its provision of ten places for the sons of nobility.　ROBERT W. DUNNING

WYLIE, ELINOR MORTON, 1885–1928, U.S. poet and novelist, born in Sommerville, N.J., and educated at private schools in Bryn Mawr, Pa., and Washington, D.C. She deserted her first husband, Philip Hichborn, in 1910 to elope to England with Horace Wylie, whom she later married. In 1923 she divorced Wylie and married William Rose Benét, the poet and critic. Her verse, which appeared in four volumes between 1921 and 1929, shows a sensitive and polished lyrical gift and reflects her interest in the metaphysical poets. She wrote four novels, distinguished by their mannered craftsmanship and high comic conception: *Jennifer Lorn: a Sedate Extravaganza* (1923), *The Venetian Glass Nephew* (1925), *The Orphan Angel* (1927), and *Mr. Hodge and Mr. Hazard* (1928).

WYLIE, PHILIP GORDON, 1902– , U.S. writer, born in Beverly, Mass. He attended Princeton but left to pursue a varied career as a press agent, advertising manager, editor, and screen writer. Wylie's novels and essays are stinging indictments of American habits and beliefs. From *Generation of Vipers* (1942) came his most controversial notion—"momism"—the excessive sentimentalizing of the idea of mother. *Essay on Morals* (1947) is an attack on organized religion. His novels include *The Innocent Ambassadors* (1957) and *Triumph* (1963).

WYNANTS, JAN, 1625?–?84, Dutch landscape painter, was born in Haarlem. Little is known of his life. Wynants' (or Wijnants') pictures are notable for their minuteness of detail, delicacy of aerial perspective, and silvery backgrounds.

WYNKYN DE WORDE, real name Jan van Wynkyn, died ?1534, English printer, was born at

Wynne

Worth in Alsace. He went to England about 1476 and was apprenticed to William Caxton in Westminster. He succeeded to Caxton's business, 1491, but, unlike his master, took no interest in the literary aspect of the work. He moved to Fleet Street, 1500, and opened a shop in St. Paul's Churchyard, 1509. He issued at least 110 books, 1493–1500, and more than 600 in 1501–?34.

¶ The counterpaunce of a dreme how Despre went to the castell of pleasure Wherin was the garden of affecyon in habyted by Beaute to whome he amerously expressed his loue upon ŷ whiche supplycacyon rose grete stryfe by spu=tacyon and argument betwene Pyte and Dysdayne. ✹

This gracefully decorated page is from a book printed by Wynkyn de Worde. The text describes how Desire went to the castle of Pleasure to profess his love for Beauty.

WYNNE, ELLIS, 1671–1734, Welsh prose writer, was born in Y Lasynys, near Harleck, studied at Jesus College, Oxford, and became rector of Llan Danwg and later of Llanfair-juxta-Harlech. His earliest work is an excellent translation of Jeremy Taylor's *Rule and Exercises of Holy Living* (1650) into Welsh under the title *Rheol Buchedd Sanctaidd* (1701). His most famous work, *Gweledigaethau y Bardd Cwsg* (Visions of the Sleeping Bard), an allegory in three parts, describing the world, death, and hell, is a Welsh prose classic. It appeared in many Welsh editions, and was translated into English by George Borrows (1860), R. Gwyneddon Davies (1897), and T. Gwynn Jones (1940).

WYNNE, ROBERT JOHN, 1851–1922, U.S. public official, was born in New York City. After a career in journalism, He was U.S. Postmaster General in the cabinet of Pres. Theodore Roosevelt, 1904–05, and U.S. Consul-General in London, 1905–10.

WYNNE, city, E Arkansas, seat of Cross County; on the W slope of Crowley's Ridge, on the Missouri Pacific Railroad and U.S. highway 64; 45 miles W of Memphis. Wynne is a trade center for an area in which peaches, rice, apples, cotton, and timber are produced. Concrete blocks are manufactured. Pop. (1960) 4,922.

WYNTOUN, ANDREW OF, 1350?–?1420, Scottish chronicler, was a canon regular in the priory of St. Andrews, Scotland, and became, ?1395, prior of St. Serf's Inch in Loch Leven. His *Orygynale Cronykil of Scotland* is a history-in-verse of Scotland from the "earliest times" until James I became king, 1406. As the first known historical work written in the Scottish vernacular, it is of special interest to philologists. Moreover, Wyntoun managed to get most of his dates right—an unusual achievement in his day. The chronicle was first edited and published, 1795, by David Macpherson (1746–1816).

WYOMING

Ranching and mining are prime industries in this western state of scenic mountains.

WYOMING, state, W United States, bounded on the NW and N by Montana, on the E by South Dakota and Nebraska, on the S by Colorado, on the SW by Utah, and on the W by Idaho; area 97,914 sq. mi., including 408 sq. mi. of inland water; pop. (1960) 330,066. Wyoming is rectangular in shape, and its boundaries are formed by meridians and parallels; its dimensions are 358 miles E-W and 278 miles N-S. It ranks 9th in area and 48th in population among the states. The state's name is probably derived from a word of the Delaware Indians, first applied to the Wyoming Valley in northeastern Pennsylvania. Wyoming's popular name, "Equality State," refers to the state's early granting of suffrage to women, 1869. The state motto is *Cedant Arma Togae* (Let Arms Yield to the Gown). The state flower is the Indian paintbrush. The state bird is the meadow lark. Cheyenne is the capital. See map in Atlas, Vol. 20. For state flag in color, see FLAG.

PHYSICAL FACTORS

Topography. Wyoming is composed of parts of two major physiographic provinces—the Rocky Mountains in the west and the Great Plains in the east—and consists of high plains and plateaus (averaging 5,000 to 7,000 ft. in elevation) broken by mountain ranges and river valleys.

The Great Plains province which includes about one third of the state's area, lies roughly east of a line from Cheyenne to Sheridan. It consists of gently rolling plains that are part of the Great Plains. The generally level terrain is broken in the northeast by the western Black Hills. Conspicuous in this section of the state is the volcanic feature known as the Devils Tower in the northeast, and the Goshen Hole depression, in the southeast.

The Rocky Mountains province is made up of mountains and plateaus that form part of the Rocky Mountains. Notable mountain ranges include the Big Horn Mountains in the north, the Absaroka Range in the northwest; the Wind River Range in the west center; the Teton, Salt River, and Gros Ventre ranges in the west; and the Laramie Mountains in the southeast. These mountains contain many lofty peaks, among them Gannett Peak (13,785 ft.), in the Wind River Range and the highest point in the state; Fremont Peak (13,730 ft.), also in the Wind River Range; Grand Teton (13,766 ft.), in the Teton

Range; Sheep Mountain (11,190 ft.) and Pyramid Peak (11,087 ft.), in the Gros Ventre Range; and Cloud Peak (13,165 ft.) in the Big Horn Mountains. Lying between the Big Horn Mountains and the Absaroka Range is the fairly level Big Horn Basin. Another level is the Laramie Basin or Plains, lying west of the Laramie Mountains. Most of the southwestern and central part of the state consists of semiarid irregular plateau, broken by sand dunes, hills, and buttes. This region is sometimes known as the Wyoming Basin and merges with the Great Plains to the northeast.

Western Wyoming lies athwart the Continental Divide which runs along the Wind River Range and the Sierra Madre (the northern extension of the Park Range of Colorado). The drainage east of the divide is to tributaries of the Missouri River, notably the Big Horn, Powder, Belle Fourche, and North Platte rivers. Drainage west of the divide is to the Colorado and Columbia rivers. Most notable is the Green River, a tributary of the Colorado, and the Snake River and its headstreams, tributaries of the Columbia River. Only about a fourth of the state drains west; the remainder lies in the catchment area of the Missouri. Since much of Wyoming has a semiarid climate, many streams are temporary. There are a number of lakes in the northwest, including Yellowstone, Shoshone, and Jackson lakes. The North Platte and Big Horn rivers have been dammed to form several large reservoirs.

Climate. Wyoming generally has a steppe type of climate. It is characterized by cold winters, fairly cool summers, and rather light precipitation. January mean temperatures are 26.7°F at Cheyenne, 19.4°F at Sheridan, and 21.3°F at Rawlins. July mean temperatures for the same stations are 67.0°F, 68.9°F, and 68.9°F, cooler conditions occur in the extensive mountain area. Average annual precipitation is generally about 15 inches, somewhat higher in the mountains, and much is in the form of snow. The Chinook wind causes temperatures to average somewhat higher on the eastern, as compared with the western, mountain slopes (see CHINOOK). The summer rainfall is light and unreliable and the growing season brief.

Plant and Animal Life. Wyoming's diversity of climate and terrain produce a wide variety of plants. The Great Plains section consists essentially of treeless plains on which the predominant vegetation is grasses. The southwestern and central plateaus and plains support sagebrush and grasses. Cacti are found in some dry localities and greasewood grows in saline areas. Wild flowers include saxifrage, fivefingers, sourdock, windflower, flax, evening star, fireweed, kinnkinnick, wintergreen, miner's candle, bearded tongue, arnica, and dandelion.

Trees are found mainly in the mountains and along streams in the plains regions. Cottonwoods and willows are particularly common along streams. Pine, juniper, and spruce occur in the mountains. The principal forest area is in northwestern Wyoming. Other mountain plants include hawthorne, mountain yellow rose, clematis, antelope brush, globe flowers, columbine, shooting star, cowslip, Jacob's-ladder, forget-me-not, and saxifrage. The uppermost mountain slopes are above the tree line and during the brief growing season are covered with many flowering herbaceous plants.

Wyoming is plentifully supplied with large game animals. Moose, elk, mule deer, American or pronghorn antelope, and grizzly and black bear are all found in the state. Other mammals include mountain lion, lynx, wolverine, coyote, prairie dog, beaver, cottontail rabbit, ground squirrel, wood rat, pocket gopher, kangaroo rat, ferret, and mole.

The state has many birds distinctive to the region. Blue-winged and cinnamon teals live on the plains; bullock orioles nest in cottonwood groves. Other common birds include the brown mourning dove, Arkansas kingbird, bronzed grackle, lark bunting, lark sparrow, brown thrasher, long-tailed chat, and western mockingbird. Sage hens are found on the plains and there are several species of hawks, owls, and other birds of prey. The Lewis woodpecker is found in foothills, and the white-throated sparrow nests at higher elevations. The junco, towhee, western tanager, vireo warbler, nuthatch, willow thrush, and several sparrows are native to the state.

SOCIAL FACTORS

Population. According to the 1960 federal census, the population of Wyoming was 330,066 (an increase of 39,537, or 13.6 per cent, over 1950), of which 56.8 per cent was classed as urban. With an average population density of 3.4 persons per square mile, Wyoming ranked forty eighth among the states; the most populous section is the southeast. There were 2,183 Negroes and 4,020 Indians in the state in 1960. Cheyenne is the largest city; other major cities, in descending order of population, are Casper, Laramie, Sheridan, Rock Springs, and Rawlins. Major religious denominations are Roman Catholic, Mormon, and Protestant.

PRINCIPAL CITIES

City	1950 Census Population	1960 Census
Cheyenne (capital)	31,935	43,505
Casper	23,673	38,930
Laramie	15,581	17,520
Sheridan	11,500	11,651
Rock Springs	10,857	10,371

Education. The state superintendent of public instruction, elected for a term of four years, has general supervision of public schools. There are also county superintendents and district school boards. Schools must be open at least three months annually for all persons aged 6 to 21, and attendance is compulsory for children from age 7 to 16 who have not completed the eighth grade. All levels of public school instruction are supported by income (including oil royalties) from a grant of land set aside as a permanent school endowment.

The University of Wyoming (1887), Laramie, is the state's principal institution of higher learning, with branches at Powell, Sheridan, and Torrington.

Public Welfare. Wyoming has a state board of charities and reform, consisting of the governor, the secretary of state, the superintendent of public instruction, the state treasurer, and the state auditor. These officers also constitute the Board of Pardons. The state maintains a general hospital at Rock Springs, a tuberculosis hospital at Basin, and a mental hospital at Evanston. The state penitentiary is located at Rawlins. The state maintains boys' and girls' reformatories.

ECONOMIC FACTORS

Agriculture. Wyoming is essentially an agricultural state, in which stock raising occupies most of the some 33 million acres of Wyoming farm land.

PRINCIPAL CROPS

Crop	Unit	1950-59 average	1960
		(in thousands)	
Barley	bushels	3,551	3,072
Beans (dry edible)	bags	819	928
Hay	tons	1,360	1,213
Oats	bushels	3,784	2,852
Potatoes	cwt.	630	672
Sugar beets	tons	500	635
Wheat	bushels	4,970	4,853

SOURCE: *U.S. Department of Agriculture*

WYOMING

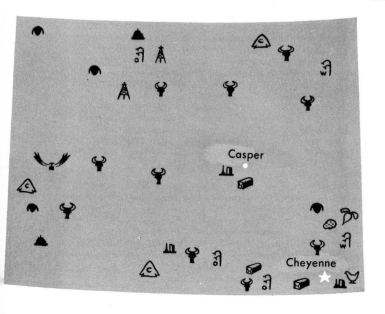

Casper

Cheyenne

Wyoming occupies a leading place among the states in the raising of cattle.

PRINCIPAL RESOURCES, INDUSTRIES, AND PRODUCTS

- Cattle
- Coal
- Food products
- Hay
- Natural gas
- Oats
- Oil refining
- Petroleum
- Potatoes
- Poultry
- Sheep
- Sugar beets
- Wheat

State Seal

State Flower
Indian Paint Brush

State Bird
Meadowlark

he Black Hills of Crook ounty contain an 865-foot Wyoming national monument ade out of volcanic rock.

The mining of coal, mainly in the western section of the state, is increasing Wyoming's mineral industry.

Lake Marie is in the Snowy Range of the southeastern part of the state. It is located close to Laramie.

The predominance of stock raising and the semiarid conditions of most of the state account for the high average farm size, which exceeds 3,000 acres. With more than 2 million sheep and more than 1 million cattle, Wyoming ranks as one of the leading producers of wool and meat. The main livestock ranching areas are the Great Plains, and the basins and plateaus of the Rocky Mountain region. Horse raising is locally important. Dairying is carried on in some irrigated sections, notably the Star Valley, in western Wyoming. Major livestock market centers are Cheyenne, Casper, Green River, Laramie, and Rawlins. Poultry raising, including turkeys, is practiced in many parts of the state, notably the Big Horn Basin and the North Platte Valley. Beekeeping and fur farming are also important.

Crop production in Wyoming is mainly for livestock feed. Most important are hay, small grains, potatoes, sugar beets, and beans. Dry farming of wheat is widespread in the eastern section of the state. However, in most areas irrigation is necessary for crop growing. The mountain areas, with their winter snows, provide numerous sources of irrigation water. Major reclamation projects are on the North Platte, Big Horn, Salt, Wind, and Shoshone rivers. Portions of Wyoming, particularly the eastern, have suffered from soil erosion. Erosion has been most severe in some areas of long-continued dry farming.

Forestry. Wyoming has about 9 million acres of commercial forest land, nearly one third of which is federally owned. The forests mainly contain softwood, principally lodgepole pine, and the main forest areas are in the mountains of the northwest. Spruce and fir are also important commercially.

Fisheries. Wyoming's extensive streams and lake fisheries are only important for recreational fishing. The state maintains numerous fish hatcheries and conducts an active stocking program.

Mining. The state is richly endowed with mineral resources, particularly petroleum, natural gas, and coal. Petroleum accounts for about three fourths of the value of mineral production. Major oil fields include Teapot Dome (naval oil reserve), Salt Creek, Byron-Garland, Elk Basin, and Lost Soldier–Wertz fields. There are enormous reserves of bituminous coal; most production is in Sweetwater, Carbon, Sheridan, and Lincoln counties. Others among the 22 mineral products of Wyoming are clays, natural gas, iron ore, bentonite, sand and gravel, gold, phosphate rock, trona, and gypsum. Over-all mineral production increased each year in 1949-60. Total value in 1965 was almost $496 million.

Manufacturing. Although little developed, manufacturing industry has great potentialities because of the abundance of mineral fuels, water power, and a variety of raw materials. The main industrial activity in the state concerns the processing of petroleum and agricultural products. There are petroleum refineries at Casper, Cheyenne, Cody, Glenrock, Greybull, Lovell, Sinclair, Thermopolis, Worland, and other cities. There are beet sugar refineries located at Lovell, Sheridan, Torrington, Wheatland, and Worland. Other agriculturally-based industries include flour milling, meat packing, and vegetable canning and freezing. Minor industries include the processing

UNION PACIFIC RAILROAD PHOTO
Wyoming's historic capital, Cheyenne, is a livestock center located at the edge of a rolling plain.

of lumber (including railroad ties) and other wood products, and the manufacture of bricks, cement, chemicals, aircraft equipment, railroad equipment, clay and glass products, leather goods, and agricultural equipment.

Transportation. Several major railroads running on 1,848 miles of track serve Wyoming. The state also has 39 municipal and 131 private airports, with the main air centers at Cheyenne, Casper, Sheridan, and Jackson. Local communities maintain 61,563 miles of highway, the state government, 5,596, and the federal government, 3,841.

Tourist Attractions. Wyoming is famous for its rugged mountains, forests, and the wide-open spaces of the plains and plateaus. Many of the most notable scenic areas are preserved in federal and state parks. The most celebrated of these is Yellowstone National Park which, established in 1872, is the oldest park in the federal park system. Most of Yellowstone's 3,350 square miles are in northwestern Wyoming. The park includes a remarkable geyser area, hot springs, and colorful pools; spectacular mountain, plateau, and valley scenery (including the noted Yellowstone Canyon and Falls); and lakes (among them the large Yellowstone and Shoshone lakes). South of Yellowstone Park, also in northwestern Wyoming, lies Grand Teton National Park containing magnificent scenery and a number of lofty snow-capped peaks of the Teton Range. It also includes the northern portion of Jackson Hole, a scenic mountain basin famed in western history. A large herd of elk roam this park.

Near Cody, in northwestern Wyoming, is Shoshone Cavern National Monument with subterranean chambers containing crystal formations and dripstone. In the Black Hills of Crook County is the Devils Tower National Monument. Fort Laramie National Monument preserves the buildings of one of the pioneer military posts on the Oregon Trail.

Among Wyoming's many state reservations are Old Fort Bridger State Park, in Uinta County, a famous way station for emigrants headed west. The park includes a museum of relics of the Old West. Saratoga Hot Springs State Park, at Saratoga, and Hot Springs State Park, at Thermopolis, preserve springs once used by Indians and now operated as health resorts.

Wyoming's forested mountains are in part protected in a number of national forests, comprising nearly 10 million acres. Many of these forest preserves are threaded by good highways and there are varied recreational facilities available, including camping, fishing, and hunting. Fishing and hunting are also available in many other locations. Game birds, mountain sheep, moose, elk, bear, antelope, and deer may all be taken in season. Many of the interesting and picturesque ranches of the state have been converted into dude ranches with riding, hunting, fishing, mountain climbing, and pack trips available. A number of towns feature rodeos and "frontier days." Cheyenne, famous for its Frontier Days celebrations in July, counts Fort Warren, Frontier Park, and the State Historical Museum among its other tourist attractions.   KENNETH THOMPSON

MINERAL PRODUCTION

Mineral	Unit	1959	1965
		thousands	
Coal	short ton	1,977	3,260
Iron Ore	long ton	503	2,337
Natural Gas	million cu. ft.	156,978	220,250
Natural Gasoline	gallons	64,586	95,090
LP Gases (liquid)	gallons	90,314	143,331
Crude Petroleum	barrels	126,050	138,314
Sand and Gravel	short ton	4,692	7,996
Stone	short ton	1,317	1,594
Uranium Ore	short ton	864	1,048

GOVERNMENT

The Constitution of Wyoming was adopted, 1889, preliminary to admission of the state to the Union in 1890. Amendments proposed by the state legislature must be approved by a two-thirds vote of all the members of each house and then be ratified by a majority of the electors voting thereon. A constitutional convention to consider amending the constitution may be called by vote of approval of two-thirds of the elected members of each house, and a majority vote of the electors at the next general elections; the convention proposals must finally be submitted to the people for their approval. Citizens 21 years of age and over who have lived in the state one year, in the county 60 days, in the precinct 10 days, and who have passed a literacy test may register to vote.

The State Legislature consists of a senate and a house of representatives. Membership in both houses is apportioned among the counties according to population. After reapportionment, there were 30 senators and 61 representatives, each county being entitled to at least 1 senator and 1 representative. The legislature must consider its own reapportionment every 10 years. Senators are elected for four years, and representatives are elected for two years. Regular sessions are held biennially beginning in January of odd-numbered years, and are limited to 40 days. The senate and house are the only fundamental lawmaking bodies in Wyoming, which does not provide for direct voter legislation through the initiative and referendum.

The Executive Officials are the governor, secretary of state, auditor, treasurer, and superintendent of public instruction, all elected for four years. Many administrative officials, including the attorney general, are appointed by the governor and are responsible to him. There is no lieutenant governor; in case of a vacancy in the governor's office the secretary of state becomes chief executive. The governor's veto power extends to all legislation, but a veto may be overridden by two-thirds of the elected members of each house of the legislature.

The Judicial Authority is vested in a supreme court of four justices elected for eight-year terms. There are district courts, municipal courts, police courts and justice of the peace courts.

Grain is cultivated near Jackson Hole. Most of it is used for feeding livestock.

TED SPIEGEL—RAPHO GUILLUMETTE

TED SPIEGEL—RAPHO GUILLUMETTE

Cattle and sheep are raised throughout most of Wyoming— on the Great Plains and in the basins of the Rockies.

HISTORY

Exploration. It is possible that the region corresponding to Wyoming may have been visited by Spaniards from New Spain (Mexico) before 1700, and by the French-Canadian fur traders, François and Louis Joseph Vérendrye, who penetrated the Black Hills country, 1742–43, but there is no real evidence that it was ever explored by white men before 1800. The U.S. government's Lewis and Clark Expedition that explored the Louisiana Purchase and Oregon country, 1804–06, passed north of Wyoming, but John Colter, who had been with that expedition, returned to the headwaters of the Missouri River as a fur trader, 1807, and explored in the country of the Yellowstone and Green rivers and Jackson Lake. Subsequently the country became known to fur traders, who both trapped there and crossed it going to Oregon country.

William H. Ashley, former governor of Missouri, established a trading post on the Yellowstone River in present-day Montana, 1822, from where he and his successors covered large parts of Wyoming. Among his best known agents were Jim Bridger, who explored Wyoming extensively, from 1822, and Jedediah S. Smith and Thomas Fitzpatrick who crossed South Pass to the Green River valley, in southwestern Wyoming, 1824. The first permanent trading post in Wyoming was Fort William (later Fort John and then Fort Laramie), built by Robert Campbell and William Sublette on the Laramie River near the junction with the North Platte River, 1834. Another early post was Fort Bridger, built in 1842. Both posts became important stations on the Oregon Trail, which was a great emigrant route during the 1840's and 1850's. Other notable explorations of the period were made by the French-American soldier-explorer Capt. B. L. E. Bonneville, 1832, and the U.S. Army's Lt. John C. Frémont, 1842–43.

Settlement. The bulk of the present state came into U.S. possession as part of the Louisiana Purchase; a section in the northwest was part of the Oregon

ROTKIN, PFI

Although much of Wyoming is semiarid, wheat is extensively dry farmed in the eastern part of the state.

The Snake River, which rises in northwestern Wyoming, winds irregularly southwestward into Idaho.

ROTKIN, PFI

country, while other small sections belonged to the Texas annexation and the Mexican cession. Although thousands of emigrants passed through the country little was done in making permanent settlements in the territory until after the Civil War, when discovery of gold in the Sweetwater Valley, 1867, discovery of coal near Evanston, 1868, and completion of the Union Pacific and Central Pacific railroads, 1869, led to a rush of immigration. Cheyenne, settled in 1867, had 6,000 inhabitants before the end of the year. Wyoming Territory was created, 1868, from parts of Dakota, Idaho, and Utah territories, and the boundaries established as those of the present state. The name derived from a Delaware Indian word, *Mecheweaming* or *M'cheuwomink* (among other spellings), meaning "big flats" or "big plains." With establishment of the territorial government, Cheyenne was made capital, 1869. During the same year Wyoming granted women the right to vote, becoming the first U.S. state, territory, or possession to do so.

Indian Wars. In the meantime, white settlement and the whites' indiscriminate slaughter of buffalo had frequently occasioned violence between whites and Indians in Wyoming. Under a treaty (1851) between the U.S. government and the Sioux, Arapaho, Cheyenne, and Shoshone Indians, the Indians surrendered parts of their lands to the government in exchange for tribal territories secured against paleface encroachment. Hostilities were renewed, however, Aug. 19, 1854, when a detachment of 28 soldiers under 2nd Lt. John L. Gratten, while investigating the killing of a cow, was massacred at a Sioux village near Fort Laramie. Sporadic outbursts ensued, and the Indian wars in Wyoming, Montana, and the Dakotas continued intermittently until late in the 1870's. By 1880, however, all Indian tribes, except the Shoshone and Arapaho, had been removed from the territory.

Statehood. During the decade 1880–90 Wyoming's population rose 300 per cent to total 92,531. The period was marked by a series of armed clashes between cattlemen and farmers and between cattlemen and sheepmen. On July 10, 1890, Wyoming was admitted to the Union as the 44th state. Early in the 1900's various conservation measures were enacted— land was set aside as forest reserve, dams were built, and steps were taken for the protection of fish and game (much earlier, Yellowstone National Park had been set aside by Congress, 1872). Twentieth century development of the state's recreational features, hunting, dude ranching, rodeos, and the like, made tourism an important business. By reason of its diversified agriculture and industry, Wyoming enjoyed a steady economic growth during the twentieth century.

In politics, the Republican and Democratic parties in Wyoming were relatively equal in strength after 1900, but after 1940 the Republicans generally held a slight majority of the state's elective offices. The Democrats won control of the state government, 1958, but the Republicans soon returned to power, 1960. Wyoming's electoral votes were cast for Democratic party presidential candidates in 1940 and 1948, for Republican candidates in 1944, 1952, 1956, and 1960. In 1960 Wyoming sent one congressman to the U.S. House of Representatives.

BIBLIOG.–American Guide Series, *Wyoming: A Guide to Its History, Highways, and People* (1946); Floyd C. Bard, *Horse Wrangler: Sixty Years in the Saddle in Wyoming and Montana* (1960); Orin H. Bonney and Lorraine Bonney, *Guide to the Wyoming Mountains and Wilderness Areas* (1960); James Chisholm, *South Pass, 1868* (1960); T. A. Larson, *History of Wyoming* (1965); Asa S. Mercer, *Banditti of the Plains* (1959); Herman H. Trachsel and Ralph M. Wade, *The Government and Administration of Wyoming* (American Commonwealth Ser., 1953); Mae Urbanek, *Wyoming Wonderland* (1964).

WYOMING, UNIVERSITY OF, a public, coeducational institution of higher learning, located in Laramie, Wyo. Established in 1886, the school offered its first instruction the following year. The university's divisions are agriculture and liberal arts, both founded 1887; home economics, engineering, and music, 1909; education, 1914; law, 1920; pharmacy, graduate studies, commerce, and adult education and community service, 1946; nursing, 1951; and physical education and intercollegiate athletics, 1956. An agricultural experimental station and an agricultural extension service are operated at Laramie. Students of demonstrated superior ability may enroll in a special honors program. Students majoring in geology, zoology, or botany may attend a summer science camp in the Snowy Range Mountains, near Laramie. An American Studies program and an Institute of International Affairs are operated by the university. The university's Rocky Mountain Herbarium contains the world's largest collection of plants of the Central Rocky Mountain region. Among the university library's collections are materials on Wyoming and western history, wool, botany, and geology, and the political papers of Wyoming statesmen. Publications include annual bulletins of the Natural Resources Research Institute, the Division of Business and Economic Research, and the College of Education Curriculum and Research Center. See COLLEGES AND UNIVERSITIES.

WYOMING MASSACRE, in the American Revolution, comprised the defeat of some 300 Continental militiamen and the massacre of many settlers in the Wyoming Valley of Pennsylvania, July, 1778, by about 1,000 Loyalist (Tory) militiamen and Iroquois Indians, all under the command of Maj. John Butler, who had invaded the Wyoming Valley from New York the month before. Col. Zebulon Butler of the Continental army, who was home on furlough, organized militiamen to protect settlers in the Wyoming Valley. Many settlers and the militia gathered at Forty Fort, near the site of Wilkes-Barre. Against Zebulon Butler's judgment, the militia left Forty Fort to meet the enemy in the open, July 3, and was overwhelmed. Many surrendered only to be massacred by the Indians. The fort soon capitulated, and some of the women and children were also massacred. As a result of the incident the Continental army carried out an expedition against Loyalists and Iroquois on the frontiers of New York and Pennsylvania, 1779; and the British, becoming belatedly squeamish with respect to Indian atrocities, somewhat curtailed the use of Indians against the colonists, but never abandoned the practice.

WYOMING VALLEY, NE Pennsylvania, in Luzerne County, drained by the Susquehanna River; about 23 miles long and 3 miles wide. The valley is an important anthracite-mining region. The chief town in the Wyoming Valley is Wilkes-Barre. During the eighteenth century the Wyoming Valley was claimed by settlers from both Pennsylvania and Connecticut, and the dispute led to the so-called Yankee-Pennamite Wars. On July 3 to 4, 1778, Tories and Indians defeated Continental militiamen at Forty Fort, near the site of Wilkes-Barre.

WYON, a family of English engravers prominent during the nineteenth century, was descended from George Wyon (died 1796), a Birmingham seal engraver and medalist. His son, Thomas Wyon the Elder (1767–1830), first a die engraver in Birmingham, worked in London from 1800 and was appointed chief engraver of seals at the royal mint, 1816. Thomas Wyon the Younger (1792–1817), a noted gold medalist, was apprenticed to his father, Thomas Wyon the Elder, before studying at the Royal Academy; he became chief engraver at the royal mint, 1815. William Wyon (1795–1851), received a gold medal of the Society of Arts, 1813, and assisted his uncle Thomas Wyon the Elder from 1816; he became chief engraver at the royal mint, 1828. William Wyon's son Leonard Charles Wyon (1826–91), became chief engraver to the royal mint in 1851. Benjamin Wyon (1802–58), another son of Thomas Wyon the Elder, was ap-

pointed chief engraver of seals in 1831. His son Joseph Sheperd Wyon (1836–73), became chief engraver of seals in 1858. After 1865 Joseph was assisted by his brother Alfred Benjamin Wyon (1837–84), who was the chief engraver of seals at the royal mint, 1873–84. Alfred compiled a work (1887) on the Great Seals of England.

WYRDES, the Anglo-Saxon fates, also known as Weirds, were represented in Anglo-Saxon mythology as a trio of sisters who preside over and determine the destinies of men. The Wyrdes ultimately derive from the Old Norse Norns; one Norn, which the Anglo-Saxons called Wyrd, is sometimes regarded as the goddess of Fate and mother of the Norns. She was a person to be feared, and even uttering her name was considered a dangerous, if not fatal, action. Of the three Wyrdes, two gave blessings while the third dispensed the evils of life. Neither the gods nor men could interfere with their power. Later the term Wyrdes came to be applied to the witches and soothsayers of Scottish folklore. The Weird Sisters in Shakespeare's *Macbeth* are direct descendants of the Wyrdes. See FATES; NORNS.

WYSE, SIR THOMAS, 1791–1862, British political leader and diplomat, was born in Ireland and was graduated from Trinity College, Dublin, 1812. In 1821 he married Laetitia, the daughter of Napoleon Bonaparte's brother Lucien, but was separated from her in 1828. Wyse advocated Catholic emancipation in Ireland, 1825, and while a member of Parliament, 1835–47, he introduced a bill for national education in Ireland, 1835, and published *Education Reform*, 1837. He served as lord of the treasury, 1839–41, secretary for the board of control of India, 1846–49, and a member of the privy council, 1849. He assumed the post of British minister at Athens, Greece, 1849. He was named a Commander of the Bath, 1850, and later, for his successful management of Greek affairs during the Crimean War, 1857, became Knight Commander of the Bath and envoy extraordinary.

WYSS, JOHANN RUDOLF, 1781–1830, Swiss writer, was born in Bern, and spent his life there as professor of philosophy and as curator of the university museum and library. He wrote the Swiss National Anthem, *Rufst du, mein Vaterland?* (1811), and published, among other works, *Vorlesungen über das höchste Gut* (1811), a philosophical treatise, and *Idyllen, Volksagen, Legenden und Erzählungen aus der Schweiz* (1815), a collection of Swiss legends and folklore. He published *Der schweizerische Robinson*, 1812 (*The Swiss Family Robinson*, 1820), and is often described as its author; according to Wyss, however, the story was written by his father, Johann David Wyss (1743–1818), and merely edited and revised by the son. This juvenile classic, admittedly based on Daniel Defoe's *Robinson Crusoe*, relates the adventures in hardiness and ingenuity of a Swiss family shipwrecked on an island near New Guinea.

WYTHE, GEORGE, 1726–1806, Colonial American patriot and jurist, was born in Elizabeth City County, Virginia. He was a delegate to the second Continental Congress, and was a signer of the Declaration of Independence. He was a judge of the chancery court of Virginia, 1778–1806, professor of law at William and Mary College, 1779–90, and a member of the convention that framed the federal Constitution, 1787. He published *Decisions of Cases in Virginia by the High Court of Chancery* (1795). Wythe died of poisoning by a beneficiary of his will.

WYTHEVILLE, town, SW Virginia, seat of Wythe County; on the Norfolk and Western Railway and U.S. highways 11, 21, and 52; about 68 miles SW of Roanoke. Rock is quarried and timber is cut in the surrounding area. Sawmills, a meat-packing plant, and plants manufacturing hosiery, shirts, and blankets are the leading industrial establishments. The settlement was established in 1792 as Evansham, then renamed for Wythe County and incorporated in 1839. Pop. (1960) 5,634.

X

1	2	3	4	5	6	7
⊖	卜	I	X	*x*	**x**	**x**

8	9	10	11	12	13	14	15	16
X	*x*	X	x	X	*X*	*x*	X	X

The letter X has descended directly from the Latin alphabet; it was taken from the Greek by the Romans who, however, could not pronounce it as the Greeks did. Some historical forms, of which there are many variations, are shown in the top row. They are hieroglyph 1, Phoenician 2, Greek 3, Roman (Trajan) 4, Irish uncial 5, Caroline 6, and Gutenberg black-letter 7. Common forms of the letter as it occurs today are illustrated in the bottom row. They are handwritten cursive capital 8, handwritten lowercase 9, roman capital 10, roman lowercase 11, roman small capital 12, italic capital 13, italic lowercase 14, sans serif capital 15, and sans serif lowercase 16.

X, the twenty-fourth letter of the modern English alphabet. Its form is that of the Greek *x*, but its sound value in the English alphabet is not the same. The Greek *x* signified the sound "ch" or "kh," while the English *x* usually represents the sound "ks" which, in Eastern Greek script, was expressed by the three horizontal lines☰ of the letter *ksi*, which was probably related to the Semitic letter *samech*.

The pronunciation of the letter *x* in English words ranges from "ks" as in *ax* to "gz" as in *example*. Initial *x* in English is usually pronounced like *z*, as in *xylophone*. The variations in French are greater, and at the end of a word *x* often remains silent, as in *cheveux*, though it may have the sound of hard *s*, as in *six*. The letter *x* is not included in the Italian alphabet. In modern Spanish, *j* is often written where *x* formerly was used; thus, for example, *Ximenes* became *Jimenes*.

In Latin, *x* was the twenty-first letter of the alphabet, but the sign X also figured in Roman numerals as the number 10. In analytical geometry, the horizontal in a system of coordinates is called *x*, the vertical is *y*. In algebra, *x* signifies any first unknown.

XANTHIPPE, the wife of the Greek philosopher Socrates, was notorious for her quarrelsome temper and shrewish disposition.

XANTHUS, ancient city, sw Turkey, about 8 miles from the mouth of the Koca (formerly the Xanthus) River, 190 miles sse of Izmir. The city was twice besieged and destroyed by fire, first by the Persians under Harpagus in 546 B.C. and again by the Romans in 42 B.C. Xanthus was first excavated in 1838 by the British archaeologist Sir Charles Fellows (1799–1860). The ruins include the theater, still in good condition, part of the Harpy Monument, and walls of the acropolis. See LYCIA.

XENIA, city, sw Ohio, seat of Greene County, about 15 miles ESE of Dayton. Chief manufactures include rope and twine, furniture, plastics, and advertising novelties. Xenia was laid out in 1803, incorporated in 1808, and chartered as a city in 1870. Located in the neighboring village of Wilberforce are Wilberforce University (1856) and Central State College (1887). Xenia has a state institution for orphans. (For population, see Ohio map in Atlas.)

XENOCRATES, 396–314 B.C., Greek philosopher, the third *scholarch* (head) of the Platonic Academy, was born in Chalcedon. Like his master, Plato, Xenocrates equated the Real with the realm of Forms (Ideas or Essences), which, following Pythagoras, Xenocrates identified as numbers. Thus he

thought of God as One and all subsequent existences as numbers more than one. Having defined the soul as a self-moving number, he made numerology the basis of his mystical theology. Among his contemporaries, Xenocrates was more renowned for his personal integrity than for his philosophy; so great was his reputation for virtue that he was exempted from taking the oath when testifying in court. He was thrice ambassador to Macedonia; after the Macedonian conquest of Athens he was offered citizenship, but he refused it.   ROBERT WHITTEMORE

XENON, a gaseous element, symbol Xe, a member of group zero of the periodic table, variously called the inert, rare, or noble gases. These, besides xenon, are helium, neon, argon, krypton, and the radioactive gas, radon.

Xenon, atomic number 54, is colorless, odorless, tasteless, and was thought to be chemically inert. Its melting point is —112°C, its boiling point is —108°C, and at 0°C and 1 atmosphere its density is 5.9 grams per liter. The atomic weight of atmospheric xenon is 131.30.

Xenon is present in the air in about one part in fifteen million. It was discovered by Sir William Ramsay and M. W. Travers in 1898. It is used in neutron and X-ray counters, bubble chambers, gas-filled thyratron and rectifier tubes, and high speed photographic lamps. Medically it has anesthetic properties. It is produced commercially by fractional distillation of air and is a by-product in nuclear reactors.

When, in 1962, xenon platinum hexafluoride $(XePtF_6)$ was made in the laboratory, it was the first time a compound of the inert gases had been synthesized. Shortly thereafter xenon tetrafluoride (XeF_4) was also synthesized, initiating the development of a more extensive chemistry of noble gases.

XENOPHANES, c. 569–c. 480 B.C., Greek philosopher and poet, the first Western thinker known to have challenged the notion that God is properly described in terms appropriate to man, and the first to proclaim the absolute One as God. Of his life little is known save that he traveled widely and lived to a great age. Born at Colophon in Asia Minor, he spent his later years, according to tradition, at Elea in southern Italy; this fact and his monism have led some to credit him with being the master of Parmenides and the true author of the Eleatic philosophy. All that is certain, however, is that he taught that there is but "one god, among gods and men the greatest, not at all like mortals in body or in mind." As he put it, "if oxen and horses and lions had hands or could draw with hands and create works of art like those made by men, horses would draw pictures of gods like horses, and oxen of gods like oxen, and they would make the bodies [of their gods] in accordance with the form that each species itself possesses." ROBERT WHITTEMORE

XENOPHON, c. 430–355 B.C., Greek soldier and historian, born in Athens. The son of a respected and well-to-do father, Xenophon reached manhood during the final disillusioning phase of the Peloponnesian War. Like other men of his generation, he fell for a time under the spell of Socrates. In 401 he joined the Greek mercenary force which Cyrus was recruiting in an attempt to wrest the Persian throne from his brother. After Cyrus was killed at the battle of Cunaxa, Xenophon rallied the soldiers and led them on their historic march to the Black Sea. The adventures of these mercenaries he recounts in his most famous work, the *Anabasis*. After subsequently joining a Spartan expeditionary force sent to Asia Minor to aid the Greek cities there against the aggression of Persia, he formed a close friendship with King Agesilaus, who took command in 396. This association with Sparta led Athens to exile him. When Agesilaus was summoned home to the Corinthian War, Xenophon accompanied him to Boeotia and fought against his native city at the battle of Coronea in 394. Sparta repaid him with a country estate near Olympia in Elis where he devoted many quiet years to literary work. About 371, political conditions forced him to leave Elis and he migrated to Corinth. Sometime after 369, when Sparta and Athens became allied, Xenophon was free to return to Athens where his last works were written. He died at Corinth.

Works. In addition to the *Anabasis*, Xenophon's principal works are the *Hellenica* and the *Cyropaedia*. The *Hellenica*, a history of Greece from 411 to 362, is a twofold work which partly completes Thucydides' unfinished account of the Peloponnesian War and partly provides a contemporary history of Greece for the early fourth century. The *Cyropaedia*, a romantic biography of Cyrus the Great, is educational in intent, holding up for admiration Persian virtues and training. Semi-historical, but also educational in aim, are the *Agesilaus*, an encomium of King Agesilaus, and the *Lacedaemonian Constitution;* both works betray Xenophon's early pro-Spartan sympathies. Other works attest to the lasting impression that Socrates made on the youthful Xenophon. The *Apology* and the *Memorabilia* both defend the memory of Socrates and contain valuable information about his life. The *Symposium* and *Oeconomicus* are imaginary discussions in which Socrates appears while the *Hieron*, another philosophical dialogue, is Socratic in manner. Xenophon's minor works include treatises on tactics, horsemanship, hunting, and public finance.

If not one of the greater authors of antiquity, Xenophon surpasses most ancient writers in the breadth of his interests. He has written at least one timeless work in the *Anabasis*. But his major value lies in the fact that he is the chief contemporary witness for much of what he records. As a historian more interested in actors than in events, he foresakes his greater predecessor, Thucydides, while anticipating the biographer, Plutarch. All his works, written in a simple, lucid style that has been much admired, reveal a man of engaging personality deeply concerned with the political and social ills of his age. GEORGE L. SNIDER

BIBLIOG.–J. B. Bury, *The Ancient Greek Historians* (1909); *A History of Greece*, 3rd ed. (1956); Werner Jaeger, *Paedeia* (1944).

XERXES I, ?519-465 B.C., king of Persia, succeeding his father Darius in 486. Having suppressed an Egyptian revolt, he prepared to renew his father's attempt to conquer Greece. Elaborate preparations were made for the greatest military expedition ever launched. A canal was dug through the isthmus of Mount Athos, and the Hellespont was bridged by boats. Herodotus numbered Xerxes' force at five million; there were perhaps one twentieth of that hyperbolical estimate. Xerxes passed unopposed into Thessaly but met tremendous—though ultimately unavailing—defense from a small force led by Leonidas of Sparta at Thermopylae (480). The heroic resistance of Leonidas on land was equalled by the exploits of Themistocles at sea: at the battle of Salamis the Persian fleet was crippled. Xerxes "the Great" now returned to Asia, leaving his general Mardonius in command. In 479 the Spartans defeated Mardonius at Plataea while the Athenians invaded Asia Minor and destroyed a Persian army at Mycale. In later years Xerxes seems to have been concerned mainly with palace politics. His ignoble reign ended precipitately when he was assassinated by his grand vizier, Artabanus.

Xerxes II, his grandson, ruled for about six weeks in 424 B.C. before sharing the same fate.

XINGU RIVER, Brazil, tributary of the Amazon River. The Xingu rises in central Mato Grosso (Serra do Roncador), flows north for 1,230 miles, and enters the Amazon at the head of its delta below Porto de Moz. The upper course of the Xingu is interrupted by waterfalls; the lower course is navigable for about 100 miles. Altamira is the river's major port.

XOCHIMILCO, town, central Mexico, about 15 miles SE of Mexico City. Its name, derived from an Aztec word meaning flower gardens, refers to the origin of the man-made islands that make up the town. The Aztecs covered rafts with soil in which a profusion of flowering plants then grew, eventually dropping their roots to the bottom of the shallow lake. The islands no longer abound with flowers, but brightly painted, flower-adorned gondolas carry tourists through the winding canals that separate them. (For population, see Mexico map in Atlas.)

Flat-bottomed *trajineras*, their names wrought in arches of flowers, ply the canals and waterways of Lake Xochimilco.

MEXICAN NATIONAL TOURIST COUNCIL

X RAY, an electromagnetic radiation of short wave length produced when a stream of highly accelerated electrons strikes a hard target, causing waves of energy to be emitted from the electrons. X rays were first observed by the German physicist Wilhelm Röntgen in 1895, when as a result of experimentation that he was conducting with electrical currents through gas-evacuated tubes, he came upon an unknown form of radiation. Röntgen noted that X rays produced a number of characteristic effects: they could produce light on a fluorescent screen; molecules would become ionized when the rays passed through a gas; they were able to penetrate through some materials and become absorbed by others; the rays could produce impressions upon light-sensitive photographic film; and they scatter in many directions when electrons impinge upon any substance.

PROPERTIES

Electromagnetic Waves. X rays are the resultant energy dissipated when electrons traveling at high speed are rapidly decelerated through head-on or glancing collisions with the atoms of the target material. The amount, or quanta, of energy expended (see QUANTUM THEORY) is dependent upon the high-speed electron velocity caused by the different electrical potential between the electron-emitting source and the target area, and the completeness of electron impact with the target surface. When an electron strikes another object head-on almost all of its energy is released, while less complete grazing with the structural atoms of the target will release proportionately smaller amounts of energy. Most of this energy is in the form of heat, with the remainder of the energy existing as widely diffused electromagnetic waves of photons similar to light but of shorter wave length (see ELECTROMAGNETIC WAVE). Electrons that are stopped with great force of impact give rise to X rays of minimum wave length. X rays exist on a continuous spectrum with wave lengths shorter than ultraviolet radiation but longer than gamma rays (see SPECTRUM). Because of the minuteness of the measurable X-ray wave lengths, they are usually measured in Angstrom units, $1 \text{ A} = 10^{-8}$ cm. On the electromagnetic spectrum, X rays for practical use measure from about .05 A to 500 A, or using the English system of measurement, X rays range from about .00000053 inch to .000000023 inch.

Ionization and Absorption. The X-ray wave length becomes important when determining the radiation action upon matter through absorption. When rays are impinged upon matter they are transmitted, absorbed, or diffused depending upon their hardness. X rays at the lower end of the continuous spectrum are referred to as soft X rays, with hardness increasing as the spectrum progresses to its far end. When the rays are absorbed, they produce heat or give rise to newly released electrons which, in turn, disseminate a new quanta of X ray called secondary radiation. This radiation will penetrate the irradiated material. X rays produced at voltages less than 70 kilovolts result in the greater part of the energy spent in the production of photoelectrons and heat (see PHOTOELECTRICITY). In this manner the rays produce the phenomenon of ionization. If the rate of ionization can be measured, it permits the evaluation of the X-ray output, or dose value. As the voltage of the cathode-anode gap in the X-ray producing tube is increased, the photoelectron production rapidly diminishes to a negligible quantity, and scattering or diffusion becomes prominent. The scattered photons form diffused X rays of increased wave length because of the Compton effect which usually speed from the region to scatter again or to be absorbed. When the applied potential in the X-ray tube exceeds a million volts some of the shortest wave length X rays become absorbed by a process similar to the photoelectric effect, known as pair production because of the simultaneous liberation of a positron, or positive electron, and a negative electron (see ELECTRON).

Penetrability. The penetrating power of hardness of X rays through materials is dependent upon the wave length of the radiation. Experimentation has shown that the shorter wave lengths of X-ray radia-

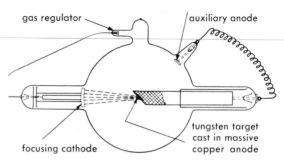

gas regulator   auxiliary anode

tungsten target cast in massive copper anode

focusing cathode

An early diagnostic gas X-ray tube used a tungsten target inserted in a massive copper anode to receive the stream of high speed electrons emitted at the focusing cathode.

tion have greater penetrating capabilities than the longer wave lengths. The ionization effect that it has on gases has been used to determine X-ray penetrating power in terms of intensity or dosage value, a necessary knowledge for medical X-ray therapy. The international unit of X-ray measurement is called the roentgen unit and is symbolized by the letter r. A roentgen is defined as that amount of X-ray radiation which will ionize one cubic centimeter of air under standard pressure and temperature to produce the value of one electrostatic unit of electric charge of either sign (see ELECTRICAL AND MAGNETIC UNITS, *Electrostatic System*). The degree of penetration that X rays may exhibit are also determined by the density of the material acted upon. Dense substances such as bone structures or metallic materials are more absorbent to the radiation than less dense material as flesh, wood, fabrics, or air.

X-RAY TUBES

X rays are usually produced from emitted electrons in a vacuum tube. The electron source, or cathode, is a material that will emit a constant flow of an electron when electrical current is applied to it and has the mechanical properties necessary for long use. The target material, or anode, is usually of high atomic number because X rays are produced in greater numbers when electrons impinge upon massive solids, although freely moving gas molecules have been used in X-ray tubes as targets. Since much of the electron-impact energy is converted into heat, the target material must be able to withstand high temperatures. The high velocity needed to speed electrons to the anode is caused by high electrical potential difference, or voltage, between the cathode and anode. Increased voltages are applied when varying wave lengths are desired for industrial and medical applications of the radiations. Voltage range from 5,000 volts needed for X rays used in crystal structure studies to 22 million volts needed for industrial inspection of castings and forgings.

There are two general types of X-ray tubes that fulfill the requirements for X-ray production: the gas-filled tubes, and the gas-free electron tube. The gas molecules in the gas-filled tube are broken down into electrons and residual ions by high voltage. The positive ions are hurled against the cathode by the electrical field, so that electrons are set free by the bombardment. A cathode-ray stream of high-speed electrons bombards the anode, producing X rays. The hardness or penetrating power of the X rays produced is determined by the amount of residual gas. As the gas in the tube diminishes during continued operation, less ionization occurs and, therefore, fewer X rays are produced. If too much gas is present in the tube, then the increased ionization causes an internal current in the tube which will not allow a sufficient electrical potential to exist between the cathode and anode, and hence, fewer electron bombardments. Early X-ray tube design

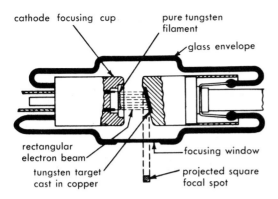

cathode focusing cup · pure tungsten filament · glass envelope · rectangular electron beam · focusing window · tungsten target cast in copper · projected square focal spot

The Coolidge hot cathode X-ray tube is used in diagnostic clinics and for low-voltage industrial radiography. The X rays pass freely through the thin glass window envelope.

provided regulators to control the releasing of small amounts of gas into the tube to reduce the high vacuum whenever necessary. Gas-filled tubes are now used only in physics laboratories, but in the early period of X-ray technology they were the only known source of X rays.

The Coolidge Hot Filament X-ray tubes have eliminated the gas tubes in industrial and medical X-ray machines. This type of tube is practically free from gas and the electrons are supplied from a hot cathode made of tungsten wire backed by a focusing plate of molybdenum. The electrons are accelerated toward the tungsten target and strike the target with the force necessary for the radiation production. Tungsten is used because of its high atomic number which gives it sufficient mass to withstand the electron bombardments, and its high melting point makes it desirable as an incandescent cathode. Water-cooling systems have been supplied to the cathodes of all classes of X-ray tubes to prevent melting when large milliampere loads are used. The constant vacuum of the Coolidge tube produces a steady stream of electrons, which will vary only with fluctuation of the cathode temperature. The hardness of the X rays then depends solely on the voltage between the electrodes. Newer X-ray tubes dissipate heat through an oil-immersion apparatus by transferring the heat produced at the anode by convection to the shell castings and finally to the surrounding air.

Electrons emitted from the filament cathode are focused toward the target anode by means of a negatively charged metallic cup of high voltage surrounding the cathode. The negative charge repels emitted electrons, allowing them to move only in the direction of the anode.

The hot filament X-ray tubes are provided with several windows made of aluminum, mica, or beryllium. These materials do not absorb X rays as readily as glass and therefore act to focus the widely scattered rays as they move from the target anode to the exterior of the tube.

The electric current needed to provide electrons moving exclusively from cathode to anode may be provided by an alternating current or a direct current source. A constant flow of electrons is present when direct current is used; alternating current allows electron flow only during the half-cycle when the filament is negatively charged. In cases where the X-ray intensity must be controlled within a narrow range, rectifiers are used to convert alternating current to direct current.

Two types of hot filament tubes are generally in use. The most widely used X-ray tube in the United States does not have interchangeable anodes and cathodes. Its vacuum is sealed at the factory and needs no auxiliary gas-evacuating equipment when in use. The tube may be used until the filament element becomes burned or the target anode becomes

altered by the continued force of the bombarding electron, which in either case will render the tube useless. A tube that permits anode and cathode replacement is used extensively in Europe. Pumping equipment to keep the tube uniformly gas-evacuated must be used with the tube since its vacuum has not been factory sealed.

High Voltage Machines must be used to utilize X rays for industrial and medical diagnostics and testing, because large electrical potentials are needed to excite the X-ray tube. Most electrical power supplies employed in X-ray machines are induction coils, voltage step-up transformers, electrostatic generators, or high frequency oscillators.

An induction coil is an open-cored step-up transformer that depends for its action on the interruption of the primary current. However, the difficulty in standardizing induction coils to serve the various demands for producing X rays of differing qualities has rendered them almost obsolete.

The closed-core step-up transformers are now generally used in X-ray work. They consist of an oil-immersed step-up transformer that is supplied with 60-cycle alternating current. Electronic rectifier tubes change the high-potential alternating current from the secondary coil of the transformer into direct current, which flows to the X-ray tube cathode. The voltage used to activate the X-ray tube must conform to the power rating of the tube. Each X-ray tube has a factory-determined maximum power rating, which if exceeded would cause damage to the tube. See TRANSFORMER.

The oscillator power supply consists of two three-element vacuum tubes or special transformers used to produce high frequency oscillations that are stepped up to high voltage by means of an air-core transformer. This system produces high potential currents up to one million volts or more.

Electrostatic generators are capable of supplying extremely high voltages and are often the power source for X-ray machines which employ high electrical potentials to produce very hard X rays. The Van de Graaff electrostatic generator is used extensively as high voltage power supply in basic X-ray research. It utilizes a continuously moving belt of insulated material that collects electric charges by induction and discharges them inside a large, hollow metal sphere, producing a high direct voltage (see ELECTROSTATICS, *Electrostatic Machines;* ELECTRON AND ION ACCELERATORS, *The Van de Graaff Generator*).

APPLICATION OF X RAYS

The Radiograph is one of the most extensively used devices employing X rays in industrial testing and medical diagnosis. Radiography exploits the ability of X rays to expose photographic film. Unlike light waves, X rays cannot be refracted and brought into sharp focus with the aid of a lens; therefore, images formed on film from X-ray penetration of an object in front of the film are shadow pictures. The shadows cast are of different densities depending upon the X rays that are neither absorbed nor scattered as they penetrate through an object. As shown previously, increased voltage applied to X-ray tubes results in radiations of shorter wave length and greater penetrating power. The atomic number and density of the material to be X-rayed also determines the amount of X-ray penetration. Materials of high atomic number and density will absorb much X-ray radiation and will leave a sharp shadow outline on film as the X rays surrounding the object penetrate through the film, activating the film chemicals and leaving areas of darkness around the lighter shadow area.

Intensifying screens used in conjunction with X-ray photographic plates increase the effect of the shadow picture. The screens are prepared with layers of fluorescent chemicals that give off blue and violet light when activated by an X-ray beam. The light given off by intensifying screens is sufficient to often allow an X-ray dosage reduction of about $\frac{1}{50}$ of the roentgen dose if they were not used.

There are several varieties and types of film, each of which has a specific application in radiography. Certain X-ray films that are designed for use without intensifying screens are more sensitive to X-ray wave lengths than regular photographic film. They have unusually thick emulsions with greater silver content and are photosensitive on both sides of the base plastic. Radiation dosage is reduced through their use. Polaroid film has been used to produce positive pictures in less than a minute by a dry process, contrasted with the half-hour or more needed to prepare an X-ray negative plate by the usual wet developing processes. See PHOTOGRAPHY.

Industrial X-Ray Inspection. The application of X-ray analysis permits control of structural aberrations in manufacturing operations. The X-ray method of testing examines forgings, castings, welds, and critical parts of machinery without changing or altering the inspected part. Blowholes and gas pockets in castings are often known to be the cause of mechanical failure; therefore, more perfect industrial machines can be produced when undesirable parts are rejected through X-ray inspection. Many manufacturing operations provide for full-scale X-ray inspections, submitting all critical materials to 100 per cent inspection in order to safeguard and insure the successful operation of the assembled machine. In other instances, it proves practical to spot-check a certain small percentage of manufactured products in order to investigate the efficacy of casting techniques and fabrication methods.

The efficiency of X-ray inspection methods depends upon how sensitive the radiograph is in showing the details of flaw structure. The selection of X-ray intensities or hardnesses which will produce the greatest penetration for a given structural piece is most important. The area of the target anode that is struck by the high-speed electrons from the cathode is called the focal spot, and the size of this area is largely responsible for the sharpness of the image on the photographic film. The distance factor from the focal spot to the film position is also an important consideration. The small focal spot in an X-ray tube is analogous to a point source of light, where in either instance a sharp shadow will be produced when the source is small rather than the hazier, more diffuse shadows caused by larger sources. X-ray tubes can be produced with focal spot sizes ranging from more than a square inch to less than 0.01 square inch; the degree of sensitivity required will determine the type of tube selected.

Medical Uses of X Rays. Diseased, atrophied, or malformed tissue can often be detected by analysis of radiographic film, or by directly viewing the body organ by means of fluoroscopy, which utilizes the ability of X rays to illuminate a fluorescent screen.

Tissue changes that result from disease or degeneration will change the density of the tissue in different degrees, depending on the severity of the destruction. Density changes, in turn, affect the penetrability of the X rays; hence, when diseased tissue radiograms, or X ray exposed films, are compared with normal, healthy tissue radiograms, an experienced diagnostician can determine the type of disease or malfunction involved and proceed to treat the ailment. As an example, a fluid-filled lung has greater X ray absorption capabilities than a healthy lung. The radiogram of a person suspected of having tuberculosis will show a darker lung area in an X-ray radiogram of that region because of the denser fluid in the lungs. Skeletal fractures and malformations are easily seen in radiograms. The soft tissues of the abdominal system can be viewed after a preparation of X-ray absorbent barium sulfate is ingested. Gastrointestinal movements may then be seen as the barium sulfate courses through the system.

X-ray treatment of disease has been increasing as newer techniques of dosage control are discovered. Certain cancerous growths have been arrested by the use of X-ray dosages which will kill the malignant cells without harming healthy tissue.

Fluoroscopy. Compounds such as barium platinocyanide and zinc sulfide will emit visible light when X rays act upon them. A screen prepared with these compounds will show the shadow of an object placed between the screen and an X-ray source in a semi-darkened room. It is also possible to combine a photographic film with the screen to preserve image impressions. X-ray fluoroscopes are used extensively in medical diagnosis. See FLUOROSCOPE.

Protection from X Rays. All well designed X-ray equipment is provided with adequate insulation to shield persons working with the apparatus from stray radiation or exposure directly to the beam coming from the tube. Instruments are provided for measuring the total value of X rays scattered in laboratories and clinics using these machines so that a check may be made at all times to determine the amount of personnel radiation exposure. According to research performed by the U.S. Bureau of Standards the maximum permissible dosage for an adult person engaged occupationally in X-ray work should not exceed a total of 0.3 roentgen per week. The measurement is taken in air to take into account the scattered and diffused radiation. Excess exposure to X-ray radiation may affect the tissue of healthy individuals. The first cells in the body to become affected are those which are rapidly reproducing, such as blood cell-forming tissue in the bone marrow and the reproductive cells in both males and females. Persons who have been overexposed to radiation will show clinical evidence of this when a blood count is made. X-ray laboratories provide all of the necessary protection for personnel, and also include special shields and radiation cones that are used in medical therapy to direct the X-ray penetration into a specific area of the body without exposing nontreated areas needlessly to the radiation.

XYLENE, or xylol, an organic compound having the formula, $C_6H_4(CH_3)_2$, and the molecular weight of 106.16. Chemically it is known as dimethylbenzene. It is a mobile, flammable liquid with a density of 0.86 grams per milliliter and a boiling point within the range of 136 to 141°C. It is obtained by the fractional distillation of coal tar. Commercial xylene, which is called xylol, is a mixture of three isomeric forms of dimethylbenzene, the ortho-xylene, the meta-xylene, and the para-xylene. These compounds differ in structure but have similar physical properties and are difficult to separate when in a mixture. All are colorless liquids. Ortho-xylene has a density of 0.8968 grams per milliliter at 20°C and melts at 25°C and boils at 144°C. Meta-xylene has a density of 0.8684 at 20°C and melts at 47.4°C and boils at 139.3°C. Para-xylene has a density of 0.854 at 20°C and melts at 13.3°C and boils at 138°C.

Uses. Xylene is used extensively as a solvent and as a starting material for the manufacture of phthalic acid and terephthalic acid. The latter is used in the fabrication of the polyester fibers such as Dacron. It is used as a solvent in rubber cements, and in the manufacture of dyes. Prolonged breathing of the vapors of xylene is injurious.

XYLOGRAPHY, the art of printing from wooden blocks upon which are engraved both text and illustrations, was practiced in China and Japan for many years before its development in Europe during the fifteenth century. The earliest dated example of the xylographer's art that has survived is the famous St. Christopher woodcut of 1423, upon which appears a caption in the form of a Latin couplet.

Xylographica, more commonly known as block books, were produced by assembling a number of xylographs into a single volume (see BLOCK BOOK). None were dated prior to 1470, but the earliest of

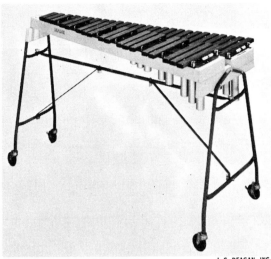

J. C. DEAGAN, INC.

The tuned bars of a twentieth century xylophone may be made from any of a great variety of materials, such as bronze, glass, bell metal, or, most commonly, hardwood.

these is thought to have antedated Johann Gutenberg's invention of movable type by some 30 years.

The block books were popular works on popular subjects—Bible stories, religious tracts, and lives of the saints. Intended as they were for the illiterate or partly literate, the texts were held to a minimum; this meant that the books could be produced more quickly, since the engraving of the letters was a laborious task. The xylographers generally followed a model, sometimes provided by old, hand-drawn (so-called manuscript) books, sometimes provided by other artisans.

Many block books achieved great popularity, going through many editions, sometimes in different languages. A much smaller number were works of great beauty; foremost among these is the *Apocalypse*, which was based on a manuscript book produced in about 1350; its pages are divided horizontally into two pictures, each of which presents some event related in the Revelation of St. John. *Ars moriendi* (?1450), which graphically illustrates the temptations that assail the dying, is thought by some to have been the work of the anonymous engraver Master E. S. The *Biblia pauperum*, which derives its name from its opening words, *Incipit biblia pauperum*, achieved great popularity. See BIBLIA PAUPERUM.

The place of xylography in the evolution of printing with movable type is disputed. Some maintain that the idea for movable type was suggested by the replacement sections of xylographs with newly carved bits of lettering. Others insist that the art of printing with movable type was an entirely independent development. To support the former view, a legend was circulated in the sixteenth century that Laurens Janszoon Coster, a xylographer of Haarlem, invented movable type about 1450.

In the second half of the century, with the development of the new printing methods, xylography declined. It continued to be used, however, in the production of ephemeral matter such as pamphlets, broadsides, playing cards, and school books.

XYLOPHONE, from the Greek *xylon* (wood) and *phone* (sound), a percussion musical instrument consisting of a series of tuned wood or metal bars laid over resonators and played by striking the bars with hard or soft mallets held in the hand. In the system of classification of musical instruments developed by Curt Sachs and Erich von Hornbostel, the xylophone is termed a "struck idiophone."

In its original form, it consisted of strips of resonant wood graduated in length and resting on belts attached to a frame, laid flat; to play the instrument,

one hit the strips of wood with a small hammer. The longer the strips of wood, the lower the pitch of the tone produced by striking it; the lengths of wood are carefully graduated so that the complete chromatic scale can be played over a range of two octaves. The strips of the modern xylophone are made of metal, bronze, or bell metal, or even of hollow glass, and an additional row of heavier strips is added at the back, so that a bass can be played. Open metal tubes are hung below the strips to increase their resonance.

The Vibraphone, an electrically operated xylophone, differs in tone from the xylophone in that a vibrato is imparted to each note by means of an electrically turned valve on top of the resonator tube.

The Marimba, an African and South American version of the xylophone, has gourds or wooden boxes that serve as resonators and a range of from three to five octaves. It is played with groups of four, six, or eight sticks.

XYZ AFFAIR, an incident in the diplomatic relations between the United States and France that culminated in an undeclared naval war between the two countries, 1797–1800. Under an alliance made between the Kingdom of France and the Continental Congress, 1778, the government of revolutionary France expected aid from the United States when war broke out between France and Great Britain, 1793 (see FRENCH-AMERICAN ALLIANCE). The United States, however, adopted a position of neutrality, 1793, and Jay's Treaty (1794) marked a *rapprochement* in relations between the United States and Great Britain (see JAY'S TREATY). In retaliation French privateers began preying on U.S. commercial shipping. With war threatening, U.S. Pres. John Adams sent Charles C. Pinckney, John Marshall, and Elbridge Gerry to France to negotiate the controversy, May, 1797. Marshall and Pinckney were Federalists who favored the British and neutrality; as a Republican (see ANTIFEDERALISTS), Gerry was more sympathetic to the French revolutionists. The French foreign minister Charles Maurice de Talleyrand-Périgord, hoping to exploit the political differences between the commissioners and thereby secure a settlement more favorable to France, officially ignored them when they arrived in Paris, October 4. On October 18 the commissioners were visited by three unofficial agents of the foreign minister, and informed that negotiations with the French government (see DIRECTORY) would be contingent upon payment to Talleyrand of 1,200,000 livres (about $250,000) and a U.S. loan to France. The commissioners notified President Adams of the proposal by letter, referring to the agents as X, Y, and Z (their actual names were Hottinger, Bellamy, and Hautval, respectively). Negotiations between the commissioners and the French agents subsequently broke down—perhaps because the commissioners lacked the authority to pay the bribe, or perhaps because they were disinclined to engage in the sordid intrigues in which European diplomats were so practiced. At any rate Marshall and Pinckney left Paris early in 1798; Gerry remained, convinced by Talleyrand that France would declare war if he refused to negotiate, but paradoxically refusing to exercise further diplomatic functions without Adams' permission. The President recalled Gerry, however, and reported the XYZ correspondence to Congress, Apr. 3, 1798. The disclosure enraged Federalists and Republicans alike, and united the nation in a censure of French policy.

The slogan, "Millions for defense, but not a cent for tribute," sometimes attributed to Pinckney as his retort to Talleyrand's agents, was not said by Pinckney but (probably) by Rep. Robert Goodloe Harper in a toast to Marshall at a Congressional dinner in Philadelphia, June 28, 1798. Pinckney's actual retort is not known with certainty, but is generally thought to have been the following: "It is No! No! Not a sixpence."

Y

1	2	3	4	5	6	7
No hieroglyph	No Phoenician form	Y	Y	V	No Caroline form	y

8	9.
Y	y

10	11	12	13	14	15	16
Y	y	Y	ɣ	y	Y	y

The letter Y has the same origin as U, V, and W. Its position in the alphabet dates from Roman times. In Old English and Middle English, the letter was frequently used instead of I. Today it is most often used in the adverbial form -ly. Some of its historical forms are shown in the top row. They are Greek 3, Roman (Trajan) 4, Irish uncial 5, Caroline 6, and Gutenberg black-letter 7. Common forms of the letter Y as it appears today are illustrated in the bottom row. They are handwritten cursive capital 8, handwritten lowercase 9, roman capital 10, roman lowercase 11, roman small capital 12, italic capital 13, italic lowercase 14, sans serif capital 15, and sans serif lowercase 16.

Y, the twenty-fifth letter of the English alphabet, in which it is pronounced "wi." As upsilon or ypsilon, ɣ is the fifth from the last letter of the Greek alphabet, in which the sign originally expressed both the sound of the "digamma" *v*, and the vowel sound ü (as in modern German); the addition *-psilon* (bare) pointed to the second pronunciation, as a vowel. As a Greek numeral, Y stood for 400 or 4,000. In the days of Cicero, when many Greek words were being absorbed into the Latin language, the Romans adopted the letter for the sound ü, and put it after the letter *x* in their alphabet; in Latin, words that include a *y* in the spelling are generally of Greek origin. In Anglo-Saxon (Old and Middle English), the sound of modern *y*, as in words such as *yes*, was formerly written with a letter that fell into disuse toward the end of the fourteenth century; subsequently this sound value in such words became that which formerly was expressed by *G* (old French *Gui*)—hence "wi" rather than "ypsilon" in later usage. Before 1800, in such English words as *ye*, *y* signified the sound "th"; thus, "ye" in "Ye Olde this or that" was pronounced "the" as in modern usage.

In chemistry, Y stands for the element yttrium. In analytical geometry (Cartesian analysis), *y* is the vertical in a system of coordinates. In algebra, *y* signifies the second unknown.

YAAN, city, central China, in Szechwan Province, in the sw region of the People's Republic of China, about 200 miles w of Chungking. Yaan is an important tea-producing center. It was the capital of the former Sikang Province, which was incorporated as part of Szechwan in 1955. (For population, see China map in Atlas.)

YABLONOVY MOUNTAINS, U.S.S.R., in the Buryat Autonomous Soviet Socialist Republic. The mountains, which run east of Lake Baikal, are among the several short, rugged ranges that form part of the watershed between the Arctic and Pacific oceans. The Yablonovy Mountains are formed from crystalline and metamorphic rocks and average 5,000 feet in elevation. The Trans-Siberian Railroad crosses the mountains near Chita.

YACHT, any of various types of water craft which are usually used for pleasure and which are relatively small and characterized by their graceful lines and sharp prow. Yachts may be powered by steam or internal-combustion engines, or be propelled by sail. A yacht is usually regarded as a luxury vessel, with accommodations for eating and sleeping aboard. Some of the most famous yachts have been racing craft. With but few exceptions, such as the royal and presidential yachts, these ships are privately owned. Since early in the twentieth century, yachting grew in popularity, both as a form of recreation and as a competitive sport, until, by mid-century, yacht clubs existed in nearly every area located on an inland or coastal waterway. See SAILING.

YAK, *Bos grunniens*, or grunting ox, native to Tibet and neighboring parts of central Asia. The wild form exists on the Tibetan plateau, at elevations of up to 15,000 feet in winter and 20,000 feet in summer. The cows and calves travel in herds of 10 to 100; the adult males are solitary, except at mating time, which occurs in winter. The wild bull, larger than the domesticated breed, stands about 6 feet at the shoulder and weighs up to 1,200 pounds. The massive animal has a pronounced hump, short legs, a long plumed tail, and long hair that hides its eyes and ears and sweeps to the ground. The yak is indispensable in Tibet. It is used as a beast of burden; it provides milk and meat; and its hair is used for fiber.

RUSS KINNE

Adult Yak

YAKIMA, a North American Indian tribe of the Shahaptian family. The tribe ranged along the Columbia, Yakima, and Wenatchee rivers in Washington. Little is known of Yakima life, but it is presumed that their customs paralleled those of the Nez Percé tribe. The Yakimas resisted a U.S. treaty of 1855 that took their land, and under Chief Kamaiakan they banded together and waged a long war against the authorities. It was not until 1859 that the treaty finally was effected. See NEZ PERCÉ.

YAKIMA, city, s central Washington, seat of Yakima County, on the Yakima River, about 120 miles SE of Seattle. The city is a trade, processing, and distribution center for an irrigated area in which fruits, vegetables, grains, forage crops, sugar beets, cattle, sheep, and poultry are raised. Yakima's chief industry is the packing of fruit, notably apples. Other industries include the manufacture of fruit sizers, sprayers, clothing, and canvas and lumber products. The city is the center of the Yakima Valley Irrigation Project, which includes a large number of mountain reservoirs. Yakima was incorporated in 1883. Yakima Valley College is located in the city. (For population, see Washington map in Atlas.)

YAKUT AUTONOMOUS SOVIET SOCIALIST REPUBLIC, U.S.S.R., part of NE Russian Soviet Federated Socialist Republic, in Siberia; bounded by the Arctic Ocean and the Laptev and East Siberian seas on the N, and by the Russian Soviet Federated Socialist Republic on the E, S, and W; area, 1,197,760 square miles. Central Yakut is a large basin through which the Lena River and its major tributaries, the Aldan and Vilyui, flow. Elevations rise westward to the Central Siberian Plateau and eastward to the Verkhoyansk and Cherski mountain ranges, where peaks rise 8,000 to 10,000 feet above sea level. On the southern border are the Patom and Aldan plateaus. The Yana and Indigirka rivers, draining eastern Yakut, flow into the Arctic Ocean, as does the Lena. Climate is of the extreme continental type, with temperatures averaging −58.2°F in January and 59°F in July. Annual precipitation averages 8 to 10 inches.

Much of Yakut is in the taiga, or evergreen forest zone; tundra prevails along the Arctic coast and on the higher slopes of the mountains. Larch is the most important timber commercially; pine and fir also are found. Soils vary, but most in the forest zone are podsol. Though the subsoil of the entire region is permanently frozen, melting of the surface layers of the relatively fertile black soils along rivers and benches supplements the meager precipitation and permits the cultivation of grains, vegetables, and natural grasses during the frost-free period, which ordinarily lasts from 90 to 110 days. Principal livestock are reindeer and cattle. Hunting, fishing, and trapping are much engaged in.

Yakut A.S.S.R. is rich in mineral deposits. Areas along the Aldan river provide at least one fourth of the gold produced in the Soviet Union; extensive coal deposits, believed to underlie most of the Lena basin, are relatively unexploited. Other mineral resources are salt, iron, tin, lead, silver, zinc, and diamonds.

Motor roads connect Yakut with the Sea of Okhotsk on the east and with the Trans-Siberian Railroad on the south. Rivers are ice-free and navigable for no more than 135 days of the year. Tiksi, near the mouth of the Lena, is a port of call on the Soviet Northern Sea Route.

History. The republic is named for the Yakuts, a Turkic-speaking people who migrated from Asia into the Lena valley in the fourteenth century. Yakut was first visited by Russians early in the seventeenth century. There was significant Russian immigration to Yakut after the 1917 Bolshevik Revolution, and the Yakut A.S.S.R. was established in 1922. Yakutsk is the capital and largest city.
DOUGLAS JACKSON

YAKUTSK, city, E U.S.S.R., Russian Soviet Federated Socialist Republic, capital of the Yakut Autonomous Soviet Socialist Republic, on the w bank of the Lena River, 1,300 miles N of Vladivostok. Industries include sawmilling, tanning, and shipbuilding. Yakutsk was founded as a fort by invading Cossacks in 1632. Under the tsars it was a station for convicts. (For population, see U.S.S.R. map in Atlas.)

YALE, ELIHU, 1649–1721, English philanthropist for whom Yale University was named in 1718, was born in Boston, Mass., and studied in London. Yale entered the service of the British East India Company in 1671 and went in 1672 to India, where he acquired considerable wealth in private trade. He was governor of Fort St. George, Madras, from 1687 to 1692. In 1699 he returned to England, having been charged with placing personal interests ahead of those of the company. In 1714 and 1718, Yale made gifts of books and money to the Collegiate School at Saybrook, Conn. The school was named for Yale on the occasion of its removal to New Haven.

YALE, LINUS, 1821–68, U.S. inventor, born in Salisbury, N.Y. He began to manufacture locks in the early 1840's and in 1851 produced the first of his own inventions, the famous Yale Infallible Bank Lock. After several versions of this lock, he introduced 11 years later his Monitor Bank Lock, the first dial, or combination, lock. To improve small key locks, he devised the cylinder lock, based on the Egyptian pin-tumbler mechanism. Yale was a partner in the Yale Lock Manufacturing Company, founded in 1868.

YALE UNIVERSITY, a privately endowed, nonsectarian school in New Haven, Connecticut. The eleven divisions of the university, each under the supervision of its own dean and faculty, include Yale College, the Graduate School of Arts and Sciences, and the Schools of Engineering, Medicine, Divinity, Law, Art and Architecture, Music, Drama, Forestry, and Nursing.

Women are admitted to the graduate and professional schools but not to Yale College, which is the undergraduate school. In the mid-1960's the total student enrollment in Yale University was over 8,000, of which approximately one half were undergraduates, one fourth students in the Graduate School, and the remainder in the professional schools. There were about 700 women students in the graduate and professional schools. Yale students come from all 50 states, the District of Columbia, Puerto Rico, and the Virgin Islands. Foreign students number about 650.

Yale is the third oldest university in the United

One of Yale University's many handsome modern structures is the Art and Architecture Building (1963).

States. In 1701, ten Connecticut clergymen met in the village of Branford and made a gift of books to found a college. Later in the year, the General Assembly of Connecticut enacted a charter for the *Collegiate School*, as it was then called. From 1702 to 1707, instruction was carried on in the home of Rector Abraham Pierson at Killingworth. Classes were held in Milford, and then Saybrook, before moving to New Haven in 1716. Two years later, the school adopted its present name in honor of Elihu Yale, an early benefactor.

The Corporation of Yale University is the final authority in the "Government, Care, and Management" of the university. It is a body of 19 trustees, consisting of the president of the university, the governor and lieutenant governor of Connecticut *ex officiis*, ten Fellows who are the "Successors of the Original Trustees," and six Alumni Fellows, elected one every year by the graduates to serve for 6 years. The president is the chief executive officer of the university.

Freshmen live on what is call the Old Campus. Sophomores, juniors, and seniors live in 12 residential colleges. Each college houses about 280 students and some faculty members. Each has its own library, common rooms, and dining hall, and its own teams, which compete in all sports with the other residential colleges. The college residence plan was instituted in 1933 with the gifts of Edward S. Harkness, a graduate.

The Yale library, which contains about 4,500,000 volumes, is one of the largest in the world. In 1963 Yale's new Beinecke Rare Book and Manuscript Library was dedicated. It is believed to be the largest building in the world devoted exclusively to rare books and manuscripts. The Peabody Museum of Natural History is one of the oldest university-connected museums in the United States. Many of its exhibits are world-famous. Yale's art gallery is the oldest university gallery in the United States. Tens of thousands of visitors throng its special exhibits several times each year. As a great teaching gallery it is invaluable to Yale's art students and to the university's distinguished Department of the History of Art. The *Yale Daily News*, established in 1878, is the oldest college daily newspaper in the United States. The *Yale Literary Magazine*, founded in 1836, was the first undergraduate magazine in the United States.

In recent years Yale's facilities and faculty in the natural sciences have been greatly increased as the result of gifts from alumni and other friends to endow new professorships and to add an entirely new science center to existing buildings. Between 1954 and 1964, 26 new buildings, designed by the nation's leading architects, were constructed at Yale.

In government and in business, in the arts and in community service, the number of Yale graduates who have attained positions of leadership and distinction is very large in proportion to the university's enrollment.   CARLOS F. STODDARD, JR.

YALTA, city and port, SW U.S.S.R., Ukrainian Soviet Socialist Republic, in Crimea Region, on the Black Sea; 450 miles SSE of Kiev. The largest of many resorts on the subtropical south coast, under the Soviets Yalta has become a convalescent and rest center for workers. The city is a processing center for grapes, tobacco, and fruit grown in the area. Livadiya Palace, formerly the tsars' winter palace and now used as a rest home by vacationing workers, was the site of the 1945 Yalta Conference.

YALTA CONFERENCE, a World War II conference attended by Pres. Franklin D. Roosevelt of the United States, Prime Minister Winston Churchill of Great Britain, and Marshal Joseph Stalin of the U.S.S.R., held Feb. 4–11, 1945, near Yalta, in the Crimean area of the Soviet Union. The conference

dealt mainly with anticipated postwar issues. Beneatha surface cordiality, the divergent aims of the participants resulted in agreements that gave way to continuing controversy.

The conferees agreed that Germany should be disarmed, demilitarized, and de-Nazified; that Germany industry should be decentralized; and that democratic political institutions should be established by the occupying authorities. France was accepted by the Soviet Union as the fourth occupying power, and previously drawn occupation zones were confirmed. The precise terms of occupation were left for future discussion.

The three powers issued a declaration guaranteeing freely chosen democratic governments to the eastern European states. They also called for a conference at San Francisco on Apr. 25, 1945, to prepare a charter for the United Nations.

Among the most strongly criticized of the Yalta agreements was that concerning Poland. The United States and Great Britain agreed to recognize the Soviet-supported Polish government i n Lublin, Poland, if it was reorganized to include political leaders from the Western-supported government-in-exile. The eastern Polish boundary was redrawn to follow the Curzon line, as Russia demanded; upon Western insistence, however, the settlement of the western Polish boundary was left for inclusion in a German peace treaty.

Equally controversial was a secret Far Eastern agreement, which provided that the Soviet Union would enter the war against Japan and conclude a friendship treaty with Chiang Kai-shek's Nationalist government, in return for the Soviet annexation of southern Sakhalin and the Kuril Islands, special rights in two Manchurian ports, and certain railway concessions in Manchuria. This agreement, which was not made public until Feb. 11, 1946, was eventually confirmed by a treaty between the Soviet Union and the Chinese Nationalist government.

Critics of the Yalta agreements charge that they violated the principles of the Altantic Charter and were in effect a surrender to Stalin, in that they sanctioned and abetted Russia's growing influence and discouraged resistance to Communist rule. Furthermore, the agreements over Poland and China were made without the consent of the two countries involved. Defenders of the agreements hold that, considering all the issues before the conference, the Soviet Union made more concessions than the United States and Great Britain; that the Soviet Union gained nothing that it might not have easily taken; that Stalin's eventual perfidy could not be foreseen; and that, in any event, the United States was in no military position to make additional demands or even to enforce the agreements made.

YALU, Korean *Amnok*, river rising high in the Changpai Mountains in Manchuria and following a course generally southwestward to its estuary at Antung, flowing into Korea Bay. The river forms the border between North Korea and China. Its total length is nearly 500 miles. Under Japanese occupation the potential of the Yalu was harnessed in several hydroelectric schemes, and factories sprang up along its often precipitous banks. During the Korean conflict the advance of UN forces toward the Yalu brought China into the war. Many of the industries dependent on the river were damaged in bombing attacks.

YAM, the tuber of several species of *Dioscorea*, a genus of tropical climbing vines. It is a staple food in Africa, southeast Asia, tropical America, and the Pacific islands. Yams may grow to 8 feet and weigh 100 pounds. In the United States the root of *Ipomoea batatas*, or sweet potato, is often called a yam.

YAMA, a Hindu god, the judge of the dead. He is depicted as green, garbed in red, holding a noose, and seated on a buffalo. In the *Rig-Veda* he is represented as the first mortal to die and be deified.

YAMAGATA, prefecture (*ken*) and city, N Honshu, Japan; area, 3,600 square miles. Yamagata prefecture produces much of Japan's rice as well as a good deal of fruit and raw silk. Lumbering and mining are carried on in its interior mountains; also, there are petroleum and natural gas deposits.

Yamagata, the capital city, processes silk and fruit and is a metalworking center. Politically important in the eighth century (a Shinto temple dates from that period), Yamagata was developed as the castle town of the Mizuno family in the nineteenth century. Yamagata University is located in the city. (For population, see Japan map in Atlas.)

YAMAGATA ARITOMO, Prince, 1838–1922, Japanese soldier and statesman. He was born of a Samurai family in Chōshū, where he received a good education and became a fighter for the Loyalist cause. After the Restoration he traveled to Europe to study military organization. His knowledge, especially of the German army, was put to use in the 1870's when, as minister of war, he created an efficient, modern Japanese army. The effect of Yamagata's military reforms was brilliantly demonstrated in the war against China, 1894–95. He served as prime minister in 1890 and from 1898 to 1900. He intervened with great diplomatic skill in the Boxer Rebellion but could ensure parliamentary majorities for his government only by bribery and threats. After 1901 his policies were carried on by his protegés, Katsura Taro and Terauchi Masataki. The death of his old rival, Ito Hirobumi, in 1909 made Yamagata's influence even greater.

YAMAGUCHI, prefecture (*ken*) and city, SW Honshu, Japan; area, 2,345 square miles. Bounded by water on three sides, Yamaguchi has one of Japan's largest deep-sea fishing catches. Mining, particularly of limestone and coal, is important in the mountain areas, and rice is grown in the fertile valleys. Vacationers are attracted by spas in the north and central areas.

Yamaguchi, the capital city, rose to prominence in the fourteenth century under the Ouchi family, who modeled their castle town after Kyoto. In the sixteenth century, St. Francis Xavier established a Christian mission there. After a period of decline, Yamaguchi became important again during the nineteenth-century Meiji Restoration. (For population, see Japan map in Atlas.)

YAMAL-NENETS NATIONAL OKRUG (district), northern U.S.S.R., about 259,000 square miles in area. The terrain is mostly tundra, but there is some forest in the south. The okrug is sparsely settled, most of the population living in the valleys of the Ob River and its tributaries. (For population, see U.S.S.R. map in Atlas.)

YANCEY, WILLIAM LOWNDES, 1814–63, Confederate politician and secessionist leader, born in Warren County, Ga. He began his law practice in Greenville, S.C., in 1883, became an Alabama lawyer in 1839, and was state legislator from 1841 to 1844 and U.S. congressman from 1844 to 1846. In answer to the Wilmot Proviso, a proposal to prohibit slavery in any territory bought from Mexico, Yancey wrote the Alabama Platform, a resolution designed to protect slavery in the territories. The Democratic National Convention rejected the platform in 1848. From that year on Yancey led the southern movement for nonpartisan organization in defending southern rights and became the foremost orator for secession. Following his speech at the 1860 Democratic National Convention, a majority of the southern delegates left the proceedings. He introduced the Ordinance of Secession at the Alabama Convention in January, 1861. He headed, in 1861–62, a Confederate commission sent to Europe in a vain attempt to secure recognition of the Confederate government, and served in the senate of the Confederacy from 1862 until his death the following year.

YANG, CHEN NING, 1922– , Chinese-U.S. theoretical physicist, born in Hofei, Anhwei Province. Dr. Yang received his B.S. in 1942 from the National Southwest Association University in Kunming and his Ph.D. in 1948 from the University of Chicago. In 1949 he joined the Institute for Advanced Studies at Princeton, N.J. In 1957, with Dr. Tsung Dao Lee, he received the Nobel prize in physics for theorizing that the law of conservation of parity is invalid in particle transformations involving weak nuclear interactions and for proposing experiments to verfiy this. See PARITY.

YANGCHOW, city, E China, in Kiangsu Province, near the Yangtze River, 35 miles ENE of Nanking. Yangchow lies on the Grand Canal and markets rice and salt. It flourished during the Sui and T'ang dynasties (589–906), and by the ninth century it was important in foreign trade. In the thirteenth century it was visited by Marco Polo. Yangchow was sacked by the Japanese in the sixteenth century, and therafter its importance declined. In 1912 its name was changed to Kiangtu, but the original name was restored in 1949. (For population, see China map in Atlas.)

YANGTZE RIVER (in Chinese, commonly *Chang Kiang* or *Ch'ang Chiang*), the longest river of China

Numerous small vessels crowd the waters of the Yangtze River at the point where it flows into the East China Sea at Shanghai.

RENE BURRI-MAGNUM

and Asia. The middlemost of China's three great rivers, it flows some 3,430 miles from its source, high in the Tibetan highlands, to its delta in the East China Sea near Shanghai. The river rises in several headstreams at over 16,000 feet in sw Tsinghai Province and flows SE, as the Dre Shu, in Tibet. It continues across the high plateau of northern Yunnan, where it is diverted northeast to the Szechwan basin. There the river descends to 1,000 feet above sea level at Ipin, the head of navigation, and its course becomes easterly as it flows between low banks through the basin, past Chungking and Wanhsien. Between Wanhsien and Ichang the Yangtze passes through its celebrated gorges, where rapids make it dangerous for navigation. Below Ichang, the head of navigation for river vessels, the river flows through the lake-filled central basin of Hupei. Here it receives the waters of two lakes, Tungting and Poyang, then turns NE at Kiukiang, passes Chinkiang, and enters the sea. Its major tributaries include the Yalung, Kialing, and Han from the north, and Wu, Siang, and Kan from the south. The Yangtze, draining more than 750,000 square miles, traverses some of China's most productive regions, which are among the most densely populated areas of the world. It is consequently the major east-to-west artery of central China, gathering approximately one half of the total trade of the country. It is navigable for 600 miles for ocean-going vessels, 1,000 miles for river vessels, and 1,500 miles for small craft. The river reaches its low-water mark in the winter months, December through March, and in the summer months the waters are swelled by melting snows and monsoon rains. The Yangtze does not flood as devastatingly as the Yellow River to the north, since the lakes in its course regulate its flow. However, record-breaking floods causing wide damage occurred in 1931 and 1954.

YANKEE, a colloquial name for a native of New England or of the northern United States in general; a derogatory name applied in the South to persons native to states which were loyal to the Union during the Civil War; and a popular name applied by people of other countries to Americans in general. The British applied the name to insurgent colonial rabble-in-arms during the Revolutionary War. The name may have derived from *Janke* (Little John), an early Dutch nickname; *Yengee*, an American Indian corruption of "English";

or it may have come from *eankke* ("coward"), a Cherokee word.

YANKEE DOODLE, a catchy song whose perennial popularity dates from the time of the American Revolution. According to legend it was first sung by the red-coated British soldiers in derision of the homespun-clad colonials. The colonials, however, turned the joke against the redcoats, by accepting enthusiastically the appellation Yankee Doodle Dandy and writing new verses more complimentary to themselves. The origin of the tune itself is uncertain. It first appeared in print about 1782.

YANKEE-PENNAMITE WARS, 1769–71, 1775, and 1784, a series of armed encounters in the Wyoming Valley of Pennsylvania between settlers from Connecticut and settlers from Pennsylvania. Land grants to two companies resulted in bitter struggles for possession of the disputed territory. In 1799 Pennsylvania finally won the area, but the Connecticut claimants received a settlement.

YANKTON, city, SE South Dakota, seat of Yankton County; on the Missouri River 58 miles sw of Sioux Falls. Industrial products include machine tools, sheet metal, and electronic components. Two colleges, Yankton College and Mount Marty College, are located in Yankton. (For population, see South Dakota map in Atlas.)

YAOUNDE, capital city of the Federal Republic of Cameroun, at an altitude of about 3,000 feet on the Cameroun Plateau. The appearance of the city is enhanced by its construction in a series of tiers. There are a variety of factories in Yaoundé—producing chiefly food products and building materials—but little heavy industry. The Cameroun Institute for Scientific Research is located in Yaoundé. The combination of tropical situation and high altitude gives Yaoundé its pleasant climate; the average temperature is about 71°F.

Yaoundé was founded in 1888, when Cameroun was a German protectorate. It has been the administrative capital since 1922 except for a period during World War II in which the government was located at Douala. (For population, see Northern Africa map in Atlas.)

YAP, archipelago, w Pacific, Trust Territory of the Pacific Islands, w Caroline Islands; 1,154

MARC AND EVELYNE BERNHEIM

A vast three-story building housing market stalls stands on the main boulevard of downtown Yaoundé, capital of the Cameroun Republic. Yaoundé is located in an agricultural region producing rubber, coffee, cacao, timber, corn, and other products. Local manufactures include soap, dairy products, and cigarettes. The city is the region's educational center.

ESE of Manila, 500 mi. SW of Guam; area about 30 sq. mi.; pop. (1950 est.) 4,652. The group, which is composed of 4 large and 10 small islands, is surrounded by a 16-mile-long coral reef, through which inlets lead to harbors and anchorages, the largest being at Tomil. The westward-sloping islands are composed of older crystalline rocks, and represent summits of an underwater chain of north- and south-trending mountains extending from Japan. Rull, 10 miles long and 3 miles wide, is the largest of the major islands and rises to 984 feet at its highest point in a low range of hills; other important islands are Tomil, Map, and Rumong. The islands are fertile and well forested with coconut and areca palms, and bamboos. Typhoons are frequent. The people are Micronesians, a group which is a mixture of Malay, northern Asiatics, Polynesians, and Melanesians. There is a Roman Catholic mission on the island. The islands are primarily a communications center with a cable and two radio stations. Vegetables and cattle are raised for local use; copra and dried bonito are exported. The Carolines were formally annexed by Spain in 1686, but were sold to Germany after the Spanish-American War (1898). During World War I, Yap was occupied by the Japanese, and following the war it was mandated, along with other former German islands, to Japan by the League of Nations. It remained under Japanese control until 1947, when the United Nations granted sole trusteeship to the United States. During World War II, Yap was an important Japanese naval and air base, and was attacked but never occupied by United States naval task forces.

YAPOK, or water opossum, an aquatic marsupial native to Central and South America. It is about 14 inches long, and has short, light gray fur, with distinctive markings of blackish brown and white, the dark markings forming diamond shapes. The hind toes are webbed, and the long tail naked and scaly. The young water opossum remain in their mother's pouch until they overgrow the pouch and must be cared for in the river-bank den. Yapoks are nocturnal animals; they feed upon water crustaceans.

YAQUI, a North American Indian tribe that is part of the Piman branch of the Uto-Aztecan family. Formerly they lived along the Yaqui River, but at mid-twentieth century they lived here and there in Sonora state, Mexico, and in southern Arizona, where they engaged in agriculture and cattle raising. The Yaquis of Mexico revolted against the Spaniards, 1740 and 1764, and until the early twentieth century were frequently in conflict with the Mexican government, which deported many of them to Istmo De Tehuantepec in the Yucatán peninsula, 1906.

YAQUI RIVER, NW Mexico, formed by the confluence of two smaller streams which rise in the W outliers of Sierra Madre Occidental. The river flows about 420 miles south and southwest through Sonora to the Gulf of California. The river is not navigable, but water is diverted to irrigate crops of wheat, corn, and rice in its lower course.

YARACUY, state, NW Venezuela, bounded by Falcón on the N, Carabobo on the E, Cojedes on the S, and Lara on the W; area 2,714 sq. mi.; pop. (1959 est.) 132,790. The state comprises two physical regions; the highlands, which are an extension of the Cordillera de Mérida, and the fertile lowlands of the Yaracuy River valley. The area has a tropical climate, which is characterized by recurring droughts on the uplands, and heavy rains from June until December in the valley. Most settlement is limited to the lowlands, where sugar cane, bananas, corn, cacao, tobacco, and cotton are grown. Coffee is grown on the more moist eastern slopes. The state has deposits of iron ore, copper, coal, and lead. San Felipe is the capital.

YARD. See WEIGHTS AND MEASURES.

YARKAND, or Soche, city, China, W Sinkiang-Uighur Autonomous Region; on the braided Yarkand River, in an oasis in the W part of the Takla

Makan; 95 miles SW of Urumchi. The city is the commercial center for an oasis, which is about 800 square miles in area. Marco Polo passed through Yarkand on his way to the court of Kublai Khan. As late as 1863 the great Moslem uprising of Chinese Turkestan began in Yarkand with the massacre of the Chinese Buddhists there. Not until 1877 did the forces of the Manchu emperor in Peking recapture Yarkand and suppress the rebellion. Pop. (1959 est.) 60,000.

YARKAND RIVER, China, in W Sinkiang-Uighur Autonomous Region, one of the chief tributaries of the Tarim Darya. The Yarkand's main source streams rise in the glaciers of Mount Godwin-Austen, Gasherbrum, and other high peaks of the Karakoram Range in India; other headwaters flow from glaciers in the western Kunlun Mountains. Descending northward from the mountains, the Yarkand flows about 600 miles northeastward around the western rim of the Takla Makan (Takla Desert) to where, with the Aksu River from the northwest, it forms the Tarim Darya. In summer, the Yarkand tends to dry up, especially in its lower course. The chief city on the river is Yarkand.

YARMOUTH, city, Canada, SW Nova Scotia; seat of Yarmouth County; on the Atlantic Ocean, and the Dominion Atlantic and the Canadian National railways; about 135 miles SW of Halifax. Yarmouth is a summer resort, a commercial center for an agricultural area, and a shipping point. Lobsters are a leading catch of the extensive fishing industry which centers there. The town has shipyards, fish curing and packing plants, textile mills, and plants which produce wood products and dairy products. Yarmouth was settled in 1761 and incorporated in 1890. Pop. (1956) 8,095.

YARN, natural or synthetic fibers or filaments twisted into one continuous strand and used in the manufacture of textile fabrics. In the production of yarn, staple fibers are carded, combed, drawn out into roving, and then spun (see SPINNING). Continuous filaments, such as those of rayon and silk, may be cut and treated as staples, or may be twisted directly into yarn. When two or more fibers are doubled, or twisted together, the yarn is said to be twofold or threefold. Yarn may be made entirely of one type of fiber, or it may contain a combination of fibers. Some yarns are twisted uniformly; others contain a pattern of loose and tight twists. The texture and design of a textile material are influenced by the type of yarn used in its manufacture. Variation in yarn, and therefore in textile, may be produced by varying the direction, twist, or the number of twists to a given length of yarn. See FIBER; THREAD.

YAROSLAVL, region, U.S.S.R., W Russian Soviet Federated Socialist Republic; bounded by the regions of Vologda on the N, Kostroma on the E, Ivanovo on the SE, Moscow on the SW, and Kalinin on the W; area 14,250 sq. mi.; pop. (1959) 1,395,000. Wheat and long-fibered flax are grown. The major industries are the manufacturing of cotton and linen goods, synthetic rubber chemicals, ships, automobiles, and trucks. The highways and railroads are well developed, and the Volga carries a considerable amount of commerce. The capital is Yaroslavl. Other important cities are Rybinsk and Rostov. In the 1930's huge dams were constructed to combat the shallowness of the Volga's channel; the great reservoir that resulted is called the Rybinsk Sea.

YAROSLAVL, city, U.S.S.R., W Russian Soviet Federated Socialist Republic, capital of Yaroslavl Region, on the Volga River; 145 miles NE of Moscow. Among the city's chief industrial establishments are motor vehicle manufacturing plants, a plant for the manufacture of synthetic rubber from potato alcohol, and chemical works. Textile mills, built there late in the eighteenth century, were improved and expanded by the Soviets. Yaroslavl has a twelfth century monastery and several seventeenth century

Byzantine Orthodox churches. Yaroslavl, founded 1024, competed with Moscow for the control of the surrounding area until falling captive to Moscow, 1463. Under the Muscovites the city became a trade and crafts center. (For population, see U.S.S.R. map in Atlas.)

YATSUSHIRO, city Japan, Kumamoto Prefecture, W Kyushu, on Yatsushiro Bay. The city exports porcelain ware. Important industries are trout fishing and the growing of citrus fruit.

YAUCO, town, SW Puerto Rico, on Yauco River, 16 miles W of Ponce. Cigars are manufactured, and coffee and sugarcane are grown. (For population, see West Indies map in Atlas.)

YAWATA, or Yahata, city, SW Japan, N Kyushū Island, in Fukuoka Prefecture; on an inlet of Shimonoseki Strait; 90 miles NE of Nagasaki. The city has direct access to the main international and coastwise shipping routes, and is on the Tokyo–Osaka–Shimonoseki Railroad and the main highway system of Kyushū. Yawata is on the northern rim of the great Chikuho coal fields, which supplies the metallurgical industry, the city's most important industry. Steel, coke, bricks, glass, cement, chemicals, motors, and fertilizer are produced in the city. During the latter part of the nineteenth century, Yawata was chosen as the site of the steel industry because it was close to the country's main coal fields and on a main sea route at a point as near as possible to the Asiatic sources of iron ore. Yawata, on Oct. 24, 1944, was the first target in Japan of a bombing attack by U.S. B-29 Superfortresses. The steel industry lagged following World War II, until the 1950's when demand for supplies by UN forces in Korea stimulated production.

YAWATAHAMA, city Japan, Ehime Prefecture, W Shikoku, on Hoyo Strait. Cotton textiles are manufactured. The city is a fishing port. (For population, see Japan map in Atlas.)

YAWL, a sailboat having a fore and aft mast to accommodate a large sail on the foremast, and a much smaller sail on the after mast. In a yawl, the after mast, variously termed the mizzen, a spanker, or a jigger, is stepped aft of the tiller or helm. In this way, a yawl differs from a ketch, which is also a two-masted boat, but with the aft mast mounted ahead of the tiller. Yawls are used mainly for pleasure sailing, racing, and fishing.

YAWS, a contagious, nonvenereal, tropical disease, caused by the spirochete, *Treponema pertenue.* It is characterized by initial lesion of the skin, mild constitutional symptoms including joint pains, irregular fever, and perhaps enlargement of regional lymph nodes, later by granular, raspberry-like lesions of the skin, and occasionally by late developing destructive lesions of the skin and bones. It is transmitted either through the bite of flies or from person to person. The skin must be broken in order for the spirochetes to enter. Diagnosis is confirmed by a positive Wassermann reaction and isolation of the spirochetes. Yaws mainly affects children and is more common in males than in females. The disease is not usually fatal except in young infants and in cases of secondary infection of skin ulcers or bone lesions. Yaws responds to treatment with the arsenicals and penicillin.

YAZOO CITY, W central Mississippi, seat of Yazoo County; on the Yazoo River; about 40 miles NW of Jackson. The town is a cotton-trading and manufacturing center and was settled about 1800. It was given its name in 1839. Pop. (1960) 11,236.

YAZOO FRAUDS, an incident of early U.S. history in which the Georgia legislature, for the sum of $500,000, granted certain lands between the Alabama and Coosa rivers—estimated to be 20 million acres, but actually 35 million acres—to four associations known as the Yazoo Companies, 1795. Since most of the members of the legislature were financially interested in the companies, it was suspected by many that the concession had not been motivated solely out of a concern for the public weal, and there were

charges of fraud; the concession was annulled by a new legislature, 1796, and the annulling act was made part of the state constitution, 1798. The companies, however, contended that the original concession remained valid. The land involved was ceded by Georgia to the United States, 1802, and a federal commission headed by Secretary of State James Madison recommended a compromise with the shareholders of the companies. The compromise was refused by the state of Georgia, and ultimately the case reached the U.S. Supreme Court. The court upheld the Madison commission's contention that since the original grant was in the nature of a contract between the state and the companies, the legislature of 1796 had acted *ultra vires* (without authority) in annulling it. Congress provided for the payment of the claims made by the Yazoo Companies, 1814, and more than $4.28 million was paid to the claimants.

YEADON, borough, SE Pennsylvania, in Delaware County; 6 miles SW of Philadelphia. Yeadon is a residential suburb located in an area that is predominantly industrial. Pop. (1960) 11,610.

YEAR, the period of the earth's revolution about the sun. The sidereal year, which is the true mechanical period of the orbit, is the period in which the sun completes its apparent path among the stars from one star around to that same star again. The interval is 365 days, 6 hours, 9 minutes, 9.5 seconds (365.25636 days) of mean solar time.

The tropical year, which is the year of the seasons, chronology, the Gregorian calendar, and civil life, is the interval of the sun's circuit from a vernal equinox back again to the same equinox; or from one solstice back to the same solstice. Since the sun's apparent motion among the stars is eastward, and the equinoxes have a slow westward motion, the tropical year is somewhat shorter than the sidereal year, namely, 365 days, 5 hours, 48 minutes, 46 seconds (365.24220 mean solar days). The calendar year is taken as 365 days in every year whose number, like 1963, is not divisible by four, and as 366 days in leap years, those years divisible by four. Century-numbered years, however, to be leap years, must be divisible by 400.

The term year is also used for periods not related to the earth's orbital motion. The eclipse year is the interval of 346.62 days between consecutive occasions when the sun is at a given node of the moon's orbit. A lunar year of 354 days based on the lunar month was used by the Jews and the Muslims.

YEARDLEY, SIR GEORGE, 1580?–1627, British colonial governor of Virginia, was born in London. He arrived in the colony of Virginia, May, 1610, and was acting governor of Virginia from the departure of Sir Thomas Dale, April, 1616, to the arrival of Sir Samuel Argall, May, 1617. He was governor of the colony, 1618–21 and 1626–27. He convened the House of Burgesses, the first legislature in North America, July 30, 1619.

YEAST, fungi belonging to the class Ascomycetes, and, specifically, members of the genus *Saccharomyces*, used in the baking and brewing industries.

Yeast cells have a large vacuole surrounded by granular cytoplasm, containing reserve food particles and a nucleus. Each colony of yeasts is composed of the descendants of a single cell. In the process of multiplication the nucleus of the original cell divides, and a swelling, or bud, arises from the cell surface. One of the daughter nuclei and some of the cytoplasm passes into the bud, which later separates from the mother cell. In this manner the yeast cells continue to divide until a colony is formed.

Under unfavorable conditions two yeast cells may unite and undergo two internal divisions to form four ascospores, which are specialized cells containing the fused nuclei resulting from division of the joint cell, enclosed within the cell wall. Single yeast cells may also form ascospores. These spores, when they are released under favorable conditions, develop into ordinary yeast cells by asexual reproduction.

When deprived of a sufficient supply of oxygen, yeasts live anaerobically in the presence of sugars. Under these conditions yeasts secrete an enzyme, zymase, which breaks up the sugars to form alcohol and carbon dioxide, and to release energy for the metabolism of the yeasts.

Commercial Yeast depends for its action upon zymase and its ability to form alcohol and gas from dextrose and fructose. Ordinary sugar (sucrose) and malt sugar (maltose) must be changed into simple sugars by the action of the enzymes present in the yeast, sucrase and maltase. There are no enzymes in yeast capable of changing starch into sugar. The enzyme diastase, however, found in flour, wheat malt, barley malt, and malt extract, changes starch into maltose, which can then be changed into simple sugars by the maltose present in the yeast. Commercial bakers control the rate of gas production in the dough by adding a carefully determined amount of malt extract.

Most commercial yeast today is cultivated in a mineral, salt, and sugar solution. The yeast cells may then be mixed with starch and compressed and shaped into cakes, which must be kept under refrigeration until they are used. Yeast may also be dried and sold as a powder which keeps without refrigeration and does not become active until water is added. Brewer's yeast, which is sold as a dry powder, and baker's yeast are made from different species of *Saccharomyces*.

YEATS, WILLIAM BUTLER, 1865–1939, Nobel prize-winning Irish poet, called "the greatest poet of our time" by T. S. Eliot, was born in Sandymount, a suburb of Dublin, the son of John Butler Yeats (1836–1922), a painter of the pre-Raphaelite school. Shortly after Yeats's birth, the family moved to London, but he was frequently sent back to county Sligo to stay with his grandparents, and much of his somewhat irregular education was received in Ireland. His parents returned to Ireland, 1881, and Yeats's father introduced him to Edward Dowden of Trinity College, who encouraged the publication of some of Yeats's earliest poetry. Returning to London, 1887, Yeats quickly became part of the hot house literary scene of the Yellow Nineties. His first success came with *The Wanderings of Oisin* (1889), a series of poems on Irish folk themes; this and his first play, *The Countess Cathleen* (1892), were well received by the critics and firmly established Yeats as an important young talent.

Mystic and Patriot. Yeats profoundly disapproved of nineteenth century rationalism and scientism and this feeling, together with some love of mystification for its own sake, led him to dabble in Rosicrucianism and theosophy, and to study East Indian theology with the self-proclaimed mystic Elena Blavatsky. At the same time he was devoted to the cause of Irish literary revival, and was the first president of the Irish Literary Society. With the help of Lady Augusta Gregory, he formed the Irish Literary Theatre, 1897, later the Abbey Theatre, a group with which he was associated for the rest of his life. Becoming a shrewd and skillful man of affairs, he fought uncompromisingly for the artistic freedom of the theater, even against the patriot and actress Maud Gonne, to whom he was devoted over the years. This practical and political experience resulted in a period of verse of a very powerful kind, and his poetry was never again to be without the direct, colloquial force of *On Those That Hated The Playboy of the Western World* and *In Memory of Major Robert Gregory*.

Yeats's "System." Yeats married Georgie Hyde-Lees, a spiritualistic medium, 1917, and credited her with being the inspiration for his philosophical "system," which is set forth in *A Vision* (1925), an ambiguous and highly symbolic work that was built up slowly out of his wife's visions, his reading in philosophy, and his knowledge of esoteric doctrines. Whatever its intrinsic merits or lack of them, this system helped him, as he said, "to hold in a single thought reality and justice." It enabled him, that is, to write both directly and symbolically. Thus the poetry of his final period, whether ostensibly occasional, as in *Among School Children*, or meditative, as in *Meditations in Time of Civil War*, or symbolic, as in *Byzantium*, is at once immediate, colloquial, and profoundly eloquent.

Yeats was a senator of the Irish Free State, 1922–28, and was awarded the 1923 Nobel prize for literature.
ARTHUR MIZENER

YEGORYEVSK, or Yegorievsk, city, U.S.S.R., W Russian Soviet Federated Socialist Republic, in Ryazan Region; 60 miles SE of Moscow. Cotton textiles are the chief manufactured product. Pop. (1959) 59,000.

YELETS, or Elets, city, U.S.S.R., W Russian Soviet Federated Socialist Republic, in Orel Region, on the Sosna River; 223 miles S of Moscow. Yelets, is a railroad junction and iron and bronze foundries, tanneries, tobacco factories, and plants which manufacture silk stuffs and laces are leading industrial establishments. It is a market for cattle and grain. The city was founded in 1646. Pop. (1959) 78,000.

YELLOW BASS, a fresh-water game fish, closely related to the white bass, belonging to the sea bass family *Serranidae*. The fin and body structure of the yellow bass is similar to the white bass; however, its body has yellow coloration with interrupted dark stripes and rarely exceeds 15 inches in length. It is generally found in lakes and rivers in the north central United States and particularly in the Great Lakes region.

YELLOW FEVER is an acute disease characterized by an onset of high fever, caused by a filterable virus transmitted to man by a species of mosquitoes generally of the *Aedes* and *Haemogogus* genera. The transmission of the disease from person to person is by a mosquito known as *Aedes aegypti*.

The severity of the disease varies from a mild transitory fever to the acute and fatal forms of yellow fever. Following an incubation period of 3 to 10 days, the onset is sudden. The classic symptoms of the first stage are fever (reaching to about 103°F), severe headache, and backache, leg pains, prostration, flushed face, and the tongue becomes pointed and bright red at the tip and edges. On the third or fourth day the temperature may fluctuate, the face becomes pale, jaundice and hemorrhage appear, depression is apparent, the tongue becomes dry and brown, the pulse rate falls, and frequent vomiting may occur. The temperature reaches normal about the seventh or eighth day, followed by a rapid convalescence in those cases that recover. However, when hiccough, black stools, copious vomiting of altered blood, and kidney failure occur, the chances for recovery are grave. Most cases are mild and few of the above-mentioned symptoms are experienced, but after each case there is established a lifelong immunity. The fatality rate is considered to be from 10 to 85 per cent, with Negroes having a lower rate than whites or Orientals.

There is no specific treatment for yellow fever. Symptomatic treatment includes absolute bed rest, administering analgesics to relieve headache; juices and alkaline waters should be given freely, and vomiting may be relieved by giving chipped ice with cocaine, and codeine intravenously. Intravenous feeding may be necessary where vomiting interferes with giving fluids by mouth. The patient having an elevated temperature can be made more comfortable by cool sponge baths and cold compresses applied to the head. Prevention of yellow fever includes elimination of the mosquito vector, preventing importation of the vector by ship or airplane, and control of individuals entering from endemic areas. Persons who are not immune should be vaccinated.

YELLOWHAMMER, a species of bunting common throughout northern Europe. The yellowhammer, *Embresiza citrinella*, is about six and a half inches in length. Its upper parts are generally colored mottled brown and the underparts yellow, the head being yellow streaked with brown, and the rump and tail colored a distinguishing chestnut. The male is more brightly colored than his mate and has a somewhat monotonous song. The nest is usually placed on the ground in hedges and ditches, and contains four or five eggs.

YELLOWHAMMER STATE, one of the two official nicknames of Alabama, probably derived from the yellowish tinge of the gray uniforms of Alabama troops during the Civil War.

YELLOW JACKET. See WASP.

YELLOWKNIFE, town, Canada, Northwest Territories, in the S central part of the District of Mackenzie; on the W side of Yellowknife Bay in the north arm of Great Slave Lake; on the Canadian Pacific Air Lines; about 600 miles N of Edmonton. The town is chiefly a center for gold mining. Fishing and trapping are other leading activities. Power for smelting is provided by hydroelectric plants on the Yellowknife River, 15 miles north, and on the Snare River, 85 miles northwest. Gold was first worked in 1938, although it had been discovered in 1898 and in 1934. The town mushroomed when new gold deposits were discovered in 1944–45. Pop. (1956) 3,100.

YELLOW RIVER, or Hwang Ho, also Huang, N China, the second largest river in the country; originates from Ngoring Nor, a lake situated at about 14,000 feet above sea level in the eastern section of the Kunlun Mountains in E central Tsinghai Province, and flows generally E to the Gulf of Chihli of the Yellow Sea; a total length of about 2,700 miles. From Ngoring Nor to the city of Lanchow in Kansu Province, the Yellow River flows east and north in a deep gorge through high rugged terrain, then generally north-northeast, and is paralleled by the Great Wall of China for about 140 miles in Kansu Province. The river passes through the sandy Ordos Desert of Inner Mongolia to the city of Paotow. It then swings southward, crosses the Great Wall of China once more, and for about 400 miles forms the border between Shensi and Shansi provinces. At the city of Tungkuan, the Yellow River flows through a deep gorge, swings abruptly eastward, emerges from the highlands, and flows generally east and northeast across the North China Plain to empty into the Gulf of Chihli.

The Yellow River is noted for the volume of silt that it carries from the Ordos Desert and the loess regions to the south. This silt has helped to build up the level North China Plain, and is constantly enlarging the river's delta. The tendency of the river to flood, together with the shifting nature of its course across the plain, has given it the name of China's Sorrow. Major tributaries of the Yellow River are the Tatung in its upper course, and the eastward flowing Wei, which enters the Yellow River as it turns eastward between Shansi and Honan provinces.

History. The Yellow River valley is believed to be the cradle of Chinese civilization, and has played an important role in the history of China. During the past 3,000 years, there were more than 1,500 instances of dike breaking, and 26 cases in which the river shifted its course. From 1191 to 1855 the river emptied into the Yellow Sea at a point 225 miles north-northwest of Shanghai. Then it changed to its present course. In 1938 the Chinese broke the dike just west of Kaifeng, in an attempt to stop the advance of the Japanese forces. The river changed its course to usurp the winter channel of the Huai River and entered the Yellow Sea south of Shangtung Province. The last dike was closed in 1947 and the river returned to its old prewar course. During 1947–55 the Pei Chin Ti and Tungping detention basins were constructed to prevent the river from breaching and shifting during extremely severe floods. In 1952 the People's Victory Canal was constructed

Location Map of Yellow River

in Honan to divert some of the Yellow River water into the Wei in order to provide irrigation for farm land and to improve navigation between Sinsiang and Tientsin. In the late 1950's a large multipurpose reservoir was constructed at Sanmen Gorge between Honan and Shansi provinces. The large reservoir behind the dam backed up both the Yellow and Wei rivers.

YELLOW SEA, or Hwang Hai, an inlet of the Pacific Ocean; bounded by China on the W and N, by Korea on the E, and the East China Sea on the S; area about 160,000 sq. mi. The sea is divided by the Liaotung and Shantung peninsulas into Korea Bay, Liaotung Bay, and the Gulf of Chihli. The Yellow Sea is generally less than 300 feet deep. It received its name from the silt which the Yellow River and other streams carry down from the interior. The main ports are Inchŏn on the Korea Coast, and Dairen, Port Arthur, Tientsin, and Tsingtao on the China Coast.

YELLOWSTONE NATIONAL PARK, the largest public park in the United States, composed of an area of 3,350 square miles of unique natural wonders, located largely in NW Wyoming, and extending for about two miles into the states of Montana and Idaho. The park is surrounded by national forests. First established as a national park, 1872, Yellowstone has been gradually enlarged to embrace the world's greatest geyser area, Yellowstone Lake, and the spectacular falls and canyon of the Yellowstone River. The region was first visited by the frontiersman John Colter, 1807–08, and 20 years later by the mountaineer James Bridger. When the region was explored, 1870, by the Washburn-Doane Expedition, the surveyors were determined that the area should be preserved for the public benefit. See NATIONAL PARKS.

The central portion of the park is a broad, volcanic plateau, with an average elevation of 8,000 feet. The plateau is rimmed by the Teton, Gallatin, Beartooth, and Absaroka mountains. Yellowstone would be inaccessible but for natural avenues formed by four river canyons. The Shoshone flows eastward, and along this river the famous Cody Road has been built. The Snake flows down through the Jackson Hole country, making a south entrance possible. To the west the Madison drains the large geyser basins and provides an entrance from that direction. The Yellowstone River, after tumbling first 109 feet and then 308 feet from the lake of the same name, has cut its way north through canyons more than 1,000 feet deep. An excellent paved highway parallels this river. The main road system in Yellowstone Park is roughly in the form of a figure 8. With the subsidiary roads there are about 300 miles of highways; foot trails, and bridle paths lead to the more inaccessible parts of the park.

Yellowstone Park includes within its borders the largest geysers in the world. Most of the geysers are located in six groups, or geyser basins, in the west and south-central portion of the park. The geysers spout water and steam from 30 to 250 feet into the air—some from open bowl-shaped basins and others from cones built up by their deposits. Extinct geysers are marked by the remains of these cones. Excelsior Geyser, active at irregular intervals, is the largest of all. It has a bowl-shaped opening, 200 by 300 feet, ejects 4,000 gallons of boiling hot water per minute, and throws a 50-foot column of water and steam 75 to 240 feet high. Giant Geyser throws a 5-foot column over 200 feet high for an hour at intervals of about 6 days. Old Faithful, the most dependable, discharges every 65 minutes on the average, spouting with each eruption some 15,000 gallons of water about 140 feet into the air. The hot springs and geysers are naturally supplied with ordinary groundwater that becomes heated by steam from hot rocks below the surface. There are about 4,000 hot springs in the area; and at widely scattered spots there are mud volcanoes, mud geysers, and colored springs.

Within the park lies Yellowstone Lake. With an area of 139 square miles, and at an altitude of 7,731 feet above sea level, the lake is the largest body of water in North America at so great an altitude. The most spectacular waterfalls are those of the Yellowstone River. There are falls in Lewis Canyon near the south entrance and on the Gibbon River near Madison Junction. The Continental Divide crosses the park.

Nine tenths of the park area are forest, chiefly conifers. The tree limit varies from 9,400 to 9,700 feet. Few of the plateau areas are bare. Pine, spruce, poplar, balsam, and cedar grow to large size. In the geyser and spring areas, many trees are covered by deposits and are buried; whole forests have thus been entombed, and petrified trees are common. Wild animals are protected by law. Deer, elk, buffalo, and bear may be approached near enough to photograph. Trout abound in the streams of the park. Visitors are not permitted to injure any living thing except in self-defense, or to remove any natural object except for scientific uses under special permit. The park is open to visitors from May to mid-October.

YELLOWSTONE RIVER, longest tributary of the Missouri River, 671 miles long. It rises in the Absaroka Range of the Rocky Mountains, Park County, NW Wyoming, and flows into Yellowstone National Park where it forms Yellowstone Lake. The river continues northwesterly, drops as several magnificent falls, passes through a giant canyon and enters Montana. It flows northeasterly past Billings and empties into the Missouri in North Dakota near the Montana border. Main tributaries are the Big Horn and Powder rivers.

YELLOWWOOD, four species of leguminous trees in the genus *Cladrastis. C. lutea,* native to North America, is grown for ornament. It grows to 50 feet and has smooth bark, bright green pinnately compound leaves that turn yellow in the fall, and white, fragrant, papilionaceous (bilaterally symmetrical) flowers in loose, drooping panicles. The wood yields a yellow dye.

YEMEN, republic, located in the southwestern corner of the Arabian peninsula, bounded on the N and E by Saudi Arabia, on the S by the South Arabian Federation, and on the W by the Red Sea; area, approximately 74,000 square miles; population, about 5 million. Yemen consists of a coastal plain (the Tihama) backed by a double range of mountains reaching a peak of 12,236 feet and separated by a plateau. To the east the mountains slope downward to the Rub' al-Khali, or "Empty Quarter" of Saudi Arabia. While the coastal plain is hot and damp, the highlands enjoy a temperate climate and considerable annual rainfall. The latter varies from 32 inches in the extreme southwest (monsoon region) to 16 inches at San'a, the capital. Important towns include the old capital Ta'izz, Ibb, Sa'ada, and Dhamar. The principal port is Hodeida; Mocha, the ancient coffee port, is little used today.

Social and Economic Features. The people are almost evenly divided between Shiites of the Zeidi sect, who occupy the highlands, and Sunnis of the Shafii sect, who occupy the lower ground. Some 300,000 Zeids, known as "Sayyids," have been considered a religious aristocracy by virtue of their putative descent from the Prophet Muhammad. The two largest tribal groupings are the Hashid and Bakil, located in the area north of San'a. Ninety per cent of the population depends on agriculture for a living. The terraced hillsides are extensively cultivated and irrigated. Yemen produces grains (mainly sorghum), coffee, fruit, honey, dates, and qat, a semi-narcotic leaf chewed throughout Yemen. The country is nearly self-sufficient in foodstuffs and exports coffee, cotton, salt, hides, and qat. The traditional coffee production, however, has fallen off because farmers have not found the crop sufficiently remunerative. Yemeni industry is limited virtually to handicrafts, and these were handicapped by the departure to Israel in 1949 of some 50,000 Jews, who formed the bulk of the artisans. Mineral and oil prospecting (the latter by a U.S. firm) has been conducted without result. Remittances from Yemenis living abroad help offset the propensity of Yemeni merchants to invest their capital outside Yemen. In an effort to overcome the traditional Yemeni reliance upon Aden as the main entrepot of trade, the government contracted with the U.S.S.R. to construct modern port facilities at Hodeida, completed in 1960. Other recent improvements have included the construction by the Chinese in 1961 of an asphalt road between Hodeida and San'a and the construction by the United States of a road from Mocha through Ta'izz to San'a, completed in 1965. The U.S. AID program has also included the construction of modern water works in Ta'izz. Yemen is without railroads but there are scheduled flights to San'a, Ta'izz, and Hodeida.

Government. The revolution of September 26, 1962, substituted a republican regime entitled the Yemen Arab Republic for the theocratic, absolutist

Location Map of Yemen

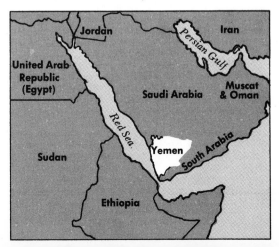

Imamate. Installed in place of the omnipotent Imam were a president, a vice president, and a prime minister, who presides over a ministerial council. Membership of the council is by appointment, and efforts are made to maintain an equal distribution between Zeidis and Shafiis. Though a constitution has been drawn up and there has been talk of convening a parliament, the primitive nature of the society and the debilitating effects of the civil war have militated against the establishment of a genuine republic. Advisers from the United Arab Republic serve in the newly established ministries, and key units of the army have been trained in the u.a.r.

History. Seat of the ancient Minaean, Sabaean, and Himyarite civilizations, Yemen once controlled the important trade route to the East as well as the incense route to the West. With the opening of alternative trade routes (Persian Gulf to Palmyra and the Red Sea), Yemen lapsed into obscurity. The end of South Arabian glory was symbolized by the breaking of the famous Marib dam in the sixth century and the outpouring of Arabs northward. With the rise of Islam, Yemen became a part of the Caliph's realm. In the late ninth century the ancestors of the current deposed Imam migrated from Iraq to Yemen and founded a dynasty which first held only religious power. In 1819 the Egyptians established control along the coast, later to be replaced by the Ottoman Turks who in 1872 captured San'a. Perpetual guerrilla warfare against Turkish rule forced the Turks formally to concede control of the interior to the Imam in 1913, and five years later the Imam became master of the whole country. In 1934 Saudi Arabian military forces compelled the Imam to relinquish the northern territory of Asir. In treaties concluded with the British in 1934 and 1951 the Yemen government, which lays claim to Aden territory, agreed to postpone the settlement of the disputed southern frontier. A loose federation with the u.a.r. was negotiated in 1958. On September 12, 1962, Imam Ahmad ibn Yahya died and was succeeded by Crown Prince Mohammad al-Badr, who promised reforms and released the hostages traditionally kept by his predecessors as insurance against tribal revolt. Eight days later a military coup headed by Brigadier General Abdullah al-Sallal unseated Badr, who fled to the hills to organize resistance. At Sallal's request u.a.r. military forces were dispatched to Yemen in an effort to suppress the Imam's forces, who were receiving support from Saudi Arabia and Jordan. Mediation efforts prevented a direct u.a.r.-Saudi military confrontation and led to the arrival in July, 1963, of a un observation mission to supervise the "disengagement" of foreign forces. The u.a.r. and Saudi Arabia agreed (1965) to end their support of the opposing sides and made a compromise settlement possible. See ARABIAN PENINSULA.

TALCOTT W. SEELYE

BIBLIOG.-Eric Bethmann, *Yemen on the Threshold* (1960); Abbas Faroughy, *Introducing Yemen* (1947); Harold Ingrams, *The Yemen* (1963); Hugh Scott, *In the High Yemen* (1942).

YEN, the monetary unit of Japan, equal to 100 sen and 1,000 rin. The Japanese Gold Standard law of 1897 set the value of the yen equal to 750 mg of gold; in 1937 the yen was revalued to equal 290 mg of gold. An official exchange rate of 360 yen per u.s. dollar was established in 1949.

YENAN, formerly known as Fushih, town, N China, in Shensi province; 165 miles NNE of Sian. Located in a narrow valley cut into the loess-covered Shensi Plateau, the town is a marketing center for cotton and cattle. There are oilfields in the vicinity. Yenan was the headquarters of the Chinese Communists from 1937 to 1949, during the campaign in which the Communists gained control of the mainland. The town is the seat of a university.

YENBO, or Yanbu' al Bahr, seaport, w Saudi Arabia, on the Red Sea, 115 miles sw of Medina. Yenbo serves as a port for Medina and is a station on the caravan route from Cairo to Mecca. (For population, see Middle East map in Atlas.)

YENISEI, or Yenisey, river, central Siberia, Russian Soviet Federated Socialist Republic; one of the world's largest rivers, with a length of about 2,360 miles and a drainage area of over 1,000,000 square miles. The Yenisei is formed by two headstreams, the Bolshoi (greater) Yenisei and the Maly (lesser) Yenisei, which rise in the Eastern Sayan Mountains, in the Tuva Autonomous Oblast. The river flows west, then north across the Sayan range and the Minusinsk Basin; as it flows to the Kara Sea, it marks the eastern boundary of the West Siberian Lowland. A rapid, narrow mountain river in its upper course, the Yenisei broadens to a width of several miles in its lower reaches. Its three major tributaries, all from the east, are the Angara, the Podkamennaya (stony) Tunguska, and Nizhnyaya (lower) Tunguska. The Yenisei is icefree and navigable from May to November in its upper course, and from June to October in its lower. The river is used extensively for floating timber. The major concentration of settlement occurs in the mining and industrial region in the foothills of the Sayan Mountains, in the vicinity of Krasnoyarsk, the largest city, and Minusinsk. The construction above Krasnoyarsk of the first of a series of hydroelectric plants, planned to exploit the Yenisei's vast power potential, was begun in 1956.

YEOMAN, a term used in feudal England to describe a man of a certain economic class or, sometimes, of subordinate military rank. Like most feudal terms, "yeoman" is incapable of exact definition. In the later Middle Ages the term was normally applied to a man of independent means but who possessed little or perhaps no land. The yeomen of England are often sentimentally regarded as forming the background of medieval English society, their sturdy independence accounting for such glorious episodes as Crécy and Agincourt.

YEOMEN OF THE GUARD, originally a royal bodyguard in England, formed at the time of the coronation of Henry VII in 1485. After the Gunpowder Plot of November 5, 1605, one of their duties was to search the vaults of Parliament. Their strength was fixed at 100 by Charles II in 1669, by which time they had already acquired their nickname, "Beefeaters." Still wearing the scarlet tunic of Tudor times, they are now a ceremonial body and include the Yeomen Warders of the Tower of London.

YEOVIL, municipal borough, Somerset, England. There was probably a Roman settlement hereabouts: certainly Yeovil is mentioned in the Domesday Book. Set amid rich farm land, it was an important market when England's prosperity was based on wool. Yeovil has long been noted for glovemaking, and today there are also light industries. (For population, see England map in Atlas.)

YEREVAN, or Erivan, city, u.s.s.r., capital of the Armenian Soviet Socialist Republic; in the eastern extension of the Armenian Range; on the Zanga Tributary of the Araks River; 33 miles NNE of Mount Ararat and 110 miles s of Tiflis. Yerevan is a railroad, highway, and airline center. It receives much of the power generated by the Armenian Zanga hydroelectric system. Aluminum, synthetic rubber, chemicals, leather, canned meat and fruits, textiles, and tobacco products are manufactured. Apricots, grapes, cotton, and pomegranates are grown in the area, and the wine and cognac industry dates from 1000 B.C. Yerevan is the cultural center of the Armenian Republic and has a university, various colleges and institutes, a public library, theaters, and a conservatory.

Yerevan is one of the oldest cities in the u.s.s.r. Under the Persians, after the downfall of Tamerlane's empire in the fifteenth century, it became the capital of Armenia. Between then and 1827, when it was conquered by the Russians, it changed hands often in struggles between the Persians and the Turks. In 1920 it was made capital of the Armenian Soviet Socialist Republic. Yerevan is undergoing intensive industrialization and seems sure to become a major industrial center of the Transcaucasians. (For population, see u.s.s.r. map in Atlas.)

YERKES, CHARLES TYSON, 1837–1905, u.s. financier, born in Philadelphia. Brilliant but unscrupulous as a manipulator of stock and bond markets, city transit systems, and city and state legislatures, he is most memorable for his gift to the University of Chicago of an astronomical observatory, in 1892. After serving 7 months in Pennsylvania on a conviction of technical embezzlement, he reorganized the city transit system in Chicago and in 1900 helped to build the subways in London.

YERKES, ROBERT MEARNS, 1876–1956, u.s. psychobiologist, born in Breadysville, Pa. He became professor of psychology at Yale in 1924, following other teaching, organization of psychological testing for the army in World War I, and service as chairman of the research information service of the National Research Council. He was named professor of psychobiology in 1929, in recognition of his interest in comparative psychology. He organized the Yale Laboratories of Primate Biology at Orange Park, Fla., in the same year, for the study of the mentality of anthropoid apes, and remained its director until 1941. It was renamed the Yerkes Laboratories in his honor in 1942. He recorded his observations in *Chimpanzees: A Laboratory Colony* (1943).

YERKES OBSERVATORY, a department of the University of Chicago, located at Williams Bay, Wisconsin, on the northern shore of Lake Geneva. The observatory houses the world's largest refracting telescope, which has a 40-inch objective lens and a focal length of 62 feet. The observatory also has a 24-inch reflector. Yerkes Observatory was a gift from Charles T. Yerkes and was officially dedicated on Oct. 21, 1897. Since then a number of attempts to build larger refracting telescopes have failed. During this time the 40-inch telescope has been used practically without interruption—on clear nights for the study of the stars, and on many clear days for the study of the sun. See TELESCOPE.

YEVPATORIYA, or Evpatoriya, city, u.s.s.r., s Ukrainian Soviet Socialist Republic, in the Crimean Region; 41 miles NW of Sevastopol. Situated on the Black Sea, the city is a fishing center and a popular resort. Meat packing and the production of salt, flour, and clothing are the main industries. Yevpatoriya was founded in the first century and named for the Pontian king Mithridates VI Eupator. The city came under Turkish control in 1475 and under Russian control with the annexation of the Crimea in 1783.

YEVTUSHENKO, YEVGENY ALEKSANDRO-VICH, 1933–   , Russian poet, generally regarded as the spokesman for the post-Stalinist literary generation. His first book of poems was published in 1952. Thereafter, his poems attacking bureaucracy and hypocrisy in Soviet life gained international popularity, as well as reprimands from orthodox Soviet critics. A collection of his verse in English translation (*Yevtushenko: Selected Poems*) appeared in

TASS FROM SOVFOTO
Yevgeny Yevtushenko

1962, followed by *A Precocious Autobiography* (1963), *Winter Station* (1965), and *Brask Station and Other New Poems* (1967).

YEW, a woody plant in the genus *Taxus*, family Taxaceae. Usually a spreading shrub, the yew sometimes grows to tree size. It is related to the coniferae, but instead of cones it bears solitary terminal pistillate flowers that develop into hard seeds surrounded by scarlet fleshy disks, or arils, known as berries. The staminate flowers may be borne on the same plant or on separate ones. The evergreen leaves are two-ranked, linear, dark green above and pale beneath. The bark is reddish and flaky. Because it grows slowly, the yew is not often used as a tree. Generally it is planted in hedges, and in old-fashioned topiary gardens it may be clipped into fantastic shapes. The heavy, tough, reddish wood is used in cabinetmaking. Before the invention of firearms it was much prized for bows because of its resiliency.

The yew is distributed throughout the northern hemisphere. The seven species are sometimes considered geographical varieties. Among them are *T. baccata*, the English yew; *T. cuspidata*, the Japanese yew; and *T. canadensis*, or ground hemlock, and *T. brevifolia*, the western yew, both American species. Hybrids and new varieties appear frequently.

JESSE LUNGER FROM NATIONAL AUDUBON SOCIETY
Japanese Yew

YEZD, or Yazd, city, central Iran, in Isfahan Province, 410 miles SE of Tehran. The city is a silk-weaving center and is noted for its silk and cotton textiles. Among its buildings are a mosque and a fort dating from the twelfth century. Yezd has been a Zoroastrian center since the Muslim conquest of

Persia, when it became a haven for persecuted followers of that religion. The city was the capital of the former province of Yezd. (For population, see Near East map in Atlas.)

YGGDRASIL, in Norse mythology, the world tree, an ash, binding the heavens, the earth, and the underworld and symbolizing existence. Its three roots extend to Asgard, the dwelling place of the gods, to Niflheim, the region of mist, ice, and snow, and to Hela, the realm of death. A dragon gnaws at its roots, an eagle sits at its summit, and between the two runs a squirrel sowing strife. A life-giving honeydew falls on the earth from its branches.

YIDDISH LANGUAGE AND LITERATURE.

The origins of Yiddish language preceded the beginnings of Yiddish literature by a few hundred years. Development of the literature was hampered by the fact that Yiddish, the vernacular, had to compete with Hebrew, the language of prayer, scholarship, and the Bible. The spoken language, on the other hand, was born of necessity and developed out of the daily experience of the people.

Yiddish language began about the eleventh century among Jewish emigrants from northern France who had settled in Germany. In adapting the local dialects, they imposed their own speech patterns and inflections. Thus, a language was formed that had overtones of Hebrew, Aramaic, and old French. When these Jews moved to other parts of the globe, Yiddish went with them; and although it was always influenced by other languages, it never lost its essential German quality. It remained a spoken language, however, until about the thirteenth century, when it first appeared in written form.

Early Yiddish literature emerged as a purely secular medium of entertainment, especially to the uneducated and to women. It was confined to stories, fables, and fairy tales patterned on the folklore and heroic epics of Europe. Rabbinic disapproval of its wholly secular nature led to the writing of didactic works, stories of holy men, devotional treatises, prayers, and pious admonitions. In the sixteenth century the *Tseno-Ureno* ("Go Out and See"), by the Pole Jacob ben Isaac Ashkenazi (1550?–1628), was so great a success that it virtually eclipsed all previous Yiddish writing. Addressed to women, the *Tseno-Ureno* was a midrashic translation of the Five Books of Moses (the Pentateuch) and came to be known as "The Women's Pentateuch." Even today, it exerts a deep and lasting influence on Jewish community and family life. An early romantic work, the *Bovo Bukh*, was written by Elyah Levita (1469–1549). The seventeenth century saw the production of Yiddish prayer books and poetry, particularly the historical epic form.

After a period of decline in the early eighteenth century, Yiddish literature and language came under attack from the *Maskilim*, proponents of the *Haskalah* (Enlightenment). The Maskilim urged the rejection of Yiddish and the use of the language of the land. However, in order to make themselves understood, they were forced to write in Yiddish. Thus they used a language based on spoken Yiddish and as a result provided a transition from the old Germanic language of the past to modern Yiddish literature.

The beginning of the nineteenth century saw an emergence of new forms and attitudes. Works of social satire and message began to appear. Isaac Baer Levinsohn (1788–1860), founder of the Haskalah movement in Russia, attacked injustice to the poor in *Hefker Velt* ("Heedless World"). Israel Axenfeld (1787–1866), Solomon Ettinger (1800–1856), and Isaac Meir Dick (1814–93) wrote exclusively in Yiddish and did much to refine and broaden the language.

The major figure in late nineteenth-century literature was Mendele Mocher Seforim, pseudonym of Sholen Jacob Abramovitch (1836?–1917). He was the center of the literary world, and all others since have either followed or opposed him. The first to create a real intimacy between author and reader, he presented, with gentleness and humor, the minutiae of Jewish life and philosophy. His works include *The Little Man, The Wishing Ring, Fishke the Lame,* and *The Travels of Benjamin the Third.* Among the modern Yiddish writers who wrote in the tradition of Mendele were I. L. Peretz (1852?–1915) and Sholem Aleichem, pseudonym of Solomon Rabinowitz (1859–1916). Both wrote numerous short, widely popular stories and novels that strongly influenced Jewish life of the twentieth century. Sholem Asch (1880–1957) is the most popular of modern Yiddish writers. He began his career with stories of Jewish community life in Poland and published his most significant work, *Moses,* in 1951. Shmuel Yosef Agnon, a 1966 winner of the Nobel prize for literature, wrote a number of his early works in Yiddish.

Except for early Purim plays and occasional works of the sixteenth and seventeenth centuries, Yiddish theater did not emerge as an art form until the late nineteenth century. Within 50 years it had reached its peak in the United States. In the early decades of the twentieth century, many Yiddish plays were produced in New York City, and Yiddish dramatists, actors, and comedians were well known and well loved.

Yiddish periodicals and newspapers flourish in several metropolitan centers today, and original works on art and the sciences continue to increase in number. Louis Finkelstein

YIN AND YANG, in Chinese thought, the polar principles ingredient in everything real, and in Reality itself considered as a unity. Thus yang is masculine, yin feminine; yang light, yin dark; yang sun, yin moon; yang outgoing, yin intaking. Every basic opposition discernible in nature or in spirit is divisible as yin or yang, and there is nothing in spirit or in nature that is not so divided. Nothing exists unrelated to its correlative opposite. The nature of things requires that Reality be regarded as a unity-in-difference. The world is once and always one and many; the "multiverse" is now and forever a universe. Thus, it must be noted, neither yin nor yang exists without the other, except, of course, as an abstraction. Robert Whittemore

YINGKOW, city, China, sw Liaoning Province, in Manchuria, on Liaotung Bay near the mouth of the Liao River, 100 miles sw of Mukden. The city is the trade center for the agricultural produce of the densely populated Liao Valley. Yingkow became the principal Liao River port and Manchuria's leading seaport in 1836, after silt accumulation made the original Liao port, Newchang, unusable. By the turn of the century, however, railroads had stimulated the growth of Talien, making it the chief Manchurian trade outlet. As a seaport, Yingkow is handicapped by navigational obstructions such as sand bars, a shallow access channel, and a harbor frozen 3 or 4 months of the year. (For population, see China map in Atlas.)

YLANG-YLANG, an essential oil steam-distilled from the flowers of a tree, *Cananga odorata,* that grows both wild and cultivated from India to the Philippines. The oil is used in expensive perfumes, especially oriental odors.

YMIR, in Norse mythology, the primeval giant, personifying chaos, who sprang from the melting ice in Ginnungagap, the primeval abyss. He was slain by Odin and his brothers, who fashioned the heavens from his skull, the earth from his flesh, and the seas from his blood.

YOAKUM, city, SE Texas, in De Witt and Lavaca counties; on the Southern Pacific Railroad and U.S. highway 77; about 98 miles E of San Antonio. The area specializes in the growing of tomatoes. Although chiefly a vegetable shipping point, the processing of wood and cottonseed oil are important, and a tannery, a cannery, a creamery, and a hatchery are in the city. Yoakum was founded in 1887 and named for a Texas historian. Pop. (1960) 5,761.

YOGA, a Hindu philosophical system that has as its end the unification (Sanskrit *yoga*, union) of the soul with the Supreme Spirit through a series of mental and ascetic disciplines, is a modification of the Sankhya school of Brahmanism. Yoga doctrines were first expounded in the *Aphorisms* of Patanjali, who lived in the second century, B.C. Yoga teaches that the soul is inhibited by the illusion of self and by the demands of the flesh, and must be liberated from the sensory world. For this purpose an individual pursues a course of meditation, concentration, and physical exercise that will overcome some of the limitations to his capacity for liberation. In any particular incarnation one's capacity for liberation is determined by the degree of liberation achieved in his previous incarnation, and complete liberation, or nirvana, is not ordinarily achieved until the soul has passed through a number of incarnations. The eight stages leading to liberation are yama (self control), niyama (religious observances), asana (appropriate postures), pranayama (breath regulation), pratyahara (control of the senses), dharana (making the mind firm), dhyana (meditation), and samadhi (profound contemplation). The yogi, in the course of his progress, is said to acquire extraordinary powers, including those of telepathy and levitation, but the demonstration of these powers is not encouraged. Seven distinct yoga systems may be distinguished as follows: (1) Hatha Yoga, which emphasizes the physical and mental exercises by which the body is brought under control; (2) Bhakti Yoga, a system of prayers and devotions; (3) Mantra Yoga, which concenrates on mystic iteration of the name of Krishna; (4) Karma Yoga, a practical philosophy of service and duty for those who cannot retire from the world; (5) Inana Yoga, a synthesis of faith and reason; (6) Raja Yoga, emphasizing mental concentration; and (7) Laya-Kriya Yoga, which is concerned with sexual union as a symbol of the union of the soul with the Supreme Spirit.

YOGHURT, a fermented milk product containing a high percentage of lactic acid. Similar in appearance and taste to sour cream, yoghurt has a very soft curd, contains little if any alcohol, and is believed by some to be of special value in the prevention and treatment of various intestinal disorders; most medical specialists in such disorders reject this belief in the special virtues of yoghurt, but acknowledge its nutritional value. Yoghurt made from the milk of cows, goats, and other animals is a popular food in the Balkans, Turkey, and Iran. It is produced commercially in the United States from pasteurized cow's milk and is distributed under various trade names. Artificially flavored yoghurt (chocolate, strawberry, and the like) is produced for those who dislike the taste of yoghurt itself, but want to eat it anyway, for health or other reasons.

YOHO NATIONAL PARK, Canada, in SE British Columbia, lying along the Continental Divide of the Canadian Rockies, on the border between Alberta and British Columbia, and adjoining the W limits of the Banff National Park and the Kootenay National Park. The area is 506 square miles. The park is said to take its name from an Indian expression *yoho*, meaning it is wonderful. The park is divided into two parts by the Kicking Horse River, which flows in a southwesterly direction through the Selkirk Mountains. Yoho is a summer sports center. Among the principal scenic points are Takakkan Falls, Twin Falls, the natural bridge over Kicking Horse River,

and Emerald, Wapta, and O'Hara lakes. The park was established, 1886.

YOKKAICHI, city, Japan, SE Honshu, Mie Prefecture, on the NW shore of Ise Bay; 47 miles E of Kyōto. The city is a major industrial center. Its chief commercial products are cotton and silk textiles, and pottery. Major imports are wool, raw cotton, oilseeds, soybeans, beancake, peanuts, and corn. Major exports are canned salmon, vegetable oils, yarns, twines and cordage, textiles, cement, pottery, enameled ware, and oil cake. The city suffered extensive damage during bombings in World War II. Pop. (1959 est.) 170,000.

YOKOHAMA, port city, Japan, central Honshu Island; on the W coast of Tokyo Bay, 17 miles S of Tokyo. It is the fifth largest Japanese city, and the capital of Kanagawa Prefecture. Its administrative area of 155 square miles is divided into 10 wards: Hodogaya, Isogo, Kanagawa, Kanazawa, Kōhoku, Minami, Naka, Niski, Totsuka and Tsurumi. Population (1960) 1,182,209.

The hilly interior of Yokohama terminates in a terrace 125 to 150 feet high overlooking Tokyo Bay. Three rivers—the Tsurumi, the Katabira, and the Ōoka—cut through the terrace and form a small compound delta along the coast. The city's port, industrial and commercial sections are in these lowlands, called Yamashita, while the residential sections are in the uplands, the Yamanote. Homes of the many foreign residents are concentrated on the southern heights, The Bluff, so-called. Steeply inclined streets link lower and upper Yokohama.

Summers in Yokohama are hot and humid, winters cold and rather dry. Average monthly temperatures range from 78°F in August to 37°F in January. Much of the 64″ average annual rainfall comes in June and July or in September. Light snowfalls are common in January and February.

Yokohama is the southern anchor of the Keihin (Tokyo-Yokohama) industrial belt which stretches along the water front northward to Tokyo. Largely built upon reclaimed land, the belt is one of Japan's two largest concentrations of large-scale heavy industry. Shipbuilding, oil refining, and the manufacture of automobiles, automotive and electrical equipment, steel, and chemicals are among Yokohama's industrial specialties.

The city's major industrial asset is its fine natural harbor, which is free of silting and protected on the south by the headlands of Hommoku Peninsula. The harbor is protected by an outer and inner concrete breakwater, with water depth varying from 25 to 45 feet. Ships may discharge cargo by lighter, or may berth at one of the eight large wharves. Shore installations include a full set of cargo-handling and warehousing facilities and specialized lumber and fuel storage areas. Serving Tokyo and central and northern Honshu, Yokohama is Japan's leading port for such imports as foodstuffs, petroleum, wool, cotton and other industrial raw materials; Yokohama is second to Kobe in exports, however, largely because Keihin's industrial output is for domestic rather than foreign consumption.

Yokohama has excellent rail and highway connections with Tokyo, with Yokosuka, the naval base city which lies immediately to the south, and with other points throughout Japan. Fast, frequent electric train service is available from Sakuragi-chō Station and Yokohama Central Station. A network of wide paved city streets has a heavy vehicular traffic. Canals that crisscross the lowlands provide easy water links with bayside industrial tracts.

Yokohama is administered by an elected major and city assembly. It has first-class water, electric, and gas service, sanitation controls, and police and fire protection. Its large public school system includes a municipal university. Among the many scenic open areas are Yamashita Park, a long esplanade laid out along the Bund, the central waterfront district;

Sankei-en, a privately developed garden of 47 acres; Sugita Gardens, noted for their spring apricot blossoms; and Hodogaya and Negishi golf courses.

History. In the seventeenth century, Yokohama was a fishing village. It experienced its initial growth after being opened to foreign trade, 1859. Developed as the outpost for Tokyo, it was linked to the capital by telegraph, 1869, and by rail, 1872. Port improvements and its function as the chief raw silk collection and export center helped it attain commercial prominence. Almost totally destroyed by the great earthquake-fire of September 1, 1923, Yokohama was soon rebuilt and by 1925 had a population of 405,000. During the 1930's accelerated industrialization was the basis for continued city growth, but all was temporarily reduced to shambles by Allied air bombing during World War II, May-July, 1945. JOHN D. EYRE

YOKOSUKA, city, E coast of central Honshu, Kanagawa Prefecture, SW side of Tokyo Bay; about 30 miles S of Tokyo. Yokosuka's primary industries are fishing and whaling, knitting, and the manufacturing of toys and kitchenware. Yokosuka is the oldest of Japan's primary naval bases. The capacious harbor has a narrow entrance, and it is almost surrounded by hills, leaving it unaffected by all but the stormiest weather.

Among the interesting sights in the vicinity is the old battleship *Mikasa*, which was Admiral Togo's flagship in the Russo-Japanese War (1904–5). Kurihama Beach near Yokosuka is the point where Commodore Perry landed, 1853, with the letter from the U.S. President to the emperor that resulted in Japan's being opened to international trade. Yokosuka's phenomenal rise to a great city paralleled that of Yokohama; and its growth was interwoven with the nation's naval expansion. (For population, see Japan map in Atlas.)

YONGE, CHARLOTTE MARY, 1823–1901, English novelist, one of the most prolific writers of the Victorian era. Most of her books reflect her High Church inclinations and morality. Her works include *The Heir of Redclyffe* (1853), *The Daisy Chain* (1856), *The Dove in the Eagle's Nest* (1866) and *The Caged Lion* (1870). She also wrote numerous school books and biographies.

YONKERS, city, SE New York, in Westchester County; on the E bank of the Hudson River facing the Palisades; N of New York City. Yonkers is both an industrial and residential suburb of New York City. It has many important factories producing chemicals and drugs, iron and steel products, elevators and other machinery products, plastic equipment, plumbing supplies, paper boxes, and stationery. The local clothing industry manufactures hats, gloves, knitwear, textiles, needlework items, coats, uniforms, and dresses. Yonkers is the site of St. Joseph's Seminary, and the Boyce Thompson Institute for Plant Research, where scientific studies are made of plant growth. Yonkers Raceway is a noted harness racing track.

Yonkers is built on the site of an Indian village Nappeckamack, which was a part of a land purchase made by the Dutch West Indies Company, 1639. After the British took over the region, 1664, the land came into the possession of Frederick H. Philipse, who established mills, and rented his land to tenants; in 1779 the estate was confiscated by the new government of the United States. The village of Yonkers began as a farm trading center; it was incorporated, 1855. Its industrial future was shaped, in part, by the establishment of the Elisha G. Otis Elevator Works, 1854, the David Saunders Machine Shop, 1857, and the Alexander Smith Carpet Mill, 1865. The city grew as its industries attracted many immigrants. Excellent rail and highway transportation supplanted the old river traffic. (For population, see New York map in Atlas.)

YONNE, department, N central France; bounded on the NW by Seine-et-Marne, NE by Aube, E by Côte-d'Or, S by Nièvre, and W by Loiret. The department's area is 2,892 square miles. The Yonne River, a tributary of the Seine River, flows through the department, from southeast to northwest draining most of the department. Agriculture, forestry, mining, quarrying, vine growing, sugar refining, and glassmaking are leading economic activities. The capital is Auxerre. (For population, see table in France article.)

YORCK VON WARTENBURG, COUNT HANS DAVID LUDWIG, 1759–1830, Prussian military figure, was born in Potsdam. He entered the Prussian army, 1772, was dismissed for disobedience, 1779, and served as a soldier of fortune with other national armies. He returned to Prussia, 1785, and was reinstated in the Prussian army, 1786. He played a successful part in the Battle of Jena, 1805, the war against France, 1806, and became second in command of a Prussian contingent of Napoleon I's army in the Russian War of 1812. Having become convinced that the French army was doomed, he neutralized his troops under the terms of the Convention of Tauroggen (1812); this action nearly led to his court-martial, but when Prussia deserted Napoleon I's cause and allied itself with Russia he was made a field marshal, 1821, and given a Prussian estate by King Frederick William III.   ALFRED DE GRAZIA

YORITOMO, 1147–99, Japanese shogun, or military dictator, was the son of the Minamoto clan warrior Yoshitomo, who was killed in battle with the Taira clan (1160). Yoritomo avenged his father's death by annihilating the Taira clan (1185), with the help of his brother Yoshitsune (1159–89). In 1192 he became the first Japanese shogun, established his capital at Kamakura, and set up a feudal system of government which lasted largely intact until the nineteenth century. Yoritomo's rule was marked by encouragement of Zen Buddhism and the warrior code of Bushido, and the institution of numerous civil and military reforms.

YORK, ALVIN CULLUM, 1887–1964, U.S. World War I hero, was born in Pall Mall, Fentress County, Tenn., reared on a mountain farm, and enlisted in the Army, 1917. On Oct. 8, 1918, during the Argonne Battle, York performed what Marshal Ferdinand Foch declared to be "the greatest thing accomplished by any private soldier of all the armies of Europe": he killed 20 or more enemy soldiers, forced the surrender of 132, and captured a hill and 35 machine guns. He received the Congressional Medal of Honor from the U.S. government and the French Croix de Guerre. After the war York returned to his native state, where he was given a farm purchased by popular subscription. A movie, *Sergeant York* (1941), was made of his life.

YORK, CARDINAL, 1725–1807, last legitimate descendant of the House of Stuart in the male line, the second son of James Francis Edward, the Old Pretender, was born Henry Benedict Maria Clement Stuart in Rome. Supporters of the Stuart claims to the English throne regarded him as the rightful Duke of York and thus third in line for the throne. Henry left France, where the Stuarts lived in exile, to help his brother Charles Edward, the Young Pretender (Bonnie Prince Charlie), in an unsuccessful attempt to regain the throne for the Stuarts, 1745. He then went to Rome, took Holy Orders, and was created a cardinal, 1747. He returned to France, and upon the death of Charles Edward, 1788, called himself King Henry IX of England. Forced to flee France during the French Revolution, he went to Venice with his only remaining assets—the crown jewels of England, which the Stuarts had taken with them into exile. After he was granted a pension by the crown he bequeathed the jewels to the Prince of Wales (later King George IV).

YORK, city, S Pennsylvania, seat of York County; on Codorus Creek, the Maryland and Pennsylvania, the Pennsylvania, and the Western Maryland railroads, and U.S. highways 30 and 111; 23 miles SSE of Harrisburg. York's chief manufactured products are refrigerating and air-conditioning equipment, hydraulic turbines, bank safes and vaults, building materials, wall and roofing paper, tire chains, bakers machinery, and pretzels. York was founded, 1741, by Thomas Cookson, a land surveyor for the Penn family, and was the first Pennsylvania town founded west of the Susquehanna River. It was incorporated as a borough, 1787, and chartered as a city, 1887. The Continental Congress met at the York Colonial Courthouse, 1777–78, while the British occupied Philadelphia. Pop. (1960) 54,504.

YORK, city, NE England, seat of Yorkshire; on the River Ouse, in the Vale of York; 190 miles NNW of London. The city of York is a county borough and forms an administrative unit separate from Yorkshire. York is the seat of an Anglican archbishop, who bears the title of Primate of England, and has ecclesiastical control of the northern section of the country. The city is an important railway junction. Glass, chocolate, leather goods, fertilizers, railroad cars, and machine goods are manufactured. The old city has narrow, twisting streets, and many historic buildings though modern suburbs extend far beyond the medieval wall, which still stands, together with four gateways, or Bars. The Cathedral of St. Peter, known as York Minster, is the largest and one of the finest medieval cathedrals in England. The Minster, founded in the seventh century, is noted for its stained-glass windows. York Castle was founded by William the Conqueror. The city was the capital of the ancient tribe of Brigantes, and was known as Caer Ebrauc, It was the capital of Britain during the Roman occupation, and the center of Roman military operations, The Romans called the city Eboracum. The Danes gave the city the name of Jorvik, from which the present name is derived. In the eighth century York was one of the major European centers of learning, and during the same period, the religious center of the country. Pop. (1951) 105,336.

YORK, English royal house established, 1385, by the creation of the dukedom of York for Edmund Langley, son of Edward III. The first Duke of York to pretend to the English throne was Richard, Edmund's grandson (see YORK, DUKES OF). His claim. which led to the Wars of the Roses, was based on his descent from Edward III on both paternal and maternal sides, and was advanced by popular support for his opposition to the policies of Margaret of Anjou. consort of the weakling Henry VI, of the rival house of Lancaster. Richard was killed in battle, 1460, but two months later his eldest son was proclaimed King Edward IV. Richard's second son, denying the legitimacy of his brother's children, overthrew Edward V, 1483, and became Richard III. This cloud on the succession made it possible for the Lancastrian Earl of Richmond, Henry Tudor, to claim the throne. He received support for his claim by promising to marry Elizabeth, daughter of Edward IV, and upon Richard's death in battle, 1485, was proclaimed Henry VII, becoming the first of the Tudor monarchs. He united the Houses of York and Lancaster by marrying Elizabeth, 1486. Although the dynastic history of the House of York was thus ended, the title Duke of York was traditionally bestowed upon the second son of ruling sovereigns of England.

YORK, BATTLE OF, a War of 1812 engagement, in which 1,600 U.S. troops captured York (later Toronto), the capital of Upper Canada (later Ontario), Apr. 27, 1813. In early Spring, 1813, a U.S. military and naval expedition, commanded by Maj. Gen. Henry Dearborn, invaded Canada. On April 27 a U.S. assault force, under Brig. Gen. Zebulon M. Pike, and supported by a Great Lakes fleet under Comm. Isaac Chauncey, overcame the York garrison of 750 British regulars and 100 Indians, under Maj. Gen. Roger H. Sheaffe. As the attackers entered the town, a powder magazine exploded, killing about 100 of them, including Pike, and 40 British. The town was captured, looted, and the public buildings were set afire. Total U.S. losses were about 320 killed and wounded; British losses were 90 killed, about 200 wounded, and 300 prisoners. The British later claimed that the burning of York justified their setting fire to Washington, D.C., Aug. 24, 1814.

YORK, DUKES OF, bearers of a title that was first conferred upon Edmund of Langley (1341–1402), fifth son of Edward III. Having gained the favor of King Richard II during the invasion of Scotland, 1385, Edmund was created Duke of York, and as such subsequently acted upon several occasions as regent of England while the king was absent from the country. During one of these absences, 1399, England was invaded by Henry of Lancaster (later Henry IV). Unable to rally his forces in defense of the king's holdings, Edmund surrendered and retired from public life. See LANCASTER.

The Second Duke of York, Edward Plantagenet (1373-1415), elder son of Edmund of Langley, was created Earl of Rutland, 1390, and became Duke of York upon his father's death. He was a close adviser of Richard II, who made him Earl of Cork during an invasion of Ireland, 1394, and Duke of Albemarle after the death, 1397, of Richard's enemy Thomas of Woodstock, duke of Gloucester. Edward deserted Richard during the 1399 invasion of Ireland and offered his services to Henry of Lancaster, but was denounced as the murderer of Gloucester, reduced to the rank of Earl of Rutland, and stripped of his vast holdings. He later was restored in the royal favor, however, and became privy councilor, 1405, and regained his former titles and lands. He was killed fighting for Henry V at the battle of Agincourt.

The Third Duke of York, Richard (1411–60), was the son of Richard, earl of Cambridge, and a direct descendant of Edward III through both paternal and maternal lines. He became Duke of York, 1415, upon the death of his uncle, Edward Plantagenet, and was well liked by both Henry V and Henry VI. The death of Henry of Gloucester, 1447, placed Richard in direct line for the throne, and during the illness of Henry VI, 1453, York became protector of the crown. But the birth of a Prince of Wales, 1453, and the recovery of King Henry, 1454, put an end to York's hopes for legal succession to the throne, and there followed years of intrigue and plots, culminating in York's march on London, September, 1460, when he formally asserted his claim to the crown before Parliament. He was pronounced heir apparent, to succeed after Henry's death, but was lured into battle by the Lancastrian forces and was defeated and slain at Wakefield December, 1460 (see WARS OF THE ROSES). He was the last hereditary duke, but the title was later to be traditionally conferred upon the second son of the reigning monarch. Richard was survived by three sons: George, duke of Clarence; Edward, later Edward IV; and Richard, later Richard III.

Richard (1472-83) second son of Edward IV, was the first to be created Duke of York while yet an infant. He was the brother of the boy king, Edward V, who reigned for only two months. Richard and his brother were declared illegitimate by their uncle, who was then Duke of Gloucester and later became Richard III. Richard had the boys confined to the Tower of London and for two decades it was not generally known whether they were alive or dead until Sir Thomas More purported to prove that they had been murdered by order of Richard III.

Among others who bore the title Duke of York were Charles I; James II of England; Frederick Augustus (1763–1827), second son of George III; George V; and George VI.

YORKSHIRE, county, NE England, bounded by Durham on the N, the North Sea on the E, Lincolnshire, Nottinghamshire, Derbyshire, and Cheshire on the S, Lancashire on the W, and Westmorland on the NW; area 6,090 sq. mi.; pop. (1951) 4,516,362. For administrative purposes the county is divided into three sections: North Riding, East Riding, and West Riding, the term Riding being a derivation of "thirding" or "thriding," a third part. The Pennine Chain trends from north to south through the western section of the county, and reaches a maximum elevation of 2,591 feet above sea level in Mickle Fell in the extreme northwest. The highland is dissected by northeast-southwest trending valleys, known as dales, which open into the broad plain of the Vale of York. In the northeast is the uplifted plateau of the Yorkshire Moors, separated from the chalk Wolds on the south by the Vale of Pickering. The River Ouse with its tributaries drains most of the county, and flows into the Humber Estuary in the southeast. The North and East Ridings are mainly agricultural, and have few large towns. Sheep grazing is common in the highlands, and in the valleys wheat, barley, fodder grasses, turnips, and potatoes are the chief crops, and dairy farming is important. The West Riding lies on a coal field, and is a major industrial region. This area has been a center of the English woollen industry for centuries, though its manufacturing industry is now more diversified. Iron and steel, machinery, electrical apparatus, and numerous consumer goods are manufactured in such centers as Leeds, Bradford, Huddersfield, and Sheffield. Hull, on the Humber Estuary, is the chief port, and a center for shipbuilding and fishing. The city of York is the county seat.

FRASIE STUDIO

The toy Yorkshire Terrier made his first appearance at an English bench show in 1861, and in the United States in 1880. He is characterized by his long, steel-blue coat.

YORKSHIRE TERRIER, a popular toy dog that is noted for his long, silky coat. A cross between the Skye and other terriers, the Yorkshire was first bred in Lancashire and Yorkshire, England, for his skill as a rat catcher in the grist mills. The Yorkshire terrier was first presented at a bench show in England in 1861, and imported to the United States about 1880. Until 1886 the Yorkshire was classed among the Scottish terriers, but in that year the English Kennel Club recognized it as a distinct breed. Since late Victorian times the Yorkshire has been allowed to forego rat catching to become a pet in England. The long, steel blue coat hangs evenly on each side of the body, which is compact, upright, and trim. These toys are born with a black body that turns a golden tan on maturity. They stand about eight inches high at the shoulders, and weigh about five pounds.

YORKTON, city, Canada, SE Saskatchewan; on the Canadian Pacific and the Canadian National railways; about 110 miles NE of Regina. Because of its position on the railway extending to Hudson Bay, Yorkton has become an important distributing center for both eastern Saskatchewan and northern Manitoba. The city has numerous wholesale warehouses,

an oil refinery, tanneries, creameries, and hatcheries; lumber and agricultural implements are manufactured. Yorkton was founded in the 1880's by settlers from York County, Ontario. The city is the site of St. Joseph College. Pop. (1956) 8,256.

YORKTOWN, SIEGE OF, the last significant military operation of the American Revolution, in which Continental and French armies and a French fleet besieged and captured the British army of Gen. Charles Cornwallis at Yorktown, Va., Sept. 28-Oct. 19, 1781 (see REVOLUTIONARY WAR, *Victory and Independence*). After the indecisive Battle of Guilford Court House, Mar. 15, 1781, Cornwallis marched northward from the Carolinas to Virginia. In May he pursued a force of continentals under Gen. Marie Joseph, marquis de Lafayette, but when the latter was reinforced by Gen. Anthony Wayne and his 1,000 infantry and six guns June 10, Cornwallis turned toward the Atlantic Coast to await instructions from Gen. Henry Clinton in New York. Clinton ordered Cornwallis to fortify Old Point Comfort and, if advisable, Yorktown, but Cornwallis neglected the former, which he deemed unsuitable. Meanwhile, Gen. George Washington and Gen. Jean Baptiste Donatien de Vimeur, comte de Rochambeau, were at Dobbs Ferry, N.Y., menacing New York City and awaiting the arrival of the French fleet of Adm. Comte François Joseph Paul de Grasse. Hoping to co-operate with Grasse in an attack upon Cornwallis, Washington set out for Virginia with about 4,000 French and 2,000 Continentals, August 19, and reached Williamsburg, September 26, where he united his forces with those of Lafayette. The French fleet, in the meantime, had turned back the British fleet of Adm. Thomas Graves off Hampton Road, September 5, and then held Chesapeake Bay to prevent British reinforcements. Washington took up a position before Yorktown, September 28, and the following night Cornwallis abandoned his outer works before the town.

Siege operations, directed by Gen. (Baron) Friedrich von Steuben, began with a bombardment, October 9. Two outer redoubts that impeded extension of rebel lines to the York River were taken, October 14, and a British counterattack was repulsed, October 15. Cornwallis attempted to cross the York River to Gloucester, October 16, but was prevented by a storm. Abandoning hope of reinforcements from New York, Cornwallis opened surrender negotiations with the Allies on the morning of October 17; the formal surrender was concluded on the afternoon of October 19. Either ill or sulking, Cornwallis was not present, and Gen. Charles O'Hara, an aide, surrendered Cornwallis' sword to Gen. Benjamin Lincoln, Washington's second in command, who two years before had surrendered Charleston, S.C. to the British. The capture of these forces practically ended the war, although more than a year elapsed before even a preliminary treaty of peace was concluded.

YORKTOWN NATIONAL CEMETERY, SE Virginia, at Yorktown; on the S bank of the York River. The cemetery, covering an area of 2.9 acres, was established, 1866. It contains the graves of 2,204 soldiers, 1,446 of which are unidentified, who fell on the Civil War battlefields in the vicinity.

YORUBA, a Negroid people of western Africa, occupying the country between Dahomey and the Niger, and parts of the lower Niger and Niger Delta. The old Yoruba kingdom was broken up, 1820, by an invasion of the Moslem Fulahs. Under influence of Islamic institutions in the north and Christian missionaries in the south, the Yoruba adopted many manners and ways of European and Middle Eastern civilization. The most famous Yoruba city is Abeokuta, Nigeria.

YOSEMITE NATIONAL PARK, California, in the Sierra Nevada, about 150 miles E of San Francisco, a 1,189-square-mile tract of mountainous country notable for the two deep valleys that cross it and for the numerous waterfalls, glaciers, peaks, and stands of giant sequoia trees. The Yosemite Valley and Mariposa Grove were first set aside as a public trust of the state of California, 1864, in an act signed by Abraham Lincoln; the area was subsequently enlarged and established as a national park, 1890. The northern portion of the park is crossed by the Tuolumne River and its tributaries, the southern portion by the Merced River and its tributaries. The main streams originate high in the mountains and are fed by glaciers, icy streams, and snow fields.

Yosemite Valley is 7 miles long, averages 1 mile in width, and is 4,000 feet above sea level. The valley's distinguishing features are the almost vertical walls, their great height, the small amount of talus at the base, and the number of magnificent falls that occur in so small an area. Its depth below the average marginal upland is from 2,800 to nearly 5,000 feet. The cliffs and domes that form the most prominent features of the walls are solid granite. El Capitan, 7,564 feet, and Half Dome, 8,852 feet, are the most striking in appearance, rising with almost vertical walls from the valley floor. Two falls, Nevada, 594 feet, and Vernal, 317 feet, interrupt the Merced. Upper Yosemite Falls tumbles 1,430 feet; and Lower Yosemite, on Yosemite Creek, completes the drop to the Merced with a 320-foot fall. Ribbon Falls on Ribbon Creek drops 1,612 feet, and Silver Strand Falls on Meadow Brook falls 1,170 feet.

The country surrounding the valley and within the park is rolling and hilly, varying from 8,000 to 10,000 feet above sea level. Notable peaks within the area are Mount Lyell, 13,090 feet, Parson Peak, 12,120 feet, and Kuna Peak, 12,951 feet. The high country is an area of granite peaks, small glaciers, and high meadows, covered with flowers during July and August. The most interesting vegetative cover is the three sequoia groves. Mariposa Grove, near the southern entrance to the park contains some 200 mature trees and many thriving young trees. Grizzly Giant, the oldest tree in the stand, is estimated to be more than 3,000 years old; it has a girth of 96.5 feet and a height of 209 feet. The park is a game refuge. There are many mammals, including bear, deer, squirrel, and chipmunk; reptiles; and about 200 varieties of birds; streams are stocked with trout from the state hatchery.

YOSHIHITO HARUNOMIYA, reign name Taisho, 1879–1926, 123rd emperor of Japan, was born in Tokyo, educated privately, and succeeded his father, Mutsuhito, 1912. Mentally unbalanced, he fortunately did little actual ruling, and his son Hirohito became regent for him, 1921.

YOUNG, BRIGHAM, 1801–77, U.S. Mormon leader and colonizer of Utah, was born in Whitingham, Vt. In 1830, at Mendon, N.Y., he obtained a copy of *The Book of Mormon*, just then published by Joseph Smith, the prophet-leader of Mormonism. He was baptized in the Mormon church, 1832, and visited Smith in Kirtland, Ohio. Thereafter he was a firm believer in Mormon principles and an ardent defender and active evangelist of the faith of Joseph Smith. He had great success in his preaching in the eastern United States and Canada. He was chosen a member of the newly organized Quorum of Twelve, which stood next to the First Presidency of the Church, 1835, headed a very successful mission in England, 1839–41, and became president of the Quorum of Twelve, 1840.

When the Mormons were driven from Missouri, 1839, Young directed their migration to Illinois, where they bought the town of Commerce and changed its name to Nauvoo, 1840. After the murder of Joseph Smith, 1844, the leadership devolved upon Young and the Quorum of Twelve. Driven from Nauvoo, 1846, the Mormons moved westward under Young's leadership until they reached the Great Salt Lake Valley, the vanguard arriving in July, 1847. The Quorum of the First Presidency, with a president

and two counselors, was reorganized with Young as president of the Church. The State of Deseret was organized, 1849, but was renamed the Territory of Utah by the U.S. Congress. Young served as territorial governor under presidential appointment, 1850–58.

Young was a great leader and an organizing genius who left his mark on almost every phase of Mormon life. He introduced irrigation; promoted agriculture; developed natural resources; founded colonies; built temples; encouraged education by establishing many schools (including the University of Deseret—now the University of Utah—and Brigham Young University); promoted the arts; encouraged recreation; organized Zion's Cooperative Mercantile Institution, 1868, the first department store in the United States; and played an important role in the construction of railroads.

Having taught and practiced the principle of polygamy, which had been introduced by Joseph Smith, Young at his death left a number of widows and 56 children. In June, 1950, his statue was placed in Statuary Hall in Washington, D.C. See MORMON; UTAH.   JOSEPH ANDERSON

BIBLIOG.–Frank J. Cannon and George L. Knapp, *Brigham Young and His Mormon Empire* (c. 1913); *Dictionary of American Biography*, Vol. XX (1936); Susa Y. Gates, *Brigham Young, the Mormon Leader and Founder of Salt Lake City* (1936); Milton R. Hunter, *Brigham Young, the Colonizer* (1940); Preston Nibley, *Brigham Young, the Man and His Work* (1936); Clarissa Y. Spencer, *One Who Was Valiant* (1940); Morris R. Werner, *Brigham Young* (1939); Ray B. West, *Kingdom of the Saints: The Story of Brigham Young and the Mormons* (1957); Leah E. D. Widstoe, *Brigham Young, the Man of the Hour* (1947).

YOUNG, CHARLES AUGUSTUS, 1834–1908, U.S. astronomer, was born in Hanover, N.H., and graduated from Dartmouth College. He was professor of natural philosophy and astronomy at Dartmouth, 1866–77, and of astronomy at Princeton, 1877–1905. He was one of the first to use the spectroscope in solar work. In 1869 he discovered the green line in the solar corona; in 1870 he observed the flash spectrum (see Chromosphere) and concluded that the bulk of the absorption producing the sun's absorption spectrum occurred in a thin layer which he called the reversing layer. At the eclipse of 1872 he added 100 chromospheric lines to the 190 then known. He was the first to photograph a prominence, 1870 and was the first to use a grating spectroscope. Among his published works are *The Sun* (1881) and *The Elements of Astronomy* (1890), and *Manual of Astronomy* (1902).
                                        EVERETT I. YOWELL

YOUNG, DENTON TRUE, known as Cy, 1867–1955, U.S. baseball player, a member of the Baseball Hall of Fame from 1937, was born in Gilmore, Ohio. He pitched in the National League for Cleveland, 1890–98, St. Louis 1899–1900, and Boston, 1911; and in the American League for Boston, 1901–08, and Cleveland, 1909–11. He won 510 games.

YOUNG, EDWARD, 1683–1765, English poet and Protestant clergyman, was born in Upham, near Winchester, and studied at Oxford. His tragedy, *The Revenge* (1721), with a plot resembling that of William Shakespeare's *Othello*, was successfully produced at Drury Lane, but his earlier play, *Busiris* (1719), received little attention, and his poems and occasional verse failed to win the patronage that he considered his due as a talented literary divine. Frustrated also in his professional and political ambitions, he finally accepted, 1730, an appointment as rector at Welwyn and lived out his life there devoting himself to the composition of his lugubrious masterpiece, *The Complaint: or, Night Thoughts On Life, Death, and Immortality* (9 vols. 1742–45), a long, didactic work in which the poet exhorts the infidel Lorenzo to reform and to return to the true faith. Despite its slovenly rhyme, excessive rhetoric, and mood of sepulchral gloom, Young's *Complaint* became one of the most popular poems of the eighteenth century in England. In

France, through a prose translation (1769) by Pierre Letourneur (1736–88), it influenced the early development of Romanticism. Among Young's other works are *The Universal Passion* (1725–28), *The Brothers* (1753), and *Resignation* (1762).

YOUNG, OWEN D., 1874–1962, U.S. corporation lawyer and economist, was born in Van Hornesville, N.Y., and studied at St. Lawrence University and Boston University Law School. He began practice in 1896, and in 1913 became counsel for General Electric Company, of which he was chairman of the board, 1922–39, 1942–44. He was chairman of the board of the Radio Corporation of America, 1919–29. Having gained public eminence as an economist by his report for Pres. Warren G. Harding on industrial stabilization, 1922, he was appointed U.S. representative, with Charles G. Dawes, at the 1924 Reparations Conference held in London. As chairman of the 2nd Reparations Conference, 1929, he devised the Young Plan, providing for payment of the German debt by 1988, through the Bank for International Settlements. After World War II Young was an advisor to Pres. Harry S. Truman in matters of foreign aid.

YOUNG, THOMAS, 1773–1829, English physician, physicist, and scholar, was born in Milverton, Somersetshire, and studied medicine in London, Edinburgh, Göttingen, and Cambridge. He began practicing in London, 1799, and was physician to St. George's Hospital, 1811–29. He was professor of natural philosophy at the Royal Institution, 1801–03, and foreign secretary to the Royal Society, 1802–29. He was secretary of the Board of Longitude and superintendent of the *Nautical Almanac*, 1818. He is best known, however, for his researches in optics: he advanced the theory of the accommodation of vision, 1793; discovered the interference of light, thus helping to establish the wave or undulatory theory of light, 1801; and was the first to describe and measure astigmatism in the human eye, 1801. He discovered the theory of capillarity, 1804, independently of Marquis Pierre Simon de Laplace. An eminent Egyptologist, he assisted in translating the inscriptions on the Rosetta Stone. Among his works are *On the Theory of Light and Colour* (1801), *Syllabus of a Course of Lectures* (1802), *Essay on Cohesion of Fluids* (1804), and *Course of Lectures on Natural Philosophy and the Mechanical Arts* (1807).

YOUNGER, COLE, real name Thomas Coleman Younger, 1844–1906, U.S. bandit leader, was born near Lee's Summit, Mo., and at the age of 17 joined William Quantrill's guerrillas in the Border War. His brothers James and possibly Robert were also guerrillas. Shortly after the war the Younger brothers joined with Frank and Jesse James in a series of spectacular bank robberies. After an attempted bank robbery in Northfield, Minn., Sept. 7, 1876, the Younger brothers were captured, tried, and sentenced to life imprisonment. Robert died in prison in 1889; Cole and James were paroled in 1901. James committed suicide a year later. Cole was pardoned in 1903 and returned to Missouri where he lectured on moral subjects and for a time ran a Wild West Show with Frank James. He wrote *The Story of Cole Younger, by Himself* (1903). DON RUSSELL

YOUNGHUSBAND, SIR FRANCIS EDWARD, 1863–1942, British soldier, diplomat, and explorer, was born in Murree, India. He studied at Sandhurst, entered the British army, 1882, and later became a lieutenant colonel, 1908. He explored Manchuria, 1886, returning across Chinese Turkestan to India and discovering the Mustagh Pass, was a British colonial agent, chiefly in India, 1890–1902, and served as British commissioner to Tibet, 1902–04, leading the famous 1903–04 expedition into Lhasa, where he negotiated a British-Tibetan treaty, Sept. 7, 1904. Younghusband lectured at Cambridge, 1905–06, was British resident at Kashmir, 1906–09, was knighted in 1904, and served as president of the Royal Geographical Society, 1919. Among his numerous publications are *The Heart of a Continent* (1898), *India and Tibet* (1912), *Dawn in India* (1930), *Everest: The Challenge* (1936), and *The Sum of Things* (1939).

YOUNG MEN'S CHRISTIAN ASSOCIATION, a voluntary, worldwide organization for the furtherance of the spiritual, social, intellectual, and physical welfare of its members and their communities. Membership is open to all, regardless of race, color, creed, or sex.

International in scope, it is active in over 80 countries and territories of the world, serving five million members. In the United States there are nearly two thousand YMCA's with four million members, one fourth of whom are women and girls. Members range in age from young children to retired adults, and they represent all major religious faiths.

The YMCA was founded in London, England, in 1844 by twelve dry goods clerks for "the improvement of the spiritual condition of young men engaged in the drapery and other trades." It quietly caught the interest of young men, and soon "Y's" were started in other cities and countries. The first American YMCA was opened in Boston, Mass., in 1851, and within seven years associations had been started from coast to coast.

The YMCA has pioneered in physical fitness, sports, and camping programs. Basketball and volleyball were first devised to supplement YMCA athletic programs, and the YMCA was the first organization to teach swimming and water safety to large numbers of people. The YMCA also developed night schools and adult education programs, originated father-and-son clubs, and was beforehand in training high school youths in citizenship. Because of its international scope it was able to devise a "Peace Corps" type of service that has brought good works to every continent.

Much of the work of the YMCA is carried out under the direction of volunteer leaders who serve on boards and committees, direct clubs and groups, and provide class instruction and leadership training. Working with a staff of professionally trained personnel, the volunteer leaders make it possible for the YMCA to serve the many people it does in as many different ways.

YMCA's in the United States, while locally independent and self-governing, maintain a National Council to act as a legislative and policy-making body for the movement. The National Council gives them a sense of national unity, speeds the exchange of new ideas and programs, and provides U.S. representation, with other national bodies, in a World Alliance of YMCA's. Major National Council publications are the *YMCA Yearbook* and *The National Council Bulletin* (monthly). JAMES F. BUNTING

The game of basketball was invented in 1891 to be a part of the YMCA winter indoor program in Springfield, Mass.
YMCA

YOUNG PLAN, a schedule of reparations payments totaling $28.8 billion to be made by Germany after World War I. The plan was designed by Owen D. Young to extend over a period of 59 years, but was cut short by the world depression of 1931. See REPARATIONS; YOUNG, OWEN D.

YOUNGSTOWN, city, NE Ohio, seat of Mahoning County; on Mahoning River, about 60 miles SE of Cleveland. Steelmaking and related activities furnish the city's main occupations. Among the city's chief manufactured products are mill machinery, bearings, furniture, cement, lamps, tires and tubes, gypsum products, paints and varnishes, electrical machinery, and meat. Youngstown developed as a result of a land purchase in the area of the Western Reserve, 1796, by John Young. The area was first settled by William Hillman, 1796. The township was organized, 1802, and incorporated, 1848. It was chartered as a city, 1867, at which time it was made a county seat. Among the city's points of interest are the Butler Art Institute, 1919, Idora Park, Mill Creek Park, which contains several small lakes, Stambaugh Auditorium, 1925, and Youngstown University, founded, 1880. Iron was first mined in the area, 1802. Pop. (1960) 166,689.

YOUNG TURKS, a political faction in the Ottoman Empire during the early years of the twentieth century, was headed mainly by young army officers, who sought both internal political reform and the re-establishment of Ottoman (Turkish) authority in southeastern Europe, the Middle East, and North Africa. In 1878 Sultan Abdul Hamid II had discarded Turkey's first liberal constitution (1876) that had provided for a parliament, freedom of speech, and equal rights for non-Turkish subjects, and suppression of political opposition, and had imposed rule by decree. There followed numerous insurrections—in Crete, 1878, in Roumelia, 1885, and in Armenia and Crete during the 1890's—and the weakened Empire lost territory, notably Tunis to France, 1881, and Egypt to Great Britain, 1882. Instrumental in many of the uprisings were Turks-in-exile who, by 1908, had gained support of a Turkish Army junta headed by Enver Pasha. On July 24 they forced Sultan Abdul Hamid II to restore the Constitution of 1876, and in Spring, 1909, exercised their control of parliament, in voting for the abdication of Abdul Hamid II and election of his brother as Sultan Mohammed V. The Young Turks proceeded to inaugurate some reforms, such as a constitutional revision (1909) by which the sultan became a mere figure head of state, but their opposition to independence movements of non-Turks led to disorders that culminated in war with Italy, 1911, which resulted in the loss of Lybia and most of the Dodecanese Islands, and in the Balkan Wars, 1912-13, which resulted in the loss of Albania, all of Macedonia, and part of Thrace. Thenceforth, the Young Turks directed their energies toward regaining not only the Empire's lost possessions, but in uniting Moslems and Turks (many of whom were under Russian rule) within the Ottoman fold. To this end the Young Turks brought the Ottoman Empire into alignment with the German-dominated Triple Alliance in opposition to the Ottoman Empire's traditional protectors, France and Great Britain, and into World War I on the side of the Central Powers, Oct. 30, 1914. See ENVER PASHA; TURKEY.

Such was the ardor for reform exhibited by the Young Turks upon their rise to power that the term "Young Turk" was subsequently applied to any young person or group aggressively advocating political change.

YOUNG WOMEN'S CHRISTIAN ASSOCIATION, an international organization whose purpose is to build a fellowship of women devoted to Christian ideals. The YWCA was originated in London, England, in 1855, growing out of a Prayer Circle for Young Women and a society to provide a home for girls and nurses returning from the Crimean War.

Work in the United States began three years later, but it was not until 1866, in Boston, that the name *Young Women's Christian Association* was used.

The YWCA movement developed rapidly in the United States. The first student YWCA was begun at the Illinois State Normal University in 1872. Work with teenage girls began in 1881. In 1906 the two national organizations of the YWCA that had developed separately, one in the Midwest and one in the East, merged.

Major YWCA programs have been devoted to education, health, recreation, provision of housing, food service, employment counseling, international affairs, the betterment of women's working conditions, and the betterment of racial relations.

The YWCA has consultative status with the Economic and Social Council; the Educational, Scientific and Cultural Organization; and the Food and Agriculture Organization of the United Nations. During World Wars I and II, YWCA groups gave aid to women's and family camps throughout the world. In 1945 the YWCA joined with the YMCA to form the YM/YWCA Service to Refugees and Displaced Persons. This Service worked with the UN Relief and Rehabilitation Administration, the International Refugee Organization, and the Office of the UN High Commissioner for Refugees.

Within the United States the YWCA is at work in approximately 5,400 locations in more than 1,000 towns and cities; it has over 2,000,000 members. The YWCA is also at work abroad in more than 70 countries, through the Mutual Service Program of the World YWCA.   IDA SLOAN SNYDER

YOUSKEVITCH, IGOR, 1912–   , U.S. ballet dancer, born in Russia. From 1938 to 1944 he was the leading dancer of the Ballet Russe de Monte Carlo. Thereafter he danced in the United States, chiefly with Ballet Theatre, and was the frequent partner of Alicia Alonso. Known for his virile elegance and fine elevation, Youskevitch excelled in classical roles, particularly in *Giselle* and *The Black Swan*.

YOUTH HOSTELS, a low-cost, overnight lodging place for hikers and cyclers.

Hostels normally provide sleeping quarters, sanitary facilities, a common kitchen, and a recreation room. Each youth hostel is in the charge of resident house parents. Hostels in the United States and Canada are chartered by American Youth Hostels (A.Y.H.), which issues membership passes to hostelers for identification. This organization in turn belongs to the International Youth Hostels Federation.

The first hostel was started in an old castle at Altona, Germany, 1910, as a low-cost overnight shelter for the school children of the near-by city. Before long, many similar hostels a day's journey apart crisscrossed Germany, and the idea rapidly spread to neighboring countries. The first youth hostel in the United States was opened, 1934, at Northfield, Mass.

American hostelers adopted the international youth hostel customs of early rising and early curfew, no drinking or smoking in hostels, simplicity of accommodations, and a welcome for young people of all nationalities, religions, and races without discrimination. Hostelers of any country may enjoy the youth-hostels privileges of a foreign country simply by presenting their youth hostels passes for admission.

YOUTH ORGANIZATIONS, social, educational, or religious institutions whose purpose is to promote the well-being of children and young people.

The increasingly complex social, economic, and political structure of Western civilization, together with rapid progress toward industrialization, urbanization, and widespread education have multiplied both the opportunities and problems of young people. The various organizations perform many functions in orienting youth to the twentieth century world. They are active in the fields of education, employment, vocational adjustment, health, and recreation, and seek to fill needs arising from the changed status of family life and the religious, political, and social movements that affect the attitudes and morale of young people. After World War II, the need in the United States for organized services to help in the readjustment of young people to peace-time living greatly increased. As a result, many youth organizations expanded their programs, and new organizations were created as new problems arose.

Most organizations joined by young people are controlled in some manner by adults. They may actually be adult associations, unions, or clubs that allow boys and girls under 21 to become members; or they may be junior divisions of adult groups; or they may be separate youth organizations sponsored and directed by adult groups. The relatively few youth organizations actually established by young people, and often called "youth movements", are distinguished from the youth-serving organizations by the fact that their directors, and working staffs, as well as their memberships are composed of young people. Even many youth movements, however, originate under the patronage of adult groups, and sometimes become subject to the control of adult organizations.

Youth-Membership Organizations. The best known and the largest of the adult-sponsored organizations for children and young people are the American Junior Red Cross, the Boy Scouts of America, the Girl Scouts, the Camp Fire Girls, Inc., the Young Men's Christian Associations, the Young Women's Christian Associations, Junior Achievement, Inc., the American Youth Foundation, the Boys' Clubs of America, Inc., the Order of the Rainbow for Girls, and Pathfinders of America. These organizations promote activities among their members that advance moral leadership, social co-operation, self-reliance, citizenship, health, homemaking abilities, and understanding of the U.S. economic system and the processes of democratic government. They are non-sectarian and some of them are designed to work in conjunction with the public schools. Many of these groups have memberships of well over a million, but numerous small communities and rural areas are not reached by any organization of this type, and only a minority of the young people of the United States belong to such groups.

Similar in many ways to these secular youth-membership organizations are the Protestant, Catholic and Jewish affiliated groups. Nearly all of the Protestant churches support such denominational or interdenominational organizations, whose common purposes are to provide acceptable social activity for their young people, foster the development of Christian character, and to furthering church welfare.

The Catholic Church has many youth movement groups and youth-serving organizations, most of which support programs of religious, civic, cultural, social, and recreational activities. Some, however, are more limited in their purposes, as, for example, promoting service to the poor, or spreading and giving application to Catholic teachings and opinion.

The Jewish youth organizations have a variety of purposes. Some are dedicated to the preservation among their young people of the values of the history, literature, and religion of the Hebrew people, while others work for the development and application of progressive social philosophy.

In addition to these general sectarian and non-sectarian classifications, there are youth-membership organizations devoted to the training and welfare of youth in specific fields. The groups whose membership is located in agricultural areas have programs directed toward meeting the needs of rural young people. The 4-H Clubs are extremely active in helping farm boys and girls receive training in farming, homemaking, rural community activities, and citizenship. The Future Farmers of America and the Youth Division of the American Country Life Association have the stated purposes of improving rural civiliza-

tion and creating more interest in the intelligent choice of farming occupations.

Other youth-membership groups with specific purposes are the Future Teachers of America which attempts to stimulate interest in teaching and educational work among high school students, and the National Music Camp, which maintains a summer school of music and arts to serve young people.

Youth Movements. Youth movements have at times arisen almost spontaneously as a response of young people to a specific, immediate, and pressing unsolved social or political problem. Many youth movements exist in the form of student organizations, political or labor associations, or associations seeking the attainment of specific goals, such as peace, world government, or consumer cooperation.

Youth-controlled political organizations, originated in Germany in the period shortly before World War II. There and in Italy, the Fascist-dominated youth groups became a military arm of the totalitarian state. In the United States, young people have for many years had their own clubs and associations devoted to sports, recreation, campus politics, and social events, that have been more or less free from adult interference. These, however, did not fall within the popular conception of youth movements. During the 1930's and '40's, depressed economic conditions and world armed conflict stimulated youth to organize to discuss public affairs and to exert their influence in determining national and international policies. Local youth councils were formed, with representatives from community religious, social, political, labor, racial, and other societies. These councils functioned as forums for discussion of local problems such as unemployment, delinquency, and political leadership. From these local groups, several national youth movements developed; some of them received widespread publicity. The American Youth Congress, which disbanded during World War II, was one of the more outstanding of these political youth movements and had as members representatives of over 60 national organizations of youth-serving and youth groups.

Adult Youth-serving Organizations. Many groups of organized adults have as their main or secondary purpose the promotion of youth welfare. Included in this category are religious groups such as the American Friends Service Committee, the Protestant Council of Higher Education, the Department of Education of the National Catholic Welfare Conference, and the Jewish Occupation Council, Inc. There are also councils, foundations, and associations devoted entirely to research and social planning directed toward solving the problems of young people. Among these are the American Council on Education's Committee on Youth Problems, the American Educational Research Association of the National Education Association, the Labor Research Association, and the Social Science Research Council.

Women's clubs, inter-racial organizations, labor unions, business and professional men's service clubs, and health and safety organizations also devote much of their time to aiding and training children and young people.

See JEWISH ORGANIZATIONS; ROMAN CATHOLIC ORGANIZATIONS; NEGRO, American Negro Organizations; EDUCATION, Educational Associations; CHILD WELFARE, Child Guidance; RED CROSS; JUVENILE DELINQUENCY; YOUTH HOSTELS; FRATERNITY; BOYS AND GIRLS CLUBS.

YOZGAT, province, central Turkey; bounded by the provinces of Çorum, Amasya, and Tokat on the N, and Sivas on the E, Kayseri on the S, and Ankara on the W; area 5,291 sq. mi.; pop. (1955) 393,235. Yozgat is the capital. Wheat, rye, barley, and grapes are the principal crops grown in the vicinity. The Yozgat area was part of the Armenoid Hittite Empire (1750–1200 B.C.). Ruins of the ancient Hittite capital Hattushash, scene of archaeological excavations, are near the village of Boghaz Keui. The Turks entered the region for the first time in the fourteenth century.

YPRES, Flemish Yperen, town, Belgium, in the province of West Flanders; 65 miles W of Brussels. Leading industries are the manufacturing of lace, linen, and thread. The Cloth Hall and St. Martin's Church both date from the thirteenth century. Ypres was a flourishing linen manufacturing town in the fourteenth and fifteenth centuries, when it was reported to have had a population of 200,000. The town was destroyed in battles during World War I, but rebuilt following the war. Pop. (1959 est.) 17,107.

YPSILANTI, city, SE Michigan, in Washtenaw County; on the Huron River; the New York Central Railroad, and U.S. highway 112; about 30 miles W of Detroit. Ypsilanti's chief manufactured products are auto parts, sheet metal, machinery, power tools, oil stoves, paper, and ladders. A French trading post occupied the site, 1809, and permanent settlers first arrived, 1832. Ypsilanti is the site of Eastern Michigan University (1849). Pop. (1960) 20,957.

YTTERBIUM, a metallic element belonging to the rare earths. The chemical symbol for ytterbium is Yb; it has an atomic weight of 173.04, and an atomic number of 70; it belongs to the Lanthanum series (see PERIODIC TABLE). Ytterbium belongs to the ytterbium group of rare earths, which also includes the elements holmium, erbium, thulium, and lutetium. Ytterbium oxide, Yb_2O_3, is found in association with yttrium oxide, Y_2O_3, in monzanite ores. The element Ytterbium was first reported in 1878, but in 1907 the distinguished French chemist Georges Urbain showed that the original substance was composed of two different elements: ytterbium and lutetium. Ytterbium has a valence of 2 or 3. In the bivalent form it is green, but the trivalent Yb_2O_3 is colorless. Ytterbium has very limited commercial applications. See RARE EARTHS. MONZANITE.

YTTRIUM, an iron-gray, lustrous powdery element, which darkens on exposure to light. Its atomic number is 39 and its atomic weight, 88.92. It has a density of 4.34 grams per milliliter at 20°C and melts at 1490°C and boils at about 2500°C. The chemical symbol for yttrium is Y or Yt and it belongs to group III B of the periodic arrangement of elements (see PERIODIC TABLE). The element exhibits an oxidation number, or valence, of 3 and exists in only one isotopic form.

Yttrium was discovered in 1794 and was obtained in a high state of purity in 1843. It occurs in the ores of gadolinite, samarskite, yttrialite, and other rare-earth minerals of which it is a member.

The metal reacts with cold water slowly to liberate hydrogen and form the white gelatinous insoluble hydroxide $Y(OH)_3$. Yttrium metal may be prepared from the trichloride, YCl_3, by reduction with metallic sodium or by the electrolysis of the mixture of the trichloride and sodium chloride. Yttrium has limited use as an alloying material in industry and has been used as a "getter" to remove oxygen and other non-metallic impurities from various metals.

YÜAN, a monetary unit used in China until 1949. The silver yuan was withdrawn from circulation, 1948, when extreme inflation had driven its black market value to a low of 12 million yuan to one U.S. dollar. It was replaced by a gold yuan officially valued at 25 cents in U.S. currency. The Peoples Republic of China (Communist China) replaced the yuan with the so-called people's currency dollar, which had no value in terms of U.S. currency throughout the 1950's and after, since the U.S. government did not maintain diplomatic or economic relations with that government.

YUAN SHIH-K'AI, 1859–1916, Chinese statesman, was born in Siangcheng, Honan Province, served in the Chinese army in Korea, 1882–85, and remained there as Chinese imperial resident, 1885–94. He was governor of Shantung, 1900-01, viceroy of Pechili, 1901–07, and was appointed guardian to the heir apparent, 1908, but retired soon afterward upon the death of the emperor and empress dowager. He was generalissimo of the imperial army during the 1911 Revolution and became premier of the provisional republic in the same year. Sun Yat-Sen resigned the presidency in his favor, 1912, and Yüan was elected president of the republic for a five-year term, 1913. Yüan soon alienated Sun Yat Sen and his followers by his efforts to increase the powers of the presidency. He suspended the parliament, 1914, promulgated a new constitution, and assumed unlimited executive powers. He attempted to make himself emperor, 1915, but the provinces in the south of China revolted, 1916, and Yüan had to content himself with the presidency.

YUBA CITY, town, N central California, seat of Sutter County; at the confluence of the Yuba and Feather rivers, on the Sacramento Northern and the Southern Pacific railroads, and U.S. highways 99 and 40; 52 miles N of Sacramento. Yuba City is a processing and trade center for an agricultural area largely devoted to producing peaches, prunes, and grain. Local industries are fruit drying and canning, fruit and nut packing, and the manufacturing of dairy products and concrete pipe. There is also a feed mill and a winery. Yuba City was founded in 1849. Pop. (1960) 11,507.

YUCATÁN, state, SE Mexico; on the Yucatán Peninsula; bounded N by the Gulf of Mexico, E and SE by the territory of Quintana Roo, SW by the state of Campeche, and W by the Gulf of Mexico; area 14,868 sq. mi.; pop. (1957 est.) 598,161. The state's name, meaning Land of the Yucca, refers to the desert plant that thrives in the rocky soil covering most of the area with the exception of the tropical region in the south. The terrain slopes gradually to the northern coast of the peninsula; in the southeastern portion are low hills known as Sierra Baja and Sierra Alta. Most of the region is dry except in the south, where there are shallow lakes and water holes. Growing and preparation of henequen is the chief industry. Extensive tropical forests in the south contain an abundance of dyewoods. Sponges are found in the sea off Yucatán. The bulk of the population is Mayan, descendants of the ancient people, many of whose ruined cities and temples have been excavated. The principal cities of Yucatán are Mérida, the capital, Progreso and Valladolid.

YUCATÁN PENINSULA, SE Mexico, separating the Gulf of Mexico from the Caribbean Sea. The peninsula is not strictly defined as to boundaries but its southern limit is usually set by the ridges extending across northern Guatemala, terminating in the east at the lower extremity of the Bahía Chetumal, and in the west at the Laguna de Términos. The peninsula includes the states of Yucatán and Campeche and the territory of Quintana Roo in Mexico and small parts of British Honduras and Guatemala.

LOS ANGELES COUNTY C. OF C.
Desert Yucca

YUCCA, a genus of plants of the family *Liliaceae*, found in Mexico, Central America, and the southern United States. These plants bear many-flowered panicles of large, showy, white, cream, violet, or red flowers, and usually thick lanceolate leaves, clustered at the summit of the woody caudex. Many species are cultivated in the greenhouses or in the open air. Several varieties of yucca are of great value to the desert Indians, who bake the flower buds, eat the fruit, and use the saponaceous roots for washing, and the fibers for basketry, sandals, and mattings.

Y. gloriosa, or Spanish dagger, a native of the southern United States, and *Y. filamentosa*, or Adam's Needle, are cultivated for ornament in the northern states and in England. One variety, the Joshua tree, *Y. brevifolia*, sometimes reaches a height of as much as 35 feet.

YUCCA HOUSE NATIONAL MONUMENT, SW Colorado, in Montezuma County, about 14 miles SW of Cortez, near Mesa Verde National Park. The monument of nine acres embraces the archaeological ruins of a prehistoric Indian pueblo village. It was established in 1919. The monument is not open to the public.

YUE-CHI, a nomadic people of Asia. In the second century B.C. they conquered the Greco-Bactrian kingdom founded by Alexander the Great. About A.D. 50 they established the Kushan dynasty in northwest India. Driven out the following century, they returned to Afghanistan and were defeated by the Huns.

YUGA, in Hindu chronology, a division of time marking an epoch in the history of the universe. Taken as a whole, each cycle of creation, existence, and destruction is known as a Mahāyuga, or Day of Brahma; each Mahāyuga alternates with the much longer night of Brahma, during which there is no world. A Mahāyuga consists of a Krita Yuga of 4,800 divine years (1 divine year = 360 human years), a Tretā Yuga of 3,600 divine years, a Dvāpara Yuga of 2,400 divine years, and a Kali Yuga of 1,200 divine years. The modern world is said to be in the very early part of a Kali Yuga.

YUGOSLAVIA, officially the Federal Socialist Republic of Yugoslavia, country SE Europe; bounded on the N by Austria and Hungary, on the NE by Rumania, on the E by Bulgaria, on the S by Greece, on the SW by Albania, on the W by the Adriatic Sea, and on the NW by Italy; area of 98,766 sq. mi.; pop. (1961) 18,549,291. Yugoslavia is the largest country of the Balkan Peninsula and consists of six constituent republics: Serbia, Croatia, Slovenia, Bosnia-Hercegovina, Macedonia, and Montenegro. Belgrade, the federal capital, and largest city, has 585,234 inhabitants. For map see Atlas, Vol. 20. For national flag in color, see FLAG.

PHYSICAL FEATURES

Topography. Yugoslavia may be divided into five physiographic provinces: (1) the Danubian Plains, or the Vojvodina in the northeast, (2) the Central and Southern Uplands and Valleys, (3) the Slovene Alps in the northwest, (4) the Dinaric Alps in the west, and (5) Dalmatia in the southwest.

The Danubian Plains, or the Vojvodina, with an elevation of less than 1,000 feet, are a continuation of the Great Alföld (Great Hungarian Plain), and are crossed by the Danube, Drava, Sava, and Tisza rivers. The Danube, which flows for 370 miles through Yugoslavia, is the main waterway of the country. The plains' soils, formed of recent alluvium and loess, are rich. The climate, like that of Central Europe, is continental; precipitation is adequate and supports a population engaged mainly in farming. Belgrade, on the Danube, has a January average temperature of 33°F, and a July average of 72°F. The annual precipitation averages 24 inches.

Central and southern Yugoslavia is a region of corridors largely dominated by the combined Morava-Vardar River valleys. The Morava drains north into the Danube, the Vardar drains south into the Aegean Sea, and together they provide a major route of travel from the Mediterranean to the Danubian Basin. In the east and southeast, the uplands are extensions of the Transylvanian Alps, the Balkan Mountains, and the Rhodope Mountains. East of Belgrade, the Danube has carved a steep-sided gorge through the Transylvanian Alps, called the Iron Gate, where for centuries rapids have impeded navigation on the river. Among the other major corridors in the region, one follows the Nisava Valley south-

westward through the Balkan-Rhodope Uplands toward Sofia, Bulgaria; another follows the Morava Valley northward toward Rumania; another follows along the Ibar and Vardar valley toward Albania in the southwest and Greece in the southeast. Most settlement is in the valleys where the soils are fertile. The uplands tend to be barren and are sparsely populated. Winters are cold and summers hot, except in the southwest where the moderating Mediterranean influence is felt.

The Slovene Alps form the southern foothills of the Alps proper. Molded by glaciers and streams, the region has a subdued relief of 2,000 feet.

Southward from the Slovene Alps extend the Dinaric Alps, which reach altitudes of 8,000 feet. The western part consists of successive longitudinal ridges of bare white limestone. Here sparse vegetation permits only sheep grazing on lower pastures despite an annual rainfall averaging 60 to 180 inches, which does not help in the formation of soil but merely dissolves the limestone and carries it away in solution via underground rivers. The hidden channels, crevices and caverns of western Yugoslavia have created the classic example of karstic topography (see KARST). To the east, however, the rivers begin to flow in valleys and a loamy soil covers the surface limestone. Most of the region drains toward the Sava. The forest wealth of the region, once considerable, has been largely depleted.

Along the Adriatic Coast (Dalmatia), the limestone ranges drop steeply toward the sea. Partial drowning of the coast has created peninsulas, embayments, and hundreds of islands. Protected from cold winds from the interior and warmed by the sea, the Dalmatian "Riviera" presents a sharp contrast to the rest of Yugoslavia. Much of the settlement, the towns and villages, are located on a narrow coastal plain which skirts the sea.

Plant and Animal Life. The Slovene and the eastern Dinaric Alps have forests of oak, chestnut, beech, and conifers; the western Dinaric Alps have mainly drought-resistant vegetation. Mediterranean scrub vegetation clothes the coastal plain, in contrast to the continental vegetation of the Danubian Plains. Dalmatia lies along one of the three principal fly routes of Europe, and birds cross Yugoslavia in migrations between Africa and northeastern Europe. The mountainous areas have typical Alpine fauna such as wolves, bear, eagles, and hawks; fresh water fish include carp, trout, and salmon. Wildlife is scarce in the more heavily populated lowlands.

Location Map of Yugoslavia

The Dalmatian coastal region, with its countless bays and islands, has very little agricultural land, but has become a noted vacation center.

Zagreb, the capital and cultural center of Croatia, is dominated by its 344-foot cathedral spires.

PRINCIPAL RESOURCES, INDUSTRIES, AND PRODUCTS

Bauxite		Olives	
Cattle		Petroleum	
Chromite		Potatoes	
Coal		Rapeseed	
Copper		Sheep	
Corn		Silver	
Dairying		Sugar beets	
Diversified manufacturing		Sunflower seed	
Goats		Textiles	
Grapes		Thermoelectricity	
Hogs		Timber	
Hydroelectric power		Tobacco	
Iron		Wheat	
Iron and steel		Wine	
Lead		Zinc	
Mercury			

Bauxite, copper, lead, and zinc form the basis of Yugoslavia's mining and smelting industries.

Forests, most of them state-owned, cover more than 30 per cent of the country. Lumbering is important, and timber is one of the chief exports.

The ancient city of Skopje, astride the Vardar River in the mountains of southern Yugoslavia, is the capital of the People's Republic of Macedonia.

SOCIAL FACTORS

People. The major ethnic groups of Yugoslavia are the Serbs, Croats, Slovenes, Macedonians, and Montenegrins. The larger minority groups are Albanians, Hungarians, and Turks. Yugoslavia recognizes three official languages: Serbo-Croatian, Slovenian, and Macedonian. Serbo-Croatian, the language of state, combines the closely related languages, Serbian and Croatian; Serbian is written in the Cyrillic alphabet, Croatian in the Latin (see SLAVIC LANGUAGES). Yugoslavia has no state religion. By tradition the Serbs and Macedonians are adherents of the Orthodox Eastern church; the Croats and Slovenes are Roman Catholics. In the south and west, where Turkish influence was strongest, there are many Moslems.

Yugoslavia is essentially a nonindustrial, agrarian country. According to the 1953 census, only 28.5 per cent of the population was urban, and there were only six cities with populations of 100,000 or more.

PRINCIPAL CITIES

City	Population*
Belgrade (capital)	470,172
Zagreb	350,829
Llubljana	138,981
Sarajevo	136,283
Skopje	122,143
Subotica	115,352

*1953

Education is controlled by the federal government. School attendance is compulsory and free for children aged 7 through 15. There are vocational and technical schools, and also the Gymnasiums, which are preparatory for university education. Among the centers of higher learning are pedagogical schools, an academy of music, and the universities of Ljubljana, founded in 1596; Zagreb, 1669; Belgrade, 1863; Skopje, 1946; and Sarajevo, 1949. After World War II much attention was given to adult education in an effort to reduce illiteracy, and to provide the technical training necessary to overcome shortages of trained manpower.

ECONOMIC FACTORS

In 1960, despite more than a decade's effort by the government to promote industry, Yugoslavia remained essentially a rather backward agricultural country. After 1955, however, there were signs of improvement. A 35 per cent increase in agricultural output in the years 1958–59 resulted in higher agricultural income; real wages in industry increased faster than productivity which, while retail prices remained stable in 1959, suggested a reduction of other costs; and the volume of foreign trade, including a larger share of manufactured exports, increased.

Agriculture. In 1945 a large-scale land reform program, begun in 1924, was completed. Large estates having been abolished and the land redistributed to peasants, the government immediately launched a program for the complete collectivization of agriculture by setting up state farms and co-operatives, or collectives. In the co-operative, the peasants pool their holdings and operate the farm under state direction; state farms are owned by the government and operated by hired labor. By 1950 there were 6,971 co-operative farms, involving 415,000 households and about 5.3 million acres of land (nearly 22 per cent of Yugoslavia's arable land). Collectivization was most successful in Macedonia and Montenegro, less so in Slovenia and Croatia. From the beginning of collectivization many peasants had balked at government control of the distribution of produce, and by 1955 the number of co-operative farms had dropped to 3,698. Although most peasants were operating their own land during the late 1950's, a federal people's assembly resolution of April, 1957, favoring closer co-operation between the state and co-operative farms and the independent peasants, indicated that the government had not abandoned its earlier goal of a socialized agriculture.

PRINCIPAL CROPS

Crop	1957	1958	1959
		1,000 Short Tons	
Corn	6,237	4,353	7,350
Plums	648	599	1,333
Potatoes	3,648	2,887	2,964
Sugar Beets	2,237	1,631	2,623
Sunflower	102	88	123
Tobacco	69	43	52
Wheat	3,416	2,700	4,561

About a fourth of Yugoslavia is suited to cropping, mainly in the Vojvodina and river valleys of the north and east. Corn and wheat are the principal crops; other grains include barley, oats, rye, and rice. Potatoes are a staple; oil-bearing crops produced in quantities adequate for local needs include sunflowers, soybeans, castor beans, and rapes; sugar beets, tobacco, hops, and chicory are commercially significant. There were 4.9 million cattle in 1958—more than before World War II, but the breeding quality was low, as was the number of fine dairy cows. Sheep and goats are raised on most farms, while transhumance (seasonal moving of animals to pasture) is widely practiced on the uplands, especially in the south. Hogs and poultry are also kept. Horses and water buffaloes are used extensively for farm work.

Forestry and Fishing. The richest stands of forest are in Slovenia, and Bosnia and Hercegovina, but in the late 1950's excessive cutting was rapidly depleting this resource. Oak is used in construction at home and for export. Beech is the main domestic firewood. Adriatic Coast waters do not support an important fishing industry, although fishing is of some local importance.

Mining and Mineral Production. Yugoslavia is not rich in mineral resources but some of its minerals, such as copper, are scarce in Europe, and are intensively exploited. The copper mines at Bor, southeast of Belgrade, are Yugoslavia's major economic asset, but the bauxite deposits along the Dalmatian Coast are also highly important. A political disagreement, 1957, between Yugoslavia's President Tito and the Soviet Union's Communist Party Secretary Nikita Khrushchev, prevented realization of a Soviet area project for making aluminum in Yugoslavia. By early in the 1960's, annual production of copper had reached almost two million tons; the output of bauxite, having doubled since 1951, amounted to almost a million tons; and iron ore production, principally from mines at Ljubija and Vares, totaled two million tons. Output of lead-zinc is important, and there are deposits of manganese, chromium, and antimony. With the acquisition of the district of Zara (Istria) from Italy, 1947, Yugoslavia gained important mercury deposits.

PRINCIPAL MINERALS

Mineral	Unit	1958	1959
Antimony	Short ton	1,835	2,514
Barite	Short ton	103,801	118,267
Bismuth	Pound	169,670	200,026
Chromite	Short ton	125,188	117,965
Copper	Short ton	38,840	42,556
Iron Ore	1,000 long ton	1,965	2,062
Lead	Short ton	99,035	101,908
Lignite	Short ton	19,597,000	21,836,000
Manganese	Short ton	11,060	8,900
Mercury	76 pound flask	12,270	13,344
Petroleum, crude	barrel	3,267,000	4,188,000
Zinc	Short ton	66,160	66,900

YUGOSLAVIA

Half way between Zadar and Split on the Dalmatian coast of Yugoslavia lies the beautiful seaport town Šibenik.

Sarajevo, capital of Bosnia and Hercegovina, is in central Yugoslavia. The murder here, June 28, 1914, of Archduke Francis Ferdinand was the immediate cause of World War I.

Mount Durmitor, the highest peak in Yugoslavia, overlooks a peaceful scene in Montenegro, on the border of Albania.

Thousands visit the busy stalls of the principal market place in Zagreb, the capital and largest city of Croatia.

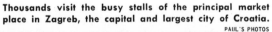

The churning water of the Pliva River in Bosnia provides power to grind flour in huts perched above the torrent. Cattle cool off by wading in the water below the falls.

Much of Yugoslavia's coal is of poor quality; in 1958, for example, a total of 18.9 million metric tons was mined, but 17.8 million tons consisted of brown coal and lignite. Bituminous coal is mined principally in the Timok Valley, in eastern Serbia. Oil and natural gas are produced in small but increasing quantities. A new oil field was opened near Sisak in Croatia, 1958, but production of fuel resources remained insufficient for the needs of the economy and future development. In the decade 1946–56 Yugoslavia's electric power capacity increased from 1,150 million kw hr to 7,356 million kw hr, of which slightly more than half was derived from hydro sources. The United States advanced credits and loans to Yugoslavia, 1958, for the construction of a thermal plant at Kosovska Mitrovica and a hydro plant at Trebinje. It was planned to build a series of hydroelectric plants on the Cetina River.

Manufacturing. In addition to the lack of fuels, the lack of capital funds and equipment have retarded industrial growth. After 1945, however, there was considerable growth, mainly in the light industries. In 1957, 300,000 of Yugoslavia's 800,000 industrial workers were employed in the metal products and machine industries, and 136,000 were employed in the textile and clothing industries. Belgrade is the chief manufacturing center, while the heavier industrial regions are located in the Vares Zenica Region near Sarajevo and along the Kupa River at Karlovac and Sisak.

Transportation and Communications. Among Yugoslavia's rivers are some of Europe's most important communication routes, but the country on the whole is a difficult one for railroad and highway construction. In 1962 there were a total of 7,370 miles of rail lines and 37,000 miles of good roads, of which the densest networks were in Serbia, Croatia, and Slovenia. Much of the western Dinaric Highland is without rail. The best connection with the Adriatic is through Italian Trieste, while Rijeka (Fiume) can be reached only on a long-winding railway. The Dinaric Alps wall hinders trade and commerce to Yugoslavia's Adriatic ports; the railroad to the Greek seaport, Thessalonika is the nation's most important outlet for ocean commerce. In 1962, Yugoslavia had more than 300 ocean-going cargo and passenger ships, representing 22 companies. Rijeka, Dubrovnik, Sibenik, and Split are the principal seaports. The main navigable rivers are the Danube, the Tisza, and the Sava.

Commerce. After World War II the nature and direction of Yugoslavia's commerce was largely determined by political circumstances. It was only after the break with the U.S.S.R., 1948, that traditional Yugoslav trade with the West was restored, and the United States, Italy, West Germany, and the United Kingdom became Yugoslavia's major trading partners. In 1963, Yugoslav imports were valued at $269 million, exports at $201 million. Exports, chiefly forest products, minerals, and some manufactured goods are exchanged for industrial fuels, machinery, tools, and foodstuffs. Yugoslavia's thriving tourist trade with both Western and Soviet-bloc nations is a significant factor in the economy.

DOUGLAS JACKSON

POLITICAL DIVISIONS

Republic	Area	Population*
	(sq. mi.)	
Bosnia-Hercegovina	19,909	3,277,948
Croatia	21,840	4,159,696
Macedonia	10,230	1,406,003
Montenegro	5,394	471,894
Serbia[1]	34,116	7,642,227
Slovenia	7,810	1,591,523

*1961 census
[1]includes Kosovo-Metohija and Vojvodina.

GOVERNMENT

Yugoslavia became a republic in 1945; its constitution was passed in January, 1946, and revised in 1953 by the Fundamental Law, in effect a new constitution. The present constitution of April 7, 1963, renamed the country as the Socialist Federal Republic of Yugoslavia, composed of the socialist republics of Bosnia and Hercegovina, Crna Gora (Montenegro), Croatia, Macedonia, Serbia, and Slovenia. All power is in the hands of the working people. Representative bodies at all levels, from federation through republics, districts, and local communes, govern social affairs. The basis of power in local communes is now wider: people from every branch of society are represented. The old council of producers has accordingly been abolished. There is universal suffrage over the age of 18. Socialization of the means of production is complete, but small peasants' holdings are permissible, and houses are often independently owned.

Yugoslavian Coat of Arms

The federal assembly has five chambers of 120 members each, dealing with different aspects of administration (federal, economic, political, education and culture, social welfare and health). There is also a 70-member chamber of nationalities, concerned with safeguarding the rights of the various peoples that make up the federation. Members of all chambers are elected for four years—half are elected every two years—and cannot be successively re-elected to the same chamber. The president may be re-elected after one four-year term. The president and members of the federal executive council are elected by and from the members of the federal assembly. President Tito, however, is exempt from these restrictions.

The constitution of 1963 was regarded by many people as an encouragement to a more liberal society. Yugoslav Communism has always been less dogmatic than the Communism of the U.S.S.R. and its adherent states; for this reason Yugoslavia has received some U.S. economic assistance. Willingness to compromise between the ideologies of East and West has not always been advantageous. The concession to "free enterprise" evident, for instance, in the peasants' freeholds has not solved problems of agricultural production shared by other Communist states.

The Judicial System comprises the supreme courts of the republics, of the autonomous province and region, and of the federal republic; and various county and district courts. The supreme courts have jurisdiction over cases appealed from lower courts; the supreme court of the socialist federal republic of Yugoslavia is the nation's court of last resort. County and district courts exercise original jurisdiction, and are presided over by judges elected by people's committees. Supreme court judges are elected by the various people's assemblies.

Local Government. Each of the republics of Bosnia-Hercegovina, Croatia, Macedonia, Montenegro, Serbia, and Slovenia has its own constitution that provides for a local government very similar to that of the federal government. The governments of Vojvodina and Kosovo-Metohija are prescribed by the Serbian constitution.

Armed Forces. In 1965, Yugoslavia's navy had 6 destroyers, more than 90 torpedo boats, and two submarines; and the air force had 650 planes, more than 500 of which were described as first-line, including jet-propelled fighters and bombers, largely of U.S., Canadian, and British manufacture. The army consisted of about 300,000 regulars plus reserves.

HISTORY

Origin of Yugoslavia. The region corresponding to Yugoslavia became a political being with the creation of the Kingdom of the Serbs, Croats, and Slovenes as a constitutional monarchy under the rule of King Peter I Karageorgevich of Serbia, Dec. 4, 1918. Previously, the history of the Yugoslavs (or South Slavs) had been the history of the separate provinces never before politically united, but related by language and a century-long struggle for independence from non-Slavic rule. In the west were Slovenia and Croatia, which had been crown lands of the Hapsburgs of Austria after 1526, and Dalmatia, which had been ruled by Austria after 1815. In the east were the sovereign states of Montenegro and Serbia (including most of Macedonia), which had been declared independent from the Ottoman Empire by the Congress of Berlin (1878), and Bosnia and Hercegovina, former Serbian territories that the Congress had mandated to Austria-Hungary.

Early in the nineteenth century, while all South Slavs were still under foreign rule, two things happened that figured prominently in the Yugoslav independence and unification movement. The first, following upon the French occupation of Slovenia, Dalmatia, and the parts of Croatia (called the Illyrian provinces), 1809–15, was the introduction of French revolutionary ideas and reforms in opposition to the existing quasi-feudal order. The second development, 1829, was the success of Serbia in gaining autonomy within the Ottoman Empire by means of two revolutions, 1804–12, and 1815–30. These inspired both additional revolts in the Balkans, and Illyrianism, a literary movement led by the Croatian writer Ljudevit Gaj (1809–72), that sought to bring linguistic and literary unity among the Serbs and Croats.

By early in the twentieth century the movement for liberation from Ottoman and Austro-Hungarian rule was powerful indeed. Serbia participated in the Balkan wars against the Turks and Bulgarians, 1912–13, in which she won much of Macedonia, and emerged a military power to threaten Austro-Hungarian rule in the Balkans (see BALKAN WARS). In Serbia two unofficial nationalistic organizations had been established to promote the cause of liberation: the National Defense and Unity or Death (the Black Hand, so-called). Among the many Austro-Hungarian Yugoslavs in service of these organizations was the Bosnian student Gavrilo Princip, who assassinated Archduke Francis Ferdinand, heir apparent to the Austro-Hungarian throne, June 28, 1914, and precipitated the international crisis that culminated in Austria-Hungary's declaration of war on Serbia, July 28, 1914. See WORLD WAR I.

For a time Serbia repulsed the Austro-Hungarian invasion, but by late 1915 the weight of German, Austro-Hungarian, and Bulgarian armies had driven the Serbs to Albania on the Adriatic Sea. In early 1916 thousands of troops were evacuated to the island of Corfu, where a Serbian government supporting the Karageorgevich Dynasty was established under Nikola Pašić. Beginning in 1916 Serbian troops from Corfu were sent to reinforce the French and British on the Salonica front in northern Greece, where an offensive launched in autumn, 1918, overwhelmed Austrian and Bulgarian armies. See SALONIKA CAMPAIGNS.

In London, meanwhile, refugees from Austria-Hungary had established a Yugoslav Committee, headed by the Croatian Ante Trumbić, which conceived a federally organized Yugoslav republic as opposed to the Serbian plan for a centralized government. At Corfu, July 20, 1917, the two factions agreed finally to form a kingdom (under the Karageorgevich Dynasty) in which Serbs, Croats, and Slovenes would be guaranteed full equality.

Making the Yugoslav Nation. From the start internal dissent beset the new regime. A Serb-dominated constituent assembly adopted a constitution, Jan. 1, 1921, providing for a strong central government that would assure Serbian control over the less-populous Croatians and Slovenes. In Serbian Macedonia, the Internal Macedonian Revolutionary Organization (IMRO) sought annexation by Bulgaria; Communists fermented general disorder in the furtherance of world revolution; and a Croatian independence movement developed, threatening dissolution of the kingdom. During 1929, Peter I Karageorgevich's son and successor Alexander I, 1921–34, took drastic steps to preserve the kingdom, suspending the constitution and dissolving parliament in January, and renaming the country the Kingdom of Yugoslavia in October. Alexander ruled by decree until September, 1931, when a new constitution was proclaimed, providing for a senate, one-half elected indirectly and the other half nominated by the king, and a chamber of deputies elected directly. In November, 1931, elections the Serbs won an overwhelming victory. Thus, Alexander had secured his position by constitutional means.

In foreign relations, Yugoslavia joined with Czechoslovakia and Rumania in an entente (1920–21) to oppose both the restoration of the Hapsburg monarchy in Hungary and Austria, and Hungarian and Bulgarian claims to former territory then part of the member nations; entered into an alliance (1927) with France to oppose Italian expansion into the Balkans; joined Rumania, Greece and Turkey in the Balkan Pact (Feb. 8, 1934). While visiting France, later in 1934, Alexander was assassinated in Marseilles, October 9, by a member of a Croatian revolutionary movement, headquartered in Hungary. The Yugoslav government denounced Hungary as somehow responsible for the assassination and war was narrowly averted. A regency, headed by Alexander's cousin Prince Paul, was instituted to rule during the minority of Alexander's son, King Peter II (1923–   ).

Early in 1936 there occurred a change in Yugoslavia's foreign policy. A barter agreement was signed with Germany in May, 1936, and a nonaggression and arbitration pact was signed with Italy in March, 1937. In 1938–39, however, such security alignments became virtually meaningless, as Germany annexed Austria and dismembered Czechoslovakia, and Italy annexed Albania. In the meantime, Serbian and Croatian leaders had been seeking to reconcile their differences; a measure of success was achieved in August, 1939, when the government was reconstructed with the Serb Dragiša Cvetković as premier, and the Croat Vladimir Maček as vice-premier.

World War II. Upon the outbreak of World War II September, 1939, Yugoslavia declared itself neutral, but was unable to resist for long German demands for political support, and joined the Rome-Berlin-Tokyo Axis, Mar. 25, 1941. However, the Yugoslav army immediately overthrew Prince Paul's regency, March 26–28, proclaimed Peter as a sovereign of legal age, and reasserted the country's neutrality. Within only a few days, German, Italian, Hungarian, and Bulgarian armies invaded the country, April 6. After two weeks of fighting the Yugoslav army surrendered and the country was partitioned among Germany, Italy, Hungary, and Bulgaria, with part of Croatia established as an Axis puppet republic under the Croatian-fascist Ante Pavelic. King Peter had fled to England, however, and a Yugoslav government in exile was established, with Gen. Dušan Simovic as premier.

Not all the Yugoslav army had surrendered, however, and from a small nucleus of survivors two underground resistance movements were organized. The first established was the Chetnek, under Col. Draža Mihajlović, a Serbian nationalist and a monarchist;

the second, established after Germany had invaded the Soviet Union, June 22, 1941, was the National Liberation Movement (NLM), or Partisan underground, led by Tito (real name Josip Brozovich or Broz), a Croatian, who had been secretary general of the Yugoslav Communist party from 1937. The two resistance groups co-operated in the summer and autumn of 1941, but neither Mihajlović nor Tito was willing to submit to the other and Mihajlović, more anti-Communist and pro-Serb than anti-Axis, apparently concluded agreements with local German and Italian commanders to co-operate against Tito-led NLM. These accommodations, together with incidents of brutality inflicted against non-Serbian Yugoslavs by some chetneks, led most Yugoslavs and the Western Allies to support Tito, who established his own Yugoslav government in the field. Tito's guerrilla fighters tied up many German troops and by the end of 1944, with some aid from the Soviet army, had recaptured Yugoslavia from the Germans.

The Communist Victory. A government representing King Peter II, still in exile, and the Communist-dominated National Front (a coalition of political parties), was formed, 1945, with Tito as premier. In the November elections, the National Front won overwhelming control of the government and proclaimed Yugoslavia a republic.

A new constitution closely resembling that of the Soviet Union was adopted, Jan. 31, 1946. Tito eliminated all opposition to his regime, and Mihajlović, tried and convicted of collaborating with Germany, was executed, July 17, 1946. In September, 1947, the Cominform (Communist Information Bureau), uniting the Communist countries of Eastern Europe in opposition to capitalism, was established with headquarters at Belgrade (see INTERNATIONAL, THE, *The Cominform*). In June, 1948, however, the Cominform expelled Yugoslavia from membership, charging that Tito had violated the principles and policies of communism. Actually Tito had diligently emulated Soviet Communism within Yugoslavia, but unlike the other Communist leaders in Europe, had refused to become a Soviet puppet, thereby challenging the U.S.S.R.'s position as the sole authority for Communist policy. The ensuing economic boycott of Yugoslavia by the Soviet Union and other Communist countries was offset by a *rapprochement* of Yugoslavia and the West, including U.S. economic aid in excess of $1 billion during the ensuing decade.

Titoism. In the meantime, internal opposition had grown against rigid centralization under the federal government of the means of production, and especially against collective and state farms. This, together with the break with the U.S.S.R. resulted in a modification in the form of government and change in the socialist doctrine. The constitution was amended, 1953, by a Fundamental Law, that decentralized political administration; abolished the Soviet-styled parliament and presidium; changed the names of the Communist party and the National Front to the Communist League and the Socialist Alliance of Working People of Yugoslavia, and gave to the state-owned businesses greater autonomy in management, production, and financing and to workers both a voice in management and a share of the profits.

A notable result of improved relations between Yugoslavia and the West was the division of Trieste between Yugoslavia and Italy, October, 1954. Claimed by both countries at the close of World War II, Trieste's political status had become an issue in the "Cold War" between the West and the Soviet Union, with the West in favor of awarding the Adriatic territory to Italy. After Tito's break with the Cominform, however, the United States and Great Britain pressed for a solution to the Trieste problem that would be agreeable to both Yugoslavia and Italy. See TRIESTE, FREE TERRITORY OF.

After the death of Soviet dictator Joseph Stalin (Mar. 5, 1953) relations between Yugoslavia and the Soviet Union improved somewhat, and in a state visit to Yugoslavia, spring, 1955, the Soviet Union's Premier Nikolai A. Bulganin and Communist Party Secretary Nikita S. Khrushchev blamed the deterioration of Soviet-Yugoslav relations on Stalin and former head of the Soviet secret police Lavrentia P. Beriya (executed for treason, Dec. 23, 1953). Nevertheless, Yugoslavia continued to follow an independent course through the 1950's. Tito bitterly criticized the U.S.S.R. for its suppression of the Hungarian revolt, autumn, 1956, but generally supported the Soviet foreign policy and was steadfastly critical of Western colonialism. Such characteristics of Yugoslav communism, or "Titoism," together with a marked rise in the country's economy in recent years impressed many economically underdeveloped countries such as India, Indonesia, the United Arab Republic, and Ethiopia, who by tradition resented exploitation by the West yet feared the Soviet Union and Communist China, and who were steadily gaining positions of greater importance through their voice and vote in the United Nations. By 1960 many observers regarded Yugoslavia as a leader among the neutral countries.   WAYNE S. VUCINICH

BIBLIOG.—Louis Adamic, *Eagle and the Roots* (1952); Robert H. Bass and Elizabeth Marbury, eds., *Soviet-Yugoslav Controversy, 1948–58* (1959); Robert F. Byrnes, ed., *Yugoslavia Under the Communists* (1957); Milovan Djilas, *Land Without Justice* (1958); Eugene Fodor, ed., *Yugoslavia, 1960* (1960); John K. Galbraith, *Journey to Poland and Yugoslavia* (1958); Ernst Halperin, *Triumphant Heretic: Tito's Struggle Against Stalin* (1958); Nagel Publishers, Inc., *Yugoslavia* (Nagel Travel Guide Ser.) (1954); Fred W. Neal, *Titoism in Action* (1958); Bernard Newman, *Unknown Yugoslavia* (1961); Eric L. Pridonoff, *Tito's Yugoslavia* (1955); Louisa Rayner, *Women in a Village* (1957); Anthony R. E. Rhodes, *Where the Turk Trod: A Journey to Sarajevo with a Slavonic Musselman* (1956); Alois Schmaus, *Yugoslavia* (1960); Dinko A. Tomašić, *National Communism and Soviet Strategy* (1957).

YUKAWA, HIDEKI, 1907– , Japanese physicist, was born in Tokyo, studied at Kyoto and Osaka universities, and was made professor of physics at Kyoto, 1939. Yukawa received the 1949 Nobel prize for physics "for having predicted, as a result of his theoretical work on nuclear forces, the existence of mesons," in a series of equations published in 1935. He was a visiting professor at Columbia University, 1949–53.

YUKON, or Yukon Territory, territory NW Canada; bounded on the N by the Beaufort Sea, an arm of the Arctic Ocean; on the E by the District of Mackenzie, Northwest Territories; on the S by British Columbia; and on the extreme SW and the W by Alaska, U.S.A.; area 207,076 sq. mi. including 1,730 sq. mi. of inland lakes; pop. (1956) 12,190. The administrative capital, and largest town is Whitehorse. See map in Atlas, Vol. 20.

PHYSICAL FACTORS

Topography and Drainage. The Yukon Plateau, in whose valleys most of the settlements are located, is the central feature of the territory. Its upland areas are from 3,000 to 4,000 feet above sea level. The broad, sloping valleys lie about 1,000 feet below the plateau. It is crossed by the territory's major river, the Yukon, formed by the Lewes and Pelly rivers near Selkirk. The Yukon joined by its main tributaries, the White and Stewart rivers near the town of Stewart River, flows north to Dawson, and from there northwest into Alaska. To the southwest of the Yukon Plateau are the St. Elias Mountains, highest range in Canada, crowned by Mount Logan whose crest, 19,850 feet above sea level, is the highest point in Canada; there are at least six other peaks in this range exceeding 15,000 feet in height above sea level. East of the central plateau the passless, linear ridges of the Selwyn and Mackenzie mountains, 7,000 to 9,000 feet high, follow much of the boundary of Yukon and the Northwest Territories. To the north of the plateau are the more rounded peaks of the Ogilvie

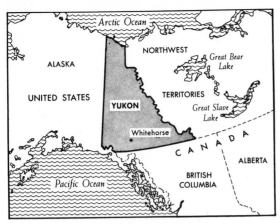

Location Map of Yukon

Range having a few high passes; still farther north are the Richardson Mountains forming the eastern part of the Brooks Range. In addition to the Yukon Plateau, there are two smaller lowland basins in the territory; north of Ogilvie Range are the poorly drained lowlands of the Peel and Porcupine rivers, while to the southeast the forested lowland along the Liard River constitutes the main topographic break north of the Rocky Mountains. The Liard River lowland is traversed by the Alaska Highway.

Climate. Records indicate that much of the Yukon has a subarctic climate, but as late as 1960 the territory's few weather stations were in the valley settlements, and weather conditions in much of the Yukon had never been charted. The uplands and mountain areas, which constitute most of the Yukon, are above tree line and probably have an arctic climate. Dawson, in west-central Yukon and just north of the 64th parallel, has severe winters, with a January monthly mean average of about −20°F. At Snag, 120 miles south southwest of Dawson, record low temperature of −81°F was recorded, 1947. Southern Yukon receives occasional warm air masses from the Pacific Ocean, and winter averages are milder; Whitehorse, at 60°41″ N lat., has an average January temperature of zero degrees Fahrenheit, which is about the same as that of Winnipeg, Manitoba, at 49°53″ N lat. Summers are relatively warm in the valleys, where some stations report July averages of about 60°F, and occasional daily maximums in the 80's. As in the rest of northern Canada and interior Alaska, precipitation in the Yukon is light, averaging 10 to 15 inches annually, although it is likely that more precipitation falls as snow on the uplands.

Plant and Animal Life. About 15 per cent of south and central Yukon is classified as productive forest, which consists mainly of spruce, pine, and fir growing in strips along the valley slopes at altitudes ranging between 2,500 and 3,500 feet. The upper slopes and the northern part of the territory have noncommercial scrub forest and tundra. About half of the Yukon is above tree line and is barren. The usual fur-bearing animals of the northern Canadian forest are to be found in the Yukon, where such small fur bearers as marten, beaver, muskrat, and squirrel support a fur-trapping industry. Most abundant of the larger animals are moose, caribou, and mountain sheep.

SOCIAL FACTORS

People. The population of the Yukon reached 27,200 at the height of the Gold Rush, 1901, but people began to drift away as the supply of easily accessible alluvial gold dwindled, and by 1921 the population was only 4,157. The building of the Alaska Highway across southern Yukon during World War II, and postwar transportation developments encouraged population increase; in the years 1951–56, for example, the population increased 33 per cent.

Most of the 10,500 white people live in Whitehorse (2,570), in small villages such as Dawson (900) and Mayo (300), in the valleys of the Yukon Plateau, and along the Alaska Highway. The 1,700 Indians of the Yukon live in the valleys and derive their livelihood mainly from fur trapping. In 1956, Yukon's department of education operated 14 public schools, and the Canadian government maintained four Indian schools. In addition there were Roman Catholic parochial schools at Whitehorse and Dawson, and several Anglican and Roman Catholic mission schools for Indian children at other settlements.

ECONOMIC FACTORS

Mining. Although the discovery of gold was the reason for the establishing of Yukon Territory, 1898, gold production was slight at mid-twentieth century. Dredging river gravels near Dawson produces about $1 million worth of gold annually. During the 1950's, Yukon's most valuable mineral resources were lead and silver, mined principally at Keno Hill, north of Mayo. Concentrates of the minerals are shipped by truck to the head of rail transport at Whitehorse, then by rail and ship to Trail, British Columbia, where they are smelted. Nickel, asbestos, tungsten, a large deposit of which was discovered, 1959, and zinc exist in the Yukon but by 1960 exploitation had been inconsequential, mainly because of high development costs. Natural gas and oil deposits believed to exist in commercially profitable quantities were discovered in the Eagle Plain area, 200 miles northeast of Dawson, 1959. It was to be expected that shipment to market would be by pipeline to the ice-free seaports of British Columbia.

Agriculture. Despite its severe climate Yukon has a potential for crop production, far exceeding the area usually under cultivation, a matter determined largely by local market. In 1956 there were less than 1,000 acres of farm land; vegetables for local consumption are grown in most of the settlements.

Forestry and Water Power. There is a reserve of potential commercial forest in the Liard lowland and in some of the southern Yukon valleys, and a few sawmills prepare lumber for the towns. Potential water power is widespread, but limited by low flow during the winter; developed hydroelectric power sites of 15,000 horsepower each are located near Whitehorse and Dawson.

Transportation and Communication. Transport services are good across southern Yukon, but scarce elsewhere. A narrow-gauge railway connects Whitehorse with the port of Skagway, Alaska. The graveled Alaska Highway crosses southern Yukon, and gravel roads extend north to Mayo and Dawson, and south to Haines, Alaska. Whitehorse is on the routes of major airlines, and charter planes will fly to other territorial settlements. Flat-bottomed, paddle-wheel steamers operated on the Yukon River and some tributaries during the first half of the twentieth century, but were unable to compete with new road and air transport after 1950. The Canadian government maintains postal service with many Yukon communities, including Old Crow on the Porcupine River, which until 1959 received mail from the U.S. Postal Service by way of Fort Yukon, Alaska. In 1959 a closed-circuit television station at Whitehorse, and Canadian Broadcasting Company radio stations at Whitehorse and Dawson were established, and construction of telephone communications connecting Whitehorse, Dawson, and Mayo were started.

J. LEWIS ROBINSON

GOVERNMENT

Yukon is governed by a commissioner appointed to an indefinite term by the Canadian national government, and under the supervision of the minister of northern affairs and national resources. The commissioner is assisted by a five-member council elected for three years. Yukon sends one representative to the Canadian House of Commons. Law and order is maintained by the Royal Canadian Mounted Police. Whitehorse succeeded Dawson as the seat of government in 1952.

HISTORY

The Yukon region was explored by Robert Campbell of Hudson's Bay Company, 1842–48, and for more than two decades thereafter remained under the company's political jurisdiction. In 1869 the company transferred all of its lands to the Canadian government, which established the Northwest Territories the same year. Prospecting for minerals was begun in the Yukon in the 1870's. Discovery of gold in the Klondike region, 1896, resulted in an influx of fortune hunters; Yukon was separated from Northwest Territories, and established as a territory with its capital at Dawson, 1898. A 1937 agreement between the Canadian government and British Columbia to make the Yukon part of British Columbia, had still to be effected in the early 1960's. The World War II and post-war years saw the radical improvement of the road system in southern and western Yukon; bridges across the Yukon, Pelley, and Stewart rivers were completed, 1959–60.

NATL. FILM BOARD

Tourists view an old steamer, a gold-rush day relic set up on the bank of the Yukon River at Carcross in Yukon Territory, Canada. The river extends well into Alaska.

YUKON RIVER, Canada and Alaska, is formed by the junction of the Lewes and Pelly rivers near Selkirk, Yukon Territory, and flows to the Bering Sea. The total length of the river is 2,100 miles, and the catchment area is some 330,000 square miles, about equally divided between Alaska and Yukon Territory. From Selkirk the Yukon flows northwest to the Arctic Circle; then forming its Great Bend, it turns at almost a right angle, flowing southwest to the sea. The upper course of the Yukon is cut into the Yukon Plateau to a depth of 2,000 to 3,000 feet. The lower course is less rugged; but below the Great Bend a gradient of about one foot to the mile is maintained. After it enters Alaska the Yukon broadens out over the tundra, until it extends 10 to 20 miles across the Yukon Flats at the Great Bend. This width is maintained for almost 100 miles, until the river is again hemmed in by the sides of the plateau. At Tanana the valley becomes a broad meadowland with isolated parts of the plateau appearing as monadnocks. The delta has an area of 9,000 square miles, across which numerous outlets flow, the most northerly, the Apoon, being the one generally used by steamers. The river's principal tributaries are the Tanana, Porcupine, White, and Koyukuk. Two very small tributaries, the Klondike and Indian in Canadian territory, have become famous for their rich gold placers. Dawson, in the Klondike region, is the chief city on the river. The Yukon is navigable and is a great highway of interior transportation.

YUMA, a North American Indian tribe indigenous to the Colorado River valley. Linguistically, the Yuma and a number of other tribes—most im-

portantly the Cocopa, Diegueño, Maricopa, and Mohave—comprise the Yuman linguistic family. It is probable that the valley of the Colorado was the principal home of the Yuma for many centuries before the Spanish first visited the area in the sixteenth century, but they also are known to have lived originally in the area south of the Gila River in what later became Arizona, and in a part of southern California later bisected by the U.S.–Mexican border. The Yuma, Maricopa, and Mohave cultivated large fields of corn and beans, irrigating these "plantations" by means of trenches. Although until recent times the Yuma lived in brush shelters and cave-like dwellings, there is reason to believe that they formerly had lived in villages of adobe houses, of which there are abundant ruins in the Colorado River valley. The Yuma population at Fort Yuma reservation, Imperial County, Calif., was 1,150 in 1950.

YUMA, city, SW Arizona, seat of Yuma County; on the Colorado River at the mouth of the Gila River; on the Southern Pacific railroad and U.S. highway 80; scheduled airline stop; 165 miles SW of Phoenix. The area about the city produces melons, vegetables, citrus fruits, pecans, wheat, and other agricultural products. Both Arizona and the federal government maintain experimental farms near by. Yuma is also the center of a diversified mining area. The area was explored by Spaniards as early as 1540. In 1854 a party of engineers constructed a plan for the town, calling it Colorado City. It was incorporated as Arizona City, 1866; and the name was changed to Yuma, 1871. The Arizona Territorial Prison, still preserved as a historic spot, was established at Yuma, 1876. During World War II, an Air Force training field was located south of the city. Pop. (1960) 23,974.

YÜNNAN, province, SW China; bounded by the Tibetan Autonomous Region on the NW, Szechwan on the N, Kweichow and Kwangsi on the E, Vietnam and Laos on the S, and Burma on the W; area 160,000 sq. mi.; pop. (1953) 17,472,737. The province has an average elevation of about 6,000 feet above sea level, and consists of a tableland, the Yünnan Plateau, which is deeply dissected by streams. Rugged mountains, which are remnants of an older plateau surface, rise above the general level of the tableland. The structural trend is from north to south, particularly in the west, where the ranges divide the narrow gorges of the Salween, Mekong, and Red rivers, which flow southward. There is a higher proportion of level land in the east. The Yangtze River flows eastward and forms much of the northern boundary of the province.

A variety of crops are grown in the province. Rice is the major summer crop in the level areas, while corn, millet, and barley are dominant in the more mountainous areas. Wheat, oilseed, and opium poppies are the chief winter crops. Cattle are raised throughout the province. Yünnan is one of the chief mining areas of China. The province is the major tin producer of the country, and coal deposits are scattered throughout the area. Antimony, tungsten, copper, lead, and zinc are also mined.

Transport is hindered by the broken terrain, but there are two significant routes in the province, which connect Kunming, the capital of Yünnan, with Mandalay in Burma and with Hanoi in Vietnam. For many centuries Yünnan formed a separate kingdom and did not become part of China until 1681.

YUZHNO-SAKHALINSK, city, U.S.S.R., E Russian Soviet Federated Socialist Republic, capital of Sakhalin Region; 600 miles NE of Vladivostok and 110 miles N of Hokkaido Island, Japan. Main industries are fur processing and pulp and paper manufacturing. Grain and potatoes are grown in outlying areas. Under Czarist Russia the city's name was Vladimirovka and under the Japanese, 1905–45, it was called Toyohara. The Soviets renamed it Yuzhno-Sakhalinsk in 1945. Pop. (1959) 86,000.

Z

1 No hieroglyph	2 No Phoenician form	3 I	4 Z	5 Ƶ	6 Z	7 Z
8 Ȥ	9 ȥ	10 Z	11 z	12 z	13 Z	14 z	15 Z	16 z

The letter Z first appears in a recognizable form as the sixth letter of the classical Greek alphabet, and thereafter as the last letter of most European alphabets. It did not occur in early hieroglyph writing of the Egyptians or in the Phoenician alphabet. Some historical forms are listed in the top row. They are Greek 3, Roman (Trajan) 4, Irish uncial 5, Caroline 6, and Gutenberg black-letter 7. Common forms of the letter Z as it occurs today are illustrated in the bottom row. They are handwritten cursive capital 8, handwritten lowercase 9, roman capital 10, roman lowercase 11, roman small capital 12, italic capital 13, italic lowercase 14, sans serif capital 15, and sans serif lowercase 16.

Z, the twenty-sixth and last letter of the English alphabet. It derives from the sixth letter, *zeta*, of the classical Greek alphabet which also signified the number seven in the Greek numerical system. Because the Romans did not use the letter until the time of Cicero (and then only in words borrowed from the Greeks), they placed it at the end of the alphabet, a position it retains in the alphabets of modern European languages. The original Semitic letter from which the Greek *zeta* was derived was the *zayin*, which was little more than a single vertical line similar to the English capital *I*.

The sound signified by the Greek *zeta* is uncertain: it was probably *ds* or, less frequently, *ts*. In modern languages the pronunciation varies considerably: voiced *s* in Latinized Slavic alphabets, in Hungarian, and in French; *ts* in German; *th* in Spanish; and *ts* in Italian. As in French, *z* in English is used to convey the voiced sound in such words as *zone* and *zeal*, or *breeze* and *gaze*. The same sound, when it occurs other than at the beginning of a word, is also conveyed by the letter *s*, as in *praise* or *surmise*. The pronunciation of the letter itself in North America is *zee*, but the British pronunciation is *zed*. The former pronunciation, *izzard*, is seldom heard.

ZAANDAM, town, Netherlands, in the province of North Holland, on the Zaan River, six miles NW of Amsterdam. There are grain mills and sawmills; paper, cement, and dyes are manufactured. (For population, see Netherlands map in Atlas.)

ZABRZE, formerly Hindenburg, city, SE Poland, Katowice province, about 45 miles WNW of Cracow and 165 miles SSW of Warsaw. Located on a coalfield, Zabrze is a railroad junction and an important industrial center. Steel, machinery, benzine, oil, glass, chemicals, wire, and tiles are manufactured. Zabrze was founded in the thirteenth century. The city came under Prussian control in 1742, and in 1915 its name was changed to Hindenburg. In 1945 the city was returned to Polish control and renamed Zabrze. (For population, see Poland map in Atlas.)

ZACATECAS, state and city, central Mexico. The state is bounded by Coahuila on the N, San Luis Potosí on the E, Aguascalientes on the s, Jalisco on the s and SW, and Durango on the NW; area 28,125 square miles. It occupies a highland zone that reaches 10,000 feet above sea level in the southern part, along the Sierra Madre Occidental. The Aguanaval River drains the state northward, and the Juchipila River flows southward. The state is noted for its mineral deposits, especially silver, gold, and copper. Major crops are wheat, corn, barley, chick-peas, chilies, sugar cane, citrus fruits, and bananas. In several cities there are food processing plants. The raising of cattle, sheep, horses, and mules also is important. Spanish colonization of the area began in 1546, following the discovery of its mineral wealth. The city of Zacatecas, founded in 1548, is the state's capital. (For population, see Mexico map in Atlas.)

ZACCHAEUS, in the New Testament, a wealthy tax collector of Jericho who climbed up into a sycamore tree in order that he might see Jesus over the heads of the crowd. Jesus called him down, lodged with him for the day, and so impressed him that Zacchaeus offered to give half of his possessions to the poor and repay fourfold if he had "wrongfully exacted aught of any man." His story is in Luke 19:1-10.

ZACHARIAS, SAINT, or Zachary, d. 752, pope from 741; born in Calabria, of Greek parentage. During an illustrious reign Zacharias increased the temporal power of the Holy See through his diplomatic treatment of the Franks and Lombards. He was directly responsible for the elevation of Pepin III—the first Carolingian—to the Frankish throne.

ZADAR, or Zara, city, W Yugoslavia, in Croatia; 120 miles SSW of Zagreb. Situated on the Dalmatian coast of the Adriatic Sea, Zadar is a trading city and a popular tourist resort. Industries include shipbuilding, distilling, and manufacturing of glass. The town was founded by the Romans in the fourth century and later was the capital of Dalmatia. It fell to Venice in 1000 but remained an object of dispute between Hungary and Venice until 1409, when it came permanently under Venetian sovereignty. Ceded to Austria in 1797, it remained Austrian during the nineteenth century except for brief French possession (1805–13). It was ceded to Italy in 1920 but reverted formally to Yugoslavia in 1947. (For population, see Yugoslavia map in Atlas.)

ZADKINE, OSSIP, 1890–   , French sculptor, born in Smolensk, Russia. He settled permanently in Paris in 1909, where he studied at the Ecole des Beaux-Arts and began carving in wood and stone. His early work was influenced by Brancusi and cubism, but he gradually became noted for his development of experimental forms of sculpture. In many of his works Zadkine creates striking results by an effective use of the play of light on concave and convex surfaces. Perhaps his most impressive work is *The Devastated City* (1953), a public monument commissioned in commemoration of the bombing of Rotterdam in 1940.

ZAGAZIG, town, Egypt (U.A.R.), 40 miles NNE of Cairo. It is a rail and canal center and supports a large cotton and grain market. Cotton ginning is an important industry. Zagazig is located in the midst of a fertile delta that was once a channel of the Nile. About a mile to the south are found the ruins of the ancient town of Bubastis. The town has a population of about 100,000.

ZAGHLUL PASHA, SAAD, c.1860–1927, Egyptian lawyer and statesman. He was appointed minister of education in 1906 and served as minister of justice from 1910 to 1912. After World War I he became the leader of the Nationalist (Wafd) party. His insistent demands for Egyptian independence from Great Britain caused his arrest (1919) and deportation to Malta. In 1924 he became premier of Egypt but resigned the same year, having failed to reach agreement with the British.

ZAGREB, city, NW Yugoslavia, capital of the constituent republic of Croatia; situated in the broad valley of the Sava River, 230 miles WNW of Belgrade. Originally the site of a Roman town, Zagreb grew from the gradual merger of two early settlements, Gradac and Kaptol, which now form the old town. The new town, developed after the seventeenth century, rapidly became Yugoslavia's second-largest city, with wide streets, open squares and parks, and modern public buildings. The city was part of the Austro-Hungarian Empire until 1918.

Zagreb is the cultural center of Croatia, possessing a university, an academy of science, a nuclear physics institute, a national theater, and various museums. It is also a major commercial center, with metal and machinery industries and chemical, leather, and textile manufactures. (For population see Yugoslavia map in Atlas.)

ZAGROS MOUNTAINS, W and S Iran, extend from the borders of Turkey and Iraq in the NW southward to the Bashagird Range; bounded by the Persian Gulf on the W and the Plateau of Iran on the E. The highest elevation is about 15,000 feet above sea level. The Trans-Iranian Railway crosses the Zagros Mountains through a series of passes between Andimishk and Arak. In ancient times the western Zagros marked the boundary between Assyria and Media.

ZAHARIAS, MILDRED DIDRIKSON, called Babe, 1912–56, U.S. athlete, born in Port Arthur, Tex. In 1950 she was named the woman athlete of the half century. She set four women's world records, including javelin and hurdle events, in the Olympic Games at Los Angeles in 1932. An outstanding golfer, she won many tournaments, including the Women's British Amateur in 1947 and the U.S. Women's Open in 1948 and 1950.

ZAHAROFF, Sir BASIL, 1849–1936, called the Mystery Man of Europe, international munitions merchant, reportedly born in Anatolia, Turkey, of Greek and Russian parentage, and educated in London. He became an international agent for several European munitions concerns and was known as a behind-the-scenes force in international politics and warmaking from the latter part of the nineteenth century to the wars of the early part of the twentieth century. He made a fortune from munitions and from international banking, oil, real estate, and other business ventures. For his aid to England and France during and following World War I, he was knighted by Great Britain in 1924.

ZALEUCUS, fl. c.650 B.C., Greek lawgiver, reputedly the author of Greece's first written legal code. A slave living in Locri Epizephyii in southern Italy, Zaleucus was chosen by the Locrians to draw up a code of law. His legislation, accepted in many cities of Italy, was notorious for its severity.

ZAMA, BATTLE OF, the decisive battle of the second Punic War, actually fought near the Numidian town of Naraggara, about 120 miles SW of Carthage, in 202 B.C.

The great Carthaginian general, Hannibal, was recalled from Italy late in 203 to oppose the Roman invasion of North Africa led by Publius Cornelius Scipio (Africanus), a general scarcely inferior to Hannibal himself. The armies were probably about equal in numbers—40,000 each—but Scipio's superiority in cavalry proved decisive after Hannibal's veterans failed to break the Roman infantry. The defeat placed Carthage at Rome's mercy, and the Carthaginians were forced to agree to humiliating peace terms.

ZAMBEZI RIVER, southern Africa, rises at about 5,000 feet above sea level in the extreme northwest of Zambia, where the borders of Zambia, Angola, and the Congo meet. The Zambezi forms a great S across southeastern Africa: it flows south through Angola and Zambia, turns east to form the border between Zambia and Southwest Africa, Bechuanaland, and Rhodesia, enters Mozambique at the town of Zumbo, and flows southeast to the Indian Ocean. Its total length exceeds 1,600 miles, and it drains an area of about 600,000 square miles. Many tributaries augment the Zambezi, the largest (in volume) being the Shire, which brings down the waters of Lake Nyasa. The Kariba Gorge, about 70 miles southeast of Lusaka, is the site of a huge dam and hydroelectric scheme, where an artificial lake 180 miles long holds about four times the capacity of the Hoover Dam reservoir. The twenty-year project was begun in 1955; the dam itself was constructed in 1955–59. The Kariba project is one manifest achievement of the defunct Federation of Rhodesia and Nyasaland.

The seasonal flow of the Zambezi varies; in the dry season the river sometimes splits into several small streams on the lower reaches. The upper basin, in Zambia, is subject to floods. Crop-growing areas—sugar, cotton, maize, sisal—cluster along the river where it flows through fertile soil, especially in Mozambique; but the tsetse fly is a grave menace to man and beast.

No large port has developed at the mouth of the river, for the Zambezi, like the Niger, is deltaic, and the mouths of the delta are obstructed by sand bars. The Kebrabasa Falls, a few miles above Tete, further restrict the utility of the Zambezi as a point of entry to the African interior. Several stretches of the river are used for internal transportation—steamers run regularly between Tete and the little port of Chinde—but these distances are relatively short. The most famous natural obstacle is formed by the Victoria Falls, discovered (1855) with dismay by David Livingstone, who had dreamed that the Zambezi would prove navigable. Livingstone explored the upper reaches between 1851 and 1853.

ZAMBIA, republic, S central Africa, bounded by the Republic of the Congo on the N, Tanzania on the NE, Malawi on the E, Mozambique on the SE, Rhodesia on the S, and Angola on the W; about 290,587 square miles in area; population about 3.5 million (1964); including 76,000 Europeans as well as some 10,000 Indians and people of mixed ancestry. The capital is Lusaka.

Physical Features

Zambia (formerly Northern Rhodesia) occupies an area somewhat larger than California and Nevada combined, and is sparsely populated. The visitor's first impression is that of immense size and limitless distance. Zambia is a landlocked country. A train from the Zambian "Copperbelt," the country's main mineralized area, has some 1,200 miles to go before it reaches Lobito, the nearest port, in Angola on the west coast of Africa. (See southern Africa map in Atlas.)

The greater part of Zambia is a plateau, some 3,000 to 5,000 feet above sea level, a flat surface broken by small hills, the result of countless ages of erosion which wore away the underlying crystalline rocks containing the bulk of Zambia's great mineral wealth. Southward from the Congo-Zambezi divide, the plateau is cut by the valleys of the Upper Zambezi and its tributaries. In the mountainous northeastern corner the land rises in places to over 7,000 feet, overlooking the western edge of the Great Rift Valley. But these highlands are isolated by the low-lying, hot, and unhealthy Luangwa valley. West of the Muchinga Mountains, which flank the Luangwa rift, lies a plateau containing the shallow Lake Bangweulu and its vast swamplands.

Zambia's vegetation is mainly of the savannah type. Much of the country is open parkland, with trees of many varieties. In the drier areas of the south (annual rainfall less than 30 inches in parts), the vegetation is more stunted. Thick thorn bush and sparse coarse grass characterize the scenery, except in the valleys and river depressions where there is sufficient water to permit heavier green forest. In the north and east the rains become heavier (over 50 inches annually in parts), and the parkland savannah merges into forest country of a type transitional between grassland and the evergreen forests of the equatorial zone.

Zambia lies within the tropics, and the lower reaches of the Zambezi, Luangwa, and Kafue rivers are hot and damp. Elsewhere height usually tempers heat, and Zambia is mostly spared that high degree of humidity and exhausting heat which make life so difficult in the tropics. Zambia has heavy summer rains and a prolonged period of winter drought (May to October). The relatively high altitude of the plateau keeps temperatures lower than usual for these latitudes: mean temperatures vary between 55° and 75° F.

One of the country's main problems is water. Many of the smaller watercourses in the south and west dry up in the season of drought. But once the rains start pouring down between November and March, some of these empty streams become raging torrents that sweep everything out of their way.

Most of the water, unfortunately, is lost, and experts calculate that hardly so much as 15 per cent remains available in rivers and streams for man's use. The larger rivers flow all the year round.

Two great African rivers—the Congo and the Zambezi—have their origins in Zambia. The headwaters of the Congo rise in the hills north of Isoka and run southwest under the name Chambeshi to the vast Bangweulu swamps and lake, where tall reeds cover huge areas. The effluent from this great expanse of water is called the Luapula. It runs in a wide semicircle, forming part of the boundary of the Congolese Republic before joining Lake Mweru on the northeastern boundary of Zambia. This lake is drained by the Luvua River, which eventually becomes the Congo.

The Zambezi winds its way from northwestern Zambia to the Indian Ocean on a course of some 1,700 miles, broken by vast gorges and rapids. The greatest drop of all is the Victoria Falls. The strength of the Zambezi has been harnessed by the Kariba Dam, behind which British, French, and Italian engineers have impounded the world's greatest man-made lake. Kariba Dam raises the river bed of the Zambezi by about 340 feet; it has created a reservoir extending about 180 miles upstream, with a surface area of about 2,000 square miles and a total water-holding capacity of 130 million acre-feet, more than four times the capacity of Lake Mead at the Hoover Dam in the United States. Natural obstacles, however, render the Zambezi almost useless for large-scale navigation; indeed, the lack of good natural communications forms one of Zambia's greatest problems.

Another great river, the Kafue, rises in the hills between Solwezi and Chingola; it flows through swampland to reach the Copperbelt, where its waters are used for industrial and mining purposes. The river swings south and west through tsetse fly country, past the uninhabited Lukanga swamps, which may one day be transformed into a great flood regulation basin, then south to the Meshi Teshi gap, before it abruptly turns east to meander some 200 miles through the vast flats, where indigenous communities raise large herds of cattle; finally it rushes through the Kafue Gorge, a great potential source of hydroelectric power, to merge its waters with the Zambezi.

Another great Zambezi tributary is the Luangwa, which rises in the mountains bordering Malawi, and runs southwest through forest and "fly" country. Much of this country is very sparsely inhabited. The dreaded tsetse fly, that today restricts cattle-keeping, in the past greatly influenced tribal migration routes and areas of white settlement. Agriculturists can breed stock only in certain areas, including the fertile flood plain of Barotseland on the Upper Zambezi, the Mazabuka Plateau in the center of the country, and parts of northeastern Zambia.

Social Features

The African people of Zambia mostly speak "Bantu" tongues; they comprise Lozi (Barotse), Bemba, Ila, Tonga, Lunda, Ngoni, Lamba, Bisa, and numerous others who speak mutually incomprehensible languages. English is the speech of the educated. See AFRICAN LANGUAGES.

In pre-colonial days the people of Zambia had no sense of political unity. They were organized into warring communities, ranging from comparatively large and highly centralized states like Barotseland in the west and the Bemba kingdom of the northeast, to small groups like the Tonga of the center who lacked any sort of state organization. The people mostly made their living by slash-and-burn agriculture, a form of shifting cultivation, which involved the use of fire to provide ash beds where crops could be planted. When the soil was exhausted, the village would seek new land, and allow the soil of their old gardens to recuperate. Some communities, like the Lozi of the Upper Zambezi, had a more intensive system of farming which made use of crop rotation and manuring. The Bantu, however, had neither horses, ploughs, nor carts; crops could not easily be stored, and the margin of survival was often precarious. When possible, the people supplemented their livelihood by means of hunting, fishing, or cattle-keeping.

Traditional forms of social organization differed a good deal from region to region. But in all tribes the basic unit of local organization was the village, and most Zambian communities practiced a matrilineal system of succession. All Zambian peoples had an idea of a Supreme Deity; but belief in spirits, especially those of departed ancestors, played a much more immediate part in the daily life of a village community. From the end of the nineteenth century onward, Christian missionaries began to enter the country. The churches pioneered the country's modern social services, especially education, and there is now a sizable Christian population. There are also dissident African churches, which try to adapt the tenets of Christianity to traditional forms of African social organization like polygamy.

Today the great majority of Africans still live in villages. But motor trucks and bicycles are now beginning to make their impact even in remote parts of the country, and many African cultivators are growing crops for sale as well as for domestic use. In addition many Africans have taken up paid employment; by 1963 there were about 225,000 African wage earners in the country. The density of population is very low; the main concentration is in the Copperbelt in the northern portion of the country. Some 17 per cent of the African population, 67 per cent of the Asian and mixed population, and 87 per cent of the Europeans live in the towns. The chief Copperbelt cities are: Kitwe-Nkana, Ndola, Mufulira, Luanshya-Roan Antelope, and Chingola-Nchanga; all have over 50,000 people. South of the Copperbelt lies Broken Hill, another mining town with a population of about 35,000. The capital is Lusaka, situated on the windswept, healthy, central plateau: population about 110,000.

European colonization ended intertribal wars. Transport and agricultural methods greatly improved; modern preventive and curative medicine brought about major advances. The African population thus began to rise rapidly in numbers. By the end of the 1950's experts estimated the country's African birth rate as among the highest in the world—59 per 1,000. Infant mortality and the general death rate remain high, but the net reproduction rate of the African population has been estimated at 1.7, a figure that entails a substantial annual increase.

At present most managerial and technical positions in the mines and the factories are still held by Europeans; some white people also work as farmers, missionaries, or in the administration. Indian people are primarily engaged in trade; the country's unskilled and semi-skilled labor force is wholly made up of Africans. But Africans have begun to move into senior economic positions; the Zambian government also endeavors to "Africanize" the upper ranks of the administration and the defense forces. High governmental priority is being given to the problem of schooling. By 1962 a total of 327,000 African children were in school. In addition there were at that time 12 teachers colleges and 20 technical and vocational institutions. There are also a college of further education at Lusaka, a college of natural resources, a government college of staff training, and a sociological research body—the Rhodes-Livingstone Institute. The government also has high hopes for a university

college to provide the country with indigenous trained manpower.

Economic Features

In 1962, out of a gross national product of £198,200,000 (c. $555,000,000), mining accounted for £93,800,000, that is to say, 47.3 per cent. Agriculture came second with £24,000,000, or 12.1 per cent; followed by distribution with £14,000,000 or 7.1 per cent; transport and communications with £10,400,000, or 5.2 per cent; and manufacturing with £10,200,000, or 5.1 per cent.

Mining. Mining is the principal source of employment for both Africans and Europeans living in Zambia; by the end of 1962 the industry employed 48,340 people, about 18 per cent of the total employed population. The mining industry supplies the larger portion of the government's revenue; it is the greatest single earner of foreign exchange. Zambia is therefore entirely dependent on world metal prices.

Copper is the main mineral resource. In 1963 the territory produced 637,278 short tons. (This figure stands for the smelter production of copper in terms of recoverable copper content, and includes refined copper produced directly from concentrates without being treated in the smelter.) Zambia is the second greatest copper producer in the non-Communist world, after the United States. Copper mining is heavily capitalized; the methods used are very modern, and financial organization is highly centralized.

Zambia also produces zinc and lead. These metals are found in great quantities at Broken Hill. In 1962 the country turned out 39,800 long tons of zinc at a value of £2,310,758 and 14,592 long tons of lead valued at £639,753. Other minerals include cobalt and limestone—used in the production of cement and burnt lime for flux and other metallurgical purposes. The country also has deposits of manganese, many of which still await exploitation. Silver and small quantities of gold and selenium are obtained as by-products of the copper mining industry; cadmium and vanadium are by-products of the Broken Hill mine. Zambia possesses great unworked resources of iron ore, coal, and other minerals, which may one day help to diversify the economy.

Farming and Forestry. The bulk of African farmers grow food mainly for their own use; in 1962 experts estimated that some 87 per cent of the total production by African cultivators was consumed within the subsistence economy. The expansion of local markets and the development of agricultural extension services and better credit facilities have, however, occasioned considerable improvements. African farmers near the railway are producing considerable quantities of maize. Especially in the eastern part of Zambia, African farmers also grow Burley and Turkish tobacco as a cash crop. Other crops include groundnuts, cassava, rice, pulses, and various fruits and vegetables.

European farmers have settled mainly along the railway line in the southern part of the country. One of the most important European crops is light, fine, flue-cured Virginia tobacco. This requires careful management from seed bed to final grading for sale. Flue-cured tobacco also demands a considerable investment of capital for the construction of tobacco barns; these are heated by furnaces carrying hot air and smoke through the barn in flues of sheet iron. The cultivation of flue-cured tobacco requires advanced financial and technical resources; it is therefore largely in the hands of white farmers. Europeans also play a major part in the territory's maize production: by 1962 African-grown sales amounted to 906,000 bags (of 200 lbs.), while European-grown production amounted to 1,489,700 bags. European farmers also grow some cotton, wheat, coffee, fodder, and green manure crops.

The country has a substantial cattle population; in 1962 Africans were estimated to own over 1,000,000 cattle, as compared with some 215,000 beasts in European ownership. Zambian Africans have also developed a fishing industry on their inland lakes.

Large areas of Zambia are covered by woodland; timber, poles, and charcoal for the mining industry are produced, and some Rhodesian teak is exported.

Communications and Manufacturing. The country's economic backbone is the railway line which runs northward from Livingstone to the Copperbelt, and thence to the Congo. Railway communications are supplemented by a fairly extensive network of roads; by 1963 some 21,500 miles of roads, ranging from bituminous-surfaced to earth, were open to traffic. There are airports at Lusaka, Livingstone, Ndola, and other centers; outlying areas are served by small airfields and landing grounds. Zambia also has a port at Mpulungu on Lake Tanganyika which handles some traffic from Tanganyika. Industry is largely concentrated along the line of rail; the country processes food; there is a small metal industry; in addition Zambia manufactures such diverse products as soft drinks, clothing, blankets, ferro-concrete pipes, and timber products.

History and Government

Zambia's earliest inhabitants were primitive hunters and food gatherers who made tools out of stone. The first agriculturists probably came in from the north at about the beginning of the Christian era, and spread out into what is now Zambia. The original Bantu settlers were followed by many other successive waves of northern immigrants. Politically the most powerful of these were the Lozi (Barotse) on the Upper Zambezi, the Lunda on the Luapula, and the Bemba in northeastern Zambia. In the nineteenth century the tide of migration was reversed, and Zambia was invaded by Bantu warrior peoples from the south, including the Kololo and the Ngoni. In addition Arab slave-traders made their way inland from the east; Portuguese and other traders came in from the west, buying up captives and ivory from indigenous chiefs, and selling guns, gunpowder, and cloth in exchange. The importation of firearms gave a new edge to internecine wars, but no single indigenous kingdom managed to dominate more than a relatively small portion of what is now Zambian territory. The Portuguese also made territorial claims which they could not enforce. In the second part of the nineteenth century British missionaries and explorers began to make their way inland; the most outstanding of these was David Livingstone. See AFRICA.

In 1890 Lewanika, Paramount Chief of Barotseland, placed himself under British protection, hoping thereby to guard his country against threats from the Portuguese in the west and from the Matabele, a warrior people inhabiting what is now Rhodesia. From 1891 to 1924 Zambia was governed by the British South Africa Company, a concern which operated under a royal charter. The Company constructed the country's railways, set up a modern system of administration, and promoted some European settlement. Northern Rhodesia, as Zambia was called from 1911 to 1964, also became a major exporter of labor, and Zambian workmen sought work as far afield as Southern Rhodesia and South Africa. In 1924 the Company's government was terminated, and the territory passed under direct imperial rule. Colonial Office rule coincided with a major economic revolution. In the early 1920's technologists discovered a process which allowed the low-grade copper resources to be worked with profit. New townships mushroomed in what is now the Copperbelt, and Northern Rhodesia became a major mineral producer. The copper industry provided markets for local farmers, and also attracted numerous white immigrants. The European colonists gained a powerful position on the local Legislative Council and entrenched their industrial position through a well-organized white miners' union. The British administration, however, resisted European claims to control the country's executive, and tried to promote African local government through methods of "indirect rule," using traditional chiefs. Educated Africans, resenting European political influence, banded themselves into "welfare societies" which in 1946 were federated on a national level. In 1948 the movement changed its name to the Northern Rhodesia African Congress, the first African political party. The local Europeans looked for political support from Southern Rhodesia, where the local settlers enjoyed self-government, and in 1953 Northern Rhodesia, Southern Rhodesia, and Nyasaland (Malawi) joined in the Federation of Rhodesia and Nyasaland, a semi-autonomous state within the British Commonwealth. There was considerable social and economic progress, but the mainly white-dominated Federal Government failed to reconcile African opposition to its regime.

The British Government lost faith in the federal experiment and in 1963 dissolved the Federation into its three constituents. Local power passed into the hands of the United National Independence Party (UNIP), a radical breakaway movement from the Congress, led by Kenneth Kaunda, a former school teacher. In 1964 Northern Rhodesia achieved full independence as the Republic of Zambia. The legislature became known as the National Assembly where UNIP holds an overwhelming majority. Executive power rests with an elected president; Kaunda became the country's first president. Early in 1965 Kaunda pronounced in favor of one-party government, but emphasized that he would not impose such a regime on the people by force. He also announced a $98,000,000 transitional development plan.

Zambia is opposed to European rule both in Rhodesia and in the Republic of South Africa. Zambia, however, depends for its coal supplies and for its southern rail outlet on Rhodesia, and must co-operate with Rhodesia over the Kariba hydroelectrical project. On the other hand, Zambia can bring pressure to bear on Rhodesia, which seeks to sell its manufactured products north as well as south of the Zambezi. Zambian planners wish to escape from the logistic dependence on the south by constructing a railway line which would link their country to Tanganyika and the Indian Ocean.

LEWIS H. GANN

BIBLIOG.—E. M. Clegg, *Race and Politics: Partnership in the Federation of Rhodesia and Nyasaland* (1960); Elizabeth Colson and Max Gluckman (eds.), *Seven Tribes of British Central Africa* (1951); A. L. Epstein, *Politics in an Urban African Community* (1958); L. H. Gann, *A History of Northern Rhodesia: Early Days to 1953* (ed. 1964); Kenneth Kaunda, *Zambia Shall Be Free* (1962); Hortense Powdermaker, *Copper Town* (1962).

ZAMBOANGA, city, Philippines, extreme W Mindanao Island, capital of Zamboanga del Sur Province, on the S tip of the Zamboanga Peninsula, 540 miles S of Manila. Zamboanga has an important port and is the center of trade and shipping for western Mindanao and the Sulu Archipelago. The surrounding area has valuable forests and produces rice, hemp, copra, sugar cane, tobacco, and sweet potatoes. (For population, see Philippines map in Atlas.)

ZAMORA, city and province, W Spain. The province is bounded by the provinces of Orense on the NW, León on the N, Valladolid on the E, and Salamanca on the s, and by Portugal on the w; area, 4,082 square miles. Zamora extends from the Sierra de Peña Negra on the northwestern border across the rolling plateau of the Meseta. The principal rivers are the Douro (Duero) and the Esla, which has been dammed to form a long, irregularly shaped lake. There are irrigated vineyards and orchards in the valleys, and wheat and sheep are raised on the plateau. There are deposits of tungsten and tin in the province.

Zamora, the capital and chief city, is located on the Douro River, 130 miles NW of Madrid. It is a trade and processing center for the province. Zamora is an ancient walled city; it contains a twelfth-century Romanesque cathedral and a municipal building dating from 1622. Possession of the city was disputed for centuries by the Moors and Christians. (For population of the city, see Spain map in Atlas.)

ZAMOYSKI, JAN, 1541–1605, Polish statesman and soldier, educated in Paris, Strasbourg, and Padua. While rector of the University of Padua, Zamoyski wrote his treatise *De senatu romano* (1563). Upon returning to Poland he became keeper of the archives and acquired considerable political influence.

After the death of Sigismund II, Zamoyski was instrumental in remodeling the Polish constitution and in securing the crown for Henry of Valois (Henry III of France) in 1573 and then for Stephen Báthory in 1575. Chief counselor to Báthory and commander in chief of the army, Zamoyski successfully led the Polish forces against Ivan the Terrible of Russia. In 1586 Stephen died, and Zamoyski used his influence to make Sigismund of Sweden the king of Poland. The new king and his minister did not get along well at first; but when relations between them improved, Zamoyski spent the later years of his life as commander in chief of the army once again. In that capacity he quelled domestic insurrection and built up the Polish defensive power against the threat of Turkish invasion.

ZANESVILLE, city, E Ohio, seat of Muskingum County, situated at the confluence of the Muskingum and Licking rivers, 52 miles E of Columbus. The city is a trade and processing center for a diversified farming area that has vast deposits of clay, limestone, sand, gas, and oil. Principal industries include the manufacture of pottery, glass, steel, fiber box containers, cement, electrical equipment, and mosaic and other tiles. A Y-shaped bridge across the Muskingum, sending its upper arms to both banks of the Licking, is the only bridge of its kind in the United States. Zanesville was the capital of Ohio from 1810 to 1812. (For population, see Ohio map in Atlas.)

ZANGWILL, ISRAEL, 1864–1926, English author, born in London, the son of a Russian Jewish refugee. Much of his early writing, including *Merely Mary Ann* (1893), which he later turned into a play, was light-hearted popular fiction. The first of his distinctive portrayals of Jewish life was *Children of the Ghetto* (1892), a panoramic novel of ghetto life. This was followed by *Ghetto Tragedies* (1893), *Dreamers of the Ghetto* (1898), and others. *The Melting Pot* (1908), a serious play about a Jewish refugee in New York City, attracted much attention, as did his earlier dramatization of *Children of the Ghetto* (1899). Zangwill was an advocate of Jewish unification and supported Zionism until 1905, when he became head of a Zionist opposition group, the Jewish Territorial Organization, which considered Palestine unsuitable for Jewish settlement.

ZANTE (Zakynthos), island province, Greece, the southernmost of the Ionian Islands, in the Ionian Sea, about 12 miles off the western coast of the Peloponnesus; area, 157 square miles. The western portion of the island is largely mountainous, rising to over 2,700 feet. In the east is a fertile and densely populated plain. The island's principal products include currants, wine, olive oil, and citrus fruits. The capital is Zakynthos. According to legend, Zante belonged to the kingdom of Ulysses (Odysseus) of Ithaca. In historical times it was a part of the Roman and then the Byzantine empires. In the fifteenth century Zante became a Venetian possession and remained so for three centuries. With the Napoleonic wars, it passed successively under French, Russian, and British rule. Along with the other Ionian Islands, it was ceded to Greece by Great Britain in 1864. (For population, see Balkan States map in Atlas.)

ZANZIBAR. See TANZANIA.

ZANZIBAR, city, Tanzania, capital of the island of Zanzibar, 23 miles across the Zanzibar Channel from the African mainland. The city developed from a Portuguese settlement on the west coast of the island in the sixteenth century, although there was an Arab trading center there earlier. The Imam Seyyid Said of Oman moved his capital there in 1840 and started the clove industry. Zanzibar soon became the world's largest exporter of cloves. During the nineteenth century Zanzibar was the chief port of East Africa until the rise of Mombasa and Dar es Salaam. Cloves and coconuts and their associated products account for almost all Zanzibar's exports. There is no heavy industry. In modern Zanzibar, Arab, African (Bantu), and European influences have met in close conjunction. (For population, see southern Africa map in Atlas.)

ZAPATA, EMILIANO, c. 1877–1919, Mexican revolutionary, born in the state of Morelos. During the revolt of Francisco Madero against the government of Porfiro Díaz in 1910, Zapata led the insurrectionists of Morelos, and at various times held independent control of that state and of Guerrero. On three occasions in 1914–15, Zapata was in temporary possession of Mexico City. His ambition was to give Mexico back to the Indians.

ZAPOROZHIE, region and city, U.S.S.R., SE Ukrainian Soviet Socialist Republic; bounded by Dnepropetrovsk Region on the N, Donetsk Region on the E, the Sea of Asov (an arm of the Black Sea) on the s, and Kherson Region on the w; area, 10,500 square miles. The region is an agricultural area specializing in the growing of cotton in the south and of wheat in the north. Other locally concentrated crops are castor beans and sunflowers in the north, and vineyards and orchards in the south. Zaporozhie was formed in 1939. Its population is predominantly Ukrainian and Russian. Chief cities are Zaporozhie, Melitopol, and Berdyansk (formerly Osipenko).

Zaporozhie, or Zaporozhye, the capital and chief city of the region, is located on the Dnieper (Dnepr) river, 270 miles SE of Kiev. It is the site of the Dneproges dam and power station. The city produces iron, steel, steel alloys, aluminum, tractors, automobiles, ball bearings, machine tools, agricultural machinery, and chemicals. Zaporozhie was founded in 1770 as a fort named Aleksandrovsk. It was renamed Zaporozhie in 1921. During World War II the Germans ravaged the city and destroyed much of its industry, but Zaporozhie has since been completely rebuilt. The area is famed as one of the homes of the Ukrainian Cossacks. (For population of city, see U.S.S.R. map in Atlas.)

ZAPOTEC, an Indian tribal group of southern Mexico. Principal tribes of the Zapotecan linguistic group are the Zapotec, the Mazatec, and the Mixtec, most of whom live in Oaxaca and surrounding states. The Zapotecs were neighbors of the Toltec and the Aztec and were intermediaries between the Maya and Aztec cultures. They were conquered by the Spanish in the 1520's. Ruins of the ancient city of Mitla contain elaborate remains of Zapotecan temples and other artifacts.

CLARK WISSLER

ZARAGOZA, or Saragossa, province and city, NE Spain. The province is bounded by the provinces of Huesca on the NE, Lérida and Tarragona on the E, Teruel and Guadalajara on the S, Soria and Logroño on the W, and Navarra on the NW. Its 6,615 square miles enclose the dry, barren plain of the Ebro River, which is flanked to the north and south by sloping plateau surfaces. The climate is characterized by extreme temperatures and by a scarcity of rainfall that causes frequent droughts. Agriculture, the major occupation, is restricted to several fertile oases in the river valley.

The city of Zaragoza, capital of the province, is located on the Ebro River, 160 miles west of Barcelona. It is the communications, trading, and industrial center for an area that extends beyond the province. Zaragoza is the seat of a university and an officer training academy and is headquarters for one of the five air regions of Spain's air force. The city was the home of Francisco de Goya. Its two cathedrals, La Seo and Virgin of the Pillar, are its biggest tourist attractions. Zaragoza, an early Roman military colony, was held by the Moors from 714 to 1118, then captured by Alfonso I, King of Aragon. The city achieved fame by its resistance to French armies during the Peninsular War (1808–14). (For population, see Spain map in Atlas.)

ZARATHUSTRA, in later Greek sources, Zoroaster; Persian prophet, visionary, and ethical teacher, founder of the Zoroastrian religion. Various legends have grown up around him in the absence of historically verifiable information. In the later sacred books of Zoroastrianism, he is described as a supernatural being, the embodiment of wisdom and truth. In the older texts, however, he appears to be a genuine historical personage.

Although scholars do not agree as to the place and time of his birth, the general opinion now is that Zarathustra was born c. 660 B.C., somewhere in eastern Persia (Bactria, Media, or Azerbaijan) and died c. 538. Little is known about his childhood, except that he began his education before the age of 7 and at 20 became a religious wanderer, seeking truth in the wilderness. In the course of his wandering he had seven visions, the first at the age of 30 and the last at 40, when he underwent his final temptation by evil spirits. Gradually gaining followers, he made a royal convert in Vistasp, a Gushtasp in eastern Persia, who was formerly identified by scholars as Hystaspes, father of Darius, but was more probably a petty king. When Tauranian tribes from central Asia invaded Persia, Zarathustra and his followers took part in holy wars against them. The prophet was killed during the second Tauranian invasion in Balkh, where, according to legend, he died at the altar.

The teachings of Zarathustra are embodied in the *Zend-Avesta*, or divine writings, of which only the *Gathas* are believed to be the actual teachings of the prophet and his immediate followers. These are primarily concerned with ethics. Zarathustra introduced monotheism to the Aryan peoples of western Asia with Ahura-Mazda, the one supreme God. Ahura (Good) struggles with Angra-Mainyu (Evil) on the battleground of the world. Ahura is destined to win this struggle, and when he does so all men will enjoy immortality in paradise. After Zarathustra died, his teachings were widely spread but were considerably altered in the process.

Friedrich Nietzsche, the nineteenth-century German philosopher, used the prophet's name for his hero, the superman, in *Also Sprach Zarathustra*. See ZEND-AVESTA.

ZARIA, town, N Nigeria. The Hausa state of Zaria was powerful in the fourteenth century under Amina, a queen of legendary notoriety. It became a great center of the slave trade and was taken over by the Fulani early in their expansion (1804). Zaria was the center of a province under colonial rule; after World War II it became an industrial center. (For population, see northern Africa map in Atlas.)

ZARZUELA, Spanish musical comedy, combining elements of opera and drama, in which spoken parts alternate with song. The name is taken from the royal hunting lodge near Madrid, where these plays were first performed. Zarzuelas are of two classes: *chico*, generally in one act; and the more fully developed *grande*, usually in three or more acts. The form dates from the 1630's (Lope de Vega's *La Selva sui Amor* is an early example), but it reached its height late in the seventeenth century in the works of Calderón and Bances Candamo. Eventually, the zarzuela became less substantial: the traditional dances often were omitted, librettos were frivolous, and the performers engaged in repartee with the audience. ANTHONY KERRIGAN

ZEALOTS, a party of Jewish patriots that originated during the reign of Herod the Great (37 B.C.–4 B.C.) as a revival of the Maccabean movement. Unlike the Pharisees, Sadducees, and Essenes, the Zealots used violence in their fanatical defense of the Torah from the threats of both heathen oppressors and Jewish compromisers. Their first organized terrorist activities began in A.D. 6, when under Judas of Galilee they protested an enforced Roman census. A succession of sporadic revolts culminated in the unsuccessful rebellion against Rome that brought the destruction of Jerusalem (A.D. 70). Thereafter the party all but disappeared.

ZEBRA, the name given to any African member of the horse tribe (family *Equidae*) marked by characteristic stripes—generally black on a white background. There are three distinct species, related to each other no more closely than they are related to the horse or the ass.

The largest is Grevy's zebra (*Equus grevyi*), which stands about 4½ feet high at the withers. Its ears are long and rounded, its stripes broad on the neck but narrow on the body, except for a broad spinal stripe. Its bray is very like the donkey's. Grevy's zebra inhabits the open plains of the Ethiopian lowlands, Somalia, and northern Kenya. The mountain zebra (*E. zebra*) is smaller—less than 4 feet tall. Its ears are pointed, its head finer; the spinal stripe is narrow, but on the thighs the stripes are broad. The mountain zebra has seldom been heard to utter. It once was common in rocky country in southern Africa, but is now practically extinct.

The quagga (*E. quagga*) resembles the mountain zebra but has smaller ears, and its stripes become diagonal toward the rear. The quagga has a distinctive cry, roughly represented by its name. The South African quagga—now extinct—had relatively ill-defined stripes. In northern species the stripes are bolder.

ZEBU, *Bos indicus*, humped cattle found in India, China, the East Indies, and East Africa. They are smaller than western cattle and have an enlarged, fatty hump, long ears, short horns, and a big dewlap. In India they are considered sacred. Crosses with western cattle have produced a hybrid resistant to Texas fever, a disease caused by the protozoan *Babesia bigemina* and transmitted by ticks.

ZECHARIAH, eleventh of the minor prophets in the Old Testament, referred to variously as the son of Iddo or of Berechiah. During the period following the Jews' return to Palestine from exile, Zechariah and the prophet Haggai were associated in the rebuilding of the Temple, which was begun in 520 B.C. and completed in 516. Having called on his people to repent of their sins, Zechariah recorded a series of oracles, or night visions (chapters 1–8), expressing his hope of a glorious future for Jerusalem—its enemies overcome, its exiles returned, its sins forgiven, its priesthood spiritually revitalized, and its line of Davidic kings restored, all through the intervention of a messiah on behalf of his people. Chapters 9–14 of the Book of Zechariah are commonly attributed to another later writer or to several later writers, because they are so different in character from the earlier chapters.

BIBLIOG.–H. G. Mitchell, "Haggai and Zechariah," *International Critical Commentary on the Holy Scriptures,* vol. 25 (1912); Sir George Adam Smith, *The Book of the Twelve Prophets* (rev. ed. 1928).

ZEDEKIAH, throne name of Mattaniah, the last king of Judah, placed on the throne in 597 B.C. as the puppet of the Babylonian king Nebuchadnezzar II, after an unsuccessful Jewish revolt. Disregarding the advice of the prophet Jeremiah, Zedekiah allied himself with Egypt and revolted against Babylonian rule in 588 B.C. Jerusalem was besieged and destroyed in 586, and Zedekiah was captured, blinded, and taken to Babylon.

ZEELAND, province, the Netherlands, forming the extreme southwest of that kingdom, below the island of Goeree and west of a north-south line drawn, approximately, through the mouth of the Scheldt. Middelburg is the provincial capital. Much of Zeeland lies below sea level; dikes and embankments protect its fertile soil from encroachments of the sea. The mass of islands, peninsulas, and waterways that comprises the province of Zeeland has been greatly affected by an enormous engineering scheme known as the Delta plan, which first took shape in 1953. When completed (in 1978) it will have shortened the Dutch coastline by over 400 miles, by means of gigantic causeways across four sea inlets. The chief purpose of the plan is to end floods. It will also conserve fresh water supplies and end the isolation of the islands.

ZEEMAN, PIETER, 1865–1943, Dutch physicist, born in Zonnemaire. He was educated at Leiden University, where later, from 1890 to 1897, he worked in research with his teacher, Hendrik A. Lorentz. He became a lecturer in physics at the University of Amsterdam in 1897, a professor of physics there in 1900, and director of the Amsterdam Physical Institute in 1908. His best known work was the discovery of the Zeeman effect: the splitting of spectroscopic lines when the source of radiation is placed in a magnetic field. Zeeman and Lorentz shared the 1902 Nobel prize in physics for investigations concerning the influence of magnetism on light.

ZEEMAN EFFECT, the splitting of spectral lines that can be observed when a light source is placed in a magnetic field. The separation of the lines increases in direct proportion to the strength of the magnetic field. The cause of the Zeeman effect was sought unsuccessfully by Michael Faraday, and was discovered by Pieter Zeeman, a Dutch physicist, in 1896.

The energy levels of an atom may be thought of as being due to the concentric orbits its electrons have while revolving around the nucleus. Each orbit corresponds to a specific energy level. When an electron moves from an orbit of higher energy to an orbit of lower energy, it radiates a light wave whose frequency is determined by the electron's resonance frequency. The resonance frequency of an electron corresponds to its period of revolution. Electrons also spin on their own axes and if there are equal numbers of clockwise and counterclockwise spins, each spectral line will be of a single frequency, that is, will be a singlet line. The simplest type of Zeeman splitting, called the normal Zeeman effect, occurs in singlet spectra.

A magnetic field will affect the path of an orbiting electron, causing it to travel helically. When a light source with a singlet spectrum is viewed longitudinally, i.e., in the direction of the magnetic field, each spectral line is symmetrically split into two lines, circularly polarized in opposite directions. When viewed transversely, the original line is seen in addition, i.e., a triplet instead of a doublet is seen, but the polarizations are changed. In both views, the line separations (expressed as differences of frequency, rather than of wave length) are linearly proportional to the strength of the magnetic field. The directions of polarization were of greatest interest in early studies of the Zeeman effect, for they were among the first indications that electrons are particles of negative, rather than positive, charge. See POLARIZATION OF LIGHT.

For atoms with unbalanced electronic spins, the Zeeman splitting is more complicated. This case is called the anomalous Zeeman effect, and cannot be explained solely in terms of the classical resonance model described above. See QUANTUM THEORY.

There is an inverse Zeeman effect, which is observed when a magnet is placed near a body that is absorbing light.

Line separation in the Zeeman effect is small, being only a few tenths of an Angstrom unit for most spectral lines when the magnetic field is 50,000 times as strong as that of the earth in middle temperate latitudes (e.g., the United States). The Stark effect is an analogous spectral line splitting due to an applied electric field, and is much greater than the Zeeman effect. EDWARD SPEYER

BIBLIOG.–F. A. Jenkins and H. E. White, *Fundamentals of Optics* (3rd ed. 1957); John H. Van Vleck, *Theory of Electric and Magnetic Susceptibilities* (1932).

ZEISBERGER, DAVID, 1721–1808, Moravian missionary in America, born in Moravia. He emigrated to Georgia in 1738 and in 1739 went to Pennsylvania, where he became a missionary to the Iroquois and Delaware Indians. He founded a Moravian mission in Ohio in 1771 and later took part in founding colonies among the Indians farther north into Canada. His writings include an English speller and an Indian grammar and dictionary.

ZEISS, CARL, 1816–1888, German manufacturer of lenses and optical instruments, born in Weimar. In 1846 he set up a factory in Jena. Having the foresight to realize that progress in building high quality microscopes depended upon progress in scientific inquiry, he engaged as research physicist Ernst Abbe, then at the University of Jena. The world renown of the Zeiss name is directly attributable to Abbe, who became a partner of Zeiss in 1875.

ZELAYA, JOSE SANTOS, 1853–1919, Nicaraguan statesman, born in Managua. In 1893 he became president of Nicaragua, after playing a leading part in the overthrow of Roberto Sacaza; he ruled dictatorially until overthrown in 1909. In an effort to re-establish the Central American Federation, he seized the Mosquitia Indian Reserve in 1894 and fomented revolution in neighboring countries in 1907–8. Latin American and U.S. opposition to his ambitions led to his downfall.

ZEN, a Japanese sect of Mahayana Buddhism that teaches self-discipline and meditation, to the end of attaining, by direct intuition, the enlightenment (*satori*) experienced by Buddha.

According to legend, Zen originated in India in the sixth century. The school of meditation was introduced into China during the early part of the sixth century by the Indian philosopher Bodhidharma, who became the first Chinese patriarch. The doctrine was subsequently transmitted from patriarch to patriarch, terminating with Hui-neng (638–713), the sixth Chinese patriarch. Under him, the doctrine developed into seven sects, which flourished most extensively in the T'ang (618–906) and Sung (960–1279) periods, and then declined in the Ming (1368–1644). Two of the sects have continued to flourish in China.

Zen was introduced into Japan several times between the seventh and ninth centuries, but it did not take hold until Eisai founded the Rinzai Sect in 1191 and Dogen founded the Soto Sect in 1227. These two sects still flourish today. A third sect that exists today, the Obaku, was founded by Ingen in 1654. After 1927, when D. T. Suzuki began to write on Zen in English, Zen came to represent the application of Buddhism to an individual's inner life, as distinct from other more social aspects of Buddhism, whose older schools had focused on the needs of life at court, in the cities, or among the aristocracy. During the middle of the twentieth century, Zen began to have considerable appeal in Western culture.

The word Zen has no exact equivalent in English or in any other European language. The Japanese *zen* derives from the Chinese *Ch'an*, which in turn derives from the Sanskrit *dhyana* (contemplation). The spiritual basis of Zen is meditation rather than a didactic canonical text. In Japan the Zen monasteries seek to direct pupils to give up questing for truth in the form of words by presenting them with paradoxes and riddles. Arduous physical discipline is also part of the program to achieve "abrupt enlightenment." The Buddha-mind is regarded as synonymous with "supreme truth"—ultimate and total intuitive knowledge of the universe. When the Buddha-mind is penetrated, the meditator has himself become a Buddha. Different sects of Zen employ a wide variety of methods of instruction, ranging from mental and physical punishment to gentle guidance.

BIBLIOG.–Heinrich Dumoulin, *Development of Chinese Zen* (1953); D. T. Suzuki, *Manual of Zen Buddhism* (1960); Alan W. Watts, *Way of Zen* (1959).

ZEND-AVESTA, the sacred document of the Zoroastrian religion, used today by the Parsees as their book of prayer and scripture. It consists of five parts: the *Yasna*, 72 chapters of priests' liturgy that includes the *Gathas* (hymns which are the oldest part of the document); the *Vispered*, 22 chapters of liturgical invocation; the *Vendidad*, 22 chapters of the Parsee priestly code; the *Yashts*, 21 invocations to *izads* (angels); and the *Khordah Avesta*, a book of private prayers. The document is written in Avesta, the language of Bactria (ancient east Iran). Parsee tradition holds that the present document is a small portion of an enormous body of work by Zarathustra, which was preserved on cowhides until it was destroyed by Alexander the Great. The remaining fragments were collected by Zoroastrian priests. "Zend" means interpretation.

BIBLIOG.–*The Zend-Avesta*, tr. by J. Darmesteter and L. H. Mills, in *The Sacred Books of the East* (1880–87); *The Avestan Hymn to Mithra*, tr. by Ilya Gershevitch (1959).

ZENGER, JOHN PETER, 1697–1746, colonial American publisher, born in Germany. He was brought to New York in 1710 and served an apprenticeship under William Bradford in the printing trade for nine years. He started in business for himself as founder of the New York *Weekly Journal* in 1733. Because of the paper's virulent criticism of the government, he was arrested, imprisoned, and tried for criminal libel. The authorities were determined to secure a conviction, and it soon became evident that the judges were similarly disposed. Andrew Hamilton, Zenger's lawyer, argued that if what Zenger had printed was true (as Zenger maintained), then it was not libelous. Zenger's subsequent exoneration was regarded as a triumphant vindication of the liberty of the press. Zenger published a verbatim record of the trial in his paper and republished it as *A Brief Narrative of the Case and Trial of John Peter Zenger* (1736).

BIBLIOG.–James Alexander, *Brief Narrative of the Case and Trial of John Peter Zenger*, ed. Stanley Katz (1963); Livingston Rutherford, *John Peter Zenger* (1904).

ZENITH TELESCOPE, a structurally modified astronomical telescope used to determine terrestrial latitudes. Physically, the zenith telescope measures the difference, in degrees, between the astronomical altitudes of two stars (one chosen slightly north of the zenith, and one slightly south). By measuring a difference rather than an absolute number, residual errors may be made to cancel out, and a high accuracy can be achieved. Using the value of this difference and known values of the declinations of the two stars, the latitude at which the measurement is being made may be calculated by the formula: Latitude = ½ (sum of the declinations) − ½ (difference of the altitudes). With modifications, the zenith telescope can be used for the accurate determination of time.

ZENO, 426–491, emperor of the Eastern Roman Empire, born in Isuria. He married Ariadne, the daughter of Leo I, and was crowned emperor on Leo's death in 474. His reign was interrupted in 475 when he was forced to yield to the usurper, Basiliscus, but he regained power the following year. Zeno recognized the barbarian rule of Odoacer in the West, but he came under increasing pressure in the East from the Ostrogoths. In 488 he persuaded Theodoric, the Ostrogoth leader, to invade Italy, and thus secured his own empire. In the Monophysite controversy, Zeno issued a letter, *Henotico* (482), in an unsuccessful attempt to settle differences between the Eastern and Western churches.

ZENOBIA, died after A.D. 272, Queen of Palmyra, wife of King Odenathus. After the death of her husband in 267, she ruled as regent for her son. Her ambition to extend the power of Palmyra over the entire East led her to challenge the power of Rome. Under the pretext of a Roman alliance, she occupied Egypt and established garrisons in Asia Minor, Syria, and Mesopotamia. On the accession of the Emperor Aurelian in 270, she openly defied Rome by naming her son king of Egypt and emperor. Aurelian immediately took steps to maintain the unity of his Eastern Empire: Egypt was retaken by Roman troops in 270, and Palmyra was conquered in 272. Zenobia and her son fled the city but were captured and brought to Rome to grace Aurelian's triumph. Granted leniency, Zenobia retired to a villa at Tivoli, where she lived with her sons and led the life of a Roman matron.

BIBLIOG.–Alexander Baron, *Queen of the East* (1956); William Wright, *An Account of Palmyra and Zenobia* (1895).

ZENO OF CITIUM, 336?–264? B.C., Greek philosopher, founder of the Stoic school of philosophy, born in Citium (Kitium), on the island of Cyprus. According to tradition, he was a merchant who was forced by a shipwreck to stay in Athens where he became acquainted with the writings of the Cynics and was so impressed by their description of Socrates's character that he gave up trade for philosophy.

Zeno conceived of the whole cosmos as the frame of reference for human ethics and politics. For Zeno, the natural and the human cosmos are one, and may be thought of as the "city of Zeus" or the "nature of things." The quest of the philosopher is for "knowledge of the divine and the human things." Since for Zeno there is a universal identity of natural and political order, the "natural law" transcends and supersedes local laws. Thus, even when the philosopher is destroyed by some local order as Socrates had been, he serenely remains a member of the divine universe.

Zeno was popular among the Athenians, who made him a citizen, presented him with a golden crown, and eventually paid for his funeral and erected a bronze statue of him in gratitude for "the sobriety and virtue" with which he had taught their young men.

ZENO OF ELEA, c.490–c.430 B.C., Greek philosopher, the son of Telutagoras and the pupil of Parmenides of Elea. In Athens he taught his master's doctrine of unity. According to tradition, he died under torture after biting out his own tongue and throwing it into the face of a Sicilian tyrant who was trying to force him to betray political associates.

Since he employed a method of indirect argumentation, Zeno is considered to be the inventor of dialectic. His philosophy attempted to refute the popular assumption of the existence of the Many, and in this attempt he opposed Heraclitus and Empedocles. He undertook to prove four propositions: (1) that the One exists as opposed to the Many; (2) that movement does not really exist; (3) that space is not real; (4) that man's senses cannot prove anything.

In order to support his doctrines, Zeno invented ingenious paradoxes, several of which have become famous. The best-known of these is the paradox of Achilles and the tortoise. The paradox supposes that Achilles, running a race with the tortoise, can never catch the tortoise if the latter is given a head-start. It proposes that we arbitrarily regard the total distance Achilles must traverse, if he wishes to catch the tortoise, as being the sum of an infinite series of geometrically decreasing distances. Mathematically this is legitimate; what the Greeks did not realize, was that a series may have a perfectly reasonable finite sum even if it has an infinite number of terms. Such series are said to be convergent. The above paradox and others similar to it were the forerunners of modern mathematical concepts of continuity and infinity.

However, it was Zeno's paradox of predication that had the most immediate effect on the succeeding generation of Greek philosophers. The paradox reads as follows: "If existences are many, they must be both like and unlike (unlike inasmuch as they are not one and the same, and like, inasmuch as they agree in not being one and the same). But this is impossible; for unlike things cannot be like, nor like things unlike. Therefore existences are not many." This paradox, which virtually denied the ability of man's senses and mind to prove anything, led to the doctrine of the Skeptics three-quarters of a century later. It remained for the One and the Many to be reconciled in the philosophy of Plato.

BIBLIOG.–John Burnet, *Early Greek Philosophy* (1920); *Zeno of Elea,* fragments ed. and tr. by Henry P. D. Lee (1936).

ZEOLITE, any of a number of minerals that are hydrated silicates of aluminum. They usually contain sodium and/or calcium, and sometimes potassium or barium. Among the best known zeolites are analcime, laumontite, natrolite, heulandite, stilbite, and chabazite. Their specific gravities are always low (2.0 to 2.4), and their hardnesses range from $3\frac{1}{2}$ to $5\frac{1}{2}$.

Zeolites are used extensively as water softeners. Their effectiveness is due to their ability to exchange their sodium for calcium and magnesium when hard water is passed over them. This property is called base exchange, or cation exchange. After a period of use, the zeolite must be regenerated (the sodium regained). Regeneration is accomplished by passing a common salt solution through it.

Zeolites usually are extracted as secondary minerals, in the form of crystals, from the cracks and cavities of basic igneous rocks. Among the areas with important zeolite deposits are Iceland, Nova Scotia, Scotland, India, South Africa, and the United States.

Artificial zeolites have been produced in a range of consistencies, from jellylike to sandy. They have been used not only as water softeners, but as gas adsorbents and drying agents as well.

ZEPHANIAH, ninth of the minor Old Testament prophets, flourished during the reign of Josiah, about 638–608 B.C. Prior to 621, and probably during the period 630–624, Zephaniah condemned his people for worshiping heathen deities and adopting foreign customs. He foretold a universal and catastrophic judgment of God on other nations—specifically, the Egyptians, Ammonites, Moabites, Philistines, and Assyrians—from which only the godly remnant of Judah would escape; and he described the glory that would be the Jews' after their delivery from captivity.

ZEPHYRINUS, SAINT, d. 217, pope from 198 until his death. During his reign, controversies as to the nature of the Trinity raged. The pope was out of his element in dealing with doctrinal matters and sought peace and unity among factions.

ZEPHYRUS, in Greek mythology, god of the west wind, son of Astraeus and Eos, brother of Boreas, Notus, and Eurus. In Roman mythology, Zephyrus is known as Favonius.

ZEPPELIN, COUNT FERDINAND VON, 1838–1917, German army officer and airship designer, born in Constance. He joined the German army in 1858 and in 1863 went to the United States, where he served with the Union army during the Civil War. Zeppelin also fought in the Austro-Prussian War (1866) and the Franco-Prussian War (1870–71). He retired from the army as a lieutenant general in 1891. Turning to airship design, Zeppelin introduced in 1900 the first of the rigid airships, soon to become known as Zeppelins in his honor. He established an airship factory at Friedrichshafen in 1908, but a series of disasters limited his financial success. See AIRSHIP.

ZERMATT, village, s Switzerland, in the canton of Valais; located in the Visp valley beneath the Matterhorn, at an altitude of 5,315 feet. Zermatt commands one of the finest views of Switzerland and is a famous mountain-climbing center. The village has a small German-speaking population, but it is frequented summer and winter by international tourists. An alpine museum is located here.

ZERO, a symbol, 0, denoting (a) the absence of a number and (b) the initial point (origin) of both the positive and negative sets of numbers. In the former sense, zero length, force, time, etc. represent no length, force, time. In the latter sense the number zero, occupying a place midway between

−1 and +1, is classed as an integer having the following properties:

$$1)\ a + 0 = 0 + a = a$$
$$2)\ a - 0 = -(0 - a) = a$$
$$3)\ a \times 0 = 0 \times a = 0$$
$$4)\ 0 \div a = 0$$

where a is a number not equal to zero. As a result of these properties the operation $a \div 0$ is meaningless. To see why, assume for a moment that it is permissible to divide by zero and examine the quotient $a/0 = b$. Multiplying both sides of the equation by 0, we obtain $a = 0 \times b = 0$, for any number b. But this cannot be true, for a was originally specified to be not zero. See NUMBER.

When in a quotient of two functions $f(x)/g(x)$ both the numerator and the denominator become equal to zero for some value of x, we have the so-called indeterminate form, "0/0". It is solved by taking derivatives, as described in the article INDETERMINATE FORM.

Other operations that have been defined for zero include the zero exponential and the zero factorial. The value of any nonzero quantity raised to the zero power is defined as unity, and so is the value of the factorial zero. Thus: $a^0 = 1$, and $0! = 1$. See EXPONENT; FACTORIAL.

The zero of a function of a variable x is the value of x for which the function is zero. At this value of x the curve of the function crosses the x axis. See FUNCTION; POLYNOMIAL.

Zero as a means of positional notation by which, for instance, we differentiate between 23, 203 and 2003 was introduced by the Babylonians about three thousand years ago, in a number system that had a basis of 60.

Zero as a number, having the properties described above, was introduced in the sixth century by the Hindus and Chinese. Use of zero as a number was not accepted in Europe, however, until the thirteenth century.

ZERO-POINT ENERGY, the kinetic energy of a system at a temperature of absolute zero. For example, the oscillating nuclei of a diatomic molecule have a vibrational energy of $\frac{1}{2}h\nu$ at absolute zero. In agreement with Heisenberg's uncertainty principle, this is the minimum energy the molecule may have.

ZEUS, the highest god of ancient Greece, called by Homer "the Father of Gods and Men." In Roman mythology, he is called Jupiter. Zeus and his pantheon were said to reside on Mount Olympus, and an almost endless series of legends each with its several variants grew up around him. The son of Cronus and Rhea, Zeus overthrew his father and the other Titans, and divided the kingdom of the universe with his brothers Hades (who ruled the underworld) and Poseidon (who ruled the sea). His wife, Hera, was also his sister; she was a fiercely jealous creature, but with ample justification, it seems, for Zeus was well-known for his amorous exploits. Zeus and Hera's children were Ares, Hephaestus, and Hebe. In many extra-marital relations and in many guises Zeus fathered other famous children, including Hermes by Maia; Apollo and Artemis by Leto; Dionysus by Semele; Helen of Troy by Leda; and Endymion by Calyce. The thunderbolt is Zeus's sign. See MYTHOLOGY.

BIBLIOG.–Thomas Bulfinch, *Bulfinch's Mythology* (rev. ed. 1962); Robert Graves, *The Greek Myths* (1955); H. J. Rose, *Handbook of Greek Mythology* (1959).

ZHDANOV, ANDREI ALEKSANDROVICH, 1896–1948, Soviet Russian official, born in Mariupol (later Zhdanov), in the Ukraine. After the revolution of 1917 he served in various party posts and became a member of the Politburo in 1939. He was in Leningrad during the heroic defense of that city

in World War II. Zhdanov's prestige rose after the war; important announcements of Soviet policy often came from him, and he was regarded as Stalin's likeliest successor. The circumstances of his rather sudden death seemed—though on slight evidence—suspicious to some people.

ZHDANOV, city, U.S.S.R., on the Sea of Asov, at the mouth of the Kalmius River in the Ukraine. Its proximity to the Donetsk Coal Basin accounts for its heavy industry. It has an excellent harbor and is a center for such activities as fish canning and shipbuilding. The city, formerly named Mariupol, was founded by Greeks from the Crimea about 1880. It was captured by the Germans during World War II. Mariupol was renamed in 1948 in honor of its most famous citizen, A. A. Zhdanov. (For population, see U.S.S.R. map in Atlas.)

ZHITOMIR, city and region, U.S.S.R., NW Ukrainian Soviet Socialist Republic. The region has an area of 11,600 square miles. Over half of the land is marshy forest. The economy is based largely on agriculture and dairying. Important crops include sugarbeets, wheat, flax, potatoes, and hops. Quartz, sand, and kaolin deposits supply raw materials for glassware and pottery factories. Lumbering is also important. The region was established in 1937.

Zhitomir, the city, is the region's capital. It is about 85 miles west of Kiev, on the Teterev River. The city is a transportation and manufacturing center; its manufactures include clothing and furniture. Founded in the ninth century, Zhitomir passed under Lithuanian rule in the fourteenth century and under Polish rule in 1569. It became a part of Russia after the second Polish partition, 1793. (For population, see U.S.S.R. map in Atlas.)

ZHUKOV, GEORGI KONSTANTINOVICH, 1896– , Soviet military leader, born in Strelkovka, Russia. He served in the tsar's army in World War I and entered the Red army after the 1917 revolution. He gained early recognition by leading tank forces against the Japanese in the Manchurian border clashes (1938–39) and against the Finns (1939–40). Promoted to general in 1940, he was chief of the Red army staff until he was relieved to conduct the defense of Moscow (1941). Zhukov organized the great victory of Stalingrad in 1943 and was made a marshal for his participation in lifting the siege of Leningrad. He personally conducted the final offensive against Germany (1943–44), captured Berlin (1945), and remained there as commander of the Soviet occupation forces until 1946, when concern over his popularity led Stalin to demote him to a series of minor regional posts. He returned to prominence after Stalin's death, becoming deputy defense minister (1953), defense minister (1955), and a member of the presidium (1957). In October, 1957, under charges of seeking absolute power for the military, Zhukov was relieved of all his important party and government posts. After Khrushchev's resignation, he reappeared at public functions.

ZHUKOVSKY, VASILI, 1783–1852, Russian poet and translator, born near Belev. From 1818 he was tutor to Alexander II. Zhukovsky's many translations of works of Western literature influenced Russian poetry. Among the authors he translated are Byron, Gray, Goethe, and Schiller.

ZIEGFELD, FLORENZ, 1869–1932, U.S. theatrical producer, born in Chicago, Ill. He began his show business career by importing musical entertainment for the Chicago World's Fair in 1893. In England, in 1896, he became manager of the famous European beauty Anna Held, whom he later married and thereafter divorced. His first theatrical review,

Follies of 1907, based on the format of the *Folies Bergères*, was spectacularly successful, and the Zeigfeld Follies then appeared annually for more than 20 years. Ziegfeld also produced successful musical comedies, among them, *Show Boat* (1927) and *Rio Rita* (1927).

ZIELONA GORA, province and city, E Poland. The province is bounded by the provinces of Szczecin on the N, Poznán on the E, Wrocław on the S, and by Germany on the W. Its area is 5,604 square miles, its terrain primarily low, rolling, and fertile. Its agriculture includes general farming (notably grapes and hops), stock raising, and forestry. There are also deposits of lignite.

Capital and manufacturing center of Zielona Góra Province is the city of Zielona Góra. It is located some 225 miles east of Warsaw. Leather goods, wool fabrics, chemicals, and metal and machine products are manufactured. (For population, see Poland map in Atlas.)

ZIGGURAT, a tower, usually in the form of a stepped pyramid, associated with the great temple complexes of ancient Assyria, Babylonia, and Chaldea. Most typical of these structures are the ziggurats built at Ur during the third millennium B.C. These are constructed of sun-baked brick set over a core of hardened reinforced clay and faced with glazed tiles. In form, the ziggurat is a series of slope-sided, rectangular platforms of diminishing sizes that are set one upon the other, with the largest at the base. Some of these towers reached a height of 300 feet. Ramps ascending each tier diagonally led to a temple or shrine at the top. The Tower of Babel is thought to have been a ziggurat.

ZILE, or Zela, also Zilleh, town, N central Turkey, in Amasya Province; about 120 miles ENE of Ankara. Tobacco is the most important commercial product. The town was first ruled by the Armenoid Hittites, and then by Pontus, Rome, and Byzantium. It was from Zile that Julius Caesar, after defeating Pharnaces II of Pontus in 47 B.C., sent the dispatch "Veni, vidi, vici" (I came, I saw, I conquered). The Turks entered Zile in the fourteenth century. (For population, see Near East map in Atlas.)

ZIMBABWE, historic ruins in Rhodesia, about 16 miles from Fort Victoria. The unexpected sight of massive stone buildings in the heart of an African forest greeted Adam Renders in 1867, but not until after Carl Mauch's visit in 1870 did Zimbabwe become known to the world at large. Since then, Zimbabwe has been a famous and controversial subject among archaeologists. The ruins are roughly divided into three groups: the "Acropolis," on a hilltop, once probably used for tribal prayer; the temple, in a nearby valley, nearly 300 feet long and over 200 feet wide with walls 30 feet high and up to 14 feet thick; and the enigmatic tower, possibly a phallic symbol, which is now 31 feet high. The ruins owe nothing to any known extra-African style of architecture, and indeed they are not noted for their design: the builders' approach was clearly empirical. The workmanship, however, is of outstanding quality. There is no decoration, and the chevron-pattern of some of the walls is no longer visible. Of relics found at Zimbabwe most interesting are the soapstone figures of birds now in various museums. The ruins were damaged—and much valuable archaeological evidence destroyed—in the years following their discovery, but they are now closely protected by the government.

The origin of the Zimbabwe ruins was long disputed: first opinions ascribed them to a period much earlier than now seems likely, and their creators were thought to have been Asians, not Africans. Their African origin is now established, and Dr. Gertrude Caton-Thompson, the most famous authority, has assigned them to about the ninth century A.D. Radiocarbon dating suggests that construction was proceeding at an even later date. Certainly most of the buildings were completed before the fifteenth century.

The origin of the word *zimbabwe* (*dzimbahwe*) is now lost; it seems to have come to mean a chief's burying ground and a place of worship. Other Zimbabwes are known, though no buildings of comparable distinction.

BIBLIOG.–Gertrude Caton-Thompson, *Zimbabwe Culture* (1931); Henrich A. Wieschhoff, *The Zimbabwe-Monomotapa Culture in Southeast Africa* (1941).

ZINC, symbol Zn, a bluish-white, lustrous, metallic element with an atomic weight of 65.37 and an atomic number of 30. It tarnishes only slightly in air, because of the thin, self-protecting coat of zinc basic carbonate it forms. It has a density of 7.14 grams per cubic centimeter at 20°C, melts at 419°C, and boils at 907°C. It has a valence of 2 in its compounds, and belongs to group II B in the periodic table. It exists in several naturally occurring isotopic forms, the most abundant of which has a mass of 64. It is a fair conductor of electricity and heat. When highly pure it reacts slowly to acids and alkalies, and in normal commercial purities it will react strongly to most acids and to strong bases.

Zinc was first recognized as a separate element early in the eighteenth century, although it had been separated and used for a variety of purposes, including coinage, as early as 500 B.C. It is not found free in nature but its ores are widely distributed over the earth's surface. The principal ore of zinc is known as sphalerite, or zinc blende (ZnS). Other common ores are smithsonite ($ZnCO_3$), willemite ($ZnSiO_4$), and zincite (ZnO).

Production. Metallic zinc is obtained from its ores either by fire refining or by an electrolytic process. Fire refining is favored in the United States, but use of the electrolytic process is growing.

Very high temperatures are needed to smelt zinc: the metallurigical reducing agent, carbon, will not reduce zinc oxide to zinc at temperatures below the boiling point of the metal. Fire refining is accomplished, for the most part, by converting the ores to oxide, and then using carbon to reduce the oxide to pure zinc in fire clay retorts, at high temperatures. The pure zinc, which forms as a vapor in the retort, is removed and condensed in receivers, as in a distilling process. The basic reactions are:

$$2ZnS + 3O_2 \rightarrow 2ZnO + 2SO_2$$
$$ZnO + C + Heat \rightarrow Zn + CO$$

In the electrolytic process for the preparation of zinc, the zinc blende (ZnS) is carefully roasted at a low temperature to form, largely, zinc sulfate, which is then leached with sulfuric acid. The resulting solution of zinc sulfate is treated with some zinc dust to precipitate any of the nobler metals that may be present and prevent their being deposited with the zinc during electrolysis. The pure solution is then electrolyzed. Electrolytically produced zinc can be from 99.9 to 99.99+ per cent pure, depending on the process control exercised.

Zinc of 99.99+ per cent purity can also be produced by fire refining through redistillation and this process is an important source of high-purity zinc.

The preceding methods have exclusively to do with the production of slab zinc (the common form) but an important segment of the industry revolves around the production of zinc oxide and zinc dust directly from the ore and from secondary materials, respectively.

An important quantity of zinc is recovered annually from scrap metals of various kinds, both old

LEADING PRODUCERS OF ZINC
(production figures in thousands of 2000 lb. tons)

	1955	1962 estimate
U.S.	1037.3	941.6
U.S.S.R.	260.0 *	440.0 *
Canada	256.5	280.2
Japan	124.1	270.4
Belgium	233.6	227.3
France	148.1	216.0
Germany	202.6	206.6
Poland	172.2	199.9
U.K.	91.2	108.9

*estimated by the U.S. Bureau of Mines

These figures relate to primary zinc recovered from domestic and imported ores and concentrates and secondary zinc recovered from scrap.

Based on figures published by the Statistical Office of the United Nations

and new. A great part of this scrap originates in brass mills, and in plants where zinc is rolled and processed. Zinc is also retrieved from the dross and skimmings of the galvanizing process. These secondary sources of zinc presently account for between five and seven per cent of the total amount of zinc produced.

Uses. The most important use of zinc is as a protective coating on other metals. In the United States, which is the world's largest consumer of zinc, approximately 40 per cent of all slab zinc produced is used for galvanizing (laying down a protective coating on steel); about 40 per cent, or slightly more, for die casting; 12-13 per cent in the manufacture of brass; about 4 per cent in making rolled zinc and various alloys; about 2 per cent for making oxide; and the balance for miscellaneous purposes.

Galvanizing. Galvanizing is the coating of cleaned steel or iron with a layer of zinc several thousandths of an inch thick. A layer of an alloy of the two metals results where they are directly in contact, with iron on the inside and zinc on the outside. Sheet steel unrolling from coils is continuously galvanized, in the major galvanizing process used in the United States.

Steel may be galvanized by electrodeposition processes applicable either to mill products or to small batches of fabricated shapes. Steel may also be coated by a process known as sherardizing, which involves controlled heating in a zinc dust pack. Steel may also be coated by being sprayed with the molten metal: this is known as metalizing.

A zinc coating protects steel in two ways: first, by acting as a barrier (in most environments zinc is at least 25 times more resistant to atmospheric corrosion than carbon steel), and second, by a sacrificial action which results in a slow corrosion of the zinc while it protects the steel galvanically. Since zinc has a relatively high electrode potential, it is anodic to iron so that when zinc and iron are placed in contact and exposed to a corrosive medium, the currents generated act to protect the steel and the medium attacks the zinc in preference to the iron.

Die Casting. Die casting is the most direct process for making molten metal into parts, and the low melting point of zinc gives it inherent advantages over other die-castable metals. In die casting, clean molten metal is injected into carefully machined die cavities under controlled pressure and temperature. The parts so produced are, essentially, ready for trimming of excess cast stock and for appropriate surface treatment. The largest use of zinc die cast parts is in the motor industry, with appliances running an important second. Zinc die cast parts are also used in machines and tools, builder's hardware, office equipment, photographic equipment, and optical and recording devices.

Brass. As mentioned above, approximately 12-13 per cent of all new zinc is used in the brass industry. See BRASS.

Rolled Zinc. Rolled zinc is particularly important in the United States for dry cell batteries and engravers' plates. Rolled zinc can be etched and soldered, and it can be finished by any conventional means of plating, painting, or low-temperature enameling.

Traces of zinc are also important to both plants and animals, though zinc and its compounds are toxic in too large quantities. Zinc containers may not be used for food.

Various zinc compounds—notably zinc oxide (ZnO), zinc chloride ($ZnCl_2$) and zinc sulfate ($ZnSO_4$)—are also commercially important and are used in the preparation of certain ointments, pigments, cements, ceramics, dyes, rubber, and arsenical sprays.   JOHN L. KIMBERLEY

BIBLIOG.–Eric Hutchinson, *Chemistry* (1959); C. H. Mathewson, *Zinc* (1959); A. M. Shrager, *Elementary Metallurgy and Metallography* (1961).

ZINCITE, the mineral zinc oxide, ZnO, usually found associated with the minerals franklinite and willemite. Although pure zinc oxide is white, the frequent presence of divalent manganese gives zincite a red to orange-yellow color and streak. Sometimes it is coated with a bluish-black film. Zincite has a hexagonal crystalline structure, a specific gravity that varies around 5.6, and a hardness of 4 to 4½. Zincite is used principally as a source of white zinc oxide. One of the few places zincite is found is Franklin, N.J.

ZINDER, town, s Niger Republic, on the fringe of the Sahara desert. Zinder was once the capital of a Tuareg state. Under French control it was the administrative capital of the territory until 1926. A trans-Saharan road links Zinder with Algiers. In the region around Zinder, groundnuts are grown for export. (For population, see northern Africa map in Atlas.)

ZINNIA, any member of a genus of the plant family Compositae, named after the German botanist Johann Gottfried Zinn (1727-59).

Zinnia elegans, the variety usually grown in gardens, is an annual, popular for the size, range of colors, and long life of its flowers; it may reach a height of three feet. The zinnia is native to the warmer parts of North America, chiefly Mexico. It is the state flower of Indiana.

Zinnias

W. ATLEE BURPEE CO.

ZINOVIEV, GRIGORI EVSEEVICH, 1883–1936, assumed name of Hirsch Apfelbaum, Soviet Communist leader, born in Elisavetgrad, Ukraine. A revolutionary in his youth, Zinoviev joined the Bolshevik faction of the Social Democratic party in 1903 and lived in exile from 1908 to 1917, when he returned with Lenin to take part in the Russian Revolution.

From 1919 to 1926, Zinoviev was the first president of the Communist International. In 1927 he was expelled from the Communist party for siding with Leon Trotsky against Joseph Stalin, but in 1928 he reversed his position and was reinstated. Accused of treasonous complicity in the murder of Sergei Kirov, Zinoviev was arrested in 1934. He was convicted and executed in the famous purge trials of 1936.

ZINZENDORF, NIKOLAUS LUDWIG, GRAF VON, 1700–1760, German religious leader, restorer of the church of the Moravian Brethren, born in Dresden. He studied at the University of Wittenberg, where he became interested in forming a Christian association that would, by benevolent activities and writings, awaken religious vitality. Zinzendorf invited persecuted members of the Unitas Fratrum, or Bohemian Brethren, to establish a colony (called Herrnhut) on his estate in Saxony in 1722. He actively participated in the reorganization of the denomination that became known as the Moravian Brethren, and wrote hymns, made contributions to Moravian literature, and established schools. After the Moravians were exiled by the government of Saxony in 1736, he traveled in Europe and America on behalf of his church, making many converts. While in the United States, between 1741 and 1743, he established Moravian colonies in Bethlehem, Nazareth, Philadelphia, Lancaster, Hebron, and York, Pa.

BIBLIOG.–William G. Addison, *Renewed Church of the United Brethren, 1722–1930* (1932); John R. Weinlick, *Count Zinzendorf* (1956).

ZION, city, NE Illinois, Lake County, situated on Lake Michigan, 6 miles N of Waukegan and 45 miles N of Chicago. The city was founded in 1901 by John Alexander Dowie as the seat of his Christian Catholic Apostolic Church and originally operated as a communal society. Zion was controlled by the church until 1935. Manufactures include television and electronic appliances and clothing. (For population, see Illinois map in Atlas.)

ZION, a hill of Jerusalem. The name apparently applied originally to a Jebusite fortress on the southeastern hill of the ancient city. The site was renamed the City of David following its capture by David (II Sam. 5:6–9), who built his palace here. Modern scholarship has cast doubt on a Christian tradition that the southwestern hill of Jerusalem was called Zion. The name also has come to refer to all of Jerusalem, to the Jews, and to their hope for their return to their homeland.

ZIONISM, the movement for the return of the Jews to Palestine and for the reestablishment and advance of the Jewish national state of Israel. In its essence, Zionism has existed in the prayers and yearnings of the Jewish people through all the centuries of the dispersion. From the Middle Ages to modern times, many groups of Jews have responded to this yearning and have gone to live in the Holy Land. But the movement known today as Zionism did not come into active being until the end of the nineteenth century. It found its first expression among the Jews of Eastern Europe.

A strong revival of the spirit of nationalism and an intensification of anti-Semitism led East European Jews to a determination to form a Jewish homeland.

Theodore Herzl (1860–1904), a distinguished Austrian-Jewish writer born in Hungary, gave direction and forceful leadership to the budding movement. At the first Zionist Congress, held in Basel, Switzerland, in 1897, Herzl formed a Zionist Organization to create "for the Jewish people a home in Palestine secured by public law." He later founded the World Zionist Organization, with subsidiary institutes, whose aim was to secure land and property in the Holy Land. Small groups of Jews already had begun to settle there, and they were supported by various philanthropic organizations and individuals. Generous support for the early settlers came from Baron Edmond de Rothschild of Paris. His holdings were taken over eventually by the Palestine Jewish Colonization Association (PICA), which carried out the work he had begun.

Before his death in 1904, Theodore Herzl had made Zionism an issue of world concern and had brought it to the attention of diplomats, heads of government, and the general public. After his death, controversies arose within the movement; some Zionists favored immediate colonization, others wished to carry on in the diplomatic tradition of Herzl. From 1905 to 1911, under the leadership of David Wolffsohn, the World Zionist Organization carried out both aspects of the work. At the 1911 Zionist Congress, Otto Warburg was elected president of the organization and headquarters were moved to Berlin. Under the new leader, colonization made substantial progress through the Palestine Office in Jaffa. Agricultural developments were founded and urban construction was begun. Plans were made for the establishment of the city of Tel Aviv. By the outbreak of World War I there were almost 100,000 Jews living in Palestine.

Chaim Weizmann, acting for the World Zionist Organization in England, was instrumental in bringing about the Balfour Declaration, which Britain issued on November 2, 1917. This was a pledge to aid "the establishment in Palestine of a national home for the Jewish people." After the war, Palestine became a Mandate of Great Britain. The terms of the Mandate, which included the Balfour Declaration, were officially sanctioned by the League of Nations. Thus the aims and ideals of Zionism were given international approval.

The subsequent British White Paper of 1939, which repudiated the Balfour pledge and drastically limited Jewish immigration to Palestine, caused extreme bitterness and often open defiance among Jews. The result was that the desire only for a national home, which had been the aim of the Zionist movement, began to crystallize into a determination to establish a Jewish state.

Zionist organizations were occupied with pleading their cause before the world and furthering it in Palestine. They spent their energies in enlisting the financial, diplomatic, and moral support of the nations, but their greatest efforts were in behalf of building the homeland and promoting the cause of Jewish immigration. Some support came from non-Zionists, but the major part of the work was accomplished by organized Zionism all over the world.

In America the strongest opposition to Zionism had come from Reform Judaism and from wealthy Jews of German and Bohemian ancestry. By the outbreak of World War II much of this opposition had weakened, and as the decimation of the Jews mounted in Europe, Zionism was accepted by many, both Jews and Christians, as the ultimate answer in providing a refuge. Numerous agencies were formed to aid the Jews in Palestine. The Jewish Agency for Palestine, created in 1929, continued to work for the enforcement of the Balfour Declaration. The Jewish National Fund bought property in the Holy Land as the "possession of the Jewish people"; in 1945–46 it owned over 213,000 acres.

Hadassah, the Women's Zionist Organization of America, devoted itself to public health and medical service.

On May 14, 1948, the State of Israel was established, with David Ben-Gurion, a famous Zionist leader, at its head. Today Zionists continue to work for the development of Israel's immigration, construction, agriculture, and industry. Largely financed by Zionist organizations outside Israel, their efforts have been phenomenally successful.

LOUIS FINKELSTEIN

BIBLIOG.–Ben Halpern, *Idea of the Jewish State* (1961); Theodor Herzl, *Diaries*, ed. Marvin Lowenthal (1962); Emil Lehman, *Israel, Idea and Reality* (1962).

ZION NATIONAL PARK, sw Utah, noted for its canyon and desert scenery, established in 1919; area, 147,034 acres. Varicolored sandstone and limestone formations have been eroded into unsual shapes resembling temples and thrones. The canyon was discovered in the 1850's by Mormon pioneers who later settled the area and named it Little Zion. See NATIONAL PARKS.

ZIRCON, a zirconium mineral, zirconium silicate, $ZrSiO_4$. It has tetragonal crystalline structure, a specific gravity of 4.7, and a hardness of $7\frac{1}{2}$. It is usually translucent, but transparent forms occur. It is commonly brown in color, although colorless, gray, pale yellow, green, and red varieties also are found. The transparent crystals are used as gems; the brownish or red-orange ones are called hyacinth or jacinth, and the colorless, yellow, and smoky ones, jargon. Opaque varieties are used primarily as a source of the metallic element zirconium and are used also to produce zirconium oxide, ZrO_2, an important refractory material. Zircon is widely distributed; it is found in practically all types of igneous rocks. Gem-quality zircon is found in Ceylon, the Ural Mountains, and Australia. Industrial zircon is found in Brazil, New South Wales, Norway, Canada, and in Maine, New York, and North Carolina in the United States.

ZIRCONIUM, Zr, a grayish-white, metallic element with an atomic weight of 91.22, atomic number of 40, specific gravity of 6.4, and valence of 4. It melts at $1857°$ C ($3374.6°$ F) and boils above $2900°$ C ($5252°$ F). There are five naturally occurring zirconium isotopes.

Zirconium metal is ductile and malleable. It resists most acids and bases. Its corrosion resistance to water and steam is not good, however, except when it is alloyed with small amounts of elements such as tin, iron, nickel, and chromium. When divided into powder or chips, zirconium is hazardous because it can burn or explode spontaneously.

Zirconium's most important use is in the manufacture of nuclear reactors. Here, once it has been freed of hafnium (an element with which it is commonly associated), zirconium offers the advantage of low neutron absorption in addition to its high mechanical strength and corrosion resistance. Zirconium also is used as a "getter" in electronic tubes, since it can absorb quantities of oxygen, nitrogen, and hydrogen. In addition, it is used in making chemical equipment, and as a bonding agent for ceramic-to-metal seals, a deoxidizer in metallurgy, and an alloying agent in a number of nonferrous alloys.

Among the many useful zirconium compounds is zirconium oxide, ZrO_2. It is the most heat resistant of all commercial refractory materials. It is also used as a paint, lacquer, resin, and ink pigment; as an abrasive and polishing agent; as a pharmaceutical agent; in X-ray photography; in metallurgy; and in making ceramics, acidproof enamel, refractory utensils, and cermets. Other important zirconium compounds are its oxychloride, pyro-phosphate, sulfate, and tetrachloride. They are used for a variety of purposes: in leather tanning, as catalysts, as water repellants for textiles, in metallurgy, and in medicines and cosmetics.

Zirconium constitutes about .028 per cent of the earth's crust. Its important ores are zircon, $ZrSiO_4$, and baddeleyite, ZrO_2. To produce zirconium by the Kroll process, the ore is converted to the carbonitride, which is chlorinated to zirconium tetrachloride. The tetrachloride is then reduced by liquid magnesium in an inert atmosphere. The van Arkel, or iodide, process yields highly pure and ductile zirconium through decomposition of zirconium tetraiodide by a hot tungsten filament in a vacuum or inert atmosphere.

BIBLIOG.–W. B. Blumenthal, *Chemical Behavior of Zirconium* (1958); W. T. Elwell and D. F. Wood, *Analysis of Titanium, Zirconium and Their Alloys* (1961).

ZITHER, a stringed musical instrument, thought to be ancient Asiatic or Greek origin, consisting of a flat, wooden soundbox over which from 30 to 45 strings are stretched. The five metal strings nearest the player carry the melody; they are plucked with a plectrum and can be stopped on a fretted finger board. The other strings, used for accompaniment, are plucked by the fingers.

In the system of classification of musical instruments, formulated by Curt Sachs and Erich von Hornbostel, zither is the name given to a subclass of instruments of the chordophone class, and as such includes board zithers, stick zithers, and long zithers. Three types of board zither are known as psalteries, dulcimers, and clavichords.

ZIZKA, JOHN, 1360?–1424, Bohemian patriot and Hussite leader, born in Troznov. Widespread military service during his early and middle years served as a prelude to his remarkably successful career as military leader of the Hussites in their war (1419 ff.) against the followers of the Romanist Sigismund, king of Germany and Hungary, who claimed the crown of Bohemia as heir of his brother Wenceslaus (d. 1419). After joining the Taborite Hussite faction and fortifying Tabor, their stronghold, Zizka in 1420 led his greatly outnumbered troops against Sigismund at Prague, where he routed the latter's army. There followed a series of military successes. While leading an attack at Rábi in 1421 Zizka was totally blinded; yet he retained his command and went on to defeat the enemy—often, as at Deutschbrod (1422), slaughtering numerically superior forces. In 1423 growing dissension between the two Hussite factions—the radical, peasant-supported Taborites and the more moderate Utraquists (or Calixtines), centered in Prague—erupted in civil war. After several confrontations Zizka marched with his Taborite troops on Prague, where a peace between the factions was concluded in 1424. Almost immediately Zizka led the combined Hussite forces in a massive attack on Moravia, which was still held by Sigismund. He died of the plague during the campaign. A brilliant tactician and innovator, Zizka created a potent peasant army by introducing the use of small arms and of armored wagons—techniques well in advance of his time. See HUSSITES.

BIBLIOG.–Frederick G. Heymann, *John Zizka and the Hussite Revolution* (1955).

ZLATOUST, city, U.S.S.R., in the Chelyabinsk oblast of the Russian Soviet Federated Socialist Republic; 74 miles w of Chelyabinsk. The city is located on the Ufa-Chelyabinsk railway in the south Ural mountains and has been an important metallurgical center since the 1750's. Manufactures include high-grade steels and alloys, machine tools, and precision instruments. (For population, see U.S.S.R. map in Atlas.)

ZNANIECKI, FLORIAN WITOLD, 1882–1958, Polish-American sociologist, was born in Swiatnice, Poland, studied at the universities of Zürich, Geneva, Paris, and Kraków, and taught at the University of Chicago, 1917–19, the University of Poznań, 1920–39, Columbia University, 1931–33, the University of Illinois, 1940–50, and Wayne University, 1950–51. Many of his fundamental works are available only in Polish, but a good idea of Znaniecki's approach to sociology can be acquired through his publications in English, of which the most significant are *Cultural Reality* (1919), *The Laws of Social Psychology* (1925), *The Method of Sociology* (1934), *Social Actions* (1936), *The Social Role of the Man of Knowledge* (1940), *Cultural Sciences: Their Origin and Development* (1951), *Modern Nationalities: A Sociological Study of How Nationalities Evolve* (1952), and *The Polish Peasant in Europe and America* (with W. I. Thomas, 6 vols. 1918–20; edit. 1960). The last named, one of the most frequently quoted works in all of sociological literature, is perhaps most significant as a methodological case history of the use of personal documents in the study of social actions. See SOCIAL SCIENCES; SOCIOLOGY, National Schools of Sociology.

ZNOJMO, town, S Czechoslovakia, in Moravia; on the Dyje River, 113 miles SE of Prague. The chief industries are the manufacturing of clay products, stoneware, and furniture, and the processing of fruits and vegetables. The town was founded in 1226. Pop. (1959 est.) 20,000.

ZOAR, one of the five cities of the Plain mentioned in the Old Testament: the other cities were Admah, Gomorrah, Sodom, and Zeboiim. First identified in the Bible as Bela (Gen. 14:2, 8), the city appears as Zoar (meaning small) following God's destruction of Sodom and Gomorrah (Gen. 19:20–29). See SODOM AND GOMORRAH.

ZOAR COMMUNITY, a communal religious settlement established, 1817, on 5,000 acres of land along the Tuscarawas River, Ohio, by a group of German separatists, under the leadership of Joseph Baumler (or Bimeler), who had come to North America from Württemberg in search of religious liberty and better opportunities of livelihood. In their religious practice, they accepted Holy Scripture as their guide, opposed ceremonies as useless and injurious, and had no ordained ministry or public prayer. They practiced "nonresistance" and, for a time, experimented with celibacy. In 1819, as a practical expedient, the group adopted a communal way of life.

The Society of Separatists of Zoar was incorporated, 1832, with about 500 members, who were classified either as novitiates or as full associates. Officers were elected by the vote of both men and women, but in practice Baumler dominated the society. The community prospered steadily for several decades, developing an industrial establishment comprising two large flour mills, a sawmill, a planing mill, a machine shop, a stove foundry, a cooper shop, a woolen mill, a brewery, a slaughterhouse, a blacksmith shop, a tile works, and so forth. By 1875 the society's total wealth amounted to about $1.5 million. After Baumler's death in 1853, however, the prosperity of the community declined. Many of the youth left the society, and few new members came into it. The society was finally disbanded and its property divided among the remaining 136 members, 1898. See COMMUNAL SETTLEMENTS.

ZODIAC, a belt extending 8° or 9° on each side of the apparent path of the sun among the stars that includes within its borders the paths of the moon and principal planets, except Pluto, which is sometimes outside the belt because of the large inclination of the plane of its orbit to the plane of the ecliptic. Some of the constellations of the zodiac may have been introduced by the Chaldeans and by the Egyptians, but its origin is usually credited to the Babylonians not later, and probably much earlier, than 2,000 B.C.

The zodiac is divided into 12 sections or signs, each comprising 30° of longitude. As all these signs except Libra are named for men or animals, the zodiac was a "zone or circle of life" or "zone of animals." Beginning with the sign Aries, which the sun enters at the vernal equinox, about March 21, the sun traverses each sign in about a month. The signs and their symbols are given below in their order from west to east around the ecliptic, and the seasons during which the sun moves through them.

Spring	Summer	Autumn	Winter
Aries ♈	Cancer ♋	Libra ♎	Capricornus ♑
(Ram)	(Crab)	(Balance)	(Goat)
Taurus ♉	Leo ♌	Scorpio ♏	Aquarius ♒
(Bull)	(Lion)	(Scorpion)	(Water-Beaver)
Gemini ♊	Virgo ♍	Sagittarius ♐	Pisces ♓
(Twins)	(Virgin)	(Archer)	(Fishes)

The spring and summer signs are north of the celestial equator, and the autumn and winter signs south of it. From the June solstice in the sign Cancer the sun moves southward through the six "descending" signs, Cancer through Sagittarius; from the December solstice in the sign Capricornus, it moves northward through the six "ascending" signs, Capricornus through Gemini.

About 2,000 years ago the signs of the zodiac were identical with the constellations of the same names. But the equinoxes, the points in which the celestial equator intersects the ecliptic, move slowly westward along the ecliptic about 50 seconds of arc each year. The vernal equinox has continued to be the "first of Aries," however, and the signs have been considered as participating in this westward motion. As a result, each sign at the present time is in the zodiacal constellation to the west of the one with which it coincided 2,000 years ago, the sign Gemini in the constellation Taurus, and so forth, so that the

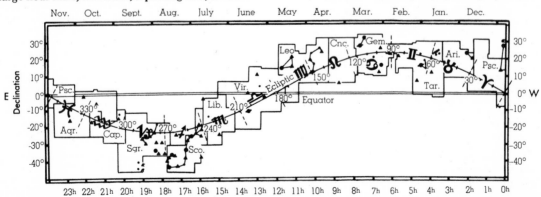

The constellations of the Zodiac are outlines and labeled with abbreviations of their names. The signs of the zodiac are marked with their symbols, and their boundaries are the dotted lines that cross the ecliptic at 30° intervals.

equinoxes, though still in the signs Aries and Libra, are now in the constellations Pisces and Virgo respectively, and the solstices in the constellations Gemini and Sagittarius. Six months from the time the sun passes through it, a constellation of the zodiac can be seen high in the night sky.

ZODIACAL LIGHT, a faint cone of luminosity that may be seen rising from a broad base on the western horizon on a clear, moonless evening after the sun has set and the evening twilight has gone. A similar cone rising from the eastern horizon before sunrise is sometimes called the "false dawn." This luminosity extends along the ecliptic and is, therefore, seen to best advantage when the ecliptic rises nearly vertically from the horizon. In midnorthern latitudes this is in March and April for the evening zodiacal light, and six months later for the morning lights. In the tropics the luminosity can often be seen extending clear across the sky. The counterglow, or Gegenschein, is a somewhat brighter area in the part of the band opposite the sun, less easy to see than the rest of the zodiacal luminosity.

YERKES OBSERVATORY

A photograph that illustrates zodiacal light requires an exposure of such duration that the trails of the stars within the camera's range form arcs across the picture.

The usually accepted explanation for these observations is that dust particles are dispersed very thinly throughout a vast region, slightly lens-shaped, that is centered at the sun and extends far beyond the earth's orbit and lies nearly in the plane of the ecliptic. Sunlight reflected from these solid particles accounts for the amount and polarization of the light received, for the direction from which it comes, and for the counterglow.

ZOË, the name of three empresses who ruled with varying degrees of power during the last years of the Byzantine Empire.

Zoë, surnamed Zaütsa, died 896, was the second of the three wives of Emperor Leo VI the Wise.

Zoë, surnamed Carbonupsina, died 919, became Leo VI's mistress sometime before or after Zoë Zaüstra's death, and married him in 906. A year before their marriage, she bore Leo a son, who later became Constantine VII Porphyrogenitus. Zoë was briefly exiled after Leo's death, 912, but soon returned to act as co-regent during her son Constantine's minority.

Zoë, 980?–1050, was the daughter of Constantine VIII. She married Romanus III Argyrus, 1028, and ruled at his side until she had him murdered, 1034. She thereupon married her lover, the epileptic Michael IV the Paphlagonian. Upon Michael IV's death, 1041, his nephew, Michael V Calaphates, assumed power and banished the ambitious Zoë from the realm. An uprising of the populace soon disposed

of Michael V, however, and Zoë returned triumphantly to rule jointly with her elder sister Theodora. She married Constantine IX Monomachus, 1042, ruling jointly with the latter and Theodora until her death.

ZOG I, or Zogu I, real name Ahmed Bey Zogu, 1895–1961, was born in Bugajet, the son of a powerful Albanian Moslem chief, and studied in Constantinople (later Istanbul). Following his service with the Hungarian army, 1914–18, during World War I, he was minister of interior, then minister of war, and premier of Albania, 1922–24. He was chosen president of the Albanian Republic, 1925, and king of that country, 1928. The Italians at first supported his throne, but deprived him of it by their invasion, 1939. Zog went into exile the same year. When Albania was proclaimed a republic, 1946, Zog was deposed *in absentia* by a Communist regime.

ZOLA, ÉMILE, 1840–1902, French man of letters and controversialist, was born in Paris. His father died when Émile was a child, leaving the family destitute except for a small holding (which was tied up in litigation) in the town of Aix-en-Provence, where Zola lived until 1858, when he went to Paris to study at the Sorbonne. Having twice failed the examination for his degree, he was forced by abject poverty to become a clerk in a publishing house. His first book, *Contes à Ninon* (1864), a series of tales in the romantic vein, was well received, and Zola thereupon determined to devote himself to writing. He attracted further favorable attention with his critical essays and incisive book reviews for the literary journal *L'Événement*, 1866, and with the novel *Thérèse Raquin* (1867), a powerful work that shows the influence of the Goncourt brothers' audaciously realistic and controversial *Germinie Lacerteux* (1865). In *Thérèse Raquin* Zola demonstrated his theory of "naturalism," a term he used to designate the systematic application of scientific method to literature.

In a series of essays entitled *Le Roman expérimental* (The Experimental Novel), 1880, modeled on Claude Bernard's *Introduction à l'étude de la médecine expérimentale* (Introduction to the Study of Experimental Medicine), 1865, Zola insisted that the method of the novelist should conform to that of the scientist—that the novelist must proceed by means of observation, hypothesis, and experimentation. To complete the scientific basis of his naturalistic theory, Zola utilized the environmental determinism of Hippolyte Taine as elaborated in the latter's *Histoire de la littérature anglaise* (History of English Literature), 1864–69, and in Prosper Lucas' treatise on *Heredity* (1868–69). Thus conceived, the function of the novelist is to present, by way of scientific documentation and analysis, characters whose psychological and moral conduct is the direct result of hereditary and environmental determinants. To illustrate his theory, Zola published, with sensational success, the 20 volumes comprising *Les Rougon-Macquart* (1871–93), a cyclical novel, inspired in part by *La comédie humaine* (The Human Comedy) of Honoré de Balzac, and purporting to present a scientific and sociological history of five generations during the Second Empire.

After completing *Les Rougon-Macquart*, Zola published the trilogy *Les trois villes* (The Three Cities), which comprised *Lourdes* (1894), *Rome* (1896), and *Paris* (1898). Of the Socialist-oriented tetralogy, *Les quatre évangiles* (The Four Gospels), Zola completed *Fécondité* (1899), *Travail* (1901), and *Vérité* (1903), but was accidentally asphyxiated in his room by gas from a defective chimney while still at work on the fourth "gospel," that on *Justice*.

Zola's famous manifesto *J'accuse* (1898) in defense of Alfred Dreyfus (see DREYFUS AFFAIR), and his continuing campaign in Dreyfus' behalf, were important factors in bringing about Dreyfus' eventual exoneration. BOYD G. CARTER

BIBLIOG.—Henri Barbusse, *Zola* (1933); Marc Bernard, *Zola* (1960); Calvin S. Brown, *Repetition in Zola's Novels*

(1952); Lee M. Friedman, *Zola and the Dreyfus Case* (1937); Frederick W. J. Hemmings, *Émile Zola* (1953); Matthew Josephson, *Zola and His Time: The History of His Martial Career in Letters* (1928); Armand Lanoux, *Zola* (1955); Winthrop H. Root, *German Criticism of Zola, 1875–1893* (1931); Robert H. Sherard, *Émile Zola: A Biographical & Critical Study* (1893); Ernest A. Vizetelly, *Émile Zola, Novelist and Reformer* (1904); Angus Wilson, *Émile Zola: An Introductory Study of His Novels* (1952).

ZOLLVEREIN. See CUSTOMS UNION.

ZOMBA, town, SE Africa, capital of Nyasaland; in Southern Province; near Lake Chilwa and S of Lake Nyasa, 360 miles W of Moçambique. Zomba is located in the Shire Highlands, and is a commercial center of an area in which cotton and tobacco are grown. Pop. (1956) 4,111.

ZOMBI, in Haitian voodoo religious belief, a human being whose soul has been stolen by sorcery. A person so victimized appears to be dead and is therefore buried; he is later dug up by the sorcerer, however, and put into a trancelike condition. Zombis have no memory and can not speak, but will obey the commands of the sorcerer who uses them as slaves or as agents of revenge. Scientific investigators believe that zombis are actually living human beings acting under the influence of hypnotism or drugs. See VOODOOISM.

ZONDEK, BERNHARD, 1891– , Israeli biochemist, was born in Wronke (later Wonki), Germany, and studied medicine in Berlin. He taught obstetrics and gynecology at the University of Berlin, 1923–29, headed the Department of Obstetrics and Gynecology at Berlin-Spandau Hospital, 1929–33, and at Rothschild Hadassah University Hospital in Jerusalem, 1933–44, and began teaching at the University of Cairo, 1944. While in Berlin, Zondek with his colleague Selmar Aschheim, isolated prolan, the gonadotropic hormone of the pituitary gland, and discovered the first reliable test for pregnancy in the human female. He received the Bublick prize from Hebrew University, 1957, and the Prize of Israel, 1958.

ZONE, a certain strip or belt of any extensive medium or substance that is found capable of delimitation by some specific character. Thus in geography certain belts with distinct boundaries of latitude, or altitude, or temperature, or depth, or moisture, or vegetation, are known as zones. In dynamic geology there are shear zones, fault zones, zones of fracture, zones of flowage, and zones of weathering, each one a very definite unit with respect to some particular geologic character or process. In stratigraphic geology the physical character of rocks make it possible to divide strata into beds; on the other hand, life forms or fossils are used to establish zones or horizons characterized by particular species which do not appear lower or high in vertical range. In accord with the evolution idea of life development, the identification of a particular zone in different areas is taken to indicate more or less perfect contemporaneity, subject only to such modification as may be attributed to local physiographic and climatic differences. See GEOLOGY.

ZONGULDAK, province, NW Turkey; bounded on the N by the Black Sea and by the provinces of Bolu on the W, Kastamonu on the E, and Cankiri on the S; area 2,876 sq. mi.; pop. (1955) 492,422. The city of Zonguldak is the capital of the province. The area's chief industry is coal mining. Zonguldak was a northern canton of the Armenoid Hittite Empire (1750–1200 B.C.). It later formed parts of the smaller Armenoid kingdoms of Phrygia, Lydia, Paphlagonia, Bithynia, and Pontus. In the medieval period it was made a part of the Byzantine Bucellarian Theme. The Turks first entered Zonguldak in the fourteenth century.

ZONGULDAK, town, NW Turkey, capital of Zonguldak Province; on the Black Sea; 155 miles E of Istanbul. The city's economy is based on coal mines and steel mills. Pop. (1959 est.) 35,631.

ZONING, the regulation by law of the character and uses of land and buildings within urban areas.

Such regulation is usually established by municipal ordinances requiring that specified urban areas be used only for specified purposes, such as residential, commercial, or industrial development. Zoning laws have been upheld in the courts as a proper exercise of the police powers of cities.

Zoning laws are enacted for several reasons. They may be part of an attempt to preserve the physical and social environment of a neighborhood, control congestion in heavily populated cities, establish efficiently planned neighborhoods, or isolate certain types of industrial establishments. Until the mid-1950's, zoning in the United States was limited chiefly to districts that were already built up. Thereafter, many new communities enacted zoning regulations among their first municipal ordinances. It has usually been undertaken to prevent the encroachment of buildings and building uses that would adversely alter the character of the surrounding environment.

History. European cities, during the Middle Ages and after, restricted trade and commerce to certain areas, but zoning in its twentieth century aspect was not practiced in Europe until about 1875, when Germany adopted a number of laws providing for the separation of manufacturing areas and residential areas, the prohibition of industry from all unauthorized areas, and the control of the height and density of new buildings. Similar regulations were soon enacted in Sweden. In both countries the laws were used to encourage the carefully planned development of densely populated urban areas. Great Britain's Town Planning Act (1909) provided for the control of new construction.

American Provisions. New York was the first large U.S. city to adopt zoning laws. Its first zoning ordinance (1916) limited the height and bulk of buildings and restricted the uses to which the buildings could be put. The height permitted for newly constructed buildings was determined by both the width of the adjacent street or streets and the proposed purpose of the buildings. During the post-World War I period most U.S. and Canadian cities enacted zoning regulations. In some places the zoning laws were part of a carefully considered program of city planning, but usually they were designed merely to preserve the character of established neighborhoods. In a few instances they were intended specifically to change the character of a neighborhood.

As municipal problems became more intense during the post-World War II period, more and more large cities and metropolitan areas used zoning laws as part of comprehensive development and renewal plans. Rapidly growing suburban areas, which were originally almost totally residential, adopted stringent zoning laws to check the spread of industrial plants and commercial establishments that attempted to locate in their vicinity. Later, however, they also began setting aside areas for industrial use. The problem of land use in crowded metropolitan areas contributed to a trend toward increasing stringency and more effective enforcement of zoning laws. See CITY PLANNING; SUBURB.

ZOO, or zoological garden, a garden or park with paddocks, houses, and cages for keeping living wild animals in captivity for exhibition and scientific study. Menageries and wild-beast shows, often combined with circuses, have been popular exhibits for many centuries. A collection of wild animals kept in an "intelligence park" is recorded in China as far back as about 1100 B.C. The circuses provided by the Roman emperors contained very large numbers of animals, but the popular interest in them was less for intelligent observation than for savage delight in watching them kill and be killed in fights between each other or with human gladiators and condemned Christians. In the Middle Ages powerful kings, feudal lords, and free cities kept menageries to provide animals for baiting and for a popular spectacle; one of the most famous of these was the menagerie kept at the Tower of London.

In the eighteenth century the growing science of zoology led to the establishment of menageries with the more serious motive of studying the animals scientifically and satisfying the universal popular curiosity about the various kinds of life in the world. One of the first of these was the Jardin des Plantes established in Paris in 1793. Thirty-three years later, in 1826, the Zoological Society of London was formed and was the first to call its menagerie a zoological garden, thereby introducing the word *zoo*.

In 1960 there were more than three hundred large and small zoos. Some of these were commercial and existed to make profits for their owners or shareholders; others were supported by state or municipal governments for the education and recreation of the public; a minority were self-supporting, but nonprofit, institutions that could devote their surplus revenues to progressive improvements, education, and scientific research. The larger zoos had well equipped veterinary departments, and some of them had up-to-date animal hospitals where sick animals were treated and research on animal welfare and management was carried out.

Modern Trends. After World War II there was an increasing growth of interest in zoos everywhere; many new zoos were founded and most of the older ones were extended or rebuilt on modern lines. The old style zoo with the animals confined in cages inside houses began to give way to the modern type where, as far as possible, animals are kept in the open air in comparatively large enclosures and separated from the public by ditches and moats instead of bars. The modern popularity of zoos was undoubtedly in part due to the television programs on them, which created zoo consciousness on the part of the public.

Among the postwar developments in zoo techniques were the establishment of walk-through aviaries, where the visitors go inside the cages with the birds. The aviaries are very large and are laid out with trees, bushes and plants, rockwork, pools, and waterfalls, among which the birds fly free and through which pathways meander for the visitors. Labeling the exhibits in zoos with notices that are informative but at the same time concise had long been a problem, but the new device of talking labels was being introduced as a means by which the visitors could listen to tape-recorded messages concerning the animals being observed. Another innovation was the large marine aquaria in which dolphins and the smaller kinds of whales are shown. These animals unexpectedly proved to be amenable to captivity and highly intelligent as well, so that they readily learn to give spectacular displays of "aquabatics."

The wild animals of the world were increasingly threatened with extermination with every year that passed, because of the rapid technical and economic development of the once underdeveloped countries. The zoos play an important part in preserving the wild animals by devising means of managing them in captivity so that they will breed and perpetuate for posterity at least a representative sample of what was destined to disappear. There were already species such as the Chinese Père David's deer which are extinct as wild animals and exist only in captivity. The wild horse of Mongolia, Przewalski's horse, the ancestor of all domestic breeds, was also nearly extinct. At the beginning of 1960 there were 59 in captivity; the zoos holding stock hoped to breed enough of these horses to return them to the wild if the Academy of Sciences of the U.S.S.R. could establish a reserve for them in their ancient home. Zoos were thus destined to take a prominent place in the conservation of the wildlife of the world.

Nearly every large city, and many of the smaller ones, in the United States and Europe has its zoo, and a number of famous ones are also located in Africa, India, the Far East, Japan, China, and Australia. In the United States the oldest zoo, opened in 1874, is in Philadelphia; the National Zoological Park at Washington, D.C., was established by act of Congress in 1889.   L. HARRISON MATTHEWS

ZOOGEOGRAPHY, the scientific study of the distribution of animals over the world. Its botanical counterpart is the plant science of phytogeography. Phytogeography and zoogeography together form the science of biogeography, the scientific study of the distribution of organisms. Broadly speaking, there are two aspects of the study of animal distribution, historical zoogeography and ecological animal geography. From the modern standpoint both fields are interdependent.

HISTORICAL ZOOGEOGRAPHY

Historical zoogeography developed relatively early. Briefly it attempted to explain present distribution of related animals on the basis of fossilized deposits of their ancestors. Study of the distribution of fossils in successive geological periods of the earth's history suggested that each group of animals arose at some particular place, the center of origin, and spread from that area through long intervals of time. The routes over which animals moved from this center were called paths of dispersal. Obstructions that deflected or stopped dispersal were termed barriers. Obviously, what was a barrier to one group of animals might be a dispersal path for another.

Consequently the study of animal distribution received great emphasis from the interest in the Darwinian theory of evolution by natural selection. Charles Darwin, in his voyage around the world in H.M.S. *Beagle*, was impressed by two principles: (1) a similarity in physical conditions between two areas does not result necessarily in a similar fauna; (2) the similarities or differences between the fauna of two regions are directly proportional to the nature of the barrier that separates them.

Between 1850 and 1900 zoogeography developed along classical lines. Darwin, Alfred Wallace, and other zoogeographers of the period were concerned chiefly with birds and mammals. Since these homoiothermal, or warm-blooded, animals are relatively independent of temperature, the unfortunate conclusion that climate was not directly or clearly correlated with animal distribution gained wide acceptance. Research was focused upon delimiting the great areas of the earth that had characteristic, and generally exclusive, faunas. Such areas, known as zoogeographic regions, cover great stretches of territory and embrace many different physiographic and climatic zones.

Generally speaking, the faunal regions of Wallace, based primarily upon the then known distribution of birds and mammals are still useful. Modern taxonomy, advances in paleontology, ecology, and more exact dating by Carbon-14 analysis have rendered Wallace's findings of less general value. Wallace described six regions. The Palaearctic Region includes Iceland, all of Europe, Africa north of the Tropic of Cancer, the northern half of the Arabian Peninsula, the Near East, and Asia north of the Himalaya Mountains, including Siberia, Japan, and most of China. The Ethiopian Region covers all of Africa and the Arabian Peninsula south of the Tropic of Cancer, Malagasy, and the Seychelle Islands, while the Oriental Region includes India, Ceylon, Burma, extreme southern China, Vietnam, Cambodia, Thailand, Formosa, Malay Peninsula, Philippines, Indonesia, and many small islands. The Australian Region is made up of New Guinea, the Solomons, the Marianas, the Marshalls, the New Hebrides, Fiji Islands, Australia, Tasmania, New Zealand and small islands of Indonesia. In the Nearctic Region are all of North America to the Tropic of Cancer, including the high Central Plateau of Mexico south of this line, nearly to the Istmo de Tehuantepec. The

Neotropical Region covers the rest of Mexico, all of Central America, the West Indies, South America, and the Falkland Islands.

Zoogeographic interest in marine life, invertebrates, the importance of climate, the essentiality of the community concept, were all to have their impact later.

Effect of Evolutionary Theory on Zoogeography. If all recent animals of a particular kind have evolved from a common ancestor in some previous geological period, then this monophyletic view requires a common ancestor and a common center of origin. This is opposed to a polyphyletic view in which the same stock is thought to have different ancestral origins. Biologists generally hold the monophyletic view.

Contemporary distribution must be explainable on the basis of past, or historical, deposits of their ancestors. The difficulty, still with us for the most part is the imperfection of the geological record. This being the case, dispersal patterns often must be deduced from present distribution and checked against fossil data where such data are available.

Deduction of Dispersal Routes. The dispersal pattern turns on the question of whether or not the ocean basins are permanent. Geological facts are not too abundant on this point, or where they are abundant their interpretation is not necessarily uniform. Fossil deposits often can be interpreted in support of permanence but sometimes also in support of impermanence of ocean basins. W. D. Matthew was an early and vigorous proponent of the permanence of ocean basins. Working chiefly with mammals, his thesis was that (1) known facts pointed to general permanency of continental outlines during later geological epochs; (2) geographic changes required to explain contemporary distribution of land vertebrates are not extensive, and generally do not affect the ocean basins as defined by the continental shelf; (3) that the general center of origin and dispersal has been from the Holarctic Region or the Palaearctic plus the Nearctic regions of Wallace.

There is good evidence for numerous small changes of the continental outlines. Such changes do not alter the continental shelf materially, but do serve to alternately connect and disconnect continental masses. Such connections are known as land bridges to biogeographers, since they serve as dispersal routes for terrestrial animals if they are formed during periods of suitable climate. Two well known examples of relatively modest land bridges are the Bering Bridge, between Alaska and Siberia, and the Panamanian Bridge, between Central and South America.

In this connection two points must be remembered. First, that when these land bridges were absent, the strait served as a water bridge for marine forms, and, consequently, when the bridges were intact for terrestrial dispersal, they served as land barriers to marine dispersal. Second, when the land bridge was absent, it served to isolate the faunas on either side.

Another method of dispersal is by natural rafts. Log-jams, caving-in of river banks, accumulations of vegetation, often held together by numerous vines, form natural rafts that are swept downstream and into the ocean, where they may be carried by oceanic currents for many miles. Sometimes such rafts have a sufficient soil cover to maintain green plants, even trees. Rafting would serve to disperse small terrestrial animals, but even large animals have been carried elsewhere in this way.

As opposed to permanence of the ocean basins, the school favoring impermanence of continents and ocean basins holds that the facts of zoogeography can be interpreted differently. In general, there are two interpretations which, if true, would presuppose profound changes in the geological past. The first of these may be called extensive land bridges. Numerous inter-continental connections have been proposed especially to explain the numerous resemblances that have been noticed among southern faunas.

The second interpretation opposed to basin permanence is the continental drift, as proposed by some. This proposes an early land mass that subsequently drifted to separate the modern continents and major islands, and that through time these terrestrial areas drifted apart to form the Atlantic Ocean and the isolation of the Antarctic land mass from other continents. The present majority opinion appears to oppose the theory of drift.

ECOLOGICAL ANIMAL GEOGRAPHY

Ecological applications to zoogeography were slowly accumulating during the period when historical zoogeography was being pursued with vigor. Gradually the early view of Wallace and others, that temperature was not of major importance in animal distribution, was discarded and the importance of climatic influences in general were recognized.

Importance of Temperature. A landmark in this recognition of temperature in animal distribution was C. H. Merriam's *Laws of Temperature Control* (1898). Merriam, however, overemphasized temperature. It was soon recognized that geographic range of a species is governed by numerous physical and biological influences, any one of which might prove limital in its effect if its intensity fell below the toleration limit of the species population. Temperature as such is not now regarded as all-important, but Merriam's classic paper had three important results: (1) it served to accelerate the view that historical zoogeography should take into account the climatic influences; (2) it initiated the life zone concept, which in its many ramifications at the hands of subsequent workers involved the zonation of the world, or parts thereof, in terms of animals, vegetation, climate, and physiography in various combinations; (3) it stimulated research along ecological lines.

Importance of Climate. Since about 1900 there has been a steadily increasing interest in the study of climate, and its application to biological problems, including the distribution of organisms. John Ball in 1910 introduced what has become known generally as the climograph method. Essentially this was a new approach, measuring climate as a characteristic of a given geographic area by plotting the mean monthly temperature against the mean monthly relative humidity to obtain a figure with 12 points, one for each month in the year. Griffith Taylor in 1918 and 1919 constructed climographs by plotting temperature and precipitation on a monthly basis, instead of temperature and relative humidity, calling them hythergraphs. Climographs furnish graphic information relative to the limiting climatic conditions for a given species over its range. Huntington in 1922 suggested that the world could be divided into zones of climatic energy. A.D. Hopkins in 1918-19 proposed the bio-climatic law, namely, that periodic events occur later northward, eastward, and upward in the spring and the reverse in the autumn, at the rate of four days for each degree of latitude, five degrees of longitude, and 400 feet of altitude. In addition to studies on contemporary climates, paleoclimatic work, especially as indicated by distribution of fossil plant materials, received growing attention.

A still more direct outgrowth of the life zone concept was the biotic province, proposed by A. G. Vestal in 1914, and currently described as a continuous geographic area that is characterized by peculiarities of flora, fauna, climate, physiography and soil, or edaphic, factors. In 1943 L. R. Dice, after reviewing previous literature on the general subject, divided North America into 29 biotic provinces based upon species of trees, birds, mammals, climate, physiography, and soil type.

Importance of Altitude. Altitude is of importance in biogeography. Air pressure decreases regularly from the normal 15 pounds per square inch at sea level upward to the highest mountain peaks, and with this steadily decreasing pressure are associated de-

ZOOGEOGRAPHY

AMERICAN MUS. OF NATL. HIST.

The paddle-like appendages and sleek, close-fitting fur of the sea lions are several of the morphological adaptations necessary for them to live in a marine environment.

U.S. FISH AND WILDLIFE SERVICE

These white pelicans of Bowdoin Lake, near Malta, Mont., have the long necks and enormous bills that are characteristic of birds that feed on fishes and other water fauna.

ERIC HOSKING, NATL. AUDUBON SOC.

The weasel family is usually found in temperate deciduous forest biomes. Adaptation within the biome is evidenced by their shedding of a summer coat for a white, winter coat.

NEW YORK ZOOLOGICAL SOC.

The gila monster is typical of animals that live in arid, desert biomes. Most of their habits are nocturnal; their homes are underground burrows, and they seek prey at night.

The American bison, whose migratory habits caused them to roam the plains in great herds, are now limited to only a few areas that are maintained in protected sections such as this one at Buffalo National Park in Alberta, Canada.

CANADIAN TRAVEL BUR.

creasing amounts of oxygen in the atmosphere, decreasing amounts of dust, and increasing cold. These and other conditions operate to stratify, or zone, organisms in general. Furthermore, the difference between soil temperature and air temperature increases with elevation. This radiant heat is important for invertebrates living in the soil, and consequently the colder north slopes have fewer such animals per unit area than do south slopes. Snow, on the other hand, tends to protect hibernating invertebrates in winter.

Mountain ranges consequently serve as barriers to dispersal for many animals, and in general the higher the range the greater the force of the barrier. This allows fewer and fewer species to pass, and consequently has a filtering effect on dispersal. On the other hand, some species, such as the puma, use mountain ranges as highways of dispersal.

Montane or alpine zonation, then, becomes an important aspect of zoogeography and has a definite relation to latitude. Alexander von Humboldt in 1850 noted that from pole to Equator the mean temperature increases about one degree F with each degree of latitude. This is known as the Humboldt Rule. F. M. Chapman in 1933, working on the bird faunas of the Andes, found a decrease in mean air temperature of about one degree F for each 300 feet increase in elevation. This is the Chapman Rule. In other words 300 feet elevation in the Andes is equivalent to about 67 miles in latitude. Chapman recognized four zones in the Andes: tropical, with a sea level of 0 to 3,000 or 5,000 feet; subtropical, from 3,500 or 5,000 or 8,000 or 9,000 feet; temperate, from 8,000 or 9,000 to 11,000 or 12,000 feet; paramo or puna, from 11,000 or 12,000 to the lower limit of the snow at between 15,000 and 16,000 feet.

Merriam in 1906 demonstrated that successive life zones in the Sierra Nevada and the White Mountains of California, adjacent mountain ranges, had similar or the same species of chipmunks, *Eutamias*. This suggests the principle of montane equivalence. Every species of animal, of course, is not confined to a distinct zone, but rather there is a zonation tendency; there are, thus, stenozonal species, those which are confined to a single zone, and euryzonal species, those that range through more than one zone.

Another application of latitude and altitude is the relation of body size as between relatively closely allied terrestrial animals. Herbert Spencer's mass-area law, that volume or mass increases as the cube of linear dimensions, while area or surface increases only as the square of these dimensions, was the basic philosophical background of this application. Homoiothermal animals, birds and mammals, expend energy and radiate heat in maintaining their relatively constant body temperatures. It follows that the colder the environment, other things remaining equal, the more energy is expended to maintain a relatively constant body temperature. Consequently a relative decrease of body surface reduces the amount of heat-radiating skin surface. It follows that the larger the animal, that is, the greater the volume to area ratio, the more economical it is physiologically to heat the body. When these facts are applied ecologically, there emerges the Bergmann Rule. This zoogeographic principle may be stated as follows: as between closely related taxonomic units, the larger homoiothermal animals are found nearer the poles, or at higher altitudes. Naturally there are exceptions to the rule, since there are numerous adjustments for otherwise conserving heat, but they are relatively few. The closely allied taxonomic units may be individuals of a subspecies, subspecies of a species, species of a genus, often genera within a family.

The reverse Bergmann Rule applies to poikilothermal land animals, such as the invertebrates, amphibians, and reptiles. These tend to be larger from poles to equator, and from high to low altitudes. There are exceptions among cold-blooded animals,

but they are relatively few. Most reptiles, amphibians, and insects are larger in the tropics than in temperate regions. As would be expected, mammals of cold climates tend to have the heat-radiating body surface reduced in several ways. They have shorter necks, shorter legs, more compact forms, including smaller ears and tails. This extension is known as Allen's Rule.

Isolation. Where two groups of closely allied forms are isolated by a barrier, the two faunas are similar without being identical. Under such conditions, the corresponding subspecies of a species, or species of a genus, tend to be distributed in pairs on either side of the barrier. This parallel occupation of similar habitats by allied stocks, such as the American moose and European elk, is known as vicariation.

Where the isolation has been continued for great periods of time, the separated faunas become very dissimilar. In the isolated portion there are few or no recent stocks entering and setting up competition for food and shelter, and the fauna has a close phylogenetic composition. In the area open to incoming dispersal of other groups, the fauna does not have this intimate phylogenetic aspect. The ancient, isolated fauna radiates into the available habitats and, although phylogenetically more closely allied, becomes adapted to various modes of life. Such species fill parallel habitat niches, corresponding to similar habitats in the area open to dispersal that are occupied by distantly related animals. This tendency to fan out and occupy available habitats is an example of adaptive radiation. It is exhibited by the marsupials of Australia, isolated at least since early Tertiary times.

Obviously some kinds of animals are more adaptive to a variety of conditions than others. In general, the dispersal power of a species is termed vagility. The degree of vagility is in inverse proportion to the number of geographic races of a species in a given area.

Isolation is produced by factors other than geography. Animals may reduce competition and obtain isolation through changes in structural adaptations or behavior; by a change in their activity pattern, for example from day-active, or diurnal, habits to night-active, or nocturnal, habits. Species may be isolated through biotic competition, that is, two closely allied species of equivalent ecological position and adaptations may be unable to penetrate each other's range, despite the absence of physiographic barriers, if each population dominates the available habitat niches and food supply. Parasitism, predation, and disease may prevent stocks from entering new areas where they would be exposed to these influences. Vegetation, lack of vegetation, soil type, salinity, water pressure, climatic factors, and other influences similarly may retard, stop, initiate, or accelerate dispersal.

Ecological processes are working continuously at the population, and at the community level to form equilibria in community distribution through space and time.

Biomes. Whereas the biotic province is strictly continuous and focuses attention upon the characteristic animals and plants as indicators of its extent, the biome is a broadly conceived formation of all the communities in a seral succession, including the climax, wherever they be located. (See ECOLOGY.) Hence the biome is not necessarily continuous. In the first place, terrestrial communities are distributed geographically with respect to broad climatic belts that are located, more or less, in great zones from poles to equator. Each climatic zone is characterized by an average range of temperature and hours of sunlight. These and other physical influences impose a corresponding zonation of vegetation. This zonation is both latitudinal and altitudinal, as would be expected from Humboldt's Rule and Chapman's Rule. Each of the biogeographic belts, including certain types of vegetation and animal life organized into

ZOOGEOGRAPHY

CANADIAN TRAVEL BUR.

Finding few natural enemies, except for the bear, in the steep, mountainous areas where they forage for food, bighorn are able to thrive on the grasses of the foothills.

The black rhinoceros, shown here with its young, is common in the African savanna. The rhinoceros migrates to moist areas in search of food during the periodic dry seasons.

WALT DISNEY PRODUCTIONS, INC.

The hyena is adapted to a life of scavenging; it follows the lion, feeding from what is left of the lion's feast.

WM. LAVARRE GENDREAU

The manatee is an example of a mammal that lives in an aquatic biome. Here it is seen emerging from a branch of the Amazon River to feed on the grasses of the bank.

WALT DISNEY PRODUCTIONS, INC.

The impalas, pictured here, and baboons maintain a mutual biological co-operation in the savanna. The baboons' keen eyesight and the impalas' sensitive smell detect danger.

self-supporting communities, has a more or less similar aspect or habitus. For example, the coniferous forests of the world have a common or dominating appearance no matter where they are found, whether in northern Wisconsin, or on the slopes of the Rocky Mountains, or in Siberia. This similarity of ecological response demonstrates the effects of climatic and edaphic influences in the present distribution of organisms over the world and is an important phase of ecological animal geography. The major biomes include the tropical forest, taiga, temperate deciduous forest, steppe, sand desert, tundra, and the great marine biome.

The tropical forest biome and its allied tropical forests covers roughly 6,000,000 square miles, mostly under 1,000 feet elevation. It lies in a fairly uniform belt on either side of the equator, usually located in the rainy, low latitude climate from about 20° N to 20° S latitude. Temperature is relatively uniform and high, with an annual mean temperature of between 75° and 80°F, and usually with a greater variation in temperature between day and night than between any two months of the year. Consequently winter and summer are absent, and instead there are wet and dry seasons. Rainfall is high, 75 to 160 inches per year, with about 72 inches as the lower limit.

Equatorial forests are of numerous types, including the true rain forest which has at least three tree strata, and many forest types that have been called jungles. The number of species populations is relatively large. Stratification within the forest community is very marked. The forest is evergreen, since the many species of trees overlap in their periods of leafing-out and flowering and fruiting. Lianas, or vines, and numerous epiphytic plants are typical. Many trees have proproots or plank-buttressed basis. Palms, bamboo, and mangroves may be locally abundant. Equatorial forests are found in three chief areas: Indo-Malaysia, central Africa, and the American forest from the Amazon Basin northward into central Mexico. As expected, the farther from the equator, the less the altitude range of such forests.

Arboreal adaptation among animals is diverse, the prehensile tail of New World monkeys, the opposable thumb and great toe in opossums, phalangers, and monkeys, and the hooked claws of sloths being notable examples. Numerous animals such as flying lizards and flying phalangers have developed parachute adjustments which allow them to volplane from tree to tree. Bats are abundant. There are various cats, chiefly nocturnal predators, such as American jaguar, civets of the Old World tropics, and the clouded leopard of southeastern Asia. Ungulates are not especially abundant, but include the small forest deer or chevrotains of Africa and Asia, and a few antelopes. Peccaries, numerous pigs, tapirs, and elephants are characteristic equatorial forest forms.

The steppe biome is characterized by perennial grasses in a well-defined sod. There are many kinds of grasslands, known as steppes, prairies, plains, pampas, or llanos. The climate is characterized by frequent but not heavy rain during the growing season. In the dry period the grasses can lie dormant, and strong winds in the dry season, or in the winter, are relatively not as injurious as they are to forest trees. The American steppe has two chief grassland types, the tall grass prairie with an annual rainfall of 20 to 40 inches and the short grass prairie with 12 to 20 inches of rain per year. The growing season is limited by moisture, since the temperature is ample for a longer period.

Grassland animals can be treated more conveniently by separating them into tropical steppe, or savanna animals, and temperate grassland animals. Tropical and subtropical grasslands, found in parts of Africa, South America and Australia chiefly, often include shrubby vegetation and scattered trees or parkland. The rain is concentrated in a hotter season and there is a well defined dry period. Where rainfall is deficient, the savanna passes gradually into sand desert, as in the transition from the Sudan to the Sahara Desert of Africa; where rain is heavy, the transition is from savanna to tropical forest, as from the Sudan to the Congo region of Africa. Kangaroos (Australia), pampas deer, armadillos, and the viscachas (South America), lions, giraffes, zebras, square-lipped rhinoceroses, certain baboons, hyenas, Cape buffaloes, and many genera of antelopes (Africa) may be mentioned as typical animals of tropical grasslands.

Temperate grasslands are well developed in Asia and North America. Steppe animals are adjusted to periods of abundance and scarcities of food and to severe changes and extremes in winter and summer. In general, there is a high proportion of gregarious, swift species; migration or hibernation is common. Typical mammals include the American bison and prongbuck of North America; Saiga antelope, several species of wild horses, two-humped camels, and gazelles of Asiatic grasslands.

The temperate deciduous forest biome is widely distributed in eastern North America, Europe, parts of Africa and Madagascar, part of eastern Asia, Japan, part of eastern coastal Australia, and New Zealand. Precipitation, between 30 and 50 inches per year, is well distributed, and the growing season is interrupted by a winter period instead of lack of rain. In the United States typical trees are oak, beech, maple, elm, tulip, poplar, and magnolia. The European bison is a deciduous forest form, now restricted in range. In North America the Virginia deer, black bear, and wildcat are characteristic of the larger mammals.

The taiga biome is the conifer forest covering much of subarctic to northern temperate North America, Europe, and Asia; it is poorly developed elsewhere, save for the Alpine zone of mountains. Rainfall is from 20 to 40 inches annually, much of it as snow in the long winter. Characteristic animals are taiga reindeer, moose, red deer and Maral stag of Asia, wapiti, tree squirrels, flying squirrels, beavers, Canadian porcupine, lynx, red fox, pine marten, sable, ermine, and mink. Numerous woodpeckers and crossbills are typical birds. The taiga is rich in heavy fur-bearers in contrast to the hot equatorial forests.

The tundra biome includes snow and ice deserts located north of the Arctic Circle, south of the Antarctic Circle, and on high mountain ranges beyond the tree line. Typical tundra is treeless, has a short summer and a very long, severe winter. The annual rainfall is never more than 10 inches, save on southwestern Greenland. Birds, with the exception of the redpoll and the ptarmigan, and mammals are either partially migratory or depend on the sea for their food. Characterisitc forms are tundra reindeer, musk ox, arctic hare, lemming, arctic fox, and the polar bear. The tundra is a desert in the sense that the water is physiologically inaccessible most of the year because it is frozen.

The sand desert biome, including numerous modifications and semi-deserts, is a desert in the sense that the water is physically inaccessible much of the time, since the annual rainfall is very scanty or even absent, usually less than 10 inches. This is a large biome. Water conservation and little perspiration; nocturnalism; estivation; fossorial habits; adjustments to protect the eyes, nostrils, and ears; and adjustments to move over the sand are but a few adaptations of animals in the desert environment. Characteristic animals include various burrowing tortoises, sidewinder rattlesnakes, one-humped camels, desert jack rabbits, Gila monsters, and certain burrowing snakes, *Typhlops*.

The marine biome embraces the seas and oceans, and consequently its study is a division of oceanography. This vast biome covers about 70 per cent of the earth's surface, including numerous seas and oceans, among which are the Atlantic, Pacific, Indian, Arctic, and Antarctic. These great masses of water are divided into a number of horizontal and vertical provinces, each with its characteristic physics, chemistry, shape, and organismal adjustment, but all are parts of a continuous, self-regulating whole.

The marine environment is divided primarily into the benthic and the pelagic. The benthic division includes all sea bottom, from the shore at flood tide to the ocean deeps. In turn, this is subdivided into the littoral system, from shore to about the 200-meter line, and the deep-sea system, from the 200-meter line to the bottom. Each of these systems is subdivided into zones. The littoral system is subdivided into the eulittoral zone, from high-tide level to the 40- to 60-meter line, which is the deepest level at which attached plants can grow; and the sublittoral zone, from the seaward limit of attached plants to the 200-meter line. Within the eulittoral zone is a well-defined intertidal subzone, which is bounded by high and low-water tidal limits. Many animals are limited to this intertidal zone, for example certain snails of the genera *Littorina* and *Acmaea*. The eulittoral in general has many habitats as a consequence of its type of bottom material, for example, rocky shores, sandy shores, and muddy shores and many intergraduations.

The deep-sea system is subdivided into the archibenthic zone, from the seaward limit of the sublittoral, roughly the end of the continental shelf, to about the 1,000-meter line, and the abyssal zone, from this 1,000-meter line to the bottom. Abyssal animals are without light, save that provided by their own bioluminescence; they live in a quiet habitat, free of most water movement, in a uniform temperature 3 or 4 degrees above freezing and under enormous water pressure. These pressures increase directly with depth, about one ton per square inch for each thousand fathoms. Deep-sea animals are chiefly detritus eaters or predators. Their skeletons are frail and their flesh generally thin and flabby. Some abyssal fishes are blind, whereas others have either telescopic eyes or eyes shaped like concave mirrors. Many have developed long tactile filaments, and many are luminescent.

The pelagic division includes all of the water above the several benthic zones. This mass is subdivided into two horizontal provinces, the neritic, or inshore province, from high-tide mark to the edge of the continental shelf at about 200 meters (in other words the water covering the eulittoral and sublittoral zones) and the oceanic province, all of the water seaward of the continental shelf. Vertically, the oceanic province is divided into an upper, lighted, zone and a lower, dark, zone. The boundary between these two is not clearly marked but is arbitrarily set at about the 200-meter depth line. Pelagic organisms consist primarily of plankton, small forms unable to move against a current, and nekton, animals able to move against a current. Plankton includes phytoplankton, such as bacteria and algae, and zooplankton, such as the numerous, minute, copepod crustaceans, including the important *Calanus finmarchicus*. Nekton is made up largely of fishes, including eel, salmon, mackerel, herring, and sharks. In addition, seals and whales among mammals, and squids among invertebrates, are nektonic.   ORLANDO PARK

BIBLIOG.–American Association for the Advancement of Science, *Zoogeography* (1958); Philip J. Darlington, Jr., *Zoogeography: The Geographical Distribution of Animals* (1957); Charles S. Elton, *Ecology of Invasions by Animals and Plants* (1958); Richard H. Manville, *Outline of Zoogeography* (1952); Marion I. Newbigin, *Principles of Animal Taxonomy* (1961); George G. Simpson, *Geography of Evolution: Collected Essays* (1965); Alfred R. Wallace, *Geographical Distribution of Animals* (2 vols.), (1876).

ZOOLOGY, the division of the science of biology that deals with the animal kingdom. Zoology is subdivided into a number of fields. These include morphology, the structure of animals viewed as a whole; anatomy, the study of form and structure by dissection; histology, the study of tissues; cytology, or cell structure; embryology, growth and development from egg to adult; genetics, the study of variation and heredity; ecology, the relationship of animals to each other, and to their environment; evolution, the problem of the origin of living things; paleontology, the study of fossil organisms; taxonomy, or classification; physiology, the study of life functions, including such subdivisions as endocrinology, reproduction, and other organs system studies; biochemistry, or the chemical composition, structure, and metabolism of living things; pharmacology, study of the effect of drugs on the organism; zoogeography, distribution of animals on earth; xenobiology, the projected study of life forms from other planets; parasitology, study of animals living on or in other organisms; pathology, the study of disease; nutrition, the use and conversion of food; and natural history, or nature study. Further specializations include studies of the various groups of animals, such as ornithology, the study of birds; mammalogy, the study of mammals; protozoology, the study of the protozoa; entomology, the study of insects; and so forth.

ZOOM LENS, a complicated system of lenses in which lens elements can be moved with respect to each other in such a way that focal length, and therefore magnification, may be continuously varied, while the image remains in the same image plane. The zoom lens enables the cameraman to achieve the effect of a close-up or long distance shot without having to move his camera nearer to or farther from the scene. It is especially useful in covering such events as athletic contests, political conventions, etc. Though used primarily for television and motion pictures, zoom lenses have also been developed for use in still photography.

ZORACH, WILLIAM, 1887–1966, U.S. painter and sculptor, born in Lithuania. He grew up in Cleveland, Ohio, studied in Paris, and settled in New York, where he exhibited in the 1913 Armory Show. After 1922 he abandoned oil painting for sculpture, evolving a highly personal and monumental style. By carving directly in wood and massive blocks of stone, Zorach was responsible for reviving in the United States the skills and practices of ancient sculptors. Two of his best-known works are *Mother and Child* (Metropolitan Museum, N.Y.) and *Spirit of the Dance* (Radio City Music Hall, N.Y.).

ZORILLA, an African mammal, *Ictonyx,* belonging to the weasel family, Mustelidae. It is about 15 inches long and has loose fur and black and white stripes from head to toe. The zorilla ranges throughout Africa and even into Asia Minor. The best-known member of the species is the South African muishond (mousehound, *I. capensis*). When attacked the zorilla ejaculates a sickly-smelling fluid and then feigns death, thus combining the defensive measures of the skunk and the opossum.

ZORN, ANDERS, 1860–1920, Swedish painter, sculptor, and engraver, born in Mora. After graduation from the Stockholm Academy of Fine Arts, where he studied sculpture and water-color painting, Zorn traveled widely in Europe, North Africa, and the Near East. Settling in England in 1882, he studied etching and created his first oil paintings. He went to Paris in 1888, where his interest in the work of the impressionists Degas and Manet began to be reflected in his own painting. In 1893 he made the first of many trips to the United States. After 1903, however, he spent most of his time in his native Mora, painting nudes, peasant subjects, and genre scenes. Zorn's fashionable portraits made him one of the most popular painters of his day, but his etchings, marked by a sensitive interplay of light and dark, now are considered his finest work.

MARTIN GROSZ

ZOROASTRIANISM, the general designation for the religion proclaimed by the prophet Zarathushtra in ancient Iran (Persia) around 600 B.C. This designation is derived from Zoroaster, the western (Greek and Latin) form of the original Iranian name Zarathushtra. Although uncertainties remain concerning some of the more important facts of Zarathushtra's life, his existence is beyond doubt. It seems safe to say that his lifetime fell between 630 and 553 B.C., that his name can be interpreted as "he who drives camels," and that he was born and worked in eastern Iran, in the area between the cities of Merv (now Mary in Russian Turkmenistan) and Herat in Afghanistan.

The preachings of Zarathushtra and the teachings of the Zoroastrian religion are contained in the Avesta, the sacred books of the Zoroastrians. These writings are in a language called Avestan, an Indo-European language closely related to the Sanskrit of India. The Avesta did not become known to the western world until the end of the eighteenth century. At that time the Frenchman Anquetil Duperron studied the sacred texts preserved by the Parsi communities in Bombay and other areas in northwestern India. From the tenth century onward, immigrant Zoroastrians from Iran had found refuge there after the collapse of the Sassanian dynasty in Iran, which followed the mid-seventh century Arab-Muslim invasion of Iran and the conversion of its inhabitants to Islam. Anquetil Duperron published his translation of the Avesta (in 1771) under the incorrect title of Zend-Avesta, the first part of which —zend, or zand—is a collective name for texts of a commentary and exegetic nature that were added to the original Avesta in later times.

Within the Avesta, the most ancient source of information for the Zoroastrian religion, several groups of writings can be distinguished: (a) Yasna (literally "sacrifice"), formulas of prayer and liturgy; part of this group is known as Gāthā (literally "chant"), writings in verse form traditionally attributed to Zarathushtra himself and written in Gāthic, a language that is slightly different from the language of the rest of the Avesta; (b) Yasht (literally "worship"), hymns of a sacrificial character devoted to the praise of individual deities; (c) Vendīdād (more correctly Vidēvdāt), or "law against the demons," by and large a collection of religious and ritual law that contains, in addition, mythological and legendary materials. Further materials are to be found in texts composed in an idiom known as Pahlavi or Middle Persian (the relationship between Avestan and Pahlavi being comparable to that between Old English and Middle English), the local language of southwestern

Iran between the third and eighth centuries. The larger number of the existing Pahlavi books were not committed to actual writing until after the Muslim conquest of Iran. Their content, however, is based on a long tradition that originated in the fourth century, when Zoroastrian orthodoxy became established in a definite form. Two of the most important Pahlavi theological books are the so-called Bundahishn—more correctly, Zandāgāhīh, or "exposition of the information" (provided by the Pahlavi version of the Avesta)—and the Dēnkart. The first is an original work on cosmology in which the scattered teachings of the Avesta on the subject are co-ordinated; the second is an extensive encyclopedia of religious lore. A third source of information consists of Zoroastrian writings in the Persian language. They came into existence after the Zoroastrian emigration from Iran to India; they represent the tradition of the Parsis (literally "Persians"), the name given to the Zoroastrians in India. So much for primary source materials of Zoroastrian origin. In addition, a considerable amount of data is provided by such secondary sources of non-Zoroastrian origin as relevant passages in Greek, Latin, Armenian, Arabic, Syriac, and Persian authors of pagan, Christian, and Muslim background.

The history of Zoroastrianism spans a period of some 2,500 years, beginning with the emergence of Zarathushtra in the early sixth century B.C. and extending to the present-day beliefs and practices of the Parsis in India. It is only natural that during that long period of time, Zarathushtra's original beliefs went through many fundamental as well as minor changes. The several sources which have been mentioned reflect these changes. By and large, three major forms can be distinguished: (1) Zarathushtrianism, the original philosophy of Zarathushtra as expressed in the Gāthā; (2) Zoroastrianism, the religious beliefs reflected in the remainder of the Avesta and, later, in the Pahlavi books; (3) Parsiism, the religion of the Parsis in India.

In Zarathushtrianism, an ethical dualism is posited with great force and insistence. It is expressed by the opposition of "truth" (*Asha*) and "falsehood" (*Drug*) and, on another level, of the "augmentative spirit" (*Spenta Mainyu*) and the "wicked spirit" (*Angra Mainyu*), whose name later became Ahriman. The Asha-Drug opposition is regulated and topped off by a monotheism expressed by Ahura Mazdā, the "wise lord" whose later name is Ohrmazd. The Spenta Mainyu-Angra Mainyu pair are represented as twin brothers, and the relationship between Ahura Mazdā and Spenta Mainyu is one of father and son. Of a somewhat similar nature is the relationship between Ahura Mazdā and the six "augmentative immortals" (*Amesha Spentas*). These entities, organs, or aspects of Ahura Mazdā are known as "good mind" (*Vohu Manah*), "truth" (*Asha*), "power, dominion" (*Khshathra*), "devotion"

A Zoroastrian house in Iran contains no furniture. Guests must sit in niches in the walls.

The Zoroastrian temple in Yezd, Iran, houses a sacred fire that has burned continuously for 2,000 years.

INGE MORATH—MAGNUM

Zarathushtra

(*Armaiti*), "wholesomeness" (*Haurvatāt*), and "immortality" (*Ameretāt*), each of which is connected with one of the elements: cattle, fire, metal, earth, water, and vegetation, respectively. Ahura Mazdā is pictured as being at the origin of the physical world and its organization.

In what has been termed Zoroastrianism, a considerable admixture of ingredients alien to Zarathushtra's original ideology can be detected. Some of these elements can be traced back to a period in which ancient Iranians and Indians still were one community, with common religious beliefs of a polytheistic nature. In fact, the Avestan hymns (*Yasht*) recommend the cult of such individual Indo-Iranian deities as Mithra (Indian *Mitra*), the god of contract, and Haoma (Indian *Soma*), the personification of the intoxicating beverage of that name, both of whom have their replica in the Rig-Veda, the most ancient (1200–1000 B.C.) collection of Indian religious writings. In the years following Zarathushtra's death the belief in these and other gods was reestablished and officially recognized, more often than not under a thin veneer of Zarathushtrian sanction. As a result of this process of integrating opposite religious beliefs, the Avesta contains writings of mixed origin and purpose, planned, perhaps, for the needs of an audience of different origin and intent.

In Sassanian times, between the third and the eighth centuries, Zoroastrianism became and remained the official state religion. It appears from the Pahlavi books that the opposition between Ohrmazd (Ahura Mazdā), the principle of good, and Ahriman (Angra Mainyu), the principle of evil, has been fully developed and is all important. The Amahraspand (Amesha Spentas) and the other Zoroastrian divinities have become Ohrmazd's created spirits and his willing servants. The antagonism between Ohrmazd and Ahriman will lead to a struggle that will last twelve thousand years, the equivalent of one cosmic year. Ahriman initiates the hostilities and is temporarily repelled. Taking advantage of his indisposition, Ohrmazd fashions creation, which has become necessary to him for use as a weapon with which to meet Ahriman. Man, by his own individual choice, sides either with Ohrmazd—by adhering to the principles of good thoughts, words, and deeds (*humat, hukht, huvarsht*)—or with Ahriman. Both Ohrmazd and Ahriman have their assistants; the first relies on the Amahraspands (*Vahuman*, "good mind"; *Artvahisht*, "best truth"; *Shahrevar*, "choice kingdom"; *Spandarmat*, "augmentative devotion"; *Hurdāt*, "wholesomeness"; and *Amurdāt*, "immortality") and gods (*yazatān*), the second on the demons (*dev*). Ahriman, then, returns

to the attack, brings death, disease, anger, envy, and other similar entities into the world, and destroys Gayōmart, father of the human race and origin of the first human couple (Mashya and Mashyānag). The dramatic, ultimate victory of Ohrmazd over Ahriman is part of what is referred to as *frashkart*, "rehabilitation, miraculization" or "transformation." This change (of the world) seals the doom of Ahriman and each of his assistants and, in addition, deals with the resurrection of the dead. Resurrection is brought about by Sōshyans, or "savior," a term that refers to the last of the three posthumous sons of Zoroaster who appear at intervals of one thousand years. The bodies of both the saved and the damned are raised from "paradise" and "hell," where they have dwelt since a previously made decision to that effect after the death of each individual. Both the saved and the damned have to go through an ordeal of molten lead, which is final punishment for the damned but causes no discomfort to the saved, "for the surging metal seems to them like warm milk." Finally, the Sōshyans secures the immortality of the resurrected and "the material world will become immortal for ever and ever."

As for Parsiism, the essential tenets of Zoroastrianism have been retained in the official Parsi beliefs, doctrines, and practices. During their stay in India, however, the Parsi theologians came in contact with other religions such as Islam, Hinduism, Sufism, Yoga, and, in the nineteenth and twentieth centuries, Christianity, theosophy, and spiritism. Although it would be wrong to emphasize the influence of these "foreign" religions, their impact is unmistakable.　M. J. DRESDEN

BIBLIOG.–Jacques Duchesne-Guillemin, *La religion de l'Iran ancien* (1962); A. V. Williams Jackson, *Zoroastrian Studies* (1928); J. J. Modi, *The Religious Ceremonies and Customs of the Parsees* (2 editions; 1922, 1937); R. C. Zaehner, *The Teachings of the Magi, a Compendium of Zoroastrian Beliefs* (1956), *The Dawn and Twilight of Zoroastrianism* (1961).

ZORRILLA Y MORAL, JOSE, 1817–93, Spanish poet and dramatist, born in Valladolid. He lived in France 1850–55, then in Mexico where he enjoyed the patronage of the Emperor Maximilian; he returned to Europe in 1866. Zorrilla was elected to the Spanish Academy, and delivered a notable inaugural discourse in verse on taking his seat in 1885. He was in economic straits throughout his life, and even his most famous work was sold for a pittance. His talent lay in recreating in dramatic form popular and historical legend—medieval tales, the wars with the Moors, religious myths. It was Zorrilla's boast that he drew all his themes from the people and then returned them to their source in more artistic form.

His greatest success in every sense is *Don Juan Tenorio* (1844). The author himself pointed out its shortcomings in an astonishing preface, but the piece nevertheless has considerable artistic merit. Its verse, though sometimes padded, is lively, infectious, and effective. The play is important principally as a part of the popular patrimony. It captured and held the popular affection through the decades and is still presented throughout Spain in the first days of November. ANTHONY KERRIGAN

BIBLIOG.–N. A. Cortés, *Zorrila: su vida y sus obras* (3 vols., 1916–20).

ZOSIMUS, SAINT, d. 418, pope from 417 until his death, successor to Innocent I. Little is known of his life prior to 417 except that he was of either Greek or Jewish origin; historians disagree. He is remembered mainly for the Pelagian controversy. See PELAGIUS.

ZOSIMUS, fifth-century Byzantine historian. His history traces the decline of Roman power from the establishment of the empire by Augustus to the capture of Rome by Alaric, 410.

ZOUAVE, originally a soldier recruited for the French Army in Algeria from the Zouaoua or Zawia, a Kabyle tribe of northern Algeria; later, a military unit, or a soldier in such a unit, whose uniform was patterned after that of the Algerian Zouaves, with their baggy trousers, short embroidered jacket, and turban. The French organized Zouave units, 1831, to aid in the conquest of Algeria. Subsequently enlistment in the Zouaves was opened to Frenchmen as well as Zouaoua, and after native Algerians in French service were organized into special infantry called *tirailleurs* (sharpshooters), Zouaves were exclusively French. Although their home garrison was Algeria, Zouaves sometimes served abroad: in the Crimea, 1853-56, in Italy, 1859, in Mexico, 1862–66, and in Europe during World Wars I and II. In the light of the successes of the Algerian independence movement early in the 1960's, the future status of the Zouaves became problematical.

The French Gen. Louis Christophe Léon Juchault de Lamoricière organized a force of Papal, or Pontifical, Zouaves, 1860, to serve the Papacy against Italian states bent on unifying Italy. Most of the Papal Zouaves were recruited from France, Belgium, and Italy, but some were from the British Isles and Canada, and a few were from the United States, such as John H. Surratt (1844-1916), who served briefly, 1866, while a fugitive under indictment for conspiring to murder U.S. Pres. Abraham Lincoln (see SURRATT, MARY E.). The Papal Zouaves fought for France during the Franco-Prussian War, 1870–71, and then were disbanded.

Zouave regiments were organized by both the Union and the Confederacy early in the U.S. Civil War; the colorful uniforms proved to be good targets, however, and those Zouaves who survived soon preferred to be dressed in the drabber blue or gray.

ZSIGMONDY, RICHARD ADOLF, 1865–1929, Nobel prize-winning German chemist, was born in Vienna, and studied at the universities of Vienna and Munich. He was lecturer at the Graz Polytechnic, 1893–97, became professor of organic and colloidal chemistry at the University of Göttingen, 1900–29, and director of the Göttingen Institute for Organic Chemistry, 1907–29. Zsigmondy invented the ultramicroscope with H.F.W. Sidentopf, 1903, the immersion ultramicroscope, 1913, the membrane filter, 1918, and the ultrafine filter, 1922. He was awarded the 1925 Nobel prize in chemistry "for his elucidation of the heterogeneous nature of colloid solutions and for the methods he has devised in this connection, which have since become of fundamental importance in modern colloid chemistry."

ZUG, or Zoug, canton, N Switzerland; bounded N by Zürich, E and S by Schwyz, and W by Luzern, from which it is separated by Lake Zug; area 93 sq. mi.; pop. (1950) 42,349. The southern part of the canton is mountainous with summits reaching 4,900 feet. In the north are the valleys of the Lorze and Reuss rivers. The Lake of Zug occupies the middle of the canton and extends southward into Schwyz. The canton is an area of pasture, forests, and orchards. Highly specialized industries such as precision engineering and woodworking are confined to the towns of Zug, the capital, Baar, Cham, and Unt-Ageri. Zug entered the Swiss Conorederation in 1352.

ZUIDER ZEE, or Southern Sea, formerly a gulf indenting the Netherlands and separated from the North Sea by the chain of the West Frisian Islands. The Zuider Zee was originally a lake surrounded by fens and marshes. In the thirteenth century the lowland separating the lake from the North Sea was inundated by the sea, leaving a fringe of islands at the mouth of the newly formed gulf. When Dutch sea power was at its height in the seventeeth and eighteenth centuries, the Zuider Zee provided the link which made Amsterdam a world port, but its shallow

depth prohibited ships of heavy draft. The advent of modern shipping led to a decline in its importance for navigation. A vast drainage project, involving the construction of polders, was begun in 1920. The old Zuider Zee has been divided into two areas: the IJsselmeer, in which large areas have been reclaimed, and the Wadden Zee. See IJSSELMEER.

ZULA, village, N Ethiopia, near the Red Sea; 33 miles SSE of Massaua. Zula is situated in an irrigated area in which cereals, sesame, and cotton are grown. Nearby are the ruins of the ancient city of Adulis. Pop. about 500.

ZULIA, state, NW Venezuela; bounded on the N by the Gulf of Venezuela, on the E by the states of Falcón, Lara, and Trujillo, on the S by the states of Mérida and Táchira, and on the W by Colombia; area 24,363 sq. mi., pop. (1959 est.) 523,568. Zulia lies in the Lake Maracaibo lowlands. The southern part of the state is hot and humid with heavy rains occurring in May–July, and September–November; the north is arid. Venezuela's major oil deposits are found in the region, especially on the eastern side of Lake Maracaibo. The state's industry ranges from the growing of cotton, sugar, and cacao in the south to goat grazing in the north. Maracaibo, the capital, is the commercial center of the state.

ZULULAND, region E Republic of South Africa, NE Natal Province; area 10,362 sq. mi. The country consists of a wide littoral fronting on the Indian Ocean and backed by the rise of the Drakensberg Mountains. Some three-fifths of the region is a native reserve, where cattle raising is the principal means of livelihood. Sugar and cotton are grown in the rich littoral plain. Zululand is inhabited by the Zulu, a Bantu people believed to have settled the country early in the seventeenth century of the Christian Era. They lived peacefully beside other Negro tribes and with European settlers until the reign of King Chaka, 1800–28, who conquered neighboring tribes and enlarged the Zulu domain to include what corresponds to Natal Province, 1818–20. Although Chaka remained friendly to Europeans, and granted Port Natal (Durban) to the British in 1824, his half-brother and successor, Dingaan, 1828–?40, massacred Pieter Retief and some other Boers in a dispute over cattle, 1837 (see BOER; DINGAANS KRAAL). In retaliation, Boers under Andries Wilhelmus Jacobus Pretorius invaded Zulu country, defeated Dingaan in a pitched battle, Dec. 16, 1838, and went on to help Dingaan's brother Umpanda secure tribal rule. Umpanda gave the British the country between the upper Tugela and the Buffalo rivers, and land around St. Lucia Bay, 1843. Harmonious Zulu-British relations continued until Umpanda's son and successor, Cetewayo, refused to accept a British adviser, whereupon the British invaded Zululand, 1879, defeated the Zulus at Ulundi, declared the Chaka Dynasty ended, and divided Zululand among several chiefs. Fighting soon broke out among the chiefs, however, and by the time of Cetewayo's death, 1884, Cetewayo's son Dinizulu, with the aid of the Boers, had control over all Zulu tribes. Cetewayo ceded Zululand's rich central agricultural land to the Boers, who set up New Republic, whereupon the British blocked Boer access to the Indian Ocean by seizing St. Lucia Bay, 1884; soon New Republic was absorbed into the South African Republic (see TRANSVAAL, *History*). The British government annexed the remaining Zululand, 1887, and ceded it to Natal, 1897, of which it was made a province. In the meantime, Dinizulu had rebelled, had been captured by the British, 1888, and had been exiled to St. Helena. He was permitted to return as Zulu king, 1898, and all went well until 1906, when the Zulus rebelled against British imposition of a poll tax. The British put down the revolt but civil unrest in Zululand continued until 1908, when Dinizulu was convicted of treason and imprisoned. When the Union (now Republic) of South Africa was formed in 1910, Zululand lost its provincial status.

ZUÑI, a North American Pueblo Indian tribe of western New Mexico. The Zuñi constitute a distinct linguistic family, but are otherwise similar to other Pueblo tribes. The first European known to have encountered the Zuñi was the Spanish priest Fray Marcos de Niza, who visited them in 1539. De Niza's reports of their wealth to the authorities in Mexico City resulted in the expedition of Francisco Vasquez de Coronado, who reached the Zuñi, 1540, and found their seven adobe villages a poor substitute for the cities of gold and turquoise that Fray Marcos' account had led him to expect (see CIBOLA, SEVEN CITIES OF). During the Pueblo revolt against the Spanish, 1680, the seven villages were abandoned; the present single pueblo was built in the 1690's on the site of one of the original seven. The population of the Zuñi was about 2,500 in 1680; in 1950, there were 2,759 Zuñi Indians living on the Zuñi Reservation, McKinley and Valencia counties, New Mexico.

BIBLIOG.—Ruth Benedict, *Patterns of Culture* (1934), *Zuñi Mythology*, 2 vols. (1935); Erna Fergusson, *Dancing Gods* (1957); Carl C. Seltzer, *Racial Prehistory in the Southwest and the Hawikuh Zuñis* (Papers, vol. 23, no. 1) (1944); Watson Smith and John M. Roberts, *Zuñi Law: A Field of Values* (Papers, vol. 43, no. 1; Reports of the Rimrock Project: Values Ser., no. 4) (1954); Edmund Wilson, *Red, Black, Blond and Olive* (1956).

ZUPPKE, ROBERT CARL, 1879–1957, U.S. football coach, was born in Berlin, Germany. He was brought to the United States, 1881, and was graduated from the University of Wisconsin, 1905. While he was head football coach at the University of Illinois, 1913–41, his teams won or tied for seven Western Conference (Big Ten) championships. He introduced the huddle and the spiral pass from center.

ZÜRICH, canton, N Switzerland; bounded N by Germany and the canton of Schaffhausen, E by Thurgau and St. Gallen, S by Schwyz and Zug, and W by Aargau; area 668 sq. mi.; pop. (1950) 777,002. Lake Zürich lies in its southern part and extends eastward between Zürich and Schwyz and between St. Gallen and Schwyz. The lake drains northwestward into the Rhine through the Limmat and Aare rivers. The canton has low mountains and fertile valleys. Much of the land is in pasture, and cattle and cereals are raised. In the south are orchards and vineyards. The mountain slopes are forested. The principal manufacturing centers are Zürich, the capital, and Winterthur. Silk and cotton mills, and plants producing machinery and railroad equipment, utilize hydroelectric power generated at plants along the Rhine River in the northern part of the canton. Most of the people are German-speaking and are Protestants.

ZÜRICH, city, N Switzerland, capital of the canton of Zürich; situated on both banks of the Limmat River where it emerges from Lake Zürich; 45 miles ESE of Basel. Zürich is the largest city in Switzerland, and the banking, cultural, and educational center of the country. The industrial area is located in the northern part of the city. Precision machinery, automotive equipment, electrical apparatus, textiles, chemicals, cement, food products, and tobacco are manufactured. Zürich is a tourist resort and has an international airport. The newer section of the city occupies land recovered from the lake, and the concert hall, the civic theater, and other public buildings are located there. Among the city's old buildings are eleventh century Grossmünster; Fraumünster, founded for nuns in the ninth century; St. Peter's; and the fifteenth century Wasserkirche which from 1631 to 1916 was the city library. The National Museum was opened in Zurich in 1898. Among the educational institutions are the University of Zürich (1523) and the Federal Polytechnic School, which was opened in 1855. Zürich is an old city, which was known to the Romans as Turicum. Huldreich Zwingli (1484–1531), a leader in the Protestant movement, was a rector of a Zürich church. Pop. (1959) 409,300.

ZÜRICH, UNIVERSITY OF, a public institution of higher education in Zürich, Switzerland, was founded by the Swiss religious reformer Huldreich Zwingli as a secondary school and theological training center, 1523, but became a university by public vote in 1832. There are faculties of theology, law and political economy, medicine, veterinary medicine, dentistry, philosophy I (liberal arts, social sciences, and education), and philosophy II (natural sciences). All instruction is in the German language.

Affiliated with the university are separate institutes for the study of the German language, dentistry, political science, and natural history. The university operates a museum of medical history and a museum of zoology, and maintains ethnological and archaeological collections and a phonetics laboratory.

ZUTPHEN, or Zutfen, city, E Netherlands, in the province of Gelderland; on the IJssel River, which flows from the Rhine River to the IJsselmeer; 57 miles ESE of Amsterdam. Zutphen is a trade center for grain and timber shipped down the Rhine River from Germany. The manufactures include leather, textiles, oil, and paper. Points of interest are a twelfth century church and the remains of the old town wall. Pop. (1959 est.) 23,793.

ZWEIBRÜCKEN, city, W Germany, in the West German state of Rhineland-Palatinate; near the French border; 18 miles E of Saarbrücken. Zweibrücken is a railroad junction, and machinery, metal products, leather, and cotton goods are manufactured. During a part of the Napoleonic period it belonged to France. It is known to scholars for an early printing press, which produced Greek and Latin classics. Pop. (1958) 33,720.

ZWEIG, ARNOLD, 1887– , German Jewish writer, was born in Glogow, Silesia, and was educated at Breslau, Berlin, Göttingen, and other German universities. During World War I he was a member of the German Labor Corps. As a prominent antimilitarist and an influential Jewish spokesman, he was banished by the Nazis, 1933, and subsequently settled in Palestine. His sardonic *Case of Sergeant Grischa* (1927), the story of a Russian war-prisoner who falls victim to Prussian bureaucracy, is the first and best known of a cycle of novels depicting the impact of war on society; later novels in the series are *Young Woman of 1914* (1931), *Education Before Verdun* (1935), and *The Crowning of a King* (1937). Among other works are *Claudia* (1912), *Ritual Murder in Hungary* (1913), *Lessing, Kleist, Büchner* (1925), *De Vriendt Goes Home* (1933), and *The Axe of Wandsbek* (1946).

ZWEIG, STEFAN, 1881–1942, Austrian writer, was born in Vienna of a wealthy Jewish family and studied at the University of Vienna. He traveled widely in Europe and Asia before settling down in

CULVER SERVICE
Stefan Zweig

Salzburg, Austria, after World War I. He went to London, 1934, to do research on Mary, Queen of Scots, and, unwilling to return to Austria, where the influence of fascism was increasing, remained in London until 1940, when he went to the United States, from where he soon moved on to Brazil, 1941. Having decided that he did not have the "immense strength [needed] to reconstruct [his] life" in this new country, Zweig and his 30-year-old wife committed suicide.

Zweig's first important literary work was the symbolic dramatic poem, *Jeremias* (1917), in which he expressed his opposition to war. Zweig, a sensitive, inward-looking personality, had an affinity for the defeated, yet as a biographer he was most attracted to triumphant creative geniuses such as Honoré de Balzac, Charles Dickens, Friedrich Nietzsche, and Lev Tolstoi. Among his works are

Paul Verlaine (1913), *Drei Meister*, 1920 (*Three Masters*, 1930), *Amok*, 1922 (Eng. tr., 1931), *Verwirrung de Gefühle*, 1926 (*Conflicts*, 1927), *Sternstunden der Menschheit*, 1927 (*The Tide of Fortune*, 1940), *Marie Antoinette*, 1932 (Eng. tr., 1933), *Triumph und Tragik des Erasmus von Rotterdam*, 1934 (*Erasmus of Rotterdam*, 1934), *Baumeister der Welt*, 1935 (*Master Builders*, 1939), *Magellan*, 1938 (*Conqueror of the Seas*, 1938), *Ungeduld des Herzens*, 1938 (*Beware of Pity*, 1939), and *Schachnovelle*, 1944 (*The Royal Game*, 1944). The posthumous *The World of Yesterday* (1943) is autobiographical.

ZWICKAU, city, E Germany, in the district of Karl-Marx-Stadt, about 40 miles S of Leipzig. The industrial picture in Zwickau is diverse: textiles, machinery, paper, china, and paint are among the manifold manufactures.

Zwickau, which is Slavonic in origin, was the site of a market as early as the twelfth century. The discovery of silver nearby in 1470 brought rapid prosperity to the merchants of Zwickau. A fine sixteenth-century guildhall still stands. St. Mary's, a fifteenth-century Gothic church, was restored in the late nineteenth century. The city is also remembered as the birthplace of the Anabaptist movement (1525) and of the composer Robert Schumann (1810). The opening of a coal field near Zwickau in 1823 marked a second burst of prosperity and expansion. Zwickau is now one of the ten greatest industrial centers in East Germany. (For population, see Germany map in Atlas.)

ZWINGLI, ULRICH, 1484–1531, Switzerland's first Protestant reformer. Born the son of a village magistrate at Wildhaus in the duchy of Toggenburg, Zwingli was educated for the priesthood and ordained in 1506. While a student at the University of Basel, he was influenced by Thomas Wittenbach, who encouraged him to study the Bible and brought him to the view that papal power was not based upon Biblical authority. The writings of Erasmus brought Zwingli by 1516 to a full appreciation of Scriptural authority. Erasmus's Christian pacifism also caused Zwingli to become an advocate of Swiss neutrality. Zwingli's consequent opposition to the Swiss alliance with France led to his dismissal fron the parish of Glarus in 1516.

Zwingli's appointment as people's priest at the Zürich Cathedral in 1519 marked the beginning of his career as a reformer. His death in a battle against the Catholic Cantons on October 11, 1531, cut short that career and marked the defeat of his plan to win the European powers to a reform of the Church, based upon the authority of Scripture. The immediate effect of Zwingli's work was confined to German Switzerland, where his teachings found support in the regions controlled by Bern, Basel, and Zürich. After the Marburg Colloquy (1529), Lutheran opposition to Zwingli's doctrine of the communion as a memorial blocked the spread of his teachings in Germany. Geneva under Calvin became the center of international Protestantism.

The success of Zwingli's work at Zürich was due to his cooperation with the Zürich magistracy. Zwingli assigned to the State a function as an instrument of the Divine purpose, with the magistrate and the pastor working together to realize God's will. As long as the magistrate recognized the authority of the Bible and the need for a reform of the Church, Zwingli was content to let him decide upon the timing of specific reforms.

This willingness to cooperate with the magistracy caused a split among his followers and led, in December, 1523, to the emergence of the first "Free Church" in modern history. The dissidents, led by Conrad Grebel, demanded the establishment of a Believers' Church, free from state interference. They later adopted the practice of adult baptism and became known as rebaptizers, or Anabaptists. Their beliefs and their supposed connection with the spread of the Peasants' Revolt in Switzerland threatened to halt the progress of the Reformation, and in 1527 Zwingli accepted the necessity of imposing the death penalty upon them. See ANABAPTISTS.

It is difficult to assess Zwingli's contribution to the Reformation. He is too often dismissed as a lesser disciple of Luther. His early sermons reflect the concerns of Erasmian humanism and Swiss patriotism. Zwingli remained a Swiss patriot but broke with Erasmus by 1522. He replaced Erasmus's conception of the Gospel as a teaching that could be learned and followed, with a theology that stressed God's will and grace. Zwingli was by this time fully aware of Luther's work and drew ideas from it. The extent of his dependence upon Luther is unclear, because it was public policy to deny that the Reformation at Zürich was the result of Luther's example. If Zwingli had claimed to follow Luther, the rest of the Swiss Confederacy would have had legal grounds to attack Zürich for supporting the doctrines of a condemned heretic. Zwingli's interpretation of the communion and his rejection of music in the church service mark his independence of Luther. And Zwingli was far more optimistic concerning the function of the State and the Christian magistrate in God's plan than was Luther.   ROBERT C. WALTON

BIBLIOG.–Oskar Farner, *Zwingli* (1952); Walther Koehler, *Huldrych Zwingli* (1952).

ZWITTER ION, also known as ampholyte or dipolar ion, a molecular complex, frequently found in solutions of amino acids, that can carry a positive charge on one end and a negative charge on the other. The stable form of certain compounds is the zwitter ion. For instance, an aqueous solution of glycine contains almost no $NH_2 \cdot CH_2 \cdot COOH$ molecules. Its stable form (the empirical formula remains the same, but the molecular configuration is altered) is the zwitter ion $NH_3^+ \cdot CH_2 \cdot COO^-$.

ZWOLLE, city, central Netherlands, capital of the province of Overijssel; 50 miles ENE of Amsterdam. Zwolle is a canal and rail center, and chemicals, metal products, textiles and dairy products are manufactured. It has a cattle and fish market and a large trade. Thomas à Kempis spent much of his life at a nearby Augustinian convent. Of interest is the Grote Kerk, a church built in 1400 whose organ is considered to be one of the finest in the world. (For population, see Netherlands map in Atlas.)

ZWORYKIN, VLADIMIR KOSMA, 1889–   , U.S. electronic engineer, born in Murom, Russia. He studied physics at the Institute of Technology, St. Petersburg, and at the Collège de France. He did radio research for the Russian Signal Corps in World War I, then emigrated to the United States in 1919 and became a citizen in 1924. He received his Ph.D. from the University of Pittsburgh in 1926. With the Westinghouse laboratories, 1920–29, he invented the iconoscope, or electronic camera, of the television transmitter and the kinescope, or cathode ray tube, of the television receiver. He directed electronic research for RCA between 1929 and 1954. In 1937 he applied his television tube to microscopy. This led to the invention of the electron microscope. After 1954 he was an honorary vice president of RCA.

ZYGOTE, a cell formed by the union of two gametes, or reproductive cells. When male and female gametes join under favorable circumstances, the zygote they form will develop into a new individual. See EMBRYOLOGY; GERM CELL.

ZYZZYVA, a genus of South American weevils belonging to the order Coleoptera. Zyzzyvas are characterized by their short, thick beak with mandibles at the tip of the snout, and an oblong body that is covered with yellow scales. The larvae are whitish grubs that are cylindrically shaped and without legs. Both the larval and adult weevils like to feed on plant structures. The genus Zyzzyva is primarily found in Brazil. See WEEVIL.